Creative Living

Basic Concepts in Home Economics

Fifth Edition

GLENCOE

The Fifth Edition of Creative Living integrates contemporary issues with complete, up-to-date home economics content, and involves students in decision-making and critical thinking.

Study guides and activity worksheets in the **Student Workbook** correlate to every chapter of the Student Text, to reinforce learning, encourage application, and build thinking skills.

The **Teacher's Wraparound Edition** is loaded with an array of teaching strategies and detailed lesson plans conveniently "wrapped" right around the student pages.

Short, self-contained chapters in the **Student Text** give you the flexibility to pick and choose the content that best suits the needs of your students

Total Teaching Program

You will find preparing for teaching easier than ever with the updated and expanded **Teacher's Classroom Resources,** a box filled with teaching strategies, activities, handouts, worksheets, and visuals.

A complete evaluation program includes **Chapter Tests, Unit Tests,** and **Testmakers.** This software provides you with a computerized bank of test items that allows you to construct your own tests, quizzes, and review sheets.

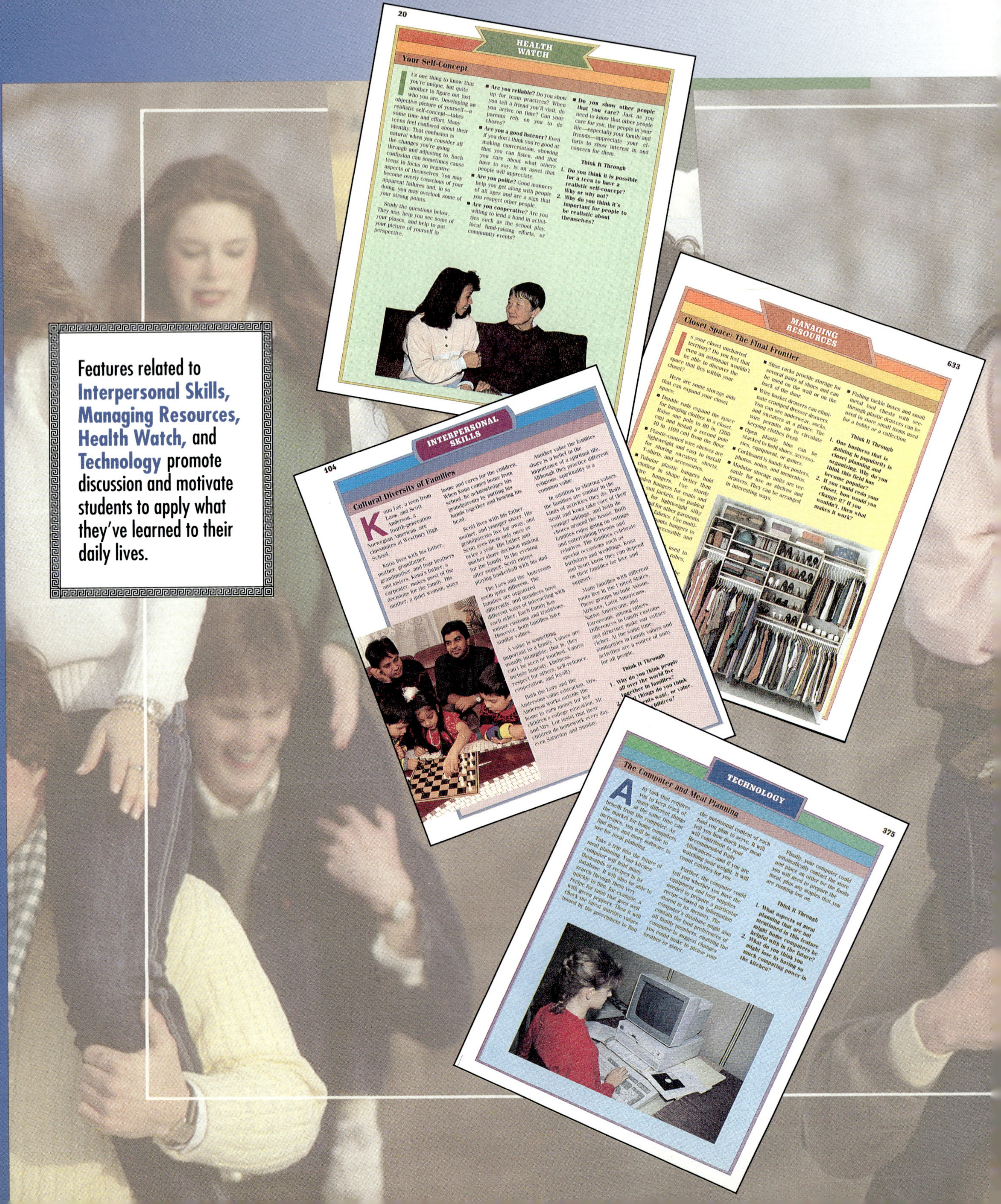

Features related to **Interpersonal Skills, Managing Resources, Health Watch,** and **Technology** promote discussion and motivate students to apply what they've learned to their daily lives.

Student Text

Seven Units divided into 75 short, stand-alone Chapters provide in-depth coverage of all the content you need to teach a comprehensive home economics course.

Each of the **Chapter Openers** sets the stage for student learning. **Chapter Reviews** help you assure students' mastery of content and promote cross-curricular learning in reading, writing, math, and science.

Teen Tips offer your students practical ideas on topics related to every unit.

Extensive **Lesson Plans** for every chapter help you organize all the teaching resources. They provide discussion starters, motivators, vocabulary builders, learning exercises, questions, activities, and academic skill-builders.

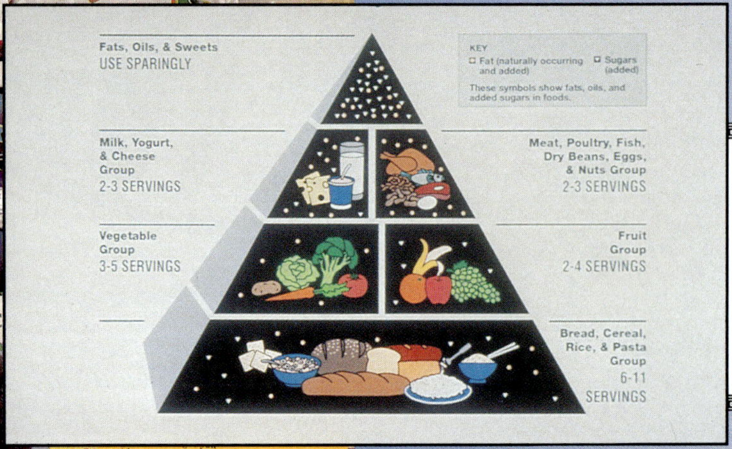

Both the **Student Text** and the **Teacher's Wraparound Edition** have been updated to include the new Food Pyramid system of categorizing food groups.

Teacher's Wraparound Edition

Teaching "Avoiding Hidden Costs" (Page 294)

This section teaches the student to be aware of various costs that are not included in the price of an item.

Checking Comprehension

✓ What other hidden costs should be considered when comparing prices? *An item ultimately costs more if it requires frequent repairs and additional parts, or cannot be exchanged if something goes wrong. Travel costs are another hidden cost.*

✓ What do you need to know about refunds and exchanges? *You need to know the store's policies and time limit for refunds and exchanges.*

Activities

Skill Builder: Writing
Tell the students the following story: Kim bought a watch at a jewelry store. After one week, it broke. She returned the watch to the store. They gave her a refund since they did not have any more of that brand in stock. She went to another store to buy the watch. After two months, the battery needed to be replaced. She went to several stores, but none carried the battery she needed. Finally, she wrote to the manufacturer. Six weeks later, they sent her a new battery and a bill for the battery, postage, and handling. Ask the students to list all the hidden costs that were involved. (*Answers: travel to return the first watch and go to another store to get a new one; travel to try and locate a battery; postage for the letter to the manufacturer; the cost of a replacement battery; postage and handling for the new battery.*)

Reteaching
Review the list of common hidden costs on page 294 in the text. Ask students to suggest other examples of hidden costs that they have discovered.

Enrichment
Sponsor a poster contest using the theme "Good Shopping Habits." Have students display posters in businesses in the area.

294 UNIT FOUR MANAGEMENT

■ Any requirements that the purchaser must meet to validate the warranty. Remember to keep your warranties and sales slips in a safe place in case you need them.

Avoiding Hidden Costs

Some costs are hidden because they are not part of the price of something. But they still must be paid. Some common hidden costs include:

■ **Travel.** When comparison shopping, don't forget to include the cost of transportation. Consider the time, energy, and money required to have your hair cut across town. It might cost less to go to a more expensive salon around the corner.

■ **Repairs.** Before buying a product, check the warranty for coverage. There may be a copy attached to the floor model. If not, ask to see one. Stores are required by law to show you warranties. Ask about the cost of repairs not covered by the warranty. If they seem high, compare them to repair costs for other models of the same products. If you buy an item that needs frequent or expensive repairs, in effect the item costs more.

■ **Additional parts.** "Battery not included" can mean another expense before the product you've bought is actually going to work. Some accessories, such as shoulder straps for schoolbags and stuff sacks for sleeping bags, are conveniences you might need as much as the item itself.

■ **Exchanges.** If something goes wrong with a product you purchased, take it back to the store with the receipt. Usually, stores have policies and time limits for refunds and exchanges. For your own protection, find out about these at the time of purchase. If you can't return a defective product, you've spent money for nothing. You'll learn more about refunds and exchanges in Chapter 32.

Accessories such as batteries are hidden costs that add to the price of some products.

Cross-Reference For additional information on returning and exchanging items, see Chapter 32 "Voicing Your Opinion".

Focus on Consumer Skills Explain to students that in this chapter they have learned ways to select products or services *before* they buy. They can help themselves become better consumers by reading, studying economic trends, taking consumer education courses, working with organized consumer groups, and learning about money management.

CHAPTER 31 REVIEW

295

Reviewing the Facts

1. What is the difference between goods and services?
2. What are the five factors that define quality?
3. Why do people sometimes pay a higher price for a product during an emergency?
4. What does suitability mean?
5. How can comparison shopping save you money?
6. What is a unit price?
7. What is a warranty?
8. How can repairs be a hidden cost?

Sharing Your Ideas

1. Have you ever made a purchase that dissatisfied you? Why were you dissatisfied? What comparison shopping techniques could you use the next time to prevent this from happening?
2. Identify five recent purchases that you or your family have made. Determine whether there are hidden costs associated with any of the products. Discuss with the class.

Applying Your Skills

1. **Evaluating Quality.** Bring to class two new shirts or blouses. Read the labels and note the prices, fibers, and care instructions. See if the labels indicate where the garment was manufactured. Also look for details such as the tailoring of collars and cuffs, and examine the pockets, buttons, and stitching. Which do you think is the better quality garment? Why? What is the difference in prices? How do you account for the difference? Write a report describing your findings.
2. **Comparing the Cost of Goods.** Go to a supermarket or store that posts unit prices for products. Examine a group of products, such as aspirin, shampoo, or cookies, and write down the unit prices for each product in the group. Draw a graph showing each of the products from the least to most expensive according to their unit prices.
3. **Evaluating Qualities.** Identify a product you are interested in buying. Find an account of the item in a consumer magazine. Read about the quality, performance, durability, safety, and features of several brands. Which one would best fit your needs?

Answers to "Reviewing the Facts"

1. Goods are material things we use; services are work performed by one person for another.
2. Performance, durability, convenience, maintenance, and safety.
3. Because they need the product or service immediately and don't have time to comparison shop.
4. How well the product fits the buyer's needs and resources.
5. By finding the best quality at the lowest price.
6. The price of an item per ounce or by count.
7. A written statement from a manufacturer or retailer promising to repair or replace a defective item or to refund the money.
8. If you buy something that needs frequent repairs, the product ends up costing you more than a similar product that does not need a lot of repairs.

Answers to "Sharing Your Ideas"

1. Answers will vary. Discussion will probably focus on products that didn't perform as expected or that broke shortly after they were purchased. If students say they kept a product they were dissatisfied with, talk about why.
2. Hidden costs usually involve travel, repairs, additional parts, exchanges, and credit terms.

COMPLETING THE CHAPTER

Summary

- When you go shopping, you can buy goods or services. Goods are material things; services are work performed by one person for another.
- When evaluating a purchase, you should compare quality, price, and suitability of each product.
- When you comparison shop you look at the prices and features of several brands.
- It is important to be aware of possible hidden costs when making a purchase.

For Review

Objective Review Questions Have students complete the "Reviewing the Facts" section on this page.

Study Guide Have students complete the Study Guide from Chapter 31 of their *Student Workbook*.

The Convenience Store Ask students to form small groups to compare the advantages and disadvantages of shopping in a small, local convenience food store or specialty store as opposed to shopping in a large chain store. Each group might choose two items, such as a pound of lean ground meat and a container of orange juice, and compare quality, prices, convenience, and so on.

For Evaluation

Questionnaire Have students develop a "Wise Consumer" questionnaire that would cover the major points of the chapter: Evaluating Purchases, Comparison Shopping, and Avoiding Hidden Costs.

Self-Appraisal Ask students to exchange the above questionnaires. They should use their classmates' questionnaires for their own self-appraisal as a "wise consumer."

Chapter Test Have students complete the test for Chapter 31 that appears in the *Teacher's Resource Book*.

Special boxes provide high-interest facts and current trends, background and in-depth information to support chapter content, additional activity suggestions, references, and additional resources.

Teacher's Classroom Resources

Glencoe has developed an expanded array of **Teacher's Classroom Resources**, a whole box filled with hundreds of ready-to-use teaching supplements that save you countless hours of preparation time.

- **Teaching with Creative Living** and **Lesson Plans** offer guidance for planning.
- Activities for **Cooperative Learning, Life Skills,** and **Extension** provide hands-on projects, worksheets, and teaching tips.
- **Chapter Tests, Unit Tests,** and **Answer Keys** provide means for accurate assessment.
- **Full-Color Transparencies** and **Blackline Masters**, both with teaching notes, are great visuals that help you keep students motivated.

Program Components	Order Numbers
Textbook	
Student Edition	0-02-675646-3
Teacher's Wraparound Edition	0-02-675647-1
Student Workbook	0-02-675649-8
Teacher's Classroom Resources	0-02-675648-X
Teaching with *Creative Living**	0-02-675656-0
Lesson Plans*	0-02-675657-9
Blackline Masters*	0-02-675659-5
Cooperative Learning Activities*	0-02-675666-8
Life Skills Activities*	0-02-675658-7
Extensions Activities*	0-02-675661-7
Foods Lab Activities*	0-02-675662-5
Clothing Lab Activities*	0-02-675663-3
Chapter Tests*	0-02-675664-1
Unit Tests*	0-02-675665-X
Answer Keys*	0-02-675668-4
Color Transparency Packet*	0-02-675651-X
Testmakers	
Macintosh	0-02-675652-8
Apple	0-02-675653-6
IBM	0-02-675654-4

* These components are included in the **Teacher's Classroom Resources.**

For more information, contact your nearest regional office or call toll-free 1-800-334-7344

GLENCOE
Macmillan/McGraw-Hill
P. O. Box 503, Blacklick, OH 43004-0543

VHE 90826-4

Fifth Edition

Teacher's Manual

CREATIVE LIVING

Basic Concepts in Home Economics

GLENCOE

Macmillan/McGraw-Hill

New York, New York Columbus, Ohio Mission Hills, California Peoria, Illinois

Send all inquiries to:
GLENCOE DIVISION
Macmillan/McGraw-Hill
3008 W. Willow Knolls Drive
Peoria, IL 61614-1083

ISBN 0-02-675646-3 (Student's Edition)
ISBN 0-02-675647-1 (Teacher's Wraparound Edition)

Printed in the United States of America.

1 2 3 4 5 6 7 8 9 VHJ 99 98 97 96 95 94 93

Co-developed by
Glencoe Division of Macmillan/McGraw-Hill and
Visual Education Corporation,
Princeton, New Jersey

Teaching with Creative Living

The Fifth Edition of *Creative Living* preserves and strengthens the outstanding features that home economics teachers have praised about the program. The primary goal of the *Creative Living* text is to offer comprehensive coverage that will fit your home economics curriculum. From the fundamentals of relationship skills to the latest in microwave techniques, *Creative Living* provides a complete home economics program. The second objective is to encourage critical thinking. *Creative Living* does much more than present the facts. Students become actively involved—through discussions and activities—in responsible decision making as reflected in their daily life choices.

In this revised and updated program:

- The chapters encourage decision-making, priority-setting, and management skills.
- The features are practical, relevant to daily life, and vital to course content.
- The learning objectives are linked with resources for mastering them and measuring student performance.
- A strong and extensive ancillary program supports the student text.
- Large, colorful illustrations and bold design help capture and maintain student interest.

In this Fifth Edition, the basic goals of *Creative Living* are carried out in components that are completely integrated for easy use by students and teachers. The program includes:

- **Student Text.** Comprehensive, up-to-date content is organized around the theme of responsible decision making. The text has an appealing format, full-color illustrations, and 704 pages.
- **Teacher's Wraparound Edition.** Lesson plans and classroom support materials are printed around a reduced-size version of the student text. This practical format is easy for teachers to use in the classroom—with no need to flip between pages or to consult other books.
- **Teacher's Classroom Resources.** A complete teaching package contains all-new supplementary materials, a total testing program, full-color transparencies, and much more.
- **Student Workbook.** Study guides and activities provide immediate review and reinforcement to support the text. The answers are in the Teacher's Classroom Resources.
- **Testmaker Software.** A computer software test bank provides a base of questions, plus room for additional questions.

The Student Text

The *Creative Living* Student Text is the core of the program. Written in a positive and practical voice, the text is supported by special features and colorful illustrations.

Units

The text is organized into seven units. Each unit concentrates on a major area of the home economics curriculum:

- **Unit 1: Focus on You.** Explores issues of concern to teens—self-concept, self-esteem, growth, and wellness. Goal-setting, decision-making, and management skills are introduced.
- **Unit 2: Your Family and Friends.** Focuses on changing relationships with family, peers, and others. Communication skills, family changes, conflicts, and emotions are explored.
- **Unit 3: Child Care and Development.** Shows the principles and skills involved in child-care responsibilities.
- **Unit 4: Management.** Examines ways to manage personal resources and presents important consumer skills.
- **Unit 5: Foods and Nutrition.** Gives guidelines for nutrition and health, and provides information on food preparation and meal management.
- **Unit 6: Clothing and Textiles.** Introduces design, fibers and fabrics, and wardrobe planning, along with garment construction.
- **Unit 7: Housing and Living Space.** Outlines housing choices and ways to care for living space.

Chapters

This edition of *Creative Living* contains 75 short, easy-to-complete chapters. Each deals with one overall concept or theme, which makes the material accessible to students and flexible for lesson planning. Each chapter includes:

- **Student Objectives.** To help you define goals for the course, clearly stated behavioral objectives begin each chapter. All review questions, activities, tests, and supplementary materials are written to support these objectives.
- **Words to Remember.** The new and significant terms used in the chapter are listed in alphabetical order. When each term is first used in the chapter, it appears in boldface type, followed by the definition. Phonetic pronunciation guides are given for difficult words. The terms are also listed and defined in the Glossary.
- **Text.** Students will enjoy the writing style—anecdotal, interactive, practical, and upbeat. The frequent use of headings and lists helps maintain interest and readability.
- **Chapter Review.** At the end of each chapter, a full page is devoted to review. This comprehensive section includes:
  Reviewing the Facts—Objective questions check students' recall of major concepts in the chapter.
  Thinking Critically— Questions spark lively discussion about the chapter content.
  Applying Your Skills—Independent activities enable students to apply what they have learned. The activities also reinforce reading, writing, math, science, and communicating skills, and are identified by symbols. These activities are suitable for classroom use and do not require extra resources.

Reading

Writing

Math

Science

Communicating

Special Highlights

To support the chapter components, the Fifth Edition of *Creative Living* has incorporated special features, which promote interest and reinforce learning. These highlights include:

- **Illustrations.** Hundreds of large, full-color photographs and drawings illuminate hands-on techniques and emphasize important concepts. These appealing illustrations and their captions foster in-depth learning.
- **Charts.** Throughout the text, charts are used to introduce new information and to reinforce material presented in the chapter.
- **Boxed Features.** The full-page boxed features focus on current issues in four areas:
  Interpersonal Skills
  Managing Resources
  Health Watch
  Technology
  These features are discussion-oriented and conclude with two discussion questions.

Teen Tips

The Teen Tips features—which follow every unit—offer practical and helpful ideas on topics as varied as "Six Ways to Feel Good About Yourself," "Study Time—Do's and Don'ts," and "Breakfast On-the-Run." These features supplement the unit content with practical information and tips that students can use in their everyday activities.

The Teacher's Wraparound Edition

For ease of use, extensive lesson plans and annotations have been developed for the Teacher's Wraparound Edition of *Creative Living*. A variety of learning exercises, questions, and activities are presented on each page in a unique format called *wraparound*. It consists of a reduced-size student text edition with the teacher's materials "wrapped around" the left, right, and bottom margins. The left and right margins are reserved for the lesson plans; the bottom margins carry the annotations.

Lesson Plans

The lesson plans help you guide students through the chapters and give you ideas for reinforcing and enriching students' learning. The lesson plans for each chapter are organized into the following components:

- **Chapter Overview.** A brief outline of the chapter allows you to quickly survey the chapter content.
- **Introducing the Chapter.** The chapter opening page includes three sections:
  Motivators—An attention-getting activity sets the stage, followed by a suggestion for using the chapter opening photograph, and an activity or discussion question that focuses on the opening paragraphs.
  Introducing the Objectives—To prepare for a basic mastery of the concepts, students are encouraged to discuss the behavioral objectives.
  Introducing Vocabulary—A short activity introduces students to the Words to Remember for that chapter.
- **Teaching the Chapter.** The teaching suggestions are organized to follow the main headings in the chapter. For each heading, there are two main components:
  Checking Comprehension—A series of review and discussion questions, with answers, that differ from the end-of-chapter review questions help measure the students' understanding of their readings.
  Activities—Additional activities include Skill Builders (focusing on critical thinking, reading, writing, math, and science), Reteaching, and Enrichment.
- **Chapter Boxed Feature.** The teaching suggestions for the boxed feature include:
  Answers to Feature Questions—Answers to the two discussion questions are provided.
  Activities—These activities enhance the feature content and encourage community involvement.
- **Completing the Chapter.** This section is divided into three parts:
  Summary—A short, bulleted list highlights the main points of the chapter and reflects the chapter objectives.
  For Review—Students are referred to the chapter review materials in the Student Text and the Student Workbook. This is followed by activities that help students review the main themes of the chapter and its overall content.
  For Evaluation—These activities are designed to help you evaluate students' comprehension of the chapter. They are followed by a referral to the appropriate test in the Teacher's Classroom Resources.
- **Chapter Review Answers.** The answers to Reviewing the Facts are printed beside the questions, while the answers to Thinking Critically are located in the bottom margin.

Annotations

The annotations appear at the bottom of the text page. They are designed to provide a wealth of information to aid in planning and presentation.

- **Chapter Resources.** Listing of the resources available in the Teacher's Classroom Resources and the Student Workbook that reinforce chapter content.
- **Real-Life Situations.** Information about current trends and high-interest topics.
- **Emphasize.** Important facts or concepts that need to be stressed to students.
- **Did You Know?** Interesting information that enhances the subject matter.
- **More About...** In-depth information to support the chapter content.
- **Focus On...** Activities and additional background information.
- **Cross Reference.** Reference to other chapters and features within the text.

Teacher's Manual

The bound-in Teacher's Manual section of the Teacher's Wraparound Edition includes an overview of the five components that make up the *Creative Living* program, suggestions for teaching the program, and a Scope and Sequence Chart.

Teacher's Classroom Resources

The third component of the *Creative Living* program is the Teacher's Classroom Resources box. The TCR includes several booklets containing reproducible masters, activities, tests, answer keys, and more. Most of these supplementary materials are designed to be reproduced for classroom use. The materials include:

- **Resources.** A list of reference books, software, and audiovisual materials for each unit can be used to augment classroom experiences.
- **Bulletin Board Ideas.** Suggestions for bulletin board displays, many with illustrations, sum up the themes of each unit.
- **Life Skills Activities.** These activities are designed to encourage higher level thinking skills. They include group work and teacher involvement. The activities fall into three categories:

  Acting Responsibly
  Thinking Critically
  Managing Your Life

- **Extension Activities.** These reproducible activities provide supplementary information that goes beyond the text.
- **Reproducible Masters.** These masters summarize and reinforce main ideas graphically.
- **Cooperative Learning Activities.** These activities are designed to encourage students to work together as a team. Students work in pairs or small groups to complete activities.
- **Foods Lab Activities.** These reproducible activities are divided into two parts.
  Food Preparation Activities give students the opportunity to practice specific cooking skills described in the chapters.
  Meal Management Projects provide menus for entire meals, along with selected recipes.
- **Clothing Lab Activities.** A similar format to the foods activities is used for the sewing activities.
  Sewing Handbook provides hands-on experience in making darts, sewing fasteners, and other construction methods. A special section focuses on techniques for using a serger.
  Sewing Projects include patterns and directions for a variety of interesting projects that utilize various skills. Two serger projects are also included.
- **Chapter Tests.** A reproducible objective test is included for every chapter. Answers are listed in the Answer Key booklet.
- **Unit Tests.** A unit test in reproducible format is given for each unit.
- **Answer Key.** This booklet contains the answers for all Chapter Tests, Unit Tests, and Life Skills Activity Sheets, as well as the Study Guides and Worksheets found in the Student Workbook.
- **Color Transparencies.** A set of 44 full-color transparencies are included, along with discussion questions and suggestions for using each transparency.

The Student Workbook

A separate workbook accompanies the *Creative Living* program. It contains study guides and worksheets for each chapter. The pages are perforated for easy removal.

- **Study Guides.** Fill-in and short answer questions help students review each chapter. Answers appear in the Answer Key booklet in the Teacher's Classroom Resources.
- **Worksheets.** The purpose of these activities is to reinforce chapter content. Designed as paper and pencil activities, they are suitable for homework assignments or individual in-class work. Answers are included in the Teacher's Classroom Resources.

The Testmaker

The *Creative Living* Testmaker is a software package that allows you to construct tests, quizzes, and review sheets. The program contains hundreds of objective questions, and you may also add questions of your own making to the test bank. At your direction, the program will create multiple versions of the same test, and also print an answer key. The Testmaker is flexible and easy to use.

Effective Teaching

Comprehensive home economics can be an exciting and dynamic course to teach. The subject matter is relevant to everyone—as students, teachers, family members, friends, consumers, workers, and citizens, each of us is touched by elements of the home economics curriculum every day.

As an experienced teacher or a new teacher, you will already have ideas and plans for teaching with *Creative Living*. Hopefully, many of the suggestions presented in the Teacher's Wraparound Edition and the Teacher's Classroom Resources will help you develop content and strategies that will be motivating and effective in the classroom. Here are some additional suggestions for using the teaching materials.

Curriculum Applications

The *Creative Living* program can be used for both one-semester and full-year courses. The short chapters provide flexibility in selecting the content that must be covered in the course. The wealth of support materials enables you to develop lesson plans that will best meet the individual needs of your students.

Adapting the Course to Slow and Fast Learners

Just as in any other course, home economics students will demonstrate wide differences in abilities and interests. Providing for individual differences is one of the more difficult and challenging tasks in teaching. While the task of adapting the course to individual needs probably will never be totally accomplished, the following suggestions will prove to be helpful:

- Because the content in *Creative Living* is so varied, all students will find topics in which they have keen interest. Be alert to such interest and capitalize on it by giving every student the opportunity to enter into the discussion, prepare activities, and participate in other ways.
- Vary your teaching methods. Not all students learn in the same way. Some learn readily through reading. Others learn best through problem solving, listening to lectures, observing demonstrations, assembling projects, participating in discussions, or completing workbook exercises.
- End-of-chapter activities are varied in both type of activity and level of difficulty. Certain questions might be assigned to committees of two or three students working together. Others could be assigned to individual students as extra credit.
- Reinforcement and enrichment activities located in the Lesson Plans for each chapter offer specific activities for both slow and fast learners.

Emphasis on Basic Skills

A good foundation in basic skills is considered essential for successful participation in today's society. Therefore, the basic skills represent a critical area of learning that needs to be addressed in all areas of education. Because the comprehensive home economics curriculum is very activity- and discussion-oriented, it is particularly suited for reinforcing and practicing the knowledge and skills your students need to acquire.

This edition of *Creative Living* integrates home economics concepts with learning experiences that spotlight basic skills in reading, writing, math, science, and communicating. Special logos are used to identify basic skills activities in the Chapter Review section, Applying Your Skills. Basic skills activities are also identified in the Lesson Plans of the Teacher's Wraparound Edition.

Here are some additional strategies for incorporating basic skills instruction into the home economics classroom:

Reading

- Students get more out of a reading assignment when the lesson is preceded with background information and followed with discussion.
- A key to promoting independent reading is to make books and other resources easily available in a classroom library.

Writing

- The most effective way to develop writing skills is to present writing assignments as a process of brainstorming, composing, revising, and editing.
- Students learn to write well through frequent practice. A well-structured assignment has a meaningful topic and a clear sense of purpose.
- Good writing assignments are often an extension of class reading, discussion, and activities—not isolated exercises.
- Prompt teacher feedback is important for written assignments.

Mathematics

- A good way to teach mathematics is to build on students' informal knowledge.
- Students learn mathematics more effectively when they use real physical objects as aids in their lessons.
- Take time to teach the skill of estimating answers. When students can make good estimates of the answer to a math problem, it shows they understand the problem.

Science

- Students learn science best when they are able to conduct experiments and witness "science in action."
- Reading about scientific principles or having a teacher explain them is frequently not enough for understanding. Causes and effects are not always obvious, and it may take an experiment to dramatize the principles.
- Scientific explanations sometimes conflict with the way students may suppose that things happen or work. To clear up misconceptions, students need the chance to predict the results of an experiment. The teacher can then explain why the original intuitive hypothesis was faulty. In this way experiments help students use the scientific method to distinguish facts from opinions and misconceptions.

Communicating

- Students can practice their communication skills by participating in small group discussions and by presenting oral reports.
- Conversation is important. A good foundation in speaking and listening skills helps students in all areas of learning.
- Teachers can play a significant role in improving students' communication skills by encouraging students to use these skills in class.

Emphasis on Critical Thinking

Critical thinking skills are encouraged through questions and hands-on activities. Questioning has always been one of teaching's most common and most effective techniques. However, questions take different forms and place different demands on students. Some questions require only factual recall; others provoke analysis. Questions meant to elicit facts are important in that students need basic information to engage in higher-level thinking processes and discussions. Such questions also promote classroom participation and provide students with opportunities to achieve a high success rate in answering questions correctly.

Critical thinking activities are identified in the Lesson Plans in the Teacher's Wraparound Edition and in the Life Skills Activities and in the Teacher's Classroom Resources.

Critical Thinking Skills Activities

- The difference between factual and thought-provoking questions is the difference between asking "What type of nutrient is found in starch?" and "Why is it important for you to know about the nutrients in food?" Each question has its purpose, but the second one intends for the students to analyze how the information affects them.
- Students learn more when the teachers ask questions that require students to apply, analyze, synthesize, and evaluate information in addition to recalling facts.
- Students' answers often improve when teachers pause for a response, giving students more time to think.

Life Skills Activities

- Questioning techniques can be reinforced with activities to give students the opportunity to practice higher-level thinking skills.

- Activities performed in small groups often encourage creative solutions to real-life problems.

Emphasis on Study Skills

The ways in which students study strongly influence how much they learn. Research has identified several study skills that students can learn how to use. Low-ability students may need to be taught when, as well as how, to use these skills. Teachers can often help students develop better study skills through vocabulary development, study guides, and review questions and activities.

Using Vocabulary Words

- To help students learn the Words to Remember for each chapter, give vocabulary quizzes.
- Teach students how to use the Glossary at the end of the student text. This will help them clarify terms when studying.
- The Student Workbook contains worksheets with vocabulary exercises that help to reinforce the meaning and usage of unfamiliar terms.

Using Study Guides

- Students tutoring other students can lead to improved achievement for both, and to positive attitudes toward coursework.
- Students should space learning sessions on a topic over a period of time, rather than cramming just before a test.
- Students should identify the main idea in new information, connect new material to what they already know, and draw inferences about its significance.
- Students should evaluate their own work using such categories as "What I already know," "What I now know," and "What I am confused about," to help improve their performance and independence.

Using Chapter Review Questions

- Answering recall questions can help students absorb and retain the factual information on which understanding and critical thought are based.
- Review questions are appropriate for homework assignments.
- Homework is most useful when teachers carefully prepare the assignment, thoroughly explain it, and give prompt feedback when the work is completed.
- Well-designed homework assignments relate directly to classwork and extend students' learning beyond the classroom.

Emphasis on Career Exploration

Career exploration is an important part of many comprehensive home economics curriculums. Six chapters in the *Creative Living* text focus on careers in the major areas of home economics. Each of these chapters begins with a discussion of the interests and skills needed for careers in the area. Then each explores various careers at three levels: entry-level jobs, jobs requiring some training, and jobs requiring an advanced degree.

In the future, American workers will need to be able to master new technologies and upgrade their skills to meet specialized job demands. Most important, they will need to demonstrate personal qualities, such as reliability, self-discipline, perseverance, and the ability to work well with others. Teachers can emphasize these important personal characteristics, which will be needed by students who go on to college as well as those who directly enter the world of work.

Integrating FHA/Hero Activities

FHA/Hero activities are an important component of many home economics programs. Suggestions for FHA activities are listed in the Teacher's Wraparound Edition on the opening pages of each of the seven units.

These activities relate to curriculum learning and can be done during the school day, after school, at night, or on the weekends. The FHA adviser training manual offers suggestions for developing co-curricular chapter activities. Additional resources are available from Future Homemakers of America, Inc.

We welcome comments from teachers and students on this and other Glencoe home economics publications. Address your letters to:

Director of Home Economics
GLENCOE DIVISION
Macmillan/McGraw Hill
3008 W. Willow Knolls Drive
Peoria, IL 61614-1083

Scope and Sequence—Unit 1/Focus on You

Topic	Chapter	
Personal Development	1 You As An Individual 2 The Teen Years 3 Your Health and Wellness 4 Examining Your Goals	Teen Tips 1, 3
Citizenship Leadership/ Entrepreneurship	5 Making Decisions	
Decision Making/ Life Management	2 The Teen Years 4 Examining Your Goals 5 Making Decisions 6 Managing Your Life	Teen Tips 1
Relating to Others	1 You As An Individual	
Communication	1 You As An Individual	Teen Tips 1
Health, Safety, and Nutrition	1 You As An Individual 3 Your Health and Wellness	Teen Tips 2
Consumer Skills		
Managing Resources	4 Examining Your Goals 5 Making Decisions 6 Managing Your Life	
Technology	4 Examining Your Goals	
Skill Development	4 Examining Your Goals 5 Making Decisions 6 Managing Your Life	
Career Exploration		

Scope and Sequence—Unit 2/Your Family and Friends

Topic	Chapter	
Personal Development	7 Relationships and You 13 Friendships 15 Decisions in Relationships 16 Your Future Relationships	Teen Tips 1, 2
Citizenship/ Leadership/ Entrepreneurship	7 Relationships and You 15 Decisions in Relationships 16 Your Future Relationships	Teen Tips 2, 3
Decision Making/ Life Management	12 Adjusting to Family Changes 15 Decisions in Relationships 16 Your Future Relationships	Teen Tips 1, 2, 3
Relating to Others	7 Relationships and You 9 Improving Relationship Skills 10 Understanding Families 11 Strengthening Families 12 Adjusting to Family Changes	13 Friendships 14 Special Relationships 15 Decisions in Relationships Teen Tips 2, 3
Communication	7 Relationships and You 8 Communication Skills 9 Improving Relationship Skills 10 Understanding Families 11 Strengthening Families	13 Friendships 14 Special Relationships 15 Decisions in Relationships 16 Your Future Relationships Teen Tips 2
Health, Safety, and Nutrition	12 Adjusting to Family Changes	Teen Tips 1, 2, 3
Consumer Skills		
Managing Resources	10 Understanding Families 11 Strengthening Families 13 Friendships 17 Careers in Working with People	
Technology	8 Communication Skills 16 Your Future Relationships	
Skill Development	8 Communication Skills 17 Careers in Working with People	
Career Exploration	17 Careers in Working with People	

TM 12

Scope and Sequence—Unit 3/Child Care Development

Topic	Chapter	
Personal Development	23 Ready for Parenthood?	
Citizenship/ Leadership/ Entrepreneurship	22 Babysitting: Earning and Learning 24 Careers Helping Children	
Decision Making/ Life Management	18 Children and You 20 The Importance of Play 23 Ready for Parenthood?	
Relating to Others	18 Children and You 19 Ages and Stages 20 The Importance of Play 24 Careers Helping Children	Teen Tips 1, 2, 3
Communication	19 Ages and Stages 21 Care and Safety	Teen Tips 1
Health, Safety, and Nutrition	18 Children and You 20 The Importance of Play 21 Care and Safety 22 Babysitting: Earning and Learning 23 Ready for Parenthood?	Teen Tips 1, 2
Consumer Skills		
Managing Resources	18 Children and You 22 Babysitting: Earning and Learning	
Technology		
Skill Development	18 Children and You 20 The Importance of Play 24 Careers Helping Children	Teen Tips 1, 2, 3
Career Exploration	18 Children and You 22 Babysitting: Earning and Learning 24 Careers Helping Children	

Scope and Sequence—Unit 4/Management

Topic	Chapter	
Personal Development	25 Managing Resources	Teen Tips 2
Citizenship/ Leadership/ Entrepreneurship	32 Voicing Your Opinion 33 Being a Responsible Consumer 34 Management and Consumer Careers	Teen Tips 1
Decision Making/ Life Management	25 Managing Resources 26 Managing Time 27 Managing Money 28 Saving and Borrowing	30 Consumer Skills 31 Price and Quality Teen Tips 1, 2, 3
Relating to Others	32 Voicing Your Opinion 33 Being a Responsible Consumer	
Communication	32 Voicing Your Opinion 33 Being a Responsible Consumer	
Health, Safety, and Nutrition	26 Managing Time 29 Advertising 33 Being a Responsible Consumer	
Consumer Skills	28 Saving and Borrowing 29 Advertising 30 Consumer Skills 31 Price and Quality	32 Voicing Your Opinion 33 Being a Responsible Consumer
Managing Resources	25 Managing Resources 26 Managing Time 27 Managing Money 28 Saving and Borrowing 31 Price and Quality	32 Voicing Your Opinion 34 Management and Consumer Careers Teen Tips 1, 2, 3
Technology	27 Managing Money 30 Consumer Skills	Teen Tips 3
Skill Development	26 Managing Time 27 Managing Money 28 Saving and Borrowing 31 Price and Quality	Teen Tips 3
Career Exploration	34 Management and Consumer Careers	Teen Tips 1

Scope and Sequence—Unit 5/Foods and Nutrition

Topic	Chapter	
Personal Development	35 Health and Fitness 53 Serving Meals and Eating Out	
Citizenship/ Leadership/ Entrepreneurship	54 Careers in Food and Nutrition	
Decision Making/ Life Management	35 Health and Fitness 37 Food Groups 38 Healthy Eating Habits 40 Planning Meals	44 Getting Ready to Cook
Relating to Others	44 Getting Ready to Cook 47 Cooking Techniques 53 Serving Meals and Eating Out 54 Careers in Food and Nutrition	
Communication	53 Serving Meals and Eating Out	
Health, Safety, and Nutrition	35 Health and Fitness 36 Nutrients 37 Food Groups 38 Healthy Eating Habits 39 Weight Control 40 Planning Meals 43 Safety and Sanitation 46 Preparation Skills	48 Microwave Cooking 49 Breads and Cereals 50 Fruits and Vegetables 51 Milk, Yogurt, and Cheese 52 Meats-to-Beans 53 Serving Meals and Eating Out Teen Tips 1, 2, 3
Consumer Skills	38 Healthy Eating Habits 39 Weight Control 41 Shopping for Food	Teen Tips 3
Managing Resources	37 Food Groups 39 Weight Control 40 Planning Meals 41 Shopping for Food 42 Kitchen Know-How 44 Getting Ready to Cook 45 Measuring Basics	46 Preparation Skills 49 Breads and Cereals 50 Fruits and Vegetables 51 Milk, Yogurt, and Cheese 52 Meats-to-Beans Teen Tips 1
Technology	40 Planning Meals 41 Shopping for Food 42 Kitchen Know-How	48 Microwave Cooking 50 Fruits and Vegetables
Skill Development	36 Nutrients 40 Planning Meals 41 Shopping for Food 42 Kitchen Know-How 43 Safety and Sanitation 44 Getting Ready to Cook 45 Measuring Basics	46 Preparation Skills 47 Cooking Techniques 48 Microwave Cooking 49 Breads and Cereals 50 Fruits and Vegetables 51 Milk, Yogurt, and Cheese 52 Meats-to-Beans
Career Exploration	54 Careers in Food and Nutrition	

Scope and Sequence—Unit 6/Clothing and Textiles

Topic	Chapter	
Personal Development	55 Clothing and You	Teen Tips 1, 2
Citizenship/ Leadership/ Entrepreneurship	57 Clothes and Fashion 68 Careers in Clothing and Textiles	Teen Tips 2
Decision Making/ Life Management	55 Clothing and You 57 Clothes and Fashion 59 Planning Your Wardrobe 60 Shopping for Clothes	Teen Tips 3
Relating to Others	55 Clothing and You 56 Design and Your Appearance 65 Adding the Details 68 Careers in Clothing and Textiles	
Communication	55 Clothing and You 56 Design and Your Appearance	
Health, Safety, and Nutrition	55 Clothing and You 57 Clothes and Fashion 63 Lay Out, Cut, and Mark 66 Clothes Care	
Consumer Skills	57 Clothes and Fashion 60 Shopping for Clothes	Teen Tips 3
Managing Resources	56 Design and Your Appearance 59 Planning Your Wardrobe 60 Shopping for Clothes 61 Selecting Patterns, Fabrics, and Notions	67 Redesigning and Recycling Teen Tips 3
Technology	58 Fibers and Fabrics 62 Sewing Equipment 64 Basic Construction	66 Clothes Care
Skill Development	56 Design and Your Appearance 58 Fibers and Fabrics 60 Shopping for Clothes 61 Selecting Patterns, Fabrics, and Notions 62 Sewing Equipment 63 Layout, Cut, and Mark	64 Basic Construction 65 Adding the Details 66 Clothes Care 67 Redesigning and Recycling Teen Tips 2
Career Exploration	68 Careers in Clothing and Textiles	

Scope and Sequence—Unit 7/Housing and Living Space

Topic	Chapter	
Personal Development	69 Living Space and You	Teen Tips 1
Citizenship/ Leadership/ Entrepreneurship	75 Careers in Housing	
Decision Making/ Life Management	69 Living Space and You 72 Caring for Living Space	Teen Tips, 1, 2
Relating to Others	69 Living Space and You 72 Caring for Living Space 75 Careers in Housing	
Communication	69 Living Space and You 71 Designing Your Space 75 Careers in Housing	Teen Tips 1
Health, Safety, and Nutrition	72 Caring for Living Space 73 Safety in the Home	
Consumer Skills	69 Living Space and You	
Managing Resources	69 Living Space and You 70 How to Organize Your Space 71 Designing Your Space 72 Caring for Living Space	74 Managing Energy Costs Teen Tips 2, 3
Technology	71 Designing Your Space 74 Managing Energy Costs	
Skill Development	70 How to Organize Your Space 71 Designing Your Space 72 Caring for Living Space 73 Safety in the Home	74 Managing Energy Costs Teen Tips 1, 3
Career Exploration	75 Careers in Housing	

Fifth Edition

CREATIVE LIVING

Basic Concepts in Home Economics

TEACHER'S WRAPAROUND EDITION

Reviewers

Joyce Armstrong, C.H.E.
Home Economics Teacher
W. W. Samuell High School
Dallas, Texas

Marie S. Bell, C.H.E.
Consumer and Homemaking Teacher
Columbia High School
Columbia, South Carolina

Mary G. Blevins
Home Economics Instructor
Mifflin High School
Columbus, Ohio

Linda L. Dannison, Ph.D., C.H.E.
Teacher Educator
Western Michigan University
Kalamazoo, Michigan

Doris H. DeSarro, C.H.E.
Home Economics Teacher
Plaza Junior High School
Virginia Beach, VA

Ruth Felty
Vocational Supervisor
Northside Independent School District
San Antonio, TX

Joan M. Fredeen, C.H.E.
Living Skills Teacher
Armstrong Senior High School
Plymouth, Minnesota

Eva Mae Lloyd
Home Economics Department Chairperson
Ballard High School
Louisville, Kentucky

Vicki A. Risinger, C.H.E.
National Future Homemakers of America Consultant
James Rumsey Vocational Technical Center
Martinsburg, West Virginia

Linda G. Smock, C.H.E.
Supervisor of Home Economics
Pinellas County Schools
Largo, Florida

Judy G. Theriot, Ph.D., C.H.E.
Teacher Educator
Nicholls State University
Thibodaux, Louisiana

Areatha Wells, C.H.E.
Coordinator, Family and Consumer Education
Racine Unified School District
Racine, Wisconsin

Fifth Edition

CREATIVE LIVING

Basic Concepts in Home Economics

Consulting Authors

Josephine A. Foster, Ph.D.
Assistant Superintendent
Alexander County Schools
Taylorsville, North Carolina

M. Janice Hogan, Ph.D.
Head, Family Social Science Department
University of Minnesota
St. Paul, Minnesota

Bettie M. Herring, Ph.D.
Director of Vocational and Adult Education
Fort Worth Independent School District
Fort Worth, Texas

Audrey G. Gieseking-Williams, Ph.D.
Former Chair, Department of Home Economics
California State University, Los Angeles

GLENCOE

Macmillan/McGraw-Hill

New York, New York
Columbus, Ohio
Mission Hills, California
Peoria, Illinois

TEACHER'S WRAPAROUND EDITION

Send all inquiries to:
GLENCOE DIVISION
Macmillan/McGraw-Hill
3008 W. Willow Knolls Drive
Peoria, IL 61614-1083

ISBN 0-02-675646-3 (Student's Edition)
ISBN 0-02-675647-1 (Teacher's Wraparound Edition)

Printed in the United States of America.

1 2 3 4 5 6 7 8 9 VHJ 99 98 97 96 95 94 93

Co-developed by
Glencoe Division of Macmillan/McGraw-Hill and
Visual Education Corporation,
Princeton, New Jersey

Contents

CLASS O
IS SO FINE,

FOOTBALL
MUMS

BUTTERICK 3082
VERY EASY / TRES FACILE
POLYESTER

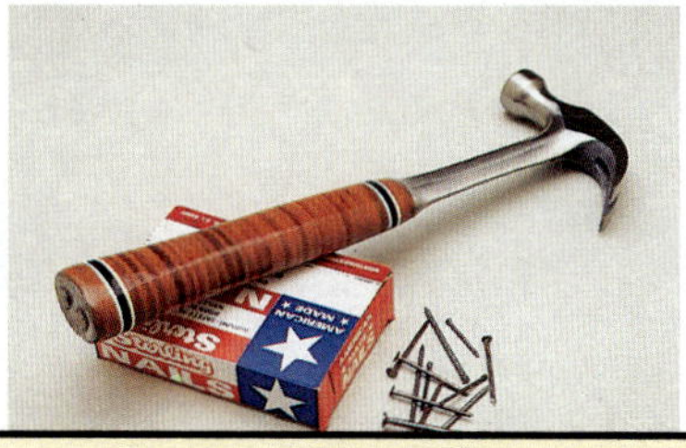

UNIT PREVIEW

Unit 1 helps students understand and accept themselves. It explores personal development and explains the benefits of establishing a realistic self-concept. The importance of high self-esteem and means of attaining it are highlighted. Decisions that affect a person's physical, mental, emotional, and social health are presented. Students learn how to use the decision-making process to set goals, evaluate resources, and make choices between conflicting goals. The management process is presented as a technique to help students plan, organize and accomplish their goals.

CONTENT DEVELOPMENT

Use these lessons to reinforce the following themes:

Content Strands	Chapters
Citizenship/ Leadership	5
Communication	1,(TT 1)
Decision Making	2,4,5,6
Health and Safety	1,3,(TT 2)
Managing Resources	4,5,6
Personal Development	1,2,3,4(TT 1,3)
Technology	4

UNIT MOTIVATORS

Decision-Making Skills

Evaluating Decisions Ask students to identify the last major decision they made. Ask: "Were you happy with your decision? What would you do differently the next time?" After students have shared their personal vignettes, explain that this unit will outline the steps of the decision-making process.

Critical Thinking Skills

Setting Goals On separate strips of paper have students list ten items (*goals*) they wish to accomplish. Have them arrange the slips of paper in the sequence in which they would like to achieve the items. Tell them that this unit will help them set and prioritize goals.

Unit One

CROSS-CURRICULAR ACTIVITY

Geography and You Post a world map on the bulletin board. Give students a paper banner and pushpin for each town where they have lived. Have them write their names on the banners and secure them to the appropriate locations on the map. Discuss how different locations have influenced their lives.

SPECIAL NEEDS

Strategies for LEP Students Have students bring to class an object or objects they associate with a favorite pastime or hobby such as a skateboard or stamp collection. Divide students into pairs and have partners tell each other about the objects. Point out how hobbies help people feel good about themselves.

FOCUS ON YOU

UNIT ONE

Focus on You

FHA ACTIVITIES

The following activities can be used with your FHA group or as public relation strategies:

Getting Acquainted Have large pieces of paper or poster board around the room with an incomplete statement at the top of each. Allow students 15 minutes to move freely around the room and complete each statement. Statements could include:

- Some things I like best are . . .
- My idea of a perfect person is . . .
- One thing I am afraid of is . . .

Discuss answers.

Building Self-Esteem Have students work in groups and develop a pamphlet on ways to develop self-esteem. Have each group make a presentation to the class and then share information with other classes.

I'm Only One Person Reproduce the handout "I'm Only One Person" (available from National Future Homemakers of America). Have students discuss how one person can make a difference in another person's life. Brainstorm ways to enhance self-concept.

UNIT CLOSURE

For Review

"**I'm Glad to Be Me**" Have students design their own "I'm Glad to Be Me" banners using fringed burlap or some other material. On their banners, encourage students to hang ribbons or awards they have won, tags showing hobbies they enjoy, and anything else that will help them feel good about themselves. Encourage them to hang their banners in their rooms at home.

For Evaluation

Unit Test Have students complete the Unit Test that appears in the *Teacher's Classroom Resources.*

Testmaker Software You may wish to design a unit test using the Testmaker software program.

COOPERATIVE LEARNING

Group Biography Divide students into several small groups. Tell groups they are to develop a biography that will include information about each group member. The biography may be in the form of an oral report to the class or a written report for the class to read. Groups might choose to use pictures or photographs to tell their group's story. Students will need to decide what information they want to include. Information should be divided into chapters such as "Our Childhood," "Our Likes and Dislikes," or "Our Plans for the Future." Each student might be responsible for a chapter and interview other group members for the appropriate information.

CHAPTER OVERVIEW

Chapter 1 focuses on the uniqueness of the individual. It explores the way that a person's characteristics as well as a person's actions set him or her apart. The chapter defines personality and the various influences on it, ending with a discussion of self-concept: what it is, how it develops, and why a realistic self-concept is important. Throughout the chapter the emphasis is on understanding and accepting oneself.

INTRODUCING THE CHAPTER

Motivators

Who Am I? Ask students to brainstorm words that describe ways in which people differ from one another, such as *tall, quiet, funny, friendly,* and *intelligent.* Ask students to choose five words that they think describe themselves. Without having students share their lists, ask whether they think that any two lists in the class are exactly the same.

Using the Photograph Have students study the photograph on this page. Then ask: "What makes this girl a unique individual? What characteristics do you think she has that set her apart from other people?"

Alike and Different Explain that although one person may be like someone else in many ways, there are always important ways in which that person is different. Encourage students to share a way in which they are like someone else and several ways in which they are different, helping them to see that no one is just like them.

Introducing the Objectives

Discuss the chapter objectives on this page. Remind students that the objectives focus on important content within the chapter.

Introducing Vocabulary

Write the terms *personality* and *self-concept* on the board. Point out that there may be a difference between the way people are (personality) and the way people see themselves (self-concept).

CHAPTER

1

You as an Individual

OBJECTIVES

This chapter will help you to:

- Explain how different characteristics combine to make each person unique.
- Describe the influence of emotions and attitudes on personality.
- Define self-concept and discuss the importance of developing a realistic self-concept.

WORDS TO REMEMBER

attitude
characteristic
environment
heredity
personality
self-concept

Chapter Resources

Teacher's Classroom Resources
- Lesson Plan
- Life Skills Activity, *Actions Speak Louder Than Words*
- Reproducible Master, *Your Unique Characteristics*
- Extension Activity, *Developing a Realistic Self-Concept*
- Chapter Test

Student Workbook
- Study Guide
- Worksheet, *Developing a Super Self-Concept*

William and Daniel are identical twins. Most people cannot tell them apart at first. Both boys are tall and slim, with brown eyes and dark curly hair. In personality, however, they are quite different, and their friends have no difficulty telling the twins apart. William is quiet and shy. He has a few close friends, but spends a lot of time alone in his room listening to music. Daniel, on the other hand, is rarely alone. He is outgoing and energetic and spends a lot of time participating in after-school activities.

You might expect that identical twins would have similar personalities as well as similar looks. After all, they have usually been brought up in the same home by the same parents. However, even twins are like the rest of us in one important respect: each is a unique individual with a personality unlike that of any other individual.

Unless you are an identical twin, there is no one in the world who looks exactly like you. More importantly, whether you are a twin, an only child, or part of a large family, there is no one who feels, thinks, and acts exactly as you do.

You Are Unique

"He had dark, brooding eyes, and when he was with people he held himself apart from them, as if afraid to be drawn in by their friendliness."

"Her admirers knew her by what she did rather than by her appearance. She was average looking—medium height, medium weight, medium brown hair. What her friends admired her for were her actions, which were always kindnesses done without a hint of seeking any type of repayment."

When authors want to describe people for us, they write about **characteristics.** These are the special features or traits that distinguish one individual from another. Characteristics may relate to a person's appearance or actions. Looking at your characteristics will help you form a picture of yourself and help you see yourself as others see you.

Your Characteristics

No single word could be used to describe you—or any human being. Each person is a complex combination of characteristics. These characteristics—physical, emotional, mental, and social—combine to make you the unique person you are.

Look at any group of people and you will discover that each individual is unique, with his or her own personality.

TEACHING THE CHAPTER

For convenience, the teaching suggestions for this chapter are arranged according to the following lesson topics:

- "You Are Unique," pages 15-17
- "Your Personality," pages 17-18
- "Your Self-Concept," pages 18-19

Teaching "You Are Unique"
(Pages 15-17)

This section shows the ways in which different characteristics combine to make each person unique.

Checking Comprehension

✓ How can examining your own characteristics be helpful? *Examination can help you form a picture of yourself and help you see yourself as others see you.*

✓ List three examples of physical characteristics. *Examples include hair color, height, eye color, facial structure, skin tone, body type.*

✓ What is the difference between emotional and mental characteristics? *Emotional characteristics have to do with your feelings, and mental characteristics have to do with your abilities, attitudes, and interests.*

✓ How does a person demonstrate social characteristics? *Answers vary but may include: getting along with other people; acting shy; or being talkative and outgoing.*

✓ Why is it true that no one person's view of you tells the whole story? *Different people see you from different viewpoints, so each person notices something different about you.*

Emphasize No single characteristic determines how others see a person. An individual may be physically attracted to someone else partly because he or she is attracted to emotional, mental, or social characteristics as well. Sometimes teens focus on the physical to the exclusion of other traits.

Activities

Skill Builder: Reading
Ask students to read a short story and list as many of the characteristics of the main character as they can discover. They should divide the characteristics into the four categories in the chapter: physical, emotional, mental, and social.

Reteaching
To help students recognize that people have many different sides, choose a well-known public figure, perhaps an entertainer. Have students give characteristics that show different facets of the person.

Reteaching
Give each student an ink pad and have them place their thumbprint on an index card. Using the thumbprint, have them create something (a word, animal, picture) that describes their individual personality. Place completed index cards on a bulletin board entitled "I'm Thumbody Special." Discuss how no two people are alike, just as no two thumbprints are alike.

Enrichment
Have students look through a number of magazines and newspapers to try to discover what physical, emotional, mental, or social characteristics are currently being promoted. Ask students to discuss to what extent individuals ought to let ideas about looks, emotional expression, attitudes, or actions affect their own personality and characteristics.

People experience a wide range of emotions. What emotions do you think this girl is expressing in each situation?

- **Your body.** People notice your physical characteristics first. You might be tall or short, straight-haired or curly-haired, dark or fair. Perhaps you wear glasses or have a turned-up nose. Your physical features affect the way people see you. Most likely, you are pleased with some but may want to change others.
- **Your emotions.** Your emotional characteristics also affect the way people see you. Perhaps you are very even-tempered, or maybe you are easily upset. You may find that your emotions swing from feeling very happy one day to feeling quite low the next.
- **Your mind.** Your mental characteristics involve your abilities, attitudes, and interests. Perhaps you are good at thinking through math problems. Do you like watching baseball, or would you rather curl up with a good book? Almost everything you say or do tells people something about your mind.
- **Your relationships.** Your social characteristics include how you get along with other people. Are you quiet and shy or talkative and outgoing? Do you like to be with large groups of people or just one or two friends?

Your Actions

Your behavior with others also helps add to the picture of who you are. Are you a good listener? Do you prefer spending time with a group of people or with only one special friend? Do you like sharing with others? Are you the leader of a group? These are social characteristics that people notice; they, too, add to the picture of who you are.

People see the world from different viewpoints, so the people who know you will probably notice different characteristics in you. Your parents may notice your kindness to a younger sister or your willingness to help with household chores. Your teachers will know that you are good in some subjects and have trouble with others. Your friends may know that you like to tell jokes or that you are good at organizing activities.

More About Emotions Increased hormone levels are in part responsible for the strong and sometimes quickly changing emotions experienced during adolescence. Chapter 2 of the text discusses hormones in more detail.

Did You Know? The minds of teens are actually different from those of preteens. At about age twelve people gain the ability to think logically—to think systematically and abstractly. This allows greater problem-solving and decision-making skills.

Nobody's picture of you is complete. Your friends at school might not know that you enjoy singing, while your friends at choir are not aware that you hate sports. Everyone sees a different side of you. To fully appreciate yourself, you must realize that you are all of the people that others see, and more.

Your Personality

Your **personality** is the combination of characteristics and actions that makes you different from every other person. Nobody has the same personality as you. The great variety in human personalities results from the interactions of heredity and environment.

Your **heredity** involves the characteristics that you inherit from your parents and ancestors. It is your heredity that determines many of your physical characteristics, such as the color of your skin, hair, and eyes, and whether you are tall or short. Your heredity also determines many of your personality traits. The way you express emotions such as happiness or anger, for example, may be strongly influenced by your heredity.

The other major influence on personality is environment. Your **environment** is everything that surrounds you. It includes your family, friends, teachers, and the neighborhood and society in which you live. Ever since you were born, your environment has helped shape your emotions, attitudes and interests.

The members of this family have inherited similar physical characteristics.

Teaching "Your Personality"
(Pages 17-18)

This section explains the influences on personality and the way personality affects emotions and attitudes.

Checking Comprehension

✓ Explain how heredity and environment shape a person's personality. *A person inherits certain characteristics and personality traits from parents and ancestors. A person's environment, or everything that surrounds him or her, shapes both emotions and attitudes.*

✓ What is the difference between emotions and attitudes? *Emotions express the way a person feels, and attitudes reflect a person's thoughts and judgments about the world.*

Activities

Skill Builder: Writing
Write on the board the sentence "Each person feels and expresses emotions in different ways." Then ask students to write a paragraph to illustrate this point.

Skill Builder: Science
Ask students to go to the library and read several articles that discuss scientific studies of the influence of heredity and environment on personality. They should write several paragraphs that summarize the articles they read.

Focus on Decision Making Explain that understanding one's own characteristics will help a person make decisions that he or she will continue to be comfortable with.

More About Heredity Differing personality traits can be seen even in newborns, who have had no real chance to be influenced by their environments. Even in the hospital nursery some are rather calm; others are excitable. Some block out their environment; others make an attempt to explore it. Heredity must have something to do with these early predispositions.

Reteaching
Have students break into groups and develop collages that show individuals expressing different emotions in different ways. Discuss the various ways in which people express basic human emotions.

Enrichment
Have students find and report on news articles that show how a person's actions reflect his or her attitude. (Protesting the dumping of chemical wastes, for example, exhibits a concern for the environment.) Students should be able to identify the attitude exhibited.

Teaching "Your Self-Concept"
(Pages 18-19)

This section describes self-concept and the importance of developing a realistic self-concept.

Checking Comprehension

✓ What is your self-concept? *Your self-concept is your own view of yourself, including your various strengths and weaknesses.*

✓ Why is your self-concept important? *It influences the way you feel about yourself and the way others see you.*

✓ Why does a person's self-concept change? *Because throughout childhood, the teen years, and adulthood people change and develop many new qualities.*

✓ What problems do teens sometimes have in forming their self-concepts? *They sometimes feel different when they're with different people, or find themselves behaving a certain way with certain people.*

✓ Why should teens work to develop a realistic self-concept? *Because that will help them to see themselves clearly, to understand their weaknesses, and to continue developing their strengths.*

Emotions

Every living person experiences the same basic emotions, yet each person feels and expresses emotions in different ways. For example, to show happiness you might yell and jump up and down. Your friend, however, might simply smile and look pleased when she feels happy. A movie that brings tears to your eyes may seem to have little effect on your friend.

The emotions you experience are part of the one-of-a-kind you. Learning to recognize, accept, and express your emotions in socially responsible ways is an important part of growing up.

Attitudes

Closely linked to your emotions are your attitudes. Your **attitudes** reflect the thoughts and judgments you have about the world around you. It is this part of your personality that makes you approve of some people or issues, but disapprove of others.

Most people's attitudes begin to form when they are children. Perhaps, as a child, you learned from your family to place a high value on helping other people. Perhaps you were taught to be honest and polite at all times.

As you grow older, some of your attitudes may change. Others are likely to remain a basic part of your personality.

Your Self-Concept

When people react to you as a person, they are responding to the set of characteristics that makes up your personality. They do not see all of those characteristics: everyone sees different things about you.

Even you don't have a complete picture of yourself. True, you know things about yourself that nobody else knows. You know what makes you sad, the kinds of people you admire, your dreams for your future. Still, it's quite likely that other people see things about you that you've never noticed.

Many factors help shape your self-concept. Your family, friends, neighborhood, school, beliefs, past experiences, skills, and talents all influence your view of yourself.

Focus on Relationship Skills Point out that adolescence is often a time of testing the attitudes held by one's parents. Being fair and reasonable will help everyone involved in a disagreement get his or her point across.

Emphasize People continue to learn new things about themselves throughout their lives. When people become parents, for example, they often learn as much about themselves as they do about children. Point out that a continuing interest in developing themselves keeps many aging people functioning well.

The particular view that you have of yourself is your **self-concept.** Your self-concept includes your views about what you like and what you think you're good at. You may see yourself as an athlete, or a computer expert, or a good cook. Your self-concept also includes what you see as your weaknesses. Perhaps you are shy about expressing your opinions, or perhaps you lose your temper easily.

Your self-concept is important to you for a number of reasons. It has an enormous influence on the way you feel about yourself. It also affects the way others see you. For example, if you think of yourself as a cheerful person and if you greet people in a cheerful, friendly manner, others will also think of you as cheerful.

How Self-Concept Develops

You start forming your self-concept when you are very young. Perhaps your grandfather often commented on your warm smile or happy laugh. Maybe your mother praised you for running fast or for helping out around the home. Your sister may have teased you about your red hair and freckles. All of these comments helped build your self-concept.

As a teen, you know that some of your childhood characteristics are changing and that you are developing many new qualities. As a result, your self-concept is changing. The way you see yourself now is different from the way you viewed yourself a few years ago. There is still much to discover about yourself.

The Importance of Self-Concept

Your self-concept—your view of yourself—is your key to becoming the person you want to be. If you are realistic about yourself, you'll know who you are and how you want to act. You'll be able to focus on your good points and to find the confidence to improve the things you don't like about yourself.

Many teens find it hard to bring their view of themselves into focus. You might find, for example, that you feel different when you're with different people. You might behave a certain way when you're with your parents, yet you might feel that you're a completely different person when you're around your friends.

Uncertainties such as these are normal, but you need to resolve them. It's important that you build a realistic self-concept over the next few years. Being realistic about yourself will help you make the decisions about your life that are right for you.

A strong, positive self-concept will help you understand who you are and why you are important. It will help you make choices and decisions that affect your life.

Activities

Skill Builder: Writing
Ask students to write one or more paragraphs about an aspect of their self-concept that they feel has changed in the past several years or is in the process of changing. If necessary, provide one or more examples to get them started.

Reteaching
To help students understand the importance of self-concept, have them think of additional examples of ways that a person's self-concept can affect the ways others see that person. The examples can be positive, as in the text, or negative.

Enrichment
Ask students to go to three family members or close friends whom they can trust to be both honest and kind. The students should ask these people to write a sentence about the student's most positive characteristic or characteristics. The students themselves should also write such a sentence. Students should then study the various comments and discuss in class the similarities and differences in the ways they see themselves and the ways others see them. Ask them if they think the exercise has helped them toward a more realistic self-concept.

Focus on Life Management Suggest that students periodically take time to examine their self-concept and their views about themselves to be sure they are maintaining a realistic self-concept.

Real-Life Situations Emphasize that the family plays a major role in influencing and shaping one's self-concept. Ask students: "How can a negative influence, such as continued criticism or abuse, damage an individual's development? How could a child or teen in such an environment overcome this influence?"

Teaching the Feature
"Your Self-Concept"

Answers to Feature Questions

1. Some students may say that it is possible for a teen to have a realistic self-concept if one is honest with oneself and knows one's strengths and weaknesses. Others may argue that at a time when so much is changing, it is not possible to have a complete picture of oneself.

2. Answers will vary, but students should focus on the idea that a realistic self-concept enables a person to form good relationships with others and to make the most of his or her capabilities.

Activities

Gaining Self-Knowledge Ask the class to brainstorm experiences and activities that could help teens get to know themselves better. (If students need help getting started, you might suggest keeping a journal, spending some time alone each day, taking on a leadership position in an activity or a sport, and so on.) When you have written 10 to 15 on the board, stop and ask the class to explain more fully how each experience or activity would help clarify self-concept.

Community Contact Divide the class into groups of three or four, and ask each group to come up with a community activity that might reflect an area of self-concept. For example, someone who is a good listener might volunteer to help with a program that works with older people who may be lonely. The group should research exactly how to get involved in such a program and then present their findings to the class.

HEALTH WATCH

Your Self-Concept

It's one thing to know that you're unique, but quite another to figure out just who you are. Developing an objective picture of yourself—a realistic self-concept—takes some time and effort. Many teens feel confused about their identity. That confusion is natural when you consider all the changes you're going through and adjusting to. Such confusion can sometimes cause teens to focus on negative aspects of themselves. You may become overly conscious of your apparent failures and, in so doing, you may overlook some of your strong points.

Study the questions below. They may help you see some of your pluses, and help to put your picture of yourself in perspective.

- **Are you reliable?** Do you show up for team practices? When you tell a friend you'll visit, do you arrive on time? Can your parents rely on you to do chores?
- **Are you a good listener?** Even if you don't think you're good at making conversation, showing that you can listen, and that you care about what others have to say, is an asset that people will appreciate.
- **Are you polite?** Good manners help you get along with people of all ages and are a sign that you respect other people.
- **Are you cooperative?** Are you willing to lend a hand in activities such as the school play, local fund-raising efforts, or community events?
- **Do you show other people that you care?** Just as you need to know that other people care for you, the people in your life—especially your family and friends—appreciate your efforts to show interest in and concern for them.

Think It Through

1. **Do you think it is possible for a teen to have a realistic self-concept? Why or why not?**
2. **Why do you think it's important for people to be realistic about themselves?**

Did You Know? Being a good listener actually helps you to become a better conversationalist. If you listen well, you will know more and be able to talk about more subjects with knowledge and authority.

Emphasize Most of us tend to forget how important it is to tell those closest to us—whom we see everyday—how much we appreciate them. It is easy to take others for granted and assume that they know how we feel.

CHAPTER

1 REVIEW

Reviewing the Facts

1. What are characteristics?
2. What four types of characteristics does every person have?
3. What are the two main influences that shape a person's personality?
4. What is environment?
5. Explain what attitudes are.
6. How do people develop a self-concept?
7. Why is it important to have a realistic self-concept?

Thinking Critically

1. What are some ways in which young people can be taught to express their emotions in socially responsible ways?
2. How might you be able to help a friend develop a realistic self-concept?

Applying Your Skills

1. **Making a List of Characteristics.** List three of your positive characteristics in each of the following categories: your body, your emotions, your mind. Then choose two of the characteristics you have listed and write one way that you could use each to help someone else.

2. **Examining Your Interests.** Make a list of your ten major interests. For each interest, decide whether you think it was a result of heredity or environment. Then calculate what percentage of your interests is based on heredity and what percentage is based on environment.

3. **Analyzing Descriptions.** Read a weekly magazine that describes people and their lives. Keep track of the adjectives used to describe the personalities of the people featured. Are there some characteristics that appear more frequently than others? How important would you say these characteristics are in your own life? Are there characteristics that are important to you that are not included in the article?

Answers to "Reviewing the Facts"

1. Special features or traits that distinguish one person from another.
2. Physical, emotional, mental, and social.
3. Heredity and environment.
4. Everything that surrounds you, including family, friends, teachers, and the neighborhood and society in which you live.
5. Attitudes reflect the thoughts and judgments you have about the world.
6. Self-concept develops from how people are treated by others and what people think their strengths and weaknesses are.
7. A realistic self-concept allows you to refine your personality, improving your weak points and reinforcing your good points. It helps you make wise decisions about your life.

Answers to "Thinking Critically"

1. Young people may be influenced by seeing their parents, teachers, or other adults act responsibly. They may be instructed by their parents or teachers in what behavior is appropriate. Other people might respond negatively to inappropriate behavior and positively to appropriate behavior by young people.
2. Answers will vary. Possible answers include complimenting the friend for having done something nice or achieving something special. Constructive criticism—with suggestions for improvement—can be helpful also.

COMPLETING THE CHAPTER

Summary

- Many different physical, emotional, mental, and social characteristics combine to create each person's unique personality.
- Each individual's personality has an effect on how he or she expresses emotions as well as on his or her attitudes toward the world around him or her.
- A person's self-concept is his or her view of self. Having a realistic self-concept allows an individual to become the person he or she wants to become.

For Review

Objective Review Questions Have students complete the "Reviewing the Facts" section on this page.

Study Guide Have students complete the Study Guide from Chapter 1 of their *Student Workbook.*

For Evaluation

Classification Provide the following list of characteristics, and ask students to classify each characteristic as either physical (P), emotional (E), mental (M), or social (S): good at math *(M)*, blue eyes *(P)*, moody *(E)*, tall *(P)*, cries easily *(E)*, talkative *(S)*, red hair *(P)*, good writer *(M)*, undemonstrative *(E)*, well coordinated *(P)*, outgoing *(S)*.

Analysis Have students write a short essay about a character in a well-known book or popular movie. The student should analyze the self-concept of a main character in the book or movie, demonstrating an understanding of what self-concept is.

Chapter Test Have students complete the test for Chapter 1 that appears in the *Teacher's Classroom Resources.*

CHAPTER OVERVIEW

Chapter 2 examines the physical, emotional, mental, and social changes that occur during the teen years. These changes often have an effect on self-esteem, the focus of the second part of the chapter. This section examines the importance and attainment of high self-esteem. A discussion of management skills as they relate to the lives of teens closes the chapter.

INTRODUCING THE CHAPTER

Motivators

What's Going On? Ask students to think about television shows that feature teens as main characters. Then have students explain how these shows portray the concerns of adolescence. Ask students if they think these are realistic portrayals.

Using the Photograph Tell students to look at the photograph on this page. Then ask: "What are the people doing in this photograph? How does their activity affect their self-esteem? Why might management skills be important in their lives?"

The Lighter Side Have students relate some humorous situations that are directly related to being an adolescent. The situations might be from their own lives or from books and movies.

Introducing the Objectives

Discuss the chapter objectives on this page. Remind students that the objectives focus on important content within the chapter.

Introducing Vocabulary

Ask students to look over the list of vocabulary terms and to tell you which one they associate most strongly with the teen years. If they cannot imagine how some of them relate, tell them that this chapter will explain their significance.

CHAPTER

2

The Teen Years

OBJECTIVES

This chapter will help you to:

- Describe the physical, emotional, mental, and social changes that take place during the teen years.
- Explain how to build self-esteem.
- Explain why you need to develop management skills.

WORDS TO REMEMBER

adolescence
hormones
management
peer group
self-esteem

Chapter Resources

Teacher's Classroom Resources
Lesson Plan
Life Skills Activity, *How in Control Are You?*
Reproducible Master, *Physical Changes in Adolescence*
Extension Activity, *Coping with Change*
Chapter Test

Student Workbook
Study Guide
Worksheet, *Identify the Change*

The teen years are often described as the best time of life. Whether or not you agree may depend on the day you are asked. Some days seem terrific; others you would like to forget.

On the plus side, you have much more knowledge and experience now than you did when you were a child. You have acquired a storehouse of information and skills. You can solve difficult problems. You've learned how to get along with many different types of people.

Still, there are times when life seems to be a real struggle. You may do graceful dives, but then sometimes stumble over your own feet (always when someone is watching). Your skin breaks out the day your class pictures are to be taken. Your emotions sometimes seem to get out of control. When you finally understand algebra, it's time to take geometry.

This is the period of life called **adolescence,** when you grow from being a child to being an adult. It is a period marked by unfamiliar feelings and new experiences. It can be a confusing time, but all these changes and feelings are signs that you're growing up.

A Time of Growth

As the most important growth stage before adulthood itself, adolescence affects your physical, emotional, mental, and social characteristics.

Physical Changes

The first changes most teens are aware of are physical. You probably noticed that some of your classmates seemed to grow taller overnight. You're probably aware, too, that certain classmates have developed far more rapidly than others. The natural differences in rates of development can be difficult to cope with. No one wants to be the first or the last person to develop an adult figure. Some of the temporary "side effects" of adolescence can also be embarrassing. Acne or a squeaky voice may seem unbearable, but it helps to keep in mind that they will pass.

The physical changes that take place during adolescence are triggered by the release of substances in your body called **hormones**. Certain hormones enable you to reach adult height and to develop adult characteristics. Sometimes, swift changes in size cause you to feel awkward until you get used to your new body. As you grow taller, the proportion of fat and muscle in your body changes. Other changes are listed in the chart below.

Changes in Adolescence

- Girls' growth spurt begins between ages 10 and 13. (At ages 11 and 12, the average girl is taller than the average boy.)
- Boys' growth spurt begins between ages 12 and 15. (In adulthood, the average man is taller than the average woman.)
- You develop more muscles and curves.
- Your legs and arms grow longer.
- Your hands and feet grow bigger.
- Your hair darkens.
- Your voice lowers.
- Your nose and chin become more sharply defined.
- Your skin becomes oilier and you perspire more.
- Your lungs and stomach can hold more air and food.
- You develop sexual maturity.

Did You Know? Both boys and girls experience a growth spurt during adolescence. Girls, however, usually begin this before boys. Most girls experience the greatest growth between the ages of eleven and thirteen-and-a-half. Boys, on the average, do not experience theirs until at least age thirteen. However, because boys generally spend a longer time growing than girls, they are usually taller in adulthood.

TEACHING THE CHAPTER

For convenience, the teaching suggestions for this chapter are arranged according to the following lesson topics:

- "A Time of Growth," pages 23-25
- "A Time of Change," page 27
- "Your Self-Esteem," pages 27-29
- "Managing Your Life," page 30

Teaching "A Time of Growth"
(Pages 23-25)

This section describes the physical, emotional, mental, and social changes that take place during the teen years.

Checking Comprehension

✓ Why do teens grow at such different rates? *Because each person's hormones are released at different rates.*

✓ What emotional changes occur during adolescence? *Teens often feel emotions more intensely than before. They may discover new emotions. Emotions may change more abruptly.*

✓ How do new mental abilities affect the way you make decisions and plans? *You begin to think in more abstract terms. You are able to imagine the consequences of actions you may make and think about alternatives. You are also able to learn from your mistakes.*

✓ What is the difference between a teen's internal and external social changes? *Internal changes come from within the individual, like being drawn to the peer group. External changes are caused by other people, like the additional responsibilities parents and teachers give and expect.*

Activities

Skill Builder: Critical Thinking
Ask students to discuss in small groups the way their friendships have changed since childhood. Encourage them to analyze the reasons they have the friends they do, the depth of sharing in the relationships, and so on. Each group should then present its conclusions to the rest of the class.

Skill Builder: Critical Thinking
Refer students to the photo essay on page 24. Ask students to explain how each photograph represents the changes taking place in adolescence. Have students use magazines to find additional photographs that depict physical, emotional, mental, and social changes of adolescence.

Physical

Emotional

Mental

Social

Adolescence is a time of growth and development as you change from a child to an adult.

Real-Life Situations Although growth in adolescence is triggered by hormones, people's health habits strongly influence their physical development. Both nutrition and exercise affect weight, posture, hair, skin, and energy levels. Thus it is important to practice good health habits during adolescence, as well as throughout your life.

Emphasize Physical, intellectual, emotional, and social maturation does not occur simultaneously. Growth rates are different for every person.

Emotional Changes

The hormones released by your body also produce emotional changes. You may feel emotions such as happiness or sadness more intensely than ever before. You may discover new emotions as well. Perhaps you feel embarrassed if someone teases you, or confused by your attraction toward someone you barely know.

Chances are that your emotions now change more abruptly than they once did. One day you may feel lonely and want to be with friends. The next day, for no obvious reason, you find you want to be by yourself.

Emotional swings such as this usually stop once the levels of hormones in your body come into balance. Fortunately, the new richness of your emotions will last into your adult years.

Mental Changes

Your teen years are characterized by mental development, too. You begin to reason and to think in more abstract terms. You may begin to ask questions such as "Why is this true?" or "Why not do it this way?" You are ready to test new ideas and to think things through for yourself.

Your new mental abilities make it possible for you to make realistic plans. You're able to imagine the consequences of actions you may take, and to think about alternatives to those actions. Equally important, you are developing the ability to reflect on the results of your decisions and to learn from your mistakes.

Social Changes

When you compare a fourth grader with a ninth grader, it's easy to see that the two interact with others in very different ways. Adolescence marks a significant change in how individuals deal with their family and friends.

Some social changes are internal—they come from within the individual. By early adolescence you probably found yourself drawn to your **peer group**—people your own age. You wanted to spend more time with your friends. You might also have found that you felt awkward around teens of the other sex.

Some social changes are caused by other people. Your parents expect more of you because you are becoming an adult. They probably expect you to take more responsibility around the house. Your teachers also have higher expectations—they expect you to take more responsibility for your own learning. Sometimes these responsibilities may conflict with what you would like to do. Learning to manage and balance your obligations is an important part of growing up.

Adolescence is a time of self-discovery, as you assume more responsibility for your decisions and actions.

Reteaching
Have students work together in groups to display pictures, such as photos from home or magazine cuttings, that portray the changes discussed in this section from childhood to adolescence to adulthood. Pictures might show differences in size, maturity, types of social interaction, and so on.

Enrichment
Explain to students that a rite of passage is a social ceremony or an event that marks an adolescent's transition to adulthood. Assign groups of students the task of reading about different cultures' rites of passage. Each group should present in class information about a rite and theorize about how the rite helps people in that culture pass from childhood into adulthood. Ask if students think our culture has any rites of passage. If so, what are they? If not, can they think of appropriate ones?

Focus on Mental Changes The feature "Changes in Thinking" on page 26 tells more about the kinds of mental changes teens go through during adolescence.

Teaching the Feature
"Help Is Available"

Answers to Feature Questions

1. Teens can ask school counselors, friends, and parents for the names of places that can help. They can also look in the yellow pages under "Suicide Prevention Service," "Support Groups," "Counseling," "Social Service Organizations," and so on. Public libraries have brochures about services for teens.

2. Answers will vary, but students should urge their friend to talk to an adult who can help.

Activities

Making a Directory Have students compile a directory of resources that can help teens in your community. The directory should include telephone numbers, addresses, and a description of the help available. Students might post copies of their directory in the school (with the school's permission).

Writing a Letter Read one or more letters from teens printed in a newspaper or magazine column that specializes in advice to young people. Have students pretend to be the columnist and write a response to the teen. Then have students compare their responses with the actual response in the newspaper or magazine. Ask students to comment on this method of getting help for problems.

Discuss Ask students to describe the qualities of a good counselor. Point out that good listening skills, a nonjudgmental attitude, and an atmosphere of trust are fundamental to all counseling situations. Emphasize that students can demonstrate the qualities of a good counselor when talking with troubled friends.

Community Contact Invite a phone counselor from a teen hot line to talk with the class. Ask the person to describe his or her training and experiences. Also ask the person to comment on the types of calls to the hot line.

HEALTH WATCH

Help Is Available

Heather often feels depressed. She is taller than all the girls in her class, and she is unhappy with the way she looks. Last summer, her best friend moved away, and just recently her parents got divorced. Lately, she has been having trouble concentrating on her schoolwork, and her grades are starting to drop. Heather wants to talk to someone, but she feels like she has no one to turn to.

Many teens like Heather suffer through their problems alone. They may think no one will understand them, or they may be too ashamed to seek help. Worst of all, they may think that no one cares. Teens should know that no matter how serious the problem—alcohol or drug abuse, family violence, divorce, depression—help is always available. Here are some ways teens can get help:

- **Teen hot lines.** Many communities have special telephone numbers troubled teens can call. Specially trained phone counselors listen to problems and suggest ways of dealing with them.
- **Support groups.** Teens facing similar situations gather to share their experiences and feelings. By seeing that others their age have problems, teens feel less lonely and embarrassed.
- **Adult counselors.** School counselors, social workers, nurses, and teachers care about young people and want to help them. Ministers, priests, and rabbis also provide counseling. These professionals can put teens in touch with human services agencies.
- **Peer counselors.** Often teens feel more comfortable talking to people their own age. Many schools and religious groups provide training so that teens can counsel other teens.
- **Drop-in centers.** Community agencies often operate centers where teens can walk in for counseling or just hang out. Some hospitals sponsor health clinics for teens.
- **Books, magazine articles, pamphlets.** "Self-help" literature is readily available. Reading books and other materials geared toward teens can be a first step toward solving a problem.
- **Parents.** Most parents want to help their children through difficult times. Even if they are unable to solve the problem, they can locate appropriate agencies and counselors and provide emotional support.

Think It Through

1. **How can teens find out about hot lines, support groups, and clinics in their community?**
2. **What would you do if you thought a friend was severely depressed?**

More About Human Services A growing trend in many communities is school-based human services centers. These centers provide all the services that students and parents need—including services for troubled teens and their families. "One-stop shopping" for human services eliminates the confusion of dealing with separate agencies, programs, and professionals as well as the need to travel to distant and separate buildings.

Did You Know? Alcoholics Anonymous is perhaps the most widespread support group in the United States. There are thousands of AA chapters nationwide. Alateen is the support group for teens dealing with family members who abuse alcohol.

A Time of Change

Each person reacts to the changes that adolescence brings in different ways. Many teens move smoothly through this period in their lives. They enjoy using their new mental abilities to solve problems. They feel stimulated by the greater demands that are placed on them. They are excited by their closer relationships with their friends.

However, many teens find the adolescent years troublesome. Their changing physical appearance makes them feel self-conscious, and the emotional ups and downs may leave them feeling confused, even depressed.

Some of the self-consciousness that teens feel is actually a result of their mental growth. As your mind matures, you become capable of imagining what other people think. You may worry, unnecessarily, that other people are being critical of you. You may believe, for example, that other people find you unattractive, think that your clothes are old-fashioned, or that you laugh too loudly. You are often mistaken—maybe those people aren't thinking of you at all, or perhaps their thoughts are positive. This will become clearer to you as you become more experienced at "reading" other people.

Your increasing intellectual abilities can help you expand your relationships with your parents, teachers, and other adults. You'll notice, in your discussions with grown-ups, that they're beginning to treat you more as an equal and to respect your point of view. However, such discussions may also create tension or lead to misunderstandings. You may find yourself questioning your parents' ideas and causing conflict within your family.

It may help you to remember that you're not the only one who is experiencing change. Just as you must adjust to the changing you, so must those around you. It's not always easy for parents to decide how much freedom and responsibility to give their teen children during the years between childhood and adulthood.

Your Self-Esteem

When you look in the mirror, are you happy about the person you see there, or do you spend a lot of time wishing you could change some of your characteristics?

The way you feel about yourself is called your **self-esteem.** You can have high self-esteem, meaning that you have a favorable opinion of yourself, even though you are aware of some faults. You can also have low self-esteem, meaning that you don't like yourself very much. Self-esteem does not just concern your physical appearance, although the way you look certainly affects the way you feel about yourself. Rather, it concerns the whole you—your feelings about your body, your mind, your emotions, and your interactions with others.

Your self-esteem is closely linked to your self-concept—the view that you have of yourself. In Chapter 1, you learned that your self-concept might be realistic: you see yourself clearly and are aware of your strengths and weaknesses. It could also be unrealistic: you focus too heavily on your faults and overlook some of your good points. People suffering from low self-esteem often have an unrealistic self-concept.

Emphasize Although the negative aspects of adolescence are frequently emphasized, the teen years can also be an exciting time of expanding horizons. Teens should avoid looking for problems that may not exist.

Focus on Relationship Skills Encourage students to try to put themselves in their parents' place. With more mature intellectual abilities, students may be able to imagine what it is like to want a child to become independent but at the same time feel a great responsibility for the child's welfare. This may help them understand why their parents act the way they do.

Teaching "A Time of Change"
(Page 27)

This section explains some of the effects of the changes that occur during adolescence.

Checking Comprehension

✓ How can self-consciousness be a result of mental growth? *As your mind matures, you become capable of imagining what other people think. You may worry that they are thinking critically about you.*

✓ Name possible positive and negative results of increased intellectual abilities. *You are able to be more of an equal with adults and have your point of view respected. But there may also be conflict if you question your parents' ideas.*

Activities

Skill Builder: Writing
Ask students to write one or two paragraphs to their parent(s) to explain why they think they are entitled to greater responsibility and freedom. (These will not actually be shown to the parents unless the teens desire.) Ask students to be specific about at least three areas in which they think they themselves, or teens in general, should be given more freedom.

Reteaching
Divide the class into two teams. Have one team brainstorm to come up with a list of problems that teens often encounter. Then have the other team suggest positive, possibly humorous, ways of dealing with the problem.

Enrichment
Divide the class into four or more groups, and have each research an organization that deals with teens. Examples might include a peer counseling program, religious youth organization, and teen alcoholism group. Have students interview someone in the organization to find out what kinds of changes they see as most significant in the lives of teens and what basic principles they use to help teens.

Teaching "Your Self-Esteem"
(Pages 27-29)

This section explains the importance of self-esteem and how to build self-esteem.

Checking Comprehension

✓ Compare and contrast the characteristics of people with high self-esteem and people with low self-esteem. *People with high self-esteem have a favorable opinion of themselves, while being aware of their faults. People with low self-esteem usually do not feel good about themselves or their relationships with other people.*

✓ How can high self-esteem help you? *You will be more confident and more able to recognize others' positive feelings about you. You will also be less likely to be influenced to do things you do not really want to do.*

✓ What should you do when someone compliments you? *Accept it; do not belittle yourself or your accomplishment.*

✓ How can you focus on your strengths? *You can write them down to remind yourself of them.*

✓ How can accepting yourself as you are help you to improve faults? *If you spend less time criticizing yourself, you will have more time to work on self-improvement.*

✓ How can you learn from mistakes? *Rather than considering yourself a failure, figure out how to avoid such mistakes in the future.*

✓ How can helping others build your self-esteem? *You will realize that you can accomplish something and will better recognize your strengths.*

✓ How will managing your life successfully make you feel? *It will make you feel competent and good about yourself.*

People who have high self-esteem usually relate well to others.

Low self-esteem is a problem for many teens. They may feel concerned about their looks. They may be upset about conflicts with the people around them. They may be confused about new kinds of friendships and new emotions. All of these problems can cause them to think less of themselves.

If you suffer from low self-esteem, you are not alone. However, it is a problem that you should begin working on immediately. If you learn to feel good about yourself, you will be more confident that you can handle the things you want to do. You will be more able to see the positive feelings that people have toward you. You will also be less likely to be influenced by others to do things you would rather not do. For example, teens who use drugs are often suffering from low self-esteem. For these reasons, developing high self-esteem is an important task for the teenage years.

Building Your Self-Esteem

There are many things you can do to develop a more positive view of yourself. Here are some of them:

- **Learn to accept praise.** When someone compliments you, don't belittle yourself or your accomplishment. People praise you because they feel you really deserve it.
- **Focus on your strengths.** Everyone has talents. You might sew well, or play the piano, or be good at gymnastics. You might be a sensitive listener or a good organizer. Write down these strengths to remind yourself of the good things others have said about you.

Focus on Health Remind students of the idea of self-concept as introduced in Chapter 1, and point out that their self-esteem is closely linked to their self-concept. Stress to students that their self-concept, or how they see themselves, has much to do with how others see them. If people consider themselves worthless, it is harder for others to see their good points.

Cross-Reference See Teen Tips "Six Ways to Feel Good About Yourself," on pages 66-67.

- **Accept yourself as you are.** Accept the fact that you are not perfect and that you have some faults. After all, you accept your friends as they are. Why should you be any harder on yourself? If you spent less time criticizing yourself, you could spend more time trying to adjust characteristics that you think need improvement.
- **Learn from what you do.** Recognize and keep developing your strengths, and try to view your mistakes as learning experiences. When you make a mistake, don't label yourself a failure. Use the opportunity to figure out how you can avoid a similar mistake in the future.
- **Use your strengths to help others.** Becoming involved in activities that help others lets you know that you can accomplish something really important. It can also reinforce your strengths.
- **Take responsibility for your own life.** Learn how to deal with the different demands that are made of you. Managing your own life successfully will make you feel very competent and good about yourself.

You can raise your self-esteem by focusing on your successes. What experiences have you had that bolstered your self-esteem?

Activities

Skill Builder: Writing
Ask students to write a description of someone they know who would benefit from a boost in self-esteem. Then have them suggest ways they could help this person.

Skill Builder: Writing
Divide students into groups and have them develop a pamphlet on ways to develop self-esteem.

Reteaching
Ask students to compare and contrast how a person with high self-esteem and one with low self-esteem might react to:

- A negative comment on a recent haircut
- A poor grade on a test
- Not making a sports team
- Having someone turn down a date
- Ending a relationship

Students should discuss the differences in the reactions that the person with high self-esteem and the person with low self-esteem would have.

Reteaching
Direct students to use "The A, B, C's of Me" activity to describe the characteristics of their personality. Using one word from each letter in the alphabet have them describe one of their characteristics. For example, A-adorable, B-bright, C-creative, etc. Remind students that all 26 words must be positive, if work is directed to help build self-esteem.

Enrichment
Have students look over the list of esteem builders on pages 28-29. First have them rate themselves on a scale of 1 to 5 (1 meaning "never" and 5 meaning "always") in terms of how effectively they think they perform each one. Then, for those that they have rated 1 or 2, they should write a short paragraph that provides ideas for improving their score.

Did You Know? Some psychologists consider chronic boredom an indicator of low self-esteem. They see boredom as the neglect and rejection of undeveloped aspects of oneself. A person who is recognizing and developing his or her own resources will not be bored.

Emphasize Help students to see that belittling a compliment also belittles the person who gave it. It calls the person's judgment into question. Instead, students need to learn how to accept compliments.

Teaching "Managing Your Life"
(Page 30)

This section explains why management skills are so important for teens.

Checking Comprehension

✓ What are the two aspects involved in management? *Management involves making decisions about the things you want to do and then accomplishing the goals you have set for yourself.*

✓ Why are goals important? *Having goals helps you to make decisions now that will help you in the future.*

✓ What is the relationship between managing your life and decision making? *If you make the decisions that are right for you, you will be managing your life well.*

Activities

Skill Builder: Writing
Have students write down three goals: one for the next 24 hours, one for the next month, and one for the next year. For the last one, have them write down at least three ways they could prepare to meet that goal.

Reteaching
Have students give examples of situations in which they have had to make management decisions (for example, as a team captain). Have them think about how these experiences might give them insight into how to manage their own lives.

Enrichment
Have students interview parents, grandparents, older siblings, or older friends who hold or have held some type of leadership or management position, either in school, on a team, or at work. They should ask the person what he or she feels are the two or three most important tasks of the leader or manager. In class, discuss the application of some of these tasks to the students' lives.

Managing Your Life

Just what is management, and why is it so important that you develop management skills? **Management** involves making decisions about the things you want to do and then accomplishing the goals you have set for yourself. By developing management skills, you begin to take responsibility for your life. That is especially important now because you will soon be making some very crucial decisions about your future.

Managing your life involves, among other things, taking charge of your health. Every day you make decisions—about food, exercise, sleep, work, and relaxation—that can have long-term effects on your health. In Chapter 3 you will learn why health is important and how to establish healthy habits.

Managing your life also involves setting goals for yourself. Having goals—about making a team, going to camp, or graduating from high school, for example—helps you make decisions now that will help you in the future. Chapter 4 focuses on goal setting and helps you figure out how to achieve the goals that you set for yourself.

Finally, managing your life means making the decisions that are right for you. When you were a child, your parents and other adults made most of the decisions about your life. Now you are beginning to make more of these decisions yourself, and eventually you will take full responsibility for your own life. Chapter 5 walks you through a decision-making process that you can apply to all your important decisions.

The teen years are not easy for anyone. Adapting to change is a challenge at any stage in life, and no other stage involves so many changes so quickly. This book is designed to help you understand the changes that occur between childhood and adulthood, and to help you develop the skills for dealing with this period in your life.

Managing your life involves making decisions about a wide variety of things—from daily tasks, such as grooming, to long-range plans for your future.

More About Managing Your Life The rest of this unit discusses life management in detail. Students are introduced to management as it applies to health, goal setting, and decision making.

Did You Know? The word *manage* comes from *manus,* the Latin word for "hand." List several management-related phrases that use the word *hand,* such as "having a hand in a process" (becoming involved) or "letting something out of one's hands" (giving up responsibility for something). Encourage students to think of others.

CHAPTER 2 REVIEW

Reviewing the Facts

1. Give two reasons why the teen years might be described as the best time of life.
2. What causes the physical and emotional changes experienced by adolescents? Name two physical and two emotional changes.
3. What are three examples of mental abilities that are developed during the teen years?
4. List six ways to build self-esteem.
5. What is management and why is it important?
6. Name three aspects of your life for which you need management skills.

Thinking Critically

1. How might you help a friend who is having a particularly difficult time adjusting to the changes of adolescence?
2. How might feeling good about yourself—having high self-esteem—affect the ways you relate to other people? Give several specific examples.

Applying Your Skills

1. **Evaluating Personalities.** Select two characters from books or television shows, one with high self-esteem and one with low self-esteem. Write a few paragraphs on how each character's level of self-esteem affected his or her actions and what it did to the lives of others around them.

2. **Generating Solutions.** Read the advice columns in at least three teen magazines, noting the kinds of problems that are covered. Select a letter and be prepared to discuss the advice that you would have given in the same situation.

3. **Describing Biological Aspects of Development.** Read the section of a life science, health, or biology textbook that describes changes in hormones during adolescence. Write two or three paragraphs in your own words to explain what occurs.

Answers to "Reviewing the Facts"

1. Any two: you have more knowledge and experience than you had as a child; you have many skills; you can solve difficult problems; you can get along with many types of people.
2. Hormones. Physical changes include growth and development of adult characteristics. Emotional changes include feeling emotions with more intensity, discovering new emotions, experiencing abrupt changes in emotions (any two).
3. Any three: ability to reason; to think abstractly; to imagine consequences of actions; to think of alternatives to an action; to reflect on the results of a decision; to learn from mistakes.
4. Learn to accept praise; focus on your strengths; accept yourself as you are; learn from what you do; use your strengths to help others; take responsibility for your own life.
5. It involves making decisions about the things you want to do and then accomplishing the goals you set for yourself. It enables you to take responsibility for your life and plan your future.
6. Taking charge of your health, setting goals, making decisions that are right for you.

COMPLETING THE CHAPTER

Summary

- During adolescence teens go through a number of physical, emotional, mental, and social changes that prepare them for adulthood. These changes require everyone to adjust.
- Teens can build their self-esteem in a number of ways that emphasize self-acceptance and focusing on strengths.
- Management skills help teens adjust to the changes they are going through and accomplish the goals they set for themselves.

For Review

Objective Review Questions Have students complete the "Reviewing the Facts" section on this page.

Study Guide Have students complete the Study Guide from Chapter 2 of their *Student Workbook.*

Class Discussion As a class, discuss the changes of adolescence and how the adjustments teens make today are different from those their parents had to make. Ask if students think things are easier or harder today.

For Evaluation

Identifying Examples Have students take a blank sheet of paper and place four headings on it: *Physical Changes, Emotional Changes, Mental Changes,* and *Social Changes.* For each category they should list two changes that occur during adolescence. Then, for one change in each category, they should think of one positive effect and one potentially negative effect.

Chapter Test Have students complete the test for Chapter 2 that appears in the *Teacher's Classroom Resources.*

Answers to "Thinking Critically"

1. You might tell your friend that you too have some of the same confused feelings and share the ways that you deal with these emotions. You might suggest that your friend participate in some activity you know he or she is good at, in order to reinforce positive feelings. You could ask other friends to include the person in group activities.
2. Students might point out that high self-esteem gives people confidence in their dealings with others. People who feel good about themselves are able to be more honest and open, which helps them establish stronger relationships. They are also better able to help other people.

CHAPTER OVERVIEW

Chapter 3 introduces the topic of wellness and helps students make wise health decisions. The chapter talks about various kinds of health (physical, mental, emotional, and social), giving examples of ways to maintain wellness in each area. A final section discusses stress, its effects, and ways of coping with it. Throughout the chapter the emphasis is on making conscious decisions about health and wellness.

INTRODUCING THE CHAPTER

Motivators

What Does It Mean to Be Healthy? Write the following unfinished sentence on the board: "A healthy person is someone who . . ." Challenge students to finish the sentence. After you have received a number of answers, ask students to copy them down for later reference.

Using the Photograph Have students look at the photograph on this page and describe what the two girls are doing. Ask: "How healthy do you think these girls are? Do you think they look after themselves? Why or why not?"

Deciding for Health Ask students what they think is the point of the story about Marcie on page 33. Stress that the jogging itself is not the point; rather, Marcie's decision to pay attention to her health, her determination to continue, and her personal benefits are the things that count.

Introducing the Objectives

Discuss the chapter objectives on this page. Remind students that the objectives focus on important chapter content.

Introducing Vocabulary

Ask students if they are familiar with the term *wellness.* (Most likely they have encountered it before.) Ask them what they picture when they think of the word and how they feel it might differ from the term *healthy.* Stress that the chapter defines the term.

CHAPTER

3

Your Health and Wellness

OBJECTIVES

This chapter will help you to:

- List the benefits of maintaining a wellness program.
- Describe the physical, mental, emotional, and social aspects of health.
- Identify ways to cope with stress.

WORDS TO REMEMBER

addictive
depression
stress
wellness

Chapter Resources

Teacher's Classroom Resources
- Lesson Plan
- Life Skills Activity, *How Are You? Very* **Well**, *Thank You*
- Reproducible Master, *Stress Chart*
- Extension Activity, *What Is Your Level of Wellness?*
- Chapter Test

Student Workbook
- Study Guide
- Worksheet, *Health and Wellness Quiz*

Marcie started jogging three months ago and now she's enjoying the results of her efforts. All her friends tell her how terrific she looks. Most important to Marcie, though, is the fact that she feels so much better. She has more energy, her skin is clearer, and she feels more confident about herself. She's determined to keep to her new regimen.

Perhaps, like Marcie, you need to take greater control of your health. In the last chapter you learned about the physical changes that take place during the teen years. You also learned that this is the time when you develop your decision-making skills. A decision to practice good health habits could be one of the smartest moves you ever make.

Why Health Is Important

Many people believe that if they're not sick, they're healthy. In fact, being healthy means a lot more than not having a disease. People who are truly healthy are physically fit, emotionally and mentally sound, and have a satisfying social life.

To emphasize the difference between a moderate and a high level of health, many people now use the word *wellness.* **Wellness** is a state of good health that you achieve by making a conscious effort to look after yourself.

Here are some of the benefits of maintaining a wellness program:

- You will look and feel better.
- You will have more energy to do the things you want to do.
- You will have a better outlook on life.
- You will enjoy being around people.
- You will enjoy being alone.
- You will be able to handle your emotions better.
- You will feel more confident.

Wellness involves four main aspects of health: physical, mental, emotional, and social. To achieve wellness, you need to pay attention to all four.

Regular exercise is beneficial for your physical health, as well as your mental and emotional health. You can make exercise a part of your social life, too.

Emphasize Remind students that they *do* have to work at maintaining a state of wellness but that it has many rewards.

Did You Know? The different facets of wellness are interconnected. Often, when people are ill, they also become depressed. And depression or high levels of stress seem to make a person more susceptible to illness.

TEACHING THE CHAPTER

For convenience, the teaching suggestions for this chapter are arranged according to the following lesson topics:

Teaching "Why Health Is Important"

(Page 33)

This section lists the benefits of maintaining a wellness program.

Checking Comprehension

✔ What is the difference between a moderate level of health and a high level of health? *A moderate level of health usually means that people are not sick. A high level of health involves wellness, a state of good health achieved by making a conscious effort to take care of physical, emotional, mental, and social health.*

Activities

Skill Builder: Critical Thinking
Ask students to discuss whether they think our society attaches a high level of importance to wellness. If so, they should give support for why they think so. If not, they should tell which things they think society considers more important.

Reteaching
Ask students to go back and reread the section about Marcie. Ask them to explain how she has experienced the benefits of wellness through her jogging program.

Enrichment
Ask students to study the list of the benefits of maintaining a wellness program (page 33). Ask them to rank the items according to which they think they need to work on most (top of list) and which they think they have already achieved (bottom of list). Ask them to keep the list and review it at the end of the chapter.

Reteaching
Ask students to compare and contrast the results of wise and foolish choices in the areas discussed in this section. Stress the impact not only on the individual, but also on family, friends, and society.

Enrichment
Have a physical education teacher or a person from a local fitness center talk in class about beginning an exercise program: how to begin, how to progress, and so on. The speaker should discuss what resources are available through both the school and the community (for example, weight rooms, swimming pools, tracks, etc.) to help students begin an exercise program.

Enrichment
Ask students to find a recent article on a program that works with addicts (of tobacco, alcohol, or other drugs) to help them fight their addiction. Ask students to report to the class on the various techniques and their success.

Teaching "Mental, Emotional, and Social Health"
(Pages 36-37)

This section describes the mental, emotional, and social aspects of health.

Checking Comprehension

✓ Explain how self-concept and self-esteem relate to mental health. *They are closely related. Your self-concept, or the way you see yourself, affects your self-esteem. In turn, your self-esteem affects your level of mental health.*

✓ What is your self-concept based on? *It is based on the positive and negative experiences you have had since childhood. It continues to change throughout your life.*

✓ How can you satisfy your need to love and be loved? *By building close relationships with your family and friends that give you a feeling of being a valued member of a group. That helps you think of yourself as a worthwhile person.*

Learn about substance abuse and its physical, mental, emotional, and social effects on individuals and families. Such knowledge can help you say "no" to using tobacco, alcohol, or drugs.

Alcohol affects the body by slowing down the nervous system. Your muscle coordination and mental judgment are affected. Alcohol abuse can cause vomiting, unconsciousness, and even death. Alcohol is also involved in one-half of all automobile accidents. Unfortunately, many teens and adults become problem drinkers or alcoholics. They come to depend on the regular use of alcohol.

The word *drugs* is used to mean many different kinds of substances, from medicine to illegal crack and heroin. Drug abuse can affect a person physically, mentally, and emotionally. It can cause severe health problems, bizarre behavior, and even death. Prescription drugs should be used only under the care of a doctor. Buying or selling illegal drugs, from marijuana to cocaine, can result in arrest, fines, and jail sentences.

Why do teens use tobacco, alcohol, or drugs when these substances are so harmful to their health? Reasons vary from a desire to act older and pressure from others to low self-esteem and personal problems. School programs, support groups, and counselors help people deal with drug problems. The best way to avoid substance abuse is never to start using tobacco, alcohol, or drugs.

Mental, Emotional, and Social Health

Physical fitness is an important component of wellness. However, to be truly healthy you need to give attention to your mental, emotional, and social health, too. The four components are interrelated.

Focus on Relationship Skills Note that mental health has to do not only with how one feels about oneself, but also with how one feels about and interacts with others. The two cannot really be separated.

Cross-Reference See Teen Tips, "Ten Ways to Say 'No' to Alcohol and Drugs," on pages 168-169.

Mental Health

Just as there are different levels of physical fitness, there are different levels of mental health. In general, people who are very healthy mentally feel good about themselves, are comfortable with other people, and are able to cope with the demands of life.

The level of your mental health is closely related to your self-concept and your self-esteem. It is not unusual for teens to be confused about their self-concept. After all, you're in a stage of transition from child to adult, and you're not sure who you are or what you want. That, in turn, affects your self-esteem. At times you feel confident and positive. You *know* you can do well in school. You feel good about your friendships. Then at other times you feel unsure about yourself. You feel clumsy and awkward. You want to try out for the soccer team but you're afraid of being rejected.

It may help if you realize that your self-concept is based on years of "input." The positive and negative experiences you've had since childhood have all affected the way you see yourself today. You can't change that perception of yourself overnight. However, as you read in Chapter 2, you can take measures to improve your self-esteem.

Emotional Health

Just as you have certain physical needs, you also have basic emotional needs. You need to give and receive love, you need to have a sense of belonging, and you need to feel worthwhile.

You can satisfy your need to love and be loved by building close relationships with your family and friends. These relationships also give you a feeling of being a valued member of a group. The approval and recognition of others help you think of yourself as a worthwhile person.

Learning to express your emotions is another important part of growing up. When you were a child, you didn't think twice about crying or throwing a tantrum. You reacted the only way you knew. Since then you have learned that there may be more appropriate ways of expressing your feelings. Sometimes, you might feel like talking things over with someone else. Other times, you might prefer to let off steam by doing strenuous exercise. Everyone has different ways of expressing emotions. Just remember that it's important that you don't bottle up your emotions.

Social Health

Your involvement in the society in which you live has an effect on your health. There are two main aspects of social health. One concerns the people with whom you have direct contact—your family, friends, neighbors, and so on. If you enjoy good, supportive relationships with the people you know, you are likely to be healthier than someone who does not.

The other aspect of social health concerns your role within society as a whole. For a society to function well, its members need to work together. There are many things you can do to contribute to the overall health of your community. You can volunteer your time to help people in need. You can take a first aid course given by your local Red Cross. You can support the local recycling effort. You can help keep your environment clean.

More About Relationship Skills The next unit discusses the skills needed to build and maintain good relationships. Good relationships with family and friends are crucial for emotional health.

Focus on Leadership Taking on a position of leadership in school is one way for teens to become active in their community. Leadership positions might range from taking charge of a club to holding office in student government.

✓ What are some appropriate ways of expressing your feelings? *Appropriate ways include talking things over with someone else and exercising.*

✓ How can your contact with others contribute to wellness? *If you enjoy good, supportive relationships with family, friends, and neighbors, you are likely to be healthier than someone who does not.*

✓ What can you do to contribute to the overall health of your community? *You can volunteer your time, take a course in first aid, support local recycling efforts, and help keep the environment clean.*

Activities

Skill Builder: Critical Thinking
Have students think about a problem in their community that they think needs attention. Have them state the problem, tell how it might be helped, and suggest ways that teens could become involved in alleviating the problem.

Skill Builder: Writing
Ask students to write several paragraphs about an incident in their childhood that had a positive influence on their self-concept. You might suggest examples such as a prize they won, a game they played well, good marks in school, and recognition of artistic or musical talent.

Reteaching
Ask students to give specific examples of ways that teens might exhibit mental, emotional, or social wellness. For example, a student might say: "A person could show mental wellness by being able to accept defeat in a school election."

Enrichment
Have students examine newspapers and/or magazines for health ads, programs and products. Ask them to clip out the articles and evaluate them according to physical, mental, emotional, or social health. Display the articles on the bulletin board.

Teaching the Feature

"Stress Can Be Good for You"

Answers to Feature Questions

1. Students might suggest that since these patients were not concerned, they may have been surprised or angered by the pain or disability suffered.

2. Students might mention stresses such as nervousness in talking with potential dating partners or fear of having a car accident. In the first case, the nervousness might cause the individual to think about what he or she is going to say, minimizing the possibility of awkwardness. In the second case, the stress might cause the person to drive more carefully or be more alert.

Activities

Making Plans Remind students that preparation is one way to deal constructively with stress. Break the class into groups, and have each group brainstorm ideas for preparing for one or more of the following common stresses: a first date, a final exam, the driving test, a speech in class, moving to a new community.

Community Contact Have students do research into the ways community groups can help people adjust to different kinds of stress. Have students look into a group of programs such as stress-relieving exercise programs, yoga or meditation groups, religious organizations, seminars on stress management, or "Welcome-Wagon" groups.

HEALTH WATCH

Stress Can Be Good for You

Most people think of stress as always bad—something to avoid. Some stress, however, can be good for you. In fact, a certain amount of stress is helpful.

One of the body's responses to stress is to prepare for action: the heart and breathing speed up, for example. If you are in danger—or even if you are preparing to run a race—these changes will benefit you. Many people find that stress gives them the boost of energy or courage needed to do a difficult task well.

Certain studies have even shown that a degree of stress can help people cope with a difficult situation. Researchers have found that people who were moderately concerned about surgery recovered better than both those who were extremely fearful and those who seemed not to be concerned at all. The slight worry apparently helped patients to construct inner defenses.

Recognizing that stress can be helpful will allow you to use it to your advantage. If you feel nervous about beginning a new job, realize that the stress may be helping you in many ways. Perhaps it will cause you to take extra care with what you do, or it may help you pay attention and remember a new procedure. Being too comfortable too soon might cause you to become careless.

Everyone encounters stressful situations in daily life. If you can see moderate stress as a helpful aid, you will find that you are taking control of situations instead of letting them control you.

Think It Through

1. **Why do you think the individuals who were not at all concerned about surgery did not do as well as those who were moderately concerned?**
2. **Choose a type of stress that you encounter in everyday life. List ways that the stress might help you perform better.**

Did You Know? The name for the body's physiological response to stress is the fight-or-flight reaction. This reaction occurs in animals and helps them either to confront extreme danger or escape danger, if possible.

Emphasize Some people allow stress to paralyze them, making them unable to cope with a situation. Tell students that recognizing the signs of stress early and realizing that one *can* cope with stress will help prevent this dangerous reaction.

Stress

Even the healthiest person feels tense and nervous on occasion. For example, you might become nervous before a team tryout, or performing in a school play, or dating someone for the first time. Serious events, such as a death, a divorce, or a major illness in the family, can leave you feeling emotionally drained.

The physical and emotional tension that is caused by important happenings or changes in your life is called **stress.** It might cause you to lose your appetite for a while, or you might suffer from headaches or sleeplessness. Usually, such effects are temporary and cause no harm. Your body is equipped to handle a certain amount of stress. In fact, stress can actually be good for you at times.

Dealing with Stress

There are many things you can do to deal positively with stress. The important thing is to recognize signs of stress early and to take action quickly.

- **Try to relax.** Sometimes just getting away from everything and spending time by yourself can help you relax. Make a point of taking time out each week to read a book, listen to music, work on a hobby, or just daydream.
- **Get some exercise.** When you are starting to feel overwhelmed, go out and run, shoot some baskets, or do some other physical activity that will help you unwind.
- **Plan ahead.** If you're nervous about an upcoming event such as a speech, take time to prepare yourself and rehearse so you feel more confident.
- **Think about the situation.** Perhaps your imagination is making it seem worse that it really is. Ask yourself, "What's the worst thing that could happen? How can I prevent that from happening?"
- **Learn from the experience.** If you're miserable because you failed an important test, think about what you can do to pass the test next time.

If the feeling of stress continues, you may need to get outside help. Although everyone feels unhappy from time to time, a prolonged feeling of stress can develop into **depression.** This can cause people to feel hopeless, to lose enjoyment of life, or to even consider suicide. If you suffer from depression, talk about your problems to someone you trust—a close friend, your parents, a teacher, or a counselor.

Remember that stress is perfectly normal, and everyone experiences it. If you take care of your health—physical, mental, emotional, and social—you'll be better equipped to deal with stress.

If you can relax during stressful times, you will feel more in control. You can also use the time to think of solutions to the problems.

Teaching "Stress"
(Page 39)

This section helps students to identify ways to cope with stress.

Checking Comprehension

✓ How can stress be both helpful and harmful for you? *It can be helpful because it is a natural reaction caused by important happenings or changes in your life that, in small doses, your body is equipped to handle. On the other hand, it is harmful if the period of stress continues or if it develops into depression.*

✓ How will planning ahead help you with something you are nervous about? *It will give you time to prepare and make you feel more confident.*

✓ How might severe depression make people feel? *It might cause them to feel hopeless and to lose any enjoyment in life. They may even consider suicide.*

✓ What should you do if you suffer from depression? *You should talk to someone you trust.*

Activities

Skill Builder: Critical Thinking
Ask students to share with classmates their ways of relaxing when stress occurs. Encourage sharing of positive ways of coping with stress.

Reteaching
Have students create collages that depict situations that could cause stress. Examples include traffic jams, speeches, and arguments.

Enrichment
Have students work in small groups and plan a stress seminar for the class. Possible speakers could include the school nurse, the health and physical education teacher, the home economics instructor, and the community health care personnel. Presentations should include topics on physical, mental, emotional, and social health.

Did You Know? Laughter is actually a form of stress. It stimulates a number of muscles, including those in the chest, stomach, and lungs. It also raises blood pressure and heart rate. It is, however, a "good" form of stress and stimulates the release of chemicals that are beneficial to the body.

Cross-Reference See "Suicide's Twelve Warning Signs" on pages 170-171.

Emphasize Some people bring on their own stressful situations by trying to do too much. Help teens to see that not every moment has to be filled with activity. They should learn to give themselves time to relax and reflect.

COMPLETING THE CHAPTER

Summary

- Maintaining wellness makes people look better, feel better, get more enjoyment out of others and themselves, and have more confidence.
- Physical wellness involves good nutrition, getting enough sleep and exercise, preventing accidents, paying attention to grooming, and avoiding harmful substances.
- Mental, emotional, and social wellness help people to enjoy and appreciate themselves as well as to contribute to life around them.
- Dealing positively with stress involves recognizing its signs and acting quickly to relax, working off tension, making plans, considering the situation, and learning from experience.

For Review

Objective Review Questions Have students complete the "Reviewing the Facts" section on this page.

Study Guide Have students complete the Study Guide from Chapter 3 of their *Student Workbook.*

Class Discussion Ask students to get out the list of what it means to be healthy created by the class at the opening of the chapter. Hold a discussion about the changes and additions they would make to that list at this point, having studied the chapter.

For Evaluation

Create a Checklist Have students create a five-item checklist of "do's" for each of the following sections of the chapter: physical wellness, mental wellness, emotional wellness, social wellness. The checklists should help them assess their degree of wellness in each area.

Chapter Test Have students complete the test for Chapter 3 that appears in the *Teacher's Classroom Resources.*

CHAPTER 3 REVIEW

Answers to "Reviewing the Facts"

1. Wellness is a state of good health that you achieve by making a conscious effort to look after yourself.
2. Any three: you will look and feel better; you will have more energy to do the things you want to do; you will have a better outlook on life; you will enjoy being around people; you will enjoy being alone; you will handle your emotions; you will feel more confident.
3. A balanced diet helps you resist disease and gives you a higher level of energy.
4. Any three: it gives you strength and endurance; it gives you greater agility; it helps release tension; it helps you maintain your weight; it makes you feel and look better.
5. Tobacco, alcohol, and drugs.
6. Person feels good about himself or herself, comfortable with other people, and able to cope with the demands of life.
7. To give and receive love, to have a sense of belonging, and to feel worthwhile.
8. Enjoying good, supportive relationships with people, and contributing to the overall health of the community.
9. Try to relax; get some exercise; plan ahead; think about the situation; learn from experience.

Reviewing the Facts

1. What is wellness?
2. Name three benefits of maintaining a wellness program.
3. Why does your body need a balanced diet?
4. Name three benefits of regular exercise.
5. What substances should you avoid when you're concerned with wellness?
6. How does a person with a high level of mental health feel?
7. What are your basic emotional needs?
8. What are the two main aspects of social health?
9. List five ways to cope with stress.

Thinking Critically

1. What could your school do to help promote wellness among students?
2. Why do you think stress has become such a major health problem in American society?

Applying Your Skills

1. **Describing a Method.** Choose one of the following stressful situations: waiting in traffic; entering a new school; having an argument with your parents; beginning a new job; having a close friend move away. List five words that would describe your physical and emotional reactions. Then write a short essay describing how you might reduce the stress that the situation created.

2. **Analyzing Your Behavior.** Make a chart to check your physical wellness habits for a week. Set up columns for wellness habits such as eating breakfast, exercising, getting eight hours of sleep, cleaning teeth, etc. Every day, make a check mark in each column if you took that step. At the end of the week, total the check marks. Then determine your wellness index by computing your total marks as a percent of the number of check marks you could have made.

3. **Observing Accurately.** With a partner, select ten emotions to express. Then play a variation of charades, with one person attempting to convey each of these emotions using only facial expressions. Are some emotions harder to express than others?

Answers to "Thinking Critically"

1. Have classes on health and wellness; provide healthy, nutritious foods in the cafeteria; have physical education classes that offer a variety of exercise options; teach students about the dangers of harmful substances; foster an attitude of caring and encouragement so students will feel good about themselves; sponsor programs in the community.
2. Answers will vary. They may include: increased competition, all the roles people perform, change being such a common part of life, belief of people that they must be perfect, all of life's conflicting demands.

CHAPTER

4

Examining Your Goals

OBJECTIVES

This chapter will help you to:

- Explain how to examine needs, wants, and values in order to determine what's important.
- Discuss different types of goals.
- Describe the resources used to accomplish goals.
- Explain how to choose between conflicting goals.

WORDS TO REMEMBER

fixed goal
flexible goal
goal
long-term goal
prioritize
resource
short-term goal
values

CHAPTER OVERVIEW

Chapter 4 explains what goals are and why they are significant. The chapter points out that in order to set goals, teens have to know what is important to them. The chapter helps teens to distinguish between types of goals, to evaluate resources, and to make choices between conflicting goals. The focus of the chapter is on taking responsibility for one's own life.

INTRODUCING THE CHAPTER

Motivators

Where's the Goal? Ask students to volunteer the name of a sport that has a specific area designated as the goal. Ask students to imagine playing such a sport without the goal. Ask: "What would be the point of the game? If the goal were moved, how would that change the way the game is played?" Help students to see that the goal defines the movement and purpose of the game.

Using the Photograph Refer students to the photograph on this page. Ask: "What is happening in this photograph? What significance is graduation? Why is a ceremony held? What other goals might the graduates have?"

Decisions, Decisions Ask students to volunteer decisions that they have made that day. Emphasize that the decisions can be minor ones. When they have called out a sufficient number, stress to students the sheer number of decisions they make daily.

Introducing the Objectives

Discuss the chapter objectives on this page. Remind students that the objectives focus on important content within the chapter.

Introducing Vocabulary

Point out that the word *goal* is included in many of the chapter's vocabulary terms. Stress that goals are the subject of the chapter and that people set many different types of goals. Add that this chapter even has a goal: to teach students about goals.

Chapter Resources

Teacher's Classroom Resources
- Lesson Plan
- Life Skills Activity, *Set Your Goals*
- Reproducible Master, *Hierarchy of Needs*
- Extension Activity, *Meeting Your Long-Term Goals*
- Chapter Test

Student Workbook
- Study Guide
- Worksheet, *Computer Terms Match-Up*

TEACHING THE CHAPTER

For convenience, the teaching suggestions for this chapter are arranged according to the following lesson topics:

- "What's Important to You?" pages 42-43
- "Setting Goals," pages 45-47
- "Goals and Choices," page 47

Teaching "What's Important to You?"
(Pages 42-43)

This section explains how to examine needs, wants, and values in order to determine what is important.

Checking Comprehension

✔ List some needs other than food, water, clothing, and shelter. *Love and companionship of family and friends, people to turn to with a problem, self-esteem builders.*

✔ Why don't most teens have to worry about satisfying their needs for such things as food and shelter? *Parents or guardians take care of these needs.*

✔ How do wants differ from needs? *Wants are not essential, but people think they will make them happier. Needs are essential for survival, such as food, water, clothing, and a place to live.*

✔ What bigger part can wants play in your life? *Wants have inspired many people to achieve their dreams.*

✔ What are your values based on? *They are based on what you believe to be important or unimportant, right or wrong.*

✔ Who and what shape your values? *People you like, respect, or admire, such as your parents and friends; what you learn in school; your religion.*

Every day you have to make many decisions. Some of them are fairly easy—like what you'll wear to school or what you'll eat for lunch. Others are more difficult. Should you buy that cassette you want or should you save your money for a new bike? Should you go swimming with your friends or should you stay home and help around the house?

As you get older, you'll find that you have to make more and more decisions, and some will require careful thought. For example, how will you decide what courses to take in school? How can you earn extra money on the weekends?

The way to make the decisions that are right for you is to examine your goals. A **goal** is a target you set for yourself to accomplish. If you think carefully about what you're trying to achieve, you'll find it easier to make decisions. Equally important, the decisions you make will help you achieve your goals.

What's Important To You?

You have a problem: you have tickets for a concert Saturday night, but now you've been invited to a friend's party on the same night and you really want to go. What should you do? One way of settling problems like this one is to sort out what's most important to you. You can do this more easily if you examine your needs, wants, and values.

Your Needs

Everyone needs certain basic things in order to survive. You need food, water, clothing, and a place to live. Needs are things that are essential—things you can't get along without.

However, you must have more than these basics for your life to be satisfying. You need the love and companionship of your family and friends. You need to know that there are people you can turn to when you have a problem. You need to do things that make you feel good about yourself and help build your self-esteem.

Right now, you probably don't have to worry about satisfying your basic needs for food, shelter, and so on. Your parents take care of that. At some time in the future, though, you will have to figure out how you are going to earn enough money to meet those needs.

The needs that you are most concerned with at present are those that help you feel good about yourself. You might feel that you need to make the soccer team, or get an A on the next math test, or be chosen for the school play.

Your Wants

Wants are things you would like to have in order to make your life more enjoyable. They have to do with preferences and desires. You might want, for example, a new leather jacket, or a CD player, or a dirt bike, or a gold chain.

Some wants are also needs. Everyone has the need to eat, for example, but when you choose pizza and your friend chooses salad, you are both satisfying your need in different ways because you have different wants. You might also argue that your desire for a leather jacket (a want) is also a need because wearing it will make you feel good about yourself. Chances are, though, that you could find some other, less expensive way to feel good about yourself if a leather jacket was beyond your means. In general, wants are not essential to your life, but you think they would make you happier.

More About Needs Psychologist Abraham Maslow classified needs into five categories: physical (such as food, clothing, shelter), safety (such as protection and security), love (such as loving, being loved, belonging), esteem (such as self-acceptance and respect for others), and self-actualization (developing to one's potential). Maslow believed that a person must satisfy the earlier categories of needs before he or she can satisfy the higher-level needs.

How might needs, wants, and values influence this teenager's goal of owning a car?

Wants also include much larger desires. You may dream about becoming a movie star, or a sport commentator, or an Olympic athlete. There's nothing wrong with such wants. Dreams such as this have inspired many dedicated people to achieve their desires.

Your Values

Some of your actions are based not on your needs and wants, but on your values. **Values** are guidelines that you have for living with yourself and others. Values are based on what you believe to be right or wrong, important or unimportant.

Your values are shaped by people you like and respect, such as your parents and friends, by what you learn in school, and by your religion. They are also influenced by people you admire, such as heroes from history, or politicians, celebrities, or athletes of today.

Perhaps you value physical fitness. It's important to you that you be strong and healthy. If so, you will be sure to exercise regularly and eat the right foods. If education is what you value, you will study hard and work toward your graduation.

Activities

Skill Builder: Critical Thinking
Have students choose five song lyrics. Ask them to study the lyrics to determine what values are expressed. Have students write several sentences about each lyric that tell about its underlying values. If there is time, discuss some of these in class.

Skill Builder: Science
Ask students to read at least one article that discusses a scientific study designed to assess the needs of animals or human beings for nurturing or physical contact. Discuss in class the implications of these studies. What happens to animals or people whose need for physical contact is denied? What does this say about the importance of this need?

Reteaching
Have students give examples of items that are advertised in newspapers, in magazines, on television, or on the radio. Ask students to categorize the items as satisfying needs or wants. (Be sure they include items that fulfill basic needs for food, shelter, and clothing.) Help students to see that a particular need might be satisfied in a variety of ways.

Enrichment
Discuss with students the importance of dreams in people's lives. Have students come up with examples of people whose dreams have helped them to achieve great things. Ask students to analyze these dreams and accomplishments to determine the values they express.

Emphasize Remind students that adolescence is a time of self-discovery. Trying on different roles is a normal part of growing up. Teens may find, therefore, that they have many different and seemingly conflicting dreams. Yet all help the individual explore a facet of himself or herself.

Focus on Decision Making Help students to see that any decisions they make that are not in line with their values are likely to be abandoned. Stress the importance of discovering and acting on one's values.

Teaching the Feature
"Acquiring Computer Literacy"

Answers to Feature Questions

1. Answers will vary. Some students might say that their family owns a computer or that someone in their family has a job working with computers.

2. Uses now: word processing or writing; keeping recipes, food inventories, and grocery lists; computer games; keeping a household inventory; budgeting and financial record keeping. Uses in the future: teaching adults and children; bank transfers; shopping; computer mail; communicating with people from computer to computer.

Activities

Computers in Your Future Ask students to do research on the computer applications used in a career in which they have some interest. If the student is interested in writing, for example, he or she should discover that many word processing programs are available, including desktop publishing programs. Have students present their findings to the class.

Community Contact Divide the class into groups of four or five, and have each group research the ways in which any of the following groups in their community make use of computer technology (some may not): library, police department, school offices, bank, supermarket, municipal offices, insurance offices. Students should ask about how the computers are used and how they make work easier. If the office does not use computers, students should ask why.

TECHNOLOGY

Acquiring Computer Literacy

If you are like most teens, you are still finding out about the world and you're not yet ready to settle on a particular career. How, then, can you set short-term goals to prepare for your future?

Experts predict that no matter what you decide to do in the years to come, computers will be a part of your life. Technology has changed the way most people do their jobs. Office workers who once used typewriters and adding machines now use word-processing computers and high-speed electronic calculators. Computers help travel agents, lawyers, and police officers to work more efficiently. Increasing numbers of factory workers are using computers to operate the machines on assembly lines. You may even be able to see technology at work at your local supermarket, which may have electronic scanners to read price codes.

How can you prepare to take your place amid this technological revolution? Here are a few suggestions:

- Become familiar with computers. Your school probably offers computer courses; if you haven't signed up for one, try to do so soon.
- Look for locations where computers are in use. If you can, ask what the computers are used for and what type of training is required to operate the computer.
- Read about computers in newspapers and magazines. Many articles describe new uses for computers, advances in computer technology, or predictions about how computers will continue to change the way we live.
- Keep an open mind. Be ready to accept change in technology and in other areas. Some people who lose their jobs because of technological advances are those who are unwilling to adapt to the new technology.

You are just beginning to plan for your future. As you set goals, keep in mind all the ways that technology has changed your life and will continue to do so in the future.

Think It Through

1. **What are some ways in which your own life has been affected by the computer?**
2. **What are some home uses of the computer now and what new uses can you suggest for the future?**

Did You Know? Using a computer game is often a good way of becoming familiar with how to operate a computer. Suggest to students that they try to gain access to a computer and to play games on it.

Focus on Technology Today there is great variety in terms of capability, sophistication, and price of computer hardware and software. Students might read computer magazines or talk to employees or managers of computer stores. Such sources can help an individual find the computer that is right for his or her needs.

Setting Goals

Analyzing your needs, wants, and values will help you set goals for yourself. At the same time, setting goals will help you satisfy your needs, wants, and values. Where do you begin? First, you must think about the different types of goals that you have.

Types of Goals

Suppose your goal is to buy a new pair of athletic shoes. This may be a need because you have worn out your current shoes, or it may be a want—you'd love to have a pair of high-tops just like your friends are wearing. A need is usually a more important reason for setting a goal than a want is.

Many goals meet a combination of needs, wants, and values. At lunch, you plan to have an apple for dessert. This would help meet your *need* for food. However, many foods could satisfy this need—one of your friends prefers a brownie. Your exact choice depends on what you *want*, but what you want may also depend on your values. If you *value* good health, you'll choose an apple over a brownie because you know it's better for you.

Short-Term or Long-Term

The way you go about reaching your goals also depends on whether they are short-term or long-term. When you have more time to do something, you usually have more options.

A **short-term goal** is something you can accomplish soon. Your short-term goals might include the following:

- Read a novel.
- Go on a hike.
- Fix your bike.
- Buy a birthday gift.
- Lose five pounds.
- Write to your grandmother.

Your goals can be short-term or long-term. This student spent several years developing his artistic skill before winning an award.

Teaching "Setting Goals"

(Pages 45-47)

This section discusses different types of goals, the resources used to accomplish various goals, and how a person goes about choosing between conflicting goals.

Checking Comprehension

✓ Give examples of short-term goals and long-term goals. *Answers will vary. Short-term goals that can be accomplished soon include doing your homework, cleaning your room, reading a magazine, or walking your dog. Long-term goals to be accomplished in the future include buying a car, growing your hair long, or knitting a blanket.*

✓ Why might you want to divide a long-term goal into several short-term goals? *It will make the goal seem more attainable.*

✓ What can you do if you do not have the resources to reach your goals? *You can establish different goals or figure out how you can get the resources you need.*

✓ Which goals are usually more flexible: those that involve just you or those that involve others as well? *Those that involve you alone are usually more flexible.*

Activities

Skill Builder: Reading
Ask students to read two short stories and to decide what goal or goals the main characters have. Ask them to decide, for each goal, whether it is long-term or short-term and whether it is fixed or flexible.

Emphasize Remind students that at any given moment they are likely to be trying to achieve a number of different goals. Some actions or decisions may further more than one goal.

Did You Know? Teens can take tests that can help to determine their aptitudes and skills. If students are vague about the areas in which they are strong, suggest that they talk to their guidance counselor about such testing.

Skill Builder: Writing
Ask students to write several paragraphs about a long-term goal they have. They should include what wants or needs it satisfies, what values it displays, and what resources they have or need for reaching it. Suggest that they also break it down into several short-term goals.

Reteaching
Ask students to demonstrate how purchasing a particular sweater may meet a combination of needs, wants, and values.

Enrichment
Have students use reference resources such as telephone directories, newspapers, community bulletins, and other sources to identify resources available in their community. Indicate the type of resource, location, telephone number, and cost. Have students combine their lists to form a resource directory for teens. Place a copy in the school library and in the home economics department.

Enrichment
Divide the class into groups, and have each work on satisfying one of the following pairs of conflicting goals. (More than one group may work on each pair.) They should define each goal as fixed or flexible and give a scenario for reaching both goals.

- You are saving money for karate lessons, but your friend asks you to sponsor him in a walk this weekend to raise money for a family whose house has burned down.
- You want to listen to your new album, but your younger brother needs help with his homework.
- You want to use your bicycle to visit a friend, but your sister needs to borrow it to go to work.

A **long-term goal** is something you plan to accomplish sometime in the future, perhaps in six months, or a year, or after you finish high school. Examples of long-term goals are:

- Make the basketball team.
- Go to computer camp.
- Buy a used car after you get your driver's license.
- Graduate from high school.

You can establish short-term goals as steps toward reaching your long-term goals. Suppose, for example, that your long-term goal is to buy a computer. You can build toward that goal by setting several short-term goals. One short-term goal will be to put aside a certain amount of money each week. Another will be to start reading magazines about computers so that you will know which computer is best for you when the time comes. Another may be to spend more time in the computer lab at school so that you'll know more about computers when you get yours. Dividing a long-term goal into several short-term goals often helps make the goal seem more attainable.

Resources

When you're deciding about your goals, you also should consider your resources. A **resource** is something that you need to accomplish a goal. There are many different types of resources:

- Your own knowledge, skills, energy, and imagination.
- Money, tools, equipment, and other possessions.
- Time.
- Other people, such as your family, friends, teachers.
- Community facilities, such as the Y, the library, and courses offered by local schools or colleges.

Resources include knowledge, skill, energy, time, money, equipment, other people, and community facilities. What resources might these students be using?

When you establish your goals, then, you must consider if you have the resources to reach them. If you don't, you have two options: you can establish different goals, or you can figure out how you can obtain the resources.

Suppose, for example, that your goal is to buy a new bike. One resource you will need is money. You have about half the money you need for the bike, but it will take you a long time to save the rest. Next, you consider some of your other resources—like your possessions. Perhaps you could raise some of the money by selling the albums that you never listen to any more, or by selling your old bike. Maybe you could offer to mow lawns during the summer to earn the extra cash.

Often, there are different ways of meeting the same goal. Examining your resources helps you consider the alternatives available to you.

Real-Life Situation More than 3,700 teenagers drop out of high school every day. Ask students what might be the life-long impact of not earning a high school diploma? How might a person's short-term and long-term goals be affected? Discuss ways that students could be encouraged to remain in school until graduation.

Emphasize Thinking in terms of fixed and flexible goals can broaden a person's thought processes. People sometimes get into a rut, thinking that the only way of doing something is the way they have always done it. If they examine their goals however, they may realize that they have more flexibility than they imagine.

Fixed or Flexible

Sometimes you'll find that your goals conflict. Perhaps you'd planned to clean up your room this afternoon, but now your father has asked you to mow the lawn. Deciding between conflicting goals is easier if you consider which ones are fixed and which are flexible.

A **fixed goal** is one that can only be met at a certain time. The lawn-mowing may be a fixed goal if the grass is so high that it can't wait another day. Fixed goals are often tied to specific dates. For example, if your goal is to sign up for a community athletics program, you must set time aside to attend the registration on the specified date.

A **flexible goal,** on the other hand, is one that has no definite time limit. Cleaning your room is a flexible goal—you can do it any time. Reading a novel for pleasure is another example of a flexible goal. If you have to read that same novel in time for a class, though, then it's a fixed goal.

Usually, goals that involve you alone are more flexible than those that involve others. Changing a plan that involves three or four people can be difficult. You will also find that long-term goals are usually more flexible than short-term goals.

Sometimes, a goal starts out being flexible but becomes fixed. If you want to work on a mid-semester assignment, it is a flexible goal for the first few weeks. As the deadline approaches, however, it becomes a fixed goal—you can't put it off any longer.

Goals and Choices

Learning to prioritize your goals is a key to taking responsibility for your own life. When you **prioritize** your goals, you rank them in order of importance. This helps you to make choices between goals when they conflict. Which goals should you go for? Which should you postpone or forget about? These are the kinds of decisions that you have to make throughout your life.

Whenever you're confused about which goals you should pursue, take time to ask yourself these questions:

- Does this goal satisfy my needs or wants?
- Is it in line with my values?
- Do I have the resources I need?
- Is it a fixed or a flexible goal?

Examining your goals carefully will help you decide which ones you should concentrate on. It will also help you figure out alternative ways of meeting conflicting goals.

Many times you have to set priorities. Some tasks have to be done at a specific time, while others are very flexible.

Did You Know? The word prioritize comes from a Latin word that means both "former" and "superior." This reflects the double purpose of prioritizing things—in terms of both time and order of importance.

Focus on Entrepreneurship Learning to prioritize goals and choices is an important quality in business decisions as well. If students decide to start a business of their own, they will use these skills daily.

Teaching "Goals and Choices"
(Page 47)

This section teaches strategies for ranking goals in order of importance to help students choose which goals to pursue.

Checking Comprehension

✓ How is learning to prioritize your goals a key to taking responsibility? *You can make choices about which goals to work toward and which ones to postpone or give up. That will help you concentrate on the things that are really important to you.*

✓ What is the purpose of prioritizing goals? *It helps you make choices between goals when they conflict.*

✓ How does examining your goals carefully help you? *It helps you to decide which ones to concentrate on and allows you to figure out alternative ways of meeting conflicting goals.*

Activities

Skill Builder: Writing
Ask students to write about a time when they had to choose between two or more goals. They should tell how they arrived at their final decision and whether they think that what they have learned in this chapter would help them to make a wiser choice next time.

Reteaching
Ask students to develop a poster or collage to portray an individual who is trying to prioritize goals. They can use pictures, diagrams, drawings, or any other visual means to get their ideas across.

Enrichment
Divide the class into groups of four or five. Ask students to reread the last section of the chapter, "Goals and Choices". Then ask them to create a fictitious teen with several conflicting goals. They should have this teen work through the four questions presented in the section and make some plans about which of the goals to pursue. Each group should present its scenario to the class.

COMPLETING THE CHAPTER

Summary

- To make decisions based on what is important to them, teens need to examine their needs, their wants, and their values.
- Goals may meet needs, wants, or values, or some combination of the three. They may also be long-term or short-term.
- Resources such as personal characteristics, money or equipment, time, other people, and community facilities can help people reach their goals.
- To choose between conflicting goals, individuals must consider whether each goal is fixed or flexible and then they must prioritize them.

For Review

Objective Review Questions Have students complete the "Reviewing the Facts" section on this page.

Study Guide Have students complete the Study Guide from Chapter 4 of their *Student Workbook*.

Class Discussion As a class, discuss the short-term and long-term goals on pages 44 and 45. For each, have students go into detail about resources that might be needed and where they might be obtained. They should give at least one resource in each of the five categories.

For Evaluation

Making a Checklist Ask students to compile a goal checklist. It should include questions that would help them clarify their goals, covering all the major points in the chapter. A sample question would be: "Does this goal satisfy a need, want, or value?"

Chapter Test Have students complete the test for Chapter 4 that appears in the *Teacher's Classroom Resources.*

CHAPTER 4 REVIEW

Answers to "Reviewing the Facts"

1. By examining your needs, wants and values.
2. Values are guidelines you have for living with yourself and others.
3. A short-term goal can be accomplished soon; a long-term goal is to be accomplished sometime in the future.
4. Knowledge, skills, energy, and imagination; money, tools, equipment and other possessions; time; other people; community facilities.
5. A fixed goal is one that can only be met at a certain time, such as a report you have to do for class tomorrow. A flexible goal is one that has no definite time limit, such as the goal of learning how to paint.
6. By prioritizing, or ranking, goals in order of importance.
7. Does this goal satisfy my needs or wants? Is it in line with my values? Do I have the resources I need? Is it a fixed or a flexible goal?

Reviewing the Facts

1. How can you sort out what is most important to you?
2. What are values?
3. What is the difference between a short-term goal and a long-term goal?
4. List the five resources you might use to accomplish a goal.
5. Define and give an example of a fixed goal; define and give an example of a flexible goal.
6. How can you choose between conflicting goals?
7. What four questions should you ask yourself when prioritizing goals?

Thinking Critically

1. Do you think the basic needs of people have changed since your grandparents were children? How about wants and values? Explain your answers.
2. What do you think is the most important resource for accomplishing a goal?

Applying Your Skills

1. **Planning Your Goals.** List four of your short-term goals and two of your long-term goals. Identify what needs, wants, and values are served by each, and whether the goal is fixed or flexible. Do you think your list will change within a year? Why or why not?

2. **Researching a Valued Person.** Study back copies of your local newspaper to find information about someone in your community whose strong values influenced people or events. Describe the values that person displayed.

3. **Weighing Your Priorities.** What is most important to you? List five long-term goals and answer the following questions for each goal. Each answer should be a number from 1 to 5 (1 = not at all; 5 = completely).
   1. How much does this goal satisfy my needs?
   2. How much does this goal satisfy my wants?
   3. How important is it that I achieve this goal?

   For each goal, add your three answers. The goal with the highest total is most important to you—you have prioritized your goals. How do your goals rate? Does the rating surprise you?

Answers to "Thinking Critically"

1. Most students will probably say that needs have not changed much—everyone still needs shelter, food, love, and so on. However, wants and values have changed a lot, especially with the current emphasis on material items and money in our society.
2. This answer will vary according to the goal the student has in mind. For instance, if the goal is to win the football game on Saturday, the student will most likely think that other people are the most important resource. If, however, the goal involves a solitary activity, the student might say that personal qualities are most important.

CHAPTER

5

Making Decisions

OBJECTIVES

This chapter will help you to:

- List different types of decisions and explain how decisions can affect people.
- Explain the five-step decision-making process.
- Discuss the importance of taking responsibility for decisions.

WORDS TO REMEMBER

alternative
decision
evaluate

CHAPTER OVERVIEW

Chapter 5 is about making decisions. It explains that there are many types of decisions and many ways of making decisions, but that every decision has an effect on the individual and on others. The chapter describes how to make wise decisions by following a five-step decision-making process. A final section emphasizes the importance of taking responsibility for one's own decisions.

INTRODUCING THE CHAPTER

Motivators

Take It or Lose It Ask students to imagine that their home is burning and they have 1 minute to decide on five things to take out of it. Have a number of students volunteer their lists, and spend some time discussing how they made their decisions.

Using the Photograph Have students study the photograph on this page. Then ask: "Where is this student and what is he looking at? What types of decisions do you think he is facing? Who might those decisions affect?"

Overruled Ask students to recall an instance in which they made a decision but were overruled by an authority figure. Call upon volunteers to describe the situation, and suggest possible reasons for the overruling. With the benefit of hindsight, do they think their decision was right or wrong? Why?

Introducing the Objectives

Discuss the chapter objectives on this page. Remind students that the objectives focus on important chapter content.

Introducing Vocabulary

Explain that the word *decision* comes from Latin roots that mean "to cut off." Ask students how that meaning might relate to making decisions.

Chapter Resources

Teacher's Classroom Resources
- Lesson Plan
- Life Skills Activity, *The Pros and the Cons*
- Reproducible Master, *The Decision-Making Process*
- Extension Activity, *Decision-Making Checklist*
- Chapter Test

Student Workbook
- Study Guide
- Worksheet, *Decision-Making Word Search*

TEACHING THE CHAPTER

For convenience, the teaching suggestions for this chapter are arranged according to the following lesson topics:

- "Decisions and You," pages 50-52
- "The Decision-Making Process," pages 52-54
- "Taking Responsibility for Your Decisions," page 54

Teaching "Decisions and You"
(Pages 50-52)

This section describes the different types of decisions and explains how decisions can affect people.

Checking Comprehension

✓ List some areas of your life in which you must make decisions. *You make decisions about family matters, friends, spending of time and money, food and clothing.*

✓ How can even minor decisions have a lasting effect on you? *Over time, the effects of certain decisions (such as nutritional decisions) can build up.*

✓ How can your decisions affect other people? *They can affect your family's and your friends' time, activities, or feelings.*

✓ How can decisions you make about friendships and dating make their mark on the lives of others? *Your choices may lead to close relationships and commitments that are just as important to others as they are to you.*

One of the differences between childhood and adolescence has to do with the number of decisions you make. When you were a child, your parents decided a lot of things for you—what you would wear, what you would eat, what movies you might watch, how you could spend your money, and so on. Now you're beginning to make these and many other kinds of decisions for yourself.

A **decision** is the choice you make between different possibilities. Decisions are directly related to your goals. As you learned in Chapter 4, goals are the targets you set for yourself to accomplish.

The decisions you make affect not only yourself but other people around you, such as your family, friends, or classmates.

Part of the process of decision making involves examining your goals so that you can figure out which ones are most important.

Some of the decisions you make are easy and you probably don't give them much thought. Others need careful consideration. After all, every decision you make, large or small, affects you and other people in your life. In this chapter you'll study a step-by-step process you can apply to your decision making, and you'll learn why it's important that you accept responsibility for your decisions.

Decisions and You

Are you the kind of person who makes decisions on impulse? Do you walk past a store window, see an item you really like, and rush in and buy it without thinking carefully about your purchase? Instead, you may be a creature of habit. Perhaps you chose to have breakfast before you got dressed this morning because you do that every morning.

Real-Life Situation Many teenagers are pressured by peers to conform in appearance and in behavior. Ask students what they could do if they are pressured by peers to make decisions that may not be best for them. Unit 2 contains additional information about values, peer pressure, refusal skills, and making responsible decisions.

Different people have different ways of making decisions. When the decisions are small ones, making a choice based on impulse or habit probably won't do you any harm. Bigger decisions, however, require a better, more organized, method of choosing.

Types of Decisions

Decisions can be of major or minor importance. They can be easy or difficult to make. They can be made by you alone, by you after you have consulted others, or by a group. Even *not* making a decision is a decision.

Decisions are part of every area of your life. You make decisions about family matters, such as how to divide telephone time or household responsibilities. You make decisions about friends too. For example, you might spend more time with one friend than another.

Other decisions concern how you spend your time and money as well as what you eat and wear. You need to organize your evenings so that you can get everything done—homework, cleaning your room, and watching a particular television program, for example. You also have to budget your money so that you save enough for special purchases like birthday presents. Food choices involve looking at nutrition, and clothing decisions are made when you purchase as well as wear garments.

The Effects of Your Decisions

Decisions vary in the ways they affect you. The small decisions you make each day may not seem important, yet the effects of some of these can build up. For example, if you choose high-calorie snacks every day, you risk gaining weight and threatening your health.

Sometimes your decisions affect others, not just you. Your family is affected when you decide to skip household duties. Your friends are affected by the way you spend your time after school and on weekends. Even the feelings of others may be influenced by your decisions. If you help with the dishes, someone in your family will probably be appreciative. When you choose a special birthday gift for someone, you show that person how much he or she means to you.

Not all decisions are small ones, however. Some can affect you for years to come. Your decisions about the use of tobacco, alcohol, and other drugs will have both immediate and long-term effects. Entire families experience deep stress when someone is involved in substance abuse. When you decide not to smoke, drink, or use other drugs, you show that you care about your own health as well as the feelings of people around you.

Other important decisions you make affect your life's work. The classes you choose to take in high school may influence what you do after graduation, whether it be a job, training, or college. Since you are likely to spend 30 or more years of your life working, choosing a satisfying career is very important. To make the right decision, you will need to examine all aspects of a potential job. Jobs with rigid hours, seasonal work, or unsteady income are not right for everyone. Those who value time spent with families or time for personal activities will need to consider how a certain career could affect these plans. Many jobs are stressful by nature, and most have stress to some degree. When people are not happy on the job, stress increases and affects their personal and family lives. As you can see, making a careful career choice can have a tremendous influence on your life for many years to come.

Activities

Skill Builder: Critical Thinking
Ask students to keep a record of their daily activities for one day. Have them identify the activities that involved the decision-making process. Ask them to think more deeply about the potentially negative effects of making decisions based on impulse or habit. Ask them to volunteer possible decision scenarios and specific effects.

Skill Builder: Writing
Ask students to write several paragraphs about a decision they made recently that had (or will have) an important effect on at least one other person. Ask them to list the ways their decision will affect themselves and the other person(s).

Reteaching
Ask students to use pictures cut from magazines to develop a collage that illustrates the variety of decisions they make each day. The collage should include illustrations of clothing choices, food choices, and activity choices.

Enrichment
Divide the class into groups, and have each group discuss one of the following decision scenarios in terms of what the decision involves, how it will affect the individual, and how it will affect others:

- You and your parents have always assumed you will go to college, but you decide that you would like to go into the military after high school.
- You decide to avoid meat and meat products in your diet.
- You decide to spend time after school each day helping your father build an addition to your house.
- You decide to join the volleyball team.
- You decide to spend less time with your friends and more time with your girlfriend or boyfriend.

Emphasize Even though many decisions are still made for teens by their parents, teens make many decisions for themselves. Practicing decision-making skills now will help them be better decision makers in the future, when they are on their own.

Cross-Reference You may wish to refer students to "Ten Ways to Say 'No' to Alcohol and Drugs," on pages 168-169.

Teaching "The Decision-Making Process"
(Pages 52-54)

This section explains the five-step decision-making process.

Checking Comprehension

✓ When should you apply the five-step process to decision making? *When the decision is a major one that requires much thought.*

✓ Ask students to read pages 52 and 53. Then ask: "What is Stephanie's problem?" *She wants to take a job at a kennel, but she does not want to let her friend Jessica down by abandoning their gardening service.*

✓ Why are alternatives important in decision making? *They give you choices for exploring different options.*

✓ Why is it sometimes helpful to discuss a problem with someone else? *Other people may think of alternatives you hadn't thought of.*

✓ What does it mean to compare possible outcomes? *It means that you consider the possible solutions, in light of your goals.*

✓ How does evaluating a decision help you make future decisions? *By seeing the strengths and weaknesses, you are able to make better decisions. It also gives you self-confidence and experience in taking control over your life.*

Thought-provoking games and activities help develop critical thinking and decision-making skills. They also help you learn about people and how you react in situations.

Decisions that are important to your future are also felt by other people. For example, a young person's decision to go to college can have a major effect on his or her parents' finances. The personal decisions you make about friendships and dating can make their mark on the lives of others, too. Your choices may lead to close relationships and commitments that are just as important to other people as they are to you.

The Decision-Making Process

Many of the decisions that you make each day don't require much thought. When you're trying to decide between a blue or a yellow T-shirt, or between two television shows, you don't spend much time thinking about your options. However, when it comes to major decisions careful thought makes sense.

Here is the basic five-step procedure for making decisions:

1. Define the problem.
2. Identify alternatives.
3. Compare possible outcomes.
4. Make the decision.
5. Evaluate the results.

For small, quick decisions, you might follow these steps in seconds, without even being aware of them. For more important decisions, you'll probably want to go through each step carefully.

How the Method Works

Here's a real-life situation that will help you understand how the decision-making process works. Stephanie and Jessica are two friends who decided to

Focus on Entrepreneurship For students still in high school, service-oriented businesses like the one begun by Stephanie and Jessica offer many advantages. Not only will students earn money, but they will gain experience in making decisions and running a business as well.

More About Alternatives Stress that although talking over alternatives with other people is helpful, it can become a way of postponing the decision. The individual must know when to stop gathering information and to begin deciding.

make extra money by working in neighborhood yards after school and on weekends. One month after they started working together, Stephanie was offered a chance to work at a local kennel. She very much wanted to do it—Stephanie loves animals and she would like to own her own pet shop one day. However, if she took the job at the kennel, Stephanie would have to stop working with Jessica. Since Jessica could not handle the gardening job alone, she would have to give it up, too. Stephanie needed to work through the decision-making model in order to figure out what to do.

- **Define the problem.** Stephanie's problem was that she wanted to take the job at the kennel but she didn't want to let Jessica down. Still, she knew she could only be in one place at a time.

  You might have a similar problem. Perhaps two of your friends have invited you to spend time with them next weekend and you only have time to see one. Perhaps you want to get to know someone who just moved into your neighborhood but you can't decide how to go about doing it.
- **Identify alternatives.** At first, Stephanie thought she had only two **alternatives,** or choices. She could take the new job and risk upsetting Jessica, or she could keep working with Jessica and forfeit her opportunity to work in the kennel. As Stephanie thought about it more, though, she realized there was a third alternative. Maybe she could find somebody else to work with Jessica.

  Often, you will find that exploring your options will help you see that you have more choices than you first thought. Sometimes, at this point, it helps to discuss your problem with somebody else. Other people may be able to suggest alternatives that you hadn't thought of.
- **Compare possible outcomes.** Stephanie then considered her three possible solutions, in light of her goals. One of her goals was to keep Jessica as a friend. They had been best friends for a long time and Stephanie valued that. If she turned down the job at the kennel she would not be endangering her friendship. Another of Stephanie's goals was to own her own pet shop one day. She knew that the experience at the local kennel would be helpful. It would help her decide if she did, indeed, want to work with animals. It would also give her valuable experience. Stephanie then thought about her third option. It would enable her to meet her goal to work in the kennel, but the risk she took was that the person who replaced her on the gardening job might also replace her as Jessica's best friend.
- **Make the decision.** In order to make her decision, Stephanie had to prioritize her goals. She decided to give top priority to her plans for a pet shop. Although she hoped to keep Jessica as her best friend, she was prepared to risk having another person take her place. She decided to accept the job at the kennel after explaining everything to Jessica.
- **Evaluate the results.** A few weeks later, Stephanie and Jessica got together for pizza one evening. They wanted to talk about Stephanie's decision and determine whether she had done the right thing. It's always useful to **evaluate,** or judge, a decision in this way—it helps with future decision making. Stephanie and Jessica spend a lot less time together now, but they are still best friends and enjoy talking about their different job experiences. Most important, Stephanie believes that she made the right choice and she expects to take a full-time job at the kennel once she finishes school.

Activities

Skill Builder: Reading
Ask students to go to the library and find an article or book on decision making. Ask them to discover what steps the article or book includes in decision making and to compare them with the steps given in the text. Ask a few students to share their findings with the class.

Skill Builder: Writing
Ask students to write a dialogue that shows how the conversation between Stephanie and Jessica might have gone on the night they met for pizza and to evaluate the decision. Encourage students to include details and to have the girls express their feelings about the decision that was made.

Reteaching
Ask students to outline the section of the chapter that discusses the five-step process. They should include in the outline not only the steps, but the application to Stephanie and Jessica as well.

Enrichment
Ask students to brainstorm important types of decisions that teens might need to make. Then divide the class into groups, and assign each group one of the decisions. Ask them to add any necessary details and then to apply the five-step decision-making process to the situation.

Did You Know? Stephanie's decision to give top priority to her future plans shows a healthy self-interest. This is not selfishness, because she continues to be concerned about the consequences of her decision.

More About Evaluation Evaluation sometimes leads to a realization that one made a wrong decision. In such cases, it is important to figure out why the decision was wrong and to learn from the mistake.

Teaching "Taking Responsibility for Your Decisions"
(Page 54)

This section teaches the importance of taking responsibility for one's decisions and taking charge of one's life.

Checking Comprehension

✓ Why is it your responsibility to make your own decisions? *It is your life, and you should take charge of it. If you let others decide things for you, you are letting them take charge.*

Activities

Skill Builder: Writing
Have students imagine that they are parents, trying to encourage their children to take responsibility for their own lives. Have them write a letter to their child, telling him or her why it is so important to make one's own decisions and accept responsibility for oneself.

Reteaching
Ask students to give examples of times in their own lives when they did not take responsibility for their own decisions—when they let someone else make a decision, put it off, or acted in some other way to deny responsibility. Ask them to describe the result of this situation and how they felt about it.

Enrichment
Explain to students that taking responsibility for their decisions means accepting the consequences when things don't work out. Discuss with the class what "taking responsibility" would mean if each of the following had happened to Stephanie:

- When she tells Jessica her decision, Jessica feels betrayed and says she never wants to speak to Stephanie again.
- Stephanie finds that after being at the kennel for several weeks, she does not like working with animals after all.
- Stephanie takes the job at the kennel and loves it. But when the two girls discuss the decision over pizza, Jessica tries to convince Stephanie to come back because the other girl isn't working out.

Whenever you make a major decision, or even a fairly unimportant one, it's a good idea to evaluate the decision's effects and to compare them with what you expected would happen. Evaluations such as this help you see your strengths and weaknesses and help you with your decision making in the future.

Taking Responsibility for Your Decisions

Sometimes it's tempting to let other people make decisions for you. That way, if something goes wrong you have someone to blame. You may also be tempted to put off making a decision. You prefer to "wait and see."

At times such as these, you may need to remind yourself that you're in charge of your own life. If you let others decide things for you, you're letting them take charge.

Imagine, for example, that Stephanie had chosen to talk over her dilemma with Jessica, and then let Jessica decide what was best. Jessica would have seen the problem from a different point of view. Her goal was to keep the gardening business going. She might have persuaded Stephanie to turn down the job at the kennel. If that had happened, Stephanie would have missed out on an important opportunity because she let someone else make a decision for her.

You know yourself better than anyone, and you know what's important to you. Making your own decisions, and accepting responsibility for them, is part of the process of growing up. As with anything else, responsible decision making takes practice. The more practice you get now, the better equipped you'll be when you need to make major decisions about your future.

When making major decisions, seek information and advice from parents, teachers, counselors, and other resources.

Emphasize Stress that if Stephanie had turned down the job at the kennel on Jessica's advice, Stephanie would be likely to feel resentment and anger at missing out on an opportunity. This would have been much more damaging to her relationship with Jessica than dropping out of the business.

Did You Know? Self-esteem and accepting responsibility are mutually supportive. When people take responsibility for their actions, they feel more competent. This boosts self-esteem, giving them the confidence to accept responsibility for future decisions and actions.

INTERPERSONAL SKILLS

Everyday Decision Making

How did you decide what to wear today? What to eat for lunch? What to do after school? Chances are you didn't follow the five-step decision-making process when reaching those decisions. If you had, you might not have found time to do much else. You probably took one of the following shortcuts:

- **Default.** You're at home studying when a friend drops by to talk. If you keep talking until it's too late to study, you've decided by default to talk rather than to study. This means that you have backed into a decision by not deciding.
- **Imitation.** You might make decisions by following the examples of others. Imitating others can lead to good decisions—you might see a new movie because a friend recommends it. Sometimes, however, imitation limits you and may even be dangerous. Imitation plays a role when teens feel they have to wear the same clothes as their friends. It also influences people to use drugs, alcohol, and tobacco.
- **Habit.** Many people make decisions purely by habit. They wake up at the same time every day or take the same route to school. Sometimes, though, habit can keep you from trying new things. If you always order a hamburger when you go out to dinner, try another food for a change.
- **Impulse.** When you decide on impulse, you don't give yourself any time to think about your decision. If you are in line at the cafeteria to buy milk and you grab some candy instead, you're acting on impulse, which means that you're doing what you feel like at that moment.

When a decision is minor, these shortcuts are harmless. However, sometimes people make a decision according to habit or by default without realizing how important the decision is and how much impact it might have on their life.

Think It Through

1. **Who are some of the people whose example might lead you to imitate decisions?**
2. **What kind of decisions should not be left to impulse or default?**

Focus on Life Management Many people try to avoid responsibility for their decisions by making them by default. They feel that because they made no clear-cut, conscious decision, what happened wasn't their fault. Sexual activity and drug experimentation often fall into this category, and the consequences of poor decisions can be serious.

Emphasize Some minor decisions can be made without the use of the five-step process. But major decisions require a lot of thought, and the five-step process helps organize your thoughts.

Teaching the Feature

"Everyday Decision Making"

Answers to Feature Questions

1. Possible answers include parents, coaches, teachers, political leaders, entertainment personalities, courageous figures who have overcome handicaps.
2. Answers should focus on those decisions that affect long-term goals or on the decisions one makes during urgent circumstances (for example, while babysitting, child develops a fever) or other situations requiring responsible action.

Activities

Preventing Poor Decisions For each of the "shortcuts," have students give examples of the types of decisions they think teens are most likely to make in this way. (Impulse decisions, for example, might have to do with consumer choices.) Have them separate those that could have important consequences and examine these decisions to discover how they can prevent taking these shortcuts in the future.

Creating a Scenario Have students create a scenario in which someone needs to make a major decision. Ask them to write the details of the scenario. Then have the students show the person making the decision. Use first a shortcut, then the five-step process. Ask students to compare and contrast the results.

Community Contact Have students interview family, friends, and other individuals to get their insights on how they make important decisions. Tell them to try to discover if any of the people they interview follows the five-step process (even if they don't recognize it as such). Discuss the relative value of the ways various people make decisions.

COMPLETING THE CHAPTER

Summary

- Decisions can be about family matters, friends, time and money, or food and clothing. They can be fairly insignificant or have a lasting effect. Both the individual and other people, especially family and friends, are affected by a person's decisions.
- The five-step procedure for making decisions involves defining the problem, identifying alternatives, comparing possible outcomes, making the decision, and evaluating the results.
- It is important that people make decisions for themselves and take responsibility for those decisions. Because individuals know themselves best, they are best equipped to make their own decisions.

For Review

Objective Review Questions Have students complete the "Reviewing the Facts" section on this page.

Study Guide Have students complete the Study Guide from Chapter 5 of their *Student Workbook*.

Class Discussion Have students try to pinpoint the most important aspect of decision making that they learned from this chapter. Ask them how they might apply this learning to their lives.

For Evaluation

Make a List Ask students to formulate a list of ten do's and don'ts (five of each) that relate to making decisions. Examples include: Do consider the outcome of every alternative. Don't make a decision on impulse.

Chapter Test Have students complete the test for Chapter 5 that appears in the *Teacher's Classroom Resources*.

CHAPTER 5 REVIEW

Answers to "Reviewing the Facts"

1. A decision is a choice you make between different possibilities.
2. Your future; your health; your family; friends; other people.
3. (1) Define the problem.
   (2) Identify alternatives.
   (3) Compare possible outcomes.
   (4) Make the decision.
   (5) Evaluate the results.
4. Because you may discover that you have more choices than you first thought.
5. By ranking them in order of importance.
6. Evaluating decisions helps you to see your strengths and weaknesses, and helps you with future decision making.
7. Because you know yourself better than anyone, and you know what's important to you.

Reviewing the Facts

1. What is a decision?
2. What is affected by the decisions you make?
3. List the five steps in the decision-making process.
4. Why is it important to think through all your options?
5. How do you prioritize goals?
6. What is the point of evaluating decisions?
7. Why should each person take responsibility for his or her decisions?

Thinking Critically

1. What are the advantages of beginning now to think about your career decisions? What might happen if you don't think about your options?
2. Do you think it's possible to improve your decision-making skills? Why or why not?

Applying Your Skills

1. **Analyzing Your Decisions.** Select a typical day and write down all the decisions you can think of that you made that day. Put a check mark beside those decisions you thought through carefully. Add the number of checks, then figure out what percentage of your decisions were thought through. Compare your findings with those of your classmates.

2. **Constructing a Story.** Write a brief story about decision making. Using Stephanie and Jessica from the chapter as models, invent two or three characters and take them through the five-step process.

3. **Evaluating a Decision.** Use an encyclopedia to learn about a court decision on a specific topic, such as prayer in school, women's rights, or a libel issue. Pretend you were the judge making the decision. Describe how you would apply the five-step process. How is this example similar to a personal decision? How is it different? What would have been the result had the judge decided differently?

Answers to "Thinking Critically"

1. Advantages include a better knowledge of yourself by the time you begin a career; the opportunity to make choices about school courses that will benefit you later; the possibility for exploring various alternatives. Otherwise your career choices may be very limited, and you might have to take a job you don't like.
2. Some students will say yes because the more you practice decision-making skills, just like other skills, the better you get. Some may say no because there are so many factors that affect situations that sometimes you make good decisions and sometimes you don't.

CHAPTER

6

Managing Your Life

OBJECTIVES

This chapter will help you to:

- Discuss reasons for developing good management skills.
- Describe the four-step management process.
- Explain why it is important to take responsibility for managing your life.

WORDS TO REMEMBER

back-up plan
flexible
implement
improvise

Chapter Resources

Teacher's Classroom Resources
Lesson Plan
Life Skills Activity, *Life-Management Skills Checklist*
Reproducible Master, *The Management Process*
Extension Activity, *Management Skills*
Chapter Test

Student Workbook
Study Guide
Worksheet, *Time Management Chart*

CHAPTER OVERVIEW

Chapter 6 is about life management. It explains that increased demands and changing roles require teens to acquire management skills. The chapter describes in detail a four-step management process, which includes planning, organizing, implementing, and evaluating. The chapter emphasis is on taking responsibility for managing one's own life.

INTRODUCING THE CHAPTER

Motivators

A Fine Mess Ask students to describe the most hectic day they ever had or the biggest mess they ever got into as a result of having too many things to do in a short amount of time. Ask them to try to analyze briefly what went wrong. Explain that this chapter will help them avoid such problems in the future.

Using the Photograph Tell students to look at the photograph on this page. Ask: "How is managing your life like assembling a complex jigsaw puzzle?"

Brian's Weekend Have students read the chapter opening paragraph on page 58. Have them make a list of all the things that Brian planned to do during the weekend. Ask them if they think Brian will be able to do them all or if he will have to change some of his plans. Explain that the chapter will give a detailed procedure for helping Brian to manage his life.

Introducing the Objectives

Discuss the chapter objectives on this page. Remind students that the objectives focus on important chapter content.

Introducing Vocabulary

Point out that some words are built on smaller words, called root words. Use the word *flexible* as an example. *Flex* is the root word, meaning "to bend." *Flexible* means "able to bend." Ask students to suggest reasons why flexibility is important for managing their lives.

TEACHING THE CHAPTER

For convenience, the teaching suggestions for this chapter are arranged according to the following lesson topics:

- "Managing a Busy Life," pages 58-59
- "The Management Process," pages 59-62
- "Responsible Management," page 62

Teaching "Managing a Busy Life"
(Pages 58-59)

This section discusses why it is important to develop good management skills.

Checking Comprehension

✓ How will sound management skills help you? *You will be better able to deal with conflicting demands on your time and energy.*

✓ How do family roles change as a person grows older? *Parents expect teens to assume more responsibility, and siblings may need more of an individual's time and energy.*

✓ What other types of roles are also more demanding? *Teens' roles of student, friend, neighbor, and community member become more demanding as they mature.*

✓ Why will management skills be even more important for teens as they enter adulthood? *Teens will take on additional, and more responsible, roles in the future.*

Activities

Skill Builder: Writing
Ask students to write a short essay (one or two pages) about the various roles they now have and the way these roles have changed in the past five years. Have them describe any additional roles they have acquired. Ask them to think in terms of more complicated relationships and increasing demands.

"You mean this coming weekend?" Brian was talking to his mother on the phone. It was Thursday and she had just told him that his grandparents were planning to attend a funeral and would be staying with them for the weekend.

Brian was happy at the thought of seeing his grandparents again. Now that they lived so far away he didn't get to see them very often. He wondered, though, how he was going to be able to rearrange his weekend around their visit.

Already, he had too much to do. He had promised to sell raffle tickets for a class fund raiser on Saturday morning. Then he had soccer practice in the afternoon and had been invited to a party on Saturday evening. He had also promised his neighbor that he would mow the lawn some time over the weekend, and he had to put in at least three hours on his science project. His mother's birthday was on Tuesday, meaning that he had to shop for a present. He'd also promised his mother that he would help with the barbecue that she had planned for a few friends on Sunday afternoon.

Now Brian had to figure out how he could squeeze still more into the weekend. After all, he wanted to spend time with his grandparents. He'd also have to clean up his room before they came—they always wanted to see his various collections. Brian had too much to do.

Managing a Busy Life

You've probably had days that were too full, and no doubt you muddled through as best you could. "Muddling through" isn't the best way to handle difficult situations, though. If you develop sound management skills, you'll be better equipped to deal with conflicting demands on your time and energy.

The need for good management skills increases as you grow older and as your various roles become more numerous and more complex. Your family roles change as your parents expect you to assume more responsibility around the home. Perhaps your brothers and sisters also need more of your time and energy than they once did.

Many teens lead very busy lives. Management skills can help you make better use of your time and energy, and help you accomplish more.

Focus on Life Management Stress that this text will help the student manage his or her life. The first chapters set the stage for management, and subsequent chapters give specific information on such things as managing relationships, resources, nutrition, clothing, and living space.

Emphasize Help students to see that now is the time to practice and perfect their management skills—when the stakes are not as high as they will be later. The consequences of making mistakes now are much less than they will be later on.

In addition, your role as a student places more demands on your time and energy than it did when you were in elementary school. Moreover, your friendships, with your own sex and the other sex, have become more complex. You're a neighbor and a member of a community—these roles carry responsibilities. Furthermore, you may be a part-time worker, a babysitter, an athlete, a scout, a member of a club.

Think, for a moment, about Brian, whom you read about at the beginning of this chapter. During one weekend he would be juggling a number of roles: son, grandson, friend, teammate, neighbor, student. Each role was making certain demands on him.

When you think about the number of roles you have and realize how much more complex your life has become, you may see why management skills are so important. Those skills will become even more important when you take on additional, and more responsible, roles in the future.

The Management Process

Whether you are sorting out a conflicting schedule, planning a party, or preparing a meal, the same management process can be applied. Management involves four steps:

- Planning.
- Organizing.
- Implementing.
- Evaluating.

This management process, just like the decision-making process that you learned about in Chapter 5, can be applied to many different aspects of your life, including your school work, social activities, and spare time.

Planning

After Brian got the phone call from his mother, he started to make a list of all the things he had to do that weekend. This is a good way to see clearly the decisions that you face. He also tried to include all the details associated with each activity: for example, helping his mother get the spare room prepared for his grandparents, checking that there was enough charcoal for the barbecue, washing his soccer uniform.

The first step of any project is planning. Planning involves assessing the situation, figuring out what resources you have, and deciding on your priorities. Writing a list is often a good way to assess the situation—it helps you see all the things you have to consider. Before you begin preparing a meal, for instance, you might find it useful to list all the steps you need to take. A food-shopping trip will be more productive if you prepare a list of needed supplies.

Another part of planning is thinking about your resources. Your resources are the things you need to accomplish your goals. They include equipment, skills, knowledge, time, energy, money, and other people.

Brian thought about the resources he would need for the different tasks on his list. His biggest problem seemed to be time: most of his time was already accounted for before he heard about his grandparents' visit. His mother had told him they would be arriving late Saturday morning. Brian decided that he needed to spend Saturday morning helping his mother get the spare room ready and cleaning up his own room. He'd promised to sell raffle tickets, though. Then Brian thought of another resource: his friends. He'd ask his friend Alan to sell raffle tickets for him. He could return the favor another time by doing something to help Alan.

Did You Know? Making a list for a shopping trip can help you avoid overspending. When you make a list, you are more likely to buy just the things on that list and not others. Without a list, you are more likely to buy things you don't need, to buy on impulse, or to be influenced by advertising ploys.

Focus on Life Management Point out to students that the feature for this chapter discusses the most valuable resource—the person himself or herself. The feature shows how learning to manage helps people make use of this resource.

Reteaching
Ask students to cut out of magazines two or three pictures that show teens in various roles. Ask them to mount each picture on a different piece of paper or cardboard and list on the board or paper at least three responsibilities that are part of the role illustrated.

Enrichment
Hold a class discussion that centers on exploring ways that students can develop their roles as neighbors and community members. In the role of neighbor, for example, students might suggest devoting an hour a week to an elderly person who can no longer do certain kinds of physical work.

Teaching "The Management Process"
(Pages 59-62)

This section describes the four steps of the management process: planning, organizing, implementing, and evaluating.

Checking Comprehension

✓ How does making a list help you to plan? *Because you can see clearly the decisions that you face and begin to assess the situation by seeing all the things you have to consider.*

✓ What should you do after you assess the situation? *You should figure out what resources you have.*

✓ Name several resources. *Included are equipment, skills, knowledge, time, money, energy, possessions, and other people.*

✓ Why is it important to think about resources, and how do you start? *It is important because it can help you prevent things from going wrong later. You start by imagining each step of the project you're planning, then picturing the resources you will need and how long each step will take.*

✓ What comes after deciding about resources? *Setting priorities.*

✓ After the students have read pages 59-62, ask: "What are Brian's top priorities?" *His top priorities are getting his own room and the spare room ready, spending time with his grandparents, attending team practice, mowing his neighbor's lawn, and helping with the family barbecue.*

✓ How are priorities determined? *They are determined by your goals, which are determined by your needs, wants, and values.*

✓ Why do you need to be organized if you want a project to go smoothly? *Because when you know what needs to be done, things are less likely to go wrong. Also, without organization, other people may not know what their duties are.*

✓ What is a back-up plan? *It is an alternative way of doing something if the original plan does not work out.*

✓ Explain the implementation stage in the management process. *Implementation follows the planning and organizing steps. It entails putting the project into action and monitoring it. During this stage, you make sure everything gets done.*

✓ Why might it be necessary to improvise? *Problems may arise while you are trying to complete a project.*

✓ What does it mean to be flexible? *To be flexible means to be able to adapt to different plans if the original plans do not work out.*

✓ Why is it important to evaluate your project? *You learn from your successes and failures.*

Activities

Skill Builder: Critical Thinking
Have students reread the section on planning, and then ask them to make a list of what they think Brian's goals are. Ask them also to figure out, from a study of Brian's priorities, what is important to him.

Skills

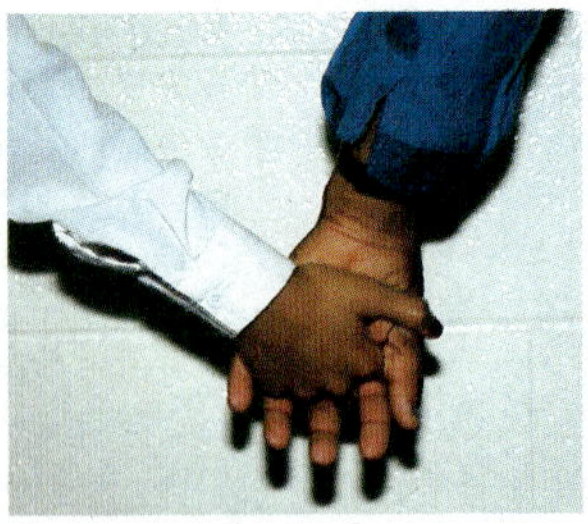

People

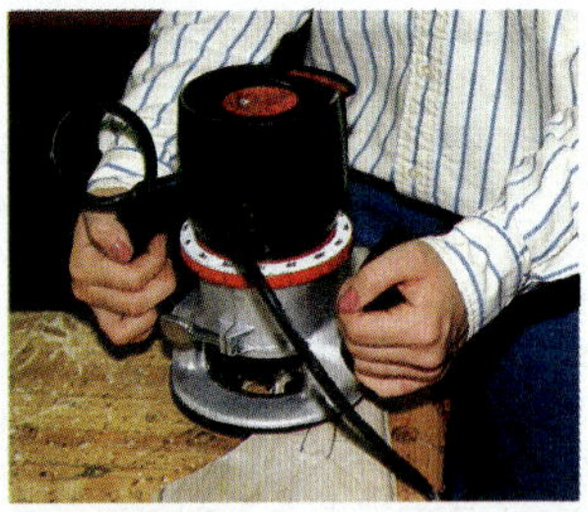

Possessions

Money

Time

Knowledge

Identifying available resources is an important part of the planning step. Which of these resources will Brian need to use during the weekend?

Thinking about resources is an important part of the management process because careful thinking can prevent things from going wrong later. You should start by imagining each step of the project that you're preparing, and picturing, in your mind's eye, what equipment or people you will need and how long each step will take. If you're preparing a meal, for example, thinking it through will help ensure that you don't discover at the last minute that you're missing a needed ingredient or utensil.

Once you've assessed the situation and figured out what resources you have, you need to set priorities. This is phase three of the planning stage.

Brian decided that his top priorities were to get his own room and the spare room ready, to spend some time with his grandparents, to attend team practice, to mow his neighbors' lawn, and to help with the Sunday afternoon barbecue. He wanted to go to the party, but it wouldn't be the end of the world if he missed it. He could put off his science project until the following weekend, though he preferred not to. If necessary, he could go shopping for his mother's present on Monday evening.

To sort out your priorities, you should follow the decision-making process described in Chapter 5. Priorities are determined by your goals, which are in turn determined by your needs, wants, and values. Brian placed a high value on helping his mother and on spending time with his grandparents, so those two items were high on his list.

Organizing

The organization stage of the management process involves developing a schedule, getting your resources together, and preparing to act. First Brian

Emphasize Help students to see that all resources, not just time, have their limitations. When considering a resource, individuals should consider its limitations—how far it will go.

Emphasize Remind students that one way to set priorities is to think in terms of fixed and flexible goals (see Chapter 4). Preparing for and spending time with Brian's grandparents is a fixed goal, as is the barbeque. Time to spend on the science project and the shopping trip are flexible goals, though ones that, if ignored, will soon become fixed.

drew up a schedule. That helped him realize that he'd be able to spend Saturday lunchtime and Saturday evening with his grandparents, if he didn't go to the party. He also realized that he had no plans for Friday night—he could work on his science project then. He could mow the lawn before the barbecue. Maybe his grandmother would like to go shopping for his mother's birthday present with him. That would allow them to spend some more time together.

Then Brian called Alan and arranged for him to sell raffle tickets Saturday morning. After that, he checked to make sure there was enough charcoal, washed his soccer clothes, and wrote down some of his ideas for presents for his mother. He'd show the list to his grandmother before they set out for the stores.

Good organization is necessary for any project to go smoothly. When you have a schedule that tells you what needs to be done when, things are less likely to go wrong. If your project involves other people, it's important that they, too, know what their duties are.

It's also a good idea to have some **back-up plans**—alternative ways of doing something if the original plan does not work out. For example, what if it rained on Sunday? Brian would gain time because he wouldn't have to mow the lawn, but he would also have to help his mother prepare food that could be served indoors.

Implementing

After you've planned and organized your project, you're ready to **implement** it, to put it into action and monitor it. During the implementing stage you make sure that everything gets done.

In an ideal world, a well-planned and well-organized project would go smoothly. Very often, though, things don't turn out exactly as you expected. Problems arise along the way, and you may have to improvise as the project progresses. **Improvising** means coming up with new ideas when some of your plans don't work.

To make the car wash a successful fund-raiser, the group spent time planning and organizing the event.

Focus on Leadership Remind students that when they are in charge of a group, they must oversee the schedule and be sure that each person knows about it and about his or her part in the schedule. Point out that it is usually better for all those involved to see the whole schedule. Then they know how their part fits into the whole.

Did You Know? The word *implement* comes from roots that mean, literally, "to fill up." Ask students how this relates to the carrying out of a plan.

Skill Builder: Writing
Have students write out a sample schedule that Brian might have used to help him organize his weekend. Have them try to guess the approximate amounts of time that would need to be spent on each activity.

Skill Builder: Writing
Ask students to imagine that they are Brian and that they are writing an evaluation of his weekend strategy. Ask them to write three or four paragraphs that take into account Brian's goals and values, the strategy's effects on Brian and others, and how the actual events worked out.

Reteaching
Ask students to look over the discussion of resources on pages 59-60. Have them think of examples of each type of resource and a situation in which each resource might be used.

Reteaching
Ask students to give examples of flexibility from their own lives. They should try to think of times when they were able to adjust successfully to unexpectedly changing circumstances.

Enrichment
Ask students to think of a task they would like to complete in the next week or two. (It can be as simple as getting ready on time every morning.) They should go through the steps of planning and organizing for this task.

Enrichment
Ask students to brainstorm ways for Brian to improvise had the following problems developed:

- Alan calls him Saturday morning and tells Brian he is sick and cannot sell tickets.
- Brian's grandparents arrive earlier than expected.
- The day of the barbeque is sunny, but the grill has been damaged and cannot be used.
- Brian's grandmother is too tired to go shopping with him.

Teaching "Responsible Management"
(Page 62)

This section explains why it is important to take responsibility for managing one's own life.

Checking Comprehension

✓ What kinds of added responsibility are teens likely to take on at home? *Responsibilities related to keeping the home clean, buying supplies, and choosing meals.*

✓ What types of increased responsibility will teens have at school? *They will have increased responsibility for managing their time and getting their work done.*

✓ What should students be doing with their management skills now? *They should be practicing their management skills on projects they undertake.*

Activities

Skill Builder: Reading
Ask students to go to the library and skim several articles or a book on management techniques. Ask them to discover the steps in the management process described and compare or contrast them with the ones in the book.

Skill Builder: Reading
Ask students to read a short story. Then have them list the responsibilities of the main character and explain how the character handles those responsibilities.

Reteaching
Ask students to volunteer examples of added responsibilities that they expect to have in the categories mentioned in the text: home life, school, relationships.

Enrichment
Ask students to consider the list they made for the reteaching exercise. Ask them to imagine how they will be able to apply the management skills they have learned to handling these added responsibilities.

For example, after Brian had mowed the lawn and had gone shopping with his grandmother on Sunday, clouds began to gather and rain started before the friends arrived for the barbecue. Brian and his mother had to put their back-up plan into action: they baked potatoes and chicken in the oven instead of on the grill, and served the food in the dining room.

Flexibility is one of the keys to good management. People who are **flexible** are able to adapt to different plans if the original plans don't work out.

Evaluating

As with decision making, it's important to evaluate your project once it is over. You learn from your successes and failures.

Overall, Brian's plans worked out well. He had managed to do all that he had wanted to do, except go to the party, and he had been able to spend several hours with his grandparents. He realized that the weekend would have been less hectic if he had been better prepared beforehand. For example, he recognized that he should have bought his mother's present earlier so that he wouldn't be forced to do it at the last minute.

After his grandparents left, Brian and his mother talked about their weekend. They had enjoyed the visit, and even though the barbecue plans had had to be changed, everyone had enjoyed their time together.

Responsible Management

In this chapter, you read about how Brian managed one weekend. In real life, of course, you have to manage every day of your life and deal with many different situations.

Over the next few years you will take more and more responsibility for managing your own life. In your home life, you will take on added responsibilities related to keeping the home clean, buying supplies, and choosing meals. That will give you experience you will need when you move into an apartment or home of your own. At school, you will find that your teachers will give you increasing responsibility for managing your time and getting your work done. In your relationships with your family and friends, you'll find that you'll be making more and more decisions for yourself.

Taking responsibility for managing your own life is an exciting prospect. During the next few years you'll have many opportunities to use your management skills. Practice applying the management process to different projects that you undertake. Practice now will help you for years to come.

Management skills can help you with added responsibilities—both now and in the future.

Emphasize Stress to students that evaluation not only points out ways that the particular project might have gone more smoothly, but also reveals general principles that help the individual avoid problems in the future. Brian, for example, learned that procrastination, which is avoidable, created part of his problem.

Focus on Relationship Skills Tell students that Unit 2 of this book, along with many of the chapter features, focuses on management skills as they relate to interpersonal relationships. Remind students that relationships are important in every aspect of life: work, home, and leisure.

INTERPERSONAL SKILLS

Community Service

Twice a week, Mark tutors second graders in math and reading at a neighborhood center. Last summer, Erin spent two weeks helping to build a house for a low-income family. Just before Thanksgiving, Amy organized a canned-food drive at school to benefit a local shelter for the homeless.

Mark, Erin, and Amy are among the thousands of young people across the country who volunteer their time to help others. They show some of the ways in which young people can be active and productive members of the community.

The United States has an ever-increasing need for volunteers. Public funding cannot supply all the human services workers necessary to meet people's needs. At the same time, the traditional source of many volunteers (homemakers) has shrunk as more women are employed outside the home. Teens are needed to fill the gap.

Young people can volunteer through school-based programs, churches, nonprofit agencies, and other organizations. They can work with a group or on their own, on an ongoing project or a short-term project. Some volunteer programs provide orientation, training, and supervision, while others are less structured.

Here are just a few ideas of how teens can provide community service:

- Read stories to younger children in an after-school program.
- Pick up litter along highways, in parks, or on your school grounds.
- Be a coaching assistant for a Little League team.
- Visit with elderly residents in a nursing home.
- Participate in a walkathon, skateathon, or readathon to raise funds for a charity.

Teen volunteers provide many benefits to the people they help. They also earn benefits for themselves. They make new friends and learn new skills. Teen volunteers say they feel better about themselves and about the world. When they see that their efforts make a difference, they feel more hopeful about the future.

Think It Through

1. **How can performing community service during high school help you in the future?**
2. **More and more high schools require students to perform community service before they can graduate. Do you think this is a good idea? Why or why not?**

Did You Know? Learning through service is becoming part of the curriculum in many elementary and secondary schools. Teachers use social service projects to teach reading, writing, and math skills. Such projects also teach young people the responsibilities of citizenship and help them realize they have the power to make changes.

Emphasize Newspapers and magazines regularly feature teens who act to meet a need. For example, two young women in Texas raise money to purchase pencils and paper for Mexican pupils and teachers. High school students in Georgia established a day care center that has operated for more than ten years.

Teaching the Feature

"Community Service"

Answers to Feature Questions

1. You can learn about different careers. You also learn to get along with a variety of people. You can develop problem-solving and communication skills. Volunteer work can be considered work experience when applying for a job.

2. Some students will think it is a good idea because it benefits both students and the community; students learn new skills; it provides valuable experience. Other students might say that community service should be voluntary and not forced; it takes time away from academic studies; it would be hard for students with part-time jobs to find time for community service.

Activities

Taking Inventory Students in your class may already be involved in community service. Ask them to describe what they do and why they do it. Students might write articles for the school newspaper describing their experiences as volunteers.

Volunteer Fair Have each student research and report on one volunteer opportunity in their school or community. Volunteer opportunities could also be through national or international groups. Encourage students to show brochures and posters related to the service opportunity.

Designing a Community Service Project Instead of joining an established volunteer effort, have students design their own project. Ask them to identify a need in their community and to plan a course of action to meet the need.

Community Contact Invite a member of Rotary International, the Lions, or another local organization to speak to the class about the group's community service. Students' parents might belong to these groups, and they could be invited to speak.

COMPLETING THE CHAPTER

Summary

- Good management skills will help teens deal with the more varied roles, added responsibilities, and sometimes conflicting demands of adolescence and adulthood.
- The four-step management process consists of planning, organizing, implementing, and evaluating.
- Taking responsibility for their own lives will give teens the experience they need to manage their time, relationships, and responsibilities in adulthood.

For Review

Objective Review Questions Have students complete the "Reviewing the Facts" section on this page.

Study Guide Have students complete the Study Guide from Chapter 6 of their *Student Workbook.*

Class Discussion Write the following maxim on the board: "Experience has shown that every man is the architect of his own fortune" (Sallust, 86-34 B.C.). Ask how this saying, in a general way, relates to the chapter. Then ask what students know about architects and their work. If necessary, provide some information and have students use this knowledge to draw an analogy between an architect and a person managing his or her life.

For Evaluation

Make a Time Line If students do not already know how to make a time line, explain the procedure. Then ask them to make a time line of Brian's weekend, showing the different aspects of his planning, organizing, implementing, and evaluating. Stress that sequence of activities is more important than any exact times.

Chapter Test Have students complete the test for Chapter 6 that appears in the *Teacher's Classroom Resources.*

CHAPTER 6 REVIEW

Answers to "Reviewing the Facts"

1. To be better equipped to deal with conflicting demands on their time; so they can assume their many different roles; so they can handle increasing responsibility.
2. Planning, organizing, implementing, evaluating.
3. Assessing the situation; figuring out what resources you have; deciding on your priorities.
4. Developing a schedule; getting your resources together; preparing to act.
5. Coming up with new ideas when some of your plans don't work out.
6. So you can adapt to different plans if the original ones don't work out.
7. Because over the next few years you will be taking on more and more responsibility for managing your life in all areas.

Reviewing the Facts

1. Why should teens develop good management skills?
2. List the four steps in the management process.
3. What three steps are involved in planning?
4. List the three steps in the organization stage.
5. What does improvising mean?
6. Why should you be flexible?
7. Why is it important to take responsibility for managing your life now?

Thinking Critically

1. Why would having good management skills help you to feel more relaxed?
2. How has your role as a student changed in the past two years? In what ways do these changes require greater management skills?

Applying Your Skills

1. **Analyzing Your Use of Time.** On a sheet of paper, list the main things you spend your time on in a typical week. Your list should include being in school, reading, sleeping, watching TV, being with friends, and so on. Estimate how much time you spend on each activity in a typical week. Then draw a circle graph to show how your time is divided.

2. **Evaluating Management's Benefits.** Make a list of the three people who are most strongly affected by the way you manage your life. For each person, list a specific example of a way that good management has or might possibly benefit that person. How can you improve your life management further to benefit these three people?

3. **Analyzing Management Skills.** Use an encyclopedia or biography and read about Lee Iacocca, Jesse Jackson, Ronald Reagan, or Margaret Thatcher to discover the role that management plays in that person's life. Describe how the person managed to get where he or she is today and how he or she relies on management skills still. Does this leader seem to apply the four-step process efficiently? Do you admire him or her?

Answers to "Thinking Critically"

1. Students should point out that when a person has good management skills, he or she feels in control. Since there are also fewer unpleasant surprises he or she can be more relaxed.
2. Students should suggest that they are getting more independence, more homework, and more choices. That requires them to have greater management skills and to make more important decisions.

TEEN TIPS

TEEN TIPS OVERVIEW

This section focuses on specific techniques to help students feel and look their best.

Six Ways to Feel Good About Yourself

This Teen Tip offers practical suggestions for feeling better when feeling down. Ideas discuss dressing to improve one's mood, maintaining a positive attitude, and using leisure time in satisfying ways.

How to Save Face

This Teen Tip discusses skin-care techniques that can help avoid or minimize problems associated with ultraviolet rays from the sun or skin blemishes.

Journaling—The New Way to Keep a Diary

In this Teen Tip students are introduced to a practice that can enable them to clarify their thoughts and deal with their emotions. Four themes for journals are described. These include: memory, imagination, dialogue, and spirituality.

These "Teen Tips" offer practical ways in which the students can more effectively cope with themselves and their world.

Introducing "Six Ways to Feel Good About Yourself"
(Pages 66-67)

Motivators

Describing the Blues Ask students to take one minute to think of and write down one word or a short phrase that describes how people feel when they feel "blue" (*for example, ugly, lonely, incompetent*). After one minute, have volunteers share their responses. List the words or phrases on the chalkboard. Save the list for later reference.

Discussion Question: Ask students: "How might a good self-image help you cope with the blues?" Have students discuss this question. Be sure to point out that a positive self-image helps one have the confidence to face problems and negative feelings when they arise and to cope with them more effectively. Note that this section will focus on ways the students can beat the blues by feeling better about themselves.

Teaching "Six Ways to Feel Good About Yourself"

Checking Comprehension

✓ Tip number one focuses on making others think you feel good about yourself when you're feeling down. Ask students: "Why do you think this is an important part of cheering up?" *If you project positive feelings about yourself, others will react positively to you, which will make you feel better.*

✓ Following the other tips can also make people respond positively to you. Ask: "What are some other ways in which these six tips are alike?" *They emphasize being good to oneself, moving ahead rather than remaining stuck on past problems or mistakes, and taking an active approach to problems rather than dwelling on them.*

TEEN TIPS

Six Ways to Feel Good About Yourself

"No one can make you feel inferior without your consent."

Eleanor Roosevelt

Sometimes you feel great—on top of the world. Other times it seems that life is just the pits. Don't worry, that's normal. On those days that you're feeling down, you have to work harder than usual at feeling good about yourself. Here are six ways that are guaranteed to lift your spirits and tell the world you're feeling great:

Look your best to feel your best. Take a little extra time and extra care in dressing, whether for school or a special event. Walk confidently so everyone will know you feel great about yourself.

Learn to relax. If you feel mentally tired after studying, a good physical workout may be what you need to unwind. On the other hand, if you've just finished mowing the lawn or working on your car, a hot bath and some music might make you feel great.

Send positive messages to yourself. If you say to yourself "I'm not popular" or "I'm not smart," you give yourself an excuse to feel bad. Instead, make a list of your strengths or the things you like best about yourself. Then give yourself a pat on the back for all your good qualities.

Did You Know? Recent research has shown that volunteering to help others is an excellent way to improve one's self-image and sense of well-being. Visiting patients in nursing homes or hospitals, running errands for shut-ins, or working for a favorite cause are examples of good "outreach" activities. Discuss the value of such projects with students and encourage them to volunteer for one that appeals to them.

TEEN TIPS

Enjoy life. Being interested in life is what is attractive to other people. If you enjoy yourself and your interests, you will be fun to be with—and it will be easier to make good friends.

Cope with problems. Accept the things that you can't change, but be able to make decisions about those things that are within your control. If you avoid making decisions, others may make them for you. Take responsibility for your own life.

Focus on what's happening right now. If you're dwelling on mistakes you made in the past, you're not helping your self-esteem. Evaluate how you handled the situations, and forgive yourself for your mistakes. Then start focusing on the present—and the future.

Activities

Skill Builder: Writing
Ask students to pretend they are their own best friend and write a letter to themselves expressing appreciation for their strengths and good points.

Reteaching
Refer to the list of words and phrases describing the blues, generated at the beginning of the lesson. Divide the class into small groups, giving each group a selection of the words on the list. Have each group decide which tips given in this section would be most appropriate for coping with each feeling on its list. Each group should choose one person to report on what the group decided.

Enrichment
Ask students to think of a recent time when they felt down or depressed. Ask them to write a paragraph or two describing the situation and how they coped with it. Ask them how they might have coped differently, having read this section.

Focus on Life Management Feeling in control of one's life is especially crucial to strong self-esteem and an ability to cope with negative moods. Have the students work in small groups to discuss and then report on why setting and achieving a goal, making a decision, or taking a positive step toward managing one's time more efficiently can make one feel better in general. Students may wish to refer to Chapters 4, 5, and 6.

Introducing "How to Save Face"

(Pages 68-69)

Motivators

Surveying Your Skin-Care Arsenal The day before teaching this section, ask students to take a skin-care product survey. Students should check their lockers, purses, bedrooms, and medicine cabinets for facial skin-care products and ask their parent(s) what products they use. Tell students to record all the different categories of products they find (for example, face cleansers, moisturizers) and also the number of different brands or variations within each category (for example, they may list three different brands of face cleanser). Have students share their results. Record the major categories of products for later use.

Discussion Question: Ask students: "Why are skin-care products so plentiful?" Students are likely to point out that skin is a factor in personal appearance, and that people are eager for products that will make them look better. Throughout the discussion of this subject, take care not to focus undue attention on those who would find this topic embarrassing.

Teaching "How to Save Face"

Checking Comprehension

✔ What does the SPF number for sunscreens mean? *The SPF number rates the sun protection factor. The higher the SPF number, the more protection provided.*

✔ What are some major causes of skin problems you just read about? *Stress, hormones.*

TEEN TIPS

How to Save Face

Did you know that the average adult has about 17 square feet of skin? Your skin serves as a waterproof covering for your body, acts as a barrier to germs, and regulates your body temperature.

How you take care of your skin affects your overall appearance—both now and when you are older.

Skin and Sun

Too much sun can result in a severe sunburn, as well as premature aging of the skin and skin cancer. How can you protect your skin and still be active outdoors?

The sun's ultraviolet rays are most damaging to skin. These rays are most intense during the middle of the day, and up to 80% of the rays can penetrate haze and light clouds. That's why you can get sunburned even on hazy or cloudy days. Also, snow and water reflect ultraviolet rays upward.

To protect your skin, avoid overexposure to the sun's ultraviolet rays. *Suntan lotions* offer little or no protection against ultraviolet light unless they contain a sunscreen. *Sunscreens* can

More About Skin Care Dermatologists and others have recently concluded that almost any amount of sun tanning is potentially damaging to the skin. Skin cancer is just one risk. Other problems that can develop, especially later in life, include many difficult-to-treat blemishes, increased wrinkling and aging of the skin, and frequently appearing, precancerous lesions that require medical treatment.

absorb some of the rays, and are rated according to their sun protection factor (SPF). The higher the SPF number, the more protection provided—the number 2 offers only minimal protection, while the number 15 provides a lot of protection. *Sun-blocking agents* deflect the harmful rays and offer maximum protection—and are good for areas that burn easily, such as lips, ears, and nose. When choosing suntan products, read the labels carefully.

Skin and Acne

What causes some people's skin to break out, while others have flawless skin through their teen years? There are several factors. For starters, heredity is involved. Just as you inherited your father's build or your mother's eye color, you also inherited your skin type and any tendency toward blemishes.

Hormones are another factor. During the teen years, rapidly rising hormone levels cause the oil glands to enlarge and produce more oil. These oil-producing glands can cause your pores to clog. When oils or bacteria get trapped in your pores, the result can be whiteheads, blackheads, or pimples.

Stress may also contribute to skin problems. That's why your face seems to break out during test week or the day before a big party.

Here are some suggestions for controlling acne:

- Wash your face morning and night with warm water and a mild soap or cleanser.
- If you wear makeup, be sure to remove all traces before you go to bed.
- Eat a well-balanced diet and get plenty of rest and exercise.
- Select cleansers and astringents, which help to clean clogged pores, carefully. Read the labels and ask the pharmacist for advice.
- If necessary, use a cream or gel containing benzoyl peroxide to help clear up pimples. Do not use too frequently, because it can dry out the skin.
- Avoid picking or squeezing any affected area as this can worsen the problem or even cause scarring.
- For a severe case of acne, contact a dermatologist, a doctor specializing in skin disorders.

TEEN TIPS

✓ Ask students to think about the chapters in this unit and describe how the topic of skin care fits in with what they've been studying. *Healthy skin contributes to self-esteem (Chapter 2). Problems can arise with the stress associated with the teen years (Chapter 2), with working towards goals and making decisions (Chapters 4 and 5), and with managing a busy life (Chapter 6). Basic good health is essential for healthy skin (Chapter 3).*

Activities

Skill Builder: Science
Have students research the definitions of the following terms and their significance to skin care: *epidermis, dermis, sebaceous glands, pH, emollient, humectant, exfoliant.*

Reteaching
Ask each student to develop a poster illustrating one skin-care tip from this lesson. Have students show and discuss their posters.

Enrichment
Refer to the list of types of products developed earlier. Divide the class into small groups and assign each group one or two product categories. The groups should visit a store and note for each category the number of brands available. They should also choose one category and catalog variations within it in terms of the cost, ingredients, and effectiveness claims for various brands. If possible, they should discuss the various products with a pharmacist or other knowledgeable person. Have the groups report in class on the variety within each product category. Suggest they make some judgment about which products are the best buys. If research in a store is not appropriate for the class, have the groups seek similar information in magazine, radio, and television advertisements for skin-care products.

Focus on Skin Care Have students research the topic of skin cancer. Topics include more detail about the possible dangers of exposure, the best means of preventing exposure, the meaning of the SPF factor on sun preparations, whether new preparations with very high numbers are actually more effective than older sunscreens with SPFs of 15, the reasons why sun exposure is dangerous, and whether the danger has increased in the past few years.

Introducing "Journaling—The New Way to Keep a Diary"

(Pages 70-71)

Motivators

Recording an Important Event Ask students to recall an important event in their lives that occurred within the past month or so. Ask them to record the event as if they were reporting it in a newspaper, although they may use the first person. Stress that they should be as objective as possible, sticking to facts and keeping discussion of feelings to a minimum. Point out that only those students who *want* to share their work will be asked to do so. Thus, they can write about any event they please. Ask for volunteers to read their work to the class. Discuss how the descriptions depict *what happened* but do not convey much about the feelings involved. Tell students to save their work for use later.

Discussion Question: Ask students: "Do you keep a diary? Why?" Bring out whether students' diaries record primarily events or feelings. Note that this section will focus on a way of writing about emotions and relationships.

Teaching "Journaling—The New Way to Keep a Diary"

Checking Comprehension

✓ What are the differences between keeping a diary and journaling? *In keeping a diary, the writer is more factual and focuses on what happened. Journaling focuses more on the emotional impact of events. Moreover, journaling can involve recording dreams, daydreams, and imaginary dialogues, as well as facts.*

✓ How can keeping a journal help the writer deal with difficult events, relationships, and emotions? *Answers may vary. Be sure to bring out that recording feelings helps the writer see problems more objectively. Imagining events helps the writer understand better what he or she wants to have happen. Imagining a conversation helps the writer understand another person's perspective and thus relate to that person.*

TEEN TIPS

Journaling—The New Way to Keep a Diary

Have you ever kept a diary of the events that happened in your life? Perhaps you went on a trip and kept a record of the things you saw and did along the way. You might have shared this diary with your friends or relatives when you came back.

Journaling is different from keeping a standard diary. Your journal is a private place where you write your thoughts and feelings. It mirrors what is going on inside your head and heart at the time.

A journal can be used to help you through difficult times, make it easier to understand yourself better, or give you a way to deal with someone who is a source of trouble to you. Because you are writing for yourself, you can use any style or form that you want to use. If you want to share your journal with anyone else, that is your personal choice.

Professionals who encourage journal writing suggest four different themes for journal entries:

Memory. Do you remember something that happened to you in the past that seems to be affecting your life now? It may be a pleasant memory of a day with your family that all of a sudden makes you feel very happy. If you write about something you remember as being uncomfortable, you may be able to deal with the memory in a more positive way.

More About Journaling A writer can use different themes within a journal, depending on his or her concerns at the time. Students need not use just one, nor limit themselves to the four mentioned in this section. Other themes might be personal reflections on current events; reactions to a play, movie, book, or concert; or thoughtful character sketches of people important in their lives. Journals may also include different styles, suitable to the writer's changing concerns, moods, and themes.

TEEN TIPS

Imagination. Do your teachers or parents ever tell you that you spend too much time daydreaming when there seems to be something more practical to do? You may be dreaming about the future or something you want that will make you feel more confident. Perhaps you dream about a special relationship in your life. Keep track of these dreams in your journal. It may help you focus on your ideas and goals.

Dialogue. Have you ever had a conversation in your mind with someone who you have a hard time communicating with in real life? It may be a parent, a brother or sister, a teacher, a friend, or a classmate. You may think that if you could only tell that person how you feel, he or she would understand you better. Try writing the conversation in the form of a dialogue. By writing the other person's side of the conversation, you may begin to understand the other person better.

Spirituality. What gives meaning to your life? Sometimes it's difficult to talk to your peers about your beliefs. Your private journal is for your eyes alone, so it is a place where you can express things that you may not feel comfortable talking about to others.

A journal may surprise you. You may discover that you are able to handle things better than you thought you could. By writing down your feelings, you will become more aware of yourself as the special person that you are.

Activities

Skill Builder: Reading

Have students read a published diary or journal and report on it. Ask them to discuss whether the book is a diary or a journal, as defined in this section, and to defend their position. Point out that people often use the terms *diary* and *journal* interchangeably, so the book's title is not a reliable guide to its genre. Also tell students that some books may not clearly fall into one of these categories and that, for such a book, they should explain why that is the case. Reports may be written or oral.

Reteaching

Have students choose one journal theme described in the "Teen Tip" and use that style to rewrite the description they did earlier. Reassure students that they will not have to share their work if they don't want to. When students have finished, ask how many chose each of the four styles. Discuss how it felt to write in this style and how using it changed the description. Ask for volunteers to read their rewritten work.

Enrichment

Have students keep a journal for two weeks. At the end of that time, discuss how students liked keeping a journal, what kinds of things they wrote about, what themes they used, and whether the activity helped them with any problems.

Focus on Imagining The theme of imagination could be expressed in a short story about the writer and other characters. A free-flowing, stream-of-consciousness style is excellent for recording dreams, daydreams, and memories. Students with special talents might use less conventional styles, such as poetry, drawings, or musical compositions. If class interest level is high, have students generate a list of additional themes and styles, and invite students to experiment with these themes and styles in journals.

UNIT PREVIEW

Unit 2 explores various types of relationships that students have with family members, friends and acquaintances. They learn how relationships can be both satisfying and rewarding. The strengths of family life are emphasized and students gain an understanding of family changes and peer pressure. They learn to use communication skills to build strong relationships and resolve conflicts. Career possibilities for those who enjoy working with people are also presented.

CONTENT DEVELOPMENT

Use these lessons to reinforce the following themes:

Content Strands	Chapters
Career Exploration	17
Citizenship/ Leadership	7,15,16
Communication	7-11,13-16
Decision Making	12,15,16,(TT 1,2,3)
Health and Safety	12,(TT 1,2,3)
Managing Resources	10,11,13,17
Personal Development	7-9,11-16,(TT 1,2)
Technology	8,16

UNIT MOTIVATORS

Decision-Making Skills

What Should You Do? Gather several letters from newspaper or magazine advice columns that deal with relationships. Cover the responses. Have students work in small groups to decide the best response to each letter. Have them compare their responses to the published answers. Which answers do they think are more helpful?

Critical Thinking Skills

Do Stereotypes Sell? Ask students: "Do you think that stereotypes are very common in advertising?" Have them make a guess and then conduct a media watch. Ask them to evaluate 25 magazine advertisements. Tally the number of men and women depicted, as well as their activities in the advertising. Does their survey support their original suspicions? Explain that this unit will explore stereotypes.

CROSS-CURRICULAR ACTIVITY

Art and Relationships Suggest that students find paintings, sculpture, and photographs that depict a relationship such as mother-child or a life-cycle event such as a wedding. They might look in art books or museum catalogs. Have them share their findings and interpret the artist's message.

SPECIAL NEEDS

Strategies for Visual Learners Have students cut out newspaper comic strips that portray different types of relationships (for example, husband-wife, employer-employee, brother-sister). Ask them to assemble their findings in a poster. Use the poster to show the types and importance of relationships.

YOUR FAMILY AND FRIENDS

UNIT TWO

Your Family and Friends

CHAPTER

COOPERATIVE LEARNING

Family vs. Friends As young people seek to become more independent, they may find themselves torn between loyalty to family and loyalty to friends. For example, teens may have to choose between going on a family outing or being with friends, or they may disagree with family members about their choice of friends. Divide the class into discussion groups of three or four students. Ask them to identify at least one source of conflict regarding families and friends. Then have them suggest ways to resolve the conflict. Call the groups together and have them report on their discussion. One person in each group can be the recorder and one person can be the reporter.

FHA ACTIVITIES

The following activities can be used with your FHA group or as public relation strategies:

Family Night Plan and organize a "family outing" event, such as playing miniature golf or a skating party. The chapter pays admission for students if they bring one other family member.

B.Y.O.B. Party As a get-acquainted activity sponsor a B.Y.O.B. Party. Have students bring their own banana and have the chapter supply items for banana splits.

Youth Conference Plan and initiate a youth conference where school psychologists or social workers visit the school and discuss peer pressure—both positive and negative. Ask them to offer helpful hints on positive decision-making skills.

Community Directory Have students make a directory of local agencies or places in the community where people could go for help. Have students decide on the type of problems that affect people in the community. Then with the use of several telephone books, have students explore the agencies where one could go for help. These could be organized, printed, and distributed during FHA week.

UNIT CLOSURE

For Review

Are You Listening? Have students explain how they could become better listeners at home and at school. Have them identify ways they could become better listeners and practice them for one week. Ask them to keep a journal and, at the end of the week, report on their success.

For Evaluation

Unit Test Have students complete the Unit Test that appears in the *Teacher's Classroom Resources.*

Testmaker Software You may wish to design a unit test using the Testmaker software program.

CHAPTER OVERVIEW

In Chapter 7 students learn general information about relationships. They also learn that relationships don't just happen—they develop through caring management. The chapter begins by mentioning different types of relationships, such as family, friends, and acquaintances. Then the importance of these relationships is discussed. Students learn that relationships are important for meeting needs, providing companionship, developing self-concept, and broadening horizons. The idea that good relationships involve both giving and receiving is emphasized. Specific ways of building positive relationships are discussed.

INTRODUCING THE CHAPTER

Motivators

Using the Photograph Have students study the photograph on this page. Then ask: "What relationships do these people have?" Then say: "Most projects involve people's cooperation. Relationships also involve cooperation."

Developing Relationships Tell students to think of a strong relationship that they have. Ask: "What do you do to help make this relationship strong? Do you listen to the other person? Do you help the person with projects or problems?" Have students list the things they do on a separate piece of paper.

Introducing the Objectives

Discuss the chapter objectives on this page. Remind students that the objectives focus on important chapter content.

Introducing Vocabulary

Explain that the word *relationship* is derived from the root word *relate*, meaning "to have some connection to." It also incorporates *relation*, or "connection through blood line." Point out that although most people think of family when they think of relationships, the word covers many kinds of connections.

CHAPTER

7

Relationships and You

OBJECTIVES

This chapter will help you to:

- Describe different types of relationships.
- Explain why relationships are important.
- Describe how successful relationships involve both giving and receiving.
- Identify skills that help to build strong relationships.

WORDS TO REMEMBER

acquaintance
compromise
relationship
respect

Chapter Resources

Teacher's Classroom Resources
- Lesson Plan
- Life Skills Activity, *From Generation to Generation*
- Reproducible Master, *Relationships Are Important*
- Extension Activity, *Build Positive Relationships*
- Chapter Test

Student Workbook
- Study Guide
- Worksheet, *The Gifts of Relationships*

A large part of your life is shaped by your relationships. **Relationships** are your connections with other people. Understanding how you interact with others is an important step in knowing who you are.

People who have good relationships are not just lucky. They learn to think before they speak and not say things that might hurt other people's feelings. They learn to see situations through other people's eyes. They learn that everyone has something to offer, whether the person is a young child, a great grandparent, a neighbor, or a best friend. People who like themselves usually treat others fairly and are liked in return.

Types of Relationships

Your relationships are not all the same. Your relationships with family members are different than those with friends. You probably get along better with some classmates than with others.

Your relationships can be divided into three groups: family, friends, and acquaintances.

- **Family.** Have you ever thought what you would be like if you had been born into a different family? Without your parents, brothers and sisters, and other relatives, you would not be the person that you are today.

  Your family helps to shape your personality: you learn how to think and act mainly from your parents. Your family teaches you values and what is important in life. It provides you with food, clothing, and shelter. More important, your family gives you love and emotional support.

- **Friends.** As soon as you were able to talk, you began to form friendships outside your family. You enjoyed running, playing, and trying new games and toys. Your playmates were your friends.

  When you started school, some of your classmates became friends. Perhaps you singled out one person as a "best friend," or you and your friends formed groups. Friends become even more important as you enter your teens.

- **Acquaintances.** You also form relationships with people you don't know very well. A schoolmate, co-worker, or neighbor can be an **acquaintance**: someone you know, but not as well as you would a good friend. An acquaintance can be someone you just met or someone you see occasionally. Sometimes these relationships develop into friendships.

  Throughout this unit you will learn to strengthen your relationships with these three groups.

The love you receive as a child helps you to form satisfying relationships as an adult.

Emphasize All relationships are different. Each relationship offers its own experiences and satisfies different needs.

Emphasize An acquaintance is someone who isn't known very well. Point out that this person could have a lot to offer and could, in time, become a good friend.

Cross-Reference Good relationships don't just happen. They take time, understanding, and caring. Suggest that students become more aware of how they interact with others by keeping a journal in which they describe their different relationships. See Teen Tips "Journaling—The New Way to Keep a Diary" on pages 70-71.

TEACHING THE CHAPTER

For convenience, the teaching suggestions for this chapter are arranged according to the following lesson topics:

Teaching "Types of Relationships"
(Page 75)

This section describes the different types of relationships.

Checking Comprehension

✓ List three groups of relationships. *Three groups of relationships are family, friends, and acquaintances.*

✓ How do friendships change from childhood to the teen years? *When children are very young, their playmates are their friends. When they go to school, classmates usually become friends. Friends become even more important in the teen years.*

Activities

Skill Builder: Writing
Ask students to think of an acquaintance they have and would like to get to know better. Have them write about ways they could get to know this person better. One example would be to get involved in activities they could do together.

Reteaching
To help students understand the different types of relationships, ask them to compare and contrast at least three connections they have to other people.

Enrichment
Have students make three columns on a piece of paper, labeling them *Family, Friends,* and *Acquaintances.* Then have them list things that each group provides for them. For example, a family provides shelter and food. Friends provide companionship. Tell students that some of their needs will be met by more than one group.

Teaching the Feature
"Older Family Members"

Answers to Feature Questions

1. Suggestions should include activities that are of interest to both, such as cooking and shopping, instruction in a grandparent's hobby or special skill, or a visit to a local historical museum.

2. Reasons might include the fact that the grandparents might offer a fresh viewpoint, might have more time than the parent to deal with the problem, or might have special insight into the situations through long experience.

Activities

Oral History Have students conduct an interview with an older member of their family. The students should prepare questions to find out what schools were like years ago. Then have students give an oral report comparing school life in the past with school life today.

When I Grow Old Ask students to imagine what it feels like to grow old. Tell them that they will experience physical and emotional changes and that some of these changes may make them feel better and some, worse about themselves. Have students write a brief profile of what they think their lives will be like when they are senior citizens.

Community Contact Have students find a community center or retirement home where they can visit and interact with older members of their community. Ask them to choose an activity (such as reading, talking, singing, playing games) that they can do with at least one older person. Then have them arrange the time to do it.

INTERPERSONAL SKILLS

Older Family Members

Teens and grandparents have much to offer one another. Still, like every relationship, the one between young and old sometimes requires extra effort.

Many teens may think of their grandparents simply as close relatives they see often, or only once in a while. That view is limited; it leaves out the fact that grandparents are individuals, too, with a wide range of abilities and experiences.

How can you find out about your own grandparents' unique characteristics and experiences? There is one simple way—you can ask them.

Duane's American history class was compiling an oral history of the local community. Duane's assignment was to tape-record an interview with his grandparents, who were known as longtime residents.

That assignment started Duane thinking about his grandparents. He loved them, but he realized he didn't know much about their lives. He decided to make a list of questions to ask them: What were they like as teenagers? How did they meet? How did they decide to settle down in this community? What made them keep on working when many others their age had retired?

Duane was delighted with the answers he received. He felt he knew his grandparents much better. His grandparents were pleased that he cared about the stories they had to tell.

Following are some hints for strengthening the ties with your grandparents. (They also apply for other older family members.)

- Ask your grandparents to recall what your parents were like as children.
- Find out if they can teach you a special skill or share a hobby.
- At family gatherings, tell them about your school and social activities.

Think It Through

1. **What are some activities that teens and grandparents could do together?**
2. **Why is it sometimes easier for teens to discuss problems with grandparents than with parents?**

Emphasize Any relationship takes a lot of work. People come from different backgrounds and have different ideas. Tell students that this is the same for relationships with older people, since the relationship is between people of different generations.

More About Aging Many young people have preconceived images of older people: they may think all older people have become forgetful or boring. In fact, as long as people exercise their ability to remember, they will retain full use of this skill—even when they are elderly. Older people can also be very creative and willing to share.

The Importance of Relationships

You will continue to form relationships throughout your life. Each relationship can enrich your life and teach you something about yourself. Relationships are important because they help meet your needs, provide you with companionship, develop your self-concept, and broaden your horizons.

Meeting Needs

Corey enjoys going camping with his family. He likes the way he and his brother joke about the dinners they cook. At night in the woods, he feels secure knowing that the members of his family are all around him. Corey's relationships with the members of his family satisfy his important emotional needs.

Your relationships with your family and friends help fulfill your need for affection, love, and a sense of belonging. You also look to your family, friends, teachers, coaches, and counselors for acceptance and approval. A hug, a pat on the back, and a word of praise help you feel appreciated and loved. Spending time together with family and friends helps you feel that you are part of a group that cares about you. Think about some of your own relationships. What emotional needs do they fulfill?

Providing Companionship

One of the reasons why relationships are so important is that they allow people to share ideas, feelings, and experiences with another person. Every relationship you have involves some level of companionship and sharing, but the level is different for each relationship. For example, Sasha may enjoy going to football games with one friend. If she wants to go to a concert, she may ask another friend. When her father became seriously ill, however, she felt most comfortable talking about it with another family member.

Friendships can enrich your life. What do you receive from your relationships with your friends?

Teaching "The Importance of Relationships"
(Pages 77-79)

This section explains why relationships are important for enrichment in many ways.

Checking Comprehension

✓ How are relationships important? *Relationships are important because they help meet your needs, provide you with companionship, develop your self-concept, and broaden your horizons.*

✓ What needs are met by family relationships? *Family relationships satisfy the need for affection, love, and a sense of belonging, acceptance, and approval.*

✓ Explain how your relationships and your self-concept are related. *The way you see yourself often comes from the way other people see you. Relationships can strengthen your self-concept.*

✓ How can relationships broaden horizons? *Relationships introduce you to new experiences and give you the confidence to try new things and discover parts of yourself you might not otherwise have known. They offer opportunities for growth.*

Real-Life Situations Due to longer life spans and our mobile society, many people will live in numerous locations during their lifetimes. Ask students what affect these two factors have on making and keeping relationships.

More About Technology Today's computer technology allows people the luxury of companionship without traveling from their homes. Using a device called a modem, computer owners can "talk" to each other via computer, building personal relationships or even professional or social clubs.

Activities

Skill Builder: Writing
Ask students to write a description of a relationship that gave them a better self-concept or that broadened their horizons.

Skill Builder: Critical Thinking
Discuss with students how relationships teach people about themselves. Ask them to share something they have learned about themselves through a relationship with another person.

Reteaching
Have students compare and contrast different relationships with family, friends, and acquaintances, noting what each one provides in terms of needs.

Reteaching
In groups have students brainstorm ways they could broaden their horizons from experiences with different people in their community, such as a blind student, deaf student, student in a wheelchair, foreign student, and so on.

Enrichment
Ask students to research family life in other cultures. Tell them to find out how important families are in that culture. Then ask them to prepare an oral report that compares and contrasts family life in America with family life from the culture they read about.

Developing Self-Concept

One way that people form their self-concepts is through relationships. How people see themselves largely comes from the way other people see them. When Tony's friend Ellen told him that she really liked his new haircut, he felt pleased. Later, however, when Kevin laughed at the shoes that Tony bought, he felt embarrassed. Tony felt intelligent when his teacher told him that his book report was good, but not so smart when his older brother yelled at him for leaving the front door unlocked.

The way people respond to you in certain situations can help to strengthen your self-concept. Suppose the children you babysit for tell you they think you are the best babysitter they ever had, or your mother thanks you for folding the laundry without being asked. In both cases, the compliments will make you feel good about yourself.

Obviously, your self-concept also affects your relationships. The way you look at yourself helps determine how you get along with others. When you feel good about yourself, getting along with others is much easier.

Broadening Horizons

Relationships do more than form the way people see themselves. Since Risa introduced Sue to Mexican food, Sue has been ordering tacos and enchiladas instead of burgers when she goes out. In this way, relationships can also introduce you to new experiences.

What is more, the comfort you feel in certain relationships—perhaps with your family or with your best friend—can give you the confidence to try new things and discover parts of yourself you might not otherwise have known about.

Getting involved in school or community activities can help you develop friendships with people who have similar interests.

Emphasize High self-esteem is important in building relationships. It is easier for other people to care about them if students care about themselves.

More About Broadening Horizons Ask students to think about the skills, interests, and knowledge they have to offer a friend. Have them list their responses on a piece of paper. Then ask them to determine which ones they acquired on their own and which ones they acquired through a friend or other resource. What does this teach them about broadening their own horizons?

Shawn didn't want to try out for the school play all by himself, but when his friend Joel agreed to try out, too, it gave him the confidence he needed. Now he is a member of the drama club and appears in club productions regularly.

Good relationships also offer opportunities for growth. Family and friends can help you learn about consideration and compromising. (See the explanation of "compromise" on page 80). They can also help you explore different ways of solving a problem. Strong relationships teach you how to listen to other people and accept their differences. In fact, many of the relationships you have now are helping you discover what makes for lasting adult relationships.

Getting Along with Others

Learning how to get along with others can benefit you and those around you. By developing certain attitudes and skills, you can improve the relationships you have and form strong ones in the future.

In order to get along well with others, you should treat them the way you want to be treated.

Giving and Receiving

In every relationship there are two actions—giving and receiving. At least one person gets something from another person. Students learn from teachers. Friends receive companionship from other friends.

We all have to give a little to get something in return. We must be aware of other people's problems, so that we can be helpful and supportive to them. In this way, they will usually be responsive to our problems when we need a shoulder to lean on.

Few relationships require one person to do all the giving and the other to do all the receiving. In fact, people usually will not stay in a relationship for long unless they get something in return for their efforts. Satisfying relationships involve giving and receiving on both sides.

Teaching "Getting Along with Others"

(Pages 79-80)

This section teaches how to build strong relationships.

Checking Comprehension

✔ Why are both giving and receiving important in relationships? *All people have to give a little to get something in return. If you are helpful and supportive when other people have problems, they will usually do the same for you. Most relationships will not last unless there is a balance of each.*

✔ How does patience help build stronger relationships? *Being patient with another person minimizes conflicts and the disagreement they cause.*

✔ Why is honesty important in relationships? *Honesty is important in relationships because it builds trust.*

✔ What happens when two people compromise? *Each person gives up a little of what he or she wants in order to come to an agreement.*

✔ Why is communication important in relationships? *It lets the other person know what you need and want, it can clear the air, it can prevent future problems.*

Activities

Skill Builder: Critical Thinking
Tell students that there is a saying: "It is better to give than to receive." Ask them if they agree or disagree with this saying. Then have them share incidents from their own lives that illustrate this saying.

Emphasize Every relationship needs some give and take. People need to give to get something in return.

Focus on Relationship Skills Have students discuss what qualities are important in helping a family member or friend through a problem. Ask them to think about which qualities they need to work on to improve their relationships.

Skill Builder: Critical Thinking
Ask students to think about what qualities they look for in a friend. Have the class combine their thoughts, listing the qualities in order of importance. Students should count how many times a specific quality was listed, then rank the qualities by the number of times they were listed, putting the one with the highest number first.

Skill Builder: Writing
Ask students to imagine that a good friend might be moving to another state. Students should write a letter to the friend, in which they offer encouragement and friendship. Ask them to think carefully about how they can help the friend deal with this major change.

Reteaching
Have students tell about the experience of building a strong relationship. Have them talk about how the connection was made, why the relationship was important, and what they did to make it stronger.

Enrichment
Guide students in a discussion about the responsibility involved in relationships. Ask them to think about the responsibility involved in caring for a pet. Have them list things that people should consider before getting a pet (such as being able to provide food, shelter, exercise, attention, and training). Then ask them to write a brief summary describing the lessons about relationships that could be learned from having a pet.

Building Positive Relationships

You can learn how to get along better with others. The following characteristics are important ones to develop:

- **Patience.** Nobody is perfect. Being patient with another person's habits and faults will minimize conflicts and the disagreement they can cause.
- **Understanding.** Try to see things through the other person's eyes. It is easy to get caught up in your own view of things and forget there is another perspective.
- **Trust and honesty.** Trust grows as a relationship grows. Naturally, you don't trust everyone in the same way or to the same extent, but trust is an important part of every relationship. Honesty is related to trust. If you want others to trust you, you must be honest with them.
- **Respect.** You can show **respect** by being polite and considerate to others. Respect is something all people need. Try to respect other people's opinions. They may be different from yours, but they are just as important to others as yours are to you.
- **Willingness to compromise.** When two people **compromise,** each gives up a little of what he or she wants in order to come to an agreement. Suppose that you want to spend the afternoon shooting baskets, but your friend wants to go to the mall to play video games. If the mall is not too far away, you might be able to get in some time at the video arcade and then go shoot baskets. Another solution would be to do what your friend wants this time, but agree that you will choose the activity the next time you get together.
- **Willingness to communicate.** Communication lets the other person know what you need and want as well as what you are feeling. It can clear the air and prevent future problems.
- **A sense of humor.** A sense of humor, especially about yourself, can get people to laugh and often can lighten an embarrassing or tense situation.
- **Acceptance.** People who get along well with others accept others as they are, with their differences and their faults.

You can practice relationship skills, such as patience, understanding, honesty, and respect, when you are with family members.

Focus on Decision Making Tell students that by accepting responsibility for their relationships they acknowledge that they have choices. They can decide to continue a relationship as it is or change it. They can also think ahead and figure out where certain decisions will lead them. Tell them to think about some of the decisions they have made with their friends recently. Ask them to discuss whether or not they took responsibility for the relationship.

CHAPTER

7 REVIEW

Reviewing the Facts

1. What are three basic types of relationships?
2. Name two needs that relationships can satisfy.
3. How do relationships provide companionship?
4. In what ways can relationships influence self-concept?
5. Describe how a relationship could provide enrichment in your life.
6. Name five qualities that are important for creating positive relationships.
7. What does it mean to compromise?

Thinking Critically

1. How do you think family relationships differ from relationships with friends? Why do you think people need different kinds of relationships?
2. Which two qualities that contribute to positive relationships do you think are the most important? Which one do you think you need the most improvement in?

Applying Your Skills

1. **Writing a Description.** Write a 100-200 word essay that describes the way your relationships have enriched your life.
2. **Writing a Scenario.** Create a fictitious situation in which two people must compromise. Write a short story or script describing how the problem is resolved.
3. **Analyzing Relationships.** Read a short story and study the relationship between the main character and another character. Are these two characters relatives, friends, or acquaintances? What needs and wants does this relationship satisfy? Is it a positive or negative relationship? Explain your answer.

Answers to "Reviewing the Facts"

1. Family, friends, and acquaintances.
2. Any two: affection, love, sense of belonging, security, acceptance, approval.
3. Relationships allow people to share ideas, feelings, and experiences with others.
4. Compliments and praise can have a positive influence on self-concept; criticism or teasing can have a negative influence.
5. Any of the following: introducing you to new experiences; giving you confidence; offering opportunities for growth; helping you learn about consideration and compromise; helping you solve problems; teaching you how to listen to others and accept their differences.
6. Any five: patience, understanding, trust and honesty, respect, willingness to compromise, willingness to communicate, a sense of humor, acceptance.
7. To give up a little of what you want in order to come to an agreement with someone.

Answers to "Thinking Critically"

1. Answers will vary. Students may suggest that family relationships develop first, that relationships with friends are usually based on common interests, and that friends are usually chosen whereas family members are not. People need different kinds of relationships because they have many interests to share. No one person can provide for all of someone else's needs.
2. Students should select two of the eight qualities listed on page 80 and be able to cite the quality in which they feel they need the most improvement.

COMPLETING THE CHAPTER

Summary

- Relationships are connections with other people.
- There are three types of relationships: family, friends, and acquaintances.
- Relationships are important for meeting needs, providing companionship, developing self-concept, and broadening horizons.
- Satisfying relationships involve both parties giving and receiving.
- Important qualities to develop for better relationships are patience, understanding, trust and honesty, respect, willingness to compromise, willingness to communicate, a sense of humor, and acceptance.

For Review

Objective Review Questions Have students complete the "Reviewing the Facts" section on this page.

Study Guide Have students complete the Study Guide from Chapter 7 of their *Student Workbook.*

Researching Relationships Relationships can go beyond personal satisfaction to include professional satisfaction through cooperation in careers. For example, Richard Rodgers and Oscar Hammerstein collaborated on numerous musicals, such as *Oklahoma!* Have students use an encyclopedia or biographies to find out what qualities made the relationship of this team or another similar team a positive one both personally and professionally.

For Evaluation

Building Relationships Ask students to list the eight qualities that help build more positive relationships. For bonus points, encourage them to include other qualities that help build strong relationships.

Chapter Test Have students complete the test for Chapter 7 that appears in the *Teacher's Classroom Resources.*

CHAPTER OVERVIEW

Communication, the process of sending and receiving messages, is the topic of Chapter 8. In this chapter students learn that communication is a vital skill in developing relationships and that messages can be nonverbal as well as verbal. Messages are sent by a person's appearance, words, tone of voice, actions, body language, and manners. Students also learn the importance of listening and ways to improve this skill. The chapter concludes with the value of sending a positive message—to oneself as well as to others.

INTRODUCING THE CHAPTER

Motivators

Means of Communication Have two students volunteer to role play a blind person and a deaf person. Then ask a third student to convey the message: "Please come with me" to the first two students. After the role play, say: "Sending or receiving a message is called communication. As you just saw, people can communicate by words, by actions, or by both. In this chapter you will learn about the skill of communication."

Using the Photograph Tell students to look at the photograph on this page. Then ask: "What are the girls in this photograph doing? What do their facial expressions and gestures tell you?"

The Two-Way Street Ask students to think of a time when they were told something but either did not hear the message or misunderstood it. Ask them what the consequences were of their failed communication. Point out that sending a message is only one part of the communication process. The message must be received for communication to actually take place. Discuss the importance of sending a clear message as well as that of receiving a message.

Introducing the Objectives

Discuss the chapter objectives on this page. Remind students that the objectives focus on important chapter content.

CHAPTER

8

Communication Skills

OBJECTIVES

This chapter will help you to:

- Define verbal and nonverbal communication.
- Describe how your words and actions, your body language, and your appearance send messages to others.
- Explain how to improve listening skills.

WORDS TO REMEMBER

body language
communicating
eye contact
first impression
manners
nonverbal
verbal

Chapter Resources

Teacher's Classroom Resources
- Lesson Plan
- Life Skills Activity, *Diary of a Communicator*
- Reproducible Master, *Sign Language*
- Extension Activity, *How to Make a Good First Impression*
- Chapter Test

Student Workbook
- Study Guide
- Worksheet, *Communication Mix-Up*

Has your best friend ever asked you "What's wrong?" before you said a word? How could your friend know something was wrong? He or she could probably sense that something was different about you. Perhaps you were walking more slowly than usual. Perhaps you were looking at the ground. Maybe it was just that you didn't say "Hi."

Communicating means sending messages from one person to another. These messages don't travel just one way—from you to others. You receive messages as well as send them. Understanding the messages you get from others requires you to listen, not just to hear. This chapter will discuss ways to improve the quality of the messages you send and receive.

The Messages You Send

When people first meet you, they receive many different messages. Communication is not always **verbal**, or using words. If you have ever seen a mime artist, you know that someone's body or facial expression can speak very clearly. The way you stand or sit, the clothes you wear, how you move, and the tone of your voice all send messages about you to others. These are types of **nonverbal** communication: communication without words.

People put together all they see and hear to create a picture of you. The images people have of someone they have just met are their **first impressions.** They use those impressions to form an opinion about the person. After meeting someone, have you ever thought "I'd like to get to know her better"? Sometimes first impressions are wrong. Someone who seems unfriendly may simply be shy. Keep this in mind, and get to know people before you decide what they are like. At the same time, remember that many people make judgments based on first impressions. After just meeting you, what judgment would people make about you?

Your Words and Actions

You also send messages with your words and the tone of your voice. Your little brother excitedly says, "Look at the picture I drew!" You answer, "That's terrific." It's *how* you say those words that is the key to your message.

Both your words and tone of voice convey messages to your listeners.

Introducing Vocabulary

Communicating, "imparting knowledge or information," is formed from the root word *communicate.* The root word is taken from the Latin word *communicare,* which means "to impart or to participate." Point out that communicating involves participation by both the sender of the message and the receiver.

TEACHING THE CHAPTER

For convenience, the teaching suggestions for this chapter are arranged according to the following lesson topics:

- "The Messages You Send," pages 83-85
- "The Messages You Receive," pages 85-86
- "A Positive Message," page 87

Teaching "The Messages You Send"

(Pages 83-85)

This section teaches by what means messages are sent: verbal, nonverbal, body language, appearance, grooming, tones of voice, actions, manners.

Checking Comprehension

✓ What factors affect your first impression of someone? *Both the verbal and nonverbal messages you receive affect your first impression, which you use to form an opinion about the person.*

✓ How does the tone of your voice affect what you are communicating? *It shows whether you really care and what other emotions you're feeling.*

✓ Why is eye contact important in communicating? *Eye contact is important in communicating because it sends a message of being interested and confident.*

✓ What message does a well-groomed appearance send? *A well-groomed appearance sends the message that a person cares about herself or himself.*

Focus on Relationship Skills Tell students that communication is an essential element in interactions among people. Divide students into pairs, and have one partner communicate an idea or skill to the other using words and actions. For example, have them define the word *relationship,* or have them give instructions on tying a shoe.

Did You Know? Scientists have taught some primates sign language. A famous gorilla named Koko knows sign language and even communicated that it would like a pet of its own, a kitten.

Activities

Skill Builder: Science
Have students research the development of the telephone. Ask them to think about how this device changed the ways people communicate. Ask: "What advantages did the telephone bring? What disadvantages?"

Skill Builder: Critical Thinking
Ask students to think about how they would communicate with people who were deaf or blind. After listening to their ideas, tell them that sign language and braille are the two systems used for communicating with people who are hearing impaired or visually impaired. Using a book on sign language, teach the class the signs for two or three words. Show the class a braille edition of a book, available from the public library. (Braille symbols are often found next to the buttons for elevators.)

Reteaching
Ask students to name one type of verbal communication and one related type of nonverbal communication. Then ask them to discuss why combining the two forms of communication is often best.

Reteaching
Have students play a guessing game where messages can be communicated only by pictures. Perhaps some of the vocabulary words from this book could be used. Tell students that they cannot use numbers, letters, or number symbols and that there can be no talking. They can nod "yes" or "no" to responses.

Enrichment
Have students research instances in which people have taught animals to communicate. Ask them to write a report on a case that they found interesting.

If your voice shows enthusiasm, your brother will be pleased that you like the drawing. If, however, you speak in a flat tone of voice and don't look up from your magazine, your brother will think that you don't really care, and he may feel hurt. Thinking before you speak can keep you from sending the wrong messages.

The way you act is another form of communicating. Your **manners** are the way you behave on the whole toward other people. They interpret your behavior as nonverbal messages you are sending. For example, if you are polite and friendly on the telephone, people will enjoy speaking with you. If you are rude, people assume that you are thoughtless.

How you react to events can also tell people about you. If you are able to solve a problem calmly, for example, people will see you as mature. If you get flustered very easily, they may think of you as childish.

People can express many feelings without saying a word. What message is this boy communicating?

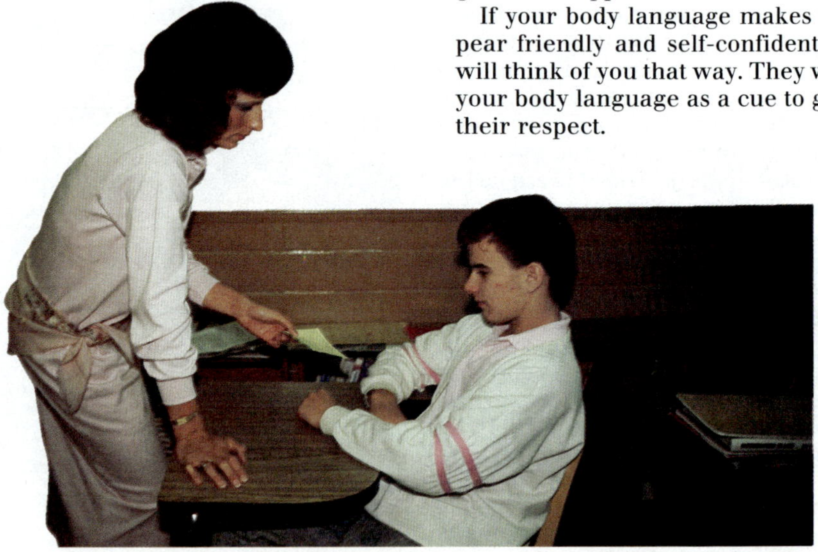

If you are concerned about how you seem to others, your family and friends can help. Ask someone you trust about the impression you make. Does your voice sound harsh or friendly? Are you usually polite to others? A good friend can give you honest answers.

Your Body Language

Body language refers to your posture and the way you move, walk, or sit. It also affects how others see you. Earl stands up straight and walks with his shoulders held high. This shows that he respects himself. Justin slouches and gives the impression that he thinks very little of himself.

An important form of body language is **eye contact:** direct visual contact with another person's eyes. Lee doesn't like to look directly at people who speak to her. She may be shy or nervous, but by avoiding eye contact, she sends the message that others should not approach her. Sheila looks directly at a new acquaintance. The message she sends is that she is interested, confident, and glad to be approached.

If your body language makes you appear friendly and self-confident, others will think of you that way. They will take your body language as a cue to give you their respect.

Real-Life Situations The science of *kinesics* explores the meaning of messages expressed, consciously or unconsciously, through body language. Ask students what their interpretation would be of the following facial expressions or body movements:
- a raised eyebrow (surprise)
- a frown (disappointment, anger)
- a smile (happy, friendly)
- a downturned mouth (sad)
- open and relaxed arms (friendly, receptive)
- crossed arms or clenched fists (anger, discomfort, or nervousness)
- tapping fingers or feet (bored, impatient)

Your Appearance

Grooming is another part of the message you send about yourself. Good grooming shows that you are trying to look your best. It includes things like brushing your hair and putting on a clean shirt. A clean, healthy appearance communicates to others that you care about yourself.

Keep in mind that appearance is more important in some circumstances than in others. For example, the type of clothes you wear matters more at an interview for a part-time job than on an outing with friends.

The Messages You Receive

"I heard you, I heard you," Anita grumbled to her friend Tanya.

"Yes, I know you heard me, but did you really *listen*?" Tanya asked in exasperation.

What is the difference? Isn't hearing the same as listening? Not at all. Hearing is merely receiving sound waves in your ears. Listening, on the other hand, involves concentrating on, understanding, and remembering what was said.

Why Listen Well?

Why should you try to become a good listener? Because being a skillful listener helps you in your daily life—at home, in school, and on your job, if you have one.

Listening can help relationships to grow. You have to listen closely to what people are saying to get to know them better.

In addition, listening well helps you to know more. You can learn about a variety of subjects in an enjoyable manner while talking to someone else. Listening is also a natural way to build your vocabulary. All these benefits can help you make a better impression on others.

Good listening skills are important, not only in school, but in all types of relationships.

More About Listening Some people do not listen well because they do not hear well. A hearing aid, a device inserted into the outer ear or attached behind the ear, helps many people to hear better. Some people avoid wearing this device even though they need it because they feel that it detracts from their appearance. However, the hearing aid can be the key to being able to appreciate everything that is going on around them. Have students think how much harder former President Reagan's job would have been had he chosen not to remedy his disability by wearing a hearing aid.

Teaching "The Messages You Receive"

(Pages 85-86)

This section teaches the importance of listening and offers ways to improve that skill.

Checking Comprehension

✓ Give an example of hearing but not listening. *Answers will vary but should include an example such as a person who hears that he or she should go to the store but does not remember what to buy when he or she gets there.*

✓ What is one way to improve concentration when listening? *Concentration when listening can be improved by eliminating distractions or moving to a quieter place.*

✓ Why should you listen with a purpose? *Deciding beforehand why you need to listen helps you concentrate.*

Activities

Skill Builder: Critical Thinking
Have students describe situations in which listening could be a life saver. Examples are hearing a fire alarm, listening to safety instructions on an aircraft, and listening to hurricane warnings.

Skill Builder: Writing
Have students create a scenario in which somebody fails to listen to important information and suffers the consequences.

Reteaching
Have students list four ways that they could improve their listening skills. Then ask them why they think it is important for them to improve their skills.

Reteaching
Have students play a word association with their name, such as "My name is Lisa and I love lemons." Explain that the first letter of the person's name should be the same as the first letter of what he or she likes. Ask students to sit in a circle. Go around the circle and have each person give his or her statement and then repeat those of each previous person. The last person in the circle has to repeat everyone's name in the circle with what they like. Variation: Halfway through the circle, turn on a record player or another type of distractor to compare how much harder it is to concentrate when there are other distractions going on in the room.

Enrichment
Divide students into small groups, and have each group brainstorm to come up with ways people can send and receive a message aside from speaking and listening, such as semaphoring (signaling with flags). Then have the groups share their ideas to see which group came up with the most original way.

To improve your listening skills, start by actively listening to what the other person is saying.

How to Listen Better

Now that you know *why* you should gain listening skills, you need to know how to do it. Here are some techniques for becoming a better listener:

- **Concentrate on what is being said.** This is the single most important part of becoming a good listener. Sometimes you can aid concentration by eliminating distractions—turning off the radio or TV while someone is speaking, or moving to a quieter area.
- **Listen with a purpose.** Most people do a job better if they know why they should do it. This is certainly true with listening. It helps to decide beforehand why you need to listen. In class, you probably want to listen well to improve your grades. You might want to listen to your friends' problems to help them find solutions. Having a purpose helps you to concentrate.
- **Be positive about listening.** Assume a positive attitude before a person starts talking so you will get something out of what you hear. Then you will be motivated to listen and remember.
- **Control your emotions.** Sometimes what the speaker is saying affects you emotionally. This can act as a barrier to listening. Suppose, for example, your mother is talking to you about when you should be in at night, and you begin to feel impatient. Your impatience may cause you to tune her out. It is better to keep your emotions in check, listen to what she has to say, and try to see things from her perspective. Then present your point of view. She will be much more likely to listen to you, and even compromise, if she knows that you have really been listening to what she has been saying.

Focus on Relationship Skills Help students develop skills in dealing with someone on the telephone whom they find hard to understand. Have students suggest tactful ways of making sure they understand what the person is saying, for example, "I didn't quite catch that. Could you repeat it a little more slowly?" If the person has a strong accent, remind students to avoid implying that the speaker is stupid or annoying. And if the person has a speech impediment, great sensitivity and patience are needed.

A Positive Message

Very often, you will have only one opportunity to make an impression. That means it is important to be sure that your image, which is made up of what you say, how you act, and the clothes you wear, creates the kind of impression you want to make.

Take a close look at the image others see. Are you communicating your real self, or are you pretending to be someone else? When you talk, act, or even dress in ways that are not natural to you, you may send mixed and even conflicting messages to others.

You also need to send the right messages to yourself. If you are sad, you may walk with your head down. It is also true that if you walk with your head down, you may begin to feel sad. On the other hand, smiling can sometimes make you feel better on a gloomy day. One way to send the right messages to yourself, then, is simply to act positively.

Of course, smiling all day is not a substitute for solving a problem that bothers you. Even so, a positive image of yourself will help you get over the smaller problems in life as well as give you strength to handle the bigger ones.

People enjoy being around others who are cheerful and happy, rather than those who are grouchy or sad.

Focus on Entrepreneurship Have students pretend they are starting a business of their own and they need investors to help finance the business. Tell them to write a short presentation about the business, and have them include a description of what they would wear to a meeting to attract investors.

More About Grooming Remind students that good grooming, which includes keeping oneself clean, is important not just for appearance, but for health, too. Attention to the skin is particularly important during adolescence, when excess oil can cause pimples. Refer students to Teen Tips "How to Save Face," pages 68-69.

Teaching "A Positive Message"
(Page 87)

This section teaches the value of sending a positive message, both in making first impressions and in general behavior.

Checking Comprehension

✓ Why is it important for people to make sure that their image creates the kind of impression they want to make? *They will have only one opportunity to make a good first impression.*

✓ How can people send messages to themselves? *People can send messages to themselves by their behavior. For example, people who smile can send a message of cheer to themselves.*

✓ How can a positive self-image help people with problems? *A positive self-image can help people get through small problems and give them strength to handle bigger ones.*

Activities

Skill Builder: Critical Thinking
Have students discuss how people dress differently for different situations. Ask them to share experiences of dressing to create a good impression. Ask them to think about how different workers dress. What kinds of colors do they use? What kinds of hair styles do different workers have? Do they wear jeans and shirts, three-piece suits, outfits for special jobs, uniforms? What do people's "work" clothes convey?

Reteaching
Ask students to collect pictures for a "Positive Image" collage. Tell them to find pictures that show people presenting themselves in a positive way.

Enrichment
Explain to the class that many companies hire public relations people and many movie stars and politicians hire image consultants to help them convey a positive image. Have the students go to the library and find out the details of one job that is concerned with images. What type of qualities and skills would a person need to do that job? Have the students discuss their findings in class.

Teaching the Feature

"Communication for People with Disabilities"

Answers to Feature Questions

1. Students should note that in this case computers allow people to fulfill a basic need: communicating with others. Machines are making it possible for people to express themselves.
2. Students' comments should point out that people will see those with disabilities more realistically. People's incorrect assumption that anyone with a physical disability is also mentally disabled may become outdated.

Activities

Learning to Communicate Have students read about a disabled person, such as Helen Keller, who learned to communicate and went on to make a valuable contribution to society. Tell students to take note of how the disabled person learned to communicate. Ask students to write a report about the person they selected.

Ideas for Communicating Divide students into small groups. Then have each group brainstorm for a new idea to help disabled people communicate. Tell them they can use imaginary futuristic technology if they want to. Then ask one student from each group to tell about their "invention."

Community Contact Although communication is difficult for many people with hearing or visual disabilities, students should know that people with such disabilities do have a lot to offer. Have students get in touch with centers that care for the disabled to find out how they can make themselves better able to communicate with people who have such disabilities. Students should give a presentation based on the information they have found and, if they have time, volunteer to work at such a center.

TECHNOLOGY

Communication for People with Disabilities

Every day we communicate in ways that we take for granted: we talk, we write, we wave hello or good-bye. For many people with disabilities, these methods of communication are difficult or impossible. With the help of technology, however, many of these people are experiencing the rewards of communicating with others. Below are just a few of the ways that technology is helping.

- Most hearing-impaired people communicate through lip reading or sign language, in which hand gestures are used to represent specific words or letters. There is also a relatively new invention that helps hearing-impaired people to communicate by telephone. A machine called the TDD, or Telecommunications Device for the Deaf, is a typewriter connected to a telephone that signals incoming calls with a blinking light. The hearing-impaired person types in a response when the light blinks, and the person making the call uses the same kind of machine on the other end to talk. The conversation is printed out as it is being typed.
- For those who are visually impaired, engineers have designed a special computer that can aid communication. The sender types out a message on a computer keyboard. The computer then translates the message into signals that control an electromechanical hand, which transfers the message to the sender's hand. Another way to send messages to visually impaired people is to use a Braille writer, a machine that writes in braille. Braille is a system of raised dots, with each letter of the alphabet having a different combination of dots.
- ERICA (the acronym for "Eye-gaze Response Interface Computer Aid") responds to the gaze of a paralyzed user rather than to touch. On the screen are a variety of choices for the user, such as displaying a book on the computer screen or requesting a cup of coffee. The user merely looks at the appropriate part of the screen, a camera records which part is being gazed at, and the message is transmitted.

These are only a few examples of the technology being used today in this area. Scientists hope that future inventions will help many people communicate easily and in more ways.

Think It Through

1. **Some people feel that computers are dehumanizing; they believe they take the human touch out of life. Would this report change their opinion? Why?**
2. **How might the new technology change people's perceptions of people with disabilities?**

Did You Know? Visually impaired people can enjoy books with the aid of audiotapes. Books and magazines can be recorded on these tapes and are available at many local libraries. Books are also printed in braille, raised dot symbols for letters and numbers.

Focus on Relationship Skills Ask students to imagine interacting with a disabled person who uses one of the devices they have just read about. Have them discuss whether the means (in this case, the technological device) would get in the way of their listening to the message.

CHAPTER 8 REVIEW

Reviewing the Facts

1. Describe the difference between verbal and nonverbal communication, using examples.
2. Why might it be unfair to make a judgment about another person from a first impression?
3. What message is communicated through good manners?
4. How does your body language affect the way people see you?
5. What are the differences between hearing and listening?
6. List three advantages of being a good listener.
7. How can you become a better listener?
8. Why should you control your emotions when you listen?

Thinking Critically

1. Do you think that making a good first impression is important? Why or why not?
2. Give two examples of situations in which listening—not just hearing—is important. Explain your choices.

Applying Your Skills

1. **Selecting Criteria.** Write five to ten "Good First Impression Guidelines" for teens. They should be appropriate for your lifestyle but also show respect for others. Illustrate the guidelines using pictures from magazines.

2. **Writing a Description.** Think about a movie or television character you have seen or a speaker that you have heard recently. Describe all the ways in which the person communicated. What methods did he or she use most effectively?

3. **Performing an Experiment.** Why can you say something to another person who acknowledges what you said—but then the person seems to forget about the conversation? This is because people often hear and respond without really listening. Perform an experiment in which the entire class sits in a circle. Think of a detailed sentence and pass it on to the next person, and so on, until the statement makes it around the circle. Did the statement change? What do you think the experiment has demonstrated?

Answers to "Reviewing the Facts"

1. Verbal communication uses words, such as speaking or writing. Nonverbal communication uses body language, such as the way you move, walk, or sit, and whether or not you make eye contact.
2. A person might not be acting in a way that shows his or her true personality.
3. Good manners show that you care about others.
4. If you look happy and self-confident, people will think of you in that positive way. On the other hand, if you look depressed and dejected, people will think of you in that way. Students may offer other examples.
5. Hearing is receiving sound waves in your ears. Listening requires concentration, understanding, and remembering what was said.
6. Any three: helps you in your daily life; helps relationships to grow; helps you to know more; helps you make a better impression on others.
7. Concentrate on what is being said; listen with a purpose; be positive; control your emotions.
8. Strong emotions can be a barrier to listening.

Answers to "Thinking Critically"

1. Some students will say yes because in certain situations, such as a job interview, you may have only one opportunity to make a good impression. Other students will say no because most people do not make a good first impression because they are shy or uncomfortable about meeting new people.
2. Answers will vary. Possible examples include listening during classes so that you do well in school; listening to your parents so that you don't get in trouble; listening in an emergency situation so that you know what actions to take.

COMPLETING THE CHAPTER

Summary

- Communicating is sending messages from one person to another.
- Communication can be verbal (with words) or nonverbal (without words).
- First impressions are the images people have of someone they have just met. Manners are the way people behave toward other people.
- People send messages with their manners and tone of voice as well as their words. People also send messages by eye contact, body language, and personal appearance.
- Listening is very important and can be improved by concentrating more, listening with a purpose, being positive about listening, and controlling emotions.
- People may get only one chance to make an impression, so they should make that impression a positive one.

For Review

Objective Review Questions Have students complete the "Reviewing the Facts" section on this page.

Study Guide Have students complete the Study Guide from Chapter 8 of their *Student Workbook.*

Speech! Speech! Have students give a short speech on the topic of communication. After each speech, have the other students discuss the speaker's message—both verbal and nonverbal. Include in the discussion the speaker's reaction to how his or her message was received.

For Evaluation

Checklist Have students list four ways to improve their listening skills.

Chapter Test Have students complete the test for Chapter 8 that appears in the *Teacher's Classroom Resources.*

CHAPTER OVERVIEW

In Chapter 9 students learn how roles and expectations affect relationships. They learn that if two people have roles that change or have different expectations, they will probably experience conflict in their relationship. Students learn to minimize conflict by controlling their feelings, communicating honestly, and showing tolerance. The chapter explains how attitudes affect relationships. It points out that people with positive attitudes tend to feel good about themselves and treat other people fairly, whereas people with negative attitudes tend to be insecure and treat other people unfairly. The chapter concludes with a discussion of prejudice and stereotypes.

INTRODUCING THE CHAPTER

Motivators

Experiencing Conflict Write the word *conflict* on the board, and ask students to define it. Summarize their definitions by saying: "Conflict is the struggle that results from opposing needs, drives, or wishes." Then have them raise their hands if they have experienced conflict in any of their relationships with people. Encourage students to discuss whether they think conflict is a natural or an unnatural aspect of human interaction.

Using the Photograph Have students look at the photograph on this page and describe what the people are doing. Ask students if this type of activity can help build strong relationships. Why? Ask: "What other activities can help build strong relationship skills?"

Role-Playing Relationships Have two students volunteer to role play the situation of friends in conflict over what to do on a Saturday afternoon. After the role play, have the rest of the class comment on how each friend handled the situation. Say: "Relationships not only involve work, but also involve skills, such as understanding others, resolving conflicts, and improving attitudes."

CHAPTER

9

Improving Relationship Skills

OBJECTIVES

This chapter will help you to:

- Describe how roles and expectations affect relationships.
- Give examples of strategies for resolving conflicts in your relationships.
- Discuss how prejudice and stereotypes hurt relationships.

WORDS TO REMEMBER

conflict
expectation
prejudice
role
stereotype
tolerance

Chapter Resources

Teacher's Classroom Resources
- Lesson Plan
- Life Skills Activity, *Conflict in Art*
- Reproducible Master, *Your Many Roles*
- Extension Activity, *Avoiding Sex Stereotypes*
- Chapter Test

Student Workbook
- Study Guide
- Worksheet, *Communication Cool-Down*

Ask yourself the following questions about relationships:

- Do I understand why my friends make the choices they do?
- Do I appreciate the ways in which my family is special?
- Can I accept that decisions that are right for me may not be right for everyone?

The answers to these questions bring out an important point: there are skills involved in getting along with others. You can work to improve these skills so your interactions with others are a source of joy, satisfaction, and personal rewards. This chapter will show you how to improve your relationship skills through understanding others, resolving conflicts, and improving attitudes.

Understanding Others

In order for a relationship to be satisfying, each person involved must work at understanding what the other one wants or needs. Relationships work best if you understand your different roles and expectations.

Roles

Roles are the parts you play when you interact with others. Remember, you have many roles. You are your parents' child, your teacher's student, your friends' friend. You might also be a team member, a musician in the band, an employee, or a neighbor.

You may have many different roles, depending on who you are with. What different roles might this girl have?

Focus on Leadership Ask students what expectations they have of leaders and public figures. Tell them that people often expect more from authority and public figures because they are supposed to set an example. Have students debate whether or not public figures should be held up as examples.

Emphasize Relationships take work and also require skills.

Introducing the Objectives

Discuss the chapter objectives on page 90. Remind students that the objectives focus on important chapter content.

Introducing Vocabulary

Tell students that *conflict* comes from the Latin *conflictus,* "the act of striking together." Point out that conflict is the striking together, or opposition, of different ideas, personalities, or actions.

TEACHING THE CHAPTER

For convenience, the teaching suggestions for this chapter are arranged according to the following lesson topics:

- "Understanding Others," pages 91-92
- "Resolving Conflicts," pages 92-94
- "Relationships and Attitudes," pages 94-95

Teaching "Understanding Others"

(Pages 91-92)

This section teaches how roles and expectations affect relationships.

Checking Comprehension

✓ What are some roles that people play? *Answers will vary but should include child, parent, teacher, student, friend, sibling, teammate, employee, and so on.*

✓ Explain the relationship between roles and expectations. *Different roles produce different expectations. As roles change, so do expectations.*

✓ What should people do if their roles and expectations differ from those of their friends? *If people's roles and expectations differ from those of their friends, they should talk about the differences and try to find ways to resolve any problems.*

Activities

Skill Builder: Critical Thinking
Encourage students to think about how expectations affect relationships by asking them to list, briefly, what they expect of their parents. Then ask them to list what they think their parents expect of them. Have them study their lists and identify possible areas of conflict. Do they think some of the expectations, in either list, are unreasonable? Ask volunteers to suggest some ways of resolving the conflicts they have indentified.

Skill Builder: Writing
Ask students to think of a relationship they have that involves some type of conflict. Have students write a letter to the person, describing their own expectations and the expectations they have for the other person. Students may also want to include some ideas they have for resolving the conflict.

Reteaching
Ask students to define *role* and *expectation* and to give examples of the two. Then have them find pictures of people in various roles and make a class collage titled "Roles People Play."

Enrichment
Ask students to write down the various roles each member of their family plays. Then ask them to see if some of the roles their family members play are similar to or the same as some of the roles the students play. Have them discuss ways they can better understand other people's roles.

Expectations

Different roles produce different **expectations,** what each person wants in a relationship. As roles change, expectations change, too. When you were a child, for example, you expected your parents to provide everything—food when you were hungry or a blanket when you were cold. As you mature, you may expect to be treated more as an adult. In turn, your parents will expect you to assume more responsibility for your own life.

Erica has been elected captain of the basketball team. She expects each team member to be interested in the game, to follow directions, and to work together with teammates. Her team members expect the captain to give directions, to treat all members fairly, and to support and encourage them.

Sometimes, the expectations of two people in a relationship differ. Beth and Amber are good friends who enjoy talking and studying together, but Beth likes to spend time with other people, too. For example, she would like to ask Carmen to come along sometimes, but Amber likes it better when she and Beth are alone.

How can Beth and Amber solve this difference in their relationship? One way is to talk about the expectations each has of the other. Once each person understands what the other wants, they can decide what to do. Beth may decide to do certain things with Amber and to see Carmen at other times.

Resolving Conflicts

At one time or another, you can expect to have **conflicts,** or problems in your relationships. Often, these conflicts occur because each person expects something different.

Eric has always looked up to his father and has spent a lot of time with him. He has always discussed his feelings and problems with his father. Lately, however, Eric has been keeping more things to himself. Even though he sometimes

When expectations differ in a relationship, problems may develop. It helps to talk about the expectations that each person has of the other.

More About Conflict Point out to students that not all conflicts are negative. Remind them that competitive sports events are conflicts. Each athlete or team has a different expectation for the outcome of the event. In this type of conflict people learn a sense of fair play and teamwork.

Did You Know? Remind students that tolerance is part of the U.S. Constitution. For example, Article I of the Bill of Rights states: "Congress shall make no law respecting an establishment of religion, or prohibiting the free exercise thereof . . ."

asks for advice, he often resents his father's giving it. Eric's father has noticed that their relationship is changing. Yesterday he said to Eric, "What's wrong with you these days? You're very moody." Eric was hurt and angry.

Changing roles and differing expectations make many demands on people in relationships. Handling these demands calls for relationship skills. Close relationships are worth preserving, even if that means compromising more than you would like. Here are a few guidelines to help you in controlling your feelings, communicating honestly, and accepting others.

Controlling Your Feelings

When people disagree with friends or family members, they should not speak in anger. If they do, they might say something that would hurt the other person. Eric was so angry at his father's remark that he almost shouted back. Instead, he turned and walked away.

In such a situation, give yourself time to cool off. Anger can be released in different ways. You might talk about the problem with another adult or with a friend. Then you could try to work the problem out with the person who made you angry when you are calm enough to control your feelings.

Communicating Honestly

Whether your relationship is with your mother, your stepfather, your best friend, your teammate, or anyone else, communicating is important. You learn what the other person expects from you, and you get a chance to tell the other person what you expect as well.

Eric's father, who had spoken out of his own hurt and anger, was not thinking about how his statement would af-

Discussing an emotional topic in a calm manner is far more productive than getting angry or shouting.

More About Honest Communication Tell students that lying makes many people feel uncomfortable. Their eyes may shift, their tone of voice may change, and their heart rate may increase. Tell students that scientists have developed a device called a polygraph, or lie detector. The lie detector, developed by William Moulton Marston, measures people's blood pressure, heart rate, breathing rate, and galvanic skin response to an electrical current when they are asked certain questions. Increases in these measurements indicate that the person may be uncomfortable with his or her response.

Teaching "Resolving Conflicts"

(Pages 92-94)

This section teaches what causes conflict in relationships and how to resolve it.

Checking Comprehension

✓ What are three skills useful in handling the demands of relationships? *Controlling your feelings, communicating honestly, and accepting others.*

✓ What can people do instead of speaking in anger? *Instead of speaking in anger, people should take time to cool off, possibly speak about the problem with another adult or a friend, and then, when they are calm, speak about the problem with the person who caused the anger.*

✓ Why should people communicate honestly? *People should communicate honestly so that they can better understand other people's feelings and expectations. Also, honest communication can earn people the respect of others.*

✓ Why is tolerance especially important in a relationship? *You have to accept people as they are to preserve relationships. It will also help you to avoid conflicts.*

Activities

Skill Builder: Critical Thinking
Point out that one of the hardest parts of talking through a problem in a relationship is getting the conversation started. Ask students to suggest some ways of broaching a difficult subject. For example, how would they begin a conversation with a friend who has made them angry? How would they begin to explain why they cannot accept an invitation from someone because they have another commitment? Discuss the pros and cons of person-to-person encounters versus the telephone for such conversations.

Skill Builder: Writing
Have students write a short story about a conflict in a relationship. Remind them to describe the conflict, the reason for it, and explain how it is resolved.

Reteaching
Have students practice resolving conflicts by role playing the following scenarios:
1. Cathy accepted a date to go bowling with Steve on Saturday, but then her mother told her she would have to babysit.
2. The teacher gave Dave a test grade that he felt he didn't deserve.
3. Dan agreed to fill in for another worker at his part-time job before his coach called a mandatory practice session.

Enrichment
Tell students that many novels revolve around a conflict. Ask them to select a novel and write a book report on the conflict on which the story is built.

Teaching "Relationships and Attitudes"
(Pages 94-95)

This section teaches how prejudice and stereotypes hurt relationships.

Checking Comprehension

✓ Compare the actions of people with a positive attitude with the actions of people with a negative attitude. *People with a positive attitude feel good about themselves and treat others fairly, without labeling or rejecting them. People with a negative attitude tend to judge others unfairly, letting their feelings of insecurity interfere with relationships.*

✓ How can society be hurt by prejudice? *When there is prejudice against an entire group of people, society loses the work of people and many individuals lose the chance to meet people who would make their lives richer.*

✓ Give an example of prejudice. *Ansers will vary but should include a case in which a person is not judged fairly, either in favor of or against the person.*

✓ List five forms of prejudice in our society. *Five forms of prejudice in our society refer to age, race, color, religion, and sex.*

fect Eric. When Eric approached him to talk things over, his father apologized. Eric also apologized for walking away angrily. As Eric explained the way he was feeling, he and his father came to understand that Eric was just trying to become more independent. Eric's father agreed to work with Eric toward that goal. They both promised to keep their communication open and honest.

Some people find it difficult to talk about their angry feelings. If that is how you feel, let the other person know it. You might feel more relaxed if you admit your feelings. If you say something like "This is hard for me to say . . .," it might actually become easier to say. In addition, expressing your feelings will show the other person that you care.

Honest communication can win you the respect of others. For example, John asked Cathy to meet him at the football game on Friday night. She really wanted to, but she had already made plans with Matt for the same evening. This left her with a decision to make.

Cathy's first impulse was to accept John's invitation. After all, this was what she wanted to do the most. "I'll just go to the game," she thought, "and tell Matt that I've been grounded so I can't go with him." Something inside her, however, made her think some more.

Lying to Matt would be dishonest. If he found out about the lie, which was likely, he would no longer trust or respect her. He would also be hurt. If John found out, he might wonder if she would do the same thing to him. The result could be the loss of two friends.

Instead, Cathy decided to honor her commitment to Matt. She turned John down because she already had plans, but she let him know that she hoped they might go another time. Although Cathy was a little disappointed, she felt right about her decision.

Accepting Others

Tolerance is the ability to accept people as they are. It is sometimes difficult to accept the fact that your friends and family don't behave exactly as you want them to. To preserve your relationships, you have to allow for people's individual traits.

Tolerance is especially important when there are problems in a relationship. If your best friend has different ideas about something that is important to you, you must learn to accept these ideas as something your friend believes in, if your relationship is to continue. Rarely does one disagreement destroy a strong relationship. Tolerance, though, will help to avoid conflicts.

Relationships and Attitudes

People's likes and dislikes are reflections of their attitudes. An attitude is a way of looking at people, events, and things. Like values, attitudes are usually learned from family and friends.

Attitudes can have a strong effect on you and your relationships. People with positive attitudes feel good about themselves and treat others with fairness. They don't label or reject people, but instead try to give everyone equal treatment. On the other hand, people with negative attitudes are often insecure, afraid, or ignorant. They let these feelings interfere with their relationships, and they often judge people unfairly.

Prejudice

Whenever groups or individuals have fixed mental pictures of what people are like, they are guilty of **prejudice**, an

Focus on Health Tell students that attitudes affect not only people's relationships, but also their health. Scientists are discovering that a positive attitude can help people recover from an illness more quickly.

Emphasize Prejudice and stereotyped thinking are products of insecurity, fear, and ignorance—not confidence, courage, and superiority.

opinion or feeling that is not based on fact. Prejudice is a form of rejection in which you decide about people before really knowing them. Whether you are prejudiced in favor of or against someone, it means that the person is not being judged fairly.

Prejudice is at work when you play favorites. The baseball coach is prejudiced if he leaves Kyle on the bench and puts Ron in every game, not because Ron is a better player but just because he is his nephew. It is a form of prejudice whenever a person is treated better on the basis of something other than ability or experience. It also almost always hurts those other people who are denied the same treatment.

When there is prejudice against an entire group of people, the society as a whole is hurt. If talented people are refused jobs or training because of their age, race, color, religion, or sex, everybody suffers. Society loses the work of people it needs, and many individuals in society lose the chance to meet people who might make their lives richer.

Stereotypes

One form of prejudice is stereotyped thinking. A **stereotype** is an unfair label that is automatically given to strangers. For example, someone may think that members of a certain group who share the same skin color or a particular way of speaking are also exactly alike in other ways.

One of the problems with stereotypes is that they sometimes cause you to act differently toward an individual than you would if you were not influenced by that image. For example, if you believe that a person confined to a wheelchair leads a boring life, you probably will stop yourself from getting to know someone you might like.

Stereotypes abound in our society and serve to limit people's experiences and possibilities. Perhaps you have heard stereotypes about races, professions, different ages or disabled people. See "Labels that Limit" on page 96.

Treating people as stereotypes rather than individuals can keep valuable relationships from beginning.

Prejudice is harmful because it limits and restricts people's opportunities. Learn to judge people as individuals, not as members of any stereotyped group.

Did You Know? The Civil Rights Acts of 1964 and 1968 prohibit discrimination based on sex, skin color, and ethnic background. These acts were passed to help end discrimination in hiring as well as wage rates and have created new job opportunities for minority groups and women.

Real-Life Situations Cliques—small exclusive groups within a peer group—are often formed during the teen years. (See Chapter 13). Cliques practice extreme forms of prejudice when they reject people who are not in their group. Ask students if cliques are strong in your school and how they handle rejection or intolerance practiced by members of cliques.

✓ Give an example of stereotyped thinking. *Answers will vary but should include a case similar to thinking that people with the same skin color are exactly alike in other ways.*

✓ Why would it be a mistake for you to stereotype people who speak with an accent? *Because you would be assuming that all people who speak with an accent are exactly alike in other ways.*

✓ What problems does stereotyped thinking cause? *Stereotyped thinking causes problems by making people act differently toward a person than they would if they didn't have the preconceived image. Stereotyped thinking also causes problems because it limits people's experience and possibilities.*

✓ What can be the result of treating people as stereotypes rather than as individuals? *It can keep valuable relationships from ever beginning.*

Activities

Skill Builder: Critical Thinking
Ask students to think of television programs about a detective, a black family, and an independent woman. Discuss the following with students: "What character traits does each have? Do you laugh at some of these characterizations when they do not fit the stereotypes? Which stereotypes do you not laugh at?"

Skill Builder: Critical Thinking
Ask students to think about ways that people can counteract prejudice and stereotypes in today's society. Have them prepare a short public service announcement promoting equality.

Reteaching
Ask students to define *prejudice* and *stereotype*. Then ask them to tell about an experience they have had or have witnessed in which prejudice or stereotyped thinking was a problem.

Enrichment
Challenge students to think of examples of tolerance, attitudes, value, prejudice, and stereotypes. Have students read their examples to the other members of the class and ask them to decide if the example is one of tolerance, attitude, value, prejudice, or stereotype.

Teaching the Feature
"Labels That Limit"

Answers to Feature Questions

1. Answers will vary. Students should point out that there will always be exceptions to any generalization that is made about people.

2. First impressions are made up of stereotypes because people usually make judgments about others before actually having had any personal experience with them. They judge them superficially by their appearance, by the way they speak, and by the way they act, without having had the chance to know their ideas and feelings.

Activities

Stereotype Flashcards Tell students that stereotypes are basically faulty generalizations. Remind them that generalizations are statements that include all people or all cases. On flashcards write generalizations that are both true and false, as most generalizations are. Then display them to the class, having students raise their hands to respond "true" or "false" for each generalization. Point out to students that anyone who answers "true" is showing prejudice. The same may hold for "false" responses.

Hold That Thought Have students discuss the problems that prejudice and stereotypes cause. Ask them to explain how they would influence younger children to avoid such negative thinking.

Community Contact Ask students to think about any prejudices or stereotypes they may have. Then ask them to attempt to learn more about the object of their negative thinking. For example, if they have a prejudice about older people, have them go to a nursing home or senior citizens' center, or get to know an older person. When the students are finished with the assignment, ask them to explain how their opinions have changed.

INTERPERSONAL SKILLS

Labels That Limit

Many general statements about people are stereotypes. Can you recognize stereotypes when you hear or read them? Here are ten general statements about people. See if you can determine why each one is a stereotype.

1. Teens are bad drivers.
2. People who wear glasses are bookworms.
3. Old people are absentminded.
4. All athletes are dumb.
5. Rural people are ignorant.
6. All doctors are rich.
7. Teenage girls only think about clothes.
8. Teenage boys only think about cars.
9. Women are too emotional to run a business.
10. Men never cry.

You don't have to let your ideas about people be governed by stereotypes. You can fight stereotypes. Here are three suggestions:

- **Avoid thinking or speaking in stereotypes.** Try to make your thoughts reflect reality.
- **Refuse to accept stereotypes.** Point out to others that their statements involving stereotypes are untrue. Mention the exceptions you know about personally.
- **Try to influence your friends.** Help them to be more flexible in their thinking. If you encourage them, they are likely to think for themselves and reject stereotypes.

Think It Through

1. **Choose two of the stereotypes listed above. Explain why they are false.**
2. **Do you think that first impressions are made up of stereotypes? Why or why not?**

Focus on Leadership Ask one student to lead a class discussion about stereotyped thinking about teens.

Focus on Consumer Skills Tell students that many advertisers rely on generalizations to sell their products. Ask students to describe a radio, newspaper, or television advertisement that employs the use of generalizations, and possibly, stereotypes.

CHAPTER 9 REVIEW

Reviewing the Facts

1. What is a role?
2. What is a common source of conflict in relationships?
3. Why should you avoid speaking in anger?
4. How can communication help prevent conflicts that arise over differing expectations?
5. What does it mean to be tolerant?
6. What is the difference between prejudice and stereotypes?

Thinking Critically

1. What role changes have you experienced in your life so far? As a result of these changes, how have your expectations and those of other people changed?
2. Discuss with the class an experience you had at one time when you stereotyped someone before knowing the person. What happened?

Applying Your Skills

1. **Analyzing Criteria.** Prepare an advertising campaign for an organization that fights stereotyping and prejudice. Examples include the American Civil Liberties Union, the National Organization for Women, or Amnesty International. Design a public service message for television and a print advertisement.

2. **Expressing Your Feelings.** Suppose that your friend Larry agreed to purchase tickets to a concert for several of his friends, including you. When Larry returns, he says that he forgot to buy a ticket for you and that the concert is sold out. Write a skit of the conversation or conversations you would have with Larry. Be sure to use the tips on how to resolve conflicts as a guide.

3. **Designing an Experiment.** Act out a scene with another classmate in which one represents a parent and the other represents a teenage son or daughter. The parent wants the teen to get home from a party earlier than the teen thinks is fair. Try to incorporate the concerns that parents have and communicate these feelings effectively. What does this show you about the roles that parents play?

Answers to "Reviewing the Facts"

1. A role is a part you play when you interact with others.
2. Often conflicts are a result of differing expectations.
3. Because you might say something that would hurt the other person.
4. When you communicate, you learn what the other person expects from you, and you get a chance to tell the other person what you expect as well.
5. To be tolerant is to accept people as they are.
6. Prejudice is an opinion or feeling about people that is not based on fact. A stereotype, which is a form of prejudice, is an unfair label given to all members of a group who may share one characteristic but are not alike in other ways.

Answers to "Thinking Critically"

1. Students will probably mention changing from dependent baby to toddler; from preschooler to student; entering adolescence and so on. Expectations that have changed include the child's lessening demands on parents and the parents' granting of added responsibilities and privileges; expectations of teachers that students in higher grades will do schoolwork without as much supervision; and so on.
2. Answers will vary. Students may recount an experience during which they stereotyped someone on the basis of sex, race, religion, age, size, or ethnic background.

COMPLETING THE CHAPTER

Summary

- Relationships work best if people understand roles and expectations.
- Changing roles and different expectations can cause conflict in relationships.
- Conflicts can be minimized by controlling feelings, communicating honestly, and accepting others.
- Positive and negative attitudes affect how people treat others.
- Prejudice (a fixed mental picture) and stereotypes (an unfair label automatically given to people) are two types of negative thinking.
- Treating people as stereotypes rather than as individuals can keep valuable relationships from ever beginning.

For Review

Objective Review Questions Have students complete the "Reviewing the Facts" section on this page.

Study Guide Have students complete the Study Guide from Chapter 9 of their *Student Workbook.*

Past Prejudices Tell students that prejudice is not a modern concept. Tell them to look back in history and they will find many instances of prejudice. Ask them to give an oral report on one case of prejudice in past times.

For Evaluation

Ignorance and Prejudice Write the following sentence on the board: "Ignorance is the mother of prejudice, whether among nations or individuals." Ask students what they think it means. Then ask whether this chapter supports this idea and what is the relationship between ignorance and prejudice.

Chapter Test Have students complete the test for Chapter 9 that appears in the *Teacher's Classroom Resources.*

CHAPTER OVERVIEW

Chapter 10 helps students understand families. The chapter explains that although the definition of *family* is different for different people, all families have certain functions, such as providing, nurturing, and guiding. The chapter explains that there are many types of families, including a married couple with no children, nuclear, single-parent, blended, and extended. The chapter also helps students appreciate their particular families. They are encouraged to remember that every family has its own style and to take time to understand the members of their families.

INTRODUCING THE CHAPTER

Motivators

What Is a Family? Write the phrase "To me, a family is . . . " on the board. Ask students to complete the sentence with a word or phrase that describes their idea of a family. After writing down different answers, say: "As you can see, the word *family* has different meanings for different people. We are going to learn more about families in this chapter."

Using the Photograph Have students study the photograph on this page. Then ask: "What is the family in this picture doing? What activity does your family enjoy together?"

Remembering Encourage students to remember and share with the class their earliest memory and why they think that event or situation had such an impact.

Introducing the Objectives

Discuss the chapter objectives on this page. Remind students that the objectives focus on important chapter content.

Introducing Vocabulary

Tell students that one meaning of the word *nurture* is "nourish." Ask students to suggest a relationship between nourishment and the family.

CHAPTER

10

Understanding Families

OBJECTIVES

This chapter will help you to:

- Define family.
- Explain how a family provides for, nurtures, and guides family members.
- Identify different types of family structures.
- Give examples of how you can develop a better understanding of parents and siblings.

WORDS TO REMEMBER

adopted
blended family
extended family
foster child
nuclear family
nurture
sibling
single-parent family
stepparent

Chapter Resources

Teacher's Classroom Resources
- Lesson Plan
- Life Skills Activity, *Birth Order: It's All Relative*
- Reproducible Master, *What Is a Family?*
- Extension Activity, *Birth Order of Famous People*
- Chapter Test

Student Workbook
- Study Guide
- Worksheet, *Family Connections*

Can you remember your first steps, or who held your hand? Perhaps not, but chances are that someone in your family was there to help you along. Back then, you learned how to talk and that it hurt to touch a hot range.

Many of your ideas, opinions, and tastes also came from your family. Do you like card games? You probably learned to play them at home. Do you love spicy food? Your family probably cooks it that way.

In addition, as you grew, your family taught you to value what is important in life. You not only developed a feeling about who you are, but also about what your place is in the world. Even after you no longer needed a hand to hold, you felt secure, a part of something. You belonged.

What Is a Family?

If you asked 12 people what a family is, you would probably get 12 different answers. A person's definition of the word *family* comes from experience, which can vary a lot. One person might say a family is a father, mother, and two sons. Another person might say that it is a mother and a daughter. A third would say that a family is a husband and wife. Even though all these definitions of family are different, they are still all correct.

A family is often defined as a group of individuals who share common values, goals, and resources. Each family member is responsible for certain decisions, and they all share emotional bonds.

No two families are the same, yet most families perform certain functions that set them apart from other groups. These functions are providing, nurturing, and guiding.

Providing

A newborn baby needs a lot of care, so it is easy to see how necessary a family is at the beginning of a child's life. The family, though, must satisfy the basic needs of all its members, young and old alike. The job of providing the physical things we need—food, clothing, and shelter—is a difficult one, and one that never ends.

Although families may have different structures, they are responsible for providing basic needs, and nurturing and guiding family members.

Emphasize Every family is different—there is no right or wrong definition of the word. Point out that every family has its own way of providing for needs, nurturing, and guiding.

Did You Know? Families were part of human life even in very early times. In the Stone Age people formed clans to help with the hunting and gathering of food.

Focus on Relationship Skills Discuss with students how they meet the needs of their family members. Ask them if they listen to other family members' problems or if they help them with certain projects or hobbies. Then ask them if there is something they could do to improve their relationship with their family.

TEACHING THE CHAPTER

For convenience, the teaching suggestions for this chapter are arranged according to the following lesson topics:

- "What Is a Family?," pages 99-100
- "Types of Families," pages 100-101
- "Appreciating Your Family," pages 101-103

Teaching "What Is a Family?"
(Pages 99-100)

This section teaches the different meanings of the word *family* and shows how a family provides for, nurtures, and guides its members.

Checking Comprehension

✔ Why are there so many different definitions of the word *family*? *There are so many different definitions of the word family because each person defines it in relation to his or her own experience. That experience is usually based on the family's common values, goals, and resources.*

✔ What needs does a family meet for its members? *A family meets its members' physical needs for clothing, food, and shelter and emotional needs for belonging, laughing, sharing, and feeling loved and cared for.*

✔ How does a family nurture its members? *A family nurtures its members by helping them to develop mentally, emotionally, and socially.*

✔ How does a family guide its members? *A family guides its members by teaching them what is right and wrong, providing values, and encouraging them to set goals, make decisions, and take responsibility for their actions.*

Activities

Skill Builder: Critical Thinking Have students speak to other members of their family. Ask them to get a definition of the word *family* from these members. Then have them discuss whether their definition of *family* is the same as or different from that of other family members.

Skill Builder: Critical Thinking
Tell students that they have just been made the head of their own family. Ask them how they would structure their family and how they would make it a strong family.

Reteaching
Remind students of the functions that families perform. Ask them to think about their own family and other families they have observed. Then ask them to compare the image of the ideal family to the realities of family life.

Enrichment
Have students research family life in a nation very different from the United States. Ask them to find out what families are like and if they perform the same functions that the chapter discusses. Have as many students as possible give a short oral report to the class.

Teaching "Types of Families"
(Pages 100-101)

This section identifies the different types of families.

Checking Comprehension

✓ Explain how the structure of families differs. *There might be two parents or one parent; there may be many children, even some from different marriages; or there might be no children. Also, grandparents, aunts, uncles, and cousins may be a part of the family.*

✓ What is special about an extended family? *An extended family may include relatives such as grandparents, uncles, aunts, and cousins living in the same household with parents and possibly children.*

✓ Are adults who are not married part of a family? *Yes, adults who are not married are part of a family—the family they grew up in.*

However, a family provides much more than physical needs. Many emotional needs are provided for as well: the need to belong, to laugh, to share with others, to feel loved and cared for.

Some families do a better job of providing for family needs than others. Usually it is not a matter of money, but rather of time, energy, and experience.

Nurturing

A family also **nurtures** its members, or helps them develop. Your family helps you grow as a person. Growing up is not just a matter of getting taller. Your mind grows just as your body does; you have to grow emotionally and socially, too. None of this happens all at once. It is gradual, and much of it happens in your family.

Your family teaches you about feelings and how to express them. At home, you can express your pride at making the track team or your disappointment at losing the school election.

You learn your first social skills from your family. Even before you could talk, you were introduced to playmates and asked to share toys. You saw how older family members got along with their friends, and people showed you how to take on new responsibilities.

Guiding

In addition, a family gives guidance to its members. Children are taught to distinguish between right and wrong. Family values help determine what kind of behavior is accceptable and what kind is not. Guidance also involves encouragement to set goals, make decisions, and take responsibility for your actions. Your family helps you learn how to live in society.

Types of Families

You have just looked at some of the ways in which families are similar. Families can also differ. One of the main ways in which they differ is in their structure.

Family Structures

All of the following groups of people are families:

- Rudolph and Yvonne Johnson have been married five years. Although they have no children, they are a family.
- The Vasquez family is an example of a **nuclear family**: two parents and one or more children sharing a household. Mr. and Mrs. Vasquez have three children: Maria, Anna, and Roberto.
- Mr. Webster heads another kind of family. He is divorced and cares for his son, Cody, and his daughter, Sherry. They are an example of a **single-parent family**: children living with one parent. Single-parent families are more common today than in the past.
- The Rosens are a **blended family**: a family that joins two separate families through marriage. Their new family consists of Mr. and Mrs. Rosen, plus Amy, Mrs. Rosen's daughter from her previous marriage, and Richard and Mindy, the children from Mr. Rosen's first marriage.

When a child gains a parent by marriage, the parent is called a **stepparent**. Mr. Rosen is Amy's stepfather and Mrs. Rosen is Richard and Mindy's stepmother. Similar terms are used for the relationships between children. Mindy is Amy's stepsister, and Richard is Amy's stepbrother.

Emphasize Point out that family structures can differ from family to family and that they may change over the years. Point out that not all changes are negative ones. For example, getting married or having children is a positive change.

More About Single-Parent Families Emphasize to students that the number of single-parent families is rising. Tell them that many communities offer single-parent clubs or activities to enable such families to interact and support each other.

Different generations enrich each other's lives.

■ Another type of family is the **extended family**, which is a family that may include grandparents, uncles, aunts, and cousins, as well as parents and children. The DeLauras are an extended family. There is Mr. and Mrs. DeLaura; their two children, Donald and Rebecca; Mrs. DeLaura's mother, Audrey Swenson; and Joe DeLaura, Mr. DeLaura's father.

These are five of the most common family structures, but many others exist as well. It is not unusual in our society for family structure to change many times. For example, single adults, or adults who are not married, are also part of a family—the family they grew up in. They may not live with their family, yet they are still part of them.

Also, when people do not live close to other family members, they may look upon close friends as almost a family group. Thus family structures are very flexible and have different variations. Every family has special characteristics that can be appreciated and enjoyed by its members.

Appreciating Your Family

Have you ever wished that your family was different? Does your dad embarrass you by telling jokes to your friends? Does your younger sister tag along wherever you go, or your older brother act like he knows everything?

Perhaps you envy a friend who is an only child and doesn't have to share or compete with her brothers and sisters. She may even seem to have a perfect relationship with her parents.

Did you ever stop to think that your friend might envy you? To her, a larger family looks like fun—there are more people to do things with and share experiences with. She may wish that she could talk to her parents the way you can talk to yours.

Family Styles

People may see family styles that are different from their own as being better or worse, but they are simply different. The fact is that all families are different—in size, in the way members interact, and in how responsibilities are divided. No one style is right. Each family finds a system that works well for its members.

✓ **If family members do not live close by, who can people look to to serve some of the functions of family?** ***When family members do not live close by, people may look to friends to serve some of the functions of family.***

Activities

Skill Builder: Critical Thinking
Have students count the number of people in their family. Ask for a show of hands to indicate who has the most family members. Then ask: "What are the advantages of a large family? What are the advantages of a small family?"

Skill Builder: Writing
Ask students to write a paragraph in which they explain what type of family structure they would most like to live in. Ask them to give reasons why they would like this family structure.

Reteaching
Ask students to list five types of family structures. Then have them find pictures showing these types of families and display them on a poster.

Enrichment
Ask students to speak to older family members. Students should ask older members to compare and contrast the structure of their family today with the structure when they were younger. Encourage students to share their findings in class.

Teaching "Appreciating Your Family"
(Pages 101-103)

This section teaches students to develop a better understanding of their parents and siblings.

Checking Comprehension

✓ How are families different? *Families are different in size, in the way members interact, and in how responsibilities are divided.*

Real-Life Situations The number of people living alone is increasing—more than 1 in 5 households consist of only one person. The greatest increase has been in the number of people ages 18-34 and people over age 65 who live alone. Ask students what factors may be influencing this trend.

Focus on Entrepreneurship Many businesses have been started by two or more family members. Family members can offer the support, trust, and similar values needed between business partners. Have students discuss the advantages and disadvantages of starting a business with family members.

✓ Why are families different? *Families are different because their members are unique, with special abilities and characteristics. The culture, customs, and religion of families also make them different from each other.*

✓ Why is it important to understand one's parents? *Because parents are people with interests, thoughts, desires, and their own dreams. Like all people, they need care and understanding.*

✓ What do children learn from their parents' nurturing and guidance? *Parents can help children build a strong self-concept by giving them love. They can also help them feel safe by caring. The guidance of parents helps children decide between right and wrong. Their sharing teaches children to give.*

✓ What is the difference between adopted children and foster children? *Adopted children have been legally made permanent members of a family. Foster children are taken from troubled homes to live with a family for a short time.*

✓ What can siblings do for each other to show that they understand each other's feelings? *Older children can try to include younger siblings in their activities. Younger children need to respect older siblings' need for privacy. All siblings should freely express their care, affection, and admiration.*

✓ How can children help overcome the feeling of jealousy toward their siblings? *Children can help overcome the feeling of jealousy toward their siblings by remembering that parents love all their children, even though they may not treat them exactly alike.*

Activities

Skill Builder: Writing
Have students write a letter to a member of their family. Tell them to ask questions that will help them better understand this family member and to include information about themselves that will help that family member better understand them.

Why are families different? Each family is unique because its members have special abilities and characteristics. For example, your grandfather makes handcrafted items, your sister plays the flute, and your father sings in the church choir. All this variety makes family life more interesting. It would not make sense for all these different people to try to follow the same pattern.

The culture, customs, and religious background of a family also make it one of a kind. Does your family always celebrate birthdays with a cake? When you go to family weddings, do you dance traditional dances that are a part of your cultural heritage, such as the Polish polka, Irish jig, or Italian tarantella?

A family's cultural pride and heritage play a very important part in family life. They influence the food you eat and the holidays you celebrate. Your cultural background also influences the role you have in your family, how decisions are made, and how responsibilities are divided. Your family style is different from the way of life of other families. Appreciating the differences helps you enjoy the ways your family is special.

Understanding Your Parents

Understanding your family means thinking about your parents' roles, too. When you were younger, you may have thought that your parents knew everything and could do anything. Now, as you grow older, you may be seeking more understanding and acceptance from your parents as you begin to make more of your own decisions.

Special celebrations, such as weddings, may reflect the culture, customs, and religious background of families.

Emphasize Culture plays a part in making families unique. Remind students that every family has its own set of traditions and customs.

Focus on Decision Making Remind students that some decisions are difficult to make. Ask them to imagine being a parent and trying to cope with a teen whose grades are falling. Have them role play being a parent who must decide whether to ignore, talk to, or punish the child for not working up to his or her ability.

As you become ready for more responsibilities, it is important to remember that parents need understanding and acceptance, too. Teens sometimes forget that parents are people with interests, thoughts, desires, and their own dreams. They are individuals with strengths and weaknesses. They, too, have good and bad days.

As you learned in Chapter 9, honest communication will help you see your parents' point of view. Getting to know your parents may help you see things differently. You will better understand why they care about where you are going, who you will be with, what you will be doing, and when you will be home.

Remember that parents' love helps you build a strong self-concept. Their caring makes you feel safe. Their guidance helps you decide what is right. Their listening proves how important you are to them. Their sharing teaches you to give.

Understanding Your Siblings

Many families include one or more children. These children may be born into the family, adopted, or stepchildren. An **adopted** child is one who has been legally made a permanent member of a new family. Some children from troubled homes are taken into families for shorter periods. They are called **foster children**.

If you have brothers or sisters, or **siblings**, it is important to understand their feelings. If you are an older child, try to include your younger siblings in your activities sometimes. If you are a younger child, you need to understand your older siblings' need for privacy.

Whether you are the oldest or youngest child, or in the middle, when you feel pleased with a brother or sister, say so. Your affection and admiration probably mean more than you realize.

Everyone who has a brother or sister feels jealous sometimes. It is important to remember that parents love all their children. In treating each child as a unique person, they may not treat them all alike.

This family consists of biological children, adopted children, stepchildren, and foster children. The parents love them all!

Skill Builder: Critical Thinking
Have students discuss their different cultural backgrounds. Then ask them to share with the class a custom, food, article of clothing, or song that is specific to their particular family.

Skill Builder: Critical Thinking
Ask students to discuss how trying to understand family members helps family relationships. Ask them to share what they do or could do to better understand other family members.

Reteaching
Ask students to use photos or illustrations to create a collage portraying their family in action.

Enrichment
Ask students to select a novel about family relationships, such as Clarence Day's *Life with Father*. Have them write a report on how the fictional family differs from their own family.

Enrichment
Invite a panel of parents from different family structures to discuss their particular family structure. The panel could consist of a mother/father group, a stepparent, a foster parent, parents of an adopted family, a parent with a blended family. Ask parents to share how they are alike or different from other families.

Real-Life Situations Adopted, foster, and stepchildren may have special concerns. Adopted children may have mixed emotions, such as resentment and wondering about birth parents, and gratitude to adoptive parents. Foster children may be concerned that parents could not care for them economically, emotionally, or socially, and be uncertain of their future. Stepchildren must share a remarried parent with a new spouse and perhaps live with new stepbrothers or stepsisters. They may be concerned about their other birth parent with whom they no longer live.

Teaching the Feature
"Cultural Diversity of Families"

Answers to Feature Questions

1. Students might answer that people live in families to protect and teach children, to provide economic support for each other, and to meet emotional and social needs.

2. Students might answer that parents want their children to be healthy and happy. Parents usually want their children to have a good education and be able to earn a good living. They may hope their children will marry someday and have children of their own.

Activities

Family Values Have each student list on a piece of paper five values important to his or her family. Then have students gather in small groups and compare values. Encourage students to share how each value is expressed in their families.

Family History Suggest that students find out about their families four or five generations back (for example, number of children, how family members earned their living). Students may be surprised to find similarities between their ancestral families and traditional families in the world today. Discuss how going from an agricultural society to an industrialized society has changed family life and structure in the United States.

Multicultural Literature Encourage students to read a book about a family from a different culture. Ask the school librarian to recommend books. Students should look for similarities and differences between the family in the book and their own families.

Community Contact Ask someone who has sponsored a foreign exchange student to speak to the class. Have the speaker describe how the student adapted to the new family life.

INTERPERSONAL SKILLS

Cultural Diversity of Families

Koua Lor, a teen from Laos, and Scott Anderson, a fourth-generation Norwegian American, are classmates at Westbury High School.

Kuoa lives with his father, mother, grandfather, grandmother, and four brothers and sisters. Koua's father, a carpenter, makes most of the decisions for the family. His mother, a quiet woman, stays home and cares for the children. When Koua comes home from school, he acknowledges his grandparents by putting his hands together and bowing his head.

Scott lives with his father, mother, and younger sister. His grandparents live far away, and Scott sees them only once or twice a year. His father and mother share decision making for the family. In the evening after supper, Scott enjoys playing basketball with his dad.

The Lors and the Andersons seem quite different. The families are organized differently, and members have different ways of interacting with each other. Each family has unique customs and traditions. However, both families have similar values.

A value is something important to a family. Values are usually intangible; that is, they can't be seen or touched. Values include honesty, kindness, respect for others, self-reliance, cooperation, and loyalty.

Both the Lors and the Andersons value education. Mrs. Anderson works outside the home to earn money for her children's college education. Mr. and Mrs. Lor insist that their children do homework every day, even Saturday and Sunday.

Another value the families share is a belief in the importance of a spiritual life. Although they practice different religions, spirituality is a common value.

In addition to sharing values, the families are similar in the kinds of activities they do. Both Scott and Koua take care of their younger siblings, and both do chores around the house. Both families enjoy going on outings and entertaining friends and relatives. The families celebrate special occasions such as birthdays and weddings. Koua and Scott know they can depend on their families for love and support.

Many families with different roots live in the United States. These groups include Asians, Africans, Latin Americans, Native Americans, and Europeans, among others. Differences in family customs and structure make our culture richer. At the same time, similarities in family values and activities are a source of unity for all people.

Think It Through

1. **Why do you think people all over the world live together in families?**
2. **What things do you think all parents want, or value, for their children?**

Emphasize Although families across cultures may share similar values, differences in values exist as well. This can be a source of conflict. Teens adjusting to the culture of the United States are often in conflict with their parents who want to preserve their traditional culture.

Did You Know? In contrast to a patriarchal or matriarchal family, an equalitarian family is one in which neither parent is the head. Parents share decision making and often solicit the opinions of their children. This type of family has become more common in the United States as more women work outside the home.

CHAPTER 10 REVIEW

Reviewing the Facts

1. Explain what a family is.
2. What are the three functions of a family? Give an example of how a family performs each of those functions.
3. List three specific ways a family provides guidance for its members.
4. What is the difference between a nuclear family and an extended family?
5. What is a blended family?
6. Why is it important to develop an appreciation of your family rather than comparing your family to other families?
7. What can you do to understand your parents?
8. What can you do to understand your siblings?

Thinking Critically

1. Identify a family tradition or custom of your family. How did it develop? Is it one that you would want to continue with your future family? Why or why not?
2. What "position" do you have in your family—oldest, middle, youngest, or only child? Name two positive and two negative aspects of this position.

Applying Your Skills

1. **Giving Some Examples.** Write a brief description of the ways you provide family members with support. How do you provide for, nurture, and guide the other members of your family?

2. **Writing a Comparison.** Think about a family television show that you watch regularly. In several paragraphs, explain the ways that this family is the same or different from real families that you know.

3. **Performing an Experiment.** Choose one of the following family positions: oldest, middle, youngest, or only child. Perform an experiment by interviewing five friends, classmates, or relatives who hold this position. Ask them how their position affected their childhood. Write down their responses and compare them. What were the similarities? What were the differences?

Answers to "Reviewing the Facts"

1. A family is a group of individuals who share common values, goals, and resources. Each family member is responsible for certain decisions, and they all share emotional bonds.
2. Providing, nurturing, and guiding. Examples include: providing food, clothing, shelter, love; helping members develop mentally, emotionally, and socially; teaching values and responsible behavior.
3. To distinguish between right and wrong; to determine acceptable behavior; to provide encouragement for setting goals, making decisions, and accepting responsibility.
4. A nuclear family includes just parents and children. An extended family includes other family members or relatives.
5. A blended family is created by the marriage of two people who have children from previous marriages.
6. Your family is a unique group of people with special abilities and characteristics. They provide you with unique cultural background.
7. Respect their individuality, get to know them, communicate honestly, remember that their love and guidance will help you.
8. Try to understand their feelings, include them in activities, understand their need for privacy, express your affection and admiration.

Answers to "Thinking Critically"

1. Answers will vary. Students might discuss a particular holiday custom or even something practiced daily, like saying grace before dinner. This custom may have been handed down from previous generations. Students should give their reasons for preferring or not preferring to continue family traditions.
2. Answers will vary. Students should give reasons or examples to support their answers.

COMPLETING THE CHAPTER

Summary

- Definitions for the word *family* vary but include "individuals who share common values, goals, and resources."
- Families perform the functions of providing for members' needs, nurturing members to help them develop, and guiding members to help them learn to live in society.
- Family structures can vary from household to household.
- Common family structures are nuclear families, single-parent families, blended families, extended families, and a married couple without children.
- Family styles differ because of the uniqueness of the members, different cultural backgrounds, and different religious backgrounds.
- It is important to appreciate one's own family for its special abilities and unique characteristics.

For Review

Objective Review Questions Have students complete the "Reviewing the Facts" section on this page.

Study Guide Have students complete the Study Guide from Chapter 10 of their *Student Workbook.*

Class Discussion Guide students in a discussion of the different types of families and how they each perform the functions of providing, nurturing, and guiding.

For Evaluation

Self-Appraisal Ask students to write a definition for each of the five types of families they learned about. Then have them look in their books and check their answers, making any necessary corrections.

Chapter Test Have students complete the test for Chapter 10 that appears in the *Teacher's Classroom Resources.*

CHAPTER OVERVIEW

Chapter 11 begins by discussing seven qualities of strong families. The chapter also explains, however, that no family is perfect and that problems will arise. A problem-solving model is introduced that includes identifying the problem, talking it over, and compromising. When outside help is needed to resolve family problems, students are encouraged to seek help from teachers, counselors, religious or youth leaders, social workers, or community organizations.

INTRODUCING THE CHAPTER

Motivators

Teamwork Write the word *teamwork* on the board, and ask students to name things they think of when they hear this word. Then ask them if they have ever thought of a family as a team. Explain that in this chapter they are going to learn about strengthening families and that pulling together as a team is one way to do this.

Using the Photograph Have students look at the photograph. Ask : "What are the people in the picture doing? What do their expressions tell you?" Then ask students to share an experience in which their family worked together as a team.

Building Teamwork Ask students why teamwork is important. Then ask them to describe a situation in which teamwork paid off for them. Guide students in a comparison between teamwork and family life: possible comparison areas are sharing responsibilities and providing support.

Introducing the Objectives

Discuss the chapter objectives on this page. Remind students that the objectives focus on important chapter content.

Introducing Vocabulary

Explain that all the vocabulary words have to do with solving problems that can occur in families. Briefly define each one, and ask students how they think each might relate to problem solving.

CHAPTER

11

Strengthening Families

OBJECTIVES

This chapter will help you to:

- Identify qualities that make families strong.
- Explain ways to communicate about family problems.
- Describe how brainstorming and compromising help to solve problems.
- List sources that will help with family conflicts.

WORDS TO REMEMBER

brainstorming
confidentiality
counseling

Chapter Resources

Teacher's Classroom Resources
- Lesson Plan
- Life Skills Activity, *Family Helpline*
- Reproducible Master, *Strengthen Families*
- Extension Activity, *Balancing Work and Family*
- Chapter Test

Students Workbook
- Study Guide
- Worksheet, *Community Helpline*

In many ways, a family is a team, and it functions just like any other team. For a baseball team to win, each player must do what he or she is best at, but they must still work together as a group. Members of winning teams communicate their plans and share responsibilities. They build confidence by appreciating one another's strengths and weaknesses and showing one another respect and trust. In fact, the players of a baseball team could not accomplish as individuals what they can accomplish as a team. A family is like that—they need to work together to be successful.

What Makes Families Strong?

Families that are vital and strong have certain qualities that help bind the family together and strengthen individual members. Here are some ways that family members provide support for one another:

- **Building self-esteem.** Families can build high self-esteem by praising each other's accomplishments. Family members need to know that they are accepted and loved as they are, with all their strengths and weaknesses. This helps them accept others.
- **Communicating effectively.** Families can aim to communicate in ways that are clear and honest. It is easy to fall into the trap of assuming that everyone else in the family knows what you are thinking. You might, for example, be upset with a friend and mope around the house, assuming that your family knows why. However, unless you tell them, they won't know, and they may become annoyed at your behavior.
- **Sharing responsibilities.** Family members can share responsibility for certain tasks such as preparing food, cleaning, and doing the laundry. Even young children can participate by setting the table, making beds, or folding clothes. Many families have rules that govern household chores along with the use of money, methods of communication, and even what happens when someone breaks the rules. Rules should be clear so everyone knows what they are. When circumstances change, family rules may need to change. For example, your curfew may get later as you get older.
- **Showing respect and trust.** Family members need to respect one another's opinions and show one another attention and concern. They can earn respect and trust by being truthful and dependable.
- **Spending time together.** The time that a family spends together is much more important than what it is they do together. They might rake the lawn, go on a hike, wash the car, make cookies, play with a board game, go biking or canoeing, or plan a vacation.
- **Establishing traditions.** Families usually have some traditions that have been handed down and are based on their ethnic or cultural background. They might also establish new traditions such as reading a favorite story or poem on a particular holiday, celebrating special occasions at a favorite restaurant, or cooking specific foods at a certain time of year.
- **Reaching beyond the family to the larger society.** Families can have a good relationship with people outside the family. They do this by maintaining an attitude of friendliness and openness toward others. Often, families become involved in some project in their neighborhood or community.

Emphasize Teamwork is important to any group with shared values and goals—a description that fits the family well.

Focus on Relationship Skills Have students think about their interactions with family members. Ask them to think about these questions: Do you think you communicate effectively? Do you spend enough time with your family? Do you build self-esteem in other members of your family?

TEACHING THE CHAPTER

For convenience, the teaching suggestions for this chapter are arranged according to the following lesson topics:

- "What Makes Families Strong?" pages 107-108
- "Handling Family Problems," pages 108-111
- "Seeking Outside Help," pages 111-112

Teaching "What Makes Families Strong?"

(Pages 107-108)

This section identifies different qualities that make families strong.

Checking Comprehension

✓ How can families build a member's self-esteem? *Families can build a member's self-esteem by praising the person's accomplishments and providing acceptance and love.*

✓ What is meant by effective communication? *Communication that is clear and honest.*

✓ What responsibilities can family members share? *Family members can share the responsibilities of household chores, such as preparing food, cleaning, and doing the laundry.*

✓ Explain how rules can be a part of family life. *Rules might govern household chores, the use of money, methods of communication, and what happens when someone breaks the rules. Rules might change when circumstances change.*

✓ What traditions can families establish together? *Families can establish traditions or practice ones that are handed down new, based on ethnic or cultural background. Specific examples might include reading a favorite story or poem on a particular holiday, celebrating special occasions at a favorite restaurant, or cooking specific foods at certain times of the year.*

This family enjoys going on weekend trips together. What activities does your family enjoy?

These seven qualities work together. The high self-esteem that a family provides, for example, allows its members to go out into the world as people who are more likely to respect themselves and to help others. Communication skills learned in the family help family members to take an active part in the larger society. In addition, sharing responsibilities helps family members to develop respect and trust for other people. Spending time together and establishing traditions contribute to the special enjoyment of family life.

No family, however, is perfect. Families are made of people, and people have weaknesses and faults as well as strengths and virtues. That means that sometimes problems arise in families.

Handling Family Problems

Problems are bound to occur in family life. Families include individuals, each with his or her own likes and dislikes, desires, and plans. There are, however, ways to deal with family problems or conflicts that can help a family grow stronger.

What's the Problem?

The first step in dealing with family conflict is identifying the source of the problem. Suppose you and your brother, Carlos, are responsible for washing the dinner dishes. You and Carlos alternate cleaning nights. You also divide the vac-

✔ How can skills learned in the family help members contribute to society? *Skills in boosting self-esteem usually result in self-respect and an interest in helping others. Communication skills help people take an active part in society. Sharing responsibilities helps people develop respect and trust for other people.*

Activities

Skill Builder: Math
Ask students to think of the cleaning responsibilities they share with the other members of their families. Then have them estimate what percentage of the cleaning chores are done by each family member. Have students draw a pie graph with divisions representing different members of the family and showing how the work is divided.

Skill Builder: Writing
Have students write a short story that describes a family reaching out to the larger community. Be sure the story shows how this strengthens the family itself as well as helps others.

Reteaching
Ask students to use pictures or illustrations to demonstrate one of the seven qualities that help to strengthen families.

Enrichment
Have students plan an activity to be shared with another family member or their entire family. After they complete the activity, ask students to give a short oral report about it. Tell them to include the following in their report: why they chose the activity they did, what they learned about the other person (or persons) while doing the activity, and what they enjoyed most about the shared time.

Focus on Leadership Ask students to become leaders in making their family stronger. Tell them to brainstorm with other members to find ways the family can spend more time together and offer more support. Then tell students to take charge in implementing the suggested improvements.

Real-Life Situations Unfortunately some families are not strong or healthy due to serious problems such as violence, drug or alcohol addiction, or emotional problems. Ask students what options are available for children or teens in such family situations.

uuming on weekends. Carlos, however, has just joined the volleyball team at school, and this week he has been getting home late because of practice. Your father asks you to clean up on Carlos's nights, too. You feel this is unfair, but you don't know what to do about the situation.

Talking It Over

Resolving family problems, like any other problems, requires communication skills. Here are a few guidelines for getting your point across.

- **Choose the proper setting.** Wait for a relaxing moment in a quiet place. Instead of stopping your father when he is getting ready for work in the morning, ask him if you can talk to him that evening when he gets home.
- **Keep to the point.** Think through what you want to say before you begin. Be direct. Your family will not get your point if you can't state it clearly. Offer a reasonable solution if you have one.
- **Keep calm.** If you are upset or angry, you will not be able to get your point across. Crying or slamming doors will not change people's minds.
- **Listen.** Listening well is just as important as speaking well. Don't think about your side of the argument when someone else is talking. Listen and try to understand the other person's point of view.
- **Avoid accusation, sarcasm, and threats.** Showing respect for another person's ideas will earn respect for your own. Saying "You're wrong!" or "That is ridiculous!" can end communication fast. Some communication experts suggest avoiding "you" statements entirely and speaking in "I" statements. Rather than saying, "You don't make Carlos wash the dishes!" you might say, "I feel like I am doing more than my share of the work."

If you want to be taken seriously, you need to present your position clearly and calmly.

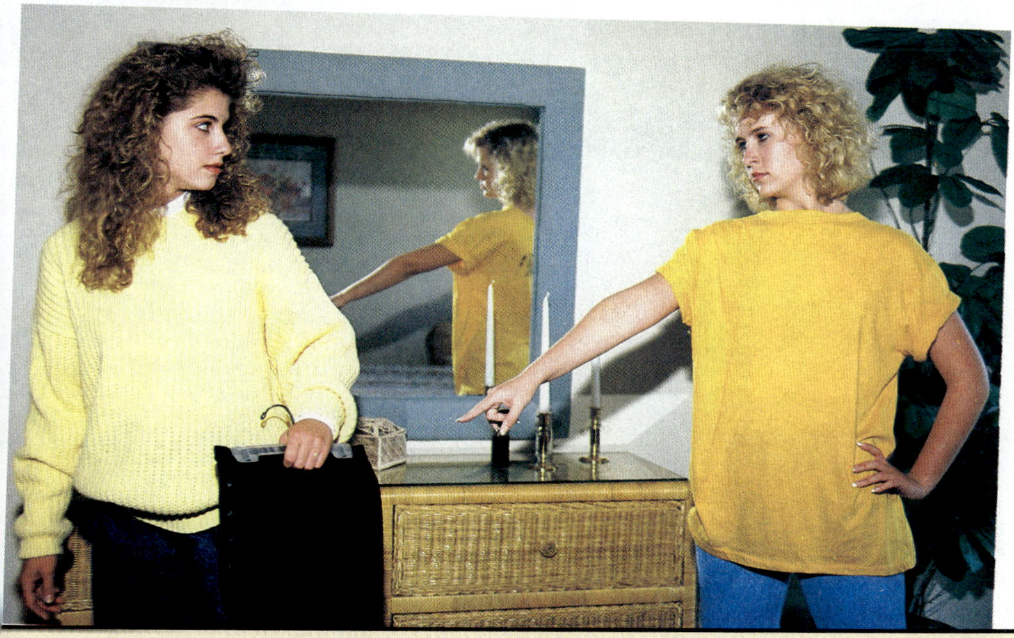

Emphasize Every family has problems and the presence of problems does not mean there is something wrong with the family.

Cross-Reference Remind students that listening is a very important part of the communication process. Stress that listening is even more important when one is trying to work out a problem. Have students review the ways they have learned to improve their listening skills on pages 85-86.

Teaching "Handling Family Problems"

(Pages 108-111)

This section describes ways to communicate about and solve family problems.

Checking Comprehension

✓ Describe the proper setting for getting a point across. *You should wait for a relaxing moment in a quiet place.*

✓ Why should you think through what you want to say before you begin? *It will help you to keep to the point and get your ideas across by stating them clearly.*

✓ What kinds of statements should you avoid when discussing a problem? *You should avoid accusation, sarcasm, and threats. Also, avoid using "you" statements and instead use "I" statements.*

✓ Why is it important not to generalize when talking over a problem? *Because doing so confuses the issue and doesn't explain the problem.*

✓ How can brainstorming help people find solutions to a problem? *Brainstorming for solutions to a problem gets ideas flowing and promotes discussion.*

✓ What are some guidelines to follow when brainstorming? *Give each person a chance to defend his or her solutions. Listen to other opinions and solutions without getting upset. Use "I" rather than "you" statements.*

Activities

Skill Builder: Critical Thinking
Ask students to brainstorm common problems that families have to resolve. Choose three or four, and ask students to act out skits of these situations. For each situation, assign the roles of parent, grandparent, siblings, and so on. Then have the "family" discuss the problem. After the skits ask the rest of the class to comment on how the family handled its problem.

Skill Builder: Critical Thinking
Have students discuss how the procedures they learned for handling a family problem might be applied to other problems, such as problems with friends, a problem in class, or even a problem in their community.

Skill Builder: Writing
Have students imagine that they are the main character in the situation described in the text. They should write a dialogue between themselves and a parent, illustrating the six guidelines on pages 109-110 for "Talking It Over."

Reteaching
Ask students to provide family problem-solving examples from television. Ask them to compare and contrast what they have read in the chapter with the way the family on television handled the problem.

Enrichment
Tell students that many books and articles have been written on how to deal with problems and how to interact with other people. Tell them that most of these books and articles offer helpful tips for improving communication. Ask them to go to the library and read an article or skim a book on this subject. They should then write a report that tells what the information taught them about communication.

- **Avoid generalizations.** When you use words such as "never" and "always," you confuse the issue and can't talk about the specific conflict you have. Saying "I always have to wash the dishes" does not explain the problem. Instead, you might say, "I am upset because I am doing my share of the washing and Carlos's, too."

Family Discussions

Some problems can best be solved by the whole family, but finding a solution that everyone accepts is not always easy. Resolving conflicts will be easier if everyone communicates openly and honestly, respects each person's opinion, listens, and allows give-and-take.

One way to find solutions is by listing as many ideas as you can think of, or **brainstorming.** This free-for-all approach to problem solving is an excellent way to get ideas flowing and to promote discussion. All it takes to brainstorm is a pen, a piece of paper, and several open minds.

Suppose your family decides to brainstorm about your conflict with Carlos. For a designated period of time, family members write down any idea they think of, without considering whether the idea is good or bad. The goal at the beginning is simply to list ideas.

Here are just a few of the solutions that might emerge:

- Carlos could do the dishes after volleyball, even though it is late and he is tired.
- Carlos could clean up after all the meals on the weekends.
- Carlos could do the dishes every evening that he doesn't have volleyball and do all the vacuuming on the weekends.

Family discussions can help solve conflicts by allowing members to share their opinions.

More About Discussions Tell students that brainstorming is one way of promoting discussion and that role playing is another. Point out that sometimes counseling sessions involve role playing to help people see different points of view or act out what they are feeling.

Emphasize Compromising is important in relationships, especially in those that are significant and in which there is a problem.

- Carlos could be given a different job entirely, one that would not interfere with volleyball. Perhaps you could do the dishes every night, but he could vacuum the whole house on the weekends.

Once family members have listed all their ideas, each person gets a chance to defend the solution he or she thinks will work best. Try to give good reasons for feeling the way you do, and listen to your family's objections without getting upset. Remember to use "I" rather than "you" statements.

Compromising

An important part of handling problems in a mature way is being able to compromise. As you learned in Chapter 7, compromising means that each person gives up a little of what he or she wants in order to find a solution that satisfies everyone. In other words, you give a little to get a little.

Suppose that as a result of your brainstorming session you and your family decide you will do the dishes every night, and Carlos will vacuum the whole house on weekends. He will not have to rush home after volleyball, and you will not have any additional chores on weekends. Usually, if each family member is willing to compromise, a workable solution can be found.

Seeking Outside Help

Sometimes, when a family has a very serious problem, even talking openly and honestly may not help. Not every family problem can be solved at home. When you have tried everything and you are no closer to solving a problem, it is time to reach out beyond the family.

Professional counseling can help families solve serious problems.

Emphasize Be sure students understand that seeking outside help for solving family problems is not a sign of weakness. It is an important and often necessary step in beginning to solve a problem.

Focus on Health Remind students that mental health is an important aspect of wellness. Point out that just as people seek expert advice for physical ailments, they should seek expert advice for problems that are harming their emotional and mental well-being.

Teaching "Seeking Outside Help"
(Pages 111-112)

This section explains when and where to get outside help for a family problem.

Checking Comprehension

✔ List three types of people or groups who can offer counseling in a community. *Any three: teachers, guidance counselors, religious leaders, youth leaders, social workers, community agencies, and crisis centers.*

✔ What are two common problems that community agencies or organizations can help families with? *Two common problems are drug abuse and family violence.*

✔ How can people find out about community agencies or organizations in their area? *People can find out about community agencies or organizations in their area by checking in the white and yellow pages of a local telephone book.*

✔ What are two common problems that hot-line services offer help with? *Two problems that hot-line services offer help with are runaway children and suicidal people.*

✔ Why is confidentiality important in counseling? *Confidentiality is important in counseling because sharing personal problems is difficult, and people need to know that the counselor will not reveal what she or he has been told.*

Activities

Skill Builder: Critical Thinking
Ask students to write a paragraph describing characteristics they think a counselor should have. You might give several suggestions to get them started, such as "a caring person," "a good listener," "an open-minded person." Have students read their paragraphs to the class. Hold a discussion on which counseling skills students think can be taught and which (if any) must be part of a counselor's personality.

Skill Builder: Writing
Ask students to write a paragraph that expresses how they imagine Lisa felt about her family situation before she approached her minister for counseling. They should then write a paragraph describing how they imagine she felt after her family began working on the problem.

Reteaching
Ask students to describe a problem a family might have that could not be solved by the family members alone. Ask them to suggest one place the family might go for outside help and to explain why they chose that particular outside source.

Enrichment
Ask students to write an article about a local counseling service. Ask them to look in the telephone book for a counseling service and to prepare questions to ask the professionals working there. After students have gathered all the information they can about the counseling service, have them write the article.

Enrichment
Suggest that students volunteer to work at an agency or on a hot line such as for child abuse, family member abuse, or rape relief. Explain that this type of orientation will help them learn ways to help people with their problems.

Enrichment
Invite guest speakers from community agencies—rape relief center, Alcholics Anonymous, or the county attorney—to come to class and explain how their agency can help with a problem. You may want to ask permission to video tape the speaker so that other classes can benefit from the presentation.

Lisa, for example, knows that her family needs help. Lisa's home has become a battleground. Her parents fight constantly. After a fight, her father often storms out, and her mother ends up drinking too much. Lisa's older sister, Alicia, has completely withdrawn from her parents and refuses to speak to them at all. What can Lisa do?

Community Counseling

Lisa can go many places to receive **counseling**, the advice and guidance given by experts, religious leaders, or support groups. She can consult:

- **Teachers and guidance counselors.** The adults you see in school every day are a good source of help. They may come up with solutions to the problem or give you the name of a community agency that offers help.
- **Religious leaders.** Many ministers, priests, rabbis, and mullahs know a great deal about counseling. They sometimes set up workshops to deal with family problems.
- **Youth leaders.** Adults who volunteer to work with young people are usually willing to help out in any way they can. If you are a scout or belong to the YWCA, YMCA, the 4-H, the Future Homemakers of America, or other organizations like these, ask your leader for help and guidance.
- **Social workers.** These people are trained to listen and to help people overcome their problems.
- **Community agencies and organizations.** Many agencies and organizations help families deal with specific problems such as drug abuse or family violence. Al-Anon, for example, has helped millions of family members who live with alcoholics. To find these groups in your neighborhood, ask at your local library or check the white and yellow pages of your local telephone directory.
- **Crisis centers.** Crisis centers have volunteers who are eager to help people with problems. Some of the centers operate telephone hot lines for people who need help immediately such as teens running away from home or considering suicide.

Making a Choice

Lisa, like many other people, feels uncomfortable and embarrassed about telling her problem to a stranger. Sharing personal problems with someone you don't know well is not easy to do. Professionals, however, know that you are discussing important feelings and will try to make you feel as comfortable as possible.

Lisa does not need to worry about her counselor telling someone else what she has said. Any professional counselor will maintain your **confidentiality**, or privacy. He or she will not reveal your problems to anyone else.

In the end, Lisa decided to talk with her minister. He suggested that she, her sister, and her parents come to a workshop being held at the church. After he talked with the whole family, Lisa's parents and sister finally agreed to attend. Together, as a family, the members were taking an important first step toward working out their problems.

Did You Know? Tell students that counseling people with problems involves more than just caring about people. Psychological counseling requires years of education and training. Briefly describe the differences between psychiatrists and psychologists. (Psychiatrists are medical doctors and are able to prescribe drugs, whereas psychologists cannot. Psychologists may be trained in one of many areas of psychology or social psychology.)

MANAGING RESOURCES

Balancing Work and Family

The struggle to balance work and family life is a reality that many families are facing today. A family may be headed by a single parent who works full time, or both parents may work outside the home. These situations require strong management skills to ensure that family members get all the attention they need.

When there are young children in the family, thought must be given to protecting and caring for them. Questions such as these may come up: Who will take care of the children when the parents are working? What will happen if a single parent has to work late? Who will take a sick child to the doctor?

Families juggle the demands of work and family by making different kinds of long-range plans. Here are some possible options:

- **Postponing work.** A parent may choose not to work outside the home while the children are young. When the children are older, the parent returns to work.
- **Flexible schedules.** Two parents schedule different working hours. Then one parent can be at home while the other parent is working.
- **Part-time work.** A parent may work part-time, perhaps during the hours when the children are in school. As the children grow older, that job may become full-time.
- **Working at home.** In some jobs, a parent can use the home as a workplace. This can be an advantage when children are young.

Trying to meet work and family obligations often leads to stress in a family. Careful planning of time can reduce the stress, but emergencies such as illness or the need for a single parent to work late may still arise. Here are two strategies that many families rely on to get necessary things done:

- **Delegating responsibilities.** When necessary, tasks usually done by one member of the family can be given to other family members who have more time. Shopping, cleaning, cooking, and laundry are tasks that can be delegated, or assigned to others.
- **Building a support system.** A support system is especially important for working parents. It includes people who would respond in emergencies: relatives, friends, neighbors, and community groups. A support group makes it possible to share the difficult job of balancing work and family.

Think It Through

1. **What could you do to provide a neighbor who is a single parent with a few hours of help?**
2. **What can young school-age children do to make it easier for the parents to balance work and family responsibilities?**

Teaching the Feature
"Balancing Work and Family"

Answers to Feature Questions

1. The help could be any number of things, such as babysitting, shopping, or just keeping in touch to see if help is needed.
2. They could do various household chores, such as folding laundry, dusting, and setting the table. They could also try to keep their room clean and orderly.

Activities

Helping Out Have students discuss how they help their families balance the responsibilities of both work and family. Ask students if they can think of any additional ways they might help, and suggest that they act on their ideas.

Research Topic Tell students that the struggle to balance work and family has become an important social issue. Ask students to research two or three articles on topics such as two-career couples, single-parent families, flex time, day care, or working mothers. Have them write a report about what they learned and present it to the class.

Community Contact Tell students that support systems are important for families that are trying to balance the responsibilities of family and work. Divide the students into small groups, and ask each group to find out what kind of support systems their community offers to families. If students need help getting started, suggest ideas such as day-care centers, single-parent groups, and businesses that offer services to help with family responsibilities. After allowing time for research, ask one person from each group to report on the group's findings.

Emphasize Point out to students that when family structures change, the struggle to balance family and work responsibilities may become more difficult.

Focus on Entrepreneurship Ask students to think of businesses they could start (such as babysitting or grocery shopping services) that would help families in their community better balance work and family responsibilities.

COMPLETING THE CHAPTER

Summary

- Families can be strengthened through building members' self-esteem, communicating effectively, sharing responsibilities, showing respect and trust, spending time together, establishing traditions, and reaching out to people beyond the family.
- Discussing family problems is important. Brainstorming—quickly listing a variety of ideas—is a good way to begin family discussions. Compromising is a necessary element in finding solutions.
- When families have tried everything to solve their problems and they still have not found a solution, outside help is needed. Teachers, guidance counselors, religious or youth leaders, social workers, community agencies or organizations, and crisis centers are all good sources for outside counseling.

For Review

Objective Review Questions Have students complete the "Reviewing the Facts" section on this page.

Study Guide Have students complete the Study Guide from Chapter 11 of their *Student Workbook*.

Debating an Issue With students, create a family scenario in which one family member is abusing drugs. Divide the class into two groups, and have them debate whether or not outside help should be sought.

For Evaluation

Constructing a Test Have students create a 20-question test that evaluates knowledge of chapter concepts. Be sure students provide answers to their questions.

Chapter Test Have students complete the test for Chapter 11 that appears in the *Teacher's Classroom Resources.*

CHAPTER 11 REVIEW

Answers to "Reviewing the Facts"

1. Building self-esteem; communicating effectively; sharing responsibilities; showing respect and trust; spending time together; establishing traditions; reaching beyond the family to the larger society.
2. Preparing food, cleaning, doing laundry, setting table, making beds, folding clothes.
3. Any three: working around the home, going out, playing games, relaxing.
4. To identify the source of the problem.
5. Choose the proper time and place; keep to the point; keep calm; listen; avoid accusation, sarcasm, and threats; avoid generalizations.
6. A problem-solving approach that gets ideas flowing and promotes discussion. Each person lists as many solutions as possible, without judging any of them.
7. If you have tried everything and are no closer to solving the problem, it is time to get outside help.
8. Teachers, guidance counselors, religious leaders, youth leaders, social workers, community agencies and organizations, crisis centers.

Reviewing the Facts

1. List the seven qualities that help strengthen family ties.
2. What are some of the household responsibilities that family members can share?
3. Name three ways that families can spend time together.
4. What is the first step in dealing with family problems?
5. What are some guidelines for handling family problems?
6. Explain what brainstorming is.
7. When should you seek outside help for a family problem?
8. List six sources of help for families in need of counseling.

Thinking Critically

1. What family traditions and rituals does your family share? Explain how these help to strengthen your family.
2. Do you think conflict is natural in a family? Why or why not?

Applying Your Skills

1. **Choosing Appropriate Examples.** Reread the seven qualities that make families strong on page 107. For each quality, write a short paragraph that gives a concrete example of how this quality might be exhibited by a real family. Do not repeat examples given in the text.
2. **Evaluating Ideas and Suggestions.** Imagine that you and your brother often argue about who should answer the telephone. Brainstorm possible solutions to this conflict. Be sure to write down everything that comes to mind, without trying to decide whether it is a good or bad idea. Then choose the idea that you think is fair to both of you, and explain why you think it is the best solution.
3. **Conducting a Survey.** Take a survey of classmates or neighbors to explore family traditions and cultures. What family traditions do they follow? How many different cultural traditions are represented in your class or community?

Answers to "Thinking Critically"

1. Answers will vary. Students may describe particular traditions or rituals for holidays, birthdays, or other occasions. These help strengthen the family by providing a common experience for family members to enjoy, look back on with pleasure, and look forward to with anticipation.
2. Most students will probably say yes because different people have different likes and dislikes, desires, and plans—and theses differences can result in problems. Some students may say no because conflict indicates that relationships aren't working.

CHAPTER

12

Adjusting to Family Changes

OBJECTIVES

This chapter will help you to:

- Explain the family life cycle.
- Describe the changes that occur in families.
- Identify ways to adjust to changes in family life.

WORDS TO REMEMBER

custody
divorce
family life cycle
traumatic

Chapter Resources

Teacher's Classroom Resources

- Lesson Plan
- Life Skills Activity, *When Someone Dies . . .*
- Reproducible Master, *The Family Life Cycle*
- Extension Activity, *Adjusting to Divorce*
- Chapter Test

Students Workbook

- Study Guide
- Worksheet, *Adding Up the Change*

CHAPTER OVERVIEW

Family changes are discussed in Chapter 12. Students learn that some family changes occur naturally over time. Changes may originate outside the family (such as job changes or moving) or may come from within the household (such as divorce or new family members). These changes may be challenging or traumatic. In any case, adjustment is needed. The chapter provides strategies for adjusting to these types of changes.

INTRODUCING THE CHAPTER

Motivators

Family Changes Ask students to think of ways that families may change. List their ideas on the board. Remind students that many factors affect families. Tell them that in this chapter they will learn about some of these factors and about ways families adjust to changes.

Using the Photograph Tell students to look at the photograph on this page and describe what is happening to the people in it. Ask: "What does the family have to do to adjust to this change?"

How Did You Feel? Ask the class to try to remember their first day in middle school or junior or senior high school. Have volunteers express their feelings about that day. Point out that change often causes many kinds of feelings, some of them conflicting.

Introducing the Objectives

Discuss the chapter objectives on this page. Remind students that the objectives focus on important chapter content.

Introducing Vocabulary

Write *family life cycle* on the board. Tell students that an individual's life cycle is made up of the stages he or she goes through during his or her existence. A family life cycle is the series of stages that a family goes through. Point out that it is normal for both individuals and families to experience change.

TEACHING THE CHAPTER

For convenience, the teaching suggestions for this chapter are arranged according to the following lesson topics:

Teaching "The Family Life Cycle" *(Page 116)*

This section describes the family life cycle.

Checking Comprehension

✓ Why should you learn about the family life cycle? *By learning about the family life cycle you can better understand the changes that your family and others go through.*

✓ What are some variations of the standard family life cycle? *People who remain single; married couples who don't have any children; single-parent families; adults who divorce, remarry, and begin another family.*

Activities

Skill Builder: Writing
Have students write one-paragraph descriptions of three fictitious families that experience the life cycle in different ways.

Reteaching
Ask students to compare and contrast different stages of the life cycle. For example, they might say: "In the first stage the couple is working for the future. In the last stage the couple is remembering the past and enjoying the present."

Enrichment
Have students interview older members of their families to find out what their family life cycle was like. Ask students to write an essay on the life cycle of one older family member and compare it to the life cycle (so far) of their present family.

Do you remember when a younger brother or sister was born or when your family moved to a new town? There are many reasons that changes like these happen in families. Some changes may occur suddenly, while others may happen slowly. Some changes occur because time passes—members of a family grow up and take on different roles. This chapter will discuss the most common family changes.

The Family Life Cycle

Just as a human being develops from a dependent baby to a toddler, an adolescent, then finally an adult, so every family goes through different stages, from birth to maturity. This growth is part of the **family life cycle**, the stages of life that the average family goes through.

Learning about the family life cycle will help you understand the changes that families go through. The chart on page 118 pictures families in the various stages of the life cycle. Of course, families vary greatly. Many families are headed by a single parent. Some couples have no children. Partners may divorce, remarry other people, and begin new families. At each stage of the life cycle, families have some common characteristics even though their experiences are different.

Factors Causing Family Changes

Some changes in a family are set in motion by factors outside the home. A parent may get a job transfer, for example, or may be the victim of an accident. Other factors come from within the family and may happen more slowly. A new baby may be born or parents may divorce. All these events require adjustments by family members.

Job Changes

A change in employment affects both the individual making the change and the rest of the family. A parent may have less time to spend at home if a new job requires additional hours or more commuting time. In some cases, a parent's new job may require a move.

Sometimes parents will change their job status. If a parent gives up an outside job to become a homemaker, the family may have to live on a smaller income. If, on the other hand, a homemaker decides to take a job outside the home, other family members may have to take on more responsibilities. Karla, for example, had to babysit a few afternoons a week for her younger sister when her mother took a job in an insurance office.

When parents lose jobs, everyone is affected. If the job provided the main or only income, the family may go through very difficult times. In addition, feelings of rejection and depression are commonly experienced by people who lose jobs.

If a parent is unemployed, everyone can help. Children might begin by showing their support. They might put off requests for new clothes or spending money until the crisis passes. Occasionally teens are able to obtain part-time jobs to help their families financially.

Moving Away

Your family may decide to move to another community. Maybe a parent's job requires it, or perhaps you are moving

Emphasize Point out to students that change is an inevitable part of the family life cycle. The change may occur naturally as family members get older, or it may occur suddenly. Note that all changes require adjustment.

Did You Know? Psychologists have researched various changes in people's life cycles and ranked them according to their effects on individuals. Death, divorce, and loss of job are ranked as the most traumatic changes that people undergo.

Part-time jobs can provide additional money or an opportunity to meet people and learn about a new community.

closer to the rest of the family. Moving is a big change. Family members must get used to a new home, new friends, and new schools.

When Jamie's father told the family that he was being transferred from Ohio to South Carolina near the coast, Jamie was not excited. He felt nervous about going to a new school. He was afraid that he would not make any new friends and that he would miss his old ones. However, the family talked about how they could make the adjustment easier for Jamie and his younger sister. Here are some of the suggestions they offered:

- Find out as much as possible about the new community and school. What courses are offered? What clubs or sports seem interesting?
- Remember that it takes time to make new friends. If possible, find other new people at school who are experiencing many of the same feelings as you. Join a club or activity, such as a newspaper, chorus, drama club, or pep club where you can meet other students with interests like yours.
- Join community groups such as youth groups at a church, temple, or YMCA.

It takes an effort to make new friends. The classmates and neighborhood kids you will be meeting already have friends, so you will have to take the initial steps. Especially in the beginning, it helps to stay in touch with old friends through letters and visits.

Divorce

Many families experience **divorce**, the legal termination of a marriage. Divorce affects not only the two people involved in the marriage, but others in the family as well. If parents announce that they are going to divorce, their child may be surprised and shocked, even if family life has been unhappy for some time. Both young children and teens may feel angry or resentful toward one or both parents for divorcing. They may be afraid that they will no longer be loved or protected.

Focus on Decision Making Ask students to pretend they are the head of a household and have been offered a new job. Tell them that the job will offer them more money and opportunity but less time for their family and relocation to another state. Have them decide whether they want the job and give the reasons for their decision.

More About Moving Tell students that some people move from one country to another. This type of move may mean adjustment to another culture. It also may mean learning another language. Ask students what other aspects of life such a move might affect.

Teaching "Factors Causing Family Changes"

(Pages 116-121)

This section describes changes involving employment, moving, divorce, new family members, illnesses and accidents, and death.

Checking Comprehension

✓ How might a new job affect an individual or a family? *The parent may have less time at home, or the family may have to move.*

✓ How could a parent's change in job status affect a family? ***If a parent gives up an outside job to become a homemaker, the family may have to live on a smaller income. If a homemaker takes a job outside the home, other family members may have to take on more and different responsibilities.***

✓ How can the loss of a job affect a family? *The loss of a job may cause financial difficulties and feelings of depression.*

✓ What can people do to adjust to a move? *To adjust to a move, people can find out as much as possible about the new community, remember that making friends takes time, join community and/or school groups, take the initial steps to make new friends, and keep in touch with old friends.*

✓ With whom can family members share their feelings about a divorce? *Family members can share their feelings with each other, with other people who have experienced divorce, or with community groups.*

✓ What kinds of adjustments might family members have to make when a new baby arrives? *Older children may need to take on more responsibility and should be especially understanding. Parents may not be getting enough sleep, so they may be more irritable and less patient than usual.*

✓ Describe the positive and negative aspects of having an aging relative come to live with your family. *Older members can contribute advice and understanding and can share in household responsibilities. But the individual may have trouble adjusting to a new area and to being more dependent.*

✓ In what ways do illnesses and accidents affect a family? *Family members may feel helpless and frustrated. Medical bills may put a strain on family finances.*

✓ What does it mean to say that a death is traumatic? *A death causes family members severe emotional shock that may take some time to heal.*

✓ How do you deal with sad feelings? *Answers will vary. Students might say that they share their feelings, have a good cry, write in their journal, listen to music, take a walk, and so on.*

The Family Life Cycle

Beginning Stage
A couple marries and establishes a home.

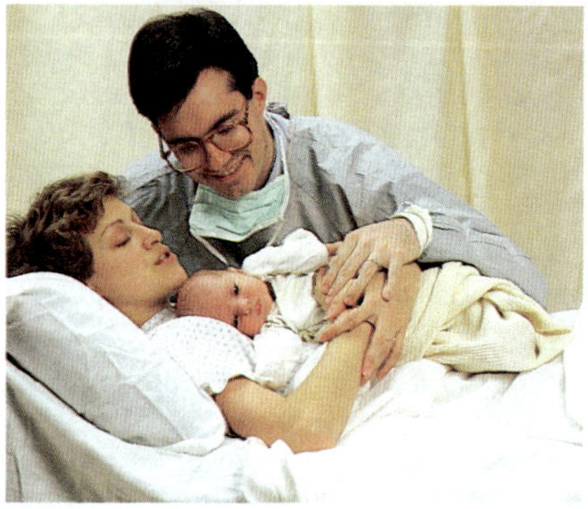

Childbearing Stage
The couple prepares for and adjusts to parenthood.

Child-Rearing Stage
As children grow, the parents work to meet their children's needs and to help them develop independence.

Launching Stage
Children gradually leave home to support themselves. Parents help children adjust to their new way of life.

Empty-Nest Stage
After the last child has left home, the couple renews the marriage relationship and adjusts to the change in their parenting role.

Retirement Stage
The couple adjusts to the aging process. They may develop new interests or renew old ones.

Focus on Relationship Skills Have students discuss ways that they could help a new family member, either a teen or an older relative, adjust to their household. Ask them to think of activities they could share with the new member to improve their relationship with the person and make the person feel more comfortable.

Focus on Health A serious illness or accident can drastically change a family. Special medical care may be necessary for the injured family member, which may put a strain on emotions, finances, and household routines. Tell students that in some cases special facilities are available to enable families to live near the hospital while a member is receiving long-term care.

Children may worry about who will care for them. This brings up the issue of **custody**, the right of caring for children granted by a court. Issues of custody often present the most painful problems in divorce.

When custody is settled, children may wish they were living with the other parent. They may hope and dream that their parents will remarry.

Children and teens whose parents are divorcing may act differently toward those around them. They may withdraw, lose interest in schoolwork, or pick fights with classmates. They may even feel guilty, as if *they* caused the divorce. It must be explained for them, however, that their parents are divorcing because of their own problems, and that the children are in no way the cause of divorce.

In some cases, children feel a sense of relief when their parents separate. This may be true especially when there has been much turmoil in the home. Divorce may also provide relief for family members who have been abused.

No matter how family members feel about the divorce, time helps everyone to adjust. Children should be urged to share their feelings with their family. They may also want to talk with other teens who have gone through the experience of divorce. This will help them adjust more easily to their situation. Community groups may also provide adults and teens with a place to share their feelings and find ways to cope with divorce.

When parents are divorcing, children need to be reassured that they are not the cause of the divorce.

Activities

Skill Builder: Critical Thinking
Ask students to think of someone who recently moved to their community. Tell them to think about the following questions: Have I been friendly and welcoming to this person? Have I treated this person as I would want to be treated if I had just moved in? Encourage students to reach out to the newcomer, finding out where the person moved from, how he or she likes the new community, and so on. Ask volunteers to report on their contact with the newcomer.

Skill Builder: Critical Thinking
Divide the class into small groups. Tell each group to imagine that the father or mother of their family has lost his or her job. Assign each group to imagine that they, as a group, are a different member of the family: father, mother, brother, sister, preschooler, grandparent, and so on. Have the group compile a list of effects of the job loss on that person and a list of ways that other family members might help him or her to adjust.

Skill Builder: Writing
Ask students to choose one of the changes discussed in this section and to write a short story about a person who experienced this change. Encourage students to use material from the chapter as they show their character adjusting to the change.

Skill Builder: Reading
Ask students to go to the library and do research on the grief process. Tell them to find out what the steps in the grief process are and to come to class prepared to discuss them. Hold a class discussion on the importance of experiencing all the stages of the grief process.

Real-Life Situations Divorce statistics vary according to the age when people marry. Although almost half of all marriages end in divorce, 3 out of 4 teenage marriages end in divorce. Ask students what factors might cause the difference in the divorce statistics.

Reteaching
Ask students to compare and contrast the effects of the changes mentioned in this section: job changes, moving, divorce, new family members, illness and accidents, and death.

Reteaching
Ask students to find and display pictures from magazines that show people going through and adjusting to the changes discussed in this section.

Enrichment
Break the class into small groups, and ask each group to go to the library and find out how often the average American family moves. Ask each group to find and read several articles that discuss the effect of family mobility on families and society. Have students report on their findings in class.

Enrichment
Ask students to talk to an older relative who is willing to discuss his or her experience of one of the changes discussed in this section. Ask students to interview the person and ask about his or her feelings, what he or she did to adjust, and what positive aspects (if any) the adult feels came out of the experience. Have students report on their findings to the class. (Be sure that students explain that the information shared will be discussed in class.)

Enrichment
Invite guest speakers, such as an attorney, family counselor, or custody caseworker to talk to your class. Have them talk about the affects of divorce on the family.

New Family Members

The coming of a baby is usually a happy event. A new baby can be a lot of fun—fun to hug and hold and play with. Still, babies are a 24-hour job. Their care takes lots of time, and this requires adjustments from every member of the family.

A new baby in your home will mean that other family members need to take on more responsibility. Older children can help feed, bathe, dress, or play with the baby. Parents, up nights with a fussy infant, may be more irritable and less patient than usual. Try to be especially understanding during this time.

New family members sometimes come through adoption or foster care. For these children also, there is a period of adjustment. If the adopted or foster child is not an infant and has become accustomed to life in a different environment, love and patience on the part of family members are very important.

If a parent remarries, adjustments in family life need to be made. Household routines are likely to change to accommodate additional people. Rivalries may occur between stepbrothers and stepsisters. Teens especially may feel resentful or jealous of the new stepparent—they may believe the stepparent is destroying the relationship they have with their own parent. Good communication is important during this trying period, and gradually many blended families can unite in a few years.

Perhaps an older relative, such as a grandparent, comes into the home. These extended family arrangements can enrich family life. Older family members contribute to the family in many ways. They are a source of support for parents, offering advice and understanding. They often share in household responsibilities such as cooking, cleaning, or child care.

Coming to live with your family may not be easy for an aging relative, however. A person who has lived in one area for many years will miss old friends and familiar sights. Accustomed to being independent, an older adult may not like feeling dependent on his or her children.

Illnesses and Accidents

When someone becomes very ill or experiences a serious accident, family life can be disrupted. The individual may be in a lot of discomfort; watching someone you love in pain can make you feel helpless and frustrated.

Illnesses and accidents are more than emotionally trying. They may also put a strain on family finances. Long-term illnesses or disabling accidents can create large medical bills. Fortunately, medicine today enables doctors to do much to heal physical and mental illness and to speed recovery from accidents.

During a time of illness, families often find strength in each other or in religious faith. You may discover qualities and strengths in others, or in yourself, that you never knew you had. Sharing their feelings and responsibilities will help families through difficult times.

Death

When Salim's Uncle Jerome died, Salim had trouble coping with his feelings. At first, Salim tried not to think about Uncle Jerome at all. Then he felt guilty about the times when he had argued with his uncle. He wished those moments had been happier ones. He felt angry, too, at his uncle for leaving him.

Salim's feelings frightened him. He felt that there was something wrong with him. All these emotions, however,

Real-Life Situations An estimated 1,300 new stepfamilies are formed every day in the U.S., according to census data and other studies. Analysis shows:

- 84% of divorced men and 75% of divorced women remarry within four years.
- 60% of the people who remarry are parents.
- 34% of children born today will live in a stepfamily before age 18.

It may take up to five years for new bonds to form between members of stepfamilies—such as between stepparent and stepchild, and between stepbrothers and stepsisters. Point out to students that good communication skills can help to make adjustments easier and solve problems within stepfamilies.

Change can be frightening to both young children and teens when a parent has an accident, becomes critically ill, or dies.

together with loneliness and sadness, are natural after a death. If someone close to you dies, allow yourself to grieve. Don't be ashamed to cry. If you ignore your feelings, you may suffer from more serious problems later on.

A death is **traumatic**: it causes family members severe emotional shock that may take some time to heal. When someone dies, everyone in the family needs care and consolation, even very small children. Sharing sad feelings is one way to deal with them. Sometimes family members need to take turns putting their own sorrow aside to comfort one another. If family members help a grieving parent or sibling, they may feel better, too.

Adjusting to Change

Changes that take place in your family may be exciting and challenging, or they may be painful and confusing. No matter what kind of situation is involved, there are ways you can adjust to them.

- **Plan ahead.** When you know that a change is unavoidable, prepare for it in advance, even if you wish it were not going to happen. If you are moving, you can learn as much as possible about the new community and school ahead of time. Perhaps you can even arrange a visit. Often, difficult changes are not as bad as you thought they would be because you prepared for them.
- **Discover something positive about the change.** This is not always easy to do. For example, what can be positive about Tom's older brother moving back home? Well, although Tom will have to once again share his room with his brother, he will enjoy using his brother's bike when he returns.

Teaching "Adjusting to Change"
(Pages 121-122)

This section describes ways to adjust to family changes.

Checking Comprehension

✓ What should you do when you know a change is unavoidable? *If a change is unavoidable, you should accept it and, if possible, prepare for it in advance.*

✓ How can you help members of your family through a change? *You can share your feelings, support others in your family, and communicate openly and honestly.*

✓ What should people do if they cannot deal with a change on their own? *If they cannot deal with a change, they should seek outside help.*

Activities

Skill Builder: Critical Thinking
Ask students to think about television shows or movies that have dealt with families that have gone through changes. Choose several that are familiar to the majority of the class. Hold a discussion on how the individuals in the shows or movies adjusted to these changes. Ask: "Did they follow any of the guidelines in the text? Did they react in ways that were damaging to themselves or others?"

Emphasize Point out to students that a very important part of adjusting to changes, especially family changes, is communication. Talking about how a change will affect the family, sharing feelings about the change, and offering support are vital to making adjustments less upsetting.

Focus on Entrepreneurship Ask students to think of a business they could start to help newcomers adjust to their community. Have them brainstorm ideas that would help someone who has just moved to their area. Then tell them to refine one of those ideas into a valuable community business.

Skill Builder: Writing
Ask students to write a letter to a fictitious person undergoing one of the changes discussed in the chapter. Ask them to give the person helpful advice, making use of the six methods of adjusting to change as necessary.

Reteaching
Have students write down an additional example for each of the six methods of adjusting to change listed on pages 121-122.

Enrichment
Ask students to write several paragraphs that describe their own family's resources for adjusting to change. Suggest such ideas as love between members, a sense of humor, and so on.

Enrichment
Have the class design a pamphlet for guidance counselors to use when new students enroll. The handbook could include information about school, clubs, sports, and other activities. Information could include the officers' names, the requirements for membership, and the advisor's name. The community activities could include the same basic information about Scouts, YMCA, Red Cross, and religious organizations for teens.

- **Share, support, and communicate.** While you are going through changes in your life, members of your family are changing, too. It helps to talk about your feelings within the family. Just having someone listen can ease your pain and confusion. Support others in your family as they try to adjust, too. When Joanne's mother was struggling to manage a job and finish her college degree, Joanne started to get up early and make breakfast for her. It was Joanne's way of showing how much she cared for and admired her mother.
- **Accept your feelings.** Changes may bring anger, sadness, or fear as well as joy or pride. You may even have conflicting feelings. When Bob's father had a serious operation, Bob was scared and angry about his father's illness, but he was also thankful that his father would eventually recover. It is important in such a situation as this that you accept the way you feel and find ways to express yourself that will not hurt you or others.
- **Stay active.** Getting involved in activities will keep you from brooding about your situation. When Suzanne's parents were getting divorced, she stayed active in the swimming team and chorus at school. Her teammates and friends helped her to cope.
- **Seek help if necessary.** Sometimes family changes may be very difficult to deal with or resolve. As you learned in Chapter 11, there are many places where individuals and families can get counseling to help them adjust more easily and successfully.

To help you adjust to family changes, get involved in school or community activities. Share your feelings with your family, your friends, or a counselor.

Real-Life Situations Support groups are available in many communities to help teens who are experiencing changes in their lives. Many schools have organizations that welcome new students or offer peer counseling. Community groups may offer support for young children or teens whose parents have divorced, remarried, or died. Others help children who are experiencing a serious illness of a family member. For example, Alateen is a group for teens who have an alcoholic parent(s), and Hospice aids family members of a person dying of cancer. Ask students what groups within your school and community offer some form of support.

HEALTH WATCH

Family Violence

Most people don't think of the home as a violent place, but family violence is a serious problem that accounts for many physical and emotional injuries. Experts who study families have collected a great deal of information about the problem. Here are some questions that are often asked about family violence and the answers that most experts support:

Q: Who are the most common victims of family violence?

A: Women and children are usually the ones abused, but some men have been victims. Elderly people are also the victims of abuse.

Q: What kinds of family violence take place?

A: Physical abuse can range from pushing and slapping to hitting and beating. Victims may suffer black eyes and broken bones. Verbal abuse is another kind of violence. Victims may be repeatedly criticized or berated by being told that they are stupid, bad, worthless, unwanted, or even hated. Such humiliation and shame results in low self-concept and self-esteem. Another form of abuse is neglect. Children may be malnourished or poorly clothed, for example. Another type of violence is sexual abuse.

Q: Is family violence a problem of a particular group of people?

A: No. The problem exists among all income levels, ethnic backgrounds, and occupational groups.

Q: What causes family violence?

A: Anger during an argument may lead to violence. Often economic problems play a part. When a parent is unemployed, family violence tends to increase. Other reasons include alcoholism, drug abuse, and mental illness.

Q: Why do some parents and stepparents abuse their children?

A: Stress within the family is sometimes the cause. When parents can't handle a stressful situation, they may take out their frustrations on their children by hurting or humiliating them. Parents who were abused when they were children often abuse their own children. You can learn more about child abuse on p. 206.

Q: Why don't women just leave home when they are victims of violence?

A: Many women worry that they will be without financial support if they leave their spouses. Others are ashamed and lack self-esteem. Many women do leave once the violence spills over and hurts their children.

Q: What kind of help is available for abused family members?

A: Counseling at community health centers is available to help families in trouble. Shelters for abused women and children have opened in many communities. Special hot lines also offer advice and support.

Q: What should teens do when they suspect violence in a family?

A: They should report any cases of suspected abuse to parents, teachers, or guidance counselors, who can then assist in getting help from experts.

Think It Through

1. **Although there is no evidence that family violence has increased, there is more discussion about the problem than ever before. What do you think is the reason?**
2. **What are some techniques you might suggest for people to try when they are angry and might be in danger of hurting someone in the family?**

Teaching the Feature

"Family Violence"

Answers to Feature Questions

1. Students might suggest that society has become more aware of the dangers of family violence because some victims have sought help from the community. Experts in family care have publicized the problem and offered help, encouraging more people to come forward.

2. Suggestions might include counting to ten slowly, leaving the room until tempers have cooled, punching a pillow, writing down things that might have been spoken, or getting professional help if the anger cannot be controlled.

Activities

Promoting Family Caring Have students work on a mural that displays family members caring for each other. Ask them to find or draw pictures that depict families caring for and helping each other. Ask them to brainstorm to find a theme or title for the class mural and then write it above the mural.

Researching Family Violence Have students select one type of family violence and research what experts have written about the topic. Then ask them to write an article that informs others of what they have learned.

Community Contact Ask students to find out what local groups or organizations help victims of family violence. Have students contact the group or organization and learn what kind of help it offers to victims of family violence. Then ask students to report on what they learned.

Emphasize Family violence can occur in any type of family, regardless of income level, ethnic background, or occupational group. Any person who experiences abuse or violence should seek help immediately, as patterns of abuse usually become more frequent and severe as time passes.

Focus on Life Management Ask students to discuss ways that they can keep their anger under control. See Teen Tips, "Ways to Let Off Steam," on pages 166-167.

Cross-Reference See "Facts on Child Abuse" on page 206.

COMPLETING THE CHAPTER

Summary

- The stages of life that an average family goes through are called the family life cycle.
- Family changes may mean that members must take on more responsibility, move to another area, or experience financial difficulties. Changes can cause happiness and excitement as well as fear and deep sadness.
- Individuals can better adjust to family changes through planning ahead whenever possible; discovering positive aspects of the change; accepting their feelings about the change; staying active; and seeking outside help, if necessary.

For Review

Objective Review Questions Have students complete the "Reviewing the Facts" section on this page.

Study Guide Have students complete the Study Guide from Chapter 12 of their *Student Workbook*.

Adjusting to Family Changes Divide students into small groups, and assign each group a category of family change (for example, moving, divorce). The groups should create a specific scenario for the change and then resolve it. Have them discuss how the change will affect various family members and how the members can adjust to the change. When the groups have completed the assignment, have a spokesperson report the group's ideas to the class.

For Evaluation

Create a List Have students create a five-item list of "do's" for individuals undergoing three of the changes discussed in the chapter. The list should help the person remember ways to adjust positively to the change.

Chapter Test Have students complete the test for Chapter 12 that appears in the *Teacher's Classroom Resources*.

CHAPTER 12 REVIEW

Answers to "Reviewing the Facts"

1. It refers to the stages of life that the average family goes through.
2. By showing support; putting off requests for new clothes and money; getting a part-time job.
3. Find out as much as possible about the new community and school; remember that it takes time to make new friends; join community groups.
4. Any three: surprise and shock; anger; resentment; fears about receiving love and protection; withdrawal from others; less interest in schoolwork; aggression toward others; guilt.
5. Changes in household routines; coping with rivalries of stepbrothers and stepsisters; resentment or jealousy toward new stepparent.
6. Grieving helps you to accept the loss; not grieving sometimes causes problems later on.
7. Plan ahead; discover something positive about the change; share with, support, and communicate with your family; accept your feelings; stay active; seek help if necessary.

Reviewing the Facts

1. What is the family life cycle?
2. How can teens help if a parent becomes unemployed?
3. What can you do to make the adjustment easier when moving to a new community?
4. List three feelings or set reactions that are common in children when their parents divorce.
5. If a parent remarries, what adjustments might the family have to make?
6. What purpose does grieving serve?
7. List six strategies for adjusting to change.

Thinking Critically

1. Families in today's society are moving more than ever before. What do you think accounts for this? What are the positive and negative consequences?
2. What could you do to help your parents prepare for a new family member?

Applying Your Skills

1. **Indicating Appropriate Methods.** Reread the material on adjusting to change on pages 121-122. Choose one type of family change discussed earlier in the chapter and rank the methods of adjusting as they apply to that type of change. Which would be the most helpful, and which the least helpful? Are there any methods of adjustment that do not apply to that type of change?

2. **Describing Adjustments.** Write a short story about a teen who must move from a small town to a major city. Describe the changes the teen experiences and the adjustments that were needed to adapt to this move.

3. **Investigating a Cause-and-Effect Relationship.** Take a poll of your classmates. Find out how many of them have experienced a major change in their family life. Describe the changes, their cause, their immediate effect, their long-term effect, and how these changes were handled.

Answers to "Thinking Critically"

1. Possible reasons include new employment opportunities, relocation of companies, desire to live in another location, desire for change. Positive consequences may be that people are seeing more of the world, meeting new people, and becoming accustomed to change. Negative consequences of frequent moves might include losing friends, difficulty in developing ties to a community, and poor school performance by children.
2. Answers may include: offering to help around the home; setting up a nursery or playroom; caring for other children while parent goes to doctor's appointments, child-care classes, or the hospital.

CHAPTER

13

Friendships

OBJECTIVES

This chapter will help you to:

- List the five qualities of strong friendships.
- Explain how to make new friends.
- Describe the characteristics of friendships in the teen years.
- Explain how to communicate effectively with friends.

WORDS TO REMEMBER

caring
clique
empathy
loyalty
reliability
self-confident

CHAPTER OVERVIEW

The topic of Chapter 13 is friendship. Students learn the five qualities of friendship (sharing, reliability, loyalty, empathy, and caring). They learn important skills for making friends, including ways to meet new people, to develop new friendships, and to build self-confidence. Teen friendships, including peer groups and cliques, are discussed. The chapter concludes with information that helps students deal with changes in friendships.

INTRODUCING THE CHAPTER

Motivators

Defining Friends Write the phrase "A friend is someone who . . ." and ask students to complete it. Discuss with students the many roles friends play in people's lives. Tell students that they are going to learn more about friendships in this chapter.

Using the Photograph Tell students to look at the photograph on this page. Ask: "Do you think these two people are friends? Why do you say so?"

Is It True? Have students read the opening paragraph of the chapter. Ask volunteers to explain what they think the statement means and then if they agree or disagree with it. Encourage a variety of opinions.

Introducing the Objectives

Discuss the chapter objectives on this page. Remind students that the objectives focus on important chapter content.

Introducing Vocabulary

Write the word *caring* on the board. Tell students that caring is the basis of all relationships. Ask them to describe an incident in their own lives that illustrates the importance of caring.

Chapter Resources

Teacher's Classroom Resources
- Lesson Plan
- Life Skills Activity, *Be a Better Friend*
- Reproducible Master, *Keys to Friendship*
- Extension Activity, *Qualities of Friendship*
- Chapter Test

Student Workbook
- Study Guide
- Worksheet, *Friendship Dialogue*

T here is an old saying that the only way to have a friend is to be one. What do you suppose the saying means?

How do you make friends? Usually, the first friends you make are those who live near you or attend your school. Often these early friendships last for years, long after school days are over.

Although you may spend time thinking about your friends, you may have given little thought to friendship itself. Have you ever wondered what makes friendships last? Friendships grow differently and at different paces. They may come easily or they may take work to develop. All friendships have some of the same qualities. You can develop satisfying and memorable friendships; some of them may even last all your life.

Qualities of Friendship

In order to answer the questions—how do you make friends and what makes friendship last—you need to know what makes a good friendship. A strong and lasting friendship is built on five qualities.

- **Sharing.** Friendships are often based on common interests. You and a friend may both work on the school newspaper, or perhaps you like to go shopping together. You can learn from your friends. You might show a friend how to change a flat tire on a bicycle, and your friend might help you find an error in your computer program. Experiences are more enjoyable if you share them. A funny movie is funnier if you can laugh at it with a friend.
- **Reliability.** If you always arrive on time to meet friends, you will be known as a reliable person. **Reliability** means being a person others can count on. If you have ever gotten homework assignments for a friend who was home with the flu, you showed your reliability.
- **Loyalty.** Suppose a friend who means a lot to you is the target of gossip. Speaking up for your friend is a sign of loyalty. **Loyalty** is being faithful to others, especially when they need it.
- **Empathy.** Just as friends can increase happiness, they can make sadness easier to bear. **Empathy** is being able to understand what someone else is experiencing. Everybody has unhappy times. Friends can encourage you if you are feeling upset about a low test grade at school. They can also help you deal with family problems. When you are feeling down, friends can help you see your situation clearly, and they can help you explore some ways to feel better.

A good friendship is based on personal qualities that are demonstrated by both persons. What qualities do you admire in your friends?

TEACHING THE CHAPTER

For convenience, the teaching suggestions for this chapter are arranged according to the following lesson topics:

Teaching "Qualities of Friendships"
(Pages 126-127)

This section describes five qualities of strong friendships.

Checking Comprehension

✓ Why is sharing an important part of friendship? *Because friendships are often based on common interests, you can learn from your friends by sharing, and experiences are more enjoyable if you share them.*

✓ What is the difference between reliability and loyalty? *Reliability means that people can count on you, and loyalty means that you are faithful to others.*

✓ What is empathy? *Empathy is being able to understand what someone else is feeling.*

Activities

Skill Builder: Critical Thinking
Ask students to make a list of the qualities they look for in friends. Then ask them to share why these qualities are important to them.

Reteaching
Ask students to give additional examples for each of the five qualities of friendship.

Enrichment
Have students keep a journal for one week of nice things they have done for their family and friends. Have them identify which of the five qualities each action was an example of.

More About Friendships Ask students if they have ever heard the maxim: "A friend in need is a friend indeed." Ask them what this statement says about friendship.

Focus on Relationship Skills Ask students to think about the qualities they have that make them a good friend to others. Ask them to pinpoint the relationship skills they need to improve.

- **Caring.** The basic quality of friendship is caring, the one from which all the others seem to grow. People are real friends when they truly care about each other. **Caring** is the emotional bond that one person feels for another. A friend who cares remembers birthdays or helps a friend rehearse for the school play. Caring means valuing your friends' feelings as much as your own. It means making the effort to be kind, trusting, and honest.

Making New Friends

You might want to make new friends for any number of reasons: because you have moved to a new area, because old friends have moved away, or even because of changes within yourself. Some people seem to have a gift for making friends easily, but there is nothing magical about it. Developing friendships is a skill, and, like most skills, it improves with practice.

How to Meet People

You can make new friends if you take the initiative, treat people with kindness, and are yourself. You should also be aware of the situations that promote friendship. Friendships generally occur between people who have something in common: the area where they live, special interests, attitudes, or activities. One way to approach making new friends, then, is to look closely at yourself. What do you enjoy doing? What is important to you? Choosing people who share your basic interests or values provides a basis for lasting friendships. Here are some ideas on how to get started.

- **Join a club or group.** Talking with someone who shares a common interest is a natural way to start a friendship. There are plenty of groups to satisfy every type of interest, whether it is drama, photography, or modern dance.
- **Join someone in an activity.** You could study with a classmate for a science test or join a neighbor in collecting canned goods for a community food bank. Working together can be an effective way to start a friendship.
- **Start a conversation.** For example, you could compliment a neighbor on something you admire or ask a classmate about the class assignment.

Shared activities, such as cleaning up a local park or playground, bring people together and lead to new friendships.

Teaching "Making New Friends"
(Pages 127-130)

This section describes ways to make new friends.

Checking Comprehension

✓ What are three reasons why people might want to make new friends? *They might want to make new friends because they have moved to a new area, because old friends have moved away, or even because of changes within themselves.*

✓ How can looking closely at yourself help you to form lasting friendships? *Examining yourself helps you to choose people who share your basic interests and values.*

✓ Why is joining a club or group a good way to make new friends? *Joining a club or group can help you make new friends because it is a place to meet people with similar interests.*

✓ What can you do to build a new relationship? *If you want to build a new relationship, don't wait for new acquaintances to make the next move. Make a second move by calling the person or by inviting him or her to do something.*

✓ What kinds of experiences bind friendships? *Finding new interests in common, sharing your own experiences and problems, and listening to the other person's experiences and problems all strengthen relationships.*

✓ Why do people sometimes have fears about meeting new people, and how can they deal with those fears? *They may be afraid because they doubt themselves and think that other people are judging them. They can deal with those fears by accepting themselves, concentrating on putting other people at ease, and acting with self-confidence.*

Emphasize When meeting new people, individuals are often very self-conscious. Point out that people tend to judge themselves much more harshly than anyone else will. Remind them that the other person is usually thinking about making a good impression, too.

Focus on Technology Tell students that the technology of computers can help them make new friends. Explain to them that many people use their computers as a means of meeting new people and joining groups that share their interests.

Teaching the Feature
"Peer Pressure"

Answers to Feature Questions

1. Answers will reflect students' own experiences with peer pressure.

2. Possibilities include: "I'm too tired to stay up." "I have to get up very early tomorrow." "I promised my parents I'd be home on time."

Activities

Role Playing Have students create role-play situations that involve peer pressure to do something that an individual does not want to do. Begin with several students role playing being at a party and pressuring one person to join in drinking alcohol. After each role play, encourage students to comment on whether the student experiencing peer pressure reacted responsibly. Encourage students also to think of other things the "pressured" student could have said or done to avoid being a follower.

Types of Pressure Remind students that peer pressure can be intensified when a particular activity seems to be encouraged by the society at large or by popular culture. First ask students to name various types of activities in which there is peer pressure to indulge (possible ideas include alcohol and other drug use and sexual activity). Ask students to what degree these activities are supported by society or by popular culture.

Community Contact Divide the students into small groups. Ask each to interview someone from a community group to find out what practical advice they give to teens on avoiding negative peer pressure. Possible groups to interview include representatives of the various religious groups in your area, mental health clinics, and guidance counselors.

INTERPERSONAL SKILLS

Peer Pressure

Many teens are strongly influenced by their friends or other teens. That influence is known as peer pressure.

Peer pressure can be a good thing when it influences you to do something that is right for you. Here are three examples of situations in which peer pressure is a positive influence:

- Aaron decides to join the FHA/HERO group because his friends are members.
- Alexandra warmly welcomes a new student because Sonya and Wes give the girl a friendly greeting.
- Kara decides to bring cans of food to a community food bank when several of her friends praise the project.

Sometimes, however, peer pressure can work against your best interests. Here are three examples of situations in which peer pressure could be a negative influence:

- Stacy is wondering whether to cut her hair after her friend Elysha comes to school with a short haircut.
- Two of Kurt's friends have been experimenting with drugs on the weekends, and Kurt is afraid of feeling left out.
- Jennifer notices a student being bullied and wants to defend him, but her friends pull her away.

Even the most determined teens may not find it easy to handle peer pressure. Everyone wants to have friends and be part of a group. If you are afraid of losing your friends or being laughed at, you might be tempted to do things that are wrong for you.

What can you do to resist peer pressure? Here are three suggestions:

- Take time to review the things you value most. If you value your health, for example, you will resist any pressure to use drugs.
- Tell those who want to pressure you your reasons for refusing to go along. Stand your ground against arguments.
- Decide what actions you will take to pursue the things you believe in, such as choosing certain groups to join or speaking out on issues of importance to you.

Think It Through

1. **Do you think peer pressure is good or bad? Discuss examples from your own experiences.**
2. **Suppose your friends try to persuade you to stay out later than you want to. What reasons can you give to resist them?**

Emphasize Peer pressure can be both positive and negative. Tell them that it is important to be able to recognize negative peer pressure. At the same time, they need to be sure of their own values.

Focus on Decision Making Remind students that making decisions for themselves is an important part of growing up. Individuals need to prevent others from making their decisions for them.

How to Develop New Friendships

Once you have established a bond with someone, how can you build a new relationship? Suppose you meet someone that you enjoy talking with. After the conversation, one of you will have to make a second move if you want to develop a friendship. If you don't hear from new acquaintances, don't assume they are not interested in you. They may be waiting for you to call, or they may simply be busy. If you make the move yourself, you could follow up with a telephone call or an invitation to do something together.

Keep in mind that friendships don't happen in an instant. It takes time to get to know and be comfortable with another person.

Each time you meet or talk to your new friends, you are likely to find new interests in common. You share your experiences and problems, and, just as important, you listen to your friends' experiences and problems. These things cement new friendships together and make them last.

How to Be Self-Confident

What is so hard about meeting new people? Why do so many people get butterflies in the stomach when faced with the prospect? Meeting strangers means facing the unknown, and it is human nature to feel a bit uncomfortable about the unknown.

Most of our fears about dealing with new people come from doubts about ourselves. We imagine that other people are judging us—finding us too tall or too short, too quiet or too talkative. Remember that people meeting you probably have similar fears. If you accept yourself as you are and concentrate on putting other people at ease, everyone will feel more comfortable.

Try to act **self-confident**, or sure of yourself, even if you don't feel that way.

It takes both time and effort to develop lasting friendships.

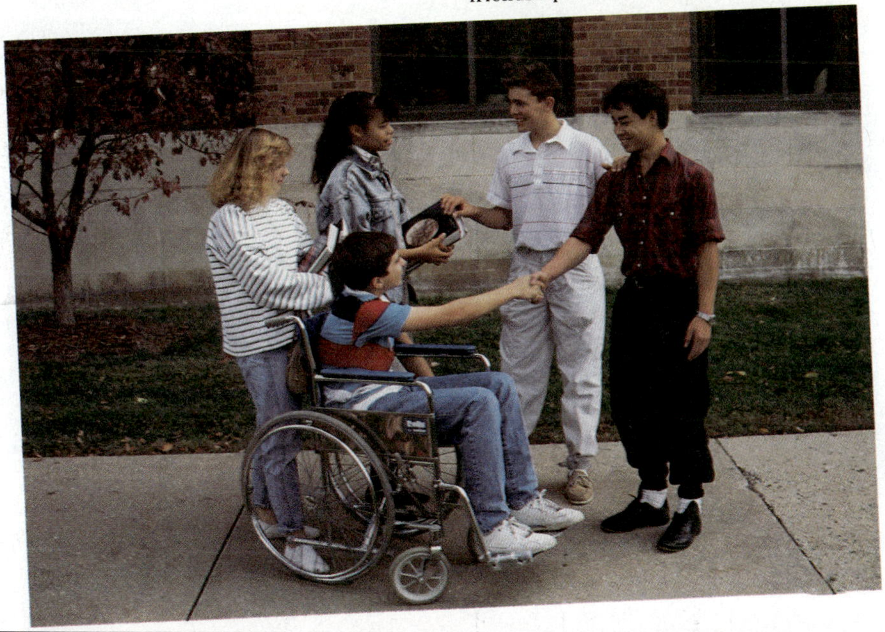

Focus on Relationship Skills Have students imagine going to a party where they do not know anyone. Have them list ideas that would help them start a conversation with a new person and perhaps develop a friendship.

Real-Life Situations Gossip is defined as a rumor or report that is personal or sensational in nature. Ask students whether they think most gossip is true or false. Ask: "What effect can gossip have on friendships? What should you do if you hear false or unkind gossip about a friend?"

Activities

Skill Builder: Writing
Ask students to think about a friendship that is very important to them. Ask them to write an account of how the friendship began and grew, as well as why it became so important to them.

Skill Builder: Critical Thinking
Point out to students that the chapter states that friendships usually occur between people who have something in common. Have students discuss why it might be difficult for a friendship to begin or to last between two people who have very little in common. Some students may have had or known of friendships between people who had very little in common. Ask them to analyze what helped these relationships overcome obstacles.

Reteaching
Have students play a game in which they must find out five or ten things about another student. Possible examples include birthplace, favorite color, middle name, and favorite television show or song. Explain that this type of information can help build relationships with others.

Enrichment
Ask students to think about their own interests. Then have them research what school or community groups are available that share or build on these interests. Encourage students to join one of the clubs or groups.

Teaching "Friendships in the Teen Years"
(Pages 130-131)

This section discusses teenage friendships.

Checking Comprehension

✓ How do childhood friendships differ from teen friendships? *Childhood friendships are based on shared activities, whereas teen friendships focus more on personal qualities.*

✓ What are some positive aspects of peer groups? *Peer groups can help people meet needs for closeness, give a sense of belonging, enable people to relax, offer support, and give opportunities to practice how to act in new situations.*

✓ What are some negative aspects of peer groups? *Peer groups can also cause pressure to act in a certain way and can limit people's views.*

Activities

Skill Builder: Writing
Ask students to write a monologue several paragraphs long that expresses the thoughts and feelings of an individual who wants to be part of a particular clique but who has been rejected by that clique. After the exercise, ask volunteers to read their monologues and discuss them in class.

Reteaching
Ask students to identify some of the cliques in their own school. Without criticizing the clique, they should state what they think is the common bond between the members of the clique.

Enrichment
Ask students to think about and make notes on the ways they feel their peer group meets their needs. (If they repeat ideas found in the text, they should try to give personal examples.) Hold a discussion in which students share their feelings about the importance of their peer group in their own lives.

When you enter a room full of strangers, walk tall and straight, look directly at other people, and smile. If you see someone you would like to speak to, say something. Don't wait for the other person to start a conversation.

Meeting new people and getting to know them may or may not lead to new friendships. Not all hoped-for friendships work out. Learning how to handle these situations is an important part of the skill of making friends.

Friendships in the Teen Years

During the teen years, the nature of friendship changes. In childhood, friendships came from sharing activities. Now personal qualities often become the focus of attention. Intense friendships that are based on sharing thoughts and feelings often develop during these years.

Peer Groups

Peer groups, groups of people of the same or similar age, are very important during the teen years. If you manage your peer relationships well, you can benefit from them in many ways.

Your peer group can help meet your need for closeness and give you a sense of belonging. You can relax among others like yourself as you talk about and think through what you value. Your peer group also provides you with support as you begin to establish your own identity. It offers opportunities to learn and to practice how to act in new situations.

There are times, however, when peer groups can have a negative influence. Peers may expect you to behave in a certain way and even reject you if you don't. This pressure is especially difficult for teens, who are often concerned with being accepted.

Sometimes friendships change and a person may feel excluded from a particular peer group or clique.

More About Peer Pressure Tell students that peer pressure often means conforming to the majority's beliefs or way of acting. Define conformity as "an action that follows existing standards or customs." Then tell them that conformity can be beneficial, as when a person follows laws. Yet conformity can also be harmful, as when someone gives in to the pressure to take drugs. The feature "Peer Pressure" on page 128 includes more information.

Emphasize Peer pressure is not just a problem for teens. Tell students that adults face pressure to follow other adults in such ways as dressing, buying goods, and voting.

Cliques

Within a peer group, there may be many **cliques**, or small, exclusive groups of people. People may form cliques without even realizing it, because they belong to the same club or sports team. Sometimes cliques are based on similar appearance or similar social or economic status.

Cliques often exclude people they think don't fit in. This can be devastating for teens who feel they need to be accepted by certain "in" groups. In fact, some teens make every effort to try to fit into groups that they want to be a part of. What the members of cliques don't realize is that by isolating themselves, they are losing opportunities to make new friends and develop new interests.

Communicating with Friends

When Ashley and Sarah started high school, they were best friends. They went virtually everywhere together, and they told each other everything.

During freshman year Sarah joined the basketball team. Ashley realized that their relationship would probably change a little during basketball season, but she didn't realize that Sarah would make new friends that she would enjoy seeing. Even though Sarah and Ashley still get together occasionally, Ashley feels left out. She wants to tell Sarah how she feels but is afraid of her reaction. She also wonders why things ever had to change.

Changing Friendships

What Sarah and Ashley are going through is common during the teen years. Changes in tastes and interests or in attitudes and beliefs can cause friends to grow apart. Sometimes those changes mean that friends just spend less time together. At other times, those changes may cause friendships to end.

Keeping Friends

Most people don't consciously work to keep their friends. In fact, many even take their friends for granted. Neither Sarah nor Ashley realized that friendship requires honest communication of thoughts and feelings.

It is important for friends to spend time together so their relationship can grow. They can benefit from sharing in each other's lives, talking about what is important to them, making new discoveries, and having fun.

Keeping friends also involves being considerate. If Sarah has to cancel plans because of basketball practice, then she should be considerate enough to tell Ashley right away and explain the situation. When friends respect each other's feelings, they are showing how much they care.

Best Friends

During the teen years, best friends take on more significance than before. You may consider just one person a best friend, or you may have several best friends. A best friend helps fulfill the need for affection and emotional closeness and helps you discover many of your own qualities. When a friend values you, it adds to your good feelings.

Sometimes teens face problems with close friendships. They can feel torn between an old friend and a new group. At times like these, it is helpful to talk the problem over with an adult.

Emphasize Honest communication is important both in making new friends and in keeping the friends one has.

Did You Know? Friendships are important beyond the teen years. Older people adjust better to stress if they have a spouse or a friend in whom they can confide.

Teaching "Communicating with Friends"
(Page 131)

This section explains how to communicate effectively with friends.

Checking Comprehension

✓ Why do friendships change? *Changes in tastes and interests or in attitudes and beliefs may cause friends to grow apart.*

✓ In what ways are best friends important? *They help fulfill needs for affection and emotional closeness and help you discover many of your own qualities. In their presence, you feel comfortable trying on new roles and testing behavior.*

Activities

Skill Builder: Reading
Point out to students that many stories and novels have been written about friendships. Ask students to find a story or short novel about the relationship between friends and give an oral book report on it.

Skill Builder: Writing
Tell students that best friends are not always peers. Ask students to write about a friend they have had or a friendship they have seen or read about that was between people of different ages.

Reteaching
Have students develop a bulletin board display that depicts friendship. Tell them to draw pictures or find photographs that show friends sharing and caring.

Enrichment
Ask students to think of a friend with whom they have lost touch. Ask them why they stopped communicating with that person. If they feel they would like to communicate with the person again, ask them to think of ways that they could renew the friendship. If they feel that the friendship cannot be renewed, ask them to explain why they feel this way.

COMPLETING THE CHAPTER

Summary

- Sharing, reliability, loyalty, empathy, and caring are important for strong friendships.
- To make new friends, it is important to know where to meet people, to know how to develop friendships over time, and to practice self-confidence.
- During the teen years, the peer group becomes very important and can have both a positive and a negative influence.
- Friendships change as people change. Maintaining friendships requires communicating, spending time together, and being considerate to each other.

For Review

Objective Review Questions Have students complete the "Reviewing the Facts" section on this page.

Study Guide Have students complete the Study Guide from Chapter 13 of their *Student Workbook*.

Debate an Issue Divide students into two teams, and have them debate whether people should be judged by who their friends are. Have them give reasons why one's choice of friends tells (or does not tell) who one is.

Better Friendships Have students write several paragraphs that explain how reading this chapter has helped them see one of their friendships in a different light or how it will help them form new friendships. Encourage details that show how the chapter material has been beneficial to them.

For Evaluation

Create a Questionnaire Have students create a list of questions about friendship that is divided into the four main sections of the chapter. The questions should allow the individual to evaluate his or her relationships.

Chapter Test Have students complete the test for Chapter 13 that appears in the *Teacher's Classroom Resources*.

CHAPTER 13 REVIEW

Answers to "Reviewing the Facts"

1. Sharing, reliability, loyalty, empathy, caring.
2. Empathy is being able to understand what someone else is experiencing or feeling.
3. Caring is the quality from which all the other qualities grow.
4. Join a club or group; join someone in an activity; start a conversation.
5. By sharing your experiences and problems, and by listening to your friend's experiences and problems.
6. Positive influences include: providing a sense of closeness and belonging; offering a relaxing group to talk to; providing support; offering opportunities to learn and practice how to act in new situations. Negative influences include: pressure to behave in a certain way; rejection.
7. A small exclusive group of people within a peer group.
8. Their tastes and interests or their attitudes and beliefs change; also, conflict can make friends grow apart.
9. Communication and consideration.

Reviewing the Facts

1. List the five qualities that help make a friendship strong.
2. Explain what empathy is.
3. Why should caring be considered the basic quality of friendship?
4. Name three ways to meet new people.
5. How can you cement new friendships?
6. What positive and negative influences can peer groups have?
7. What is a clique?
8. Why do some friends grow apart during the teen years?
9. What two elements are essential to keeping friends?

Thinking Critically

1. What would you do or say to help a very shy person make friends?
2. Describe the qualities your best friend has that are most important to you.

Applying Your Skills

1. **Writing a Dialogue.** With a classmate, write a dialogue between two people who are interested in initiating a conversation in order to build a friendship. Act out the dialogue in class.

2. **Ranking Ideas.** Reread the qualities of friendship on pages 126-127 and rank them in your own order of importance. Be prepared to discuss your choice for the most important quality and the ranking of the others.

3. **Resolving a Problem.** With a partner, create a fictional situation in which two close friends are having a disagreement. Act out the roles of the friends. Remember to be open and honest but also to respect each other's feelings. Did you resolve the problem? Did you remain friends?

Answers to "Thinking Critically"

1. Students might suggest trying to build the shy person's self-confidence by complimenting him or her on a specific achievement. Another way is to introduce the person to others with similar interests.
2. Answers will vary. Students may describe their best friend as a good listener; as being reliable and loyal; as participating in activities that they also enjoy.

CHAPTER

14

Special Relationships

OBJECTIVES

This chapter will help you to:

- Describe ways that teens become interested in and attracted to the other sex.
- Identify what teens can gain from dating.
- List and describe common problem areas in relationships.

WORDS TO REMEMBER

infatuation
platonic
unrequited love

CHAPTER OVERVIEW

Chapter 14 discusses romantic relationships, stressing that people are ready for these kinds of relationships at different times. It explains the ways that attractions first express themselves and shows that dating, whether in a group or as a couple, allows opportunities for learning about others and oneself. The last section of the chapter discusses coping with problems from unrequited love, poor communication, disagreements, and outgrown love.

INTRODUCING THE CHAPTER

Motivators

Friendship versus Romance Divide students into small groups, and have them brainstorm similarities and differences between friendships and romantic relationships. Ask them to choose three similarities and three differences and report on them to the class.

Using the Photograph Have students look at the photograph on this page. Ask: "What is happening in this photograph? How are the young man and young woman reacting?"

Differing Timetables Explain to students that throughout life people develop physically, mentally, emotionally, and socially at different rates. Those variations are also common in dating. Have students talk to older friends or relatives and ask them when they started dating. Then have the class discuss their findings and compare variations.

Introducing the Objectives

Discuss the chapter objectives on this page. Remind students that the objectives focus on important chapter content.

Introducing Vocabulary

Write the word *platonic* on the board, and pronounce it for students. Tell them that it refers to a type of love defined by Plato, a Greek philosopher. Plato felt that this type of love transcends physical desire for an individual and concentrates on the spiritual or the ideal.

Chapter Resources

Teacher's Classroom Resources
- Lesson Plan
- Life Skills Activity, *Dear Dateline*
- Reproducible Master, *Is It a Crush or Is It Love?*
- Extension Activity, *Dating Guidelines*
- Chapter Test

Student Workbook
- Study Guide
- Worksheet, *Cross Your Heart*

TEACHING THE CHAPTER

For convenience, the teaching suggestions for this chapter are arranged according to the following lesson topics:

- "New Interests and Attractions," pages 134-135
- "Dating," pages 136-137
- "Problems with Relationships," pages 137-139

Teaching "New Interests and Attractions"

(Pages 134-135)

This section describes the beginnings of interests in and attractions to the other sex.

Checking Comprehension

✓ What kinds of new relationships are teens likely to develop? *Teens are likely to become attracted to the other sex, feeling both strong emotions and sexual attraction. Then they may develop romantic relationships or friendships with the other sex.*

✓ What is the difference between a platonic relationship and infatuation? *A platonic relationship is a close friendship that is not romantic. An infatuation involves romantic feelings that are usually short-term and one-sided. Both types of relationships are common among teens.*

✓ How do infatuations allow people to explore relationships in a safe way? *They are safe because the other person is not required to respond.*

✓ What should teens keep in mind when they begin to reach out to members of the other sex? *They should remember that their shyness is normal and that other people are probably not judging them but are concerned about how they themselves appear.*

Imagine a group of teens your age. Bruce thinks about girls a lot, but his shyness keeps him from asking a girl out or even approaching one for friendship. Leann is interested in boys, but her parents don't let her date yet. Brett has no great interest in the other sex; he enjoys spending time with his male friends. Zack would love to have a girlfriend. So far, however, no one he has been interested in has shown any interest in him.

Every one of these teens is different, and all are normal. There is no timetable, no set of steps to follow, that dictates when and how teens should take interest in and interact with the other sex. No one but you can say when you are ready for romantic relationships.

New Interests and Attractions

At some point during their teen years, most people become attracted to the other sex, even if they decide to do nothing about it right away. They feel strong emotions as well as sexual attraction. Such feelings may start to be expressed in friendships.

Just Friends

When Trea was in grade school, all her closest friends were girls. Now she has formed a close friendship with Nathan, a boy she knows from the debating team. Neither of them is interested in getting romantically involved yet, but they really enjoy being together. Trea says that Nathan helps her understand boys better. Nathan finds that he can relax with Trea because their relationship doesn't have the demands or the pressures of a romantic relationship.

Sometimes friendships like the one between Trea and Nathan *do* turn into romantic relationships. More often they are just **platonic** relationships—close friendships that are not romantic.

One-Sided Relationships

Whether you call them crushes, puppy love, or **infatuations**, most people experience intense, but usually short-term, feelings of love for someone who may not even know the yearnings exist. Usually the crush is on someone who is unattainable, such as a friend's older sibling, a teacher, or a rock star. The

Many teens experience crushes or infatuations. Such experiences help you begin to understand what love is all about.

Emphasize Teens differ widely as to when they begin to have romantic relationships and what kind of relationships they have. Emphasize that there is no standard that they have to meet to be "normal."

More About One-Sided Relationships Tell students that infatuations are only one type of one-sided relationship. Another type is one in which one person does all the giving and the other does all the taking. Also, a relationship is one-sided when one person is in the relationship simply because the other person has something he or she wants.

person experiencing the crush daydreams about the object of the crush and often becomes fascinated with the details of his or her life.

Such one-sided relationships are part of learning to love. Respect and admiration are important elements in a love relationship. Also, an infatuation allows you to explore relationships in a safe way, since the other person is not required to respond.

If you get a crush on someone, you may be told that a crush is not real love. That is not exactly true. Unlike mature love, a crush *is* limited and one-sided, yet it is a kind of love. In any case, the feelings of excitement, yearning, sadness, and despair are very real to you.

First Steps

Children's first steps are wobbly and unsteady, and often they fall, but it is only through this experimentation that they learn to walk. The beginning steps that you take in relationships with the other sex are a little like that. It is normal to feel awkward about telephoning someone to talk or to get together, or even approaching someone you like at school for a conversation. Tess can talk to most boys with ease. When she speaks to Dave (whom she would like for a boyfriend), however, she feels tongue-tied.

Because of such fears and shyness, the first interactions between teens often occur in groups. In Camille's high school, a popular meeting place is the mall. Separate groups of boys and girls spend Saturdays there, talking, laughing, and having fun. Sometimes one group tries to attract the attention of another group, often through teasing and flirting. They may spend time talking in small groups.

As you begin to reach out, remember that any shyness you might feel is normal. You are learning how to talk and act with the other sex. Other people are probably not judging your every move; more likely, they are concerned about how they appear to you.

Many teens feel shy or awkward when they first talk to someone they like. It takes time for relationships to grow.

Activities

Skill Builder: Critical Thinking
Divide students into pairs, and have them role play how they might start a conversation with a person of the other sex. After each role play, ask the class to evaluate how each person overcame any awkwardness in the situation. Ask if anyone has suggestions for further reducing shyness in the situation.

Reteaching
Ask students to volunteer additional examples that illustrate platonic love and infatuation.

Enrichment
Ask students to name the places in their community, other than school, where teens can meet one another. Ask students to suggest other places the community could provide where teens could meet on a casual basis.

Focus on Relationship Skills Remind students that the more experience they gain interacting with members of the other sex, the less awkward and the more confident they will feel.

More About Flirting Ask students to define *flirting*. Ask what purpose they think it serves. Explain that flirting can be a harmless way of relating to and showing interest in someone else. Remind students, however, that teens need to be aware of how seriously others are taking their flirting and to take care not to cause misunderstanding or hurt.

Teaching "Dating"

(Pages 136-137)

This section describes the advantages of dating.

Checking Comprehension

✓ Why is dating valuable? *Dating helps you to learn to evaluate others, to discover what kinds of characteristics you like in someone else, to determine what characteristics you might want in a mate, and to learn how to share your interests, opinions, and feelings.*

✓ What are the advantages of dating in a group? *In a group, a person usually feels less self-conscious, and each person has less responsibility for keeping the conversation going. Also, some parents allow teens to go on group dates but not on individual dates.*

✓ How can going steady benefit teens? *Going steady can help them get to know another person well, feel secure, and feel good about themselves.*

✓ How can going steady be a disadvantage? *It can rob people of the chance to meet and date others and to learn what they like in a person. It may also have a negative effect on friendships with those of the same sex.*

Activities

Skill Builder: Reading
Tell students that dating customs vary from nation to nation. Ask them to choose a foreign nation or culture and research its dating rituals. Ask them to find out at what age people start dating and what kinds of activities dates involve. Have them give a report to the class that compares and contrasts American dating customs with the ones they read about.

Reteaching
As a class, compare dating as a group to dating as a couple.

Enrichment
Ask students to think of the negative effects that going steady can have on friendships with people of the same sex. Students should suggest ways of behaving that might reduce these negative effects.

Dating

In time, these first contacts give way to dating relationships. Though the point at which you begin dating is not important, dating itself is a valuable activity. Through dating you:

- Learn to evaluate others.
- Learn what kinds of characteristics you like in another person.
- Learn how to determine the characteristics that are best for you and those you want in a mate.
- Learn how to share your interests, opinions, and feelings.

Dating helps you learn about the other sex as well as about yourself. There is one more purpose of dating that should not be forgotten: having fun!

Going Out in Groups

Sometimes dating starts with a group of friends who have fun together. Teens might meet for bowling, skating, parties, or movies. In a group date, people can relax and have fun with both males and females.

In fact, that is one of the advantages of a group date: you will feel less self-conscious with your friends around. It is easier to talk in a group. Each person has less responsibility for keeping the conversation going. In addition, some parents will not allow young teens to go out on an individual date, but they may allow them to go on a group date.

Dating as a Couple

Nadia was always surprised at how nervous she felt on a first date with someone new. Making conversation seemed especially difficult.

Perhaps the most popular thing to do on a first date is to see a movie, because you can relax while you are watching the film instead of worrying about making conversation. In addition, the movie gives you something to talk about later. Your separate opinions can tell you a lot about each other.

Group dating provides fun opportunities to get to know other people better.

Did You Know? Tell students that dating customs have changed over the years. In the nineteenth century a man and a woman who were dating needed a chaperon present whenever they were together.

Focus on Technology Tell students that in recent years computer dating and video dating services have become popular. On the basis of information given them, computers can match people according to their similar characteristics, likes, and interests. Video dating services allow people to see a videotape of a prospective date.

Remember that the object of the date is to learn about the other person and to have fun. Don't worry about doing everything right. If you concentrate on making the other person comfortable, you will find you have a better time.

Some teens prefer to date different people. This gives them the advantage of gaining lots of experience in getting to know and understand many types of people. Sometimes a couple decides to date each other exclusively. This is sometimes referred to as going steady. It has some advantages. You get to know another person well, you derive a feeling of security, and your self-esteem is boosted. Yet going steady can also rob you of the chance to meet and date many people and to learn what you really like in a person. It may also have a negative effect on your same-sex friendships.

Problems with Relationships

It seems odd that love, which is something that is supposed to make people feel happy, can also bring sadness or hurt. Yet it is because loving and being loved mean so much that having something go wrong causes unhappiness. Knowing how to handle problems with relationships can help you cope with them and make better decisions.

When Love Is Not Returned

Rock stars sing about it, movies show it, soap operas thrive on it: **unrequited love**, or love that is not returned. Loving someone who does not love you in return is painful. Your friends and family may tell you to forget about the person, but you end up thinking about him or her all the time.

Ryan thought Lily was the only girl for him. After a few dates, however, she told him that she didn't think they should go out anymore because she didn't feel as strongly about him as he did about her. For a while, he tried to win her over. He knew her schedule, and he would turn up after her classes and at her table at lunch. After some time, however, he began to feel resentful and angry at her. He began to see faults that he had not seen before.

What happened to Ryan is normal. As a defense against the pain of unrequited love, Ryan experienced feelings of anger and resentment, which helped him to stop pursuing Lily. Eventually he could focus his attention on another girl, who cared for him in return.

Poor Communication

When Gina said to Tory, "I really like being with you," she only meant that she felt comfortable with him. When Tory heard those words, though, he thought Gina was saying she wanted an exclusive relationship with him. He was hurt when she explained that was not it at all.

Misunderstandings like these often happen when people are just starting out in a romantic relationship. They even happen to people who have been in a relationship for some time. Unfortunately, people don't always say what they mean. People don't always hear what others say, either; instead, they may hear what they *want* others to say.

It is important to be as honest and clear in your communication as possible. If there is a problem, discuss it. When the other person is speaking, listen. If you aren't sure what the message is, ask. Open communication is the best way to keep a relationship going strong.

Teaching "Problems with Relationships"

(Pages 137-139)

This section describes areas that often cause problems in relationships.

Checking Comprehension

✓ What is unrequited love? *Unrequited love is love that is not returned.*

✓ Explain why open communication is important to relationships. *Open communication is the best way to keep a relationship going strong. Without good communication, people have misunderstandings and problems. This can happen whether they are just starting out in a romantic relationship or whether they have been in a relationship for some time.*

✓ What is a power struggle in a relationship? *A power struggle occurs when two people in a relationship want to be in control.*

✓ How can a power struggle be resolved? *To resolve power struggles, people need to sit down and talk about what they want and how they are willing to work together.*

✓ Why might couples fight frequently? *They may enjoy the attention and feelings of making up after the quarrel is over. Others may provoke fights as a kind of test of love.*

✓ Why do teens sometimes outgrow relationships? *During the teen years, teens are growing and changing very quickly. Teens may change in different ways.*

✓ What are some of the qualities of love? *Caring about the whole person, giving as well as taking, and enduring the test of time.*

Emphasize Point out to students that differences and disagreements themselves do not cause the end of a relationship. Often, what ends the relationship is the inability to communicate, discuss, and cope with differences.

Real-Life Situations Acquaintance rape, or "date rape," is being more widely reported. Most assaults take place in the victim's or someone else's home. It is important for students to know that communication skills can help to clarify any confusion about each person's values, expectations, and limits—preventing an assault before it starts.

Activities

Skill Builder: Critical Thinking
Remind students that there are positive aspects of each of the problems discussed in this section. Ask students to think about and share the things they think a person could learn—both about oneself and about someone else—from experiencing such a problem. For example, after getting over unrequited love, individuals might realize they are strong enough to recover from a painful experience.

Skill Builder: Critical Thinking
Divide students into small groups, and ask each group to suggest possible different meanings of each of the following statements. Encourage them to examine the consequences of misunderstandings of each statement:

- "I love you."
- "You are my best friend."
- "I want to spend more time with you."
- "I want more time for myself."
- "I want to date other people."
- "I want our relationship to be more serious."

They might come up with additional statements that could create misunderstandings in relationships.

Skill Builder: Writing
Ask students to think about the way people use the word *love.* Ask them to think of ways they have heard people use it in the last week or so. (They may suggest "loving" such things as foods, classes, books, or seasons, as well as people.) Ask students to write several paragraphs that explain what they think love is and whether or not they think that using the word for a variety of other emotions makes it less meaningful.

Disagreements and Quarrels

Disagreements in relationships can begin for many reasons. Sometimes two people have different values or ideas about what is important. You will learn more about relationship problems in Chapter 15.

Sometimes a power struggle is the underlying problem. Power struggles come from the desire of the two people in a relationship to be in control. Sometimes one person will give in for a time. Soon, however, he or she tires of putting up with this and begins to fight back, perhaps in subtle ways. Jon, for example, really enjoys playing basketball, both on the school team and in more informal games with friends. He expects Robin to come and watch him. In fact, that is how most of their dates are spent. Robin didn't mind at first. When she did get upset, however, she didn't tell him directly. Instead, she started coming to the games and bringing her homework with her. Sometimes she would disappear for long stretches during the game.

Power struggles occur in some relationships. To solve them, people need to sit down and talk about what they want and how they are willing to work together. Unless Jon is willing to be less domineering, or Robin is willing to give in gladly, their relationship will probably end.

In another kind of disagreement, the two parties will fight about almost everything. Luke and Penny's friends joke about their quarrels. One day one friend said to another, "They seem to create situations just so they can break up. Do they really like fighting?"

"I think what they really like," said the other friend, "is making up after the fight." For some people the attention and feelings that go with making up make the quarrel worthwhile. Others, not confident in their partner's love, provoke fights as a kind of test. Games like these may be fun for a while, and they are one way to experiment with relationships. In the long run, however, they are a waste of time. Most people outgrow relationships built on games like these.

Frequent disagreements or quarrels may mean that the relationship is not based on mutual interests or values.

More About Game Playing Tell students that starting a quarrel to get attention or to test people is not the only form of game playing some people engage in. Ask students to think of other games that people play, such as acting annoyed at someone but insisting that nothing is wrong.

Real-Life Situations Sometimes abuse or assault occurs in dating relationships. Slapping and hitting are forms of violence. Too often, abuse in a dating relationship does not end when the couple is married, but rather escalates into family violence. As in all abuse cases, help should be obtained for both the victim and the abuser.

Outgrown Love

"I don't really understand what happened. I thought I loved Libby," said Doug. "But the relationship just doesn't seem to be working anymore. What's wrong with me?"

There really is not anything wrong with Doug, or Libby either. During your teen years you are growing and changing very quickly. Two teens in a relationship may change in different ways. When this happens, one person usually becomes dissatisfied with the relationship before the other. The often painful process of breaking up must then take place.

Breaking Up

Breaking up is not easy. Sometimes a relationship ends by mutual agreement, but more often one person wants to end it before the other. In such cases, one person usually feels hurt and may be angry while the other feels guilty. There are ways, though, you can make breaking up easier on you and the other person. (See "Ending a Relationship" on page 140.)

With every relationship you experience in your teen and young adult years, you will probably ask, "Is this love?" No one can really explain to anyone else what love is. Some say that when you are in love, you care about the whole person, not merely his or her looks or talent. You want to give as well as take. Whatever real love is, it should endure the test of time. It should not be here today, gone tomorrow. Maturity will help you define love and determine what role it will play in your future.

From every relationship—no matter how long it lasts—you can learn about yourself and the qualities that you seek in your future mate.

Reteaching
Have students choose one of the problem areas discussed in this section and write dialogue that reflects a couple resolving the problem.

Enrichment
Ask students to reread a story or short novel that deals with unrequited love or outgrown love. Ask them to write a description of how each person involved acts and feels. Then ask them to evaluate how the individual copes with the problem.

Enrichment
Ask students to role play a couple breaking up due to a: power struggle; outgrown love; poor communications; or quarrels and disagreements.

Focus on Health Tell students that sometimes when there are problems in a relationship or a relationship ends, people stop eating and sleeping properly. Discuss with students the importance of maintaining healthful habits throughout situations that are stressful.

Focus on Relationship Skills Tell students that although ending a relationship is painful, it is often necessary. In fact, it may be kinder to end the relationship than to let the person be deceived about one's feelings. Tell students that it often helps to imagine being in the other person's place. They should try to imagine how they would want to be dealt with in a similar situation.

Teaching the Feature
"Ending a Relationship"

Answers to Feature Questions

1. Possible answers: Stay busy with friends and activities; talk it over with friends, family, or other people you trust; take up a sport or hobby; start dating other people; avoid places and things that remind you of the other person.

2. Some students will probably say that it depends on why they broke up. Others may say yes because they had a lot in common, or no because it would be too painful.

Activities

Role Playing Have students create role-play situations that involve breaking up a relationship. They should include a situation in which the break-up is mutual as well as one in which it is not. Have them act out the various situations, allowing time afterward for the comments of other students.

Class Discussion Ask students to think about how they would feel if someone they cared deeply about decided to end their relationship. Ask questions such as: "How would you react? Would you be angry? Would you pretend you didn't care?" Have them discuss positive and negative ways of handling the end of a relationship that they do not want to end.

Community Contact Break the class into groups, and ask them to find out what groups in their community can be resources to teens as they begin romantic relationships. To start them thinking, suggest that they consider groups that provide activities for teens, counseling services that deal with both physical and mental health, and groups that help teens deal with feelings of sadness or depression over the end of a relationship.

INTERPERSONAL SKILLS

Ending a Relationship

During the teen and early adult years, people often have several close relationships with the other sex. That means that some of them will end. There are ways to make the experience of breaking up less painful.

If you are the one ending the relationship, do it with honesty and sensitivity. Express your feelings, but try not to make the other person feel unlovable. Try to use "I" statements rather than "you" statements. Instead of saying, "You're too possessive," say, "I don't want to tie myself down to one person just yet." Avoid blaming and insulting the other person. Be kind, but firm.

If you are on the other side of the relationship, avoid pressure, sarcasm, or threats. Trying to keep a relationship from ending by clinging to the other person is bound to make him or her resentful. It will also make you feel worse about yourself.

After a breakup, give yourself time to recover from the hurt and disappointment. You will eventually regain your self-confidence and feel happy again. Don't expect, however, to remain friends with the person you broke up with. Although this is sometimes possible, more often it creates jealousy. Also, it may keep you hoping for a reconciliation when none is possible.

Though breaking up is hard, don't be afraid to try having a relationship again. Breaking up does not mean that your love was a waste. The experience of loving and being loved is part of you now. You have even learned from breaking up that you can bear the pain, and that it passes.

Think It Through

1. **What do you think are some ways to get over the hurt of breaking up?**
2. **If you broke up with someone, would you want to remain friends? Why or why not?**

Emphasize Point out to students that ending a relationship is something that everyone has to deal with at sometime or another. Having a relationship end does not mean that there is anything wrong with the people involved.

Focus on Entrepreneurship Ask students to think about a service that would help teens cope better with problems in relationships. The service might publish helpful information, offer a type of counseling, or set up a hot line.

CHAPTER 14 REVIEW

Reviewing the Facts

1. What is an infatuation?
2. Why do early interactions between teens often happen in groups?
3. List three reasons why dating is important.
4. Name one advantage and one disadvantage of going steady.
5. Explain why good communication is important in a relationship.
6. What are two reasons why disagreements occur in relationships?
7. Why do teens sometimes outgrow their partners in a love relationship?

Thinking Critically

1. Do you think there are pressures on teens today to begin romantic relationships early? Explain your answer.
2. How might the following aspects of an early dating relationship lead to poor communication: shyness, nervousness, and lack of knowledge of each other?

Applying Your Skills

1. Analyzing a Problem. Think of a book you have read or a movie or television show you have seen that has portrayed some troublesome aspect of relationships between teens of different sexes. Write a paragraph in which you describe ways that poor communication played a part in the problem, and give several suggestions for how communication might have been improved.

2. Writing a Dialogue. Derek and April have been going out for about a year. During a six-week vacation in California, April realizes that she wants to go out with boys other than Derek. She still likes Derek but does not want to tie herself down to one boy just yet. Write a dialogue in which April breaks this news to Derek in a sensitive manner.

3. Making Inferences. Usually Natalie asks Jake to come to her track meets. Jake used to go all the time. All of a sudden Jake is busy on some of the days of the track meets. Should Natalie infer something from this behavior? Explain your answer. What should Natalie and Jake do?

Answers to "Reviewing the Facts"

1. Intense, but usually short-term feelings of love for someone.
2. Teens often feel awkward or shy talking one-on-one to someone they are interested in. They are less self-conscious in groups.
3. Any three: learn to evaluate others; learn what characteristics you like in another person; learn how to determine the characteristics that are best for you and those you want in a mate; learn how to share your interests, opinions, and feelings.
4. Advantages include: getting to know another person well; a feeling of security; boost in self-esteem. Disadvantages include: eliminating the opportunity to meet and date many people; a possible negative effect on same-sex friendships.
5. Helps to avoid misunderstandings, to solve problems, and to keep a relationship going strong.
6. Any two: different values or ideas about what is important; power struggle; enjoyment of making up after a quarrel.
7. Teens are growing and changing very quickly and two teens may change in different ways.

Answers to "Thinking Critically"

1. Most students will probably say yes. They might cite pressure from other teens; examples in movies, magazines, television, and other forms of the media; possible pressure from parents; inner pressure to feel important, popular, or loved.
2. Students may point out that such people might be afraid to reveal their true selves at first and instead pretend to be what they think the other person wants them to be; they might not express themselves as clearly as they would with someone they knew well; they might be thinking about their shyness or nervousness and not listen to the other person.

COMPLETING THE CHAPTER

Summary

- In the teen years most people become attracted to the other sex. Sometimes this may be expressed in a platonic relationship, sometimes in an infatuation. Feelings of shyness are common when beginning relationships.
- Through dating, people can learn to evaluate others, discover what kinds of characteristics are important to them and what kinds of traits they want in a mate, and learn how to share interests, opinions, and feelings. Dating can be done in groups or as a couple.
- Problems can occur in relationships from unrequited love, poor communication, disagreements and quarrels, and outgrown love.

For Review

Objective Review Questions Have students complete the "Reviewing the Facts" section on this page.

Study Guide Have students complete the Study Guide from Chapter 14 of their *Student Workbook.*

Class Discussion Have students list examples of comic strips or of humorous movies or television shows that portray some of the issues in this chapter. After students have given a number of examples, discuss the value of humorous portrayals. Point out that humor can help people gain perspective on their situation and have the courage to begin again.

For Evaluation

Making a List Ask students to create a list of ten "Points to Remember" that have to do with beginning, enjoying, and ending romantic relationships. The list should reflect what they have learned from the chapter.

Chapter Test Have students complete the test for Chapter 14 that appears in the *Teacher's Classroom Resources.*

CHAPTER OVERVIEW

Chapter 15 discusses decision making in relationships. Students learn that their values have an important effect on their relationships. The struggle between values and relationships is called inner conflict. To deal with inner conflict and peer pressure, students are taught to know their values, practice self-control, and think about the consequences of their decisions. Students also learn that emotions affect relationships and that anger, jealousy, and sexual feelings can cause problems in relationships. Students are reminded that how people express their emotions shows how much respect they have for themselves and for others.

INTRODUCING THE CHAPTER

Motivators

Decisions Write the word *decisions* on the board, and define it as "the choices people make." Ask students to share some simple decisions they made today (such as what to wear or what to eat). Then ask them if they have ever had to make a difficult decision. Have them imagine they have two tickets to a concert and two of their close friends want to go. Ask them how they would decide who should go to the concert. After discussing several students' responses, say: "In this chapter you will learn about making decisions in relationships."

Using the Photograph Have students look at the photograph on this page, and ask: "What might these teens be saying to each other? Is the situation relaxed or tense?" Explain that a situation can become uncomfortable when you have to choose between your values and your relationships.

Responsible Decisions Have students read the chapter opening paragraphs on page 143. Ask them to summarize the incident between Andy and Vince. Then ask: "Did Andy make a responsible decision? Why or why not?" Have students write a description of how they think Andy felt about making his decision.

CHAPTER

15

Decisions in Relationships

OBJECTIVES

This chapter will help you to:

- Identify ways of dealing with inner conflicts and peer pressure.
- Explain how to decide what is right for you.
- Discuss how to handle emotions, such as anger, jealousy, and possessiveness, in relationships.

WORDS TO REMEMBER

conscience
jealous
self-control

Chapter Resources

Teacher's Classroom Resources
- Lesson Plan
- Life Skills Activity, *It's Up to You*
- Reproducible Master, *Refusal Skills*
- Extension Activity, *What Do You Value?*
- Chapter Test

Student Workbook
- Study Guide
- Worksheet, *Journey to the Center of Yourself*

Andy and Vince were walking home from school when Vince asked Andy if he wanted to go to a party that night and drink a few beers. Vince had moved to town a few months ago. Andy had immediately liked him and thought that he and Vince could become good friends. Now Andy was surprised and couldn't stop thinking about the offer. After a few minutes he told himself, "If Vince does it, then it must be OK." He decided to ask Vince about it.

"I didn't know you drank," Andy said.

"Yeah, and it's great," Vince exclaimed. "Why don't you come try it?"

Suddenly Andy remembered what the football coach had said: "If I ever catch any of you guys drinking alcohol or doing drugs, you're off the team for good."

"No, I don't think so, Vince," Andy finally replied. "Coach said that if he ever caught any of us doing any of that stuff, we would be off the team for good."

"Oh, come on," Vince said. "Nobody will ever find out."

"Nope," Andy said. "It's not worth taking the chance."

Relationships and Values

Andy turned down the drinks because of his values. To him, being on the football team meant more than drinking beer. He and his parents had discussed teenage drinking, and he knew they were opposed to it. He also knew that drinking under the age of 21 was illegal in his state. Andy's values have an effect on his relationships. Although he may not develop a close relationship with Vince, he has strengthened the trust of his parents and coach.

Throughout the teen years, relationships change. Values change, too, as people make more decisions for themselves and figure out what is really important to them.

Inner Conflict

It is common for teens to feel torn between their relationships and their values. Many of them have not decided what is most important to them. They may experience conflicting feelings when faced with a decision, and, after making one, they may be overcome with doubts.

Andy was undecided at first, until he remembered the coach's warning. Even though Andy's feelings may have been in favor of going along with Vince, his mind told him that he didn't want to risk being kicked off the football team or having his parents or the police find out about the drinking.

Your values can help you sort out conflicting feelings when you make decisions.

More About Relationships and Values Tell students that values affect relationships in many ways. Point out that people tend to start and build relationships with other people who share their values. Also, some people learn new values from people who are important to them.

Focus on Technology Scientists have discovered that people can exercise self-control over such physical functions as relaxation, heart rate, and blood pressure. Called biofeedback, the process involves the use of a machine to read physiological activity of a person and the training of the person to control these activities.

Introducing the Objectives

Discuss the chapter objectives on this page 142. Remind students that the objectives focus on important chapter content.

Introducing Vocabulary

Write *conscience* on the board, and pronounce it for students. Tell them that the word comes from the Latin word *conscientia,* "to be conscious." A conscience is an awareness of the moral goodness or responsibility of an act. It is the "little voice" inside a person.

TEACHING THE CHAPTER

For convenience, the teaching suggestions for this chapter are arranged according to the following lesson topics:

- "Relationships and Values," pages 143-144
- "Relationships and Emotions," "Respect for Yourself and Others," pages 145-146

Teaching "Relationships and Values"
(Pages 143-144)

This section identifies ways of dealing with inner conflicts and peer pressure and ways of deciding what is right for you.

Checking Comprehension

✓ How are values, inner conflict, and conscience related? *Your values, or the things that are important to you, may cause you to feel inner conflict if your relationships do not enhance your values. Your conscience is often a part of that inner conflict, and it is like a "little voice" that tells you whether, according to your values, you are doing what is right or wrong for you.*

✓ Why is self-control important? *Self-control is important because it stops people from depending on others to make decisions for them and because it makes people feel better about who they are and what they can do.*

Activities

Skill Builder: Writing
Have students write a scenario similar to those with Andy and with Cassie that shows a teen dealing with peer pressure in a responsible way. Have them share their writing with the class.

Skill Builder: Critical Thinking
Divide students into two groups, and have them debate which is more likely to prevent a person from acting a certain way: fear of the consequences or knowledge that the act is wrong. Give each group time to discuss their thoughts and come up with examples to illustrate their argument.

Reteaching
Ask students to give examples of the things teens might be tempted to do as a result of peer pressure. Write their suggestions on the board; then ask students to rate them right or wrong, according to their own values.

Enrichment
Have students design posters that promote the suggestions for making tough decisions they read about. Tell them to paraphrase the suggestions in a catchy phrase or illustrate them with an attention-getting drawing.

Enrichment
Invite a police officer to class to tell about the outcome of shoplifting, using drugs, or being arrested for driving while intoxicated.

Teaching "Relationships and Emotions" and "Respect for Yourself and Others"

(Pages 145-146)

This section discusses how to handle anger, jealousy, possessiveness, and sexual feelings in relationships. It explains how to make a choice that earns respect.

Checking Comprehension

✓ Give three examples of the different shadings of the emotion love. *Love for parents, love for friends, and love for someone special.*

At times you may, like Andy, feel as if there are two or even three people inside you. Your feelings may tell you to do one thing, your mind another.

Everyone has a **conscience**, the "little voice" that tells you whether, according to your values, what you are doing is right or wrong. When Cassie's friend tried to convince her that cheating on a test was OK, Cassie's conscience told her that it was wrong but she did it anyway. Afterward, Cassie felt very guilty.

A conscience isn't any help if it merely produces guilt. Your conscience should be helping you to develop **self-control**: an inner control over your own behavior. With self-control, you don't depend on someone else to look out for you. You become responsible for yourself, and you begin to feel better about who you are and what you can do.

Peer Pressure

Many teens find that their decisions are strongly influenced by their friends. Andy almost gave in to Vince's pressure because he wanted to be better friends with him.

A good friend will respect your values and not pressure you into making decisions that might be wrong for you.

In order to deal with peer pressure you need to know what your values are. Then you can make the decisions that are right for you.

Because Andy valued being on the football team and maintaining his parents' trust, he resisted the pressure to drink alcohol. Some teens might resist drinking because they value their health or because they don't want to be arrested. The important thing to remember is to act according to your values or what *you* think is right.

Deciding What Is Right

When you know what your values are, you can decide what is right for you. However, when you feel pulled in two different directions, those decisions may seem more difficult than ever. What can you do so that the tough decisions are easier to make? The following suggestions can help:

- **Think about the possible outcomes.** For example, shoplifting or using an illegal drug even once may result in your getting arrested.
- **Think about the physical consequences.** Smoking cigarettes, marijuana, or crack has serious physical effects. People have died from using cocaine just once.
- **Think about the emotional consequences.** What if you have lied to a friend? How will you feel when that friend discovers you haven't told the truth?

Once you have made a choice, how do you communicate your decision so that others respect it? Andy said no and then explained why. Explaining your reasons can be an effective way to say no. See "Refusal Skills" on page 147 for more information on this subject.

Focus on Decision Making Tell students that deciding how to handle a strong emotion is an important part of maturing. Ask them to decide how they would handle a strong feeling of anger if a very close friend did not support them in an election for class president.

Focus on Health Each year, millions of cases of sexually transmitted diseases (STDs) occur in the United States. Since such diseases can affect anyone who is sexually active, it is important that people make responsible decisions regarding their sexual activity.

Relationships and Emotions

Emotions are a part of all relationships. At times, you may feel love, joy, or enthusiasm. There might also be times that you will feel annoyed, impatient, or depressed. Emotions can have many different shadings as well. You might feel one kind of love for your parents, another kind for your best friend, and even a third kind for someone special.

It is even possible to experience several different emotions at the same time. Have you ever been excited and scared at the same time? What is most important is how you express the emotions you have.

Anger

Everyone experiences angry feelings occasionally. In relationships, it is important to learn how to express that anger responsibly.

When you have a disagreement with a friend, the thing you should *not* do is speak in anger. You will only be tempted to say something that will hurt the other person. You may even say something you don't really mean, which will drive you and your friend further apart.

When you are angry with anyone, avoid name-calling and threats. You should also learn how to express your anger in a nonviolent way.

Give yourself time to cool off. This does not mean that you should not express your anger. You might talk about the problem with your parents or with another friend. Try to work the problem out with your friend when you are calm enough to be able to control your feelings.

During the teen years, you may feel deep emotions about someone special. How might such emotions influence your decisions?

Although anger is a common emotion, it is important to learn how to express your anger in nonviolent ways.

✓ Is it possible to experience more than one emotion at the same time? Explain your answer. *Yes, it is possible to experience more than one emotion at the same time. For example, a person can feel excited and scared at the same time, as in starting high school.*

✓ Should anger be expressed in a relationship? *Yes, anger should be expressed in a relationship, but it should be expressed responsibly and nonviolently when you are calm.*

✓ Why might a person feel jealous? *Answers will vary but should illustrate reasons for a person to feel hurt or resentful, such as being excluded from something he or she wants.*

✓ What problems can a lack of understanding of or control over sexual feelings cause? *Pressure by one person on another to get sexually involved, sexually transmitted diseases, and teen pregnancy.*

✓ Why is it especially hard for teens to make tough decisions? *They are faced with so many conflicting emotions they have never felt before.*

✓ What is important to keep in mind when making decisions about emotions? *Emotions are changeable, and the way that people handle emotions shows how much respect they have for themselves and for others.*

Activities

Skill Builder: Critical Thinking
Have students select a popular movie that many of them have seen and that involves a relationship between teens. Ask them to analyze the relationship. What was good about the relationship? What kinds of things caused tensions? Was one of the partners jealous or possessive? Why? Ask students if they thought the partners behaved in a responsible way.

Skill Builder: Writing
Have students write a poem about a strong emotion they have felt. It can be a short poem, similar to a haiku, or a song. Encourage them to see that writing about an emotion can help them understand it.

Emphasize Emotions can be strong, but they are changeable. Very few decisions in a person's life should be made solely on the basis of emotions.

Cross-Reference See Teen Tips "Ways to Let Off Steam" on pages 166-167.

More About Emotions Ask students if anyone has ever told them they could tell what they were feeling by the look on their face. Tell them that facial expressions often indicate a person's emotion. For example, when people are surprised, their eyes widen; when they are angry, their eyes narrow a bit.

Reteaching
Ask students to give examples of the kinds of things that make them feel angry or jealous. Then have them suggest reasons why the emotions of anger and jealousy might run particularly high during the teen years. Ask volunteers to explain how they have learned to control these emotions.

Reteaching
Have students give examples of situations that might result in conflicting emotions. Get them started by suggesting that they think of situations that involve new experiences, such as learning to drive or starting a new job.

Enrichment
Explain to students that conflict can be either helpful or harmful to a relationship. Have students discuss the differences between two types of conflict. Explain that one difference is the *focus* of the disagreement. For example, if the agrument involves name calling or fault finding, the results are likely to be harmful. However, if the quarrel can stay focused on one area of disagreement until it is resolved, the conflict might be helpful to the relationship. Have students suggest constructive and destructive ways to manage anger, jealousy, or possessiveness.

Enrichment
Ask students to think of adults they know who have had to handle a strong emotion, such as anger at losing a job or grief over a death. Ask students to discuss how the person handled his or her emotion.

Jealousy and Possessiveness

Relationship problems can also occur because of other strong emotions like jealousy and possessiveness. You are **jealous** when you feel hurt or resentful if a boyfriend or girlfriend spends time with or pays attention to someone else. You may also get these feelings when he or she does something that does not include you.

When making decisions about relationships, always maintain respect for yourself and for the other person.

These emotions are normal parts of relationships, and everyone has them. That does not mean they should be ignored or exaggerated. If they build up, they can threaten a relationship.

Special Considerations

There are also other important emotions and actions that can affect relationships. For example, dating brings new responsibilities as well as new experiences. In the teen years, the same hormones that bring physical maturity may also cause strong sexual feelings. Lack of understanding of or control over sexual feelings can lead to problems such as pressure by one person on another to get sexually involved, sexually transmitted diseases, and teen pregnancy.

It is important to base decisions about these subjects on both a personal sense of responsibility and a respect for others. Emotional or physical pressure on another person to become more physically involved than he or she wants is unfair and selfish.

Feelings can be very strong in the teen years, but part of growing up is learning how to control your own feelings and express them in ways that are good for everyone.

Respect for Yourself and Others

Teens are faced with so many conflicting emotions they have never felt before that it may be especially difficult for them to make decisions sometimes. Those emotions can be both exciting and frightening at the same time. It is important to keep in mind that emotions are changeable, and that what you do with them shows how much respect you have for yourself and for others.

Real-Life Situation Teen pregnancy has become a major social concern in the United States. Each year, one out of 10 teenage girls becomes pregnant, and almost 1/2 million teenagers give birth. More than 1/5 of these teenage mothers have two or more children. Ask students what might be the short- and long-term outlook (physical, emotional, social, financial) for teenage mothers and their babies.

Emphasize Tell students that people are not automatically given respect—they must *earn* it. Stress that how they handle their emotions can earn them respect—from themselves and from other people.

INTERPERSONAL SKILLS

Refusal Skills

If friends try to talk you into doing something you don't really want to do, you need to be prepared. You have to make sure that other people really understand and accept your refusal. If you are in a situation where you need to say no, you can use these four steps to refuse firmly.

- **Step 1: Plan ahead.** You need to decide in advance what you will do in case certain situations arise. Doing this allows you to make up your mind without pressure from other people. You can also be ready to stand up for your own beliefs and values. For example, if your parents are going to be away on Saturday night and your friends ask if they can come over and have a party, you will be prepared to say no because you have made an agreement with your parents not to do this. You can also plan ahead by asking yourself some specific questions such as: Is it safe? Is it legal? Can it hurt me or anyone else?
- **Step 2: Say no.** It is important to say no and to mean it. Look straight at the other person. Don't smile, because your smile will communicate yes. Keep your voice steady, and watch your body language. Don't send confusing messages or the other people involved will doubt your statement.
- **Step 3: If necessary, repeat your refusal and give reasons why.** There may be times when saying no is not enough. You should be prepared for a put-down, but don't get into an argument. Give your reasons calmly but firmly. For instance: "It's against school rules," "I wouldn't feel right doing it," "I might get hurt," "It's illegal," or "I've promised my parents that I will not do that."
- **Step 4: Suggest an alternative.** Put on your own pressure by suggesting another activity, one that is fun, healthy, safe, and legal. If that does not work, you should get away from the pressure as soon as you can. You might even say that you have already made plans to do something else.

If you use the four steps, you will let your friends and acquaintances know that you are not rejecting them or their friendship. You are just making your own decisions. More often than not, your friends will respect you for making your decisions.

Think It Through

1. **Suppose a friend dares you to join a group that plans to pocket several items at a department store just for fun, and then return the items afterward. Use the four steps to tell your friend why you don't want to take part.**
2. **What could you do if a friend threatened to end the friendship with you after you refused to do something you didn't want to do?**

Teaching the Feature
"Refusal Skills"

Answers to Feature Questions

1. Students should give a response that incorporates all four parts of the refusal technique.
2. Possibilities include trying to persuade the other person to remain friends, allowing time for the person to reconsider before trying to renew the friendship, and making other friends who will respect your right to differ with them.

Activities

Ways to Say No Have students brainstorm to find ways of saying no to something they really don't want to do. Give them suggestions such as: "I'm sorry, but I'm busy." "You can do it, but I really don't want to." "Thanks, but I wouldn't have fun doing that." Have students evaluate each response.

Role Play Have students role play situations in which one student tries to convince another to do something he or she doesn't want to do. For example, have one person try to convince another to drink alcohol. Encourage each student to be as persuasive as possible. The other person should be prepared to give reasons for his or her refusal.

Community Contact Suggest to students that being involved in various activities might help them deal better with peer pressure. Then have students find out what activities their community offers for teens. Ask them if they have any suggestions for other activities that would help teens feel better about themselves so that they could make their own decisions.

Emphasize Saying no alone is not enough. Students must also show that they *mean* no. Eye contact, tone of voice, and posture can all be used to communicate refusal.

Cross-Reference See Teen Tips "Ten Ways to Say 'No' to Alcohol and Drugs" on pages 168-169.

Focus on Life Management Have students review the decision-making process in Chapter 5. Point out that following that process will help students develop their refusal skills. For example, weighing the pros and cons of a decision will help them see good reasons for saying no to something they don't want to do.

COMPLETING THE CHAPTER

Summary

- Relationships are affected by values and emotions.
- Inner conflict is the struggle between values and relationships, and conscience is the "little voice" that says whether something is wrong or right.
- To make decisions, think about the possible outcomes and the physical and emotional consequences.
- Emotions such as anger and jealousy need to be handled in a way that is good for everybody.
- Decisions about sexual feelings should be based on both a personal sense of responsibility and a respect for others.
- Emotions are changeable. How people handle emotions shows how much respect they have for themselves and others.

For Review

Objective Review Questions Have students complete the "Reviewing the Facts" section on this page.

Study Guide Have students complete the Study Guide from Chapter 15 of their *Student Workbook.*

Decisions in Life Ask students to share and compare the kinds of decisions they made five years ago with the ones they make as teens. Ask: "Do you find your decisions are getting more difficult?" Ask them to think about future decisions they will have to make, such as going to college or finding a job. Have them discuss why decisions seem to get more difficult as people get older, encouraging them to see the relationship between maturing, responsibility, and decision making.

For Evaluation

Questions About Relationships Ask students to make a list of the questions they would ask themselves if they were thinking of getting involved in a relationship with someone.

Chapter Test Have students complete the test for Chapter 15 that appears in the *Teacher's Classroom Resources.*

CHAPTER 15 REVIEW

Answers to "Reviewing the Facts"

1. The part of you that tells you when something you do goes against your values.
2. The inner control that you develop over your own behavior, enabling you to be responsible for yourself and to feel better about yourself and what you can do.
3. What your values are so you can make decisions that are right for you.
4. Possible outcomes, physical consequences, and emotional consequences.
5. Give yourself time to cool off before talking about the problem; avoid name-calling, threats, and violence.
6. Being hurt or resentful if a friend spends time with or pays attention to someone else.
7. A personal sense of responsibility and a respect for others.

Reviewing the Facts

1. Explain what your conscience is.
2. Describe self-control and how it helps you handle inner conflicts.
3. What do you need to know in order to deal with peer pressure?
4. What three things should you think about when you are deciding what is right for you?
5. What should you do when you are angry?
6. Define jealousy.
7. When making decisions about dating, what should you base your decisions on?

Thinking Critically

1. What do you think is the relationship between self-esteem and self-control?
2. Do you think anger and jealousy should be expressed? Why or why not?

Applying Your Skills

1. Analyzing a Sequence of Events. Write a paragraph describing a time when you felt pressured by your peers. Try to analyze what you did on the basis of whether you thought about the three suggestions on page 144.

2. Dissecting Behavior. Write a paragraph about a television show you have seen or a book you have read in which one or more characters took responsibility for their emotions. Discuss specifically what the characters did that showed responsibility.

3. Discovering Cause-and-Effect Relationships. Have you ever been asked to do something that you didn't want to do? Describe the situation. How did it arise? How did it make you feel? What was the outcome?

Answers to "Thinking Critically"

1. Students should suggest that self-esteem and self-control are interrelated. For example, if you have a high level of self-esteem, you usually have a lot of self-control. You don't depend on others for decisions because you take responsibility for your own decisions. Usually the more responsible you are, the better you feel about yourself. In contrast, low self-esteem may result in lack of self-control.
2. Some students may answer yes because if one person in a relationship has these feelings and holds them in, they can destroy the relationship. Others may answer no because their expression of anger or jealousy could cause problems in themselves.

CHAPTER

16

Your Future Relationships

OBJECTIVES

This chapter will help you to:

- Explain the benefits of new friendships at school and at work.
- Describe the elements of a successful love relationship.
- Discuss how family relationships can change.
- Define the roles of a leader and a good citizen.

WORDS TO REMEMBER

citizen
parliamentary procedure
role model

Chapter Resources

Teacher's Classroom Resources

- Lesson Plan
- Life Skills Activity, *Follow Your Leader*
- Reproducible Master, *Four C's of Love*
- Extension Activity, *Achieving Independence*
- Chapter Test

Students Workbook

- Study Guide
- Worksheet, *Smooth Sailing with the Four C's*

CHAPTER OVERVIEW

In Chapter 16 students learn about the relationships they can expect to make in the future. They learn how the relationships they have in school can help them prepare for the relationships they will build in the next part of their life, when they go to college or start work. The chapter discusses love relationships focusing on the four C's (caring, commitment, communication, and compromise). Students also learn how their family roles and the roles of their family members change as they become more independent. Lastly, relationships with community and nation are discussed. Students learn the skills and qualities that make a good leader and citizen.

INTRODUCING THE CHAPTER

Motivators

Lifelong Relationships Write *love, work,* and *community* on the board. Tell students to think about their relationships in these areas. Have them discuss ways in which they are currently preparing to deal with these future relationships. To start the discussion, remind them that dating is helping them learn about future relationships developed through love, work, and community bonds.

Using the Photograph Have students look at the photograph on this page. Ask: "What are the people doing in this picture? How old do you think the people are? How do you imagine your friendships will be when you are this age?"

Introducing the Objectives

Discuss the chapter objectives on this page. Remind students that the objectives focus on important chapter content.

Introducing Vocabulary

Write *role model* on the board. Ask students to define the phrase. Tell them that a role model is someone you admire and whose behavior you use as an example. Explain that copying another person's admirable behavior is a good way to learn the behavior yourself.

TEACHING THE CHAPTER

For convenience, the teaching suggestions for this chapter are arranged according to the following lesson topics:

- "Friendships," pages 150-151
- "Love," pages 151-152
- "Family," page 152
- "Neighborhood, Community, and Nation," pages 152-154

Teaching "Friendships"

(Pages 150-151)

This section explains the benefits of new friendships at work and at school.

Checking Comprehension

✔ List four relationships that can be developed at school. *Any four: friends, teachers, guidance counselors, coaches, librarians, and other adults.*

✔ What can be learned from relationships developed at school? *People can learn to get along with those in authority. They can also develop skills in listening, understanding, and following directions.*

✔ If you go to college, what should you remember when dealing with roommates or when seeking new friends? *Speak honestly, listen patiently, and be considerate. Also, keep a sense of humor and be yourself.*

✔ What can be learned from relationships developed at work? *People can learn to build friendships with people who are different from themselves. They can learn to follow suggestions and to accept criticism of their work.*

✔ What are the pros and cons of working in a group or team? *Some of the pros are that team members get to interact with others and share ideas and responsibilities. The cons include sharing responsibility for problems.*

Your teen years are a time of preparation. In getting ready to be an adult, you learn how to be a friend and how to be a member of a family. The success of your future relationships might depend on what you learn now.

Of course, no one knows what your future relationships will be like. Everyone takes a different path. You may stay in your town and remain friends with the people you know now. You may go to college in a new city and decide to stay there. Perhaps you will go away for a period—in the armed services, for example—and then return to your hometown to work at another job.

Whatever you do, wherever you go, there will always be people with whom you can form satisfying relationships.

Friendships

As you get older, you and your friends may grow apart. Sometimes, a friend moves away and it is harder to keep the closeness over a long distance. Sometimes, you grow apart because of a change in interests. Changes in your life don't mean that you *must* lose your current friends, though. You can talk about your new experiences whenever you are together. At the same time, you may develop new friendships with people at school or at work.

New Relationships at School

When you think of your relationships at school now, you probably think of your friendships. However, your relationships with teachers, counselors, coaches, librarians, and other adults are also opportunities for growth.

Your relationships with these adults help you to learn how to get along with those in positions of authority. You also learn, through these contacts, skills in listening, understanding, and following directions that are crucial in all parts of your life. These people are your **role models**, people you admire and whose behavior you use as an example.

After high school, perhaps you will go to college away from home and live in a dormitory with a roommate. Both you and your roommate will need to adjust to living with someone who has different habits. Getting along will be easier if you speak honestly, listen patiently, and are considerate. A sense of humor helps, too.

Finding new friends at college—especially at a big school—may seem impossible. Actually, though, it is like making friends in school now. As you read earlier, you can meet people in classes, at the cafeteria, in special clubs, or on teams.

In seeking these friendships, remember to be yourself. You have built a self-concept and identified your interests. Now act on what you have learned.

New Relationships at Work

People spend so much time at the place where they are employed that they often make friends of the people they meet there. Of course, being friendly at work does not mean chatting all day, but it does mean being pleasant, cooperative, and considerate of others.

The people you work with have different opinions and personalities, but you will have to get along with all of them, not just the ones you like. A positive aspect of getting along with co-workers is that you may develop friendships with people who are different from you.

Emphasize Making and keeping friendships is a lifelong activity.

More About Role Models Some people are strongly influenced by role models. Ask students what career they would like to choose and whether their choice was influenced by a role model.

Focus on Relationship Skills Tell students that, like other relationships, relationships at work have their share of problems. Have students role play work situations such as asking an employer for a raise, talking to a co-worker about not smoking, and reprimanding an employee for always being late.

You will also have to learn to follow suggestions and to accept criticism of your work. If you remember that your boss is discussing your *work*, not judging your character, you will find criticism easier to accept. It is natural to make a few mistakes, and your boss wants to help you learn from those mistakes. Just be sure that you aren't making the mistakes because you are afraid to ask questions.

Finally, you may often find yourself working in a group or team. Team workers share ideas and responsibility, and this means sharing responsibility for both success *and* failure.

Love

Sometimes a friendship will undergo a change and turn into a love relationship. Love is based on the give-and-take of two people so that the deepest needs of both people are met.

The Four C's

For love to grow and develop, it helps to follow the four C's. These are caring, commitment, communication, and compromise.

- **Caring.** The most satisfying part of a love relationship may be the caring. Knowing that someone else cares makes you feel more secure and worthy. You can show how much you care, too, by helping when your partner is feeling low or has a problem.
- **Commitment.** A strong relationship also depends on both people's making a commitment. Each partner must want to make the relationship work. Love relationships don't just happen; they require teamwork.
- **Communication.** Commitment requires communication. Talking honestly can help solve the problems that arise. Just talking is not enough; you must listen, too.
- **Compromise.** To settle differences, both partners must be willing to compromise. They must be willing to give a little so that they can reach a solution that satisfies them both. The result is a stronger relationship.

An enduring, lasting love is based not just on physical attraction, but on qualities such as trust, understanding, and respect.

Emphasize Building a strong love relationship takes work as well as caring.

More About Marriage Not every marriage is the same. Depending on individual personalities and the partners' goals, different roles are taken on. Sometimes a wife may be the homemaker; other times a husband may fill that role. More often both wife and husband take care of home responsibilities including any children.

Activities

Skill Builder: Critical Thinking
Divide students into pairs, and have them role play meeting a college roommate and working out sharing space for their possessions. When students are finished, have them describe their feelings about the compromises they needed to make.

Reteaching
Ask students to list two skills people can learn from relationships developed at school and two things people can learn from relationships developed at work.

Enrichment
Review with students how friendships change over the years. Ask them to list changes they look forward to, such as meeting different people. Then ask them to list qualities of friendships that they would like to stay the same over time.

Teaching "Love"
(Pages 151-152)

This section describes the elements of a successful love relationship.

Checking Comprehension

✓ How could you help show your partner that you care? *Answers will vary. Students might say that they could show it by helping when their partner is low or has a problem, by showing kindness and consideration, or by treating their partner with respect.*

✓ Why does a love relationship require commitment? *Because for a relationship to work, two people must be prepared to work together.*

✓ Why is good communication important in a love relationship? *Both persons must express their caring, discuss any problems that occur, and listen to the other person.*

✓ Why is the ability to compromise important in a love relationship? *Two people will not always agree, and they must settle the difference or problem in a way that satisfies both people.*

✓ Why is getting married a major decision? *It is a major change in one's life, requiring a lot of adjustment. Marriage means practicing caring, commitment, communication, and compromise every day.*

✓ Explain the ways single people may find fulfillment. *They may dedicate themselves to a career and have satisfying relationships with old friends, new friends, and family members.*

Activities

Skill Builder: Critical Thinking
Divide students into small groups, and have them brainstorm about four "don'ts" in a love relationship. Have the group share their ideas.

Reteaching
Have students give examples of the four C's that help to strengthen a love relationship.

Enrichment
Have students ask married friends or relatives what difficulties, amusing or otherwise, the two partners encountered in the first year of marriage. Have them interview people who have been married for varying lengths of time.

Teaching "Family"
(Page 152)

This section discusses how family relationships change as family members grow more independent and move away.

Checking Comprehension

✓ How can a family member's independence change family relationships? *The person may move out and away from his or her family. Also, the person will not play the same roles with family members that he or she used to.*

✓ Even when a person is living independently, why is it important to maintain family ties? *It is comforting to have family members willing to lend a hand if needed.*

Marriage

Deciding to marry someone is a major decision. It means being willing to practice the four C's every day. It usually also requires a lot of adjustment by each person, especially during the first year. If both partners work hard, however, they can get over the rough spots. The joy that may result can make it all worthwhile.

Of course, not everyone chooses to marry. You may prefer to dedicate your life to a career. Single people can still have satisfying relationships with other people: old friends, new friends, and family members.

Family

Your family relationships also will change in the future. You may start to care for younger siblings or perhaps help take care of your grandparents. When you move away from home, however, you begin a whole new stage in your life. Your family will not play exactly the same role as it did before.

Independence and Moving Out

In many other countries, grown children live with their parents until they are married, and sometimes even after. In our society, though, young adults often leave their homes and become independent. They live on their own or with roommates and begin setting up their own household.

It can be an exciting time, doing what you want on your own schedule. This new freedom carries its responsibilities, however. You will have to manage your money to meet your expenses for food, clothing, shelter, and leisure activities, for example.

As you meet the new challenges, you gain more confidence in yourself. You prepare yourself to take on even more new experiences. Still, it can be comforting to have family members who are willing to lend a helping hand.

New Family and Old

If you marry, you will probably acquire more than just a spouse. New relatives are likely to be involved. Your spouse's family may be very different from your own, and your family may seem strange to your spouse. In fact, accepting one another may be difficult for everyone at first.

Remember that your spouse draws strength and love from his or her family, just as you do from yours. A good relationship with your new relatives is important to you and to your marriage.

Neighborhood, Community, and Nation

Beyond your family, school, and workplace, you are a part of your neighborhood, your community, and your nation. Your relationships in these larger groups will also help determine your future.

Groups consist of leaders and followers, and all groups need both. There are times you may assume the role of leader, such as when you serve as a student council officer or get your group involved in an after-school project. At other times you may be a follower, as when you help with a car wash or participate in a community walkathon.

Different skills are required of each position, and each is needed to get the job done. Whether you are a leader or a follower, you relate to the group in different ways.

Real-Life Situations More young adults are continuing to live at home or returning to the "empty nest" to live with their parents. Some of their reasons include lack of employment, high housing costs, financial problems, divorce, and rearing of young children. Ask students what impact this might have on each family member.

Focus on Relationship Skills Tell students to pretend they are moving out of their family's home and into an apartment. Ask them to list the qualities they would look for in a future roommate.

Being a Leader

A good leader uses the best talents of a group to achieve the group's goals. These might range from running a bake sale to cleaning up a park. Whatever the project, an effective leader enables group members to work together efficiently to reach the goal.

What characteristics make a leader effective? The following five skills are very important.

- **Management.** A leader must know and follow the management process: planning, organizing, implementing, and evaluating. Good leaders don't do it all themselves; they use the special talents of everyone in the group to get things done.
- **Motivation.** To use the resources of the group fully, a leader must be aware of the talents and abilities of each member, as well as sensitive to the ways that each person can best be motivated. Some people, for example, work well with little direction. Others require more help in getting started. An effective leader understands people's talents and abilities and tailors management to each person's needs.
- **Problem solving.** A good leader solves the problems that naturally arise when people work together. Creative thinking, conflict resolution, and decision-making skills are all necessary for good leadership.
- **Communication.** A good leader communicates effectively. He or she must be able to explain to the group what needs to be done and how each person can help do it. A leader needs to listen to suggestions, problems, and complaints, and to communicate praise and encouragement to group members.
- **Conducting meetings.** A good leader gives group members at a meeting an opportunity to voice their opinions following rules developed first by the English Parliament. This democratic method, known as **parliamentary procedure,** permits the reaching of a majority decision. Knowing parliamentary rules can help you become a leader at school and at work.

Leadership skills, just like other skills, can be learned and developed.

Focus on Leadership Review the skills a good leader needs. Then ask students to think of other skills or qualities that may be important for a leader to be effective. To start the discussion, ask students if compassion or empathy is a good quality for a leader.

Focus on Decision Making Divide students into small groups, and select one person to be the leader of each group. Then have each group decide how to raise money for a class trip. Encourage them to use parliamentary procedures so that each member of the group gets to voice his or her opinion and the group arrives at a majority decision.

✓ How can marriage change family relationships? *By adding new family members that each person will have to learn to accept. It may also place stress on old family relationships.*

Activities

Skill Builder: Critical Thinking
Have students imagine they are moving into a place of their own. Ask them to list the new responsibilities they will have, such as paying bills and cooking food. Conclude the activity by discussing what is exciting and what is scary about living on one's own.

Reteaching
Have students develop a class mural that illustrates how family relationships change over the years. Tell them to find pictures of people in various stages of life—as infants, toddlers, teens, spouses, parents, grandparents. The pictures should show people relating to each other in various ways.

Enrichment
Have students read a book about a teen growing up and/or gaining independence, such as *Across Five Aprils* by Irene Hunt. Have students write a book report when they have finished reading the book.

Teaching "Neighborhood, Community, and Nation"
(Pages 152-154)

This section defines the qualities of a good leader and a good citizen.

Checking Comprehension

✓ How can you tell if a leader is effective? *A leader enables group members to work together efficiently.*

✓ What should a leader know about management? *A leader should know the steps in the management process, and use the talents of everyone in the group.*

✔ What skills help a leader solve problems? *Creative thinking, conflict resolution, and decision making.*

✔ Define the term *parliamentary procedure. Parliamentary procedure is the democratic process, based on the rules of the English Parliament, that gives people in a meeting the opportunity to voice their opinions and reach a majority decision.*

✔ What qualities make a good citizen? *Respect, cooperation, responsibility and participation.*

Activities

Skill Builder: Critical Thinking
Have students pretend they are the leader of a group (their class) that is planning a group community project, such as cleaning up litter in a park, raising funds for a historic marker, planting flowers in a public area, or other specific tasks. Ask them to think of things they could do to achieve this goal. Remind them to think about the abilities of various class members that will help the group meet its goal.

Reteaching
Ask students to select a local or national leader and to give examples of how that leader has used the five leadership skills.

Enrichment
Have students think of qualities that make a good follower. Explain that both leaders and followers are needed to make a society function and that followers are sometimes leaders and vice versa.

Enrichment
Ask students to design a bulletin board in the hall to recognize a good citizen of the school. Have students select a person who has done something for the school and feature his or her photograph on the bulletin board for a week.

Being a Good Citizen

A **citizen** is a member of a group such as a school, a community, or a nation. Your role as a citizen is the role of follower and group member. You already know what it means to be a good citizen within your family, and you have discovered how working together helps everyone.

What makes a good citizen? Several qualities stand out:

- **Respect.** A citizen respects other people, their individuality, their needs, and their property. Some property is shared by all people in a group. The earth, for example, belongs to all of us. By trying to live in ways that minimize pollution, you act as a good citizen of the world who respects this common heritage. Being respectful also means acting honestly and obeying the rules or laws of the group.
- **Cooperation.** No group can achieve its goals if the members do not cooperate with each other and share ideas and resources. Part of good citizenship is working together with others to achieve a common goal, such as running the student government smoothly and effectively.
- **Responsibility.** Being a good citizen means thinking before you act—you need to consider how your action will affect others. It also means taking responsibility in your daily life. For example, your walking your dog on a leash will be appreciated by others in your neighborhood.
- **Participation.** Part of being a good citizen means pitching in with the group for everyone's good. As a citizen of the United States, for example, you participate by staying informed and by voting when you come of age. At some point in your life, you may decide to open up your own business, buy a home, or invest in the stock market. All of these actions contribute to the nation's economy.

Being an effective leader or citizen benefits everyone. Doing your job well will make you feel good about yourself, and it will make others feel good about you. You will know that you can make a difference in the world of the future by controlling your own life and affecting the lives of others for the good of all.

One of the responsibilities of citizenship is voting in every election.

More About Being a Good Citizen Tell students that being a good citizen involves helping community workers whenever they can. Some neighborhoods have started a program called Crime-Watch, in which neighbors look out for and report any neighborhood crime.

Focus on Life Management Remind students that being good citizens will make them and others feel better about themselves. Being good citizens will also let them know that they can make a difference in the world. Ask students to write how they would like to manage their lives to make a difference in the world.

INTERPERSONAL SKILLS

Leadership

In 1963, a 16-year-old boy from Hope, Arkansas, stood in the Rose Garden at the White House and shook the hand of President John F. Kennedy. It was a thrilling moment for the teen—a moment that inspired his own political ambitions. Thirty years later, that boy—William Jefferson Clinton—became the forty-second president of the United States.

As a teen, Bill Clinton participated in a program of leadership training known as Boys' State. Members of Boys' State get together every year at state capitals or university campuses. Delegates become citizens of an imaginary state, similar in political structure to their own state government. After campaigning for election to various government offices, they debate issues and pass laws. Every summer, two representatives from each Boys' State meet in Washington, D.C., to conduct a mock federal government known as Boys' Nation. Bill Clinton was a member of Boys' Nation when he met President Kennedy.

Boys' State and its parallel organization, Girls' State, give young people experience running for political office. Teens have other opportunities for political campaigning as well. At school, you could run for a class office such as president or secretary. You could campaign to be elected a student council representative or an officer of a school organization such as the Drama Club or Spanish Club.

Youth groups at churches and synagogues and community groups such as 4-H clubs and Future Homemakers of America also elect leaders. In addition, the Democratic and Republican parties have student organizations.

Running for political office in your school or community can be a valuable experience. President Clinton no doubt applied his experience from Boys' State to his political campaigns.

While you may or may not run for president of the United States, you will certainly have opportunities for leadership roles in community groups you belong to as an adult. Being a leader will give you an opportunity to solve problems and make changes that will improve people's lives.

Think It Through

1. **How would you go about organizing a campaign to be elected president of the student body at your school?**
2. **Why do you think many adults are reluctant to run for community or government offices?**

More About Boys' State The Illinois American Legion developed the first Boys' State in 1934, and the program was endorsed nationally in 1935. Local American Legion posts sponsor participants nominated by their high schools. Nationwide, about 25,000 to 30,000 boys participate annually.

Did You Know? Hillary Rodham Clinton also developed leadership skills as a young person. By the time she was 16, she had organized a neighborhood Olympics, child care for migrant workers, and a voter-registration project. She was president of the student government at Wellesley College and the first student to speak at a commencement there.

Teaching the Feature
"Leadership"

Answers to Feature Questions

1. Students can use their knowledge of school and community campaigns to answer the question. They should recognize that it would be important to know the duties of the office and be able to demonstrate their qualifications. They should have a clear idea of what they would hope to achieve in office. They should expect to assemble campaign workers and decide how they would get their message across—speeches, posters, buttons, and so on.

2. Answers will vary. Students may say that many adults feel they have neither the time nor the leadership skills to hold office. People may think that campaigns are too costly and time-consuming.

Activities

If I Were . . . Have students think of a school office they would like to hold. Then have them list things they would do if elected to that office. Ask volunteers to read their platforms to the class.

Research Have students find out whether their school has rules for the conduct of campaigns for school offices. For example, the school might limit the amount of time for campaigning. If the school does not have such rules, suggest that students formulate a campaign procedure and present it to the student government for adoption.

Anatomy of a Campaign Invite a candidate for school board, city council, state legislature, or other political office to speak to the class. Ask the speaker to describe what goes into running a campaign.

Community Contact Encourage students to work on the campaign of a candidate whose views on the issues are similar to their own. Political campaigns need young people to stuff envelopes, answer telephones, distribute brochures, and do research.

COMPLETING THE CHAPTER

Summary

- Over the years friendships will change, and new ones, perhaps at college or at work, will be formed.
- Four elements for a strong love relationship are caring, commitment, communication, and compromise. Marriage includes practicing these four C's every day.
- Family relationships change as members become independent and move out. Also, marriage adds new family members to existing ones.
- Followers and leaders need different skills. Good leaders can manage, motivate, solve problems, communicate, and conduct meetings using parliamentary rules.
- Good citizens respect others, participate in civic activities, cooperate with others, and act responsibly.

For Review

Objective Review Questions Have students complete the "Reviewing the Facts" section on this page.

Study Guide Have students complete the Study Guide from Chapter 16 of the *Student Workbook*.

Class Discussion Have students think about various relationships in life. Tell them to think of the relationships they have today and those they will have in the future. Ask: "What skills are needed in all relationships, regardless of whether it is a work, love, family, or friend relationship?" Start the discussion by reminding them of the importance of communication skills.

For Evaluation

Essay Have students answer one of the following essay questions.

1. How do relationships with friends change?
2. What skills build a strong love relationship, and why?
3. What are the pros and cons of being independent?
4. What skills does a good leader need, and why?

Chapter Test Have students complete the test for Chapter 16 that appears in the *Teacher's Classroom Resources*.

CHAPTER 16 REVIEW

Answers to "Reviewing the Facts"

1. You can learn important information and skills from teachers; also how to get along with people in authority.
2. People in the workplace are together for many hours and may work closely together as a team.
3. Caring, commitment, communication, compromise.
4. Any two: you may care for younger siblings or for grandparents; move away from home; begin your own family.
5. Because the skills of both leaders and followers are needed to get jobs done.
6. Management, motivation, conducting meetings, problem solving, communication.
7. A citizen is a member of a group such as a school, community, or nation.
8. A group can achieve its goals only if its members cooperate with each other and share ideas and resources.

Reviewing the Facts

1. How can your relationships with teachers help you in the future?
2. Why do friendships often start in the workplace?
3. What are the four C's of a strong love relationship?
4. What are two ways in which your family relationships can change as you grow older?
5. Why are leaders and followers needed to get a job done?
6. What five qualities are important for good leadership?
7. Define the term citizen.
8. Why is cooperation within a group important to good citizenship?

Thinking Critically

1. List two things that you learn in your relationships at school that you expect will also help you at work.
2. How can you be a good citizen of your family? At school? In your neighborhood? Give two examples for each.

Applying Your Skills

1. **Evaluating Change.** There are advantages and disadvantages for people when they move out of the family home and become independent. Make a list of five advantages you can think of and a second list of five disadvantages. Then write one or more paragraphs stating your conclusions about the process of becoming independent.

2. **Applying Characteristics.** Reread the section on being a leader. Think of a goal your school or community wants to achieve, such as cleaning up the local playground. How could you use the five qualities that effective leaders possess to accomplish that goal?

3. **Supporting Theories.** Think about a couple you know who has been married for several years. How do the four C's fit into this relationship? Then think about some of the couples in your school. How do the four C's fit into those relationships? Compare your answers for the couples still in school. Explain your answer.

Answers to "Thinking Critically"

1. Possible answers include any two: how to take direction; how to work with others on a project; how to take criticism; how to get along with someone in authority.
2. Possible answers for family: ask before you borrow something; take care of family possessions; help with family chores. Possible answers for school: don't cheat on exams; take care of school building(s) and grounds; participate in class discussions. Possible answers for neighborhood: be friendly and respectful to neighbors; don't litter or write graffiti; be aware of neighborhood concerns.

CHAPTER

17

Careers in Working with People

OBJECTIVES

This chapter will help you to:

- Identify the interests and skills required for a career in working with people.
- List personal goals and achievements.
- Give examples of jobs that involve helping people.
- Distinguish between entry-level jobs and jobs that require training.

WORDS TO REMEMBER

aide
clergy
client
entry-level job
objective
personal inventory

Chapter Resources

Teacher's Classroom Resources
- Lesson Plan
- Life Skills Activity, *Try a Career on for Size*
- Reproducible Master, *Do I Want to Work with People?*
- Extension Activity, *Careers Helping People*
- Chapter Test

Student Workbook
- Study Guide
- Worksheet, *People Helping People*

CHAPTER OVERVIEW

Chapter 17 discusses careers that help people with relationships. Students are asked to make an inventory of their interpersonal skills valuable in this area. Students then learn about various jobs that involve helping people. Entry-level jobs include companions, aides to social workers, and hot-line operators. Jobs requiring some training are police officers, day-care workers, and physical therapist assistants. Jobs as family therapists, social workers, clergy, and psychologists require more advanced training.

INTRODUCING THE CHAPTER

Motivators

Helping Ask students to share experiences of helping other people with problems. After some examples have been discussed, say: "Some people choose a career that involves helping other people. People in these careers need special skills and qualities. This chapter will teach you about the special skills needed for a career that helps people, and it will teach you what kinds of jobs are available in this field of work."

Using the Photograph Ask students to look at the photograph on this page and describe what the people are doing. Ask: "Are you or would you like to be involved in the activities of a teen center? Why or why not?"

How Can People Help? Divide students into small groups, and have them brainstorm ideas that would help their fellow classmates (such as tutoring) or their family members or neighbors (such as becoming a day-care worker).

Introducing the Objectives

Discuss the chapter objectives on this page. Remind students that the objectives focus on important chapter content.

Introducing Vocabulary

Write *inventory* on the board, and pronounce it. Ask students to help define the term. Say: "An inventory is a survey of assets or goods. A personal inventory is a survey of a person's own assets or goods. How can having a personal inventory of your skills and qualities help you select a career?"

TEACHING THE CHAPTER

For convenience, the teaching suggestions for this chapter are arranged according to the following lesson topics:

Teaching "Helping People: Which Qualities Are Needed?"

(Pages 158-159)

This section identifies the interests and skills required for a career in working with people.

Checking Comprehension

✓ Define the term *client*. *A client is a person who is given help and information by a professional.*

✓ Why should a person in a career that helps people be a good listener? *Most of his or her working hours would be spent listening and talking to people with problems.*

✓ Why should professionals allow their clients to make independent decisions? *If they force their clients to take a certain action, it is very likely to fail.*

✓ Why are negotiating skills important to people working in careers that help people with relationships? *Problems in relationships involve compromise. The professional should be able to get each party to see the other's side so as to encourage compromise.*

Very often people need help in improving their relationships with others. Consider the following situations:

- Looking for new friends, you join a youth group at a community center, where a young adult plans activities for teens with common interests.
- Your best friend's family begins weekly meetings with a family therapist to help settle some conflicts peacefully.
- Your elderly neighbor has suddenly become a widow and hires a companion to avoid loneliness.

These are only a few of the situations that may require the help of workers with certain skills. Helping people improve their relationships with others can be the basis of a rewarding career.

Helping People: Which Qualities Are Needed?

Ask yourself some questions to find out whether you have the personal qualities that could lead to a career in helping people improve relationships. Many of the jobs focus on helping a **client**, a person who is given help and information by a professional. Most of your working hours would be spent listening to people with problems. Do you have many of the following qualities?

Interests and Skills

- **Do you relate well to people?** You need to understand people's fears and hopes, how they learn, and why they act as they do. Some of this knowledge comes from studying, but much is learned on the job.
- **Are you a good listener?** You need to learn about the particular client who wants help. You must be able to let the clients tell their story, while you keep an open mind.

This teenager enjoys tutoring other classmates. What qualities would she need for a job that focuses on helping others?

Emphasize It is important for people to know their interests and skills so that they can choose a career that will satisfy them and bring them personal gratification.

Focus on Health Tell students that finding a job that is personally satisfying is important. Stress from jobs has become a leading problem for workers, causing high blood pressure, ulcers, and heart attacks. Clinics and seminars have been developed all over the country to try to help people deal with job stress.

- **Can you allow the client to make independent decisions?** You must be careful to let the client choose what to do. If you force a client to take a certain action, it is very likely to fail.
- **Are you assertive?** If you are positive and confident, a client will be more inclined to trust your ability to help with problems.
- **Can you negotiate well?** With individuals, and especially with families, you may need to help clients see all the sides of a conflict. It is important for you to help them discuss their problems and reach a compromise.
- **Are you interested in people?** Listening to people with problems is often very demanding. Although you must be prepared to put a lot of energy into this type of work, the results can be very rewarding. One reward is the satisfaction of helping a client deal with a problem.
- **Do you have empathy?** You must have empathy, the ability to understand what the client is experiencing. You may feel that your client's problems are minor, but the client is likely to disagree. Being able to see a problem from the client's point of view is essential.
- **Can you be objective?** To help a client, you must be **objective**, or able to listen without becoming emotionally involved. Balancing empathy and objectivity is a great challenge.
- **Can you handle conflict?** By being calm, you can put a client who is very upset at ease. Often, this helps the client see solutions to the problem.
- **Are you trustworthy?** Since clients may reveal deep and important secrets, they need to feel confident that you will keep those secrets.

A Personal Inventory

Even if you are not ready to choose a specific career, it is a good idea to examine your goals and achievements. Then you will be more prepared in the future to decide which careers you might be suited for.

Making notes about what you discover about yourself will help you develop a **personal inventory**, or a review of your interests and skills. The chart below shows a method of organizing details about your interests, skills, and your future goals.

Finding Out About Yourself

What I like to do: ______________________

What I am good at: ______________________

Activities I enjoy: ______________________

Work I have done: ______________________

My goals for the future: ______________________

Jobs I think I would enjoy: ______________________

Emphasize Tell students that there is a difference between *empathy* and *sympathy.* Empathy goes beyond sympathy and calls for an active response of help.

Did You Know? Tell students that most helping professions are bound to uphold the confidentiality of their clients. Doctors have a code of ethics outlined in a promise called the Hippocratic Oath. Some lawyers and journalists have gone to jail because they would not reveal the information their clients or sources gave them.

✔ When dealing with a client, why is empathy an important quality? *Empathy is important because you need to be able to understand what the client is experiencing. Being able to see a problem from a client's point of view is essential.*

✔ Why should professionals be trustworthy? *To gain the trust of their clients and to honor the confidences their clients have shared, which may be deep and important secrets.*

✔ Why is it beneficial to develop a personal inventory of your skills and interests? *A personal inventory will better prepare you to decide which careers are best suited for you.*

Activities

Skill Builder: Writing
Have each student write a questionnaire that will help people assess their interests and skills. When they have completed the assignment, have them exchange questionnaires with another classmate. Then have them complete the questionnaire. You may want to discuss what students learned about themselves through completing the questionnaire.

Skill Builder: Critical Thinking
Ask students to think of someone they know who has a job that involves helping people. Ask volunteers to describe the person they are thinking about and to list the qualities that make him or her effective in the job.

Reteaching
Ask students to list ten skills or qualities that they should have before choosing a career that helps people.

Enrichment
Ask students to interview an adult who has a job that interests them. Tell them to find out what skills and qualities are required for a job such as the one that person has. Also tell them to find out what the job is really like—not just what the image of the job is. After they have completed the interview, ask students if they are still interested in that kind of job.

Teaching the Feature
"Fully Qualified"

Answers to Feature Questions

1. Students should note that homemaking is not easily defined. Also, because homemakers don't go off to an office or receive a paycheck, people often take their performance for granted. They don't realize how many skills, interests, and abilities are involved.

2. Students should consider the following: it would be necessary to break down the components of a homemaker's job and define what each is worth; figure out how much you would pay for comparable services; and determine where the money would come from to pay homemakers.

Activities

Class Debate Divide students into two groups, and have them debate whether a wife should be entirely responsible for homemaking or whether a husband and wife should share homemaking responsibilities.

Homemakers' Skills Have students list the skills that homemakers acquire that give them valuable experience for jobs outside the home.

Community Contact Divide students into small groups, and have them brainstorm for a community service that they could provide to help homemakers. For example, they could run a "gofer" service and do errands for busy homemakers. They may also provide some type of housecleaning service or help with plants and gardening. A third service might be to start a club for homemakers at which these workers could share their concerns and problems.

MANAGING RESOURCES

Fully Qualified

Nina Johnson and her mother are sitting in the living room of their home.

"Mom, Tim just told me that his mother is getting her master's degree in business administration. Isn't that great?" Nina says.

"Yes, it's wonderful. She certainly deserves it after working so hard," Mrs. Johnson replies.

"Why don't you go back to school, Mom? You're just as smart as Tim's mother. You should have a career, too," Nina says.

"I already have one. I'm a homemaker," Mrs. Johnson says.

"That's not a real career, like being a lawyer or a big executive. You know what I mean," Nina says. She stands up and gets her trombone. "So long, Mom," she says, waving. "I have band rehearsal at school."

After Nina leaves, Mrs. Johnson thinks for a minute, takes a notepad from the table, and begins to write. When she has finished, she folds the paper, puts it in an envelope with Nina's name on it, and leaves it in Nina's bedroom.

When Nina returns from school, she finds the envelope on her dresser. She tears it open and begins to read.

Memo to Nina from Mom:

Do you know anyone who could fill this job I heard about? There is a position available for a mature individual with at least fifteen years of experience in the following areas:

- **Instructor.** Giving direction to others.
- **Consultant.** Serving as a major source of information on a wide variety of subjects.
- **Scheduler.** Planning and organizing tasks to achieve specific goals.
- **Financial Planner.** Making budgets, distributing income, and paying expenses.
- **Manager of Human Resources.** Having chief responsibility for the health and safety of other human beings.

After reading the note, Nina looks for her mother. She finds her in the dining room. "Mom, what is this?" She holds up the note. "Are you really applying for this job?"

"No, I don't have to. I've had that job for fifteen years."

Nina looks at the note again and says, "Oh, I get it. You really do all those things as a homemaker, don't you?"

"I like to think so," Mrs. Johnson replies. "And I would like to hold on to my career as a homemaker. I think it suits me."

"You're right. I guess I just didn't think of it that way."

Think It Through

1. **Why is it hard for some people to accept the idea that homemaking is a career?**
2. **How would you go about paying homemakers for the work they do?**

Emphasize It is very easy to take someone for granted who is always there. Ask students to stop and think if they are taking the homemakers in their families for granted.

More About Homemaking Homemaking used to be more physically demanding than it is today. Clothes and dishes were washed by hand. Carpets were cleaned by beating them with a broom, and cooking could begin only after a fire had been built. Today, inventions such as vacuum cleaners and microwave ovens perform jobs more efficiently.

Jobs Working with People

You may have already decided that you want a job helping people deal with relationships. To prepare for such a job, you need to know how much training is required at each job level.

Some people are hired for **entry-level jobs**, or those jobs for which little or no experience is needed. Jobs at the next level require some training. That training could be education in a community college or technical school, work in an apprenticeship program, or on-the-job training.

The third group of jobs requires at least a degree from a four-year college. Some jobs call for higher degrees as well, such as master's, doctorate, or medical degrees.

Entry-Level Jobs

A companion may help a person who is elderly, disabled, or recovering from illness. If you work as a companion, you might keep house, prepare meals, and even entertain the client. Companions can work full-time or part-time. They may live in the home of the person they care for, in which case they might get room and board along with a wage. Experience working in a hospital can be helpful for this job.

Government agencies hire social worker aides. **Aides** are workers who assist higher-level workers with their jobs. Some ask clients questions to learn whether they are eligible for income or jobs programs. Others explain programs to clients and provide information. Social worker aides also can work part-time or full-time. Typing skills can be valuable for this job.

Many support groups have hot lines, telephone numbers that people can call for emergency help. Some hot lines help people who are thinking about committing suicide. Others assist people with drug problems. Since they offer important care to people who need it right away, hot-line workers need to be calm and understanding. Most programs train their workers, but college courses in counseling will help.

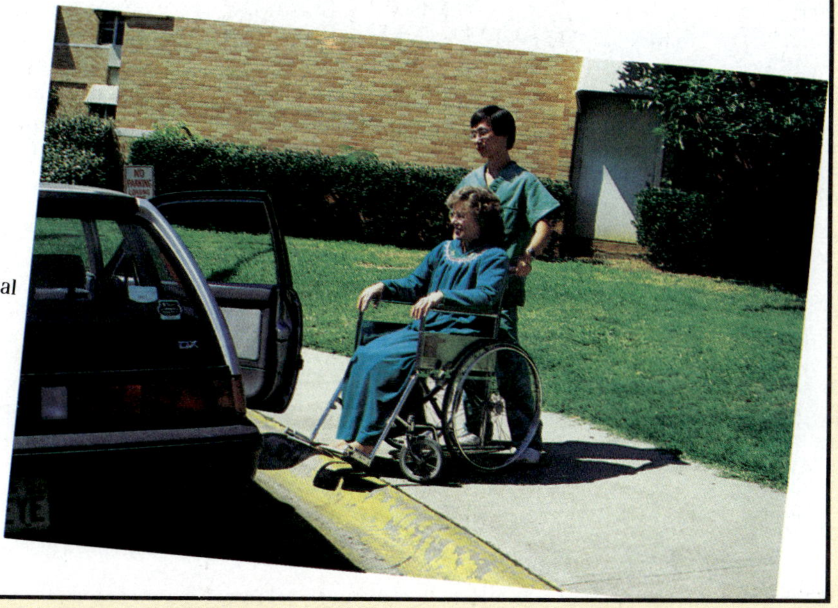

Medical assistants provide health care services at medical offices and hospitals.

Did You Know? Some companion-type jobs require a person to care for another's pet. This is known as dogsitting or catsitting or even birdsitting.

Focus on Entrepreneurship Ask students to think about what is involved in working in a child care center. Tell them to list responsibilities they could take on if they did volunteer to work at a child care center.

Teaching "Jobs Working with People"
(Pages 161-163)

This section gives examples of jobs that involve helping people.

Checking Comprehension

- Explain what a companion does. *A companion helps other people who are elderly, disabled, or recovering from an illness.*
- Describe the functions that aides perform. *Aides assist higher-level workers. They can perform typing duties, explain programs to clients, and provide general information.*
- What is a hot line, and what do hot-line workers do? *A hot line is a telephone number that people can call for emergency help in a crisis. Hot-line workers must be able to help people who are thinking about committing suicide, have a drug problem, or are otherwise in a crisis situation.*
- Explain a medical assistant's job. *A medical assistant works with doctors and nurses in providing health care.*
- What must a person first do to become a police officer? *To become a police officer, a person must first pass a test.*
- Explain what physical therapist assistants do. *Physical therapist assistants help people who are recovering from illness or injury. They use equipment, exercise, and massage to help patients overcome their physical problems or pain.*
- Where can family therapists work? *Family therapists can work for clinics and hospitals or in their own private practice.*
- What do social workers do? *Social workers help individuals and families deal with problems. They can provide advice and counseling as well as hold classes for clients.*
- How do religious workers train for their job? *Training for religious workers varies from religion to religion, but most have studied at a religious school and have a college degree.*

✓ What training is required to be a psychologist? *Psychologists have a college degree and usually an advanced degree. They also get extra training by talking with patients and helping them resolve problems.*

Activities

Skill Builder: Writing
Have students select one of the jobs they have just read about and write a letter of inquiry to a prospective employer, stating why they would like the job. Remind them to tell the employer about the skills and qualities they have that would make them a good person to hire.

Skill Builder: Critical Thinking
Have students think of other careers that help people. One example would be lawyers. Ask students to list skills and qualities they think would be needed for each career they mention.

Reteaching
Have students write down three jobs (one at each level) that help people. Then have them describe what each job entails.

Enrichment
Invite two or three people who have jobs working with people to come to the school and give presentations to students. Suggest that students prepare questions for the guest speakers ahead of time.

A medical assistant works with doctors and nurses in providing health care: you might handle office records, do lab work, or do simple physical tests on patients. Most medical assistants work in doctors' offices, though some are employed by hospitals. Usually, they are trained on the job, but some junior colleges offer courses.

Jobs That Require Training

Among their many duties, police officers sometimes handle emergency family problems. In such instances, it is very important for them to act calmly, since situations involving family violence can be dangerous. To become a police officer, you must first pass a test. Then you will be trained in a police academy. The number of jobs in police work is expected to grow in the future, so there will be many openings for applicants.

Many police officers are called upon to handle emergency family problems.

Child care workers care for preschool children whose parents work. These workers help the children grow emotionally, socially, and mentally. Because many families are now headed by a single parent who works, or by two parents who both work, the demand for child care workers is growing. Training can be obtained on the job, although some employers require a degree from a two-year or four-year college.

Physical therapist assistants help people who are recovering from illness or an injury. Physical therapist assistants use equipment, exercise, and massage to help patients overcome their physical problems or pain. They might also instruct patients in using wheelchairs or braces. Training is given in two-year colleges.

Jobs That Require an Advanced Degree

Some jobs require a college degree or additional study. Sometimes a master's degree is needed and sometimes even a doctorate.

Families that are having conflicts often turn to family therapists. These highly trained people work with the whole family rather than with one or two individuals. They can work for clinics and hospitals, or in private practice. Family therapists must have a college degree and usually a master's degree.

More About Psychologists Psychologists are divided into several fields of study. Social psychologists research areas of human behavior and thought. Clinical psychologists counsel people with problems. Industrial psychologists use their expertise to help workers in various areas of business.

Focus on Life Management Ask students to think about a career they would like to have. Then have them write down a course of action that would help them find out more about the career in which they are interested.

Social workers help individuals and families deal with problems, such as obtaining help from various agencies. They can provide advice and counseling, as well as hold classes for clients. Social workers may be based in schools, hospitals, or government agencies. Most have a college degree and a master's degree as well.

Many people turn to a religious worker or a member of the **clergy** such as priests, ministers, rabbis, and mullahs when they need help. These people can be important sources of comfort and advice. Training for religious workers varies from one religion to another, but a college degree and study at a religious school are the usual requirements.

Psychologists study how the mind works. They offer counseling to clients who want therapy. Psychologists may work in a hospital or have their own practice. These professionals have a college degree and usually an advanced degree. They also get extra training by talking with patients and helping them resolve difficulties.

Following Up

The more you plan and prepare ahead in pursuing your career goals, the better off you are. Here are three suggestions to follow if you think you might be interested in a career helping people:

- Talk to school guidance counselors. They can help you determine whether you would be happy in a career that involves dealing with people's problems. They might also suggest ways for you to gain a little experience to help you decide.
- Ask students who have spent time caring for small children or for people with disabilities to share their experiences with you. You will then have a better idea of what it means to meet the needs of people who may not be independent.
- Volunteer for several hours a week at a child care center, hot-line service, or other facility in your community that provides aid to people. Having direct contact with social service centers can help you decide whether a career helping people is a good choice for you.

Religious leaders can provide counseling for both individuals and families.

Real-Life Situations Volunteers provide valuable services to community organizations, health care facilities, and voluntary agencies. Groups such as Boy Scouts, Girl Scouts, and 4-H have volunteer leaders. Parent-teacher organizations (PTO, PTA), recreational athletic teams, and booster clubs depend on volunteer help. Many towns have volunteer fire departments and ambulance corps. Programs such as Meals-on-Wheels, Hospice, and Foster Grandparents provide special services. Volunteers work at hospitals, nursing homes, and special-care facilities. Many agencies, such as the American Red Cross, March of Dimes, and United Cerebral Palsy Association, depend upon volunteer help. Ask students what volunteer groups aid your community.

Teaching "Following Up"

(Page 163)

This section offers suggestions for finding out more about careers that help people.

Checking Comprehension

✓ How can talking to a guidance counselor or an experienced person help people decide about a career? *Talking to such a person can give people more information about a career. They can also get a better idea of what training is needed for the job.*

✓ How can volunteer work help people decide about careers? *Volunteer work gives them firsthand knowledge of the job. Volunteer work can also give people job experience they can apply to future jobs.*

Activities

Skill Builder: Writing
Ask students to think about the skills and qualities that are important for teaching. Then ask them to find out what kind of training a teacher needs. Then tell them to write a brief essay about why they would like to be a teacher or why not.

Reteaching
Have students tell you three ways to find out more about a career in helping people.

Enrichment
Ask students to think of a way they could help people—babysitting, tutoring, being a companion, helping in a day-care center. Ask them to find time to perform one of these activities and share the experience with the class.

Enrichment
Invite a guest speaker to come and talk about a job interview. Have the person explain what to do and not to do, and what to expect. Have them discuss what rights the interviewer has, ie. what can be asked about marriage status, age, number of children, etc.

Introducing "Ways to Let Off Steam"

(Pages 166-167)

Motivators

I really got angry when . . . . Write this phrase on the chalkboard. Ask students to complete the thought by writing a description of one situation in which they became angry. Reassure them that anger is a normal and acceptable feeling. Call on volunteers to read their responses to the class. Have students save their work for use later.

Discussion Question: Ask students: "What do you do when you get angry?" Allow several students to respond. They may start by relating how they handled the situation described in the previous activity, but let them also talk about other ways they customarily deal with anger. Point out that recognizing and dealing with anger is important, but that "exploding" or "blowing your top" is not usually the most appropriate or effective response. Tell students that this section will suggest ways in which they can calm down and gain time to deal with anger more effectively.

Teaching "Ways to Let Off Steam"

Checking Comprehension

✓ Which techniques will help you avoid "blowing up" immediately in reaction to something that angers you? *Numbers 1 (counting), 2 (deep breathing), and 3 (calling a time out).*

✓ Anger is a physical emotion that gives you a great deal of energy. Which techniques focus primarily on using up some of the energy? *Numbers 2 (deep breathing), 7 (exercising), and 9 (hugging pillow).*

✓ What purpose do you think is served by the techniques of writing about your anger and calling a friend? *These techniques aim primarily at helping you begin to communicate and understand the anger.*

TEEN TIPS

Ways to Let Off Steam

Anger is perfectly normal, and "blowing off steam" can be a healthy way to clear the air. When you are angry and don't express it, tension builds. Anger held inside too long can cause headaches, backaches, and stomach troubles. Unexpressed anger can even cause depression.

If you put off dealing with anger, you may end up hurting others or getting into trouble. Often, bottled-up anger results in a big explosion when it comes. An angry outburst usually makes it harder to solve the problem that caused your anger.

Here are ten helpful ways to let off steam:

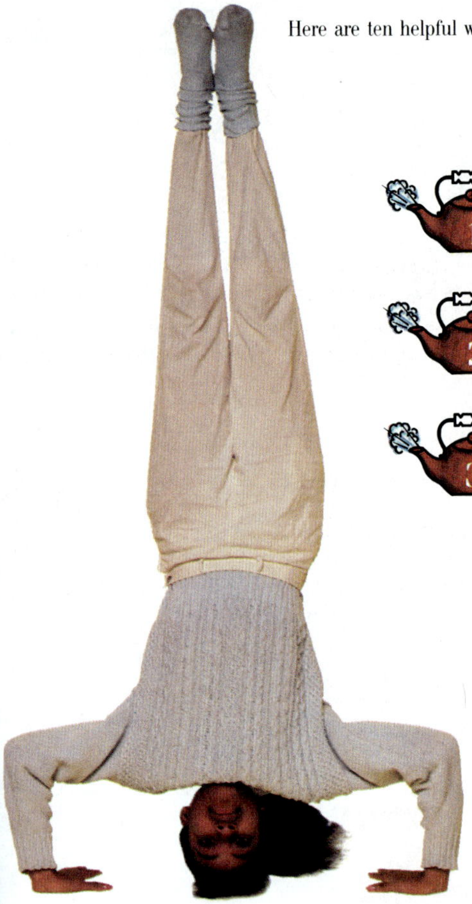

1 Count to 10. Better yet, count to 20. Or say the alphabet out loud.

2 Breathe deeply, concentrating on your breathing, until you feel calmer.

3 Call a time-out. Go into another room or outside until you cool off.

Emphasize Ask students what they've heard about anger from their parents or other authority figures. Some students will probably have encountered such misconceptions as the belief that anger is unfeminine or unmasculine and that expressing anger is not "nice." Discuss these and any other misconceptions that surface. Suggest that students construct imaginary dialogues in which they refute someone who believes one of the misconceptions about anger.

TEEN TIPS

4. Get a pencil and notebook and write down what you're feeling. What caused the anger?

5. Put on your favorite tape or turn on the radio and play some quiet music.

6. Phone a friend. If you can't reach a friend, phone for the weather.

7. Do some sit-ups, go for a run, or ride a bike.

8. Splash some cold water on your face or take a hot bubble bath.

9. Hug a pillow.

10. Lie down on the floor and concentrate on a spot on the ceiling.

Focus on Relationship Skills The ability to express anger appropriately is an essential interpersonal skill. The work students did in the previous unit on communicating about feelings can be considered in light of communicating about anger. Students might wish to role play situations showing anger between friends.

Activities

Skill Builder: Writing
Have students research and write short reports on the body's production of adrenalin, focusing on its role in anger and its effects on the body.

Reteaching
Have students refer to the situations they described at the beginning of the lesson. Ask them to think about which techniques for letting off steam might have been useful in dealing with this situation. Call on volunteers to name the techniques they chose and discuss why these would have been effective in the situation.

Enrichment
Divide the class into two groups. Give one group the statement "Anger can be useful" the other "Anger can be scary." Point out that both statements are accurate; then ask each group to list statements that support its statement. Students may do library research on their topics, discuss them with school counselors or other adults, or simply discuss them among themselves. Instruct each group to prepare a report summarizing what they've learned and to choose a spokesperson to report to the class. Discuss each group's report. Encourage students to talk about how they feel about their own anger.

Introducing "Ten Ways to Say 'No' to Alcohol and Drugs"
(Pages 168-169)

Motivators

What causes substance abuse? Ask students to consider why drug and alcohol abuse is so common among teenagers today. Be sure to point out that teens who engage in substance abuse may do it to escape from painful realities. Ask students to consider whether such behavior really solves any problems.

Discussion Question: Ask students: "Why is it hard to say 'no'?" Discuss the question and record responses on the chalkboard. (Possible answers include difficulty in withstanding peer pressure, the desire to seem "cool," the need to be accepted, and the desire to escape from problems.)

Teaching "Ten Ways to Say 'No' to Alcohol and Drugs"

Checking Comprehension

✓ Which techniques do you think are the most useful, and why? *Answers will vary. Accept any that include a reasonable rationale.*

✓ Which techniques do you think would be the most difficult to do, and why? *Again, accept any answer that is reasonable and supported.*

TEEN TIPS

Ten Ways to Say "No" to Alcohol and Drugs

Imagine this: You've been hanging around with a group of friends and having a great time. You really like these people because you seem to have a lot in common. Then you discover that the group wants you to drink alcohol or take drugs. How can you say "no" to your friends?

Here are ten ways to resist peer pressure:

1 **Just say "No."** Keep your response short and your voice firm. Let your facial expression tell your friends exactly how you feel about their pressure. Shake your head and say:
"I'll pass."
"I'm not interested."
"Forget it."

2 **Leave the situation.** You don't have to explain your reasons for saying no. When you walk away, your actions speak louder than words.

3 **Ignore the offer.** Pretend to read a book. Be distracted by someone else. Just don't listen.

Focus on Decision Making Have students consider the interpersonal dynamics that occur when one friend urges another to use drugs or alcohol, or to do anything else potentially harmful. Discuss what might make one person urge another to use drugs or alcohol and what might make a person agree to do so. Ask students to think about whether a really good friend would ask another to join him or her in a clearly harmful activity. Also invite students to think about what they would do if they knew a friend or relative was engaging in substance abuse.

TEEN TIPS

4 Make an excuse. Think of something you could or should be doing instead.
"I've got other plans."
"I have to practice ____________." (the piano, football, dancing, etc.)
"I promised I'd be home by _______ o'clock."

5 Change the subject. Pick a topic that will get their interest or take them by surprise.

6 Make a joke. Use humor and say: "Are you kidding? If I did that, my reputation might improve."
"Sorry, I'd like to but I need to spend more time with my plants."
"No thanks. I'm not into body pollution."

7 Act shocked. Show that you can't believe what your friends have asked you to do. Roll your eyes, let your mouth drop open, and say:
"I can't believe what I just heard."
"I know you didn't mean that. How did I pick such crazy friends?"

8 Try flattery. Say something kind and thoughtful to one of your friends.
"You're too smart to really mean that."
"You're too good a friend. I don't want to see you do anything crazy and get hurt."

9 Suggest a better idea. Suggest something else to do—say it with excitement and enthusiasm.
"Hey, I've got a good idea. Let's go get pizza or burgers."
"Why don't we ____________?" (go biking, practice shooting baskets, play a video game, etc.)

10 Return the challenge. If someone calls you a "chicken" because you won't ;join them, throw the challenge right back with a comment such as:
"Scared to do it by yourself?"
"Yeah, I'm a chicken. Anybody smart would be."
"I'd rather by a chicken than a jailbird."

Activities

Skill Builder: Critical Thinking
Have students collect magazine and newspaper advertisements for cigarettes and alcohol. Ask them to evaluate these advertisements, focusing on what the ads appeal to (for example, the desire to look glamorous or to appear more masculine). Discuss the students' conclusions in class. Ask students what relationship might exist between the prevalence of such ads and the problem of drug and alcohol abuse, particularly among teenagers. Be sure to point out that advertisements encourage teenagers to feel smoking or drinking makes them appear glamorous and grown-up. You might wish to expand the discussion to advertisements for over-the-counter medications, such as painkillers or diet pills. Discuss whether such advertisements encourage people to rely too much on taking pills and how this might relate to serious drug and alcohol abuse.

Reteaching
Have students role play saying "no." Divide the class into pairs, and assign each pair one technique described in this section. One student will play the person offering drugs or alcohol; the other, the "refuser." Let the pairs develop a realistic scenario for their role play, and then have them act it out. Volunteers may present their role plays before the entire group. You may also have the pairs switch roles and act out a second scenario. Discuss how students felt using their particular technique in the role play and how effective they feel it would be in a real situation.

Enrichment
Bring in a speaker from a drug and alcohol rehabilitation facility, a counseling office, the police department, or any other appropriate group to discuss the problem of substance abuse and ways of saying "no." As an alternative, students can interview people who work with substance abusers and write newspaper-type interviews for the class to read.

Cross-Reference You may wish to have students read Chapter 3, "Your Health and Wellness" to review the harmful effects of substance abuse.

Introducing "Suicide: Twelve Warning Sings"
(Pages 170-171)

Motivators

What would you do if . . .? Ask students to discuss what they would do if a friend said to them, "I feel so terrible that I can't go on." Let students discuss the question for a few minutes, then comment that a statement like this, and many other actions or statements, might indicate that someone is considering taking his or her own life.

Discussion Question: Ask students: "What movies or television shows have you seen or books have you read that have dealt with suicide?" Let students share their experiences for a few more minutes. Then ask them how they felt about the movie, show, or book. Point out that suicide is a leading cause of death among young people and that discussing it is one way of dealing with the problem and preventing its spread. Tell the students that this section will focus on recognizing when someone is feeling suicidal.

Teaching "Suicide: Twelve Warning Signs"

Checking Comprehension

✓ What are some similarities among these 12 signs? *Many indicate sudden changes in usual behavior and interests. Many indicate that the person is feeling depressed and lacking self-esteem.*

✓ A lack or loss of self-esteem is often the cause of suicidal thoughts. Which of the signs described here most clearly indicate such a loss? *Withdrawal from friends or job; loss of interest in appearance; substance abuse; crying and depression; a sense of failure, shame, or guilt.*

Suicide — Twelve Warning Signs

Each year, more than 8,000 teenagers commit suicide. Suicide is now the third leading cause of death for 15- to 24-year-olds. Many teens who commit suicide feel unable to handle the pressures in their lives—at home, at school, or with their friends.

For many teens, attempting to commit suicide is a way of asking for help or of getting attention. Many teens who tried suicide later admitted that they hoped they would be found before it was too late. Fortunately, they were—others were not so lucky.

Professional counselors feel that many suicides can be prevented if help is obtained when warning signs appear. How can you know if someone is feeling suicidal? Here are some warning signals:

- A sudden change in behavior characterized by withdrawal, rebellion, irritability, or taking extreme risks.
- A dramatic change in eating or sleep patterns—eating or sleeping too much or too little.
- Social withdrawal—dropping out of activities, quitting a job, or spending less time with friends.
- Sudden drop in grades or performance; lateness or absence from school or work.

TEEN TIPS

Emphasize Discuss appropriate responses to a person who appears to be considering suicide. Emphasize that students should not try to act as counselors, but should encourage the person to seek professional help. Point out that usually the concern should be communicated to an adult, and as quickly as possible. In this regard, discuss the question of confidentiality. Help students see that they should avoid promising secrecy when facing potential suicide attempts. Discuss whether such promises, if made, should be disregarded. Point out that enduring anger over a broken promise would be easier to bear than the knowledge that one might have prevented a friend's suicide.

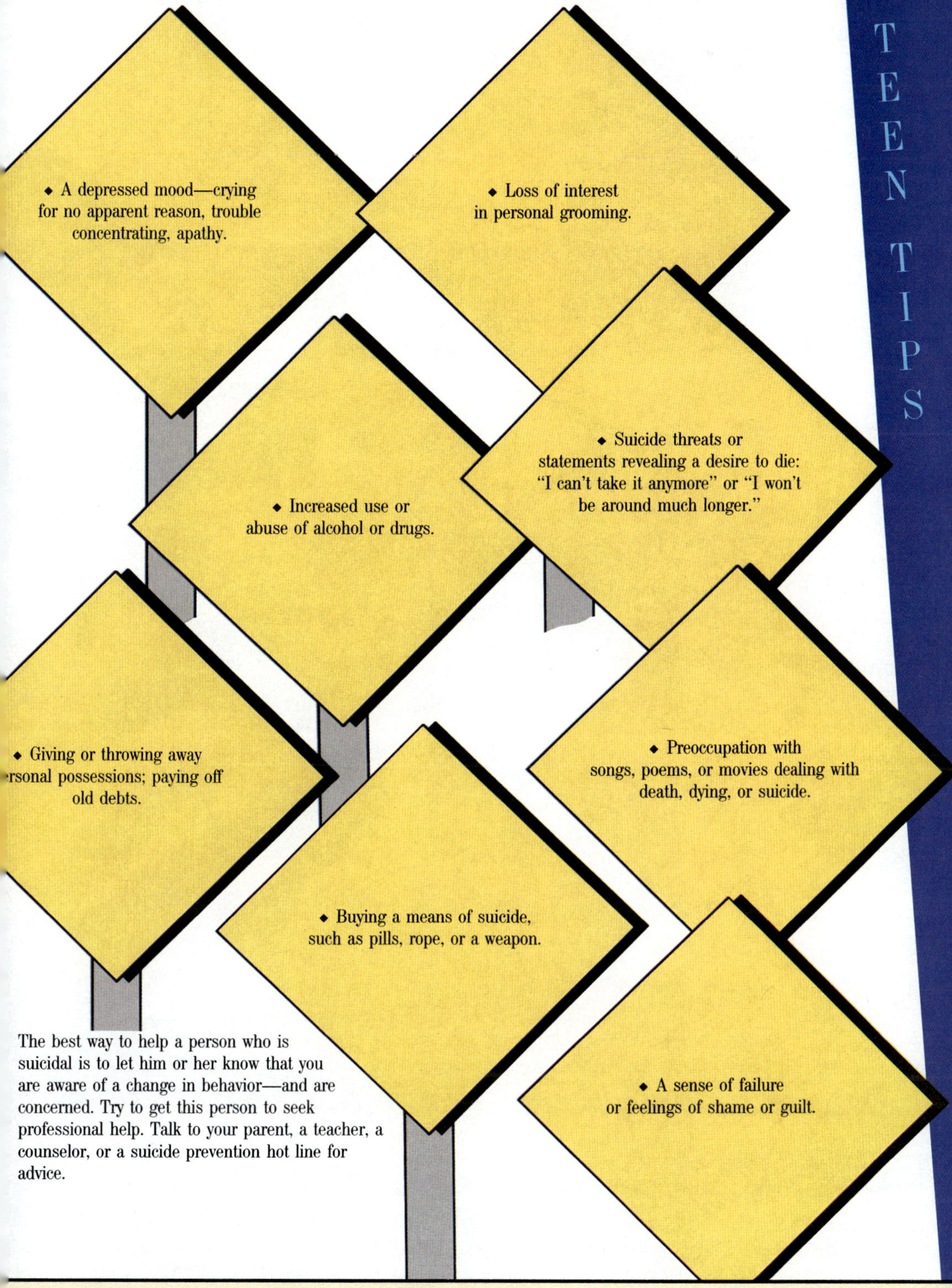

The best way to help a person who is suicidal is to let him or her know that you are aware of a change in behavior—and are concerned. Try to get this person to seek professional help. Talk to your parent, a teacher, a counselor, or a suicide prevention hot line for advice.

Focus on Communication Much has been written on communicating about feelings. Encourage students to research this topic and report their findings to the class. If this subject is of special interest, students can develop role plays or skits to illustrate techniques for responding to emotionally upset people.

TEEN TIPS

✔ What feelings do you think are associated with suicidal thoughts? *Loss of self-esteem; feelings of loneliness, hopelessness, frustration, sadness, grief; pressure to succeed.*

✔ What should you do if you think someone is considering suicide? *Let the person know you are aware of a change in behavior, and encourage him or her to get professional help.*

Activities

Skill Builder: Writing
Ask students to review the twelve warning signs. Direct them to write one or two sentences that summarize these signs. Have volunteers read their summaries to the class and evaluate them.

Reteaching
Ask students to choose one warning sign and imagine a friend is exhibiting it. Have them write a description of the friend's behavior in detail and their reaction. Suggest that writing a dialogue could be very appropriate for this activity. Call on volunteers to share their work with the class. Class members can discuss the behavior described.

Enrichment
Divide the class into small groups to discuss how they would feel toward a person who seemed suicidal. Encourage students to be completely honest in their discussion, and point out that natural feelings include not only sympathy but also such feelings as anger, fear, or guilt. Tell the groups each to choose a spokesperson who will summarize and present the group's findings to the class. Discuss each group's findings. If you wish, some or all groups can focus on feelings about people who actually commit suicide.

UNIT PREVIEW

Unit 3 deals with child development and child care. Students learn how to meet a child's needs and make decisions and plan activities appropriate to the child's stage of development. Students learn that safety is the primary responsibility of a caregiver. They discover the benefits of babysitting include the opportunity to earn money and to learn more about children. Parenthood is presented as a rewarding part of many people's lives that involves financial and emotional costs. Students also explore jobs and careers that involve working with and for children.

CONTENT DEVELOPMENT

Use these lessons to reinforce the following themes:

Content Strands	Chapters
Career Exploration	18,22,24
Citizenship/ Leadership	22,24
Communication	19,21
Decision Making	18,19,20,23
Health and Safety	18,20-23,(TT 1,2)
Managing Resources	18,22
Personal Development	18,20,22,23

UNIT MOTIVATORS

Decision-Making Skills

Which Toys? Suggest that students investigate the toys available for children in their area. Have them draw, describe, or provide pictures of toys that they would recommend to parents. They should write a brief note for each toy explaining the ages for which it is appropriate and why they think it would be a useful and entertaining toy.

Critical Thinking Skills

Classify and Evaluate Jobs Have students use the classified section of a newspaper to find jobs that involve children. Have them classify the jobs according to whether they involve working with or for children. Then have students select the job that most appeals to them. Have them write a list of duties they think the job requires and explain how the employment would suit their characteristics.

CROSS-CURRICULAR ACTIVITY

Physical Education and Child Care Have students demonstrate exercises and games for building motor skills in young children (for example, running, marching, skipping, rolling a ball). They can ask a preschool teacher or a physical education teacher for suggestions.

SPECIAL NEEDS

Strategies for Students Having Difficulty Arrange for students to tutor children at a nearby elementary school. Students might listen to the children read a story, help them practice their multiplication tables, or drill them on vocabulary words. Students will gain self-esteem by being able to help others.

CHILD CARE AND DEVELOPMENT

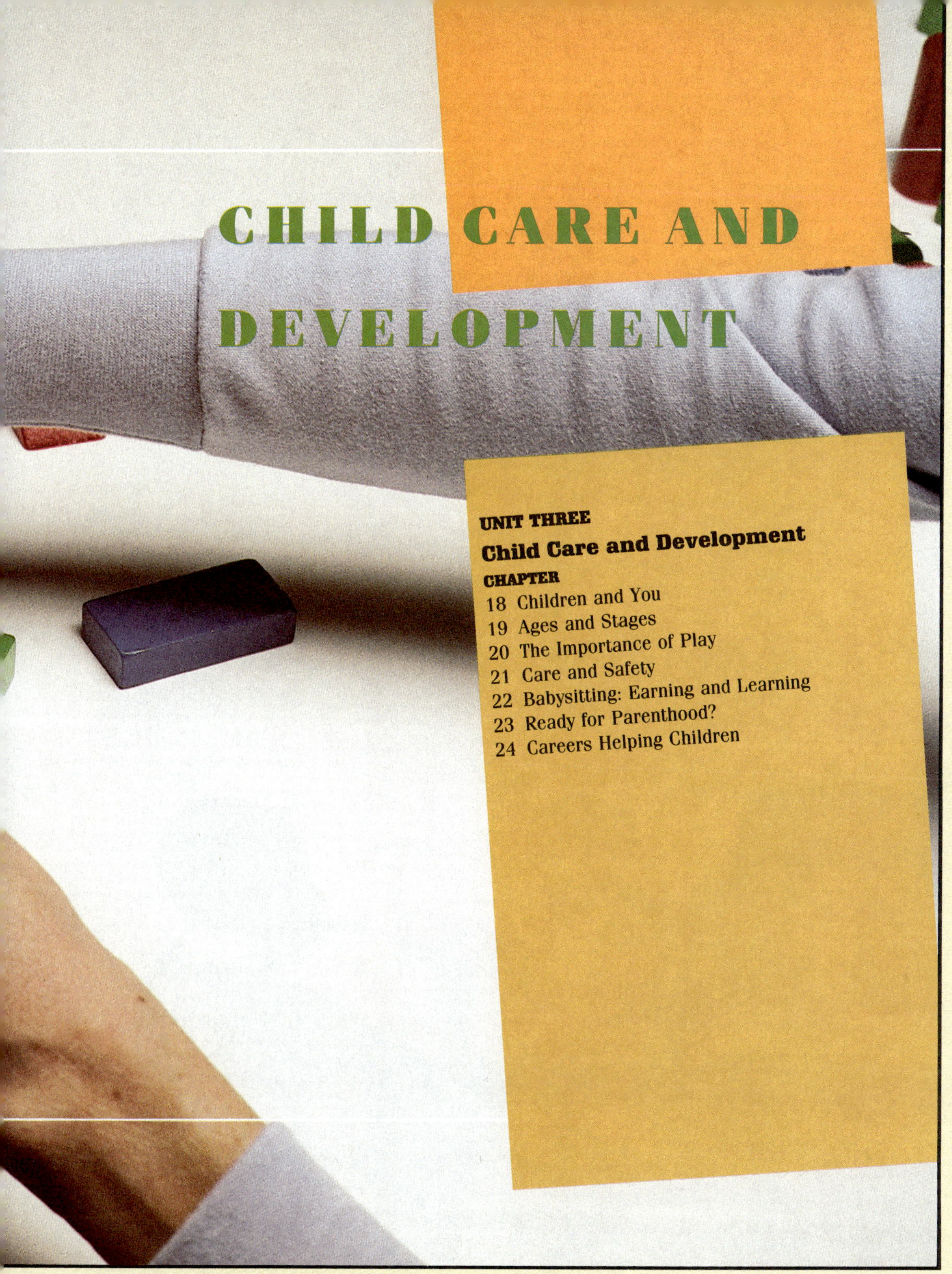

UNIT THREE

Child Care and Development

COOPERATIVE LEARNING

My Book About. . . Divide students into several small groups. Have them design and make a book to teach a concept to a young child. For example, they might make a book to teach a child the alphabet or colors. The book might teach a child to count, to tell time, or to manipulate fasteners (shoelaces, snaps, buttons, zippers, and so on). Books could be constructed using a variety of materials, including construction paper and cloth. Each member of the group should be responsible for making one or more pages of the book. Completed books might be presented to children in day-care center.

FHA ACTIVITIES

The following activities can be used with your FHA group or as public relation strategies:

Safety Handbook Have students prepare a "safety workbook" to use with a younger group of children. Ask the Board of Education to run copies and give them out at the elementary school. Have students use various formats for the worksheets, such as a connect-the-dots, word search, or coloring book. Emphasize that all pages should contain the safety theme.

Babysitting Services On a Saturday or during the holidays, open a free babysitting service for parents. Have students prepare educational games, songs, and activities that could be played with the children.

Children and Television Have students observe four or five children's programs on television. Ask them to develop a list as to why the programs are good or not good for children. Have them compare their responses to their classmate's and compile a list of all programs viewed by class members. They should develop a "Nielsen's" rating for children's programming, using a rating scale of 1-5 (1 = excellent; 5 = poor).

UNIT CLOSURE

For Review

Letter to Future Child Suggest that students write a letter to their future child. In the letter have students explain what they would do as a parent to meet their child's physical, mental, and social needs.

For Evaluation

Unit Test Have students complete the Unit Test that appears in the *Teacher's Classroom Resources.*

Testmaker Software You may wish to design a unit test using the Testmaker software program.

CHAPTER OVERVIEW

Chapter 18 introduces students to the term *caregiver* and explains the difference between main caregivers (usually parents) and part-time caregivers (for example babysitters, nannies). It explores the rewards of caregiving and emphasizes the need for decision-making skills. The three basic parenting skills—providing physical care, nurturing, and giving guidance—are explored in detail. Students learn about the management skills needed in parenting as well as about the personal qualities caregivers need.

INTRODUCING THE CHAPTER

Motivators

What Is a Parent? Write the phrase, "A parent is someone who . . ." on the board. Ask students to complete the sentence in as many ways as they can. Explain that their answers indicate that parents have many roles and that this chapter will be exploring what parents and other caregivers do.

Using the Photograph Have students study the photograph on this page. Then ask: "What situation is shown here? What personal qualities can you detect in this caregiver?"

Who Is a Caregiver? Explain that almost everyone is a part-time caregiver at sometime in his or her life. Prove this by asking for a show of hands from students who either have had babysitting experience or have cared for younger siblings.

Introducing the Objectives

Discuss the chapter objectives on this page. Remind students that the objectives focus on important chapter content.

Introducing Vocabulary

Tell students that they will see the word *caregiver* many times in this chapter. Point out the roots *care* and *give* and explain that a caregiver is literally someone who gives care.

CHAPTER 18

Children and You

OBJECTIVES

This chapter will help you to:

- Explain the rewards of caregiving.
- Identify the needs of children that are met by parenting.
- Explain the difference between parenting and parenthood.
- Explain the roles of nurturing and guidance in a child's development.
- Describe the resources used in parenting.

WORDS TO REMEMBER

caregiver
guidance
nurture
parenting

Chapter Resources

Teacher's Classroom Resources
Lesson Plan
Life Skills Activity, *On-the-Scene Parenting*
Reproducible Master, *Parenting Tasks*
Extension Activity, *What Is Parenting?*
Chapter Test

Student Workbook
Study Guide
Worksheet, *What Is a Caregiver?*

Monica is feeling good; she is happy about the money she has earned babysitting and pleased that her day has gone so well. She is proud of the way she has handled the Vega children. Mrs. Vega even complimented her on her work and told her that she recommended her to a neighbor who needed a babysitter two days a week.

Monica thinks of herself as a babysitter, but she can also be called a caregiver. A **caregiver** is someone who takes care of children or who cares for people who are sick or elderly. Because Monica works only occasionally, she is called a part-time caregiver. The people who take the main responsibility for rearing children, usually the parents, are called main caregivers.

Many people, including grandparents, older brothers and sisters, and babysitters, can be caregivers. Have you had any experience being a caregiver?

Rewards of Caregiving

Many young people enjoy working as part-time caregivers. They often begin to learn the skills they need to take care of children by caring for younger brothers and sisters. Then, when they feel comfortable enough to manage other people's children, they seek jobs as babysitters, camp counselors, and similar occupations. The skills they develop and the trust adults place in them help to build their self-esteem.

Through her babysitting job, Monica is earning extra money, learning skills for the future, and showing that she is a dependable and responsible employee. Monica's goals in this job are to take good care of the children, to please her employer, and to earn money.

If she has children of her own someday, she will find that her child-care goal is somewhat different. She will still want to do a good job, but for different reasons. Her goal then will be long-term: to rear happy, healthy children who will grow into responsible, well-adjusted adults.

Emphasize Getting a recommendation from an employer is important. Suggest that students ask for a written recommendation when they babysit. That way they will have something they can use to reassure potential new employers.

Focus on Decision Making Suggest that students refresh their memory of the decision-making process by re-reading the relevant section in Chapter 5.

TEACHING THE CHAPTER

For convenience, the teaching suggestions for this chapter are arranged according to the following lesson topics:

Teaching "Rewards of Caregiving"

(Pages 175-176)

This section teaches the rewards to be gained from caring for children.

Checking Comprehension

✓ What do part-time and full-time caregivers have in common? *They both have to make many decisions.*

✓ How do Monica's responsibilities as a babysitter compare with the responsibilities of a parent? *Her current responsibility is limited. As a parent, her responsibility would last over years and be more complete.*

Activities

Skill Builder: Critical Thinking
Ask students to compare and contrast the roles of full-time and part-time caregivers. What are the main similarities? What are the main differences?

Reteaching
To help students understand that caregivers need decision-making skills, ask them to list some of the decisions they had to make when they worked as babysitters.

Enrichment
Discuss with students the current rates of pay for babysitting in their community. Have students compare methods of payment and decide on what they think is a fair rate for the job.

Teaching "What Is Parenting?"
(Pages 176-178)

This section teaches how parenting meets the needs of children, explains the difference between parenting and parenthood, and explores nurturing and guidance.

Checking Comprehension

✓ What does *parenting* mean? *Meeting children's physical, emotional, mental, and social needs.*

✓ List some people who can share parenting responsibilities. *Parents, babysitters, grandparents, older siblings, child care center employees.*

✓ What kinds of food should caregivers provide for children? *Nutritious meals and snacks that provide all the vitamins, minerals, and nutrients that growing bodies need.*

✓ What factors should caregivers consider when choosing clothes for children? *Clothes should keep children warm and dry; they should be appropriate for the weather and (for older children) be easy to put on and take off.*

✓ How can caregivers help ensure that children get the rest they need? *They can develop a routine for daily naps and a regular bedtime.*

✓ What hygiene skills should a caregiver teach young children? *To wash themselves, to brush their teeth, to go to the bathroom by themselves.*

✓ Why do caregivers have to protect children from accidents? *Because children are not aware of the dangers of stairs, electric outlets, or poisons.*

✓ What kinds of stimulation do infants need in order to learn? *Chances to see, hear, touch, taste, and smell.*

✓ How can caregivers show children that they really care about them? *By giving love, affection, and a sense of security.*

✓ Compare the roles of parents and part-time caregivers in setting limits. *Parents set limits. Part-time caregivers remind children of what the limits are and make sure children stick to them.*

If you are either a part-time or full-time caregiver, you have to make many decisions. The decision-making skills that you learned in Chapter 5 can help you.

When Monica sat for the Vega children, she had to decide:

- What can I do to stop the baby's crying?
- How will I give her a bottle and fix lunch for the older child at the same time?
- What activities are fun for a two-year-old?

By making decisions such as these, Monica is developing her management skills.

As a part-time babysitter, Monica was responsible for the Vega children for only a few hours. If she were the children's parent, she would be responsible for them for years, and she would have to make dozens of decisions daily that would affect them throughout their lives.

What Is Parenting?

Parenting involves taking care of children in all the ways that children require. It means meeting children's physical, emotional, mental, and social needs.

Parenting is not the same as *parenthood*, which means to be a father or mother of a child. Many people use parenting skills, including parents and babysitters. In some families, parenting is shared by the parents, grandparents, older brothers and sisters, and child caregivers. Parenting involves three basic skills: providing physical care, nurturing, and giving guidance.

Physical Care

- **Food.** Caregivers are responsible for providing nutritious meals and snacks to help children grow and develop. They should offer a wide variety of foods to ensure giving children a balanced diet with all of the vitamins, minerals, and nutrients that growing bodies need.

  Infants begin by drinking either milk from their mother or formula. During the first year, they begin eating strained foods and, later, food cut in small pieces. As they get older, children can eat the same meals as adults.

  Caregivers should avoid giving children rich, spicy, or fried foods, which can upset a child's digestion, or foods that are high in sugar, salt, or fat. They should also avoid giving very young children foods like nuts and popcorn, which can get stuck in a child's throat.
- **Clothing.** Caregivers must provide proper clothing for children so that they are kept warm and dry. Infants need fresh diapers—often! Other good clothes for infants include T-shirts and one-piece outfits such as footed sleepers.

  Once children are able to dress and undress themselves, they need clothes that they can put on and take off easily. Whatever their age, children need clothing that is appropriate for the weather. For example, in cold weather a child needs to wear a coat, hat, boots, and mittens. In addition, caregivers are responsible for making sure that the children's clothing is kept clean and in good repair.
- **Rest.** Children need more sleep than adults. They need naps during the day and many hours of sleep at night. It is

Emphasize Babies and young children are utterly dependent on their parents and on other caregivers, not only for their immediate needs, but also for their health and development for years to come.

Did You Know? Infants who are not breast fed are given formula—a mixture of milk or milk substitutes and added nutrients. Strained foods are usually added to a baby's diet between 4 and 6 months of age. Strained fruits, vegetables, and meats have been processed so they are smooth and somewhat runny. They can be purchased or prepared at home.

up to the caregiver to keep the children on the same routine each day and night so they can get the rest they need.

Newborns can sleep in cradles or carriers. Once they are larger, they should sleep in cribs. Since they can hurt themselves by hitting the crib sides, the crib should have padded bumpers. Washable sheets and a waterproof pad covering the mattress are also necessary.

- **Hygiene.** Children need to be bathed and washed when they are infants. Once they are older, they should be taught to wash themselves and brush their teeth, but even after they learn these things, they will still need supervision. When they are ready, young children also need toilet training so they can learn to go to the bathroom by themselves.
- **Safe environment.** Children are not aware of the dangers of stairs, electric outlets, or poisons. Adults must protect them from accidents that their exploring can cause. Chapter 21 explains how to make the home safe for children.

Nurturing

Caregivers are also responsible for nurturing children. To **nurture** means to help children learn, and it involves providing love, support, attention, and encouragement.

Children are constantly learning because the whole world is new to them. To help them learn, they need stimulation: chances to see, hear, touch, taste, and smell. Infants learn by exploring with their senses. Older children build on this base as they experience even more. They learn a variety of skills, from walking and talking to reading and climbing. They also must learn how to get along with others. Children first learn how to relate to family members, then how to relate to friends. Chapter 20 offers some ideas on how to help children learn.

Children need a safe, stimulating environment where they can play and explore their surroundings.

More About Hygiene Point out that most children are toilet trained between eighteen months and three years of age but that there is no set age at which a child should be toilet trained. Babysitters should check with parents about their children's toilet habits.

Did You Know? Eating habits are established very early in life. Babies who are encouraged to eat sugary foods may develop poor eating habits. Young children should be discouraged from adding salt to their food so that they do not develop a "salt habit."

Activities

Skill Builder: Science
Ask students to research the nutritional needs of babies. Suggest that they select an age—six months, nine months, twelve months—and that they find out how much food a baby of that age needs each day and what kinds of foods are most appropriate.

Skill Builder: Critical Thinking
Divide the class into small groups, and have each group brainstorm ideas for one of the following:

- Setting limits is an important part of parenting. Come up with a list of the kinds of limits parents must set.
- Suggest ways for making washing and grooming into a fun activity for young children.
- Create a learning project for a young child that could make use of scraps of fabric, colored paper, ribbon, or other safe materials.

Skill Builder: Writing
Have students write a jingle about safety in the home or on the playground. Have them share the jingle with the class and practice singing with a group of small children.

Reteaching
Have students develop a collage of pictures taken from magazines to illustrate the various parenting skills. Alternatively, develop three separate collages—to illustrate physical care, nurturing, and guidance.

Enrichment
Ask students to go to the library and select an article on parenting in a current family magazine. Have selected students present summaries of their articles to the class and evaluate them as resources for caregivers. Ask students to comment on the suggestions made in the articles.

Enrichment
Ask a local organization such as the Chamber of Commerce or Parents and Teachers Association to sponsor a schoolwide essay contest that compares the differences between parenting and parenthood. Have all essays brought to the home economics classroom before or after school.

Teaching "Resources for Parenting"
(Page 179)

This section teaches that caregivers need knowledge, skills, and certain personal qualities.

Checking Comprehension

✓ How can a caregiver know what to expect from a child at various ages? *By understanding the stages of development that children reach at various ages.*

✓ How can you show children you respect them? *You can take care to act in a way that sets a good example.*

Activities

Skill Builder: Critical Thinking
Explain to students that parenting skills require common-sense solutions to everyday problems. Describe the following situations, and have students suggest how they would resolve them. Then ask: "Which parenting skill did you use?"

- It is 5:00 p.m. and the three-year-old child says he is hungry. You know his mother will be home to give him supper by 5:30.
- The two-year-old you are taking care of has just been scratched by the family cat. The wound is not deep, but it is bleeding, and the child is crying.
- Two four-year-olds are playing near a swing set in the backyard. They argue over who gets to ride on the red swing first.

Reteaching
Have students describe particular problems they have had to deal with as caregivers. Let the class decide which kinds of skills were needed to deal with the problem.

Enrichment
Ask students to interview someone they know who has had experience in caring for children. They should ask how the person prepared for the role of a caregiver. What was the most serious problem the caregiver faced, and how did he or she solve it? Have the student prepare a brief report on the interview.

Caregivers also provide children with love, affection, and a sense of security. Children need someone to comfort them when they are hurt or upset. They need to know that the people who are responsible for them really care about them. Showing affection can be as simple as saying a few kind words when a child scrapes a knee or praising a drawing when a child proudly displays it.

Guidance

Finally, caregivers need to provide **guidance** to children. In other words, they need to help children understand what type of behavior is acceptable and what type is not. For example, kicking a younger brother or sister is not acceptable. Young children do not yet know right from wrong. If given complete freedom, they may be confused about what to do and may be frightened.

Caregivers help children by setting limits: they tell them when to go to bed, what to eat for a snack, which programs to watch on TV. Of course, children may *test* limits and purposely do the wrong thing. They are not trying to be bad; they only want to make sure that the caregiver meant it.

Setting these limits is the responsibility of the parents. Part-time caregivers simply remind children what the limits are, and they get the children to stick to them. Of course, it's the responsibility of the part-time caregivers to find out from the parents what the limits are.

Nurturing involves comforting children when they are unhappy, hurt, or scared.

Emphasize Caregivers need a *combination* of book learning and experience. Neither one is adequate alone.

Focus on Relationship Skills Have students select words from the text to start a list on the chalkboard of personal qualities that good caregivers need. Then have them suggest other words or terms that could be added to the list.

Resources for Parenting

When you parent a child, you are, in effect, a manager. You are responsible for the child's needs, activities, and behavior. Parenting is demanding work. It requires knowledge, skills, and personal qualities such as understanding, patience, love, and respect. Some of these things can be learned in classes and by reading. Others must be learned through experience.

Knowledge

Effective parenting requires knowing about children. You wouldn't expect a one-year-old to speak in complete sentences. Similarly, you wouldn't expect a five-year-old to write a book report. A caregiver (whether it is the parent or babysitter) must understand the stages of development that children reach at various ages. Then, he or she will know what to expect from the child and how to respond.

Skills

If you become a caregiver, you must learn more than just how to take care of children physically. Along with bathing an infant and dressing a two-year-old, you may need to know how to stop an argument between two children, how to deal with a child's fears, and how to help with a child's homework. You will also need to be able to plan appropriate activities, communicate positively, and act wisely and quickly in an emergency.

Personal Qualities

As a caregiver you need certain personal qualities in order to deal effectively with children. Basically, you need to have an understanding of the needs and abilities of children so that you know what to expect from them. You also need patience so you can remain calm even in the most difficult circumstances, such as when a child repeatedly throws food on the floor. In addition, you need to love and respect children.

Are you concerned about what you are teaching children by the example you set? That is a sign that you respect them. There is a good chance that the children who are shown respect will, in turn, learn to show respect to others.

A realistic understanding of yourself is the key to deciding whether you would make a good caregiver. That means knowing your strengths and weaknesses. For example, if a child became frustrated or angry because she couldn't tie her shoes, how would you react? Would you be patient and sympathetic?

Approaches to Parenting

In the past, most people believed that everyone automatically knew how to be a good parent. Now society recognizes that parenting involves skills and abilities that are usually learned through practice.

This does not mean that there is only one correct approach to parenting. Different parents have different values and philosophies that affect the way they rear their children. What works for one family may not work for another, but there are some characteristics that are common to every successful approach.

Whatever the approach, for it to succeed, parents must provide for their children's physical, mental, social, and emotional needs. They must also give children care, guidance, and a loving and supportive atmosphere.

Real-Life Situations A child's self-concept begins forming in infancy. If a parent or caregiver responds positively to an infant's cries with food or comfort, the baby begins to feel like a worthwhile person. During early childhood, children develop basic attitudes about themselves. If they receive attention and praise from caregivers, they will believe that they are good people who can accomplish many things. However, if they are continually told that they are bad or stupid, they will develop a poor self-concept and may begin to match their behavior according to people's expectations. Thus it is never too early to help a child develop a good self-concept.

Teaching "Approaches to Parenting"

(Page 179)

This section emphasizes that different parents approach parenting in different ways.

Checking Comprehension

✓ How has society's view of parenting changed? *In the past most people believed everyone knew how to be a good parent; now people recognize that skills and abilities of parenting are usually learned through practice.*

✓ What determines the different ways parents raise their children? *The parents' values and philosophies.*

Activities

Skill Builder: Critical Thinking
Repeat the statement from the text "What works for one family may not work for another." Ask students what they think it means, within the context, and ask them to give examples that illustrate it.

Reteaching
Help students understand that parental values affect the way children are raised by giving some specific examples. Explain, for example, that the value that parents place on education, exercise, relaxation, nutrition, the environment, and other issues will all affect the way that they raise their children.

Enrichment
Arrange for a visit to a child care center in your community. Ask students to observe the activities as the teachers, aides, and assistants interact with the children. Have students take notes and list some of the personal qualities they observe in these caregivers. Before the trip, alert the students that they will be asked to select one "situation" or "incident" (such as one child taking another's toy, a crying child, disruptive behavior) and report on how the situation was handled. Ask students to discuss how they would have handled the same situation.

Teaching the Feature
"Parenting Skills: A Learning Process"

Answers to Feature Questions

1. Answers will vary. Students may suggest that they would like to know more about working with physically and/or emotionally impaired children; making toys and games for children; planning children's parties; "kids in the kitchen"; planning and preparing meals with children in mind. Sources of information might include the local library, local child care facilities, and parents of young children.

2. Talk with people who have had experience in the child care field. Read about people who are professionals in the field and those who may have begun their own child care businesses. Visit and/or volunteer at a child care center. Sign up for a course on child care.

Activities

Games for Children Have students work in groups to prepare lists of games that they have played successfully with children. The lists should include brief descriptions of how the games are played. Ask for a volunteer to combine the lists into one master list that can be copied and distributed to students.

Programs for Learning Have students identify and research a child care class in their community. Ask them to find out facts such as what subjects are covered, how many weeks or months the course lasts, when it is offered, and how much it costs.

Community Contact Suggest that students who are interested in obtaining babysitting jobs design fliers to promote themselves that they can distribute to neighbors. Before students design their fliers, discuss the information that should be included.

MANAGING RESOURCES

Parenting Skills: A Learning Process

Knowledge is the most important resource that you can use as a caregiver. The more you know about how children develop and behave, and the more parenting skills you learn, the better you will be at meeting the needs of the children you care for. Here are some ways that you can acquire the knowledge you need to be a good caregiver:

- **Ask your own parents or other knowledgeable adults.** Your parents are experienced caregivers who can provide you with a lot of useful information and help. Don't be embarrassed to ask them for help if you find yourself in a situation you can't handle. It is much better to get help from experienced adults than to make a mistake that might harm or endanger the children you are caring for.
- **Read about caregiving.** Your library and local bookstores have dozens of books and magazines on child care that offer sound advice and very specific information about how to care for children of all ages. Some books tell you about games you can play with young children, others tell you how to make nutritious snacks, and still others advise you about how to handle illnesses and emergencies.
- **Take a course.** Check around your community to see who offers child care courses. The Red Cross holds babysitting classes, and the Girl Scouts offer child care merit badges. Some school districts, hospitals, and community service organizations also offer child-care courses.
- **Learn by doing.** Volunteer at a child care center, nursing home, or hospital where you can learn caregiving skills under the supervision of trained professionals. Volunteering is also an excellent way to find out whether you are interested in a caregiving career.

Think It Through

1. **List five topics related to children that you would like to know more about. Where would you go to find this information?**
2. **If you were considering a child care career, what would you begin doing?**

Emphasize When you are babysitting, if you encounter a problem that you feel you cannot solve, call your parents or a close neighbor for advice or ask one of them to come over and help.

Did You Know? Children remember and look forward to special games or activities that they share with caregivers. That activity could be as simple as a favorite story before bed or a game of hide-and-seek. What matters the most is that the caregiver is consistent and enthusiastic about sharing that activity.

CHAPTER

18 REVIEW

Reviewing the Facts

1. How do the responsibilities of a main caregiver and a part-time caregiver differ? How are they similar?
2. What are some of the rewards of caregiving?
3. What is the difference between parenting and parenthood?
4. What are the three basic parenting skills?
5. What physical needs do children have?
6. Name two ways to nurture a child.
7. What is guidance? Why do children need it?
8. List three personal qualities that you need to be a good caregiver.

Thinking Critically

1. What resources do you possess that would help you be an effective caregiver? What additional resources do you need?
2. If you were interviewing people for the job of caregiver, what two questions would you ask first? Why?

Applying Your Skills

1. **Recalling a Decision.** Identify a person in your life who has provided a parenting role in your development. How did the person prepare for the role of a caregiver? What was the most serious decision the caregiver faced in your presence, and how did he or she handle it? Write a brief report.

2. **Planning for a Babysitting Job.** Assume that you have been hired to babysit for a two-year-old child. Read the section of a child development textbook, a parenting book, or an encyclopedia that describes the developmental stage of toddlers. What limits would you need to set for the child? How could you provide a nurturing environment?

3. **Selecting Important Qualities.** Imagine that you are a parent and that you are looking for someone to take care of your child two afternoons a week. Write a want ad for your local newspaper listing the personal qualities of a caregiver that you think are most important.

Answers to "Reviewing the Facts"

1. A main caregiver is responsible for a child for many years; a part-time caregiver is responsible only for a few hours. Both must take care of the child's needs and must make many decisions.
2. Immediate rewards include: earning money; learning skills; demonstrating dependability and responsibility. Long-term rewards include: rearing happy, healthy, and responsible children; feeling good about helping others.
3. Parenting involves taking care of children. Parenthood means to be a father or mother of a child.
4. Providing physical care, nurturing, and giving guidance.
5. Food, clothing, rest, hygiene, safe environment.
6. Any two: providing love, support, attention, encouragement, stimulation, a sense of security, affection.
7. Guidance means teaching children acceptable behavior and right from wrong. Without guidance children may be confused about what to do and may be frightened.
8. Any three: understanding of needs and abilities, patience, love, respect.

Answers to "Thinking Critically"

1. Answers should suggest personal qualities such as good decision-making skills, ability to act quickly and wisely in an emergency, creativity, patience, warmth, self-confidence, self-respect, experience with child care, and so on.
2. Some students will be concerned about what the caregiver knows, while others may care most about the caregiver's personal qualities. Emphasize that questions like "What would you do if . . . ?" may be more effective than "Are you patient?"

COMPLETING THE CHAPTER

Summary

- Caregiving enables young people to develop parenting skills, earn money, and show that they are responsible employees.
- Parenting involves providing physical care, nurturing, and giving guidance.
- Parenting means taking care of children; parenthood means being a father or a mother.
- Nurturing involves providing love, support, and attention, and guidance involves setting limits.
- Effective parenting requires knowledge, skills, and certain personal qualities.

For Review

Objective Review Questions Have students complete the "Reviewing the Facts" section on this page.

Study Guide Have students complete the Study Guide from Chapter 18 of their *Student Workbook.*

Class Discussion Write the following old adage on the chalkboard: "Do as I say, not as I do." Discuss the meaning of the phrase and its implications for parents.

Debate an Issue Some people say parenting is an instinct, whereas others believe that the more a person can learn about how children develop and behave, the better parent that person can be. Ask students to discuss this issue based on what they have read and on their personal experiences.

For Evaluation

Classification Have students copy from the chalkboard the list of sentences about parents that you prepared earlier ("A parent is someone who..."). Ask them to add any other sentences they can think of, now that they have read the chapter. Then have them classify each sentence as either physical care (P), nurturing (N), or giving guidance (G).

Chapter Test Have students complete the test for Chapter 18 that appears in the *Teacher's Classroom Resources.*

CHAPTER OVERVIEW

Chapter 19 introduces students to the developmental tasks of childhood and explains how development occurs in stages. Students learn about the physical, mental, and social tasks that children master at each of the four developmental stages: infant, toddler, preschooler, school-age. The chapter also explores the characteristics of children with special needs and explains how these children can be encouraged to develop to their fullest ability.

INTRODUCING THE CHAPTER

Motivators

Memories Ask students to share any single incident about their first two years of life that their parents may have described. Students may wish to discuss possible reasons why each incident stands out in the parents' memories.

Photo Collage Have students prepare a developmental collage using pictures cut from magazines. The pictures should show children from early infancy through school age. They should be arranged in sequence so that students can observe growth and change. You will be referring to these pictures again later.

Using the Photograph Have students study the photograph on this page. Then ask: "What positive emotions are being expressed here? How does the parent encourage the child? What feedback does the parent receive from the child?"

Introducing the Objectives

Discuss the chapter objectives on this page. Remind students that the objectives focus on important chapter content.

CHAPTER

19

Ages and Stages

OBJECTIVES

This chapter will help you to:

- Explain how development occurs in stages.
- List the four stages of development.
- Describe the physical, mental, and social characteristics of each stage.
- Explain how children with special needs can learn to develop to their full potential.

WORDS TO REMEMBER

developmental tasks
fine-motor skills
gross-motor skills
hand-eye coordination
parallel play
reflex
stages

Chapter Resources

Teacher's Classroom Resources
- Lesson Plan
- Life Skills Activity, *That's Good Advice*
- Reproducible Master, *Stages of Development*
- Extension Activity, *Stages, Ages, and Tasks*
- Chapter Test

Student Workbook
- Study Guide
- Worksheet, *The Secret of Ages and Stages*

Most nine-month-old babies can crawl, and by the time they are a year old, most are able to walk. Two-year-olds can speak a few words, and by the time they are three and a half, they can talk in sentences. Walking, talking, drawing, eating with a knife and fork, and learning colors and letters are all examples of **developmental tasks**: the skills and abilities that children acquire as they grow.

Nearly all children master these tasks in the same order. They crawl before they walk and speak in single words before they talk in sentences. Children build on what they've already learned. Walking becomes running and scribbling becomes drawing.

A major function of caregivers is to encourage and help children master these developmental tasks. If adults do not help children in such tasks as learning to talk, the children will not grow and develop properly.

Stages of Development

Researchers have found that children, after birth, go through four developmental stages:

- Infant (birth to one year).
- Toddler (one to three years).
- Preschooler (three to five years).
- School-age (five to ten years).

These **stages** are periods during which the child can perform certain tasks. The chart on page 184 shows what some of the developmental tasks are for the first three stages of development. It is important to remember that the ages given are just averages. Some children develop more rapidly and some more slowly. One child may walk at nine months and another may not walk until fourteen months. However, both are developing normally.

Remember, too, that the stages are not rigid categories. An infant does not suddenly become a toddler the day after his first birthday. The change is very gradual. Still, you can refer to this table as you read the chapters in this unit to learn what things a young child has probably learned.

Infant

For the first year of a baby's life, growth and development are very rapid. Most of the changes are fairly predictable and occur in the same sequence.

Physical Development

Although she is only a few days old, Gloria is already quite a complex individual. She has strong **reflexes**, or automatic, involuntary responses. If you stroke her cheek, she turns her head toward your hand and sucks. If you place your finger in her palm, she will curl her tiny fingers and grasp it tightly. Gloria cries to signal unhappiness. She can see, hear, taste, smell, and touch.

As she gets older, Gloria will learn about shapes and textures by putting objects in her mouth. Bringing objects to her mouth will help her develop **hand-eye coordination**, the ability to get her eyes and her muscles working together so that she can make complex movements. Batting a baseball or eating with a fork are examples of movements that require good hand-eye coordination.

Did You Know? *Identical twins* occur when the egg splits apart soon after fertilization. Identical twins are always the same sex and have very similar characteristics. If the split is not complete, *Siamese twins* result—their bodies are joined together at some part. *Fraternal twins* occur when two eggs are fertilized by different sperm. Fraternal twins may be the same sex or opposite sexes. *Triplets* can be identical (egg splits into three parts), fraternal (three eggs develop), or both (one egg splits into two parts; a second egg develops). Multiple births of more than two babies are rare—although fertility drugs have increased their occurrence.

Introducing Vocabulary

Explain the words *gross-motor skills* and *fine-motor skills.* Explain that motor skills or motor control means the control of muscles or organs that cause parts of the body to move. *Gross* means large and refers to large muscles. *Fine* means small and refers to small muscles. Ask the students to distinguish between fine-motor skills and gross-motor skills. Ask: "Which kind of skill does it take to crawl across the floor? Which kind is used in fitting one object into another?"

TEACHING THE CHAPTER

For convenience, the teaching suggestions for this chapter are arranged according to the following lesson topics:

- "Stages of Development," page 183
- "Infant," pages 183-185
- "Toddler," pages 186-187
- "The Preschooler and the School-Age Child," pages 187-188
- "Children with Special Needs," pages 188-189

Teaching "Stages of Development"
(Page 183)

This section teaches that children go through various stages of development on their way to becoming adults. Examples of tasks typical of each stage are presented.

Checking Comprehension

✓ What are the age ranges for the four stages of development? *Infant—birth to one year, toddler—one to three years, preschooler—three to five years, school-age—five to ten years.*

✓ Why is it important to remember that the ages given for the different stages of development are just averages? *Because children develop at different rates—some more rapidly, some more slowly.*

✓ How can the chart of "Stages, Ages, and Tasks" on page 184 be helpful to you? *You can refer to it as you read the chapters in this unit to discover what a young child has probably learned.*

Teaching "Toddler"
(Pages 186-187)

This section teaches the physical, mental, and social development of toddlers.

Checking Comprehension

✔ What were signs of Manuel's gross-motor skills development? *First he walked and climbed stairs. As he became steadier, he wanted to run everywhere.*

✔ What will Manuel's fine-motor skills allow him to do? *They will allow him to feed and dress himself and, later, to draw or write.*

✔ What changes in verbal skill will Manuel go through in his toddler years? *He will go from speaking single words to speaking short phrases and finally whole sentences.*

✔ What do children learn about objects in the toddler stage? *They learn about relationships between objects and what objects are meant to do.*

✔ What is parallel play? *The natural tendency for toddlers to play alongside each other, rather than together.*

✔ Why does frustration often develop in children at around age two? *They are struggling with their dependency on others on the one hand and their desire for independence on the other.*

Activities

Skill Builder: Critical Thinking
Ask students to think of specific examples of ways that parents or caregivers can help toddlers form their self-concepts and develop high self-esteem. For example, a student might say: "Caregivers could praise a child for accomplishing a task."

Reteaching
Give each student a large-size pencil or crayon and an unlined sheet of paper. Have them use the opposite hand from what they usually write with to draw a picture of their house and write their name. Discuss gross-motor and fine-motor skills.

Reading aloud helps a child learn to talk. The child can listen to the sounds of the words and imitate them.

Toddler

Physical growth usually slows a bit as an infant becomes a toddler. During this stage, however, children master an amazing number of physical, mental, and social skills.

Physical Development

Manuel's first steps were a thrill for him and his family. Once Manuel felt steady, he wanted to walk everywhere, including up every flight of stairs. After he became more sure of himself (he was then one and a half to two years old), he often wanted to run everywhere as fast as he could. His gross-motor skills were improving every day.

Manuel was also beginning to gain more control over his smaller muscles, such as those in his hands. He was developing the **fine-motor skills** he will need to be able to feed and dress himself and, later, to draw and write. Of course, Manuel's parents encouraged these efforts—even though they had to pay special attention to some skills, such as Manuel's being able to climb out of his crib and high chair.

Mental Development

Much mental growth occurs during the toddler years. Manuel will go from speaking single words to saying short phrases and finally whole sentences. He will build on his knowledge of cause and effect by noticing that if he lets something go, it falls.

As a toddler, Manuel will learn a lot about size and space and about how objects relate to one another. He will learn which object is larger and which is smaller and which objects go on top of

Did You Know? A toddler's messiness at mealtime can stem both from a child's need to explore and experiment with the foods and from underdeveloped muscles and poor eye-hand coordination.

Cross-Reference See Teen Tips "Tidbits Toddlers Love to Eat" on pages 234-235.

Emphasize Toddlers learn each new skill by trial and error, a lengthy process. Parents and caregivers can easily become impatient waiting for a child to zip up a jacket or put on a shoe. But for the child to learn, the caregiver should resist offering help too quickly. Whenever possible, allow the child to complete a task at his or her own speed.

or inside other objects. During this stage, children may spend a lot of time putting blocks and toys together and taking them apart, or playing with groups of objects, such as pots and pans. Manuel will also learn what tasks objects are meant to do. He will learn, for example, that spoons help you eat and sweaters keep you warm.

Social Development

Sometimes parents are concerned because their toddlers aren't interested in playing with other children. However, this is natural for children this age. Toddlers tend to play alongside each other, rather than together. This is called **parallel play**.

Around the age of two, children get caught in a struggle between their dependency on others and their desire for independence. The struggle usually shows up in fits of frustration. Often, Manuel wants to do everything for himself and realizes that he can't. At the same time, he resents his parents' efforts to help. When he isn't able to feed himself, climb into his high chair, or put together a puzzle, he may have a temper tantrum because he is frustrated. Adults can help by providing children with objects to assist them: low tables, step stools, and clothes they can put on by themselves. Adults should also be patient and allow children enough time to do things by themselves.

Little by little, Manuel is beginning to acquire the ideas that will form his self-concept: the knowledge that he is unique, that he has his own feelings, that others have certain feelings about him. Many of Manuel's early attitudes about himself will come from people who care for him. Caregivers must help children to feel good about themselves and must promote their self-esteem.

The Preschooler and the School-Age Child

Preschoolers and school-age children practice and refine their physical abilities. They also ask lots of questions and develop their communications skills. In addition, they develop friendships and become more independent.

Physical Development

From the age of four until the teen years, the changes that occur in children's bodies are not as dramatic as those that took place in infancy. During the preschool years and middle childhood, children continue to get bigger and stronger and to have more control over their bodies and emotions.

Children at these stages eat the same food as adults. By the time they start school, they can handle such personal tasks as bathing and dressing. They also learn to be aware of their own feelings of wellness and illness.

Mental Development

The exploring and testing that began during infancy will continue as a child grows. This is a time for exploring, asking questions, and thinking about things.

The preschool stage is when children refine their thinking processes. They learn to count and name colors, and many children also learn to identify the letters of the alphabet. By three or four, preschoolers have mastered the ability to speak in sentences, and many of them can print their own names.

Emphasize Like adults, children have individual preferences. Children will not like to eat every food that they are given. Caregivers will have to be flexible and creative when faced with mealtime choices.

Did You Know? Preschoolers respond well to praise and enjoy winning, but they are emotionally unprepared for losing. Preschool is not the time to begin competitive games and sports.

Reteaching
Explain to students that toddlers learn about size and space and about how objects relate to one another. Ask students to suggest common household items (other than those mentioned in this section) that may be used to stimulate mental development.

Enrichment
Have students draw a "perfect" room in which a toddler can develop fine-motor skills and gross-motor skills freely. Have them display their drawings. Ask them to explain why certain objects were included—toys, cushions, play equipment, balls, tunnels, puzzles, and shapes.

Teaching "The Preschooler and School-Age Child"
(Pages 187-188)

This section teaches the physical, mental, and social development of preschoolers and school-age children.

Checking Comprehension

✓ What physical changes occur in children's bodies during the preschool years and middle childhood? *Children grow bigger and stronger and have more control over their bodies and emotions.*

✓ List two things that children may learn to do in the preschool stage. *Any two: learn to count, name colors, learn the alphabet, print their names, speak in sentences.*

✓ How might the development of imagination affect a child? *He or she may brag or have scary dreams.*

✓ What social behavior do children learn in child care, nursery school, and kindergarten? *How to get along in a group, how to share, how to play together, how to argue, how to compete.*

Activities

Skill Builder: Critical Thinking
Arrange for a nursery school, kindergarten, first-grade, or second-grade teacher to supply samples of work done by his or her students. These could include art projects, writing samples, or arithmetic exercises. Ask students to point out how the samples display the child's physical, mental, emotional, or social development.

Reteaching
Arrange to have the class visit a kindergarten class. Have students observe the preschoolers as they play alone or as they relate to other children. Then have students compare the preschoolers' play patterns to the information they learned in the chapter. Have the students discuss what they saw. Did the children interact with one another as they expected them to?

Enrichment
Arrange to have your class visit a kindergarten class in your school district. Ask each student to focus on a single child (or small group of children). Students should observe and make notes describing the various skills being demonstrated by the youngsters. Have students categorize their observations as illustrating physical, mental, or social development.

Teaching "Children with Special Needs"

(Pages 188-189)

This section teaches the physical, mental, and social development of children with physical or learning disabilities, as well as gifted children.

Checking Comprehension

✔ Contrast mentally retarded children with those who have learning disabilities. *The capabilities of mentally retarded children develop slowly or stop at a low level. Children with learning disabilities are of normal or even high intelligence. They just have difficulty mastering certain skills.*

School-age children build on these skills to master more complex tasks. They learn arithmetic and reading, and they refine their fine-motor skills so they can draw and write.

Children in these stages are able to sit still doing one thing for a longer time than toddlers can. These are also the years when children's imagination plays an important role, when children may brag or have scary dreams.

Social Development

During the preschool years, a child begins to learn what it means to enjoy the company of others. Around age four or five, a child is likely to single out another child as a best friend.

In day care, nursery school, and kindergarten, children learn social behavior: how to get along in a group, how to share, how to play together. Children at this stage also learn how to argue and how to compete. Winning contests becomes very important to them.

Belonging to a group is important for school-age children, but during this time they continue to need close family relationships. It is important that they have acceptance from family members, and encouragement and reassurance from caregivers.

Children with Special Needs

Some children need special attention. They may be mentally, physically, or emotionally disabled. In some cases, the disabilities are present at birth; in others, they occur as a result of an accident or illness. Other children may have certain learning difficulties or may be unusually bright. All these children are children with special needs.

Physical Development

It's important to remember that children with physical disabilities are children *first.* They have the same basic needs as other children—to be loved, to be cared for, and to be stimulated. Like any child, Paul, who uses a wheelchair, needs to develop self-confidence. Colette, who wears leg braces, is just as concerned about what she wears as any other child. Emil's hearing loss affects some parts of his life, but not his involvement in sports.

Children with physical disabilities may need special exercise or equipment, but they still need to be given the chance to help themselves as soon as possible. Help them learn to wash and dress themselves. Give them chores that they are capable of doing so that they will feel better about themselves.

Mental Development

The mental development of children with special needs varies greatly. Some children are mentally retarded. Their mental capabilities may develop very slowly, and development may stop at a low level. Other children have learning disabilities. Still others are mentally gifted. All of these children need special attention.

Children who are mentally retarded must be given every chance to develop their skills, abilities, and interests. They may be slower in completing a developmental task, but eventually many are able to do it. Encouraging these children, as well as rewarding them for what they do learn, can lead to further learning. Whenever possible, emphasize what children *can* do.

Children with learning disabilities are of normal intelligence, and some may even be very bright. They just have diffi-

Real-Life Situations Dyslexia (dis-LEX-ee-uh) is a learning disability that makes it difficult for children to process information—especially visual information—in the brain. Dyslexia causes problems with reading, writing, spelling, and math. Children with dyslexia have difficulty following visual instructions, sounding out words, and carrying out activities in sequence. Although intelligent, they may be treated as if they cannot learn. This may cause frustration and discouragement in the classroom and with homework. Many schools now provide special help for children with dyslexia.

Children with disabilities have the same needs and go through the same stages of development as other children.

culty mastering certain mental skills. Some children find reading or mathematics difficult, for example, because letters or numbers appear inverted or backward to them. These children require extra help in school so they can keep up with their classmates.

Children who are unusually intelligent need special attention, too. Many schools offer extra projects or special classes to stimulate and interest gifted children. This enables the children to do challenging work and still take part in regular school activities.

Social Development

Children with special needs have the same social and emotional needs that all children do. They need to make friends and to learn how to get along with others. As with all children, the way they feel about themselves will influence their relationships with others.

Sometimes a child's social behavior can indicate an emotional disturbance. For example, children who are very withdrawn, or constantly afraid, or very aggressive may be emotionally disturbed. Such children might need professional counseling.

All children, regardless of their abilities, share a common need. They all need to feel loved and accepted by their family and friends.

✓ How are unusually intelligent children helped in school? *They may be offered extra projects or special classes to stimulate them.*

✓ What social and emotional needs do all children share? *The need to make friends and learn how to get along with others.*

✓ When might a child need professional counseling? *If the child's social behavior indicates an emotional disturbance.*

Activities

Skill Builder: Writing
Bring in several (at least five) photos cut from magazines illustrating children with different types of physical disabilities doing different tasks. Have students select a photo to study. Then ask them to write a one-paragraph description, telling how the child might accomplish the task in comparison with how a child without the disability might do it.

Reteaching
Help students develop a sensitivity for the special-needs child by simulating a blind student. Take turns blindfolding students and have them experience walking, tasting, and using a braille book to read. Ask students to share their thoughts and feelings about the experience.

Enrichment
Ask students to discuss the value of early diagnosis of problems in mental development or learning disorders.

Real-Life Situations There are many different kinds of birth defects that occur during the prenatal period of development. Some are very mild or correctable; others result in severe handicaps or death. Some are apparent at birth; others not until months or years later. Although birth defects are rare, here are some selected ones: cerebral palsy, cleft lip and/or palate, congenital heart defect, cystic fibrosis, Down syndrome, hemophilia, muscular dystrophy, sickle cell anemia, spina bifida, Tay-Sachs disease. For additional information about birth defects, contact the March of Dimes, 1275 Mamaroneck Ave., White Plains, NY 10605. Or contact individual volunteer agencies for specific birth defects.

Teaching the Feature
"Tempering a Tantrum"

Answers to Feature Questions

1. Answers will vary, but students may suggest: keep the child busy and interested; follow the child's routine; be patient to allow the child time to figure something out independently; provide objects that encourage independence; plan time for physical activities; give simple instructions.

2. Answers will vary. Students might suggest that children are beginning to assert their independence, are easily frustrated, resent efforts to help when they cannot do things themselves, and so on. Students may suggest that children be taught to talk about their frustration and ask for help if needed. Children might also hit a pillow, throw a ball, or engage in some other physical activity when frustrated.

Activities

Time-out Explain to students that "time-out" is often suggested as a way to respond to tantrums or other misbehavior. With time-out a child is removed from the problem situation for a short time, until he or she settles down. Have students discuss with what ages and situations the time-out method of discipline works best.

Expectations When thirteen-year-old Owen was asked to babysit for Stephanie, a bright, lively eighteen-month-old, he was not sure what to expect. He was told by her mother that she had special needs since she was born without her left hand. Owen was to take charge of her for the entire day. Ask students to suggest what special precautions or appropriate activities they would prepare.

Community Contact Ask students to explore resources in your community that provide assistance to families of people with learning disabilities. Have them compile a list of the names and telephone numbers of the local groups. The entire class list could then be donated to the school library.

INTERPERSONAL SKILLS

Tempering a Tantrum

Have you ever seen a child throw a temper tantrum? Tantrums often occur when children become frustrated because they cannot do something they want to do, such as unbutton a coat. Tantrums may also happen when children are denied something they want, such as a toy or an ice-cream cone. They may fall on the floor and cry and kick for several minutes. Some also bang their heads against the floor or pull their hair.

If you are caring for a child who throws a tantrum, here are some ways to handle it:

- **Try to distract the child.** If children have a tantrum because they want something, try to offer another object. Turn the children's attention to something else to help them forget what they wanted.
- **Remain calm.** Remember that occasional temper tantrums are normal behavior for children in the toddler stage. Stay calm and talk soothingly. Losing your own temper and yelling at the child will not stop the tantrum; it will only make things worse.
- **Ignore the tantrum.** Many experts believe the best way to deal with a tantrum is to ignore it. If you walk out of the room, the child has no audience and gets no reward for the tantrum. Usually it will soon stop.
- **Physically restrain the child.** When children bang their heads against the floor or act violently during a tantrum, they may harm themselves physically. These children need to be held or hugged tightly until the tantrum subsides.
- **Remove the child from the situation.** Many children throw tantrums in the middle of a shopping mall or supermarket. The best thing to do is pick the child up and leave. If you take children home whenever they have a tantrum in a public place, they soon learn that one of the costs of tantrums is losing the pleasure of an outing.

Think It Through

1. **If you were caring for a young child, what are three things you would do to help avoid a temper tantrum?**
2. **Why do you think that temper tantrums are most likely to occur in children between the ages of two and four? How can tantrums be redirected into more socially acceptable behavior?**

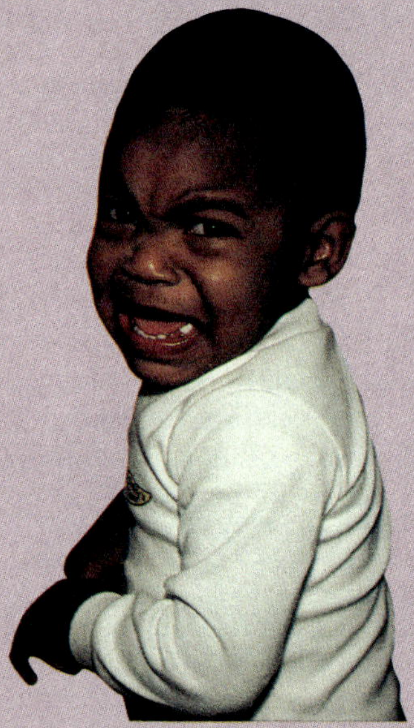

More About Tantrums Here are some additional ways to keep children from having temper tantrums. First, let the child make some decisions. Many times the child wants to feel in control. If you give him or her two or three choices, he or she will feel less frustrated. Second, follow the child's routine. This helps to alleviate tantrums that are based on confusion. Children like to know what to expect, and they feel more secure when they have normal routines for eating, playing, and going to bed.

CHAPTER 19 REVIEW

Reviewing the Facts

1. What are the four stages of children's development?
2. Define *reflexes* and give two examples of reflexes that infants possess.
3. What is hand-eye coordination? Give an example.
4. What can an infant learn by shaking a rattle?
5. What is object permanence? At what age does a child learn about it?
6. What is the difference between gross-motor skills and fine-motor skills? Give an example of each.
7. At what stage does parallel play become common?
8. Describe the mental development that occurs during the preschool stage.
9. What is the main thing to remember about children with special needs?

Thinking Critically

1. Why are caregivers so important to a child's development?
2. Why do you think that children who are unusually intelligent need special attention?

Applying Your Skills

1. **Classifying Activities.** Make a list of ten activities that you remember from your early childhood. Then beside each activity on your list, state if it was a physical, mental, or social task. Identify those activities that helped build fine-motor skills and those that helped build gross-motor skills.

2. **Listing Services.** Use the local telephone directory to find out what programs are available in your community to help meet the needs of gifted and disabled children. Prepare a list of all the places that offer such services.

3. **Sequencing Events.** With two other students, make a time line showing the physical, mental, and social changes that take place in a child between the ages of one and three. Each student should be responsible for recording one type of development.

Answers to "Reviewing the Facts"

1. Infant, toddler, preschooler, and school-age child.
2. Automatic, involuntary responses. A baby turns his head when his cheek is stroked, and curls his fingers and grasps tightly when you place your finger in his palm.
3. The ability to get the muscles and the eyes to work together. Eating with a fork.
4. Cause and effect.
5. The realization that people and objects continue to exist when they are out of sight. 8 to 12 months.
6. Gross-motor skills refer to the development of the large muscles of the body, such as the arm and leg muscles. Fine-motor skills refer to the control of small muscles, such as those in the hands and fingers.
7. Toddler stage.
8. Refine their thinking process; learn to count; name colors; identify letters of alphabet; speak in sentences; print own name.
9. That they are children first and have the same basic needs as other children.

Answers to "Thinking Critically"

1. Students should mention that children learn by watching others, they need help and encouragement to grow and develop properly, and many of their early attitudes about themselves come from their caregivers.
2. Students might suggest that these children need challenging activities to stimulate them and hold their interest.

COMPLETING THE CHAPTER

Summary

- Children go through four early developmental stages: infant, toddler, preschool, school-age.
- Infants grow and develop rapidly.
- Toddlers master many physical, mental, and social skills.
- Preschoolers refine their thinking processes and physical and social skills in preparation for school.
- All children, regardless of their abilities, must feel loved and accepted by their family and friends.

For Review

Objective Review Questions Have students complete the "Reviewing the Facts" section on this page.

Study Guide Have students complete the Study Guide from Chapter 19 of their *Student Workbook.*

Memories—Class Discussion Ask students if they have any written records of their earliest accomplishments—their first smile, first tooth, first step, and so on. Ask them how they feel about hearing about these milestones. Why do parents often keep books, records, albums of their child's development?

Create a Book Ask students to prepare a record book to be given to a newborn baby's parents. The students may be as creative and artistic as they wish. Be sure they include space to record the major tasks of development. They may have checklists, calendars, fill-in-the-blank spaces.

For Evaluation

Classification Draw a chart on the chalkboard listing "Infant," "Toddler," and "Preschooler." Then list about 15 tasks (taken from the chart on page 184) on the board. Ask students to classify each task under the appropriate heading.

Chapter Test Have students complete the test for Chapter 19 that appears in the *Teacher's Classroom Resources.*

CHAPTER OVERVIEW

Chapter 20 explains the importance of play for a child's physical, mental, and social development. Students are given examples of how children in each stage of development learn through play. The chapter gives suggestions on how to choose suitable play activities for infants, toddlers, and preschoolers. Students learn about the effect of passive activities on children. They examine the important safety points to consider when choosing toys and equipment.

INTRODUCING THE CHAPTER

Motivators

Childhood Memories Ask students to try to think back as far as they can into their early childhood. Ask them to describe their favorite toy or game. Have them explain to the class why they think that this particular toy or game was so important to them that it remains in their memories.

What Is Playing For? Ask students if there is a serious side to the play of children. Elicit from them the ideas that play is vital to a child's development. Ask students to think of a play activity that teaches something critical about a child's approach to the world.

Using the Photograph Have students study the photograph on this page. Then ask: "What situation is shown here? How are the caregivers interacting with the child?"

Introducing the Objectives

Discuss the chapter objectives on this page. Remind students that the objectives focus on important chapter content.

Introducing Vocabulary

Explain to students that *role-playing* is pretending to be someone else. Children enjoy acting out real-life situations. They may dress up in old clothes and pretend they are fire fighters or ballerinas. For some children, dramatic play through puppets can allow the freedom of self-expression without actually having to do the talking.

CHAPTER

20

The Importance of Play

OBJECTIVES

This chapter will help you to:

- Explain how children learn through play.
- Give examples of activities that can help children develop physically, mentally, and socially.
- Choose play activities suitable to a child's age and stage of development.

WORDS TO REMEMBER

passive activity
role playing
sensory toy

Chapter Resources

Teacher's Classroom Resources
- Lesson Plan
- Life Skills Activity, *Exploring Children's Television*
- Reproducible Master, *Television Tips*
- Extension Activity, *Toys for Children*
- Chapter Test

Student Workbook
- Study Guide
- Worksheet, *Toy Judge*

Playing comes so naturally to children that you may never have given it much thought. If you sometimes take care of a younger brother or sister or your neighbors' children, you've probably noticed how children enjoy playing.

When children play there is more going on than just amusement. Playing teaches children about their environment and how to interact with others. It also influences how they grow. Only recently have experts realized the great importance of play in children's learning.

Play and Development

Playing helps children develop in many different ways. It helps them develop physically by giving them the opportunity to exercise their muscles and improve their fine- and gross-motor skills. Play also helps children to grow mentally. When they put puzzles together, stack blocks, and play with nesting toys, they are also learning about sizes and shapes, colors, and counting. Board games and books help them learn numbers and letters. Play also helps children develop socially because it gives them practice in sharing and taking turns.

Children change as they grow and develop, and so does their play. An infant develops his fine-motor skills by grasping toys and bringing them to his mouth. A preschooler improves her fine-motor ability by making drawings.

When you know about the stages of development, you can provide children with opportunities to play that match their skill levels. Remember, though, that children develop at different rates and have different interests. One child can be ready for one kind of play before another child of the same age. To get the best results, adapt your play suggestions to children's actual skills.

How Infants Play

Infants play by exploring the world through their senses. Adults can help them to do this by spending time with them, by playing games with them, and by providing them with safe, interesting objects that they can enjoy and learn from.

Young children learn through their senses. They need toys they can see, touch, suck, and hear.

Did You Know? If you're creative when caring for children, you can use their toys in new ways. Arrange stuffed animals in a "zoo" or a "circus," make a school for animals, set up an animal puppet show, and so on.

Focus on Consumer Skills A creative caregiver doesn't have to spend a lot of money on children's toys. Household objects can be used in many ways—paper towel rolls make great tunnels, spools of thread make colorful buildings, and so on.

TEACHING THE CHAPTER

For convenience, the teaching suggestions for this chapter are arranged according to the following lesson topics:

- "Play and Development," pages 193-197
- "Passive Activities," pages 197-198
- "Playing in Groups," page 198

Teaching "Play and Development"

(Pages 193-197)

This section teaches the role of play in the development of the child.

Checking Comprehension

✓ How does play help children develop physically? *It gives them the opportunity to exercise their muscles and improve their fine- and gross-motor skills.*

✓ How does play help children develop socially? *They practice sharing and taking turns.*

✓ Why is it important to adapt play suggestions to a child's individual skill level? *Children develop at different rates and have different interests.*

✓ List one way to stimulate the sense of touch and one way to stimulate the sense of hearing. *Touch—any one: cuddling, holding, providing different textures and shapes or teething rings. Hearing—any one: singing, playing music, talking, reading.*

✓ What are sensory toys? *Objects to touch that have different textures, shapes, sounds, and colors and safe objects to put in infants' mouths.*

✓ Once infants can sit up, what can you do to help them discover their world? *Prop them up safely so that they can enjoy different sights and sounds around them.*

✓ Why do toddlers need space to walk and run? *To help them develop their gross-motor skills and expend energy.*

✓ Name four toys toddlers love. *Any four: dolls, vehicles, balls, books, play telephones, and housekeeping toys.*

✓ How can you help toddlers develop language skills? *By talking and reading to them and by explaining things in simple terms.*

✓ Why shouldn't you be surprised if a toddler takes a toy from another child? *Children of this age haven't learned to share and take turns and can not be expected to do so on their own.*

✓ Why are coloring books, crayons, modeling clay, dolls and changeable clothing, and construction sets good toys for preschoolers? *These toys help develop fine-motor skills.*

✓ How can you teach preschoolers social skills through play? *You can help them resolve their disputes and take turns. Role playing helps them express their feelings and practice behaviors.*

Activities

Skill Builder: Critical Thinking
Students are learning how important play is for children's development. Have students consider the advantages and disadvantages of organized (or structured) play as contrasted with free play. Briefly discuss the students' views on this issue in class. Then have them decide on which type of play they consider to be most important. Have them work in small groups to develop a list of the advantages of their side of the issue. Then have students present their cases to the class.

Skill Builder: Writing
Ask students to write a brief dialogue between two toddlers with one shovel in a sandbox.

Skill Builder: Science
Ask students to prepare a list of sensory "tests" they would be able to try with an infant. These would include "experiments" such as having the infant hear different sounds; touch objects of varying texture; and look at different colors or patterns, of course. They should then share their proposed tests with the class.

Here are some suggestions on how to play with infants:

- Stimulate their senses by holding and cuddling them, by singing and playing music for them.
- Talk and read to them so they become familiar with words.
- Surround them with **sensory toys**: objects to touch that have different textures and shapes, rattles and squeak toys they can listen to, brightly colored objects and mobiles they can look at and watch, and teething rings they can put in their mouth.
- Once they can sit up (at about five months), prop them up in a comfortable, safe chair, or in a playpen, or on the floor, so they can enjoy different sights and sounds.
- Play games with them like peekaboo, funny faces, and hide-and-seek.
- Give them new toys occasionally so they can make new discoveries.

How Toddlers Play

Toddlers are busy developing their gross-motor skills, so they need lots of space to walk and run. At this age, children love large dolls, wooden or soft plastic vehicles, balls, books, play telephones, and housekeeping toys, such as shopping baskets, vacuum cleaners, and brooms.

Here are some hints for playing with toddlers:

- Set aside time for active play so they can exercise their muscles and use up their store of energy.
- Be prepared to change games or activities when toddlers become bored or restless.
- Help toddlers develop language skills by talking and reading to them. Using simple terms, describe what you are doing or what you see on a walk.
- Children at this age have not yet learned to share or take turns, so don't be disturbed if they try to take toys away from other children or hit them. Be patient and correct their behavior in a gentle way.

Young children like to imitate adults. Can you explain how going shopping might influence this child's physical, mental, and social development?

Did You Know? When a child receives new toys, some old toys should be stored away for a time. With an overabundance of toys, the child can be overwhelmed and confused with choices. If a small group of toys is put away every few weeks and retrieved on a rotating basis, they will seem fresh and fun and more interesting to the child.

Emphasize Babies and toddlers need to be able to explore their environment in order to learn about their surroundings and to gain self-confidence. Parents should make the home safe for exploration (see Chapter 21) and not keep a baby or toddler always confined to a crib or playpen.

HEALTH WATCH

Choosing Toys and Equipment

If you have ever gone shopping for a birthday present for a child, you will know that there are literally thousands of toys to choose from. Your first concerns were probably to find something that the child would enjoy, and that was suitable for the child's age. There is another important factor that you need to consider when buying a toy for a child: is it safe?

Here are some important safety points that you need to consider when choosing toys:

- Does the toy have any small parts that a young child could swallow or that could get stuck in the child's ears or nostrils? (Young children *do* put things in unlikely places!)
- Are the decorations, such as the eyes on stuffed animals and dolls, firmly attached so that the child can't pull them off?
- Are there any sharp edges or points that could cause cuts?
- Is the toy strongly constructed, so it won't break? Broken toys might have sharp and dangerous edges.
- If the toy is made of fabric, is it washable? If not, it could become unhygienic.
- If the toy is for a crib, is it designed for safety? You should avoid anything that has strings that could get wrapped around a baby's neck.

Choosing equipment for children demands a similar attention to safety. When buying cribs, playpens, swings, and jungle gyms, caregivers need to pay attention to what *might* happen, and to make their purchase cautiously.

For example, when choosing cribs, buyers should make sure that the bars or slats are no more than 2 1/2 inches apart. With wider spacing, the infant could get his or her head lodged between the bars. Buyers should also ensure that the mechanism that allows the side of the crib to be dropped cannot be accidentally released.

Swings and jungle gyms should be strongly constructed. There should be no rough edges or exposed bolts, and no parts that could pinch or trap a young child.

Ensuring safety is an important responsibility of caregivers. Remember, when you are buying toys, or taking care of children, those children don't know what can harm them. It's up to you to protect them, by choosing safe toys and equipment.

Think It Through

1. **In what ways can product labels help you determine if a toy is safe?**
2. **What safety measures would you take if you were babysitting for children who had a jungle gym?**

Teaching the Feature
"Choosing Toys and Equipment"

Answers to Feature Questions

1. Product labels on toys might suggest what age the toy is appropriate for and might offer suggestions for safe use. Labels on soft toys may state if the product is washable.

2. Students should suggest checking that the jungle gym is sturdy, checking for any rough spots or exposed bolts, making sure children do not try anything too risky, supervising the children at all times.

Activities

Party! Party! Divide students into small groups and ask them to plan an entire birthday party for their "four-year-old niece or nephew" and eight friends. Have them plan the length of the party and scheduled activities as well as describe games to be played, food to be served, and any prizes or treats the children will take home as souvenirs. Finally, have them "select" an appropriate gift for the birthday child. Ask students to explain why they chose that particular gift.

Safe Toys Have students cut out pictures from magazines showing different types of toys. Then have them mount the cutouts on three large poster boards marked "Safe for under three years old"; "Safe for three to six years old"; "Safe for over six years old." Have students look over the boards and see if they disagree with any safety decisions. If they do, have them explain why.

Community Contact Suggest that students look through their homes to find toys that they might recycle and bring them to class. They should write a safety tag for each toy, suggesting the age, use, and what a child might learn from this toy. These could be donated by the class to a local hospital or day-care center.

Emphasize When selecting toys and equipment for children, keep in mind both the age and the individual development of each child.

Did You Know? It's not a good idea for adults to take too active a part in children's play life. If they do, children may come to depend on adults for entertainment. Or the children might have trouble developing independence and self-sufficiency.

Reteaching
Have the students list some common household items that would make good, safe playthings for infants and toddlers.

Reteaching
Play a game that preschoolers might enjoy, for example, ring-around-the-rosy. Ask students how they feel about playing this game at their age. You may wish to reinforce the importance of age-appropriate play by asking them to try other games such as peek-a-boo or pat-a-cake.

Enrichment
Arrange for students to visit a child care center, a nursery school, or an elementary school to observe children at play. Ask them to take notes and come back to class prepared to discuss what they think the children were learning through play.

Enrichment
From scrap materials, have students create an original toy to be used by infants. Students may wish to work individually or in small groups. Toys should be shown to the class. They should decide: Is the toy safe for infants? What can infants gain from using the toy?

Enrichment
Have students prepare a list of interesting outings and activities in your neighborhood that would be fun for a toddler. These could be simple, such as a walk to the library or a visit to the grocery store, or more complicated—for example, a walk to a park to look for different shapes of leaves. Tell students to include activities that would allow for a release of toddler energy.

How Preschoolers Play

Preschoolers are proud of themselves and their abilities. Their muscles are developing rapidly, and their favorite words are "Watch me!" as they run, jump, and climb.

Preschoolers are also mastering many fine-motor skills. Good toys for this age group include blunt-edged scissors, coloring books and crayons, finger and poster paints, modeling clay, plastic and wooden construction sets, dolls with changeable clothes, small cars and trucks, tricycles, and swings and jungle gyms.

Children at this age tire quickly. Some still take a daily nap, and all need a change of pace at the end of an hour of active play. That is the time for gluing a collage or looking at a book.

Because preschoolers' abilities are increasing quickly, they want and need many opportunities for learning. Here are some suggestions:

- Taking them on walks through the neighborhood or to the local store. Talk about whatever you see along the way.

Preschoolers like to dress up in old clothes and pretend to be other people. This role playing helps them develop emotionally and socially.

Emphasize Children of all ages enjoy books. For a one-year-old, choose short books with large, simple pictures. They like rhymes, objects they can name, and textures they can touch. Two-year-olds like simple stories about families and familiar experiences. Three-year-olds enjoy longer stories that use their imagination or help them learn about things. When reading to a child, use gestures, facial expressions, and even different voices. Let the child turn the pages. Ask the child questions as you read, or let the child act out special parts. Children who enjoy books when they are young are more likely to enjoy reading throughout their lives.

- Encouraging questions and safe exploration.
- Helping them resolve their disputes and learn to take turns with their favorite toys when they are playing in groups.

Can you remember dressing up in your mom's or dad's old clothing and playing house? Maybe you had clothes or props for playing cowboys or pirates. Preschoolers are very interested in using their imagination. They enjoy **role playing**, pretending to be someone else. Role playing helps them express their feelings and practice the behaviors they are learning. Providing children with old clothes and props will amuse them for a long time.

If the children are old enough to read simple books, let them read to you or to younger children. Help them with words they don't know and praise them for the parts they do well. Don't be too quick to help, though. They may just need a little more time to figure out a word.

Here are some tips on reading:

- Choose books and stories that are appropriate for the child's age. Most children have favorite books they love to have read to them again and again.
- Let the children look at the pictures in the book you are reading for as long as they like.
- Ask questions about the pictures or the story in order to involve the child. Let the child turn the page.
- Act out the stories when you're done.

Passive Activities

Passive activities are those that you watch or listen to, but do not join in. Watching a baseball game is passive, as is watching television or listening to a story.

Although passive activities don't get children into the action, they still affect them. Children learn how to do things by imitating people they watch, and their ideas and attitudes are affected by what they see and hear.

Reading Books

Young children love to be read to. They especially like it when you vary the pitch of your voice and use facial expressions and body movements to act out the characters in a book. Try to get them to join in whenever possible. They can cheer for heroes, boo the bad guys, and repeat simple rhymes as you read.

Watching Television

Some caregivers use television to keep children busy. They might let children watch television so they can do other things without any interruption. It's important to keep in mind that television programs can have a great impact on children. They may contain violence or scary situations that children do not understand.

Watching television can be a good change of pace for children, but, like anything, too much of it can be harmful. Children should not be watching television because they can't think of anything else to do. Challenge yourself to find interesting activities for children instead of relying on television.

If the children do watch television, you should get into the habit of sitting and watching it with them. Be ready to discuss what is going on and to explain situations that may confuse them. Turn off the set or turn to another channel if the program is not suitable for children.

Emphasize It is good to involve children in passive activities near bedtime. Students may wish to discuss why this is important.

Cross-Reference You may wish to refer students to "The Quiet Times" on pages 236-237.

Emphasize Television can be both a positive and negative influence. Children should watch television only in moderation, choosing the more worthwhile programming. Many cartoon shows for children contain violence, and young children cannot distinguish between fantasy and reality. Commercials also have a strong impact on children's wants.

Teaching "Passive Activities"

(Pages 197-198)

This section teaches how children learn by being read to or watching television, sports, or other activities in which they do not directly participate.

Checking Comprehension

✓ How can you get children to join in when you are reading to them? *They can be asked to comment on the characters, repeat simple rhymes, say names of characters aloud, or comment on the illustrations.*

✓ If you decide to allow a child to watch television, why is it important to watch with the child? *You need to able to discuss and explain any situation that may be confusing or disturbing.*

Activities

Skill Builder: Reading
Ask students to make a list of the books they enjoyed listening to or reading when they were very young. Ask them to react to these books now. Would they select these books to read to another young child?

Skill Builder: Critical Thinking
Tell students that the average child spends several hours a day watching television. Ask students to think of three ways in which children can be interested in active pursuits instead of watching too much television.

Reteaching
Have students give examples of television programs that might have *positive* effects on children. Then have them give examples of television programs that might have *negative* effects on children.

Enrichment
Have students work independently or in groups to do one or more of the following:

- Write and illustrate a book for a toddler or preschool child.
- Sew a fabric book for an infant or toddler.
- Develop a puzzle or game for a preschool child.
- Write a computer program that will be a game for a preschool child.

CHAPTER OVERVIEW

Chapter 21 discusses ways in which a parent or caregiver can meet the physical, mental, and social needs of children within a safe environment. It introduces the need to control children's activities by establishing rules and setting limits and communicating these rules to children in a positive way. The main focus of this chapter is on safety and preventing accidents. First aid for many types of childhood accidents and maladies is discussed in detail.

INTRODUCING THE CHAPTER

Motivators

Childproof Write *childproof* on the chalkboard, and ask students for its definition. Have them suggest some ways to make an ordinary house childproof.

Using the Photograph Have students study the photograph on this page. Then ask: "What safety precautions should the babysitter take when children are playing outdoors? What other outdoor activities would be suitable for a child of this age?"

Setting Limits Explain to students that setting limits is an important part of parents' responsibilities. Have students consider whether parents should always have to explain or give a reason for a limit. What kind of limits do students' parents still set today? What kinds of limits do students now set for themselves?

Introducing the Objectives

Discuss the chapter objectives on this page. Remind students that the objectives focus on important chapter content.

Introducing Vocabulary

Write the term *first aid* on the board. Ask students why they think it's called first aid. Elicit the explanation that the term is used to describe help or emergency treatment given in the first moments after an accident, before regular medical treatment is obtained.

CHAPTER

21

Care and Safety

OBJECTIVES

This chapter will help you to:

- List and describe ways to meet children's physical, mental, emotional, and social needs.
- Discuss the importance of setting limits and communicating positively.
- Describe the basics of accident prevention and first aid for children.

WORDS TO REMEMBER

child abuse
childproof
distract
first aid
Heimlich maneuver

Chapter Resources

Teacher's Classroom Resources
- Lesson Plan
- Life Skills Activity, *"Read Me a Story, Please"*
- Reproducible Master, *Positive Communication*
- Extension Activity, *First Aid*
- Chapter Test

Student Workbook
- Study Guide
- Worksheet, *Caregiver to the Rescue*

When you care for children, you have to be able to meet all of their needs. Children need someone to feed and dress them, to teach them about their world and the people in it, and to comfort them when they are hurt or upset.

As a parent or caregiver, you help guide children's behavior by setting limits and sticking to them. In doing this, you will make the children feel comfortable and loved, and give them opportunities to play and learn.

You are also responsible for keeping the children in your care safe. This means not only protecting them from obvious dangers such as electrical outlets and sharp objects, but also protecting them from people who might want to hurt them. If you do your job well in all these areas, you will help the children you care for to grow, to learn, and to become confident and self-reliant.

Caring for Children

In Chapter 18 you learned that parenting means taking care of children and meeting all their needs. Whether you are a babysitter, a camp counselor, or a nanny, for some period of time you will be doing the parenting for the children in your care. The children will look to you to provide them with many of the things their parents provide, from a glass of milk to a bedtime story. You must meet their physical, mental, emotional, and social needs.

Meeting Physical Needs

Think back to the ways you have been cared for in your life. When you were a small child, you were helped at special times in your day: mealtime, bedtime, bathtime, and playtime. With this help, you could have your physical needs for sleep, food, cleanliness, and exercise satisfied.

Here are some tips for helping you meet the physical needs of the children in your care:

- **Bedtime.** Getting children to bed is often the caregiver's most difficult task. Younger children may be fussy and tearful at bedtime, and older children may try to persuade you to let them stay up later. It helps to follow the children's usual bedtime routine. A warm bath, a bedtime snack that includes milk, and a bedtime story often help children to relax and go to sleep. Once they are asleep, check on them often.
- **Mealtime.** If you are going to make a simple meal for the children, find out from their parents what foods to serve and how to prepare those foods. If you are expected to use a microwave oven or other appliances, make sure you

When caring for children, you must meet all their needs. Bedtime might involve nurturing and guidance, as well as physical care.

Cross-Reference See Teen Tips "Baby Basics" on pages 232-233.

Focus on Health Accidents take more young lives in America than any disease. Thus, parents and caregivers must be alert to the safety needs of infants and children—both inside and outside the home.

Emphasize Nursery furniture must be checked for safety. Space between the slats of cribs and playpens should be no more than 2 1/2 inches. Paint should be nontoxic and lead-free. There should no exposed bolts or rough edges. The top of the crib sides should have a plastic covering (teething rail).

TEACHING THE CHAPTER

For convenience, the teaching suggestions for this chapter are arranged according to the following lesson topics:

- "Caring for Children," pages 201-202
- "Rules and Limits," pages 203-204
- "Keeping Children Safe," pages 204-207

Teaching "Caring for Children"

(Pages 201-202)

This section teaches how to provide for the physical, mental, and social needs of children.

Checking Comprehension

✓ Name one thing to do when serving a meal to children. *Any one: find out what foods to serve and how to prepare them, know how to use appliances, follow the usual routine.*

✓ In what ways can a caregiver make children relax and feel comfortable at bedtime? *A bedtime story or song, a warm bath, or a warm glass of milk and a snack are ways to help children to go to sleep. It is important to follow the child's usual routine.*

✓ What are the two most important things to remember when you are giving a young child or an infant a bath? *Make sure the temperature of the water is warm, but not too hot; and never leave the child alone in the tub, not even for an instant.*

✓ How can a caregiver help a child learn and develop language skills? *By talking and reading to the child.*

✓ Name two ways that a caregiver can give children emotional support and guidance. *Any two: praise their work, encourage them, give them love and attention, respond quickly when they are upset or hurt, comfort them.*

✓ What social skills can a caregiver help a child with? *A caregiver can help a child learn to get along with others and to communicate.*

know how to operate them or ask the parents to show you. You should follow the children's normal mealtime routine. Have them eat in the same place and at the same time as they usually do.

- **Bathtime.** When you are bathing toddlers or infants, never, ever leave them alone in a bathtub, not even for an instant. In addition, before you place a child in bathwater, check the temperature of the water to make certain it is warm, but not hot. Drowning and scalding are two very common childhood accidents.
- **Playtime.** When you play games with children or read to them, you provide companionship and you help them learn about their world. If children are playing together, you need to monitor their play and intervene if they start squabbling, name-calling, or hitting each other. Use such incidents as opportunities to teach children how to share and take turns.

Whatever activity you are engaged in as a caregiver, you need to keep the children safe. As much as possible, a child's environment should be made **childproof**, or safe for children. Childproofing should be done by parents, but a babysitter who knows what to look for can help make sure a child is safe.

Here are some things that should be done to childproof a home:

- Dangerous objects, such as glass knickknacks, scissors, and matches should be placed out of reach.
- Plastic caps should be placed over any unused electrical outlets.
- Gates should be installed at the top and bottom of stairs until children can climb the stairs safely.
- Any cabinets or closets that contain medicines or dangerous substances should be kept locked.

Meeting Mental Needs

Caregivers can help children learn about the world and develop their mental skills in these ways:

- By playing games that are appropriate to a child's skill.
- By changing to a new game when a child tires of what he or she is doing.
- By talking to the child to help him or her learn and develop language.

You can review some of the play ideas in this unit to help you meet children's mental needs.

Meeting Social and Emotional Needs

Children look to caregivers for emotional support and guidance. Be ready to praise a drawing or a project that a child has done. Encourage a child who becomes tired or frustrated with a game or toy.

You can help children socially and emotionally in other ways:

- Give them love and pay attention to them; this helps them feel loved and secure.
- Respond quickly when they are hurt or upset.
- Teach them to get along with others—by sharing toys, for instance.
- Help them learn to communicate.

Young children may cry when their parents leave. Be understanding. Often, you can quiet them by interesting them in a toy or a song. They usually get over their unhappiness quickly.

Children who wake up frightened need to be reassured that they are safe. Never make fun of their fears. Comfort them by talking or singing to them, or by holding or rocking them.

Activities

Skill Builder: Writing
Have students develop a checklist of items needed and steps to be taken before a baby is put into the bath. Have students consider how this list may change as the child grows older.

Skill Builder: Critical Thinking
Ask students to choose one room in their home. Have them survey the room for safety. Have students determine: Is the room childproof? What would have to be done to make the room childproof? They may wish to sketch the room "before" and "after" childproofing, or they may present their findings in one or two paragraphs.

Reteaching
Lead the class in a discussion to help students understand the importance of following a child's normal routine. Have them give examples for mealtime and bedtime routines.

Reteaching
Have students give examples, taken from previous discussions and from their reading, of play ideas for developing mental and language skills at various age levels.

Enrichment
Explain to students that the physical needs of children are met differently in different cultures. Have them go to the school library to research care of children in another culture. Suggest that they look up kibbutzim (where children are raised in a communal setting in Israel), select an African tribe, or research a South American Indian family. Have them share their findings with the class.

Enrichment
Have students bring in pictures of children receiving various kinds of attention from caregivers. Ask students to classify the pictures by identifying which need or needs are being met—physical, mental, or social. Ask students why it might be difficult to limit the classification of some pictures to one category.

Emphasize Children need nutritious food for proper growth and development. Poor nutrition can affect physical and emotional health.

Focus on Health Babies should not go to sleep sucking a bottle of milk or juice. The long exposure to the milk or juice can cause tooth decay.

Real-Life Situations Children can be seriously injured or killed in an auto accident if not buckled into a car safety restraint. Infants need a bucket-type carrier in which they recline backwards. Toddlers should use a special seat with a harness or protective shield. Children over age four, depending on their size, can be secured by regular seat belts.

These caregivers are helping the children develop their mental skills as they learn about animals. What rules or limits might the caregivers have set?

Rules and Limits

Children need to have limits placed on what they can do and where they can go. Setting these limits is the parents' responsibility, but other caregivers must uphold them. It is always important to ask parents what limits they have set.

Setting Limits

Some limits are set to protect the children's safety. You should refuse to take children in, or near, dangerous areas that cannot be childproofed.

If the children are going to be outdoors near water, make sure that you review their parents' rules for water play. If they are going to use bicycles or other wheel toys, show them exactly where they can ride and review bicycle safety rules with them. Such boundaries and rules prevent accidents.

Limits also apply to behavior. For example, children learn what time to go to bed or how they should play together.

Communicating Positively

Children like to try out forbidden activities when someone new is in charge of them, but they need to know that the limits hold true at all times. Be firm about what is and is not permitted.

One way to handle this problem is to focus on what children may do, rather than on what they may not do. "You can run all the way to . . ." is a more positive way of suggesting limits than starting every sentence with *Don't*. See the chart on page 204 for examples of how to give children positive directions.

Of course, sometimes you can't enforce a limit by gentle reasoning. When a child chases a ball into the street, you don't have time to reason with him. You must take immediate and complete control. Either call out a sharp command or grab him, or do both.

Teaching "Rules and Limits"
(Pages 203-204)

This section teaches the reasons and procedures for setting and enforcing rules and limits.

Checking Comprehension

✓ Compare parents' and caregivers' roles in setting and enforcing limits. *Setting limits is the parents' responsibility, but caregivers must know what the limits are and then uphold them.*

✓ What is the best way to tell a child about limits placed on him or her? *By communicating them in a positive way.*

✓ What is the purpose of providing distractions for children? *Interesting and safe activities can keep them from becoming restless and bored and getting into trouble.*

Activities

Skill Builder: Writing
Ask students to write a paragraph describing a situation in which it would be appropriate for the caregiver to take complete control over the child, rather than using gentle reasoning.

Skill Builder: Critical Thinking
Have students play the roles of parent and child. Before the role playing begins, ask the student playing the "child" to state how old he or she is. The students should develop short skits in which the "parent" must set limits.

Emphasize Children who know their limits feel secure.

Emphasize When setting limits, parents must keep in mind the limited knowledge the child has attained at a particular age and stage of development.

Real-Life Situations Spanking seldom helps a child learn proper behavior. Most child-care experts recommend that spanking be used very seldom, if at all. Too often spanking is used to vent a parent's anger and frustration. The child learns that hitting, rather than self-control, can be used in conflict situations.

Reteaching
Ask students to compare and contrast several positive and negative ways of communicating limits to children. You might want to begin with an example of a sentence beginning with "Don't . . ." and ask students to suggest a positive version of the same message.

Enrichment
Have students discuss the importance of creativity when relating to children—especially as it relates to setting limits and providing distractions. Have them creatively extend the list of positive and negative ways of communicating limits to children.

Teaching "Keeping Children Safe"
(Pages 204-207)

This section teaches accident prevention and elementary first-aid procedures.

Checking Comprehension

✔ Which items in a household can be potentially dangerous for infants and children? *Any of the following: small toys or objects; toys with breakable or sharp parts; plastic bags; stairs; electric outlets or wires; furniture that isn't sturdy; the range and oven; knives and breakable dishes or glasses.*

✔ What potential dangers should you look for when you take children outside or to the park? *(1) Make sure they don't run into the street; (2) make sure they use park equipment safely; (3) watch them at all times near a pool or body of water.*

✔ Give examples of childhood injuries or symptoms of illness for which you should call an ambulance immediately. *If a child has trouble breathing, is badly burned, has a broken bone, or is bleeding severely.*

Positive Communication

Children respond better to positive statements than to negative ones. They will also be happier if they are told what they can, rather than what they can't do.

What to Say	What Not to Say
"Let's read a story."	"Stop running around!"
"You can play here in the living room."	"Get out of the kitchen!"
"You can phone George to say hello."	"Don't go out!"
"You can play on the swings."	"Stay off the jungle gym!"
"Let's play with the toy truck."	"Put down your brother's toys!"
"Pet the dog gently."	"Don't hit the dog!"
"You can stay up until 8:00."	"You have to go to bed soon."

Providing Distractions

A good way to prevent arguments over limits is to provide distractions. Children who are busy with safe, interesting play are far less likely to become restless and get into trouble. You can **distract** children, or lead them away from something they shouldn't do, by interesting them in another activity.

Planning interesting activities is important. If it is raining and you are stuck indoors, try an art project. You can organize a finger-painting session, which preschoolers enjoy, with a minimum of effort and supplies. You can help children build something with their blocks.

If you take the children outside, organize races and games or take them for a walk, perhaps to a nearby park. Have a picnic lunch or play on the swings and jungle gym. When you can keep children busy in these ways, you prevent the arguments and fights that result from boredom.

Keeping Children Safe

Keeping children safe is your most important job. When children miss a meal or go to bed later than usual, little harm is done. When they are not protected from danger, however, serious and even fatal accidents can occur.

Fingerpainting is a good activity to amuse preschoolers on a rainy day.

Real-Life Situations Young children should be taught what to do in case of an emergency, although they should not be frightened unnecessarily. They should learn their name, address, and telephone number in case they are ever lost. They should learn how to telephone for help, and how to get out of the home in case of a fire. They should be warned never to go off with strangers. Some parents establish a "code" in case a friend has to pick up the child at a school or day-care center. Unless the adult says the code word, the child is forbidden to leave with the adult.

Preventing Accidents

Children don't understand the dangers that surround them, and in their eagerness to learn and explore, they will try anything. Babies put things in their mouths; toddlers poke things into electrical outlets or wander into busy streets; preschoolers may be fascinated by water or fire; and older children may wander off in stores or crowds.

To prevent possible accidents, follow these guidelines:

- Don't give babies small toys or objects that they could accidentally swallow. Toys should not have any breakable or sharp parts. Give babies playthings that are large and soft.
- When changing diapers, never leave an infant alone on a table. He or she may turn over and fall off.
- Keep plastic bags away from children to prevent suffocation.
- Restrict crawling babies and toddlers to places they can explore safely. Don't let them play on stairs, with electrical outlets or wires, or with any breakable or dangerous objects.
- Take toddlers off any piece of furniture that isn't sturdy. Also take them off if they are reaching too far and might lose their balance.
- In the kitchen, keep children away from the top of the range and oven so they can't burn themselves.
- Keep knives and breakable dishes away from children.
- Outside, always watch toddlers to prevent their running out into the street or riding their wheeled toys into the paths of automobiles.
- At a playground, make sure children use the equipment safely. It is very easy for a child to slip or fall off a piece of playground equipment.
- At a public pool, keep your eye on the children at all times and call the lifeguard immediately if any child is in trouble in the water. If you are watching children at a home with a pool, be especially alert. Small children can slip away from you and drown in a pool in a matter of moments.
- In a car, a child should always ride in a child car seat, no matter how short the trip. The safest spot for a child is in the middle of the backseat.

Gates can restrict babies and toddlers from exploring areas where they might get hurt.

✓ What should you do if the child you are watching cuts himself or herself? *Apply direct pressure to stop the bleeding; then wash and apply an antiseptic to the cut. Put on a bandage. If the cut is deep, call the doctor.*

✓ What symptoms signal a possible allergy to an insect bite? *Shortness of breath, fainting, and stomach pain.*

✓ What should you do if a child has swallowed a poisonous substance? *Immediately call the poison control center and report the name and quantity of the substance. Do what the center says. Take the container with you to the doctor or hospital. If you are babysitting, notify the parents.*

Activities

Skill Builder: Critical Thinking
Have students relate ways in which they or their parents dealt with an emergency situation with a child. This might be a personal experience the students remember from childhood. Have them consider: How was the emergency handled? Would they have handled the situation differently?

More About Preventing Poisoning Keep household cleaners stored above floor level, not below the sink. Never reuse bottles or food containers for household cleaners. Use childproof locks on cabinets and medicine cabinets. Keep medicines out of reach and locked if possible. Children learn by imitating, so avoid taking medicine in a child's presence. If you are using a poisonous product and are interrupted by the doorbell or phone, take the product with you, so the child cannot get into it. Read all labels carefully before using a product so that you know what to do in the event of accidental poisoning.

Teaching the Feature
"Facts on Child Abuse"

Answers to Feature Questions

1. Students might make a number of suggestions, such as better support for parents and education for parents and caregivers.
2. Answers will vary but might include: They might not want to get involved. They might not be positive. They might be afraid to ruin their relationship with the family.

Activities

Reasons for Abuse Lead the class in a discussion about the various kinds of child abuse and their causes. Ask students to talk about possible reasons why people abuse their children. What measures can students suggest for helping parents who abuse their children?

Discussing Cases of Abuse Have students select a newspaper article or a series of articles about a case involving child abuse. Ask them to find out what the outcome was. Then have students discuss how the courts deal with people suspected of child abuse and what other action might be taken.

Community Contact Ask students to do research in their community to compile a list of support groups and service agencies that would aid families under stress. The completed list could be given to the local library in booklet form.

HEALTH WATCH

Facts on Child Abuse

Sometimes children are physically or emotionally mistreated. That mistreatment is called **child abuse,** and it involves more than just an occasional scolding or spanking. Child abuse has long-lasting effects on the physical, emotional, mental, and social health of its victims.

Child abuse occurs in all levels of society: among rich and poor, and among all races and ethnic groups. Parents who are under extreme stress are more likely to abuse their children than are other parents. Financial problems, family problems, and drug and alcohol abuse are sometimes causes of abusive behavior.

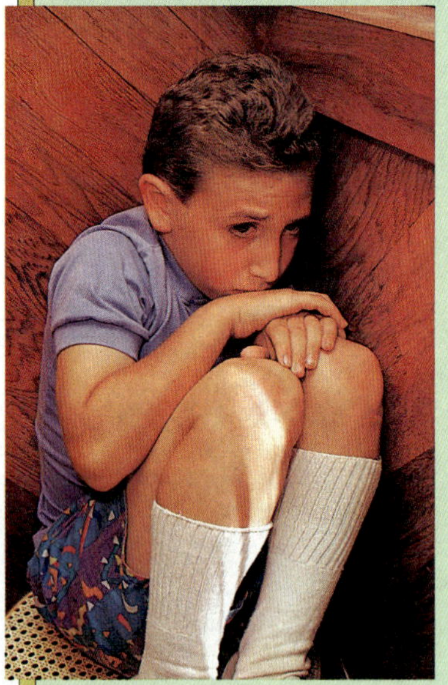

Child abuse can be divided into the following categories:

- **Neglect.** A parent or guardian fails to give a child basic love and care. The parent may not feed or clothe the child or provide medical care. The child may be left unattended for long periods of time.
- **Physical abuse.** The abuser physically injures a child in some way. Beating, scalding, scratching, or burning are some types of physical abuse.
- **Sexual abuse.** An adult forces or persuades a child to have sexual contact with him or her. Usually the abuser is a person the child knows well, such as a family member or neighbor.
- **Emotional abuse.** Emotionally abused children may be constantly yelled at, intimidated, ridiculed, or humiliated. They may be continually made to feel bad about themselves and may suffer from a loss of self-esteem. They may even be told, "You're stupid. I hate you."

Abuse tends to be repeated and to increase in frequency and severity unless help is obtained. Child abuse can be treated and the cause prevented. Help must be given to both the abused child and the abuser to stop the pattern and to prevent it from recurring.

A child who is being abused may bear visible signs of neglect or physical abuse. Signs of sexual and emotional abuse are usually harder to identify, but the children may give unconscious signals. Abused children may not want to go home. Some abused children are withdrawn, while others act like bullies. Some may even give hints, such as saying that a "friend" is being hurt.

If you suspect that a child is being abused, seek guidance from your parents or from an adult you can confide in, such as a teacher, a counselor, or a member of the clergy. Most communities have resources to help deal with child abuse. Every state and county has an agency to protect children. Various hot lines are available, on the city and national level, for calling and reporting the abuse or for getting advice about what to do.

Think It Through

1. **What do you think could be done to help cut down on the number of cases of child abuse?**
2. **Why do you think some people are afraid to report suspected incidents of child abuse?**

Emphasize Most parents get angry and feel frustrated at times, but they have developed ways to cope. Some ways of maintaining control include taking deep breaths, counting to ten, and, if possible, seeking help with the child from a friend, neighbor, or relative.

Focus on Relationship Skills Ask students to think about how they cope with stressful situations. What stress-reducing steps could they take in a crisis situation? Ask for volunteers to share their ideas.

Giving First Aid

Children dash around with abandon, unaware of the many dangers that surround them. As a result, they tend to hurt themselves fairly often, though usually in very minor ways. As a caregiver, you should know the basics of **first aid**: emergency care or treatment given to an ill or injured person.

In case of very serious illness or injury, or if you feel uncomfortable administering first aid, call an adult for help Call an ambulance immediately if a child has difficulty breathing, is unconscious, is badly burned, has a broken bone, or is bleeding severely.

First Aid

Always contact the parents if there is a serious injury or illness.

Scrapes and bruises Clean scrapes with soap and water; apply antiseptic and bandage. For bruises, apply a clean washcloth wrung out in cold water.

Nosebleed Keep child seated and leaning forward. If head is tilted back, child may choke. Apply direct pressure by pressing on bleeding nostril. Apply a cold towel to nose and face.

Earache Pain can be relieved by covering the ear with a warm towel or heating pad set on low. Call doctor.

Cuts Apply direct pressure to stop bleeding. Wash and apply antiseptic and a bandage. If cut is deep, call doctor.

Bites (insect) For minor bites, wash the area and apply antiseptic or calamine lotion. For bee, hornet, or wasp stings, scrape against the stinger with a flat object, like a piece of cardboard, until you pull out the venom sac. Wash area thoroughly with soap and water. **Caution:** Some people are highly allergic to stings. If child is short of breath or faint or has stomach pain, call doctor immediately.

Bites (animal or human) Wash the wound with water; clean with soap and water, and cover with gauze. Call doctor.

Burns For minor burns, immediately run cold water on the burn for about five minutes and apply a clean, dry dressing. For major burns, rush to hospital immediately. Do not try to remove burned clothing.

Sprains Don't allow child to walk. Elevate foot and apply a cold pack. Call doctor.

Choking First, look into the throat to see if something is caught there. Next, try to get the child to cough up the object. If these methods don't work, you can use the **Heimlich maneuver.** This procedure works by your using pressure to force the object that is interfering with breathing from the throat. For older children and adults, stand behind victim and place your fists just below her rib cage. Have her lean forward while you give one quick, upward push against her abdomen. This forces the air in her lungs to expel the object. Repeat if necessary. If the object doesn't come out, seek help immediately.

For infants and toddlers, turn child face down over your arm. Using the heel of your other hand, give four quick blows between the child's shoulder blades. Turn child over, supporting his head, neck, and back. Position your two fingers below the rib cage and above the navel, and give four quick thrusts. Repeat if needed.

Poisoning If a child swallows a poisonous or irritating substance, call the nearest poison control center immediately. Report the name and quantity of the substance and follow the center's instructions. Take the container with you if you go to the doctor or hospital.

Electric shock Don't touch the child until his or her contact with electricity is broken, or you will get a shock, too. Turn off electricity if you can, or pull or push child away from source of shock with a stick, cloth, or rope, but never with anything metal. If child is not breathing, apply mouth-to-mouth respiration if you know how. Call ambulance immediately.

Focus on Health All children should be immunized to protect them from serious diseases—polio, diphtheria, whooping cough (pertussis), tetanus, measles, rubella (German measles), and mumps. A vaccine, given orally or by injection, helps the body produce antibodies that fight off the disease. The first immunizations are usually given to infants at age two or three months. Some, such as those for tetanus, must be renewed throughout your life. Parents should keep a record of the child's immunizations as many states require certain ones for all school-age children. Ask students if they know which diseases they are immunized against.

Skill Builder: Reading
Ask students to read about what types of accidents often occur to children. Ask them to compile some statistics specifically identifying age groups, types of injuries, and places where injuries occur. Ask students to summarize their findings.

Reteaching
Have students prepare two posters illustrating the Heimlich maneuver, one for older children and one for infants and toddlers.

Enrichment
Students should design a pocket-sized first-aid device in any compact form, such as a card, wheel, chart, or list. They should include local emergency telephone numbers (such as poison control and hospital) and some suggested first-aid steps to deal with various emergencies.

Enrichment
Have students make a first-aid kit. Ask them to explain why they selected the items for their kits. Suggest that they show the kit to a paramedic or other health official and ask him or her to rate the kit.

COMPLETING THE CHAPTER

Summary

- Caregivers help children meet their physical, mental, and social needs.
- Parents must set limits to guide children's behavior and provide for their safety.
- Parents and caregivers need to provide a safe environment for children and prevent accidents and harm whenever possible.
- Caregivers must be able to give first aid for common household accidents and to know when to call for help.

For Review

Objective Review Questions Have students complete the "Reviewing the Facts" section on this page.

Study Guide Have students complete the study guide from Chapter 21 of their *Student Workbook*.

Safety Poster Ask students to develop posters on child safety. The posters might illustrate various situations—for example, in the home, in the street—in which safety measures are needed. Students should make up appropriate slogans for their posters.

For Evaluation

Outdoor Fun Ask students to write a brief description of a planned outing full of safe and interesting activities for a toddler.

Group Input Ask students to look at the list you made earlier on the chalkboard of ways to childproof a home. Ask them to add any other ways of childproofing that they can think of, now that they have read the chapter.

Chapter Test Have students complete the test for Chapter 21 that appears in the *Teacher's Classroom Resources*.

CHAPTER 21 REVIEW

Answers to "Reviewing the Facts"

1. Bedtime, mealtime, bathtime, playtime.
2. Any three: place dangerous objects out of reach; place plastic caps over electrical outlets; install gates at stairs; keep dangerous substances locked up.
3. Any four: praise; encourage; love; pay attention to; respond quickly; teach how to get along with others; help to communicate; be understanding; reassure; comfort.
4. To prevent arguments and stop children from getting into trouble.
5. Any four: don't give small objects that could be swallowed; never leave infant alone on changing table; keep plastic bags away; restrict children to safe places; take toddlers off unsteady furniture; keep children away from range; keep knives and breakable dishes away; prevent running into the street; make sure equipment is used safely; watch closely at a pool; use a car seat.
6. When there is a serious illness or injury, or if you feel uncomfortable administering first aid.
7. A technique for forcing objects out of the throat or windpipe.

Reviewing the Facts

1. List four daily activities that give caregivers opportunities to help children meet their physical needs.
2. What are three things parents can do to childproof their home?
3. Describe four ways that a caregiver can meet the emotional and social needs of a child.
4. Why is it a good idea to provide children with distractions?
5. What are four safety guidelines to follow to prevent possible accidents?
6. When should you call an adult for help with first aid?
7. What is the Heimlich maneuver?

Thinking Critically

1. Imagine that a niece (a toddler) is coming to stay at your house. What would you need to do to make the house childproof?
2. What kinds of accidents are most likely to happen to the children in your neighborhood? What could be done to prevent such accidents?

Applying Your Skills

1. **Planning a Meal.** Look through cookbooks and get ideas for nutritious meals that could be served to young children. Plan a lunch or dinner and explain how it would be attractively served.

2. **Preparing a Brochure.** Put together a brochure about childproofing that could be distributed to prospective parents. Explain the importance of childproofing a home, then provide a list of step-by-step procedures that parents could follow.

3. **Developing Questions.** When you care for somebody else's child, you need to know what rules and limits the parents have set. Make a list of the questions you should ask parents so that you can enforce their rules while they are absent.

Answers to "Thinking Critically"

1. Answers vary but may include placing all dangerous objects out of her reach; placing gates at the stairs; locking up any dangerous substances.
2. Answers will vary depending on the neighborhood. If there is a lot of traffic, then children might wander in front of cars or trucks. In order to prevent this, more people would need to be educated about the danger, and caution signs erected along the road. Other neighborhoods might have potential dangers such as lakes or ponds, railroad tracks, old mines or wells, swimming pools, or construction sites.

CHAPTER

22

Babysitting: Earning and Learning

OBJECTIVES

This chapter will help you to:

- Explain how to run a babysitting business.
- List the information you need to be a responsible babysitter.
- Describe ways to handle the problems babysitters may have.

WORDS TO REMEMBER

day-care center
family day care
licensed
reference

Chapter Resources

Teacher's Classroom Resources
- Lesson Plan
- Life Skills Activity, *Are You Prepared to Care?*
- Reproducible Master, *Babysitter's Emergency Card*
- Extension Activity, *Babysitting Job Sheet*
- Chapter Test

Student Workbook
- Study Guide
- Worksheet, *Babysitting Dollars*

CHAPTER OVERVIEW

This chapter describes the management skills involved in running a babysitting business, including negotiations with parents. It stresses decision-making skills and the responsibilities a caregiver incurs. The information a caregiver needs, both for normal child care and for emergencies, is explored in some detail. Finally, the chapter discusses careers in child care.

INTRODUCING THE CHAPTER

Motivators

In What Ways Is a Babysitter Like a Parent? Ask the class to think about the parents' responsibilities toward their children that were discussed in Chapter 18. Then have them decide which of those responsibilities are passed on to a babysitter who is hired to watch their children.

Using the Photograph Have students study the photograph on this page. Then ask: "What kind of relationship do you think the people in the picture have? What responsibilities will the babysitter have while the parents are gone? How could the babysitter prepare for her job?"

Discussion Question Remind students that they know that a babysitter takes on the parents' responsibilities, but ask them about the *rewards* of the job.

Introducing the Objectives

Discuss the chapter objectives on this page. Remind students that the objectives focus on important chapter content.

Introducing Vocabulary

Write the term *day care* on the board. Point to its two roots—*day* and *care*. Explain that many parents rely on other caregivers to provide for their child's physical, mental, and social health. Point out that when the term *day care* is used as an adjective, as in *day-care center,* it is usually hyphenated. Ask students to think of other words that follow this practice. Point out that day-care centers are commonly called child care centers.

TEACHING THE CHAPTER

For convenience, the teaching suggestions for this chapter are arranged according to the following lesson topics:

- "Running a Babysitting Business," pages 210-212
- "Dealing with Problems," pages 213-214
- "A Job Well Done," page 214

Teaching "Running a Babysitting Business"
(Pages 210-212)

This section teaches the students that babysitting, like any other responsible job, requires people to manage their time and be organized. Babysitters must have a clear agreement with the parents on what is expected of them on the job.

Checking Comprehension

✔ What business experience can you gain from babysitting? *You learn about earning money, managing time and resources, and dealing with employers.*

✔ What is a good method for sitters to use to make sure they do not forget an appointment? *They can keep a calendar of social and work dates right by the telephone.*

✔ Describe what you should settle with parents about rules and limits. *You should find out what the rules and limits are and how you should enforce them.*

✔ What are some examples of things a responsible caregiver should not do while the parents are away? *Entertain friends, talk too long on the telephone, leave the house untidy, answer the door to a stranger.*

✔ How should you handle an employer who wants you to do household work? *You can explain politely that your rate does not include housework and that such work takes your attention away from the children.*

One thing has become very clear to fourteen-year-old Caitlin in the last several months: she loves children. Because of this interest, Caitlin has thought about different caregiver roles. Caregivers can be parents, foster parents, family members, child care workers, and babysitters. All of these people need skills as they care for children, either on a short- or long-term basis. Caitlin hopes to have several caregiving roles in her future.

For now Caitlin is satisfied to be with the children she babysits. While parents are away for short periods of time, Caitlin takes on the responsibility for their children's safety, welfare, and happiness. When a child is sick or unhappy, she meets the child's needs and feels good about her success.

Babysitting offers Caitlin several rewards. Not only is she earning money, but she is also preparing herself for her future roles. She especially wants to be a child care worker, someone who has a regular job caring for children. Caitlin realizes that much of what she does now as a babysitter will help prepare her for this career.

Running a Babysitting Business

Babysitting gives you practice in caring for children, making decisions, and dealing with new people and new situations. It can help you decide if you would like a career working with children, and it can also be fun. One other benefit that you can gain from your jobs is that you may develop close relationships with the children you care for.

Babysitting is a business. You will earn money and gain experience in managing your own time and resources. If you are organized and if you understand what the job requires, you should be very successful.

If you want your child care jobs to multiply, you will have to be businesslike in your dealings with each of your employers. Your rates, hours, and responsibilities should be clear to both you and your employer before you start work. Then both parties should stick to the agreement.

Making and Keeping Appointments

One of the biggest mistakes you can make as a babysitter is to forget an appointment. Almost as bad in parents' eyes is a last-minute cancellation.

To prevent these mistakes, keep an appointment calendar next to the telephone at home. Write everything you are scheduled to do in it: club meetings, a friend's birthday party, swim team practices, and all your child care jobs. Then when someone calls to offer you a job, you will be able to check your calendar and tell at a glance whether you are free that day at that time.

If you have to cancel, let your employers know as early as possible. If you find someone capable to take your place, they will appreciate it and will remember that you are a responsible person.

Agreeing on Rates and Hours

When parents call, clearly state what you charge for your services. You won't seem very businesslike if you tell your employers to pay you what they think is fair. Also, it is possible that you will end up being underpaid.

Find out what others in your area charge and set the same rate. You may want to charge extra for difficult jobs, such as those that involve large families, infants, or late hours.

Focus on Management Ask students to share with the class the changes they would make in negotiating with parents and being prepared for child care in the light of the suggestions in this chapter.

Emphasize Not only should caregivers have emergency numbers like fire, ambulance, and doctor at hand, but they should also make sure they know the telephone number and address where they are employed. They should have this information near the telephone in case of an emergency.

When caring for children, always get needed information from parents before they leave. Be sure you know where they can be reached in emergencies.

You should also establish the length of the job. Find out what time to arrive and what time the parents expect to return home. Make arrangements for transportation. Will the parents be picking you up? How will you get home? By being clear about these details from the start, you will prevent confusion later on.

Getting the Information You Need

When parents hire you to care for their children, you become their employee. Like any employee, you have a responsibility to carry out your duties competently. To do this, you need to obtain certain information.

Before the parents leave, make sure you find out the following:

- What is the schedule for mealtime and bedtime?
- What foods are the children allowed to have for meals and snacks?
- Do they take any medicines?
- Do they have any allergies or fears?
- What are the rules for watching television?
- Where are the children's rooms and bathrooms?
- Where are the light switches?
- How do you work the appliances you will need to use?
- Where are flashlights and first-aid supplies kept?
- Where are the fire escapes?

You should also find out what rules and limits the parents want you to follow with their children. You need to know, for example, if it is acceptable to take away privileges when a child misbehaves. Sometimes, it helps to go over rules with the parents while the children are there. Then the children know that you are aware of the limits.

It is also essential that you get the phone numbers of the following:

- Place where you can reach a parent.
- Fire department.
- Police department.
- Child's doctor.
- Local poison control center.
- Nearest hospital emergency room.
- Local ambulance service.
- Nearby family member or friend.

The chart on page 212 shows what this "emergency card" would look like.

Focus on Safety When caring for children in a large home, keep lights on in several rooms. The house will look occupied. In an apartment, be sure you know the location of stairways and fire escapes.

Activities

Skill Builder: Science
Remind students that although babysitting is an art, it is also a science. Ask students to consider the elements, based on observation, that are involved in running a child care service. Working in pairs, have students make up a form on which they could record their observations about a child's age, stage of development, feeding behavior, upsets, if any, and so on. Ask them to consider how such observations would improve the service.

Skill Builder: Math
Have the students compute possible earnings for different kinds of babysitting situations. Have them build in additional charges for staying after midnight, for several children rather than one child, and for any additional tasks they think they might be asked to do.

Reteaching
Ask students to create a want ad that lists the personal characteristics needed by a caregiver.

Enrichment
Have students take turns role playing an interview with a babysitter in which one student is the parent and another is applying for the babysitter's job.

Teaching "Dealing with Problems"
(Pages 213-214)

This section teaches the students how to deal with unexpected illness or emergencies, as well as with children who are unhappy when they are left with a babysitter.

Checking Comprehension

✓ Give examples of unexpected situations that can arise when you care for children. *Crying, illness, accidents, fire.*

✓ How should a caregiver respond to a crying child? What are possible reasons for the child's crying? *The caregiver should respond quickly and try to find out why the child is unhappy. The child could be hungry, tired, hurt, or upset because parents left.*

✓ If you are asked to care for a sick child, what should you know about managing the illness while the parents are away? *You should have detailed instructions on any medicine you have to administer—how often, how much.*

✓ What is the most important rule to follow in case of fire or another emergency? *Stay calm! If you panic, you'll frighten the children.*

Emergency Information Card

Parent's names ______

Phone number where parents can be reached ______

Fire department ______

Police department ______

Poison control center ______

Child's doctor ______

Ambulance ______

Hospital emergency room ______

Nearby relative or friend ______

name ______

number ______

Acting Responsibly

Your employers may tell you to make yourself at home, but that does not mean that you can behave exactly as you would in your own home. Here are some do's and don'ts:

- Check with the parents about snacks and about using the phone, the television, and the stereo.
- If you do use the phone, keep your calls short. You would not want to tie up the line, because the parents might be trying to reach you.
- Don't entertain friends on the job. Your job is to watch the children, and friends would be a distraction.
- While the parents are out, you are responsible for their house. You should leave it as neat as you found it. If you prepare a meal or a snack for the children, you should clean up the dishes. Help them put away any toys or games they have played with.
- Take a few precautions. Keep all doors and windows locked. Never open the door to strangers. Don't give information over the phone. Don't tell the caller who you are, where the parents are, or when they will be back. Ask to take a message and get the caller's name and number. If the message is very important, you can call the parents and tell them.

Doing Work, Not Favors

While employed, your job is to care for the children, not to clean the house or do the laundry. Some chores, like cleaning up the children's dishes after a snack, should be done. If your employers expect extra favors, however, like taking out the garbage or cleaning the living room, explain politely that your rate does not include housework. Also point out that the extra work takes you away from the children.

You have a right to expect certain things from your employers. If they find themselves out later than planned, they should call to let you know. If they don't, tell them in a friendly way that you would appreciate a call next time. They should also provide you with the information and instructions you need to do your job.

Did You Know? Parents can ease the problems of leaving a child with a caregiver. The parents could play peek-a-boo with infants, helping them learn about separation. Parents could explain to an older child ahead of time that they will be away from the home but will return at a specified time. Parents should have a new caregiver meet the child, if only for a few moments, before they leave. Parents should describe the child's routine in detail to the caregiver.

Dealing with Problems

When you care for children, you are responsible for their safety and welfare. Part of that responsibility includes being prepared to handle unexpected situations, such as crying, illness and accidents, fire, and other problems.

Crying

Young children may cry when their parents leave. Be understanding and try to get them interested in something else, such as a toy or a song. They usually get over their unhappiness very soon.

At other times, children may cry because they are tired, hungry, hurt, or upset. If this happens, you should respond quickly. Ask them what is wrong, and try to solve the problem if possible. Children need someone to comfort them and to reassure them.

Illness and Accidents

Sometimes, you may be asked to care for a sick child. You should get detailed instructions from the parents about how to manage the child's illness while they are away. Be sure you know when to administer medication and how much to give the child, and follow the instructions on any medicine bottle or pill vial very carefully.

If you are caring for a sick child, you will need to find some quiet play activities to amuse him or her. Play board games with the child, provide coloring books and crayons, or give the child blunt scissors, old magazines, and paste with which to make collages. Older children can build models, work on jigsaw puzzles, or do craft projects. When children are sick, their attention span is shorter, so you may have to change activities more frequently.

As you learned in Chapter 21, accidents sometimes happen, and you have to be prepared to handle them. One general rule to remember for any problem or emergency is *stay calm.* You may feel upset, but acting excited or panicky will only frighten the child and make things worse.

Review the first-aid tips on page 207, and always keep the list of emergency telephone numbers near the phone. Then, if an accident occurs, you can easily find the right number to call.

After feeding children, be sure to leave the kitchen as clean as you found it.

Real-Life Situations Most babies and young children have a special method of comforting that they like best. Some like to be held and rocked. Others are comforted by sucking on a thumb, fist, or pacifier. Many children have a special stuffed toy or blanket that they like to hold. When you are caring for children, it helps to know how best to comfort a child.

Activities

Skill Builder: Critical Thinking
Ask students to imagine that they are babysitting for two children, one three-year-old and one six-year-old. Write the following situations on the chalkboard, and have students suggest what they would do *first:*

- The three-year-old is crying because his parents have just left.
- The toast in the toaster oven catches fire and begins to burn.
- The telephone rings and someone asks to speak to one of the parents.
- The six-year-old falls off her bike and skins her knee. She's sobbing, and her knee is bleeding.

Skill Builder: Writing
Have students as a class develop a letter to send to the U.S. Department of Health and Human Services asking for information and pamphlets on babysitting, child safety tips, toys and games for young children, and so on. Select a student to type and send the final letter.

Reteaching
After reviewing the first-aid section of Chapter 21, the class should discuss the steps a caregiver should take in the event of a common household accident or injury.

Enrichment
Remind students that occasional emergencies can arise from threatening weather. Have them read in the library the information they might need to cope with such an emergency, such as a tornado or hurricane. Have them compile a list of procedures to follow for the weather conditions most likely to occur in the region in which they live.

Enrichment
Have students create a form for parents to fill in and leave with a babysitter.

COMPLETING THE CHAPTER

Summary

- Babysitting is a business and must be carried out in an organized and responsible fashion.
- Parents and sitters should agree on rates, hours, and responsibilities before the job starts.
- A sitter should get specific information from the parents about the children's mealtime, bedtime, medicine, and restrictions, as well as about the location of various rooms and safety devices in the house.
- A sitter is responsible for the safety and welfare of the children and must be prepared to handle unexpected situations and emergencies.
- Babysitting is a good way to find out if you might want a job working with children.

For Review

Objective Review Questions Have students complete the "Reviewing the Facts" section on this page.

Study Guide Have students complete the Study Guide from Chapter 22 of their *Student Workbook*.

Preferences Ask students to consider their own experience and to state which age group they prefer to care for and to give reasons for their choice.

Class Debate Have students debate the pros and cons of licensing of day-care facilities. Suggest that they research the legal requirements governing day care in your state before the debate.

For Evaluation

Checklist Ask students to prepare a checklist of things to do before accepting any caregiving job.

Are You a Good Caregiver? Ask students to write a short essay in which they evaluate their own interests and personality for suitability as a responsible babysitter.

Chapter Test Have students complete the test for Chapter 22 that appears in the *Teacher's Classroom Resources*.

CHAPTER 22 REVIEW

Answers to "Reviewing the Facts"

1. Any four: practice in caring for children; practice in making decisions; practice in dealing with new people and situations; better understanding of careers; close relationships with children; fun; money.
2. Rates, hours, and transportation.
3. Any three: bedtime and mealtime schedules; meals and snacks; medications; allergies and fears; television rules; location of bedroom and bathroom; light switches; how to work appliances; flashlights; first-aid supplies; fire escapes.
4. Any five: where parents can be reached; fire department; police; doctor; poison control center; hospital; ambulance service; nearby family or friends.
5. Don't tell the stranger that you are a babysitter; don't say where the parents are or when they will be home. Take a message; if important, call the parents.
6. Provide quiet playthings; play board games; change activities often to prevent boredom.
7. Stay calm.
8. Find all children and go to nearest exit. To avoid smoke inhalation, cover mouths with damp cloths and stay close to the floor. Feel closed doors for heat before opening. After getting out, call fire department from a neighbor's home.

Reviewing the Facts

1. Name four benefits that you gain from babysitting.
2. What three topics should you discuss with parents when they call to hire you to care for children?
3. Give three examples of information you need to obtain from parents when babysitting for their children.
4. List five telephone numbers you should keep by the telephone when you care for children.
5. What should you do if you are babysitting and a stranger calls?
6. What can you do to amuse a sick child?
7. What is the most important rule for handling accidents when you are caring for children?
8. What should you do if a fire breaks out while you are babysitting?

Thinking Critically

1. Amanda has her own babysitting business. Tonight, she is babysitting for the Martins for the first time. She arrives on schedule, but the Martins are running late and don't have time to give her the information and phone numbers that she needs. What should Amanda do?
2. If you were asked to babysit for an infant but had never done so before, what would you do?

Applying Your Skills

1. **Finding Average Rates.** Calculate the average rate for babysitting in your community by asking five people their hourly rate. Use this information to set your own pay rate for future jobs.
2. **Writing an Ad.** Write an ad or flyer to publicize your services. Include information about your age, experience, and the hours you are available. What other information would you include?
3. **Compiling Emergency Information.** Consult your local telephone directory for the numbers of the police and fire departments, poison control center, and hospital. Make a checklist of emergency telephone numbers to take with you each time you care for children.

Answers to "Thinking Critically"

1. Answers will vary. Some students may say that Amanda should insist that the parents give her at least a phone number where they can be reached. Other students may say that Amanda should tell the parents that she can't babysit for them unless they give her all of the information she needs.
2. Answers will vary. Some students might say that they would turn down the offer. Others might ask the parents if they could bring along a friend or relative who knows how to care for an infant.

CHAPTER

23

Ready for Parenthood?

OBJECTIVES

This chapter will help you to:

- Describe some of the challenges of being a parent.
- Discuss the financial and personal costs of parenthood.
- Describe the rewards of parenthood.

WORDS TO REMEMBER

emotional maturity
fetus
financial stability
premature birth
prenatal

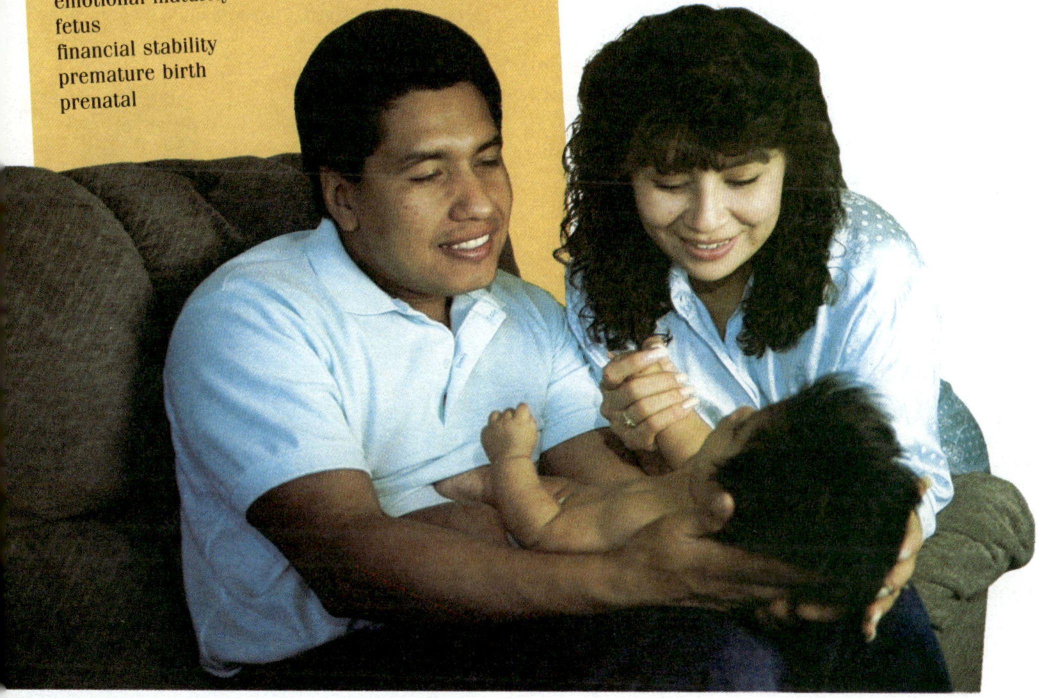

Chapter Resources

Teacher's Classroom Resources
- Lesson Plan
- Life Skills Activity, *Do You Know the Costs of Having a Baby?*
- Reproducible Master, *Ready for Parenthood?*
- Extension Activity, *Teen Pregnancy*
- Chapter Test

Student Workbook
- Study Guide
- Worksheet, *Parenting—For Real*

CHAPTER OVERVIEW

Chapter 23 discusses the challenges of parenthood. It provides an overview of the adjustments that parents must make when they have a baby. The chapter describes some of the financial and personal responsibilities associated with parenthood. It emphasizes the importance of emotional maturity for parents. The chapter concludes with a description of the special satisfactions and rewards parenthood can bring.

INTRODUCING THE CHAPTER

Motivators

Parents Have a 24-Hour Job Write this sentence on the chalkboard, and ask students to explain what they think this statement means. Ask: "Do you agree with the statement?"

Using the Photograph Refer students to the photograph on this page. Ask students to describe the emotions that are displayed by the expression on the parents' faces. Have students brainstorm other emotions that new parents might feel.

Rewards of Parenthood Ask the class: "What do you think are some of the rewards of parenthood?"

Introducing the Objectives

Discuss the chapter objectives on this page. Remind students that the objectives focus on important chapter content.

Introducing Vocabulary

Write the words *prea, natalis,* and *prenatal* on the board. Explain to students that the word *prenatal* has two roots: *pre,* a prefix from the Latin *prae,* meaning "before," and *natal,* from the Latin *natalis,* meaning "to be born." Thus *prenatal* means "before birth." Ask students what the word *postnatal* means.

TEACHING THE CHAPTER

For convenience, the teaching suggestions for this chapter are arranged according to the following lesson topics:

- "The Challenge of Parenthood," pages 218-219
- "The Responsibilities of Parenthood," pages 219-220
- "The Rewards of Parenthood," page 221

Teaching "The Challenge of Parenthood"

(Pages 218-219)

This section teaches that parenthood changes a couple's life dramatically and that many of their dreams and plans may have to be postponed.

Checking Comprehension

✔ Give examples of some of the challenges that new parents face. *Any of the following: postponing career or education plans; more responsibilities and more work; less time for other activities and other people.*

✔ Why were these young people luckier than many parents of their age? *They loved each other and their baby. They also had advice and help from their parents.*

Activities

Skill Builder: Writing
Ask students to list the equipment that parents need to buy when they have a baby. Ask them to include everything they can think of, no matter how small, from crib to diapers.

Reteaching
Invite an outstanding recognized parent from the community to talk about the rewards and challenges of being a parent. Have students develop questions to ask the speaker.

Parents have a 24-hour job. They have complete responsibility for their child's health, safety, and development every day over the course of many years.

Parents have to invest a lot of time, energy, and money in their children, and they often have to postpone some of their plans and dreams. However, parenthood has many rewards. Seeing their children's accomplishments and helping them develop into happy, productive adults brings great joy to parents.

The Challenge of Parenthood

Donna and Mario had fallen in love. They knew they were young for marriage, but they wanted to get married anyway. Their parents asked them to wait. Donna's parents knew she wanted to go to college and become a teacher, and Mario's parents knew he planned to go to a local community college to study accounting.

Despite their parents' concerns, however, Donna and Mario got married right after they graduated from high school. They rented a small apartment, and Donna went to work in a department store. Mario took a part-time job at a garage and enrolled in classes at the community college.

Dreams and Realities

Two months later, Donna became pregnant. Neither of them had planned it that way or had even thought much about having a baby. Donna quit her job before the baby was born and postponed plans for college. Mario quit school and got a second job driving a truck.

In spite of these changes in plans, they were both excited. They were in love with each other, and they looked forward to having a child to care for and share their happiness. They wanted to help this new person grow and learn. They were a little scared, but they had each other and a lot of hope.

The Baby

Once Jan arrived, Donna's and Mario's lives changed completely. They still had their love, of course, and some fun, too, but they had many more responsibilities as well. It was hard for them to believe that anything as small as an infant could require so much work.

A lot of time and energy goes into being a parent. Changing diapers is only one of the many daily tasks that parents must do for a baby.

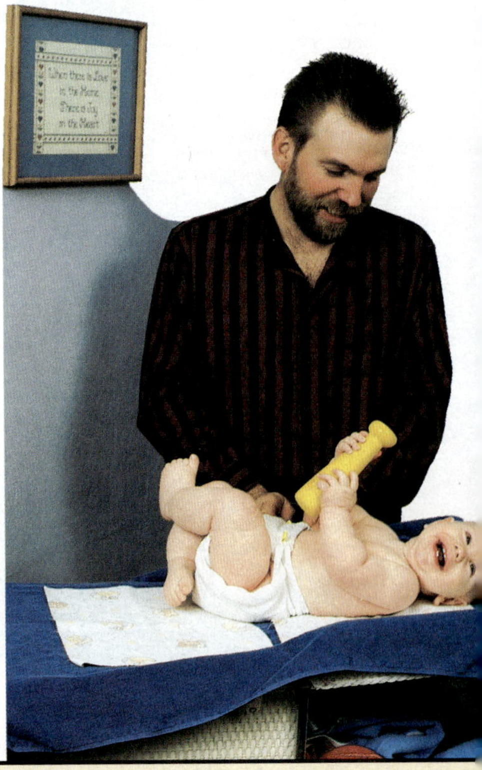

Focus on Relationship Skills After the birth of a child, the parents' relationship changes. The couple focus on the child's demands and needs, rather than on each other. A couple must make a conscious effort to relate to each other as *individuals* as well as parents.

More About Couple's Time A couple must make a point to set aside time to be alone together. The time together can take on many forms—a quiet walk, a cup of coffee, a date with dancing or dinner. This time should not be spent talking about the baby, but rather about each other, talking about feelings and aspirations.

There was washing and diapering and feeding around the clock. The list of needs seemed to go on and on. Donna and Mario found they had to rearrange their lives around Jan's needs. Still, they were lucky. They cared for each other and for their baby. They were able to get help and advice from their parents, and they were smart enough to use that advice to help them over the rough spots.

The Responsibilities of Parenthood

Having a child affects a parent's life in many ways. When a new baby arrives, both parents must consider their child in everything they do. They must also adapt to their new financial and personal responsibilities.

Financial Responsibilities

Parenthood involves financial responsibilities for the present and the future. There are doctor's bills to pay and baby food to buy. Babies require a lot of special baby furniture and equipment, such as cribs and car seats. They outgrow their clothing very quickly.

While two may live in a small apartment happily, three people need more space; this may mean moving to a larger and more expensive apartment. In addition, if both of the baby's parents want or need to go back to work after the child is born, they have to pay for child care.

For this reason, it is important for parents to have **financial stability**. They need to be able to meet all their expected, everyday living costs, which increase significantly when a couple has children.

Personal Responsibilities

Because caring for an infant is a full-time job, there may be little time left over for outside activities. Mario and Donna found that they had less time to spend with their friends. A child needs constant care and attention; you can't punch a time clock at five o'clock and quit working for the day.

Basic supplies for a baby include clothing and diapers, as well as equipment for eating, sleeping, bathing, and traveling. Some items can be borrowed to reduce costs.

Enrichment
Explain to students that the impact of having children is felt not only when a baby is born, but also throughout the couple's entire lives. Have students look at the scenario describing Donna and Mario on pages 218 and 219. Then ask them to write a paragraph describing what Donna's and Mario's lives might be like in five years. This activity may take the form of an essay or a dialogue. Ask for volunteers to share their predictions in class.

Teaching "The Responsibilities of Parenthood"
(Pages 219-220)

This section discusses the financial and personal responsibilities of being a parent.

Checking Comprehension

✓ What are some typical financial responsibilities for the parents of a new baby? *Doctor's bills, baby food, clothes, cribs, car seats, and, possibly, a larger apartment and child care.*

✓ Why is it important for parents to have financial stability? *They need to be able to pay for all expected, everyday living costs, which are considerably higher after they have children.*

✓ How might caring for a baby full-time change a couple's personal lifestyle? *They may have less time and energy for outside activities, friends, education, and each other.*

✓ Why is emotional maturity so important for parents? *It helps them make the necessary emotional adjustments of parenthood, such as giving love without expecting it back immediately and looking beyond one's own needs.*

Emphasize Parenting brings changes in lifestyles.

Did You Know? The estimated cost of raising a child to age eighteen in the late 1980s was $100,000 to $200,000.

Real-Life Situations Fewer than 50 percent of women who have a baby before age eighteen ever earn their high school diploma. To help more young mothers continue their education, some schools now have special programs for teen parents. The schools provide child care while the parents attend classes.

Activities

Skill Builder: Math
Ask students to bring in a local newspaper. Using ads from the paper and giving guidance, help students to prepare a monthly budget for a young couple and their new baby. Students should assume that their rent is $325 per month, utilities not included, and that their income is $1,000 per month. What will they need the rest of the money for?

Skill Builder: Critical Thinking
Explain to students that parents often change very much as they go through the processes of becoming parents. Ask students to write a brief essay or report on how the role of parenthood can be made more meaningful, before as well as after the baby is born.

Reteaching
Ask students to compare and contrast the personal lifestyles of a young couple before and after they become parents. How does a typical weekend change?

Enrichment
Suggest that students prepare a shopping list for parents of a newborn. They might use fliers from the local grocery stores, magazines, and store catalogs or make a trip to the supermarket and a department store. Then ask students to suggest other sources of supplies and equipment (such as buying used items or borrowing from friends and relatives). How much money could be saved?

Caring for a baby also takes a lot of energy. Parents of young infants often find that they are too tired for other activities or interests.

One of the biggest adjustments that new parents face is the change in their personal lifestyle. Because parents are responsible for providing for all of a baby's needs, they have to deal with limits on their personal freedom. Young adults who are just beginning to get to know themselves and to find out what they want out of life may be affected even more by this adjustment. For example, Donna and Mario want to continue their education, but they have decided to postpone their plans until their baby is older.

For many people, having a baby may mean having to postpone or change a rewarding and fulfilling career. Fortunately, babies grow to be toddlers, then preschoolers. Once children are older, parents can spend more time on their own interests, and parents and children can always enjoy doing things together.

Parenthood may require many emotional adjustments, too. One parent may feel left out if the baby occupies most of the partner's time. Those feelings may be difficult to deal with if a young couple has not spent much time together before becoming parents.

Also, loving an infant may seem like a one-way street. The baby can't talk about love or other feelings, but a smile or a hug helps keep you going.

To meet these emotional demands, parents need something more important than money—they need **emotional maturity**. They must be secure enough in their own self-image to be able to meet the emotional demands and responsibilities they face.

This maturity includes being able to give love without expecting it back right away. It also means being grown up enough so that they don't think of their own needs all the time.

Sometimes one parent feels left out after the arrival of a new baby. What could parents do to solve this problem?

Did You Know? Three out of every four teenage marriages result in divorce. Divorce statistics decline as the marriage age level rises.

Did You Know? Over one million children in America live with teen parents. More than half of these children live with single parents, generally the mother.

Real-Life Situations In many communities special efforts are being made to make teenage fathers feel more responsible for their children. Many young men do not realize their financial responsibility for supporting their child, even if they are not married to the baby's mother.

The Rewards of Parenthood

There is more to parenthood than the costs. Some moments make up for everything. Listen to the way parents speak of their children. Watch the light in their eyes when they say, "Do you know what my little Christopher did yesterday?"

Children are long-term investments. The bond formed by love and shared experience, by two lives helping each other develop, is emotionally very rewarding for parents.

Children also change the way you think about yourself and your world. Before you became a parent, you needed to think only about yourself and, if you are married, about your partner. When you become a parent, you think more about the future. What kind of a world will it be when your children are grown? Is that the kind of world you want for them? If not, what can you do to change it?

Helping children learn brings special satisfaction. Parents thrill to see their children master new skills. From the infant who begins to walk to the student graduating from high school, children give joy to their parents.

Parents enjoy watching a child grow, and they find it fascinating to observe all the changes. Seeing a child develop his or her self-concept leads parents to think about themselves, and, in fact, parents learn and grow along with their children.

Becoming a parent may be the most rewarding step to take in life. Parenthood involves a lot and requires even more than you expect, but for those who are ready for it, parenthood makes their lives richer and more satisfying.

Parents gain joy and satisfaction in helping their children learn about the world, master new skills, and develop positive self-concepts.

Teaching "The Rewards of Parenthood"
(Page 221)

Checking Comprehension

✓ How does becoming a parent change the way you think about yourself and your world? *Instead of just thinking about yourself and your partner, now you must think about the child and the future. What kind of world will your children grow up in?*

✓ How do parents get satisfaction from their children? *From helping them learn new skills; watching them grow and change; growing and learning along with them.*

Activities

Skill Builder: Writing
Have students write a humorous paragraph describing the life of young parents with a baby. They may wish to illustrate their prose.

Skill Builder: Critical Thinking
Ask students to consider when is a good time to plan for children. Ask them to think about what considerations they would give to financial security, stable relationships, careers, and so on.

Reteaching
Lead the class in a discussion of what it means to have emotional maturity. Ask them to give examples of this maturity either from incidents in their own lives or from fictitious situations.

Enrichment
Have students plan a panel discussion on teen pregnancy. Ask them to form committees to decide which outside resource persons to invite and the format of the panel discussion.

Did You Know? Some humorists note that the job of parenting is interesting, but the hours long, the work hard, and the pay is hugs and kisses.

Emphasize Parenthood can be nourishing to the mind and spirit. Parents can observe and try to capture the fresh, uninhibited open mind of a child. The skill of childlike (not childish) thinking is a rare treat to capture. Observing the magic, hope, and special way of thinking that a child displays is one of the most precious rewards of parenting.

Teaching the Feature
"Caring for the Unborn"

Answers to Feature Questions

1. By helping the mother to care for herself, by giving her both physical and emotional support, and by not making a lot of demands on her.
2. Women will find it easier to maintain healthful habits during pregnancy if they start them prior to pregnancy. Also, they will be healthier at the time they conceive the child.

Activities

Interview a Mother Suggest that students conduct an interview to find out how a woman they know cared for her unborn child. Did she have regular prenatal appointments with her doctor? What foods did she eat? Was she on a special diet? Did she need to rest a lot? Were there certain substances or activities she avoided? If so, what were they? How else did she care for the baby when she was pregnant?

Healthy Moms/Healthy Babies Ask students to develop a poster or flier explaining the importance of good nutrition for pregnant women. This should be colorful and attractive as well as informative.

Community Contact Ask students to find out what services are available in the community to help pregnant women and teens. The list might include clinics, food assistance programs, and social services. Suggest that they offer the posters made for the preceding activity to the services they list.

HEALTH WATCH

Caring for the Unborn

The responsibilities of being a parent don't begin when a baby is born. They start long before that. From the moment a child is conceived, the mother must begin caring for herself to ensure that her child gets the best possible start in life. This helps to prevent a **premature birth**, a birth that occurs before development is complete.

Here are some ways that an expectant mother can care for herself and her unborn child:

- Every pregnant woman should begin receiving regular **prenatal** (pree-NAY-tul), or before birth, medical care as soon as she realizes she is pregnant. If the first prenatal visit has not taken place before pregnancy, it should come during the early weeks. The mother should then return monthly until the seventh month, when more frequent examinations are recommended. Pregnant women can develop several physical problems or conditions, which can be life-threatening to the **fetus** (FEE-tuss), or the unborn child, if they are not treated. These include high blood pressure and German measles.
- The most important factor in prenatal care is good nutrition. If a pregnant mother wants to help her baby develop properly, she must eat a balanced diet consisting of food from the basic food groups.
- Expectant mothers should also get plenty of rest and moderate exercise. They should avoid becoming overtired and relax whenever necessary.
- Pregnant women should not take any medication without consulting their doctors. During pregnancy, both prescription and over-the-counter drugs such as aspirin can affect the growth of the fetus or cause a malformation as the fetus is developing.
- Alcohol, tobacco, and illegal drugs should be avoided. The use of these substances can result in serious problems such as low birth weight and birth defects.
- A pregnant woman should avoid having sexual contact with people who have sexually transmitted diseases such as syphilis, gonorrhea, genital herpes, or AIDS. She could pass it on to her unborn child, who could become seriously ill, deformed, or even die.
- If a woman is pregnant, she should tell medical personnel, dentists, and orthodontists, so that special precautions can be taken when X rays are needed. The radiation from X rays and other sources can be dangerous to an unborn child.

Think It Through

1. **How can the father participate in the care of the unborn child?**
2. **Many doctors recommend that women quit smoking and drinking alcohol and eat healthy foods *before* they become pregnant. Why do you think they make this recommendation?**

Did You Know? Babies born to teens who are under the age of sixteen are twice as likely to be underweight as the babies of mothers aged twenty to twenty-four. Low birth weight is the greatest threat to the life of a newborn.

Emphasize Stress the importance of regular prenatal care throughout pregnancy.

More About Caring for the Unborn Doctors can check the condition of the fetus by using high-frequency sound waves. Those waves are bounced off the fetus to create an image on a screen. The image shows the size, shape, and position of the fetus.

CHAPTER 23 REVIEW

Reviewing the Facts

1. Why is parenthood more demanding than a nine-to-five job?
2. How does parenthood affect a couple's material resources?
3. Why is financial stability an important factor in starting a family?
4. What are two ways that parenthood affects a couple's social life?
5. Give two examples of the emotional adjustments new parents may have to make.
6. What is emotional maturity?
7. Describe two of the rewards of parenthood.

Thinking Critically

1. Why is emotional maturity especially important for parents? What could happen when people who are not emotionally mature become parents?
2. Discuss some of the ways that young adults find out what is important to them and develop a sense of self. How can becoming parents hinder that process?

Applying Your Skills

1. **Comparing Costs.** Use a mail-order catalog to calculate the costs of equipping a home for a baby. Prepare two price lists: one for essential items and one for desirable but nonessential items. Add up your totals and compute the difference. What other alternatives could be used to obtain equipment? How would these costs compare?

2. **Exploring Effects.** Imagine that your long-term goal is to be a computer programmer; then imagine that while you are still in vocational school, you are about to become a parent. Write a short essay describing how you think parenthood would affect your goals.

3. **Developing a Survey.** Think about the questions you could ask parents in order to discover more about the pleasures that children bring. List your questions in a logical sequence. Use your list to conduct a survey of four or five parents.

Answers to "Reviewing the Facts"

1. Because parenthood is a 24-hour-a-day job and a parent's responsibilities never end.
2. Their present and future financial responsibilities increase.
3. A couple needs to be able to meet all their living costs, which increase significantly when a couple has children.
4. They may have less time to spend with friends; may have less energy and be too tired for other activities and interests.
5. Coping with jealousy and accepting the fact that babies can't tell you about their feelings.
6. Being secure enough in one's own self-concept to meet the emotional demands of others.
7. Any two: enjoying children's accomplishments; loving; sharing; thinking about yourself and the world in a different way; helping children learn; watching children grow and develop.

Answers to "Thinking Critically"

1. Emotional maturity is important because parents must be able to meet the emotional demands and physical needs of their children. Parents who are not emotionally mature may abuse or neglect their children, abandon them, or fail to provide them with the social and moral guidance they need.
2. Answers may vary. Students may talk about jobs and careers, travel, material possessions, volunteer work, friendships, further education, and so on. Becoming parents means that young adults may have to give up or postpone some of these things until they have met the needs of their children.

COMPLETING THE CHAPTER

Summary

- Being a parent is very challenging. It can change a couple's lifestyle and priorities.
- There are many responsibilities involved in being a parent. These responsibilities are partly financial, as living costs increase considerably when children are born.
- Parents also have personal responsibilities and may find that limits on their freedom and emotional adjustments are required.
- There are rewards to being a parent, but it requires emotional maturity and lots of hard work.

For Review

Objective Review Questions Have students complete the "Reviewing the Facts" section on this page.

Study Guide Have students complete the Study Guide from Chapter 23 of their *Student Workbook.*

Single Parents Ask students to identify some of the difficulties that a single parent may have raising a child that a two-parent family would not have.

Dreams/Realities Have students use an artistic medium to illustrate the dreams versus the realities of parenthood.

For Evaluation

Changes and Parenthood Ask students to make a list of the changes parenthood can bring to the lives of the parents.

Energy Adaptation Remind students that caring for an infant requires energy. Ask them to list the daily activities of an infant that would demand energy from the parents.

Chapter Test Have students complete the test for Chapter 23 that appears in the *Teacher's Classroom Resources.*

CHAPTER OVERVIEW

This chapter discusses the characteristics and skills required for careers working with children and gives detailed information on a number of jobs that involve working directly and indirectly with them.

INTRODUCING THE CHAPTER

Motivators

Who Works with Children? Students should name as many careers related to children as they can. Start students by suggesting teacher, pediatrician, physical therapist, camp counselor, and so on. Encourage them to think of jobs that involve indirect contact as well as direct contact with children. Save this list for the "Evaluation" activity at the end of the chapter.

Using the Photograph Have students study the photograph on this page. Then ask: "What job is this man performing? What job skills are evident from seeing him work with children?"

Introducing the Objectives

Discuss the chapter objectives on this page. Remind students that the objectives focus on important chapter content.

Introducing Vocabulary

Ask students: "What does the word *pediatrician* mean?" Explain to students that the root of *pediatrician* comes from the Greek word *paidos*, meaning "child."

TEACHING THE CHAPTER

For convenience, the teaching suggestions for this chapter are arranged according to the following lesson topics:

- "Characteristics for Careers Working with Children," pages 225-226
- "Jobs Working with Children," and "Getting a Job" pages 226-228

CHAPTER

24

Careers Helping Children

OBJECTIVES

This chapter will help you to:

- Identify the personal qualities a person needs to work well with children.
- Describe some jobs that involve working directly with children.
- Discuss some kinds of jobs in which people work for children.

WORDS TO REMEMBER

creativity
dietitian
pediatrician

Chapter Resources

Teacher's Classroom Resources
- Lesson Plan
- Life Skills Activity, *Meet the Caregivers*
- Reproducible Master, *Do I Want to Work with Children?*
- Extension Activity, *Careers Helping Children*
- Chapter Test

Student Workbook
- Study Guide
- Worksheet, *Caregiver Career Search*

Children make a lot of noise and have a lot of energy, and they constantly demand attention. Working with children can be exhausting, but when they smile at you or at something they have learned, the work seems worthwhile. People who enjoy working with children often have such characteristics as an interest in children, creativity, sensitivity, and a sense of humor.

Being a parent means working with children. Parents have the full-time responsibility for their children's health, safety, learning, and happiness, but parents can't do everything themselves. They need teachers, doctors, coaches, child care workers, writers, and many other kinds of people who work with young children and teens. Perhaps you will want to perform one of these jobs when you become an adult.

Characteristics for Careers Working with Children

Before exploring some actual jobs and careers that involve working with young children or teens, let's find out what characteristics are needed. Some of these personal traits are mental and some are emotional.

Interests and Skills

- **Are you interested in children and how they learn and grow?**
- **Can you treat each child as an individual, with his or her own unique qualities?**
- **Do you have creativity? Creativity** is the ability to use your imagination to do things in new ways. This characteristic can help you think of new and interesting activities for children.
- **Do you respect children as people?** You must show children that you respect their feelings and that you take their needs seriously.

This teacher is using her creativity and enthusiasm to interest the young children in a story. She enjoys helping them learn new concepts and skills.

Emphasize Child care workers must be selected carefully since a person's influence on a child may leave a lasting impact.

Did You Know? The school guidance office is a good place to begin exploring career aptitudes and interests. Students can find books and pamphlets and take a personality inventory with guidance from school counselors.

Teaching "Characteristics for Careers Working with Children"

(Pages 225-226)

This section teaches the particular talents and skills required for careers that involve working with children.

Checking Comprehension

✓ Why is creativity an important talent for a person who works with children? *It can help people think of new and interesting activities to do with children.*

✓ Why is it important to respect children as individuals? *Respecting their feelings will help children see that you think they are important and should be taken seriously. This is important in forming self-concept and self-esteem.*

✓ Why is it important for people who work with children to have a sense of humor? *They can help children learn to laugh at themselves and see the funny side of minor mishaps and frustrations.*

✓ What other traits would be important when working with children? *Being patient, calm, tolerant, enthusiastic, adaptable, sympathetic, interested, willing to learn.*

Activities

Skill Builder: Science
Explain to students that many psychologists specialize in child development. Ask them to suggest ways that the scientific method could be used in studying the development of children.

Skill Builder: Writing
Ask students to write a brief story for children. Encourage them to illustrate the story as well.

Reteaching
Ask students to work in small groups to develop a poster or collage depicting people in various careers related to children.

Enrichment
Invite a professional person (for example, a pediatric dentist, caseworker, child psychologist) to your class to discuss why he or she decided to work primarily with children. Have students develop a list of questions to ask the guest.

Enrichment
Have students put on a play showing what the world looks like from a child's perspective. Afterwards, discuss why people who work with children need to understand their point of view.

- **Are you patient, tolerant, and calm?** These qualities can help you play repetitive games and settle arguments.
- **Do you have a sense of humor?** If you do, you can help children learn to laugh at themselves and see the funny side of their mistakes.
- **Are you enthusiastic and willing to join with children in their play?** Playing with them shows them that you think they are important.
- **Are you adaptable?** Child care workers need to switch activities when children tire of what they are doing.
- **Are you sympathetic?** Can you put yourself in the children's place? Are you able to imagine what the world looks like from their perspective? If so, you will be able to calm their fears and respond to their needs more effectively.
- **Are you willing to learn about children?** To understand a child's behavior and needs, you must know what to expect at each stage of development.

If you have these qualities, you may be interested in some of the careers described below. Although this is just a sampling of the many jobs available, it should give you a basic idea of the variety of work you can do.

Jobs Working with Children

Many people work directly with young children or teens. Some provide day care or health care. Others help children learn or play.

Other people work in jobs related to children or teens. Some may create or sell products for children, such as clothes or toys. Others may work behind the scenes in schools, hospitals, or camps.

Entry-Level Jobs

A nanny cares for the children of a working parent or parents. This work is usually done in the child's home. (A child care worker, whom you read about in Chapter 17, does similar work in a child care center.) A nanny usually lives with the family, cares for the child in the evenings as well as the day, and receives free room and board as well as a salary. Babysitting experience and home economics courses are helpful for this job.

Camp counselors work with children at summer camps. They teach the children new skills, such as swimming, boating, and crafts, and they care for children who often are experiencing their first time away from home. Camp counselors are usually high school or college students. They may also work in day camps, where the campers go home every night. Scouting and babysitting experience is useful training for being a camp counselor.

Cafeteria workers prepare food and serve it to children in the school lunchroom. These workers should enjoy cooking and being with children. Patience and friendliness are a big help, too. Many mothers find this a convenient job, because it allows them to work when their children are at school and to be home after school is out.

Jobs That Require Training

A teacher's aide helps a teacher either with paperwork or with actual instruction in the classroom. The training needed for this job varies from one school system to another. Many two-year colleges offer a course of study leading to a degree for teacher's aides. With more course work, the aide can eventually become a teacher.

Focus on Life Management Suggest to students that they keep records of dates, places, and names and addresses of supervisors for any volunteer work they have done. These experiences can help when applying for a job in the future. Students should record their activities and responsibilities.

Emphasize People considering a career with children must have enough stamina to work under the pressures and demands of the day. They should have proper rest, a nutritious diet, and maintain good general health. The demands of jobs working directly *with* children and working *for* children differ in some ways.

Cafeteria workers are responsible for preparing nutritious meals for students.

A team coach works with children who enjoy athletics. Many coaches are hired by school systems, but some work for the community parks department. Coaches have a very important role. They instruct children not only in the basic skills of a particular sport, but also in good sportsmanship. The training for this job includes experience in sports and, usually, a certain number of college credits. Coaches who are also teachers need college degrees.

Children's book authors write books for children. They may write picture books for toddlers or novels for teenagers. There is no single way of becoming a writer, though most writers have college degrees. However, the most important requirements are the desire to write and the creativity to capture children's interests.

Coaches are employed by schools and recreational departments. If you like sports and working with people, a coaching job may be for you.

Teaching "Jobs Working with Children" and "Getting a Job"

(Pages 226-228)

This section looks at entry-level jobs, jobs requiring extra training, and those requiring an advanced degree. It explains what students can do now to prepare for a job working with children.

Checking Comprehension

✓ What is the difference between a child care worker's job and a nanny's job? In what ways are they the same? *A child care worker cares for the children in a child care center during the working day. A nanny cares for the children in their own home; he or she usually works day and night and receives room and board in addition to a salary. Nannies and child care workers do similar work in caring for children.*

✓ What would be good experience for someone who wanted to be a camp counselor? *Babysitting and scouting; knowing how to teach swimming, boating, crafts.*

✓ What skills and interests are desirable in cafeteria workers? *Cafeteria workers should enjoy cooking and being with children and should be friendly and patient.*

✓ If you enjoyed sports and working with children, what jobs might you consider? *Coaching in schools or community parks, camp counseling.*

✓ What are important skills and requirements for authors of children's books? *The desire to write and creativity or imagination.*

✓ Name three jobs dealing with children that require college degrees and, in some cases, advanced degrees. *Any three: teacher, children's librarian, pediatric nurse, pediatrician, or dietician.*

Did You Know? The Bureau of Labor Statistics, Washington, D.C., can provide you with information as to which child-care jobs will be in demand in the future.

Activities

Skill Builder: Writing
Have students write a brief paragraph describing the "ideal" nanny. They may be as creative and poetic as they wish.

Skill Builder: Critical Thinking
Hold a discussion in which students consider qualities that would be especially important for a pediatrician or pediatric nurse. Be sure they consider the fact that these professionals interact directly with both their young patients and the parents of their patients.

Reteaching
List the various levels of jobs related to child care on the board: entry-level jobs, jobs that require training, jobs that require advanced degrees. Then have students suggest various careers and have them categorize these under the appropriate heading.

Enrichment
Invite to class an instructor in child development or child-care training from an area college. Ask that person to discuss the topics covered in the curriculum and to describe the preservice training offered to students at the college.

Jobs That Require an Advanced Degree

How heavy is the earth? How many breeds of dogs are there? These are the kinds of questions asked of children's librarians. Whether they work in a school or a public library, librarians help children find books and information and teach them how to use reference materials. Children's librarians also purchase books and magazines for libraries. A children's librarian needs to have a college degree and often a master's degree as well.

The doctors who care for children are called **pediatricians**. Like all doctors, they have extensive training in both college and medical school, as well as in an internship at a hospital. They may have their own practice or work in a hospital or clinic. Some nurses also specialize in caring for children. These pediatric nurses may work for a doctor, advising parents about how to cope with childhood illnesses and other problems, or they may work on a hospital ward caring for gravely ill youngsters.

Children spend more time with their teachers than with any other adults except their parents. Teachers are responsible for helping children learn mental concepts and skills that they will need to succeed later in life. Even though teaching often means spending long hours at home planning lessons and grading papers, teachers receive a great deal of satisfaction from their careers. Teachers need a college degree and usually a teacher's certificate. Many also go on to get a master's degree.

A school dietitian plans and directs the purchase and preparation of the food in the school cafeteria. A **dietitian** is a person who has studied food and nutrition and their relationship to health and fitness. The aim of the school dietitian is to provide food that appeals to children, satisfies their nutritional needs, and meets the school's budget. Dietitians usually have a college degree in nutrition or food service, and most have a master's degree in food service. Management training is also a helpful background to have in this profession.

Pediatricians examine and treat children and advise parents about child care.

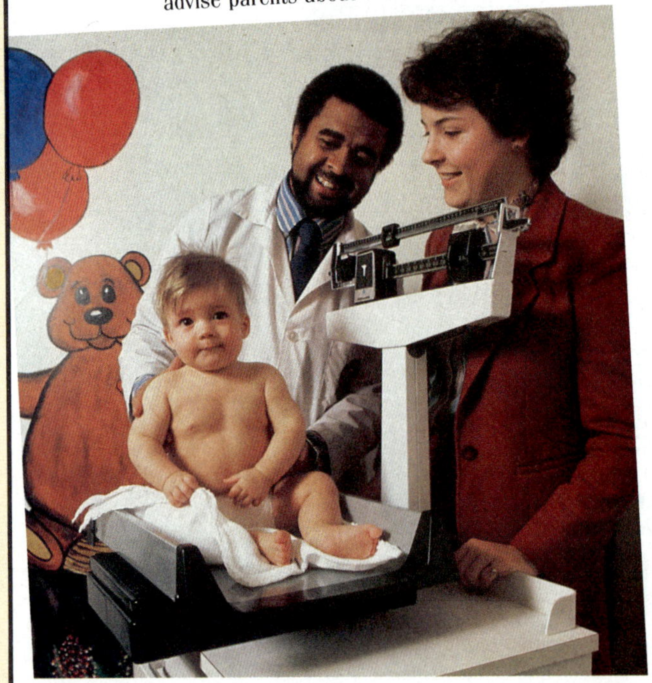

Getting a Job

If you think you might like a career working with young children or teens, you can start preparing now. While you are still in high school, you can get some basic experience by babysitting, scouting, or working as a camp counselor. Any experience you can gain will probably help you get the job you want.

Focus on Life Management Point out to students if they are considering an extensive, long-term babysitting job, they should have their employer *write out* the terms of employment. This will allow them to see exactly what is expected of them. Flexibility should be built in, since as the child changes, the nature of the job will change as well.

Did You Know? Some vocational programs offer child-care career skills or on-the-job training programs in which students can attend class part-time and work with children part-time.

INTERPERSONAL SKILLS

Volunteer to Learn

One of the best ways to find out whether you would want a career working with or for children is to do volunteer work that involves being with youngsters. Volunteer work gives you the opportunity to develop the skills you need to work with children, but it does not impose more responsibilities on you than you can handle.

If you can't figure out how to get two children to stop fighting or what to do for a child who is sick, you can always call on the other people around you for help. By watching the other workers, you learn how to care for children, how to remain calm in the face of emergencies, and how to control your own anger and frustration when things are going badly. Here are some ways you can volunteer:

- Become a candy striper or volunteer worker at a children's hospital or in the children's ward of your local hospital. Sick children demand a lot of extra attention, and they will sharpen your skills at providing them with amusement and comfort.
- Volunteer at a day-care center, Sunday school, or a children's group at a church or synagogue. You could also work in a summer recreation program for children. You will learn how to manage groups of children as you lead them in games and activities. You will probably also learn how to treat minor injuries, such as scrapes and insect bites, which commonly occur when children play outdoors. Working with groups of children will also help you develop the skills you need to handle the fighting, bickering, and name-calling that sometimes erupt among children.
- Volunteer to help the parent of an infant for an afternoon a week. You will learn how to bathe, feed, and handle a small baby, and you will see how much time and attention even the smallest child needs and demands.

Think It Through

1. **If you were to choose one type of volunteer work discussed above, what would it be and why?**
2. **In addition to learning child-care skills, what else can you learn by volunteering to work with young children?**

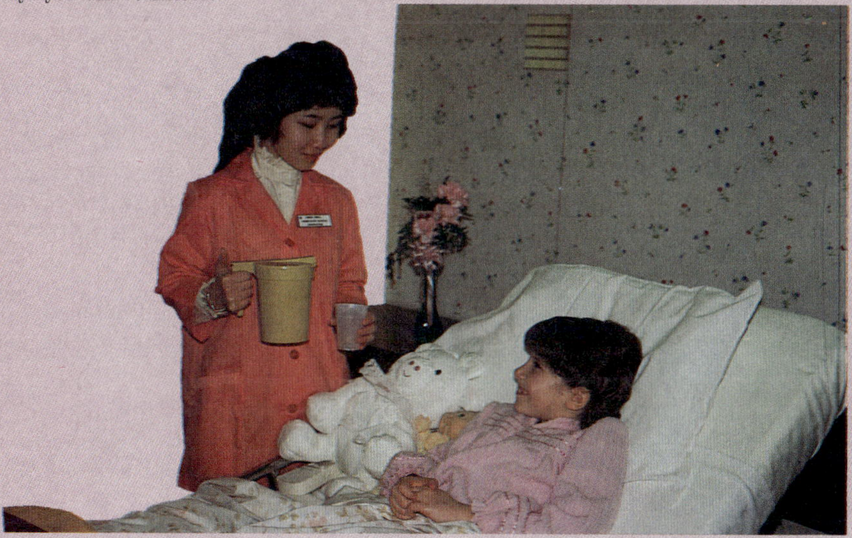

Teaching the Feature
"Volunteer to Learn"

Answers to Feature Questions

1. Answers will vary depending on students' interests. Some may prefer to work with sick children at a hospital, and others might like working at a Sunday school. Be sure students explain the reasons for their preference.

2. Students might suggest responsibility, time-management skills, empathy, and how to work with other adults.

Activities

Students as Volunteers Have students relate to the class any experience they may have had doing volunteer work with children. Ask them if they might share some of their most rewarding experiences and some of their most challenging experiences.

Conduct a Survey Suggest that students contact two or three organizations that use volunteers as a significant part of their work force to find out how many volunteers they need, how many they have, and what percentage of the total work force they make up. Have students discuss the results.

Community Contact Invite the volunteer coordinator of a local hospital to speak to your class about the need for volunteers, the jobs that volunteers do, and the procedures for becoming a volunteer. The volunteer coordinator might explain how volunteers are recruited. Students may try to publicize the need for volunteers and launch a campaign in the school for hospital volunteers.

Emphasize Volunteer work serves many purposes. Volunteers learn new skills, receive enrichment, and provide the community with valuable services that are needed.

Cross-Reference See more information about volunteer work in "Real-Life Situations" on page 163.

Did You Know? Many hospitals, political organizations, community services, and religious organizations would not be able to function without the work that volunteers do. In fact, many of those organizations are made up almost entirely of volunteers.

COMPLETING THE CHAPTER

Summary

- People who work with children need to have certain skills and talents. For example, they need to be creative, enthusiastic, and adaptable.
- Many jobs involve working directly with children, including nanny, camp counselor, coach, librarian, pediatrician, pediatric nurse, teacher.
- Jobs that involve working for children but not directly with them include school cafeteria worker, children's book author, and dietitian.

For Review

Objective Review Questions Have students complete the "Reviewing the Facts" section on this page.

Study Guide Have students complete the Study Guide from Chapter 24 of their *Student Workbook.*

Career Questions Have students select one career related to children. Ask them to list five or six questions they would ask a person already in that field.

For Evaluation

Aptitude Test Ask students to develop a checklist or quiz that would help identify a person's talents and skills for working well with children.

Classification Use the list developed by the class in the "Motivator" activity at the beginning of this chapter. Write the elements of the list on the chalkboard. Have students make three headings on paper: (1) Entry-Level Jobs; (2) Jobs That Require Training; (3) Jobs That Require an Advanced Degree. Ask students to classify each career under the appropriate heading.

Chapter Test Have students complete the test for Chapter 24 that appears in the *Teacher's Classroom Resources.*

CHAPTER 24 REVIEW

Answers to "Reviewing the Facts"

1. Any four: an interest in children and how they learn; ability to treat children as individuals; creativity; respect for children; patience; tolerance; calmness; sense of humor; enthusiasm; adaptability; sympathetic; willingness to learn about children.
2. Any two: nanny, camp counselor, cafeteria worker.
3. A nanny usually cares for children in the parents' home, while a day-care worker cares for children at a nursery, preschool, or day-care center.
4. Helps the teacher with paperwork or instruction in the classroom.
5. To be able to interest children in the books.
6. Both specialize in caring for children. They may work in a doctor's office, hospital, or clinic.
7. They plan and direct the purchase and preparation of food served in school cafeterias, and try to provide food that is both appealing and nutritious.
8. Babysitting, scouting, or working as a camp counselor.

Reviewing the Facts

1. Name three personal qualities that are useful for working with children.
2. Name two entry-level jobs that involve working with children.
3. What is the difference between a nanny and a day-care worker?
4. What does a teacher's aide do?
5. Why is creativity important for writers of children's books?
6. What jobs do pediatricians and pediatric nurses do?
7. How do school dietitians help children?
8. What experience could you get now to help you know if you would like a career working with children?

Thinking Critically

1. Discuss your own experiences in working with children. What were the most rewarding and the most difficult parts of the job?
2. Think of some of the people you know who work well with children. What words would you use to describe them? What special qualities do they have that make them good at their job?

Applying Your Knowledge

1. **Evaluating Children's Books.** Read three children's books by different authors. Rate each book on creativity and interest. Write a brief report comparing the books and tell which book you think a child would enjoy most.

2. **Creating an Advertisement.** Suppose that you work for an advertising agency. Write a toy advertisement that would appeal to parents of young children. Illustrate your ad with drawings or photographs.

3. **Identifying Special Qualities.** Write a description of your favorite teacher. Explain why you think this person does a good job. What special qualities does she or he have?

Answers to "Thinking Critically"

1. Students who have worked with children may cite the shared affection or the fun as the most rewarding parts of the job; and getting children to listen and follow rules as the most difficult parts.
2. The words and qualities students might suggest include: kind, patient, trustworthy, mature, sympathetic, loving, self-confident, tolerant, calm, flexible, and other qualities.

TEEN TIPS OVERVIEW

This section focuses on practical suggestions for three important aspects of child care.

Baby Basics

In this Teen Tip students look at the common tasks of feeding, diapering, and bathing that can seem formidable to the inexperienced. Step-by-step instructions will increase students' confidence as babysitters or parents' helpers.

Tidbits Toddlers Love to Eat

This Teen Tip offers fresh ideas for making attractive, nutritious meals that appeal to children's sense of fun as well as to their taste buds.

The Quiet Times

This Teen Tip presents a variety of ways for entertaining children at bedtime, naptime, or any other time that requires calm and quiet activities.

These "Teen Tips" support the contents of "Child Care and Development" by giving students ideas they can make use of whenever they are responsible for young children.

Introducing "Baby Basics"
(Pages 232-233)

Motivators

Discussion Question: Ask students: "Is it hard to care for a baby?" Discuss this question, drawing on students' experiences. Bring out that many people think caring for a baby is difficult and discuss what might make it difficult. Emphasize that caring for a baby is not difficult if a person knows how to feed, diaper, and bathe a baby.

What Do I Know? Ask students to jot down one tip they would give a friend that would help him or her feel more comfortable feeding, diapering, or caring for a baby. Tell students that this section will go into detail about feeding, diapering, and bathing a baby and may answer their concerns.

Teaching "Baby Basics"

Checking Comprehension

✔ If you had to sum up caring for a baby in just a few key words, what might you say? *Answers will vary but may include: use gentle actions; always use safety precautions; and keep a baby clean, dry, and fed.*

✔ Why should you never leave a baby alone on a table when changing diapers? *The baby can quickly turn over and fall.*

✔ Some babies don't like getting baths at first and protest quite vigorously. What might you do to bathe such a baby and get him or her over the dislike of baths? *Answers will vary but might include: get the baby used to a bath gradually, first by giving a sponge bath next to the tub and then by putting the baby into the bath just to be rinsed, just for a short time; amuse the baby with songs or games; give the baby bath toys.*

TEEN TIPS

Baby Basics

How to Feed Babies

Here are some hints on how to feed a bottle to a baby:

- Warm the milk by setting the bottle in warm water for one or two minutes.
- Always check the temperature of the milk by shaking the bottle upside down so that a few drops fall on your wrist.
- Make sure that the neck of the bottle is full of liquid so the baby takes in less air.
- Midway through the feeding, burp the baby to release any air in the stomach. Cover your shoulder with a towel in case some milk comes up. Hold the baby against your shoulder and pat firmly but gently on the baby's back. The baby can also sit on your lap as you pat gently on the back.

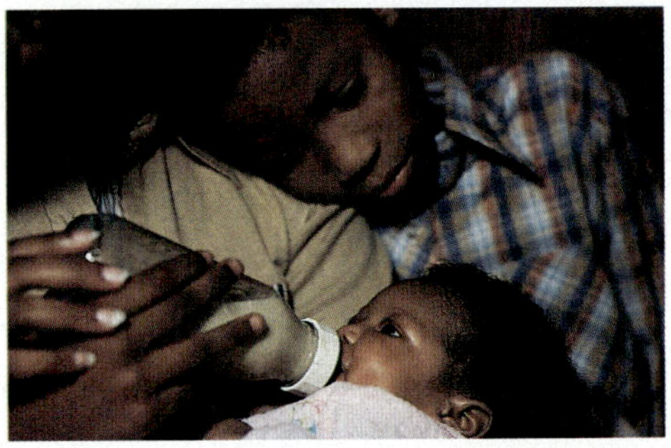

Emphasize Safety is a key consideration when feeding, diapering, or bathing infants. Ask students what possible dangers this activity might entail. If necessary, prompt students by asking them to think about how "squirmy" infants can be and how dangerous leaving an unattended baby on a changing table or in even a few inches of water can be for children, especially infants. Record the possible dangers.

How to Diaper Babies

Parents may use either cloth or disposable diapers. Here are some diapering tips:

- Use a clean, flat surface such as a changing table, crib, or towel on the floor. Have all supplies nearby before you begin.
- Never leave the baby alone on a table—she may turn over quickly and fall off.
- Remove wet or soiled diaper and clean the baby using warm water or diaper towels. Be sure to wipe from front to back. Apply powder, oil, or ointment if parents use it to prevent diaper rash.
- Lift baby's legs by holding both ankles with one hand, and slide clean diaper underneath. Fasten a cloth diaper with pins; a disposable diaper with the attached tapes.
- Place wet or soiled diaper in a diaper pail, if cloth, or in the garbage, if it is disposable.

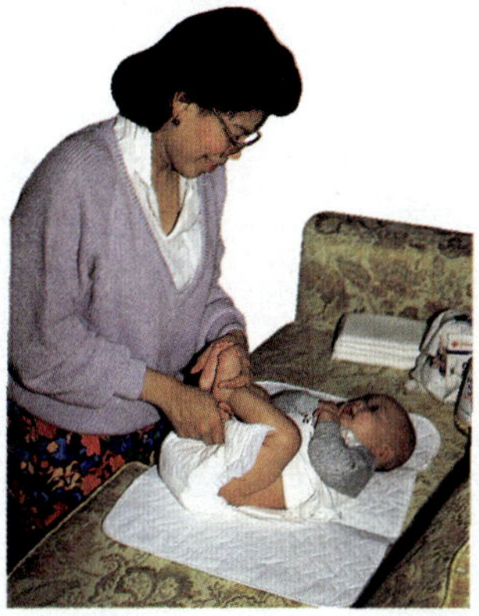

How to Bathe Babies

Bath time can be fun, but safety is very important. Here are some bathing tips:

- For an infant, use a small tub or sink lined with a towel. Fill with water up to the level of the baby's navel when placed in the bath.
- Test the temperature of the water by using your elbow—it should be warm and not hot.
- Hold the baby securely, keeping the head out of the water and away from the sink fixtures.
- Wash the head and face first, using a face towel and a mild baby soap. Rinse and dry the head. Then wash and rinse the rest of the body, remove the baby from the water, and wrap in a towel to dry.
- Older babies and toddlers can sit up in the bathroom tub in a small amount of warm water. To wash hair, use a baby shampoo and rinse by pouring water on the head but away from the face.
- Never leave a baby alone in water—not even for a second!

TEEN TIPS

More About Safety With the students, develop a list of safety pointers to diminish these hazards when working with children. Include the following:

- If you turn away to get something, keep one hand on the baby.
- Hold the baby especially firmly when he or she is soapy or wet.
- Never leave the baby alone in the bath even for a few seconds.
- In an emergency, put the baby on the floor so that he or she can't fall.

✓ How can you check the temperature of milk in a bottle? How can you burp a baby? *Check the temperature of milk by shaking the bottle upside down so a few drops fall on your wrist. There are two ways to burp a baby: hold the baby against your shoulder or have the baby sit on your lap, then pat the baby on the back.*

Activities

Skill Builder: Math
Ask students to take a survey of baby supplies and care products on the market. They should look at formulas, diapers, special soaps, shampoos, lotions, powders, and any other products of this type or materials made especially for feeding, diapering, and bathing babies. Tell students to note how many such products are available; the number of brands of each item and comparative prices; and the ingredients in the various products. Encourage them to discuss these products with a pediatrician, pharmacist, or parent to evaluate the value and convenience of each item. Students may work individually or in groups and should discuss their findings with the class as a whole.

Reteaching
Have students refer to the tip they wrote down at the beginning of the lesson. Ask if this section has answered any concerns and made them more comfortable with the prospect of feeding, diapering, and bathing a baby. Ask those who gave advice to comment on whether what they wrote duplicated material in the tips, conflicted with it, or added to it.

Enrichment
If possible, have a parent visit your class and demonstrate feeding, diapering, or bathing a baby. Additionally or alternatively, obtain a baby doll and have students take turns practicing how to feed, diaper, or bathe a baby. As another alternative, ask students to develop posters illustrating the step-by-step procedures described here.

Introducing "Tidbits Toddlers Love to Eat"
(Pages 234-235)

Motivators

Appealing Meals Ask students what makes meals appealing, in addition to foods they like. Point out that visual appeal and variety in taste and appearance are important aspects of attractive meals.

Discussion Question: Ask students: "What considerations are important in feeding small children?" Discuss this question, drawing on students' babysitting or other child-care experiences. Point out that children need nutritious food that they enjoy as well as a pleasant, calm atmosphere for meals. Point out that one way of maintaining calm is to avoid fighting to get the child to eat, and note that this section describes foods toddlers are likely to want to eat.

Teaching "Tidbits Toddlers Love to Eat"

Checking Comprehension

✔ What do you think is the taste appeal of these various recipes? *These recipes use such ingredients as honey, raisins, peanut butter, and granola in fairly limited quantities to perk up "good-for-you" foods such as carrots, oatmeal, and apples. Point out that the foods are tasty without relying on large quantities of fat or sugar.*

✔ In addition to taste, what else about these various foods is likely to appeal to children? *Some are amusing (for example, "Devilish Eggs"). Some offer a variation on standard fare (for example, "Bunny Food"). Some come in small portions, which children enjoy (for example, "Meat Loafies"), and some have special visual appeal (for example, "Rainbow Pasta").*

Tidbits Toddlers Love to Eat

Mealtime should be a happy time for toddlers and preschoolers—and for the people who care for them. Sometimes a new name or a new presentation makes food more fun to eat. Here are ten examples:

TEEN TIPS

More About Meals for Children Mealtime for everyone, but especially for young children, should be tranquil and pleasant; yet it often is quite the opposite. Discuss why mealtimes should be pleasant. Point out that a calm and happy atmosphere contributes to good digestion and that young children who learn to associate conflict with meals can develop poor eating habits. If they learn, for example, to eat more than they want just to avoid conflict with a caregiver, they may overeat and develop a lifelong weight problem.

TEEN TIPS

- **Bunny Food**
  Combine grated carrots with raisins. Mix with some mayonnaise, or a little honey and lemon juice.

- **Baked Banana Boat**
  Peel firm bananas and place in a greased baking dish. Brush with a little butter or margarine, and bake at 350°F for 12-15 minutes. When done, make a groove the length of the banana and fill with honey. Let cool before serving.

- **Devilish Eggs**
  Add a face to deviled eggs—using strips of green pepper or carrot for eyes, nose and mouth.

- **Yummy Apples**
  Peel and core a whole apple. Mix peanut butter with raisins or granola. Stuff the peanut butter mixture into the hole of the apple and slice into eighths to serve.

- **Personalized Pancakes**
  Using a teaspoon of pancake batter, draw a letter or number *backwards* on a hot pan or griddle. When the letter is browned, pour more batter over the letter so the pancake completely surrounds it. Bake until bubbles appear, then turn and brown the second side. The letter or number will be darker on the finished pancake.

- **Oatmeal Faces**
  On the top of a bowl of hot cereal, such as oatmeal or farina, make a face with chocolate chips or raisins for eyes, peach slices for mouth and ears, a dot of jelly for a nose.

- **Finger Food Buffet**
  Place finger foods such as fresh strawberries, cheese cubes, and hard-cooked egg wedges in an empty ice cube tray—for a fun-to-eat snack or meal.

- **Meat Loafies**
  Bake meat loaf mixture in muffin tins. Freeze individual meat loaves and reheat in a toaster oven or microwave oven.

- **Rainbow Pastas**
  Serve multicolored pasta (tomato, spinach, egg) in a sauce with multicolored vegetables.

- **Bean Dip**
  Combine chick peas, lemon juice, oil, garlic powder, and water in a blender or food processor. Blend or process until smooth. To serve, spread dip on crackers, breadsticks, or celery pieces.

Activities

Skill Builder: Math
Divide the class into groups of two or three and assign each group two of the recipes. Have students research the approximate cost of making these recipes. First, students need to decide how much of each ingredient they would use to make a recipe. (They may need help with this.) Then they should figure out the cost of that quantity of each ingredient and calculate the cost of the total recipe. Have each group report on its research to the class, and discuss the relative costs of these foods.

Reteaching
Work with the class as a whole to plan children's menus for two days. For each meal, have the class include one of the recipes described here. In addition, have students suggest what else might be served. Discuss how the different dishes suit different meals. Point out also that—especially for children—foods can be served at meals the foods are not usually associated with. For example, "Yummy Apples" could make a tempting if unconventional breakfast.

Enrichment
Have students search through housekeeping, child-care, and food magazines for pictures of foods and for recipes that might appeal to children. Have them make posters illustrating two to four suggestions. The posters should include a few words about why each item would appeal to children (for example, "includes peanut butter"), a recipe or general directions for preparing the item, and an illustration of it. Students can provide the recipe and draw the illustration, or they can cut these items out of magazines.

Cross-Reference Develop a list of things that can interfere with a pleasant mealtime atmosphere, particularly when young children are present. Encourage students to come up with as many possibilities as they can. Be sure to include such factors as very young children's tendency to play with their food or throw it. Have each student choose one of the factors listed and research how it might be overcome. Sources include child care books (for tips on managing very young children at the table), Unit 3 of this book, or other sources about family relationships. Have students share the results of their research with the class.

Introducing "The Quiet Times"
(Pages 236-237)

Motivators

Class List What's your favorite activity to do with children? Ask students to answer this question, and record their answers on the chalkboard. Save the list for later use.

Babysitting Troubles Ask students if they've ever had trouble getting children to calm down. Invite students to share their experiences with the class. Tell them that this section will provide suggestions that may help the next time they need calming activities for children.

Teaching "The Quiet Times"

Checking Comprehension

✓ Name some suggested activities that might be best for children before a nap or bedtime. Why are they especially appropriate for such times? *Examples include reading or making up stories; listening to music; counting or reciting the alphabet. Such activities are largely passive, require little physical movement, and don't use special materials.*

✓ Which activities might be especially appropriate for younger children? *Answers will vary but may include reading stories; identifying animals or shapes; playing with clay or Playdough; singing songs; playing with books or toys that teach how to manage fasteners, and so on.*

✓ Which activities are especially good for stimulating creativity? *Examples include making up stories; finger painting with whipping cream; drawing; and making collages, patterns, clay or Playdough figures.*

TEEN TIPS

The Quiet Times

Children need a balance of active and quiet play for healthy growth. Quiet play is especially important if you're caring for a child who doesn't want to settle down for a nap or bedtime. Try some of these calming activities for quiet times:

- Read a story aloud.
- Make up stories—and include the child as one of the characters in the story.
- Draw pictures to illustrate the stories.
- Identify shapes.
- Identify animals in pictures. (If the children decide to make animal noises, this activity may not be so quiet!)
- Finger paint with aerosol whipping cream on a cookie sheet.
- Play card games—Go Fish, Concentration, Old Maid, Crazy Eights.
- Do a jigsaw puzzle.

Emphasize Working with stories is an especially enjoyable quiet activity, and it helps children gain language and reading skills. Have students try one or more of the approaches on these pages and report to the class on their success.

TEEN TIPS

- Make a collage—cut out pictures from magazines and paste them on colored paper.
- Cut out shapes and make abstract designs.
- Make shapes with clay or Playdough.
- Make paper airplanes, hats, and boats.
- Place paper over a coin and rub with a pencil until the picture can be seen.
- Play guessing games such as "I'm thinking of an animal" or 'I'm thinking of a place."
- Listen to music—even two-year-olds love "Peter and the Wolf."
- Cut a potato, carrot, or turnip in half and carve out a design. (You do the cutting with the knife.) Brush with poster paint or use an ink pad, and stamp the design on note paper or wrapping paper.
- Make flashcards with objects to identify.
- Play with a book or toy that teaches how to manage clothing fasteners, such as zippers, snaps, buttons, and shoelaces.
- Count or recite the alphabet.

More About Storytelling Share the following techniques with the students and suggest they add their own ideas to the list.

- Start a story, then have the children continue it. Give each child a set amount of time and then move on, or take another turn yourself.
- Read part of a book, then ask the children what will happen next, or what they would do if they were the character. Older children can write their responses.
- Have children act out a story you've read or perform a puppet show about it.
- Have older children pretend they are characters in the story and write letters to other characters. Or have the children write letters from themselves to characters in a story.

Activities

Skill Builder: Writing

Have students develop and write detailed instructions to tell another person how to do one activity suggested in this section. Have students share their instructions with the class. The class can critique the instructions, focusing on whether they are clear, complete, and easy to follow.

Reteaching

Have students refer to the activities listed at the beginning of the lesson. As a class, decide which are appropriate for quiet time, and why. Discuss how those that are not quiet might be modified to suit times when calmer activities are required.

Enrichment

If possible, have the class visit a day-care facility, nursery school, or kindergarten and spend enough time to see a variety of activities. Have the students observe and make notes about the activities the children engage in, paying attention to the variety of activities, the level of activity each requires, the sequence of these activities, and the children's reactions to them. Have students write reports commenting on how effective they think the various activities, their sequence, and timing were. Alternatively, encourage students to try one or two activities that are new to them the next time they take care of children. Have the students report on the success of the activity and how they might change it the next time.

Unit Four

UNIT PREVIEW

In Unit 4 students learn how to use resources wisely. They discover the four types of resources: human, material, community, and natural. Time and money management are covered in detail. Students learn the benefits of saving money, establishing credit, and using money wisely. Students learn how to comparison shop, evaluate advertising, and judge quality of products and services. In addition, management and consumer-related careers are outlined.

CONTENT DEVELOPMENT

Use these lessons to reinforce the following themes:

Content Strands	Chapters
Career Exploration	34
Citizenship/ Leadership	32,33,34
Communication	32,33
Consumer Skills	28-33
Entrepreneurship	(TT 1)
Decision Making	25-28,30,32,(TT 1,2,3)
Health and Safety	26,29,33
Managing Resources	25-28,30-32,34, (TT 1,2,3)
Technology	27,30,(TT 1,3)

UNIT MOTIVATORS

Decision-Making Skills

What to Buy? Have students practice making group decisions by forming a buying committee with several classmates. Ask them to select a product that would be useful in the classroom, such as a computer. Using consumer magazines and other sources of information, they should decide the features, brand, and model that would be best for the class. After selecting the product, discuss how compromises were reached during the selection process.

Critical Thinking Skills

Analyze Advertising Display advertisements from magazines aimed at teens. Have students identify the kinds of products that are advertised most often and list the techniques commonly used to create interest in a product. Ask students to identify misleading claims.

CROSS-CURRICULAR ACTIVITY

Mathematics and Management Have each student write a word problem related to managing money or purchasing goods and services. For example, a problem might require figuring the amount of change due after a purchase. Compile students' problems into a worksheet for the class to solve.

SPECIAL NEEDS

Strategies for Gifted Students Have students write a newspaper column on money matters for teens. The column might feature ways teens can earn money. It might evaluate services and products for teens. Suggest that students submit their columns to the business section of the local newspaper.

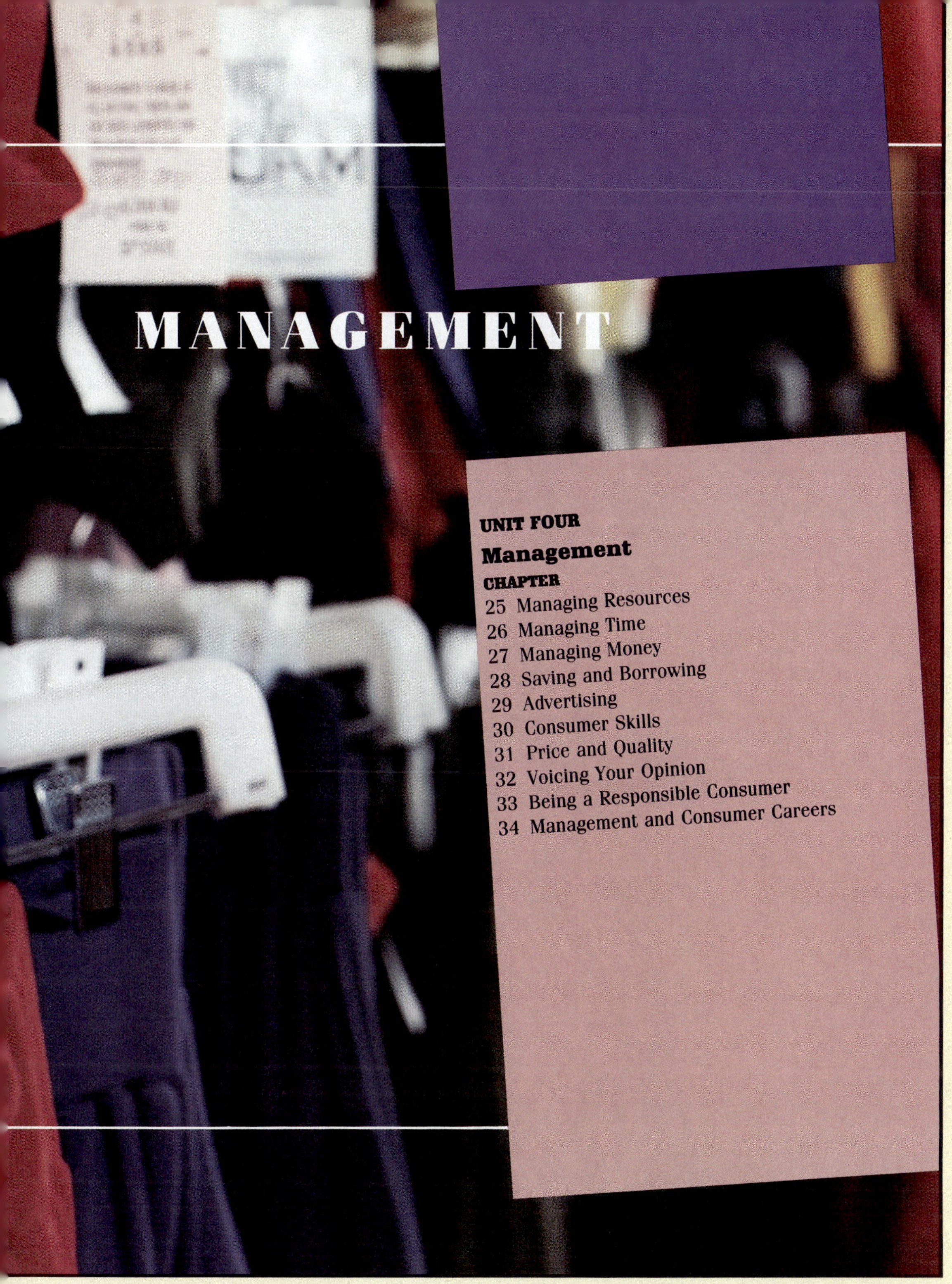

MANAGEMENT

UNIT FOUR

Management

CHAPTER

COOPERATIVE LEARNING

Managing a Project Divide the class into groups and have each group plan a fundraising project, such as a car wash, bake sale, or talent show. The proceeds might go toward a class trip, a charity, or new equipment for the school. In deciding on an event, students should consider the resources they have available and the resources they will need to obtain. Each group member should be responsible for planning at least one aspect of the event such as supplies, work assignments, publicity, and finances. After time for discussion, have one person from each group report on the group's plans. Encourage students to implement their plans if possible.

FHA ACTIVITIES

The following activities can be used with your FHA group or as public relation strategies:

Better Management Fair Sponsor a Better Management Fair for the school. Invite resource people to discuss and give help for better time and money management.

Financial Fitness Center Have students take the "Financial Fitness" Quiz in the "Financial Fitness" peer education program of the Future Homemakers of America, Inc. Or have students set up a Financial Fitness Center (in the student lounge, library, a classroom, or hallway). Announce hours so that a student can come and take the quiz.

Good Shopping Habits Sponsor a poster contest using the theme, "Good Shopping Habits." Display posters in businesses in the community.

Small Claims Court Have the FHA chapter visit a small claims court to find out how cases involving consumer problems are handled.

UNIT CLOSURE

For Review

Catalog or Store? Have students look through a mail-order catalog and choose one item they might like to purchase. Have them compare the price, quality, and warranty to a similar item in a store. Have them evaluate the advantages and disadvantages of buying through a catalog and through a store.

For Evaluation

Unit Test Have students complete the Unit Test that appears in the *Teacher's Classroom Resources.*

Testmaker Software You may wish to design a unit test using the Testmaker software program.

CHAPTER OVERVIEW

Chapter 25 introduces the concept of resources and identifies four types: human, material, community, and natural. It discusses the need to manage resources and then investigates strategies for doing so. Students learn that wise use of resources involves setting goals as well as using decision-making skills.

INTRODUCING THE CHAPTER

Motivators

What Resources Do We Need? Ask students to list ten things they need in their lives. Point out that their answers are examples of resources. Explain that this chapter explores four types of resources and how students can manage them wisely.

Resources Tell the class that a resource is anything that helps them reach their goals or meet their needs. It may be material (money or personal possessions) or nonmaterial (friends, teachers, time).

Using the Photograph After students have looked at the photograph on this page, ask: "What resources does the magician need?" Possible answers include supplies, skill, knowledge, and energy.

Introducing the Objectives

Discuss the chapter objectives on this page. Remind students that the objectives focus on important chapter content.

Introducing Vocabulary

Explain to students that the word *resource* comes from the Old French *ressoudre,* "to rise again." A resource is a means of supplying some want or deficiency. Ask students to name some ways that human beings can be resources.

TEACHING THE CHAPTER

For convenience, the teaching suggestions for this chapter are arranged according to the following lesson topics:

- "Your Resources," pages 241-245
- "Managing Resources," page 246

CHAPTER

25

Managing Resources

OBJECTIVES

This chapter will help you to:

- Identify human resources and describe their benefits.
- Give examples of material, community, and natural resources.
- Determine how to manage your resources to achieve your goals.

WORDS TO REMEMBER

barter
community resource
conserve
human resource
material resource
natural resource
pollution

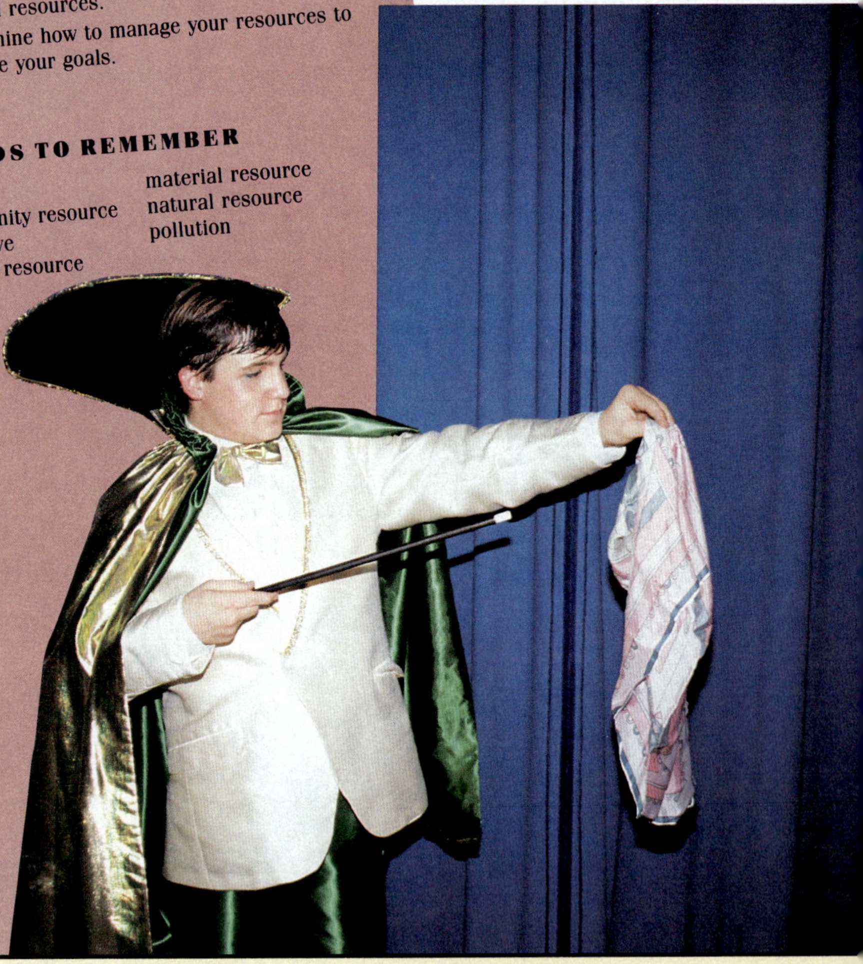

Chapter Resources

Teacher's Classroom Resources
- Lesson Plan
- Life Skills Activity, *Getting to Your Goal*
- Reproducible Master, *Your Resources*
- Extension Activity, *Creativity: The Extra Ingredient*
- Chapter Test

Student Workbook
- Study Guide
- Worksheet, *You're Richer Than You Think*

Sharon never seems to have enough time and money to do the things that interest her. On the weekends she is tired from her hectic week and doesn't feel like cleaning her room or making plans for the upcoming week. She usually has little of her allowance left to spend.

Sharon's friend Charlie doesn't seem to have the same problems. He always seems to have the money and time to do the things he wants. Sharon saw Charlie taking photos at school with an expensive-looking camera. She watched him playing an electric guitar in the school's talent show. Charlie also finds time to help coach a Little League baseball team.

One day, Sharon asked Charlie jokingly how he was able to do so many things. Charlie explained that he had no secrets but that his older brother taught him one important thing—how to manage the resources he has.

Charlie had borrowed the camera from his older sister in exchange for babysitting services, Sharon learned. He had rented the guitar from the music store and was taking guitar lessons in return for cleaning up the store. Charlie's healthful diet and adequate rest give him the energy to do many things during his spare time, such as coaching the team.

You might decide that you, like Charlie, could benefit by learning how better to manage your resources. Resources are the things you use to help you meet your goals. By managing your resources more effectively, you will find you can better achieve your goals and feel more in control of your life.

Your Resources

You have many resources that you can use to accomplish your goals. You might have a special talent, such as a pleasant singing voice or the ability to fix a machine that breaks down. You may have an outgoing personality or a great sense of humor. Your friend may be good with numbers and have a good memory for people's names and famous dates. Time, money, possessions, family and friends, and even your community are other available resources.

Individuals and families have differing amounts of resources available to them, but one resource can often be substituted or traded for another. This flexibility can help you and your family make the best use of your resources.

This boy is using several resources to help him accomplish his goal of becoming an artist. Can you name at least three of the resources?

Teaching "Your Resources"
(Pages 241-245)

This section focuses on human, material, community, and natural resources.

Checking Comprehension

✔ What human resources are available? *Knowledge, skills, imagination, energy, time, family, and friends.*

✔ How does imagination help meet human needs? *By enabling people to solve problems or make decisions before taking action.*

✔ How can you use your knowledge as a resource? *You apply your knowledge, or the information you have gained from experience, in hundreds of ways every day.*

✔ How can people replenish their supply of energy? *By getting enough rest, eating nutritious foods, exercising, and avoiding harmful substances.*

✔ What resources does the family provide? *It helps people meet their basic needs for food, clothing, and shelter as well as love, companionship, and support.*

✔ Name some possessions that enable people to use other resources more efficiently. *Answers include sewing machine, bicycle, lawn mower.*

✔ Why is money known as a medium of exchange? *It can be traded for goods and services.*

✔ How do community resources help people? *By enabling them to enjoy life, improve their skills or knowledge, and achieve their goals.*

✔ List several familiar community resources. *Schools, libraries, medical facilities, police, gymnasiums, places of worship, social service organizations, museums, zoos, theaters, restaurants, stores, parks.*

Emphasize There is no such thing as commitment without time. Ask students to think of a goal they want to commit themselves to and determine how much time they are willing to devote to it.

Focus on Life Management Ask students to think of friends or relatives who always seem to have enough time, money, or other resources, regardless of income or daily schedule. How do you think these people manage?

✓ What do community resources provide that other resources do not? *They offer experiences that would not otherwise be available to the individual or family.*

✓ List two natural resources. *Any two: air, water, soil, plants, minerals, petroleum.*

Activities

Skill Builder: Writing
Have students write a paragraph describing a time when a friend served as a resource. What needs or goals did the friend help them meet?

Skill Builder: Math
Have students compute the amount of time they spend getting ready for school in the morning. How long does each individual task take? What percentage of that time could they save by doing some things the night before?

Skill Builder: Critical Thinking
Have students consider their usefulness as a human resource. In what ways do they help other people? Suggest that students start by listing all the people they can think of who rely on them in some way.

Skill Builder: Critical Thinking
Write the following sentence on the chalkboard: "Money cannot buy everything." Ask students to explain why they agree or disagree. See if they can name examples of resources that cannot be obtained with money.

Skill Builder: Reading
Have students gather fliers, brochures, or other literature describing resources in their community. After they have read this material, ask them to give a brief summary of the services each resource offers.

Human Resources

Human resources may be the easiest to draw upon because they are easily available and everybody possesses some. Human resources include knowledge, skills, imagination, energy, time, family, and friends.

- **Knowledge.** Knowledge, the information you acquire from your experience, includes the things you know about and the things you know how to do. Can you diaper a baby? Do you know how to use a computer? Have you learned the capital cities of the fifty states? These are different kinds of knowledge. You acquire your knowledge from your family, from school, from watching television, and from observing the world around you. You use your knowledge every day in hundreds of ways, but it never gets used up.
- **Skills.** Skills are your abilities to perform specific actions or techniques. Skills can be mental or physical. Walking on a balance beam is a physical skill, whereas working out mathematics problems in your head is a mental skill. The more you practice your skills, the better you will perform them.
- **Imagination.** Imagination is another valuable human resource. Have you ever tried to work out a problem in your mind, such as how to retrieve a box from a high shelf or how to redecorate your room on a tight budget? Those tasks require imagination. Your imagination helps you solve problems and make decisions by letting you think the situation through before you have to use any other resources. Artists and writers use imagination to envision the stories and pictures they will create.
- **Energy.** Energy is the power that allows you to get things done. You always use some mental or physical energy to accomplish a task. You can replenish your supply of energy by following four steps: get plenty of rest, eat nutritious foods, exercise, and avoid harmful substances. Following these steps will help prevent you from feeling tired; you will be better able to utilize your other resources.
- **Time.** Time is a resource that affects everything you do—working, resting, and playing. You would probably agree that time is often used up much too quickly. You probably know people who accomplish a lot. How do they do so much? In the next chapter you can learn some specific techniques for managing your time more effectively.
- **Family and friends.** Family and friends are irreplaceable resources. Your family helps you meet your basic needs for food, clothing, and shelter. Family members also have skills and knowledge that you can draw on. Your family is a resource that provides love, companionship, and support.

  Friends provide companionship and support. It's nice to have friends you can rely on when you need someone to talk to and laugh with. They often have skills that you don't have, and you can sometimes trade your skills for theirs. For example, if you help a friend with her homework, she may help you redecorate your room.

Material Resources

Material resources are objects that you can use to provide or make other things. They include possessions and money.

Focus on Human Resources Ask students to think of examples of a person whose imagination was his or her greatest resource. How did he or she use imagination to get things done?

Did You Know? Human beings use imagination to solve problems and reach decisions. Certain animals also show problem-solving abilities. In laboratory situations, chimpanzees, for example, can figure out how to use a stick or several boxes to get bananas that are out of reach. Some birds drop shellfish from a height in order to crack open the shells. Compared to animals, humans exhibit considerable ability to solve problems and make decisions by purely mental means, which gives them a great advantage.

hours the night be
study 20 minutes e
Managing your w
helps you make tin
other way of manag
to rely on three use
a schedule, and a li

Using a Calendar

A common tool fo
tivities is a ca
monthly, or yearly
pointments, importa
birthdays, and so
keep a calendar fo
ahead at a time.
To use a calenda
down all of the eve
you have scheduled
wall or desk calenda
practice every Tue
evening, put that
work schedule, clu
appointments, baby
events, and anythin
to set aside time fo
As other activities
those on the calenda
Whenever you wa
or do something wit
cific day and time, y
calendar and see if
Another advantage
dar is that you don'
dates and times or t
getting an activity o

Making a Schedule

A **schedule** can be
tool for managing yo
a daily or weekly pla
and length of each of
are already familiar
ules that show when

Focus on Managem
times they might lo
that the calendar
ment tool. Have st
might need two cal
one for home) once

Community Resources

Community resources are people and facilities in your community that help you enjoy your life, improve your skills, and achieve your goals. For example, schools are staffed with many people who serve as resources. Teachers, coaches, and counselors help you to increase your knowledge and improve your skills. Schools offer you opportunities to explore a wide variety of interests—such as art, foreign languages, child care, and computers—and also provide facilities such as libraries and gymnasiums that you can use.

People go to church, synagogue, and other places of worship for spiritual support and a sense of belonging. Individual religious leaders and other members provide guidance and friendship. Teen groups and functions provide opportunities to have fun and meet people.

People and places in your city or town provide many other resources. You can use the services of doctors, dentists, police officers, social service workers, child caregivers, and volunteer agencies. You can explore the varied offerings of museums, zoos, parks, movie theaters, libraries, restaurants, and stores. All these places enrich your life by enabling you to experience things you couldn't provide on your own, such as Bengal tigers, French paintings, and Vietnamese food.

Natural Resources

Air, water, soil, trees, minerals, and petroleum products are all **natural resources** that we use every day. We use water and soil to grow our food, trees to make paper and lumber for our houses, and gas and oil to heat our homes and fuel our cars. It is important to save, or **conserve**, our natural resources so that we don't use them up faster than we can replace them. Natural resources are important to us in other ways as well. They often provide a sense of beauty that improves our quality of life.

Community resources include members of your school staff, such as guidance counselors. What other people and places in your school can serve as valuable resources for you?

Did You Know? One example of a community resource is the Red Cross. The American Red Cross was founded in 1881 by Clara Barton, who introduced the idea of disaster relief in peace time. The Red Cross provides volunteer blood bank services and maintains a system of local, national, and international disaster preparedness and relief.

Did You Know? Tell students that more th
half the trash collected in the United State
paper. Paper products are made from one
our natural resources: trees. If America
would recycle paper, they could help c
serve trees while decreasing the amount
garbage that needs to be disposed of.

Other people are valuable resources. They can help you in many ways, from teaching you a new skill to providing support and friendship.

- **Possessions.** Possessions are the things you have or own. Some possessions, like the furniture in your room, can be used for years before they have to be replaced. Others, such as loose-leaf paper, ballpoint pens, or the film for your camera, need to be replaced often. Taking good care of your possessions can make them last longer.

Some possessions can help you use other of your resources more efficiently. A bicycle speeds travel and conserves time. Other possessions, such as a sewing machine or lawn mower, help you increase certain resources. By sewing, you can have more clothes. By using your lawn mower to mow other people's lawns, you can increase the amount of money you have.

- **Money.** Money, another material resource, is known as a "medium of exchange" because it can be traded for almost anything. Your skateboard would not be accepted by the owner of a pizza shop in exchange for a pizza. The shop owner would rather have money, which he can then use to buy supplies.

Money is a resource that you can earn by working or performing a service. Some teens receive money as a weekly or monthly allowance from their parents. Learning to manage money by saving and spending wisely will help you to better meet your goals. Although money is useful, it cannot buy everything. Money can't buy the fun you have with your friends or the love of your family.

Reteaching
To help students better understand the human resources they rely on, have them work individually or in groups to create collages showing the variety of human resources available to them.

Reteaching
Have students tell about some of the ways they earn money. What are some of the ways in which they use their earnings or allowance?

Reteaching
Call upon students to give examples of the resources their school provides, both to the student body and to the community.

Reteaching
Ask students to give examples of how paper and paper products are often wasted. Tell them that two principle illustrations of this practice are supermarket grocery bags and disposable diapers. Point out that in Europe shoppers usually own a cloth or mesh shopping bag that they use over and over again.

More About Money Many items have been used as a medium of exchange. Native Americans traded furs and hides to obtain supplies from European settlers. On the Pacific island of Yap, huge stone disks once served as money. In the United States, paper money was held in low regard until the government promised to redeem it for its full value.

Emphasize Point out that possessions serve a variety of purposes. See if the students can identify what needs some of their possessions fulfill.

Teaching the Feature
"There's Only One World"

Answers to Feature Questions

1. Answers will vary. Students might suggest not using Styrofoam or air-conditioners; boycotting fast-food restaurants that use Styrofoam containers; planting trees.

2. There were no viable alternatives; people didn't believe the situation would really become so dangerous; large companies have influence and want to continue making a profit from those products.

Activities

Resource Interrelatedness Have students do some research on the need for preserving tropical rain forests. What is happening to these rain forests and what are the results? Ask students how rain forests help to preserve the ecology of the whole planet.

Whose Earth Is It, Anyway? Ask students to specify some of the reasons why people have wasted, destroyed, or polluted natural resources. What assumptions are these people making about the nature of our resources? Ask students to list these assumptions and tell why they are mistaken.

Recycling Have students work individually or in small groups to list items that can be recycled. Lead a class discussion about how recycling benefits the individual and the community.

Community Contact Ask students to find out about recycling centers in their community. Then have students make posters advertising these centers, telling their location, hours, and what kinds of things they recycle. Finally, have students place the posters in the areas that they believe are most appropriate.

There's Only One World

Do you like to spend time in the sun, or visit beaches or woods? Can you imagine a world where you can't do those things? That kind of world may be in our future. Why? Because people are misusing our natural resources.

Poll
prop
beac
wast
natio
caus
Fore
burn
maki
dama

Na
fuel,
oil, a
threa
exam
dioxi
layer
surro
calle
the e
futur
caps

An
cause
chemi
those
fast-fo
Freon
Those
the sh
earth
ultravi
could
growth
people
suscep

Here
do to u
more e

More About Pollution The Environmental Protection Agency (EPA) was created in 1970 by the U. S. government to enforce federal laws aimed at keeping the air and water clean. Pressure from the EPA has resulted in the banning of aerosol sprays because of the damage they do to the Earth's atmosphere. In addition, car emissions are now tested once a

Skill Builder: Wr
Have students w
short compositio
would do with th
day.

Reteaching
To help students
the benefits of tim
them to list the t
done in the past
ran out of time.

Enrichment
The political sci
Parkinson wrote:
to fill the time ava
tion." Write this "
the chalkboard ar
they think it mea
disagree? Ask th
cific examples
experience to sup

Teaching "Maki For You"
(Pages 250-252)

This section tea
breaking large tas
and by using ca
and lists.

Checking Comp

✓ How can large t
manageable? *By
smaller units.*

✓ What three too
management? *A c
and a list of things*

✓ Why is it usefu
plans and obligatio
*enables you to see
time, you don't ha
dates and times o
ments, and you
important activitie*

✓ What is a sched
*daily or weekly pl
and duration of yo*

CHAPTER OVERVIEW

Chapter 29 discusses how advertising affects people. Students learn that advertising provides information and also shapes tastes, habits, and attitudes. The chapter describes the most common advertising media and the methods advertisers use to persuade people to buy goods and services. Strategies are offered to help the consumer evaluate advertisements wisely.

INTRODUCING THE CHAPTER

Motivators

Advertisements Everywhere Ask students to volunteer the names of products or services for which they have seen or heard an advertisement in the last 24 hours. Write these responses on the board. Then stress to students the sheer number of advertisements that bombard them daily and the need to sift through these claims for useful information.

Using the Photograph Ask students to note the placement and size of this advertisement. Have them suggest the types of people who would notice the ad—commuters, young people on their way to school, shoppers. Ask students to consider what kind of ad they notice most often.

Advertising Can Help Ask students to share experiences that they have had that are similar to Brian's on page 273. Point out that Brian might have missed the sale if he hadn't seen the advertisement in the newspaper.

Introducing the Objectives

Discuss the chapter objectives on this page. Remind students that the objectives focus on important chapter content.

Introducing Vocabulary

Write the expression *bait and switch* on the board. Ask students if they know what each noun means. Then discuss the meaning of the phrase when applied to advertising.

CHAPTER
29

Advertising

OBJECTIVES

This chapter will help you to:
- List the advantages of advertising.
- Identify two types of advertisements.
- Describe several kinds of advertising techniques.
- Identify sources of reliable information about products.
- Discuss several strategies to evaluate advertisements.

WORDS TO REMEMBER

bait and switch
direct mail ad
image ad
information ad
media

Chapter Resources

Teacher's Classroom Resources
- Lesson Plan
- Life Skills Activity, *Be an Advertising Analyst*
- Reproducible Master, *Information vs Image*
- Extension Activity, *Evaluating a Food Advertisement*
- Chapter Test

Student Workbook
- Study Guide
- Worksheet, *Commercials Are Calling You*

The ad in Sunday's newspaper for Whitney's Sporting Goods Store caught Brian's eye. The tennis racket he had been wanting was on sale for almost half the regular price.

After school on Monday, Brian and his friend Randy went to the store to look at the tennis racket. As Brian paid for it, he remarked to Randy, "I'm sure glad I saw that ad. I thought it would take me another three months to save enough money to buy this."

Advertisements can be very helpful to shoppers because they provide a wealth of information about products. However, some advertisements can also be very misleading. To shop wisely, you need to learn how to separate the facts from the fiction in the advertisements you see and hear every day.

The Pros and Cons of Advertising

The ability to make decisions about where and when to spend their money gives people great power in the marketplace. If too few people buy a product, that product will be taken off the market and its manufacturer may go out of business. All manufacturers and stores want you to spend your money on their products, so they compete for your dollars by offering attractive packaging and by advertising.

Advertisements are everywhere, in newspapers and magazines, on radio and television, on buses and roadside signs, sometimes even on the clothes you wear. They are all designed to make you want to buy the product or service they display.

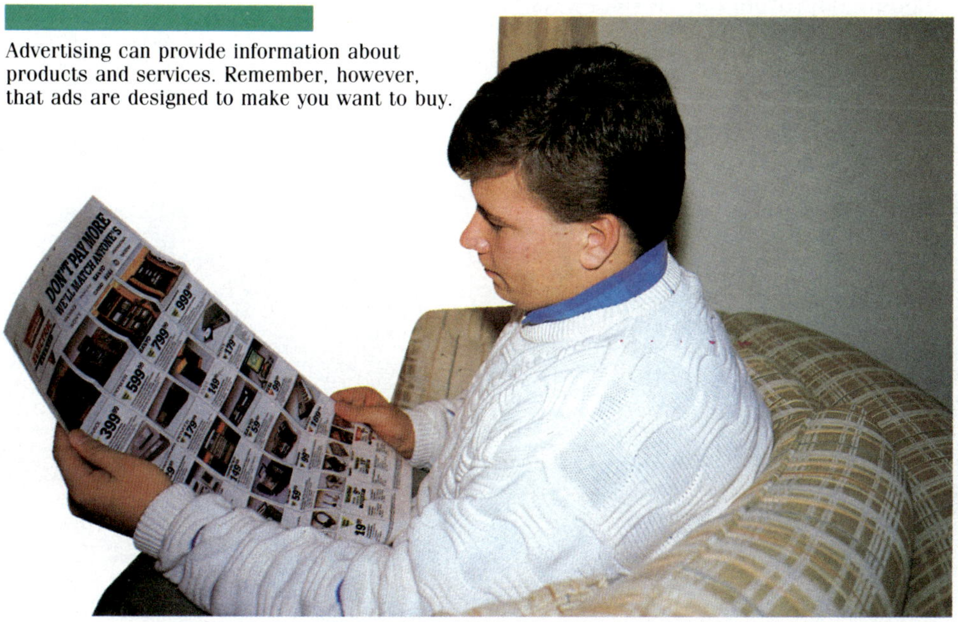

Advertising can provide information about products and services. Remember, however, that ads are designed to make you want to buy.

Focus on Consumer Skills Discuss with the class how casting votes in an election compares with casting a vote with dollars when purchasing items. Explain that manufacturers and retailers use these "dollar votes" to determine their marketing and sales strategies, production and expansion projections, investments, and so on.

Emphasize Many people find out about new ideas, discoveries, and inventions through advertisements.

Emphasize Advertisements or announcements that promote ideas for the common good are called public service announcements (PSAs).

TEACHING THE CHAPTER

For convenience, the teaching suggestions for this chapter are arranged according to the following lesson topics:

- "The Pros and Cons of Advertising," pages 273-275
- "Evaluating Advertising," pages 275-278

Teaching "The Pros and Cons of Advertising"

(Pages 273-275)

This section describes some of the types and advantages of advertising as well as some of the methods advertisers use.

Checking Comprehension

✓ Why do buyers have so much power in the marketplace? *The decisions buyers make about what products and services they will spend their money on influences the survival of these commodities in the marketplace.*

✓ Besides companies that sell products and services, what other groups advertise? *People running for political office and special interest groups.*

✓ What type of ad is usually used to promote a special sale? *An information ad.*

✓ To what kinds of wants do image ads appeal? *They appeal to the desire to be more popular, better looking, or smarter.*

✓ Name the three most common advertising media. *Print, electronic, and direct mail.*

✓ Compare the effects of ads in newspapers with those in magazines. *Newspaper ads reach local residents; magazine ads reach readers nationwide. Magazine ads can also reach specific interest groups.*

✓ What kind of advertising makes use of catalogs and advertising circulars? *Direct mail advertising.*

Activities

Skill Builder: Writing
Have students write a paragraph describing their favorite ad. Have them explain why the ad is especially appealing to them.

Skill Builder: Critical Thinking
Ask each student to look through newspapers or magazines and cut out an image ad. Ask students to tell what image is being promoted by the ad, what this appeals to in the individual, and what the ad uses to promote this image.

Reteaching
Ask students to suggest the most effective advertising medium for the following: a sale at a local appliance store; a special at a local restaurant; the release of a new collector's postage stamp; a discount on student holiday travel; a state senator's political campaign; a new soap product.

Enrichment
Have students form small groups and choose an item such as a bike, watch, computer, or television set. Have them prepare both an information and an image ad for the item. Ask the groups to share their ads with the class and to point out the differences between the two. Ask the other students to discuss the effectiveness of both ads.

The Purposes of Advertising

When you buy a soft drink, do you ask for a certain brand? Do you look for a particular restaurant chain when you go out to eat? You probably learned about both through advertising. Another major purpose of advertising is to make people familiar with products, services, or ideas—to provide us with information.

Companies that make or sell products advertise. People running for political offices and special interest groups supporting various causes do, too. The American Cancer Society has used advertising very effectively in recent years to get out the message that smoking is harmful to your health.

Advertising also shapes our tastes, habits, and attitudes. For instance, a television advertisement for a new movie not only lets you know that the movie has arrived at local theaters but it also attempts to make you want to see that movie by showing a few funny or dramatic scenes from the movie.

Types of Advertisements

All advertisements aren't the same. They fall into two basic types—information ads and image ads:

- **Information ads.** An **information ad** provides specific information about a product such as its size, color, price, and features. Stores usually use this kind of ad in their catalogs or in newspapers when they want to promote special products or sales.
- **Image ads.** These are the kinds of ads that feature rock stars selling sun glasses or beautiful women driving sports cars. **Image ads** attempt to associate the product with a popular image so that you'll want to try it. Image ads also try to appeal to you to buy the product by making you think that if you do, you will be more popular, better looking, or smarter. Many magazine and television ads are image ads.

Which ads are information ads and which are image ads?

More About the "Cons" of Advertising Critics of advertising say it appeals to base motives, creates wants, and makes people buy things they cannot afford.

Did You Know? Ad agencies and the media themselves often set standards to prevent false or misleading advertising practices.

Advertising Media

Advertising **media** are the means by which ads are broadcast or displayed. The three most common advertising media are print (newspapers and magazines), electronic (radio and television), and direct mail. To advertise in a newspaper or magazine, the advertiser must purchase space in the publication in which the ad will appear. Newspapers are useful to local advertisers, like supermarkets and department stores who want to reach nearby residents.

Magazines, on the other hand, can reach millions of readers nationwide. The ads they carry are called national ads. Advertisers who want to reach a specific group of people, such as cooks or stamp collectors, can advertise in magazines devoted to these specialties.

When advertisers want to buy an ad on radio or television, they buy time instead of space. For example, they can buy 15 or 30 seconds of time in the middle of, or between, programs in which to air their ads. The national ads that appear on television can reach 30 or 40 million viewers at one time.

Direct mail ads are the kind of ads that are delivered by the postal service. These include catalogs from mail-order houses, advertising circulars for local supermarkets and stores, and any other advertising you get through the mail.

Other kinds of advertising include store window displays, roadside billboards and neon signs, point-of-sale displays, and bus and taxi signs. Clothes that carry the designer's name or symbol are a form of advertising also.

Evaluating Advertisements

Will a new pair of designer jeans really make you more popular, as the ad suggests? Probably not, but the "popularity ploy" is just one of many methods that advertisers use to persuade you to buy things you may not really need or want. Here are some other common advertising techniques:

- **Attention-getting headlines.** "Buy!", "Save!", "Lose 25 pounds in one week!" These kinds of headlines lure you into reading the rest of the ad and often promise you some benefit.

Many point-of-sale displays include attention-getting signs. What advertising information would be most helpful to this consumer?

Did You Know? Advertising slogans sometimes become a part of everyday speech. Testimonial ads show us which public figures consumers identify with. Thus the words, songs, and people in ads become a part of America's popular culture.

Did You Know? Some stores will meet the advertised price of a competitor if the consumer can supply proof with a legitimate current ad.

Teaching "Evaluating Advertisements"

(Pages 275-278)

This section describes some common advertising techniques and tells how to obtain and evaluate reliable information about products.

Checking Comprehension

✔ List five common advertising techniques. *Attention-getting headlines, testimonials, product characters, emotional appeals, and slogans.*

✔ What should the consumer be aware of when examining advertisements? *The consumer should keep in mind that advertisers use various creative techniques that may not reflect the nature or quality of the products advertised.*

✔ Name two agencies that regulate advertising. *The Federal Trade Commission (FTC) and the Federal Communications Commission (FCC).*

✔ What can happen if advertisers are found to have violated federal advertising laws? *They may have to pay a fine or run a new ad that corrects false claims.*

✔ How can friends give you information about products they use? *You can ask friends what they like or dislike about the product, how much it costs, and whether they would recommend it to others.*

✔ How can consumer magazines help you? *They can give you information about products that they have tested and rated.*

✔ How can you separate fact from opinion in advertisement? *You need to read and listen carefully.*

✔ What is the purpose of a bait and switch advertisement? *It lures you into the store so that you will be persuaded to buy something more expensive than the one advertised.*

Activities

Skill Builder: Writing
Have students write five attention-getting headlines. Share several with the class. Ask which would entice people to read the rest of the ad.

Skill Builder: Reading
Have students go to the library and bring back examples (or copies) of newspaper or magazine ads that are over 30 years old. Have students comment on any areas in which they suspect that the advertisement is less than truthful and suggest how a modern advertisement might present the product.

Skill Builder: Critical Thinking
Ask students to choose three advertisements and to evaluate them to separate the facts from the opinions in the ad. Each student should report to the class on an advertisement.

Reteaching
Have each student bring in or describe five advertisements. List the five common advertising techniques on the board: attention-getting headlines, testimonials, product characters, emotional appeals, and slogans. Ask students to review the ads and put them in the appropriate category. Explain to students that some ads will fit into several categories.

Reteaching
Ask students to create fictitious advertisements with which they can illustrate each of the four strategies for evaluating ads mentioned in this section.

- **Testimonials.** Your favorite athletes, actors, or rock stars tell you how great a product is.
- **Product characters.** Cartoons or fictional characters are frequently associated with a product. For example, cartoon characters are often used to advertise breakfast cereal to appeal to children.
- **Emotional appeals.** These ads tell you that you'll be happier, healthier, more beautiful, or more popular if you use a certain product.
- **Slogans.** Ads use a slogan over and over again until it (and the product) sticks in people's minds.

Advertisers can use any and all of these methods, but the consumer should be aware that they are creative techniques and don't necessarily represent the nature or quality of the products they advertise.

Before truth-in-advertising laws, ads made claims for miracle cures. Today advertisers must be able to prove what they say in their ads.

Truth in Advertising

A hundred years ago, advertisers could make the most outlandish claims for their products and buyers had no way of knowing whether those claims were true or not. Today, advertisers can be challenged legally for making false or grossly misleading claims about their products. Advertising is regulated by several U.S. government agencies, including the Federal Trade Commission (FTC), and, if the ads are aired on radio or television, the Federal Communications Commission (FCC). These agencies can force advertisers to prove their claims or to pay fines if they violate federal laws. The FCC can even make an advertiser run a new ad to correct false claims made in earlier ads.

Sources of Information

Despite federal regulations, advertisers often exaggerate in an attempt to persuade you to buy their products. However, you don't have to rely solely on ads to gather information about products. One way to get information about products is to ask your friends questions about the products they use, such as "What do you like or dislike about a product?" "How much did it cost?" and "Would you recommend this product to others?"

You can also look for information in consumer magazines, such as *Consumer Reports* and *Consumer Research*, which test and rate many different products to see how well they perform and how closely they meet advertising claims. The *Consumer Index*, available in most libraries, lists which products and services have been reviewed in the consumer magazines.

More About False Claims If a mistake is made in a published advertisement and it is not an obvious misprint ($3.95 for a color television instead of $395), you may be able to get the item for the printed price if you bring the ad into the store with you.

Did You Know? At one time traveling salesmen sold "patent medicines" that were said to cure all kinds of physical problems. Some were merely flavored syrups, others consisted primarily of alcohol; and a few contained poisonous substances.

HEALTH WATCH

Read That Label!

After weeks of allergy testing, the doctor gave Allison a list of foods and fibers that she was allergic to. Allison wondered how she could avoid buying products that contained the items on the list. She discovered that product labels provide important information about both the contents and safety of a product.

- **Food.** The Federal Food and Drug Administration (FDA) requires that food manufacturers list the weight, ingredients, additives, and added nutrients contained in their products on their packages and cans. Ingredients must be listed by weight in descending order, so if the first item on a list of ingredients is flour, the product contains more flour than any other ingredient.
- **Clothing.** Clothing sold in the United States must have a label showing what fibers were used in making the item and a care label that must include information on how the garment should be cleaned and whether it can be bleached or pressed.
- **Furniture.** Furniture that is stuffed or covered with fabric must have a label showing what materials were used and whether the material is flame-resistant.
- **Household cleaners.** Some household cleaners, painting supplies, and lawn-care products are poisonous, irritating, flammable, or explosive near heat. The labels on these products usually give safety and storage information.

Think It Through

1. **Rachel was trying to choose between two breakfast cereals. The first four ingredients listed on one cereal box were whole wheat, sugar, rice flour, and soybean oil. The first four ingredients listed on the other box were whole wheat, wheat bran, raisins, and sugar. Which cereal do you think Rachel should choose? Why?**
2. **Do you think that product labels give enough information? Do they give too much information? Explain your answer.**

Teaching the Feature
"Read That Label!"

Answers to Feature Questions

1. Rachel should choose the second box of cereal. Since it lists sugar as the fourth rather than the second ingredient, it is likely to have less sugar in it. Also, the second cereal does not list an oil among its first four ingredients, which may mean it contains less fat than the first.

2. Product labels do provide much information. They include details on ingredients, nutritional information, and last sale date (for foods); type of fabric used and care of fabric (for clothing); and what to do in case of accidental ingestion of the product (for household cleaners and medicines).

Activities

Studying Labels Ask students to choose a product and bring the label to class. This may be a label from clothing, food, furniture, or household cleaners. Have students study the information provided on the label and list the different categories of help it provides—for example: nutrition, safety, accident information, washing instructions. Have several volunteers share their findings, then discuss in class what other information might be useful on a label.

Community Contact Have students prepare informational posters or typed sheets on the importance of reading labels. These should first be displayed and discussed in class. Then they can (with permission) be posted on school bulletin boards or in a local community center, library, or supermarket.

Did You Know? Canned fruits and vegetables are graded A, B, or C by government agencies. All grades are of equal nutritional value, but they differ in appearance. Grade A fruits, for example, are all the same color, size, and shape. Grade C fruits may include broken pieces or different color shadings. These grades do not always appear on the label.

Emphasize Reading labels requires some effort on the part of the consumer. This effort will be rewarded, however, with the best value for the dollar.

Enrichment
Break the class into small groups. Each should select a product and study consumer magazines for information about it. Then they should go to a store and compare various brands of the item. Each group should prepare a report telling what they have learned.

Enrichment
Divide the class in half. One half represents the advertisers, and the other half the consumers. The advertisers should break into groups of two or three. Each group should come up with an advertisement that is designed to sell a product using exaggeration, statements of opinion, testimonials, and so on. As each group presents its commercial, the consumers should analyze it and consider whether they should buy the product.

Strategies for Evaluating Advertisements

Here are some strategies to use to help you evaluate what advertisements are telling you:

- Read and listen carefully to separate the facts from the opinions in an ad. The ingredients in a pizza are facts. The idea that eating a pizza will make you and your friends feel terrific is simply the restaurant's opinion.
- Remember that the famous people who appear in commercials are well-paid for telling you how wonderful a product is. Actors and rock stars may sincerely like the products they are advertising, but they do not necessarily know about the nutritional content or effectiveness of one product over another.
- Remember that advertisements only talk about the best features of a product. If a product tends to break down under certain conditions, the advertiser isn't going to tell you that.
- Watch out for **bait and switch** advertisements. These are ads that offer a model of a product at a very low price. When you get to the store, however, you discover that it has run out of the item or that the item is of very poor quality. Then the salesperson steers you toward a more expensive model.

When you read, watch, or listen to advertisements, remember that the advertisers are doing everything possible to persuade you to buy their products. It is up to you to separate the facts from the techniques used to impress you. Don't be easily convinced that products are good, just because an advertisement says so. To be a wise shopper, you have to take the responsibility for finding out what you need to know. The information is out there, but you have to analyze it before you purchase a product.

When gathering information about products or services, evaluate ads carefully to separate facts from advertising techniques.

Focus on Consumer Skills Skilled consumers study advertisements carefully to determine if value is truly being offered. Even if the price is good, an item is not a bargain if it is not useful to the consumer. The impulsive purchase of a "bargain" may result in later regrets.

Real-Life Situations Television commercials often use stereotypes when they portray people in different activities. The stereotypes may be related to sex roles, age, ethnic background, or occupation. Ask students to identify current commercials that reinforce typical stereotypes (elderly grandparents) and those that do not (males cooking or doing laundry).

CHAPTER 29 REVIEW

Reviewing the Facts

1. What are two main purposes of advertising?
2. Name two kinds of advertisements.
3. What is the difference between an information ad and an image ad?
4. What do the words "advertising media" mean?
5. What is direct mail advertising?
6. What is a testimonial?
7. What do magazines such as *Consumer Reports* do?
8. What does "bait and switch" advertising mean?

Thinking Critically

1. What ads do you pay the most attention to? What advertising techniques are being used? Do they influence your buying decisions? Why or why not?
2. Luis saw an ad for a local discount store that advertised a bicycle for $59, but when he went to the store, the department manager claimed that that model was sold out. Instead, Luis was urged to buy another model that cost $79. What would you do if you were Luis?

Applying Your Skills

1. **Writing an Analysis.** Choose a product, such as a television, compact disc player, lawn mower, automobile, or microwave oven, and look up a recent article on that product in *Consumer Reports* or *Consumers' Research*. Using the information in the magazine, write a report explaining which brand or model you would buy and why.

2. **Comparing Advertising Techniques.** Cut out or photocopy three or four advertisements from a national magazine. Analyze each ad for factual information and for persuasive messages. Make two lists. List the facts contained in each ad on the first list and the opinions or persuasive messages contained in each ad on the second list. Which list is longer?

3. **Composing an Advertisement.** Choose a familiar product, such as a brand of soft drink or a favorite snack food. Create a 15- to 30-second radio ad or a full-page magazine ad. Use one or more of the advertising techniques described in the chapter.

Answers to "Reviewing the Facts"

1. Any two: to make you want to buy a particular product or service; to provide information about products, services, or ideas; to shape tastes, habits, and attitudes.
2. Information and image ads.
3. Information ad provides specific information about a product, such as size, color, and price. Image ad associates a product with a popular image, such as good looks, popularity, and intelligence.
4. The means by which ads are broadcast or displayed.
5. Advertising that is delivered by the postal service.
6. An ad in which an actor, athlete, or other celebrity endorses a product.
7. They test and rate products for performance and adherence to advertising claims.
8. When a store advertises a low-cost product to get a customer to come in, then attempts to steer the customer to a more expensive model.

Answers to "Thinking Critically"

1. Answers will vary. Students may mention ads with rock stars; ads that show teenage actors or models having a good time; ads that show products teenagers are most interested in, such as clothing, food, cars, sports equipment, and so on. Students should identify specific advertising techniques—headlines, slogans, testimonials, emotional appeals, or product characters.
2. Answers will vary. Some students might say they would buy the bicycle because the price is still reasonable. Some might ask for a raincheck.

COMPLETING THE CHAPTER

Summary

- Advertisements are designed to make people want to buy a particular product or service. Ads provide information and also shape tastes and attitudes.
- The two basic types of advertisements are information ads and image ads. These messages reach the public in print media, electronically, and through direct mail.
- Advertisers use many creative techniques to convince people to buy their products or services.
- Advertising is regulated by several federal agencies.
- Reliable product information may be obtained from several consumer magazines.
- Consumers need to evaluate advertisements carefully to make wise purchasing choices.

For Review

Objective Review Questions Have students complete the "Reviewing the Facts" section on this page.

Study Guide Have students complete the Study Guide from Chapter 29 of their *Student Workbook*.

On Sale Now . . . Ask students to cut out at least two different sale ads for a basic product, such as soap, shampoo, toothpaste, milk, or bread. They should tell the class which products they would be most likely to purchase and give reasons for their choice.

For Evaluation

Classifying Advertisements Bring in a variety of advertisements. (If possible, have a television available so that students can also watch several commercials.) Ask students to classify each advertisement into the categories discussed in the chapter: print, broadcast, or direct mail; and information or image.

Chapter Test Have students complete the test for Chapter 29 that appears in the *Teacher's Classroom Resources*.

CHAPTER OVERVIEW

Chapter 30 explains how planning purchases can help make the best use of a consumer's major resources—time, money, and knowledge. The advantages and disadvantages of several different kinds of stores are described, as are other ways to shop. Students are taught the importance of knowing when to buy, why stores have sales, and how to read sale ads carefully.

INTRODUCING THE CHAPTER

Motivators

"You Get What You Pay For . . ." Ask the class to comment on this phrase. Ask them to consider their experiences to explain their point of view. Have them give examples of past purchases that may or may not have lived up to their expectations.

Using the Photograph Refer students to the photograph on this page. Then ask them to suggest the things these shoppers should consider when comparing items for purchase. List the suggestions on the chalkboard.

Getting the Most for Your Money Refer students to the opening paragraphs on page 281. Explain that Angela was a knowledgeable consumer. She found a jacket that she liked, but she felt it was too expensive. Instead of giving up or giving in, she looked around for a less expensive version of the jacket. Ask the class if they have ever done this. Then have them suggest other ways of being a smart shopper.

Introducing the Objectives

Discuss the chapter objectives on this page. Remind students that the objectives focus on important chapter content.

Introducing Vocabulary

Write the words *impulse buying* on the chalkboard. Explain that impulse, in this case, means to act on the spur of the moment. Ask students to describe situations in which they have given in to impulse buying. Ask them also to describe how they felt about their actions after the purchase.

CHAPTER

30

Consumer Skills

OBJECTIVES

This chapter will help you to:

- Describe how planning your purchases can make the best use of your resources.
- List the advantages and disadvantages of different types of stores.
- Evaluate sales and sales ads.

WORDS TO REMEMBER

clearance sale
consumer
department store
discount store
factory outlet
impulse buying
mail order
specialty store

Chapter Resources

Teacher's Classroom Resources
- Lesson Plan
- Life Skills Activity, *Bargain Hunting Expedition*
- Reproducible Master, *Shopping by Mail or Phone*
- Extension Activity, *Where Should I Buy?*
- Chapter Test

Student Workbook
- Study Guide
- Worksheet, *Smart Shopper . . . or Budget Bungler?*

Angela was shopping in a local department store when she noticed a denim jacket she really liked. The jacket was very expensive, however, and Angela decided to wait and see if she could find a similar jacket for less money somewhere else.

A week later, Angela was in a nearby clothing store when she saw another denim jacket for sale. She read the labels and learned that this jacket was very similar in quality and workmanship to the one she had seen in the other store but it was a good deal cheaper. This time, Angela decided to buy the jacket. She felt good about the purchase because she was sure she had made the right decision by waiting.

Planning Your Purchases

Without even being aware of it, Angela had planned her purchase of the jacket. She made a better decision than she would have if she had bought the first jacket she saw.

When you plan your purchases, you use the same strategies you learned about in Chapter 25. You set a goal by deciding what you want to purchase, and you decide how to use your resources to achieve the goal.

As a **consumer**, or a person who buys and uses things, your major resources are money, time, and knowledge. If you do not have enough money to buy the product you want, you can earn, save, use credit, or shop around for a less expensive model. If you don't have the time to shop around, you may end up spending more money for an item.

As Angela demonstrated, planning your purchases means using knowledge as well as time and money. You have to know when and where to shop and how to compare goods. You will find that knowledge can save you time and money. For example, you may want to buy a particular model bicycle because you researched bicycles in consumer magazines and found the model that suits you best. If a local store offers that model in a special sale, then you can buy it at a good price without having to spend a lot of time in stores.

Knowing Your Stores

Different kinds of stores serve different purposes. People can save time and money by shopping at the most appropriate store.

- A **specialty store** sells only a certain kind of merchandise, such as tapes and records, sporting goods, or shoes, and therefore offers a wider selection of those items.

Speciality stores usually offer a wider selection of choices than stores that carry a variety of merchandise.

TEACHING THE CHAPTER

For convenience, the teaching suggestions for this chapter are arranged according to the following lesson topics:

- "Planning Your Purchases," page 281
- "Knowing Your Stores," pages 281-284
- "Understanding Sales," page 285-286

Teaching "Planning Your Purchases"

(Page 281)

This section explains that consumers must plan purchases by using strategies that put their time, money, and knowledge to best use.

Checking Comprehension

✓ Name four things consumers can do if they do not have enough money to purchase a product. *Earn or save money, use credit, shop for a less expensive model.*

Activities

Skill Builder: Math
Explain to students that Sam's Department Store is advertising a special sale. Any item that remains unsold after today gets marked down 20 percent on Wednesday; if it's still in the store the next Wednesday, it will be marked down 35 percent off the original price; on the third Wednesday, the item will be sold at 50 percent off the original price. If Mindy sees a jacket priced at $85 on Tuesday, how much money would she save if she waited until Wednesday to buy it? Until the next Wednesday? Until the third Wednesday? *(Answers: $17, $29.75, $42.50).*

Reteaching
Ask students to explain the three main resources a consumer has. Then have them describe how to set goals and plan purchases using those resources.

Enrichment
Ask the class to consider what risks Mindy would be taking (see the Math Skill Builder above) by waiting to purchase the jacket. Have the class role play different shopping situations.

Emphasize Before going out to make a purchase, ask yourself if you really need and want the item.

Did You Know? Even if you do not have time to compare prices by going to several stores, you may be able to telephone the stores to find out if they carry the item and to compare prices.

Emphasize The lowest-price item may not necessarily be the best bargain. Check for price *and* quality.

Teaching "Knowing Your Stores"

(Pages 281-284)

This section explains the differences between several kinds of stores. It also describes other ways to shop, such as mail order, shopping clubs, direct sales, and so on.

Checking Comprehension

✓ Describe some advantages and disadvantages of shopping in department stores as compared to discount stores. *Department stores offer variety, credit-card privileges, and special services such as gift wrapping and delivery. Discount stores often lack the variety and special features of department stores, their merchandise may be of lesser quality, but their prices are usually lower.*

✓ What is a factory outlet? What are the advantages and the disadvantages of shopping there? *It is a store in which the manufacturer of a product sells goods directly to the shopper. Prices are low, but merchandise might be imperfect or out of style.*

✓ What makes mail-order shopping convenient? *A person can shop from home, without need for transportation.*

✓ What is a shopping club? *A kind of mail-order shopping service that usually sells one kind of merchandise.*

✓ Why do you need to examine carefully items purchased at a flea market or garage sale, or through a classified ad? *You cannot return defective goods and may not even be able to locate the seller again.*

✓ Why is it important to know when to buy merchandise? *Various kinds of products customarily go on sale at particular times of the year.*

✓ What kinds of defects or problems may be present in sale items? *The item may be out of fashion, out of season, or in the case of food, no longer fresh.*

- A **department store** offers shoppers a wide variety of goods, often in different price ranges, under one roof. Department stores issue their own credit cards and offer many services such as gift-wrapping and home delivery.
- A **discount store** carries nationally advertised brands at reduced prices. They usually also carry lines of clothing and shoes that are cheaper and of lesser quality than found in department stores.
- A **factory outlet** is a store in which the manufacturer of a product sells goods directly to shoppers. Prices are low,but the goods may be slightly imperfect or out of style.

Mail-order companies are businesses that send catalogs to people who can order various products from them. Some mail-order companies sell all kinds of merchandise, whereas others specialize in certain types of goods, such as sporting equipment, clothing, cooking utensils, or garden seeds.

Several major department store chains issue mail-order catalogs that enable people to use the telephone or mail to purchase many of the same goods that are sold in their stores. Many magazines also include advertising sections in which people can shop by mail. Mail-order shopping is a convenient way for teens to shop when they have no transportation to get to stores.

Other Ways to Shop

Stores aren't the only places where you can shop. You can also buy from mail-order companies and shopping clubs. You can shop by telephone, by direct sales in your home, and even by television. (See "Remote Control Shopping" on page 283.)

Shopping by mail is very convenient, although you may have to wait several days or weeks to receive your order. Read product information carefully and fill out the order form accurately.

Real-Life Situations Mail-order shopping is one of the fastest growing industries in the country. To shop successfully by mail, follow these tips:

- Read the catalog or ad carefully—descriptions, colors, sizes, quantities, and prices.
- Be sure to include all necessary information on the order form to prevent delays.
- Pay only by check, money order, or credit card—never send cash through the mail.
- Some companies have a toll-free 800 number.
- Note the shipping and return policies so you know when to expect delivery (must be within 30 days or you can cancel the order) and how to return merchandise.
- Keep a record of your order.

TECHNOLOGY

Infomercials

While searching through television channels with the remote control, Dan landed on a talk show that sounded interesting. The host was interviewing an ex-football star. After a few minutes, Dan noticed that the host and the football star were spending a lot of time talking about exercise equipment. Then Dan realized he was watching an infomercial.

An infomercial is a 30-minute television advertisement for a product. While 30-second ads concentrate on developing a product's image, infomercials present detailed information about a product. Many infomercials follow the format of television talk shows. Often the ads feature celebrities promoting the product. Like home-shopping shows, infomercials provide an 800 number so that viewers can order the product.

Weight-loss products, kitchen items, self-improvement tapes, books on money-making opportunities, and teeth whiteners are among the most commonly advertised products in infomercials. Political candidates have begun to use infomercials to explain their positions on campaign issues.

Compared with 30-second ads, infomercials are relatively inexpensive to produce. Production standards tend to be lower for infomercials, and they usually run late at night or early in the morning when air time costs less.

Infomercials started in 1984 when the federal government removed restrictions on program-length television commercials. The infomercial industry grew rapidly, mainly because an increasing number of cable and independent channels needed programming to fill air time. They also needed the money from the sale of air time.

Infomercials now sell millions of dollars worth of merchandise each year. Small businesses and entrepreneurs are the main users of these ads. However, as automobile manufacturers, insurance carriers, and other major companies see the success of infomercials, they are expected to start using them too. Industry observers also predict that more infomercials will be seen during daytime and prime-time hours and on major television networks.

It is easy to forget that infomercials are commercials and not unbiased news reports. To guard against charges of consumer fraud, responsible producers of infomercials identify each program as a paid ad at the beginning and end of the show and at every ordering opportunity.

Think It Through

1. **Why do you think people are willing to sit through 30-minute commercials?**
2. **You're thinking about ordering a pair of sunglasses you saw on an infomercial. What should you consider before ordering the product?**

Emphasize Many products currently advertised on infomercials offer instant or effortless success, fame, and beauty. The audience for these products usually does not want to put forth effort or wait a long time to see results.

Did You Know? Infomercials are the fastest-growing segment of the television direct-response industry. Besides the cost-effectiveness of putting these ads on the air, the 800 numbers that accompany them provide advertisers with immediate consumer feedback.

Teaching the Feature
"Infomercials"

Answers to Feature Questions

1. Answers will vary. Students might say that people find infomercials interesting and entertaining, that infomercials feature products people want to buy, or that watching an infomercial is less time-consuming than shopping in a store.
2. You should use the same precautions as when shopping for any other product. Be sure you have done some comparison shopping so you know you're getting the best product for the lowest price. Be sure the product comes with a warranty and a money-back guarantee. Realize, too, that if you're dissatisfied with the product, you will need to spend time and money returning it.

Activities

Watching an Infomercial Tape one or more infomercials for viewing in class. Discuss the format of the show, the type of product being advertised, the target audience, and the techniques used to motivate buyers. Analyze the information presented. Ask students to tell why they would or would not buy the product based on the infomercial.

Writing a Letter Ask students to imagine that they ordered the sunglasses. After waiting two months, they still have not received them. They called the 800-number but got no response. Divide students into groups and assign one of the following to each group: television station, Better Business Bureau, state attorney general, National Infomercial Marketing Association. Tell each student to write a letter of complaint to his or her respective organization. Ask volunteers to read their letters to the class.

Community Contact Invite a local manufacturer or entrepreneur to speak to the class on ways to advertise a product or service. Have the person discuss the pros and cons of using infomercials.

A shopping club is a kind of mail-order shopping service that usually sells one kind of merchandise, such as books or records. When you join a shopping club, you may be offered a low-cost introductory bargain, such as four books for one dollar. In return, you agree to make a minimum number of additional purchases at regular prices within a specified time period, usually one year. See "Clubs Are More Than You Bargain For" on page 291.

In direct, or door-to-door sales, the salesperson brings products such as vacuum cleaners, encyclopedias, cosmetics, and magazine subscriptions to your home. Direct sales are a convenient way to shop, but you need to be cautious. Sales representatives may try to pressure you to buy on the spot without giving you time to compare the prices and quality of their products to similar ones.

Other ways to shop include cooperative (co-op) organizations that buy in bulk at wholesale prices and pass the savings on to their members. Food co-ops are the most common of these kinds of organizations.

You can also shop at thrift shops, garage sales, and flea markets, which are places that sell used and new merchandise at low prices. In addition, people sell cars, household furnishings, and a variety of other items through the classified advertisements in newspapers.

You can sometimes discover great bargains at flea markets and garage sales or in the classified ads, and occasionally you can find a true treasure such as an antique, an old record, or an out-of-print book. Shop carefully at these places. Examine anything you plan to buy very thoroughly because you cannot return defective goods. In some cases, you may not be able to find the seller again, and you may end up spending money on a worthless product.

Knowing When to Buy

You probably wouldn't like it if you bought a shirt at a store for $20 only to learn that the same shirt was marked down to $15 for a special sale the following week. That's why knowing when to buy is as important as knowing where to shop. This means knowing what time of year stores customarily hold sales on various kinds of products. For example, you can purchase bath and bed linens on sale during the annual January white sales. You can often get good buys on winter and summer clothing when you buy them at the end of that season.

Knowing when to buy also means that you know when *not* to buy. When you go into a grocery store or discount store, you may have the urge to engage in **impulse buying**, purchasing things that you hadn't intended to. Store managers deliberately display goods to tempt you to buy on impulse. For example, you will find gum, candy, magazines, and inexpensive items such as batteries and key chains right at the checkout counter on the chance that you'll decide to buy them while you wait.

To help avoid impulse buying, make a shopping list and stick to it. If you're not sure whether to buy a particular item, such as a sweater, wait. A store may be willing to hold an item aside for you for several hours. This allows you time to check other stores.

When you are shopping, you should be aware that sale items are sometimes out of fashion or out of season. Sometimes clothing is discounted when a particular color, style, or length is no longer fashionable. In the case of food, sale items may have passed their peak of freshness and may not be worth buying. Many food items have only a limited shelf life left (that is, time during which they can be legally sold). If a food item is dated, don't buy it after that date.

Activities

Skill Builder: Critical Thinking
Remind students that making a list can help them plan before they shop. Ask them if they make a list before they go to the store. If so, when? If not, why? How do they think a list could be helpful?

Skill Builder: Writing
Ask students to choose a product they would like to buy. Then have them create a sale advertisement for the product. They should include where and when the merchandise is on sale and any other pertinent information about the item (colors, price, size). Information about store services, such as free gift-wrapping, accepts credit cards, and deliveries could also be included. Tell them that their ad should be as realistic as possible.

Reteaching
Ask students to list the various places that consumers can shop. Write the list on the board as items are suggested. Then ask students to name particular stores, mail-order companies, and so on that they or their families have used in shopping.

Enrichment
Have students work in small groups to create a chart listing different kinds of shopping facilities and comparing the advantages and disadvantages of each.

Enrichment
Have students visit local stores and make a list of the items displayed at the checkout counters. Then ask students to compare their lists. Were certain items consistently displayed there? Ask students to suggest other places in the store that are highly visible and might encourage impulse buying.

More About Consumer Cooperatives Cooperatives can provide their members with several financial benefits. Not only do they usually offer items at lower prices than retail, but they also allow profit sharing. This means that when the cooperative makes money, the profits are divided among its members, often in the form of refunds on purchases.

Counter displays encourage impulse purchases.

Understanding Sales

Stores use sales for two purposes—to attract new and regular customers, and to clear out merchandise that may be selling poorly or slowly. Stores also hope that you will buy regular-price items as well as the sale merchandise.

When Stores Hold Sales

You'll often see sales at certain times of the year. Summer clothes, for example, go on sale in July. Many sales traditionally are held on or around holidays such as Easter and Labor Day. Stores that are closing have going-out-of-business sales to get rid of their remaining stock.

Stores also hold **clearance sales** when they are seeking to get rid of old stock to make room for new items. Car dealerships, for example, have sales on last year's models when the new models come out. Some stores schedule sales when they know more people will be out shopping—back-to-school and Christmas sales—to try to lure these shoppers to their stores. And stores also hold sales at the end of a season to move leftover seasonal or dated merchandise.

Is It a Bargain?

When reading ads for sales, be sure to question these phrases.

- **List price.**The list price, the manufacturer's suggested selling price, is seldom the retailer's actual selling price.

Focus on Consumer Skills Explain that consumers should evaluate sale claims to be sure the store is offering a true discount. Some retailers may run frequent sales on a particular item. The so-called sale price may be what the regular price really should be.

Did You Know? One way to prevent impulse buying is by taking only as much money with you as you plan to spend. Also, if you take something to the checkout counter that you have picked up on impulse and you really do not want it, do not hesitate to put it back.

Teaching "Understanding Sales"
(Pages 285-286)

This section describes the various types of sales held by stores. It then lists several points to remember when shopping for bargains.

Checking Comprehension

✓ Name some times that stores traditionally hold sales. *Around holidays such as Easter or Labor Day; before going out of business; during heavy shopping periods, such as when school begins and at Christmas; at the end of a season.*

✓ What is a "special purchase" item? *Merchandise sold at a lower price, especially for a sale. The item may not be of the store's usual quality.*

✓ How could using a rebate or coupon cost you more money than you would otherwise have spent? *The product you purchase with the coupon might be priced higher than the brand you usually use.*

Activities

Skill Builder: Critical Thinking
Assign students to look through local newspapers and cut out five advertisements for sales. Have students identify the type—or theme—of the sale. Have them explain what attracted them to these particular ads.

Skill Builder: Reading
Have students bring in examples of sales ads that might, at first glance, be misleading. Ask them to underline or highlight the key words in each ad.

Reteaching
Using the ads brought to class from the previous activity, ask students to circle the key phrases: list price, below manufacturer's cost, comparable to, special purchase. Have students note which phrase was found most often.

Enrichment
Ask students to use consumers' magazines to develop a calendar of sales. This should indicate the best time to buy certain items. For example, white sales, or sales on linens and sheets, are traditionally held in August and January.

Enrichment
Break the class into small groups. Have the students assume they are the advertising managers for a major store of their choice. Ask each group to design an ad (or series of ads) to stimulate sales, reduce inventory, and clear space for new stock. They may choose any time of year and conduct any type of sales campaign. Display the ads in the classroom. Ask students to comment on where they would most likely "shop."

Enrichment
Have students bring in several pieces of direct mail advertising that have been sent to their home. Discuss the kinds of products advertised and ways the products might be different from items sold in a local store. Discuss what are some of the advantages and disadvantages of buying through direct mail.

- **Below manufacturer's cost.**This phrase suggests that both the manufacturer and the retailer have lost money on the product, which isn't likely. Check the merchandise. Is it out of date? Are parts for it available?
- **Comparable to $49.95 value.**A statement like this is just the opinion of the advertiser. The merchandise may be worth only the $29.95 you pay for it.
- **Special purchase.**Special purchase items are merchandise sold at a lower price than usual, especially for a sale. These may not be of the store's usual quality.

Points to Remember at Sales

Sales can offer excellent bargains for consumers who evaluate merchandise carefully.

- Is the product worthwhile? Examine the item carefully and check the label to see if it says "as is," "seconds," or "irregular." All of these phrases indicate that the product has a flaw, but if the flaw is minor, it may still be a worthwhile purchase. Labels that say "final sale" or "as is" mean the product is not returnable.
- Is the sale price really lower than the usual price? Some stores will advertise that a product that "regularly sells for $9.95 is now $5.95." In some cases, the store never sold the item at the higher price and never intended to. The lower price therefore is not a sale price but the store's regular price.
- Do you really need or want the product? Discount stores often put a large selection of products on sale, knowing that shoppers will be tempted to buy several items that they don't really need.
- Are coupons, rebates, or special offers really saving you money? In some cases, even with the coupon or saving, the product may cost more than the brand you usually use.

When buying items on sale, evaluate them for quality and price. If you are a careful shopper, you can get very good bargains at sales. When is a sale item not a good bargain?

Did You Know? Sometimes an item sold as irregular or "as is" has only cosmetic defects. This just affects the way the product looks, not its performance. Indeed, the product may carry the same warranty as a regular-priced item.

CHAPTER 30 REVIEW

Reviewing the Facts

1. Name the three main consumer resources.
2. What is the difference between a specialty store, a department store, a discount store, and a factory outlet?
3. Name three ways you can shop without leaving home.
4. Why should you shop carefully when buying goods at a flea market or garage sale?
5. What are two reasons why stores use sales?
6. What is a clearance sale?
7. Why is the statement "comparable to a $40 value" misleading?
8. List four things you should remember when buying merchandise.

Thinking Critically

1. If you were interested in buying a radio, would you buy it in a store, through direct mail, or at a flea market or garage sale? Explain your answer.
2. Years ago, door-to-door sales were more common than they are today. What might be some reasons for their decline?

Applying Your Skills

1. **Calculating Expenses.** Make a list of three items that you plan to purchase. If you waited and bought the items during a 15 percent clearance sale, how much money would you save?

2. **Justifying a Choice.** If you were buying a pair of running shoes, what type of store would you choose—a department store, a discount store, or a specialty store? Which kind of store would you expect to offer the greatest selection? the lowest prices? the highest quality shoes? Write a brief report in which you tell which kind of store you would patronize to purchase running shoes. Explain why.

3. **Designing an Ad.** Design a sales ad for a mountain bicycle that is regularly priced for $225.00 and is discounted 30 percent.

Answers to "Reviewing the Facts"

1. Time, money, and knowledge.
2. Specialty stores sell only one kind of merchandise. Department stores offer a wide variety of goods, often in different price ranges. Discount stores carry name brands at reduced prices. A factory outlet sells the manufacturer's goods directly to shopper.
3. Any three: mail-order catalogs; shopping clubs; door-to-door sales; television shopping shows.
4. You cannot return items, and you may not be able to find the seller again.
5. To attract new and regular customers; to clear out merchandise that may not be selling.
6. A sale to get rid of old stock and make room for new goods.
7. Because it is only the advertiser's opinion, not a fact.
8. Is the product worthwhile? Is the sale price really lower than the usual price? Do you really need or want the product? Are coupons, rebates, or special offers saving you money?

Answers to "Thinking Critically"

1. If buying it at a store, you could examine the model but you might pay a higher price. If bought through direct mail, you would have to wait days or weeks for delivery but the price might be lower. If bought at a flea market or garage sale, the price might be very low but you could not return it if problems occurred.
2. Answers will vary, but students might mention that modern transportation has made is easy for people to go to stores to shop; mail order and televsion shopping programs—provide people with other ways to shop at home; more people are in the work force, so fewer people are at home.

COMPLETING THE CHAPTER

Summary

- Through planning, a consumer can best decide how to use resources effectively.
- Different kinds of stores serve different purposes.
- Consumers can buy merchandise through mail-order companies, shopping clubs, telephone, direct sales, television, cooperatives, and classified ads, and at thrift shops, flea markets, and garage sales.

For Review

Objective Review Questions Have students complete the "Reviewing the Facts" section on this page.

Study Guide Have students complete the Study Guide from Chapter 30 of their *Student Workbook*.

Shopper's Scrapbook Ask students to cut out newspaper ads from various kinds of stores—department store, discount store, specialty store, and factory outlet. Have students make a scrapbook, categorizing the ads under each store type. Ask students to share their scrapbooks, and explain how the ads reflect differences in these types of stores.

Bargain Hunting Have students form small groups. Ask each group to select an item that the group will pretend to "purchase." Group members should divide shopping searches. One member may look at classified ads, another at a flea market, another at a department store or specialty store, and so on. Have students report on their hunt for bargains. Explain that they should keep track of the amount of time they spent finding the item at each source, the quality and condition of the item, any warranties or guarantees, and the cost of the item.

For Evaluation

Smart Shoppers List Ask students to develop a list of effective shopping techniques used by wise consumers.

Chapter Test Have students complete the test for Chapter 30 that appears in the *Teacher's Classroom Resources.*

CHAPTER OVERVIEW

Chapter 31 opens with an example of why careful shopping is so important. It suggests ways for a wise consumer to compare the price, quality, and suitability of goods and services. Later the chapter considers the components of comparison shopping: price, performance, contents, durability, convenience, maintenance and warranties. In addition, students are taught to evaluate hidden costs, such as travel expenses and the cost of repairs and additional parts.

INTRODUCING THE CHAPTER

Motivators

What Is an Educated Consumer? Ask students to define an educated consumer. Explain that an educated consumer compares products and reads labels before making any purchase.

Using the Photograph Have students refer to the photograph on this page. Then ask, "What is the teen checking for in the store? What other things should you look for before buying a product?"

What Is a Warranty? Ask students to define *warranty* or look up the definition in a dictionary or in the glossary in the back of the text. Have them explain why it was foolish for Jason to purchase a tape player without a warranty.

Introducing the Objectives

Discuss the chapter objectives on this page. Remind students that the objectives focus on important chapter content.

Introducing Vocabulary

Write *goods* and *services* on the chalkboard and ask students to explain the difference between the terms. Ask students to name a few examples of each.

CHAPTER

31

Price and Quality

OBJECTIVES

This chapter will help you to:

- Judge the quality of a product or service.
- Choose the most appropriate product to satisfy your wants and needs.
- Explain the purpose of comparison shopping.
- Give examples of hidden costs.

WORDS TO REMEMBER

comparison shopping
goods
service
Underwriter's Laboratory
unit price
warranty

Chapter Resources

Teacher's Classroom Resources
- Lesson Plan
- Life Skills Activity, *Warranty Wise*
- Reproducible Master, *Signs of Quality*
- Extension Activity, *Be a Successful Shopper*
- Chapter Test

Student Workbook
- Study Guide
- Worksheet, *Searching for Consumer Satisfaction*

Jason bought a portable tape player for a very low price at a going-out-of-business sale. He thought he had a real bargain, but the tape deck kept snagging and ripping his tapes.

Jason attempted to return the tape player and get his money back, but the store had gone out of business. In addition, the tape player did not come with a warranty from the manufacturer.

Jason was stuck with a bad buy because he had been overly influenced by the price of the tape player and he neglected to examine it for quality. Has this ever happened to you? You can learn how to be a better consumer by looking closely at both price and quality.

When you go to a store to shop, you can buy goods or services. **Goods** are material things, such as clothes and records, that you can use. A **service** is the work performed for one person by another. The person who cuts your hair provides a service, as do doctors, dentists, gardeners, travel agents, and plumbers.

Evaluating Purchases

Whenever you shop, you have to choose from a variety of goods and services. How then do you choose? What do you look for and what should you avoid?

You can compare the price and quality of goods by examining them, by reading about them, and by talking to people who have used the items. Were other people pleased with their purchases? Would they buy the same items again? It is a little harder to compare the price and quality of services. To compare the price of a service, you can ask several people who provide the same service to give you their price lists or estimates of their charges. To compare quality, you have to look at the work the people who are providing the service have already done for others.

If money were no object, you could always buy the highest-quality item available. For most people, however, money is limited. They often have to make trade-offs or compromises between what they can afford and what they really need or want. The best trade-offs result from planning before you shop. Planning requires thinking about quality and price.

Quality

What is quality anyway? How can you tell when a product is of poor or high quality? Quality depends on five factors:

- **Performance.** How well does the product work? Is the video game fun? Is the cereal nutritious as well as delicious?
- **Durability.** How strong, sturdy, or well made is the product? Will the sweater shrink after being washed? Will the schoolbag hold your books, or will it fall apart in a few weeks?
- **Convenience.** Is the product easy to open, close, use, and store? Do you have to fight those boots to get them on? Does the shampoo bottle tend to pour more than it should?
- **Maintenance.** How much care will a product require during its lifetime? Will the watch need expensive repairs if you get it wet? Does the portable television come with a warranty? Are there service centers nearby in case repairs are needed?

Emphasize Price is not always a guide to quality.

Emphasize *Plan* before you shop.

Did You Know? Buying services may be more difficult than buying goods, since you cannot see, touch, or examine services before purchasing them.

TEACHING THE CHAPTER

For convenience, the teaching suggestions for this chapter are arranged according to the following lesson topics:

Teaching "Evaluating Purchases"
(Pages 289-290)

This section teaches how to make choices when shopping for goods and services, and how to evaluate products on the basis of quality, price, and suitability.

Checking Comprehension

✔ How can a shopper compare the price and quality of goods? *By examining them; by reading about them; by talking to people who have used the same items.*

✔ Compare and contrast *durability* and *convenience. Both are factors to consider when determining quality. Durability has to do with how well made a product is. Convenience has to do with how easy it is to use.*

✔ What is the Underwriter's Laboratory? *An agency that tests and approves electrical products for safety.*

✔ What should you do if you buy a product that can't be tested or tried in the store? *Make sure the item can be returned if it is defective; save the sales receipt.*

✔ How can planning ahead help you get the most for your money? *Planning ahead enables you to shop carefully. If you wait until the last minute, you might be forced to settle for a high-priced item.*

✔ How can you choose the most suitable model from all those offered? *You should have some idea of what your needs are before you shop.*

- **Safety.** Are there any potential hazards involved in using the product? Is the handle of the typewriter case strong enough? Does that hair dryer come with the Underwriter's Laboratory (UL) seal of safety? The **Underwriter's Laboratory** is an agency that tests electrical products for safety.

Sometimes you can't answer all these questions before you buy a product. You can't try a hair dryer or play a compact disc in the store, for example, so it is always a good idea to make sure you can return the product if it proves to be defective. That is why it's important to keep sales receipts. You'll learn how to return damaged or defective goods in Chapter 32.

Safety is an important factor in judging the quality of a product. Electrical products should carry labels assuring they have met inspection standards.

Price

You need to consider several things when you decide how much you're willing to spend on a product. A higher price doesn't always mean better quality, and paying a low price at a discount store may not be a bargain if you have to travel far to get to the store.

Emergencies may cause you to pay more. If your glasses break and only an expensive repair shop is open, the price may be less important than getting your glasses fixed in a hurry. Your need for a product is as important a consideration as its price.

You'll usually get more for your money when you plan ahead. If those $6 pierced earrings are a perfect gift for your sister, buy them now if you can afford it. Six months from now, when her birthday arrives, you might pay $10 for a last-minute gift that you like less.

Suitability

Having some idea of what you need before you shop can make all the difference when you're in the store looking at rows and rows of products. This will help you select a suitable model—one that meets your needs and resources.

You won't always want or need the highest-priced, best-quality item. For example, if you shop for an electronic keyboard, you can choose from a small, inexpensive one with few features or one costing several hundred dollars. The high-priced keyboard includes many extra features and is intended for professional musicians who play in bands.

If you are a professional musician or if you are aspiring to be one, you might choose the expensive keyboard. If you just want a keyboard to play for fun, you should probably choose a much less expensive one with fewer features.

Activities

Skill Builder: Reading
Have students go to the library and do research on the Good Housekeeping Seal of Approval: what it is, how products that carry it are selected, and so on. Ask several students to report on their findings and then discuss in class how this designation helps the consumer.

Skill Builder: Critical Thinking
Have students draw a chart that can be used to evaluate their purchases. Have them first make three columns titled: "Goods and Services," "Satisfied," and "Not Satisfied." In the first column they should list goods (food, clothing, appliances) or services (a haircut, dry cleaning) they have purchased in the past two weeks. Then they should indicate whether or not they were satisfied with each item on their list. Ask them to discuss how the chart might help them shop more wisely in the future.

Reteaching
Ask students to suggest ways to compare goods and services. Have them list the five elements on which quality depends.

Enrichment
Ask students to bring in the service manuals that came with any large purchases they or their parents made in recent months. Have them study the maintenance instructions and discuss how clear the guidelines are. Is the product easy to maintain? Have they and their parents been following the maintenance instructions? If not, why?

Emphasize Buying is essentially a matter of making choices.

Did You Know? Businesses use market research to find out why consumers buy certain items, and what new products are likely to be popular or unpopular. This is done because a business's success depends on consumer satisfaction and repeat purchases.

MANAGING RESOURCES

Clubs Are More Than You Bargain For

When Jeremy joined a record club, he thought he had found a real bargain. He not only got to select eight albums or tapes for one low price, but also was promised a monthly magazine on all the hottest new releases. A few months later, after Jeremy had a chance to discover some of the hidden costs, he felt disappointed.

Record and book clubs are very popular. When people join a club, they get to select a large number of records, tapes, or books from a list of current favorites. The club then sends all those selections for a very small charge. There's a catch, though: Members are usually required to purchase a certain number of full-priced items within a given time period. In addition, there are other hidden costs that consumers aren't usually aware of when they join.

- How do club prices compare with similar products bought in a store? If a club's prices are higher, it may be better to buy the items locally.
- Are costs for handling and postage added to the price? If so, those charges usually put the total cost of the item above the retail price.
- How does the quality of club products compare? For example, the quality of the paper used in a book can be much thinner than in a similar book bought at a bookstore.
- What do you have to do if you don't want the club to send you the items featured in its monthly catalog? You may have to return a postcard with the appropriate boxes crossed off. If you forget to send the postcard back, or if it gets lost in the mail, the club will send you all its featured selections of the month.
- What do you have to do if you don't want to keep the items? Usually, you are responsible for packaging the returns and mailing the items back.
- If the club has special sales or bonuses, do these items go towards fulfilling your membership requirements? If not, you may have to purchase full-price items instead.

Think It Through

1. **Do you think Jeremy made a good choice in joining the record club? Why or why not?**
2. **Why do you think record and book clubs are so popular?**

Teaching the Feature

"Clubs Are More Than You Bargain For"

Answers to Feature Questions

1. Answers will vary. Some students may say that Jeremy made a good choice because he still got eight inexpensive records. Others might say he made a bad choice because the club will cost him more money in the long run.
2. Most people believe they are getting a good deal in the initial offers. Also, in areas in which there are few specialty stores, clubs are very convenient.

Activities

Five Books for $1.00 Ask students to look through popular magazines to bring in examples of book clubs, computer clubs, video cassette clubs, and so on. Ask students what part of the ad appealed to them most. Then have students explain why they think the offer is a good one or a bad one.

Community Contact Ask students to compile a list of local consumer protection groups. They may use telephone books, library reference files, municipal offices, the local Chamber of Commerce, and other resources. If possible, invite a local consumer advocate to talk to your class about how to be an informed shopper. Present the class list to your guest, and ask if he or she has any additions.

Did You Know? If merchandise that is being returned gets lost in the mail, the consumer must either pay for the lost items or provide proof, such as a post office or UPS receipt, that the merchandise was indeed mailed.

Emphasize The postcards that are returned to book or record clubs once or twice a month must have stamps on them. That's a minimum expenditure of 12 stamps per year.

Teaching "Comparison Shopping"
(Pages 292-294)

This section teaches how to compare the prices, features, and performance of products before purchasing them.

Checking Comprehension

✓ What is comparison shopping? *Comparing prices and features of several brands or models before buying.*

✓ How can unit prices help you? *The unit price tells you how much you are paying per ounce or by count, allowing you to select the best value.*

✓ Why might you want to buy an expensive model of a product? *It might have special features that you could use; it might be of better quality.*

✓ Why might you decide *not* to buy an expensive model of a product? *It may not be better than cheaper models; it may have features you do not need; or it may have gotten a low rating from a consumer magazine.*

✓ Why should you look at care instructions on clothing labels when considering the cost? *If the item requires dry cleaning, it will cost you additional money in the long run.*

Comparison Shopping

If you're about to make an expensive purchase—a home video game system, for instance—you probably won't want to buy the first one you see. More than likely you'll want to look at several models and compare the features and prices of each before you buy. Such **comparison shopping** is a good habit even if the product is a relatively small item, like a box of cereal. It's even more important when buying a high-priced item.

In Chapter 29, you learned how to compare products by researching them in articles in consumer magazines and by reading the labels on similar products. Your comparisons should include price, performance, contents, durability, convenience, maintenance, and warranties.

Price and Performance

You may think that a difference of a dime on a food purchase isn't that much, but what are the reasons for the 10-cent difference? Read the labels of two similar products carefully. Is the nutritional value the same? Is there as much in one package as in the other? Should you buy the larger or smaller size?

Using **unit prices**, or the prices of items per ounce or by count, will help you find the best value. Unit prices are usually found on the store shelf under the item.

Suppose that 15 ounces of your favorite shampoo costs $3.69, and 12 ounces of a new brand is $3.39. You wonder if the new brand is cheaper. Reading the unit prices of the two shampoos shows that your brand costs less. The other is priced at $4.52 per pint, but yours is only $3.94 per pint.

Prices are a good way to compare products, but at the same time you should consider performance. You may

Remember that the most expensive model is not always the one that best suits your needs or wants.

Emphasize It is important to read all labels, tags, or other consumer information before purchasing any item. Pay special attention to warning labels.

Did You Know? When comparing goods or services, you should check the reputation of the product and the firm or manufacturer. This is done by asking other people, reading articles in consumer publications, or calling consumer agencies.

Unit prices help you compare prices for the same quantities of similar items.

want to buy a more expensive model of a product such as a typewriter because it has more features or works better. To compare performance, start by looking up the product in the *Consumer Index*. Read all you can find about different brands and models. A more expensive brand may not be better. It might not have the features you want, or it may have features you don't need. It might have gotten a very low rating from a consumer magazine.

Next, go to the store and ask for a demonstration. You may prefer the sound of one keyboard over another.

Contents and Durability

Labels and packages will tell you about the contents of most products, but whenever you can, you should also get a "hands-on" feel for what you're buying. Try on clothes and shoes and examine them carefully to see how well they're made. Check tools and machines to see if they are sturdy and well constructed. You can't always depend on manufacturers' sizes or brands to determine the quality. Look at labels on food packages to see whether the item is as nutritious as you would like.

Convenience and Maintenance

Another factor to consider when choosing one brand of product over another is instructions for its assembly and care. If you're buying something that you'll need to assemble yourself, be sure that the instructions are included in the package. Ask at the store if someone will be available to answer questions should you have trouble with the item you have purchased.

Look for care instructions on clothing labels, and consider the cost of such care before you make your purchase. Most wool clothing, for instance, requires dry cleaning. Appliance packages should come with service manuals. These booklets describe how to use and care for the appliance properly.

Warranties

A **warranty** (or guarantee) is a written statement from the manufacturer or retailer, promising to repair or replace a defective product, or to refund your money. Because warranties vary from company to company and from state to state, you should examine them carefully. A warranty should include the following information:

- Name and address of the company.
- An exact statement of what is covered. Does the company agree to pay for parts and labor, or only parts?
- The length of time of the coverage.
- The procedure to be followed in case of a defect. For example, who will pay shipping costs to send the product back?
- Whom the owner must contact to get the warranty fulfilled.
- The length of time the company has to take action on a problem.

Activities

Skill Builder: Math
Write the following list on the chalkboard and have students calculate the unit price for each (rounded off to the nearest cent):

	Price	Unit Price
Potatoes		
5 lbs.	$1.59	______ lb.
Toothpaste		
6.4 oz. tube	1.99	______ oz.
Aspirin		
100 tablets	1.39	______ tablet
Vegetable oil		
24 oz.	1.49	______ oz.
Canned tuna		
6.5 oz.	.99	______ oz.
Sugar		
5 lbs.	2.09	______ lb.

(Answers: potatoes, $0.32/lb; toothpaste, $0.31/oz.; aspirin, $0.01/tablet; vegetable oil, $0.06/oz.; canned tuna, $0.15/oz.; sugar, $0.42/lb.)

Skill Builder: Critical Thinking
Explain to students that unit pricing adds to the cost of products because supermarkets must buy the equipment for making the pricing labels and pay people to do the unit pricing. Ask students if they would prefer to shop at a store that charges less for its goods but doesn't provide unit pricing. Do students think that they would have the discipline to figure out the unit prices on their own?

Reteaching
Bring in a warranty from an appliance, cassette player, or some other item. Make photocopies of the warranty and have students underline and label the information referred to on pages 293-294. Ask students to note whether the information is easy to understand.

Enrichment
Ask students to go to the grocery store and select one food item that comes in several different brands, such as mayonnaise or peanut butter. Students should make a list of three or four brands, the size of each jar, and the retail price. They should record the unit price of each item and decide which brand and size is the best value.

More About Warranties Explain that many products come with warranties. It is up to informed consumers to determine whether the warranty offered for a specific product meets their needs. A *limited* warranty promises replacement or repair of certain parts for a maximum of one year. It usually does not include labor costs. Under a *full* warranty, the consumer can expect a defective product to be repaired or replaced within a reasonable amount of time, usually set by federal guidelines. Consumers may choose to purchase, at additional cost, an *extended* warranty. These are often offered by the sellers of major electronic items, such as VCR units, computers, washers, kitchen appliances, and so on.

Teaching "Avoiding Hidden Costs"

(Page 294)

This section teaches the student to be aware of various costs that are not included in the price of an item.

Checking Comprehension

✓ What other hidden costs should be considered when comparing prices? *An item ultimately costs more if it requires frequent repairs and additional parts, or cannot be exchanged if something goes wrong. Travel costs are another hidden cost.*

✓ What do you need to know about refunds and exchanges? *You need to know the store's policies and time limit for refunds and exchanges.*

Activities

Skill Builder: Writing

Tell the students the following story: Kim bought a watch at a jewelry store. After one week, it broke. She returned the watch to the store. They gave her a refund since they did not have any more of that brand in stock. She went to another store to buy the watch. After two months, the battery needed to be replaced. She went to several stores, but none carried the battery she needed. Finally, she wrote to the manufacturer. Six weeks later, they sent her a new battery and a bill for the battery, postage, and handling. Ask the students to list all the hidden costs that were involved. *(Answers: travel to return the first watch and go to another store to get a new one; travel to try and locate a battery; postage for the letter to the manufacturer; the cost of a replacement battery; postage and handling for the new battery.)*

Reteaching

Review the list of common hidden costs on page 294 in the text. Ask students to suggest other examples of hidden costs that they have discovered.

Enrichment

Sponsor a poster contest using the theme "Good Shopping Habits." Have students display posters in businesses in the area.

- Any requirements that the purchaser must meet to validate the warranty.

Remember to keep your warranties and sales slips in a safe place in case you need them.

Avoiding Hidden Costs

Some costs are hidden because they are not part of the price of something, but they still must be paid. Some common hidden costs include:

- **Travel.** When comparison shopping, don't forget to include the cost of transportation. Consider the time, energy, and money required to have your hair cut across town. It might cost less to go to a more expensive salon around the corner.
- **Repairs.** Before buying a product, check the warranty for coverage. There may be a copy attached to the floor model. If not, ask to see one. Stores are required by law to show you warranties. Ask about the cost of repairs not covered by the warranty. If they seem high, compare them to repair costs for other models of the same products. If you buy an item that needs frequent or expensive repairs, in effect the item costs more.
- **Additional parts.** "Battery not included" can mean another expense before the product you've bought is actually going to work. Some accessories, such as shoulder straps for schoolbags and stuff sacks for sleeping bags, are conveniences you might need as much as the item itself.
- **Exchanges.** If something goes wrong with a product you purchased, take it back to the store with the receipt. Usually, stores have policies and time limits for refunds and exchanges. For your own protection, find out about these at the time of purchase. If you can't return a defective product, you've spent money for nothing. You'll learn more about refunds and exchanges in Chapter 32.

Accessories such as batteries are hidden costs that add to the price of some products.

Cross-Reference For additional information on returning and exchanging items, see Chapter 32 "Voicing Your Opinion".

Focus on Consumer Skills Explain to students that in this chapter they have learned ways to select products or services *before* they buy. They can help themselves become better consumers by reading, studying economic trends, taking consumer education courses, working with organized consumer groups, and learning about money management.

CHAPTER 31 REVIEW

Reviewing the Facts

1. What is the difference between goods and services?
2. What are the five factors that define quality?
3. Why do people sometimes pay a higher price for a product during an emergency?
4. What does suitability mean?
5. How can comparison shopping save you money?
6. What is a unit price?
7. What is a warranty?
8. How can repairs be a hidden cost?

Thinking Critically

1. Have you ever made a purchase that dissatisfied you? Why were you dissatisfied? What comparison shopping techniques could you use the next time to prevent this from happening?
2. What types of products might come with a warranty? Why do you think manufacturers provide warranties on these products?

Applying Your Skills

1. **Evaluating Quality.** Bring to class two new shirts or blouses. Read the labels and note the prices, fibers, and care instructions. See if the labels indicate where the garment was manufactured. Also look for details such as the tailoring of collars and cuffs, and examine the pockets, buttons, and stitching. Which do you think is the better quality garment? Why? What is the difference in prices? How do you account for the difference? Write a report describing your findings.

2. **Comparing the Cost of Goods.** Go to a supermarket or store that posts unit prices for products. Examine a group of products, such as aspirin, shampoo, or cookies, and write down the unit prices for each product in the group. Draw a graph showing each of the products from the least to most expensive according to their unit prices.

3. **Evaluating Qualities.** Identify a product you are interested in buying. Find an account of the item in a consumer magazine. Read about the quality, performance, durability, safety, and features of several brands. Which one would best fit your needs?

Answers to "Reviewing the Facts"

1. Goods are material things we use; services are work performed by one person for another.
2. Performance, durability, convenience, maintenance, and safety.
3. Because they need the product or service immediately and don't have time to comparison shop.
4. How well the product fits the buyer's needs and resources.
5. By finding the best quality at the lowest price.
6. The price of an item per ounce or by count.
7. A written statement from a manufacturer or retailer promising to repair or replace a defective item or to refund the money.
8. If you buy something that needs frequent repairs, the product ends up costing you more than a similar product that does not need a lot of repairs.

COMPLETING THE CHAPTER

Summary

- When you go shopping, you can buy goods or services. Goods are material things; services are work performed by one person for another.
- When evaluating a purchase, you should compare quality, price, and suitability of each product.
- When you comparison shop you look at the prices and features of several brands.
- It is important to be aware of possible hidden costs when making a purchase.

For Review

Objective Review Questions Have students complete the "Reviewing the Facts" section on this page.

Study Guide Have students complete the Study Guide from Chapter 31 of their *Student Workbook*.

The Convenience Store Ask students to form small groups to compare the advantages and disadvantages of shopping in a small, local convenience food store or specialty store as opposed to shopping in a large chain store. Each group might choose two items, such as a pound of lean ground meat and a container of orange juice, and compare quality, prices, convenience, and so on.

For Evaluation

Questionnaire Have students develop a "Wise Consumer" questionnaire that would cover the major points of the chapter: Evaluating Purchases, Comparison Shopping, and Avoiding Hidden Costs.

Self-Appraisal Ask students to exchange the above questionnaires. They should use their classmates' questionnaires for their own self-appraisal as a "wise consumer."

Chapter Test Have students complete the test for Chapter 31 that appears in the *Teacher's Classroom Resources.*

Answers to "Thinking Critically"

1. Answers will vary. Discussion will probably focus on products that didn't perform as expected or that broke shortly after they were purchased. If students say they kept a product they were dissatisfied with, talk about why.
2. Answers will vary, but students might mention appliances, electronics equipment, cameras, cars, and so on. Manufacturers may be required by law to provide warranties on certain products. In addition, manufacturers want to keep consumers happy so that they will buy more products.

CHAPTER OVERVIEW

This chapter makes students aware of their rights as consumers and teaches them how to make a complaint, either in person or through the mail. It also discusses taking legal action and seeking help from various kinds of consumer agencies.

INTRODUCING THE CHAPTER

Motivators

Who Cares What You Think? Ask students if they think that consumers' opinions are valued. Have them suggest reasons why stores and manufacturers should listen to their customers' complaints and praise.

Using the Photograph Ask students to study the photograph on this page. Then ask: "What are some reasons why the customer might be returning this item? What could the customer do to make the return/refund as fast and simple as possible?"

Have You Ever Been a Dissatisfied Customer? Ask students if they ever bought a faulty or damaged product. Did they handle the problem as Jeff did, or did they handle it differently? Ask them to explain.

Introducing the Objectives

Discuss the chapter objectives on this page. Remind students that the objectives focus on important chapter content.

Introducing Vocabulary

Tell students that they will be learning about the Better Business Bureau in this chapter. Then briefly describe how the bureau works to protect consumers. Have students find out where the nearest one is.

CHAPTER

32

Voicing Your Opinion

OBJECTIVES

This chapter will help you to:

- List the rights of consumers.
- Explain how to make a complaint in person and by letter.
- Identify and describe sources of help for consumers.
- Explain why consumers should voice their opinions.

WORDS TO REMEMBER

Better Business Bureau (BBB)
redress
small claims court

Chapter Resources

Teacher's Classroom Resources
- Lesson Plan
- Life Skills Activity, *Consumer Hot Line*
- Reproducible Master, *Your Consumer Rights*
- Extension Activity, *Writing a Letter of Complaint*
- Chapter Test

Student Workbook
- Study Guide
- Worksheet, *Caveat Emptor*

Jeff had saved $35 to buy a video game disk for use on his home computer. When he and his friends tried to play the game, it wouldn't work. Just to make sure it was the disk and not the computer that was at fault, Jeff tried several other disks on the computer and each one worked fine.

Jeff took the disk, along with the sales receipt, back to the store where he bought it. When he explained the problem, the store manager gave him his money back.

Jeff was exercising his rights as a consumer. When you aren't happy with a purchase you've made, you do have certain rights. At such times, it's important to know how to voice your opinion so that you can obtain those rights.

Your Consumer Rights

When you purchase a product that is damaged, inferior, or unsafe, you have a right to make a complaint and to be heard. In the last 25 years, the U.S. Government has enacted many laws to protect the rights of consumers. These rights include:

- **The right to safety.** Consumers are protected from the selling of dangerous products.
- **The right to be informed.** Consumers are protected from misleading advertising. They can ask for all the facts needed to make good choices.
- **The right to choose.** Consumers are given the chance to make their own choices.
- **The right to be heard.** Consumers can speak out when they aren't satisfied. They have a voice in the making of consumer laws.
- **The right to consumer education.** Consumers have the right to learn about consumer issues.
- **The right to redress. Redress** means consumers have the right to get a wrong corrected.

When You Have a Complaint

Consumers expect manufacturers and sellers to be fair. They expect to be offered goods and services at fair prices, and they expect the things they buy to perform well. Consumers must also be fair by voicing their opinions only when their complaints are real ones.

For example, Donna bought a wool-blend sweater. The care label on the sweater said, "Hand wash, using a cold-water wash product." Donna followed the directions and washed the sweater by hand in cold water, but it shrank. Donna has a real complaint against the sweater manufacturer.

Generally, a complaint is fair if you purchased a product that was damaged, or if it was not sold at the advertised price. You would also have a right to complain if a service you paid for was not done correctly.

Complaining in Person

If you do have a fair complaint, act soon. A delay in making a complaint makes it harder for you to solve the problem. First, find your sales receipt and warranty. Always save these because they can help you state your case.

Then follow these five steps:

1. Check to see if the problem is covered by the warranty. If so, follow the directions listed on it. If not, take the next four steps.

Did You Know? An excellent source of government publications for consumers is the Consumer Information Center, Pueblo, Colorado 81009.

Emphasize Although laws vary by state, agencies on the state, county, and municipal levels work to protect consumers. Restaurants and food services are inspected and licensed; hairdressers are licensed; banking, credit, and insurance companies are regulated, as are places that sell alcoholic beverages.

TEACHING THE CHAPTER

For convenience, the teaching suggestions for this chapter are arranged according to the following lesson topics:

Teaching "Your Consumer Rights"
(Page 297)

This section emphasizes that consumers are protected by a number of laws and have the right to complain when they have purchased damaged, unsafe, or inferior merchandise.

Checking Comprehension

✔ How is the right to safety similar to and different from the right to be informed? *Both rights protect consumers. The right to safety protects them from the selling of dangerous products, while the right to be informed protects them from false or misleading advertising.*

✔ What does the right to redress mean? *Consumers have the right to get a wrong corrected.*

Activities

Skill Builder: Writing
Ask students to choose one of the consumer rights listed on page 297. Have students write a short story or paragraph about a consumer exercising one of these rights.

Reteaching
Have students give examples of the rights of consumers and briefly describe what each of them means.

Enrichment
Invite a representative from the district office of the Federal Trade Commission or the state attorney general's staff to speak to the class about their responsibilities. Have students develop questions to ask the guest.

Teaching "When You Have a Complaint"

(Page 297-299)

This section teaches students when it is appropriate to make a complaint, and how to do so in person. In addition, detailed steps are provided for writing a letter of complaint.

Checking Comprehension

✓ Generally, when is a consumer complaint considered to be fair? *When the item purchased was damaged, the service provided was not done properly, or the consumer was not charged the advertised price.*

✓ When you have a problem with merchandise, what should you check for in the warranty? *You should see if the problem is covered by the warranty. If it is, follow the instructions given.*

✓ Why are store employees usually eager to settle customers' problems? *Because a satisfied customer will return in the future.*

✓ When is it appropriate to write a letter of complaint to the product manufacturer? *If the visit to the store does not resolve the problem.*

✓ Who should you address the letter to and why? *Your letter is more likely to be read if you address it to a particular person, such as the president of the company.*

✓ Should you include the sales receipt, warranty, or bills with your letter? *No! Send photocopies of these documents but keep the originals yourself.*

Activities

Skill Builder: Writing
Ask students to refer to the problem experienced by Donna on page 297. Students should write a detailed plan of action that will enable Donna to complain in person about her damaged sweater.

2. Write down exactly what's wrong with the product. Use these notes to guide you as you explain the problem.
3. Go to the store where you made your purchase. Ask a salesperson to help you or to direct you to someone who can, such as the store manager or store owner. Bring your receipt and warranty. Some large stores have a customer service department for handling customer complaints.
4. Explain your problem clearly and briefly. Be polite, firm, and willing to compromise. Remember that the store employee will probably want to settle the problem. A satisfied customer means future sales.
5. Propose a solution to the store employee. You may want the product to be repaired, to receive a replacement, or to get your money back.

Writing a Letter of Complaint

The problem may not be solved by visiting the store. If it isn't, it's time to write a letter. Send your letter to the company that makes or sells the product or supplies the service. Whenever possible, address the letter to a particular person, such as the president, rather than "To Whom It May Concern." This makes it more likely that your letter will be read.

You are the head of a recording company. One day, you receive the following three complaint letters. How would you react to each one?

741 Planter Way
Dallas, Texas 75218
March 15, 19____

Ms. Joan Snelling
President
Top Quality Records
32 Platter Drive
Columbus, Ohio 43224

Dear Ms. Snelling:

Last week I bought the tape, Reaching for the Stars, made by your company. Unfortunately, my copy is broken.

I took the tape back to the store, Sound Effects, but the manager said that he had no more copies and suggested I write to you. I'm enclosing a copy of the sales slip.

I would like a new copy of the tape please. Also, please tell me what to do with the broken copy.

Thank you for your help.

Sincerely,

Wanda Ramirez

775 West 82 Street
New York, New York 10024
March 15, 19____

Company Head
Top Quality Records
32 Platter Drive
Columbus, Ohio 43224

Dear Company Head:

Your company made Reaching for the Stars, but my copy is broken.

I want my money back.

Yours truly,

Barbara Palatino

13 Weston Court
St. Louis, Missouri 63116
March 15, 19____

President
Top Quality Records
32 Platter Drive
Columbus, Ohio 43224

Dear President:

I bought the tape, Reaching for the Stars. It is broken and will not play properly.

Please send me a new copy of the tape or a refund. I would like your help in this.

Thank you very much for your time and attention.

Sincerely,

Alan Yamashita

Did You Know? Many major firms have a toll-free telephone number specifically set up to answer consumer questions. To find out if a firm has a toll-free number, call the information operator, 1-800-555-1212.

Focus on Consumer Skills Consumers can find the name and address of a company's customer relations manager or other officers of the company in the local library. Many firms are listed in *Standard and Poor's Register of Corporations, Directors, and Executives.*

If the company is local, check your phone book for name and address. For a national company, go to the library. You can find the company's address in a business reference book or in a consumer complaint guide.

A complaint letter should have the following information:

- Your name and address.
- The date you are writing the letter.
- The name, job title, and address of the person you're writing to.
- The product or service name, style, and model number.
- The name and address of the store where you made your purchase, and the date you bought it.
- What sales receipts, bills, or warranties you are including with your letter (always send copies of these papers, not the originals).
- A simple and brief explanation of why you are unhappy with the product or service.
- A statement telling how you would like the problem solved.

Taking Further Action

In most cases, visiting the store or writing a letter will settle the problem, but sometimes these actions are just not enough. In those cases, the consumer can get help from other sources.

Consumer Agencies

Most large companies have public relations or customer relations departments that are staffed by people who are paid to help dissatisfied customers. Some companies have toll-free 800 numbers. You can use this number to call the company. Ask to speak to someone in the public relations department.

If the company fails to satisfy you, you can contact the **Better Business Bureau (BBB)**. This is an organization formed by businesses. Member businesses promise to abide by strict business standards, and the Better Business Bureau in turn tries to resolve consumer complaints against its members and other businesses in the community. There are 178 branches of the BBB helping consumers. Check for your nearest branch.

If you cannot resolve a consumer complaint through the store or manufacturer, you can contact a consumer agency for assistance. The Better Business Bureau tries to resolve complaints between consumers and member businesses.

Did You Know? If you have a complaint about professional services, contact the licensing agency or other state agency, or the ethics committee of the appropriate professional association.

Focus on Entrepreneurship The Better Business Bureau, Inc., is a private organization financed by businesses. One BBB service is voluntary arbitration, which helps settle consumer problems. Under arbitration, a panel (or individual) listens to both sides of a complaint, weighs the evidence, and reaches a decision that is binding on both parties.

Skill Builder: Writing
Ask students to imagine that a classmate or friend has a legitimate complaint with which the store refuses to help. Problems might include purchasing a do-it-yourself kit with several parts missing, cottage cheese that was spoiled, or headphones with a loose earpiece. Students should imagine they are helping the friend write a letter of complaint, making sure to include all of the important components.

Reteaching
Ask students to tell the class about a purchase with which they were dissatisfied. Then have students recommend appropriate courses of action for making a complaint in person and through the mail.

Enrichment
Ask students to take turns role playing the dissatisfied consumer (Donna), the store clerk who sold her the sweater, the store manager, and the president of the manufacturing firm that produced the product.

Teaching "Taking Further Action"
(Pages 299-302)

This section teaches the role of consumer agencies as a source of advice and assistance to the dissatisfied consumer. Students are told how consumers can band together to generate unfavorable publicity for a company or manufacturer. They also learn how consumers can take legal action, when it is warranted, to get a problem resolved.

Checking Comprehension

✔ What services are provided for dissatisfied customers by large companies? *They have customer service or public relations departments, and may have toll-free numbers to call for assistance.*

✔ Who belongs to the Better Business Bureau, and how does it help consumers? *This is an organization of businesses that work together to maintain strict standards and to resolve complaints against its members.*

CHAPTER OVERVIEW

Chapter 33 discusses how to be a good consumer by being honest, fair, and considerate. Shoplifting and vandalism are discussed, along with the responsibility to use products safely and to preserve natural resources.

INTRODUCING THE CHAPTER

Motivators

How Do a Dishonest Consumer's Actions Affect You? Ask students to suggest ways in which dishonest shoppers might have an impact on them. How could those actions affect prices and store security practices?

Using the Photograph Refer students to the photograph on this page. Then ask: "What is this girl removing from the garment? What is the purpose of the device? Is it usually effective?"

Was Marlene a Responsible Consumer? Lead the class in a discussion of why Marlene was a responsible consumer. Ask the students what might have happened if she had not returned the watch.

Introducing the Objectives

Discuss the chapter objectives on this page. Remind students that the objectives focus on important chapter content.

Introducing Vocabulary

Ask students if they know what *vandalism* means. Explain that vandalism comes from the name Vandals, the Germanic tribe that destroyed Rome in A.D. 455. A modern vandal is a person who willfully destroys property of value or beauty.

TEACHING THE CHAPTER

For convenience, the teaching suggestions for this chapter are arranged according to the following lesson topics:

- "Being Honest," pages 305-307
- "Being Fair," page 307
- "Being Considerate," pages 307-308
- "Being Responsible," pages 308-309

CHAPTER

33

Being a Responsible Consumer

OBJECTIVES

This chapter will help you to:

- Identify dishonest consumer actions and describe their impact on the public.
- Explain the consumer's responsibility to be fair and considerate.
- Discuss how consumers can use products safely.

WORDS TO REMEMBER

return policy
shoplifting
vandalism

Chapter Resources

Teacher's Classroom Resources
Lesson Plan
Life Skills Activity, *Using Resources Responsibly*
Reproducible Master, *Be a Responsible Consumer*
Extension Activity, *Irresponsible Consumer Behavior*
Chapter Test

Student Workbook
Study Guide
Worksheet, *Fair Exchange*

This year Marlene did her Christmas shopping by mail order. She sent away for several gifts from a catalog. When she opened the box from the mail-order company, she discovered not only the gifts she had ordered but a very expensive watch. When Marlene looked at the shipping receipts enclosed in the box, she realized that a clerk at the mail-order firm had accidently packed another order in with hers.

Marlene knew that she could keep the watch and no one would ever know what had become of it. At the same time, she remembered how long it had taken her to save for the gifts she had bought, and how much they had cost her in time and energy as well as money. She realized that eventually someone—the company, the shipping clerk, or the other customer—would have to pay for the lost watch as well.

Marlene promptly returned the watch to the mail-order company with a written explanation of how she had received it by mistake. By taking this action, Marlene was acting as a responsible consumer.

Being Honest

Consumers expect merchants to be honest with them. If a can of food is spoiled, they expect it to be taken off the shelves. If they ask the difference between one guitar and another, they expect an honest answer. Consumers, in turn, should be honest with sellers.

Honest or Dishonest?

Honest consumers pay the price that is marked on an item. Some consumers put saving money ahead of honesty. They may switch price tags, putting a lower price on the item they plan to buy. This practice is unfair to other consumers, who paid the correct price. In fact, this cheating makes prices higher because the store has to make up the money it loses this way by charging more for the product.

If a store cashier gives a customer too much change, an honest consumer returns it. It would be unfair for the store to charge too much for a purchase; keeping extra change is just as unfair. It could be costly for the cashier, too. Some stores make cashiers pay for missing money out of their own pockets.

No Shoplifting

Have you ever entered a store where you were asked to leave your shopping bag at the cashier's counter? The owners wanted to be sure that you wouldn't hide anything in your bag. They were trying to prevent **shoplifting**, or stealing goods from stores.

Some people believe that shoplifting is harmless, that it only hurts businesses and stores, not people. Nothing could be further from the truth; shoplifting hurts everyone. Such stealing costs $24 billion each year. That figure covers the cost of the goods stolen, the cost of security systems aimed at preventing shoplifting, and the cost of taking shoplifters to court. Store owners pay for some of these things, but consumers pay for most shoplifting costs by having to pay higher prices. In the end, everyone pays for the dishonesty of a few.

To try to stop shoplifting, stores are taking extra steps. They are putting special tags on clothes. These tags are removed by the cashier when the garment is purchased. If not, the tags sound an alarm if the clothing is taken out the door.

Teaching "Being Honest"

(Pages 305-307)

This section teaches that honesty is as important for consumers as it is for merchants. Shoplifting is examined in detail, along with its effect on businesses, stores, and consumers.

Checking Comprehension

✓ If a customer switches price tags on an item and pays the lower price, how can this affect consumers? *The store may have to make up its losses by charging more in the future.*

✓ Why is it false to say that shoplifting is harmless? How does it affect people? *Shoplifting hurts businesses, stores, and consumers. Merchants are forced to pass their losses on to consumers through higher prices.*

✓ What are the possible consequences of being caught shoplifting? *Shoplifters who are arrested may be fined or imprisoned if they are adults, or placed in a correctional facility if they are minors.*

Activities

Skill Builder: Math
Tell students the following story. A clothing store owner has been victimized by shoplifters. She has decided to hire a security guard for 50 hours a week at $8 per hour, and install an alarm system that costs $1,200. The owner's normal stock for one year includes 2,200 items of clothing. If the owner divides her costs equally into all her merchandise for one year, how much more will each item cost? *(Answer: $10).*

Reteaching
Ask students to think of ways that consumers could act honestly.

Enrichment
Have students imagine that they own their own business or store. Then ask them to describe ways in which they might try to prevent shoplifting.

Emphasize Consumer rights imply consumer responsibilities.

Did You Know? More and more merchants are making it a policy to prosecute all shoplifters, regardless of age.

Emphasize Penalties for shoplifting can be severe and felt for a lifetime.

Focus on Mental Health Shoplifting, vandalism, and other forms of antisocial behavior may be a sign of an emotional or mental disturbance that may require professional care.

Teaching the Feature
"Taking a Bite out of Crime"

Answers to Feature Questions

1. Students who answered yes might say that they told an adult or that they didn't do anything. All students would probably say that if they saw someone shoplifting now they would report it to a store employee or an adult because thefts cost the store money and the stores raise their prices on all merchandise to compensate.

2. Answers will vary. Most students will probably say that the most difficult step would be having to tell an adult about their friend's shoplifting because they are betraying their friend's confidence—even though telling is in the friend's best interest.

Activities

Role playing Ask students to form small groups to prepare skits illustrating either: witnessing a shoplifter (a person not known to you); seeing an acquaintance shoplift; knowing about a theft; witnessing vandalism. Students should take roles of store manager, security guard, witness, bystander, or shoplifter.

Community Contact Ask a community relations officer from your local police department to visit your class, possibly to observe the skits from the previous activity and/or to describe the local penalties for shoplifting and vandalism. Or—invite a few local merchants to see the skits. Ask them to comment. How would they have changed some of the scenes?

INTERPERSONAL SKILLS

Taking a Bite Out of Crime

Imagine that you are in a large department store when you notice a nearby shopper taking wallets off a counter and stuffing them into a shopping bag. The person is shoplifting and you are the only one who notices. Would you know what to do? Here are the steps you should take:

- Do not speak to the shoplifter or indicate in any way that you have seen the theft.
- Make a mental note of what the person looks like and what he or she is wearing.
- Report the theft to the nearest salesperson or store employee. Do not point or stare at the shoplifter but describe him or her to the employee.
- Tell the salesperson what items were taken and where the shoplifter hid them. The salesperson will probably check to make certain that the items are missing.
- Remain in the area until you know you are no longer needed. The sales clerk may ask you to wait to talk to a store security guard, or you may be asked to be a witness in the event the shoplifter is arrested.

Reporting a stranger for shoplifting is one thing, but what would you do if you knew a close friend were shoplifting? Here are some suggestions:

- Avoid going to stores with your friend. If your friend is caught, you will be suspected of being an accomplice and you might be arrested as well.
- Talk to your friend. Find out if he or she is troubled about something. People who shoplift sometimes have emotional problems that require professional help.
- Ask your friend to think about what would happen if he or she were caught.
- If you are convinced that your friend is continuing to shoplift tell your parents, guidance counselor, or other trusted adult. Your friend may resent you for telling, but if you remain silent, the chances are that sooner or later your friend will be caught and suffer much worse consequences.

Think It Through

1. **Have you ever witnessed anyone shoplifting? If so, what did you do? What would you do if you saw someone shoplifting now? Why?**
2. **Which step would be the most difficult for you to follow if you saw a friend shoplifting? Why?**

More About Stopping Theft Among the new antitheft devices being used to prevent shoplifting is a dye capsule. This capsule is attached to a tag on each item. If the tag is removed improperly, the capsule bursts, staining the item and the thief with an indelible colored dye.

Did You Know? Some communities have education programs provided as a community service by the local police department. The theme of "taking a bite out of crime" is presented by a person dressed in the costume of McGruff-the crime-fighting dog.

Shoplifting is a crime that is punishable by a fine and/or imprisonment.

Some stores hire security guards and use mirrors or cameras. Many stores are no longer letting shoplifters go with only a warning. When people are arrested for shoplifting, they are taken to a police station where they are questioned, fingerprinted, searched, photographed, and held until they can raise bail. If they are convicted, they can be imprisoned and fined. Children and teens also face stiff penalties for shoplifting. A judge may place shoplifters in a correctional facility or require them to perform a community service. Shoplifters may also acquire a criminal record that can cause them problems later in life.

Being Fair

Consumers expect stores to sell their goods at fair prices and to give them good service. They expect sellers to answer complaints fairly. Consumers should also be fair toward sellers.

Many stores have a **return policy**, a specific set of rules for returning or exchanging merchandise. A customer can return an item in exchange for another item, or perhaps for a cash refund. Whenever you buy an item in a store you are also agreeing to abide by the store's return policy. You should make a point of finding out what the policy is when you make your purchase, especially if you are buying an expensive item.

Fair consumers use the store's return policy when they need to—perhaps to return something that doesn't fit. Unfair consumers try to take advantage of this policy. They buy a sweater, wear it once or twice, and then return it. In the long run, this behavior hurts consumers. Handling too many returns and giving refunds force a store to raise its prices. Some stores adopt very strict policies—such as exchanges only, no refunds—to discourage returns.

Being Considerate

A considerate consumer remembers that the store and merchandise belong to someone else. Littering makes a store unpleasant for everyone. When trying on clothes, do so carefully so they don't become torn or stained.

Vandalism is an even more serious problem. This is when someone mars or destroys someone else's property, such as spraying paint on a store building or breaking products. Just like shoplifting, vandalism forces store owners to raise prices.

Focus on Consumer Skills The retailer has the responsibility to sell safe, undamaged merchandise. The consumer has the responsibility to be a considerate shopper and never return merchandise damaged by misuse or neglect.

Emphasize If a consumer buys an item clearly labeled "as is," or "damaged," there is no right to complain if the item is not perfect.

Emphasize Returning goods is a privilege, not a right.

Teaching "Being Fair"
(Page 307)

This section teaches students how to be fair in their dealings with stores, and what they can reasonably expect as consumers. It introduces the concept of a return policy and how a fair consumer agrees to abide by the store's return policy.

Checking Comprehension

✓ Name two ways in which consumers expect stores to deal fairly. *Consumers expect fair prices and good service, and to have complaints answered fairly.*

✓ Why should a consumer check the store's return policy when making a purchase? *Whenever a consumer buys something, he or she is agreeing to abide by the store's return policy.*

✓ How might an unfair consumer take advantage of a return policy? Who does this hurt? *By using or wearing the item and then returning it. This type of behavior could result in the store's raising prices, which would hurt all consumers.*

Activities

Skill Builder: Critical Thinking
Tell students that abiding by a store's return policy is just one way for a consumer to be fair. Ask them to think of other ways they can be fair as consumers. If they are unfair, how might it affect merchants and consumers?

Reteaching
Have students imagine that they own a store. Ask them to make up a return policy that will outwit unfair consumers. Then ask them to explain how their return policy works.

Enrichment
Ask students when shopping in retail stores during the next week to write down the return policy of one store. If the policy is not clearly posted, students should request information from customer service or a cashier. Compare area return policies in class.

Teaching "Being Considerate"

(Pages 307-308)

This section stresses the importance of being a considerate consumer, showing respect for other shoppers as well as for the store and the merchandise. It also briefly discusses how vandalism can lead to stores' raising prices.

Checking Comprehension

✓ In what other ways can a consumer be inconsiderate? *By littering in the store; by staining or tearing clothes when trying them on; by breaking open packages without a store clerk's help (resulting in parts of the product being lost or soiled).*

Activities

Skill Builder: Reading
Have students find an article in a local newspaper or magazine that discusses an act of vandalism. Ask them to report on their articles to the class. Discuss how the vandalism affected the business owner and the community.

Reteaching
Have students describe vandalism. Ask them to relate any acts of vandalism they may have encountered, such as opened boxes of cookies; kit with missing parts; damaged packaging, and so on.

Enrichment
Have students interview a local business owner on the economic impact of vandalism in his or her store as well as in the community at large. Have students present their findings to the class, using charts if possible.

Teaching "Being Responsible"

(Pages 308-309)

This section emphasizes that consumer responsibility continues even after a product is purchased. The responsible consumer should use dangerous products with caution and should stay informed regarding product safety. Consumer responsibility also includes the careful use of natural resources, such as trees, or products made from these resources, such as paper.

When shoppers open boxes, they sometimes lose, damage, or soil parts of a product.

Considerate consumers also think of others. Have you ever brought home something new, only to find that one piece was missing? The piece could have been lost when a thoughtless shopper opened the box in the store. If you need to see the product, ask the store clerk to show you a floor sample, rather than opening the box yourself. The person who buys the product wants it to be new, not dirty and incomplete.

Being Responsible

Consumer responsibility goes beyond how you act in stores. It also includes how you use the products you buy, and how you use both your own resources and the resources of the whole nation.

Using Products Safely

Consumers should follow manufacturers' instructions. Many products, such as lawn mowers and floor cleaners, can be very dangerous if they are used improperly. A responsible consumer is aware of the possible dangers and uses products carefully.

Consumers should stay informed about safety problems. News reports and articles tell the public about products that are found to be unsafe, such as dangerous toys and tainted foods. Many foods and medicines have special safety seals to prevent people from tampering with products on store shelves. Don't buy products with broken safety seals. If you notice a torn or opened box, point it out to the manager.

Emphasize Each citizen plays an important role in the conservation of resources. Local recycling laws encourage efficient use of resources. Visit your local recycling facility and learn about how to package trash for recycling.

By staying alert and informed, consumers can protect themselves. They can also protect each other. If you hear of a product with a safety problem, tell your friends and neighbors. Then call the company that manufactures it, and report it. If the person you speak to is not interested in the problem, you can contact one of the agencies listed in Chapter 32.

Using Resources Responsibly

In this chapter and in Chapter 25 you learned that there are some steps you can take to become a responsible consumer. You have read about using human, material, and community resources carefully and honestly, but what about the natural resources that go into making these other resources?

For example, right now you are reading your textbook. This book is made out of paper, which is made from trees, a natural resource. However people don't always use resources, such as paper, responsibly. They often throw paper wrappers on the street. They use vast quantities of newsprint that they usually don't recycle. If this continues, manufacturers will have to use more trees to produce more paper, and eventually trees will be rare and so will paper.

You don't have to worry yet; the forests are not out of trees. Still, people need to change their habits in order to use all of their natural resources responsibly. If everyone were to act as a responsible consumer, all of society would benefit. Being honest, fair, and considerate makes relations between consumers and sellers better. In addition, consuming natural resources responsibly makes the world a cleaner, healthier place to live.

Because natural resources—just like other resources—are limited, they must be used responsibly. How can you help conserve natural resources?

Checking Comprehension

✓ What should consumers know about the packaging of products such as foods and medicines? *Many of these products have safety seals to prevent tampering with the products in the stores. A responsible consumer should report a torn seal or opened box to the store manager.*

✓ What can responsible consumers do to help save natural resources, such as trees? *They can try not to waste paper and they should recycle usable paper.*

Activities

Skill Builder: Writing
Ask students to think of any safety problems that they might have encountered with a household item. Have them write a "consumer advisory" or develop a new safety label suggesting how the item should be used safely.

Reteaching
Ask students to suggest ways in which they can use resources more responsibly. List these on the board.

Enrichment
Have students read an article on product safety in a magazine such as *Consumer Reports.* Then ask students to check for similar products at home that might be potential problems.

Did You Know? Some people mark the publicity received by Ralph Nader in the mid-1960s regarding the unsafe features of the Corvair as the beginning of the active U.S. consumer movement.

Cross-Reference See "There's Only One World" on page 244.

More About Consumer Power Consumers demonstrate their economic power by the choices they make when purchasing goods and services.

COMPLETING THE CHAPTER

Summary

- Consumers should be honest, fair, considerate, and responsible in their dealings with stores, businesses, and other consumers.
- Dishonest practices, such as switching price tags or shoplifting, can cause stores to raise prices.
- Shoplifters face stiff fines or penalties, plus a criminal record.
- Consumers should be fair when returning or exchanging merchandise.
- Inconsiderate actions include littering, damaging merchandise, and vandalism.
- Responsible consumers should use products carefully and conserve natural resources.

For Review

Objective Review Questions Have students complete the "Reviewing the Facts" section on this page.

Study Guide Have students complete the Study Guide from Chapter 33 of their *Student Workbook.*

Consumer Behavior Ask students to cite one example each of how a consumer can act: honestly, fairly, considerately, and responsibly.

Safety First Have students find and read warning labels or safety labels on one or two items in their homes (or in a store). Ask students if they would add anything to that label. Ask them to suggest any other common household items that they believe require a warning label. Have students suggest how to encourage people to be more careful.

For Evaluation

Consumer Qualities Ask students to make a list of all the responsibilities a consumer has. Have them write an example next to each item on their list.

Chapter Test Have students complete the test for Chapter 33 that appears in the *Teacher's Classroom Resources.*

CHAPTER 33 REVIEW

Answers to "Reviewing the Facts"

1. Cost of stolen goods; cost of security systems; cost of taking shoplifters to court.
2. Hire more guards; use cameras, mirrors, and special tags that set off alarms; hold shoppers' bags at the counter.
3. The rules that a store has for the return or exchange of merchandise.
4. The marring or destruction of someone else's property.
5. Any three: don't litter; don't damage merchandise; don't open boxes; don't vandalize; don't shoplift.
6. The food or medicine may be tainted or poisoned.

Reviewing the Facts

1. What are three ways that shoplifting costs businesses and consumers money?
2. What can stores do to prevent shoplifting?
3. What is a return policy?
4. What is vandalism?
5. Name three ways that consumers can be considerate to store owners and other shoppers.
6. Why shouldn't you buy a food or medicine package that has been opened?

Thinking Critically

1. A friend tells you that she is going to buy an expensive dress to wear to a dance. She is planning to return the dress after having worn it only once. What would you say to your friend?
2. Robert bought his little brother, Mark, a remote-control car for his birthday. Mark had only played with the car a few minutes when it hit a bump in the street and lost a wheel. Would it be fair for Robert to return or exchange the car? Why or why not?

Applying Your Knowledge

1. **Writing an Article.** Write an article for the school newspaper warning teens about the consequences of vandalism and shoplifting.
2. **Researching a Topic.** Look through newspapers and magazines to find articles about product safety. Write a brief report summarizing what you have learned about product safety.
3. **Planning a Strategy.** Make a list of things that you and your family could do to cut down on the amount of natural resources you waste each week. Compare this list with your classmates' lists.

Answers to "Thinking Critically"

1. Students should tell the friend that doing this would hurt not only the store but also the consumers who shop there. The store may have to raise prices or adopt a stricter return policy.
2. Some students will say it is fair to return the car because it appears to be poorly built since it broke under normal usage. If the car broke after weeks of rough usage, Robert would not be justified in returning it. Other students might say that hitting a large bump or hole in the street is the customer's fault, not the manufacturer's.

CHAPTER

34

Management and Consumer Careers

OBJECTIVES

This chapter will help you to:

- Explain how interests and skills influence management and consumer career choice.
- Discuss different kinds of management careers.
- Describe several different kinds of consumer-related jobs.

WORDS TO REMEMBER

capital
entrepreneur
telecommunication

Chapter Resources

Teacher's Classroom Resources
- Lesson Plan
- Life Skills Activity, *Entrepreneur Profile*
- Reproducible Master, *Would I Like to Manage?*
- Extension Activity, *Management and Consumer Careers*
- Chapter Test

Student Workbook
- Study Guide
- Worksheet, *Consumer Careers*

CHAPTER OVERVIEW

Chapter 34 examines many different types of management and consumer-related careers. It begins with a thorough look at the characteristics, interests, and abilities necessary for pursuing careers in these two fields. Within the management and consumer career sections, the chapter describes specific jobs, grouped according to the level of education and amount of job training required.

INTRODUCING THE CHAPTER

Motivators

Managing and Consuming Write on the board the titles: "I Am a Manager" and "I Am a Consumer." Ask students to volunteer examples from their daily life of ways that they act as managers and consumers. Explain that this experience will help them if they decide to pursue some of the careers explained in this chapter.

Using the Photograph Have students study the photograph on this page. Then ask: "What does the person shown in this picture do for a living? What are some of her responsibilities? What do you think are some of the rewards of her job?"

Living to Work Ask students to react to the statement that they will spend about a third of their life working. Explain that this is why it is so important for them to enjoy the kind of work they do. Ask them if they can think of a management or consumer career that they would enjoy. Then have them explain their reasons.

Introducing the Objectives

Discuss the chapter objectives on this page. Remind students that the objectives focus on important chapter content.

Introducing Vocabulary

Ask students to look up the definition of *telecommunication* in the dictionary. Ask them to explain the meaning of the prefix *tele-* and to give some examples of words that begin with this prefix (telegraph, telephone, television).

✔ What kinds of services are provided by financial advisers? *They help people manage their money and set financial goals.*

✔ Compare personnel managers with environmental scientists. *Personnel managers manage people, and environmental scientists manage resources.*

Activities

Skill Builder: Writing
Ask students to imagine that they manage a retail store in their community (a drugstore, a clothing store, hardware store, grocery store). Ask them to write a dialogue between themselves and a person applying for an entry-level position in their store.

Reteaching
List the following jobs on the board: stock clerk, administrative assistant, farm worker, hairstylist/shopowner, personnel manager. Ask students to suggest what skills a person would use in each of these careers.

Enrichment
Ask students to go to the library and do research on a famous entrepreneur. Ask students to find out what business the person started and, if possible, how he or she got the idea for the business. Ask them to report on the person to the class, and to try to identify at least one quality that helped make this person a success.

A wide variety of workers is involved in managing natural resources. Fish hatchery workers, park groundskeepers, and farm workers, for instance, are outdoors much of the time. Depending on where they live, these people may be seasonal workers—very active in some months, but less so in others.

Jobs That Require Training

If you enjoy working with numbers, you may want to become a bookkeeper. These workers keep financial records so that managers know how much money is being spent and in what way. Bookkeepers are trained in two-year college programs.

People who want to be their own bosses become **entrepreneurs** (AHN-truh-preh-nors). They open a new business to provide a product or service that they think people will want to buy. Being an entrepreneur is challenging and rewarding. You work for yourself instead of for other people, you set your own goals, and the money you make depends on how profitable your business becomes. Being an entrepreneur also presents many responsibilities and pressures, and it can also be risky. Entrepreneurs usually use their own savings to get the business going. If the new business does not do well, they can lose everything.

Many people start a business based on something they learned about in school, like hairstyling. Others learn by working for someone else first. Someone who works in a bookstore, for example, may eventually open his or her own store. Many business owners take courses in business management and financial planning to increase their knowledge so they can operate their businesses more successfully. Several government agencies and business groups also provide training and advice to new business owners.

Businesses around the globe can communicate almost instantly with each other thanks to the telecommunications revolution. **Telecommunications** workers install and repair electronic systems that transmit voices, images, and information from one place to another. These include telephones, televisions, computers, and satellites. People who work in telecommunications jobs need specialized technical training to perform their jobs.

Entrepreneurs own their own businesses. They can achieve many rewards but must also assume the financial risks.

Cross-Reference See Teen Tips "Using Sense to Make Dollars" on pages 320-321.

Did You Know? Personnel managers at some companies perform "exit interviews" of employees who leave the company. From these interviews the managers try to gain insight into how to choose employees more wisely and how to serve future employees better.

Jobs That Require an Advanced Degree

Many people and groups turn for money information to financial advisers. These experts in managing money help clients set financial goals. Then they write a savings or investment plan to meet those goals. Advisers have a college degree in business, finance, home economics, or economics. This career is expected to become very important in the future.

Most businesses have a personnel manager to help plan the company's employee needs. These managers make rules about hiring and firing and how workers should act on the job. They handle the health and life insurance policies provided by the company for the workers. They often have a college degree in business or a related area.

Environmental scientists plan how people use natural resources. They study an area to identify its resources and try to predict how long these resources will last. They may study how people and industry affect plant and animal life in an area. These scientists have at least four years of college and many have graduate degrees as well.

Consumer-Related Careers

Many people work with and for consumers. They provide goods and services, or they help consumers get the most for their money.

Entry-Level Jobs

A person interested in working in a bank often starts out as a bank teller. A teller handles deposits and withdrawals for bank customers. Tellers must be very careful in their work to avoid making mistakes.

Comparison shoppers work for large stores. They travel to competing stores to check the prices and quality of similar products. Then they report to their managers. The store uses these reports to plan its own pricing and advertising.

Market survey interviewers ask people what they like. They take surveys at public places such as shopping malls to find out how people will respond to a new advertising campaign or a new product. They should be friendly and willing to work with the public.

Market survey interviewers seek out people to test new products or new advertising campaigns.

More About a Career as a Consumer Advocate People become consumer advocates after studying law, political science, home economics, or government administration. Some have training in research, public information, or community education. All levels of government offer public service jobs for consumer advocates. In the private sector, consumer advocates work for citizens' groups or lobbyist organizations. Further information about a career as a consumer advocate can be obtained by writing to the Consumer Federation of America, 1314 Fourteenth Street, NW, Washington, D.C. 20005.

Teaching "Consumer-Related Careers"
(Pages 315-316)

This section describes careers in which people work with and for consumers and consumer agencies.

Checking Comprehension

✓ How do store managers use the reports made by comparison shoppers? *They use the reports to plan pricing and advertising.*

✓ What kinds of qualities are needed by market survey interviewers? *They need to be friendly and to be able to work with the public.*

✓ What does a consumer writer do? *A consumer writer writes articles about new products or how to manage resources.*

✓ How do lawyers work for consumers? *They study laws and court decisions about product safety and consumer rights. They may represent a consumer group or write books or articles giving valuable advice.*

✓ Name two jobs that a home economist might perform. *Any two: work for a public school, work for the government answering consumer questions and developing family living programs, work for a bank or gas company, write pamphlets about appliance care and use, work for a store or manufacturer.*

Activities

Skill Builder: Critical Thinking
Ask students to read about one of the careers in this section that they have particular interest in. Ask them to state which of their personal characteristics might help them perform the job well.

Reteaching
Ask students to make a collage that shows people doing one or more of the jobs described in this section.

Enrichment
Break the class into small groups and ask each group to make up an interests-and-skills inventory that would help a person find out whether he or she might be suited to a consumer-related career. The inventory might take the form of a checklist, questions, or rating charts.

Teaching "Getting a Job"
(Page 316)

This section gives practical advice on obtaining a job in management or a consumer-related field.

Checking Comprehension

✓ How will an advanced degree help you obtain a position that has greater responsibility? *An advanced degree will help you in getting more experience and gaining more knowledge.*

Activities

Skill Builder: Writing
Ask students to choose one of the careers discussed in the chapter. Then ask them to write out a possible plan of action for someone who wanted to make that his or her career. The plan might include both on-the-job training and advanced education.

Reteaching
Ask students to give examples of jobs mentioned in the chapter that require just a high school diploma, technical training or some college, an advanced degree.

Enrichment
Ask students to interview a person who holds one of the jobs described in the text. Have them ask the person how he or she got into the field, what kind of education or training he or she thought was most valuable, and what advice he or she would give to someone trying to enter the field.

Jobs That Require Training

Many magazines and newspapers print articles about new products or how to manage resources. The consumer writers who write these articles learn about these topics from research and from their own experience. They must be able to write clearly so that their readers understand what they say.

Credit managers work in banks or stores. They read the loan applications made by consumers and businesses. They must decide whether the person or business will be able to pay back the money borrowed. Some credit workers have attended college. Most of their experience, however, is received through on-the-job training.

Jobs That Require an Advanced Degree

Many lawyers work on behalf of consumers. They study laws and court decisions about product safety and consumer rights. They may practice alone or work as part of a consumer group. Some write books or articles giving consumers advice. These professionals go to college and then go to law school for three years to earn a law degree.

Home economists have college degrees. They perform a wide variety of jobs. Some teach in public schools, of course, and nearly every county in the United States employs a home economist through the Cooperative Extension Service to answer consumer questions and to develop family living programs. They also organize 4-H clubs.

Many businesses such as banks and electric and gas companies hire home economists to advise families about how to manage their resources. Home economists also write pamphlets, explaining how to use and care for appliances. Stores and manufacturers also hire home economists. They work with the public, explaining new products or new uses for old products.

Training in home economics, then, opens up many career possibilities. If you like managing and you like working with people, it may be for you.

Getting a Job

If you think you might decide to pursue a career in a management or consumer-related field, there are many things you can start planning to do. Most of the jobs described in this chapter require high school diplomas. Technical training or some college education is necessary for some of these positions. Advanced degrees will aid you in getting more experience and gaining more knowledge in order to obtain one of the more specialized positions that have greater responsibility.

Did You Know? America's service industries have a growing concern with customer satisfaction. Therefore, the job of service-quality manager will be in demand in the future. The service-quality manager ensures that each customer is a satisfied customer.

Emphasize Usually, the more education and training a person has, the more income that person will earn.

Did You Know? In the next 20 years, the minimum requirement for most jobs will be a high school education. A growing number of jobs will require a college degree.

MANAGING RESOURCES

Make It Your Business

Have you ever considered becoming an entrepreneur? Have you ever wondered what it takes to start your own business? No matter what type of business you're thinking of, a lawn service or dog walking service, you'll need three basic resources: money, knowledge, and time.

- **Money.** You will need some money to start your business and keep it going until you start making money. You will need to use this **capital,** the money you invest in your business, to buy supplies—such as a lawn mower and gasoline to power the mower in a grass-cutting business, for example. You may need to save this money, borrow it from someone, or go into business with a partner who can provide some money.
- **Knowledge.** Entrepreneurs need to know a great deal about the kind of business they are starting. For example, if you are starting a babysitting business, you need to know how to care for infants and children, how to entertain them, and how to deal with emergencies. Many entrepreneurs acquire the knowledge they need by taking courses, by doing the same job for others, or by turning their hobbies into paying businesses.
- **Time.** A new business needs time to become established. It takes time to make people aware that you are available to walk dogs or cut lawns. You may have to advertise to attract customers. Some teens hand out flyers or cards to announce their businesses. Once you have customers, you have to do your job well so that they will want to hire you again. You have to be willing to put as much time into your business as it takes to become successful.

Running your own business is hard work, but it is also very satisfying. You make all of your own decisions about the business and you earn money by using your own resources and abilities.

Think It Through

1. **Why do you think many people prefer to start their own businesses while others don't?**
2. **Give an example of a business that you think would be a hit in your neighborhood. What would it take to start this business?**

Teaching the Feature

"Make It Your Business"

Answers to Feature Questions

1. Many people who become entrepreneurs do so because it is exciting. They work for themselves, not for other people. They set their own goals and make their own decisions. The company is theirs to run and any of the profits are theirs to keep. But being an entrepreneur has many responsibilities and pressures. It is also very risky. If you don't like risks and taking responsibilities, you would not want to start your own business.

2. Answers will vary. Students might suggest a car wash, babysitting service, or an errand-running service. They need to consider how much money, time, and knowledge would go into planning and then running the business.

Activities

My Own Business Ask students to write a paragraph that begins as follows: "I would (would not) like to start my own business because . . ." Remind students to assess their own interests and skills before beginning their essay.

Community Contact Ask students to find an entrepreneur in their own community and interview him or her. Students might ask the interviewees when they got the idea for their business, what training or education helped them in starting it, what difficulties (if any) they had, and why they like owning their own business. Have students report on their findings to the class.

Emphasize Explain to students that the amount of money required to start a business varies widely depending on what kind of business they choose. Someone who wanted to start a typing service would need only a typewriter and supplies. Other businesses need much more expensive equipment.

Did You Know? Henry Ford not only formed his own automobile company but also pioneered a major contribution to modern industry—the moving assembly line. His ideas changed methods of production throughout industry.

COMPLETING THE CHAPTER

Summary

- People in management and consumer-related careers need to know how to communicate well, perform well in math, make decisions and solve problems, set goals and make plans, make and keep schedules, lead others, and work with others.
- Entry-level positions in management include stock clerks, administrative assistants, and resource management workers. Positions that require extra training include bookkeepers, entrepreneurs, and telecommunications workers. Advanced degrees are required for financial advisers, personnel managers, and environmental scientists.
- Entry-level positions related to consumers are bank tellers, comparison shoppers, and market survey interviewers. Positions that require extra training include consumer writers and credit managers. Lawyers and home economists must have advanced degrees.

For Review

Objective Review Questions Have students complete the "Reviewing the Facts" section on this page.

Study Guide Have students complete the Study Guide from Chapter 34 of their *Student Workbook.*

Looking at the Future Lead students in a discussion of whether they think there will be more or less demand for management and consumer-related jobs in the future. What possible new jobs can they suggest?

For Evaluation

Making a List Have students list some of the mental and social characteristics useful in management and consumer careers. Ask students to suggest qualities other than those mentioned in the text.

Chapter Test Have students complete the test for Chapter 34 that appears in the *Teacher's Classroom Resources.*

CHAPTER 34 REVIEW

Reviewing the Facts

1. Name three skills needed by people in management and consumer-related jobs.
2. What do administrative assistants do?
3. What is an entrepreneur? List one possible risk that entrepreneurs take.
4. What do telecommunications workers do?
5. What do financial advisers do?
6. What are two characteristics that a market survey interviewer needs to have?
7. Name two consumer-related jobs that require college degrees.

Thinking Critically

1. If you could have any job in this chapter, which would you want? Why? What skills or interests do you have that would prepare you for the job?
2. What's the relationship between management in business and everyday management?

Applying Your Skills

1. **Researching Career Information.** Check the classified ads in your local Sunday newspaper for job opportunities in management and consumer-related fields. Clip out five ads and circle the education or experience requirements. Be prepared to discuss the ads in class.
2. **Organizing Consumer Careers.** Make a list of the jobs discussed in this chapter. On another piece of paper, make a chart with three columns. Title each column with one of the following: Entry-level jobs, jobs requiring training, jobs requiring an advanced degree. List these and other consumer-related and management jobs in the appropriate category.
3. **Preparing Questions.** Prepare a list of questions you as an interviewer would ask a person applying for a position in the management or consumer field.

Answers to "Reviewing the Facts"

1. Any three: communication; math; decision making and problem solving; setting goals; making and keeping a schedule; leadership; working well with people.
2. Help managers by preparing reports, scheduling meetings, and communicating with other workers.
3. A person who starts a new business. Failure and the loss of the money they invested in their business.
4. Install and repair electronic communications systems for businesses.
5. Help people and companies manage their money.
6. Friendly and willing to work with the public.
7. Lawyers and home economists.

Answers to "Thinking Critically"

1. Answers will vary, but students should compare their own attitudes, skills, interests, and goals with those outlined for particular jobs. They should be able to discuss their strengths and abilities that would be helpful in the career.
2. Managers in businesses need to be able to set goals, plan, make decisions, keep a schedule, and solve problems to keep a department running efficiently. These skills are also necessary in everyday life. Appointments need to be kept, chores must be completed, and activities and schedules have to be coordinated.

TEEN TIPS OVERVIEW

This section focuses on three topics that develop students' management skills.

Using Sense to Make Dollars

This Teen Tip suggests a wide variety of projects teenagers can undertake to gain both a measure of financial independence and a greater degree of control over their work lives. Related activities emphasize considerations in planning and starting such enterprises.

Study Time Dos and Don'ts

This Teen Tip offers practical tips for increasing productivity, eliminating or minimizing distractions, and organizing time for maximum efficiency.

Beyond Computer Games

This Teen Tip discusses the use of computerized spreadsheets and schedules in managing time and money.

These reinforce the contents of "Management" by providing practical suggestions for making the most of the precious resources of possessions, time, money, and talent.

Introducing "Using Sense to Make Dollars"

(Pages 320-321)

Motivators

Thinking About Working Ask students to write a brief description of a job they would like to have now or in the next year. Tell them to include the type of work, the hours, how much they would earn, and what other people would be involved. Ask them to be realistic about the money and time involved. Encourage the students, however, to "dream" about the type of work and the people involved, particularly their boss. Stress that they should not limit themselves to jobs they know are available, such as baby-sitting or working in a fast-food restaurant. Discuss the descriptions with the class. Be sure to bring out that many people's ideal job involves being their own boss.

Definition: Entrepreneur Point out that being an entrepreneur is one way of doing something you like and being your own boss. Define the term: "A person who organizes, operates, and assumes the risk for a business venture." (*The American Heritage Dictionary of the English Language)* Tell students that they can be entrepreneurs even at their age, and that this section will suggest how.

Teaching "Using Sense to Make Dollars"

Checking Comprehension

✔ Being an entrepreneur means using resources well. Name some jobs that use the resource of a specific talent. *Examples include jobs that involve cooking, sewing, or handicrafts. Accept other reasonable answers.*

✔ Some jobs listed require the resource of money to buy supplies or raw materials. Identify some of these jobs and state what that expense is for. *Examples include jobs that involve preparing and selling food (for ingredients and packaging materials); selling or wearing costumes (materials, props); selling handicrafts (raw materials).*

TEEN TIPS

Using Sense to Make Dollars

Would you like to earn extra money and still be your own boss? Here are 55 ideas for increasing your income—and learning how to run your own business:

- **Help People**
  - Tutor younger children
  - Be a mother's helper after school for a working mom
  - Pack for people who are moving
  - Shop and run errands for people who can't leave home
  - Deliver balloons or specialty baskets
  - Walk kids to school and home again

- **Provide a Service**
  - Coordinate a baby-sitting service
  - Bake cookies, brownies, or nutritious muffins
  - Walk dogs
  - Take care of pets when people are out of town
  - Wash and groom pets
  - Water and take care of plants
  - Start a telephone wake-up service
  - Make clothing repairs and alterations
  - Address and stuff envelopes

More About Setting Goals Point out that no business plan is complete without a statement of what is to be accomplished. Goals should be specific and measurable, that is, anyone should be able to tell if the goal has been met. (A sample start-up would be to obtain five lawn-mowing service clients.) Business goals should also include a time frame (to get five lawn-mowing service clients by May 1).

- **Clean Things**
  - Clean homes
  - Wash windows
  - Clean barbeque grills
  - Wash and wax cars and boats

- **Do Yard and Garden Work**
  - Mow lawns
  - Weed gardens
  - Turn sprinklers on and off
  - Rake leaves
  - Shovel snow

- **Holiday Projects**
  - Make and sell pinecone or candy wreaths
  - Wrap gift packages
  - Deliver valentines
  - Make Halloween costumes
  - Deliver gifts as the Easter Bunny or Santa Claus
  - Hold a holiday boutique to sell craft items

- **Recycle Things**
  - Repair, redesign, and sell used clothing
  - Organize a garage sale
  - Sell used toys
  - Reclaim scrap lumber for craft projects
  - Collect and sell jars and bottles
  - Sell used books and magazines
  - Collect and sell sea shells and pinecones

- **Make Things to Sell**
  - Start plants from cuttings
  - Make wooden or stuffed toys
  - Decorate T-shirts, sweatshirts, sneakers
  - Make wall hangings for children's rooms

- **Use Your Computer**
  - Publish a newsletter
  - Write computer programs
  - Publish a list of babysitters
  - Word process reports and papers
  - Publish a cookbook
  - Maintain mailing lists for clubs and organizations
  - Design craft projects and write instructions

- **Party Services**
  - Be a disc jockey
  - Take pictures at parties and family occasions
  - Be a clown for children's parties
  - Run a party clean-up service
  - Be a waiter or waitress
  - Organize and run children's birthday parties
  - Decorate cakes

TEEN TIPS

Activities

Skill Builder: Math

Point out that to make money, you need to make a *profit*. Define profit as "what's left of earnings after subtracting all the expenses of running the business." Present the following situations to give practice in figuring profits.

- In April, Jill took in $20.25 from selling cookies. It cost her $4.15 to make and package the cookies. What was her profit? *($16.10)*
- Trent makes $7.00 an hour tutoring children in math. His bus fare for each hour of tutoring is $.80. Students provide their own supplies. He tutors for three hours every week. What is his weekly profit? *($18.60)*

Reteaching

Develop with the class a list of the "pluses" and "minuses" of being in business for oneself. Discuss whether, to them, the "pluses" outweigh the "minuses" and why. Lead students to consider whether being an entrepreneur actually appeals to them.

Enrichment

Have students draw up business plans for starting one of the businesses suggested. Plans should include how they would advertise or get clients; what they would charge; where and how they would do the work; how they would keep track of expenses, earnings, profits, time spent, and materials needed; and a time schedule for getting started. Students interested in the same job may work together, or the activity may be done individually. Have students share their plans with the class, and have the class offer constructive criticism.

Focus on Realistic Goals Of course, goals should also be realistic. Businesses often have more than one goal. Usually there is a financial objective (to earn $100 profit by the end of the third month). Goals can also concern business volume or growth (help four families pack to move in May; get six new clients by June 30). And they can include personal objectives (to learn a new computer program in June). Have students complete the business plans begun earlier (in the "Enrichment" Activity) by adding goals. Review the goals with the class. Be sure the goals are specific and measurable and include a time frame.

Introducing "Study Time—Do's and Don'ts"

(Pages 322-323)

Motivators

Identification: Study Problem Comment that just about everyone finds some aspect of studying that's a problem: a particular subject; a specific activity, such as writing papers; a procedural problem, such as trouble scheduling or concentrating; or a mechanical problem, such as lack of good study space. Ask students to make notes about one such problem that they would like to work on. Tell them that this section gives suggestions that might help them with these and other problems.

Discussion Question: Ask students: "Do you follow a routine for studying?" Call on volunteers to describe their routines and talk about how and why they developed. Maintain a nonjudgmental tone in this discussion. Point out that most people find that a routine helps them study more effectively but that some people do well without one, or with an unconventional routine.

Teaching "Study Time—Do's and Don'ts"

Checking Comprehension

✔ Which suggestions would be most useful if you have a problem managing your time? *Studying when you're most productive, outlining priorities, setting realistic goals, noting what you want to accomplish, scheduling time, allowing for breaks, stopping others from interrupting, organizing what's been done.*

✔ Several techniques have to do with the physical circumstances of studying. Why is that an important part of studying efficiently? *Physical comfort helps increase energy and eliminates distractions caused by discomfort or posture.*

TEEN TIPS

Study Time Dos and Don'ts

DON'T sleep, eat, or watch TV where you study.

DO sit in a comfortable chair at a desk or table where you have a good light.

DON'T get *too* comfortable. Easy chairs, sofas, and beds tell your body "It's time to relax."

DO study in a quiet place when you need to concentrate. If there's background noise that disturbs you, wear headphones and listen to quiet music.

DON'T listen to loud music while you study.

DO take the first 10 minutes to outline your priorities. What is due tomorrow? What is due in two days? What is due next week?

DO study when you're most productive. Some people are "morning people" and others are "night people."

DO use a regular study area. When you study in the same place every day, your body becomes trained to respond.

DO schedule your time. Estimate how long it should take you to accomplish each task.

DON'T let others misuse your time. If family members interrupt your study time, they may need a gentle reminder. Try hanging a "Do Not Disturb" sign on the door.

More About Planning Many business training programs address the question of whether to tackle easy or difficult tasks first. Some people advocate starting with the most challenging, to eliminate any anxiety that surrounds them and to make everything else seem easier by comparison. Others think it is better to begin with a relatively easy task, to build up a feeling of accomplishment and confidence before facing harder jobs. What constitutes the best approach actually depends on the individual and on the specific tasks. Ask students to discuss their opinions on this matter and to explain why they generally prefer one approach over the other.

DO study your most difficult subjects first.

DO break up big projects, such as book reports and term papers, into small segments to do each day. Then you won't have to panic at the last minute to get the project done.

DON'T let the phone interrupt your study time. Tell the caller that you are studying and will return the call during your break.

DO allow for breaks. Use this time to do some exercises. Touch your toes. Do side bends. Roll your shoulders to get the kinks out.

DO set realistic goals. Say to yourself, "I'll study for an hour, then I'll watch TV for 30 minutes, then I'll study for 40 minutes and have a snack." It usually doesn't work to say, "I'll study for 4 hours straight."

DON'T waste time. If you find you aren't accomplishing anything, take a minute to evaluate what you're doing. Are you trying to avoid an unpleasant task? Face the task and get it over with.

DO spend the last 10 minutes to organize what you have done. Check your priority list again to be sure that you've completed everything you had planned.

TEEN TIPS

✓ In the second unit, you learned about good communications skills with family and friends. How might such skills help you get more out of your study time? *Skillful communications techniques could help you negotiate with family members to arrange for good study space and would help you stop family and friends from interrupting your study time.*

Activities

Skill Builder: Time Management
Have students develop study schedules for a day, a week, or even an entire month, depending on the student and the kinds of assignments he or she has. Schedules should include brief notes on the goals for the time period, the order of tasks to be done, and an estimate of the time each will take. Discuss and critique the schedules with the class.

Reteaching
Ask students to discuss their study habits in light of the suggestions given in this section. Ask them what they seem to be doing right and how they might improve their routines as a result of this lesson. Students may also write up plans for changing their study habits.

Enrichment
Have students refer to the specific study problem they identified at the beginning of the lesson. Ask them to create posters illustrating how one tip or a group of tips (like all those having to do with eliminating noise distractions) could help solve the problem they identified. Display the posters.

Introducing "Beyond Computer Games"

(Pages 324-325)

Motivators

Computers, Budgets, and Schedules Ask students if they or anyone they know uses a computer to work on a budget or to schedule time. Discuss any examples the students bring up. Point out that most businesses today use computers to manage their finances and schedules, and note that this "Teen Tip" will discuss how the students can do the same.

Discussion Question: Ask students: "What is a budget?" Discuss this question. Students may begin by defining a budget as a way of limiting their expenses, as in being "on a budget." Point out that *budget* can have other, slightly different meanings. A budget can mean the amount of money you have to spend, for a specific item or for a specific time period. A budget can also be a list of all the expenses a business, family, or individual is likely to have and a record of all the money that is likely to come in during a specific time period. Point out that budgets of this last kind are particularly useful for planning and managing business, family, or personal finances.

Teaching "Beyond Computer Games"

Checking Comprehension

✓ What are the advantages of using a computer to figure budgets or plan schedules? *Using a computer saves considerable time, especially when using a spreadsheet. In addition, students might also note that computers produce very neat and readable budgets and schedules, and that the programs themselves can help you plan better because they include topics and ideas you might not have thought of.*

TEEN TIPS

Beyond Computer Games

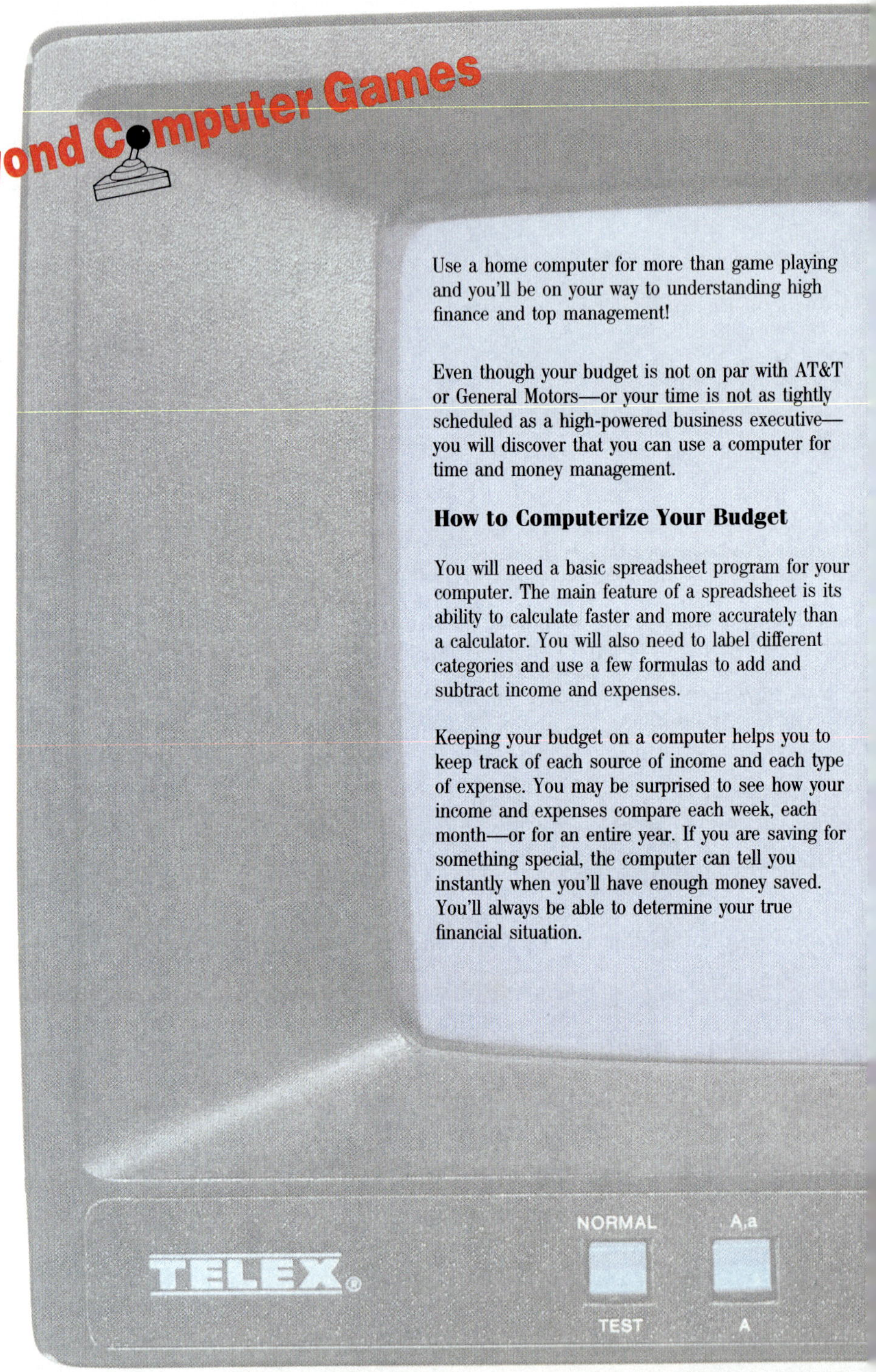

Use a home computer for more than game playing and you'll be on your way to understanding high finance and top management!

Even though your budget is not on par with AT&T or General Motors—or your time is not as tightly scheduled as a high-powered business executive—you will discover that you can use a computer for time and money management.

How to Computerize Your Budget

You will need a basic spreadsheet program for your computer. The main feature of a spreadsheet is its ability to calculate faster and more accurately than a calculator. You will also need to label different categories and use a few formulas to add and subtract income and expenses.

Keeping your budget on a computer helps you to keep track of each source of income and each type of expense. You may be surprised to see how your income and expenses compare each week, each month—or for an entire year. If you are saving for something special, the computer can tell you instantly when you'll have enough money saved. You'll always be able to determine your true financial situation.

Focus on Management The principles of money and time management that underlie the use of spreadsheets and scheduling programs can be applied even if a computer or the appropriate software is not available. Of course, without using a computerized spreadsheet, it is much harder and more time-consuming to figure out such factors as how much profit a business would make at the end of a year or how much one would have to earn a month to meet a specific financial target by a certain date. Discuss how such calculations might be made without a computer, manually or with a calculator.

FOODS AND NUTRITION

UNIT FIVE

Foods and Nutrition

CHAPTER

COOPERATIVE LEARNING

Potluck Dinner Divide students into groups and conduct a "potluck" dinner. Explain that at a potluck dinner everyone brings a dish to share. There is no set menu. Tell students to be prepared to describe a favorite dish—salad, main dish, or dessert—to their group. They should be able to list the ingredients in the dish, tell how the dish is prepared, and comment on its nutritional value. If the dish has an ethnic origin, they should mention that as well. Students might bring a picture of the food or demonstrate some aspect of its preparation.

FHA ACTIVITIES

The following activities can be used with your FHA group or as public relation strategies:

Mealtime Funtime Have students visit a first-grade or second-grade classroom and prepare a lesson on physical fitness and healthful snacks. Have them prepare nutritious snacks and nutritional games for the children.

Five Food Groups Differences Visit a community group (senior citizens, scout troop, and etc.) and present a skit or play outlining the nutritional differences among the food groups.

"Lose-a-thon" Sponsor a "Lose-a-thon" in the school. Have a weekly weigh-in after students have secretly recorded their present weight and how many pounds they need to lose. "Lose-a-thon" group meetings should include discussion on the pitfalls and successes.

Shopping Lists As a community resource, have students develop a shopping pad for consumers to use for efficient shopping. Ask a local community group to fund the printing cost. Place the shopping pads in the local supermarkets with the chapter's logo on each pad.

UNIT CLOSURE

For Review

Food Mobiles Have each student choose one nutrient and make a mobile explaining its importance, food sources, and benefits to the body. Have them add pictures and use hangers to display the mobiles in class.

For Evaluation

Unit Test Have students complete the Unit Test that appears in the *Teacher's Classroom Resources.*

Testmaker Software You may wish to design a unit test using the Testmaker software program.

CHAPTER OVERVIEW

Chapter 35 discusses the basics of fitness—good nutrition and exercise. It outlines the various needs that food fulfills—energy needs, emotional needs, social needs, and physical needs. It suggests that students analyze their own eating and exercise habits to evaluate how they are contributing to their general health and fitness. The chapter also explores the nutritional variety available in the United States as a result of the ethnic, religious, and regional differences that exist here.

INTRODUCING THE CHAPTER

Motivators

Food Feelings Have students describe their favorite food and talk about how it makes them feel. Do their mouths water? Do they feel hungry just thinking about the food? Do they feel good? Anxious? Loved? How do they feel when they eat the food?

Using the Photograph Have students study the photograph on this page. Then ask: "What does this picture tell you about the concern for the athletes' health and fitness?"

Exercise Styles Have students discuss the exercise habits of family members and how they reflect family members' interests, personalities, commitment to fitness, and so on.

Introducing the Objectives

Discuss the chapter objectives on this page. Remind students that the objectives focus on important chapter content.

Introducing Vocabulary

Point out that people often speak of "going on a diet" when they want to lose weight. Stress that the word *diet* does *not* refer only to weight-loss programs: a person's diet is everything that a person eats. A healthful diet includes a variety of nutritious foods. Tell students that the prefix *aero-*, as in the word *aerobic*, refers to "air" or "atmosphere." Other words using the *aero-* prefix are *aerodynamic* and *aerogram* (an air-mail letter).

CHAPTER

35

Health and Fitness

OBJECTIVES

This chapter will help you to:

- Identify ways in which food satisfies physical, emotional, social, and health needs.
- Explain some ways in which food and exercise contribute to fitness.
- Evaluate your eating habits.

WORDS TO REMEMBER

aerobic
appetite
diet
hunger
nutrition
stamina

Chapter Resources

Teacher's Classroom Resources

- Lesson Plan
- Life Skills Activity, *Are You a Couch Potato?*
- Reproducible Master, *Food Meets Your Needs*
- Extension Activity, *How Much Exercise Do You Need?*
- Chapter Test

Student Workbook

- Study Guide
- Worksheet, *The Food in Your Life*

Herschel wants to help his friend Ty. They are both on the school basketball team, but Herschel is a first-string player, while Ty spends a lot of time on the bench. Ty wants to improve his game. He has some great moves and shoots well from outside, but he tires too quickly.

"Coach said I would make the starting lineup if I could keep up with everybody else," Ty told Herschel. "He told me to cut down on junk snacks like candy and cookies. But I need the snacks, especially now with all this exercise—why else would I get so hungry? Food provides energy, right? Still, you don't snack like I do, Hersh, so how come you seem to have more energy?"

Herschel didn't know what to say. Not only does he play more during games than Ty, he also trains more on his own. Still, he actually eats less than Ty.

Herschel, too, had always thought that people ate food to meet their energy needs. Then shouldn't he need more food than Ty? Is their information about energy wrong?

What Food Does for You

Herschel and Ty are not wrong. Food *does* supply the energy that people need for their activities. However, it also contributes many other things to our lives. In addition to physical needs, food can meet emotional and social needs as well. It also plays a vital part in the growth and repair of body tissues.

Physical Needs

Your body is active all the time. Food provides you with all the energy you use—energy for walking, talking, writing, and more strenuous activities. Food also helps your heart to beat, your body to maintain its temperature, and the cut on your finger to heal.

If you go without eating, you will become tired, listless, unable to concentrate—and hungry. **Hunger** is the body's physical signal that it is short of energy and needs food. However, people often feel the urge to eat without being hungry. This is because we use food to satisfy emotional needs, too.

Studying and concentration take energy—which is best provided by nutritious food.

Real-Life Situations Hunger is defined as a physical signal for food. However, "world hunger" refers to starvation by many people in different areas of the world. Famines and limited food supplies are increasing due to many complex situations. These include: the world's rapidly growing population outpacing food production; changing weather conditions in certain areas; rising costs of importing needed food and fertilizer; poor farming practices; inadequate storage and transportation systems; and so on. Many agencies and organizations are trying to aid the hungry through food-aid programs, agricultural assistance, and nutrition education.

TEACHING THE CHAPTER

For convenience, the teaching suggestions for this chapter are arranged according to the following lesson topics:

- "What Food Does for You," pages 329-330
- "The Importance of Fitness," pages 332-333
- "Analyzing Your Own Eating Habits," page 334

Teaching "What Food Does for You"

(Pages 329-330)

This section teaches how food fulfills physical, emotional, social, and health needs.

Checking Comprehension

✓ What do you need energy for? *You need energy for walking, talking, writing, and more strenuous activities, as well as healing and thinking.*

✓ What happens if you go without eating for a long time? *You will become tired, listless, unable to concentrate—and hungry.*

✓ What are two situations in which the urge to eat may not be motivated by hunger? *You might have a second helping of a dish because it is your favorite food. Or you might go into a bakery on impulse because of the smell of freshly baked bread and the beautiful display of pastries in the window.*

✓ What social pleasures do people get from food? *Some people get a great deal of satisfaction from preparing and cooking food for others. And most people enjoy the social pleasure of getting together to eat, regardless of actual hunger.*

✓ What may happen to your appetite when you are tense or upset? *You may eat excessively to comfort yourself, or you may lose your appetite entirely.*

✓ What are some special occasions that center around food? *A birthday, Thanksgiving, the Fourth of July.*

✓ Why do we need food to combat diseases and to heal properly? *Because food provides the raw materials that help build and repair all parts of the body and mind.*

Activities

Skill Builder: Writing
Have students write a description of a family celebration that centers around a big meal or special foods.

Skill Builder: Critical Thinking
Have students watch television commercials about food and determine which need the food claims to fill in the advertising. Some cereals, for example, claim to meet your energy needs, and snack foods are often shown in party atmospheres fulfilling social needs.

Reteaching
Tell students that most people have a "comfort food" that they eat when they're "down" or tense. Ask students what their comfort foods are and when they tend to eat them.

Enrichment
Ask students if they would forgo eating if their energy and health needs could be met by taking food pills. Have them discuss what they would miss about eating.

Emotional Needs

The urge to eat often comes from your emotions. You might have a second helping of meat loaf because it is your favorite food. You might go into the bakery on impulse because you smell the freshly baked bread and see the beautiful display of pastries in the window. These reactions are automatic, as is the urge to eat because it's lunchtime. This desire to eat is called **appetite**.

Your appetite is linked to your emotions in many ways. Food gives people a sense of security and well-being. When you are tense or upset you may eat excessively to comfort yourself—or you may lose your appetite entirely.

Social Needs

Eating also plays an important part in our social lives. Preparing and cooking food for others can be very satisfying. Most people enjoy the social pleasure of getting together to eat.

In fact, people spend a lot of time around the dining table enjoying each other's company. Do you sometimes sit and talk to a relative or friend at the table? Do you often stop with friends for pizza or ice cream after school?

In addition, of course, special social occasions often center around food—a birthday cake, a Thanksgiving dinner, a cookout on the Fourth of July. Food is a social experience. It is more than just a way to soothe your emotions or satisfy hunger.

Health Needs

Another major benefit you gain from food is health and well-being. When people don't get enough of the right kinds of food for a long time, they may get sick and even die.

Young people need certain foods to grow normally. Your body cannot combat diseases or heal properly unless it is well nourished. This is because food provides the raw materials that help build and maintain a healthy mind and body.

Families and friends enjoy getting together for a meal or to celebrate a special occasion.

Emphasize The text suggests that loss of appetite can occur in times of emotional upheaval. Point out that it is one of the symptoms of clinical depression. But loss of appetite can also be a symptom of physical illnesses like head colds or flu.

Did You Know? Some people eat to alleviate stress, using nervous nibbling or compulsive bingeing to respond to problems or tension. See Chapter 3 for information about managing stress, and Chapter 39 for information about the eating disorders—anorexia nervosa and bulimia.

HEALTH WATCH

U.S.A.: Land of Food Opportunity

Have you ever been surprised to see one of your friends enjoy a meal you never imagined she or he would eat? All people have favorite foods, and they aren't always what you would expect.

Your idea of what tastes good is based largely on what you eat in your own home, what you see on TV ads, and what your friends eat when you go out together.

However, taken together, American families probably eat a wider variety of foods than any other people in the world. There are several reasons for this:

- **Ethnic background.** Because the United States is a nation of immigrants, foods from many countries are eaten here—not only in ethnic restaurants but in people's homes. There are sausages from Germany, pasta from Italy, tortillas from Mexico, rice dishes from China and Japan—to name a few.
- **Religious customs.** The United States is also home to many religious groups, each with their own customs. Families often eat special foods on their religious holidays—egg dishes at Easter, matzoth during Passover. Some religions encourage the eating of fish; others have rules that forbid the eating of pork, shellfish, or any type of meat. Some religious groups fast—or do not eat—on certain holidays or at certain times of the year.
- **Regional traditions.** Many food specialties developed in different regions due to the foods that were plentiful there and the ethnic backgrounds of the settlers. Today, although most foods are available in all parts of the United States, certain dishes are still associated with a specific region: New England clam chowder, Southern fried chicken, Texas barbeque, Creole gumbo, or sourdough bread from San Francisco.

As a result, the United States offers a wide choice of healthful foods. True, *your* tastes have been shaped by your family, with its special ethnic, religious, and regional traditions. Our country, however, offers many opportunities to broaden your tastes. Take advantage of these opportunities; sampling the variety is not only fun, it's good for your health and fitness.

Think It Through

1. **What foods are considered typical of where you live? Why do you think that they became popular in your region?**
2. **Why do you think people are often unwilling to try new foods? Give some reasons for and against eating something you have never tried before.**

Teaching the Feature

"U.S.A.: Land of Food Opportunity"

Answers to Feature Questions

1. Answers will vary depending on where the students live. In the Northeast, they might mention steak sandwiches, scrapple, or hoagies; in the South, grits, smoked ham, pecan pie; in the West, salmon, berries, game meats. These foods probably became popular because of their availability or because certain ethnic groups settled in those areas.

2. People may not try a food because they don't think they will like it; because other people they know have expressed their dislike for it; or because the food looks, or smells unappealing. Trying new foods can be fun; people might find they really like the food; or it might prompt them to learn about other cultures and traditions. On the other hand, if you experiment with new foods and are unhappy with the results, this might keep you from trying other foods in the future.

Activities

Ethnic Foods Encourage students to make a survey of the ethnic restaurants in their area and to try a kind of ethnic food (Greek, Vietnamese, and so on) that they've never tried before.

Religious Customs Have students identify the religions that subscribe to the dietary restrictions discussed in this feature and investigate the origins of the religious dietary customs.

Community Contact Have students plan a regional food festival. Students might solicit recipes for regional favorites (chili, crabcakes, gumbo) from area residents, prepare them, and allow other students to taste them. You might have students do this same activity for a different area of the country as well.

More About Ethnic Foods Most countries have foods identified with them, such as: Great Britain—roast beef, fish and chips. France—onion soup, bouillabaisse, crepes. Germany—sauerbraten, sausages, sauerkraut. Italy—antipasto, minestrone, pasta, spumoni. Scandinavia—herring, pork, lingonberries. Middle East—shish kebabs, couscous, phyllo. India—curry, dal, yogurt, flat breads. Africa—millet meal, yams, black beans. China—stir-fried dishes, rice, hot pot. Japan—sushi, tempura, sukiyaki, seaweed. Mexico—tortilla, tacos, tamales, frijoles. Caribbean—plantains, rice and beans. South America—ceviche, beef, stews, cassava.

Teaching "The Importance of Fitness"
(Pages 332-333)

This section teaches that fitness can be achieved through good nutrition and regular exercise and discusses the benefits of fitness.

Checking Comprehension

✓ Aside from enabling you to participate in physical activities, how does fitness improve other aspects of your life? *You look better, you feel calmer and more relaxed, you are less likely to suffer injuries.*

✓ How can you practice good nutrition? *By eating the right combinations of food.*

✓ What physical benefits does good nutrition have? *Good nutrition helps you to control your weight; to avoid many illnesses; and to make your skin, hair, and nails look their best. It also enables you to grow to your full height and allows your muscles to develop to their full potential. Your body can also manufacture the thousands of new cells that it needs every day.*

✓ Name three kinds of exercise that do not involve sports. *Walking to a friend's house instead of taking a bus, bicycling to the store to pick up groceries, washing down the kitchen floor at home.*

✓ How can exercise lessen emotional dependence on food? *By helping with stress.*

✓ What parts of your body are strengthened by push-ups, knee bends, and sit-ups? *Push-ups and full knee bends strengthen your arms and legs, and sit-ups tighten your stomach muscles.*

✓ What is stamina? *Stamina means staying power or endurance.*

✓ How do endurance exercises improve your ability to use oxygen? *Endurance exercises build up your blood circulation system, including your heart and lungs, increasing the amount of oxygen that your body can use.*

The Importance of Fitness

Fitness, which can be achieved through good nutrition and regular exercise, is important for everyone, not just for athletes like Ty and Herschel. When you are fit, you are strong and healthy enough to participate in a wide range of physical activities. Because your body is conditioned, you are less likely to suffer injuries.

Fitness improves other aspects of your life, too. You look better, and you feel calmer and more relaxed.

Good Nutrition

The way that your body uses food is called **nutrition**. When you eat the right combinations of foods, your body receives all the nourishment it needs; this means you are practicing good nutrition. Much research has been done to find out exactly which combinations of foods are most healthful. You will learn some of the results of this research in the next few chapters.

Without good nutrition, your body cannot manufacture the thousands of new cells that it needs every day. Good nutrition can help you to control your weight, avoid many illnesses, and reach your full height. Eating right and getting enough exercise is the key to strong muscles and healthy looking skin, hair, and nails. Understanding nutrition is an important part of managing your own life.

Regular Exercise

Exercise doesn't mean only sports and the activities you do in physical education class. When you walk to your friend's house instead of taking a bus, that is exercise, as are bicycling to the store and washing the kitchen floor at home. If activities such as these are not a part of your daily routine, however, set aside time for exercising regularly.

Regular exercise not only helps you become physically fit, it often gives you the opportunity to be with friends. In addition, as you read in Chapter 3, exercise can help you deal with stressful situations in your life. By helping with stress, exercise can lessen emotional dependence on food. People often feel fewer appetite urges when they exercise regularly.

Not only are you being good to your dog by going for a walk, you are doing yourself a favor by getting some exercise.

More About Good Nutrition Studies have shown a correlation between adequate nutrition and mental health. A child who is undernourished will have trouble concentrating in school. Adults who do not eat properly may suffer from depression and apathy. Good nutrition does lead to good mental health.

Emphasize Fitness, like happiness, is difficult to define. Sometimes we do not realize how much better we would feel if we improved our eating habits and got regular exercise until we try it and see.

Cross-Reference See Chapter 3 for additional information on health and wellness.

Types of Exercise

Regular exercise can contribute to your fitness in three important ways:

- **Strength.** Many types of exercise are designed to make you stronger. Weight training and similar activities usually benefit particular parts of your body. For example, push-ups strengthen your arms, full knee bends strengthen your legs, and sit-ups tighten your stomach muscles.
- **Endurance.** Endurance exercises increase your **stamina**, or staying power, by building up your blood circulatory system. They strengthen your heart and lungs, increasing the amount of oxygen that your body can use. Some activities that promote endurance are called **aerobic** (uh-ROH-bic) exercises because they improve your ability to use oxygen from the air. They include running, swimming, cycling, fast walking—in fact, any exercise that requires sustained regular movement for 30 minutes or more, with *no* rests. Endurance is probably more important than strength for general fitness, because it means that your whole body is working efficiently. It also helps your body make better use of the food you eat.
- **Flexibility.** Exercises that increase flexibility, such as stretching, are important to fitness. They help to make you more agile—whether you are dancing or playing football. If your body is flexible, you are less likely to pull a muscle during exercise.

Before you begin an exercise program, check with your doctor to be sure you do not have a condition that could be aggravated by strenuous exercise. Start each workout with warm-up activities such as stretching and bending. This helps to prevent muscle pulls and other injuries. When you are finished, a cool-down period of stretching or slow movement lets your body return to a relaxed state.

Each type of exercise provides different benefits for your body.

Did You Know? The best way to determine your exercise level is to monitor your pulse rate. Your pulse can be taken on your wrist or the side of your neck—count for one minute. To determine how hard to exercise, you can check your target pulse rate. This is the rate within which you should work for the most benefit from exercise. To identify your target pulse rate, first compute your maximum pulse rate by subtracting your age from 220. Then multiply this number by 70 percent and by 85 percent. For example, if you are age 14, your maximum pulse rate is 206 (220-14)—the most your heart should beat a minute. Your target rate is between 144 (70 percent) and 175 (85 percent) beats per minute.

✓ How long must you sustain aerobic exercise for it to be effective? *To be effective, sustained regular exercise must be maintained 30 minutes or more, with* ***no*** *rests.*

✓ Why is endurance more important than strength? *Endurance is probably more important than strength for general fitness because it means your whole body is working efficiently, making better use of the food you eat.*

✓ How does flexibility help you to exercise effectively? *If your body is flexible, you are less likely to pull a muscle during vigorous exercise. You are also more agile.*

✓ Why is a cool-down period after exercising important? Contrast this with a warm-up period before exercising. *A cool-down period lets your body return to a relaxed state. A warm-up period helps prevent injuries.*

✓ What should you do before starting an exercise program? *Check with your doctor to be sure you have no condition that could be aggravated by strenuous exercise.*

Activities

Skill Builder: Writing
Have students view a television exercise show or an exercise video and describe it. Ask students to tell what kind of exercises are done and what benefit they have.

Reteaching
Ask students to keep track of all exercise they get on a daily basis (dancing, bike riding, walking up stairs, and so on) without an exercise program. Do they feel they are getting enough exercise? Why or why not?

Enrichment
Have students evaluate how they feel immediately prior to exercise and then again right after exercising. What benefits (physical and emotional) does exercise have for them?

Teaching "Analyzing Your Own Eating Habits"
(Page 334)

This section teaches students to analyze their own eating habits and to plan for good nutrition.

Checking Comprehension

✓ What is the best way to become aware of eating habits? *To keep a record for a week or two of each time you eat and exactly what you eat, including what you were doing at the time.*

✓ What can a record of your eating habits tell you? *When you review this record, you will see how frequently you eat and what foods you choose.*

✓ What is an example of a bad eating habit? *You might find that you eat candy and fried foods, for snacks instead of more healthful foods such as fruits, yogurt, or popcorn.*

Activities

Skill Builder: Writing
Have students make a list of five good eating habits and five bad eating habits. Students should explain why the habits are good or bad for them.

Skill Builder: Reading
Ask students to read a diet plan (or book) to see if the diet is a healthful one or not. Does the diet include a balance of healthful foods, or does it encourage bad eating habits (such as skipping meals or eating only one kind of food)?

Reteaching
Have students discuss the factors in their lives that contribute to bad eating habits. Are there situations (irregular meal schedules, lots of snack foods in the kitchen) or people who encourage unhealthful habits? What can be changed to allow for better nutrition?

Enrichment
Help students to set up a plan for eating healthfully. Encourage them to stick to the plan for a week and then report to the class about how they did.

Analyzing Your Own Eating Habits

By paying attention to your eating habits, you can learn if you are choosing foods that help promote health and fitness. A healthy **diet**, the food and drink you typically consume, will help you feel and look good.

The best way to become aware of your eating habits is to keep a record of everything you consume for a week or two. Exactly what did you eat, and how much? What time of day was it? What were you doing at the time? When you review this record, you will see how frequently you eat and what foods you choose. You might discover there are certain times that you always eat—such as when you watch television.

When analyzing your eating habits, be sure to include snacks as well as regular meals.

To help you analyze your eating patterns, here are some questions you can ask yourself:

- Do you usually eat three meals a day?
- Do you ever skip meals?
- What foods do you enjoy the most?
- What foods do you seldom eat?
- When do you snack?
- What do you order when you eat out?

Your answers to these kinds of questions can make you more aware of your eating habits. Some of these habits may be very good; for example, you might always eat a nutritious breakfast. Other habits, however, may be bad; you might find that you eat candy and fried foods for snacks instead of more healthful foods like fruits, yogurt, or popcorn.

As you read the rest of this unit, you will learn which foods are better for you and why. You will learn the importance of exercise and good eating habits, and how you can control your weight and improve your fitness. You will also find out how to prepare meals and snacks for yourself, your family, and your friends. You will thus be more able to take responsibility for the foods you eat and get the maximum benefits that food can provide.

Did You know? The word *diet* comes from the Greek *diaita,* which means "to lead one's life." A diet in many ways is the way you lead your life. A healthful diet is a big part of a healthful lifestyle.

Emphasize Some bad eating habits are a result of the way food was used as a punishment or reward during childhood. If sweets were used as a reward when you were young, you may use them to reward yourself now that you are older. If food was a symbol of love, you may not be able to deny yourself food without feeling deprived.

CHAPTER 35 REVIEW

Reviewing the Facts

1. What four needs does food supply?
2. What is the difference between hunger and appetite?
3. How are your emotions linked to your appetite?
4. What does it mean to be fit?
5. List two benefits of being fit.
6. How do exercise and good nutrition contribute to a person's fitness level?
7. What types of exercise would you choose if you wanted to increase your strength? Your stamina? Your flexibility?

Thinking Critically

1. What is your personal definition of fitness? Compare it to a classmate's. How is it similar? In what ways does it differ? Why do you think people may have different definitions?
2. Why do you think it is important to begin an exercise session with a warm-up and end it with a cool-down period? What could be some hazards if you did not warm up and cool down?

Applying Your Skills

1. **Analyzing Your Diet.** Keep a record of what you eat for a week: when, what, how much, and why. Do you see any patterns in your eating habits? Were you surprised at any aspects of your diet? Do you eat a variety of different foods, or do you eat the same ones over and over again?

2. **Developing a Workout.** Develop a personalized 30-minute workout including exercises that build strength, stamina, and flexibility. Include a warm-up and cool-down period. What percent of your program consists of strength exercises? What percent are endurance exercises? What percent promotes flexibility? Go over your program with a physical education teacher, then present it to the class.

3. **Drawing Conclusions.** Make a list of the exercise you get in an average week and a record of everything you eat in a week (see activity #1). What might be the relationship between your physical fitness and the amount of exercise and the foods you eat? What changes might you make in your lifestyle?

Answers to "Reviewing the Facts"

1. Physical, emotional, social, health.
2. Hunger is a physical need; appetite is an emotional desire.
3. Food gives a sense of security and well-being; when tense or upset, you may eat excessively or lose your appetite.
4. Being strong and healthy enough to participate in a wide range of physical activities.
5. Any two: able to participate in physical activities; less likely to suffer injuries; look better; feel more calm and relaxed.
6. Good nutrition helps you grow, control your weight, avoid many illnesses, and look healthy. Exercise helps you become physically fit—strength, endurance, and flexibility; deal with stress; and control your weight.
7. Strength: weight training, push-ups, knee bends, sit-ups. Endurance: aerobic exercises such as running, cycling, fast walking. Flexibility: stretching.

Answers to "Thinking Critically"

1. Students' personal definitions of fitness may include being healthier; being more able to withstand illnesses; looking and feeling better; growing to one's full height; having well-developed muscles. Definitions will differ depending on people's values and goals.
2. Students should say that a warm-up period allows the body to gradually stretch out and prepare for the added stress of exercise. A cool-down period allows the system to slowly relax after the demands of a workout. Hazards include pulled muscles, muscle cramps, hyperventilation, erratic pulse, dizziness, or nausea.

COMPLETING THE CHAPTER

Summary

- Food supplies the energy and the raw materials we need for good health and fitness.
- Food also fills emotional and social needs.
- Fitness can be achieved through good nutrition and regular exercise.
- Exercise can help to develop strength, endurance, and flexibility.
- Analyzing your eating habits is a good way to begin to improve your health and fitness.

For Review

Objective Review Questions Have students complete the "Reviewing the Facts" section on this page.

Study Guide Have students complete the Study Guide from Chapter 35 of their *Student Workbook.*

Eating Habits Survey Have students conduct a survey of the eating habits of the student body, asking such questions as those suggested in this chapter. As a result of the survey, students can identify the most prevalent bad eating habits of their peers.

Developing Tastes Have students talk about the things that have contributed to their tastes in food. What factors besides family preferences have influenced which foods are their favorites, and which ones they will not even try?

For Evaluation

Substantiation Ask students to substantiate (offer proof of) one of the following statements from the text:

- "Food is a social experience."
- "Fitness can be achieved through good nutrition and regular exercise."
- "A healthy diet will help you feel and look good."
- "The United States offers a wide choice of healthful foods."

Chapter Test Have students complete the test for Chapter 35 that appears in the *Teacher's Classroom Resources.*

CHAPTER OVERVIEW

Chapter 36 explains the importance of nutrients in food. It presents the six classes of nutrients—carbohydrates, proteins, fats, water, vitamins, and minerals—and describes how they contribute to general health. Students also learn about calories and life management skills to use calories to their own advantage.

INTRODUCING THE CHAPTER

Motivators

Breakfast of Champions Tell students that many people consider breakfast to be the most important meal of the day. Have students tell what they had for breakfast and evaluate whether or not they think it was a healthful breakfast.

Using the Photograph Have students study the photograph on this page. Then ask: "How do you think food affects the activities and life styles of these teens?"

Food for Thought Explain that this chapter is concerned with the components of food—with the various nutrients that food provides. Ask students to give examples of types of food that they believe to be particularly healthful and to explain why they think the food is good for the body. Write the students' ideas on the board, and be prepared to go back to the list at the end of the chapter.

Introducing the Objectives

Discuss the chapter objectives on this page. Remind students that the objectives focus on important chapter content.

CHAPTER

36 Nutrients

OBJECTIVES

This chapter will help you to:

- Explain the importance of nutrients in food.
- List the six classes of nutrients and their functions.
- Identify foods that are good sources of carbohydrates, proteins, fats, water, vitamins, and minerals.

WORDS TO REMEMBER

amino acid
calorie
carbohydrate
cholesterol
fiber
mineral
nutrient
protein
vitamin

Chapter Resources

Teacher's Classroom Resources
- Lesson Plan
- Life Skills Activity, *Your Bones Are on the Line*
- Reproducible Master, *Nutrients for Your Body*
- Extension Activity, *Vitamins and Minerals at a Glance*
- Chapter Test

Student Workbook
- Study Guide
- Worksheet, *Nutrition on the Menu*

Nutritionists are scientists who study food and its effects on the body. They have found that food contains many nourishing substances, or **nutrients.** These nutrients are all needed for your health; if your diet lacks any, you won't feel your best and may even become sick.

More than 40 key nutrients have been identified. They can be grouped into six classes: carbohydrates, proteins, fats, water, vitamins, and minerals. Knowing about nutrients and the foods that contain them will help you plan for a healthy life.

Carbohydrates

Starches and sugars are two main categories of **carbohydrates,** nutrients that provide your body with ready energy. However, your body cannot store them in large quantities. If you need energy but haven't eaten carbohydrates recently, your body has to make energy from other body tissues.

Therefore, foods containing carbohydrates should be a major ingredient in your diet—especially grains, vegetables, and fruits. These foods are complex carbohydrate foods; they contain other nutrients besides starch or sugar, making them particularly valuable.

How can you include carbohydrates in your diet?

- **Starches.** Rice, potatoes, and grain products such as bread and pasta are examples of foods high in starch. Starch is digested to form a simple sugar called glucose, which is a major source of energy for your body.
- **Sugars.** Glucose can also be formed from the sugar in fruits. To most people, however, sugar means refined sugar, which is found in foods such as cakes, candy, cookies, and many soft drinks. Refined sugar is a poor source of energy because it lacks other nutrients. Too much refined sugar can lead to weight gain and dental problems and it can cause complications in diseases such as diabetes.

Grains—breads, cereals, pasta, rice—are excellent sources of carbohydrates. The starch in these foods provides energy for your body.

Focus on Health Many people are critical of the amount of refined sugar in breakfast cereals. A cup of a popular cereal contains four teaspoons of sugar, and even a "healthful" cereal often has three teaspoons of sugar per cup. Suggest that students check their breakfast cereal to see how much sugar it contains.

Did You Know? Athletes in endurance sports such as marathon running sometimes use "carbohydrate loading" to maximize their performance. The athlete eats a carbohydrate-rich diet for the three days prior to competition to increase glycogen (stored glucose) and raise energy levels.

Introducing Vocabulary

Tell students that many of the words associated with nutrition come from Latin. Consider that *nutrient* and *nutrition* both come from *nutrire* (meaning "to feed"). The word *vitamin* comes from the Latin *vita,* which means "life." The term *calorie* is derived from *calor* (meaning "heat") because a calorie is actually the amount of heat required to raise the temperature of 1 kilogram of water by 1 °C.

TEACHING THE CHAPTER

For convenience, the teaching suggestions for this chapter are arranged according to the following lesson topics:

- "Carbohydrates," pages 337-338
- "Proteins" and "Fats," pages 338-339
- "Water" and "Vitamins," pages 339-341
- "Minerals," pages 342-343

Teaching "Carbohydrates"
(Pages 337-338)

This section teaches about the two categories of carbohydrates—starches and sugars—and tells students what foods are good sources of this energy-producing nutrient.

Checking Comprehension

✔ What happens if you don't eat carbohydrates often enough? *If you need energy but haven't eaten carbohydrates recently, your body has to make energy from other body tissues.*

✔ What are complex carbohydrate foods? *They are foods that contain nutrients other than starch or sugar, making them particularly valuable.*

✔ Name four foods that are high in starches. *Rice, potatoes, bread, and pasta are examples of foods high in starches.*

✔ What problems can refined sugar cause? *Too much refined sugar can lead to weight gain and dental problems. Sugar has been linked to diabetes and heart disease.*

An important benefit of eating certain carbohydrate foods is that they contain indigestible threadlike cells called **fiber**. Fiber is not strictly a nutrient, but it is important because it helps to move food through the digestive system. Whole-grain cereals and breads are excellent sources of fiber, as are fruits and vegetables, especially the peels and seeds.

Fiber can also promote a feeling of fullness, making you less hungry. This is helpful if you are trying to lose weight.

Proteins

Anyone who is growing needs a diet high in **proteins**, the nutrients necessary for building and repairing body tissues. Proteins are the basis of all the body's cells, and form the major part of hair, nails, and skin. The body includes more proteins than it does any other nutrient except water.

Though your body needs many different types of protein, all proteins are made from the same basic chemicals. These chemicals are called **amino acids**, and 22 different kinds have been identified.

While it is useful to have most of the amino acids present in your food, only 9 are absolutely necessary—the other 13 can be created by your body from other food substances. These nine are called the essential amino acids. The foods that contain them—animal proteins like meat, poultry, eggs, and milk—are said to have complete proteins.

Vegetables, fruits, and grains have incomplete proteins. They contain many amino acids, but not all of the essential ones. You can get the essential nine, however, by combining certain incomplete proteins, such as beans with rice, or nuts with whole grains. This is called protein complementing. People who do not eat meat or dairy products can use protein complementing to get the nutrients necessary for good health.

Complete proteins come from animal sources, such as meat, poultry, fish, eggs, and milk. Incomplete proteins come from plant sources, such as grains, vegetables, and fruits. Combining certain incomplete proteins, such as rice and beans, is called protein complementing.

✓ What are four good sources of fiber, and what does fiber do? *Whole-grain cereals and breads are excellent sources of fiber. So are fruits and vegetables, especially the peels and seeds. Fiber helps move food through the digestive system and promotes the feeling of fullness.*

Activities

Skill Builder: Reading
Have students read the labels on several kinds of food and note the carbohydrate content. Using students' suggestions, compile lists of foods that are high in starch or high in sugar.

Skill Builder: Science
Ask students to research how sugar is refined and to find out about the different kinds of refined sugar. Have them write a brief report on their findings.

Reteaching
Have students make a list of all the foods containing carbohydrates that they like to eat regularly. Suggest that they underline the foods that are most nutritious.

Enrichment
Ask students to pay careful attention to cereal advertisements on TV and to note the ones that make a special point of talking about fiber. Students should then compare those cereals with cereals not advertised as high in fiber. Do they notice a difference in fiber levels?

Teaching "Proteins" and "Fats"

(Pages 338-339)

This section teaches about proteins (the tissue builders) and fats. Students learn how amino acids help the body build cells and how fats are used for reserve energy. Students are warned about having too much fat in their diet.

Checking Comprehension

✓ What functions do proteins serve in the body? *Proteins form the basis of all the body's cells and form the major part of hair, nails, and skin.*

Did You Know? Experts recommend that carbohydrates make up about 55 percent of a person's daily calorie intake: 45 percent should come from starches and sugars that occur naturally in foods, such as potatoes and oranges; only 10 percent from refined or processed carbohydrates in foods such as cakes and candy.

More About Cholesterol There are two kinds of cholesterol: "bad" cholesterol (LDLs—low-density lipids) and "good" cholesterol (HDLs—high-density lipids). HDLs actually decrease a person's risk of heart disease. HDL cholesterol levels can be raised by exercise, weight control, and avoidance of cigarette smoking.

Fats

Some fats are necessary for good health. The body uses them for reserve energy. Fats also allow your body to store and use other nutrients, such as vitamin A, and they help regulate body temperature. Without fats in the diet, skin and hair problems can develop.

However, too much fat in your diet is stored as fatty tissue and may make you overweight. It can lead to serious health problems.

Fats are present in most foods, especially meat, butter, salad dressings, nuts, milk, cheese, baked goods, and snack foods. Some fats are visible—such as butter or the layer of fat on meats. Other fats are hidden in foods such as egg yolks, french fries, hard cheeses, ice cream, and chocolate. Fats are also obtained from excess carbohydrates, which are converted to fat if not immediately needed for energy. Nutritionists recommend that fat intake be reduced for better health.

There are two types of fats: saturated and unsaturated. Saturated fats are found in the animal fats in meat, milk and butter, as well as in tropical oils such as coconut and palm oils. Saturated fats are particularly undesirable in the diet because they may lead to high levels of cholesterol in the blood. **Cholesterol** (kuh-LESS-tuh-rahl) is a white, waxlike substance that plays an important part in transporting and digesting fat. However, high cholesterol levels can lead to heart disease, high blood pressure, hardening of the arteries, and other health problems.

Unsaturated fats are better for you. They are found in vegetable oils which come from fruits and vegetables like corn or olives. Whenever possible, unsaturated fats should be substituted for saturated fats.

Water

Close to 75 percent of your body is water. Water is found in all cells and is the basic material of your blood. It transports nutrients throughout your body and carries away waste products. It also helps to move food through the digestive system and to regulate the temperature of your body.

Your body loses water continually, so it is important that you take in enough. Foods especially high in water are milk, soups, many fruits, and vegetables such as lettuce and celery. Health care professionals also recommend drinking between six and eight glasses of water daily. You need more water when it is hot and after you exercise or do physical work.

Your body needs six to eight glasses of water a day.

Emphasize Water is one of the most important nutrients even though it has no calories. People can live several weeks without food but only a few days without water. Even a 10 percent loss of water can cause serious medical problems.

Focus on Consumer Skills There are now many popular spring waters on the market. Some taste studies have concluded that they are no more tasty than most tap water, and nutritionally they are no better for you.

✓ How many amino acids are there, and how many are essential? *Twenty-two kinds have been identified. Nine are absolutely necessary; the other thirteen can be created by your body from other food substances.*

✓ What is the difference between complete and incomplete proteins, and what kinds of foods are in each category? *Complete proteins are in foods such as meat, poultry, eggs, and milk that contain the nine essential amino acids. Incomplete proteins are in foods such as vegetables, fruits, and grains that contain many amino acids but not all the essential ones.*

✓ Why are saturated fats undesirable? *Because they may lead to high levels of cholesterol in the blood.*

✓ Name two vegetables that contain fat. *Corn and olives contain vegetable oils, which are a type of fat.*

Activities

Skill Builder: Reading
Have students read about vegetarianism. Then ask them to discuss its advantages and disadvantages. Ask them if they would consider becoming vegetarians. In what ways does it appeal to them?

Skill Builder: Writing
Ask students to imagine that they know someone whose diet is far too high in saturated fats. Suggest that they write a letter to this person, in which they explain why excess fats are undesirable and suggest practical ways of cutting down on fats.

Reteaching
Have students make a chart of substitutions that they could make to reduce saturated fats in their diets and replace them with unsaturated fats (for example, vegetable oil for butter).

Enrichment
Invite a representative from the American Heart Association to give a presentation on diet and nutrition. Students might use the information they gain to develop a poster to alert other students to the dangers of saturated fats.

Teaching the Feature
"The Truth About Calories"

Answers to Feature Questions

1. The body will not get all the nutrients it needs. Weakness or illness might result.

2. Possible answers include exercise with a friend, set a schedule, join a gym, take an exercise class.

Activities

Calorie Cutting Have students make a plan for cutting 50 calories a day. It might mean cutting out an after-school snack or switching from ice cream to ice milk. Have students calculate how many calories they would eliminate over the course of a year.

Diet Books Have students read different diet books or plans and evaluate whether the diets seem to be healthful. Students should try to talk to people who have followed the diet to find out how successful they were at losing weight, whether they liked the diet, how they felt when they were on the diet, and whether they gained the weight back or gained even more weight.

Fitness Program Have students plan an exercise program that fits their interests, that is varied enough not to be boring, and that they think they can stick to. They should estimate the time involved to make sure it is reasonable and list equipment (bicycle, weights, jogging shoes) and costs involved.

Community Contact Arrange to have a fitness or an aerobics instructor speak to the class about exercise classes and clubs in their community. Have him or her talk about the costs and services of each.

HEALTH WATCH

The Truth About Calories

What is a calorie? You hear a lot about calories, but you may not know what they are. A **calorie** is no more than an amount of energy; specifically, a measure of heat. A food's calorie count is the amount of energy the food provides. This energy may be used by the body or stored as fat.

In terms of calories, not all nutrients are created equal. There are four calories in every gram of protein and four in every gram of carbohydrate (starch or sugar). In every gram of fat, however, there are nine calories. Water, vitamins, and minerals, on the other hand, have no calories at all.

Let's look at an example. One 5-ounce (150g) baked potato has approximately 100 calories—it consists mostly of carbohydrates and has no fat. A 5-ounce steak, which is 80 percent fat, has 550 calories. Five ounces of butter has 1,000 calories!

Many people try to lose weight by counting calories, but it is important to understand that this is only half the story. Body weight is really a reflection of the energy balance in your body. If you eat more calories than your body uses up, the extra calories are stored as fat. If, on the other hand, you eat fewer calories than you use, your body burns stored fat to make energy. For most people the problem is not so much the calories that go in, but rather those that do *not* go out. In other words, they may not overeat so much as under-exercise.

If you are trying to lose weight, don't just count calories. Instead, eat to get the most out of your calories. Choose foods that are nutrient-rich. At the same time, exercise to be sure you are burning calories as well as taking them in.

Exercise has benefits beyond the calories used during the activity. In a half-hour bicycle ride, you might use up 250 calories, but your exercise keeps on working for you. It helps your body burn calories faster all day long.

Think It Through

1. **What do you suppose is the danger in fad diets that call for a person to eat only one or two kinds of food for a period of time?**
2. **How might teens who don't get regular exercise encourage themselves to exercise?**

Did You Know? Fast-food restaurant fare is often very high in calories. You would have to bicycle for over an hour to work off the calories in one popular brand of hamburger. Just think how long you would have to work out to get rid of a chocolate shake (383 calories) and fries (220 calories), too! See Teen Tips "Fast Foods: Cutting the Calories" on pages 494-495.

Emphasize The number of calories one needs to take in is directly related to the amount of energy one needs to expend. An extremely active teen (one who is participating in a sport, for example) may need as many as 5,000 calories a day. See Chapter 39 for information about weight control.

Vitamins

Vitamins are nutrients that help the body stay healthy, function properly, and make use of other nutrients. They are needed in very small amounts. Vitamins do not provide energy or form tissues, but if you don't get enough of each, you may become seriously ill. Vitamins can be water soluble or fat soluble.

Water-Soluble Vitamins

The B vitamins and vitamin C are water-soluble vitamins. That means that they are easily absorbed and can move through the body in water. However, since water is constantly being lost from the body, you need fresh supplies of these vitamins every day.

Citrus fruits are an excellent source of vitamin C.

There are eight B vitamins. They are especially important in helping nerve and brain tissue to develop and work well. They also aid in digestion. The most important of the group are thiamine (B_1), riboflavin (B_2), and niacin. B vitamins are found in milk products, meats, and breads and cereals.

Vitamin C, also called ascorbic acid, helps the body build cells. This makes it important in healing cuts and bruises. It also helps form strong teeth and bones and healthy gums. Vitamin C is found in many fruits and vegetables. Citrus fruits (such as oranges and grapefruits), strawberries and cantaloupes are excellent sources. Vegetables high in vitamin C include broccoli, raw cabbage, and turnip greens.

Fat-Soluble Vitamins

Vitamins A, D, E, and K are fat-soluble. This means that they travel through the bloodstream in droplets of fat. They can also be stored in fat cells for long periods of time.

Vitamin A is found in yellow and dark green vegetables, such as carrots, sweet potatoes, broccoli, and spinach. You need it for good vision, healthy teeth and gums, and strong bones. It also helps the body resist infections.

Vitamin D, another key substance in the formation of bones and teeth, helps you use minerals like calcium and phosphorus. Your body makes its own vitamin D if it gets enough sunlight. The dairy industry helps by adding vitamin D to many milk products.

Vitamin E helps keep red blood cells healthy. It is found in vegetable oils as well as foods such as grains, nuts, and green leafy vegetables. Vitamin K, which helps your blood to clot, can be obtained in vegetables such as broccoli and cauliflower.

Real-Life Situations Advertisements abound for vitamin and mineral supplements. Although doctors may recommend supplements for young children, pregnant women, and people with certain health problems, most nutrition experts say that people who are healthy and eat a balanced diet do not need to take daily supplements. People should read health articles and ads carefully to distinguish facts from claims. For example, some ads claim that particular vitamins or minerals can work "miracles," healing and preventing all types of illnesses. Some promote megavitamins, or large amounts of vitamins to cure colds or other illnesses—but large doses may be harmful to the body.

Teaching "Water" and "Vitamins"

(Pages 339-341)

This section teaches that water and vitamins are essential to keeping the body working properly.

Checking Comprehension

✓ What foods have a high water content? *Foods especially high in water are milk, soups, and many fruits and vegetables, such as lettuce and celery.*

✓ What are the most important B vitamins? *The most important of the group are thiamine (B_1), riboflavin (B_2), and niacin.*

✓ Why is vitamin C important, and in what foods is it found? *Vitamin C helps the body build cells, heal cuts and bruises, and form strong teeth and bones and healthy gums. It is found in many fruits, such as oranges, grapefruits, strawberries, and cantaloupes, and in many vegetables, such as broccoli, raw cabbage, and turnip greens.*

✓ How do fat-soluble vitamins go through the body? *They travel through the bloodstream in droplets of fat.*

✓ Which vitamins help form strong bones and teeth? *Vitamins C, A, and D.*

✓ What foods are high in vitamin E? *Vitamin E is found in vegetable oils as well as foods such as green leafy vegetables, grains, and nuts.*

✓ What does vitamin K do? *It helps your blood to clot.*

Activities

Skill Builder: Science
Explain that many people believe that vitamin C helps cure the common cold. Have students investigate this claim by reading health books and periodicals, then have them present their findings to the class. Ask them: "Is there any hard evidence that vitamin C *does* cure the common cold?"

Skill Builder: Reading
Ask students to read first-aid books to find out about the symptoms and treatment of dehydration.

Reteaching
Have students list all the foods mentioned in this section as important sources of vitamins. Beside each item on the list, students should write the vitamin that food contains.

Enrichment
Explain that people who eat a healthful diet normally get all the vitamins they need. Yet many Americans spend a considerable amount on vitamin supplements. Suggest that students undertake research to discover the effects of too many vitamins.

Teaching "Minerals"
(Pages 342-343)

This section explains why minerals such as calcium, iron, and sodium are necessary for good health.

Checking Comprehension

✓ What is osteoporosis, and what can you do to prevent it? *Osteoporosis is a condition in which bones lose their density and become brittle. You can help prevent it by taking in enough calcium and by exercising regularly.*

✓ What is anemia? *It is a condition in which blood cannot carry enough oxygen. It causes low resistance to infections and a lack of energy.*

✓ What might happen if you eat too much salt? *It may lead to high blood pressure and swelling of the hands and feet.*

✓ What foods are high in potassium? *Orange juice and bananas are good sources of potassium.*

Vitamins at a Glance

Vitamin	Source	Function
Vitamin A	Yellow and dark green vegetables: carrots, sweet potatoes, broccoli, and spinach	Builds good vision, healthy teeth and gums, and strong bones
Vitamin B thiamine (B_1) riboflavin (B_2) niacin	Milk products, meats, breads, and cereals	Helps nerve and brain tissue to work well; aids in digestion
Vitamin C (ascorbic acid)	Fruits: citrus fruits (such as oranges and grapefruits), strawberries, cantaloupe. Vegetables: broccoli, raw cabbage, and turnip greens	Helps body build cells—important in healing cuts and bruises; helps form strong teeth and gums
Vitamin D	Your body makes it and it is in many milk products	Helps you use minerals like calcium and phosphorus; forms bones and teeth
Vitamin E	Vegetable oils as well as foods such as grains, nuts, and green leafy vegetables	Helps keep red blood cells healthy
Vitamin K	Vegetables like broccoli and cauliflower	Helps blood to clot

Minerals

Minerals are simple substances that form parts of many tissues and are needed to keep body processes operating smoothly. Your body contains large amounts of some minerals and tiny quantities of others. All are vital to your health.

Calcium and Phosphorus

Calcium and phosphorus work together in the body as a team. They are essential for building and maintaining strong bones and teeth. Both help keep the nervous system working properly.

Calcium also helps normal growth to take place and keeps muscles healthy. It must always be present in the blood so that your heart beats regularly and blood clots normally.

Although calcium is found in many foods, it is not uncommon for teens to take in too little calcium. This is particularly true of girls, who need more calcium than boys.

A condition known as osteoporosis can develop later in life if you skimp on calcium foods when you are young. When osteoporosis occurs, bones lose their density and become brittle. Such bones are much more likely to fracture. Osteoporosis is a special problem for older people, especially women. However, by taking in enough calcium throughout your life and exercising regularly, you can help to prevent osteoporosis.

Emphasize Calcium is a mineral that is needed throughout life, not just by young children. Calcium, along with phosphorus, is necessary for the growth, hardening, and repair of bones. Both minerals are stored in the bones for use by the body. If a person's diet is deficient in these minerals, the body takes away some of the mineral supply in the bones to provide the minerals to the nerves, muscles, and blood. This weakens the skeleton and increases the chances of bone fractures.

Did You Know? People with osteoporosis are very susceptable to hip fractures and compression of the spine, causing a curvature of the spine and loss of height.

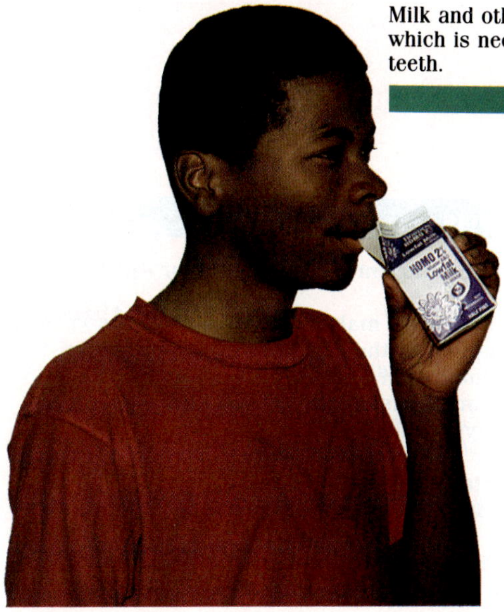

Milk and other dairy products provide calcium, which is needed for building strong bones and teeth.

Dairy products such as milk, cheese, and yogurt are the best sources of calcium. Dark green leafy vegetables and canned fish with soft bones (such as sardines and salmon) provide calcium also.

Phosphorus also helps the body use other nutrients. Good sources of phosphorus are milk, cheese, yogurt, meats, fish, poultry, and whole-grain breads and cereals.

Iron

Iron is vital for building red blood cells. When people do not get enough iron, they develop anemia—their blood cannot carry enough oxygen, causing a lack of energy and low resistance to infections. Liver, spinach, and raisins are good sources of iron.

Sodium

Sodium—found in table salt—plays an important part in controlling the movement of water in your body. Too much of it can disrupt the system, leading to high blood pressure and swelling of the hands and feet.

Unfortunately, sodium is widely used in processed food; not only chips and pretzels but even canned soups, catsup, and soft drinks. People often use extra salt to flavor their food, but today many individuals are cutting down on their sodium intake. See "Kicking the Salt Habit" on page 359.

Other Minerals

Other important minerals include potassium, magnesium, zinc, and iodine. Potassium regulates muscle contractions, transmission of nerve signals, and fluid in the cells. Your body may lose potassium when you perspire heavily, exercise strenuously, or become ill. Orange juice and bananas are good sources of potassium.

Magnesium helps the body use proteins and carbohydrates. It also helps regulate the nervous system. Good sources include whole-grain cereals and breads, dried beans, and green leafy vegetables.

Zinc is used to make insulin, which helps the body use glucose. People who eat no meat or eggs may get too little zinc. Iodine, available in iodized salt and seafood, helps the thyroid gland work properly. If the diet lacks iodine, a goiter, or enlarged thyroid gland, may develop.

Activities

Skill Builder: Science
Have students conduct research into the mineral content of various canned and frozen foods in their homes. Suggest that they study labels, then list the minerals, such as calcium, iron, sodium, and phosphorus. Beside each mineral on the list give the name of a product that contains it.

Reteaching
Have students list all the foods mentioned in this section as important sources of minerals. Beside each item on the list, students should write the name of the mineral that food contains.

Enrichment
Have students bring in recipes that use foods high in iron, such as liver and spinach. Suggest that students share their recipes with their friends.

More About Sodium Since sodium is used as a preservative in processed foods, it is present in surprisingly high quantities in such foods as canned soups (900-1,800 mg a cup), cheese (400 mg an ounce), and pickles (1,400 mg in one dill pickle). When looking at labels, consumers should look not only for salt but also for sodium additives like sodium phosphate and sodium nitrate. Another controversial sodium additive, used in many Chinese restaurants, is monosodium glutamate (MSG). See "Kicking the Salt Habit" on page 359.

TEACHING THE CHAPTER

For convenience, the teaching suggestions for this chapter are arranged according to the following lesson topics:

- "Guidelines for Selecting Foods," pages 354-355
- "Meal Patterns," pages 355-357
- "Eating Habits and Your Future," pages 357-358

Teaching "Guidelines for Selecting Foods"

(Pages 354-355)

This section teaches how to use food groups to plan a healthful diet. Dietary guidelines are provided that help students establish healthful eating habits.

Checking Comprehension

✓ From which food group do you need the largest number of servings each day? *The bread, cereal, rice, and pasta group—6–11 servings.*

✓ Why is it important to eat a variety of foods in each food group? *By varying your diet, you're more likely to eat all the nutrients you need.*

✓ How do the guidelines suggest you maintain a healthy weight? *By eating nutritious foods, eating in moderation, and exercising.*

✓ What do foods high in fiber do to keep you healthy? *Fibrous foods, such as fruits, vegetables, and whole-grain products, keep your digestive system in good order.*

✓ Of the seven Dietary Guidelines for a healthful diet, which are "do's" and which are "don'ts"? *Do: Eat a variety of foods; maintain desirable weight; eat foods with adequate starch and fiber. Don't: Eat food containing saturated fats and cholesterol; eat too much sugar; eat too much sodium; drink alcoholic beverages.*

Carl doesn't feel hungry when he first gets up in the morning. He never wants to eat breakfast, but every morning his mother fixes him breakfast anyway. "Eat something!" she always tells him. "You can't do well in school on an empty stomach."

Carl's mother is right. It's very important to eat a good breakfast because breakfast restores your body's energy and nutrient levels after several hours of sleep. Other meals and snacks are important too. Food is the fuel your body uses for energy throughout the day.

To be healthy, you must eat enough foods to meet your body's daily energy needs. Not just any foods will do, however. Your body must get vitamins, minerals, and other essential nutrients. Making the right food choices is a major step toward enjoying a healthy, active life.

Choose healthy snack foods, such as a piece of fruit. Try to avoid snacks that are high in sugar, salt, or fats—usually these are high in calories too.

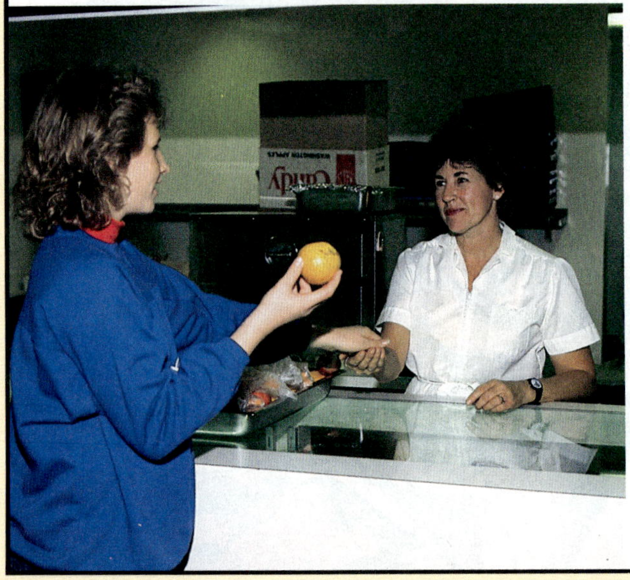

Guidelines for Selecting Foods

In this chapter, you will learn how to select nutritious meals and snacks. Two guidelines—the Food Guide Pyramid and the Dietary Guidelines—can help you make wise choices.

Using the Food Guide Pyramid

In Chapter 37, you learned that the Food Guide Pyramid lists the number and size of servings needed daily for each of the five food groups.

- 6–11 servings from the bread, cereal, rice, and pasta group.
- 3–5 servings of vegetables.
- 2–4 servings of fruits.
- 2–3 servings from the milk, yogurt, and cheese group.
- 2–3 servings from the meats-to-beans group.

Using the Dietary Guidelines

As you have learned, the Food Guide Pyramid is a good way to keep track of the foods you need day by day. In addition, a set of **Dietary Guidelines** has been developed by the United States government. These recommendations for improving your eating habits offer a number of suggestions:

- **Eat a variety of foods.** Most foods contain several nutrients but no food provides all the nutrients in the amounts you need. When choosing foods within a food group, don't limit yourself to only a few foods. For example, if you eat only carrots and green beans from the vegetable group, you will not get all the nutrients you need.

Focus on Health Suggest that students refresh their memories about the five basic food groups and why they form the basis for healthful eating habits. See Chapter 37.

Did You Know? In recent years, people have become aware that eggs are high in cholesterol. On the basis of that information, many people have reduced the number of eggs they eat for breakfast. But it's not the whole egg that is a problem. All of the 274 mg of cholesterol in the egg are in the yolk. The white of an egg has no cholesterol at all.

- **Maintain desirable weight.** Eating nutritious foods and exercising can help you achieve and maintain your ideal weight. Being overweight or underweight can cause health problems (see Chapter 39). Try to always eat in **moderation**—neither too much nor too little.
- **Avoid too much fat, saturated fats, and cholesterol.** These can contribute to high blood pressure and heart disease. Choose lean meats and poultry and trim off excess fat and skin. Switch to low-fat or skim milk, limit the number of eggs you consume to two a week, and broil or bake rather than fry foods.
- **Eat foods with adequate starch and fiber.** Starchy foods, such as potatoes, pasta, and bread provide lots of carbohydrates for energy. Fibrous foods, such as fruits, vegetables, and whole-grain products, keep your digestive system in good order.
- **Avoid too much sugar.** Sugar can lead to cavities in your teeth and weight gain. Eat less sugar, honey, syrup, and foods that contain sugar. Read food labels for ingredients such as sucrose, glucose, maltose, dextrose, lactose, fructose, and syrups.
- **Avoid too much sodium.** Too much salt contributes to high blood pressure. Don't add extra salt to food, and limit the amount of salty foods and snacks that you eat.
- **Avoid alcoholic beverages.** Drinking alcoholic beverages is illegal for young people. Alcoholic drinks are high in calories and provide few nutrients—they are part of the "others" group. More important, alcohol can cause serious health problems. Also, pregnant women who drink alcohol can harm their baby's health.

Meal Patterns

What you eat affects your health, and how you eat does, too. Do you often eat on the run, or skip breakfast, or eat lots of snack foods instead of regular meals? These and other eating habits are likely to affect your energy and fitness.

Mealtimes should be relaxed. They should give you a chance to unwind and enjoy time with your family and friends. You should be able to eat slowly, enjoy the taste of your food, and digest it comfortably. Slow eating allows time for your stomach to sense that it's full. If you eat too fast, you often eat more than you really need.

Families follow different meal patterns. Some eat breakfast followed by a light lunch and a large dinner. Others have their main meal at midday and eat a light supper in the evening. No matter what pattern your family follows, stick to a regular schedule of meals and snacks. Your body can then prepare itself to digest meals at specific times. If you miss one of these regular meals, it disturbs your system.

Any food is fine for breakfast as long as it's nutritious. Some people prefer traditional breakfast foods, such as milk and cereal, while others enjoy a sandwich.

✓ Compare the problems resulting from eating too much salt, sugar, and saturated fats and cholesterol. *Too much salt can result in high blood pressure; too much sugar can lead to weight gain and cavities; too much saturated fat and cholesterol may contribute to heart disease, and high blood pressure.*

Activities

Skill Builder: Writing
Have students analyze the Dietary Guidelines as they apply to their lives. They should write a paragraph for each of the seven guidelines in which they describe whether or not they adhere to the guideline's recommendations. They should also explain what improvements they should make based on each guideline.

Skill Builder: Science
Have students study the process by which sugar causes tooth decay and then draw a diagram to illustrate this process.

Reteaching
With students, look at the weekly menu of the school cafeteria. Then have students construct a bar graph to show the number of servings from each of the five food groups.

Enrichment
Ask students to design a poster to promote and illustrate the Dietary Guidelines. Suggest that the less artistic students use pictures cut from magazines as illustrations.

Teaching "Meal Patterns"
(Pages 355-357)

This section teaches that following a regular meal pattern is important for good health. It offers some suggestions for what to eat at breakfast, lunch, and dinner, as well as for snacks and when eating out.

Checking Comprehension

✓ Why is it important to eat slowly? *Eating slowly enables you to enjoy the taste of the food and digest it comfortably, and it allows time for your stomach to sense that it is full.*

Emphasize Point out that the easiest way to make a dietary change may be gradually. Use whole milk with skim for a while instead of switching from whole to skim all at once. Reduce salt used in cooking, then at the table.

Cross-Reference See Chapter 3 for information about alcohol abuse.

Did You Know? Point out that the word *breakfast* indicates the purpose of the meal—to *break* the *fast* (period without eating) that we all undergo while we sleep at night.

Cross-Reference See Teen Tips "Breakfast On-the-Run" pages 492-493.

✔ Why is a regular meal schedule important? *It helps your body prepare itself to digest meals at specific times.*

✔ Why is breakfast a particularly important meal? *Because you have not eaten for many hours and because carbohydrates and water-soluble vitamins, which are not stored in the body, must be replaced every day.*

✔ What can you have for breakfast instead of bacon and eggs? *You could have a cheese sandwich, soup, yogurt, a piece of chicken, or peanut butter on toast for breakfast.*

✔ Why are you hungry at midday? *By midday, your body has used up much of the energy it gained from breakfast.*

✔ Compare your energy requirements for dinner with those of your other meals. *Your energy requirements for dinner are not as great as they are for lunch and breakfast, since, at dinnertime, the day's activities are generally over.*

✔ What are the three guidelines for snacking? *Don't snack too close to a meal, choose snacks from the five basic food groups, and consider snacks as a part of your total daily intake.*

✔ How can you avoid junk foods as snacks and at fast-food restaurants? *Be creative with snack ideas and choose a food with more nutrients and less sugar, salt, and fats. At a fast-food restaurant, choose the salad bar, pizza, tacos, or broiled rather than fried foods.*

✔ How can you avoid fats and oils if you're eating fried chicken? *If you order fried chicken, remove the skin and breading and eat only the meat.*

✔ What beverages should you choose, and which ones should you avoid when eating out? *Drink milk and fruit juice and avoid milk shakes and soft drinks, which are loaded with calories.*

Breakfast

The day's first meal is particularly important because you have not eaten for many hours. Carbohydrates and water-soluble vitamins are not stored in the body—they must be replaced every day. A good breakfast will restore these nutrients and energize you for the day ahead.

You don't have to limit your food choices only to breakfast foods. Instead of cereal and milk or bacon and eggs, you could have a cheese sandwich, soup, yogurt, a piece of chicken, or peanut butter on toast.

Lunch

By midday, your body has used up much of the energy it gained from breakfast. You need a healthy lunch to keep going through the rest of the school day. Whether you pack your own lunch or purchase lunch at the school cafeteria, make sure that it has servings from the five food groups.

A good lunch could include a sandwich made with meat, cheese, or peanut butter on whole-grain bread; carrot sticks; a piece of fruit; and a container of milk. What do you usually eat for lunch?

Dinner

Dinner allows you to eat the remaining number of servings you need from the five food groups. You should not skip dinner. However, it is not necessary to make it the largest meal of the day, since most of your day's activities are behind you.

Snacks

As a growing teen, you may find you get hungry between meals. Snacks can provide quick energy and help satisfy your hunger until the next meal. Here are some guidelines:

- Snack midway between meals. If you snack too close to a meal—you'll spoil your appetite.
- Choose snacks from the five basic food groups; avoid foods in the "other" group like chips and candy.
- Remember that snacks are part of your total daily food intake—consider serving size and calories.

Be creative with snack ideas. Alternatives to junk food can give you more nutrients and less sugar, salt, and fats. If you have missed one of your food-group servings, you can make up for it with a snack. Try:

- A fresh apple, orange, or banana.
- Plain yogurt with fresh fruit.
- Celery sticks with peanut butter or cream cheese.
- Whole-grain cookies, breads, and muffins.
- Raw vegetables with a yogurt dip.
- Plain, unsalted popcorn.
- Dry-roasted, unsalted nuts.
- Ice milk.
- Pizza.

Eating Out

Most restaurant menus make it possible for you to select healthy foods while eating out. To avoid excess fat, choose an **entrée** (AHN-tray), or main dish, that is broiled or baked rather than fried. Order side dishes such as a baked potato and tossed salad instead of french fries. Choose fresh fruit for dessert.

Cross-Reference See Teen Tips "50 Snacks under 75 Calories" on pages 490-491 and "Fast Foods: Cutting the Calories" on pages 494-495 for additional information about food choices.

More About Eating Out Many restaurants are responding to people's desire to eat healthfully by providing special menu offerings that are low in salt, fats, and calories. The American Heart Association has worked with restaurants to make these healthful choices available to diners around the country.

A salad bar can be a low-calorie, low-fat alternative to many fast foods. Which salad bar items give the most nutrition for the fewest calories?

With care, you can eat nutritious foods at fast-food restaurants also. Pizza and tacos include foods from three and often all four food groups. Broiled hamburgers have less fat and calories than fried ones. If you order fried chicken, remove the skin and breading and eat only the meat.

Some fast-food restaurants offer a salad bar where you can make your own salad. Choose fresh salad greens and vegetables—macaroni and potato salads are much higher in calories. Go lightly on the salad dressing.

Choice of beverage in a restaurant is also important. Milk shakes and soft drinks are loaded with calories; fruit juice and milk have greater nutrient density.

Eating Habits and Your Future

If you regularly eat fewer than the required number of servings in each group, you run the risk of becoming malnourished. A **malnourished** person is not getting enough of the nutrients essential for growth and development. Get into the habit of thinking about what you eat each day. Are you getting the number of servings that you need from each food group?

Your food needs as a teen are greater than at any other point in your life. You are more active than many adults and, more important, you are still growing. Growth requires extra energy, as well as nutrients to build body tissue.

Infants obtain most of the energy and nutrients they need from milk. As they are introduced to solid foods, they must get nutritious meals and snacks. During

More About Changing Nutritional Needs In addition to changing needs in amounts of food, our nutritional needs change as we grow. Children and teens need higher amounts of calcium and protein for growing bones. Women need more iron than men because of a monthly loss of iron during menstruation.

Real-Life Situations Surprisingly, many people are malnourished. Some are poor and are unable to buy enough food for a nutritious diet. Others eat too much of the wrong kinds of food—and may actually be overweight, though malnourished.

Activities

Skill Builder: Math
Have students keep track of their mealtimes for a week and prepare a table showing the times that they ate each meal. Then have them study the table to see where the greatest irregularity occurred. Ask volunteers to suggest reasons that some meals occur less regularly than others and then suggest ways of making mealtimes more regular.

Skill Builder: Critical Thinking
Have students bring in restaurant menus and practice choosing healthful foods from them. Students should be prepared to explain their choices and tell why they are nutritious. Ask students to think about special requests they might make while ordering that would make their choices even more healthful (for example, hold the dressing, broil instead of fry).

Reteaching
Point out that brunch is a combination of breakfast and lunch, usually served from 10:00 a.m. to 1:00 p.m. Have students discuss the kinds of food that could be served as part of a healthful brunch.

Enrichment
Have students try some of the healthful snacks suggested in this section and identify the food groups they belong to.

Teaching "Eating Habits and Your Future"
(Pages 357-358)

This section teaches how people's nutritional needs change as they grow.

Checking Comprehension

✓ Why do teens need more food than other age groups? *Because teens are more active than many adults, but, more important, teens are still growing.*

✓ Compare the nutritional requirements of infants, teens, and adults. *Infants can get most of the energy and nutrients they need from milk, teens require extra nutrients and energy, adults need fewer calories than teens.*

✓ Why does a construction worker need more food than an office worker of the same age and size? *A construction worker is more active than an office worker and needs more calories.*

✓ Why is good nutrition important for a pregnant woman? *Because the baby relies on her for all nutrients; as the baby grows and develops, the woman's need for nutrients increases.*

Activities

Skill Builder: Reading
Ask students to review RDA tables in the back of their books to see how dietary needs change in different age groups.

Skill Builder: Math
Have students use the RDA tables in the back of their books to determine the approximate number of calories required at different stages of life and in different circumstances (pregnancy, and so on). Ask students to chart those calorie requirements.

Skill Builder: Critical Thinking
Since it is important for people to learn good eating habits when they are young, ask students to suggest ways we can educate young children about the importance of eating nutritiously.

Reteaching
Have students discuss the eating habits they developed when they were young and how they've changed as they've grown.

Enrichment
Ask students to plan a daily menu for a toddler, including nutritious meals and snacks that would be appealing to a three- or four-year-old and that would meet nutritional needs.

the toddler, preschool, and elementary school years, children develop their eating habits. It is important for them to learn to eat a variety of foods, to eat regularly, and not to overeat.

Adults, whose growth has ended, usually need fewer calories than teens. If they continue to eat the same amount of food as they did while they were still growing, they will probably gain weight. The amount of food adults require depends on their age, body size, and how active they are. For example, a construction worker will need more food than an office worker of the same age and size.

Good eating habits are especially important when a woman is pregnant and if she is nursing her baby. Her need for nutrients increases as the baby grows and develops. She should get some extra protein and additional servings from the milk-milk products group. Poor nutrition during pregnancy, as well as the use of tobacco and alcohol, affect the health of both the mother and the child.

Older adults continue to need well-balanced diets. They should choose nutrient-rich foods and snacks to maintain their health and avoid weight gain. Good nutrition and exercise are essential for a long and healthy life.

A pregnant woman needs to increase her daily servings of some food groups—especially milk-milk products and meats-to-beans. She also needs an additional 300 calories per day.

Emphasize A pregnant woman should eat balanced, nutritious meals and avoid the use of alcohol, tobacco, and drugs to help prevent health problems for herself or her child. See "Caring for the Unborn" on page 222.

Cross-Reference See Teen Tips "Tidbits Toddlers Love to Eat" on pages 234-235.

Focus on Relationship Skills Toddlers and preschoolers tend to be picky eaters. Their interest in food decreases, and they often refuse to eat. Forcing a child to eat usually doesn't work and creates very unpleasant mealtime scenes. Think about ways that you can persuade a child to eat, or arrange mealtimes to minimize conflict while ensuring a healthful diet for the child.

HEALTH WATCH

Kicking the Salt Habit

Salt was very precious in ancient times because it was difficult to mine and transport. The ancient Chinese used it as money, and the word "salary" comes from "salarium," the salt allowance given to Roman soldiers as part of their pay.

Salt is no longer so rare or precious. In fact, it is by far the most common additive in our diet. Our bodies must have some salt, but most Americans consume two to four teaspoons (10 to 20 mL) every day—more than 20 times more than they actually need!

Common table salt is the chemical sodium chloride. The sodium it provides works with potassium from other foods to control movement of fluids and nutrients in your body. However, too much of a good thing can be dangerous. Overuse of salt leads to high blood pressure, which can contribute to heart disease, strokes, and kidney failure.

Start now, in your teen years, to prevent these often fatal diseases from striking you. Cut down on obviously salty foods like potato chips, pretzels, and crackers. Go easy on pickled foods, cured meat, and sausage, all of which contain a lot of salt. When you shop for groceries, study the nutritional information on the package or can. Avoid foods that show high levels of sodium (Na), sodium propionate, sodium bicarbonate, soda, or monosodium glutamate (MSG). These are all forms of salt that your body probably doesn't need.

In addition, you could look for alternative, safe flavor enhancers. You can use herbs and seasonings instead of salt to make favorite foods more appetizing.

Think It Through

1. **What are your favorite fast foods? Why? What can you do to reduce the amount of salt you take in from eating fast foods?**
2. **What are your favorite convenience foods? How can you find out how much salt they contain? What foods could you substitute for the salty convenience foods you like?**

Substitute Flavor Enhancers

Food	Seasoning
Baked potato	Basil, Thyme, Oregano, Paprika
French fries	Vinegar
Salad greens	Basil, Chives, Dill, Tarragon
Tomato	Basil, Celery seed, Oregano, Sage, Thyme
Meat roasts	Pepper, Paprika, Thyme, Garlic, Parsley
Fish, seafood	Vinegar, Lemon juice, Thyme, Oregano, Parsley

Teaching the Feature
"Kicking the Salt Habit"

Answers to Feature Questions

1. Answers will vary. Students may say they shouldn't use salt shakers or packets on fast foods; they could ask for unsalted fries; they could remove the breading and skin from fried chicken; they could switch to other less salty fast foods, such as salads or roast beef sandwiches; they could cut down on the amount of fast foods they eat every week.

2. Answers will vary. Students should read the labels on convenience foods and try to choose foods with less salt. Some companies put out lines of low-sodium soups, lunch meats, and other products that they could purchase instead of their high-sodium counterparts. They could try to cut down on the use of convenience foods and switch to fresh foods instead.

Activities

Substitute Flavor Enhancers Have students try (or at least smell) some of the flavor enhancers mentioned in this feature to see that there are alternatives to salt and pepper. Ask students to add to the list any flavor enhancers their family uses in place of salt (such as grated cheese.)

Community Contact Have students meet with the school administration or cafeteria staff to talk about reducing the amount of salt in the school lunches. As a radical measure, talk about the possibility of removing all salt shakers from the cafeteria on a trial basis.

Did You Know? Point out to students that the ingredients are listed on food labels in the order of amount contained in the food. The substance present in the greatest amount is listed first, and so on, in descending order. So if salt is one of the first ingredients listed, you know the food is salty.

Focus on Life Management To evaluate your salt intake, shake the salt shaker onto a paper towel instead of your food for one meal and then measure how much salt you would have consumed.

COMPLETING THE CHAPTER

Summary

- The easiest way to select healthful foods is to use the five basic food groups.
- The U.S. Department of Agriculture has suggested that people eat a variety of foods; maintain a healthful weight; eat foods with enough starch and fiber; avoid fats, sugar, and sodium, and avoid alcoholic beverages.
- Establishing regular meal patterns is an important part of healthful eating.
- Eating snacks and eating out can be part of a healthful lifestyle if nutritional choices are made.
- Good eating habits should be developed at a young age and carried through a whole lifetime.

For Review

Objective Review Questions Have students complete the "Reviewing the Facts" section on this page.

Study Guide Have students complete the Study Guide from Chapter 38 of their *Student Workbook.*

Personal Evaluation It takes a concerted effort to change eating habits. Have students begin by making one or two resolutions that will get them on the road to healthful eating.

Class Discussion Have students discuss the dilemmas that new products create for consumers. They should consider the proliferation of convenience foods, microwave foods, artificially sweetened products, and so on.

For Evaluation

List Have students list ten "do's" and ten "don'ts" that will help people establish healthful eating habits.

Chapter Test Have students complete the test for Chapter 38 that appears in the *Teacher's Classroom Resources.*

CHAPTER 38 REVIEW

Answers to "Reviewing the Facts"

1. Eat a variety of foods; maintain desirable weight; avoid too much fat, saturated fats, and cholesterol; eat foods with adequate starch and fiber; avoid too much sugar; avoid too much sodium; avoid alcoholic beverages.
2. Because no food provides all the nutrients in the amounts you need.
3. Any three: choose lean meats and poultry; trim off fat and skin; switch to low-fat or skim milk; limit the number of eggs; broil or bake rather than fry foods.
4. For energy and good digestion.
5. To give you time to digest your food, enjoy the taste, and feel full.
6. Carbohydrates and water-soluble vitamins are not stored in the body and must be replaced daily.
7. Provide quick energy; satisfy hunger between meals; supply some of your food-group servings.

Reviewing the Facts

1. List the seven Dietary Guidelines.
2. Why should you eat a variety of foods?
3. What are three ways you can reduce saturated fats and cholesterol in your diet?
4. Why do you need to eat starchy and fibrous foods?
5. Why is it important to eat slowly?
6. How can eating breakfast help you meet your body's daily nutritional needs?
7. What benefits can snacks provide?

Thinking Critically

1. Your parent has to leave very early tomorrow morning, and you will have to get your younger brother or sister off to school. Plan a breakfast that will energize you both for the day. Why did you choose these foods?
2. Describe your regular routine for eating meals. Is it a healthy routine, based on what you now know? How can you improve it?

Applying Your Skills

1. Examining Your Eating Habits. Keep a diary in which you list all the foods you eat each day for a week. (If you did this in Chapter 35, use the record you made then.) Determine from the diary how many servings you chose each day from each of the five food groups. Did you choose the correct servings, or did you choose more from one food group and less from the others? Did you eat a lot of foods that contain saturated fats, salt, and sugar? Write a brief report explaining how you plan to correct any bad eating habits.

2. Planning a Course of Action. Use the five basic food groups and the Dietary Guidelines to plan nutritious and varied meals for a week. Consult cookbooks and nutrition books to help you plan your meals.

3. Graphing Information. Use a line graph to demonstrate the number and size of servings needed daily for each of the five food groups. On the same graph, chart your food intake for one day. Compare the positions of the lines. What does this tell you about your eating habits?

Answers to "Thinking Critically"

1. Answers will vary. Some examples might be fresh fruit or fruit juice followed by cereal and milk, soup, sandwich, left-over meat or pizza, yogurt or cheese, blender drink, peanut butter, whole-grain muffin, bagel, and so on. They should also have a glass of milk.
2. Answers will vary. Some may eat on the run; others might sit down with their family for breakfast or dinner. Unless the students answer that they eat slowly and have well-balanced meals, they are not following a healthy routine. They should allow more time for meals, and follow the Food Guide Pyramid and the Dietary Guidelines.

CHAPTER

39

Weight Control

OBJECTIVES

This chapter will help you to:

- Explain the relationship between fitness, basal metabolism, and weight control.
- Compare reasons for going on a weight-loss or weight-gain diet.
- Define and describe two serious eating disorders.
- Evaluate different approaches to weight control.

WORDS TO REMEMBER

anorexia nervosa
basal metabolism
bulimia
dieting

Chapter Resources

Teacher's Classroom Resources
- Lesson Plan
- Life Skills Activity, *Food Is the Media's Mixed Message*
- Reproducible Master, *Calories Burned in Various Activities*
- Extension Activity, *Why Do People Overeat?*
- Chapter Test

Student Workbook
- Study Guide
- Worksheet, *Diet Information—or Misinformation*

CHAPTER OVERVIEW

Chapter 39 discusses weight and fitness. It encourages students to take responsibility for maintaining a healthful weight by controlling diet and exercising. It helps students determine their ideal weight and see how the food they eat and the amount of exercise they get can be adjusted to allow for weight gain or loss. Students are also made aware of eating disorders, such as anorexia nervosa and bulimia, and are encouraged to avoid crash diets.

INTRODUCING THE CHAPTER

Motivators

Good Bodies Have students talk about celebrities (TV and movie stars, athletes, politicians) they think have good bodies. Have them discuss how these people maintain their bodies and if it is realistic for "regular" people to aspire to good bodies like these.

Using the Photograph Have students study the photograph on this page. Then ask: "What are these people doing? What do you notice about their weight? What, do you think, is the purpose of this photograph?"

Personal Evaluation As an exercise in self-awareness, ask students to write a brief evaluation of their own weight and fitness level. They need not share that evaluation with others.

Introducing the Objectives

Discuss the chapter objectives on this page. Remind students that the objectives focus on important chapter content.

Introducing Vocabulary

Point out to students that *anorexia* comes from the Greek: *an-* means "without" and *orexis* means "appetite." The term *bulimia* also comes from Greek: *bous* means "ox" and *limos* means "hunger"; this applies because bulimics demonstrate an enormous appetite when overeating.

TEACHING THE CHAPTER

For convenience, the teaching suggestions for this chapter are arranged according to the following lesson topics:

- "Weight and Fitness," pages 362-363
- "What Affects Your Weight?" pages 363-364
- "Changing Your Weight," pages 364-367
- "Changing Your Habits," page 367

Teaching "Weight and Fitness"
(Pages 362-363)

This section teaches how weight relates to diet and fitness and explains how to determine ideal weight.

Checking Comprehension

✓ Why are many athletes relatively heavier than other people? *Because they have less fat and more muscle than other people and muscle is heavier than fat.*

✓ Compare expectations of ideal weight for people with large and small body frames. *People with larger body frames should expect to be heavier.*

✓ Why might family background have an effect on weight? *Scientists believe that a tendency toward being thin or being overweight may be inherited.*

✓ What do weight charts show? *Weight charts show ideal weights for males and females of different heights, ages, and body frame types.*

✓ What are the best ways for you to determine your ideal weight? *Judge by how you feel; ask others; consult your family doctor.*

Activities

Skill Builder: Science
Have students investigate how the amount of body fat and the muscle mass of a person can be measured. Then ask the students to discuss their findings.

Have you ever gazed in a mirror, wishing you were as slim as the model on the cover of your favorite magazine? Do you sometimes flex your arm muscles in secret, imagining they are stronger and heftier?

Comparing your appearance with others is a normal part of adolescence. Often, however, those "others" are models, actors and actresses, or athletes who spend a lot of time and money maintaining their weight and appearance. Concern about looking perfect can cost you time and cause you dissatisfaction. Also, it distracts you from a more important issue—weight as it relates to fitness.

Weight and Fitness

In Chapter 35, you read about the importance of being fit. Fitness makes you feel good and look your best. It gives you strength, endurance, and flexibility, and it helps promote high self-esteem.

Your weight is affected by the same two things that influence your fitness—the foods you eat and the exercise you get. With the right mix of nutritious foods and exercise, people can achieve and maintain a healthy weight.

Individual Differences

Healthy weights differ for different people, however. Many athletes have less fat and more muscle than other people. This makes them relatively heavier because muscle is heavier than fat. However, other people may *look* heavier, because their bodies have a little more fat.

Your ideal weight is dependent on different factors, such as your age, height, bone structure, and muscular development.

Cross-Reference Suggest that students reread the sections on fitness in Chapter 35 for information about specific kinds of exercise programs.

More About Individual Differences It has been argued that we are born with body types that predispose us to fatness or leanness. A scientist named Sheldon grouped people into three body types: endomorphs, mesomorphs, and ectomorphs. An endomorph is round and soft; the mesomorph has heavy bones and muscles; and the ectomorph is slight and has fine bones. Endomorphs are more likely to gain weight than are ecotmorphs.

Physical activity isn't the only factor that affects a person's ideal weight. Several other things make a difference:

- Your age, sex, and height affect your weight. In general, adults weigh more than teens, and men weigh more than women of the same height. The taller a person, the more he or she can weigh.
- Bone structure also makes a difference. People with larger body frames should expect to be heavier. You can judge the size of your frame by looking at your wrist. If it is slimmer than most people your age, sex, and height, you have a small frame. If it is sturdier you have a large frame.
- Your heredity may affect your ideal weight. Scientists believe that a tendency toward being thin or being overweight may be inherited.

An Ideal Weight for You

If people are so different, how can you decide how much you should weigh? One clue is how you feel. If you feel mentally and physically good most of the time, you may be at your ideal weight. Other clues include how your family and friends evaluate your appearance.

You can consult charts and graphs showing ideal weights for males and females of different heights, ages, and body-frame types. However, the best way is to talk to your family doctor.

What Affects Your Weight?

To maintain your ideal weight, the food you eat should supply exactly the right amount of energy to meet your needs. Several factors are involved in this balance: basal metabolism, exercise, food, and calories.

Basal Metabolism

Your **basal metabolism** (BAY-sul muh-TAB-uh-liz-uhm) means all the automatic functions of your body, including breathing, tissue repair, blood circulation, and growth. It consumes well over half the energy most people use up in a day—more than they use for exercise and other activities.

The energy used for basal metabolism differs for different people. Do you eat a lot of food and yet not gain any weight? This could mean that your basal metabolism uses energy at a high rate. Other people have smaller food needs, because their metabolisms are lower.

Your activity level also affects your metabolism. After vigorous exercise, your body continues to use up more energy, even when you are resting. The

Exercise will help you firm up, look good, and have more energy.

More About Basal Metabolism Basal metabolism is determined by a type of measurement called calorimetry. This measures the amount of oxygen breathed into the lungs and the carbon dioxide breathed out to determine the number of calories burned within the body. The measurement is taken when the individual is lying absolutely still, in a comfortable temperature, 12 hours after the last meal.

Reteaching
Have students consult a weight chart to see how weight is affected by the factors of sex, age, height, and body frame.

Enrichment
Ask students to compare their body frame and weight with those of other people in their extended family (grandparents, parents, cousins, siblings). Have them list similarities and inherited characteristics.

Teaching "What Affects Your Weight?"
(Pages 363-364)

This section explains how basal metabolism differs among people and how it affects weight.

Checking Comprehension

✔ What is basal metabolism? *Basal metabolism means all the automatic functions of your body, including breathing, tissue repair, blood circulation, and growth.*

✔ Compare the food needs of a person with a high metabolism to a person with lower metabolism. *A person with a high metabolism needs more food than a person with a lower metabolism.*

✔ How does activity level affect metabolism? *After energetic activity, your body continues to use up more energy, even when you are resting. The more exercise you get the higher is your basal metabolism.*

✔ When and why does the "starvation reflex" occur? *It occurs as the body adapts to having fewer total calories to burn. Your metabolism slows down and your body loses weight more slowly.*

✔ If you increase your exercise, what must you do if you want to maintain the same weight? *You must eat more food.*

Activities

Skill Builder: Math
Have students use the calorie chart in the Appendix to count the calories they consumed yesterday. Then have students compare their calories with those of others in the class.

Skill Builder: Critical Thinking
Have students assess their metabolic rates. Would they characterize them as fast or slow? Is their metabolism similar to that of other people in their families?

Reteaching
Have students reread this section and then list the factors mentioned that affect an individual's weight.

Enrichment
The text suggests that people instinctively adjust food intake to match exercise. Have students discuss whether their own experience seems to support this idea.

Teaching "Changing Your Weight"
(Pages 364-367)

This section teaches how to develop new exercise and eating habits to lose or gain weight. It also discusses anorexia nervosa and bulimia.

Checking Comprehension

✓ Why is developing new exercise and eating habits an important part of weight change? *Current habits have resulted in overweight or underweight. If habits are not changed, pounds can creep back.*

✓ What is the relationship between stress and weight? *Stress may cause overeating in some people and loss of appetite in others.*

✓ What does an effective weight-loss diet do? *It cuts the amount of calories in the foods you eat to fewer than the calories your body is using.*

more exercise you get, the higher is your metabolism. On the other hand, when people are starving their metabolism becomes lower. This "starvation reflex" occurs as the body adapts to having fewer calories to burn. It helps explain why some people have difficulty losing weight.

Exercise, Food, and Calorie Balance

Besides your basal metabolism, your weight is affected by the exercise you get and the food you eat. To maintain your weight, the calories your body burns up must equal the calories in the food you eat. If you increase your exercise, you will need to eat more to stay the same weight. If you get less exercise, you will need to eat less. Fortunately, most people instinctively adjust food intake to match their exercise, so their bodies maintain their weight.

Calories Burned in Various Activities

Activity	Calories burned per hour
Basketball	360–660
Bicycling (5 mph)	240
(10 mph)	420
Dancing, fast	240–360
Soccer	600
Housework, light	240–300
Karate and judo	700
Mowing lawn (hand mower)	450
Reading	125
Running (5 mph)	600
(8 mph)	1020
Swimming, most strokes	360–750
Table tennis	300–420
Walking, leisurely	300
Watching TV	125

Changing Your Weight

It may be, however, that you need to change your weight. An important part of adjusting—and then maintaining—your weight is developing new exercise and eating habits. Your present habits have resulted in your becoming overweight or underweight, so changing those habits is the way to reach your new goal. However, if you plan to lose or gain more than a few pounds, consult your doctor first.

The Importance of Exercise

Whether you plan to lose or gain weight, exercise should play an important part in any weight-change program. Exercise will make your body more fit. It will also help you to deal with stress, which causes overeating in some people and loss of appetite in others. Finally, exercise can provide the satisfaction of knowing that you are taking good care of yourself. All of these are pluses whether you are seeking weight loss or weight gain.

Dieting to Lose Weight

If you increase the exercise you are doing, you may find that changing your eating habits isn't necessary. Your body will use up more calories—perhaps enough to result in a weight loss. The chart on this page indicates how many calories are burned per hour in various activities.

Weight loss can also be helped by **dieting**, which means controlling your food intake for a specific purpose. An effective weight-loss diet cuts the amount of calories in the foods you eat to below the calories your body is using.

Did You Know? Consider these facts when planning your diet:

- Eating fewer than 800 calories a day can be dangerous.
- It takes 3,500 calories above the number of calories required for basic activity to form one pound of fat. In contrast, it takes 3,500 fewer calories to lose one pound.
- Dieting slows the body down, lowering the metabolic rate as the body adjusts to less food. Exercise can raise the metabolic rate and increase weight loss.

Cross-Reference See Teen Tips "50 Snacks Under 75 Calories" on pages 490-491, and "Fast Foods: Cutting the Calories" on pages 494-495.

HEALTH WATCH

Fad Diets Aren't Worth Their Weight

"I lost 45 pounds in two months, and I kept the weight off." "With these pills, I wasn't hungry between meals." Do these lines sound familiar? They come from advertisements for popular fad diets. These diets are often seen in books and magazines.

People follow fad diets because they believe the diets will help them lose weight or make them healthier. In reality, most such diets fail to accomplish either goal. They sometimes even cause serious illness.

Crash diets are diets that promise quick and easy weight loss. They are almost always dangerous to your health, and usually fail. They encourage bad eating habits because they may exclude one or more food groups.

Some popular diets tell people to eat large amounts of protein, but almost no carbohydrates. People on these diets seem to lose weight—at first—but most of what is lost is water. As soon as the dieter goes back to normal eating, the water weight is regained. If people stay on these diets for a long time, the body even begins to break down muscle to get needed glucose.

Some weight-loss diets are based on the mistaken idea that certain foods, such as grapefruit, help the body burn fat. This is not true, and people on this kind of diet can suffer from weakness, dizziness, low blood pressure, and intestinal upsets.

People may also purchase diet pills or candy to lose weight. These substances are supposed to reduce the appetite, so the dieter eats less. Once dieters go off the pills or candy, they usually regain any weight they lost.

Some advertised diets, however, *are* healthy and effective. You can tell which ones are good by checking if they are based on principles of good nutrition and if the weight loss they promise is slow.

Think It Through

1. **Do you know anyone who is on a popular weight-loss diet? What is the diet called? How successful has it been? What details do you know about the diet? Does it seem nutritionally sound to you?**
2. **There are many fad diets that advertise weight loss, but few that advertise weight gain. Why do you think this is? What is the most common type of weight-gain advertisement?**

Teaching the Feature
"Fad Diets Aren't Worth Their Weight"

Answers to Feature Questions

1. Answers will vary. Students should identify as nutritionally sound only those diets that clearly promote the food-groups concept or equivalent.

2. Answers will vary. Weight loss is a more common concern in the American population, so more money can be made from it. Weight gain is associated more with exercise than eating; muscle building ads are the most common type for weight gain.

Activities

Outrageous Claims Have students collect examples of outrageous claims made by fad diets and discuss why those claims cannot realistically be met. Why do people fall for such claims in the first place? Have students discuss why dieters are such vulnerable targets for fraudulent claims.

Diet Pill Danger Ask students to check out the ingredients of over-the-counter diet pills to determine whether they are safe to use. What dangers do diet pills present, both physically and psychologically?

Community Contact Arrange to have a physician talk to the class about several popular diets. Are they nutritionally sound? Why or why not? What diets would he or she recommend? Why?

Emphasize The more extreme a diet is, the more potentially dangerous it is. The most severe diet regimen is fasting—not eating at all. Although a fast causes weight loss, it may result in death from heart failure.

Did You Know? Overeaters Anonymous is a nonprofit organization modeled after Alcoholics Anonymous. Members admit that they eat compulsively and regard each day as a new challenge to control their eating. Members provide a support group for each other.

What are two ways to cut down on calories? *One way to cut down on calories is to stop eating high-calorie snacks, such as soda and potato chips. Another way is to refer to a calorie chart when choosing foods.*

What does your body need, even when you're dieting? *Your body needs all the nutrients even though you are eating less food.*

How can people who are underweight gain weight? *They should plan meals around foods they like; eat more frequently; try to eat larger portions; and snack on high-calorie, nutritious foods.*

Compare strategies for weight loss with those of weight gain. *Both require patience, change of habits, and effort.*

What should be avoided when gaining weight? *Avoid any solutions, such as steroid drugs, that promise speedy results.*

How does dieting sometimes lead to eating disorders? *Some people become so obsessed with control over their bodies that they resort to drastic measures.*

How do people with bulimia control their weight? *They have sudden bouts of secret overeating, then, out of guilt and fear of gaining weight, they get rid of the food by using laxatives or forcing themselves to vomit.*

Activities

Skill Builder: Critical Thinking
Have students discuss why so many diets (and dieters) fail. How many people do they know who are always on a diet but never lose weight? What do they think are the causes? Ask students if they know people who lose weight but always gain it back. What might be the cause of that?

Skill Builder: Reading
Ask students to use the library to read about anorexia nervosa or bulimia and to prepare a short report for the class.

Here are three important points to consider when trying to lose weight:

- Some people can cut down their calorie intake by no longer eating high-calorie snacks like soft drinks and potato chips. Others find it helpful to refer to a calorie chart when they select foods for meals and snacks.
- Your body needs all the nutrients even though you are eating less food, so stick to the Daily Food Guide and choose foods that are high in nutrients and low in calories. For example, choose lean poultry or fish rather than red meat. Eat fresh fruit for dessert rather than fruit pie.
- Be content to lose weight slowly—one or two pounds per week. Crash diets (see page 365) are hard to stick to and can cause physical problems. Many people who lose weight this way find the pounds creeping back again because they haven't altered their habits. If you slowly adjust your eating and exercise habits as you diet, you will find it easier to maintain your new weight. You'll be able to enjoy some treats, too.

Dieting to Gain Weight

When people are underweight, it may be caused by a variety of reasons. Perhaps mealtimes make them tense. If so, an exercise program may help them to relax and enjoy mealtimes more. They should plan meals around foods they like, eat more frequently, and try to eat larger portions. They can snack on high calorie, nutritious foods such as milk shakes, cheese, and whole-grain sandwiches.

If you are underweight, think whether other parts of your life may be affecting your weight. Are you getting enough sleep? Do you try to do too much every day? If so, try to slow down, and leave yourself enough time for eating and sleeping.

Also, be patient. As with weight loss, rapid weight gain is undesirable and should not be expected. It takes time to build healthy muscle. Avoid any solutions—such as steroid drugs—that promise speedy results. These could be very dangerous to your overall health.

Even though you are dieting, be sure to eat a variety of foods from the four basic food groups. This boy enjoys low-fat cheese and fruit as an after-school snack.

Real-Life Situations The use of steroids is rapidly increasing, especially among athletes at all levels. Anabolic steroids are natural or synthetic testosterone used to promote rapid muscle development. Although some female athletes are suspected of using steroids, its abuse is primarily by young males who desire a large, muscular body build that might enhance their athletic ability and be admired by peers. However the use of steroids is very dangerous as it can cause physical and psychological side effects, such as liver and kidney disorders, temporary acne and baldness, hypertension, decreased sperm count, aggressive behavior, depression, irritability, and even death.

Eating Disorders

Occasionally, some people become so obsessed with control over their bodies that they resort to drastic measures. The result may be anorexia nervosa or bulimia, two serious eating disorders that can cause severe health problems and even death. Most victims of eating disorders are females in their teens or early twenties, though some males are affected too.

- **Anorexia nervosa.** This disorder can result in starvation. Typically, people with **anorexia nervosa** (an-uh-REK-see-uh ner-VOH-suh) believe they are overweight even when they are painfully thin. They force themselves to diet still further, even though parents and friends try to get them to eat more.
- **Bulimia.** People who suffer from **bulimia** (buh-LEE-mee-uh) may be normal weight, but they maintain that weight in a very damaging way. They have sudden bouts of secret overeating, perhaps eating a gallon of ice cream at one time. Then, out of guilt and fear of gaining weight, they get rid of the food by using laxatives or forcing themselves to vomit. Both these methods of losing food are very damaging to the body.

If you recognize your own behavior in one of these descriptions, or if you think that a friend may be anorexic or bulimic, it's important to contact a counselor or doctor. Victims of these disorders can be helped by professional counseling.

Changing Your Habits

For less serious problems with weight control, you can often change your habits by yourself. Willpower is important, but if you focus on weight-control techniques that make you feel good, your goal will be easier to achieve. For example, if you are an individualist, your best form of exercise may be running. If you are sociable and like music, aerobic dancing classes may be more to your liking.

Look for small things about your new diet program that you enjoy. Maybe you've noticed that you like the taste of the food more when you eat slowly. Perhaps the taste of salad without dressing struck you as surprisingly good, particularly if you sharpen it with a little onion or radish. Focus on elements in your weight-control program that give you pleasure—it will make permanent results far more likely.

The most successful method of losing weight is to increase exercise and decrease calorie consumption. Go for a walk, jog, jump rope, or do aerobic exercises.

Focus on Relationship Skills Sometimes the people around a dieter (friends, family, acquaintances) subconsciously sabotage the person's diet. They fear they will "lose" the person if he or she succeeds in losing weight, so they make it harder for the dieter to succeed. Have the students think about this phenomenon and discuss it.

Emphasize Anorexia nervosa affects approxiamtely 1 in 150 to 200 teenage girls. Anorectics tend to be above average in intelligence but have lost any real perception of body size; they cannot see that they are becoming skeletal.

Reteaching
Ask students to think of different ways of completing the phrase, "A wise dieter . . ." Their answers should reflect the content of this section of the chapter. You could start them by giving the example: "A wise dieter loses weight slowly."

Enrichment
Ask students to interview people who are on diets and summarize their diet regimens. Have the students evaluate the plan. Has it been successful so far? Is it healthful? Can the dieter stick to it?

Teaching "Changing Your Habits"
(Page 367)

This section explores attitudes toward dieting that can lead to successful weight loss or gain.

Checking Comprehension

✓ What is an important factor in any program of weight control? *Willpower is important.*

✓ How can you make dieting easier? *If you focus on weight-control techniques that make you feel good, your goal will be easier to achieve.*

Activities

Skill Builder: Critical Thinking
Ask students to think about other circumstances in which willpower is an important ingredient. Have students talk about whether they think they have a lot of willpower and about people whose willpower they admire. Do they think they can acquire more willpower? If so, how?

Reteaching
Ask students to list five positive things about maintaining a healthful program of weight control and fitness.

Enrichment
Encourage students to provide support for friends and family members who are trying to gain or lose weight. Ask them to discuss ways they can make it easier for a friend to stick to a diet.

COMPLETING THE CHAPTER

Summary

- Weight is affected by age, sex, height, bone structure, and also heredity.
- You will feel better if you are fit and maintain your ideal weight.
- Basal metabolism consumes energy for the automatic functions of your body.
- The calories you eat must be balanced with the exercise you get.
- Dieting should be done slowly and without sacrificing nutrition.
- Anorexia nervosa and bulimia are eating disorders that stem from concerns about weight control.
- It is desirable to maintain a positive attitude when changing eating habits.

For Review

Objective Review Questions Have students complete the "Reviewing the Facts" section on this page.

Study Guide Have students complete the Study Guide from Chapter 39 of their *Student Workbook.*

Survey Have students conduct a survey of family and friends to see how many want to lose weight, how many want to gain weight, and how many are satisfied with their weight. Then ask the class to tally up the results and discuss which category has the most and which has the least.

Awareness Campaign Have students make a collage or poster to inform fellow students on the components of healthful dieting or on the symptoms and dangers of eating disorders.

For Evaluation

Assessment Have students summarize a well-known diet plan and evaluate whether it is healthful or not.

Design Have students design a healthful diet and exercise program for weight gain or loss, including hints for the dieter about attitude and individual differences.

Chapter Test Have students complete the test for Chapter 39 that appears in the *Teacher's Classroom Resources.*

CHAPTER 39 REVIEW

Answers to "Reviewing the Facts"

1. Weight and fitness are both affected by the foods people eat and the exercise they get.
2. Age, sex, height, bone structure, and heredity.
3. If you feel good, look good, match recommendations on charts, and your doctor approves.
4. If your basal metabolism is high, you may be able to eat a lot and not gain weight; if it is low, you may have difficulty losing weight.
5. Makes your body more fit; helps you deal with stress which can affect eating; provides satisfaction; uses up calories.
6. Any three: finding a diet that is suited to you; getting the nutrients you need; being content to lose weight slowly; avoiding crash diets.
7. Plan meals around foods you like; eat more frequently; eat larger portions; snack on high-calorie, nutritious foods; exercise to help relax; get enough sleep; slow down; be patient; avoid steroids.
8. Anorexia nervosa—victims think they are overweight, even if they aren't, and diet to lose more weight. Bulimia—victims overeat and then vomit or use laxatives.

Reviewing the Facts

1. What is the relationship between fitness and a healthy, ideal weight?
2. What factors affect a person's ideal weight?
3. Identify some ways you can tell if you are at your ideal weight.
4. What does basal metabolism have to do with weight and weight control?
5. How does exercise contribute to weight control?
6. Describe three important concerns for a weight-loss diet.
7. What are some sound strategies for weight gain?
8. Name and describe two serious eating disorders.

Thinking Critically

1. What aspects of American life can you think of that contribute to people's being overweight? Try to think of at least four.
2. If you had a friend who appeared to have an eating disorder, how might you try to help him or her?

Applying Your Skills

1. **Researching a Topic.** In the library, find three books or magazine articles that describe weight-loss diets. Read the diets carefully, and use your nutrition knowledge to decide how sound each one is. Then write a report on them, including your opinion on how easy it would be for a person such as you to succeed at each diet.
2. **Computing Calories.** Your friend is dieting with your help and advice. In the first week of summer vacation he did a lot of physical work: three hours cleaning house, five mowing lawns, two each day swimming, and riding 20 miles on his bicycle (five mph). With the chart on page 364, figure out how many calories he used. Then use a table of food values to calculate portions of nutritious meals and snacks that total the same number of calories. Write a note to your friend telling him what extra he could eat on his diet, and why.
3. **Promoting a Strategy.** Write a script in which you encourage a friend to lose weight. Suggest healthy ways of losing weight as well as the disadvantages of fad diets.

Answers to "Thinking Critically"

1. Suggestions might include: lack of exercise because of sedentary jobs; excess fat and sugar in the diet; advertising that promotes high-calorie snack foods; habit of driving rather than walking or biking; watching too much television; eating too-large portions at home or in restaurants; and so on.
2. Answers will vary, but students might suggest trying to talk to the friend and explain the nature and danger of eating disorders, talking to a counselor about how to help, or referring the friend to a counselor for guidance.

CHAPTER

40

Planning Meals

OBJECTIVES

This chapter will help you to:

- Explain the main considerations for planning a healthful and appetizing meal.
- Describe five ways in which to make meals appealing.
- Use newspapers, magazines, and cookbooks as planning tools.
- List the types of resources needed to carry out a recipe.
- Develop a shopping list for quick and efficient shopping.

WORDS TO REMEMBER

food preference
ingredient
portion
recipe
staple

Chapter Resources

Teacher's Classroom Resources
- Lesson Plan
- Life Skills Activity, *Pointers from Meal Planners*
- Reproducible Master, *Meal Planning Checklist*
- Extension Activity, *Family Food Spending*
- Chapter Test

Student Workbook
- Study Guide
- Worksheet, *Rate-a-Recipe*

CHAPTER OVERVIEW

Chapter 40 outlines the process of meal planning. The most important considerations in meal planning are nutrition and meal appeal. Meals should represent the five food groups and blend food flavors, colors, shapes, textures, and temperatures. The next step is to choose a recipe from a cookbook, newspaper, magazine, or recipe file. Recipes should be evaluated to see if they are complete and suit the family's needs. The last step is to make a shopping list to be used at the grocery store, listing ingredients as well as staples.

INTRODUCING THE CHAPTER

Motivators

Who Plans the Meals? Have students talk about who usually does the meal planning in their families and what kind of input other family members have.

Using the Photograph Have students study the photograph on this page. Then ask: "What is this person doing? Why is planning like this important?"

A Great Meal Ask students to describe a meal they have really loved and then to try to pinpoint why it had such appeal.

Introducing the Objectives

Discuss the chapter objectives on this page. Remind students that the objectives focus on important chapter content.

Introducing Vocabulary

Point out that the word *recipe* was first used to refer to medical prescriptions because the pharmacist had to combine different ingredients to make the medicine that the doctor prescribed. It is still sometimes used that way, but it is more often used in connection with food preparation.

TEACHING THE CHAPTER

For convenience, the teaching suggestions for this chapter are arranged according to the following lesson topics:

- "Meal Planning Considerations," pages 370-372
- "Sources of Recipes," page 372
- "Choosing a Recipe," pages 372-374
- "Making a Shopping List" and "Keeping Your Plan Flexible," page 374

Teaching "Meal Planning Considerations"

(Pages 370-372)

This section explains the factors that should be considered when planning meals. Nutrition and appeal are the main considerations. Meal appeal is achieved by blending food flavors, colors, shapes, textures, and temperatures.

Checking Comprehension

✓ Why should a meal planner ask if there will be small children or older people at a meal? *Because they may need special foods served at certain times.*

✓ What is the heart of most meals? *The heart of most meals is a combination of proteins and carbohydrates.*

✓ How can the dairy group be included in a meal? *The dairy group could be included as a dessert, as a drink, or even as a topping on the main course.*

✓ Name two successful combinations of flavors. *Sweet flavors can often be paired with savory ones; strong flavors go best with mild ones.*

✓ What are some vegetable combinations that provide color contrast? *Carrots and string beans or tomatoes and spinach.*

✓ Why don't creamed chicken, mashed potatoes, and applesauce make the best combination? *Because they all have almost the same texture.*

In Nick's family, his father takes the main responsibility for meal planning. Each week he looks over the food supply, decides what the family will need for the week, and makes a shopping list. Sometimes Nick or his elder brother shop, but it is his father who determines what they will have each day. He follows a routine—a pot roast on Sunday, cold cuts on Monday, and so on.

At breakfast each morning, Melanie's family discusses what they will eat that night and who will buy the food. When they decide to have fish and vegetables, her father stops at the supermarket. Her mother buys meats at the butcher near where she works; and sometimes Melanie picks up pizza on her way home from school.

Meal planning is a very important step in food preparation. A good plan will ensure that you and your family eat a variety of nutritious meals that taste good and are within the family's budget.

When planning meals, you need to consider many different factors. Explain why this meal would be nutritious and appealing to a young child.

Meal Planning Considerations

If you're like most teens, you are already responsible for preparing some family meals, and may even do so on a regular basis. It should come as no surprise that there are many things to consider such as:

- How many people will be eating?
- What type of meal will it be (breakfast, lunch, dinner)?
- What foods will be included (appetizer, main course, side dishes, desserts, beverages)?
- How much of the family budget can go toward the meal?
- What items must you shop for?
- What time will the meal be served?
- What can be done ahead of time?
- Will anyone be late and need food kept hot?
- Will there be any small children or other family members who need special foods served at certain times?

In addition, you could ask what people's **food preferences** are—what foods they like best. You should also find out if there are any foods that some people cannot or will not eat.

However, two of the most important considerations for planning a healthful and appetizing meal are nutrition and appeal.

Real-Life Situations Some meals are planned to use up "leftovers" from previous meals. Pieces of meat, poultry, and fish can be used in casseroles, sandwiches, and salads. Cooked vegetables can be added to soups, stews, salads, casseroles, and omelets. Cooked pasta can be used in casseroles and salads, or topped with a tomato or cheese sauce.

Did You Know? The taste buds of your mouth detect only salt, sweet, bitter, and sour. The distinction of flavors is actually made from smelling the food rather than tasting it. That's why food tastes different when your nose is clogged by a cold.

Nutrition

As you have read in earlier chapters, good nutrition is vital for everyone, so as you plan one or more meals, don't forget the four basic food groups. All four groups don't have to be included in each meal. However, during the day everyone should get the required number of servings from each group: four servings of breads and cereals, four of fruits and vegetables, two or more of milk and milk products, and two from the meats-to-beans group.

The heart of most meals is a combination of proteins and carbohydrates. Some examples are meat and potatoes, beans and rice, chicken and noodles, macaroni and cheese, or a tuna salad sandwich.

To round out these basic meals, add fruits and vegetables—as appetizers, salads, side dishes, or desserts. The dairy group could be included as a dessert (yogurt or ice cream), as a drink (plain milk or milkshake), or even as a topping on the main course (cheese on pizza or a casserole).

Meal Appeal

Have you ever had a meal that looked and tasted just delicious? How did the cook achieve this success? A well-planned meal successfully blends food flavors, colors, shapes, textures, and temperatures.

- **Flavor.** The right combination of flavors makes a meal more enjoyable. Sweet flavors can often be paired with savory ones (applesauce and pork; cranberry sauce and turkey). Strong flavors go best with mild ones (tomato sauce on spaghetti; salsa on tacos; cheddar cheese on crackers). Two very strong flavors in the same meal are rarely successful.
- **Color.** Think about what colors you'll include in your meal. A meal with only one color is far less appealing than one with a variety. If you plan to serve two vegetables, match carrots with string beans or tomatoes with spinach. A lemon wedge, a slice of orange, or a sprig of parsley can also provide an attractive color contrast.

Which meal has more appeal? Can you explain why?

More About Color Contrast As this section suggests, garnishes such as parsley, lemon wedges, or orange slices can be used to provide color contrast and add to the visual appeal of a meal. Some other colorful, edible garnishes to consider are cherry tomatoes, carrot curls, radishes, and pickles.

More About Appeal Herbs and spices can be used to add taste and color to foods. Herbs include parsley, oregano, chives, basil, and marjoram. You can use 3 to 4 times as much fresh herbs as dried. Spices include cinnamon, pepper, cloves, and paprika. Some herbs and spices are made into special combinations, such as curry and chili powder.

Activities

Skill Builder: Critical Thinking
Have students make a list of food combinations that would go together and would create a pleasing contrast in each of the following areas: color, flavor, temperature, shape, texture.

Skill Builder: Critical Thinking
Ask students to look at a restaurant menu that lists complete meals (as opposed to a la carte) and to rate the meals according to their appeal. Students should justify ratings according to the criteria noted in this section.

Skill Builder: Writing
Ask students to plan a lunch for one or more of their friends. As the first step in planning the meal, they should write answers to the questions posed at the beginning of this section. (You may want to have students follow through on this meal plan throughout the chapter—choosing recipes and making a shopping list.)

Reteaching
Have students analyze their favorite dinner menu to see if it provides a contrast of flavors, colors, textures, and so on.

Enrichment
Have students try a variety of foods and classify the textures (crispy, chewy, smooth, crunchy, soupy, and so on). Students should analyze their own food preferences to see if one type of texture is predominant.

Teaching "Sources of Recipes"
(Page 372)

This section teaches where to find recipes—in cookbooks, in newspapers, in magazines, on food packages, or from family and friends.

Checking Comprehension

✔ What are recipes? *They are detailed instructions for preparing foods.*

✔ Name two kinds of cookbooks. *General cookbooks and specialized ones, such as those for ethnic foods, desserts, or vegetarian meals.*

Teaching "Making a Shopping List" and "Keeping Your Plan Flexible"
(Page 374)

This section teaches the advantages of making a logical shopping list and of staying flexible about the list once you get to the store.

Checking Comprehension

✓ What are staple foods? *They are basic food items that are used regularly and that do not spoil easily.*

✓ What are two ways of organizing a shopping list? *List the same type of foods together, such as all meats and all milk products, or list foods in the same order as they are arranged in the store.*

Activities

Skill Builder: Critical Thinking
Give students a long shopping list, and have them organize it in a logical manner. Ask them to explain the logic in their method.

Skill Builder: Reading
Have students read a grocery store circular and discuss how the information in it could be used in meal planning and making a shopping list. They should identify bargains, special offers, what is in season, new foods, and so on.

Reteaching
Have students use five dinner menus (theirs or yours) and assemble a shopping list that includes all the ingredients that would allow them to make the recipes in their kitchen at home. For example, if one of the recipes calls for nutmeg and there is no nutmeg in their cabinets, they should plan to purchase some. Amounts of each item should be on their lists.

Enrichment
Provide students with a commercially prepared shopping list. Have them analyze the logic of the list and note any obvious flaws (food categories or items missing, mix-ups about where things are on the list, and so on). Have students comment on whether such a list would be helpful, and encourage them to have their family try using the list to see how it works out.

- **Money.** Plan your meal within the family food budget.
- **Skill.** Don't take on a project that's more complex than you are ready for.
- **Supplies and equipment.** Check the refrigerator and kitchen cabinets for necessary ingredients. Be sure you have all the tools and appliances that you will need.

Making a Shopping List

Once you've chosen your recipe, check over the list of ingredients. Will you need to make a trip to the store for some of them? If so, make a shopping list—write down which items you will need to buy, along with the amounts needed.

You will find it more economical to plan several meals at a time. Check with other family members who prepare meals to see whether there are items that they will need. Also, look over supplies of **staple** foods—the basic food items, such as flour and sugar, that are used regularly and that do not spoil easily.

Shopping will be easier if you organize your list logically. List the same types of food together, such as all meats at the top of the list and milk products next. You can also list foods in the order that they are arranged in the store.

Keeping Your Plan Flexible

While you are checking your supplies, try to stay flexible. Perhaps you have some perishable foods on hand that will not stay fresh much longer, such as vegetables or fruits. If you can adapt your meal plan to use these in place of what you originally planned, you will be using your food resources more effectively.

Flexibility will make you a better shopper, too. Perhaps you will decide to buy a little extra in case a family member brings a friend home, or you may want to take advantage of a bargain you see when you are shopping. You may choose to substitute chicken for turkey if it's on sale. Green beans might look fresher than the broccoli that you had planned to serve. For more about shopping for food, see the next chapter.

Before starting to prepare a meal, check the refrigerator and kitchen cabinets to make sure that you have all of the ingredients you will need.

Emphasize When making a shopping list, be sure to check cabinets to see what ingredients you have on hand. This is especially necessary when more than one person does the cooking. You may think there is a box of rice in the cabinet, not knowing that someone else has used it.

Did You Know? Surveys have shown that a person who goes into a supermarket without a list and plans to buy three items will usually walk out with eight to ten purchases. Making a list can save not only time but money.

TECHNOLOGY

The Computer and Meal Planning

Any task that requires you to keep track of many different things at the same time can benefit from the computer. As the market for home computers increases, you will be able to find more and more software to use for meal planning.

Take a trip into the future of meal planning. Your kitchen computer will hold many thousands of recipes in its database. It will also be able to search through them very quickly to find, for example, a recipe for lamb that goes well with green peppers. Then it will check the latest nutritive values issued by the government to find the nutritional content of each food you plan to serve. It will tell you how much your meal will contribute to your Recommended Daily Allowances—and if you are watching your weight, it will count calories for you.

Further, the computer could tell you whether you have the equipment and food supplies needed to prepare a particular recipe—based on information stored in its memory. The computer's database might also contain the food preferences of all family members, enabling the computer to suggest changes you could make to please your brother or sister.

Finally, your computer could automatically contact the store and place an order for the foods you will need to prepare the meal, plus any staples that you are running low on.

Think It Through

1. **What aspects of meal planning that are not mentioned in this feature might home computers be helpful with in the future?**
2. **What do you think you might lose by having so much computing power in the kitchen?**

Teaching the Feature
"The Computer and Meal Planning"

Answers to Feature Questions

1. Computers of the future might figure out special diets for people with weight or medical problems, remember what foods each family member has eaten at home during the last week and recommend variety for the next meal, multiply or divide the recipes it has in store so that they can be served to any number of people, share favorite recipes with a neighbor's home computer.

2. Answers will vary. Some students will say "nothing"; others will suggest that there will be a loss of spontaneity in meal planning, which is an essential element in good cooking.

Activities

Recipe Input Have students look at recipes to see what information from the recipe could be input into a computer and how it could be useful to a meal planner.

Time Saving Ask students to estimate the amount of time that could be saved in the various stages of meal planning (planning the meals, choosing recipes, making a shopping list) by using a home computer.

Software Survey Have interested students examine existing software to see what is available that may be of use to the meal planner. Have them report to the rest of the class.

Community Contact Arrange to have a computer salesperson or professor talk to the class about software for meal planning. Have him or her explain the programs, their uses, availability, and cost.

More About Computer Memory Many of the computer applications that apply to meal planning use the computer's memory. We cannot be expected to remember everyone's food preferences, favorite recipes, the nutritional content of all foods, or what food supplies and equipment are in the home. The computer is a great tool for keeping track of such information, but it is the creativity of the human mind that actually puts that information together to make appealing meals.

COMPLETING THE CHAPTER

Summary

- Meals should be planned with the family's needs (nutrition, budget, food preferences, and time) in mind.
- Meal appeal is based on blending food flavors, colors, shapes, textures, and temperatures.
- Recipes can be found in cookbooks, in magazines and newspapers, and on food packages; they are also passed on from person to person.
- Recipes should be chosen because they sound as if they will taste good, because they are complete, and because you have the resources needed.
- Making a shopping list is a very effective way to organize food shopping.
- Being flexible when shopping allows for more economical and smarter food-buying decisions.

For Review

Objective Review Questions Have students complete the "Reviewing the Facts" section on this page.

Study Guide Have students complete the Study Guide from Chapter 40 of their *Student Workbook.*

Class Discussion Have students talk about how lifestyle affects meal planning. Ask them to consider single people living alone, families that eat at different times, people who don't have time to cook elaborate meals, and so on.

For Evaluation

Assessment Have students assess two menus, pick one, and justify their choice (based on nutrition and meal appeal). Then have them choose between two recipes and justify that choice (based on the recipe and the resources it requires).

Chapter Test Have students complete the test for Chapter 40 that appears in the *Teacher's Classroom Resources.*

CHAPTER 40 REVIEW

Answers to "Reviewing the Facts"

1. Nutrition and appeal.
2. Flavor, color, shape, texture, and temperature.
3. Cookbooks; newspapers and magazines; food packages or cans; relatives and friends.
4. Good taste; complete information about the ingredients, yield, equipment, and step-by-step instructions.
5. Time, money, skill, supplies and equipment.
6. Make a shopping list.

Reviewing the Facts

1. What are two important considerations when you are planning meals?
2. Name five qualities of foods that you can vary to make an appealing meal.
3. What sources can you consult if you are looking for recipes?
4. What should you look for in a good recipe?
5. What four resources should you consider in planning a meal?
6. What is the next step to take after choosing a recipe?

Thinking Critically

1. Which of the five qualities that affect meal appeal is it most important to vary for a successful meal? Which is the least important to vary? Why did you choose these answers?
2. What are some possible consequences of not planning properly for a meal?

Applying Your Skills

1. **Evaluating Recipes.** Compare recipes for spaghetti from three different sources—a package, a can, and a cookbook. Which looks as if it would be tastiest? Which looks easiest to make? What are the preparation times for the three recipes? Write a summary of what you find, and be sure to include the recipes themselves and to identify their sources.
2. **Making a Plan.** Prepare a shopping list for your family. Plan five meals and include the ingredients for each one on the list. Also include any staples, cleaning and household supplies, snacks, and other items your family customarily uses during an average week. Rearrange the list to follow the layout of the supermarket where your family shops, or according to groups of foods. Write a brief summary based on the list and share it with the class.
3. **Writing a Checklist.** You are having a friend to dinner next week. Make a detailed checklist outlining all of the things you must accomplish to make the meal a success.

Answers to "Thinking Critically"

1. Students will probably choose taste, or perhaps texture, as the most important variable in meal appeal. Shape will probably be least important to them. They could explain their choices by saying that food is primarily for tasting, rather than for looking at.
2. Students might mention that they might not have all of the necessary ingredients or resources, they might not have prepared enough food, or the meal might not be ready on time.

CHAPTER

41

Shopping for Food

OBJECTIVES

This chapter will help you to:

- Select the most appropriate store for your food shopping needs.
- Evaluate the quality and freshness of foods.
- Compare the nutritional value and price of foods.
- Describe how to get the best food buys.

WORDS TO REMEMBER

additive	generic product
brand	preservative
expiration date	pull date
	universal product code

Chapter Resources

Teacher's Classroom Resources

- Lesson Plan
- Life Skills Activity, *Is Bigger Better?*
- Reproducible Master, *Nutrition Label*
- Extension Activity, *What Are Additives?*
- Chapter Test

Student Workbook

- Study Guide
- Worksheet, *It's on the Label*

CHAPTER OVERVIEW

Chapter 41 tells students about the decisions involved in shopping for food. It offers suggestions about how to choose where to shop, how to judge food for quality and freshness, and how to read labels to make wise food-buying decisions. The chapter also advises how to locate the best food buys and how to evaluate the use of additives and preservatives in food.

INTRODUCING THE CHAPTER

Motivators

Food Shopping Routines Have students talk about their family's food shopping routines: Where is food bought? How often is shopping done? How long does it take? Are coupons used?

Using the Photograph Have students study the photograph on this page. Then ask: "What are these shoppers doing? What should shoppers consider before choosing fresh fruits and vegetables?"

Decision Making at the Food Store Point out that the person in the photograph has to make a choice about what to buy. Have students talk about what kinds of choices have to be made at the grocery store and what might influence those decisions.

Introducing the Objectives

Discuss the chapter objectives on this page. Remind students that the objectives focus on important chapter content.

Introducing Vocabulary

Point out that additives are substances that are added to food as it is being processed. Additives are used for many reasons (which you'll explore in this chapter). Some of the things that are added to foods are preservatives, which keep foods from spoiling.

TEACHING THE CHAPTER

For convenience, the teaching suggestions for this chapter are arranged according to the following lesson topics:

- "Planning Where to Shop," pages 378-379
- "Judging Food for Quality and Freshness," pages 379-380
- "Reading Labels," pages 380-381
- "Locating the Best Buys," page 383

Teaching "Planning Where to Shop"

(Pages 378-379)

This section describes the different kinds of places where people can purchase food and examines the advantages and disadvantages of each.

Checking Comprehension

✓ What are the two main advantages of supermarkets? *Lower prices and a wider selection than most other kinds of food stores.*

✓ What is a convenience store? *A small store with a limited selection of basic items that is open for many hours each day.*

✓ Why do some people choose to go to specialty stores? *Because specialty stores offer high-quality goods and a wide selection of their specialty.*

✓ How do a supermarket, a discount supermarket, and a superstore differ? *Discount supermarkets usually have lower prices, stock fewer brands, and offer fewer services than regular supermarkets. Superstores are gigantic supermarkets which offer many goods and services in addition to groceries.*

You've probably gone food shopping with a parent dozens of times, and may have gone by yourself for a few items needed to prepare a meal. You know that food shopping requires lots of decision making.

Some planning must be done beforehand—such as where to shop and what items are needed. Other decisions are made in the store. How fresh is the lettuce? What is the date on the yogurt container? Should I buy canned or frozen peas? How do prices compare? Efficient food shopping helps you select good quality foods and also saves you money.

Specialty food stores, such as this fruit and vegetable store, sell one kind of food product. Their prices are usually higher than supermarket prices, but they offer a wide variety of high-quality food.

Planning Where to Shop

Different kinds of food stores fill different customer needs, but prices, quality, and service can vary widely. Where you shop often depends on what you need and when you need it.

Supermarkets

Supermarkets are large stores that sell many brands of food and household products. They usually have counters where you can buy fresh cold cuts, salads, and pastries. The two main advantages of supermarkets are that they have lower prices and a wider selection than most other kinds of food stores.

Some communities have discount—or "no-frills"—supermarkets. While these stores have lower prices, they may stock fewer brands of basic items and may offer fewer services than regular supermarkets. At many discount supermarkets, customers select some items from cardboard boxes or barrels. They may also have to bag their own groceries or bring their own shopping bags to take their purchases home.

Gigantic supermarkets, also known as superstores, sell small appliances, books, automotive supplies, and many other goods, in addition to groceries. Superstores often feature fresh fish counters, gourmet foods, salad bars, and restaurants. They may also have small shops, such as a florist or a video rental outlet.

More About Convenience Stores and Supermarkets In recent years, supermarkets have made several moves in an effort to compete with the popularity of convenience stores. The appeal of convenience stores has been long hours and quick service. Now supermarkets have extended their hours—many are open 24 hours a day. They also provide express checkout lines for customers with only a few items.

Convenience Stores

A convenience store is a small store with a limited selection of basic items that is open long hours. Some serve customers 24 hours a day and are open on holidays when other food stores are closed. Convenience stores are handy if you need to pick up a few food products quickly, but prices are usually higher and their selection is more limited compared to supermarkets.

Specialty Stores

Stores that sell only one type of product, such as meat, or fruits and vegetables, or baked goods, are called specialty stores. Their prices are usually higher compared to supermarkets, but they attract customers because they offer high-quality goods and a wide selection of their specialty.

Other Places to Shop

Some towns have a farmers' market, where shoppers can buy fruits and vegetables directly from the farm. The food is very fresh and prices may be quite low. Fresh fruits and vegetables are also sold from roadside stands right next to farms.

Some people belong to food co-ops (or cooperatives). A co-op is a group of shoppers who join together to purchase large amounts of basic food items at discount prices.

Judging Foods for Quality and Freshness

Wherever you decide to shop, you will find that successful shopping requires informed decision making in the store. The foods available may vary from day to day, and prices are continually adjusted also.

Judging Quality

The first thing you should do in selecting food items is to judge their quality. For example, you will want to choose the freshest fruits and vegetables, since they can lose nutrients while being stored and shipped to stores. Look for firmness, adequate color to indicate ripeness, and lack of bruises and breaks. Tips on buying fresh foods in the four food groups are included in Chapters 49 through 52.

Warning Signs

You can protect yourself from purchasing spoiled or tainted processed foods by looking for these warning signs:

- Bulging and dented cans may contain dangerous bacteria.
- Rusty cans may be old and have rust on the inside.
- Frozen-food packages that are soft or wet may be thawing.
- Frozen-food packages that are stained, covered with thin sheets of ice, or irregularly shaped may have thawed and been refrozen.

Emphasize For high-quality, nutritious food, it is commonly believed that it is best to shop the periphery (around the edges) of the supermarket. That's where the fresh fruits, vegetables, meat, poultry, seafood, and dairy products are located. These foods are the least processed and often have the highest nutritional value.

Cross-Reference See specific information about selecting breads and cereals on pages 444-445; fruits and vegetables on pages 452-453; milk, yogurt, and cheese on pages 459-461; and meat, poultry, fish, dry beans, eggs, and nuts on pages 467-469.

Activities

Skill Builder: Critical Thinking
Have students compile a list of the food stores in their community or neighborhood. Then ask them to classify the stores into the categories used in this section.

Reteaching
Have students make a chart illustrating the pros and cons of the various types of stores. Students should consider hours, prices, closeness to home, and other relevant factors.

Enrichment
Ask students first to consider the kinds of food stores currently available in their community, and then to determine which type (of those described in this unit) their community most needs. Ask volunteers with different answers to explain their choice.

Teaching "Judging Food for Quality and Freshness"
(Pages 379-380)

This section teaches some general rules for judging quality and freshness and offers warning signs for identifying tainted foods. It also discusses product dating.

Checking Comprehension

✓ How should you check to see if fruits and vegetables are fresh? *Look for firmness, adequate color to indicate ripeness, and lack of bruises and breaks.*

✓ What might bulging or dented cans indicate? *The cans may contain dangerous bacteria.*

✓ What signs indicate that frozen food packages have been thawed? *The packages may be soft or wet, stained, or covered with thin sheets of ice, or irregularly shaped.*

Activities

Skill Builder: Critical Thinking
The tampering scandals of the 1980s forced manufacturers to seal food packages in ways that would discourage people from adding foreign substances to the packages. Ask students to describe some of the tamper-proof packages they have seen.

Reteaching
Ask each student to bring in an empty food package. Then pass the packages around for students to locate the product dating labels and tell what kind they are and what they mean.

Enrichment
Have students investigate and report on the different kinds of food poisoning caused by dented or rusty cans or by frozen food that is not properly stored.

Teaching "Reading Labels"
(Pages 380-381)

This section teaches about the information available on food packages, including basic information, brand names, and nutrition labels.

Checking Comprehension

✓ In what order are ingredients listed on food labels? *Ingredients are listed by weight: the ingredient that weighs the most is listed first.*

✓ What nutrients are specifically noted on a nutrition label? *Grams of fat, cholesterol, sodium, carbohydrates, and protein per serving.*

✓ What is the difference between preservatives and other additives? *Preservatives keep foods fresh and tastier longer. Other additives make foods taste or look better.*

✓ What agency tests additives to make sure they are safe? *In the United States, all additives must be approved by the Food and Drug Administration (FDA).*

Product Dating

Dates stamped or printed on food packages can also help you to judge freshness. There are two major types of dates used on food products.

- The **pull date** is the last day a product may be sold. A label may say, "Do not sell after November 17."
- The **expiration date** is the last day a product can be used safely. This kind of label says, "Do not use after July 1994."

Other types of dates include the *pack date,* which states when the product was made or packaged, and the *freshness date,* which tells when the product will taste best or be most nutritious.

Reading Labels

Food labels tell you a lot about the contents and nutritional value of a product. This enables you to compare the features of different brands.

Basic Information

Almost every food label, by law, must contain the following information:

- Name of product.
- Weight of contents.
- Name and address of manufacturer, packer, or distributor.
- Ingredients.

Ingredients are listed in order by weight—the ingredient that weighs the most is listed first. A can of stew that lists beef first, for example, will have more meat than one listing potatoes first. Some standard foods such as catsup, mayonnaise, and peanut butter, however, do not have to list ingredients.

Nutrition Labels

By law, foods that have had nutrients added and products that are advertised as being nutritious must have nutrition labels. These labels include:

- Serving size and number of servings.
- Calories per serving and calories from fat.
- Grams of fat, cholesterol, sodium, carbohydrates, and protein per serving and their percentage of daily value.
- Key vitamins and minerals and their percentage of daily value.

What information can you find on this food label?

Nutrition Facts
Serving Size ½ cup (114g)
Servings Per Container 4

Amount Per Serving	
Calories 90	Calories from Fat 30
	% Daily Value*
Total Fat 3g	**5%**
Saturated Fat 0g	**0%**
Cholesterol 0mg	**0%**
Sodium 300mg	**13%**
Total Carbohydrate 13g	**4%**
Dietary Fiber 3g	**12%**
Sugars 3g	
Protein 3g	

Vitamin A 80%	•	Vitamin C 60%	
Calcium 4%	•	Iron 4%	

*Percent Daily Values are based on a 2,000 calorie diet. Your daily values may be higher or lower depending on your calorie needs:

	Calories	2,000	2,500
Total Fat	Less than	65g	80g
Sat Fat	Less than	20g	25g
Cholesterol	Less than	300mg	300mg
Sodium	Less than	2,400mg	2,400mg
Total Carbohydrate		300g	375g
Fiber		25g	30g

Calories per gram:
Fat 9 • Carbohydrates 4 • Protein 4

More About Product Dating Pull dates are found on breads, dairy products, and delicatessen meats. Freshness dates are used on meats and some snack foods, while expiration dates are most commonly seen on containers of milk and packages of yeast.

More About Labeling Regulations The FDA exempts more than 300 food items from labeling ingredients because the food manufacturers have agreed to use a standard recipe. Tomato products, margarine, jellies, and cheese are among these products.

- Recommended daily intake of nutrients for a 2,000-calorie diet and a 2,500-calorie diet.
- Number of calories per gram of fat, carbohydrate, and protein.

Food Additives

A list of ingredients may indicate that a food contains **additives.** These are substances that are added to the food before it is sold. Additives can serve a variety of purposes. Food colors, sweeteners, and flavorings are all intended to make foods taste or look better. Additives help baked goods rise, keep ice cream smooth, and help soft foods like candy retain moisture.

Some additives are **preservatives,** which keep foods fresh and tastier longer. In the United States, all additives must be approved by the Food and Drug Administration (FDA), a federal agency. Because information about food additives is included on the labels of packaged goods, you can avoid some or all additives if you wish.

You can also look for foods that have been organically grown without chemicals. Such foods generally cost more than foods grown by standard procedures that use chemical fertilizers or pesticides.

Brands

A **brand** is a particular name of a product; it is usually the first piece of information you notice on the package label. The brand name belongs to the company that makes that food product; no other company may use the same name or trademark. There are several brands of nearly every food product.

When you shop for food, you may encounter three different kinds of brands. National brands are sold across the country and are advertised on radio and television and in magazines. Store or house brands are products that have been produced by the supermarket chain that sells them. These usually cost less money than national brands. A third kind of brand, the **generic product,** is plainly packaged and is usually the cheapest of all brands.

You may find differences in quality among brands. These may be important to you for some products, such as canned vegetables or paper towels, but not for others, like relish.

Although the prices of different brands of food may differ, the quality is usually quite similar.

Did You Know? Caffeine is a stimulant that can be addictive. It increases blood cholesterol, dilates arteries to the heart, and constricts blood vessels to the brain. Everyone knows that coffee and tea contain caffeine, but watch also for high caffeine levels in cola drinks and chocolate.

More About Additives Food colorings are the most controversial additives because their use in foods is cosmetic. While improving the appearance of the food, they may also mask poor quality. Some synthetic food dyes (derived from coal tars) are even suspected of causing cancer.

Activities

Skill Builder: Math
Ask students to compare the prices of several food items available in national, store, and generic brands. Have them write down how much can be saved by buying one brand over another.

Skill Builder: Science
Ask students to read the labels on several food products and try to identify the additives. Then have them research the additives to find out what purpose they serve.

Skill Builder: Critical Thinking
Point out to students that they would think that the first listed ingredient on a can of vegetable soup would be a vegetable but it isn't; it's water. Have students list what they think is the first ingredient of some other products, such as spaghetti sauce, pancake syrup, chocolate cake mix, grape drink, and hot chocolate mix and then check their assumptions by reading food labels.

Reteaching
Have students compare two labels from different brands of the same kind of product. Have them list the ingredients in order by weight and compare the two lists. Then have them compare the serving size and number of servings; the calories per serving and the calories from fat; and the number of grams of protein, carbohydrates, and fat per serving.

Enrichment
Ask students to read food labels with a "critical eye" and bring in examples of label information that might be deceptive. Students should be sensitized to words like "brand new," "natural," or "20 percent more nutritious."

Enrichment
Have selected students visit a health food store and talk to someone about additive-free food alternatives. Students should compare prices for organically grown foods with those in which chemicals and pesticides have been used in the growing.

Teaching the Feature

"Packaging"

Answers to Feature Questions

1. Answers will vary. Manufacturers may use excess packaging to make their products appear more attractive, or to make them bigger in order to prevent shoplifting. Overpackaging may also increase consumer confidence in the safety of a product.

2. Most students will say that some product packaging is needed. It is used to identify manufacturers, to keep products safe and sanitary for consumers, and to keep products from being damaged.

Activities

Scavenger Hunt Have students look at home for products that demonstrate source reduction in packaging. If possible, have them bring these products to show the class. Students also might look for products that demonstrate "source expansion" or products that have added to their packaging. Throwaway plastic microwave trays in packages of instant rice would be an example.

Research Remind students of the other 2Rs—reuse and recycling. Have them research and report on ways manufacturers are applying these principles in their packaging. For example, reuse—detergent manufacturers sell concentrated refills for 64-ounce plastic fabric softener jugs. Recycle—manufacturers use recycled paper for cardboard packaging.

Community Contact Suggest that students meet with the manager of a local supermarket or drugstore to discuss source reduction in packaging. Students might find out what local merchants are doing to reduce excess packaging.

MANAGING RESOURCES

Packaging

People who care about the environment practice the 3Rs: reduce, reuse, recycle. Let's concentrate on the first R—reduce. It should receive first priority. *Reduce* means to use less raw material and energy. Environmentalists call this source reduction.

Source reduction can be applied to product packaging. Many products that people buy are overpackaged. For example, individually wrapped doughnuts placed in a plastic tray placed inside a cardboard box wrapped in cellophane are definitely overpackaged!

Overpackaging wastes the water, trees, petroleum, and other natural resources used to create the packaging materials. Excess packaging contributes to other environmental problems as well. When unnecessary packaging is discarded, it adds to the tons of solid waste already needing disposal. Excess packaging creates more cellophane wrappers, plastic trays, and cardboard liners to litter streets and highways. Of course, costs for unnecessary packaging are passed along to the consumer.

The situation is improving, however. Many manufacturers are starting to cut back on packaging waste. Here are a few examples:

- Some cookie manufacturers have eliminated the plastic inner tray in a bag of cookies.
- Some rice makers put loose rice directly in a box, no longer using a plastic inner bag.
- Some manufacturers of contact lens solutions use a small seal to secure box tops instead of cellophane outer wrap.
- Fast-food restaurants use paper wrappers instead of styrofoam containers for sandwiches.

You don't have to wait for manufacturers. Here are some source-reduction methods you can take when making shopping decisions.

- Select products that use fewer packaging resources. For example, choose the deodorant that just comes in a plastic bottle rather than the one that comes in a plastic bottle inside a cardboard box.
- Buy products in the largest practical size. This minimizes the overall amount of packaging you'll have to get rid of.
- Buy products such as fruits and vegetables loose rather than shrink-wrapped in a cardboard or foam tray.
- Bring your own tote bag when you go food shopping. This eliminates the need for new paper or plastic bags every time you shop.

Think It Through

1. **Why do you think manufacturers overpackage their products?**
2. **Is no packaging the best packaging? Explain your answer.**

More About Packaging In many instances, manufacturers are reducing, reusing, and recycling their packaging as a marketing tactic. Polls show that consumers are more inclined to buy products that claim to protect the environment.

Did You Know? On the bottom of most plastic packaged-goods containers you'll see the "arrows-chasing-arrows" recycling emblem with a number in the middle. The number is part of the resin-coding system of the Society of Plastics Industry. The system enables recycling center operators to separate the various resins since they can't be recycled readily if mixed together.

Locating the Best Buys

The choices you make in a food store are usually between different brands or different versions of the same food. Do you want fresh fish, frozen fish, canned fish, or a complete fish dinner? Will you buy a ready-made cake, a cake mix, or flour, eggs, sugar and baking powder to make a cake from scratch? Your decisions will be based on several factors such as the products' price, the amount of time you have, and your skills and preferences. Here are some general guidelines that may help you make shopping decisions:

- Decide if convenience is worth the extra money. Fresh foods which have been cut up generally cost more. Chicken parts are usually more expensive than a whole chicken. Shredded cheese usually costs more than a solid piece of cheese.
- Compare different forms of foods—fresh, canned, frozen, dried—to see which is the best buy. Consider taste, convenience, cost, preparation time, and storage.
- Take advantage of seasonal foods. Fresh fruits and vegetables in peak season will be high quality and often low in cost.
- Evaluate the extra expense of prepared foods. Frozen dinners, fresh salads, and packaged cookies are convenient but usually cost more than preparing the food from scratch.
- Learn to substitute one food for another. Buy cheaper cuts of meat or less expensive protein sources like poultry, eggs, and beans.
- Take advantage of sale items. If you need the item and have the storage space, you can save money by buying products on sale.
- Compare unit price labels, which are usually posted on the store shelves under each item. These help you to choose between different sized packages of similar items. For more on unit prices, refer to Chapter 31.
- Keep to your shopping list. Avoid impulse buying, especially at special displays and at the checkout counter.
- Use coupons for items that you usually buy. Coupons are found in newspapers, advertising fliers, and on some product packages and containers. Some supermarkets offer double or even triple value for coupons. That means that the store subtracts two or three times the coupon discount from a product's price.

Unit prices list the price per ounce, helping you to compare the cost of similar items. Coupons also help you save money—but only if they are for products that you will use.

Did You Know? Food manufacturers send representatives to the supermarkets to bargain for shelf space in locations that appeal to impulse buyers—at the end of an aisle and on eye-level shelves. They position their most expensive products in those locations, so remember to check the prices of items on upper and lower shelves, too

Focus on Consumer Skills Keep these money-saving tips in mind:

- Eat before you shop so you're not tempted to buy extra "goodies."
- Use coupons only for those products you would have bought anyway.
- If you're at the store just to "pick up a few things," don't get a cart. It encourages impulse buying.

Teaching "Locating the Best Buys"
(Page 383)

This section teaches ways to save money at the food store by making wise food-buying decisions. Comparison shopping, comparing unit prices, avoiding impulse buying, and using coupons are all ways to get the most for your money.

Checking Comprehension

✔ What are four factors to consider when trying to locate the best buys? *The price, the amount of time you have, your skills, and your preferences.*

✔ What is the main disadvantage of convenience foods? *They are usually more expensive than other types of foods.*

✔ Why might you select canned or frozen foods rather than fresh foods? *Canned and frozen foods may take less time to prepare and can be stored for a much longer time.*

✔ Which protein sources are cheaper than meat? *Poultry, eggs, and beans.*

✔ Where is the unit price listed? *Unit prices are usually posted on the store shelves under each item.*

✔ Where does most impulse buying take place? *At special displays and at the checkout counter.*

Activites

Skill Builder: Math
Have students compare the unit prices and costs of vegetables in fresh, canned, and frozen forms. Also ask them to compare the cost of an RDA serving of different protein sources (fish, chicken, beef, pork, beans).

Reteaching
Have students list five ways to locate the best buys at the food store.

Enrichment
Have students look at supermarket fliers to see what sales are available and discuss whether they would take advantage of these discounts.

COMPLETING THE CHAPTER

Summary

- Consumers must decide whether to shop at a supermarket, convenience store, specialty store, or some other kind of store.
- Food should be judged for quality and freshness, and consumers should note whether food appears spoiled or if it is on the shelf after its pull date or expiration date.
- Food labels provide basic information and nutritional information, as well as a list of additives.
- Shoppers can locate the best buys by comparison shopping, avoiding impulse buying, and using coupons.

For Review

Objective Review Questions Have students complete the "Reviewing the Facts" section on this page.

Study Guide Have students complete the Study Guide from Chapter 41 of their *Student Workbook.*

Food Shopping Excursion Have students do the family food shopping (or accompany the person who does it). The students should use as many of the suggestions offered in this chapter as are practical (judging food quality, using coupons, comparing unit prices, and so forth). Students should write a report on the excursion.

Be a Smart Shopper Students might role-play a radio call-in show: "Be a Smart Shopper." "Shoppers" call in questions to a panel of "experts" on food shopping. Students then reverse roles.

For Evaluation

Assessment From the information in the chapter, have the students assess a store (supermarket, convenience, or specialty) in terms of prices, hours, and quality.

Identify Have students identify the different parts of a food label taken from a product (brand name, pull date, weight of contents, and so on).

Chapter Test Have students complete the test for Chapter 41 that appears in the *Teacher's Classroom Resources.*

CHAPTER 41 REVIEW

Answers to "Reviewing the Facts"

1. Any three: supermarkets have lower prices, wider selection; convenience stores are open long hours; specialty stores offer high quality; farmer's markets offer freshness, low prices; co-ops have discounted prices.
2. Canned: bulging, dented, or rusty cans. Frozen: packages that are soft, wet, stained, covered with ice, or irregularly shaped.
3. Pull date is the last day a product can be sold; expiration date is the last day a product can be used safely.
4. Name of product; weight; manufacturer; ingredients.
5. Detailed information about the nutrients in a food; required by law if the product is advertised as nutritious or has nutrients added.
6. National brands are sold across the country and widely advertised; store or house brands are produced for the supermarket chain; generic products are plainly packaged and usually the cheapest.
7. Any five: decide if convenience is worth the extra money; compare different forms of foods; take advantage of seasonal foods; evaluate cost of prepared foods; substitute one food for another; take advantage of sales; compare unit prices; keep to a shopping list; use coupons.

Reviewing the Facts

1. Name three kinds of food stores. What is one advantage of each?
2. What warning signs should you look for to avoid buying tainted canned and frozen goods?
3. What is the difference between a pull date and an expiration date on a food package?
4. What four pieces of information are found on all food labels?
5. What are nutrition labels, and when are they required by law?
6. What is the difference between a national brand, a store brand, and a generic product?
7. List five guidelines to help you make wise shopping decisions.

Thinking Critically

1. Rising food prices have a major effect on an average family's budget. What can people do to keep food costs down while ensuring that their families eat a nutritious diet?
2. What would you do if the supermarket where you and your family shop had frozen-food packages that were often soft and wet?

Applying Your Skills

1. **Making a Comparison.** Read and compare the nutritional labels on two brands of the same product. How large are the serving sizes? How many servings per package? Which product has more calories, protein, carbohydrates, and fats per serving? Which has more vitamins and minerals? Report your findings to the class.

2. **Computing Costs and Savings.** Clip coupons from your family's newspapers and magazines. Decide which ones you would probably use if you did your family's food shopping. How much money would you save if you used the coupons? What would be the savings if you received double the face value?

3. **Sharing Information.** Create a poster about helpful tips for buying food that would aid teenage shoppers. Use one or more ideas from this chapter or from other sources.

Answers to "Thinking Critically"

1. Higher prices would probably mean having to switch to cheaper cuts of meat, preparing more meatless meals, not using convenience foods, elminating nonessentials such as soft drinks and snack items, and looking more carefully for bargains. All of these measures would still ensure nutritious meals.
2. Some students might say that they would report the problem to the store manager. Others might decide to purchase their frozen food elsewhere or even not to shop at that supermarket at all.

CHAPTER

42

Kitchen Know-How

OBJECTIVES

This chapter will help you to:

- Explain kitchen storage principles.
- Describe how to plan work areas for maximum efficiency.
- Discuss how to use and care for kitchen appliances.
- List ways to conserve energy in the kitchen.
- Describe how to use the kitchen efficiently and responsibly.

WORDS TO REMEMBER

appliance
perishable
rotation
utensil
work center
work triangle

Chapter Resources

Teacher's Classroom Resources

Lesson Plan
Life Skills Activity, *Appliance Shopping Spree*
Reproducible Master, *The EnergyGuide Label*
Extension Activity, *Small Appliances*
Chapter Test

Student Workbook

Study Guide
Worksheet, *Energy Wise*

CHAPTER OVERVIEW

Chapter 42 explains how to use the kitchen efficiently for food storage and preparation. It outlines how to plan work centers and care for appliances, and how to conserve energy when using them. Guidelines are also given for using the kitchen responsibly and for cooperating with others in cooking and cleanup.

INTRODUCING THE CHAPTER

Motivators

Kitchen Appliances and Utensils Have students name as many kitchen appliances (large and small) and as many utensils as they can.

Using the Photograph Have students study the photograph on this page. Then ask: "What appliances, equipment, tools, and utensils can you identify in this kitchen?"

Successful Cooking Have students discuss what they would consider a successful cooking experience. Also, ask them to share some successful experiences they have had in the kitchen and to identify why the undertaking worked out so well.

Introducing the Objectives

Discuss the chapter objectives on this page. Remind students that the objectives focus on important chapter content.

Introducing Vocabulary

Tell students that rotation, described here in connection with storing foods, is the process of alternating the use of an object to get the most from it. Other things that are rotated are tires and crops.

TEACHING THE CHAPTER

For convenience, the teaching suggestions for this chapter are arranged according to the following lesson topics:

- "Using the Kitchen for Food Storage," page 386
- "Planning Work Areas," pages 386-387
- "Kitchen Appliances," pages 389-390
- "Using the Kitchen," page 390

Teaching "Using the Kitchen for Food Storage"

(Page 386)

This section teaches how food should be stored so that it will not spoil and it can be found easily.

Checking Comprehension

✓Explain the system of rotation. *Use older supplies first. If you purchase a new carton of eggs, for example, store the new carton in back of or under the old.*

✓ How should leftovers be stored? *Leftovers should be wrapped in airtight packages of aluminum foil, plastic wrap, sealed plastic bags, covered bowls, or storage containers.*

✓ Where should cartons of milk, bags of onions, and cans of soup be stored? *Milk should be stored in the refrigerator; onions should be stored in a dry, dark, cool closet; and cans of soup should be stored on shelves together.*

Activities

Skill Builder: Critical Thinking
Ask students to analyze the way packaged and canned foods are stored in their own homes and to suggest possible ways of improving the method of storage. Have volunteers explain their suggestions to the class.

Reteaching
Give students a recipe and have them list where each item from the recipe should be stored in the kitchen.

Kitchens are workshops which surround you with equipment for working with food. You accomplish many tasks with **appliances,** kitchen equipment run by electricity or gas. For example, you store foods in a refrigerator, cook foods on a range or in an oven, and may wash dishes in a dishwasher. You may also use small appliances, such as a mixer, blender, or toaster, to prepare and cook foods. In addition, many **utensils,** such as knives, spoons, and other small tools, are needed to complete tasks in the kitchen.

In your kitchen at home you probably work alone or with another person. The foods laboratory that you use in school is more like a restaurant kitchen, with many people working on food preparation and cooking at the same time. In this chapter, you will learn how to organize equipment for work in the kitchen at home and at school.

Using the Kitchen for Food Storage

When you return from a shopping trip, your first task is to put the food away. Food should be stored where it will not spoil and you can find it easily. A large portion of most kitchens—the refrigerator, the freezer, and a lot of shelf space—is devoted to storing food. Storing foods properly can save you money and time.

Many fresh foods are **perishable** foods—they tend to spoil easily. Perishable foods should usually be stored in the refrigerator or freezer. Try setting up a system of **rotation,** so older supplies are used before newer ones. If you purchase a new carton of milk, for example, store it in back of any older ones. This helps ensure that you will use the older milk first.

Leftovers should be wrapped in airtight packages of aluminum foil, plastic wrap, sealed plastic bags, or covered bowls. You can purchase plastic storage containers with airtight lids which are specially designed to store refrigerated and frozen foods.

Not all foods should be kept in the refrigerator. Some perishables, such as potatoes and onions, do better in a dry, dark, and cool closet. Packaged and canned goods can be stored on shelves. Put soups together in one place, cereals in another; this will make everything easier to find.

Planning Work Areas

Food storage is only one task performed in the kitchen. Two other major kitchen tasks are food preparation and cooking. You can organize the kitchen for these tasks by thinking of it as divided into three areas.

Work Centers

Work centers are organized areas where the main kitchen tasks can be performed. A *food storage center* is most convenient if storage supplies like plastic bags and bowls are kept near the refrigerator. The main shelves for canned and packaged foods should be nearby. A surface for putting down grocery bags and wrapping foods is also important.

For a *food preparation center,* you need counter space to work. There should be nearby storage space for the equipment and utensils that are used to

More About Refrigeration For best food storage, the refrigerator should be kept between 32° and 40°F (0° and 4° C). The meat and dairy areas should be coldest (32°-35°F) (0°-2° C). In most refrigerators, the areas at the bottom and on the door are the warmest. The freezer section of the refrigerator should be kept at 0°F (-18° C). At these recommended temperatures, fruit and vegetables will keep in the refrigerator for one to two weeks, milk for about five days, and cooked meat for four days or so. Food will keep in the freezer for much longer—three to nine months. See a chart of refrigeration storage on page 396.

A kitchen can be organized most efficiently by storing equipment, tools, and supplies near the area where they are used most frequently.

prepare food, such as bowls, knives, and measuring spoons. You could also use space for small appliances like blenders and mixers—and the sink should be close by for washing foods and keeping equipment clean.

Finally, the range and oven are important elements in the *cooking center.* Cabinets in the cooking center are convenient for storing pots, pans, lids, and hot pads. Utensils and supplies used during cooking can be placed here too. You may want to keep pepper, herbs, and spices nearby so you can add them to food as you cook.

The Work Triangle

As you have learned, the kitchen has three major work centers. The storage center is linked to the refrigerator. The food preparation center should be near the sink. The cooking center is around the range. The arrangement of these three centers in the kitchen is known as the work triangle. An ideal work triangle has equal sides, but is not too small or large.

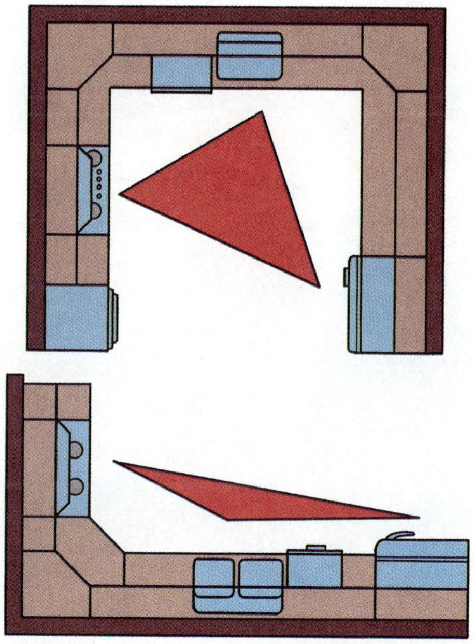

The U-shaped kitchen is usually considered the best work triangle, but the L-shaped kitchen is also easy to use. What other kitchen layouts have you seen? Why might an island be used in a large kitchen?

Did You Know? Kitchens in colonial times were sometimes in separate buildings, apart from the living quarters. They centered around a giant hearth where food was cooked. Another separate area—a smokehouse—was used to store food.

Did You Know? The most effective layout in a kitchen creates a triangular traffic pattern. The refrigerator, sink, and range form the three points of the triangle. Experts say that the three sides of the triangle should measure no more than a total of 22 feet to avoid excessive walking between work centers.

Enrichment
Have students evaluate the uses and merits of the following kinds of food storage materials: storage bins, plastic bags, plastic food containers, wrapping materials (freezer paper, waxed paper, plastic wrap, aluminum foil), and canisters.

Teaching "Planning Work Areas"
(Pages 386-387)

This section teaches about the work centers for food storage, food preparation, and cooking and how they can be organized for efficiency.

Checking Comprehension

✓ What resources would you expect to find in a food storage center? *Storage supplies, such as plastic bags and bowls; the main shelves for canned and packaged foods; a surface for putting down bags and wrapping foods.*

✓ What resources would you expect to find in the cooking center? *The range and oven, cooking utensils and supplies, cabinets for storing pots and pan, herbs and spices.*

Activities

Skill Builder: Math
Have students make a diagram of their kitchen at home, identify the work centers, and indicate the work triangle. Is it ideal? How does it compare to the kitchens pictured in the book?

Skill Builder: Writing
Have students write a description of their "ideal" kitchen in which they explain how the work centers are organized, where things are stored, and so on.

Reteaching
Have students make a detailed list of things to be stored in each work center in the kitchen.

Enrichment
Ask students to draw floor plans for ideal kitchens. They should indicate the location of major appliances, the work centers, counter space, cabinets, and so on.

Teaching the Feature
"Smarter Appliances for Easier Living"

Answers to Feature Questions

1. Possible answers include: self-checking appliances could help you find a problem early and prevent a larger repair bill; ovens that turn off automatically save energy; computer cookbooks could make cooking more convenient.
2. Students' answers will depend on their own priorities. Some students may be attracted to machines that respond to their voice; others may like machines that can be preset to that the individual can go to work or elsewhere while food cooks; others may like machines that take over mundane tasks.

Activities

Appliance Check Have students read the instruction manuals of the appliances in their kitchens at home to see what capabilities the units have. Students should analyze if (and why or why not) their family has taken full advantage of what each appliance can do.

Microwave It! Ask students to investigate the increasing popularity of microwave ovens and the kinds of kitchen utensils and containers that have come into use as a result of the microwave. What problems still remain with microwaves? Students may also explore the reluctance of some consumers to use a microwave oven (or other "smart" appliances).

Community Contact Have selected students visit a local appliance store and talk to a salesperson about state-of-the-art kitchen appliances. What can today's refrigerators, ovens, and ranges do? How do computerized options affect the price and energy efficiency of the appliance?

TECHNOLOGY

Smarter Appliances for Easier Living

Perhaps it seems like something out of a science fiction novel—appliances that turn themselves on and off and sense when your food is done—then tell you! But computer technology has brought this kind of magic into the kitchen. With the use of microprocessor chips, or micros, appliances are becoming "smarter" all the time.

Here are just a few of the innovations that are now available:

- **Self-checking appliances.** Some refrigerators have a light that signals a power failure, a door left open, or an overheating problem. Some dishwashers can tell you about a blocked drain.
- **Intelligent appliances.** Dishwashers, ovens, and coffee makers can be set to start whenever you want them to. Even older appliances can be "educated" when you plug them into a central remote-control panel or a presetting device. Someday it may be possible to control appliances with your voice.
- **High-tech microwaves.** Some microwave ovens use a moisture sensor to tell when a food is ready. In other models, preprogrammed labels saying "baked potato" or "frozen dinner" make cooking as easy as pressing a button.
- **Computer cookbooks.** Are you stumped about what to make for dinner? Tell your computer software program what ingredients you have on hand. In seconds on your screen you'll have a list of recipes you can make using those ingredients. Tired of writing out your shopping list? Input a week of menus and the computer will produce a shopping list including everything you need to prepare those meals.

Maybe you don't feel like cooking tonight. Just say "pizza," and your preprogrammed, voice-activated telephone will start dialing your favorite restaurant—one that delivers!

Think It Through

1. **How could some of the appliances named save you money as well as time?**
2. **Which of the appliances mentioned appeals the most to you? Why?**

Emphasize There is a human element to all smart appliances. The coffee maker that is preset to start must first be set up to make coffee; the refrigerator that warns of an open door cannot close it; and the computer cookbook can find a recipe but not execute it. Although these appliances make life easier, they still require human effort and creativity.

Did You Know? If you are not going to use the capabilities of a smart appliance, you are better off buying the "no-frills" model because it will be less expensive and less likely to need repairs.

Kitchen Appliances

No matter how your kitchen is set up, your major appliances are basic necessities. This chapter discusses ways to use and care for these appliances to help you work efficiently. (Specific preparation and cooking techniques are covered in chapters 46 and 47.)

Types of Appliances

The most important appliances in every kitchen are the refrigerator, the range, and the oven.

- **The refrigerator.** Many fruits, vegetables, meats, and dairy products are stored in the refrigerator. Most refrigerators have special areas for vegetables, meats, and eggs. Refrigerators usually have a freezer section as well, where frozen foods are stored until they are used. Some kitchens include a separate freezer where large quantities of frozen foods can be kept for many months at a time.

  Caring for refrigerators and freezers means keeping them clean. If a freezer is not self-defrosting, it must be routinely defrosted to keep it operating efficiently.
- **The range.** The cooking surface with three or four gas or electric units is called the range. It may be on top of the oven or located nearby. A range top should be cleaned after each use. Safety while working with the range is especially important, since high temperatures can cause burns or even a fire.
- **The oven.** The oven is used for baking and roasting foods and may also be used to keep foods warm. It is usually located under or near the range. Like other appliances, it requires periodic cleaning to keep it working efficiently. Both ranges and ovens need to be kept clean for safety reasons as well; grease and food spills can cause fires.

Kitchens generally include the three appliances just listed. Other common appliances are dishwashers, microwave ovens, garbage disposals, and trash compactors.

Then there are the many small appliances available to make cooking easier—toasters, toaster ovens, blenders, food processors, electric skillets, and mixers. Many of these appliances have multiple uses. Toaster ovens, for example, can both toast and bake. Food processors do several different preparation tasks, and some mixers have grinding or dough-kneading attachments. These appliances should be wiped off or cleaned after every use.

Many portable appliances are very practical and useful. Some, such as the coffee maker, can also be used for serving.

More About the Range The range has undergone many innovations in recent years. In addition to gas and electric fuel sources, ranges are now available with quartz halogen burners. There are also innovative features such as a range-top hibachi and other types of grills.

Focus on Consumer Skills Many single-use appliances, such as hot-dog cookers, ice cream makers, and bread bakers, are available. Before purchasing this type of product, you should ask yourself how often you will use it and whether it will be worth the cost. Some small appliances merely take up valuable space in the kitchen.

Teaching "Kitchen Appliances"
(Pages 389-390)

This section teaches how to use and care for major kitchen appliances—the refrigerator, range, and oven.

Checking Comprehension

✔ How should a freezer be cared for? *It should be kept clean, and if it is not self-defrosting, it must be routinely defrosted to keep it operating efficiently.*

✔ What is the oven used for? *The oven is used for baking and roasting foods, and may also be used to keep foods warm.*

✔ Name some small kitchen appliances. *Toasters, toaster ovens, blenders, food processors, electric skillets, and mixers.*

✔ How does the EnergyGuide label help the consumer? *This label allows the buyer to compare the energy consumption of various models of appliances.*

✔ How can you save energy when using the refrigerator? *Don't open the refrigerator or freezer door repeatedly or leave it open any longer than necessary.*

✔ What are three ways to save energy when using the oven? *Preheat the oven only if the recipe calls for it; cook two or more items in the oven at the same time; heat small things in a microwave or toaster oven rather than the oven itself.*

Activities

Skill Builder: Critical Thinking
Ask students to list what they should take into account when deciding whether to purchase a small kitchen appliance.

Skill Builder: Math
Have students chart their family's use of kitchen appliances such as toaster, microwave, coffee maker, or blender. Their charts should indicate the approximate number of minutes a week each appliance is used. What would be the projected yearly use for each?

Appliances and Energy

All appliances use energy in some form. The way you use and care for your appliances, however, can have an effect on how much energy they consume.

Major appliances come with an EnergyGuide label. This label allows the buyer to compare the energy consumption of various models.

There are other ways that you can make the kitchen more energy efficient. They include the following:

- Don't open the refrigerator or freezer door repeatedly. Take all that you will need and then close the door as soon as possible.
- Preheat the oven only if the recipe calls for it.
- Cook two or more items in the oven at the same time.
- Heat small things—such as frozen dinners—in a microwave or toaster oven rather than the oven itself.
- Run the dishwasher only when it is full.
- Use the shortest possible washing cycle of your dishwasher, and let the dishes air dry.

The EnergyGuide label gives information about the energy costs of appliances. Consumers can use this information to compare the energy efficiency of various models.

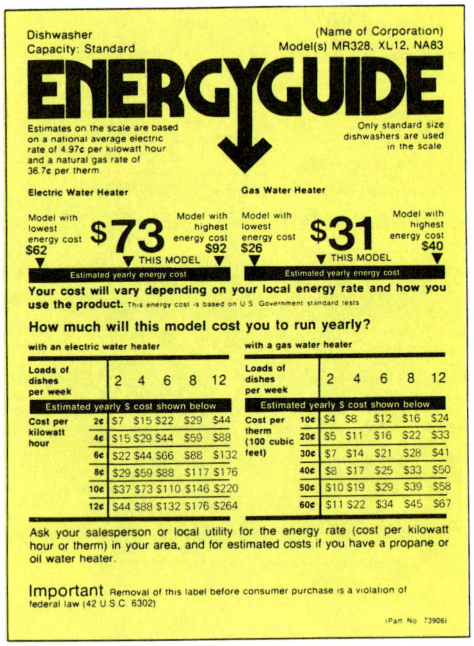

Dishwasher
Capacity: Standard

(Name of Corporation)
Model(s) MR328, XL12, NA83

ENERGYGUIDE

Estimates on the scale are based on a national average electric rate of 4.97¢ per kilowatt hour and a natural gas rate of 36.7¢ per therm.

Only standard size dishwashers are used in the scale

Electric Water Heater

Model with lowest energy cost $62 — $73 THIS MODEL — Model with highest energy cost $92

Estimated yearly energy cost

Gas Water Heater

Model with lowest energy cost $26 — $31 THIS MODEL — Model with highest energy cost $40

Estimated yearly energy cost

Your cost will vary depending on your local energy rate and how you use the product. This energy cost is based on U.S. Government standard tests

How much will this model cost you to run yearly?

with an electric water heater

Loads of dishes per week		2	4	6	8	12
	Estimated yearly $ cost shown below					
Cost per kilowatt hour	2¢	$7	$15	$22	$29	$44
	4¢	$15	$29	$44	$59	$88
	6¢	$22	$44	$66	$88	$132
	8¢	$29	$59	$88	$117	$176
	10¢	$37	$73	$110	$146	$220
	12¢	$44	$88	$132	$176	$264

with a gas water heater

Loads of dishes per week		2	4	6	8	12
	Estimated yearly $ cost shown below					
Cost per therm (100 cubic feet)	10¢	$4	$8	$12	$16	$24
	20¢	$5	$11	$16	$22	$33
	30¢	$7	$14	$21	$28	$41
	40¢	$8	$17	$25	$33	$50
	50¢	$10	$19	$29	$39	$58
	60¢	$11	$22	$34	$45	$67

Ask your salesperson or local utility for the energy rate (cost per kilowatt hour or therm) in your area, and for estimated costs if you have a propane or oil water heater.

Important Removal of this label before consumer purchase is a violation of federal law (42 U.S.C. 6302)

(Part No. 73906)

Using the Kitchen

Whether you are in the foods laboratory at school or in your own home, there are guidelines that help you work more efficiently and responsibly. Keep the following ideas in mind as you work in the kitchen:

- **Learn how to use various tools and appliances.** Later chapters will describe which tools are the right ones for which jobs. Before you use an appliance at home, read the instruction manual. The manual for a dishwasher, for example, will tell you the best ways to load it to get dishes clean.
- **Cooperate with others.** The kitchen belongs to everyone in your home and the foods laboratory belongs to all the students. At home, ask permission before using ingredients. Wherever you are, share responsibilities for preparation, cooking, and cleanup. When working with another person, try to plan so that you don't get in each other's way.
- **Keep the kitchen clean.** Clean the dishes, tools, and small appliances you use, and put away any foods or ingredients you have gotten out. Large appliances should be wiped down regularly. Try to leave the kitchen as clean as, if not cleaner than, you found it.

Reteaching
Ask students to list all the appliances mentioned in this section of the chapter, then rank them in order of importance. Have students place a number 1 beside the appliance they consider the most important, a number 2 beside the next most important, and so on. Afterward have students compare their lists.

Enrichment
Have students choose two or three of the energy-saving suggestions from the chapter and try to institute them at home. Students should then report to the class on their success and analyze why it is sometimes hard to establish energy-saving habits.

Teaching "Using the Kitchen"
(Page 390)

This section teaches how to use the kitchen responsibly by learning how to use utensils and appliances, by keeping the kitchen clean, and by cooperating with others.

Checking Comprehension

✔ What responsibilities should be shared when working with others in the kitchen? *Share responsibilities for preparation, cooking, and cleanup.*

Activities

Skill Builder: Reading
Have students read an instruction manual for a small appliance and outline the booklet's contents.

Reteaching
Have students make a list of cleaning tasks that need to be done after working in the kitchen.

Enrichment
Ask students to make a list of rules for using the kitchen safely and efficiently. They should include rules for the safe and energy-efficient use of kitchen appliances, rules for keeping the kitchen clean, and rules for cooperating with others.

Cross-Reference See Chapter 31 for information about evaluating appliances for quality, durability, convenience, maintenance, safety, price, performance, and warranties.

Cross-reference See Chapter 74 for additional information about managing energy costs in the home.

Focus on Relationship Skills Have students work together in the food lab (or ask them to work jointly with someone at home) to prepare a meal, then discuss the ways they needed to work cooperatively in the kitchen. See "Cooperating in the Foods Lab" on page 406.

CHAPTER 42 REVIEW

Reviewing the Facts

1. What are the three main work centers in the kitchen?
2. What kitchen items would you store in drawers and cabinets by the food preparation center?
3. What is the work triangle?
4. Why should you keep the range and oven clean?
5. What are three things you can do to conserve energy in the kitchen?
6. What are three rules you should follow when you use the kitchen?

Thinking Critically

1. Think about how your family stores food, dishes, and utensils in your kitchen. How could you rearrange these items to create work centers and to save time and energy when working in the kitchen?
2. What kinds of cooperative behavior, other than those mentioned in the text, can you think of that would contribute to smoother operations in the foods laboratory, or in your kitchen at home?

Applying Your Skills

1. **Evaluating Data.** Select a type of small kitchen appliance that your family is thinking of buying, or that you would like them to buy. Find a recent report about it in a consumer magazine, and compare the different brands for quality, features, cost, and, if possible, care and warranty information. Report to the class which one you think your family should buy, and why.

2. **Collecting Information.** Study the owner's manual or manufacturer's instructions for two major appliances (either from home, or in your home economics laboratory). Analyze the two documents, and write a report describing the kinds of information that they provide. Note whether they cover the same general topics, and indicate which document is likely to be more helpful, and why.

3. **Diagramming an Efficient Work Center.** Diagram the way you would set up your kitchen for maximum efficiency. Include the storage of tools and supplies, as well as the placement of major appliances.

Answers to "Reviewing the Facts"

1. Food storage center, food preparation center; and cooking center.
2. Equipment and utensils for preparing food, such as bowls, knives, and measuring spoons.
3. The arrangement of the three major work centers in the kitchen indicated by the refrigerator, sink, and range.
4. So they will work more efficiently and safely; grease and food spills can cause fires.
5. Any three: keep refrigerator and freezer doors closed as much as possible; preheat oven only when recipe requires; cook more than one item in the oven; heat small things in microwave or toaster oven; run dishwasher only when full; use short washing cycle of dishwasher if possible.
6. Learn how to use various tools and appliances; cooperate with others; keep the kitchen clean.

Answers to "Thinking Critically"

1. Answers will vary. Students should think in terms of what foods, dishes, tools, and supplies are needed at each work center.
2. Answers will vary, but students may suggest some of the following ideas: always return food and equipment to its correct storage location; let others know when supplies of a particular staple are getting low; be ready to step aside if someone is carrying a hot container past you; volunteer to clean up an area when you are not busy.

COMPLETING THE CHAPTER

Summary

- Food should be stored where it will not spoil, in the proper containers, using the rotation system.
- The kitchen has three work centers: one for food storage, one for food preparation, and one for cooking.
- The work centers in the kitchen form a work triangle.
- The refrigerator, range, and oven are the major kitchen appliances. They, and smaller appliances, should be used carefully and kept clean.
- The EnergyGuide label helps consumers buy energy-efficient appliances. Appliances should be used in ways that conserve energy.
- To use the kitchen responsibly, learn how to use tools and appliances, keep the kitchen clean, and cooperate with others.

For Review

Objective Review Questions Have students complete the "Reviewing the Facts" section on this page.

Study Guide Have students complete the Study Guide from Chapter 42 of their *Student Workbook*.

Describe Have students describe the rules for responsible use of the kitchen and tell why each of the rules is important.

For Evaluation

Classification Have students classify all the appliances mentioned in this chapter by listing them under one of the following three headings: "Necessary," "Desirable but not Necessary," "Luxury".

Follow Through Have students plan the preparation of a meal, listing each task and identifying the work center where it would be carried out. They should also list all of the utensils and appliances that would be used and the cleanup that would be required.

Chapter Test Have students complete the test for Chapter 42 that appears in the *Teacher's Classroom Resources.*

Teaching "Make a Schedule"
(Pages 404-407)

This section explains how to make a schedule for preparing and cooking a meal.

Checking Comprehension

✓ What should you consider in estimating the preparation time of a meal? *How much time it will take to chop, mix, and assemble the ingredients before cooking time begins; what equipment needs to be assembled beforehand; what ingredients need to be processed beforehand; and how long each item will take to cook or chill.*

✓ How does determining a sequence for the preparation tasks help you? *By enabling you to work efficiently and to make the most of your time. If you are working with others, the tasks can be divided more productively if a sequence has been worked out.*

✓ Why is it important to dovetail tasks? *To save time and perform tasks more efficiently.*

Make a Schedule

Once you have read the recipe or directions, your next step is to work out a schedule so all the foods will be ready on time.

Note the Times

Estimate preparation time—the time it will take you to chop, mix, and assemble the ingredients before cooking begins. In addition, you may need to prepare equipment beforehand—to preheat the oven or grease a baking pan. These tasks also take time.

Some recipes may call for ingredients that have already been prepared, such as hard-cooked eggs, crisp bacon, or firm gelatin. Check how long it will take each item to cook or chill. If the recipe does not contain this information, consult other recipe books or talk with someone who has used a similar recipe.

Plan the Sequence

Next, you need to decide exactly what steps you will take and in what order, or **sequence**. Should you measure out all the ingredients beforehand, or as you need them? Is there anything you can do while waiting for the water to boil or the meat to brown? Deciding on a sequence helps you to work productively and make the most of your time.

When working with others, you need to divide the tasks efficiently. Everyone should have something to do. For example, you might prepare the pasta while someone else makes the sauce. In the foods laboratory, learning to assign tasks and work together is very important.

A Sample Schedule

Julie and Binh plan to prepare and serve the following meal to two of their friends:

Macaroni and Cheese
Garden Salad
Apples
Milk

They plan a simple salad of lettuce, carrots, and cucumbers, so they have only one detailed recipe to follow—"Creamy Macaroni and Cheese." (See page 405).

Before they started preparing the meal, Julie and Binh sat down to plan their schedule. They figured that the macaroni and cheese would take about an hour to prepare. They decided to make the salad while the macaroni and cheese was baking. Here is the schedule they planned:

11:00
Binh: Heat water for macaroni. Wash apples, put in bowl, place in refrigerator. Grease casserole.
Julie: Measure ingredients for cheese sauce and grate cheese.

11:10
Julie: Preheat oven. Make cheese sauce.
Binh: Place macaroni in boiling water. Melt butter and mix with bread crumbs for topping. Set table.

11:25
Binh: Drain macaroni and put in casserole.
Julie: Pour sauce on macaroni and add topping.

11:30
Julie: Put casserole in oven. Wash and dry lettuce, break up leaves, put in salad bowl.
Binh: Wash and shred carrots. Wash and slice cucumbers. Add to salad and refrigerate.

11:50
Binh: Add dressing to salad and place bowl on table.
Julie: Set out apples.

NOON
Julie: Bring casserole to table.
Binh: Pour milk.

Emphasize Making a schedule not only increases cooking efficiency, it also helps prevent accidents and cooking failures.

Cross-Reference See Chapter 26 for information about time management.

Focus on Consumer Skills Some preparation tasks can be shortened by buying convenience foods available in grocery stores. For example, you can buy packages of chopped nuts, premade pie shells, or instant stuffings and rice mixes to speed your cooking tasks.

CREAMY MACARONI AND CHEESE

8 oz.	(240 g)	elbow macaroni
¼ cup	(50 mL)	butter or margarine
¼ cup	(50 mL)	flour
½ tsp.	(2 mL)	salt
¼ tsp.	(1 mL)	pepper
2 cups	(500 mL)	milk
1 cup	(250 mL)	grated cheddar cheese
Topping:		
½ cup	(125 mL)	dry bread crumbs
1 Tbsp.	(15 mL)	butter or margarine, melted

Exact Amounts — Ingredients listed in order of use

Cook macaroni according to package directions and drain. Place in greased 1½ qt. (1.5 L) casserole.

To prepare sauce, melt butter or margarine in 1 qt. (1 L) saucepan over low heat. Add flour, salt, and pepper and stir until mixture is smooth and bubbly. Remove pan from heat and add milk. Stir mixture over medium heat until boiling, then stir one minute longer. Reduce heat. Add cheese and stir until melted. Pour cheese sauce over macaroni and mix.

Combine bread crumbs and melted butter, and sprinkle mixture over macaroni and cheese. Bake uncovered at 375°F (190°C) for 30 minutes, or until top is brown and sauce bubbles. Makes 4 servings.

Pan Size — Time — Temperature — Step-by-Step Instructions — Servings

Making a schedule helps you manage the meal preparation so all the foods will be ready to eat at the same time.

Focus on Leadership Ask students to imagine what scheduling responsibilities a restaurant manager has. Ask students to list what qualities they think such a person would need to perform his or her supervisory tasks.

Activities

Skill Builder: Critical Thinking
Reorder the following sequence of tasks for preparing tuna salad; then ask students to sequence them in a logical order: 1) read recipe carefully; 2) chop up celery and onions and set aside; 3) open can of tuna and put in bowl; 4) combine ingredients; 5) stir in salad dressing; 6) refrigerate.

Skill Builder: Writing
Have students write a schedule, in the same format as the chapter's sample schedule, for preparing to cook a meal of salad, spaghetti, garlic bread, and chocolate pudding. (Provide package directions for the pasta and pudding as well as a written recipe for the garlic bread.) Remind students to consider what tasks can be done ahead of time, and in what sequence they should perform the tasks so all the foods will be ready at mealtime.

Reteaching
Give students a recipe for cookies or cake. Then divide the class into groups of two or three and have each group write down how they would allocate the tasks for maximum efficiency. Explain that they should also sequence their tasks in the proper order.

Enrichment
Have students observe someone preparing to cook a meal. Ask students to write down the schedule and sequence that the cook followed. Then ask students to interview the cook about how he or she organized the preparation tasks.

Teaching the Feature

"Cooperating in the Foods Lab"

Answers to Feature Questions

1. Students could do other important tasks until the machines is free. Students might offer to do a favor for someone using a food processor in return for being allowed to use the machine. Students could slice, chop, or mix in ingredients using tools other than the food processor.

2. This is a good rule because it would be unfair for you to start off at a clean work center, then leave it dirty for the next student. Such a rule shows respect for others and it teaches good work habits. The student might explain to the person who left the work center dirty that he or she was being unfair to the rest of the class. If the student gets no response, the incident should be reported to the teacher.

Activities

Promoting Cooperation Have students create posters that promote courteous and safe behavior for group cooking in a foods lab. Help students get started by telling them to think of a good rule for cooking in a foods lab (such as cleaning up after cooking), and illustrate it with drawings or pictures, a catchy title, and/or a caption.

Supervising Group Cooking Tell students to imagine they are supervising a group of people who are baking chocolate chip cookies. Provide each student with a recipe, and have individuals assign tasks that others could do to make baking the cookies a quicker, more efficient job. Remind them that tasks should include beforehand preparations, such as chopping nuts or melting margarine, as well as cleanup afterward.

Community Contact Have a local restaurant or cafeteria manager speak to the class on how professional kitchens operate. Ask him or her to explain how tasks are divided among workers.

INTERPERSONAL SKILLS

Cooperating in the Foods Lab

Working in a foods laboratory is different from doing tasks by yourself in your own kitchen. You are working in a group, and that means cooperation; you have to take turns, share ingredients, and wait to use some appliances and tools. Here are a few guidelines that will help you:

- Plan your work ahead of time. Decide what has to be done when. Make a list of the ingredients, equipment, and utensils you will need.
- Share preparation with other students so you can get all your work done faster. For example, if your group is making beef stew, one student can trim and cube the beef while a second chops the onions. A third student can peel and slice the carrots, and a fourth can peel and cut up the potatoes.
- Follow all rules and procedures that your home economics teacher has established. These rules are important for safety and sanitation.
- Remember that laboratory time is limited. If you waste time, you and your classmates may not be able to finish preparing a recipe.
- Be courteous to other students. Show the same good manners you would in any social situation. Wait patiently for your turn at the range, or volunteer to help others when you have nothing to do. This will contribute to making the foods laboratory an enjoyable experience for everyone.

Think It Through

1. **What would you do if you needed to use one of the home economics laboratory's food processors, but other students were using all of the available appliances and the class period was nearly over?**
2. **Your teacher has a rule that students must clean up each work center as soon as they finish using it. Why is this a good rule? What would you do if you saw a student leave a work center without cleaning it up?**

Did You Know? Large professional kitchens provide work stations for various tasks. For example, there may be a station where workers prepare foods for cooking. There may also be a bake work station for preparing breads and desserts, a hot-food station for hot foods and final cooking, and a cold-food station for cold foods and appetizers.

Focus on Health Cooperation during group cooking is important so that there is less confusion and better handling of food, and thus fewer accidents.

Simplify Your Work

Once you've made a plan, look it over to see if you can make it simpler or more efficient. Some things to look for are:

- **Can you dovetail any tasks?** When you **dovetail** tasks, you combine them in such a way that one task overlaps another, saving time. Check the schedule on page 404—while the macaroni is cooking, the cheese sauce and crumb topping can be prepared.
- **Are you doing the job in the most efficient way?** When you are chopping onions, cut up peppers and celery, too. If you need to use flour, sugar, and baking powder, measure them all at the same time, and keep them in a bowl or on wax paper until needed.
- **What can you prepare ahead of time?** Sometimes you can prepare food earlier in the day or even the day before you plan to serve it. Perhaps you can bake a cake in the morning for dessert that evening. You can make potato salad one day to eat the next.
- **Is your plan flexible?** Even though you plan for all items to be completed at the same time, some foods may get done before others. However, most foods can be kept warm in the oven or on the range or kept cold in the refrigerator.

Assemble the Equipment and Ingredients

The final stage before preparation and cooking can begin is assembling the equipment and ingredients.

1. Clear the kitchen counters to give yourself room to work. For good sanitation, wipe off the counters and range to make sure they are clean.
2. Lay out the equipment and utensils you will need. Many recipes call for special pans, such as cake pans or cookie sheets, or they require bowls or casseroles of a certain size or capacity. For microwave cooking, you will need microwave-safe dishes or containers (see Chapter 48). In addition, some recipes require you to measure, cut, or mix ingredients. For each task, locate the right tools or appliances to do the job. You will learn how to do these tasks in the following chapters.
3. Lay out the ingredients you will need, including herbs and spices. However, keep refrigerated items in the refrigerator until you are ready to use them.
4. Plan to clean up as you work, so you won't have so much to do afterward. Fill a dishpan or one-half of a double sink with hot sudsy water. Rinse bowls, utensils, and pans immediately after using them, and place in the hot water to wash or to soak until you have time to wash.

Assembling all the necessary ingredients and equipment ahead of time will make the preparation and cooking steps much easier.

Focus on Technology Many appliances have been invented to help speed up cooking tasks and make the job more efficient. Many of these appliances perform more than one job. For example, a blender can mix different foods or it can chop ingredients. Have students discuss the multiple uses of a food processor. See Chapter 46.

Focus on Consumer Skills Before buying a new kitchen appliance, certain considerations must be made. These include cost, use, safety, and reliability. See Chapter 31 for information about evaluating purchases on quality, performance, and price.

Teaching "Assemble the Equipment and Ingredients"
(Page 407)

This section explains the importance of assembling equipment and ingredients.

Checking Comprehension

✓ Why should you fill a dishpan with hot sudsy water when you're preparing to cook? *To wash bowls and utensils as soon as you are finished so you won't have so much work to do afterward.*

Activities

Skill Builder: Math
Tell students that cooking for groups often means cooking large quantities of food, which in turn means buying food in large quantities. Some food stores allow consumers to buy in bulk. Tell students that, in most cases, the larger the amount of food you buy, the less the food costs per individual serving. Have the students calculate the following example: A can of pet food costs $.39 when you buy only one can. If you buy a case (24 cans) for $7.20, how much will each can cost you? ($.30)

Skill Builder: Reading
Provide a carrot cake recipe for students to read. Ask them to list the equipment and ingredients they would assemble before baking the cake. Remind them to note any special utensils or procedures the recipe calls for.

Reteaching
Have students give examples of various equipment and ingredients they would need to assemble before baking a cake, boiling pasta, or preparing a garden salad.

Enrichment
Ask students to evaluate a meal that they or another person cooked at home. Ask students to note whether more careful scheduling of tasks would have resulted in a tastier or better-timed meal. Encourage students to share what they have learned from their own or someone else's experiences.

COMPLETING THE CHAPTER

Summary

- Reading the recipe or package directions and understanding its abbreviations and cooking terms is the first step in planning a meal.
- Next, prepare a schedule, listing the times and the sequence of the steps to follow.
- Preparation of food can be simplified by dovetailing tasks, checking for efficiency, preparing ahead of time, and being flexible.
- A final step in preparing a meal is to lay out the equipment and ingredients that are needed to cook the meal.

For Review

Objective Review Questions Have students complete the "Reviewing the Facts" section on this page.

Study Guide Have students complete the Study Guide from Chapter 44 of their *Student Workbook.*

Tacos Anyone? Divide students into two groups and have them read a package recipe for tacos. Have one group use the directions for a conventional range and oven to make the tacos, and have the other group use the directions for a microwave oven. Ask each group to make plans for preparing their tacos. Plans should include a schedule for completing each step, a description of tasks to be completed by different group members, and a list of equipment and ingredients. Have each group evaluate the other's plans.

For Evaluation

Self-Appraisal Ask students to perform a self-appraisal of their group's plans for preparing tacos in the preceding activity. Tell students to evaluate whether or not their group understood the package directions and made an efficient schedule.

Chapter Test Have students complete the test for Chapter 44 that appears in the *Teacher's Classroom Resources.*

CHAPTER 44 REVIEW

Reviewing the Facts

1. What five pieces of information should a recipe include?
2. What are abbreviations? What are the abbreviations for tablespoon, pound, and milliliter?
3. Name one important item to note when reading package directions.
4. Why is it important to understand all of the terms in a recipe?
5. What is the purpose of making a schedule for preparing a meal?
6. List three things you should consider when simplifying your work plan.
7. What are the four steps to follow during the final stage of getting ready to cook?

Thinking Critically

1. Karen's lunch for her friends, described at the start of this chapter, was a disaster. If you planned to make the same meal for your friends, what would you do differently?
2. Why do you think it is important to study the recipe or package directions well before you are actually going to prepare the dish?

Applying Your Skills

1. **Making a Schedule.** Assume that you intend to cook the following meal for three friends: hamburgers, corn on the cob, salad, and pudding. Consult cookbooks for the cooking times for each of these foods and make a schedule, similar to the one Binh and Julie planned in the chapter. Show each step you would take to complete this meal. Be prepared to present it to the class.

2. **Evaluating Seasonings.** Make a list of the herbs and spices you find in the home economics laboratory. Then go through some cookbooks and find recipes that use these spices or herbs. Make a chart showing the seasonings and the recipes they are used in.

3. **Assessing Formats.** Look at the recipe formats presented on page 402. Then look through cookbooks and identify which formats were used. Why do you think some formats are more popular than others? Which do you find easiest to follow, and why?

Answers to "Reviewing the Facts"

1. Name of the food; name and amount of each ingredient; directions for assembling and cooking the food; oven setting; number of servings.
2. Shortened forms of words. T. or Tbsp., lb., mL.
3. Any one: if any additional ingredients are needed; special directions for your area (high-altitude) or cooking method (microwave).
4. If you make a mistake in the preparation, cooking, or measurement of ingredients, you can ruin the entire recipe.
5. To make certain that all the foods are ready to eat at the same time.
6. Any three: Can you dovetail tasks? Are you being efficient? What can you prepare ahead? Is your plan flexible?
7. Clear the counters and range top; lay out equipment and utensils; lay out ingredients; plan to clean up as you work.

Answers to "Thinking Critically"

1. Answers should center on planning ahead. Since students already know the menu, they should check that all the ingredients are available. They should also check that the kitchen is clean. The best plan for a novice would probably be to prepare the salad first and refrigerate it, then heat the soup and leave it on a slow heat, and finally prepare the sandwiches.
2. Students should mention that they need to make sure that they have all of the necessary ingredients and equipment, that they understand what they have to do, and that they will have enough time to prepare the dish.

CHAPTER

45

Measuring Basics

OBJECTIVES

This chapter will help you to:

- Identify customary and metric terms of measurement.
- Describe measurement utensils and their use in the kitchen.
- Demonstrate how to measure liquid and dry ingredients accurately.
- Adapt recipes for smaller or greater amounts.

WORDS TO REMEMBER

customary system
equivalent
metric system
volume

Chapter Resources

Teacher's Classroom Resources
- Lesson Plan
- Life Skills Activity, *Measuring Techniques*
- Reproducible Master, *Measuring Tools*
- Extension Activity, *Equivalents*
- Chapter Test

Student Workbook
- Study Guide
- Worksheet, *Measuring Match-Ups*

CHAPTER OVERVIEW

Chapter 45 teaches students how to measure. It defines measuring terms—for volume, weight, temperature, length, and time—and describes the equipment that is used to determine measurements. Specific instructions are given for accurately measuring liquid and dry ingredients, some of which require special techniques. Instructions are also provided for adjusting recipe measurements.

INTRODUCING THE CHAPTER

Motivators

Measure It! Ask students to think about circumstances (outside of the kitchen) in which they measure something (for example, they might weigh themselves in the morning, take their temperature when they feel sick, measure the length of a football pass, and so on). Point out that being able to measure things properly is a valuable skill—especially in the kitchen.

Using the Photograph Have students study the photograph on this page. Then ask: "What measuring utensils do you see here? What others are commonly used in the kitchen?"

Imprecise Measurements Have students list some precise measurements (two teaspoons, four inches) and some that are imprecise (a pinch, a handful).

Introducing the Objectives

Discuss the chapter objectives on this page. Remind students that the objectives focus on important chapter content.

Introducing Vocabulary

Point out that the Metric system is so named because its fundamental unit of measurement is the meter.

When you watch experienced cooks, it often seems that they follow their instincts as they prepare food. A pinch of this combined with a dash of that results in something delicious. However, even an experienced cook relies on recipes for most food preparation. Following a recipe starts with careful measurement of the ingredients. If you don't measure precisely, the food won't turn out the way you expected.

Measuring Terms

Before beginning to cook, you need to understand the terms used for measuring food. This section explains the most common measurement terms and their abbreviations.

Two different systems of measurement may be used to give the ingredient amounts in a recipe. The standard one in the United States is the **customary system**, which measures in teaspoons, tablespoons, cups, pints, quarts, ounces, and pounds. Most of the world, however, uses the **metric system**, which measures in grams and liters. The metric system is also used by scientists, nutritionists, and other health professionals in this country. Remember that the two systems are just different ways of expressing amounts. It is helpful to know how to measure using both systems.

See "Measure for Measure: Equivalents" on page 414 for a comparison of customary and metric measurements. Both systems can be used for measuring volume, weight, temperature, and length.

Measurement by Volume

The most usual method of measurement for cooking in America is measurement by **volume**—the amount of space taken up by an ingredient.

Common terms for volume measurement include:

- Customary—teaspoon (tsp. or t.), tablespoon (Tbsp. or T.), fluid ounce (oz.), cup (c.), pint (pt.), quart (qt.), and gallon (gal.).
- Metric—milliliter (mL) and liter (L).

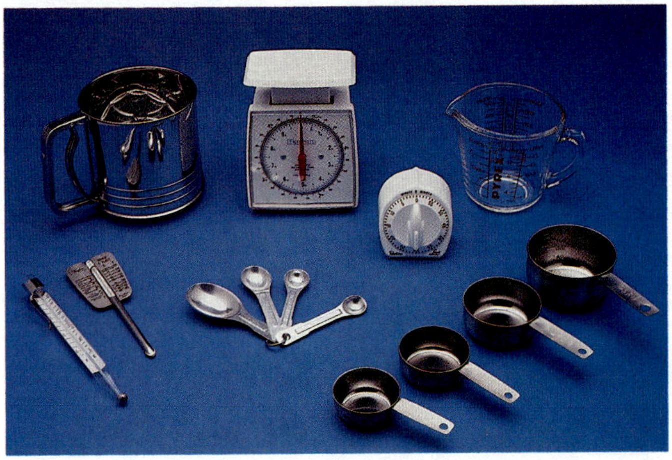

How many of these tools can you identify? See page 412 for a description of each.

TEACHING THE CHAPTER

For convenience, the teaching suggestions for this chapter are arranged according to the following lesson topics:

- "Measuring Terms," pages 410-411
- "Measuring Equipment," page 411
- "Measuring Accurately," pages 411-415
- "Adjusting Measurements," page 415

Teaching "Measuring Terms"
(Pages 410-411)

This section explains the customary and metric systems of measurement and discusses the methods of measurement by volume, weight, and other standards.

Checking Comprehension

✔ Where is the metric system used? *Most of the world uses the metric system. It is also used by scientists, nutritionists, and other health professionals in the United States.*

✔ How are the metric and customary systems of measurement similar? *They can both be used for measuring volume, weight, temperature, and length.*

✔ What is the difference between volume and weight? *Volume is how much space is taken up by an ingredient; weight is how much the ingredient weighs.*

Activities

Skill Builder: Reading
Have students read five recipes and list all of the indications for measurement, including volume, weight, temperature, length, and time.

Skill Builder: Critical Thinking
Ask students to discuss the problems caused by the United States using a different measurement system from the rest of the world and the problems that would result if the United States were to try to switch systems.

Did You Know? The metric system was first proposed in France by Gabriel Mouton in 1670. It was put into practice more than 100 years later, in 1795.

More About Metric The metric system is a decimal system, that is, one in which all derived units are multiples of ten.

Cross-Reference See Chapter 44 for information about recipes and common abbreviations for measurements.

Measurement by Weight

Solid ingredients in recipes are often described in terms of their weight. Most packaged foods, such as meat, poultry, pasta, and canned foods list the weight on the package. For other ingredients you can sometimes use **equivalents**, or comparison facts. These can help you convert weight measurements into volume.

The following are common terms for measuring weight:

- Customary—ounce (oz.) and pound (lb.).
- Metric—gram (g) and kilogram (kg).

Notice that ounce is used both as a volume measure (for liquids) and as a measure of weight. You may have to figure out which is called for when you read the recipe.

Other Types of Measurements

Volume and weight are not the only types of measurements needed in cooking. Temperature is measured in degrees—degrees Fahrenheit (°F) in the customary system and degrees Celsius (°C) in the metric system.

Length measurements may be used in recipes to indicate the size of a vegetable, the thickness of a cut of meat, or the size of a pan. In the customary system, length is given in inches (in.). For metric recipes, millimeters (mm) or centimeters (cm) are used.

Time is also important in cooking. To prepare a recipe successfully, the cooking or baking time should be followed carefully. Time is measured the same way in both systems—hours, minutes, and seconds.

Measuring Equipment

There are many tools used for measuring, and each plays a vital part in food preparation. Learning how to select and use the proper equipment will make measuring easier and more accurate for you.

On page 410 you will see pictures of various measuring utensils. Volume is measured with liquid measuring cups, dry measuring cups, and measuring spoons. A kitchen scale is used to determine weight. Oven thermometers show the temperature of the oven while food is cooking. Special meat and candy thermometers are available to check the temperature of those foods. You can keep track of cooking or baking time with a timer.

Measuring Accurately

Correct measurements depend on using the right equipment in the proper way. Cups and spoons used for drinking and eating can vary considerably in size. That is why special measuring cups and spoons should always be used for measuring ingredients.

When you measure most ingredients, you can either pour the ingredient into the measuring utensil or dip the utensil into the ingredient, whichever is more convenient. If you are dipping, wash and dry the cup or spoon before you measure a different ingredient. If you are pouring, never hold the utensil over the bowl in which you are mixing. You might pour too much, and the extra amount that falls in the bowl could affect the results.

Measuring techniques differ depending upon whether the ingredient is liquid or dry. Some techniques are even special for particular ingredients.

Focus on Consumer skills When choosing a thermometer (oven, meat, or candy), select one that is clearly marked and easy to read. Candy and oven thermometers should have a clip that attaches them to the pan or the oven shelf.

Emphasize Using the illustrations on page 412, have students describe the characteristics and use of liquid measuring cups, dry measuring cups, and measuring spoons. Which ones should be used for larger amounts of liquids and solids? Which should be used for smaller amounts of liquids and solids?

Reteaching
Have students list the customary and metric terms of measurement from the chapter under the following categories: volume, weight, temperature, and length. (Volume: teaspoon, tablespoon, fluid ounce, cup, pint, quart, gallon, milliliter, and liter. Weight: ounce, pound, gram, and kilogram. Temperature: degrees Fahrenheit and degrees Celsius. Length: inches, millimeters, and centimeters.)

Enrichment
Have students find some cookbooks that offer both customary and metric measurements in their recipes and ask the students to name some advantages of listing both types of measurement.

Teaching "Measuring Equipment"

(Page 411)

This section describes the measuring equipment used when cooking or preparing food.

Checking Comprehension

✓ What equipment is used to measure volume? *Volume is measured with liquid measuring cups, dry measuring cups, and measuring spoons.*

✓ What is a kitchen scale used to measure? *It is used to measure ingredients by weight.*

✓ What are three type of thermometers? *Oven, meat, and candy thermometers.*

Activities

Skill Builder: Writing
Have students examine a recipe and list all the measuring equipment they would need to prepare the food.

Introducing Vocabulary

Write the word *garnish* on the board and define it as to decorate or add savory touches to food. Tell students that a wide variety of foods can serve as garnishes. Commonly used garnishes include lemon wedges, sprigs of parsley, radishes, and nuts. Ask students to suggest other ideas.

TEACHING THE CHAPTER

For convenience, the teaching suggestions for this chapter are arranged according to the following lesson topics:

- "Preparing Food" and "Cutting Techniques," pages 418-421
- "Mixing Techniques," pages 421-424
- "Special Techniques," page 424

Teaching "Preparing Food" and "Cutting Techniques"

(Pages 418-421)

The first section identifies the tasks involved in getting food ready for cooking or serving. The second section describes cutting methods and tools as well as safety precautions for using the tools.

Checking Comprehension

✓ What tasks are involved in preparing food for a meal? *Getting cold foods ready for the table and hot foods ready for cooking; cutting and/or mixing ingredients; and knowing what equipment to use, what recipe terms mean, and how to perform certain preparation tasks.*

✓ How is a paring knife different from a chef's knife? *A paring knife is a small knife used for peeling and cutting foods, especially fruits and vegetables. A chef's knife has a long, triangular blade that is used for slicing, chopping, mincing, and dicing foods.*

✓ How should soft fruits and vegetables be peeled? *By cutting lightly into the food with a paring knife and lifting the skin away.*

Have you ever seen a professional chef prepare food? In some Japanese restaurants, you can watch as the food is prepared and cooked at your table. The skillful way in which the chef cuts vegetables becomes an impressive display of showmanship. A chef who can do this knows a great deal about techniques as well as equipment.

How does your knowledge compare? Do you know the difference between dicing and mincing? Can you distinguish between blending and folding? Each term names a technique for using certain equipment in specific ways to get the right results.

Preparing Food

Preparing food means getting cold foods ready for the table and hot foods ready for cooking. The steps you must follow often involve cutting or mixing ingredients. Your recipe will guide you through the preparation techniques required. However, you need to know what equipment to use, what the terms mean, and how to perform certain tasks.

Cutting Techniques

For the preparation jobs that involve cutting food into slices or smaller pieces, many specialized tools and appliances have been developed. Learning about each will help you choose the right equipment for each job. You will also need to know the terms that describe different cutting tasks. Since cutting involves using sharp tools, safety rules must always be followed.

Cutting Tools and Equipment

A well-stocked kitchen has several types of knives, each of which can be used for many tasks. Other tools—from shears to peelers to cutting boards—are needed for special cutting jobs. In addition, cutting appliances like the blender and the food processor can handle many tasks. See these tools on page 419.

Cutting Terms and Tasks

Cutting tools are helpful only if you know how to use them for different tasks.

- **Peel.** Use a knife or peeler to **peel** or remove the skin of fruits and vegetables. For soft fruits and vegetables, such as peaches and tomatoes, use a paring knife. Cut lightly into the food and lift the skin away. Dipping the fruit or vegetable in boiling water for 30 seconds will make peeling easier. A paring knife can also be used to cut away the skin of firm fruits, such as apples and oranges.

  Use a peeler for firm vegetables, such as carrots, cucumbers, and potatoes. This cuts a much thinner peel, leaving more of the vitamins that are concentrated just under the skin. A peeler can also be used to cut vegetables into thin, decorative strips. These can be used in a salad, or as a **garnish** to add color to other foods.

PEEL

Emphasize Stress the importance of knowing the correct cutting techniques for different types of foods. Always use a sharp knife—it makes the job easier and actually causes fewer accidents than a dull knife.

More About Cutting Techniques Boning means to cut closely along the bone to separate the meat from the bones and joints. A special knife, called a boning knife, is used for this job. This knife has a thin lightweight blade that narrows to a sharp point.

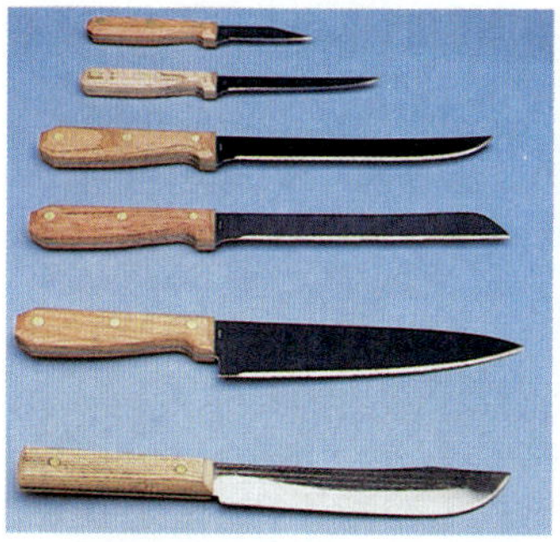

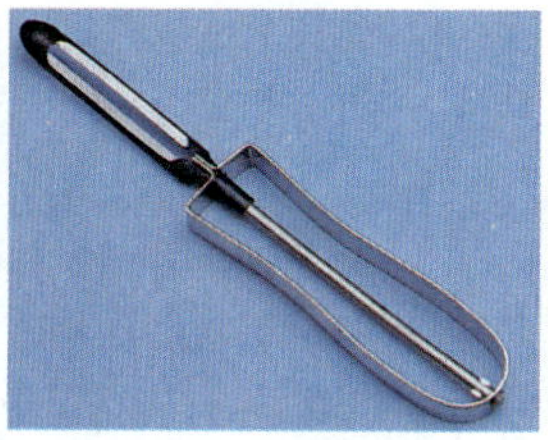

Peeler. Swivel blade is used to remove the skin from fruits and vegetables.

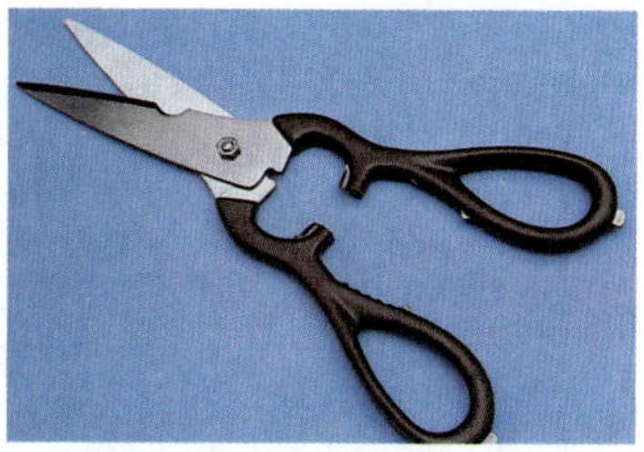

Kitchen Shears. Sturdy scissors used to cut foods such as meat, poultry, vegetables, pastry, and dried fruits.

Paring Knife. Use to peel fruits and vegetables.
Utility Knife. Use to cut and slice cheese and vegetables.
Slicing Knife. Use to slice meats and poultry.
Bread Knife. Has serrated edge for cutting bread and cake.
Chef's Knife. Use to slice, chop, mince, and dice fruits and vegetables.
Butcher Knife. Use to divide large cuts of meat or vegetables.

Cutting Board. Wooden or plastic board used to protect countertop when cutting or chopping foods. (Plastic should be used with meat or poultry.)

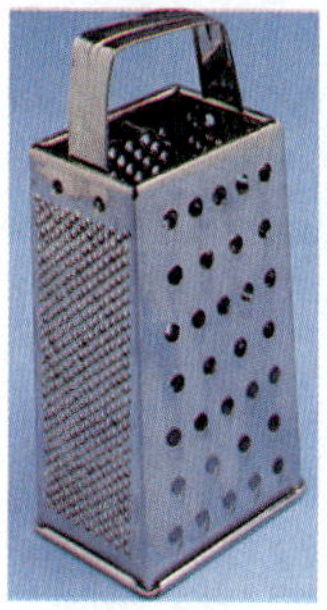

Grater. Sharp-edged holes are used to shred and grate vegetables and cheeses.

Food Mill. Used to puree foods.

Food Processor. Appliance used to slice, chop, mince, shred, and grate foods; knead dough; and mix ingredients.

Blender. Appliance used to chop, blend, and liquify foods.

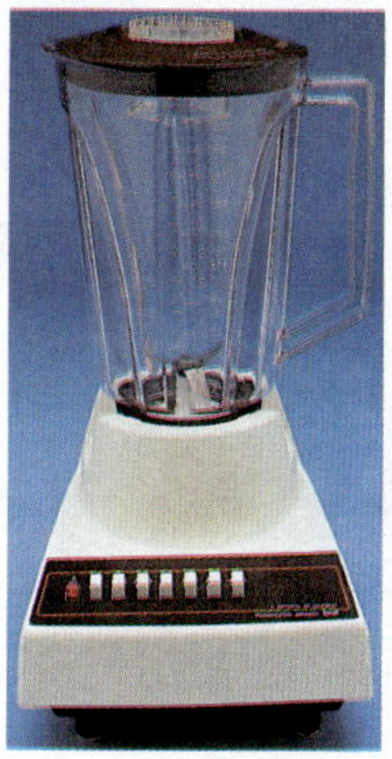

✓ What is the difference between chopping and mincing? *To chop, you cut food into small pieces; to mince you keep chopping until the food bits are even smaller—as small as you can make them.*

✓ Name two cutting tools that can shred food. *A grater and a food processor.*

✓ Why are dull knives a danger? *Because they slip easily and can cut your fingers.*

✓ How should knives be washed? *One at a time—don't place them in soapy water where they cannot be seen.*

Activities

Skill Builder: Writing
Ask students to choose one of the cutting tools mentioned in this section and write a brief description of it. Their description should explain what the tool looks like and what it is used for. Students should include examples of foods that could be cut with that particular tool.

Did You Know? There is a special knife that is only used for sectioning citrus fruits. This citrus knife has a blade that is serrated on both sides, and a rounded tip that curls upward.

Focus on Health To prevent cutting injuries when using knives, be sure to use the correct knife for the task. For example, do not use a light-bladed knife to cut heavy foods, like watermelon. The knife might break or slip out of your hand, causing injury.

Skill Builder: Critical Thinking
Ask students to brainstorm safety rules for using cutting tools. Ask them to organize their ideas into a list and write the list on poster boards. Tell students to display the boards in the foods lab.

Reteaching
Ask students to give examples of three cutting techniques and the tools necessary for performing these techniques.

Enrichment
Have students make a list of the cutting tools that are in their kitchens at home. Then ask them to describe what cutting techniques these tools can be used for and to offer safety precautions for using the tools.

- **Slice.** To slice food—carrots or meat, for example—cut it into thin, flat pieces using a sharp knife and a cutting board. Steady the food with your other hand or with a fork.
- **Chop and mince.** To **chop** is to cut food into small pieces. Tools used for chopping can range from a chef's knife to a food processor. Some foods, such as parsley, can even be chopped with kitchen shears. Food can be chopped coarse, medium, or fine. To mince, keep chopping until the food bits are as small as you can make them. Foods such as onions, garlic, and ginger give the most flavor when chopped or minced.
- **Cube and dice.** Use these techniques to cut food into small cubes or squares that are all the same size. You can cube cheeses, cooked meats, and vegetables. Slice the food in one direction, then grasp the slices all together and cut them in the other direction. Finally, grasp the resulting strips together, lay them on their sides, and cut again to make cubes. To dice, make the cubes very small.
- **Shred.** To **shred** is to grate or cut food into fine pieces using a grater. Foods such as carrots, cabbage, and cheese are often shredded or grated. Food processors are also excellent for shredding.
- **Puree.** To **puree** (pyu-RAY) is to cut or mash food so fine that no solid pieces remain. Foods such as vegetables are usually cooked first before being pureed. Small amounts of some foods can be pureed in a blender.

CUBE

SHRED

PUREE

SLICE

CHOP

Focus on Technology For cutting large amounts of food (such as lettuce or cabbage), an appliance called a vertical cutter can be used. It is a much larger, heavier version of a blender. This appliance can also be used to mix pie dough or cake batter.

Focus on Technology There is a machine, called a salad maker, that slices, shreds, or grates raw vegetables and fruits to be used in salads. Salad makers can be manual or electric.

Cutting Safety

Cutting usually requires the use of knives or other hazardous equipment, so it's important to follow safety precautions to avoid accidents.

- Keep knives sharp. Dull knives slip easily and can cut your fingers.
- Always cut with the blade of the knife slanting away from you.
- Use a cutting board each time you use a knife.
- If you drop a knife, let it fall. Never try to catch it on the way down.
- Wash knives one at a time. Never place them in soapy water where they cannot be seen.
- When working with a food processor or blender, don't put your hand or a tool inside while the blades are moving or the motor is turned on.

Safety is very important when using appliances with motor-driven blades.

Mixing Techniques

Food preparation often requires combining one ingredient with another—or mixing. Ingredients must be combined in the correct way for the recipe to turn out well.

Mixing Tools and Equipment

Mixing is usually done with a variety of mixing bowls and spoons. Some mixing tasks, however, require specialized equipment, such as an electric mixer. How many of the items shown on page 422 would you use to make a cake?

Mixing Terms and Tasks

Mixing tasks differ according to the speed at which the mixing is done, and whether any air is introduced into the mixture.

- **Stir and combine.** These are slow mixing techniques usually done with a spoon. To stir, you use a circular motion to mix the ingredients.

Stirring can be done with a wooden or metal spoon.

Teaching "Mixing Techniques"
(Pages 421-424)

This section explains different mixing techniques and tools, and offers several tips for mixing foods.

Checking Comprehension

✓ Why is mixing important in food preparation? *Because if ingredients are not combined correctly the recipe will not turn out well.*

✓ How do mixing tasks differ? *By the speed at which the mixing is done, and by whether any air is introduced into the mixture.*

✓ What utensils can you use to cut shortening into pastry dough? *A pastry blender or two knives.*

✓ Compare blending and beating. *Blending is mixing two or more ingredients thoroughly with a spoon or wire whisk so they lose their original appearance. Beating is mixing ingredients thoroughly with a spoon, wire whisk, rotary beater, or electric mixer so that air is introduced.*

✓ What is the difference in food preparation between beating and whipping? *Beating involves strong, circular motions. Whipping is very rapid beating which incorporates so much air that it increases the volume.*

✓ What utensils and appliances can be used for mixing ingredients? *Mixing bowls, mixing spoons, wire whisks, pastry blenders, rubber scrapers, rolling pins, rotary beaters, and electric mixers. Blenders and food processors can also be used to mix ingredients.*

✓ How do whipped egg whites affect a cake mixture? *They make it lighter.*

More About Mixing How ingredients are mixed affects their texture after cooking. For example, cake batter that has been well beaten will give the cake a lighter, fluffier texture. And if the ingredients of a meat loaf recipe are mixed well, the meat dish will have a smooth, even texture.

Did You Know? Your hands can serve as good mixing tools, especially for shredding salad greens or mixing ingredients for meat loaf. Be sure your hands are clean, and as an extra precaution, wear plastic gloves.

✓ What is a rolling pin used for? *To roll out dough for pies, pastry, biscuits, and cookies.*

✓ What two models do mixers come in? *Hand-held and stand models.*

✓ List five tips for mixing ingredients. *1) Choose the right size bowl. 2) Choose the best tool or appliance available for the mixing task. 3) Place a wet cloth under the mixing bowl to keep it from sliding. 4) When adding dry ingredients to a wet mixture, add only a small amount at a time, mixing until the dry ingredients disappear. 5) Use a rubber scraper to remove food from the bowl.*

Activities

Skill Builder: Math
Divide students into two groups and provide each group with a bowl. Tell students that they will be making pastry dough. Then have each group measure 3/4 cup of flour using a 1/8 measuring cup. Using the same measuring cup, have each group measure 1/4 cup of shortening and add it to the bowl. Finally, have each group measure 1/8 teaspoon of salt and add it to the mixture.

Mixing Bowls. Available in different sizes, usually as a set, and used for mixing food. Made of glass, metal, plastic, or pottery.

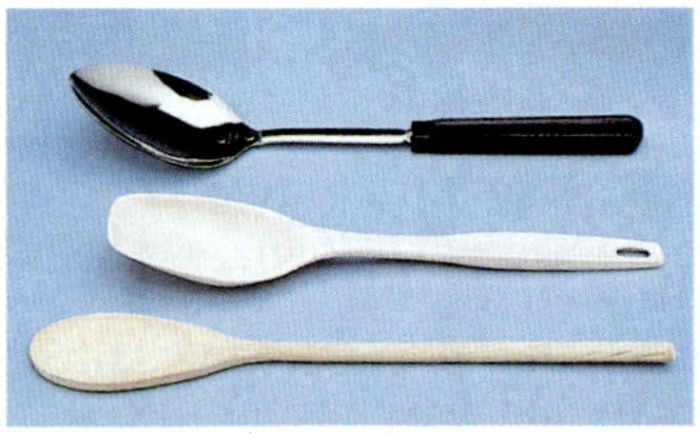

Mixing Spoons. Made of wood, plastic, or metal; used for combining ingredients.

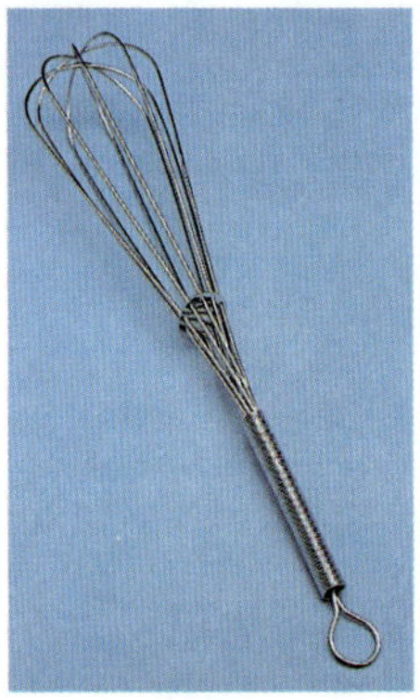

Wire Whisk. Used for blending, stirring, and beating.

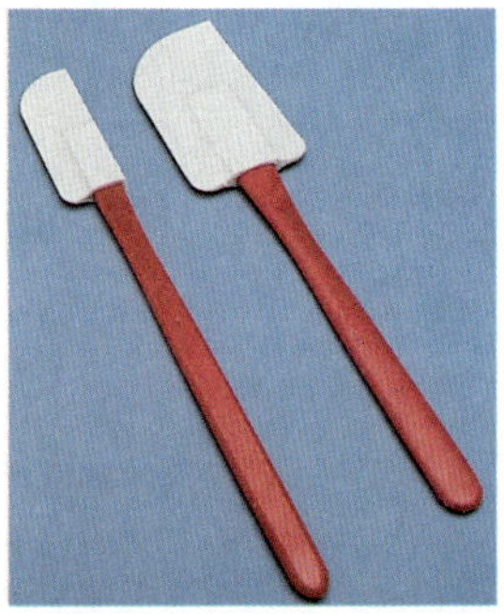

Rubber Scraper. Used to fold ingredients and to scrape food from bowls and pans.

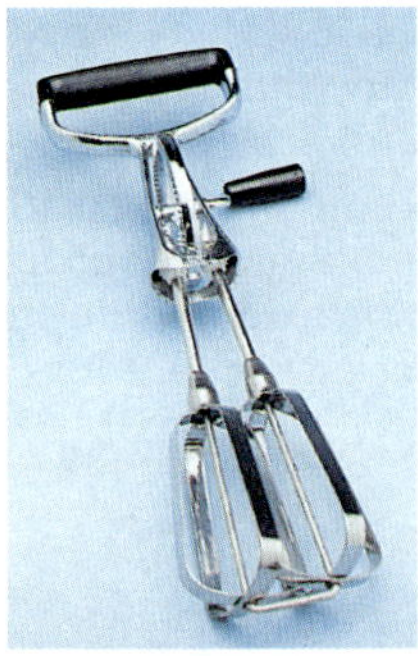

Rotary Beater. Used for beating ingredients, especially eggs and thin batters.

Electric Mixer. Appliance used to mix, beat, and whip ingredients. Comes in hand-held or stand models.

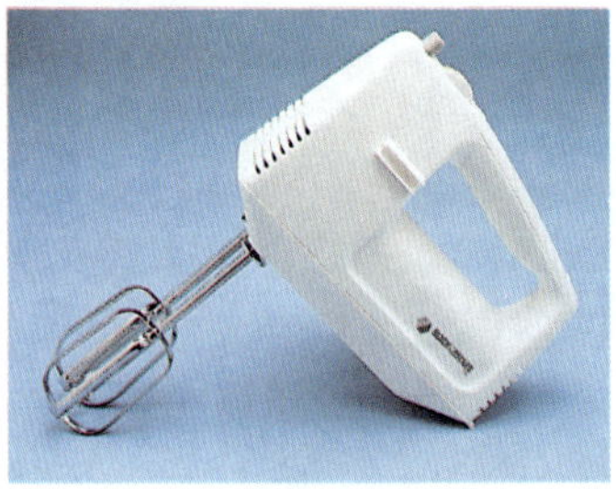

Pastry Blender. Used to cut shortening into flour for biscuits and pie crusts.

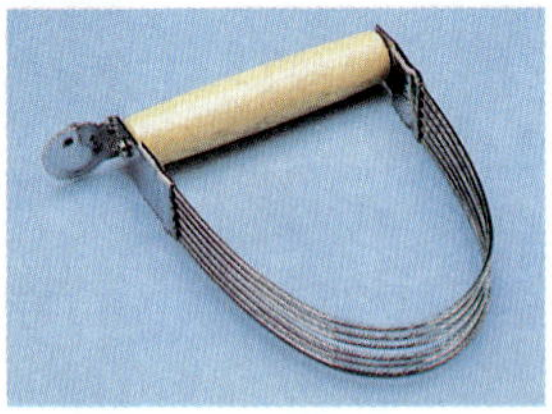

Rolling Pin. Used to roll out dough for biscuits, pies, pastries, and cookies.

Cross-Reference Blenders and food processors can also be used for mixing ingredients. See page 419.

Focus on Technology Some mixers come with different attachments for different mixing techniques. There can be attachments for beating, whipping, or for blending doughs. Some mixers do not have cords—they run on rechargeable batteries.

- **Cream.** Sometimes a fatty ingredient like shortening must be mixed with another ingredient like sugar until the mixture is very creamy and smooth. Creaming is done with a spoon, rotary beater, or electric mixer.
- **Blend.** To **blend** means to mix two or more ingredients thoroughly with a spoon or wire whisk so that they lose their original appearance.
- **Beat.** To **beat** is to mix ingredients thoroughly so that air is introduced. Beating involves a strong, circular motion. When you do it by hand with a spoon or wire whisk, you use a quick over-and-under motion that lifts the mixture on each rotation, adding air. You can also use a rotary beater or electric mixer.
- **Whip.** Whipping is a very rapid beating that incorporates so much air that it increases the volume. For example, whipped cream is twice the volume of the original heavy cream. To whip, use a wire whisk, rotary beater, or electric mixer.
- **Fold.** You use a spoon or rubber scraper to fold—or slowly combine—air-filled ingredients. For example, whipped egg whites can be folded into a cake mixture to make it lighter. If you stir them together, some of the air will be lost.

Fold gently with a spoon or rubber scraper.

Use a whisk to blend, beat, or whip.

Use a rotary beater to cream, beat, or whip.

An electric mixer has multiple speeds for various mixing tasks.

Focus on Health It is important to properly store cut and mixed foods so that they will not spoil or attract bacteria. Until they are ready for cooking, cut fruits and vegetables should be kept in airtight containers or tight plastic wrap. Cover bowls of dough or batter with plastic wrap so air cannot get in and dry the mixture.

Skill Builder: Critical Thinking
Ask students what tool(s) they would use to mix the ingredients for pastry dough in the preceding activity. Then ask students to decide what technique they would use to mix these ingredients.

Skill Builder: Science
Divide students into two groups and have each group mix the ingredients from the first activity in this section, using the technique selected from the second activity. Then tell each group to select a utensil to make the dough flat. After each group has rolled out their dough, ask two volunteers to place the two pieces of dough in separate pie pans and wrap it for storage in the freezer.

Reteaching
Have students give three examples of mixing techniques and the tools necessary for performing the techniques.

Enrichment
Have students make a list of mixing tools and appliances that are in their kitchens at home. Then ask students to describe what mixing techniques these tools and appliances can be used for and to offer tips for using equipment.

Teaching "Special Techniques"
(Page 424)

This section identifies two special techniques used for food preparation.

Checking Comprehension

✓ Describe the technique of separating an egg. *Tap the egg lightly on the edge of the bowl, just enough to crack one side of the shell. Gently separate the halves of the shell so some of the egg white will slip into the bowl. Transfer the yolk carefully from one half of the shell to the other, allowing more white to drop into the bowl until only the yolk remains.*

✓ What is breading? *Breading food means covering it with a light layer of flour, crumbs, or cornmeal before cooking it.*

Activities

Skill Builder: Science
Divide students into two groups and give each group two bowls. Have two volunteers from each group separate one egg each, putting the egg whites in one bowl and the egg yolks in the other bowl. Have another volunteer from each group cover and chill both the egg whites and the egg yolks.

Skill Builder: Critical Thinking
Divide students into two groups. Have one group use the bag method of coating chicken breasts, and the other use the method of dipping the chicken into flour, then a beaten egg, and then bread crumbs. Ask students to compare and contrast the two methods. Have them discuss which method took more time and which resulted in more evenly breaded chicken. Ask students whether or not they would recommend covering food with packaged breadings, using the bag method.

Reteaching
Ask students to develop a list of instructions either for separating eggs or for breading food. Point out that their instructions should be numbered and should indicate the sequence that the reader would have to follow.

Enrichment
Have students find a recipe that requires either separating eggs or breading food. Ask them to make the recipe and share their experiences in performing the techniques.

Salad tongs can be used to toss and serve salads.

- **Toss.** To make a tossed salad, you tumble the ingredients lightly together using a spoon and fork.
- **Cut-in.** When pastry is made, the shortening is cut-in, or mixed with the dry ingredients using a pastry blender or two knives (see "Making Do" on page 425).

Mixing Tips

Here are some tips to help you when mixing.

- Choose the right size bowl for the job. Base your decision on the amount of ingredients and the method of mixing. Beating or whipping will require a larger bowl than stirring.
- Choose the best tool or appliance for the job. You might use a food processor to chop a large amount of cabbage for coleslaw, but a chef's knife to chop one onion.
- Place a wet cloth under the mixing bowl to keep it from sliding.
- When adding dry ingredients to a wet mixture, add only a small amount at a time, mixing until the dry ingredients disappear.
- Use a rubber scraper to remove food from a mixing bowl.

Special Techniques

Some other techniques used in food preparation deserve special mention. Here are some guidelines to help you master these techniques.

- **Separating eggs.** To separate an egg, or divide the white from the yolk, tap the egg lightly on the edge of a bowl, just enough to crack one side of the shell. Gently separate the halves of the shell so some of the white slips into the bowl. Transfer the yolk carefully from one half of the shell to the other, allowing more white to drop into the bowl until only the yolk remains.

- **Breading.** Foods such as fish or chicken are sometimes breaded, or covered with a light layer of flour, crumbs or cornmeal before cooking. Roll the food in seasoned crumbs, or place crumbs in a paper or plastic bag, add the food, close the bag tightly, and shake.

More About Special Techniques Dusting means lightly sprinkling a food with another dry ingredient. Seasoning means sprinkling a food with herbs or spices to add flavor. Coating means covering food with flour, sugar, crumbs, or nuts. Foods such as onion rings can be dipped in batter before frying.

Did You Know? When separating more than one egg, you should use three bowls. One for saving the separated whites; one for saving the separated yolks; and one for catching the whites as you separate them. If a yolk should burst and spill into all the whites, you would not be able to use them as planned.

MANAGING RESOURCES

Making Do

In a perfect world, all kitchens would be stocked with every useful tool. However, in your kitchen at home, and even in your school foods laboratory, some equipment may not be available. Even if a particular tool is around, someone else might be using it.

When this happens, you can usually substitute another tool for the one you preferred. For example:

- **Peeler.** If a peeler is unavailable when you need it, a sharp paring knife can be used to remove the skins of firm vegetables. Work slowly and carefully, however, so you peel away only the necessary amount of skin. Going slowly will also help you avoid cutting yourself.
- **Wire whisk.** If a whisk is unavailable, a fork or rotary beater can be used for beating foods such as eggs. To blend a smooth sauce or to beat a cake mix, you might use a long-handled spoon.
- **Sifter.** If you can't find a sifter, use a fine mesh strainer to sift flour and other dry ingredients. Gently tap the strainer or stir the ingredients until they pass through the mesh.
- **Pastry blender.** A pastry blender is used for cutting shortening into flour, but you can also do the same job with two table knives. Hold one knife in each hand with the blades down. You will have better control if you extend your forefinger along the back of the blade. Cross the knives in an X and cut through the mixture repeatedly, pulling the knives apart as you cut. Between cuts, use the sides of the knives to push the ingredients together again.

These are just a few of the ways that you can substitute one tool for another. You may be able to think of more. The more familiar you become with the kitchen and with cooking, the better you will get at making emergency substitutions.

Think It Through

1. **You have just looked at some substitutions for common tools. What are the advantages of using the right tool if you can get it?**
2. **Name two hand tools that could do some of the work done by a food processor.**

Teaching the Feature
"Making Do"

Answers to Feature Questions

1. Possible answers include: convenience, ease of use; safety; does a better job in terms of appearance of food; and so on.
2. Possible answers include: chef's knife; paring knife; kitchen shears; grater.

Activities

Improvisation Ask students how they would remove noodles from soup if they did not have a slotted spoon. Remind them that their substitute utensil must enable them to pick up the noodles, but not the broth. Then ask students how they would shred carrots if they did not have access to a food processor. Have students comment on each other's ideas for substitute utensils.

New Inventions Ask students to brainstorm ideas about a tool or appliance for separating eggs. Tell students that their invention should be a workable alternative to the manual separation of eggs.

Community Contact Have students visit a local store that specializes in kitchen utensils and appliances. Ask them to note the various products the store sells, and encourage them to talk to the store manager or clerk to get more information about each product.

Focus on Consumer Skills Have students discuss the importance of comparison shopping for kitchen tools and appliances. Encourage them to think about the advantages of buying a general tool or appliance that performs several tasks, rather than one special tool or appliance that performs only one task.

COMPLETING THE CHAPTER

Summary

- Getting food ready to cook or serve usually requires cutting and mixing techniques.
- Special tools and appliances are available for specific food-cutting chores. Safety precautions must be taken when using cutting tools and appliances.
- Careful mixing of ingredients is important if the recipe is to turn out well.
- Mixing techniques differ according to the speed at which the mixing is done and whether any air is introduced into the mixture.
- Other preparation skills include: separating eggs, and breading.

For Review

Objective Review Questions Have students complete the "Reviewing the Facts" section on this page.

Study Guide Have students complete the Study Guide from Chapter 46 of their *Student Workbook*.

Recipe—What and How To stress the importance of the information in this chapter, ask students to bring in a favorite recipe from home. Point out that almost all recipes use one or more of the tools or techniques mentioned in this chapter. Have students study their recipe carefully. Ask them to list all the techniques and tools from this chapter that they would use to complete the recipe.

For Evaluation

The Right Tool for the Job Emphasize to students the importance—for safety and efficiency—of using the right tool for each job. Read the following list of food preparation tasks, and ask students to suggest the right tool for:

1. peeling a peach
2. slicing carrots
3. slicing a tomato
4. slicing bread
5. chopping onions
6. shredding cheese

Chapter Test Have students complete the test for Chapter 46 that appears in the *Teacher's Classroom Resources*.

CHAPTER 46 REVIEW

Answers to "Reviewing the Facts"

1. Any four: paring knife—to peel; utility knife—to cut and slice; slicing knife—to slice; bread knife—to slice bread; chef's knife—to slice, chop, mince, dice; butcher knife—to divide large pieces; peeler—to peel; kitchen shears—to cut; grater—to shred and grate; cutting board—to protect countertop; food mill—to puree; blender—to chop, blend, liquify; food processor—to slice, chop, mince, shred, grate, knead, mix.
2. For peeling fruits and soft vegetables.
3. Any four: keep knives sharp; slant knife blade away; use cutting board; let a knife fall; wash knives separately, keep hands away from blades of blender or food processor.
4. Both add air to the mixture.
5. Beating introduces air into the mixture; creaming does not.
6. To divide the white from the yolk.
7. Place food and crumbs in a paper or plastic bag, close bag tightly, and shake.

Reviewing the Facts

1. Name and describe the uses of four cutting and chopping utensils.
2. When would a paring knife be used instead of a peeler?
3. List four safety rules for cutting foods.
4. What do the mixing methods whipping and beating have in common?
5. What is the difference between beating and creaming?
6. What does it mean to separate an egg?
7. Describe an easy way to bread food.

Thinking Critically

1. If you were making a stew with meat and vegetables, which preparation tasks would you do and in what order?
2. Compare a grater with a food processor for the task of shredding cheese. What might be the advantages and disadvantages of each?

Applying Your Skills

1. **Identifying Words.** Prepare an 18-word matching exercise, using the food preparation terms you have learned in this chapter. Instead of the definitions given in the chapter, use a brief description of a food or the name of a particular food as the clue to the term. For example, whipped cream (whip). Exchange papers with a classmate, and see how many preparation terms you both know and how often you came up with the same foods for the same terms.

2. **Making Comparisons.** Prepare two identical bowls with ingredients for scrambled eggs. Pour one into a blender and mix it for 15 seconds. Whisk the other one by hand for 15 seconds. Do you think there will be any difference when the two mixes are cooked? Make a prediction, and then test it by cooking the two mixes. Was your prediction correct? Write a report, and present it to your class.

3. **Writing a Recommendation.** Your friend asks your advice on what three cutting tools to purchase for a kitchen. Consider how often you and your family use different cutting tools at home. Write your recommendations, giving specific reasons for each of your selections.

Answers to "Thinking Critically"

1. Possible order: peel the potatoes and other vegetables that need peeling, cut up vegetables, cut up meat if necessary.
2. A food processor is easier to use and shreds cheese much faster than a grater. However, a food processor is more difficult to clean because is has several small parts. In addition, a food processor is more expensive and more dangerous to use.

CHAPTER

47

Cooking Techniques

OBJECTIVES

This chapter will help you to:

- Identify equipment used for cooking and baking.
- Describe different kinds of cooking using moist heat, dry heat, and fat.
- Determine when foods are done.

WORDS TO REMEMBER

braise
broil
casserole
poach
sauté
simmer
steamer
stir-fry

Chapter Resources

Teacher's Classroom Resources
- Lesson Plan
- Life Skills Activity, *Where Did I Go Wrong?*
- Reproducible Master, *Cooking Tools*
- Extension Activity, *The Right Tool for the Task*
- Chapter Test

Student Workbook
- Study Guide
- Worksheet, *A Day in the Life of a Restaurant Worker*

CHAPTER OVERVIEW

Chapter 47 describes the cookware and bakeware used to prepare food. It introduces the methods of cooking food with moist heat (boiling, simmering, poaching, braising, stewing, steaming, and pressure cooking), with dry heat (roasting, baking, and broiling), and with fat (sautéing, pan-frying, stir-frying, and deep-fat frying). It also gives guidelines for telling when food is cooked.

INTRODUCING THE CHAPTER

Motivators

How Can I Cook It? Let Me Count the Ways Have students talk about all of the ways that the following foods might be cooked: egg (boiled, fried, poached), ground beef (fried, grilled, broiled, baked), potato (boiled, baked, fried). Point out that this chapter will describe the various cooking methods they have just listed.

Using the Photograph Have students study the photograph on this page. Then ask: "How were these foods prepared? What other ways could they have been cooked?"

The Shape It's In Ask students to think about how the shape of bakeware determines the shape of the food (such as meat loaf, cupcakes, quiche). Could these foods be prepared in different shapes? How would the recipe have to be adjusted?

Introducing the Objectives

Discuss the chapter objectives on this page. Remind students that the objectives focus on important chapter content.

Introducing Vocabulary

Point out that many of these cooking terms are of French origin—*sauté, braise,* and *casserole* among them. Over the years, French cooking was considered the height of elegant cuisine (another French word).

TEACHING THE CHAPTER

For convenience, the teaching suggestions for this chapter are arranged according to the following lesson topics:

- "Cooking Equipment," pages 428-429
- "Cooking with Moist Heat," pages 430-431
- "Cooking with Dry Heat" page 432
- "Cooking with Fat," and "How to Tell When Food is Cooked," page 434

Teaching "Cooking Equipment"
(Pages 428-429)

This section explains the cookware and bakeware used to prepare food. It describes the uses and materials of pots, pans, casseroles, and other cookware.

Checking Comprehension

✓ How can you decide what to heat food in? *It depends on what you are preparing and the cooking method you have chosen.*

✓ Why does most cookware have lids and handles? *The lids retain steam and nutrients during cooking. The handles are for safe and easy handling when hot.*

✓ Which cookware materials are durable? *Stainless steel, cast iron, and glass-ceramic are durable.*

✓ What is the main disadvantage of aluminum pots? *They may stain.*

Have you ever had a boiled steak or an egg roasted in its shell? What about broiled spaghetti? You can probably tell just by imagining it that these foods would taste wrong, and look wrong, too. The steak would be watery and not browned. The egg would probably explode. The spaghetti would be crisp and inedible. Why?

There are many different ways to apply heat to foods. Some methods suit some foods, and some suit others. This chapter explains the different equipment used to heat foods, and describes the different techniques for cooking. In chapters 49 to 52 you will learn more about which techniques to use for which foods.

Wooden spoon. Use to stir hot foods.
Long-handled fork. Use to lift or turn hot foods.
Slotted spoon. Use to lift food out of a liquid.
Steamer. Use inside a covered saucepan to steam vegetables.
Ladle. Use to dip out soup or stew.
Tongs. Use to lift and turn hot foods without piercing.
Turner. Use to flip foods such as pancakes and hamburgers.
Strainer. Use to drain liquid from fruits or vegetables.
Colander. Use to drain liquid from cooked pasta.
Cooling rack. Use to cool cakes, cookies, and breads.

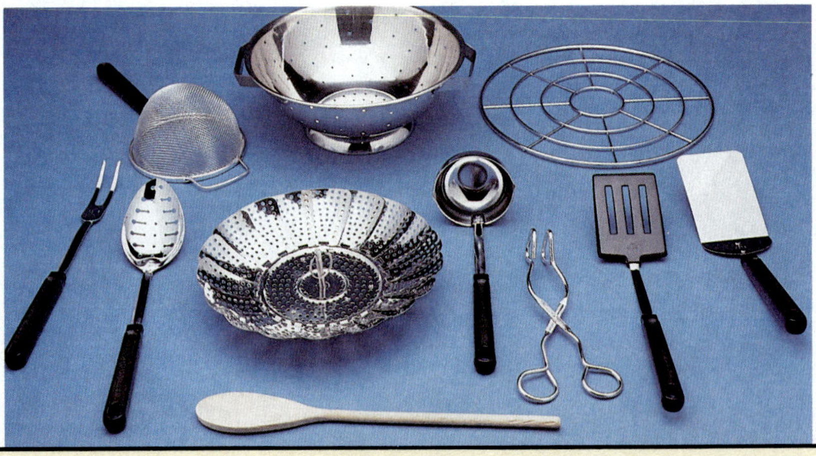

Cooking Equipment

Will you heat food in cookware or bakeware? It depends on what you are preparing and the cooking method you have chosen.

Cookware and Bakeware

Cookware—pots and pans used on top of the range—comes in many sizes. Most have lids to retain steam and nutrients during cooking. Cookware also has handles for safe and easy handling when hot. A pot with small handles on each side is lifted with both hands. A saucepan that has a long handle can be lifted with one hand. Even though handles may not get hot, you might touch a hot lid or pan accidentally. Use a hot pad or mitt to prevent accidents and burns.

Bakeware consists of containers that are used in the oven. Like cookware, these come in many sizes. Some dishes, or **casseroles**, can be used for both cooking and serving. Casseroles usually have lids and small handles. Other pieces of bakeware may have a ridge around the edge to allow for easy gripping. Hot pads or mitts are essential when removing bakeware from the oven.

Cross-Reference See Chapter 48 for information about microwave cooking.

Emphasize Cooking materials conduct heat in different ways. Some heat more evenly than others, and some heat more quickly than others. Some experts suggest that when baking in glass containers rather than metal ones, you reduce the oven temperature by 25° F.

Know Your Materials

Cookware and bakeware can be made from different materials. Each type of material has its own characteristics. These affect how food cooks, how long the cookware or bakeware will last, and how it should be cleaned.

Many pieces are made of aluminum or stainless steel. Aluminum is lightweight, heats rapidly and evenly, but may stain. Stainless steel is durable, heats slowly and unevenly, but is easy to clean. Some metal pans have nonstick surfaces to make them easier to clean.

Enamel pots and pans are attractive but chip easily and cannot be scoured. Cast-iron pots and skillets are durable and heat well, but they are heavy and may rust.

Some pieces, especially bakeware, are made of glass or glass-ceramic. Many can go from freezer to oven to table, but they may not heat evenly. Glass is inexpensive but can break. Glass-ceramic is attractive, durable, and easy to clean.

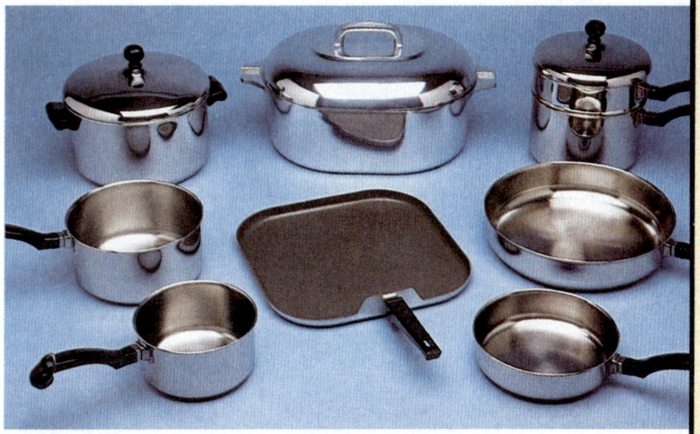

COOKWARE

Saucepan. Comes in several sizes; has one long handle and lid. Used for cooking foods in liquids.
Pots. Large pans with two handles and lid. Used for cooking pasta, soups, corn-on-the-cob.
Dutch oven. Large heavy pot and lid used for slow cooking of meats and poultry.
Double boiler. Two saucepans, one inside the other, used for heating foods that burn easily.
Frying pan or skillet. Low-sided pan, usually with lid; comes in several sizes. Used for frying.
Griddle. Flat surface used for cooking eggs and pancakes.

BAKEWARE

Roasting pan. Large shallow pan with rack. Used for roasting meat and poultry.
Broiler pan. Shallow pan with slotted tray for fat to drip through when broiling meats.
Casserole. Dish used for baking and serving.
Cake pan. Round, square, or rectangular. Used for cakes, brownies, and bar cookies.
Muffin pan. Has individual cups for muffins or cupcakes.
Pie Pan. Round pan with sloping sides for pie.
Loaf pan. Deep, rectangular pan for bread, cake, or meat loaf.
Baking sheets. Large, flat, metal pan (sometimes with narrow sides) for cookies.

Focus on Consumer Skills Nonstick surfaces on cookware make both cooking and cleanup easier. Fried or baked food is more easily removed from nonstick cookware, and dirty pans don't need to be scrubbed to remove leftover food.

Focus on Safety Pots and pans should have heat-resistant handles. Lids should fit tightly to hold in steam. Knobs should be heat-resistant and easy to grasp. The bottom should be flat, and not be able to tip over when empty.

Activities

Skill Builder: Math
Using a mail-order catalog or newspaper ads, have students compare the costs of similar pots (1-qt., frying pan) made of different materials. Features such as nonstick surfaces or decorative designs should be taken into account.

Reteaching
Have students list one advantage and one disadvantage of each of the cookware materials listed: aluminum, stainless steel, enamel, cast iron, glass.

Enrichment
Ask students to list as many special cookware and bakeware items as they can think of (bundt pan, roasting pan). Gourmet shops, catalogs, and cookbooks are good sources for ideas.

Teaching "Cooking with Moist Heat"
(Pages 430-431)

This section explains the methods of cooking with moist heat and tells the differences between them.

Checking Comprehension

✔ What is the difference between boiling and simmering? *When boiling food, the water is boiled, or heated to 212° F, When simmering, the food is cooked in liquid at temperatures just below the boiling point.*

✔ Why is simmering more nutritious than boiling? *Fewer nutrients are lost when food is simmered rather than boiled.*

✔ Which moist-heat cooking method is best for tender foods? *Tender foods are sometimes poached.*

✔ Which moist-heat methods are recommended for vegetables? *Simmering, stewing, steaming, and pressure cooking.*

✔ Describe how food is steamed. *A small amount of water is boiled, then the food is put in a steamer above the water. The pan is covered with a tight-fitting lid, and the steam cooks the food in the steamer.*

Cooking With Moist Heat

Moist-heat cooking methods use liquid or steam to cook the food. Boiling, simmering, poaching, braising, and stewing all use liquid. Steaming and pressure cooking use steam.

Boiling, Simmering, and Poaching

In boiling, simmering, or poaching, the food is partially or completely covered with water or gravy as it cooks. To boil foods such as spaghetti and noodles, first bring the water to a boil—212°F (100°C). Bubbles should rise continuously to the surface of the water and break. Add the pasta and cook until softened. Boiling is not used for most foods, however, because this heating method robs food of nutrients, and it often results in overcooking.

To **simmer** means to cook food in liquid at temperatures just below the boiling point. A few bubbles should rise slowly but not break the surface of the liquid. Foods lose fewer nutrients when simmered rather than boiled, so vegetables are frequently simmered.

To **poach** means to simmer in a small amount of liquid so the food keeps its original shape. Tender foods such as fish, eggs, and fruit are sometimes poached.

When a liquid simmers, the bubbles do not break the surface.

Because boiling can toughen many foods and destroy nutrients, use this method only for foods such as pasta or corn. Be careful not to overcook.

Use a wooden spoon—not metal—when stirring hot foods.

Cross-Reference See Chapter 43 for safety information about preventing burns, scalds, and fires when cooking in the kitchen.

More About Boiling Water boils at 212° F (100° C) at sea level. One mile above sea level (as in Denver, Colorado), water boils at 198° F (90° C). At higher altitudes, there is lower atmospheric pressure that causes a change in boiling point. Instructions for cooking at high altitudes are often included in recipes.

Braising and Stewing

You can braise or stew foods that require long, slow cooking for tenderness or taste. Sometimes the food is browned, or cooked in a little oil first, for added color and flavor.

To **braise** food—a pot roast, for example—place it in a small amount of liquid in a pan that has a tight-fitting lid. Cook it slowly in the oven or on top of the range until tender. Check occasionally to be sure the liquid is not drying up.

Stewing is similar, but the food is cut into small pieces and covered with water before cooking. Braising and stewing are used for less tender cuts of meat and for poultry, vegetables, and some fruits.

Steaming and Pressure Cooking

Steaming helps preserve the nutrients in food. The most common method is to boil a small amount of water in a pan, then put the food in a **steamer**, a metal basket that holds the food above the water. After the pan is covered with a tight-fitting lid, the water continues to boil and the steam cooks the food in the basket. Steaming is recommended for cooking vegetables.

Pressure cooking requires an airtight pan in which the food cooks quickly by means of hot steam that is under pressure. The manufacturer's directions should be followed carefully. This method is used for less-tender meats, poultry, and vegetables such as potatoes and carrots.

Braising is a good method for cooking less tender cuts of meat.

Stews may be cooked for several hours to achieve maximum tenderness and to blend the flavors.

Steaming is recommended for cooking vegetables. The food is held above the water and retains nutrients such as water-soluble vitamins.

More About Braising When cooking on top of the range, the liquid should simmer just enough to create steam. If steam escapes around the edge of the pan lid, the liquid is boiling. Reduce heat and add more liquid if necessary. If the liquid is allowed to evaporate, the food will scorch and stick to the bottom of the pan. When braising in the oven, check the liquid occasionally also.

More About Moist Heat Special plastic vapor-proof cooking bags are available for cooking less tender meats in the oven. A small amount of liquid is added to the bag with the food. Follow instructions carefully to prevent bursting or splattering.

Activities

Skill Builder: Critical Thinking
Have students make a daily menu (breakfast, lunch, and dinner) that uses as many moist-heat cooking methods as possible. The students might plan poached eggs and stewed fruit for breakfast; boiled pasta for lunch; and braised meat, steamed vegetables, and boiled potatoes for dinner.

Reteaching
Ask students to explain the difference between boiling and simmering and between braising and stewing.

Enrichment
Stews are a popular food all around the world. The French have their pot-au-feu and boeuf bourguignonne, the Poles love their bigos, the Hungarians are famous for goulash. Have students research the popular stews of other countries and report to the class.

Teaching "Cooking with Dry Heat"

(Page 432)

This section teaches how to bake, roast, and broil.

Checking Comprehension

✔ What are the sources of dry heat? *The heat may come from hot air in the oven or a direct source such as a broiler or grill.*

✔ Why is the inside of baked food softer than the outside? *Because the outside cooks first.*

✔ Where can food be broiled? *You can broil food under a broiler or on an outdoor grill.*

✔ What kind of meats are broiled, and what kind are stewed? *Tender meats are broiled, and less tender cuts are stewed.*

Activities

Skill Builder: Science
Have students discuss ways to save energy when using the oven.

Skill Builder: Critical Thinking
Ask students to think of a food that can be roasted, baked, and broiled, such as chicken. Then ask them to describe how each would be done and how they eat it at home. What is their favorite way to eat that food?

Reteaching
Ask students to list the similarities and differences between roasting, baking, and broiling.

Enrichment
Have students investigate equipment used in outdoor cooking—grills, utensils, and so on. They should report on design, cost, safety features, and special features.

Teaching "Cooking with Fat" and "How to Tell When Food is Cooked"

(Page 434)

This section teaches about the methods of cooking with fat, including sautéing, panfrying, stir-frying, and deep-fat frying. It also lists ways to tell when food is properly cooked.

Checking Comprehension

✓ What is the difference between sautéing and stir-frying? *Sautéing is a slow way of frying, and stir-frying is done very quickly.*

✓ Why should extra fat that accumulates in the pan be poured off during the cooking process? *Because fat adds calories and makes the food soggy.*

✓ Why would you have to test a food even if you've used the time listed in the recipe? *The time may vary from oven to oven.*

Cooking with Dry Heat

Cooking with dry heat means cooking without liquid. The heat may come from hot air in the oven or from a direct heat source such as a broiler or grill. Dry-heat cooking includes roasting, baking, and broiling.

Roasting two or more foods together in the oven saves energy.

Roasting and Baking

Roasting and baking are methods of cooking food uncovered in the oven. The term *roasting* is usually used to describe cooking meat or poultry by this method. *Baking* refers to cooking foods such as potatoes, fruit, fish, breads, cakes, cookies, and pies.

When food is roasted or baked, the outside cooks first and often becomes brown or crisp. The inside is usually softer.

Baking is used for many foods, such as pies, cookies, cakes, muffins, and breads.

Broiling

To **broil** means to cook food directly with a glowing heat source. You can broil food under a broiler or on an outdoor grill. As the food broils, any fat released drips away. The outside of the food browns quickly. Broiling is often used for tender meats such as steaks and hamburgers, chicken, and some fruits and vegetables.

Tender meats, such as hamburgers, can be broiled indoors or out.

Did You Know? Some ovens have "hot spots," places that are hotter than the set temperature. It helps to know where these spots are so that you can adjust cooking times or positions.

Emphasize Frying uses high temperatures, but fat should not be heated until it smokes. All fats have a smoking point, a point at which they break down and begin to taste and smell bad. Butter, olive oil, and margarine begin to smoke at lower temperatures than other fats. You can raise their smoking point by blending them with other vegetable oils.

INTERPERSONAL SKILLS

Working in a Restaurant Kitchen

Have you ever been in the kitchen of a busy restaurant? You might be surprised at the feeling of pressure. Everyone is working to meet the customers' needs. Certain principles and procedures help the staff work efficiently and safely. Kitchen organization and teamwork are two of these principles. Here are some others:

- **Cooperation.** Workers need to help one another and follow general rules. If someone spills some oil while making a cake, another worker could offer to help clean it up. To avoid accidents, everyone needs to observe traffic rules within the kitchen—keeping to the right in any passageway, and correctly using doors marked "entrance" and "exit."
- **Communication.** Kitchen workers need to warn each other about dangers and problems, such as spills, obstacles, and broken equipment. Also, they need to let others around them know their intentions. For example, people carrying hot food should announce when they are passing behind other workers by saying, "Behind you."
- **Keeping cool.** The kitchen is a hot place. Workers should keep paper and clothing away from flames and use hot pads whenever necessary. They need to know what to do if a fire starts, and learn where fire extinguishers are and how to use them. They must also know where to get help if someone is hurt.

Keeping cool has another meaning as well. In a restaurant kitchen, many things are happening at once, and tempers may flare. To be effective, kitchen workers need to practice remaining calm no matter what is said to them. They'll work more safely and efficiently if they have themselves under control.

Think It Through

1. **What problems could be caused by workers not putting tools and utensils back where they belong?**
2. **Describe a potentially dangerous kitchen problem and how it could be prevented through good communication.**

Teaching the Feature

"Working in a Restaurant Kitchen"

Answers to Feature Questions

1. Possible answers include: food preparation could be delayed; people could become angry; accidents could occur if tools or utensils are stored in an unexpected or inconvenient place.
2. Students may think of such problems as an obstacle placed on the floor (tell others about it so that they won't trip); a piece of broken equipment (inform manager and others); and so on.

Activities

Do's and Don'ts Have students prepare a list of rules that could be posted on the wall of a restaurant kitchen to remind employees of the importance of cooperation, communication, and keeping cool.

Role Play Have students role play the following situations in which a kitchen worker would have to try hard to keep cool.

- A waiter comes into the kitchen complaining about how long it is taking for an order to be filled.
- The manager comes into the kitchen to tell the head chef that a restaurant critic has just walked in. They must plan a strategy.
- During the lunch rush, one of the workers must quickly decide who will take over the sick worker's jobs.

Community Contact Have students make posters on guidelines for safety in the cafeteria kitchen. They can either focus on one of the three guidelines from the feature or explain all three. After they have been completed, have the cafeteria manager talk to the students about safety practices and then choose a poster to display in the cafeteria.

More About Communication Many kitchen workers use a special kind of shorthand language to communicate with each other. A waitress talking to a short-order cook might say, "Run it through the garden," and the cook would know to add lettuce and tomato to the dish. If the waiter asks for eggs "up," the cook will prepare the eggs sunny-side up, and the cook knows that a hot dog with "the works" has all the available condiments on it.

Activities

Skill Builder: Math
Explain to students that frying food adds calories to the food because of the fat it is cooked in. Ask students to choose one type of food, such as eggs, and, using calorie charts, compare the calories when it is fried and when it is cooked another way. What is the difference in calories? What percentage increase is that?

Skill Builder: Writing
Have students write a description of a few of their favorite foods: when they are undercooked, when overcooked, and when done just right. Ask students to identify which method(s) would be most effective in judging doneness.

Skill Builder: Critical Thinking
Ask students to compare the appropriate cooking times of various vegetables and notice the range. Ask them to name some factors that would determine how long the vegetables would need to be cooked (size, hardness, and so on).

Reteaching
Ask students to explain the difference between sautéing and panfrying and between stir-frying and deep-fat frying. Have them give examples of foods that could be cooked using each method.

Reteaching
Have students name three foods not mentioned already in which the doneness would be judged by each of the methods discussed here. (Pancakes, some cookies, and waffles can all be judged by appearance, for example.)

Enrichment
Have students debate the pros and cons of using fat to cook, taking nutrition, taste, health, and cost into account.

Enrichment
Ask students to bring in recipes that give suggestions on how to tell when the food is cooked. They should especially look for recipes that use methods other than those listed in this section.

Cooking with Fat

Sautéing, panfrying, stir-frying, and deep-fat frying are methods of cooking with fat. The food cooks fast and gets a crisp, brown crust. However, some of the fat gets sealed into the food, adding calories.

- **Sautéing or panfrying.** To **sauté** (saw-TAY) means to cook food, such as onions, mushrooms, and peppers, slowly in a little fat until tender but not brown. Panfrying is used to cook tender meats such as chops, chicken, eggs, and vegetables until brown. Extra fat from foods like bacon should be poured off during cooking.
- **Stir-frying.** To **stir-fry** is to cook food very quickly in very little fat until the food is just tender. This method is used for vegetables and thin slices of meat, poultry, and fish. Many oriental dishes are stir-fried.
- **Deep-fat frying.** This method is used to cook foods, such as french fries and doughnuts, in a deep kettle of hot oil or shortening.

When Food Is Done

How do you judge when food is cooked properly? Here are some suggestions:

- **Check the appearance.** Many foods can be judged by the way they look. Toast is brown when it is done. Sautéed onions become transparent.
- **Pierce the food with a fork.** Do this for vegetables, such as potatoes, carrots, beans, and asparagus. The fork should insert and pull out easily.
- **Use a thermometer.** Insert a meat thermometer in the center of a roast before cooking. When the recipe temperature is reached, the meat is done.
- **Use a wooden or metal tester.** When cakes are done, a toothpick or skewer inserted into the center will come out clean. Use a knife for custards.
- **Test a sample.** Remove a piece of vegetable or pasta, let it cool slightly, and taste. Vegetables should be crisp; pasta should be slightly chewy.
- **Use the time listed in the recipe.** Many recipes give estimated cooking times, though actual time may vary.

SAUTÉ

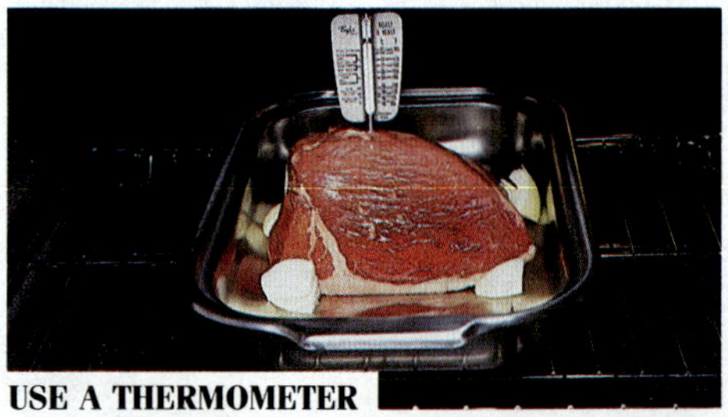
USE A THERMOMETER

STIR-FRY

PIERCE WITH A FORK

Focus on Safety Never pour water on a grease fire. This will only spread the flames. Do not grab for the pan. You may spill grease and cause severe burns. Turn off the heat immediately, and cover the pan with a lid, or pour baking soda or salt over the fire. The fire will die out from lack of oxygen.

Did You Know? Some turkeys are sold with a built-in thermometer. It pops up when the turkey is done. Another way to test the doneness of turkey is to move a leg around. When it moves easily in the socket, the turkey is done.

CHAPTER 47 REVIEW

Reviewing the Facts

1. What is the difference between cookware and bakeware?
2. Name three materials used for making cookware and bakeware. What are the characteristics of each?
3. Why is simmering a good cooking method?
4. What is the difference between braising and baking?
5. What is the difference between stewing and broiling?
6. What is one point to remember about cooking with fat?
7. What are three ways to tell when food is cooked?

Thinking Critically

1. Assume that you are helping a friend shop for cookware and bakeware to furnish his or her kitchen in a college apartment. Which cooking equipment and utensils would you consider essential, and which would you advise could wait to be purchased at a later date? Why?
2. Foods such as potatoes, fish, and eggs can be cooked in several different ways with equal success. Assuming that you like the taste of each method equally, which cooking technique would you favor and why?

Applying Your Skills

1. **Writing Descriptions.** Using a catalog from a mail-order company that sells kitchen supplies, find at least four items that you would like to have in your "dream" kitchen. Note the prices, and write a short paragraph on each item describing its usefulness to you.

2. **Using Reference Materials.** Go to the library and look up the history of dry-heat cooking, from prehistoric to the present time, across cultures. Be sure to find information on peoples of desert, tropical, and temperate lands, and find out how they bake, roast, or broil. Make illustrations of their "ovens" or cooking utensils. Label these items and write a brief description of how each is used.

3. **Forming Hypotheses.** Cookware is used on top of the range, while bakeware is used in the oven. Why do you suppose that pots and pans are not used in the oven? Why are baking pans and cookie sheets not used on the range top? What would happen if they were?

Answers to "Reviewing the Facts"

1. Cookware includes pots and pans used on top of the range. Bakeware consists of containers used in the oven.
2. Any three: aluminum—lightweight, heats rapidly and evenly, may stain; stainless steel—durable, easy to clean, heats slowly and unevenly; enamel—attractive, chips easily, can't be scoured; cast iron—durable, heats well, heavy, may rust; glass—inexpensive, may break; glass-ceramic—attractive, durable, easy to clean.
3. Retains more nutrients than boiling.
4. Braising is a moist-heat method using a small amount of liquid; baking is a dry-heat method.
5. Stewing is a moist-heat method in which the food is covered with water, broiling is a dry-heat method of cooking with a direct heat source.
6. Some of the fat gets sealed into the food, adding calories.
7. Any three: check the appearance; pierce with a fork; use a thermometer; insert a tester; taste a sample; follow the time in the recipe.

Answers to "Thinking Critically"

1. Answers will vary. Essential cooking equipment and utensils would probably include: saucepan, pot, frying pan, wooden spoon, long-handled fork, and turner.
2. Answers will vary. Students may prefer moist-heat methods for tenderness; dry-heat methods for cooking ease; or frying for speed (the least desirable answer). Energy costs may also figure in their answers.

COMPLETING THE CHAPTER

Summary

- Cookware is used on the range; bakeware is used in the oven.
- Cookware and bakeware are often made of different materials, each with advantages and disadvantages.
- Moist-heat cooking methods use liquid or steam to cook the food.
- Cooking with dry heat means cooking with hot air or a direct heat source.
- Some cooking methods use hot fat to cook foods.
- You can tell when food is cooked by checking appearance or texture, using a thermometer or a timer, or testing a sample.

For Review

Objective Review Questions Have students complete the "Reviewing the Facts" section on this page.

Study Guide Have students complete the Study Guide from Chapter 47 of their *Student Workbook.*

Choose a Method Have students choose a cooking method for each of the foods in this nutritious dinner: pork tenderloin, zucchini, wild rice, biscuits, and a fruit dessert. They should plan a variety of methods. You may ask them to find actual recipes that could be used to carry out their plans.

Health Alert Have students identify the most healthful methods of cooking. What methods would be appropriate for people on low-fat diets, weight-reduction plans, and other special diets?

For Evaluation

Synthesis Ask students to select a recipe, study it carefully, then describe the cookware and bakeware that they would need and the cooking methods that they would employ.

Chapter Test Have students complete the test for Chapter 47 that appears in the *Teacher's Classroom Resources.*

CHAPTER OVERVIEW

Chapter 48 discusses microwave functions and techniques. Students learn the scientific principles that enable a microwave oven to work. They also learn what settings and cookware to select when using a microwave oven. The microwave cooking techniques discussed in this chapter include stirring, rotating, covering, puncturing, shielding, and standing time. Also discussed in this chapter are variables, such as the food type, volume, shape, and starting temperature, that affect the time of cooking. Finally, the chapter discusses the safety considerations of cooking with microwave ovens.

INTRODUCING THE CHAPTER

Motivators

What Is a Microwave Oven? Ask for a show of hands to find out how many students use a microwave oven at home. Ask them to share their experiences. Then ask students to write down any questions that they have about using microwave ovens. Explain that this chapter focuses on microwave ovens. Ask students to hold on to their questions—you will refer to them later.

Using the Photograph Ask students to look at the photograph on this page. Then ask: "What is the student putting in the microwave oven? What do you notice about the container? About the oven?"

Microwaves in the Workplace Help students understand the value of knowing how to use microwave ovens by pointing out that many employers now provide them for the use of their staff. Ask students to give examples of places where they have worked (including babysitting assignments) that a microwave oven has been available.

Introducing the Objectives

Discuss the chapter objectives on this page. Remind students that the objectives focus on important chapter content.

CHAPTER

48

Microwave Cooking

OBJECTIVES

This chapter will help you to:

- Describe the uses of the microwave oven.
- Explain how microwaves cook food.
- Describe various techniques for cooking with microwaves.
- Name the variables in microwave cooking and tell how they affect the cooking time.

WORDS TO REMEMBER

arcing
microwave
rotate
shield
standing time
variable

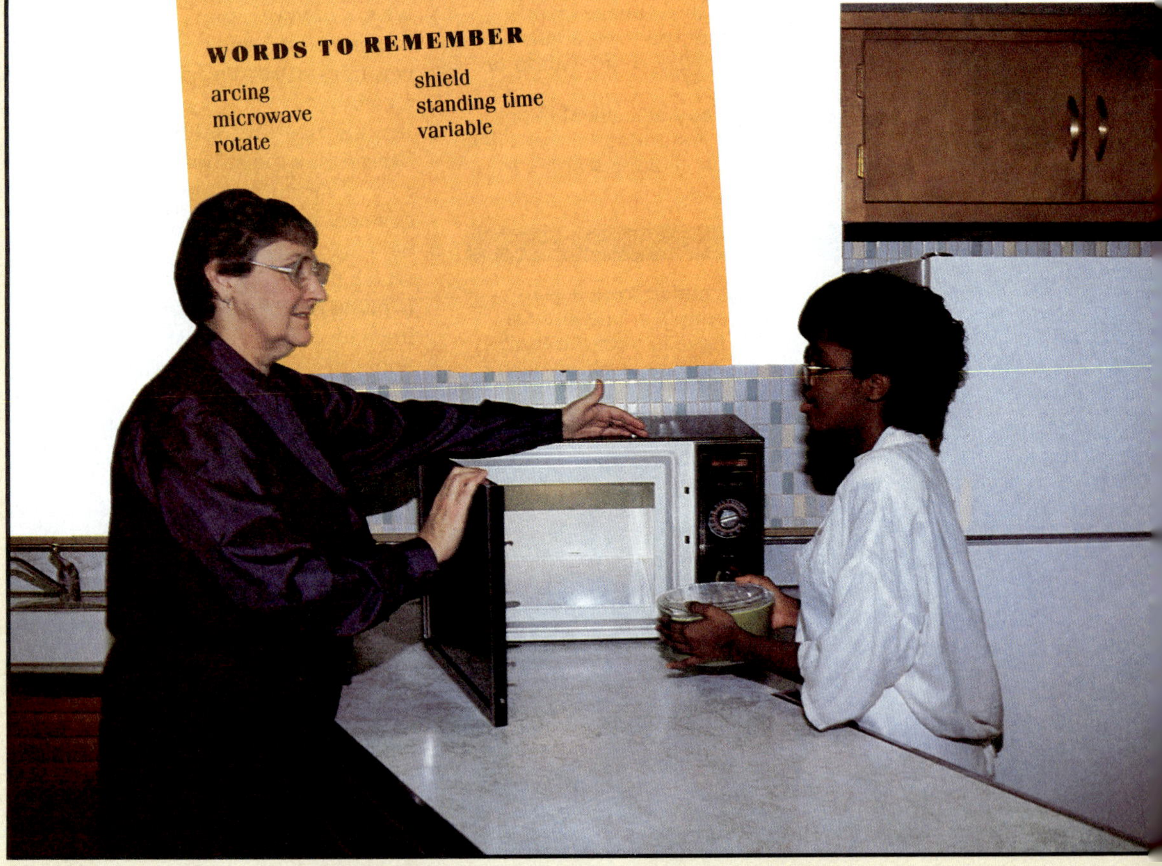

Chapter Resources

Teacher's Classroom Resources
- Lesson Plan
- Life Skills Activity, *Make It in the Microwave Oven*
- Reproducible Master, *How Microwaves Work*
- Extension Activity, *Utensils for Microwave Cooking*
- Chapter Test

Student Workbook
- Study Guide
- Worksheet, *A Few Words About Microwave Cooking*

In recent years, microwave cooking has become popular in the home kitchen because the microwave oven performs many cooking tasks faster and more easily than a conventional oven does. Using a microwave oven, you can cook a meal in a matter of minutes or prepare a snack in seconds. Microwave ovens are cleaner and more economical than conventional ovens. They also have an added advantage in hot weather—they do not heat the kitchen.

To make the best use of microwave cooking, you need to know when to use a microwave oven and when to use other cooking methods. Most microwave ovens are best suited for cooking relatively small amounts of food; large amounts usually call for a conventional oven or range top. Microwave ovens are particularly useful for preparing quick snacks such as hot cereal, soup, melted cheese sandwiches, nachos, or popcorn. They are also ideal for reheating cooked foods and defrosting frozen foods.

Some microwave ovens have different power settings. Although higher power cooks foods faster, some foods cook better at a lower power.

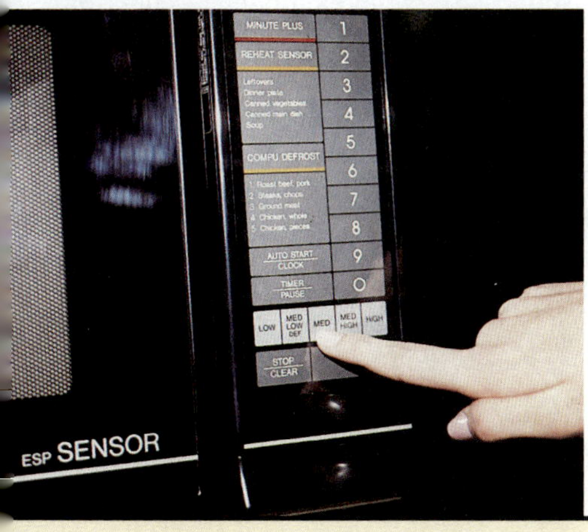

How a Microwave Oven Works

Microwave ovens vary in size, features, and power, but they all work in a similar way. They differ from conventional ovens in that they themselves do not get hot. With microwave cooking, only the food gets hot.

When you turn on a microwave oven, you activate a magnetron tube that produces microwaves. A **microwave** is a type of energy wave that operates at a very high frequency. A stirrer, or fan, at the top of the oven spreads the microwaves around the oven.

Microwaves can penetrate most materials except metal. The walls of the microwave oven are lined with metal. The microwaves bounce off the oven walls and penetrate the food, causing its molecules to vibrate and rub against each other. This causes friction, producing the heat that cooks the food.

Microwaves cook foods without greatly changing their appearance and texture. Usually this is an advantage—broccoli and carrots, for example, retain their bright colors. For foods which are traditionally baked, however, microwave cooking may be perceived as a drawback because foods do not brown in this type of oven.

Settings

Microwave power is measured in watts. The maximum power of most microwave ovens is 500 to 700 watts, but some recipes may call for lower power settings. You can usually control the amount of power you use for different tasks and recipes—the more power used, the faster most foods will cook.

The power control on the microwave may be a single dial or a control panel.

Emphasize Although microwave ovens have made cooking easier and faster, their use requires time to learn certain cooking techniques and safety considerations. Manufacturers' instructions should *always* be followed.

Did You Know? Microwaves penetrate foods from the outside to a depth of about one inch. Small foods are penetrated to the center from all sides, and larger foods heat from the outer layers to the center. Some foods, such as eggs, appear to cook more on the inside because the microwaves are drawn to the fat in the yolk.

Introducing Vocabulary

Write *microwave* on the board. Tell students that *micro* is a prefix meaning "small" or "short." Have students give examples of other words that begin with this prefix (*microscope, microorganism, microfilm*). Explain that *microwaves* are very short high-frequency radio waves. Microwave ovens cook food by the heat produced when the microwaves penetrate the food.

TEACHING THE CHAPTER

For convenience, the teaching suggestions for this chapter are arranged according to the following lesson topics:

- "How a Microwave Oven Works," pages 437-438
- "Microwave Techniques," pages 438-439
- "Variables in Microwave Cooking" and "Safety Considerations," page 441

Teaching "How a Microwave Oven Works"

(Pages 437-438)

This section explains how a microwave oven works, its settings, and the proper cookware.

Checking Comprehension

✓ What is a microwave? *A microwave is a type of energy wave that operates at a very high frequency.*

✓ How does a microwave oven work? *In a microwave oven, the microwaves bounce off the oven walls and penetrate the food, causing its molecules to vibrate and rub against each other. This causes friction, producing the heat that cooks the food.*

✓ Compare and contrast the different kinds of power controls on a microwave oven. *The power control may be a single dial or a control panel. The numbers on one kind of power control represent the fraction of the power used. Other microwave ovens may have control panels with such settings as low, medium, and high.*

✓ What is the range of maximum power of most microwave ovens? *500 to 700 watts.*

✓ Why are microwave-safe ceramic, glass, and plastic unaffected by microwaves? *Microwave-safe ceramic, glass, and plastic are unaffected by microwaves because their molecules are not disturbed enough by the microwaves to cause friction, and therefore heat. They are also heat resistant, so the heat generated by the food itself does not crack or melt them.*

✓ What cautions should be followed in choosing cookware for microwave ovens? *Metal pans and bowls should never be used because they could cause arcing.*

Activities

Skill Builder: Science
Tell students they are going to test a dish to see whether it is safe for microwave cooking. Have one student put a glass bowl in the microwave oven. Then have another measure 1 cup of water in a glass cup and put the cup on or beside the glass bowl. Heat the water on high for 1 minute. Ask students to see if the dish became hot or if only the water became hot. Tell students that if the dish is hot, it can't be used for microwaving.

Skill Builder: Critical Thinking
Have students imagine they are about to purchase a microwave oven. Have them discuss what factors (such as cost, size, features, or warranties) they should consider before buying the appliance.

Reteaching
Have students explain how a microwave oven works and what settings are important on its control panel. Then have them list three considerations for selecting cookware to be used in a microwave oven.

Enrichment
Tell students that microwaves operate radios, remote controls, and mobile telephones as well as microwave ovens. Have students use encyclopedias to find out how the microwaves make one of these devices work.

This control is usually numbered from one to ten; each number represents the fraction of power used. Thus, number one gives you one tenth or 10 percent of the available power, and number ten gives you 100 percent. Some models have low, medium, and high settings, with the percent of power provided by each setting varying among brands.

In addition to selecting a power setting, you also need to decide how long to cook the food. Another control on the microwave oven enables you to key in the exact cooking time required.

Cookware

Not all cookware is suitable for microwave cooking. Ceramic, glass, plastic, and paper containers are usually appropriate, but you should look for a label indicating that they are microwave-safe.

Microwave-safe ceramic, glass, and plastic are unaffected by microwaves. Their molecules are not disturbed enough by the microwaves to cause friction, and therefore they do not get hot. They are also heat resistant, so they do not crack or melt when the food becomes hot. Ceramic dishes that are not microwave-safe may shatter in a microwave oven.

Special microwave cookware is available, but you can use many dishes and containers that you already have. Check for labels that state "microwave-safe."

Metal pans and bowls should never be used. Because microwaves cannot pass through metal, some parts of the food will not be heated. More serious, metal containers may cause **arcing** (ARK-ing), sparks that can damage the oven and start a fire.

Some dishes have metallic trim or a metallic glaze, and they too should not be used. Even recycled paper sometimes contains metal. Metal *can* be put in many microwave ovens, but only with great care, as you will read later.

Microwave Techniques

For most microwave cooking, you need to use certain techniques when preparing and cooking the food. Because food heats up so fast in a microwave, moisture can escape very quickly and foods can burst. Also, evenness of cooking is a concern.

Stirring and Rotating

Microwaves penetrate food to a depth of about an inch from all of its surfaces. The heat generated by the microwaves is then conducted toward the center of the food. That is why the center of a large piece of food, or of a container of soup or stew, takes longer to cook than the outer edges.

More About Microwave Techniques Tell students that although they may not want to use a microwave oven to prepare an entire meal, they can still use it to speed up preparation of a conventionally cooked meal. For example, a microwave oven can save time in melting or boiling ingredients in a recipe.

More About Microwave Cookware Tell students that they can use paper plates and hot drink cups for heating foods and beverages in the microwave oven. Some products are made from paper that is freezer-proof and safe for both microwave and conventional ovens up to 400 degrees.

You can help soups, stews, and other foods containing liquids to heat up evenly by stirring them occasionally. For best results, stir from the outer edge toward the center. When food can't be stirred, you may need to **rotate** it. Turn the dish a quarter- or half-turn in the oven. This allows the microwaves to penetrate the food evenly on all sides.

In some cases you may need to rearrange food pieces or turn them over. For example, you would rotate a tuna casserole, rearrange baking potatoes, and turn over a ham.

Covering

Most foods should be covered in a microwave oven to hold in moisture and to prevent spattering. Choose the cover according to the type of food:

- White paper towels or napkins work well for covering bacon, sandwiches, and appetizers.
- Waxed paper is often used on meats or vegetables to hold in some of the moisture while letting steam escape.
- Microwave-safe dishes with lids are ideal for vegetables and casseroles.
- Vegetables can also be covered with plastic wrap. However, because plastic wrap forms a tight cover, it must be pierced or turned back at one corner to keep it from bursting.

Puncturing

Foods that are encased in a skin or seal should be pierced before they are placed in a microwave oven. Otherwise, steam will build up inside the food and cause it to burst. A quick jab or two with a fork or a small slit with a knife will prevent the pressure buildup. Puncture whole potatoes, egg yolks, hot dogs, and vegetables in plastic pouches.

Shielding

As a rule, you should not place metal in a microwave oven. However, you can use small pieces of aluminum foil to **shield** parts of food that might overcook. For example, you might shield the small end of chicken drumsticks, or the corners of a rectangular casserole. Be careful that the foil does not touch the sides of the oven and cause arcing. Check the instruction manual for any cautions.

Standing Time

A mistake that many people make when cooking in a microwave oven is to ignore the standing time called for in a recipe. **Standing time** is the time you should allow for the food to continue to cook after the microwave oven is turned off. You may think that the food is just sitting there, but the food molecules are still moving inside. Standing time is almost as important as cooking time for the food to turn out just right.

Recipes usually call for a cooking time slightly less than what is needed for doneness. Then, during standing time, the center of the food can cook some more, yet the outer edges do not dry out.

Whole potatoes must be pierced before being cooked. After they are removed from the oven, potatoes can be wrapped in tinfoil to retain moisture as they continue cooking during standing time.

Teaching "Microwave Techniques"
(Pages 438-439)

This section describes various techniques for cooking with microwave ovens.

Checking Comprehension

✔ List four materials that can be used for covering foods in a microwave oven. *White paper towel or napkin, waxed paper, microwave-safe lids, and plastic wrap can be used for covering foods in a microwave oven.*

✔ What happens if foods encased in skin or seal are not pierced before being cooked in a microwave oven? *If foods encased in skin or seal are not pierced before being cooked in a microwave oven, steam builds up inside the food and causes it to burst.*

✔ What precautions should be taken when using aluminum foil for shielding food in a microwave oven? *Use only small pieces of aluminum foil for shielding edges of casseroles or the small ends of drumsticks. Do not allow foil to touch the side of the microwave oven which can cause arcing.*

✔ What is standing time? *Standing time is the time you should allow for the food to continue to cook after the microwave oven is turned off.*

Activities

Skill Builder: Critical Thinking
Have students imagine they are going to microwave hot dogs. Ask them what techniques they would use (such as puncturing and rotating) to cook the food.

Reteaching
Have students describe four techniques of microwave cooking.

Enrichment
Divide students into groups, and have them prepare to toast pumpkin seeds or almond slivers on a pie plate. Tell both groups to cook the seeds or nuts on high for 5 to 6 minutes.

More About Shielding Tell students that another way of shielding foods is to use sauces to cover meat or vegetables.

Emphasize Stress that many frozen foods come in plastic pouches, which must be punctured before being heated. Others must be covered with plastic wrap, with the corner turned back.

Focus on Technology Tell students that some microwave manufacturers produce a turntable, called a carousel, that automatically and constantly rotates food being cooked in a microwave oven.

COMPLETING THE CHAPTER

Summary

- Microwave ovens have become popular because they cook faster and more easily than conventional ovens and because they are also cleaner and more economical.
- Microwave ovens have settings that control the amount of power and the time required to cook foods.
- Only microwave-safe cookware should be used in a microwave oven.
- Certain techniques, such as stirring, rotating, covering, puncturing, and shielding, are needed for cooking food in a microwave oven.
- Variables that affect how long foods should be cooked in a microwave oven are food type, volume, shape, and starting temperature.
- As with other appliances, safety must be considered when using a microwave oven.

For Review

Objective Review Questions Have students complete the "Reviewing the Facts" section on this page.

Study Guide Have students complete the Study Guide from Chapter 48 of their *Student Workbook.*

Class Debate Divide students into two groups, and have them debate the pros and cons of microwave cooking.

Answers to Students' Questions Ask students to look at the question they wrote before reading this chapter. Ask: "Has your question been answered by the information in this chapter?"

For Evaluation

Microwave Information Have students write a letter to someone who has never used a microwave oven in which they explain what it is, how it works, and what kinds of foods it is most suited for. Encourage them to finish their letters with a brief summary of the pros and cons of microwave cooking.

Chapter Test Have students complete the test for Chapter 48 that appears in the *Teacher's Classroom Resources.*

CHAPTER 48 REVIEW

Answers to "Reviewing the Facts"

1. Ceramic, glass, plastic, and paper containers—look for microwave-safe labels. Metal pans and bowls and dishes with metalic trim should not be used.
2. Stirring helps foods cook more evenly by moving the cooler food particles from the center toward the warmer outer edges.
3. Rotate the food a quarter- or half-turn; rearrange food pieces; turn pieces over.
4. To prevent steam from building up inside and bursting the food.
5. Type of food, volume, shape, and starting temperature.
6. Remove covers over microwaved food carefully; use microwave-safe dishes; do not use an extension cord on the oven; keep the oven in good working order.

Reviewing the Facts

1. What cookware can be used for microwave cooking? What material should you not use for microwave cooking?
2. Why is it sometimes necessary to stir food at intervals during microwave cooking?
3. When foods cannot be stirred, what can you do to help them cook faster and more evenly?
4. Why should you puncture food or plastic wrap before placing it in the microwave oven?
5. What are four variables in microwave cooking, and how do they affect cooking time?
6. Give four safety precautions to follow when cooking with a microwave oven.

Thinking Critically

1. If you had to choose between either a microwave oven or a conventional oven, which would you choose, and why?
2. If you were in charge of the household cooking and had a microwave oven in the kitchen, for what purposes and foods would you use it?

Applying Your Skills

1. **Supporting Decisions.** Bring to class several cookbooks or magazines containing microwave recipes. Make a list of some of your favorite foods, and from that list choose at least five that could be cooked in the microwave oven. From the cookbooks or magazines, find two microwave recipes for each food. Decide which recipe of each pair is most suitable for your family. Explain what your choices are and why you selected them.
2. **Explaining Techniques.** From the cookbooks or magazines that you have brought to class, find examples of rotating, stirring, covering, puncturing, shielding, and leaving to stand. For each of the five recipes you selected in Activity 1, check to see which of these techniques are used. Using your recipes as examples, write a paragraph or two explaining how two of these techniques are used in microwave cooking.
3. **Comparing Results.** Cook broccoli, carrots, and baked apples in a microwave oven and by conventional methods. Compare the appearance and taste of each item. Which method of preparation do you prefer, and why?

Answers to "Thinking Critically"

1. Answers will vary. Advantages of a microwave oven include its speed and its superior ability to preserve nutrients; also, there's no preheating and it does not heat the room. A conventional oven might be preferred because food requires less attention when cooking, and large amounts of food can be cooked easily.
2. Answers will vary. They might cook quick breakfasts for family members, prepare snacks, heat beverages, steam vegetables, cook casseroles and small meats, prepare appetizers for entertaining, warm rolls, reheat left-overs and so on.

CHAPTER

49

Breads and Cereals

OBJECTIVES

This chapter will help you to:

- Identify and select foods in the breads-cereals group.
- Explain how to store breads and other cereal foods.
- Describe the best methods of cooking breads and other cereal foods.

WORDS TO REMEMBER

knead
quick bread
yeast bread

CHAPTER OVERVIEW

Chapter 49 discusses selecting, storing, and cooking foods in the breads-cereals group. Students learn how grain is processed through milling, refining, and enriching procedures. Then various grain products, such as breads, breakfast cereals, rice, pasta, and flour products, are described. Next students learn how to store these foods. This chapter explains procedures for cooking foods in the breads-cereals groups in water, by baking, and by microwaving.

INTRODUCING THE CHAPTER

Motivators

What Did You Eat? Tell students that the breads-cereals group includes various types of bread, muffins, cereals, rice, and pasta. Add that there is a good chance they selected something from this food group for their breakfast or lunch that day. Ask students what they had for breakfast (and/or lunch) and which of those items are from the breads-cereals group. Ask if students have ever had, or considered having pasta for breakfast, cereal for lunch, and so on.

Using the Photograph Tell students to look at the photograph on this page. Then ask: "What foods are in this picture? Which of these foods do you eat? Can you name other foods in the breads-cereals group?"

The Food of Life Remind students that grains are the main source of nutrients for well over half of the world's population. Tell them to use an encyclopedia to find out how other cultures use grain products in their diet. For example, Mexicans use cornmeal to make tortillas.

Introducing the Objectives

Discuss the chapter objectives on this page. Remind students that the objectives focus on important chapter content.

Chapter Resources

Teacher's Classroom Resources
- Lesson Plan
- Life Skills Activity, *Feeding the World*
- Reproducible Masters, *How to Make Muffins, How to Make Biscuits*
- Extension Activity, *Types of Pasta and Their Uses*
- Chapter Test

Student Workbook
- Study Guide
- Worksheet, *Invent a Better Breakfast*

Introducing Vocabulary

Write the words *yeast bread* and *quick bread* on the board. Point out that these are two different kinds of bread and that the difference is based on the ingredients used to make the bread rise. Tell students that yeast is a tiny plant that feeds on sugar in dough and grows, causing the dough to rise. Quick breads, on the other hand, use baking soda or baking powder to make the dough rise during baking.

TEACHING THE CHAPTER

For convenience, the teaching suggestions for this chapter are arranged according to the following lesson topics:

- "Selecting Breads and Cereals," pages 444-445
- "Storing Breads and Cereals," page 447
- "Cooking Breads and Cereals," pages 447-449

Teaching "Selecting Breads and Cereals"

(Pages 444-445)

This section identifies foods in the breads-cereals group.

Checking Comprehension

✓ What should be kept in mind when selecting breads and cereals? *Your decisions may be based on personal taste, convenience, and nutrition. How the grain was processed should be considered when selecting breads and cereals.*

✓ Why are the bran and germ removed during milling? *The bran and germ are removed during milling to give the flour a finer texture and to make it last longer.*

✓ Why is flour enriched? *Refining removes important nutrients, such as iron and B vitamins. Federal law requires that nutrients lost in processing be replaced.*

Among the five food groups, the breads-cereals group holds a special place. Cereal grains like wheat and rice are the main source of nutrients for well over half the world's population. In addition to providing carbohydrates for energy, they supply protein and important vitamins and minerals. They are a valuable source of fiber, too.

Many food products come from grains—breads, breakfast cereals, pasta, biscuits, muffins, tortillas, pancakes, waffles, and even pizza crusts. Grains and grain products should be a part of everyone's diet because of the nutrients they provide.

Some breakfast cereals are ready-to-eat, while others need either cooking or mixing with hot water.

Selecting Breads and Cereals

You will find a wide variety of breads and cereals to choose from in most markets. Your decisions may be based on personal taste, convenience—and also nutrition. An important question to ask is, how was the grain processed to make the product you are choosing?

Many products sold in America are made of white flour. This type of flour has been refined, meaning that the bran and the germ are removed during milling to give the flour a finer texture and to make it last longer. See "Whole and Hearty" on page 446 for an explanation of the parts of a grain.

Together with the bran and the germ, refining removes important nutrients, such as iron and the B vitamins. The flour is then enriched—federal law requires nutrients lost in processing to be replaced—and may also be fortified with additional nutrients.

Whole-grain products are made from the entire grain, including the bran and germ. They do not have to be enriched. Whole-grain products often have a distinctive, nutlike taste, and are higher in fiber than refined flour products.

Breads

There are many types of breads—white, whole wheat, rye, pumpernickel, and oat bran are just a few examples. Bread products include rolls, muffins, and biscuits, as well as loaves.

In addition to bread that has been commercially baked, you can buy bread mixes or ingredients to make the bread yourself. For extra convenience, you can also buy frozen bread products such as waffles or rolls. These merely need thawing or heating to be ready to eat.

Focus on Health Stress to students the importance of getting 6-11 servings a day from the breads-cereals group. Ask them to reread appropriate sections of Chapter 37 to remind them of why the breads-cereals group is so important.

More About Rice Regular white rice is the most popular type and the least expensive. Brown rice has more nutrients, but does not keep as well and takes longer to cook. Converted rice has been partly cooked before milling so it retains more nutrients, but takes longer to cook. Precooked rice has been cooked and dehydrated so it cooks quickly.

Breakfast Cereals

Breakfast cereals are made from grains such as wheat, oats, corn, rice, and barley. Some are ready to eat—wheat flakes or corn puffs, for example—and can be served with milk and fruit. Others are cooked in water or milk and served hot. Some hot cereals are instant—you only have to add boiling water.

Read the labels carefully for nutrition and ingredient information. Many breakfast cereals contain large amounts of sugar and salt, and are high in calories. However, many cereals are fortified with added nutrients, and whole-grain cereals are also available.

Rice

White rice has had its outer coverings, the hull and bran, removed by polishing. Because most of the vitamin B and fiber is in the bran layer, enriched rice, like enriched bread, has had the vitamins put back in. You can also buy brown rice, which has been hulled but is unpolished. Much of the nutritious, fiber-rich bran is retained in brown rice, which has a nutlike flavor similar to whole wheat.

Other rice products include rice that is packaged with a sauce or seasoning packet, and instant rice which can be cooked quickly. These rices usually cost more than regular rice.

Pasta

Macaroni, spaghetti, and noodles are also in the breads and cereals group. These products are called pasta, which comes from the Italian word for dough. Most pasta keeps its shape and stays firm even after it has been cooked because it is made from a special flour called semolina.

Pasta comes in all sizes and shapes—from thin strands of spaghetti to little shells and pieces that look like wagon wheels. Some pasta products have spinach or tomatoes added to the dough for color. They all usually taste the same, but the difference in texture or appearance may be important in your recipe.

Flour

You can purchase several kinds of flour for making bread products. All-purpose flour is used for general baking and cooking. Self-rising flour is an all-purpose flour with baking powder and salt added for baking.

Other types of flour include whole-wheat flour, rye flour, oat flour, and buckwheat flour. Cornmeal is used for baking corn bread, tortillas, and hush puppies. Other grain products are discussed in the feature on page 446.

Pasta comes in assorted shapes and is a good source of carbohydrates.

✔ How are whole-grain products different from those made of refined flour? *Whole-grain products are made from the whole grain, including the bran and germ. They have a nutlike flavor and are higher in fiber.*

✔ What grains are used in making breads and breakfast cereals? *There are many types of bread: wheat, rye, pumpernickel, and oat bran are just a few examples. Breakfast cereals are made from grains such as wheat, oats, corn, rice, and barley.*

✔ What is the difference between white rice and brown rice? *White rice has its outer coverings, the hull and bran, removed and it has to be enriched. Brown rice has been hulled but much of the fiber-rich bran is retained.*

✔ What is the difference between all-purpose flour and self-rising flour? *Self-rising flour is an all-purpose flour with baking powder and salt added.*

Activities

Skill Builder: Writing
Write the following topic sentence on the board, "Foods from the breads-cereals group should be a vital part of everyone's diet." Then list the following words: *milling, refining, whole-grain, enriched, pasta, semolina.* Have students write a two-paragraph essay beginning with the topic sentence and using each word.

Reteaching
Ask students to find pictures of foods in the breads-cereals group and arrange them in a collage.

Enrichment
Have students find out what conditions are necessary for growing grains. Then have students use a world map to indicate where most of the world's grain supply comes from.

Focus on Technology Pasta has become such a popular food that many manufacturers market small machines to enable people to make homemade pasta in their own kitchens. Homemade or fresh pasta takes less than five minutes to cook compared to the 10 to 15 minutes for store-bought pastas.

Focus on Consumer Skills Tell students to look for the word *enriched* on labels of pasta packages. This means that the products are a valuable source of B vitamins and iron.

Did You Know? Wild rice is not a rice but a grain of tall marsh grass. It has a crisp texture and nutlike flavor, and is very expensive because of its limited supply.

Teaching the Feature
"Whole and Hearty"

Answers to Feature Questions

1. Students might suggest to the person that whole-grain breads have more nutrients, that they have more interesting taste, that they are more satisfying. Students' individual choices will reflect their reasons for choosing one food over another.

2. Students might suggest whole-wheat waffles or pancakes, whole-wheat cereals, whole-wheat bread for toast, or whole-wheat muffins.

Activities

Finding Additional Information Have students choose one of the grain products in the feature to research. They should find out where it is popular and how it is prepared and then choose a recipe made with it that they would like to try.

New Twists to Old Recipes Ask students to list foods they eat at home that they could substitute one of the featured grains for. Then have them bring in a recipe they would alter and explain how they would change it.

Community Contact Have selected students contact the American Cancer Society. Ask them to find out the value of a high-fiber diet in reducing the risks of getting cancer. Ask them to prepare a poster on their findings and display it in health clubs or in community centers.

HEALTH WATCH

Whole and Hearty

A grain of wheat measures no more than one quarter of an inch, yet wheat has been a staple food throughout the world for thousands of years. How can you get the most out of this important source of energy, nutrients, and fiber?

A grain of wheat has four parts and is crammed with nutrients. The germ, which is at its core, contains vitamins and minerals that your body needs to stay healthy. Surrounding the germ is the endosperm, with nutrients to nourish the seed if it were allowed to sprout. These include starchy carbohydrates for energy, and most of the grain's protein. Outside the endosperm are layers of bran, covered by an outer protective case called the hull. The germ, bran, and hull all contain cellulose, or fiber.

The germ, the endosperm, and the bran are all retained in whole-wheat flour, which can be used in bread, graham crackers, pasta, and even pizza crust. Here are some other healthful grain products:

- Wheat berries, or whole-wheat kernels, can be cooked much like rice and served in similar ways.
- Bulgur, or cracked wheat, is the pasta of the Middle East and can be used in place of pasta or rice.
- Wheat germ can be sprinkled on cereal, yogurt, or ice cream.
- Barley, which usually has the bran removed, can be used in soups or served as a side dish.
- Grits, or ground white corn, are used as cereal or instead of rice or mashed potatoes.
- Kasha, or ground buckwheat with the bran removed, is used in Eastern European cooking instead of rice.

These grains can provide lots of nutrients. They are delicious and fun to eat as well!

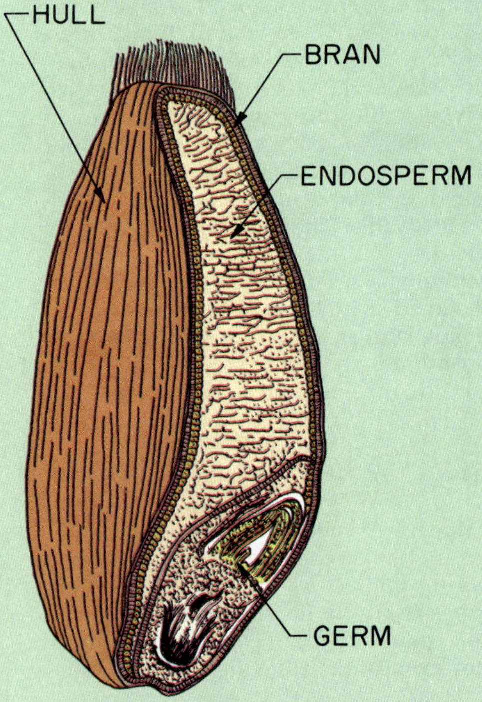

Think It Through

1. **What arguments would you use to convince someone who eats only white bread to try whole-grain varieties? Which argument would be most likely to convince you?**
2. **What breakfast foods can you think of that are made with whole grains?**

More About Wheat Germ Wheat germ is removed from grains because it contains oil that can become rancid and cause spoilage. But wheat germ is available in vacuum-packed containers in grocery stores. It can be added to other foods to increase their nutritional value and add fiber and bulk to your diet.

Focus on Consumer Skills Bulgur, grits, kasha, and other grain products are available in grocery stores as well as health food stores. Look for them the next time you are at the supermarket and check the prices—they are often a bargain compared to more common grains.

Storing Breads and Cereals

One of the advantages of products in the breads and cereals food group is that they can easily be stored. Many items keep well for long periods of time without refrigeration.

Breads

Bread tastes best when it's fresh, but it can also keep for some time. Always wrap breads tightly and store them in a cool, dark place, such as a breadbox or cabinet. In hot weather, keep bread in the refrigerator to slow down the growth of mold. Refrigeration will cause breads to get stale quickly, so do not store them this way unless it is necessary. Refrigerator rolls should remain refrigerated after you bring them home from the store.

Bread freezes well if it is tightly wrapped. It can be kept in the freezer for several months. Bread products that come frozen should be kept in the freezer until they are used.

Cereals, Rice, Pasta, and Flours

Dry cereals keep well in tightly closed packages or airtight containers. Rice, pasta, and flours also stay fresh for a long time if kept air-tight. Refrigeration is not needed for most cereal products except in hot, humid weather or if insects are a problem. However, whole-grain flours should be refrigerated.

Cooking Breads and Cereals

Breads and cereals may be cooked in liquids, baked, or heated in the microwave oven. Learn how to prepare them correctly, so the finished food will have good taste, texture, and appearance.

Cooking in Liquids

Many cereal products, including rice, pastas, and hot breakfast cereals, are cooked in water, and sometimes other liquids. They expand to two or three times their original size when fully cooked, so it is important to use a large enough pot.

Nutrients, especially the B vitamins, escape into the liquid during cooking. The key to preparing cereal products, therefore, is to use just the right amount of liquid. The package will tell you how much water or broth to use and how long to cook the product.

Rice and breakfast cereals absorb all the liquid used to cook them, so no nutrients are lost. Do not rinse rice before or after cooking, because the water may wash away nutrients.

Cook pasta in a large pot so it can move around freely and not stick together. First bring the water to a boil and then slowly add the pasta so the boiling does not stop.

Emphasize Cereal boxes and bread bags should be opened carefully so that they can be resealed to keep air out and maintain freshness longer.

More About Storing Pasta If stored properly, macaroni and spaghetti will keep up to one year, and noodles will keep for about six months.

More About Freezing Breads Home-baked breads and rolls should be cooled to room temperature before freezing. The breads should be wrapped in aluminum foil, plastic wrap, airtight plastic bags, or freezer wrap, with all the air pressed out of the package. Breads can be frozen for up to three months before losing their flavor.

Teaching "Storing Breads and Cereals"
(Page 447)

This section explains how to store breads and other cereal foods.

Checking Comprehension

✓ What is one advantage of products in the breads and cereals food group? *They can be easily stored, and many items keep well for long periods without refrigeration.*

✓ In general, how should breads be stored? *In general, breads should be wrapped tightly and stored in a cool, dark place such as a breadbox.*

✓ How should bread be prepared for freezing? How long can it be kept frozen? *Bread should be wrapped tightly before being frozen. Bread can be kept in the freezer for several months.*

✓ In general, how should dry cereals be stored? *In general, dry cereals should be stored in tightly closed packages or airtight containers.*

✓ How should whole-grain flours be stored? *Whole-grain flours should be stored in the refrigerator.*

Activities

Skill Builder: Science
Suggest that students seal one slice of bread in a plastic bag and store it in a cool, dark place at room temperature. At the same time, they should seal another slice of bread in a plastic bag and store it in a refrigerator. Ask them to compare the quality of the two slices of bread after several days.

Reteaching
Have students write directions for storing breads and cereals during summer and winter months.

Enrichment
Have students describe ideas for containers in which to store breads, cereals, and pastas. Ask them to think about the shape of the various foods and how that shape could affect the various containers.

Teaching "Cooking Breads and Cereals"
(Pages 447-449)

This section describes methods of cooking breads and cereals.

Checking Comprehension

✓ Why should you use a large pot when cooking rice and pasta? *You should use a large pot when cooking rice and pasta because they expand to two or three times their original size when fully cooked.*

✓ Why are nutrients lost when pasta is cooked but not when rice is cooked? *Rice absorbs all the liquid used to cook it, but pasta is cooked in more water and some of the nutrients are discarded with the extra cooking water.*

✓ What happens when pasta is overcooked? *Texture and nutritive value are destroyed.*

✓ What happens when breads are baked? *Chemical and physical changes take place. The dough rises or puffs up because ingredients in the dough release gases.*

✓ What are some examples of quick breads and yeast breads? *Examples of quick breads are muffins, biscuits, pancakes, waffles, and banana bread. Common yeast breads include white bread, whole-grain bread, raisin bread, rolls, and pizza crusts.*

✓ Why do yeast breads take longer to make than quick breads? *The dough of yeast breads must be kneaded and allowed to rise several times before it is put in the oven.*

✓ Why does it take the same amount of time for rice and pasta to cook in a microwave oven as it does for them to cook on a range? *Rice and pasta take as long to cook in a microwave oven as they do on a range because time is needed for them to absorb the liquid and soften.*

Pasta should be cooked until just tender, or "al dente" (meaning "to the tooth" in Italian). Drain pasta in a colander but do not rinse after cooking.

In contrast, pasta is cooked in a large amount of water and then drained. Use 2 quarts (2 L) of water for every 8 ounces (250 mL) of pasta. Add the pasta slowly.

Pasta is done when it has expanded and softened. Overcooking destroys the texture and nutritive value. The pasta must be drained, using a colander. Do not rinse it or additional nutrients will be lost.

Baking

When you bake muffins, biscuits, or a loaf of bread, chemical and physical changes take place. The dough rises or puffs up because ingredients in the dough release gases. There are two basic types of breads—quick breads and yeast breads. Each type uses different ingredients to make the dough rise.

Quick breads use baking soda or baking powder to rise. These ingredients work fast, so that the bread is ready for baking right away. Examples are muffins, biscuits, pancakes, waffles, and banana bread. Most quick breads are made by combining the dry ingredients in one bowl and the liquid ingredients in another. The liquid is poured all at once into the dry ingredients, and the mixture is stirred only until the dry ingredients are moistened. Overmixing will cause the baked product to be tough.

Muffins, biscuits, and pancakes are quick breads.

Focus on Decision-Making Tell students that they can vary recipes by using different kinds of pasta. However, when substituting, uncooked pasta should be measured by weight, *not* by the cup.

Did You Know? Tell students that wheat flour is best for making yeast breads since it contains gluten, which stretches during kneading and traps gas formed by the yeast, producing a light, airy bread. Whole-wheat flour has less gluten and makes heavier, smaller breads.

Some biscuits are made by cutting the shortening into the flour mixture with a pastry blender or two knives. Then the liquid is added. After the ingredients are mixed together the dough is **kneaded.** To knead dough, press and fold it by hand several times. Then the dough is rolled, or flattened with a rolling pin, and the biscuits are cut out and baked.

Quick breads should be baked or cooked until lightly brown. When they are done, they spring back when touched lightly.

Yeast breads rise through the action of yeast, a tiny plant. They take longer to make than quick breads because the dough must be left to rise, often for half an hour or more, before it is put in the oven. Common yeast breads include white bread, whole-grain bread, raisin bread, rolls, and pizza crusts.

To make a yeast bread, combine the ingredients according to the recipe. When the yeast is mixed with warm water, it becomes active and slowly releases the gas that makes the dough rise.

After the flour and other ingredients are combined, most yeast breads are kneaded for at least eight to ten minutes. Then the dough is allowed to rise, punched down, shaped, and allowed to rise a second time. This process may be repeated more times for heavier breads. Finally, the dough is put into the oven.

You can test yeast breads for doneness by rapping the crust with your knuckles. A hollow sound means the bread is done.

Microwave Cooking

A microwave oven can be used to defrost or warm prepared rolls, pancakes, waffles, bagels, and other breads. Baking in a microwave is also possible, though microwave baked breads are pale in color, not brown. Chopped nuts, cinnamon and sugar, or frosting can be added as a topping.

Hot breakfast cereals can easily be cooked in a microwave oven. Make sure, though, that your dish is microwave-safe—and large enough to allow for expansion of the cereal.

Rice and pasta take as long to cook in a microwave oven as they do on the range. Time is needed for them to absorb the liquid and soften. However, precooked rice and pasta can be quickly reheated in a microwave.

Most yeast doughs are kneaded for about 8 to 10 minutes. This develops the gluten which forms the structure of the bread. Then as the yeast releases carbon dioxide gas, the dough rises.

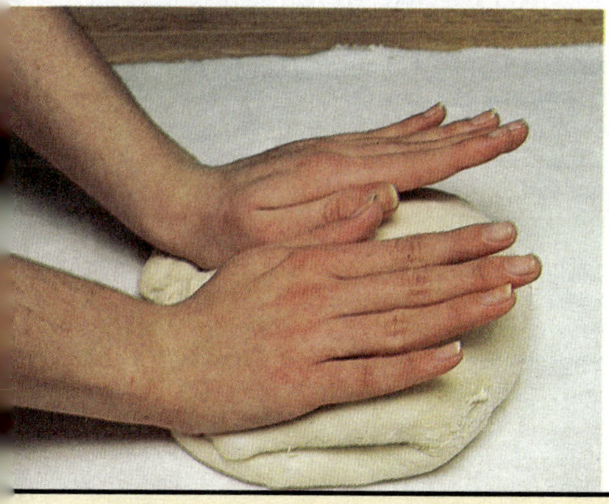

More About Quick Breads The "muffin method" is used for making muffins, loaf breads, and pancakes. The ingredients should be mixed together only until the dry ingredients are moistened. Small lumps will still remain in the batter. If the batter is overmixed, the baked product will have large tunnels inside and a peaked crust.

Did You Know? Baking muffins in cupcake liners makes for easy removal of the muffins and quick clean-up of the muffin tin. Some liners can be used without a muffin tin and simply placed on a flat baking sheet.

Cross-Reference See Chapter 48 for more information about microwave cooking.

Activities

Skill Builder: Reading
Have students read bread recipes and identify them as quick breads or yeast breads.

Skill Builder: Writing
Ask students to write out a recipe for a food in the breads-cereals group that they like and share it with the class. They might combine all of the recipes in a class cookbook that can be added to in later chapters of this unit.

Skill Builder: Critical Thinking
Have students discuss the pros and cons of using a microwave oven to cook foods from the breads-cereals group. What foods from this group have they cooked in a microwave oven? What would they like to try? What wouldn't work at all, and why?

Skill Builder: Math
Tell students to imagine that they are cooking pasta for a family get-together. The pasta is packaged in 1-lb. boxes. If they are having ten people and plan to serve each a 2-oz. cooked serving, then how many boxes do they need? *(One box because the 16-oz. box of dry pasta will double when cooked.)* How many ounces of dry pasta should they cook? *(10 oz.)* If they need 2 qt. of water to cook 8 oz. of dry pasta, then how much water do they need to cook the pasta for their group? *(2qts. 2 cups.)*

Reteaching
Have students describe the correct process for cooking each of the following: rice, spaghetti, muffins, raisin bread.

Enrichment
Have students prepare oatmeal, pasta, or rice, using two of the methods described in this section. Then have students discuss their reasons for choosing the methods they did, and have them compare the results they get.

COMPLETING THE CHAPTER

Summary

- Cereal grains like wheat and rice are the main source of nutrients for well over half the world's population.
- Foods in the breads-cereals group include breads, cereals, rice, pasta, and flour products.
- Selecting foods in the breads-cereals group should include considerations such as personal taste, convenience, nutrition, and how the grain was processed.
- In general, breads and cereals should be sealed in airtight containers and stored in cool, dry places.
- Breads and cereals can be prepared by cooking them in water, baking them, or cooking them in the microwave oven.

For Review

Objective Review Questions Have students complete the "Reviewing the Facts" section on this page.

Study Guide Have students complete the Study Guide from Chapter 49 of their *Student Workbook.*

Planning a Meal Have students plan a meal using two foods from the breads-cereals group. Ask students to describe how they plan to select, store, and cook the bread and cereal foods.

For Evaluation

Bread-Cereal Summary Have students pick one group of foods (pasta, rice, bread, or cereal) and do a summary of the information presented in the chapter. List products, storage recommendations, and cooking techniques.

Comparison Have students compare (1) refined and whole-grain flour and (2) storing bread in summer and winter.

Chapter Test Have students complete the test for Chapter 49 that appears in the *Teacher's Resource Book.*

CHAPTER 49 REVIEW

Answers to "Reviewing the Facts"

1. Enriched means that the nutrients lost in processing have been replaced; fortified means that additional nutrients have been added.
2. Nutrition and ingredient information.
3. In hot weather; if refrigerator rolls. Frozen bread products should be kept in the freezer.
4. Use just the right amount of liquid; do not rinse before or after cooking; do not overcook.
5. Quick breads use baking soda or baking powder to rise and can be baked right away. Yeast breads rise through the action of yeast, and must be kneaded and allowed to rise one or more times before baking.
6. Quick breads should be lightly brown and spring back when touched lightly. Yeast breads give a hollow sound when tapped.
7. Defrost or warm prepared foods; cook hot breakfast cereals; reheat cooked rice and pasta.

Reviewing the Facts

1. What is the difference between bread and cereal products that have been enriched and those that have been fortified?
2. When buying cereals, what can you find out by looking at the label?
3. When should breads be stored in the refrigerator?
4. What can you do to conserve nutrients in pasta and rice when cooking them?
5. What is the difference between quick breads and yeast breads?
6. How do you test quick breads and yeast breads for doneness?
7. What is the best use of a microwave oven for bread and cereal products?

Sharing Your Ideas

1. You make a pasta salad for lunch, but when you are eating it you find that the pasta is mushy and it breaks when you try to pick it up on your fork. What might you have done to cause this? Did it affect the nutrient value? What should you do next time?
2. What reasons do you think that people have for baking their own bread at home when so many varieties can be bought in the store?

Applying Your Skills

1. **Researching Processes.** Another type of rice is *converted* rice. Using the resources of your classroom and the library, find out what converted rice is. Why is the conversion process used? Does it relate to the way that rice is normally cooked? Explain the process to the class.

2. **Giving Instructions.** Prepare a chart that gives simple instructions on making bread. Divide all the steps into three parts: preparing the dough; kneading; rising. Write the steps for each part in a list on one half of a sheet of paper. Create simple illustrations of each step on the other half.

3. **Identifying Objects and Phenomena.** Several types of bread rise through the action of yeast. Use an encyclopedia to learn what yeast is and how it works. In one small bowl, mix yeast with warm water. In another bowl, mix yeast, warm water, and sugar. Then explain what happens.

Answers to "Sharing Your Ideas"

1. The pasta was overcooked because it was boiled too long. Nutrient value has been lost in overcooking. The student should follow the package directions carefully, since cooking times and amount of water needed vary according to the shape and size of the pasta.
2. Answers will vary. Students may suggest that people get enjoyment from baking bread. They know exactly what ingredients are in the bread and how fresh it is. They may get a sense of accomplishment and may feel they can bring a home-baked bread as a gift.

CHAPTER

50

Fruits and Vegetables

OBJECTIVES

This chapter will help you to:

- Identify and select foods in the fruits and vegetables groups.
- Explain how to store fruits and vegetables.
- Describe the best methods of cooking fruits and vegetables.

WORDS TO REMEMBER

concentrate
produce
seasonal
spoilage

CHAPTER OVERVIEW

Chapter 50 discusses selecting, storing, and preparing fruits and vegetables. Students are made aware of the advantages and disadvantages of fresh and processed fruits and vegetables and the storage requirements of the various forms of these foods. The chapter presents ways of preparing and cooking fruits and vegetables—cooking with moist heat, baking, stir-frying, and microwave cooking.

INTRODUCING THE CHAPTER

Motivators

Twenty Questions Have students play a "twenty questions" guessing game of fruits and vegetables. Students will ask, "Is it red?" "Is it sweet?" "Can I eat it raw?" to get enough information to guess what fruit or vegetable the person has in mind.

Using the Photograph Have students study the photograph on this page. Then ask: "What does the photograph show? What different kinds of produce do you see?"

Favorite Things Ask students to write down their five favorite fruits and their five favorite vegetables. Tell them to keep their lists—they will refer to them later.

Introducing the Objectives

Discuss the chapter objectives on this page. Remind students that the objectives focus on important chapter content.

Introducing Vocabulary

Point out that *concentrate* and *produce,* as they are used in this chapter, are nouns, not verbs.

Chapter Resources

Teacher's Classroom Resources
- Lesson Plan
- Life Skills Activity, *At the Produce Market*
- Reproducible Master, *Save the Nutrients*
- Extension Activity, *Vitamin C Facts*
- Chapter Test

Student Workbook
- Study Guide
- Worksheet, *Tutti Frutti*

TEACHING THE CHAPTER

For convenience, the teaching suggestions for this chapter are arranged according to the following lesson topics:

- "Selecting Fruits and Vegetables," pages 452-453
- "Storing Fruits and Vegetables," page 455
- "Preparing Fruits and Vegetables," pages 455-456

Teaching "Selecting Fruits and Vegetables"

(Pages 452-453)

This section teaches how to select fruits and vegetables in their fresh and processed (frozen, canned, dried, juice) forms.

Checking Comprehension

✓ Why are fresh fruits and vegetables more nutritious than processed ones? *In general, fresh produce is more nutritious because processing may destroy some of the nutrients.*

✓ Why is it advantageous to buy produce in season? *Buying produce in season can save you money, and it also assures you that the food is fresh. Out-of-season produce will probably be more expensive, less nutritious, or both.*

✓ Why is it sometimes necessary to buy processed fruit? *Because the produce you want may not be available, is in poor condition, or is expensive and out-of-season, or because you want to stock up or prefer the convenience of processed foods.*

✓ Compare frozen and fresh fruits. *Frozen fruits have a softer texture than fresh and retain almost as many nutrients.*

✓ What options do people who buy canned fruits have? *Canned fruits come in many forms, such as whole, halved, sliced, or in pieces. Some are sold in a sugar syrup, others in their own juice.*

Plants have provided people with important foods for thousands of years. Early people wandered over great distances to find roots, stems, leaves, berries, and fruits to eat. Today, however, refrigerated transportation brings a wide array of fruits and vegetables right to your neighborhood stores.

Fruits and vegetables are valuable sources of vitamins and minerals. Oranges, tomatoes, and green peppers, for example, are rich in vitamin C. Carrots, cantaloupes, and apricots contain a lot of vitamin A. Collard and turnip greens are valuable sources of vitamins A and C, calcium, and iron.

In addition, fruits and vegetables provide carbohydrates—starches and sugars. They also are excellent sources of fiber.

The way fruits and vegetables are handled, processed, and cooked can affect these nutrients. Thus, learning how to select, store, and prepare fruits and vegetables will do more than improve the taste of your meals and snacks—it will add to their nutritional benefits, too.

Selecting Fruits and Vegetables

There are probably more varieties of fruits and vegetables than of any other food. Most people can easily name ten fruits and vegetables that can be found in the produce section of their local supermarket. **Produce** (PRAH-doos or PRO-doos) is a term used to describe fresh fruits and vegetables. In fact, new transportation techniques are increasing the variety of produce in supermarkets, as described in "Strawberries in December" on page 454.

You can buy fruits and vegetables in several different forms—fresh, frozen, canned, and sometimes dried. Many types of juices are available too.

Fresh

Fresh fruits and vegetables—crisp, tart apples, steaming baked potatoes—have tastes and textures that many people find irresistible. In general, fresh also means more nutritious, because fruits and vegetables may lose some of their nutrients during processing. However, some of the vitamins in fresh produce deteriorate after harvest. So you should select fruits and vegetables that look fresh and crisp, and have not wilted.

Fruits and vegetables should also have a healthy color, with no bruises, spots, or sticky areas. Fruit that is soft to the touch may be overripe. For maximum juiciness, fruit should feel firm but not hard.

Examine fresh vegetables and fruits for color, ripeness, and texture. Don't buy any that are wilted, bruised, spotted, or damaged—they have lost nutrients and will not keep well.

Focus on Health Tell students that some people follow a fruitarian diet. They eat only raw or dried fruits, seeds, and nuts. Because it is so low in protein, it can be a dangerous diet regimen.

Did You Know? Fruits and vegetables are 80 to 95 percent water. Water does, however, serve many vital functions—it transports nutrients in the blood and plays an important role in digestion and elimination.

Some produce is **seasonal**, meaning that it is more plentiful at certain times of the year, when it is usually less expensive. For instance, fresh corn is available in the summer but rarely in the winter. Buying produce in season can save money, and it also assures you that the food is fresh. Out-of-season produce may have been artificially ripened, or have traveled a long distance; either way, it will probably be more expensive, less nutritious, or both.

Processed

Perhaps you want a particular kind of produce, but its fresh form is either unavailable, in poor condition, or expensive and out of season. Maybe you want to stock up on fruits and vegetables so you don't have to go to the store so often. You may just prefer the convenience of processed foods—frozen, canned, or dried.

- **Frozen.** Frozen fruits and vegetables retain almost as many nutrients as fresh produce, and they keep their flavor and color better than canned products. However, frozen fruits usually have a softer texture than fresh fruits. Frozen vegetables are available whole, cut in pieces, and in special sauces.
- **Canned.** Fruits and vegetables in cans also come in many forms, such as whole, halved, sliced, or in pieces. Which form you choose depends on how you will use the item. Whole fruits and vegetables usually cost more than those in pieces. Most canned fruits are sold in a sugar syrup. For fewer calories, look for fruits packed in their own juice.
- **Dried.** Many fruits and vegetables are available dried, from raisins and apricots to mushrooms and onions. They can all be used in cooking, and dried fruits can be eaten as snacks.
- **Juices.** Apples, oranges, prunes, and tomatoes are just some of the many fruits and vegetables that are made into juices. Juices may be sold fresh, canned, or as frozen **concentrates**—juice products from which most of the water has been removed. Concentrates may be less costly than other forms of juice.

Many fruits and vegetables are available in several different forms. Your choice depends on how and when you plan to use the food, as well as availability and price.

✓ Name two fruits and two vegetables that are available in dried form. *Raisins, apricots, mushrooms, and onions are available dried.*

✓ What is a concentrate? *It's a juice product from which most of the water has been removed.*

Activities

Skill Builder: Critical Thinking
Ask students to name three vegetables that are available in juice form and three fruits that are available fresh, canned, frozen, dried, and as a juice.

Skill Builder: Writing
Have students write a list of all the snacks they can think of that consist of foods from the fruit and vegetable groups. You might want to suggest that a master list of all the snacks be compiled and circulated.

Reteaching
Have students list all the advantages and disadvantages of buying fruits and vegetables in each of the following forms: fresh and processed—frozen, canned, dried, and as juices.

Enrichment
Suggest that students conduct an inventory of all the fruits and vegetables stored in their homes. Their inventory should be divided into five sections: fresh, frozen, canned, dried, and juices. From a show of hands, find out which category is most popular.

Cross-Reference See Chapter 37 for additional information about various types of fruits and vegetables and the nutrients they supply.

Did You Know? It is primarily water-soluble vitamins, the eight B vitamins, and vitamin C that leach out into cooking water and are lost.

Teaching the Feature
"Strawberries in December"

Answers to Feature Questions

1. Greater variety of tastes could appeal to people who like only a few fruits or vegetables; people can get a wider variety of nutrients by eating different types of produce.

2. Foods grown closer to home are cheaper since transportation and packaging costs are not too high. Such foods may also be fresher and less bruised. Students might want to support local farmers.

Activities

Try It! You'll Like it! Encourage students to try one of the new produce items mentioned in this section. Ask those who have already tasted some unusual items to describe their impressions to the class.

A Day in the Life of . . . Ask students to write an imaginary account of a day in life of an apple, a strawberry, or some other fruit that is in transit from farm to market. Suggest that they describe, in their accounts, the packaging, loading, and jolts that their chosen fruit receives in its journey from one destination to another.

Community Contact Have students prepare handouts about unusual fruits and vegetables. Their handouts should include a picture, a description, and recommendations for choosing and preparing the item. Suggest that they post their handouts at appropriate places in the community.

TECHNOLOGY

Strawberries in December

Strawberries in December? Blueberries in February? Yes, these summer pleasures can brighten up a dreary winter weekend, thanks to modern technology.

Alongside the familiar fruits and vegetables, you may also find new and strange-looking varieties. The kiwi fruit from New Zealand and Australia; the carabola, or star fruit, from South America; winged beans from the Philippines; and the chayote, or vegetable pear, from Mexico are among the new "residents" of the produce sections in today's supermarkets.

How is it possible to have this rich variety of fresh produce from thousands of miles away? Improvements in the following areas help to bring produce from all over the world to your local markets, from January to December:

- **Storage.** Warehouses and storage facilities can accommodate varied produce for longer periods because of refrigeration equipment that adjusts automatically to maintain the proper temperature.
- **Transportation.** Airplanes, boats, and trucks, have specially insulated refrigerator compartments for shipping produce long distances. The temperature is controlled automatically while fruits and vegetables are in transit.
- **Packaging.** Perishable produce is protected from jolting and bruising in transit. Individual fruits are wrapped and separated from each other with molded plastic wrapping, and containers are insulated with foam.
- **Computerization.** A microprocessor chip can record and time the number of jolts, collisions, or any serious disturbances of a shipment of produce in transit. The little computer is enclosed in a piece of hard beeswax that has been molded in the shape of a fruit or vegetable; it is then packaged with the produce. It provides information that can lead to improved packaging, or a change in the transportation method.

Think It Through

1. **What are some advantages of more fruits and vegetables being available in supermarkets year round?**
2. **Now that techniques have been developed to transport produce great distances, are there any advantages in buying fruits and vegetables that have been grown locally?**

More About Out-of-Season Fruit Now that fruits and vegetables are available year round, we have lost sight of when they are in season. The following fruits and vegetables are in season during the summer, but we can now get them even in December: corn, eggplant, lima beans, okra, peas, tomatoes, apricots, berries, melons, cherries, peaches, and plums.

Emphasize Many of our eating traditions (pumpkin pie at Thanksgiving and strawberry shortcake at Memorial Day picnics, for example) were originally based on when certain foods were available. Now they can be eaten all year long.

Storing Fruits and Vegetables

Storing fruits and vegetables properly helps prevent **spoilage**, damage that happens when food is too old to eat or contains bacteria or mold.

- **Fresh.** In general, fresh fruits and vegetables need refrigeration. Lettuce and other leafy vegetables, should be refrigerated in airtight containers to retain their moisture. Bananas and a few other products do much better stored at room temperature.

  You can wash and dry fresh fruits and vegetables before storing. However some, like berries, are best kept as dry as possible until they are served.

  Most fresh produce should be used within a few days of buying it. Apples, though, can stay fresh for three or four weeks, while oranges and other citrus fruits can keep for five weeks in a plastic bag in the refrigerator. Potatoes and onions can be kept a long time—two or three months—in a cool, dry, dark place. If you have a question about a specific product, ask the produce manager at your supermarket.
- **Frozen.** Frozen products keep well for several months if the temperature in the freezer or freezing compartment is no higher than 0°F (-18°C). If the freezer or freezing compartment is not this cold, frozen foods should be stored for only a few days.
- **Canned.** Canned fruits and vegetables keep for a year or more if they are stored in a cool, dry place—70°F (21°C) is recommended.
- **Dried.** Dried and freeze-dried products do well on the cupboard shelf, tightly wrapped. In humid weather, dried fruit should be refrigerated.
- **Juices.** Juices should be stored according to the package directions.

Preparing Fruits and Vegetables

Nutrition and flavor are the words to remember when preparing fruits and vegetables.

Serving Fresh Produce

Fresh fruits and vegetables may be eaten as snacks, in salads, as appetizers, as side dishes, or for dessert. Produce such as apples, grapes, celery, and tomatoes can simply be washed and served. Other produce, such as oranges, bananas, and carrots, are peeled before being eaten.

Some peeled fruits and vegetables darken in color if not eaten or cooked immediately. This is especially true of apples, bananas, peaches, and avocadoes. To prevent this, sprinkle the cut surfaces with lemon juice and wrap the produce in plastic or another airtight covering. You can also put them in a bowl of water with lemon juice added.

Salad greens should be washed, drained thoroughly, and torn into bite-size pieces before tossing. To prevent wilting, add dressing to greens just before the salad is served.

Before using fresh fruits and vegetables, wash them carefully under cold running water to remove dirt, bacteria, and pesticides.

Did You Know? You can ripen an avocado by burying it in a bowl of flour; you can ripen green bananas by wrapping them in a wet dishtowel. Most fruits ripen best in a paper bag.

More About Storage Consider these additional storage hints:

- Lemons stored in a tightly sealed jar of water in the refrigerator will be juicier.
- Lining the bottom of the vegetable compartment of the refrigerator with paper towels absorbs excess moisture and keeps produce fresh longer.

Teaching "Storing Fruits and Vegetables"
(Page 455)

This section teaches how fruits and vegetables can be stored for maximum freshness.

Checking Comprehension

✓ How does spoilage occur? *Spoilage happens when food is too old to eat or contains bacteria or mold.*

✓ How does the storage of berries and lettuce differ? *Berries are best kept as dry as possible until they are served; lettuce needs to be kept in an airtight container to retain its moisture.*

✓ Name two fresh fruits and two vegetables that can be stored for a long time. *Apples, oranges, potatoes, and onions.*

✓ Compare the storage requirements of frozen, dried, and canned products. *Frozen foods may be kept for several months at temperatures below 0°F (-18°C); dried and freeze-dried foods should be kept tightly wrapped on a shelf; canned goods may be kept for a year or more in a cool, dry place.*

Activities

Skill Builder: Writing
Have students bring in one recipe for a fruit and one recipe for a vegetable. Ask them to write a paragraph for each one, explaining what form they would buy the fruit or vegetable in and how long and where they would store it before preparing it. Does the recipe appeal to them? Why or why not?

Reteaching
Have students make a chart on which they list guidelines for storing the following kinds of foods: fresh apples, fresh spinach, frozen broccoli, canned beets, dried apricots, and a carton of orange juice.

Enrichment
Ask students to take the temperature of the various places where fruits and vegetables are stored in their kitchens at home to see if they conform to the guidelines suggested in this section.

Teaching "Preparing Fruits and Vegetables"

(Pages 455-456)

This section explains how to prepare fresh produce and gives hints on cooking with moist heat, baking, stir-frying, and microwave cooking.

Checking Comprehension

✓ What can you do to keep peeled fruits and vegetables from darkening? *Sprinkle cut surfaces with lemon juice and wrap the produce in plastic or another airtight covering. Or put the produce in a bowl of water with some lemon juice added.*

✓ Why is it important to cook produce at a low, even temperature with little water and with a tight-fitting lid? *To prevent the steam from escaping with valuable nutrients.*

✓ How should food be prepared for cooking in a microwave oven? *Cut pieces into equal sizes and pierce any unpeeled produce with skin to prevent bursting. Usually, the food should be stirred or rearranged once or twice for even cooking.*

Activities

Skill Builder: Science
Peel two apples, two potatoes, and two peaches at the beginning of class. Use lemon juice on one of each, and leave the others out. Have students compare the color of the fruits and vegetables at the end of class to see how they differ.

Reteaching
Ask students to write instructions for cooking a vegetable (such as asparagus or peas) in its fresh, frozen, and canned forms. Students should aim for minimum loss of nutrients.

Enrichment
Ask students to find unusual recipes using fruits and vegetables—a vegetable dessert or a fruit side dish, for example. Have them also look for recipes that incorporate fruits or vegetables in interesting ways—fruit glazes on meats or edible vegetable garnishes, for example.

Cooking with Moist Heat

Vitamin A, vitamin C, and the B vitamins are easily destroyed or dissolved by water, heat, and air, so follow the cooking suggestions given in Chapter 47. Use a heavy-bottomed pan so fruits and vegetables can cook at a low, even temperature. Add a minimum amount of water and cover the pan with a lid. This prevents the steam from escaping with valuable nutrients.

The general rule is, the less water used, the better the result will be. Steaming is ideal for most vegetables. Any water leftover from cooking vegetables contains valuable nutrients and is good to save for use in soups and stews.

Canned vegetables are already cooked and only need to be heated. The water from canned vegetables can also be saved if you wish.

Baking

Baking is an excellent way to cook many fruits and vegetables; it preserves the nutrients well. You can bake pears, apples, potatoes, and all forms of squash. Sometimes a very small amount of liquid is added to the pan to prevent the skins from becoming too dry. Potatoes, however, are baked entirely dry after their skin has been pierced to release steam.

Stir-Frying

Stir-frying—cooking quickly in very little fat—is another good method of preparing vegetables. Stir-fried vegetables should remain a little crisp and not be overcooked. You can test for doneness by poking them with the point of a knife or a sharp fork.

Microwave Cooking

Fruits and vegetables can be cooked to perfection in a microwave oven. Very little water, if any, is needed so nutrients are not lost. Because microwaves cook fruits and vegetables from within, there is no change in the color, flavor, or texture.

Cut pieces into equal size and pierce unpeeled apples, potatoes, and other foods with skins to prevent bursting. Usually the foods should be stirred or rearranged once or twice for even cooking. Fruits and vegetables should be taken out of the microwave while they are still slightly crisp and allowed to stand a few minutes. Be careful not to overcook them. (See Chapter 48 for the general rules of microwave cooking.)

Microwave cooking is an ideal way to cook vegetables. For fresh vegetables, you can add a very small amount of water—no more than two tablespoons. Don't add water to frozen vegetables. Cover with plastic wrap and pierce, or pierce a plastic pouch. Check the manual for cooking times.

Cross-Reference See Chapters 47 and 48 for additional information on cooking methods.

Did You Know? If raw vegetables aren't stored properly, they can lose vitamins. The nutrients lost in cooking vegetables in water can be recaptured by using the water to make gravy, sauce, or soup.

Focus on Health Even washing fruits and vegetables can destroy valuable vitamins and minerals. Therefore, it is better to rinse produce under running water, rather than soaking it. If produce is caked with dirt or has been exposed to pesticides or chemical fertilizers, however it may have to be scrubbed or even peeled.

CHAPTER 50 REVIEW

Reviewing the Facts

1. Name five forms in which you can buy fruits and vegetables.
2. What important fact related to nutrition should you consider when buying fresh produce?
3. Describe features to look for when you are buying fresh produce.
4. What does the term *seasonal* mean?
5. Name advantages of buying fresh fruits and vegetables, of buying frozen, and of buying canned.
6. How long can you store most fresh produce?
7. Why is steaming vegetables preferable to boiling them?
8. Why is microwave cooking a good method of cooking fruits and vegetables?

Thinking Critically

1. What steps would you suggest to encourage young people to eat a wider variety of fruits and vegetables?
2. Deep-fat frying is a common way of cooking some vegetables. Why do you think this might not be the ideal method?

Applying Your Skills

1. **Comparing and Evaluating Costs.** Bring to class the weekly food advertisements from your local newspaper. Compare the prices of the fresh, frozen, and canned forms of one fruit and one vegetable. Estimate an equivalent amount, remembering that with fresh produce you may discard some of the fruit or vegetable before you use it. Which form is least expensive? Is the fresh form currently in season in your area? Write a brief report on your findings.

2. **Using Reference Materials.** Select your favorite fruit or vegetable, and find a recipe that uses it as an appetizer, a side dish, and a main dish or dessert. Make a poster showing the versatility of the fruit or vegetable and listing the various recipes.

3. **Choosing a Cooking Method.** If you were cooking dinner for your family or friends, what vegetable would you serve? Which method would you use to cook it? Why? Write a brief summary of your answers.

Answers to "Reviewing the Facts"

1. Fresh, frozen, canned, dried, and juice.
2. Some of the vitamins deteriorate after harvest, so select fruits and vegetables that look fresh and crisp, and have not wilted.
3. Healthy color; no bruises, spots or sticky areas; firm but not hard.
4. Produce is more plentiful at certain times of the year when it is usually less expensive.
5. Fresh: crisp tastes and textures; most nutritious. Frozen: better color and flavor then canned; convenient to use; can be stored for a long time. Canned: available in many forms; convenient to use; can be stored for the longest time.
6. Most should be used within a few days. Apples and citrus fruits can keep for several weeks; potatoes and onions can be kept for several months.
7. Fewer nutrients are lost.
8. Fruits and vegetables retain their color, flavor, and texture, and most of their nutrients.

Answers to "Thinking Critically"

1. Answers will vary. There are now many new and different types of fruits and vegetables. Many fruits and vegetables can be found in several forms or cooked with foods that teens like. Companies could advertise fruits and vegetables in ways similar to those for snack foods.
2. Deep-fat frying leads to excess fat in a person's diet and is not recommended by the Dietary Guidelines. Sometimes vegetables, such as onion rings, are coated in batter—which also retains excess fats after frying. Sautéing vegetables has similar disadvantages.

COMPLETING THE CHAPTER

Summary

- Fruits and vegetables are good sources of carbohydrates, vitamins, and minerals.
- Produce is available fresh or in processed form—that is, frozen, canned, dried, or as a juice. Each form has its advantages.
- Fresh produce should be refrigerated; frozen food is kept in the freezer; and dried and canned food can be stored in cabinets.
- Some fresh produce can be served without cooking.
- Fruits and vegetables can be cooked with moist heat, baked, stir-fried, or cooked in a microwave oven.

For Review

Objective Review Questions Have students complete the "Reviewing the Facts" section on this page.

Study Guide Have students complete the Study Guide from Chapter 50 of their *Student Workbook.*

Favorite Things—Part 2 Ask students to refer to the lists of favorite fruits and vegetables that they wrote at the beginning of this chapter. Ask how many now want to change their lists. Ask volunteers to give reasons for wanting to change.

For Evaluation

Chart Have students chart the availability, forms, uses, storage, and cooking methods for a common fruit (the apple) and a common vegetable (the carrot).

List Have students list the advantages of steaming produce; eating fresh produce; and buying produce in season. Then have them list the disadvantages of peeling vegetables and buying frozen fruit.

Chapter Test Have students complete the test for Chapter 50 that appears in the *Teacher's Classroom Resources.*

CHAPTER OVERVIEW

Chapter 51 gives an overview of the milk products available—milk, cream, cheese, ice cream, yogurt, and so on. It discusses the various forms in which these milk products are sold—liquid, dry, frozen, and solid. Storage requirements are discussed, and guidelines for cooking milk and cheese are provided.

INTRODUCING THE CHAPTER

Motivators

Product Review Explain that this chapter focuses on foods that are made from milk. Ask students to name as many of these milk products as they can, and have a volunteer write their suggestions on the board. Point out that the list already demonstrates the wide variety of foods in this group and that it will probably be longer by the time students finish the chapter.

Using the Photograph Have students study the photograph on this page. Then say: "This young calf will one day produce milk. What other animals give milk? Have you ever had milk from an animal other than a cow?"

Alternatives to Milk Explain that some people cannot drink milk because their bodies react negatively to it. Ask for a show of hands of students who do not like drinking milk. Then point out that certain milk products do not produce the same effects as milk. People who do not drink milk should make sure that they include enough milk products in their diets to compensate.

Introducing the Objectives

Discuss the chapter objectives on this page. Remind students that the objectives focus on important chapter content.

Introducing Vocabulary

Point out that *pasteurization* is named for Louis Pasteur, a French chemist who discovered the process by which disease-producing microorganisms could be destroyed in the process of partially sterilizing milk.

CHAPTER

51

Milk, Yogurt, and Cheese

OBJECTIVES

This chapter will help you to:

- Identify and select foods in the milk, yogurt, and cheese group.
- Explain how to store milk, yogurt, and cheese.
- Describe the best methods of cooking milk and milk products.

WORDS TO REMEMBER

coagulate
dehydrated
homogenized
pasteurized

Chapter Resources

Teacher's Classroom Resources
- Lesson Plan
- Life Skills Activity, *Check Out Some Cheeses*
- Reproducible Master, *Dairy Food Safety*
- Extension Activity, *Getting More Calcium*
- Chapter Test

Student Workbook
- Study Guide
- Worksheet, *Are You a Cheese Wiz?*

The milk group is unique among the food groups in that it includes products made from just one substance: milk. In the United States, *milk* usually means cow's milk. In some other countries, people drink milk that comes from goats.

Milk is an excellent source of many nutrients. It provides complete proteins, carbohydrates, and fats—the last in varying amounts depending on how the milk is processed. Milk is also an excellent source of calcium and phosphorus. Together, these two minerals make bones and teeth strong.

Milk is a good source of riboflavin, a B vitamin, as well as vitamin A. (Since vitamin A is fat soluble, milk from which the fat has been removed must be fortified with vitamin A.) Most milk is also fortified with vitamin D, a nutrient that must be present for calcium to be used by the body. Because vitamin D occurs naturally in very few foods, adding it to milk makes it possible for people to get enough.

Selecting Milk Products

Milk products come in many varieties. You can buy whole milk or milk with less fat. You can choose from yogurt and hundreds of cheeses. In addition, there are many delightful flavors of ice cream available.

Milk

You can buy milk in liquid form or **dehydrated**, meaning that some or all of the liquid has been removed. Milk sold as a liquid is usually **pasteurized** (PASS-chuh-ryzed), or heated and cooled to kill harmful germs. It is also **homogenized** (huh-MAHJ-uh-nyzed), to blend the creamy fats into the liquid. Some or all of the fats may be removed, making lowfat milk or skim milk.

- **Whole milk.** Whole milk has all the original nutrients of milk, and at least 3.5 percent fat.
- **Lowfat milk.** Lowfat milk has less fat than whole milk, but more than skim

Milk is available in several different forms. What are the characteristics of each? Which ones have you used?

Cross-Reference See Chapter 37 for nutritional information about milk and milk products.

More About Butter Butter is made from cream which is churned to separate out the butterfat. Salt and coloring may be added. Unsalted (sweet) butter has no added salt.

More About Dairy Substitutes Margarine is made from vegetable oil. Though the fat is unsaturated, it has the same amount of fat and calories as butter. Nondairy creamers, made with vegetable oil and milk or soybean protein, can replace cream in coffee. Whipped toppings, made of sweeteners and vegetable oil, substitute for whipped cream.

TEACHING THE CHAPTER

For convenience, the teaching suggestions for this chapter are arranged according to the following lesson topics:

- "Selecting Milk Products," pages 459-461
- "Storing Milk Products," page 463
- "Cooking Milk Products" pages 463-464

Teaching "Selecting Milk Products"

(Pages 459-461)

This section teaches about the variety of milk products—whole, lowfat, skim, evaporated, condensed, and nonfat dry milks, as well as cream and half-and-half.

Checking Comprehension

✓ List the liquid forms of milk and the dehydrated forms. *Whole milk, lowfat milk, skim milk, cream, and half-and-half are the liquid forms of milk. Dehydrated forms include evaporated, condensed, and nonfat dry milk.*

✓ What is done to milk to homogenize it? *The creamy fats of the milk are blended into the liquid.*

✓ Arrange whole milk, lowfat milks, and creams according to their fat content. *Skim milk has the least fat; next are 1 percent, 2 percent, whole milk, half-and-half; and cream has the most fat content.*

✓ What is cream? *Cream is the fat in milk. It rises to the top of the container if milk is not homogenized.*

✓ How are evaporated milk and condensed milk sold? *They are sold in cans.*

✓ What is sweetened condensed milk used for? *It can be used in baked desserts and candy.*

✓ What is the nutrient value of nonfat dry milk? *Nonfat dry milk contains all the nutrients found in skim milk with about half the calories of whole milk.*

✔ Name two uses of nonfat dry milk. *It can be used for cooking and, with water added, for drinking.*

✔ What determines the type of cheese? *The type of cheese depends on what milk it is made from and how it is made.*

✔ Name one fresh cheese and one aged cheese. *Cottage cheese is a fresh cheese. Swiss or Parmesan cheeses are both aged.*

✔ How much cottage cheese or cheddar cheese must you eat to equal the calcium you would get in a cup of milk? *One-and-a-half cups of cottage cheese or two 1-inch cubes of cheddar cheese provide the same amount of calcium as a cup of milk.*

✔ What is the difference between cream cheese and Camembert? *Cream cheese is mild in flavor, and Camembert is tangy.*

✔ What are processed cheeses? *These are mixtures of different cheeses, sometimes combined with flavorings.*

✔ Name three cultured milk products. *Yogurt, sour cream, and buttermilk.*

✔ What is a culture? *A culture is a colony of harmless bacteria used to turn milk and cream into cultured products.*

✔ What is the difference between the cultured milk products discussed in this section? *They are made from different milk products—yogurt from whole or skim milk, sour cream from cream, and buttermilk from skim milk.*

milk. Lowfat milk comes in different varieties—2 percent and 1 percent fat content are common. Although lowfat milk is a little higher in calories than skim milk, many people prefer its flavor and texture.

- **Skim milk.** Skim milk is whole milk from which almost all the fat has been removed. It has most of the nutrients supplied by whole milk, except for fat, and it is fortified with Vitamin A.
- **Cream.** Cream is the fat in milk. It rises to the top of the container if milk is not homogenized. An ounce of cream contains 110 calories. An ounce of whole milk, in contrast, has only about 20 calories.
- **Half-and-half.** Half-and-half is a mixture of cream and milk. It offers some of the rich taste and texture of cream with less fat and fewer calories.
- **Evaporated milk.** Canned evaporated milk is whole milk that has been heated to remove more than half the water content. If you add the right amount of water, you have a product like fresh whole milk.
- **Sweetened condensed milk.** Canned sweetened condensed milk has half the water removed and sugar added. It is a rich concentrated milk that can be used in baked desserts and candy.
- **Nonfat dry milk.** This is milk from which all the moisture and most of the fat has been removed before packaging. Nonfat dry milk is an inexpensive powder that contains all the nutrients found in skim milk with about half the calories of whole milk. It can be used for cooking and, with water added, for drinking.

Cheese can be used for appetizers, dips, salads, sandwiches, sauces, in cooked foods, and with fruit for dessert.

Focus on Consumer Skills Gourmet shops and even supermarkets offer cheeses from around the world—Brie and Roquefort from France, Muenster from Germany, fontina and mozzarella from Italy, Edam from Holland, and, of course, Swiss from Switzerland.

Did You Know? Nonfat dry milk has been added to some brands of lowfat milk to increase its protein content. They are labeled as "high protein" or " protein fortified."

Cheese

Cheese is made from the milk of cows or goats. The type of cheese depends on what milk it is made from and how it is made. There are more than 400 types of cheeses, with over 2,000 different names. Some cheeses are fresh, such as cottage cheese, and must be used within a short time. Other cheeses, such as Swiss and Parmesan, are aged or ripened for as long as two years. Each type of cheese requires a specific length of time to develop.

Cheese is a milk product and is a good source of complete proteins, carbohydrates, and calcium. For example, the calcium content of 1 cup (250 mL) of milk can be provided by 1 1/2 cups (375 mL) of cottage cheese or by two 1-inch (2.5 cm) cubes of cheddar cheese. However, cheeses are higher in calories than milk is, although lowfat varieties are now available. Almost all cheeses can be put into one of four groups:

- **Soft.** These range in flavor from mild types such as cottage cheese, cream cheese, and ricotta to the tangy French Brie and Camembert.
- **Semisoft.** Mild cheeses such as Muenster, Gouda, and Mozzarella are semisoft. So are many strong-flavored blue cheeses.
- **Hard.** Hard cheeses range from mild to sharp flavors, such as Cheddar, Swiss, and Parmesan.
- **Processed.** These are mixtures of different cheeses, sometimes combined with flavorings such as pepper, olives, or pineapple.

Other Milk Products

Some milk products are formed by adding new ingredients to milk, while others are developed through a freezing process.

- **Cultured milk products.** The taste and texture of milk and cream can be changed by the addition of certain harmless bacteria. These bacteria, grown in colonies called cultures, turn milk and cream into products that have a tangy taste and a thick texture. That is why yogurt, sour cream, and buttermilk are called cultured milk products. Yogurt can be made from either whole or skim milk, sour cream is made from cream, and buttermilk is made from skim milk.
- **Frozen milk products.** Ice cream, ice milk, and frozen yogurt are all popular desserts made from milk. Ice'milk and frozen yogurt contain less fat and fewer calories than ice cream. However, all three are sweetened with sugar and contain more calories than liquid milk or regular yogurt.

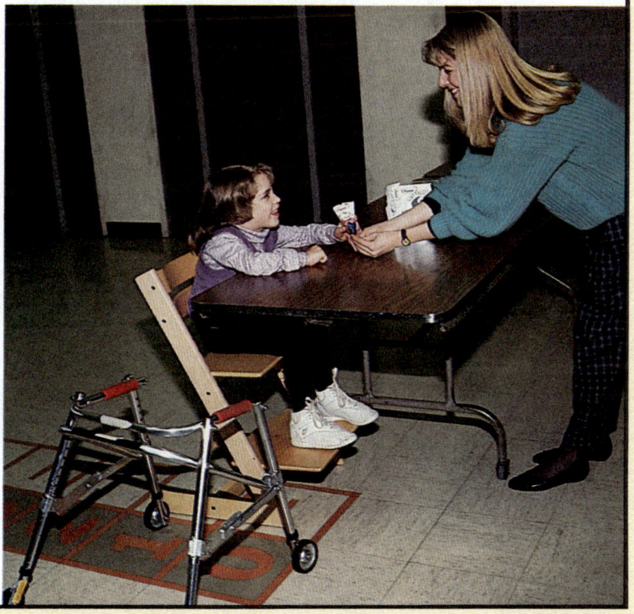

Milk and milk products are excellent sources of calcium, which is needed for strong bones and healthy teeth.

More About Cheese Fresh cheese is produced when heat or lactic acid is added to milk to separate it into chunks of curd and liquid whey. Cream or milk is added to the curd to make cottage cheese, riccota, and other fresh cheeses. Aged cheeses are made by adding bacteria culture to the curd and allowing the cheese to ferment. The consistency of the cheese depends on the amount of whey left in it, and the flavor depends on the aging conditions and the type of milk used.

Activities

Skill Builder: Critical Thinking
Ask students to give examples of nondairy products that are thought of as being in the milk category. (Coffee lighteners and nondairy dessert toppings are some of these, as are margarine and products made from soybeans.) When possible, ask them to list the ingredients of the nondairy products.

Reteaching
Ask students to explain the difference between whole milk, lowfat milk, cream, and cheese.

Enrichment
Milk intolerance, or lactose intolerance, is one of the most common food allergies. Have students read about milk intolerance—why it occurs, how it can be treated, what nutritional decisions must be made by people who suffer from this food allergy.

Teaching the Feature
"The Truth About Yogurt"

Answers to Feature Questions

1. Possible answers include boredom with plain milk; different texture of yogurt; tangy taste; fruit or other flavorings that make it more appetizing.

2. Possible answers include emphasis on weight control; emphasis on eating healthfully; convenience (can carry it easily, eat it quickly); recent reports about the importance of calcium intake.

Activities

Yogurt in Recipes The feature suggests a number of ways in which yogurt can be substituted for other ingredients. Have students discuss the advantages of using such substitutions and suggest other recipes or dishes in which yogurt can be substituted to create a more healthful alternative.

Origins of Yogurt *Yogurt* is a Turkish word. Have students research the origins of yogurt and how it came to be such a popular food in the United States.

Community Contact Have students meet with the cafeteria staff to suggest that yogurt be made available to students in the lunchroom to provide an alternative to milk and ice cream. If yogurt is already available, ask students to evaluate the amount of sugar (and calories) in the yogurt. Recommendations could be made to the cafeteria staff about switching to a less fattening brand or type of yogurt, if appropriate.

HEALTH WATCH

The Truth About Yogurt

Over the years, many claims have been made about yogurt—if you believe one company's commercials, yogurt is the key to long life. Even though this claim may be exaggerated, no one questions that yogurt is a nutritious and highly beneficial food.

Nutritionally, yogurt almost exactly matches the milk from which it is made; and milk is one of the most nutrient-rich of all foods. Like milk, yogurt has calcium, phosphorus, B vitamins, and high-quality protein.

The cultures in yogurt release lactase, a chemical that allows milk to be digested. People who cannot digest milk can usually eat yogurt.

For those who like to eat yogurt straight from the cup, there are hundreds of varieties—whole milk, lowfat, and nonfat yogurt; yogurt flavored with fruits or other flavorings; liquefied, custardized, and frozen yogurt.

Many people consider yogurt a low-calorie food. Plain yogurt contains only a fraction of the fat and cholesterol of ice cream. However, many flavored yogurts have sweetened fruit sauces added. Though low in fat, these yogurts are relatively high in calories. A healthier alternative is to add fresh fruit to plain yogurt.

Plain yogurt can also be used in place of sour cream on baked potatoes, and in salad dressings, dips, and dessert toppings. It can also be substituted for some of the mayonnaise in potato salad. Yogurt is a nutritious snack food and a healthful addition to any meal.

Think It Through

1. **Why might a person choose to eat eight ounces of yogurt rather than drink an eight ounce glass of milk?**
2. **Why do you think yogurt has become so popular in the last two decades?**

Focus on Life Management Yogurt can be a healthful part of any meal of the day. You can have it at breakfast instead of cereal, as a light lunch, or as dessert after a nutritious dinner. It is also a healthful snack any time of the day.

Emphasize The presence of the bacteria *Lactobacillus acidophilus* in yogurt causes it to be helpful in aiding digestion. It breaks down milk sugar into lactic acid. The acid environment helps in the absorption of minerals and prevents the growth of harmful bacteria.

Storing Milk Products

Once you get milk products home, keeping them fresh is important. Most dairy products are perishable. Storing them properly helps you use them safely, enjoy their flavor, and avoid wasting money.

Milk

All fresh milk should be kept in the coldest part of the refrigerator to retain nutrients and freshness for as long as possible. Putting the milk container away as soon as you have used what you need is important, since warmth and light both harm fresh milk. Warmth allows the growth of harmful bacteria, while light destroys the riboflavin, a B vitamin in milk. Cream and half-and-half should also be refrigerated.

Evaporated and sweetened condensed milk are canned and can be stored for long periods of time on the shelf. Once you have opened the cans, however, refrigerate any unused portions and use them within a day or two.

Nonfat dry milk keeps well on the shelf as long as it is kept away from moisture. When you add water to dry milk and restore it to a liquid, refrigerate it immediately after use, just as you would fresh milk.

Cheese and Other Milk Products

All cheese should be kept in the refrigerator. Soft cheeses, like cottage cheese, keep for a few days if tightly covered. Hard cheeses, like Cheddar and Swiss, remain fresh for weeks or even months if they are tightly wrapped.

Cultured milk products also need refrigeration. They keep longer unopened than fresh milk, but once opened, they spoil quickly. Use them by the dates stamped on their packages.

The freezer, of course, is the place for ice cream, ice milk, and frozen yogurt. If the freezer temperature is above 0°F (-18°C), the product should be used within a few days.

Cooking Milk Products

Proteins **coagulate** when they are heated. This means that they change from a fluid state to a thickened mass. In order to prevent proteins from becoming tough and stringy at high temperatures, low heat is the rule for cooking milk and milk products. Often, the difference between success and failure is a matter of a few degrees; all the stirring in the world won't save a cream sauce that's been cooked at too high a temperature.

Low-temperature cooking and frequent stirring keep the proteins in milk from coagulating.

Did You Know? Milk and most cheeses can be frozen for up to three months, whereas frozen milk products such as ice cream and ice milk are best if used before they've been in the freezer for a month.

Cross-Reference See Chapters 47 and 48 for information about cooking techniques.

Did You Know? The nutrient value of milk is slightly affected when heated, and milk becomes an incomplete protein after boiling. Pasteurization occurs at a very low temperature and does not cause this loss.

Teaching "Storing Milk Products"
(Page 463)

This section teaches how milk products should be stored to avoid spoilage.

Checking Comprehension

✓ Why is it important to store milk products carefully? *Most dairy products are perishable and spoil very easily.*

✓ How are warmth and light harmful to milk? *Warmth allows the growth of harmful bacteria. Light destroys the milk's riboflavin.*

✓ Where should cheeses and cultured milk products be stored? *They should all be kept in the refrigerator.*

Activities

Skill Builder: Science
Have students list some physical signs of spoilage of milk products that they may have observed. (The sour smell of milk and mold growing on cheese, for example.)

Skill Builder: Critical Thinking
Explain to students that there is a type of liquid milk that has a much longer shelf life. That milk—called UHT for Ultra High Temperature—can be stored on a kitchen shelf for months. Ask students to think about situations in which that milk would be useful. (Examples might include camping, hiking, shelters, blizzards, electrical blackouts, other natural disasters, picnics, boating, and other times when refrigeration is not available.)

Reteaching
Have students write a brief essay explaining how to store the following: milk, nonfat dry milk, cottage cheese, and ice milk.

Enrichment
Ask students to walk through the dairy section of their local supermarket and note the variety of products. They should pay attention to the way these products are stored and marketed.

Teaching "Cooking Milk Products"

(Pages 463-464)

This section teaches about some of the problems involved in cooking with milk and cheese and offers hints for ways to avoid those problems.

Checking Comprehension

✔ What happens when proteins coagulate? *They change from a fluid state to a thickened mass.*

✔ Why should you cook milk products in heavy pans? *Because milk can burn easily, and heavy pans allow slow, even cooking.*

✔ Why is it a good idea to cover the pan when cooking milk? *It discourages a skin from forming and helps retain milk nutrients.*

✔ What are three ways to prevent cheese from toughening as it cooks? *Chop, grate, or slice the cheese before adding it to a recipe, cook over low heat, and stir constantly.*

Activities

Skill Builder: Writing
Have students write a list of foods on which cheese toppings would be tasty or are frequently used (for example, pizza, tacos, hamburgers, spaghetti). They might even specify the kinds of cheeses that make good toppings for various kinds of food.

Reteaching
Have students list five guidelines they should follow when cooking with milk or cheese, such as cooking milk in a heavy pan.

Enrichment
Have students compare milk and cheese dishes in cooked and uncooked versions to see how the dish is changed by cooking and which version they prefer. For example, students might try cold and hot chocolate milk or a cheese sandwich, cold and grilled.

Cooking Milk

Because milk can burn easily, cook milk products in heavy pans that allow slow, even heating. This keeps the milk from burning on the bottom of the pan and prevents it from boiling over.

Low temperatures also prevent proteins from forming a skin over the top of the milk. If a skin does develop, beat it back into the milk so the valuable proteins will not be lost. Covering the pan will also discourage a skin from forming. At the same time, this will help retain the milk nutrients, since light quickly destroys riboflavin.

To cook milk and milk mixtures in a microwave oven, follow the same general rules but watch the mixture very closely. Because milk boils over easily, the glass or bowl you use should be no more than two-thirds full. Puddings will scorch if they are in the microwave too long.

Cooking Cheese

Cheese can be served uncooked, melted in a sandwich, or added to a creamy sauce. It can also be sprinkled on top of casseroles or vegetables near the end of the cooking period. Baking or broiling quickly melts the cheese.

Cheese, like milk, toughens when overcooked. To prevent this, chop, grate, or slice the cheese before adding it to a recipe. Low heat and constant stirring also help.

The same principles apply if you cook cheese in a microwave. Cheese dishes and toppings need to be watched for signs of overcooking or toughening.

A double boiler can be used to heat milk. The heat from boiling water in the lower pan cooks the food in the upper pan without scorching or curdling it.

Cheese can be grated and sprinkled on top of casseroles to provide color, taste, and added nutrition.

Emphasize Not all cheeses are good for cooking. The more pungent cheeses (like Brie, fontina, and blue cheese) are better used as an appetizer with crackers or as a dessert with fruit. Milder cheeses combine better with other food flavors in recipes. You can substitute one cheese for another, but use cheeses of similar texture for best results.

Focus on Health The traditional cure for insomnia—drinking a glass of warm milk—is probably a myth. Milk does contain tryptophan, an amino acid that naturally aids people in falling asleep, but it does not seem to matter whether the milk is hot or cold for the tryptophan to do its work.

CHAPTER 51 REVIEW

Reviewing the Facts

1. Name four forms of liquid milk. What are the differences among them?
2. What are the four basic types of cheese?
3. What produces a cultured milk product? What is its effect on the taste of milk?
4. Name three popular frozen desserts made from milk. Which one contains the most butterfat?
5. How should you store fresh milk?
6. What is the rule of heating that applies to cooking milk and milk products? Give the reason for this rule.

Thinking Critically

1. What might be some of the advantages and disadvantages of adding cheese to vegetables and sauces?
2. Why might it be a good idea to keep a supply of evaporated and dried milk on hand?

Applying Your Skills

1. **Using Reference Materials.** Use an encyclopedia to research the way Swiss and Cheddar cheese are made. Write a paragraph describing the steps involved in each one. Be sure to tell how the holes develop in Swiss cheese.

2. **Comparing Costs.** Check newspaper advertisements or food stores for the prices of whole milk, nonfat dry milk, and evaporated milk. How much evaporated and how much dry milk is needed to prepare one gallon of milk? Compute the costs of a gallon of milk made from these two sources. Then compare the costs per gallon for both to the price of a gallon of whole milk. Which one of the three is the most expensive? Can you think of any reasons for the price differences?

3. **Performing an Experiment.** There are many types of milk, all with different qualities. Obtain small amounts of as many types as possible, and pour each one into a separate cup that has been labeled on the bottom. Rearrange the cups, then taste. Try to correctly identify the types of milk. Document your procedures and results.

Answers to "Reviewing the Facts"

1. Any four: whole milk has at least 3.5 percent fat; lowfat milk has less fat than whole milk—1 or 2 percent; skim milk has almost all the fat removed; cream is the fat in milk; half-and-half is a mixture of cream and milk.
2. Soft, semisoft, hard, and processed.
3. Harmless bacteria added to milk and cream; the taste is more tangy.
4. Ice cream, ice milk, and frozen yogurt. Ice cream contains the most butterfat.
5. Keep in the coldest part of the refrigerator.
6. Use low heat because milk and milk products contain proteins, which coagulate and become tough and stringy at high temperatures.

Answers to "Thinking Critically"

1. Possible advantages include: more flavor; added protein; increased quantity; added color. Possible disadvantages include: cheese may become tought if cooked too long or at too high a temperature; added fats; increased calories.
2. Students should point out that if they run out of fresh milk either evaporated or nonfat dry milk can be reconstituted easily and quickly. These forms of milk can also be used in many recipes.

COMPLETING THE CHAPTER

Summary

- Milk products are a good source of calcium, phosphorous, and vitamins A, B, and D.
- You can buy milk in liquid form or dehydrated—whole, lowfat, skim, cream, half-and-half, evaporated, condensed, or nonfat dry.
- Cheese comes in soft, semisoft, hard, and processed forms.
- Cultured milk products (yogurt, sour cream, and buttermilk) and frozen milk products (ice milk, ice cream, and frozen yogurt) are also good sources of calcium.
- Almost all milk products require refrigeration.
- Milk and cheese should be cooked over a low heat to avoid coagulation.

For Review

Objective Review Questions Have students complete the "Reviewing the Facts" section on this page.

Study Guide Have students complete the Study Guide from Chapter 51 of their *Student Workbook.*

Product Review—Part 2 Ask students to study the list of milk products on the board and to suggest any other products that should be added to it, in light of what they have read in the chapter.

Scrapbook Have students work on a class scrapbook illustrating the benefits and uses of dairy products. They can include packages from milk products with storage and serving suggestions and nutritional information; recipes; pictures of dishes using cooked cheese and milk; and advertisements of the benefits of cheese, milk, and other sources of calcium.

For Evaluation

List and Store Have students list each of the milk products discussed in the chapter and suggest how to store each properly.

Chapter Test Have students complete the test for Chapter 51 that appears in the *Teacher's Classroom Resources.*

CHAPTER OVERVIEW

Chapter 52 describes the variety of protein sources—meats, poultry, fish, eggs, nuts, and beans. Tips are given on how to select these foods in their various forms—fresh, frozen, canned, and dried. Proper storage techniques are described as well. The chapter recommends ways to cook the foods of this group with moist heat (stewing, boiling, poaching) dry heat (baking, roasting), and fat (sautéing, stir-frying, deep-fat frying), as well as microwave cooking.

INTRODUCING THE CHAPTER

Motivators

Where's the Beef? People have been eating less beef in recent years. Ask students to analyze their families' beef-eating habits. Are they eating less beef than before? What protein sources are they substituting for beef?

Using the Photograph Have students study the photograph on this page. Then ask: "What different foods do you see here? What do these foods have in common?"

Different Strokes The amount of protein sources consumed varies in different parts of the country. Have students talk about why more beef is eaten in Texas and more shellfish in Maine, Maryland, and Louisiana. Ask them which protein foods are especially popular in their part of the country.

Introducing the Objectives

Discuss the chapter objectives on this page. Remind students that the objectives focus on important chapter content.

Introducing Vocabulary

Point out that when talking about meats, *cut* is a verb and a noun. Butchers cut meat into salable portions called cuts. Among the cuts of meat is the cutlet— a 2-inch section of the tenderloin flattened into a thin piece of meat. Cutlets are made from pork, veal, beef, and lamb.

CHAPTER

52

Meats, Poultry, Fish, Eggs, Nuts, and Beans

OBJECTIVES

This chapter will help you to:

- Identify and select foods in the meats, poultry, fish, eggs, nuts, and beans group.
- Explain how to store foods in the meats-to-beans group.
- Describe the best method of cooking foods in the meats-to-beans group.

WORDS TO REMEMBER

cut
marbling
processed meat
variety meat

Chapter Resources

Teacher's Classroom Resources
- Lesson Plan
- Life Skills Activity, *Cooking for Company*
- Reproducible Master, *Do You Know Beans?*
- Extension Activity, *Choose the Proper Method*
- Chapter Test

Student Workbook
- Study Guide
- Worksheet, *Meats-to-Beans Basics*

The milk group depends on one substance—milk—for all its products. In contrast, the meats-to-beans group includes foods as varied as pork, Cornish game hens, flounder, eggs, and navy beans.

The meats-to-beans group is a major source of protein in your diet. Even after you have finished growing, your body will continue to need protein every day. Proteins are the nutrients that maintain healthy muscles, tissues, and cells in your body. Most foods in this group also contain iron and important vitamins, such as the B vitamins or vitamin A.

Selecting Meats, Poultry, Fish, Eggs, Nuts, and Beans

You have a great range of choice when you are shopping for foods from the meats-to-beans group. Do you want a steak, a chop, a roast, or ground meat? Do you prefer beef, lamb, or pork? Would you rather have poultry or fish? What about **variety meats**, which are organ meats such as liver, heart, and kidney? If none of these appeal to you, what about eggs for an omelet or beans for a casserole?

Meats

Beef, veal, lamb, and pork are the most common types of meats. Beef and veal come from cattle, lamb from sheep, and pork from hogs. Meat is a good source of complete protein, B vitamins, and iron. However, it also has saturated fat, so choose lean cuts and trim away excess fat.

Each type of meat is sold in many different **cuts**, sections or parts, such as loin chops, spare ribs, flank steaks, and ground chuck. The name of each cut indicates what part of the animal the meat is from (for example, the flank or the chuck), and how it has been prepared (as a steak or as ground meat). **Processed meats** have been seasoned, smoked, or prepared in some other way before they are brought to the store. They include hot dogs, bacon, sausages, ham, and luncheon meats.

Both the type and cut of meat determine its flavor and tenderness. Expensive cuts of meat are usually more tender, because they are taken from parts of the animal that have less connective tissue and get less exercise—the

When comparing the costs of different cuts of meat, compare the price per serving rather than the price per pound. Although boneless cuts usually cost more per pound than similar cuts with bones, they provide more meat per pound and may be the better buys.

TEACHING THE CHAPTER

For convenience, the teaching suggestions for this chapter are arranged according to the following lesson topics:

- "Selecting Meats, Poultry, Fish, Eggs, Nuts, and Beans," pages 467-468
- "Storing Meats, Poultry, Fish, Eggs, Nuts, and Beans," page 469
- "Cooking Meats, Poultry, Fish, Eggs, Nuts, and Beans," pages 470-471

Teaching "Selecting Meats, Poultry, Fish, Eggs, Nuts, and Beans" *(Pages 467-468)*

This section teaches about the variety of choices in the meats-to-beans group and gives suggestions on how to make wise decisions when selecting meat and poultry.

Checking Comprehension

✓ What is another name for variety meats? *Variety meats are also called organ meats, such as liver, heart, and kidney.*

✓ Why are expensive cuts of meat more tender than other cuts? *Because they are taken from parts of the animal that have less connective tissue and get less exercise.*

✓ How much fat should there be in a piece of meat? *High-quality pieces of meat will have marbling (fine streaks and flecks of fat within the lean area of the meat). But excess fat should be trimmed from meat before cooking.*

✓ How can you tell if meat is fresh? *Check the meat's color. Meat that looks brown and dry is probably not fresh.*

✓ Name three types of fish. *Saltwater, freshwater, and shellfish.*

✓ Describe the difference between whole, dressed, and filleted fish. *Only the scales and insides have been removed from whole fish; the head, tail, fins, scales, and insides have been removed from dressed fish; fillets have had all the above as well as the bones removed, and have been cut into steaks or boneless strips.*

More About Buying Beef All beef sold in the United States is inspected by the USDA, but not all beef is graded. Grading is a voluntary program, and about half of the beef is graded. The grade most widely sold at retail is USDA Choice.

Focus on Health Have students reread the information in Chapter 37 that outlines the serving information for these protein foods.

✓ What does the head chef do? *The head chef acts as manager of all kitchen activities. He or she also has experience with cooking and may plan the menu and even create new dishes.*

✓ How does a chef learn his or her profession? *Some attend a culinary institute, take vocational courses, or learn from other chefs.*

✓ How can editors and writers help the public learn about food and nutrition? *They write articles explaining new ways of using food or describing the latest discoveries in nutrition.*

✓ What is a dietitian? *A dietitian is a scientist who uses information about nutrition and food preparation to plan meals.*

✓ Compare the training of food editors with that of dietitians. *Food editors have college degrees, often with training in home economics, English, and journalism. Dietitians have college degrees in home economics or dietetics and must serve an internship in a hospital, college, or business.*

Activities

Skill Builder: Writing
Give students an opportunity to experience the work of a food writer. Suggest that they undertake research into an aspect of food or nutrition that interests them and then write a short article about it for the school newspaper.

Reteaching
Encourage students to talk about their own experiences in the area of food service, as a waiter, waitress, dishwasher, hostess, and so on. What skills have they used in those jobs? What has been most satisfying and least enjoyable about the work? Why would or wouldn't they consider a job like this on a permanent basis?

Enrichment
Have students look at the classified ads in the local newspaper to determine what kinds of opportunities are currently available in the food service area. Ask students which seem particularly appealing and why.

Many chefs receive their training by taking special courses or by working under a more experienced chef.

Jobs That Require an Advanced Degree

Editors and writers help the public learn about foods and nutrition. They write newspaper and magazine articles explaining new ways of using food or describing the latest discoveries in nutrition. They also write books, and they prepare reports for food manufacturers.

Most editors and writers have college degrees, often with training in home economics, English, and journalism.

Dietitians are scientists who plan meals using information about nutrition and food preparation. They know the importance of serving meals that are appealing as well as nutritionally balanced. They usually work for schools or hospitals. Dietitians have a college degree in home economics or dietetics and must serve an internship in a hospital, college, or business.

Getting a Job

Have you found that the information in this chapter describes a career you would like to pursue? If so, there are things you can do to prepare yourself to find a job.

Many of these careers require a high school diploma. While you are still in school, however, you can often get a part-time job as a waiter, waitress, or stock clerk. This will give you a feel for the work and hands-on experience.

Some of the more involved careers, like dietitian or food technologist, require a college education or specialized training. The more education you have, the more responsibility you'll be prepared to handle. This will make you very valuable to your future employers.

Cross-Reference See "Working in a Restaurant Kitchen" on page 433 for additional information about the skills needed by chefs and kitchen workers.

Cross-Reference For additional information about skills needed to succeed on the job, see "Success on the Job" on page 671.

INTERPERSONAL SKILLS

Special Order: Your Career in Food Service

"Two cheeseburgers, a small order of french fries, and a *job*, please!" said Josie when she went to the fast-food restaurant for dinner. She had seen a "Help Wanted" sign as she walked in. It was an opportunity to learn more about the food-service field.

You too could take advantage of such an opportunity. Employee schedules in fast-food restaurants are usually flexible because managers realize that students can only work part-time. Many of their teenage employees work after school and on weekends, and then full-time during the summer.

Usually you will be hired as an entry-level, general fast-food worker, to be assigned to different work stations. One day you may be responsible for cooking the hamburgers, while the next day you may be in charge of the french fries.

Doing a good job and conveying your interest to your supervisors can help you get **promoted**, or advanced, to a position of higher rank and greater responsibility, such as assistant manager. Assistant managers supervise general workers, keep track of inventory, count money in the cash registers, and deal with any customer complaints. When the restaurant gets busy, they often pitch in to help the general workers.

Later you could be appointed store manager, overseeing all of the restaurant employees. Store managers look after everything from maintaining the health and cleanliness standards of the store, to hiring and firing employees. A successful store manager might one day become an executive who manages a whole region or takes care of services like advertising and transportation.

As an employee in a fast-food restaurant, you will gain valuable experience, work with people your own age, and make money. So go ahead, put in your order for a food-service career!

Think It Through

1. **In what ways do you think being a fast-food worker could prepare you for a food-service career? Would you consider taking such a job? Why or why not?**
2. **What points would you bring up if you were trying to convince your superior that you deserve a promotion?**

More About Flexibility Jobs in fast food service offer the benefit of flexibility of location, hours, and job responsibilities. Fast food franchises can usually be found throughout a region or the whole country. If you move, you can get a job at the franchise in your new location. Since fast food restaurants are usually open long hours, you can work after-school or evening hours during the week, then switch to other hours on the weekend. There are many food preparation tasks to be done, and you can change tasks from day to day or week to week.

Teaching the Feature

"Special Order: Your Career in Food Service"

Answers to Feature Questions

1. Like any job, a fast-food job teaches you responsibility. You need to get to work on time and look presentable. You need to work efficiently and quickly to keep your job and possibly get promoted. You learn to interact with other people. More specifically, you will be working with food, learning how to cook certain items, learning about sanitation and safety practices, and learning how to keep the food fresh. These skills will be very important should you choose to pursue a career in food services. Students' answers as to whether they would take such a job will vary, but they should take into account the benefits of a job in a fast-food restaurant.

2. To get a promotion, you must convince your employer that you are working hard, that you are doing a good job, that you are on time and neat, that you are interested in getting experience and in learning everything you possibly can, and that you are responsible.

Activities

Career Ladder A career ladder is a sequence of jobs through which an employee can be promoted. Have students diagram the career ladder that this section suggests might operate at a fast-food restaurant.

Fast-Food Work Force Have selected students visit a fast-food restaurant and note the employees (at the counter and behind the scenes) and what tasks they are doing. Could they tell who the manager was? Was the restaurant adequately staffed?

Community Contact Invite food service workers from various facilities in your community to describe their jobs to the class, explain how they got their jobs, and answer students' questions. Help students prepare a list of questions ahead of time.

COMPLETING THE CHAPTER

Summary

- Skills like attention to detail, calmness, and creativity and features such as cooperativeness and a pleasant personality are essential in food careers.
- Canner and stock clerk are examples of entry-level jobs in food processing.
- Training is required to be a supermarket manager, a meat cutter, or a quality-control inspector.
- Agricultural researchers and food technologists both try to improve the quality of the food we eat.
- Food service workers include waiters, waitresses, dishwashers, hosts, hostesses, and chefs.
- Editors, writers, and dietitians all inform people about food and nutrition.

For Review

Objective Review Questions Have students complete the "Reviewing the Facts" section on this page.

Study Guide Have students complete the Study Guide from Chapter 54 of their *Student Workbook.*

Job Survey—Part 2 Review with students the list of food and nutrition jobs that you wrote on the board at the beginning of the lesson. Almost certainly, students will now be able to offer other ideas to expand the list. Add their suggestions to the list, then have students classify the jobs as entry-level, jobs that require training, and jobs that require an advanced degree.

For Evaluation

Description Have students list five characteristics needed to succeed in food and nutrition careers and tell why they are important.

Chart Have students compile a chart listing six jobs in the area of food and nutrition along with the jobs qualifications and principal responsibilities.

Chapter Test Have students complete the test for Chapter 54 that appears in the *Teacher's Classroom Resources.*

CHAPTER 54 REVIEW

Answers to "Reviewing the Facts"

1. Any four: ability to pay attention to detail; ability to be calm under pressure; creativity; ability to get along and work well with others; having a pleasant and friendly personality; interest in food and food preparation.
2. Food processing and food service.
3. The amount of each product in stock.
4. Try to improve existing methods of processing food.
5. Prepares the food; manages kitchen activities; plans the menu; creates new dishes.
6. Plans meals using information about nutrition and food preparation.
7. You should get a high school diploma, and work part-time to gain on-the-job experience. Research the field and plan to get as much training or education as is necessary for the career of your choice.

Reviewing the Facts

1. List four interests and skills useful for a career in foods and nutrition.
2. What are the two general fields foods and nutrition can be divided into?
3. What is a store's inventory?
4. What does a food technologist do?
5. List some functions of a chef.
6. Describe the work of a dietitian.
7. How can you prepare for a job in food processing or food service?

Thinking Critically

1. Would you prefer working at a food-processing plant that uses a lot of machinery, or one that requires people to work by hand? What do you see as the advantages of each method for the worker, the plant owner, and the public?
2. What are some traits a waiter or waitress should have? How could these be important to the server, the customer, and the restaurant?

Applying Your Skills

1. **Researching a Topic.** Choose any career in this chapter and read about it in a book selected from your school library. Write a short summary including a job description, education and training requirements, and salary information.

2. **Making a Plan.** Pretend you are opening a new restaurant. Describe how you would go about hiring workers and what skills they would need. Research how you would go about getting supplies. Write a paper describing your findings.

3. **Analyzing a Situation.** Choose any career in this chapter, and pretend you were hired for such a position. Describe a situation that you might encounter on your first day on the job. How should you handle the situation? What skills would you need?

Answers to "Thinking Critically"

1. Answers will vary. Using machinery can be faster and less tedious, but dangerous. Working by hand is slower, but can be more satisfying because it yields a specialized product. Owners can produce more machine-made products with fewer employees, but hand-made or hand-packaged products can get premium prices. Customers will pay less for machine-made products, but may prefer hand-made specialty items.
2. Waiters and waitresses should be pleasant, efficient, quick, and organized. The customer will be pleased, more pleasant and probably eat there again—making the owner happy.

TEEN TIPS OVERVIEW

This section focuses on making healthful food choices to suit teenager's lives and concerns.

50 Snacks under 75 Calories

This Teen Tip lists a wide variety of snack foods in amounts that supply under 75 calories. This list enables students to make intelligent choices based on their hunger, nutrition, and calorie needs.

Breakfast On-the-Run

This Teen Tip shows that time pressures need not interfere with good nutrition. Many suggestions go beyond traditional fare and appeal to people who "don't like breakfast."

Fast Foods Cutting the Calories

This Teen Tip looks at how teenagers can eat well in some of their favorite spots without having to limit themselves to salad bars.

These "Teen Tips" present ways in which students can apply the nutritional concepts of "Foods and Nutrition" to the realities of their daily lives.

Introducing "50 Snacks under 75 Calories"

(Pages 490-491)

Motivators

Discussion Question: Ask students: "When and why do you snack?" Discuss this question, considering whether students snack more during the day or at night, and because they're truly hungry, or bored, or need some quick energy. Point out that considerations like these determine the healthfulness and intelligence of snack choices.

The Week's Snacks Ask students to write down all the snacks they can recall having in the past week, along with the time of day they were eaten. Ask a few volunteers to share their lists. Tell students they'll look at the lists later, in light of information in this section, which focuses on snack foods.

Teaching "50 Snacks under 75 Calories"

Checking Comprehension

✔ Assume you want to keep your calorie intake down but are quite hungry. Name some snacks on the list that would be best for you, and why these would be good choices. *Answers should include foods that, because they are low in calories, can be eaten in fairly large quantities (such as most vegetables or fruits) and those that may supply more calories per ounce but satisfy hunger because they are filling (for example, any of the protein foods, a baked potato, lowfat milk).*

✔ Snacks are part of your total nutritional intake every day. Which of the snacks listed would be good choices if you had mostly fruits and vegetables at your regular meals? *Foods from the bread, cereal, rice, and pasta group; milk, yogurt, and cheese group; or meat, poultry, fish, dry beans, eggs, and nuts group.*

TEEN TIPS

50 Snacks under 75 Calories

Do you need a quick snack after school or to get you through the evening? All of these snacks are under 75 calories—but you have to watch some amounts carefully, or the calories will add up fast!

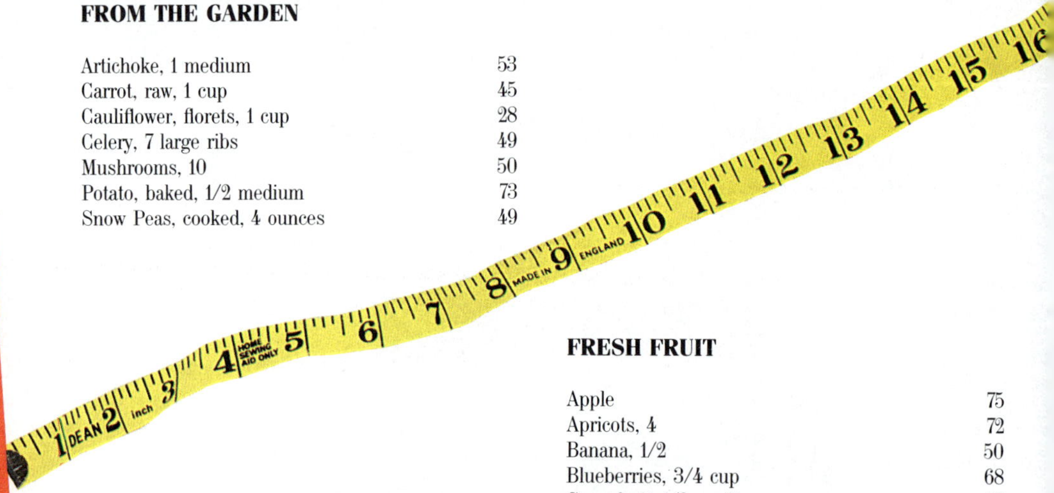

FROM THE GARDEN

Artichoke, 1 medium	53
Carrot, raw, 1 cup	45
Cauliflower, florets, 1 cup	28
Celery, 7 large ribs	49
Mushrooms, 10	50
Potato, baked, 1/2 medium	73
Snow Peas, cooked, 4 ounces	49

FRESH FRUIT

Apple	75
Apricots, 4	72
Banana, 1/2	50
Blueberries, 3/4 cup	68
Grapefruit, 1/2 medium	40
Grapes, 1 cup	70
Kiwi	60
Orange	60
Peach	40
Strawberries, 1 cup	55
Watermelon, diced, 1 cup	42

SAY CHEESE

Cottage Cheese, low-fat, 1/3 cup	67
Parmesan, grated, 2 tablespoons	55
Provolone Cheese, 1/2 ounce	50

Emphasize Point out to students that they will need to make a conscious effort to choose nutritious, low-calorie snacks, rather than merely eat whatever is available or attractive. But also emphasize the good taste of the snacks mentioned here.

More About Fresh Fruit Remind students that certain kinds of fruits are more readily available fresh in particular months, when they are usually less expensive. Some fruits are available frozen and many are available canned. Canned fruits may have added sugar, however, boosting their calorie count—choose those in natural juices.

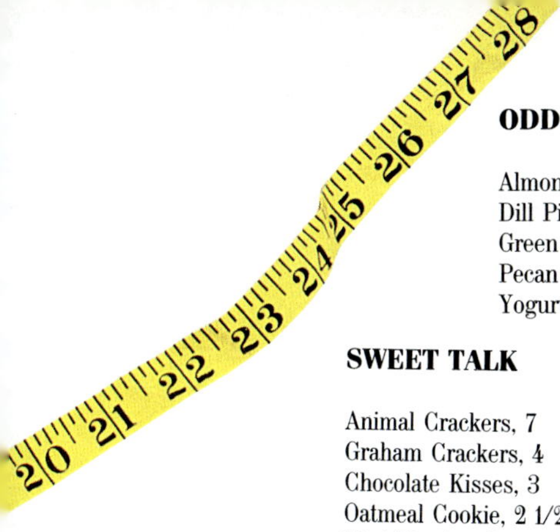

ODDS 'N' ENDS

Almonds, 8 whole	48
Dill Pickle, medium	8
Green Olives, 15 large	68
Pecan Halves, 9	72
Yogurt, low-fat, lemon, vanilla, coffee, 4 ounces	75

SWEET TALK

Animal Crackers, 7	74
Graham Crackers, 4	60
Chocolate Kisses, 3	72
Oatmeal Cookie, 2 1/2" diameter	60
Mini Marshmallows, 24	40

MUNCHIES

Date-Nut Bread, 1 ounce slice	40
Goldfish Crackers, 25	75
Popcorn, unbuttered, 3 cups	69
Potato Chips, 6	66
Pretzel Logs, 3" unsalted, 3	59
Raisins, 1 ounce	75
Rice Cakes, 2	70
Rye Toast Crackers, 4	64
Taco Chips, 1/2 ounce	64

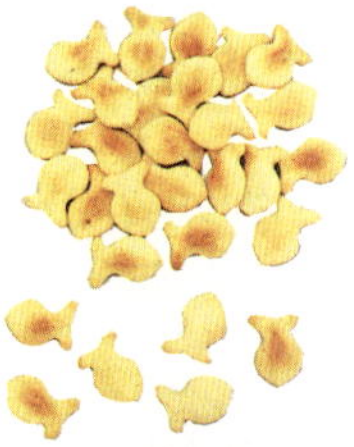

SIPPERS

Milk, low fat, 8 ounces	75
Apple Juice, 6 ounces	60
Beef Bouillon, 1 cup	30
Orange Juice, reconstituted, 6 ounces	68
Tomato Juice, 1 cup	45

POWER FROM PROTEIN

Chicken Roll, 2 ounces	75
Ham, extra-lean, 2 ounces	74
Hard-Cooked Egg, medium	72
Peanut Butter, 2 teaspoons	60
Shrimp, 10 medium	37

TEEN TIPS

✓ Which snacks would be appropriate if you had eaten mostly high-protein and high-fat foods at meals, like eggs, hamburgers, or chicken. *Any fruits and vegetable, which supply vitamins, minerals, and fiber with little fat.*

Activities

Skill Builder: Math
Divide the class into small groups and assign each group one or two of the snack categories. Have them research the cost of the snacks within their category or categories by finding out the cost of a standard-size package of the food and then figuring out the cost of the portion listed.

Reteaching
Work with the class as a whole to determine which nutrients are supplied by each snack within one or more of the categories. Then compare the cost per serving of the snack, as determined above, with the nutritional content and decide which foods among those analyzed supply the most nutrients for their costs. Finally, have students compare the snacks they recorded at the beginning of the lesson to those listed here. Ask volunteers to comment on whether they might choose snacks differently now that they have considered this information.

Enrichment
Have students develop a collection of more "under seventy-five calorie" snacks. They can look in magazines and cookbooks for advertisements and/or recipes, and include their favorite pre-packaged or restaurant snack foods. Have them prepare a card for each snack, listing the food, the calorie and nutrition content, and the recipe, if appropriate. Students can share their collections in class.

Emphasize The Dietary Guidelines recommend reducing the amount of fat, sugar, and salt in the diet. Many prepared snack foods, such as chips, candy, cookies, and non-diet soft drinks, are very high in fat, salt, and/or sugar. For healthy eating it's important to choose snack foods as carefully as foods eaten during a meal.

Emphasize The amounts of some snacks are very small in order to be less than 75 calories. If larger amounts of these snacks are eaten, the calorie count can increase dramatically.

Introducing "Breakfast On-the-Run"
(Pages 492-493)

Motivators

Surveying Breakfast Habits Four days before teaching this section direct students to keep a record of the breakfasts they and members of their family eat for the next three days. Ask them to record what is eaten and how long people spend at breakfast. To introduce this lesson, have students share their findings. Discuss why breakfast is important, and have students evaluate the healthfulness of some of the breakfast habits they noted.

Discussion Question: Ask students: "Why do so many people neglect breakfast?" Discuss this question, bringing out that people often say they don't have time for breakfast. Also bring out that some people don't feel like eating in the morning, and that many people don't like traditional breakfast foods. Tell students that this section will suggest breakfasts that can overcome these objections to this important meal.

Teaching "Breakfast On-the-Run"

Checking Comprehension

✔ Which ideas do you think most successfully address the problem of limited time for breakfast? *Answers may vary but should include suggestions that take no cooking and little preparation, such as a leftover chicken leg, open-faced sandwiches, trail mix made in advance, and a muffin and individually wrapped cheese.*

✔ Which of these suggestions do you think might appeal most to people who don't like traditional breakfast food? *Answers will vary but might include pizza, a chicken leg, sandwiches, and stuffed celery.*

TEEN TIPS

Breakfast On-the-Run

No other meal is skipped as often as breakfast. Often the reason is "I don't have time." Yet breakfast gives you the energy you need to start the day. Here are 15 breakfast ideas that take only a minute or two to prepare:

1 Toss your favorite fruit juice in a blender and add milk or yogurt, a banana, and some ice. If desired, add a dash of cinnamon or nutmeg.

2 Sprinkle grated cheddar or mozzarella cheese on an English muffin or pita bread. Pop in a microwave or toaster oven until the cheese melts.

3 Top a bowl of yogurt with granola, wheat germ, coconut, or raisins—or all four!

4 Spread peanut butter on rice cakes or whole-wheat bread and sprinkle with sunflower seeds.

5 Warm up a leftover slice of pizza. You'll get three or four of the basic food groups in one quick breakfast.

6 On a cold morning, nothing beats a bowl of hot cereal. Try the instant varieties that cook in a microwave oven. Top with a banana or fresh strawberries.

Did You Know? "Power breakfasts" have become popular among business people in urban areas, rivaling the traditional position of lunch or dinner as the meal over which business is discussed. Some hotel dining rooms offer elegant (and expensive) "executive" breakfasts featuring elaborate and rich foods such as omelettes, pancakes, and waffles made with a variety of ingredients; smoked fish; or steak and eggs. Have students consider the nutritional content of such meals and the possible affects of eating them early in the day (for example, fullness or sleepiness) and comment on what people at "power breakfasts" might choose as lighter alternatives.

7 Raid the refrigerator and eat a leftover chicken leg.

8 Make an open-faced sandwich with leftover meat or a sliced hard-cooked egg. Top with a slice of cheese and melt quickly in a microwave or toaster oven.

9 Add sliced peaches or berries to cold cereal.

10 Make a homemade trail mix ahead of time. Combine 3 cups Chex cereal, 1 cup sunflower seeds, 1 cup nuts, and 1 cup raisins. Spread on a baking sheet and bake 8-10 minutes at 375°F. Store mix in individual plastic bags and enjoy for breakfast with a frozen yogurt bar.

11 Stuff celery with peanut butter or cottage cheese mixed with raisins.

12 Grab a whole-grain muffin and a slice of individually wrapped cheese to eat on the way out the door.

13 Keep low-fat yogurt and yogurt drinks in convenient serving-size containers in the refrigerator. Eat the yogurt with a banana, orange, apple, pear, or grapes.

14 Try cream cheese and a tomato slice on a bagel.

15 Keep a supply of emergency rations such as peanut butter, whole-grain crackers, and raisins in your locker for when you need a morning pick-me-up. That way you can avoid the candy machines.

TEEN TIPS

Activities

Skill Builder: Math
Have each student figure out the calorie and nutritional content of three or four of the breakfast suggestions. This activity will require estimating amounts of specific ingredients for the breakfast suggestions. Students can then figure out calorie counts per serving and also determine the nutrients each breakfast supplies in the greatest quantities.

Reteaching
Using the nutritional analyses developed above, consider which of the suggested breakfasts would be best for people concerned about limiting their intake of fat, sodium, sugar, and/or calories; which would supply the most protein, fiber, vitamins, or minerals; and which are most balanced in terms of including all food groups.

Enrichment
Divide the class into small groups and assign each one a "quick" breakfast product sold today, such as cold cereals, instant hot cereals, liquid breakfasts, and microwave or toaster-oven products such as waffles and toaster "tarts." Have the groups research the number and variety of products available; the nutritional content of each, concentrating particularly on the amount of fat, sugar, and additives in each; and their price. Have the groups share their findings and comment on the relative nutritional value and cost of these breakfast products.

Focus on Caffeine Caffeine is a major part of breakfast for many people, but from a health point of view it has drawbacks. Students can research this ingredient and report on its potential ill affects. A related project would be to report on the many hidden sources of caffeine, including pain killers, chocolate, and cold medicines.

Introducing "Fast Foods: Cutting the Calories"

(Pages 494-495)

Motivators

Fast-Food Restaurant Menus A few days before teaching this section, discuss what fast-food restaurants the students regularly eat in. Assign a few students to each restaurant mentioned and ask them to bring to class a list of the foods available. To introduce this lesson, discuss what foods on the various menus students particularly like. Ask them to speculate on the nutritional and caloric content of these foods.

High-Calorie Ingredients Using copies of a standard calorie table, ask students to look up the caloric value of the following: mayonnaise, mustard, cheese (American, blue, cheddar, and Swiss), butter, Russian or Thousand Island dressing, sour cream, catsup. Record the calorie content of these foods. Ask students to figure out how many calories they would add to a basic hamburger if they add a tablespoon of mayonnaise or mayonnaise-based sauce, an ounce of cheese, and a serving of catsup. Point out that fast foods are high in calories partly because of the relishes and sauces people add to them. Tell students that this section will suggest ways they can reduce the caloric content in their favorite fast foods.

Teaching "Fast Foods: Cutting the Calories"

Checking Comprehension

✓ From earlier activities, and from what you've read, what general category of food seems most likely to add calories to fast foods? *Fats—and foods high in fat, mayonnaise, cheese, and oils.*

Fast Foods Cutting the Calories

Did you know that a fried chicken dinner—or a burger, fries, and a shake—can have more than half the calories you need for an entire day! Many fast foods are high in fat, salt, and sugar, but must you always limit yourself to the salad bar? Here's some help in making good choices when you're choosing from a fast-food menu:

TEEN TIPS

- Order what you want on your burger. Fast-food beef is usually lean, but the special sauces and mayonnaise boost up the calories and fat content. Instead, top your burger with lettuce and tomato.
- Skip the french fries and order a baked potato or mashed potatoes instead. Remember, however, that adding lots of butter, sour cream, or gravy quickly increases the calorie count.
- Watching the sodium? Hold the pickles and don't add extra salt to your food.
- Order skim milk instead of a milkshake.
- Save 85 calories on the fast-food chicken by not ordering the extra crispy. Cut even more calories and fat by removing the breading and skin from the chicken.

More About Salad Bars The very name *salad bar* suggests nutritious choices tailor-made for the weight conscious. Eating at a salad bar however, does not automatically guarantee a healthful, low-calorie meal. The dressings available tend to be mayonnaise-based or high in oil content and can turn a bowl of lettuce and vegetables into something close to a hamburger in terms of calories and fat. Moreover, salad bar ingredients themselves are not necessarily low in calories. Garnishes such as cheese, bacon bits, olives, and fried croutons should be used sparingly by dieters.

- Looking for all four basic food groups in one item? Order pizza or tacos.

- Try some chili—it has less calories than a burger.
- Skip the snack-type fruit pies and other sugary desserts. Eat a piece of fresh fruit instead.
- Use caution even at the salad bar. Prepared salads made with mayonnaise or dressing, such as potato salad or pasta salad, can be high in calories. Choose salad greens, plain vegetables, and a low-calorie dressing.

TEEN TIPS

Did You Know? Prepared items such as cole slaw, tuna or chicken salad, or three-bean salad can be loaded with mayonnaise or dressings high in fat and sugar content. More elaborate prepared foods, such as fried chicken, ribs, or meatballs, are found in some salad bars. Their calorie content doesn't drop just because they're served alongside containers of lettuce and broccoli! Have students visit salad bars in local restaurants and report on the nutritional value of the choices.

✓ From what you've read, what method of cooking seems to be best to avoid if you're counting calories? Why do you think this is so? *Deep fat frying—which is how french fries and fried chicken are cooked. Foods absorb a great deal of fat in deep fat frying. Breading, which often goes along with deep fat frying, adds more calories.*

Activities

Skill Builder: Critical Thinking
Have students study magazine, radio, and television advertisements for fast-food restaurants. Tell them to focus on what the ads seem to appeal to and what aspects of the restaurant's food they emphasize. Have the students evaluate the advertisements in terms of what they do to encourage or undermine healthful eating habits.

Reteaching
Discuss the information in this section in relation to the students' preferences in fast foods, discussed earlier. Have them state how they could cut calories in their favorite foods. Note that the principles can easily be applied to foods students may enjoy that were not covered in this section. Discuss how students might reduce the calories in Mexican foods (*cut down on the amount of cheese and go easy on fried foods*); Chinese foods (*avoid fried noodles or dumplings and other dishes with a high oil content; cut down on soy sauce to reduce sodium intake*); pizza (*don't have extra cheese, choose mushrooms or other vegetable toppings over high-fat sausages*); and any other popular foods.

Enrichment
Extend the above activity to the "real world." Ask students to write down brief plans for cutting calories in fast foods they commonly eat. Have them put these plans into effect over the next two weeks. Tell students to keep track of what they do. Discuss how the calorie-cutting measures affected the students' enjoyment of the foods.

UNIT PREVIEW

Unit 6 gives students an understanding of how clothing helps a person express individuality and make a good impression. The elements of design are presented as techniques to help students highlight their best features. Fibers, fabrics, and finishes are explained. Students learn to evaluate the quality, fit, and construction of garments. Basic sewing tools and skills for making a sewing project are presented. The unit also discusses clothing care and repair, and offers suggestions for redesigning and recycling clothes. Specific jobs related to the clothing and textile industry are discussed.

CONTENT DEVELOPMENT

Use these lessons to reinforce the following themes:

Content Strands	Chapters
Career Exploration	68
Citizenship/ Leadership	57,68
Communication	55,56
Consumer Skills	57,60,(TT 3)
Decision Making	55,57,59,60
Health and Safety	55,57,63,66
Managing Resources	56,59,60,61,67
Personal Development	55-57,59,(TT 1,2)
Technology	58,62,64,66

UNIT MOTIVATORS

Decision-Making Skills

Which Product? Display an assortment of detergents, bleaches, or fabric softeners on a table. Ask students to explain how to use each item. Tell them that they will learn about clothing care in this unit.

Critical Thinking Skills

Analyze Design Choices Ask students to briefly describe the ten clothing items they wear most often. Have them analyze the garments in terms of line, shape, space, texture, and color. Ask: "What conclusions can you draw about your choice in clothing?"

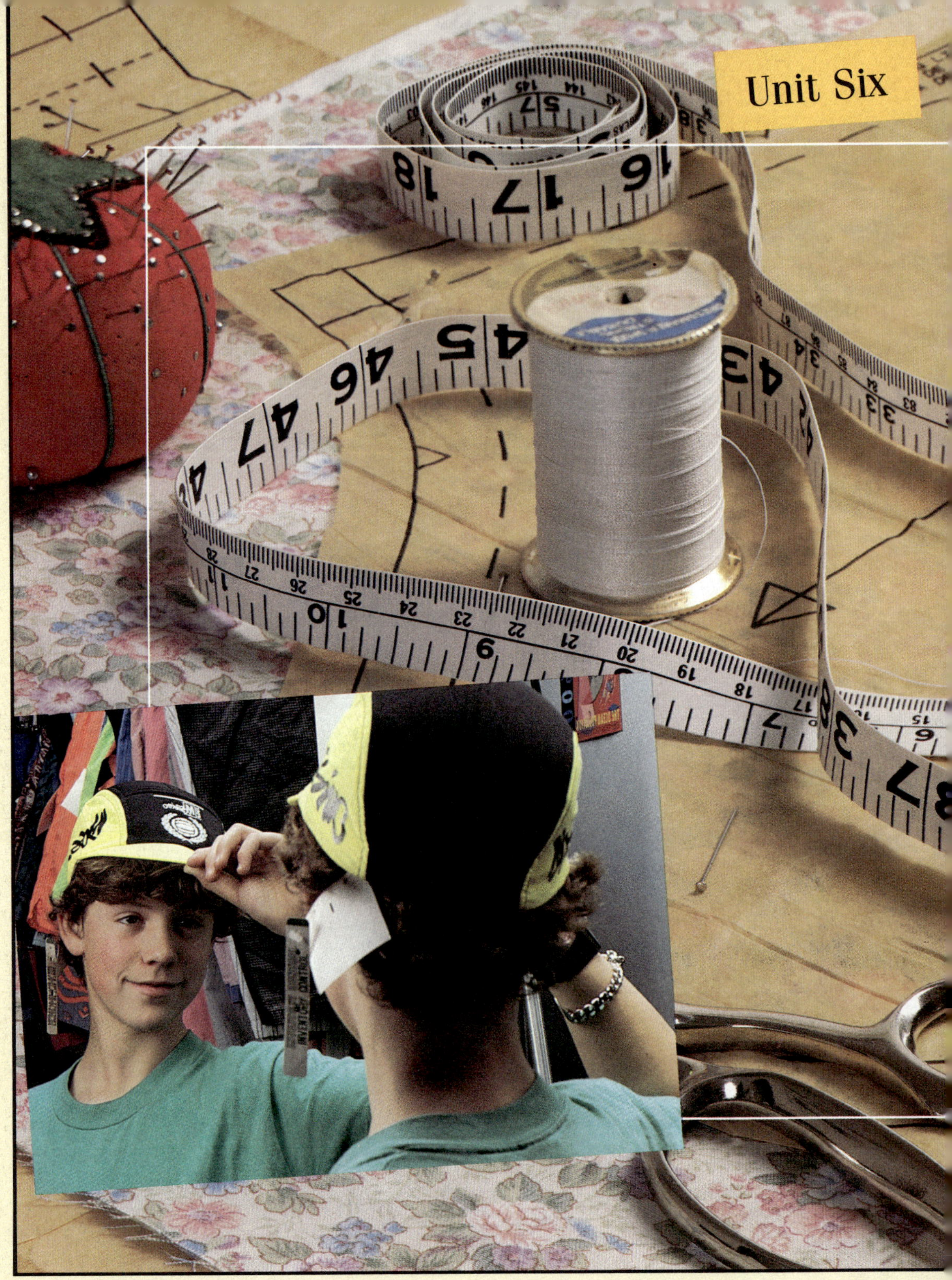

CROSS-CURRICULAR ACTIVITY

Psychology and Clothing Note that many schools and businesses enforce dress codes. Ask students to explain the psychological intent of dress codes (for example, to improve people's performance, to project a certain image). Have students explain why they approve or disapprove of dress codes.

SPECIAL NEEDS

Strategies for Tactile/Kinesthetic Learners Have students collect and label swatches of fabric: flannel, denim, cotton, linen, corduroy, and so on. They might use their swatches in a bulletin board display. Besides learning to identify fabrics, students should learn each fabric's characteristics and uses.

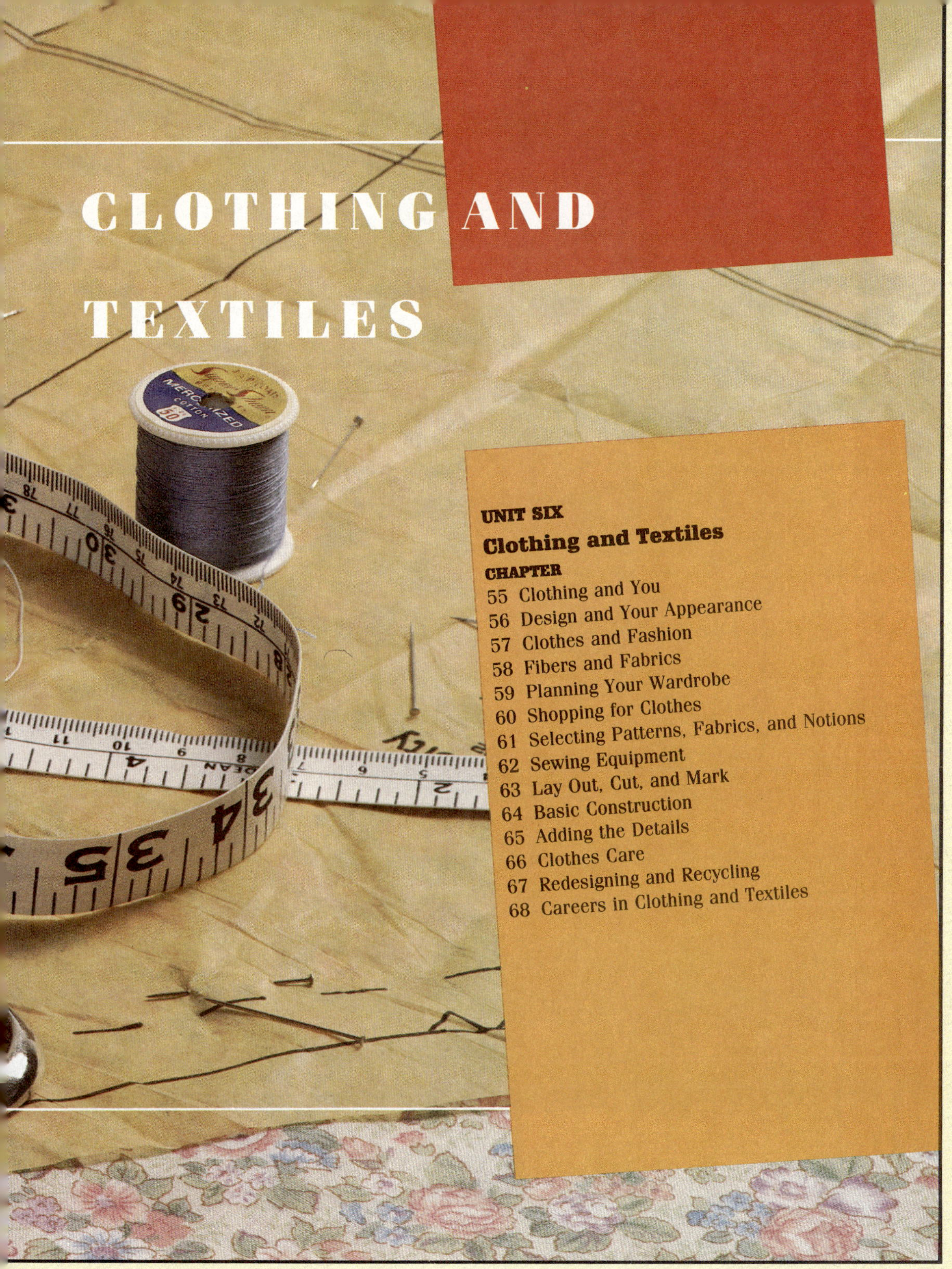

CLOTHING AND TEXTILES

UNIT SIX

Clothing and Textiles

COOPERATIVE LEARNING

Sewing Repair Shop Divide students into groups of five. Tell them that every adult should know how to make basic repairs to his or her clothing. Assign one of the following repair skills to each group member: sewing on a button, repairing a ripped seam, darning a sock, mending a hole, fixing a ripped hem. Each group member will be responsible for learning the skill and teaching it to other group members. Students can practice on actual clothing or on swatches of material. The entire group will be evaluated on how well each member can perform all five repair tasks. You might suggest that students assemble sewing repair kits containing needle and thread, a small scissors, and a thimble.

FHA ACTIVITIES

The following activities can be used with your FHA group or as public relation strategies:

Fashion From the Past Organize a fashion show demonstrating various fashion/fads of the 20's, 30's, 40's, 50's, and 60's.

Sewing Projects Set up an assembly line (manufacturing type) to make school pennants, holiday stockings, or patchwork items. Then arrange a "store" and sell the items as a money-making project.

Nursing Home Projects Make wheelchair carry-alls for a nursing home using a variety of decorative stitches and seam finishes.

Repair-Your-Wardrobe Clinic Have a repair-your-wardrobe clinic. Have each member bring one or two garments to repair—hems, zippers, rips and tears, buttons. As a money-making project, have them offer an alteration service in the school.

UNIT CLOSURE

For Review

Buy or Sew? Have students look through catalogs to find a ready-to-wear garment they would like to own. Have them write down the price and a description of the garment. Then find a pattern for a similar garment, and figure out the cost of making that garment. Include the price of the pattern, fabric, and notions. Compare the costs of the two garments. Ask them to list the factors other than price that they would consider before deciding whether to sew or buy ready-made.

For Evaluation

Unit Test Have students complete the Unit Test that appears in the *Teacher's Classroom Resources.*

Testmaker Software You may wish to design a unit test using the Testmaker software program.

CHAPTER OVERVIEW

Chapter 55 describes personal, environmental, and social factors that affect clothing choices. It explores the concept of appropriateness of dress in relation to climate, weather, activities, occupations, and social contexts and suggests that appropriate dress shows respect for others. Students learn that in addition to affecting their appearance and the impression they make on others, their clothing decisions communicate personality and self-concept, individuality and conformity, role and status, and group membership.

INTRODUCING THE CHAPTER

Motivators

What Do Your Clothes Tell Others About You? Have students write lists or essays answering this question. Ask them to save their responses for reassessment after completing the chapter.

Using the Photograph Refer students to the photograph on this page. Then ask: "What is happening in the picture? What factors might someone consider in deciding what to wear?"

Self-Concept Tell students that their clothing choices reflect their self-concept. Define self-concept as the particular view you have about yourself. Ask students to give examples showing how clothing choices might reflect self-concept.

Introducing the Objectives

Discuss the chapter objectives on this page. Remind students that the objectives focus on important chapter content.

Introducing Vocabulary

Write the words *conformity* and *individuality* on the board. Discuss with students the meanings of the words and their relationship as concepts. Introduce the word *appropriate.* Ask students to suggest synonyms (*suitable, fitting, proper, apt, correct*). Point out that ideas about appropriateness sometimes conflict. Allow students to develop a definition of appropriate dress on which all can agree.

CHAPTER

55

Clothing and You

OBJECTIVES

This chapter will help you to:

- Discuss factors that affect individual and family apparel choices.
- Identify the ways that clothing decisions affect your appearance.
- Describe ways to select clothing for comfort.
- Analyze how clothing decisions are affected by groups.

WORDS TO REMEMBER

appropriate
conform
formal clothes
individuality
status

Chapter Resources

Teacher's Classroom Resources
- Lesson Plan
- Life Skills Activity, *Evaluating Your Time*
- Reproducible Master, *Clothing Communicates*
- Extension Activity, *Dressing Comfortably*
- Chapter Test

Student Workbook
- Study Guide
- Worksheet, *Making Clothing Choices*

The first decision you have to make nearly every day of your life is what to wear. One day you want to feel comfortable, and you don't really care what others think of your clothes. On another day you dress so you can fit in with your friends. Some days you have to dress up for a special occasion. There are also days when nothing in your closet seems to suit you.

Experimenting with clothing is part of finding out about yourself. As you try different styles and fashions, you learn what kinds of clothes make you feel comfortable—with yourself and with others.

The choices you make about clothes depend on many things:

- Your self-concept.
- Your personality.
- Your coloring and body type.
- The climate you live in.
- Your activities and interests.
- The groups you belong to.

Clothing Choices

Some clothing choices depend on your activities. You need certain clothing for school, other outfits for special occasions, and some comfortable clothes for exercise or relaxation. You may also select clothes based on the weather. Heat, cold, sun, rain, and snow all affect your choice of clothing.

Some choices are not so clear-cut. You may need to make a decision between what you want and what you need, considering the amount of money that you have to spend.

In making these choices you have to decide what is important to you. Do you want to dress like your friends or in your own way? Do you want clothes that are easy to care for, or are you willing to iron some items? Do you like to sew, or would you rather buy your clothes ready-made?

Your clothing choices can tell others something about your personality, your interests, and your values.

Focus on Decision Making Remind students that choices involve an evaluation of needs, goals, and values. Have students apply the information in Chapter 5 to decisions about clothing choices and appearance.

Cross-Reference See Chapters 1 and 2 for information about self-concept and self-esteem.

Cross-Reference For information about grooming, see Chapter 3 and Teen Tips "How to Save Face" on pages 68-69.

TEACHING THE CHAPTER

For convenience, the teaching suggestions for this chapter are arranged according to the following lesson topics:

- "Clothing Choices," pages 499-500
- "Clothes and Your Appearance," pages 500-501
- "Clothes and Comfort," pages 501-502
- "Clothes and Groups," and "Clothing Decisions," pages 502-503

Teaching "Clothing Choices"
(Pages 499-500)

This section teaches the kinds of needs or wants that affect clothing choices.

Checking Comprehension

✓ What four factors determine an individual's clothing choices? *Needs for different activities; needs for different weather conditions; amount of money to spend on clothing; wants that are important to you.*

Activities

Skill Builder: Writing
Ask students to write short essays on the following topic question: What three considerations are most important to you in choosing clothing, and why?

Reteaching
Clarify the idea of wants and needs as an economic concept. In allocating scarce resources, people must make choices to meet their basic needs before they can make choices to satisfy their wants. Students might review Chapters 25 and 27. Ask for examples of clothing that might be regarded as needs as opposed to wants.

Enrichment
Ask each student to evaluate a recent clothing choice. What were the reasons for this choice? What wants or needs did the choice satisfy? Students might wish to discuss why conflicts about clothing choices sometimes arise between parents and their children.

The other members of your family may have different factors to consider when selecting their clothing:

- **Occupation.** Where a family member works influences the kinds of clothing chosen. A person who works outdoors has different needs from an office worker, and someone who wears a uniform to work does not need as large a wardrobe as someone who works in an office or retail store.
- **Type of community.** The type of community your family lives in can affect clothing choices. For example, small towns usually have a more casual style of dress than large cities.
- **Family structure.** People have different needs at different times in their lives. Young children, who quickly outgrow their clothes, are often dressed in inexpensive, practical outfits. Many older children are involved in activities such as sports and dancing, which require special clothing. A family member who has retired might prefer casual clothing to business attire. A family member who is disabled might have special clothing needs.
- **Values.** Family values also influence clothing choices. Some families value easy care in clothes. Others like handmade items, such as hand-knitted sweaters. Still others might favor designer labels.

Clothes and Your Appearance

Clothes are like the wrapping on a package. When you meet people for the first time, you often make a judgment about them based on the way they are dressed, just as you might guess what is in a package according to the way it is wrapped.

Your clothing tells others about your lifestyle, your interests, and how you feel about yourself. Your willingness to select your clothes carefully and keep them in good condition indicates that you feel good about yourself and take pride in your appearance.

Expressing Your Personality

Your clothes also express your personality. If you wear unusual clothes that set you apart from the crowd, you may like to show your **individuality,** the ways in which you are different from others. You think for yourself and enjoy being original.

When you wear the same type of clothing that your friends wear you dress to **conform**—to be like the people around you. Being part of the group makes you feel comfortable. Can you conform and still be an individual? Even if everyone in your group wears jeans and T-shirts to an event, the design, style, and color of your T-shirt is your special choice.

The colors you choose often reflect your inner feelings and preferences. When you wear cool, quiet colors such as soft blue or green, you may be showing a calm mood. Bold, bright colors and splashy prints show the fun-loving, outgoing side of your personality.

Making You Look Better

You can use your clothing to change your appearance. Some designs make your shoulders look broader or your body seem slimmer. Color and accessories can call attention to your best features. For example, you might use a wide belt to highlight your slim waist or a shirt with a contrasting collar to accent your face.

Teaching "Clothes and Your Appearance"
(Pages 501-502)

This section teaches the impressions clothes make and how impressions can be altered.

Checking Comprehension

✓ What is one of the first things you notice about people when you meet them for the first time? *The clothes they are wearing.*

✓ What does paying careful attention to the way you dress show? *That you feel good about yourself and care about your appearance.*

✓ What is the difference between individuality and conformity? *Individuality means that you wear clothes that set you apart from the crowd; you think for yourself and enjoy being original. Conformity means that you dress to be like the people around you; being part of a group makes you feel comfortable.*

✓ What aspects of clothing might reflect your moods or inner feelings? *Colors, fabrics, patterns, and accessories.*

✓ What aspects of clothing might draw attention to your best features? *Design, color, and accessories.*

Activities

Skill Builder: Critical Thinking
Ask students if they have ever made judgments based on outward appearances. Have them explain if those judgments turned out to be correct or incorrect. Ask them to suggest errors that they might make when basing their opinions on first impressions. How might that adversely affect their relationships?

Reteaching
Have students work in small groups to list qualities of dress that show you feel good about yourself and care about your appearance. Groups might share and discuss their lists. Ask students to identify three ways in which they use clothing to express individuality and three ways they use clothing to conform.

Real-Life Situations Being part of a family can affect clothing needs and wants, purchases, and responsibilities. The clothing needs of a growing child or a parent entering the workforce may take priority over the wants of other family members. Responsibility for selecting and caring for clothes may be given to one person or shared by family members.

Cross-Reference See Chapter 8 for additional information about first impressions.

Emphasize Ask: "Can you conform and still be an individual?" Stress the relative nature of the two terms and the idea that individuality and conformity are not mutually exclusive. Have students offer examples.

Which styles and colors are best for you? You can learn how to select clothing that will accent your best features.

Colors play an important part in the way you look. The same style can have different effects in different shades, depending upon your skin tone and hair color.

Learning how color and design can change your appearance will help you make clothing decisions. You'll be able to choose clothes that express your personality and help you look your best. Chapter 56 has more information about using color and design to enhance your appearance.

Clothes and Comfort

Comfort has a lot to do with clothing choices. It's hard to be good-tempered if you're shivering with cold, or if the sandals you're wearing on city streets are made for use on the beach.

Dressing for Climate and Weather

If you are like most people, you will switch on a weather report or glance outside before deciding how to dress for the day. On a cold day, you might wear a parka, a hat, gloves, and boots for comfort. Underneath your parka you might wear a sweater and a shirt. Wearing several layers of clothing helps the body to retain heat.

If the weather is warm, you will probably wear light-colored, loose-fitting clothing. You will wear less clothing than in cold weather, so that body heat can escape. In hot climates people often cover their heads to protect themselves from the sun. Raincoats and umbrellas offer protection from the rain.

Did You Know? People wear clothes for a variety of reasons. Some of these reasons are physical; others are emotional or social.

- Protection—clothes provide protection from the weather and injuries.
- Modesty—clothes cover different parts of the body; standards of modesty vary according to activities and cultures.
- Identification—clothes can identify people as members of a group, or by occupation or activity.
- Status—clothes can show the level of a person's importance.
- Decoration—clothes and jewelry can improve a person's appearance and express their uniqueness.

Enrichment
Have each student create an annotated scrapbook of illustrations, clippings, or samples for greater self-awareness. Scrapbooks might include examples of the ways they currently use clothing to express individuality, to conform, to suggest positive or negative moods, to express their personality, or to call attention to their best features.

Teaching "Clothes and Comfort"
(Pages 501-502)

This section teaches the conditions that influence the kinds of clothing worn.

Checking Comprehension

✓ What two factors should you consider in dressing for comfort? *Climate and weather; activities.*

✓ In responding to climate, what purpose do clothing choices serve? *Staying warm enough or cool enough for comfort.*

✓ What kinds of clothes might be required at a job? *Work clothes, a uniform.*

✓ Give some examples of clothing that is used for health and safety. *Answers will vary. Students might list helmets, hard hats, goggles, padding, fireproof suits, bulletproof vests, and so on.*

Activities

Skill Builder: Writing
Have students keep a log of their clothing choices in relation to their activities. Ask students to develop a list of all the activities in which they usually participate during a given month. Then have students describe their clothing choices for each activity in terms of the following categories: casual wear, semiformal wear, formal wear, uniform, special-purpose clothing. Students might add descriptions of specific apparel in each category.

Reteaching
Have students create collages illustrating one of the following themes: climate affects clothing choices throughout the world; different activities require different clothing choices; some activities require special clothing for health, safety, and job performance.

Enrichment
Assign students to research and report the scientific explanation for each of the following phenomena: several layers of clothing keep you warmer than single layers; light-colored clothes keep you cooler than dark-colored clothes; loose-fitting clothes keep you cooler than tight-fitting clothes; head coverings can protect you from both extreme heat and extreme cold; all people require protection from over-exposure to the sun.

Teaching "Clothes and Groups" and "Clothing Decisions"
(Pages 502-503)

This section teaches circumstances in which clothing is worn to conform to a group style of dress.

Checking Comprehension

✓ Give three examples of clothes that identify you as a member of a group. *Any three of the following: club jackets, special accessories, band uniforms, team uniforms, and so on.*

✓ How can clothing be used to show status? *Some clothing shows favored position within a group, such as uniforms, emblems, badges, or costly designer clothing.*

✓ How can you find out what is appropriate to wear for a special occasion? *Ask the host or hostess, or ask other guests what they plan to wear.*

Dressing for Activity

You also select clothing based on what you do. In a given day, you probably participate in a variety of activities. You may go to school, practice with a sports team, work at a job, play in the marching band, go out on a date. The clothing that is appropriate for one activity may not be suitable for another. Casual clothes are fine for school, but you may need to dress less casually at work. Some jobs and sports require a uniform.

Certain activities call for clothing that serves a specific purpose. A helmet protects a bicyclist's head, and shoulder pads cushion the shocks endured by a football player. Like athletes, some laborers need protective clothing, such as hard hats, fireproof suits, or plastic aprons.

Clothes and Groups

The people around you also influence your clothing choices. You are a member of many groups—your friends, your family, a club or athletic team, or a religious organization. Clothes have always been useful in identifying certain people in a community. Police and fire fighters, for example, are known by their uniforms. The business executive's suit, the cheerleader's outfit, and the bride's white gown all identify these people and what they are doing.

Belonging to a Group

Being comfortable in a group is important to nearly everyone. When you're dressed like the others in your group, you feel confident that you are a part of that group.

Sometimes people in a group dress identically, as when members of a school athletic team or band wear uniforms. Clubs may have matching jackets or sweaters. When you wear these special clothes you are identified and recognized by others as belonging to a particular group. Wearing a uniform also carries a special responsibility. You represent the entire group—the band, team, or school. Your actions tend to influence what other people think of the group as a whole.

Sometimes clothing shows favored position, or **status**, within a group. The leader of a marching band may wear a tall fur hat. Scouts wear badges on their uniforms to show that they have mastered certain skills. Some people believe that designer labels indicate status.

Respecting Others' Feelings

You usually choose what you wear based on how you feel. However, there are times when you choose clothes to show your respect for others.

If your family has a large celebration—such as a party for your grandparents' anniversary held in a restaurant—your parents want to feel especially proud of you. Dressing less casually than you usually do is an easy way to show that you care about your parents' and grandparents' feelings.

On special occasions, you are expected to wear a certain kind of clothing. Dressing in an **appropriate** manner, that is, in clothes suitable for the occasion, is important. For many of these occasions, dressing appropriately means dressing up.

- **Parties.** The person who invites you may tell you whether it is a dressy or casual party. Otherwise, ask the person who is giving the party or check on what your friends are wearing.

Cross-Reference For information about peer groups and peer pressure, see "Peer Pressure and Clothes" on page 500, as well as Chapter 13 and its feature, "Peer Pressure."

Did You Know? Research shows that people's ideas about appropriate dress for different activities are strongly and subconsciously influenced by television advertising. This is true even when advertising is for products other than clothes. Invite students to discuss the effect of television ads on their clothing choices.

Uniforms identify members of a particular group and help to create a special image for the group.

- **Weddings.** Members of the wedding party often wear **formal clothes**—tuxedos for the men and long dresses for the women. The guests, however, are not required to dress formally. Females can wear knee- or calf-length dresses. For a male guest, a jacket, shirt, and tie is generally accepted.
- **Funerals.** At one time, black was considered the only proper color for funerals. This is no longer the rule everywhere; simple, dark- or neutral-colored designs are now considered appropriate.
- **Religious services.** Some groups have strict rules about dress. If you're not sure what to wear to a service or inside a particular house of worship, ask a member of the congregation.
- **Trips to stores and restaurants.** You may not be permitted to enter certain places if you are dressed inappropriately. Stores in many areas are forbidden by law to admit customers who are barefoot or without shirts. Restaurants require shirts and shoes. Some insist on ties and jackets for men.

Clothing Decisions

In the following chapters of this unit, you'll learn how to make important decisions about your clothing. You'll find out how to choose fashions and designs that are right for you and how to plan your wardrobe. You'll discover what to look for when buying clothes and which stores to shop in. You'll learn how you can make your own clothes and choose the patterns and fabrics that are best for you. In addition, you'll find out how to care for your clothes so they'll look better and last longer.

Activities

Skill Builder: Writing
Write the term *status symbol* on the board. Define *symbol* as a sign representing an idea. A status symbol is a sign of one's status. Have students brainstorm a list of clothing features that serve as status symbols in their community and school. Suggest a relationship between status symbols, social cliques, and clothing fads. Students might ask parents about clothes that were "in" when the parents were in high school.

Skill Builder: Writing
Ask students to find and cut out a clothing advertisement that uses status as a selling point. Then have them write a paragraph or two about their reaction to the ad, whether they would like to buy the item and why, and how the advertisers used status to appeal to consumers.

Reteaching
Ask students to visualize the group of friends they most associate with in school. Have students think about or respond in writing to the following questions: To what extent and in what ways do you and your friends conform to a group style of dress? What information or image does your group style communicate to others?

Enrichment
Ask students to find a sociology book in the library and to read about the different kinds of groups, roles, and status levels in society. Have students pool their information and discuss the use of clothing and accessories as outward signs of roles, status level, and membership in groups.

Focus on Relationship Skills Present students with hypothetical situations in which they are expected to dress differently from the way they would prefer. How might students compromise to retain their individuality while showing respect for others' feelings? Point out that making compromises is an important interpersonal skill.

Emphasize Dress codes differ regionally and historically. Ask students to describe changes in dress codes for school, for religious services, or for other traditional contexts.

Teaching the Feature
"Peer Pressure and Clothes"

Answers to Feature Questions

1. Students might mention such things as the peer group's making them more aware of the importance of taking care of their appearance, introducing them to new styles, the peer group commenting on their best features or suggesting colors or styles that would look good on them, giving them confidence to choose their own clothes.

2. Students are most likely to mention conflicts with parents or friends. Students will probably express either uncomfortable reactions (fear, feeling out of place, awkwardness, and so on) or feelings of self-confidence (pride, freedom, and so on).

Activities

Skits Have students develop skits showing positive and negative aspects of peer pressure concerning clothing choices. Students might also act out situations in which parents and teens have conflicts over clothing choices. Skits should fairly represent different points of view and should stress conflict resolution.

Examine Your Clothing Ask students to go through the clothing they have at home. Have them list the items under two categories: those that they chose in order to fit in with peers and those that they chose for other reasons. Then ask them to add the number of items in each category. Which category was larger? What does that say about the influence peer pressure has on them?

Community Contact Have the class present skits to younger students as a peer education service.

INTERPERSONAL SKILLS

Peer Pressure and Clothes

How much time do you and your friends spend talking about clothes, shopping together, or reading the fashion magazines to see what other people your age are wearing? Keeping up with the current clothing styles may be an important interest that you share with your peers.

Clothing expresses the behavior, tastes, and interests of a group. If a style is popular with a group you belong to, you will probably want to wear it to show that you are part of that crowd. You may even change your style of clothing in order to gain acceptance in a group.

A group of peers can have a positive influence on your clothing choices. Your peers can, for example, help you journey toward independence. Perhaps your parents no longer choose your clothing or tell you what to wear. Shopping with your friends can help you adjust to this new responsibility.

Your peers can also help you develop your self-concept. When you dress to identify with a group, you are making a choice about who you want to be. You are showing that you care about yourself and how you look.

Peers can also help you learn appropriate behavior. By dressing like the group you learn the acceptable standards for your age, lifestyle, and society. From your friends you learn how to deal with new situations.

Although a group of friends can provide positive support, a group may also have a negative influence. The group may pressure you to adopt a style that causes conflict with your parents or another group to which you belong.

Some groups may put pressure on you to wear only designer labels. If you don't wear a certain brand, you will not be considered part of the group. What if you simply cannot afford expensive designer jeans?

In addition, peer pressure to conform can suppress your individuality. In all the choices you make, be sure to pay attention to your own feelings and values. If they are different from what the group demands, you may need to say no—or find another group that better reflects what is important to you.

Think It Through

1. **What positive influences has your peer group had on your appearance?**
2. **Describe an occasion when you had a conflict with someone because you expressed your individuality through your clothing. How did you feel about it?**

Did You Know? A strong source of fashion peer pressure is the clothing worn by actors, actresses, and singers and the styles worn in particular movies, videos, and television shows.

Emphasize The fashion industry depends on people conforming to fashion trends. Those changing trends are one of the main reasons that many people buy new clothes every season.

CHAPTER 55 REVIEW

Reviewing the Facts

1. List five factors that affect clothing choices.
2. What does your clothing tell other people about you?
3. How is your personality expressed through your clothing?
4. What type of clothing do you need for a hot climate? What type of clothing dò you need for a cold climate?
5. Why does wearing a uniform carry a special responsibility?
6. Give an example of clothing that shows status.
7. What is meant by dressing appropriately?
8. List four occasions for which it is usually necessary for people to dress a certain way.

Thinking Critically

1. Give three examples other than those discussed in the chapter in which appropriate dress is important. Discuss why.
2. How have your clothing tastes changed in recent years? Can you identify the reasons why they have changed?

Applying Your Skills

1. **Writing a Description.** Write a humorous short story in which a character finds himself or herself in a social situation wearing inappropriate clothing.
2. **Using Reference Materials.** Select a country that interests you. In the library, research the traditional clothing for males and females of that country. Find out how the clothing reflects the climate, lifestyle, and culture of the country. Are traditional clothes still worn today? Prepare a report for the class. Include drawings or photos.
3. **Presenting Two Sides of an Issue.** List two activities or jobs that require a uniform, and explain the advantages or disadvantages of the uniform in each example.

Answers to "Reviewing the Facts"

1. Any five: self-concept; personality; coloring and body type; climate; activities and interests; groups you belong to ; amount of money to spend; occupation; type of community; family structure; values.
2. Your lifestyle; your interests; how you feel about yourself; your personality; your feelings your preference.
3. By showing individuality, you show you think for yourself and enjoy being original. By conforming in dress, you show you like being part of the group. Soft colors may show a calm mood; bright colors may show an outgoing personality.
4. Hot climate: loose-fitting, light-colored clothing; hat for protection from sun. Cold climate: heavy sweaters, coats, hats gloves, boots, several layers of clothing.
5. Since you are identified with the group, your actions in public represent the entire group.
6. Any one: uniform, emblems, badges, designer labels.
7. Wearing clothes that are suitable for the occasion.
8. Any four: parties, weddings, funerals, religious services, trips to stores and restaurants.

COMPLETING THE CHAPTER

Summary

- Others initially judge you by your appearance.
- Your self-concept and personality influence your clothing choices.
- Clothing choices express both individuality and conformity.
- Dressing for comfort involves consideration of climate and activity.
- Your membership and status in groups affect your clothing choices.
- It is desirable to dress appropriately and to respect others' feelings about dress.

For Review

Objective Review Questions Have students complete the "Reviewing the Facts" section on this page.

Study Guide Have students complete the Study Guide from Chapter 55 of their *Student Workbook.*

Class Discussion Write the following quotation on the chalkboard: "Clothes make the man." Suggest that the word *person* might substitute for the word *man.* Ask students what they think the quote means, whether or not they agree, and why.

For Evaluation

Motivator Follow-Up Ask students to reassess their initial responses to the question, "What do your clothes tell others about you?" Have students write essays revising their answers according to what they have learned in this chapter.

Assessing Clothing Choices Ask students to choose two reasons from the chapter content that they use to make specific clothing choices. Then have them write a paragraph for each reason explaining why that reason is important to them.

Chapter Test Have students complete the test for Chapter 55 that appears in the *Teacher's Classroom Resources.*

Answers to "Thinking Critically"

1. Students may give examples such as a job interview; a dance with a theme; a sporting event in which they are participating; dinner at a fancy restaurant. Students may explain that it is practical to dress a certain way; the type of dress is dictated by the occasion; it's important to show respect for others.
2. Answers will vary. Reasons may include changing schools; becoming a member of a new group; growing out of old clothes; moving to a new climate; spending more time with a peer group; gaining the self-confidence to select their own clothes.

CHAPTER OVERVIEW

Chapter 56 explains line, shape, space, texture, and color as the five design elements to consider in making clothing choices. Students learn design terminology and the characteristics of color. The chapter provides examples, suggestions, and applications to help students relate design elements to their body type and appearance.

INTRODUCING THE CHAPTER

Motivators

Describe Your Best Outfit Ask students to write a detailed description of one outfit they wear that attracts compliments. Why do they look better in that outfit than in others? Have students save this analysis for reassessment after completing the chapter.

Using the Photograph Ask students to point out design elements in the photograph on this page. Then ask: "How does design seem to affect each person's appearance?"

Design Tell students that this chapter explains principles of design. The term *design* refers to an overall pattern or composition that is planned and created as a visual presentation. All designs rely on five main "ingredients" (design elements). Have students infer these elements and point out examples of design in the classroom. Write students' responses on the chalkboard to check against chapter content.

Introducing the Objectives

Discuss the chapter objectives on this page. Remind students that the objectives focus on important chapter content.

CHAPTER

56

Design and Your Appearance

OBJECTIVES

This chapter will help you to:

- Identify and describe the main design elements in clothing.
- Give examples of ways to use line, shape, space, and texture effectively.
- Describe how to use color to achieve a special look.

WORDS TO REMEMBER

analogous color scheme
complementary color scheme
hue
illusion
intensity
monochromatic color scheme
proportion
texture
value

Chapter Resources

Teacher's Classroom Resources
- Lesson Plan
- Life Skills Activity, *You're the Fashion Consultant*
- Reproducible Master, *Design Lines*
- Extension Activity, *The Message of Colors*
- Chapter Test

Student Workbook
- Study Guide
- Worksheet, *Working With Color*

Rita was trying to decide what to wear to school. She wanted to look especially nice, and she was looking forward to wearing the blouse she had just bought. As she tried on the blouse with a few different skirts, she realized that it just didn't look as good on her as it did in the store window. For some reason, her old plaid blouse seemed to give her face more color and sparkle. Maybe that's why she got compliments every time she wore it.

Have you ever wondered why you look better in some clothes than others? Why doesn't everyone look great in the same outfit? You will discover the answers to these questions as you study the elements of design as applied to clothing.

Elements of Design

Deciding what to buy and which article of clothing to combine into an outfit are some of the most common clothing decisions you will make. To choose wisely, you need to be aware of the basic elements of design and how they can be used to create pleasing effects in clothing.

If you look carefully at any garment, you can pick out the five elements of design:

- Line.
- Shape.
- Space.
- Texture.
- Color.

All five design elements affect the way clothing makes you appear to yourself and others.

Line

The stripes on a shirt, the creases in a pleated skirt, and the seams on a pair of jeans are examples of line. Line defines the form of a garment. Line can also be used to create an **illusion**—an image that fools the eye.

Vertical lines can make you look taller and thinner. Because these lines lead the eye up and down, the distance from side to side seems less significant.

Horizontal lines have the opposite effect. They lead the eye from side to side, making the wearer seem shorter and broader. Wide waistbands and belts and wide horizontal stripes are lines that make you look heavier.

Diagonal lines can give the illusion of either height or width, depending on their length and angle. Curved lines, such as the curved front of a vest, create a softer effect than either vertical or horizontal lines.

Shape

The outline of a garment is its shape. A leotard closely follows the shape of the body. A dress that is loose and full creates a triangular shape. A shirt that hangs straight from the shoulders creates a boxy shape. The shape of a garment can cover up or draw attention to certain parts of your body. As you choose clothing, you need to consider the way the garment's shape accents your best features or hides those that are not your best.

Space

Space is the area between or inside lines. One way to think of space is as the entire area within a garment. Garment lines break up this total space. Pockets,

Did You Know? Fashion designers and artists draw human figures based on standard anatomical proportions. The figures, called croquis (CRO-kees), are used to illustrate clothing designs.

Did You Know? Clothing is sometimes named for the shape of the garment, for example: (dresses) A-line, sack, trapeze; (tops) T-shirts, box jacket, halter; (pants) bell-bottom, flared, balloon. Ask students for other examples.

Introducing Vocabulary

The "Words to Remember" for this chapter include technical terms. Distinguish those that refer to color from those that refer to design. Point out the relationship between *analogous* and *analogy,* which both refer to parts that correspond or are similar in some way. Distinguish *complementary* from *complimentary.* The root word, *complement,* means something that completes or makes up a whole. Also differentiate *illusion* from *allusion* and *monochrome* from *polychrome.* Have students look up *chroma* and its extensions in a dictionary. Point out that such commonly used words as *proportion, intensity,* and *value* have special meanings in the context of design.

TEACHING THE CHAPTER

For convenience, the teaching suggestions for this chapter are arranged according to the following lesson topics:

- "Elements of Design," pages 507-509
- "Understanding Color," and "The Whole Effect," pages 509-511

Teaching "Elements of Design"

(Pages 507-509)

This section teaches the main elements of design and their component parts.

Checking Comprehension

✔ What are four kinds of line in design? *Horizontal, vertical, diagonal, and curved.*

✔ How can lines create illusions? *By directing attention to some features and away from others.*

✔ What is meant by the space in a design? *The area between or inside lines.*

✔ If you wanted to appear thinner, what types of clothing design elements would you choose? *You would do best to choose vertical lines, a shape that isn't tight, small patterns, and smooth fabrics.*

Activities

Skill Builder: Math
Figure drawings are based on standard body proportions. For female figures, the head, from the top to the base of the chin, is one-eighth of the height of the figure. The line of the underarms is one-quarter of the height from the top. The waist is three-eighths from the top. The hip line at the widest part is one-half of the height, and the knee line is one-quarter of the height from the soles of the feet. Have students graph and label these proportions for a figure drawing 4 inches (10 cm) in height.

Skill Builder: Critical Thinking
Based on the elements of clothing design discussed in this section—color, line, shape, space, and texture—have students describe an outfit they would design to make the most of their positive points while minimizing features they don't like.

Reteaching
Have students use magazine clippings to create a scrapbook illustrating line, shape, and space. For line: On one page, sketch and label examples of the four types of line. On the facing page, paste clippings of clothing designs illustrating the use of each type. For shape: On another page, draw a triangle with an apex at the top, a triangle with the apex at the bottom, a square, a vertical rectangle, an oval, and a figure eight. On the facing page, paste clippings of clothing illustrating each shape. For space: Draw four vertical rectangles. Divide one rectangle into quarters, one horizontally into thirds, one horizontally in half, and one vertically into sixths. On the facing page, paste examples of each kind of space.

Enrichment
Draw these illusions on the chalkboard. Explain that a change in line direction can change the apparent length of a line.

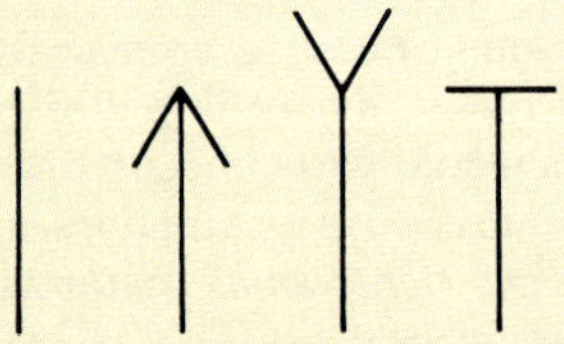

Have students find pictures of clothing that represent the different lines.

Emphasize Design elements apply to the features of a garment as well as to the garment itself. Have students collect examples of the use of line, shape, and space in collars, neck openings, pockets, and sleeves.

seams, buttons, and trim divide a garment into different shapes. For example, a belt at the waist of a dress breaks the dress up into two spaces.

Proportion is the relationship between spaces within a garment. Proportion in a man's suit would be the length of the jacket in relation to the length of the pants.

By changing the proportions of your clothes, you can change the way you look. For example, a short, waist-length jacket can make your legs look longer. A long, hip-length jacket can make your legs seem shorter and your upper body look longer.

Patterns within an outfit have proportion, too. These should be appropriate in size to the person wearing the clothing. Large plaids and prints look better on a tall person. A short person should choose smaller plaids and prints.

Texture

Texture is the way a fabric looks and feels. Leather is smooth and slippery. Denim is rough and rugged. Corduroy is ribbed and bulky. Texture can also create illusions. Bulky fabrics usually make you look heavier. Smoother fabrics tend to make you look slimmer.

Not all textures are equally appropriate in all situations. Some textures, such as bulky, ribbed sweaters, are traditionally casual. Fabrics that reflect light and have a shimmery texture—such as velvet, satin, and taffeta—are dressy and suitable for formal occasions.

Color

You will learn about color and its many effects in the following section.

Understanding Color

If you ever told a friend that your new shirt was light, bright, fire-engine red, you were describing the shirt's color. Color is an element of design which is described in terms of hue, value, and intensity.

Hue is a specific color name such as green, red, or blue-violet. A color wheel is an arrangement of basic hues. It shows how the colors are related to each other. Although there are hundreds of hues, they are all blends of the three primary colors: red, yellow, and blue.

A secondary color results when two primary colors are mixed in equal amounts. Orange, green, and violet are the secondary colors. Orange is a mixture of red and yellow, and appears on the color wheel halfway between these hues. Green is a mixture of blue and yellow, and violet is a mixture of red and blue.

Other hues can be made by mixing the primary colors in different amounts. For example, both pine trees and olives are green, but they are two different hues. The green of a pine tree has more blue than yellow in it. The green of an olive has more yellow than blue in the blend.

White, black, and gray are considered neutrals. They are not included on the color wheel, but they are used to create different values of a hue. **Value** is the lightness or darkness of a color. Darker values result when black is added to a hue. These darker values are shades of the hue. Burgundy is a shade of red. When white is added to a basic hue it creates a tint of that color. Pink is a tint of red.

Intensity is the brightness or dullness of a color. Hot pink and lemon yellow are bright. They are high in intensity. Subdued colors like navy blue and rust are low in intensity.

Emphasize Stress that all colors are made up of the primary colors. Have students look around the room for a variety of hues, shades, and tints of a secondary color. Then ask students to identify the dominant constituent colors (red, yellow, blue, white, black) in each of their samples.

More About Color Remind students that color names are subjective. People disagree about color distinctions. Have students give examples of color names (for example, peach, mustard, pigeon brown, Nile green). Why are such names imprecise? Ask students if they ever disagreed with someone about whether a color was green or blue.

Teaching "Understanding Color" and "The Whole Effect"

(Pages 509-511)

This section teaches the concepts of hue, value, and intensity. It describes the common types of color schemes and their uses and effects.

Checking Comprehension

✓ What three kinds of information are used to describe a color? *The color's hue, value, and intensity.*

✓ What is the difference between primary colors and secondary colors? *Primary colors are the ones from which all other colors are derived. Secondary colors are colors that result from the equal mixture of two primary colors.*

✓ How is a tint different from a shade? *A tint is a lighter value of a hue created by adding white; a shade is a darker value of a hue created by adding black.*

✓ Which is the most intense color, forest green, lime green, or olive green? *Lime green.*

✓ Compare and contrast the three types of color schemes. *A monochromatic color scheme uses variations of the same color, an analogous color scheme uses colors that are closely related, a complementary color scheme uses colors that are direct opposites on the color wheel.*

✓ What kinds of colors create the illusion of larger size? *Light, bright, warm colors.*

✓ What purposes can contrasting colors in an outfit serve? *To break up an outfit, to create emphasis, and to draw attention away from certain features.*

✓ Why should you consider your personal coloring when selecting colors to wear? *It helps you choose which values and intensities of a color look best on you.*

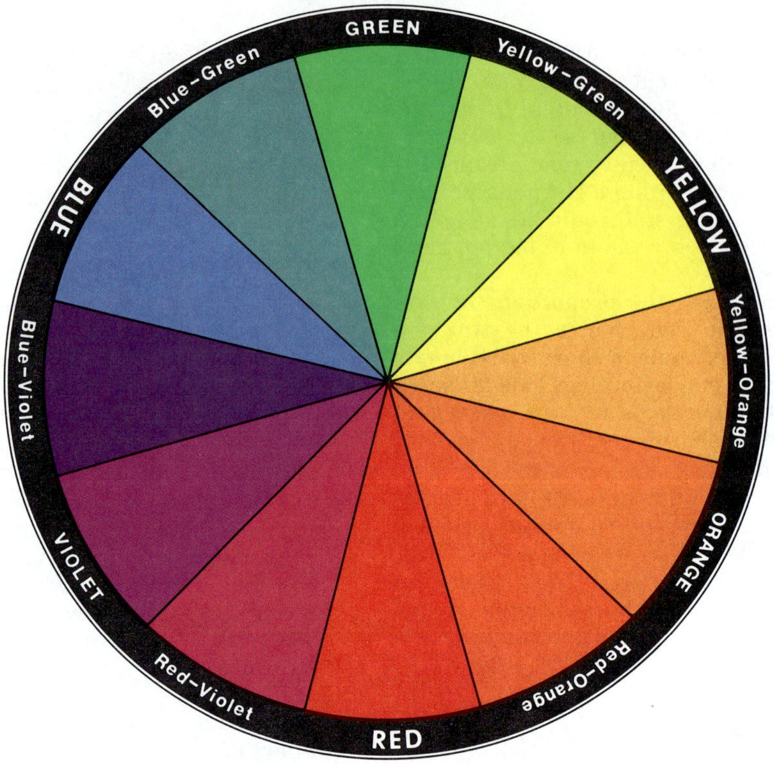

THE COLOR WHEEL
All the colors on the color wheel are blends of the three primary colors—red, yellow, and blue.

Color Schemes

How do you put colors together for a pleasing effect? The color wheel is useful for making up combinations or color schemes. There are three common color schemes.

A **monochromatic color scheme** uses variations of the same color. If you wore a light blue sweater and dark blue pants, your outfit would be monochromatic.

An **analogous color scheme** uses colors that are closely related, such as yellow, yellow-orange, and orange. If you topped your blue pants with a blue-green sweater, your color scheme would be analgous.

A **complementary color scheme** uses colors that are direct opposites on the color wheel, such as red and green. Different values and intensities can also create an interesting effect. Suppose you decide to use the complementary colors blue and orange in an outfit. With pants that are navy blue (a shade of blue), you may choose a peach (a tint of orange) sweater for a pleasant complementary color combination.

Visual Effects of Color

Like the other four elements of design, color can be used to create illusions. Colors that are light and bright

Activities

Skill Builder: Critical Thinking
Tell students that use of color is both symbolic and a nonverbal form of communication. Colors symbolize countries, schools, teams, holidays, and emotions. The colors of building interiors, vehicles, signs, products, and packaging are carefully chosen to create certain effects. Ask students for specific examples. Invite them to observe and discuss the psychology, associations, and symbolism of color.

Skill Builder: Critical Thinking
Tell students that the appearance of a color is affected by the colors near it. The same color can look different depending on its surroundings, or field. Have students experiment with color swatches to see how this is true. For example, students might view violet swatches on fields of yellow, red, blue, and a variety of neutral colors. Ask what the phenomenon has to do with choosing color schemes. Students might add to their scrapbooks examples of color influences and of neutral colors.

Reteaching
Have students use crayons, paints, or other coloring devices to create a color wheel 4 inches (10 cm) in diameter at the center of a large sheet of paper. Students should then clip from magazines swatches of ten colors they particularly like. Have them compare the swatches to the colors on the wheel and arrange each swatch in the appropriate marginal area to show hues, tints, and shades of a color. Students should evaluate their color choice in terms of primary and secondary colors, color values, and color intensities.

Reteaching
Have students find examples of clothing in magazines illustrating the three color schemes described in the chapter. Students might create scrapbooks with two examples of each type. For each example, students should indicate on a small color wheel the location of the colors shown.

Focus on Entrepreneurship People's interest in determining their best colors has encouraged new businesses run by color consultants. Color consultants sell color-charting services, advice, and products. Some use computers to assist in color typing and color matching. Ask students if they know anyone who has performed or used such a service.

Focus on Technology Show students color separations for the reproduction of a picture. Color separations show the amount of red, yellow, blue, and black in a picture. You might invite a printer to explain how color separations are made.

tend to make a person look larger. Warm colors, such as red, yellow, and orange, also give the appearance of added weight. Darker shades and less intense colors tend to minimize size, as do the cool colors, blue, green, and violet.

If you wear a solid color outfit, you will probably seem taller. Contrasting colors, such as a yellow shirt and dark blue pants, break up the outfit and can make you appear shorter.

Contrasting colors can also create emphasis, or a center of attention. For example, a bright contrasting scarf or tie at your neckline draws attention to your face. Contrast can emphasize your best features and draw attention away from other areas.

When choosing colors to wear, consider your personal coloring. Your eyes, hair, and skin have their own combinations of tones. Your wardrobe can include a variety of colors, but you should learn which values and intensities of a color look best on you: a clear green, forest green, mint green, blue-green, or olive green. Some people look best in bright, bold colors. Others find that softer, paler colors are most attractive. Ask a friend to help you analyze what looks best on you.

The Whole Effect

Your appearance is created by the lines, shapes, and spaces found in your clothing, combined with texture and color. When you know how these elements work together, you can choose clothes that are right for you.

Take a look at some of your favorite outfits. What features make them look especially good on you? Could using the same design elements in the same way work for other outfits?

Don't be afraid to try a style or color that you've never worn before. You may discover a look that suits you perfectly.

Study your skin, eyes, and hair coloring to determine which colors look best on you. What colors do you recommend that each of these teens wear?

Enrichment
Have students research color theory and conduct experiments to show how color is a property of sunlight. Prisms, raindrops, and soap bubbles make the color of light visible. To prove that black is the absence of light, display brightly colored objects and gradually eliminate all light sources. Even white objects will appear black if they are not reflecting any light. Other experiments can show how different colors reflect and absorb light and can seem nearer or farther away, or larger or smaller. Some students might report on how people perceive color and why people are susceptible to optical illusions.

Enrichment
Ask students to find information about the classification of hair colors, eye colors, and skin tones. What are some methods of determining which color schemes are most compatible with one's hair color, eye color, and skin tone? Students might work in groups to share information and draw conclusions about their best and worst colors.

Enrichment
Have students go in pairs to clothing stores and each try on one style, one color, and one color scheme that they have never worn before. Students' illustrated reports of their experiments should include their own and their partner's reactions.

Cross-References See Teen Tips, "Create Your Color Palette" on pages 612-613.

Real-Life Situations Some people are color-blind and are not able to tell all colors apart. Some may confuse reds and greens but be able to see a wide range of yellows and blues; others may confuse some reds and greens with some yellows. Only a very few people can see no color at all. People can be easily tested for color blindness by identifying colored shapes buried in a jumble of dots. More than 4 out of every 100 males and 1 out of every 200 females are color-blind.

Teaching the Feature

"Understanding Clothing Traditions"

Answers to Feature Questions

1. Traditional clothing—like special foods and customs—promotes cultural identity and pride.

2. Answers will vary. Students might suggest that the United States is too diverse to be portrayed in one national costume. Others might select a cowboy outfit or some other style of dress from the nation's history as a national costume. Still others might suggest that jeans and a T-shirt would be the traditional U.S. clothing style.

Activities

Research Have students use library resources to find out about traditional clothing styles of a country or an ethnic group. They should try to find out reasons behind a particular way of dressing. Have them report their findings to the class, using drawings or photographs to illustrate the clothing style.

Guest Speaker Invite a member of the community or an exchange student to model his or her traditional dress. For example, you might invite a woman of Indian descent to demonstrate how a sari is worn.

Making Comparisons Divide students into several groups. Give each group a supply of fashion magazines and pattern books. Tell them to look for clothing designs that have been influenced by traditional styles. Students might assemble their findings into a bulletin board display.

Community Contact Encourage students to attend a festival or event at which an ethnic group might wear traditional clothing. Examples might be a Hmong New Year's celebration, a German Oktoberfest, or a St. Patrick's Day parade. Have students describe to the class the clothing they saw.

INTERPERSONAL SKILLS

Understanding Clothing Traditions

Sombrero. Kilt. Sari. Moccasins. What countries or groups of people come to mind when you hear these words? If you answered Mexico or Spain, Scotland, India, and Native American, you would be right. These represent only a few examples of traditional clothing.

Traditional clothing means the style of dress associated with a country or group of people. Such clothing styles have generally developed over hundreds of years. Today, the people in most industrialized countries wear clothes similar to those seen in the United States. Traditional clothing is worn only for special events. In less developed countries, traditional clothing continues to be worn every day.

A great variety of traditional clothing styles exists throughout the world. Different purposes for wearing clothes have led to diversity in clothing styles.

People wear clothes for protection against the sun, wind, cold, and rain. Thus, climate influences clothing styles. In the warm climate of Mexico, a straw sombrero with a wide brim acts as a sunshade. In the cold climate of northern Finland, a wool hat pulled over the ears provides warmth.

Clothes also provide protection for certain types of activities. Brazilian cowboys wear chaparreras, or leather leggings, to keep their legs from getting chafed while riding horseback. Moccasins allowed Native Americans to go quietly through forests without alerting their prey.

People wear clothes as a means of communication. By wearing a certain type of clothing, people identify themselves as belonging to a particular group. The plaid in Scottish kilts, for example, varies from clan to clan. Clothes can also communicate a group's beliefs. The plain dark clothes of Amish people reflect beliefs about personal adornment.

Of course, traditional clothing is not worn only by the people associated with the clothing. Many fashion designers incorporate traditional clothing into their designs.

Think It Through

1. **Why might traditional clothing styles be important to a group of people?**
2. **What do you think a traditional clothing style for the United States would look like?**

More About Traditional Clothing Traditional styles also differ according to the materials and equipment people have available for making clothes. Australians may wear a lot of wool clothing because of the abundance of sheep in their country. People living in villages in India may wear simple clothing because they have only hand-powered equipment available for weaving cloth and they must sew their clothes by hand.

Focus on Relationship Skills Knowing about traditional clothing can help you understand and appreciate people from different cultures. A variety of clothing styles makes a richer, more interesting society.

CHAPTER 56 REVIEW

Reviewing the Facts

1. What are the five elements of clothing design?
2. How do vertical and horizontal lines in clothing affect a person's appearance?
3. How can proportion affect the way you look?
4. Define texture. How does texture in clothing affect a person's appearance?
5. Name the primary and secondary colors.
6. What is the difference between value and intensity? Give examples of each.
7. Give an example of each of the three common color schemes.
8. What aspects of your own appearance should you consider when choosing colors to wear?

Thinking Critically

1. In terms of shape, space, and proportion, how would you describe the "look" of today's clothing? Find drawings or photographs in current fashion magazines to illustrate the elements of design in today's fashions.
2. Suppose your friend Cliff has asked you to go shopping with him and help him pick out some clothes. He is somewhat uncomfortable about his height because he is taller than most people in his class. What kinds of styles and colors would you suggest that he choose? What should he avoid?

Applying Your Skills

1. **Writing a Description.** Find a picture of an outfit in a newspaper or magazine. Write a description of the clothing in terms of the five elements of clothing design.
2. **Comparing and Contrasting Colors.** Colors are affected by different types of light. Examine several colored fabrics under incandescent light, fluorescent light, and natural sunlight. Describe any difference in value and intensity of each color. What similarities do you observe?
3. **Conducting a Survey.** List the colors on the color wheel. Then list 20 adjectives that might be used to describe different colors. Ask five boys and five girls individually to choose which of the adjectives they associate with each color. Write down their responses. Were their answers similar or different? Do you see any trends in their choices?

Answers to "Reviewing the Facts"

1. Line, shape, space, texture, color.
2. Vertical lines make a person look taller and thinner; horizontal lines make a person look shorter and broader.
3. By changing the proportion, you can change the way you look.
4. Texture is the way a fabric looks and feels. Bulky textures make a person look heavier; smoother textures make a person look slimmer.
5. Red, yellow and blue; green, orange, and violet.
6. Value is the lightness or darkness of a color—burgundy (shade); pink (tint). Intensity is the brightness or dullness or a color—hot pink and lemon yellow (bright); navy blue and rust (dull).
7. Monochromatic (variation of one color—dark and light blue. Analogous (closely related)—yellow and orange; blue-green and green. Complementary (opposites)—red and green; purple and yellow.
8. Your height and weight, the color of your eyes and hair, your skin tone.

Answers to "Thinking Critically"

1. Answers will depend on current fashion.
2. Possible styles and colors to choose: horizontal lines; cool, less intense colors; outfits with contrasting colors. Possible styles and colors to avoid: vertical lines; small patterns; warm, intense colors; solid-color outfits.

COMPLETING THE CHAPTER

Summary

- People can make better clothing choices by considering the five design elements of line, shape, space, texture, and color.
- Vertical, horizontal, diagonal, and curved lines create different effects.
- The shape of a garment, the spaces within it, the proportion of the spaces and the texture of fabric affect appearance.
- Colors consist of hues, values, and intensities and include tints and shades of a hue.
- Three common color schemes are monochromatic, analogous, and complementary.

For Review

Objective Review Questions Have students complete the "Reviewing the Facts" section on this page.

Study Guide Have students complete the Study Guide from Chapter 56 of their *Student Workbook.*

Decision Making Have students recommend clothing choices for the hypothetical person described below. Students should explain their choices in terms of the five elements of design and illustrate their plans with drawings or samples.

At below-average height, Brian wouldn't mind appearing a little taller. Brian is very slim but regards his slim hips as one of his best features. He wonders if he could have a more broad-shouldered look.

For Evaluation

Motivator Follow-Up Have students review the "Describe Your Best Outfit" exercise, which they did at the beginning of the chapter. Ask students to reevaluate their descriptions according to what they have learned.

Scrapbooks Have students combine their scrapbook projects, design a cover folder, and submit for evaluation.

Chapter Test Have students complete the test for Chapter 56 that appears in the *Teacher's Classroom Resources.*

CHAPTER OVERVIEW

Chapter 57 explains the role of social and technological change in the creation of fashions. Students learn how the garment industry, the media, designers, and celebrities initiate fashion changes. The chapter explores the historical and functional origins of clothing designs and the impact of consumer demand on clothing markets. The chapter concludes with suggestions for distinguishing classics from fads and for investing wisely in a wardrobe.

INTRODUCING THE CHAPTER

Motivators

What Determines Your Options? Point out that although there is a great variety of clothing styles, only certain styles are available in stores in any given year. Ask: "Who or what determines what the alternatives will be? How do clothing styles begin, change, and end?" Write students' responses on the chalkboard to check against chapter content.

Using the Photograph Ask students to identify the clothing styles shown in the picture. How do they know about theses styles? Students might note that their parents wore these styles and that young people today are interested in the fashions of the 1950s and 1960s. Have students seen anyone wearing similar styles lately? Fashions of the past often resurface as nostalgia fads.

Fashion Tell students the word *fashion* comes from Middle English and Old French words meaning "a making" which comes from the Latin verb for "to make." Synonyms are *style, mode,* and *vogue,* which also refer to prevailing customs of dress. Someone who is fashionable conforms to the current style. *Style* and *mode* can also refer to standards of beauty and elegance. A style that is in vogue is widely accepted for a limited time. A fashion plate is someone who always wears the latest fashions. High fashion refers to the expensive designs worn by the rich and famous.

CHAPTER

57

Clothes and Fashion

OBJECTIVES

This chapter will help you to:

- Explain why fashions change from year to year.
- Identify several ways in which fashions get started.
- Distinguish between a classic fashion and a fad.
- Describe how to display good judgment in building a wardrobe.

WORDS TO REMEMBER

classic
designer
fad
fashion
garment industry

Chapter Resources

Teacher's Classroom Resources
- Lesson Plan
- Life Skills Activity, *Create a Fashion Newsletter*
- Reproducible Master, *Fashion Changes*
- Extension Activity, *Clothing Trademarks of Famous People*
- Chapter Test

Student Workbook
- Study Guide
- Worksheet, *Do You Know Your Fashion Facts?*

A **fashion** is a style of clothing that is accepted in a society at a given time. During any one period, certain lengths, shapes, colors, proportions, and fits are favored above others. The fashion of the day sets broad guidelines that help people decide which clothes they will purchase and wear.

Today, hundreds of millions of dollars are spent on advertising to promote a certain fashion. Nevertheless, you must be careful not to build your wardrobe based on commercials and other types of persuasion. Rather, your clothing purchases should reflect:

- Your tastes.
- Your need to express yourself.
- Your lifestyle.
- Your need for comfort.

What similarities and differences are there between these two outfits? What social changes do they reflect?

What Makes Fashion Change?

Fashion changes quickly. A certain style suddenly becomes popular and everyone seems to be wearing it. Skirt lengths go up or down; pant legs get wider or narrower; jackets are longer or shorter. Today, a new look may not replace a previous fashion, but merely add another alternative from which to choose.

Social Changes

One reason that fashions change is that people change. They have different clothing needs from those of their parents and grandparents.

When your parents, grandparents, and great-grandparents were teens, life was much more formal than it is today. Now the emphasis is on comfort and leisure, and fashion has changed to reflect this fact. Today's clothes have been adapted to the active lives people lead.

More About Social Change World War II greatly affected home-front fashions. Mobilization required the rationing of fabrics, which were needed for soldiers' uniforms and parachutes. In 1942, United States passed a law that made it illegal to manufacture clothing with patch pockets, cuffs, or wide hems.

Focus on Technology Computers allow greater speed and variety in designing fabrics and clothes. Three-dimensional computer-aided design (CAD) programs permit simulations of weaves, textures, colors, and patterns. Computer graphics can show designs modeled "in the round."

Introducing the Objectives

Discuss the chapter objectives on page 514. Remind students that the objectives focus on important chapter content.

Introducing Vocabulary

Review the "Words to Remember." Point out that *classic,* used as a noun, means a work considered to be of the highest rank or excellence and therefore having lasting value. Ask for examples of works that are regarded as classics. *Fad* originally referred to a whim, hobby, or fancy undertaken with great zeal for a short time. Ask for examples of recent clothing fads.

TEACHING THE CHAPTER

For convenience, the teaching suggestions for this chapter are arranged according to the following lesson topics:

- "What Makes Fashion Change," pages 515-516
- "How Do Fashions Start?," pages 516-517
- "Fashions and Fads," pages 517-519

Teaching "What Makes Fashion Change"
(Pages 515-516)

This section teaches the factors that influence changes in fashion, such as changes in style of living and new technology.

Checking Comprehension

✔ How does social change affect clothing styles? *Changes in styles of living create different wants and needs.*

✔ How does technological change affect fashion? *New fibers and manufacturing methods create new possibilities.*

✔ What new technology increases the rate of change? *High-speed communications systems and computers.*

Activities

Skill Builder: Science
Have students research and report on the history of technological changes affecting the textile and garment industries. General topics might include mass production methods and machines (for example, spinning, weaving, knitting, die cutting, bonding, mercerizing) and the application of specific inventions (for example, button, elastic, sewing machine, zipper, cellulose, plastic, aluminum, adhesives, hook-and-loop tape, manufactured fibers, and dyes.)

Reteaching
Ask students for examples of fashion changes reflecting each of the following social changes: Women entered the work force outside the home (for example, business suits for women); more emphasis was given to social equality between men and women (for example, unisex clothes); people had greater mobility and more opportunity for travel (for example, lighter-weight, wrinkle-resistant clothes); greater emphasis was placed on comfort (for example, women's pantsuit, leisure suit for men); people expressed greater interest in health and fitness (for example, jogging suit).

Enrichment
Have students select a period in European or American history and research the fashions of the time. Alternatively, students might research a country's traditional native dress. Students' illustrated written or oral reports should include an analysis of the social and cultural factors affecting clothing styles.

Teaching "How Do Fashions Start?"

(Pages 516-517)

This section teaches the influences on fashion of the garment industry, the media, designers, celebrities, and consumer demand.

Checking Comprehension

✓ What does the garment industry include? *The many companies involved in manufacturing clothing.*

Technical Changes

Some new fashions result from changes in technology. The new fibers and fabrics that can now be produced are easier to care for and more comfortable to wear than the fabrics available to previous generations. For example, knit and stretch fabrics can be used for all types of clothing. Special finishes make fabrics wind-resistant and water-resistant.

Besides creating new fabrics, technologists have changed the way fashions are produced. The development of high-speed communications and computers has enabled clothing manufacturers to see and copy fashions from anywhere in the world. A new fashion can be put into production and shipped to hundreds of stores much more quickly than before.

How Do Fashions Start?

Fashion ideas come from many different sources. Much of current fashion, however, is a reflection of our society and of the things that our society considers important.

The Garment Industry

Clothing fashions are created by the **garment industry**—the many companies involved in manufacturing clothing. A **designer** is a person who creates new styles. Designers get their ideas from many sources—history and current events; books, movies, and television; and styles of other countries. Designers also create new styles of their own based on what they feel will be acceptable to the public.

At one time high fashion—the expensive clothing created by world-famous designers—was made entirely by hand in France, which was then the center of the fashion world. The influence of the Paris fashion market is not as strong today as it used to be. Many other fashion centers, including London, Milan, Tokyo, New York, Los Angeles, and Dallas, produce original clothes.

Designer labels have become popular in recent years, mostly because they are considered to be status symbols. Many people believe that wearing such labels shows that they are in fashion. Famous labels and symbols may mean that clothes are particularly well made or well designed, but this is not always true. They are, however, usually more expensive.

Some designer labels are so popular, in fact, that counterfeit, or imitation, clothing bearing a fake label may be produced. These fashions are often made from cheaper fabrics or with poorer construction methods than are the designer fashions.

Personalities and the Media

Fashion is influenced by famous people. Millions of people notice what movie and television stars, rock singers, politicians, and athletes wear. Some fashions become popular because they're seen on a hit television show or movie.

People and events in the news also affect fashion. Clothing associated with a particular ethnic group may become fashionable if members of the group are featured in the news long enough for their fashions to capture the imagination of the public. Concerts, videos, and television bring fashions to the public instantly. Before you know it, they're available in many stores.

Emphasize The garment industry is very large and complex. It involves more than two million workers, of whom designers and fashion models are only the most visible. The three main tasks of the industry are to make textiles, to make clothing, and to sell clothing to stores.

More About Designers Students might report on the contributions of a well-known fashion designer, such as, Cristobal Balenciaga, Bill Blass, Pierre Cardin, Coco Chanel, Liz Claiborne, Oscar de la Renta, Christian Dior, Perry Ellis, Hubert de Givenchy, Halston, Kenzo, Calvin Klein, Ralph Lauren, Issey Miyake, Mary Quant, and Yves Saint Laurent.

Blue jeans originally were considered work clothes. What other current fashions started as clothing worn for work or sports?

Groups of People

Blue jeans, overalls, and cowboy boots started out as practical work clothes. Then people began to wear these familiar garments in a new way—and they became fashionable.

Fashions like these start when a few people try out a new idea. Soon it seems that everyone is wearing the same thing. Often, no one knows who first created the fashion.

Consumer Demand

When there is a need for a different type of clothing, manufacturers start producing it. The popularity of certain sports activities and the current interest in physical fitness, for example, have created a demand for clothing that is both comfortable and functional.

Some sports, such as bicycling and running, involve speed and require a wide range of body motion. Clothing for these sports has been designed to cut down on wind resistance and increase speed. The clothes are made of stretch fabrics to provide ease of movement and comfort. Bicycle shorts and leotards are examples of fashions that allow the wearer to move freely.

Sweatsuits, T-shirts, jogging outfits, and rugby shirts were designed for active sports, but now have become fashion items. One of the reasons for their popularity with people of all ages is their comfort.

Fashions and Fads

Some fashions are popular for short periods and then suddenly lose their appeal. Other fashions are enduring favorites for several decades, even generations.

Focus on Consumer Skills Remind students of the significance of demand and supply in a market economy. Tell them that they have contributed to consumer demand without even being aware of it. Have students explain what you mean and give examples from personal experience.

Focus on Relationship Skills Have students interview older relatives about past fashions and fads. Students might pool their data to develop a historical profile.

✓ How is high fashion different from fashion? *High fashion is expensive clothing created by world-famous designers. Fashion is a style of clothing that is accepted in society at a given time.*

✓ Who else aside from designers influences fashions? *Famous people, people and events in the news.*

✓ What role does the media and the entertainment industry play in changing fashion? *Television, print media, movies, and live public performances bring fashion statements to the attention of people.*

✓ Explain the effect that consumer demand has on fashion. *When consumers need and want a certain type of clothing, manufacturers start producing it. For example, the physical fitness movement has caused a need for comfortable, functional exercise gear.*

Activities

Skill Builder: Writing
Write the following topic sentence on the board: "Fashion ideas come from many different sources." Then list the following words: *designers, history, status symbols, celebrities, media.* Ask students to write a three-paragraph essay beginning with the topic sentence and using all the words in appropriate contexts.

Reteaching
Ask students to describe a clothing choice they made that may have been influenced by an athlete's endorsement; high-fashion advertising; a designer label; an admired public figure or performer; a movie or television program; ethnic, racial, national or regional pride.

Enrichment
Assign each student one of the following celebrities to research. Have students write essays describing clothing styles associated with the celebrity: George "Beau" Brummel, Amelia Bloomer, Jean Harlow, Elvis Presley, James Dean, Jacqueline Kennedy, the Beatles, the Beach Boys, Cyndi Lauper, Michael Jackson, Florence Griffith-Joyner.

Teaching the Feature
"Extremes in Fashion"

Answers to Feature Questions

1. People today have access to various media sources—magazines, television, and newspapers—that may expose health hazards. Government agencies might require standards for some fashions.

2. Some students might say yes and mention people who wear only natural fibers or certain styles. Most students, however, will probably say no, stating that people think more about the way clothes look, whether or not they are in fashion, or how much they cost.

Activities

Understanding Sources of Danger Have students give examples of aspects of clothing that relate to health and safety. How can clothing contribute to accidents? How can clothing make you ill? Students might note that loose clothing can become caught in machinery (for example, pant legs in bicycle spokes) or can accidentally ignite (for example, sleeves on a range-top burner). Long clothing and unreliable footwear can cause falls. Some clothing materials are highly flammable or melt easily (for example, in the dryer). Animal fibers and fabrics treated with chemicals can cause allergic reactions. Overly tight clothes can cause infertility in men, in addition to the conditions described in the feature. Airtight, moisture-retaining fabrics increase the risk of bacterial and fungal infections, including yeast infections.

Community Contact Have a group of students write or phone the Consumer Product Safety Commission in Washington, D.C. (1-800-638-2772). Students should ask to receive information about the commission's agenda and the laws that have been passed to protect people from unsafe or unhealthy clothing and fabrics. Ask the class to review and discuss this information.

HEALTH WATCH

Extremes in Fashion

If the Surgeon General had been around throughout history, there might have been labels on certain clothing that said: "SURGEON GENERAL'S WARNING: The wearing of this fashion may be hazardous to your health."

You can blame the button for the development of some extreme fashions. The introduction of buttons in the thirteenth century made it possible to cut garments to fit the shape of the body. By the fourteenth century, men and women were tightly lacing and binding their bodies with stiff undergarments called corsets so that they could fit into the fashionable clothes of the time.

The dangers of the corset were many. It caused deformities of the spine, respiratory and digestive problems, and pregnancy complications. In the late 1800s doctors encouraged abolishing the corset.

In the 1920s the ideal fashion figure was a thin, boyish body. Women tightly bandaged their chests to get a stylish straight-up-and-down look. Even though most women no longer wore corsets, starvation diets became a fad. Later, very high "spike" heels for women increased the potential for ankle injuries. In addition, wearing such heels required posture adjustments that often led to back strain.

Although today's fashion trend is toward a natural look, ultra-slim fashion models and body-conscious fashions still promote fashion-related health hazards, such as fad diets.

When you choose fashions, try to think about your health as well as what is in style. Fashions will come and go, but a healthy body is an asset for your whole life.

Think It Through

1. **Why might it be easier for people today to recognize dangerous fashion trends than it was for people in previous centuries?**
2. **Do you think their own health is a consideration for most people when they choose clothes? Explain.**

Did You Know? Small waistlines have been a desirable trait since the Cretan civilization existed around 2000 B.C. The people's waists were kept to a maximum of 12 in. by soldering belts on male and female children at the age of six.

Emphasize Use common sense when evaluating new fashion trends for safety. No fashion is worth risking your health or your safety.

Classics vs. Fads

Some styles are **classics**—they stay popular for a long time. Classics were probably worn by your parents or grandparents. They may be part of your wardrobe, too. Examples of styles that have been around for years are blazers, pullover sweaters, pleated skirts, and polo shirts.

Other fashions may gain popularity quickly, but then lose their appeal. Fashions that are very popular for a short-time are called **fads.** Hi-top sneakers with colorful laces and oversized sweaters are clothing fads that have been popular with teens in the recent past.

Other styles seem to go through fashion cycles—periods when they are in and out of fashion. Short skirts, for example, were popular in the 1920s, then again in the 1960s. They came back in style in the 1980s.

Building Judgment

It takes experience to be able to tell which styles will stay popular for a while and which will disappear quickly. One way to learn about fashion trends is to talk to one of your parents, an older friend, or even an experienced clothing salesperson. Writers in fashion magazines also give their opinions about trends. Usually styles that are simpler and less innovative are likely to last longer: a basic skirt, a solid-color blazer, or a classic shirt with a conservative collar and cuffs.

Consumer Strategy

Most wardrobes contain both fashions and fads. Fad items carefully chosen can add sparkle to your wardrobe. Although some fad items are not expensive, others cost a lot of money. In that case, a fad may be a very poor buy.

You can compromise by selecting classic styles when you make an expensive clothing purchase, and by looking for bargains when you buy fad items. T-shirts are examples of inexpensive fad clothes that can keep your wardrobe up-to-date at little cost. You can also follow fads when buying accessories, the smaller items that are not part of your basic outfits. Belts, scarves, and jewelry can perk up your clothes for a reasonable amount of money. You can look fashionable without spending more than you can afford.

Some clothing styles are classics that never go totally out of fashion. Others are fads that may be popular for only a short time.

Emphasize Ask students to suggest reasons for fashion cycles, such as the reappearance in the 1980s of the padded shoulders of the 1940s. Show students examples of the following clothing features: bustles, wing collars, crinolines, pedal pushers. Ask students if they think the style will become fashionable again, and why or why not.

Did You Know? The women's pantsuit was introduced in 1966 but was not at first accepted in all contexts. Women in pantsuits were not allowed in some restaurants.

Teaching "Fashions and Fads"
(Pages 517-519)

This section teaches the difference between classics and fads, discusses cyclical styles, and concludes with strategies for consumers.

Checking Comprehension

✓ Which is an example of a fad, pleated skirts or oversized sweaters? *Oversized sweaters.*

✓ What are fashion cycles? *Periods when a style is in or out of fashion.*

✓ How can you learn which clothes are fashion trends? *You can learn by talking to parents, older friends, or an experienced clothing salesperson. Also, fashion magazines often have articles about popular trends.*

Activities

Skill Builder: Critical Thinking
Discuss with the students the distinction between fads (for example, dog-leash belts, tie-dyed shirts, platform shoes) and design features that come and go (for example, tie and lapel widths, waistline and hemline heights). Ask students to predict which current styles they think will turn out to be fads and why. Then have students propose theories explaining why fads appeal to only a few and last for only a short time.

Reteaching
Have students evaluate their wardrobes to estimate the percentage of clothes that are fashionable, faddish, classic, and out of fashion. Students should be able to give at least one example of clothing or accessories they have that fit each category. What kinds of clothes do students hope to add to their wardrobes in the near future, and why?

Enrichment
Have students read reviews in fashion magazines and forecasts of fashion trends. What new and classic designs will be available as ready-made clothes next year? Ask students to describe two or three high-fashion designs they think they would like to wear.

COMPLETING THE CHAPTER

Summary

- Although influenced by fashion, clothing choices depend on personal taste, the need for personal expression, individual lifestyle, and individual needs for comfort.
- Fashions change as a result of social and technological changes.
- Fashions are created by designers in the garment industry.
- Fashion designs are influenced by famous people through mass entertainment and mass media.
- New fashions develop when practical clothes are adapted for nonwork use.
- Fashion designs are influenced by consumer demand.
- Some fashion designs are classics or fads; others cyclically reappear.

For Review

Objective Review Questions Have students complete the "Reviewing the Facts" section on this page.

Study Guide Have students complete the Study Guide from Chapter 57 of their *Student Workbook.*

Application Have students plan and create a fashion collage, visually presenting chapter content. Picture ideas might include historical and international costumes, garment industry workers, world-famous designers, high-fashion models, designer labels, record album covers of fashionable stars, public figures who influenced fashion, practical clothes that became fashionable, family photos showing changing hemlines and styles, classic designs, fads, price tags, and so on.

For Evaluation

Motivator Follow-Up Have students revise their explanations of how clothing styles begin, change, and end, based on what they have learned.

Chapter Test Have students complete the test for Chapter 57 that appears in the *Teacher's Classroom Resources.*

CHAPTER 57 REVIEW

Answers to "Reviewing the Facts"

1. A style of clothing that is accepted in a society in a given time. Social changes and technological changes.
2. Any one: new fibers and fabrics are easier to care for and more comfortable; special finishes make clothing more useful; technology brings new fashions to the public faster.
3. History and current events; books; movies; television; styles of other countries; own imagination.
4. Their clothing is seen by millions of people on television, in videos and movies, and at concerts.
5. Any three: blazers; pullover sweaters; pleated shirts; polo shirts.
6. Classics stay popular for a long time; fads are popular for only a short time.
7. You can choose classics for more expensive items and fad items as accessories.

Reviewing the Facts

1. Define the term *fashion.* List two reasons why fashions change.
2. Name one way that advances in technology affect fashion.
3. Where do designers' fashion ideas come from?
4. How do famous people influence fashion?
5. What are three examples of clothing classics?
6. What is the difference between a classic and a fad?
7. How can you mix fashion and fad items effectively in your wardrobe?

Thinking Critically

1. Name a popular television star, movie star, or rock star who started a fashion trend. What is the fashion? When people wear this fashion what are they saying about the person who started the fashion? What are they saying about themselves?
2. Particular fashions tend to project special images. Choose a fashion popular with teens in recent years. Why do you think it was popular? What image does the fashion project?

Applying Your Skills

1. **Judging Historical Information.** Look through a book on the history of fashion and choose two illustrations. Describe each fashion to the class and tell about the time in which each fashion was popular. Could these designs be popular today? How could they be modified for today's lifestyles.

2. **Writing an Evaluation.** Read an article in a newspaper or magazine about current fashions. In your opinion, which of these fashions will be short-lived fads and which could become classics? Explain the reasons for your choice.

3. **Comparing Prices.** Look through newspapers, magazines, or catalogues for clothing with designer labels. Record the prices of three items. Then find three similarly styled garments or accessories that do not have designer labels. What is the difference in prices? How much would you save by buying the lower-priced item?

Answers to "Thinking Critically"

1. The answer will depend on who is popular at the time. People wear this fashion because they admire the star or his or her style. People copy the fashion of the star because they want to be identified with the person, group, talent, or lifestyle.
2. The answer will depend on recent fashions. Images might include fitness, wealth, interest in the outdoors, elegance, and so on.

CHAPTER

58

Fibers and Fabrics

OBJECTIVES

This chapter will help you to:

- Summarize the characteristics of various natural and manufactured fibers.
- Identify woven, knitted, and nonwoven fabrics.
- Describe how color applications and finishes affect clothing care.

WORDS TO REMEMBER

blend
dyeing
fabric
fiber
finish
manufactured fiber
natural fiber
yarn

Chapter Resources

Teacher's Classroom Resources
Lesson Plan
Life Skills Activity, *Know Your Fabrics*
Reproducible Master, *Fabric Construction*
Extension Activity, *Fiber Characteristics*
Chapter Test

Student Workbook
Study Guide
Worksheet, *Familiar Fabrics and Fibers*

CHAPTER OVERVIEW

Chapter 58 introduces students to the characteristics of fibers, yarns, and fabrics. Students learn about natural and manufactured fibers, yarns, and blends. The chapter explains weaving, knitting, and bonding as three methods of fabric construction. Information about dyes, printed designs, and finishes is included. The chapter concludes with suggestions for using care labels.

INTRODUCING THE CHAPTER

Motivators

Did You Ever? Have students share experiences of clothing frustrations, disappointments, and disasters. Most students will have experience with shrunken, scratchy, knobby, faded, snagged, unraveled, color-bled, stretched-out, wrinkled, shiny, frayed, or stained clothes. Tell students this chapter will help them avoid these problems in the future.

Using the Photograph Refer students to the photograph on this page. Then ask: "What is the woman in the photograph doing?"

Fibers Tell students that, according to archaeologists, the earliest use of fibers for making cloth (for which there is evidence) was made by farmers of about 10,000 years ago. The oldest surviving fabrics are fishnets and linen cloth woven from plant fibers.

Introducing the Objectives

Discuss the chapter objectives on this page. Remind students that the objectives focus on important chapter content.

Introducing Vocabulary

Organize the "Words to Remember" into an outline or chart showing the order of fabric construction. Subsume *natural fiber* and *manufactured fiber* under *fiber*, followed by *yarn*, *fabric*, and *finish*. Have students use reference materials to define the following words, which also appear in the chapter: *knit*, *bond*, *weave*, *loom*, *warp*, *pile*, *fusible*, *preshrunk*, and *napping*.

TEACHING THE CHAPTER

For convenience, the teaching suggestions for this chapter are arranged according to the following lesson topics:

- "Fibers," pages 522-523
- "Yarns," page 524
- "Fabric Construction," pages 524-525
- "Colors and Finishes," and "Care Labels," page 525

Teaching "Fibers"
(Pages 522-523)

This section teaches the differences between natural and manufactured fibers.

Checking Comprehension

✓ Give three examples of sources of natural fiber. *Any three: the seed pod of the cotton plant; the stalk of the flax plant; the hair of sheep, camels, goats, and rabbits; the silkworm's cocoon; the stems of china grass.*

✓ What is a manufactured fiber, and what are its advantages? *A manufactured fiber is a fiber formed all or in part by chemicals. One advantage is that those fibers make fabrics easy to care for.*

Activities

Skill Builder: Science
Have students examine natural and manufactured fibers under a microscope and draw or describe what they see. Specimens might include raw cotton, flax, sheep wool, raw silk, acetate, or other wood-pulp-based fiber, and nylon, polyester, or other petroleum-based fiber. Unlike natural fibers, manufactured fibers tend to appear uniformly even and smooth. Have students examine a strand of their own hair. Which fiber does it most closely resemble? *(the animal-protein fiber—wool)*

Steve bought a warm-up suit that looked great in the store, but he got very little use out of it because it was not comfortable to wear. Kim spent a week sewing a pair of shorts in just the color she wanted, only to give them to her younger sister a few weeks later because they shrank when she washed them. What could have prevented these mistakes?

There are more things to know about clothing than how it looks on a hanger or even how it looks on you. One of the most important considerations is the fabric. Knowing about fabrics can help you:

- Be a smarter shopper.
- Look and feel better in your clothing.
- Get more satisfaction from the things you make.
- Care for garments correctly so they look better and last longer.

The natural fibers come from plants and animals.

Fibers

Fibers are the basic components of all fabrics. They are the tiny strands that, when twisted together, make up yarns. Fibers are made into yarns, yarns into fabrics, and fabrics into clothing. There are two kinds of fibers: natural and manufactured.

Natural Fibers

Natural fibers come from plants or animals.

- Cotton is the most common plant fiber. It comes from the seed pod of the cotton plant.
- Linen is another common plant fiber that comes from the stalk of the flax plant.
- Wool is from the fleece of sheep. Camels, alpacas, goats, and rabbits also provide hair that is used for speciality wool.
- Silk is made by an insect—the silkworm. The fibers come from a cocoon that the silk worm spins around itself.
- Ramie comes from the stems of china grass.

Did You Know? Mohair and cashmere are natural fibers made from the hair of Angora goats and Kashmir goats.

Emphasize All fibers have advantages and disadvantages, and all fibers have uses for which they are best suited.

Each natural fiber has its own special characteristics, but they all absorb moisture and allow air to reach your skin. They are comfortable to wear, keeping you warm in winter and cool in summer. Natural fibers usually require more care than manufactured fibers.

Manufactured Fibers

Until the end of the last century, all fabrics were made of natural fibers, but today many fabrics are made of **manufactured fibers.** These are fibers formed all or in part by chemicals.

Characteristics of Natural Fibers

Fiber	Characteristics
Cotton	soft, comfortable, absorbent strong even when wet takes finishes well wrinkles & shrinks unless treated easily laundered
Wool	warm, retains body heat resists wrinkles naturally water repellent can shrink with heat and moisture can be damaged by moths usually drycleaned; sometimes washable
Silk	natural luster soft, flexible, but strong can be damaged by perspiration usually drycleaned; sometimes washable
Linen	comfortable, absorbent strong, but stiff wrinkles & shrinks unless treated easily laundered
Ramie	very strong, stiff natural luster absorbs moisture often combined with other fibers washable

Many manufactured fibers were made to replace or copy natural fibers. For instance, nylon was made to look like silk and acrylic is a substitute for wool in sweaters and blankets. One advantage of manufactured fibers is that they are easy to care for.

Characteristics of Manufactured Fibers

Fiber*	Characteristics
Acetate Celanese Chromspun	attractive silk-like look soft, drapeable may wrinkle and fade, heat sensitive, usually drycleaned
Acrylic Acrilan Creslan	soft, lightweight yet warm blends with other fibers for added bulk resists wrinkles does not cause allergy heat sensitive drycleaned or laundered
Nylon Antron Cantrece	very strong, holds shape well doesn't absorb moisture heat sensitive washable, dries quickly
Polyester Dacron Fortrel Kodel Trevira	resists wrinkles blends with other fibers for wrinkle resistance holds oily stains washable, dries quickly needs little or no ironing
Rayon Avril Fibro	absorbs moisture soft and comfortable may wrinkle or shrink unless treated usually drycleaned, sometimes washable
Spandex Lycra	excellent stretch and recovery combines with other fibers for stretchability washable, avoid chlorine bleach

*Listings under each fiber type are trademark names.

Did You Know? Metallic yarns are made of aluminum foil that is bonded to or coated with clear plastic.

Focus on Technology Machines for spinning fibers are capable of producing a great variety of yarns with different sizes, shapes, weights, and textures. Variety depends on the number and types of fibers and the degree of twist or spin.

Reteaching
Have students suggest two or three fibers that would be most suitable for each of the following uses: sportswear, party dress, bathing suit, winter coat, knapsack, sleepwear. In each case, ask students to explain the reasons for their choices.

Enrichment
Have students work as a group to develop a chart of "Fiber Superlatives," like a "Senior Superlatives" page in a high school yearbook. Which natural and manufactured fibers would students nominate "Softest," "Most Hypoallergenic," "Stretchiest," "Most Wrinkle Resistant," and so on?

Teaching "Yarns"
(Page 524)

This section teaches how fibers are combined to form yarns and blends.

Checking Comprehension

✓ What is the name for yarn made of two or more kinds of fibers? *A blend.*

✓ If you wanted a shirt that did not require ironing, which blend would you choose: 70 percent polyester and 30 percent cotton, or 60 percent cotton and 40 percent polyester? *Seventy percent polyester and 30 percent cotton.*

Activities

Skill Builder: Critical Thinking
If a polyester-and-cotton blend is easier to take care of than 100 percent cotton, why do you think many people choose 100 percent cotton shirts? For what kinds of occasions do you think a blend would be more appropriate? For what occasions would 100 percent cotton be advisable?

Reteaching
Using spun yarns of different fibers, give each student a short length of yarn. Each student separates or untwists the yarn into its constituent fibers and then gives one or two fibers to another classmate. Students combine or retwist the fibers to make a yarn blend.

Reteaching
Have each student develop a list of personal clothing needs, based on activities and seasonal requirements. Students should rate each needed item with a plus sign (+), indicating that their wardrobes meet the need, or with a minus sign (–), indicating that additions to their wardrobes are needed. For each minus sign, students should describe the specific reasons an addition is needed. Students should then assess the reasons and star (*) opportunities for choosing additions that will meet more than one need.

Reteaching
Have students complete their long-term wardrobe plans. Ask students to suggest advantages and disadvantages to buying, sewing, redesigning, and trading clothes.

to shop. To determine whether a specific item is important to your wardrobe, answer these questions:

- What do you really need?
- Will you be able to wear the new item for different occasions?
- Will you be able to wear the new item with other clothes in your current wardrobe?
- Can you make your wardrobe more versatile by adding accessories?

If you are going to be matching a new piece of clothing to an old one to make an outfit, you should decide which colors and fabrics will go with the item you already have.

Although you can combine colors any way you like, be aware that some combinations look better than others. For example, you probably would not want to wear a black top with navy. That combination isn't interesting because it lacks contrast. Why not add excitement by choosing a bright color instead, such as red or yellow?

Fabric and texture combinations need to be planned, too. Some textures do not work together as well as others. You may want to try to match a fabric you already have or find one that is compatible with it. Two good combinations are corduroy with tweeds and velvet with satin.

When you shop for the new addition, try to take along the article of clothing that you plan to wear with it to make sure that your new clothes will go well with what you already have. Also, think again what you like about your current wardrobe. When you are sure of the colors, textures, and styles that you prefer, you will choose additions that will please you.

A wardrobe plan can help you make decisions about what new clothes and accessories to add to your wardrobe.

Emphasize Adding to your wardrobe should be the *last* step. Some planned additions will prove unnecessary after you have experimented with what you have.

Focus on Relationship Skills Invite students to bring an unwanted article of clothing to class to negotiate a trade. What factors must be considered in ensuring a satisfactory trade? What are the steps in the negotiating process?

Trading clothes with a relative or friend is one way to add new items to your wardrobe.

Making the Additions

You can add to your wardrobe in four ways: buying, sewing, redesigning, and trading.

- **Buying additions.** You can buy ready-to-wear clothes from stores and catalogs. By buying ready-to-wear clothes you are able to build your wardrobe with little work. Chapter 60 has information on how to shop for clothing.
- **Sewing additions.** You can choose to make your clothes. Being able to sew gives you a chance to make a garment that's exactly what you want. When you gain experience, you might even design your own clothes.

  Sewing has another benefit, too. It allows you to make minor changes in ready-to-wear clothing. You can also take advantage of bargains by fixing used or discounted clothes. Chapters 64 and 65 introduce you to basic sewing skills.
- **Redesigning.** You can put the clothes that you no longer wear to use. Go back to your wardrobe list and look at those items you have outgrown or don't like. Could you lengthen or shorten something to make it wearable again? Would a change of style make a sweater more appealing? Chapter 67 has more ideas on how to turn old clothes into new.
- **Trading.** You may have something that you don't wear because you don't like the color, or it doesn't go with anything else in your wardrobe, or it just isn't comfortable. Could you trade it for something that you need with a friend or a family member?

Enrichment
Ask students to sketch and describe two articles of clothing (one top and one bottom) with which they would like to find clothes to combine. Have students prepare samples of colors, fabrics, textures, and styles that would go well with each article. What might go well with *both* articles?

Enrichment
Ask students what they will do with the clothes they don't wear. What are all the alternatives? Clothes might be discarded or given to a family member or a friend. Serviceable clothes might be donated to charitable organizations, church fairs, community fund-raisers, or relief centers for victims of floods, earthquakes, or famines. Unusable clothes might be sent to recycling facilities, cut up for household use, or saved for sewing projects. Clothes in excellent condition can be sold in yard sales, flea markets, or consignment stores.

Focus on Entrepreneurship Some students might be interested in establishing a schoolwide clothing exchange.

Cross-Reference See Teen Tips "T-Shirt—Make It Unique" on pages 614-615.

Teaching the Feature
"Buying Coordinated Pieces"

Answers to Feature Questions

1. Answers will vary. Some students might say a sweater and jacket that would coordinate with pants or skirts. Others might say pants and a shirt in a particular color that would coordinate with other clothes in their wardrobe.

2. Some students will say yes because they like what they have and feel they have enough. Others might say no because they don't have enough items or potential combinations of items. Students might suggest adding particular items to round out their wardrobe.

Activities

Scrapbooks Have students make scrapbooks of magazine clippings. They should make at least one page for each of the "Points to Remember When You Go Shopping." Have them label the bottom of each page and, in a sentence or two, explain how the clippings illustrate one of the points.

Knowledge Is a Resource Have students reassess their wardrobe plans in terms of the information in the first four chapters of Unit 6. Have they applied their new knowledge about themselves, about design and color, about fashion, and about fabrics?

Community Contact Make arrangements to have a professional wardrobe consultant or fashion coordinator come to speak to the class about wardrobe planning. Ask students to have their wardrobe plans with them so that the speaker can comment on them.

MANAGING RESOURCES

Buying Coordinated Pieces

Building a wardrobe is easier when you plan it around **coordinated pieces**—garments that can be worn together in several different ways. You will have a maximum number of outfits for a minimum amount of money.

Classic items are basic to a coordinated wardrobe. To think that classics are boring is a mistake. Classics can be selected in fabrics and colors that are suited to your personal style. Buy the best quality in fabric and workmanship that you can afford. Then, buy or sew some trendy pieces or accessories that add spice to the classics.

Here are some points to remember when you go shopping:

- Can the jacket be worn with two pairs of pants? You get more wear out of a jacket when you have two or more bottoms to wear with it.
- Shirts and blouses with a finished bottom edge can be worn out and belted or worn as lightweight jackets.
- Cotton knit T-shirts are classics; mix with jeans, pants, and skirts. Sweaters can be worn in different seasons and change the mood of an outfit.
- Patterns can be mixed together. However, the decision to mix should be evaluated by current fashion. To coordinate prints, plaids, and stripes, use different patterns that contain the same or related colors or use the same patterns in different colors. Small patterns are easiest to mix.

How many combinations can you get from these items?

Think It Through

1. **If you could add two items to your wardrobe, what would they be? With what would they coordinate?**
2. **Do you think you have a good wardrobe? Why or why not? If not, what could you do to improve it?**

Did You Know? For people who don't feel comfortable coordinating items in their wardrobe, there are now unisex sportswear lines designed to take the guesswork out of mixing and matching. Every piece is designed to work with all the others.

Emphasize Color and pattern are the biggest factors affecting whether items can be coordinated. When in doubt, buy solids in black or white—they go with almost any colors or patterns.

CHAPTER

59 REVIEW

Reviewing the Facts

1. What is a wardrobe inventory?
2. Why should you look carefully at the clothes in your wardrobe that need to be repaired?
3. What is the advantage of mixing and matching different clothing items?
4. Before adding an item to your wardrobe, what four questions should you ask yourself?
5. Name two ways to add to your wardrobe without buying new clothes.
6. Give two advantages of sewing your clothes.

Thinking Critically

1. What do you think is the most versatile item in a typical teen's wardrobe? Why?
2. How could you make the clothes you are wearing right now more versatile?

Applying Your Skills

1. Judging Versatility. You have been invited to your cousin's wedding and plan to purchase an outfit for this special occasion. Study catalogs or store circulars and choose an appropriate outfit. From the illustration and description, how versatile would it be for other occasions? How could accessories be used to increase its versatility?

2. Writing Descriptions. Choose your favorite season of the year. Using what you have learned in Chapters 55–59, plan a wardrobe that you could wear during this season. Describe each garment in terms of type and color (for example, red shirt) rather than specific brands or styles.

3. Making a Budget. Using a wardrobe plan, determine which items of clothing you will need to purchase during the next six months. List an approximate price for each item. What is the total of the estimated costs? How could you distribute these costs evenly over the six-month period? If necessary, how could you reduce some of these costs?

Answers to "Reviewing the Facts"

1. A detailed list of the clothes you own.
2. They might need only simple repairs or cleaning before they are wearable again.
3. To stretch your wardrobe by creating new combinations and outfits.
4. What do I really need? Will I be able to wear the item for different occasions? Will it go with my other clothes? Can accessories make my wardrobe more versatile?
5. Any two: sewing; redesigning; trading.
6. Any two: you can make something exactly the way you want it; you can make minor changes in ready-to-wear clothing; you can take advantage of resale clothing or discounted items by fixing them.

COMPLETING THE CHAPTER

Summary

- Planning your wardrobe helps you get the most out of your clothing choices.
- A wardrobe inventory helps you determine your clothing needs.
- Combining clothes and accessories in new ways can stretch your wardrobe.
- Wardrobe additions should be based on need and versatility.
- In adding to your wardrobe, you must decide whether to buy, sew, redesign, or trade clothes.

For Review

Objective Review Questions Have students complete the "Reviewing the Facts" section on this page.

Study Guide Have students complete the Study Guide from Chapter 59 of their *Student Workbook.*

Motivator Follow-Up Have students revise their responses to the question "How do you build your wardrobe?" in light of what they have learned from this chapter.

Class Discussion Ask students how clothing designers, manufacturers, and retailers help them to build versatile wardrobes. Many clothing lines are designed, made, and sold as "separates" or "coordinates." Retail stores suggest combinations by the way clothing is displayed on racks and on mannequins.

For Evaluation

Wardrobe Plans Have students submit their plans for evaluation. Have they followed the steps outlined in the chapter?

Chapter Test Have students complete the test for Chapter 59 that appears in the *Teacher's Classroom Resources.*

Answers to "Thinking Critically"

1. The most versatile items might be a shirt, a sweater, or a pair of jeans that can be worn with many other garments or dressed up with various accessories. Answers should include specific explanations of the garment's versatility.
2. Students might suggest ways to mix-and-match items with other garments, or new ways of accessorizing the outfit.

CHAPTER OVERVIEW

Chapter 60 prepares students for making good decisions in clothing purchases. Students learn where and when to shop, how to determine their sizes, how to evaluate clothing quality, and how to maximize value for their money. Students are encouraged to check the fit, comfort, fabric, construction, and cost of clothing choices. The chapter includes instructions for estimating cost per wearing and a checklist for buying clothes.

INTRODUCING THE CHAPTER

Motivators

Questionnaire Have students answer the following questions in writing: Where do you prefer to shop for clothes? When do you usually go clothes shopping? What size clothes do you wear? How do you determine the quality of clothing items? How do you determine their value? What was the best clothing bargain you ever bought? Save answers to questionnaires for students to revise after completing the chapter.

Using the Photograph Refer students to the photograph on this page. Then ask: "What do the tags tell you? What other information can you learn by examining a garment?"

Discussion Ask students to describe articles of clothing they bought but rarely wear. What might they have done to be better shoppers? Students' responses should anticipate some of the suggestions they will read in this chapter.

Introducing the Objectives

Discuss the chapter objectives on this page. Remind students that the objectives focus on important chapter content.

Introducing Vocabulary

Introduce the concept of *cost per wearing,* which will be new to most students. The value of this estimate can be compared with the value of estimating the cost per meal for a food budget or the cost per mile of owning, maintaining, and operating a car.

CHAPTER

60

Shopping for Clothes

OBJECTIVES

This chapter will help you to:

- Explain how to prepare to shop for clothes.
- Identify the places where you can buy clothing.
- Discuss how to determine your size.
- Describe how to evaluate clothes for fit and quality.

WORDS TO REMEMBER

cost per wearing
end-of-season sale
facing
hem
inseam measurement
seam
size range
trimmings

Chapter Resources

Teacher's Classroom Resources
- Lesson Plan
- Life Skills Activity, *Comparison Shopping*
- Reproducible Master, *Check Your Choice*
- Extension Activity, *Sources of Clothing*
- Chapter Test

Student Workbook
- Study Guide
- Worksheet, *Garment Checklist*

Have you ever bought a skirt that you felt you "couldn't live without," only to have it pushed to the back of your closet in a short time? Have you ever bought a sweater at one store—only to see it three days later at another store for less money? Have you ever bought a pair of slacks in "your size" that just didn't fit? What about the brand new shirt that came apart at the seam and frayed when it was washed?

We can all answer "yes" to at least some of these questions. Buying wearable clothes takes skill. You should know:

- What you want.
- Where to buy.
- How to find your size.
- How clothes are made.

The more you know about clothes, the more success you'll have in shopping and finding the right garment for you.

Getting Ready to Shop

The first step is to write down exactly what you have decided to buy. Next to each item, write what you plan to wear it with and possible colors and fabrics. This information is part of a wardrobe plan. You might wear or bring along the clothes you're trying to match when you go shopping. If you want to match a color or fabric and cannot bring the whole garment along, take samples such as the belt or a tiny piece of fabric cut from the inside. If you plan to wear a specific pair of shoes with your new purchase, bring them along when you try on the new clothing.

There are still two decisions to be made before you begin shopping: you must decide where to shop, and you must decide how much you can afford to spend. Then you will know how much money to take with you.

Where to Shop

Where you buy your clothes will determine the selection you'll find, the prices you'll pay, and the quality you can expect. Convenience and atmosphere are also factors to consider when deciding where to shop.

- **Department stores.** These stores are divided into sections that offer many clothing styles and sizes for men, women, and children. They also sell accessories. Most offer extra services, such as credit cards, gift wrapping, and free delivery. Department stores may have slightly higher prices than some other stores, but they almost always have certain items on sale.

Stores differ in type of merchandise, prices, and services offered. This specialty store carries one particular brand of clothing.

Focus on Consumer Skills Discuss shopping malls, which often house department stores, specialty shops, discount stores, and factory outlets under one roof. Have students visit a shopping mall, and discuss the advantages and disadvantages of the mall as a place to shop for clothes.

Focus on Technology Have students read "Remote Control Shopping" on page 283. If possible, have students view shopping programs on network television or shoppers' networks on cable television or home computers. How does the system work? How is it different from mail-order merchandising? What are some advantages and disadvantages of shopping electronically for clothes?

TEACHING THE CHAPTER

For convenience, the teaching suggestions for this chapter are arranged according to the following lesson topics:

- "Getting Ready to Shop," pages 537-539
- "Know Your Size," pages 539-540
- "Evaluating Your Choice," pages 540-542

Teaching "Getting Ready to Shop"
(Pages 537-539)

This section describes the different types of stores and places to buy clothing. It also discusses the best times to shop.

Checking Comprehension

✓ What two decisions must be made after writing down what you have decided to buy? *You must decide where to shop and how much money you can spend.*

✓ What factors should you consider when deciding where to shop? *You should consider the type of selection you want, the prices, the quality of the merchandise, the convenience, and the atmosphere.*

✓ What are some advantages and disadvantages of shopping in specialty stores? *They have good selections of one type of clothing; extra services are available, but prices tend to be higher.*

✓ What is a factory outlet? *A store run by a clothing factory or manufacturer.*

✓ Name three factors you must consider when ordering clothes from catalogs. *Ordering the correct size, waiting for delivery, paying shipping costs.*

✓ What is a consignment shop? *A store in which your used clothing can be resold; you receive a percentage of the sale price.*

✔ What are some advantages and disadvantages of buying clothes at garage sales or rummage sales? *Clothes might be very inexpensive but must be examined carefully and cannot be returned.*

✔ What should you know about sales to get the most from them? *Don't buy an item on sale if you have no use for it; don't buy regularly priced items just because you are in a store with a sale; the time of year affects prices and selection; make yourself aware of a store's sale schedule so you can plan major purchases.*

Activities

Skill Builder: Math
Rosa had $30.00 for clothes. She went to a discount store advertising 40 percent off the ticket price on blazers. She found just what she wanted in a white blazer marked $29.95. How much did Rosa pay for the blazer? *($17.97)* How much money did she have to put toward another purchase? *($12.03)* Rosa next visited a consignment shop, which used different-colored tags to indicate markdowns, based on how long an article had remained in the store. White tags were full price; yellow tags were 20 percent off; and blue tags were 40 percent off. In this way, the shop owner hoped to sell older items to make room for new consignments. Rosa looked at skirts and found two she liked that would go with her new blazer. One was $9.00 and had a white tag, and the other was $15.00 and had a blue tag. Which skirt should Rosa buy? (Either; both cost $9.00) How much of her clothing budget did she have left? *($3.03)*

Skill Builder: Writing
Have students write two or three paragraphs about a store in which they shop for clothing. Ask them to explain what type of store it is, what type of services the store offers, and what they like or dislike about shopping there. Then have them suggest ways the store could be improved to suit their needs better.

- **Specialty stores.** These stores sell only one type of clothing, such as sportswear, shoes, children's apparel, or a particular brand of clothing. A specialty store may carry labels that most department stores do not stock. Prices may be higher than at a department store, but many specialty stores offer extra personal services and handle special orders.
- **Discount stores.** These stores sell clothing and other items at lower prices than department stores. Discount stores do not always carry the same merchandise as department stores. Don't expect to find the *same* item for less, but you can probably find a *similar* item. Discount stores offer fewer services than department stores.
- **Factory outlets.** These stores are run by a manufacturer or factory. Prices are low because few customer services are offered. Some factory outlets may look like warehouses and may not accept returns or exchanges. You'll find a mix of merchandise in these stores, from high-quality clothes to clothing that is labeled *seconds* or *irregulars.* These have flaws or are otherwise not perfect. If the flaws aren't noticeable, the item may be worth buying. You may also have the sewing skills to repair some of the imperfections.
- **Mail-order catalogs.** These books and pamphlets are sent out by many stores and companies. They are convenient to use, but you'll have to wait from a few days to several weeks for your order to be delivered. A decision about which size to order should be made carefully. Catalogs usually explain how to measure for your correct size. Catalog prices vary and you will usually have to pay mailing or shipping charges. It's a good idea to compare prices with those in local stores.
- **Resale shops.** These shops sell secondhand garments that often look new. Some may specialize in antique clothing or designer clothing. A resale shop may be sponsored by a charitable organization, or it may be a consignment shop where the person bringing the clothing to be sold will get a percentage of the selling price. The clothing cannot be returned.
- **Garage sales, yard sales, and rummage sales.** These are other sources of used clothing. Clothing items at these sales can often be purchased for a few dollars or less. You have to check very carefully to be sure that items are not stained or worn beyond repair since they cannot be returned.
- **Flea markets.** These can offer everything from first-quality merchandise to seconds and irregulars. Some items labeled as "designer" may be poor-quality copies. Prices are usually below retail store prices, but many flea markets do not allow customers to try on or return items.
- **Art and craft fairs.** These can be sources of original, one-of-a-kind designs. You may find hand-painted, quilted, patchwork, hand-woven, and hand-knitted garments, as well as handcrafted jewelry and accessories. Although you will pay a premium price for these unique designs, a special item may be worth the extra cost.

When to Shop

Stores generally market clothes for different seasons, so the time of year will affect prices and selection. At the beginning of each season, prices tend to be at their highest, but more clothing is available. During the season, the selection decreases and prices usually go down.

Emphasize Retailers' schedules for seasonal sales encourage advance planning when shopping for clothes. Schedules affect the availability of certain kinds of clothes as well as their prices. In some areas, winter clothes are on display before summer is over, and bathing suits might not be available again until the following spring.

Focus on Entrepreneurship Some students might be interested in organizing a clothing rummage sale or flea market to benefit the school. Others might wish to experiment with consigning clothes to resale shops.

Cross-Reference See Chapter 30 for more information about stores, other ways to shop and sales.

Most stores hold some type of clearance sale at the end of each season to make room for new merchandise.

In addition, stores usually hold sales at regular times throughout the year. If you are aware of the sale schedule, you can plan ahead for larger purchases such as a winter coat. Sales are important to anyone buying clothes, but remember that stores hope you'll also buy their regularly priced items when you shop during a sale. Keep in mind, too, that no item is worth buying if you have no use for it, no matter how much of a bargain it is.

Here are traditional types of sales:

- An **end-of-season sale** is held to clear out merchandise to make room for the next season's styles. Winter coats, sweaters, and ski clothes go on sale in February; bathing suits and summer sportswear go on sale in July.
- Annual holiday sales, such as those on Columbus Day or Washington's Birthday, aim to bring in business on a day when more customers can shop.
- Markdowns, or reduced-price items, are almost always available. These are clothes that, for some reason, didn't sell as fast as planned. The longer an item remains in the store, the more it is marked down.
- Special purchases are items that the store has bought for a lower than usual price. The store then passes on the savings to their customers.

Know Your Size

Knowing what size you wear involves knowing which **size range** or category you fit into. If you shop in the right size range, you'll get a better fit. For teens there are several possible size ranges.

Size Ranges

There are so many terms used in sizing clothes today. Here are some guidelines to use when trying to decide which size range will fit you best.

- **Female sizes.** Most females wear either a misses or a junior size. Misses sizes are even-numbered (4, 6, 8, 10, 12, 14, 16) and designed for a well-proportioned figure. Junior sizes are odd-numbered (3, 5, 7, 9, 11, 13, 15) and cut for a trimmer, shorter-waisted figure. Teen sections in some department stores carry clothes made for developing teen figures.
- **Male sizes.** Male clothing comes in men's and boys' sizes. Some stores have special teen departments with clothing sized for this age group. Boys' and mens' pants are sold by waist and **inseam measurement**—the length of the pants leg from the bottom to where the two legs meet.

Cross-reference See Chapter 29 for more information about types of advertising, such as information ads and image ads.

Cross-Reference See Chapter 30 for more information about types of stores, other ways to shop, and sales.

More About Sizes Because sizes vary according to manufacturers, a female with a 32-inch bust might wear a misses size 8, a junior size 9, a junior petite size 7, a teen size 9/10, a numerical size 32, or the general size small. Show students a measurement chart indicating size range characteristics and size equivalents.

Skill Builder: Critical Thinking
Ask students what kinds of enticements advertisers offer to get people to attend store sales. Then have students create posters or a bulletin board display showing advertisements for different kinds of store sales. Some kinds other than those mentioned in the text might include factory closeouts, surplus or overstock sales, inventory sales, grand opening sales.

Reteaching
Have students review Chapters 27 and 31 on managing money. Ask them to establish a budget for making additions, based on the wardrobe plans they developed in Chapter 59. Identify the factors that determine price, and review the differences between wholesale, retail, and sale prices. Have students discuss how they can get what they need while staying within their budgets. What are their options of where and when to shop?

Enrichment
Have students bring in mail-order catalogs in order to compare and contrast the services offered by different mail-order houses. With students working in groups, have them develop a chart on which they can indicate delivery costs, sizing information, return policies, and so on. Then have students discuss the differing services and costs. Which mail-order companies seem to offer the best deals?

Teaching "Know Your Size"
(Pages 539-542)

This section teaches how to know what size clothing is best.

Checking Comprehension

✓ What is the difference between misses and junior sizes? *Misses sizes are even-numbered sizes from 4 to 16 and are designed for a well-proportioned figure. Junior sizes are odd-numbered sizes from 3 to 15 and are cut for a trimmer, shorter-waisted figure.*

✓ By what measurements are boys' and men's pants sold? *Waist and inseam measurements.*

✔ Name two size ranges made for body shapes other than average. *Any two of the following: petite, women's, slim, husky, tall, short.*

✔ Name a size that fits two or three standard sizes. *Extra-small small, medium, large, extra-large.*

Activities

Skill Builder: Math
Divide the class into groups of four or five students. Groups should be all male or all female. Have each group calculate the average height and the average clothing size for the group. List their findings on the board, and ask students to calculate the average height and size for the class males and the class females.

Reteaching
Have students inventory by category the sizes of the clothing in their wardrobes and chart the size of each blouse, skirt, dress, sweater, pair of pants, and other items. Ask what conclusions students can draw from their inventories. Have students suggest reasons for size variations.

Enrichment
Have students work in groups to make a list of the kinds of clothing to buy that allow for growth. For example, buy clothing with large seam allowances, elastic waistbands, and so on. Ask them to take into account the fabrics and features of the garments such as raglan sleeves rather than set-in sleeves. Explain that this information can be useful to them since many of them are still growing.

- **Special sizes.** Some manufacturers make special sizes such as *petite, women's, slim, husky, tall,* and *short,* to better fit different body shapes.

Finding Your Size

Sizes in ready-to-wear clothing are based on the measurements of typical bodies, but no one is typical, so finding the right size can be difficult. Unless you're familiar with a particular label or brand name, never buy clothing without trying it on.

Some clothing is marked *extra-small, small, medium, large,* or *extra-large.* These categories will fit two or three standard sizes. For example, a small will fit sizes 6 and 8; medium fits sizes 10 and 12. It's best to try these on because there can be a great variation in manufacturers' sizing.

If you are having trouble choosing between two sizes, it's smart to buy the larger size. Because you're probably still growing, you will be able to wear the item longer.

You can also allow for growth by looking for skirts and pants with wide hems. You'll be able to let them down later to lengthen the garment if you grow taller. Elasticized waists that leave room for expansion are good ideas, too.

Evaluating Your Choice

How can you tell whether you are getting good value in a garment you are considering buying? What do you look for? Fit, comfort, fabric quality, construction details, and cost all determine the value of a garment.

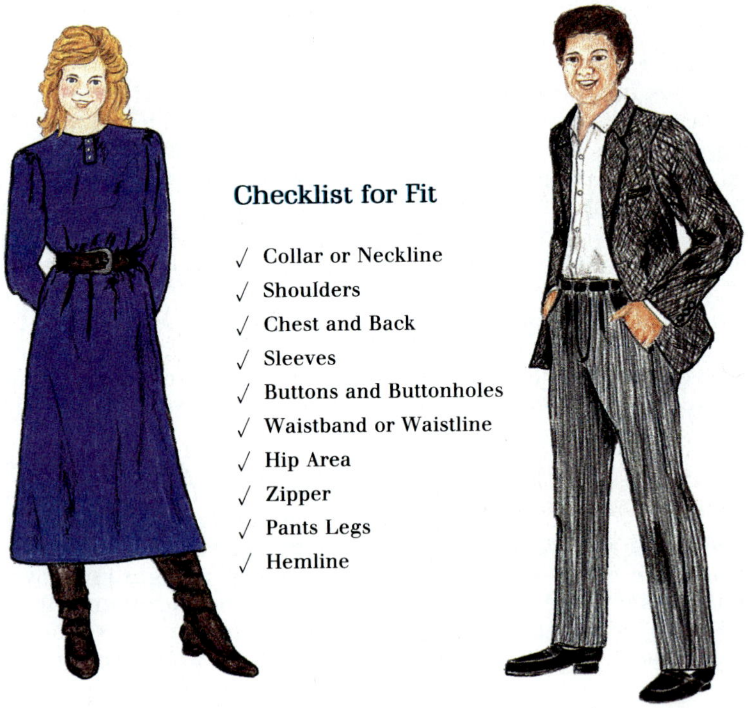

More About Buying Shoes When shopping for shoes, have both feet measured as some people have one foot that is larger than the other. Shoes have a number and letter size. The number refers to length; the letter to width. Try on both shoes and walk around to check fit. You should be able to wiggle your toes—a shoe should extend 1/2 inch beyond your longest toe. The heel should be snug without rubbing. The last (the form of the shoe) and the instep (the arch) should fit the shape of your foot. Don't buy shoes that are uncomfortable. Leather shoes and boots will soften with wear; plastic will not.

Checking the Fit

To find out if a garment fits properly, you'll have to try it on. When you are in the dressing room, don't just stand still. Move around, sit down, reach up, bend over. If you cannot do any of these things easily, or if the garment sags, gaps, or pulls anywhere, it's probably too large or too small. If it doesn't fit right, don't be discouraged. Remember what you learned earlier in the chapter—clothing is manufactured according to typical body measurements as well as the manufacturer's own specifications. Try another size.

Never compromise on fit. An uncomfortable garment will end up at the back of your closet and never be worn. Avoid buying too small a garment in the expectation that you will lose weight. Poor fit also leads to broken zippers, split seams, and worn fabric.

Checking the Fabric

You really like the jacket you found. It fits nicely and goes well with your pants. What questions about its quality should you consider before making it your final choice? First take a look at the fabric:

- **Wrinkling.** Grab a handful of fabric, crush it in your hand, and release it. Do the wrinkles stay or fall out quickly? If the wrinkles don't fall out, the garment will look rumpled when you wear it.
- **Pattern.** If the fabric is a plaid or a print, check that the pattern is straight and even all around. The pattern should run in the same direction in all pieces. Plaids should match at the seams.
- **Wearing qualities.** Hold the garment up to the light. If patches of light come through the fabric unevenly, it will probably wear unevenly. The tighter the knit or weave, the better the garment will hold its shape.
- **Care information.** Look at the labels for the fiber content and care information. You want clothes that you wear often to be made of easy-to-care-for fabrics.

Checking the Construction

Next look at how the jacket is made. Check its construction in these areas:

- **Seams.** First, check each **seam**, the line of stitching that joins the pieces of the garment together. Make sure they're straight and smooth with no puckering. Stitches should be secure so the seams won't come apart. Check the inside of the garment, too. The seams should be finished, with no raw edges to ravel.

Examine the way a garment is constructed inside, as well as outside. Look for straight, smooth seams that won't pull out, and for pucker-free facings and hems.

Teaching "Evaluating Your Choices"

(Pages 540-542)

This section teaches how to evaluate fit, fabric quality, construction, and cost.

Checking Comprehension

✔ How can you tell if a garment fits properly when you try it on? *Move around in it; sit down; reach up; and bend over. See if the garment sags, gaps, or pulls anywhere when you do those things.*

✔ How can you tell if a fabric will wrinkle easily? *Squeeze the fabric tightly and release. If the wrinkles don't fall out, the fabric is not wrinkle-resistent.*

✔ What construction details should you examine closely? *Seams, edges and corners, hems, fastenings, and trimmings.*

✔ What is a good seam? *One that is straight, smooth, securely stitched, and finished inside so as not to ravel.*

✔ What are some questions to ask about cost before making a purchase? *Is it within your budget? Will it last or be used long? How does the price compare with that of similar items? Can you buy it elsewhere for less?*

Activities

Skill Builder: Critical Thinking
Jamie wants a good pair of jeans and is willing to pay as much as $35 for them. He plans to wear them for school, for work, and for fun. Jamie's parents suggested he buy a pair of dry-clean-only dress pants for only $20. What can Jamie say to his parents to persuade them that the jeans are a better value?

Skill Builder: Writing
Have students bring in an item of clothing that they recently purchased. Ask them to examine the fabric as outlined in the chapter for wrinkling, pattern, wearing qualities, and care information. Then ask them to write an evaluation of the fabric based on those tests. Would they buy it again after checking those points?

Focus on Relationship Skills Ask students to discuss customer service in stores and communication between customers and sales personnel. How might sales personnel help in making clothing choices? What is the best way to ask for or avoid assistance? What is the best way to make complaints?

Focus on Consumer Skills Have students find out about layaways, and charge accounts at selected local stores. What are the advantages and disadvantages of each? What are store policies about check cashing, returns, credit, warranties, and customer complaints?

Skill Builder: Writing
Have students use the same item of clothing they brought in for the last activity to check the construction in the following areas: seams, edges and corners, hems, fastenings, and trimmings. Tell them to follow the guidelines for evaluation listed in the chapter and then write up their results. Would they purchase the item again?

Reteaching
Ask students for examples of garment features that determine a garment's value to you. How do you know if it fits? How do you determine comfort? How can you tell the quality of fabric? How do you evaluate construction details? How can you tell if the price is right for you?

Enrichment
To give students experience in comparison shopping, have them select an article of clothing and check the quality and price of the article in several stores. Ask students to submit reports including checklist answers or conclusions about comparison shopping.

- **Edges and corners.** Collar points and lapels should be flat and smooth without bulk or puckers. Some edges, such as necklines and armholes, have **facings**—extra pieces of fabric sewn on the outside and turned to the inside to finish an edge. Facings should lie flat and be anchored so they won't show when the garment is worn.
- **Hems.** The **hem** is the bottom edge of fabric turned up and sewn to the wrong side of the garment. Hemmed edges should be smooth. Stitches should be invisible from the right side, with no wrinkles or puckers.
- **Fastenings.** Make sure zippers are sewn in securely, and that they slide evenly and smoothly. Buttonholes should be even and without loose threads. Check that buttons, hooks, eyes, and snaps are firmly attached.
- **Trimmings.** Look at any **trimmings**. These are the decorations sewn on a garment. They should be attached with even, secure stitches. Topstitching thread should match the fabric, unless done for contrast. It should be even, without any puckers.

Cost

The overall cost of a garment is very important. Some questions to ask when purchasing an item are:

- Is the price within your budget?
- How long might you wear it or how long might it last?
- Can you buy something similar for less?
- Can you get it cheaper somewhere else?
- Could you save money by waiting for it to be put on sale?
- Could you make the item?

The more times you wear a garment, the more value you will get from the money you spent on it. One way of finding that value is to compute the **cost per wearing**. This is the total of the purchase price and the cost of cleaning divided by the number of times you wear a garment. See the chart below.

Although cost is important, you also need to evaluate your purchases as to your needs and wants, color and design, fit and quality. If all these factors are met, you can be sure of making good choices.

Estimating Cost Per Wearing

Suppose you buy a dressy sweater and a pair of pants. The sweater had been marked down to $24.99. The pants cost $25.00.

Through the year you wear the pants 39 times, but you wear the sweater only 5 times. The next year you wear the pants another 25 times until they are too short and too tight. The sweater still fits and you wear it 5 more times.

You have the sweater drycleaned three times in two years, for a total of $8.25. The pants are washable, so their cleaning cost is only a fraction of the family laundry—about 50 cents a year.

To figure the cost per wearing for each garment over two years, add the purchase price and the cleaning cost then divide by the number of wearings.

Sweater: $24.99 + $8.25 =
$33.24 ÷ 10 = $3.32

Pants: $25.00 + 1.00 =
$26.00 ÷ 64 = $0.41

The cost per wearing of the sweater is eight times that of the pants. The pants are a better value than the sweater, even though they were not marked down. When you consider buying a garment, weigh its price against the cleaning cost and the number of times you expect to wear it.

More About Evaluating Clothes Other construction details to consider are darts, tucks, gathers, pleats, sleeves, pockets, and linings. See Chapters 64 and 65 for additional information about construction.

Cross-reference See Teen Tips "Designer Jeans—Worth the $$$?" on pages 616-617.

Focus on Life Management Ask students to develop guidelines for appropriate behavior while shopping. What complaints do retailers have about the way customers use their facilities and merchandise? What measures do stores take to protect their investment?

MANAGING RESOURCES

Choosing Accessories

Accessories include items such as scarves, shoes, boots, gloves, hats, belts, socks, jewelry, sunglasses, ties, handbags, backpacks, and tote bags. They are a way to brighten your wardrobe. They also help you express your unique personality and creativity. Use accessories to:

- Update a classic or favorite outfit with the latest fashion colors.
- Make a quick change from a school outfit to a party outfit.
- Add color and life to neutral colors.
- Focus attention wherever you want it.

Check fashion magazines, catalogs, and pattern books to see the new trends in colors and accessories. In one season you may see that wide belts are being shown in bright, fluorescent colors. In another season, the emphasis may be on natural accessories, such as wood jewelry or rope belts. These are small items that can inexpensively update and accent your wardrobe.

Some other accessories are not so inexpensive. It's possible to spend more for a pair of leather boots than for a coat, and a silk scarf can cost more than a blouse. When you are deciding how much money to spend on accessories, it is best to spend more money on items that will last for several seasons and limit fad purchases to low-priced items.

- Select accessories that are appropriate for a person of your size. If you are short, a large tote bag may make you look even smaller.
- Use accessories to set the tone of your look. A whimsical piece can put a little humor into your appearance.
- Classic leather belts are 3/4″ to 1 1/4″ wide. Collect them in a variety of colors.
- Carry a list of the garments you have and their colors when you shop. Fabric samples from your clothing will help you match accessories.
- Think of new ways to wear accessories you already own. Try wearing a tie or a scarf as a belt. Or twist two scarves together and knot.

Think It Through

1. **What are some additional ways of using accessories you already own, such as belts, scarves, hats, or ties?**
2. **What is your favorite accessory and why?**

Teaching the Feature
"Choosing Accessories"

Answers to Feature Questions

1. There are many possibilities. Some suggestions include wearing a colorful scarf around the neck or over the shoulder, tying a scarf around a hat, wearing several narrow belts together, coordinating suspenders with a long tie or a bow tie.

2. Answers will vary. Students might say a piece of jewelry because it was a gift or shoes or belts that go with a lot of their clothes.

Activities

Footwear Remind students that shoes, boots, and other footwear can accessorize clothing. Ask them to consider the shoes, boots, and other footwear they own. How often do they wear each pair? Are there some they wear frequently? Or seldom? What do they like about the ones they wear a lot? What do they dislike about the ones they don't wear? Discuss the importance of quality, comfort, and correct fit in footwear choices.

Scrapbooks Have students use magazine clippings to illustrate the uses of accessories described in the chapter and the suggested guidelines for choosing accessories. Students might illustrate how accessories can enhance or detract from a person's appearance. Students might also focus on one type of accessory, such as shoes, belts, or hats.

Community Contact Arrange to have a salesperson who works in the accessory department of a local store speak to the class about the use of accessories, what accessory fads are popular now, and what accessories are classics. Ask him or her to bring examples in each category to show to the class.

Did You Know? The rubber shoe became a popular accessory during the nineteenth century. It was the forerunner of today's tennis or athletic shoe.

Emphasize An outfit can be easily and inexpensively updated by adding accessories.

COMPLETING THE CHAPTER

Summary

- Before shopping, decide what to buy and when and where to shop.
- Places to shop include department, specialty, and discount stores; factory outlets; and resale shops. Mail-order catalogs and various informal sales are also options.
- End-of-season sales, holiday sales, and markdowns are sources of bargains.
- Always try on clothes because of variations in sizes and fit.
- Evaluate clothing according to fit, comfort, fabric quality, construction details, and cost.
- To evaluate fabric quality, check for wrinkling, pattern matching, wear, and care requirements.
- To evaluate construction quality check seams, edges and corners, hems, fastenings, and trimmings.
- Evaluate clothing cost according to budget and cost per wearing.

For Review

Objective Review Questions Have students complete the "Reviewing the Facts" section on this page.

Study Guide Have students complete the Study Guide from Chapter 60 of their *Student Workbook.*

Motivator Follow-Up Return questionnaires for students to revise according to what they have learned.

Classification Write two column headings on the board, "Before You Shop" and "Before You Buy." Ask students to complete the chart.

For Evaluation

Consumer Reports Have students write a consumer report on an article of clothing they have evaluated. Reports should draw conclusions about the article's value and state the students' final decision.

Chapter Test Have students complete the test for Chapter 60 that appears in the *Teacher's Classroom Resources.*

CHAPTER 60 REVIEW

Answers to "Reviewing the Facts"

1. Any two: decide what you want to buy; where to shop; how much to spend.
2. Any six: department stores; specialty stores; discount stores; factory outlets; mail-order catalogs; resale shops; garage, yard, and rummage sales; flea markets; art and craft fairs. Advantages include: wide selection; special services; lower prices; unusual or original designs. Disadvantages include: higher prices; low-quality items; few services; shipping costs; having to wait for order; no returns.
3. Any three: end-of-season sales; annual holiday sales; markdowns; special purchases.
4. Female sizes include juniors and misses. Male sizes include boys' and mens'.
5. Because of great variations in manufacturers' sizing.
6. Move around—sit, reach, bend.
7. Wrinkling, pattern, wearing qualities, care information.
8. The lower the cost per wearing, the better the value.

Reviewing the Facts

1. What are two things you should do to get ready for a shopping trip?
2. List six places where you can buy clothing. What is one advantage and one disadvantage of each?
3. Name three traditional types of clothing sales.
4. What are two female and two male clothing size ranges?
5. Even if you know your size, why should you always try on clothing before buying?
6. When checking the fit of a garment, what should you do?
7. What are four factors to check when evaluating fabric quality?
8. How does the cost per wearing help you determine the value of a garment?

Thinking Critically

1. When planning a wardrobe, why does it help to read advertisements in a newspaper or special store circular?
2. Which of the following are most important to you when you are shopping for clothes: *price, style, fit, color, fiber content and care, appearance, quality*. Which characteristics, if any, are least important to you?

Applying Your Skills

1. **Analyzing Quality.** Examine a garment that you recently purchased. Check the quality of the fabric and construction, and write a brief quality analysis of the garment. Did you make a good purchase?

2. **Judging Advertising Techniques.** Collect five clothing ads from newspapers or catalogs. Compare the information they give. How does each persuade customers to buy?

3. **Drawing Conclusions.** Where do you buy most of your clothes? List the reasons why you shop where you do. Which factors—convenience, price, quality, service, selection, advertising, and peer pressure—have the greatest influence on you, and why? How does your list of reasons compare with those of your classmates?

Answers to "Thinking Critically"

1. To learn: what items and styles are available; how prices compare; what the new fashion looks are; which colors, fabrics, and sizes are available; what accessories are being worn with the fashions; what is on sale or what special purchases are available.
2. Answers will vary. Discuss with the students why smart shoppers consider *all* of these elements when purchasing clothing.

CHAPTER

61

Selecting Patterns, Fabrics, and Notions

OBJECTIVES

This chapter will help you to:

- Determine the correct pattern size to buy.
- Explain how to select a pattern.
- Use the information on the pattern envelope.
- Suggest factors that affect your choice of fabric and notions.

WORDS TO REMEMBER

bolt-end label	pattern
figure type	pattern catalog
notions	view

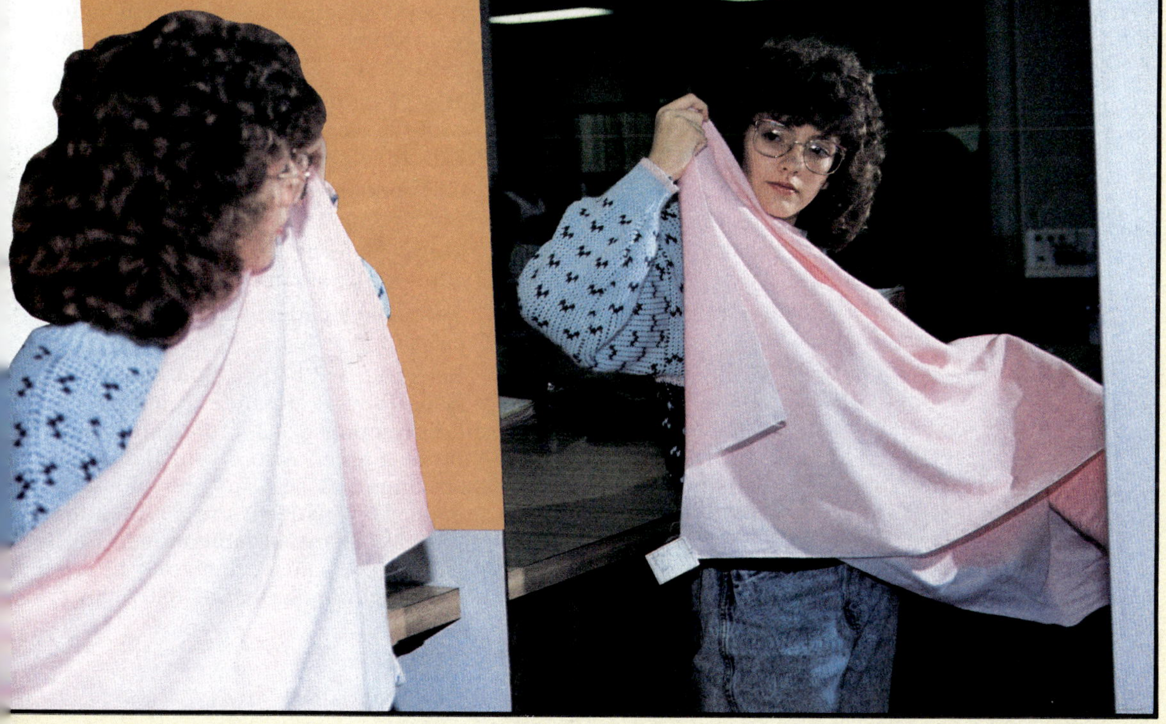

Chapter Resources

Teacher's Classroom Resources

- Lesson Plan
- Life Skills Activity, *What's in a Pattern?*
- Reproducible Master, *What's on the Back?*
- Extension Activity, *Taking Measurements*
- Chapter Test

Student Workbook

- Study Guide
- Worksheet, *I've Got a Notion*

CHAPTER OVERVIEW

Chapter 61 instructs students in taking measurements and determining figure types and pattern sizes. Students learn how to use pattern catalogs, choose patterns, and read pattern envelopes. Students assess their skills and apply their knowledge in selecting fabrics and in evaluating fabric quality. The chapter also offers guidelines for determining the cost of a sewing project and for selecting notions.

INTRODUCING THE CHAPTER

Motivators

Discussion Ask students to describe past sewing efforts. Some will have had some experience sewing with a needle and thread. Fewer will have made clothing from patterns or used a sewing machine. Ask: "What are some advantages of sewing your own clothes?"

Using the Photograph Have students study the photograph on this page. Then ask: "What is the girl doing? What can she learn from doing this?"

Demonstration Disassemble an article of discarded clothing to show that it was made from a pattern. Have students trace and label the clothing parts on the board. Tell them the pattern they select for their sewing project will contain similar labeled parts.

Introducing the Objectives

Discuss the chapter objectives on this page. Remind students that the objectives focus on important chapter content.

Introducing Vocabulary

Tell students that the word *pattern* comes from a Medieval Latin word *patron,* which meant someone worthy of being imitated. A pattern is a plan worthy of imitation. How does the definition apply to dress patterns?

TEACHING THE CHAPTER

For convenience, the teaching suggestions for this chapter are arranged according to the following lesson topics:

- "Body Measurements," pages 546-547
- "Selecting a Pattern," pages 548-549
- "Selecting a Fabric," pages 551-552
- "Selecting Notions," page 552

Teaching "Body Measurements"

(Pages 546-547)

This section teaches students how to take body measurements to determine figure type and how to select the correct pattern size.

Checking Comprehension

✓ What is a pattern, and what information does it give? *A pattern is a set of written directions and paper pieces for putting together a sewing project. The pattern tells you how much fabric you need and shows you how to lay out and cut the pieces.*

✓ What can you do to make taking body measurements easy and accurate? *Ask a friend or relative to help, wear smooth-fitting clothes, wear shoes you will wear with the garment, tie string or narrow elastic around your waist, stand straight and tall, for measuring around the body be sure the tape measure is parallel to the floor, pull the tape snugly but not too tight, double-check measurements before writing them down.*

✓ What is a figure type? *A size category determined by height and body proportions.*

When you sew you can choose from the hundreds of patterns, fabrics, and colors available to make the item you want. You can make it in the exact size that you need, and in the color that does the most for you and your wardrobe. You can also sew accessories, gifts, and practical items like backpacks, duffel bags, and pillows. You can get satisfaction and pride from sewing something to wear or use. You may even be able to earn extra money with your sewing skills.

Body Measurements

The first step in making clothing is selecting a pattern. A **pattern** is a set of written directions and printed paper pieces that show you how to put a sewing project together. The pattern also tells you how much fabric you need and shows you how to lay out and cut the pieces. To know what size pattern is right for you, you must first know your body measurements.

Taking Measurements

Here are a few things that you can do to make measuring easy and accurate:

- Ask a friend or relative to help you take your measurements and write them down for you.
- Wear smooth-fitting clothes, a leotard, or underwear when measuring. Do not measure over a bulky sweater or jacket.
- Wear shoes. That will make your posture close to what it will be when you wear the clothing.
- Tie a string or piece of narrow elastic around your waist. You'll use it to locate your waist and for measuring the length of your back, hips, and legs.
- Stand straight and tall.
- For measurements around the body be sure that the tape measure is parallel to the floor.
- For accurate measurements, pull the tape measure snugly, but not too tight, around your body.
- Before writing down any measurement, double-check it. See page 547 for the measurements to take.

Figure Types and Pattern Sizes

To help you choose the correct pattern size, compare your measurements with the pattern size charts. These charts are found in the back of a **pattern catalog,** a book that shows all the patterns available from one company.

Pattern sizes are divided by **figure types,** size categories determined by height and body proportions. The major pattern companies use common figure types. Which description most closely describes your figure type?

- **Misses** patterns are designed for the well-developed figure about 5′5″ to 5′6″ in height.
- **Girls** patterns are for the petite figure, 5′1″ or shorter.
- **Mens** patterns are for the average adult build, about 5′10″ tall.
- **Teen-Boys** patterns are for boys who are still growing.

Because each body is built differently, it is not always possible to match your measurements exactly to a pattern size. Choose the size within your figure type that comes closest to your measurements. A few patterns are not identified by size but by measurements, such as by waist size for pants. Others may be sized small, medium, large, and extra-large.

Emphasize Posture and technique are important when taking body measurements. Suggest what can happen to size and fit if you don't stand straight and if you pull the measuring tape too tight.

Did You Know? Pattern sizes are not the same as ready-to-wear clothing sizes. A store-bought item in size 8 might be a pattern size 6 or 10, based on body measurements and figure type.

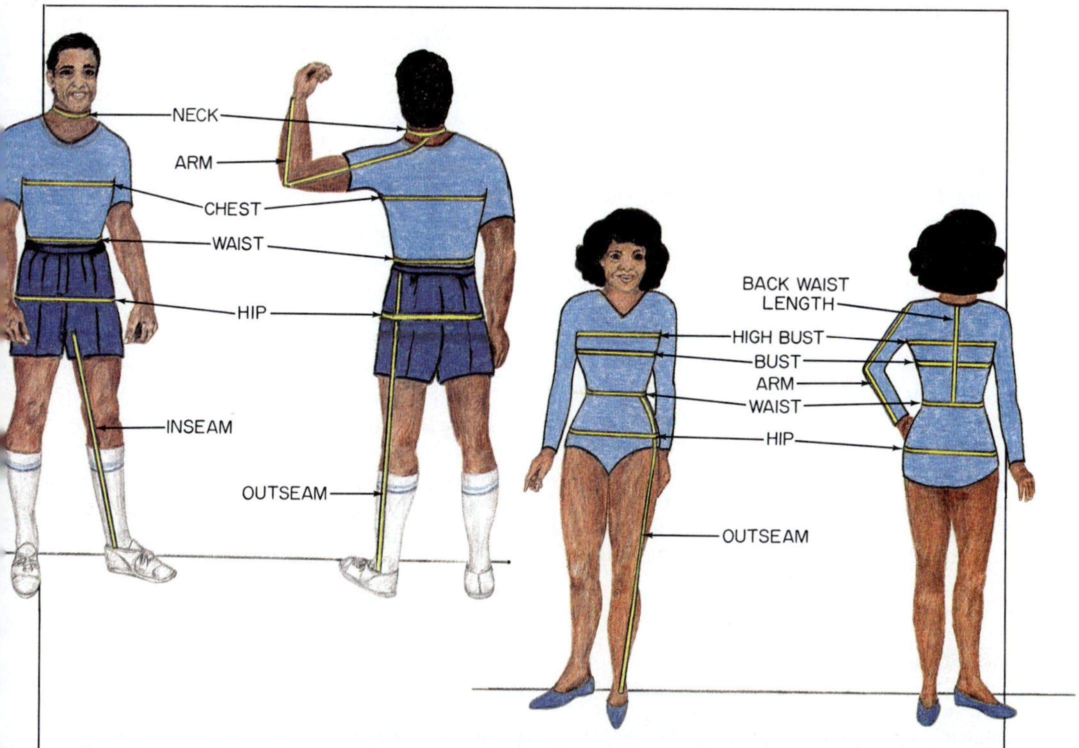

Measuring Up

Height Stand tall against the wall, barefoot. Have another person make a mark level with the top of your head. Measure from this point to the floor. For pants and skirt measurements, it is best to wear shoes.

High Bust For females, measure around body, under the arms. This measurement is not found on pattern size charts. It is used for comparison with bust measurement to help select pattern size.

Bust For females, measure at fullest part of bustline. If bust measure is 2 in. (5 cm) or more larger than high bust, use the high bust measurement to select pattern size.

Chest For males, measure the fullest part of the chest.

Waist For females, measure where string or elastic falls. For males, measure around the natural waist where a belt or waistband feels most comfortable.

Back Waist Length Measure from the base of the neck to the waistline.

Hips Measure around the fullest part of the hips. For females, this is 7–9 in. (18–23 cm) below the waist. For males, this is usually about 8 in. (20 cm) below the waist.

Outseam Measure along the outside of the leg from waist to desired length of pants.

Inseam For males, measure along inside of leg from crotch to desired length of pants. Or measure a pair of pants that fit well, measuring from bottom of one leg to where the two legs meet.

Neckband For males, measure around the fullest part of the neck, adding ½ in. (1.5 cm) for wearing ease.

Sleeve Bend arm up. Measure from base of neck across center back to elbows, across elbow crook, and up to wrist bone.

Did You Know? The first paper pattern was developed by a Ebnezer Butterick, a Massachussetts tailor. His wife used it to make his shirts, and soon friends began buying the patterns. By 1865, the Buttericks had moved to New York City and were selling patterns by mail to customers from all over the world. In 1870, James McCall, a tailor and an author of a system for drafting patterns, began to sell dress patterns in New York City.

Activities

Skill Builder: Math
Supply pattern catalogs for students to study. Have students compare their measurements with the pattern size charts in the catalogs.

Reteaching
Have students develop a poster showing how to take accurate measurements.

Enrichment
Have students take their body measurements at home with the help of a friend or relative. They should use the chart in this chapter as a guideline for measuring. Then ask them to use those measurements to determine their figure types. Ask students to record all measurements in both inches and centimeters.

Teaching "Selecting a Pattern"
(Pages 548-549)

This section gives guidelines for choosing patterns, including using pattern catalogs, selecting a style, assessing sewing skills, and interpreting the information on the front and back of a pattern envelope.

Checking Comprehension

✓ How are garment patterns categorized in pattern catalogs? *By type of garment, by figure type or size range, by sewing skill, by special categories.*

✓ Where can you see patterns in a store? *In pattern catalogs or on special display racks in fabric stores.*

✓ How does the pattern catalog help you determine if a style is right for you? *By showing different views; by showing the lines, shapes, and length of the design; and by describing the fit.*

✓ What information is given on the front of the pattern envelope? *Drawings and photographs of the pattern views, figure type and size, pattern number, and price.*

✓ What shopping information is given on the back of a pattern envelope? *Garment description, sketch of each back view, size chart of body measurements, fabric yardage needed, suitable fabrics, and notions needed.*

Activities

Skill Builder: Critical Thinking
Have students examine two or three patterns, each from different manufacturers. How do the patterns differ? Which brand of pattern do the students prefer and why?

Skill Builder: Reading
Have students read a sample pattern envelope and write the following information: pattern number, number of views, figure type or size range, size, design details, yardage, recommended and not recommended fabrics, notions, and pattern price.

Selecting a Pattern

Pattern catalogs provide lots of information about patterns. First, look for the type of garment or item you want to sew. Clothes patterns usually are grouped according to the type of garment (such as sportswear or dresses) or by figure type (such as men and boys, or children). Other categories are based on sewing skill, such as easy-to-sew patterns. Catalogs also have sections for gifts, home decorating, toys, accessories, and crafts.

Each catalog page has illustrations or photographs showing how the project will look when sewn. This often includes a number of views. A **view** is a different version of the pattern. For example, a sweatshirt pattern might include views for long and short sleeves.

Don't overlook patterns that may be shown on special display racks in the store. These may be best-selling patterns, seasonal selections, or easy-to-sew patterns.

Choosing for Style

When you buy a pair of pants or a shirt in a store, you can see the style, color, and fabric together. You can also try the item on to see how it looks and feels. With patterns, you have to rely on the way the pants or shirt look in the pattern catalog. Study the photograph and illustrations carefully. Check the design lines, the shape, the length, and the fit. What details are there? Read the description under the pattern. This will tell you how it fits. Is it snug-fitting or loose? Pattern catalogs also feature a drawing of the back of the garment.

You may still wonder if the garment will look good on you. One clue might be whether the item is similar to something you have worn in the past. If not, look for a similar garment in a store and try it on. Be sure to select a pattern that you really like. Half the fun of sewing is showing off what you've made.

Choosing for Your Sewing Skills

When picking a pattern, consider your sewing skills. If you are a beginner, look for patterns marked "easy to sew" or "very easy." The number of pattern pieces is a clue to the difficulty of the pattern. The fewer the pieces, the easier the pattern. Details such as shirt cuffs, collars, fly-front zippers, extra darts, tucks, and topstitching make a pattern more difficult to complete. Easy-to-sew patterns include few of these details.

When you look through a pattern catalog, study the illustrations to get an idea of what the finished item will look like. Read the descriptions for information about sewing difficulty.

Did You Know? If your measurements fall between two sizes, select the smaller size if the design is full or loose fitting. Select the larger size if the design is closely fitted.

Focus on Decision Making Have students learn the names of style details they like. For example, neckline and collar styles include boat-neck, cowl-neck, crew-neck, stand-up collar, round collar, notched lapels, and others. Sleeve styles include puffed, dolman, drop-shoulder, and raglan.

8959
17 PIECES

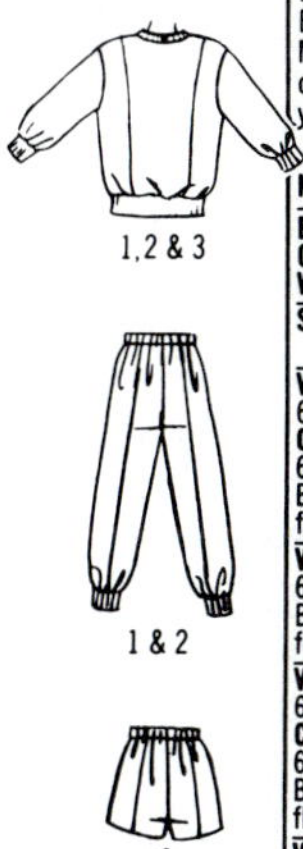

1, 2 & 3

1 & 2

3

MISSES', MEN'S OR TEEN BOYS' KNIT PANTS, SHORTS AND TOP: Long sleeved crewneck top has side sections and ribbed knit bands. V. 1 top has pockets and contrast sleeves and side sections. V. 3 top has contrast side sections. Pants and shorts have side sections and elastic waistline casing. Pants have ribbed knits bands. V. 1 pants and V. 3 shorts have contrast side sections.

Fabrics—Knits only such as: sweatshirt knits, velour, stretch terry, cotton interlock. Bands in stretchable ribbed knit fabric. (SEE PICK-A-KNIT® RULE FOR BANDS ONLY.) Not suitable for obvious diagonals. Extra fabric needed to match plaids, stripes or one-way design fabrics. For pile, shaded or one-way design fabrics, use with nap yardages/layouts.

Notions: Thread, straight seam tape. Look for Simplicity notions.

BODY MEASUREMENTS						
Chest/Bust	30-32	34-36	38-40	42-44	46-48	Ins.
Waist	26-27	28-30	32-34	36-39	42-44	"
Sizes U.S.A. ONLY	X-Small	Small Small	Medium Medium	Large Large	X-Large X-Large	
View 1 Top and Pants						
60"**	1½	1⅝	1⅝	1¾	1¾	Yds.
Contrast side sections and sleeves (top and pants)						
60"**	1½	2	2	2	2	Yds.
Bands—Stretchable ribbed knit fabric—18" to 20" tubular **OR** 36" to 40" flat**	⅝	⅝	⅝	¾	¾	Yd.
View 2 Top and Pants						
60"**	2⅝	3¼	3¼	3¼	3⅜	Yds.
Bands—Stretchable ribbed knit fabric—18" to 20" tubular **OR** 36" to 40" flat**	⅝	⅝	⅝	⅝	¾	Yd.
View 3 Top and Shorts						
60"**	1½	1½	1½	1⅝	1¾	Yds.
Contrast side sections (top and shorts)						
60"**	⅞	1⅛	1⅛	1⅜	1⅜	Yds.
Bands—Stretchable ribbed knit fabric—18" to 20" tubular **OR** 36" to 40" flat**	½	½	½	⅝	⅝	Yd.
View 1, 2 or 3 Elastic—1¼ yds. of 1" wide						
Pants side length V. 1 or 2	43	43½	44	44½	45	Ins.
Shorts side length V. 3	15	15½	16	16½	17	"

*without nap **with nap ***with or without nap

The back of the pattern envelope includes information about design details, measurements, fabrics, and notions.

Using the Pattern Envelope

The pattern department in most stores is self-service. That means you find the pattern you want in the large file drawers that hold the patterns by number. After you find the right number, be sure to select the correct size. Most stores will not allow you to exchange or return a pattern.

Once you have chosen your pattern, take a good look at the pattern envelope. The outside of the envelope contains important information.

- **Front of the envelope.** The front of the envelope shows the same drawings and photographs of the pattern views that were in the catalog. You will also find the figure type and size the pattern is made for, along with the pattern number and the price.
- **Back of the envelope.** On the back of the envelope, the garment description lists the design details that may not be obvious in the illustration. A sketch is given of the back of each pattern view, along with a size chart of the body measurements for each pattern size.
- **Other information.** The back of the pattern envelope is your shopping list. The yardage chart shows how much fabric you'll need for each pattern size. It will tell you whether you need extra material for napped fabric, such as corduroy, velvet, and velveteen. Under the heading "Suggested Fabrics," it will list the types of fabric that are appropriate for the pattern. It will also say whether a fabric such as a plaid or diagonal is not suitable. Finally, you'll find information on the notions that you will need to buy. **Notions** are the supplies needed to complete a project. They include thread, zippers, buttons or other fasteners, elastic, seam binding, hem tape, and trimmings.

Skill Builder: Critical Thinking
Ask students to select from pattern catalogs an easy and a difficult pattern. Have students compare and contrast the patterns. How many pattern pieces are needed for each? What sewing skills are needed?

Skill Builder: Critical Thinking
Have students compare and contrast pattern catalogs from two or three different manufacturers. Do some catalogs have patterns that are "trendier" than others? Do some have more sections than others? What are they? Do some catalogs specialize in particular types of clothing? If so, what are they?

Reteaching
Draw three columns on the board with the headings "Numbers," "Pictures," and "Words." Ask students to list in the appropriate columns the kinds of information presented in each of these ways in pattern catalogs and on pattern envelopes.

Enrichment
Have students select a pattern and study the list of supplies needed. They should then take an inventory of the supplies already available in their own home. Then ask students to prepare a list of the supplies they would need to buy. Help students figure out how much these supplies would cost. How many would be one-time-only purchases?

Did You Know? Developing a pattern is a complicated task. First, the designer sketches a proposed design. Then a croquis, or drawing showing the various views and suggested fabrics, is made. The design is draped in muslin on a dress form, then stitched into a garment that is worn by a model to check fit and appearance. A master pattern is made to use as the guide for grading, or converting the pattern into different sizes. Photographs or sketches are made, fabric layouts are developed, step-by-step sewing directions are written, and information is gathered for the pattern envelope. Finally, the pattern pieces and guide sheets are printed, folded, and inserted into the printed envelope.

Teaching the Feature
"Deciding Whether to Make or Buy"

Answers to Feature Questions

1. Answers will vary. Some students might suggest that a sewing project would be the preferred choice, even if it costs more, because they would be giving something unique and special to their family.

2. If the ready-to-wear item is priced cheaply enough, it is a saving of time and energy to purchase it, even if it requires minor adjustments or repair.

Activities

Comparing Costs Ask students to select a garment in a clothing store and record its price. Then have students find the same style of garment in a pattern catalog and the same type of fabric in a fabric store. Can the garment be sewn for the same price or less?

Community Contact Arrange to have a dressmaker or tailor speak to the class about the quality and cost of the clothes he or she produces. The speaker should also discuss working hours and labor charges. Suggest that students prepare some questions ahead of time.

MANAGING RESOURCES

Deciding Whether to Make or Buy

Do you enjoy shopping and have good luck finding what you need at the right price? Maybe you feel you can have more clothes for less money when you sew.

Ask yourself these questions when you are deciding whether to make or buy. Then, consider the following:

- **Time.** Does it take more time to shop or to sew? How much time do you have?
- **Money.** Can you save money by sewing the item or can you find it on sale for the same price or less?
- **Skill.** Do you have the sewing skills necessary to complete the project?
- **Sewing equipment.** Will you have to invest in new tools and sewing supplies?

One way to determine what to sew and what to buy is by degree of difficulty. Plan to sew garments that can be simply constructed. Sometimes you can make something in less time than it takes to shop for it.

It makes sense to sew when you cannot find what you want in ready-to-wear. It also makes sense to sew when you can copy an expensive item. For example, you can make a simple belt from a braid trim or an interesting ribbon for about one-fifth the cost of a similar, ready-made belt.

You may decide to sew something that you can wear often. You will get the most wear out of seasonless fashions that can be worn year round. You may decide to sew something that is expensive to buy but that you will wear only once or twice, such as a prom or bridesmaid's dress.

It makes more sense to buy than to sew when you don't have the time to make what you need, and the pattern details or fabric is beyond your sewing skills. Other times you may find a garment that seems just right—the color, fit, design lines, and price tag are perfect for you.

You may find something great in a perfect fabric at an ideal price, but it requires some minor adjustments of detail or fit. Then you can use your sewing skills to improve something that you buy.

Think It Through

1. **Do you think your family would rather receive ready-made gifts or a gift you sewed? Why?**
2. **Why is purchasing a ready-to-wear item sometimes a better use of your resources than sewing one?**

Focus on Technology Large manufacturing companies use computer-aided design (CAD) to design patterns on computers.

Emphasize When you cannot find what you want in the stores or when you cannot afford it, sewing is the alternative.

Did You Know? Patterns can be useful for people whose proportions are not perfect. An individual could combine a size 10 skirt with a size 8 bodice for a dress that fits perfectly. Some patterns are available in mutiple sizes—with two or more sizes on each pattern piece.

Selecting a Fabric

The array of different fabrics in a store can appear overwhelming. There are so many fabrics to choose from that you may not know where to start.

What the Pattern Tells You

Luckily, the pattern envelope tells you what type of fabric will be most suitable for a particular pattern. A lot depends on the shape and style of the garment. A soft fabric, such as challis, will be suggested for a soft, gathered shape. For casual clothes, the envelope will suggest a more durable, sturdy fabric. Dressier fabrics will be recommended for a special-occasion item, such as a formal for a prom.

Using Your Knowledge

Ask yourself some questions about which fabric is right for your project. Here are a few guidelines that will help you decide.

- **Your own experience.** Your feelings about yourself and the clothes you wear will help you make a decision about fabric. What feels comfortable and seems to express your personality? What will the item be used for and where will it be used? For instance, backpacks need durable, sturdy fabric, and placemats require medium-weight washable fabric.
- **Seasonal wear.** What time of year do you plan to wear the item? You wouldn't want a heavy wool for summer or a lightweight cotton fabric for winter. If you plan to wear the garment often, you want to buy a fabric that wears well.
- **Fabric care.** If you don't want to spend a lot of time hand-washing and ironing, pick an easy-care fabric. If your budget is limited, avoid a fabric that needs drycleaning. You will find the fiber content, recommended care, the fabric width, and price per yard on the **bolt-end label**. When you pay for the fabric ask the salesperson for a sew-in care label for your garment.
- **Sewing difficulty.** Some fabrics are easier to work with than others. Fabrics with a one-way design or a nap are more time-consuming to lay out because all pattern pieces must be placed in the same direction. Then, when the pieces are sewn together the nap will retain the same look throughout the garment.

Plaids need to be matched at the seams and are more difficult to lay out and cut. Fabrics that ravel easily can be frustrating to work with. Lightweight silky fabrics are slippery to lay out and cut. They may need special sewing techniques. Firmly woven or knitted fabrics are easier to handle.

Looking for Quality

Find a mirror and drape some of the fabric over your shoulder to see how it looks on you. Consider not only the color and design, but also the softness or firmness. Does it drape nicely for a garment with soft gathers? Is it crisp enough for the details in the pattern that you have selected.

When you've found a fabric that you like, examine it for flaws. These may be torn threads, snags, holes, or grease stains. Crumple it in your hand to see if the wrinkles disappear when you release it. If it's a knit, stretch it across the cut edge and see if it goes back into shape after you let go.

Emphasize Yardage charts on the back of pattern envelopes tell how much fabric is required, depending on the fabric width.

Did You Know? The easiest type of fabric to work with is one that is firmly woven or knitted, is medium weight, and has small all-over print so tiny sewing mistakes won't show.

Focus on Consumer Skills Have students choose three different fabrics they could use with a selected pattern to achieve three completely different looks. Have they chosen a versatile pattern? What would each look cost to make?

Cross-Reference See Chapter 58 for more information about fabrics.

Teaching "Selecting a Fabric"
(Pages 551-552)

This section offers students guidelines for choosing fabrics, evaluating fabric quality, and deciding how much fabric to buy.

Checking Comprehension

✓ What determines the appropriateness of a fabric to your project? *Personal preference, seasonal requirements, fabric care, and sewing difficulty.*

✓ What information will you find on the bolt-end label? *Fiber content, recommended care, fabric width, and price per yard.*

✓ How can you tell what your project will cost? *Multiply cost per yard of fabric by the number of yards and add the cost of notions and pattern.*

Activities

Skill Builder: Math
Mary Beth chose a floral print cotton-polyester blend for $2.98 a yard. The pattern envelope said she needed 3 yd. for view A of the skirt she planned to make. She also needed 1/4 yd. of interfacing for the waistband, which was $.96 a yard; an 8-in. plastic zipper for $1.98; a large spool of all-purpose thread for $1.10; two buttons, which came on a card of two for $.67; and a package of hem tape for $.99. The pattern cost was $2.50. How much will Mary Beth's project cost? *($16.42)*

Reteaching
Ask students to review Chapter 58 on fibers and fabrics and Chapter 60 on shopping for clothes. How does the information in those chapters relate to this section's discussion of evaluating the quality of fabric?

Enrichment
Have students study bolt-end labels in a fabric store and answer the following questions: What are the standard widths in which fabric is sold? What is the range of prices for fabric by the yard? What are two of the least expensive and two of the most expensive fabrics? What are remnants?

Teaching "Selecting Notions"
(Page 552)

This section offers guidelines for choosing appropriate notions and thread.

Checking Comprehension

✔ How do you know what notions you need? *The pattern envelope lists them.*

✔ What color notions should you buy? *Thread, zippers, seam binding, and bias tape should match or be slightly darker than the fabric. Buttons should match the color or be contrasting for accent.*

✔ Name three specialty threads. *Cotton, silk, rayon, and nylon threads; threads for embroidery, quilting, topstitching, and sewing on buttons.*

Activities

Skill Builder: Writing
Write the following topic sentence on the board: "Notions should coordinate with your fabric." Ask students to write a short essay beginning with the topic sentence.

Skill Builder: Critical Thinking
Have students think of ways they can use notions to update items of clothing they own. Ask them to make suggestions for using notions to make clothes they sew more interesting.

Reteaching
Ask students why all-purpose thread is a good buy. Have them study thread details and notions in the clothing they are wearing.

Enrichment
Ask students to survey the notions available in a fabric store. Have students develop a list or display of all the different kinds of notions and their uses.

Buy the best quality fabric that you can afford. You waste time and money by working with poor quality fabric. You want to enjoy your sewing and end up with something that lasts and is a pleasure to wear.

Deciding How Much Fabric to Buy

Check the chart on the back of the pattern envelope to find out the amount of fabric to buy. Look at the correct size of the pattern, the view you'll be using, and the width of the fabric. The envelope will also tell you if extra fabric is needed for napped or plaid fabrics.

Estimate the total cost of the project by multiplying the cost per yard of the fabric by the number of yards you need. Add the cost of the pattern, buttons, zipper, and thread. If that total cost is more than you planned to spend, look for a less expensive fabric or shop at another store.

Before buying a fabric, check for characteristics—such as drapability, wrinkle resistance, or stretchability—that could affect your sewing project.

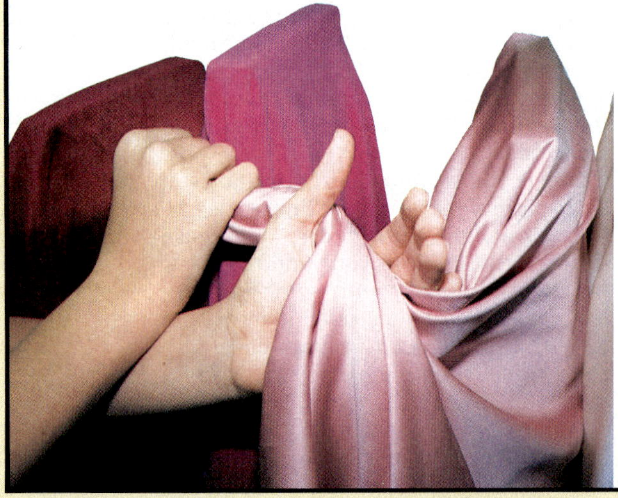

Selecting Notions

When you're buying a pattern and fabric, also buy your notions. The pattern envelope lists the notions that you'll need.

Choosing Colors

Notions should coordinate with your fabric. When buying thread, zippers, seam binding, or bias tape, pick a color that matches or is slightly darker than the fabric. Buttons can match the color of the fabric or contrast with it for accent. If you're unsure about what style or color notions to buy, look at some ready-to-wear clothing for ideas.

Choosing Thread

The thread you use depends on the fabric you are working with. All-purpose thread, such as cotton-wrapped polyester and 100 percent polyester can be used for almost all fabrics. These threads are strong, stretch slightly, and don't shrink. They're especially good for knit and stretch fabrics, as well as fabrics made from manufactured fibers.

If you will be using a serger or overlock machine, buy special serger thread on cones. Because three or four spools of thread are used at once, serger thread is finer and more lightweight than all-purpose thread.

Specialty threads are available for machine embroidery, quilting, topstitching, and sewing on buttons. In addition, there are cotton, silk, rayon, and nylon threads for other specialty sewing.

More About Thread Cotton-covered polyester thread is best for sheer, lightweight, and medium-weight fabrics made of manufactured fibers or blends. Mercerized cotton is best for sheer, lightweight, or medium-weight fabrics made of natural fibers. Heavy-duty cotton and cotton-polyester threads are available for heavy-weight fabrics.

More About Zippers Whitcomb L. Judson's slide fastener was the forerunner of today's zipper. It was first shown at the 1893 Chicago Exposition. The product was very different from a modern zipper—it ran sideways, or perpendicular, to the opening that was to be closed. When the fasteners were first marketed, sales were low because they opened under stress and sometimes tore the fabric.

CHAPTER

61 REVIEW

Reviewing the Facts

1. Why is it helpful to know how to sew?
2. Before picking out a pattern, what do you need to know about yourself?
3. What are two female figure types and two male figure types?
4. Name two non-clothing projects included in pattern catalogs.
5. Why does a page in a pattern catalog often have several different drawings or photos?
6. What are two clues that would help you determine that a pattern might be easy to sew?
7. Where do you find suggestions for the kind of fabric that is suitable for a pattern?
8. List three things to consider when selecting a fabric.

Thinking Critically

1. How can sewing help you use all five design elements to create an illusion that highlights your good features?
2. Why is it a good idea to estimate the cost of a project before making a final decision on the type of fabric you will use?

Applying Your Skills

1. **Taking Body Measurements.** Have a friend or classmate take your measurements, following the guidelines on pages 546–547. Using the pattern size charts found in a pattern catalog, determine the best figure type and pattern size for you to use.

2. **Computing and Comparing Costs.** Go to a fabric store and select a pattern for a sewing project. Also, choose the fabric and the notions. Record the prices and calculate the total cost of the project. Don't forget the cost of the pattern. Could you have purchased a garment of similar style and quality for less money in a department store? At a discount store? On sale?

3. **Predicting Results.** Look through several crafts or women's magazines (for example, *McCall's*, *Woman's Day*, *Family Circle*). Choose a project that you would like to make. Are the instructions clearly written? Are the terms similar to those in pattern instructions? Do you have the necessary skills to complete the project?

Answers to "Thinking Critically"

1. When you sew you have more control over the use of the design elements because you can combine them in the way they work best for you. You can choose fabrics in the colors and textures that are most flattering. You can choose pattern styles that feature the best lines, shapes, and proportions for your body shape.
2. If you have compared the price of sewing with the cost of a similar ready-to-wear item, you may find that it is going to cost you more to sew than to buy the item. The quality of the fabric may be worth the extra cost, or the cost per wearing may be so high that the garment will not be practical.

COMPLETING THE CHAPTER

Summary

- To select patterns, you must know your size, which is determined by taking measurements and finding your figure type.
- Pattern catalogs show what patterns you can buy and give information about sizes, styles, and sewing difficulty.
- Pattern envelopes provide all the information you need to start your project, including recommended fabrics, yardage, and notions.
- Fabric selection depends on the pattern, personal preference, project use, fabric care considerations, and sewing convenience.
- You should buy the best-quality fabric you can afford; you should estimate the total cost of your project before buying.
- Notions, including thread, should coordinate with your fabric.

For Review

Objective Review Questions Have students complete the "Reviewing the Facts" section on this page.

Study Guide Have students complete the Study Guide from Chapter 61 of their *Student Workbook.*

Classifying Information Write two column headings on the board: "Before You Shop for Fabric," and "Before You Buy Fabric." Have students complete the chart, numbering the items in each column to show the sequence of steps they should take in preparing to sew.

For Evaluation

Decision-Making Analysis Have students describe in writing the clothing project they would most like to undertake next and the reasons for that decision.

Chapter Test Have students complete the test for Chapter 61 that appears in the *Teacher's Classroom Resources.*

CHAPTER OVERVIEW

Chapter 62 introduces students to the sewing machine, explaining its parts, operation, accessories, and care. Students learn key sewing machine terms and also read about the serger and other advances in sewing technology. The chapter includes descriptions of tools and equipment used for measuring, cutting, marking, sewing, and pressing.

INTRODUCING THE CHAPTER

Motivators

The Sewing Machine in History Tell students that Elias Howe was a New England farmer whose hobby was inventing machines. The sewing machine he invented in 1845 ran by a hand-turned wheel. It was later improved and mass marketed by another inventor, Isaac Singer. Historians say the machine changed American life. Ask students how. Point out that more clothing could be made in a shorter time. Custom-tailoring businesses declined; the first ready-to-wear shops appeared; women found employment opportunities in the garment industry.

Using the Photograph Direct students' attention to the photograph on this page. Then ask: "What do you notice about the sewing machine? What is happening as the fabric is moved through the machine?"

Sewing Techniques Explain that even though there are many technological advances in the area of sewing, some tasks are still done the old-fashioned way. Prove this by asking for a show of hands from students who have stitched a hem or sewn a button on by hand.

Introducing the Objectives

Discuss the chapter objectives on this page. Remind students that the objectives focus on important chapter content.

CHAPTER

62

Sewing Equipment

OBJECTIVES

This chapter will help you to:

- Describe the parts of the sewing machine and the serger.
- Use a sewing machine.
- Identify and describe the purposes of many pieces of sewing equipment.

WORDS TO REMEMBER

bobbin
feed
lockstitch
looper
serger

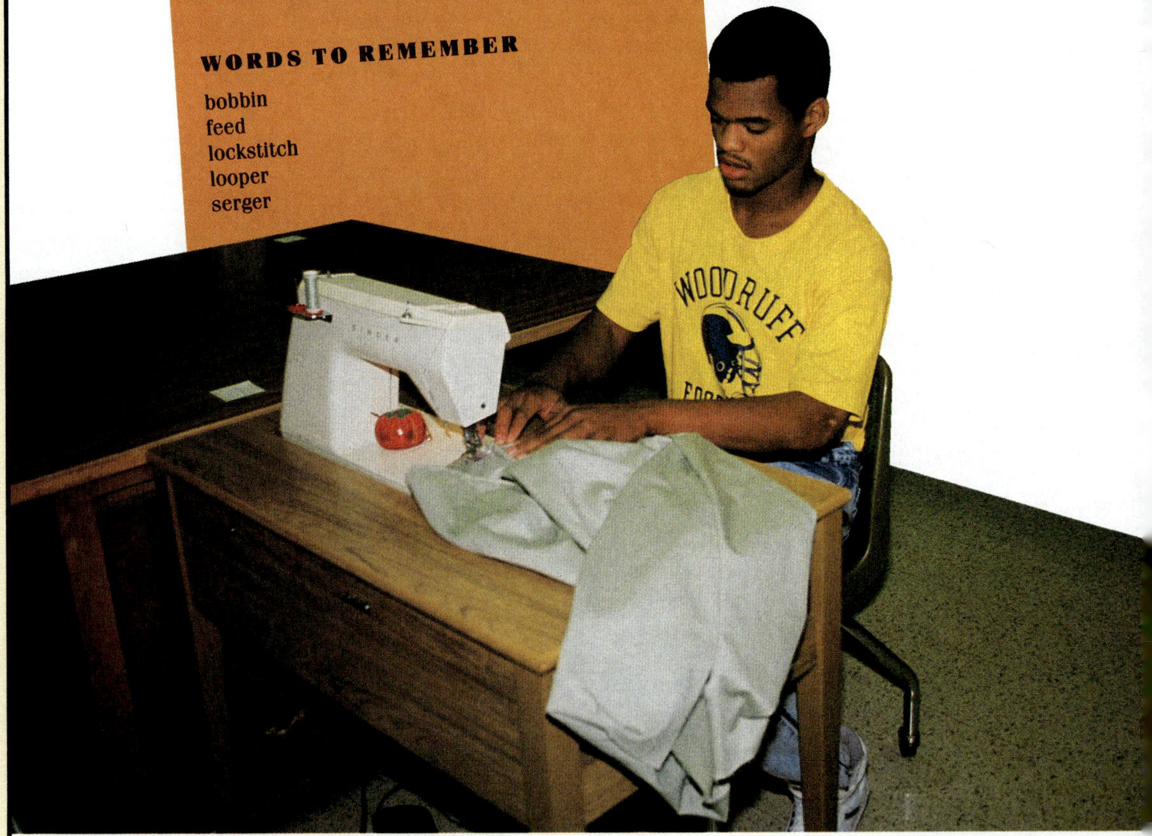

Chapter Resources

Teacher's Classroom Resources
- Lesson Plan
- Life Skills Activity, *Smart Sewing Machine Shopping*
- Reproducible Master, *Parts of the Sewing Machine*
- Extension Activity, *Correcting Stitching Problems*
- Chapter Test

Student Workbook
- Study Guide
- Worksheet, *Sewing Machine Parts*

Many centuries ago, people sewed clothes using long thorns and strips of leather to attach pieces of animal skin together. The results were crude, but sufficient for the way most primitive people lived. Until the 1800s all sewing was done by hand. Then, in 1845, a Massachusetts machinist named Elias Howe invented a workable sewing machine. His invention revolutionized the making of clothing.

We've come a long way since then. We now have electronic, computerized sewing machines that allow you to complete sewing projects with speed and efficiency. **Sergers**, high-speed overlock machines developed for industrial sewing, are now available for home use, helping even more do-it-yourself sewers to achieve professional results.

The Sewing Machine

A sewing machine is the most important piece of sewing equipment. Although sewing machines vary in capabilities and accessories, each machine has the same basic parts and controls. Refer to the chart on page 556 as you read the information in this chapter.

How It Works

Sewing machines join pieces of fabric together with a **lockstitch.** This stitch requires a thread above the fabric to meet another thread coming from below the fabric. The top and bottom threads should link or lock in the middle of the fabric layers. A special tension control on the sewing machine helps form a balanced stitch.

The fabric is moved along by a part of the machine called the **feed**. The feed positions the fabric for the next stitch. The process is repeated over and over again to create a row of stitching.

The machine is operated by a foot or knee control. You can also turn a hand wheel to raise and lower the needle as you begin and end stitching.

Threading the Machine

Each sewing machine model is threaded a bit differently. The basic steps, however, are the same for all machines. The thread goes from the spool to the upper tension control to the take-up lever and down to the needle. Thread guides keep the thread from tangling along the way. You can find diagrams in your machine's manual that will explain how to thread that particular machine.

You must also wind and insert the **bobbin**, a small spool that holds the bottom thread. Wind the bobbin on the machine and insert it in the bobbin case according to the directions in your machine's manual.

Adjustments

You must adjust the type and length of your stitches to suit each sewing job. There are four main types of stitches:

- Regular stitch is a medium-length stitch used for most purposes.
- Basting stitch is a long stitch used for holding layers of fabric together temporarily. It is also used for gathering.
- Reinforcement stitch is a short stitch used to strengthen the stitching area at a corner or point.
- Zigzag stitch is a sideways stitch used to finish seam allowances, make buttonholes, and sew special seams.

Introducing Vocabulary

Tell students that they will find new words in this chapter describing the parts and functions of sewing machines. Refer them to the chart on page 556. Tell students that they must know these terms in order to follow directions for operating a sewing machine.

TEACHING THE CHAPTER

For convenience, the teaching suggestions for this chapter are arranged according to the following lesson topics:

- "The Sewing Machine," pages 555-557
- "The Serger," page 559
- "Other Sewing Tools and Equipment," pages 560-561

Teaching "The Sewing Machine"
(Pages 555-557)

This section describes how sewing machines work and how they are threaded, adjusted, accessorized, and maintained.

Checking Comprehension

✓ Explain what a lockstitch is. *A sewing machine stitch that joins pieces of fabric together. A thread from above the fabric meets another thread from below the fabric. The top and bottom threads link or lock in the middle of the fabric layers.*

✓ What is the function of the feed? *It moves the fabric into position for the next stitch.*

✓ How do you thread a sewing machine? *Each model is threaded a bit differently, but the basic steps are the same for each machine. The thread goes from the spool to the upper tension control to the take-up lever and down to the needle.*

✓ What four kinds of stitches do sewing machines make? *Regular, basting, reinforcement, and zig-zag.*

Emphasize For sewing projects to turn out right, students must make machine stitches that interlock correctly and that suit the sewing task.

Focus on Technology Early sewing machines had to be operated by hand. Later, a treadle was added, which people could move up and down with their feet. Pulleys and gears connected the treadle to the balance wheel, freeing people's hands for other sewing tasks. After the invention of electric motors, sewing machines were fitted with motors to drive the balance wheel. People could turn the power to the machine off and on by using a pedal, lever, or switch.

Teaching the Feature
"The Language of Sergers"

Answers to Feature Questions

1. Answers will vary according to students' levels of interest in this area.

2. Some advantages are: it stitches much faster than a conventional machine; it eliminates seam finishes as an extra step because it stitches and finishes a seam at the same time; you don't have to fill a bobbin; stitches are all the same length and are even because stitches are formed on the stitch fingers.

Activities

Who Needs It? Ask students to suggest the kinds of people who could make the best use of a serger. Point out that many of the features of these machines would not be required by people who sew only occasionally. However, because sergers stitch so fast, they can be real timesavers for professional sewers or tailors, and for people who do a lot of sewing at home.

Community Contact Have students check to see if there are local people who use sergers for professional dressmaking or alterations. They may do dressmaking and alterations in their home, for a department store, or at a dry cleaner. Have students ask these professionals what the advantages and disadvantages of the serger are in their profession.

TECHNOLOGY

The Language of Sergers

It may seem that another language is used to describe serger parts and techniques. Knowing the terminology will make it easier to understand the differences between a serger and a conventional sewing machine. Here are some of the terms commonly used with sergers:

- **Cones.** Sergers use cones instead of spools of thread. A serger can have up to five cones of thread instead of only one spool. Because sergers use more thread than conventional sewing machines do, cones are practical because they hold up to 1,000 yards of thread. In comparison, a large spool holds only about 175 yards of thread. Serger thread is lighter weight than all-purpose thread.
- **Loopers.** Sergers have loopers instead of bobbins. One advantage to this is that you don't have to worry about running out of bobbin thread. You can always see how much thread you have left.
- **Thread guide holder.** This looks like a mini television antenna on the back of the machine. Each thread goes through a loop on this holder before it goes through its own set of tension dials.
- **Tension dials.** These dials are different from the tension control dial on a conventional sewing machine. On a serger these dials are used to change the pattern of the stitch. On a conventional machine, you adjust the tension to create a balanced stitch.
- **Thread guides.** These are used to help with the threading. To change threads, a new thread can be tied to the old one and pulled through each thread guide. This is easier than rethreading the machine because each thread goes through up to eight guides.
- **Stitch finger.** This is a metal prong on the needle plate or the presser foot. This prong determines the width of the stitch and prevents the overedge stitches from pulling too tight around the edge of the fabric. When you are serging, stitches form around the stitch finger and the fabric edge at the same time.
- **Tail chain.** On a serger you start with a thread tail chain, made without fabric under the needle. This tail chain is created as the loopers wrap the thread around the stitch fingers. At the end of the row of stitching, continue running the machine until you have several inches of tail chain behind the needle.

Think It Through

1. **Do you think you would enjoy working on a serger? Why or why not?**
2. **What do you think are the advantages of using a serger?**

Emphasize The serger does not replace the conventional sewing machine. Both machines may be used to construct a garment. Special methods have been developed for using a serger to sew many garment details. Depending on the style or the fabric, some garments may be sewn entirely on the serger; others may also require the use of a conventional machine.

More About Sergers Phrases that are used with serging are "Pull up the antenna," "Don't get your tail caught in the door," "Close the doors," "Left is loose, right is tight," "Put the knife down," and "I've got a tension headache."

The Serger

The serger, or overlock machine, trims, sews, and overcasts in one step. It creates the special stitches that you see on seams of ready-to-wear garments. Sergers sew at extremely high speed and can form up to 1,500 stitches per minute.

Sergers are known as 2-thread, 3-thread, 4-thread, or 5-thread, depending on the number of threads used to make the stitch. Each thread goes through a separate tension disc. Sergers do not have bobbins. Instead they have **loopers** that perform like bobbins do in conventional sewing machines. The looper threads loop around each other and are interlocked with the needle thread, or threads. Depending on the model, sergers may have one or two needles. A well-adjusted serger stitch interlocks exactly on the cut edge of the seam.

Another difference between sergers and sewing machines is the cutting knife. There are small knife blades on the serger that work like scissors to trim the fabric to the width of the stitch.

In addition to stitching seams, sergers can do narrow rolled hems, similar to the hems on napkins or silk scarves. With other adjustments they can produce a blind hemming stitch and a flatlock stitch. The flatlock stitch is a flat seam that can be used to decorate lingerie, T-shirts, and sweatshirts.

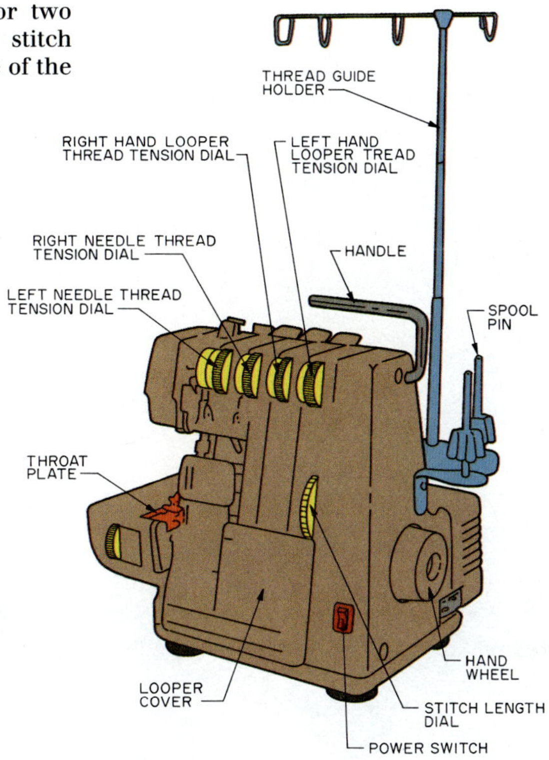

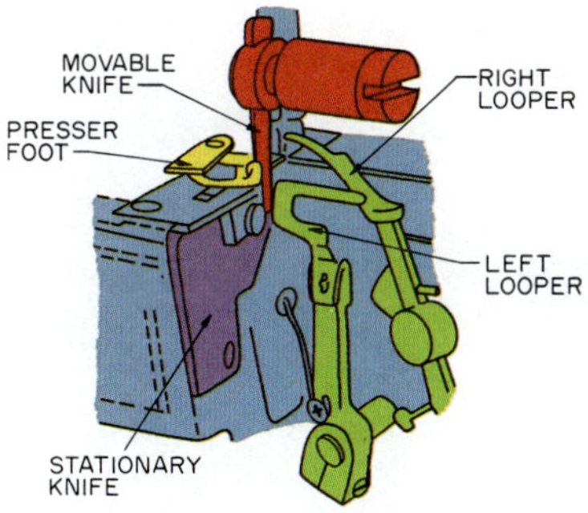

The serger can stitch, trim, and overcast a seam in one step. What are the similarities and differences between a serger and a conventional sewing machine?

Teaching "The Serger"
(Page 559)

This section explains the differences between sergers and regular sewing machines and identifies some advantages and disadvantages of using a serger.

Checking Comprehension

✓ What does a serger do that distinguishes it from a regular sewing machine? *It trims, sews, and overcasts in one step at very high speed.*

✓ List two specific ways in which sergers differ from sewing machines. *Any two: Sergers use from two to five threads; sewing machines use two. Sergers do not have bobbins like sewing machines; they have loopers. Sergers also have a cutting knife that works like scissors to trim the fabric to the width of the stitch; sewing machines don't have any feature resembling this.*

✓ What do loopers do? *Loop thread around each other before interlocking with the needle threads.*

✓ What is a flatlock stitch? *A flat seam stitch used on lingerie, T-shirts, and sweatshirts.*

Activities

Skill Builder: Critical Thinking
Have students examine the seam and hem stitches in clothing they are wearing. What seams and hems do they think were made on a serger? What leads them to think so?

Reteaching
Have students develop a chart comparing and contrasting sergers with regular sewing machines.

Enrichment
Ask students to visit stores where sewing machines are sold and to request a demonstration of the serger. Have students report and discuss their impressions.

Did You Know? Sergers were originally developed in the early 1900s by manufacturers of military uniforms made of serge. Serge is a kind of cloth woven in a twill pattern from woolen fibers. Sergers enabled manufacturers to quickly provide a great many uniforms at a price the government could afford.

Emphasize A serger stitch interlocks exactly on the cut edge of the seam, in the middle of the fabric layers. A regular sewing machine stitch interlocks in the same place but at some distance from the cut edges of the seam.

Teaching "Other Sewing Tools and Equipment"
(Pages 560-561)

This section identifies additional equipment needed for sewing, including tools for measuring, cutting, marking, pinning, hand stitching, and pressing.

Checking Comprehension

✓ What is a yardstick or meter stick used for? *For measuring fabric, checking grain lines, marking hems, and drawing long lines.*

✓ How are pinking shears different from regular shears? *Pinking shears have zigzag-shaped blades that finish the edge of firmly woven fabric and prevent raveling. Regular shears have long, straight blades.*

✓ How do you use tracing paper and a tracing wheel? *You lay tracing paper down on the fabric and transfer the pattern markings by using the tracing wheel along the lines.*

✓ What is an advantage of chalk over liquid marking pencils? *Chalk brushes or irons off of fabrics, whereas liquid pencil marks must be washed off before pressing.*

✓ Why might you need a press cloth? *To prevent shiny marks on fabric caused by an iron's heat.*

Other Sewing Tools and Equipment

You will need additional supplies to do sewing projects. These special tools are used for measuring, cutting, marking, pinning, hand stitching, and pressing.

Measuring Tools

- **Tape measure.** You need this to take body measurements. It should be flexible and 60 in. (1.5 m) long.
- **Yardstick/meter stick.** This is used to measure fabric, check grain lines, mark hems, and draw long lines. The sticks are 36 in. or one meter (39.5 in.) long and are made of wood.
- **Ruler.** A 12 in. (30.5 cm) ruler with 1/8 in. (3 mm) markings can be used to measure and mark lines. A see-through plastic ruler is practical.
- **Sewing gauge.** This is a 6 in. (15 cm) ruler with an adjustable sliding marker that is used to measure small areas, such as seams or hems.

Cutting Tools

Scissors and shears should cut along the whole blade. Buy good cutting tools, which will last a long time. Oil and sharpen your cutting tools regularly to keep them in good working order.

- **Shears.** These have long blades, and the two handles are shaped differently. They are used to cut fabric.

Which of these sewing tools and equipment can you name?

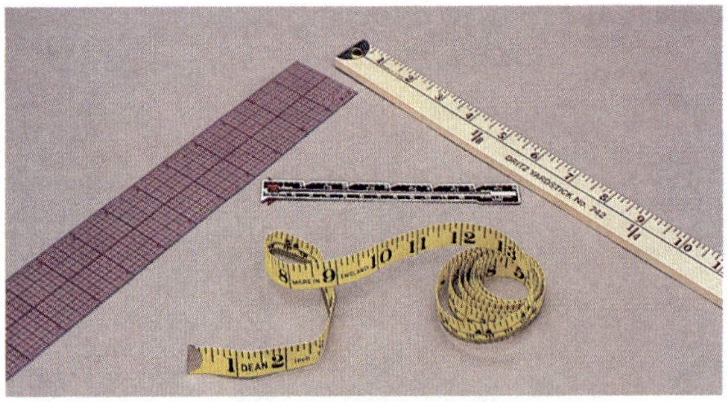

MEASURING

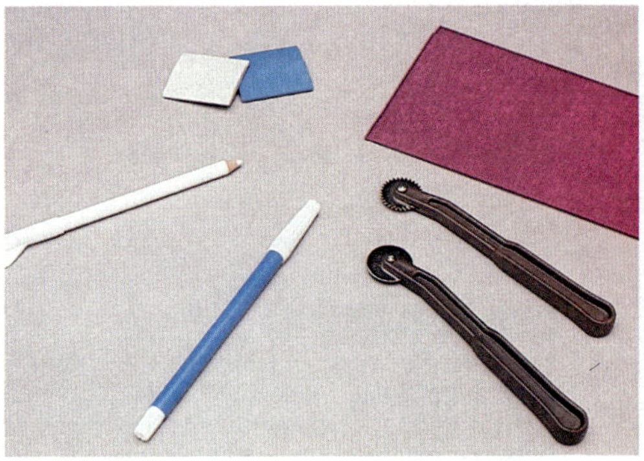

MARKING

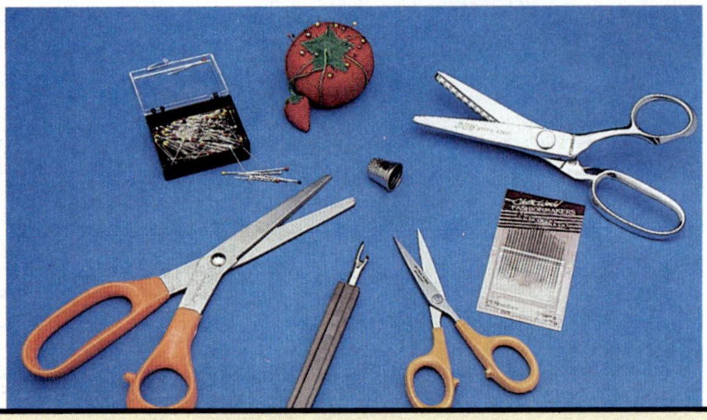

CUTTING AND SEWING

PRESSING

More About Consumer Skills There are many different types of sewing tools on the market. Some are necessary for even beginning sewers to have—others are used only for very specialized tasks and can be added as a person's skills and interest grows. If you take good care of your sewing tools, they will last for many years.

Emphasize Always use a measuring device that is appropriate to the task. A project quickly becomes difficult if you use a yardstick to measure a 5/8-inch seam and a 6-inch sewing gauge to measure pattern length.

Cross-Reference See "Safe Use of Sewing Tools" on page 566.

Bent-handled shears are easiest to use because the fabric can stay flat on a surface as you cut.

- **Scissors.** These are smaller than shears and are used for trimming and clipping. Both handles are the same shape.
- **Pinking shears.** These shears have zigzag-shaped blades. They can be used to finish the edge of firmly woven fabrics and help prevent raveling.
- **Seam ripper.** This penlike object has a sharp, pointed end and small blade for removing stitches.

Marking Aids

Here are some of the marking tools that are used to transfer pattern symbols to fabric.

- **Tracing paper.** This comes in several colors. Choose a color that will show up on the fabric without being too dark. Double-faced tracing paper allows you to mark two layers of fabric at one time.
- **Tracing wheel.** This device is used with tracing paper to transfer pattern markings. Wheels with sawtooth edges can be used for most fabrics. Smooth-edged wheels are best for delicate fabrics.
- **Chalk.** Chalk can be used to mark most fabrics. The markings can be brushed off or will disappear when pressed with an iron. Chalk is available as colored squares, pencils, or powder.
- **Liquid marking pencils.** These make quick work of marking tucks, darts, pleats, and pocket locations. Use the type that washes off with water. Pressing may set the marks permanently, so remove the marking before pressing the area.

Small Equipment

Some additional items are essential for pinning and hand sewing.

- **Pins.** These are used to fasten the pattern to the fabric and to hold fabric layers together for stitching. Pins with colored heads are easy to see and use.
- **Needles.** Needles for hand sewing come in a variety of sizes and lengths. The smaller the number, the larger the needle. Sizes 7 and 8 are good for most purposes.
- **Pincushion.** This is better than a box for holding pins because the pins can't spill onto the table or floor. Magnetic pin holders are convenient to use and are handy for picking up spilled pins.
- **Thimble.** A thimble made of metal or plastic is used to push the needle through the fabric when hand sewing. Wear it on your middle finger.

Pressing Equipment

Pressing as you sew will make your sewing easier and more accurate.

- **Steam iron.** An iron that steams and sprays at any setting, not just the high settings, gives best results.
- **Ironing board.** Your ironing board should have a well-padded, clean cover. It also should be adjustable for your height.
- **Press cloth.** For some fabrics, a press cloth is needed to prevent shiny marks caused by the iron's heat. It can be dampened to provide additional steam for hard-to-press fabrics.
- **Tailor's ham.** This firm cushion, shaped like a ham, is used for pressing curved seams and darts.

More About Pins Silk pins are designed for delicate fabrics and are very fine so that the fabric will not show puncture marks. Pins of any type or size should be brass or stainless steel dressmaker pins, because steel pins rust easily and can leave rust marks in fabric. Pins can damage sewing machine mechanisms, which is a good reason for using a pincushion rather than placing pins on the machine base. Pincushions can be worn on the wrist for convenience.

Activities

Skill Builder: Math
Have students work with tools for measuring fabric length and width and for measuring the gauge of stitches. Ask students to solve the following problem: A fabric piece to be gathered measures 24 in. *(about 61 cm).* If you make 72 stitches across the piece, what gauge (number of stitches per inch) are you using? *(3 per inch)* If gathering should reduce the length of the piece by 50 percent, how long should the gathered piece be? *(12 in. [about 30.5 cm]).*

Reteaching
Have students practice using the tools and equipment described in this section. Ask students to exchange tools round-robin fashion and to keep a checklist of items used. Give extra practice with items students find most unfamiliar or difficult to use.

Enrichment
Have students examine the patterns they selected and predict how they might use the tools described in this section to make their sewing projects. Ask students to save their predictions to check against the information in the next chapter.

COMPLETING THE CHAPTER

Summary

- Sewing machines have similar basic parts and controls, such as the needle, feed, and tension control, for joining pieces of fabric together with thread.
- Sewing machines are threaded with top threads and bottom threads that interlock in the middle of the fabric layers.
- Sewing machines adjust for the length and tightness of stitches.
- Sewing machine needles come in different sizes and types for different fabrics.
- Sewing machines have attachments for special tasks, such as sewing zippers.
- Sewing machines need regular maintenance and careful handling.
- Sergers trim, sew, and overcast in one step—at high speeds.
- Sergers use two to five threads; they have loopers instead of bobbins and knife blades for trimming.
- Measuring tools include tape measures, yardsticks or meter sticks, rulers, and sewing gauges. Cutting tools include shears, scissors, pinking shears, and seam rippers. Marking tools include tracing paper, tracing wheels, chalk, and liquid marking pencils.
- Other equipment includes pins, needles, pincushions, and thimbles.
- Pressing equipment includes a steam iron, ironing board, press cloth, and tailor's ham.

For Review

Objective Review Questions Have students complete the "Reviewing the Facts" section on this page.

Study Guide Have students complete the Study Guide from Chapter 62 of their *Student Workbook*.

For Evaluation

Label A Diagram Give students a blank diagram of a sewing machine, and ask them to label as many parts and features as they can.

Chapter Test Have students complete the test for Chapter 62 that appears in the *Teacher's Classroom Resources*.

CHAPTER 62 REVIEW

Answers to "Reviewing the Facts"

1. In 1845, by Elias Howe.
2. By a lockstitch—the top and bottom threads are locked together in the middle of the fabric layers.
3. The feed.
4. It should be unplugged, covered or put away in its cabinet or case, cleaned regularly, and oiled occasionally.
5. Trims, sews, and overcasts.
6. Any three: tape measure, yardstick or meter stick, ruler, sewing gauge.
7. Shears have long blades and handles that are shaped differently; scissors are smaller and have handles that are the same shape.
8. Any three: tracing paper, tracing wheel, chalk, liquid marking pencil.

Reviewing the Facts

1. When and by whom was the sewing machine invented?
2. How does the sewing machine join pieces of fabric together?
3. What part of the sewing machine moves the fabric along?
4. How should a sewing machine be cared for between uses?
5. What are the three things that a serger does in one step?
6. List three measuring tools used in sewing.
7. What is the difference between shears and scissors?
8. Name three useful marking tools.

Thinking Critically

1. When purchasing a sewing machine or a serger, what factors do you think you should consider?
2. How can knowing how to use a sewing machine be valuable?

Applying Your Skills

1. **Writing Instructions.** Make up a game to identify and explain the important terms in this chapter. Be sure to develop a key for reference later. Terms should include parts of the sewing machine and serger, and sewing tools and equipment.

2. **Compare Costs.** List any sewing tools and equipment that you already have. What additional tools would you need to begin a sewing project? Estimate the cost of these tools, and add the total to the cost of the item you would like to make. Would it be more or less expensive to buy a ready-made item? What other options might you have?

3. **Comparing Techniques.** Demonstrate the use of various sewing tools and equipment on different types, weights, and colors of fabrics. For example, cutting with shears, scissors, and pinking shears; marking with tracing paper, chalk, and pencils; and pressing with and without a press cloth. How do the results differ? What recommendations can you make for different fabrics?

Answers to "Thinking Critically"

1. Answers may include: your sewing needs; the type and amount of sewing that you expect to do; the price, quality, and particular features of different models; the reputation of the dealer.
2. Advantages include: saving money by making clothes and other items rather than buying them ready-made; being able to make clothes that are specifically created for the individual; being able to alter and repair clothes; making money by selling hand-sewn items or alteration services; developing a lifelong skill.

CHAPTER

63

Lay Out, Cut, and Mark

OBJECTIVES

This chapter will help you to:

- Adjust a pattern to fit your body shape.
- Prepare the fabric and lay out the pattern pieces.
- Cut out and mark the fabric pieces.

WORDS TO REMEMBER

directional cutting
ease
grain
layout
seam allowance
selvage

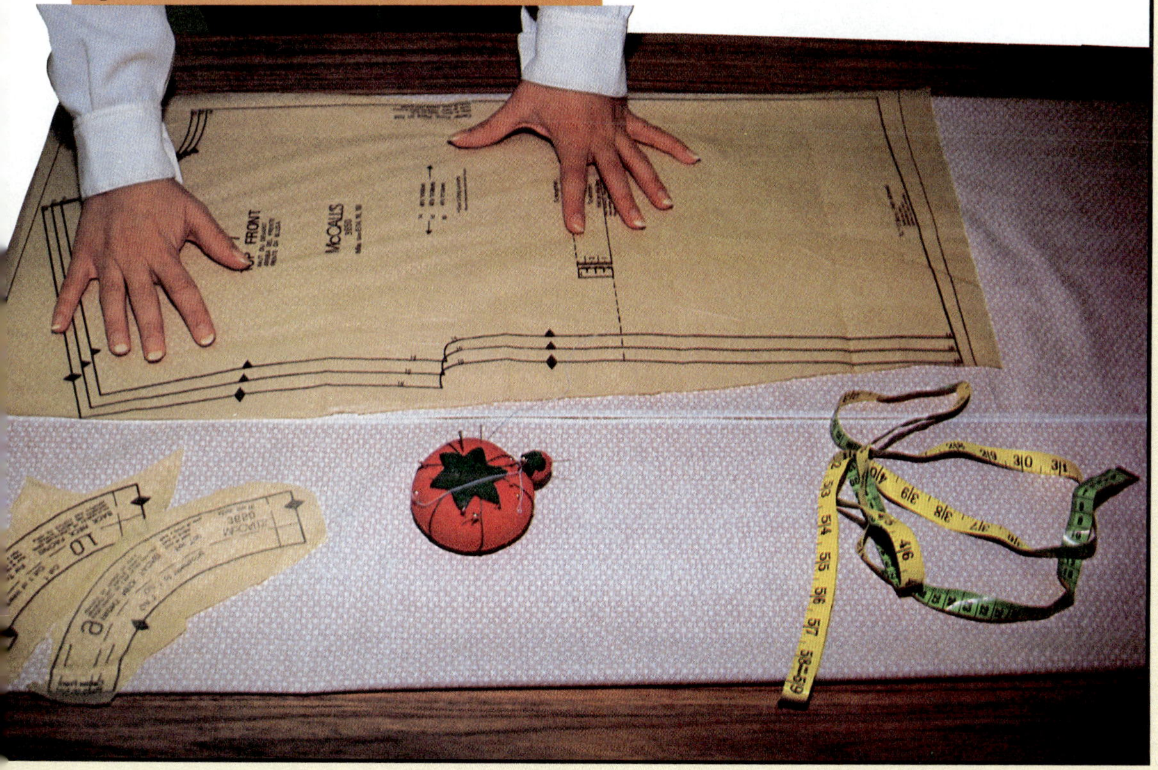

Chapter Resources

Teacher's Classroom Resources
- Lesson Plan
- Life Skills Activity, *Stop! Before You Cut . . .*
- Reproducible Master, *Patterns and Pattern Terms*
- Extension Activity, *Sewing Safety*
- Chapter Test

Student Workbook
- Study Guide
- Worksheet, *Identify Pattern Markings*

CHAPTER OVERVIEW

Chapter 63 instructs students in the procedures for preparing to sew. Students learn how to check and adjust their patterns; prepare fabric; lay out, pin, and cut their patterns; and transfer pattern marks to the fabric pieces. The chapter presents definitions of pattern terms and diagrams of preparation steps.

INTRODUCING THE CHAPTER

Motivators

What Next? Have students bring their patterns and fabric to class. Ask them to make a list of all the steps they expect to take before using the sewing machine. Have students save their lists to revise after completing the chapter.

Using the Photograph Direct students' attention to the photograph on this page. Then ask: "What is the person in the picture doing? Why do you think it is important to do that? What do you think the person will do next?"

Doll's Dress Using a pattern for a doll's dress, demonstrate the steps described in this chapter. Ask students: "What am I doing?" Clarify their observations by giving the correct sewing terms, for example, "Yes, now I'm doing the *layout.*" Have students identify each sewing tool you use. Check their comprehension by asking, "Why do you think I'm doing this?" or "Why do you think I'm doing it this way?"

Introducing the Objectives

Discuss the chapter objectives on this page. Remind students that the objectives focus on important chapter content.

Introducing Vocabulary

To help students remember the meaning of the word *selvage*, point out that it comes from "self edge," meaning the edge of the fabric "itself" where a narrow woven border prevents raveling. Other pattern terms appear in the chart on page 564.

TEACHING THE CHAPTER

For convenience, the teaching suggestions for this chapter are arranged according to the following lesson topics:

- "Preparing Your Pattern," page 565
- "Preparing Your Fabric," page 567
- "Lay out and Cutting" and "Marking the Fabric," pages 567-568

Teaching "Preparing Your Pattern"

(Page 565)

This section explains how to use a pattern guide sheet and instructs students in comparing their body measurements with pattern measurements and adjusting the pattern as needed.

Checking Comprehension

✓ What information is on the pattern guide sheet? *Step-by-step information for cutting, marking, and sewing the garment or accessory. The front of the guide sheet contains general instructions, information about pattern symbols, and diagrams for laying out the pattern pieces.*

✓ What should you do with pattern pieces before laying them out? *Press them, write your name on them, and compare your body measurements with those listed on the back of the pattern envelope to see if you have to make adjustments.*

✓ What is a pattern's seam allowance? *The space between the cutting line and the stitching line.*

✓ What effect does ease have on pattern measurements? *It makes pattern measurements larger than body measurements.*

✓ How can you lengthen a pattern? *By cutting at the adjustment line and adding extra tissue paper or by adding to the bottom of the pattern.*

You are now probably anxious to start sewing. You have your pattern, fabric, notions, and sewing equipment; you're ready to start the sewing process.

In this chapter, you will learn the four steps to go through before you can actually begin sewing on the machine.

The four steps are:

1. Preparing your pattern.
2. Preparing your fabric.
3. Laying out the pattern pieces and cutting the fabric.
4. Marking the fabric.

The result of careful preparation will be a garment that looks good and fits well.

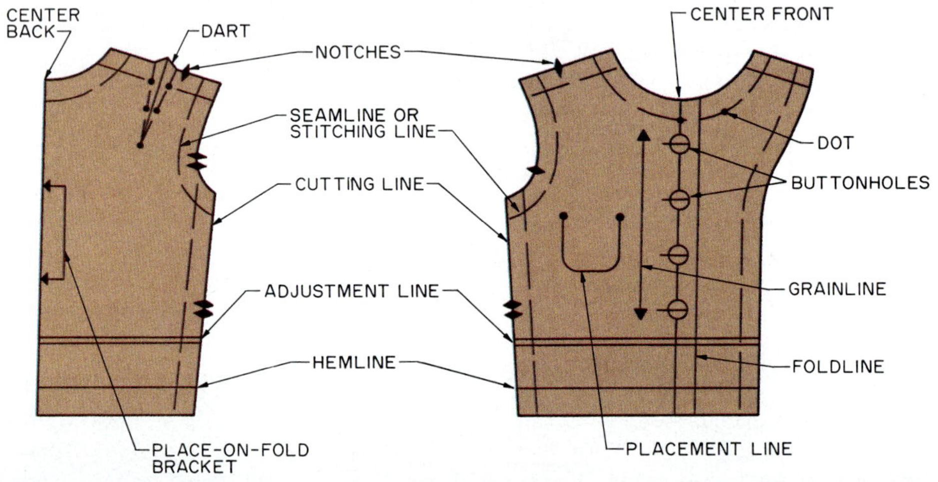

Patterns and Pattern Terms

Adjustment line A double line, where the pattern may be lengthened or shortened.

Buttonholes Marked by lines that show the exact location and length.

Center front and center back Solid lines that show the center of the garment.

Cutting line The heavier outer line, along which you cut.

Dart Consists of two broken lines and corresponding dots.

Dots Used for matching seams and construction details.

Foldline A solid line showing where the fabric is to be folded.

Grainline The heavy solid line with arrows at each end that shows the direction of the grain.

Hemline A solid line indicating the finished edge of the garment.

Notches Diamond-shaped symbols along the cutting line that are used for matching seams.

Placement line Line showing the exact location of pocket, zipper, or trim.

Place-on-fold bracket The symbol which shows that the pattern piece is to be placed along a fold of fabric.

Seamline or stitching line A broken line ⅝" inside the cutting line (unless otherwise noted).

Emphasize The various lines and symbols on the pattern pieces serve as guides during cutting and sewing. Some pattern pieces will have many markings and symbols; others will have only a few. Stress that it is important to recognize and understand these pattern symbols and terms.

Did You Know? To compare pattern piece sizes with body measurements, you measure the front and back pattern sections, add together, and double the total. The result should equal your body measurement plus the ease allowance.

Preparing Your Pattern

First, take out your pattern guide sheet. This sheet gives you step-by-step information for cutting, marking, and sewing the garment or accessory. The front of the guide sheet contains general instructions, information about pattern symbols, and diagrams for laying out the pattern pieces. Circle the layout for your pattern size, view, and width of fabric.

Now, take out the pattern pieces that you'll need. Press them with a warm, not hot, dry iron to make them smooth and flat. Write your name on all your pattern pieces, the pattern envelope, and the guide sheet.

Next, find the measurements that you took before you bought the pattern. Compare them with those listed on the pattern envelope to see if you'll need to adjust the pattern to make it fit better.

Checking Pattern Measurements

If your body measurements do not exactly match those listed on the back of the pattern envelope, you may have to make adjustments. You must change the pattern so that the finished garment will fit you properly.

If there's a difference of an inch (2.5 cm) or more between your measurements and the size measurements on the envelope, you'll probably have to make adjustments. You can check with your instructor to be sure, because if a pattern style is loose or full, adjustments may not be necessary.

You can also compare your measurements to those of the pattern by actually measuring the pattern pieces. Measure only from seam to seam. Don't include the **seam allowance**. This is the fabric between the line for cutting and the line for stitching. The seam allowance is 5/8 in. (1.5 cm) from the cutting line. If your pattern has three sizes printed on it, the seam allowance line is not marked. You will have to measure it yourself.

Remember that the pattern includes **ease**. This is extra room that a pattern allows for clothing to fit comfortably. Because of the ease, pattern pieces measure larger than size measurements. The difference might be 3 to 4 in. (7.5 to 9.5 cm) at the bust, 3/4 to 1 in. (2 to 2.5 cm) at the waist, and 2 in. (5 cm) at the hips. Thus, a pattern for 34 in. (87 cm) hips would actually measure 36 in. (92 cm). Patterns for bathing suits and leotards will have little or no ease because they fit close to the body.

Simple Adjustments

Lengthening or shortening a pattern is the easiest adjustment to make. An adjustment line is printed on some pattern pieces to show where they can be lengthened or shortened; others can be adjusted at the lower edge.

Shorten a pattern piece by taking a tuck at the adjustment line or at the bottom. If a pattern must be made longer, cut it apart at the adjustment line. Insert and tape a strip of tissue paper between the two pieces, or add it to the bottom of the pattern. Don't forget to adjust the front and the back.

Adjusting for width is a little more complicated. An increase or decrease of 1 in. (2.5 cm) or less can be done at the side seams. Just draw new seamlines parallel to the old, adding tissue paper if necessary. If you have to add or subtract more than 1 in. (2.5 cm), get assistance from your instructor. Multi-sized patterns have three separate cutting lines. You may be able to make a width adjustment by using two sizes. Blend gradually from one size to the next in areas where you need to adjust the width.

More About Patterns Patterns came into use in the second half of the nineteenth century. Patterns were needed to mass-produce ready-made clothing. Pattern use spread to the general public from the garment industry along with the spread of the sewing machine.

Did You Know? For loosely fitted garments, minor differences in body measurements and the measurements listed on the pattern envelope can be overlooked. For tightly fitted garments, the measurements should correspond very closely.

Activities

Skill Builder: Science
To help students understand the concept of ease, have them measure the bust, waist, and hips on pattern pieces for different garments and different sizes. Then have them compare those measurements with the measurements given on the pattern envelope. In most cases, they should find that the measurements they have taken are larger than those given on the envelope. Ask them if the pattern pieces are larger by a consistent number of inches. If so, how many?

Reteaching
Have students practice the steps outlined in this section. Review the pattern guide sheet. Have them compare body measurements with pattern measurements. Have students identify the seam allowance, cutting line, and adjustment line on pattern pieces and make decisions about adjustments.

Enrichment
Ask students why there are limits to the amount of pattern adjustment you can make. Demonstrate the effects of radical adjustments on garment proportions and shape. For example, with radical side seam adjustments, sleeves won't fit the armholes and the garment might be out of proportion with the shoulders or other elements.

Teaching "Preparing Your Fabric"

(Page 567)

This section explains how to preshrink fabric and straighten its grain before laying out the pattern.

Checking Comprehension

✔ How do you know if you should preshrink your fabric? *If the bolt-end label lacks information or says the fabric will shrink more than 1 percent.*

✔ What happens if you don't straighten the grain? *The hemline might hang unevenly, or the garment might twist to one side.*

Teaching the Feature
"Safe Use of Sewing Tools"

Answers to Feature Questions

1. Students might suggest posters, inspection, and discussions.
2. Other safety tips include not running or fooling around in the sewing room; supervising children and pets; checking the sewing machine stand for sturdiness.

Activities

Classifying Information Have students identify the safety rules that relate to each of the following goals: to prevent burns; to prevent electric shock; to prevent cuts and punctures; to prevent falls and bruises; to protect equipment from damage; to prevent equipment loss. Some safety tips can be listed under more than one purpose.

Designing for Safety Have students visit the library to look at home interiors in homemaking and housing design magazines. Have students find designs for sewing rooms or sewing areas in homes. Then have them make a collage of good safety features. How do the designs reflect the safety tips described in the feature?

Community Contact Arrange to have a residential interior designer speak to the class about designs for sewing areas. Ask the designer to review the students' collages and comment on feasible safety features.

HEALTH WATCH

Safe Use of Sewing Tools

You will prevent accidents and injuries in the sewing room by following a few general safety tips.

- Keep pins in a pincushion or magnetic pin holder, never in your mouth or stuck in your clothes.
- Keep scissors, shears, and seam rippers closed when you are not using them.
- When passing scissors or shears to another person, pass them with the handle out.
- Keep your tools and supplies in your sewing box when they are not being used.
- Use a magnetic pin holder to pick up loose pins around your sewing machine. Be careful not to drop pins.

Using a sewing machine:

- Keep the sewing machine cord out of the way so that no one trips over it.
- If you are learning how to use a sewing machine or serger, use a slow speed until you are comfortable enough to sew faster.
- Keep your fingers away from the needle of the sewing machine and the cutting knives of the serger.
- Do not lean your face too close to the machine when stitching in case the needle breaks.
- Remove pins as you come to them. Do not stitch over them as they might break or dull the sewing machine needle.
- When you are not using the sewing machine, unplug the cord from the outlet and then disconnect the cord from the machine.
- Close the sewing machine carefully or cover it when you are finished sewing.

Using an iron:

- Don't touch a hot iron anywhere but on the handle.
- Keep your fingers and face away from the steam.
- Place the iron cord so that the iron cannot be accidentally pulled off the ironing board.
- Rest the iron on its heel when not in use.
- Unplug the iron when finished. Empty any water from it. Be sure the iron has cooled completely before putting it away.

Think It Through

1. **If you were a sewing instructor, what steps would you take to ensure that your students were following safe sewing practices?**
2. **How many more sewing safety tips can you list?**

More About Safety Sewing machine needles are less likely to break if you use the type that is meant for the kind of fabric you are sewing with. Also, hot irons should not be placed near paper or plastic products that can catch on fire or melt.

Emphasize Do not leave children or pets unattended when irons, sewing machines, or sewing equipment is in reach.

Preparing Your Fabric

The next step is to decide if your fabric needs to be preshrunk or straightened. Read the label on the bolt of the fabric to check if the material has been preshrunk. If the label says it will shrink more than 1 percent, or if no information is given, you should preshrink the fabric before cutting out the pieces. To preshrink washable fabrics, wash and dry the fabric according to the care instructions. Fabrics that cannot be machine or hand washed must be taken to a drycleaner for preshrinking.

Straightening grain is another step in preparing your fabric. Fabric **grain** is the direction in which the yarns run. Lengthwise and crosswise grains should meet at right angles. If the fabric is not straightened before the pieces are cut out, the hemline may hang unevenly or the garment may twist to one side. To check grain, first straighten the fabric ends. For a woven fabric, pull a thread across the width of the fabric and cut along this crosswise thread or cut along a woven stripe or other woven line. For a knit, cut along a row of loops.

Next, fold the fabric in half, matching lengthwise and crosswise edges. If the fabric isn't smooth, and the corners do not match exactly, it is off-grain. You may be able to straighten it by steam pressing. Pin the fabric along the **selvages**, the finished edges of the fabric, and along both ends. Press from the selvage to the fold. Fabrics that have a permanent finish can't be straightened.

To be sure the pattern piece is exactly on grain, measure from each end of the arrow to the selvage. If the distances are not equal, move the pattern and remeasure.

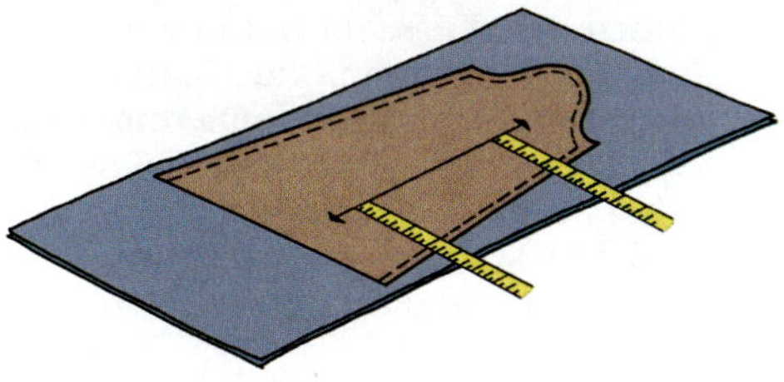

Layout and Cutting

The laying out and cutting of pattern pieces and fabric should be done in a comfortable place. It is best to work on a large, flat surface such as a table topped with a cutting board.

Laying Out the Pattern

The pattern **layout** is a diagram that shows how to place the pattern pieces on your fabric. Its purpose is to help you use fabric as economically as possible, with little waste. Special layouts may be given for fabrics with a nap or directional print.

Follow the layout that you circled on the pattern guide sheet. Fold your fabric as shown on the layout, with the right sides together. Smooth the fabric flat on a surface that is large enough to hold the fabric width. Then follow the layout as you arrange your pattern pieces on the fabric. To avoid mistakes, lay out all the pieces before starting to pin and cut.

First, pin any pattern pieces placed along the fold line. These pieces have a bracket arrow on a straight edge. Next, pin the pattern pieces that have grainline arrows in the center of the pattern piece.

Smooth out each pattern piece and pin it diagonally at the corners. Then place pins about 6 in. (15 cm) apart at right angles to the edges. Make sure that the pins don't extend into the cutting lines.

✓ How do you straighten grain? *By folding lengthwise and steam pressing from the selvages to the fold.*

Activities

Skill Builder: Writing
To help students understand and remember the concept of grain, ask them to write two sentences in which they use the term *against the grain.* The first sentence should use the term in a literal way, and the second sentence should use the term in a figurative way.

Reteaching
Help students identify the grain in the fabric they selected for their sewing projects, and have them practice the steps outlined in this section.

Enrichment
Have students find out through research or experiments which fabrics are more susceptible to grain problems and why.

Teaching "Layout and Cutting" and "Marking the Fabric"
(Pages 567-568)

This section explains the use of layout diagrams and the proper techniques for laying out patterns, pinning them to fabric, and cutting out the fabric. This section also presents alternatives for transferring pattern marks to cut fabric.

Checking Comprehension

✓ Are pieces with bracket arrows and pieces with grainline arrows placed the same? If not, where are they placed? *No. Pieces with bracket arrows are placed along the fold, and pieces with grainline arrows are placed with the arrows exactly on the grain.*

✓ How can you tell if a pattern piece is on the grain? *If the distances between each point on the grainline arrow and the selvage are equal.*

✓ What should you do before using any marking system? *Test marks on a scrap of your fabric.*

Did You Know? To help determine the right side of fabrics, fold back one edge and compare the two surfaces. The right side will have a more pronounced weave, more nap, a brighter and clearer print, or be shinier. For knitted fabrics, stretch a crosswise cut edge—the edge will usually roll to the right side of the fabric.

Did You Know? Blocking is another term for straightening the grain of fabric by steam ironing.

Emphasize Stress to students the importance of laying out and pinning all pattern pieces before starting to cut out.

✓ Explain how to cut out pattern pieces. *First, double-check the layout. With your free hand, hold the fabric flat on the table. Using sharp shears, cut with long even strokes, following the cutting line. Use the point of your shears to cut corners, curves, and notches.*

Activities

Skill Builder: Writing
Have students write an analysis of whether they thought the directions on their pattern were clear and complete. Did they understand the layout? Was it clear how many times to cut each pattern piece? Were cutting lines and notches clearly marked? What problems, if any, did they have?

Skill Builder: Critical Thinking
Ask students why fabric should always be folded with the front of the fabric facing itself (right sides together). Point out that this practice makes it easy to transfer marks to the wrong side of the fabric and protects the fabric face.

Reteaching
Have students study their pattern guide sheets and circle the correct layout for their projects. Then have them study the pieces and identify foldline arrows, grainline arrows, seamlines, cutting lines, and notches. Have students practice the steps outlined in this section for laying out, pinning, and cutting their patterns.

Reteaching
Have students identify dots and darts and any other marks on their pattern pieces that need to be transferred to the fabric. Then have students choose a marking method and practice the steps outlined in this section.

Enrichment
Invite students to try to invent a more efficient layout for their pattern pieces than the one recommended in the pattern guide. Remind students that foldline and grainline instruction must be followed.

Enrichment
Ask students to predict the functions of dots and darts and their effects on the finished garment.

Cutting

Before cutting your fabric, double-check the layout. Are all your pieces laid out? Are grain lines accurate?

Use sharp shears to cut accurately and evenly. With your free hand, hold the fabric flat on the table. Cut with long, even strokes, following the cutting line exactly. If the pattern is printed with more than one size, be sure to cut on the line that is your size. Use **directional cutting**, which is cutting with the grain of the fabric. The direction may be shown on the pattern by arrows on the stitching line or by illustrations of tiny scissors positioned on the cutting line.

Use the points of your shears to cut corners, curves, and notches. Always cut notches *outward* from the cutting line. Cut two or three notches together as one long notch.

Double-check to be sure that you have cut each pattern piece as many times as necessary. Do not remove the pattern from fabric pieces after cutting. Now the pieces must be marked.

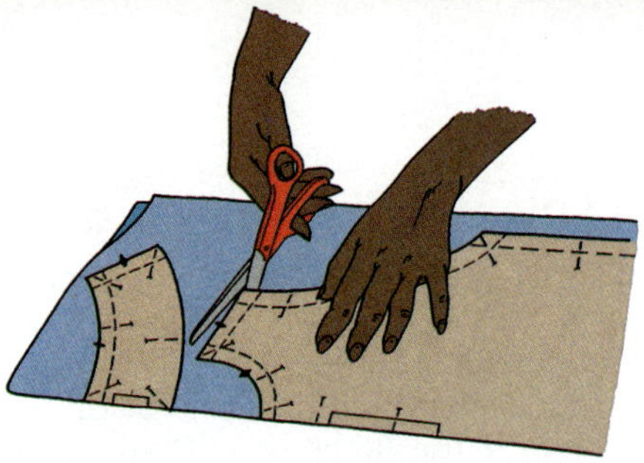

Use sharp shears and cut with long, even strokes on the pattern's cutting line.

Marking the Fabric

Each pattern piece is printed with markings that must be transferred to the wrong side of your fabric. You will use these markings as you stitch the pieces together. Choose the marking method most suitable for your fabric, testing it first on a fabric scrap.

- **Tracing paper and wheel.** Slide the tracing paper under the pattern so that the color is against the wrong side of the fabric. If you have two layers of fabric to mark, use two pieces of tracing paper, or fold one in half. Roll the tracing wheel once along the line that you want to mark. Use a ruler to keep the lines straight. Mark dots with an X.
- **Pins and chalk.** Push a pin through pattern and fabric at the symbol to be marked. Then make a chalk mark on the wrong side of both fabric layers at the pin marking.
- **Fabric markers.** Special liquid marking pens allow temporary markings to be made on fabric. Some markings can be removed with a bit of water; others fade within a few hours. Test such markers on a scrap of your fabric to be sure the markings come out.

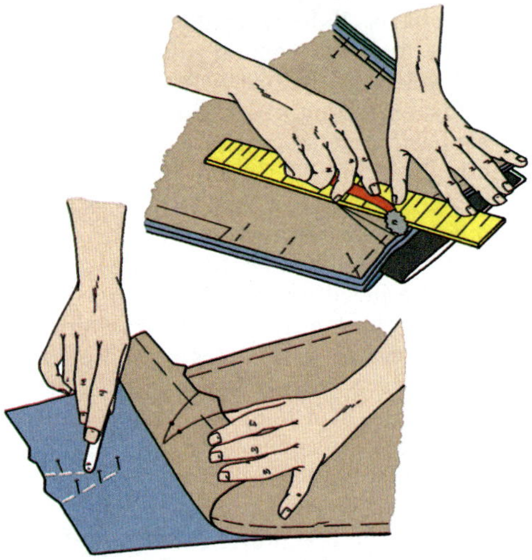

Use a tracing wheel with tracing paper, pins and chalk, or a liquid marking pen to transfer pattern markings to fabric.

More About Marking Tailor's tacks can be used for sheer and bulky fabrics. Make several loose stitches at each mark, remove pattern, pull fabric layers apart, cut threads between layers.

Emphasize Use the lightest color of tracing paper, also called carbon paper, that will show on the fabric—colors may not wash out easily.

CHAPTER 63 REVIEW

Reviewing the Facts

1. What are the four steps to take before sewing a garment?
2. Why do pattern pieces measure slightly larger than the size measurements?
3. Describe two simple adjustments you can make to a pattern.
4. Why should you straighten fabric that is off-grain?
5. What does the pattern layout show you? Where is it found?
6. Which pattern pieces should be placed on the fabric first?
7. Describe how to cut around notches on the cutting line.
8. Why is it important to transfer markings to your fabric?

Thinking Critically

1. What do you think would happen if you began to sew without properly adjusting the pattern? Without following the pattern layout? Without marking the fabric pieces?
2. Which of the methods of marking fabric do you prefer? Why?

Applying Your Skills

1. **Identifying Details.** Using two or three pieces from any pattern, identify, list, and define all the markings and pattern terms printed on the pattern pieces.

2. **Creating a Safety Poster.** Create a poster that emphasizes one or more safety tips to follow when using sewing tools and equipment. Use stick figures, cartoons, or pictures to illustrate the safety tips.

3. **Solving Measurement Problems.** Marsha is making a skirt. Her measurements are 1 in. (2.5 cm) larger at the waist and hips than those shown for the pattern size. She also needs to make the skirt 1½ in. (3.8 cm) longer. The skirt pattern has three pieces—a skirt front, a skirt back, and a waistband. How must it be adjusted so the skirt will fit Marsha?

Answers to "Thinking Critically"

1. If the pattern isn't adjusted, the garment may not fit properly. If the layout isn't followed, all the pattern pieces may not fit on the fabric. If the fabric pieces aren't marked, they might not be stitched together correctly.
2. Answers will vary. Some students may like the tracing wheel and paper because the marks are clear; others may say it makes too heavy a mark or tears the pattern pieces. Chalk is easy to remove but may not be as clear and may rub off; the pins may fall out. Marking pens are easy to use but may bleed on some fabrics and may not wash out.

COMPLETING THE CHAPTER

Summary

- The pattern guide sheet gives directions for cutting, marking, and sewing, and it includes layout diagrams.
- Before laying out pattern pieces, compare pattern measurements with body measurements and consider adjustments.
- Adjustments can easily be made to the length and width of pattern pieces.
- Before laying out pattern pieces, prepare fabric by preshrinking and straightening the grain.
- Lay out and pin pattern pieces, beginning with foldline pieces, and then cut on the cutting line using directional cutting and taking care with notches.
- Before removing pattern pieces, transfer pattern markings to the wrong side of the fabric, using tracing paper and wheel, pins and chalk, or liquid markers.

For Review

Objective Review Questions Have students complete the "Reviewing the Facts" section on this page.

Study Guide Have students complete the Study Guide from Chapter 63 of their *Student Workbook.*

For Evaluation

Simulation Distribute unlabeled diagrams of a pattern piece, and have students add the following labels to the appropriate pattern features: seamline, cutting line, seam allowance, adjustment line, grainline, foldline bracket, notches, dots, darts. Have students draw lines on plain pieces of paper, simulating fabric construction, and label the selvage, lengthwise grain, and crosswise grain. Have students fold the "fabric," lay out and glue the pattern piece, cut, and transfer markings.

Chapter Test Have students complete the test for Chapter 63 that appears in the *Teacher's Classroom Resources.*

CHAPTER OVERVIEW

Chapter 64 takes students through the next steps in their sewing projects, beginning with staystitching. Students learn how to sew darts, tucks, gathers, pleats, and seams, and how to construct facings and interfacings. The chapter emphasizes the concept of unit construction and the importance of pressing work throughout the construction process.

INTRODUCING THE CHAPTER

Motivators

What Next? Have students examine their cut and marked fabric pieces. What do they think they will do next? Introduce the concept of unit construction. Then ask students to identify the units in their patterns and to list them in the order in which they think the units will be constructed. Have students save their lists for reassessment after completing the chapter.

Using the Photograph Direct students' attention to the photograph on this page. Then ask: "What do you think these people are constructing?"

Doll's Dress Continue the demonstration begun in Chapter 63. Identify the units, and list the steps in the construction sequence. Have students study their pattern guide sheets to see what units they will assemble first.

Introducing the Objectives

Discuss the chapter objectives on this page. Remind students that the objectives focus on important chapter content.

Introducing Vocabulary

Have students review the "Words to Remember." Ask students in what contexts they have heard the word *bias* or *biased*. Students might say that biased means "slanted," "nonobjective," or "prejudiced." Show how bias-cut fabric stretches to distort the shape of the piece. Recall that *warped* is a similar expression derived from a sewing term.

CHAPTER

64

Basic Construction

OBJECTIVES

This chapter will help you to:

- Define the unit method of construction.
- Explain ways that fabric pieces are shaped to fit the body.
- Demonstrate techniques for stitching and finishing seams and facings.
- Distinguish between pressing and ironing.

WORDS TO REMEMBER

bias
dart
directional stitching
gather
pressing
staystitching
tuck
unit construction

Chapter Resources

eacher's Classroom Resources
- Lesson Plan
- Life Skills Activity, *Ask the Expert*
- Reproducible Master, *Step-by-Step to Sewing Success*
- Extension Activity, *The Language of Sewing*
- Chapter Test

Student Workbook
- Study Guide
- Worksheet, *Scrambled Construction Terms*

Now that you have marked all your fabric pieces, spread them out and look at them. Can you see how to put the pieces together and where to stitch? Are there areas that are marked for pleats, gathers, tucks, or darts? Markings make your job easier and your work more accurate.

You are now ready to assemble—or construct—your project. Soon you'll see it begin to take shape using a basic technique called unit construction. In **unit construction,** you prepare the separate pieces first, then assemble them in a specific order. For example, a shirt has a back, two fronts, two sleeves, and maybe a collar. Each part is a unit and each unit is constructed separately. Then you simply put them together.

Staystitching

Before you start assembling your project, you have to prepare the pieces to prevent them from pulling out of shape while you're working with them.

Look for all edges that are curved or cut on the **bias.** Bias is any curve or angle that is not cut on the lengthwise or crosswise grain of the fabric. Bias-cut edges stretch as you work with them, so you'll need to put a row of stitching on these curved edges to keep them from losing their shape.

This row of stitching is called staystitching. **Staystitching** is a line of machine stitches sewn through one layer of fabric. The stitches are placed in the seam allowance, 1/2 in. (1.3 cm) from the edge of the fabric. You should stitch in the same direction as the grain, usually from the wide section of the piece to the narrow part.

Shaping to Fit the Body

Darts, tucks, pleats, and gathers are used to shape a flat piece of fabric to fit the shape of your body. Each creates a different effect.

- **Darts.** A **dart** is a triangular fold of fabric stitched to a point. Darts help shape the fabric to body curves. They're usually located at the waistline, the bustline, the back of the shoulder, and the elbow. Darts can also be used to shape curved areas in hats and tote bags.

  On the outside of your garment, darts will look like short seams. They should not have bubbles or puckers at the points. Darts in the right and left sides of a garment should be the same

Fold the dart in half, matching markings, and pin. Stitch from the wide end to the point. Tie a small knot at the point.

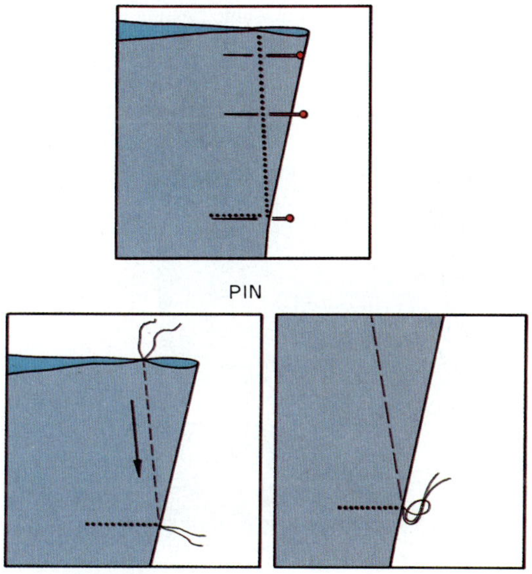

Emphasize Staystitching is done through each layer of bias-cut fabric separately. The purpose is to reinforce individual pieces, not to join them.

Did You Know? An easy way to identify the direction of the grain is to run your finger along the cut edge of the fabric. The direction that smooths the yarns against the fabric is with the grain. This is the direction in which to stitch.

TEACHING THE CHAPTER

For convenience, the teaching suggestions for this chapter are arranged according to the following lesson topics:

- "Staystitching," page 571
- "Shaping to Fit the Body," pages 571-572
- "Assembling the Pieces," pages 572-575
- "Pressing," page 575

Teaching "Staystitching"

(Page 571)

This section explains the reasons and procedures for staystitching.

Checking Comprehension

✔ What is a disadvantage of using bias-cut edges, and how can you prevent it? *One problem is that the edges stretch as you work with them. You can prevent it by staystitching.*

✔ Where should staystitching be done? *On one layer of fabric in the seam allowance, 1/2 in. (1.3 cm) from the edge.*

✔ In what direction should you staystitch? *In the direction of the grain, from the wider to the narrower part of a piece.*

Activities

Skill Builder: Math
Your fabric stretches about 1/8 in. per inch on the bias. One of your pieces has a bias-cut edge about 24 in. long. How much length will you add to this edge if you fail to staystitch before working on the piece? *(about 3 in.)*

Reteaching
Have students practice the steps explained in this section. Ask students to measure 1/2 in. (1.3 cm) from the fabric edge and staystitch all bias-cut edges.

Enrichment
Have students experiment with sewing machine stitches to determine which stitch length works best for staystitching their fabric.

Teaching "Shaping to Fit the Body"
(Pages 571-572)

This section explains how to sew darts and describes how tucks, gathers, and pleats help shape a garment.

Checking Comprehension

✓ Where do darts usually appear on a garment? *At the waistline, bustline, back of the shoulder, and elbow.*

✓ Why should darts in the left and right sides of a garment be the same length and the same distance from the center? *So that the left and right sides of the garment will look the same.*

✓ How should darts be pressed? *Vertical darts should be pressed toward the center; other darts should be pressed downward.*

✓ How is a tuck like a dart? *A tuck is also a fold that gives shape.*

✓ How are gathers created? *By sliding the fabric along a line of basting stitches until the larger piece of fabric fits the smaller one.*

Activities

Skill Builder: Math
The skirt pattern guide says that there should be 6 pleats per side, front and back. How many pleats will there be in all? *(24 pleats).* Assume that the skirt will have a 24-in. waistband. If the front and back pieces of fabric each measure 24 in. (60 cm), how wide should each pleat be to fit the waistband? *(About 2 in. or 5 cm)*

Reteaching
Have students use fabric scraps to make samples of darts, tucks, gathers, and pleats. Students might show the variety of shaping devices, such as vertical, horizontal, and diagonal darts; broad and narrow tucks; tight and loose gathers; and stitched and unpressed pleats.

Enrichment
Ask students to find examples of the use of darts, tucks, gathers, and pleats in garments shown in magazines or old catalogs. Students might make scrapbooks illustrating these uses of shaping in garment construction.

length, and they should be the same distance from the center. Vertical darts should be pressed toward the center of the garment. Horizontal and diagonal darts are usually pressed downward.

- **Tucks.** Like a dart, a **tuck** is a small, stitched fold used to give shape. However, a tuck doesn't taper at the end; it makes a small, unpressed pleat in the fabric. Tucks may be stitched on the inside for shaping, and on the outside for decorative detail as well as shaping.
- **Gathers.** Soft folds of fabric stitched into a seam are called **gathers**. They are created by sliding the fabric along a line of basting stitches in order to fit a larger piece of fabric to a smaller one. Gathers can be used at a waistline, cuff, shoulder, or sleeve. Ruffles on clothing, pillows, and placemats are also gathered.

Stitch two rows of machine basting next to the seam line in the seam allowance. Pull up both bobbin threads at one end and gently slide fabric along threads. Repeat at other end until fabric is proper length. Distribute gathers evenly.

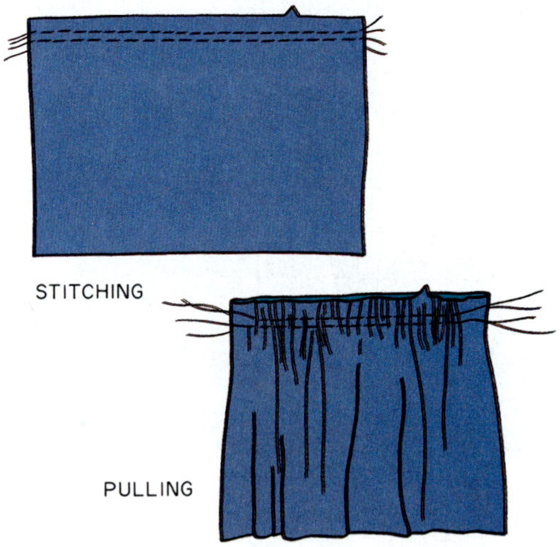

- **Pleats.** Stitched pleats, such as on a classic pleated skirt, give the same close fit as darts. Unpressed pleats, such as on shorts and trousers, give the ease of gathers. Both styles of pleats result in a straight, vertical line. Accurate marking and stitching are important to be sure that the width of each pleat is even.

Assembling the Pieces

After you have staystiched the pieces and built in the shape, you are ready to start assembling your garment. You begin with the seams.

Stitching Seams

Pin the two layers of fabric together with the right sides facing each other, matching the notches. Use a regular stitch length and **directional stitching,** that is, stitching with the grain of the fabric. This will keep your seams from stretching as you work on them. Backstitch at the beginning and end of each seam to secure the stitching. Most seams are 5/8 in. (1.5 cm) wide, unless the pattern has different instructions.

Press the seam before going on to the next one. First, press the seam flat, just as it was stitched. Then, press the seam allowance open.

Finishing the Seams

Seams need to be finished to prevent fabric edges from fraying or raveling and to create a neat appearance. There are four ways that seam allowances can be finished.

Emphasize Care must be taken in pressing not to leave an impression of the dart on the outside of the fabric.

More About Pleats Accordion pleats are thin, even pleats, one folded over another. Knife pleats are narrow and turned in the same direction all around the body. Box pleats are two knife pleats that are folded to face each other on the inside of the garment. Kick pleats—two knife pleats folded away from each other on the inside—are usually placed at the bottom of garments.

- **Pinked or stitched-and-pinked.** Trim the edges with pinking shears. For fabrics that ravel easily, stitch 1/4 in. (6 mm) from the edge and then pink.
- **Zigzagged.** Zigzag by machine near each raw edge, using a narrower stitch for lightweight, closely woven fabrics and a wider stitch for heavy, bulky, or loosely woven fabrics.
- **Hemmed.** This method, also called clean finishing, can be used on light- and medium-weight fabrics. Turn the edge of the seam allowance 1/8 in. (3 mm) under and press. Then stitch along the edge of the fold.
- **Bound.** This method is good for medium- and heavy-weight fabrics. Put double-fold bias tape or sheer bias tricot strips over each raw edge. Place the slightly narrower folded edge of tape on top, and stitch through all the layers.
- **Serged or overlocked.** Stitch a regular width seam with the sewing machine. Overedge each side of the seam allowance using the serger. You can also stitch and overedge seam at the same time on the serger. These seams will only be about 1/4 in. (6 mm) wide, so mark seams accordingly.

Stitching Facings

Facings are cut in the same shape as the edges and used to finish a raw edge such as a neckline, armhole, or waistline. A facing is stitched to the right side and turned to the inside of the garment. Separate pieces for facings are included in the pattern.

The type of fabric and the amount of raveling determines what seam finish to use.

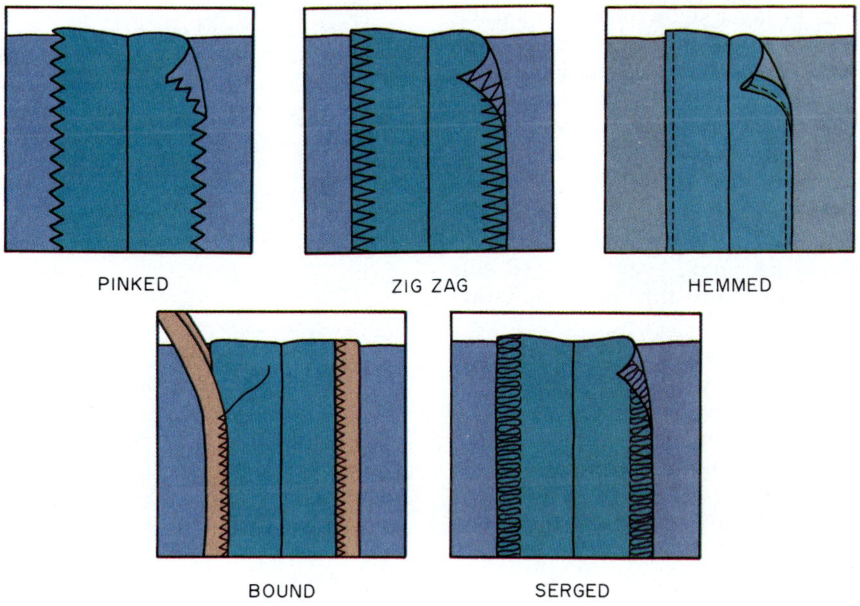

More About Seams The kind of seam commonly seen on jeans and other action wear is called a flat-felled seam. Both edges of the seam are enclosed and topstitched as part of the garment's design. Another kind of "double" seam, the French seam, makes the seams on sheer fabrics look neat.

Did You Know? If you are working with a fabric that will not ravel, seam edges can be "pinked" with pinking shears and stitched near the pinked edge.

Emphasize To trim seams that meet at sharp angles, cut off the corner seam allowance diagonally to make the angle point less bulky when the fabric is turned.

Teaching "Assembling the Pieces"

(Pages 572-576)

This section explains how to stitch seams and to finish seams using one of five methods. Students also learn how to stitch and assemble facings and interfacings.

Checking Comprehension

✓ In what direction should seams be stitched? *In the direction of the grain of the fabric.*

✓ Why should you backstitch at the beginning and end of each seam? *To secure the stitching.*

✓ How is a facing attached to a garment? *It is stitched to the right side of the garment and then turned to the inside.*

✓ Why do seams need to be finished? *To prevent fabric edges from fraying or raveling; to create a neat appearance.*

✓ Where are facings commonly used? *Necklines, armholes, waistlines, and front openings on jackets and shirts.*

✓ How do you make a facing lie flat and smooth? *By trimming, grading, clipping, or notching the seam allowance.*

✓ When should you grade seam allowances? *When the fabric is thick or the seam has three or more layers.*

✓ What should you do to make inward-curving seams lie flat? *Clip by making small, evenly spaced cuts.*

✓ What should you do to make outward-curving seams lie flat? *Notch by cutting V-shaped wedges in the seam allowance.*

✓ How do you make the facing lie flat after it has been turned to the inside? *By understitching, topstitching, or tacking it.*

✓ What is the purpose of interfacing? *To prevent stretching and to give faced edges extra body and shape.*

Activities

Skill Builder: Science
Have students experiment with stapled paper to explore the physical limitations of turned facings. Ask students to cut four long, curved shapes, as in a pattern piece for armhole openings. Two shapes are carefully stapled together on the convex side of the curve and two on the concave side. Staples simulate stitches and should be parallel to the edge. When students fold the papers, as in turning facings, they discover that the seam allowances will not fit in the folds and that the pieces will not lie flat. Have students find which technique (trim, grade, clip, or notch) works best in each case.

Reteaching
Have students practice the five methods of finishing seams and decide which way is best for their projects. Then ask students to stitch their front, back, and side seams and to press and finish the seams. Have students practice the steps outlined in this section for assembling and sewing facings.

Enrichment
Have students create samples from fabric scraps for a bulletin board display of the alternative methods of finishing seams and facings. Students might add samples of various kinds of interfacings.

Trimming, grading, clipping, and notching are done to help facings lie flat and smooth by reducing fabric bulk. These steps are often necessary when stitching collars, necklines, armholes, and waistbands.

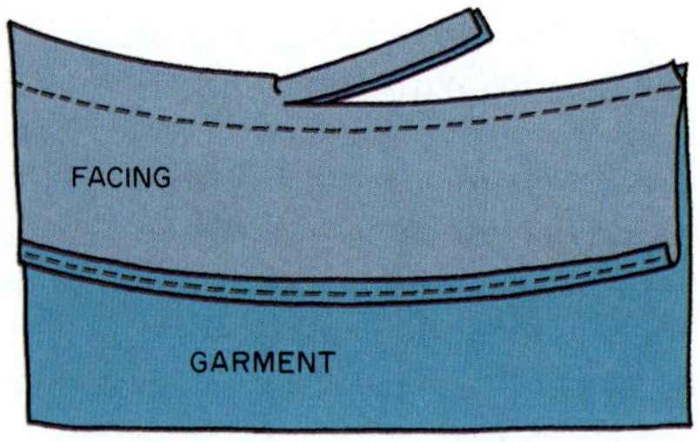

TRIMMING

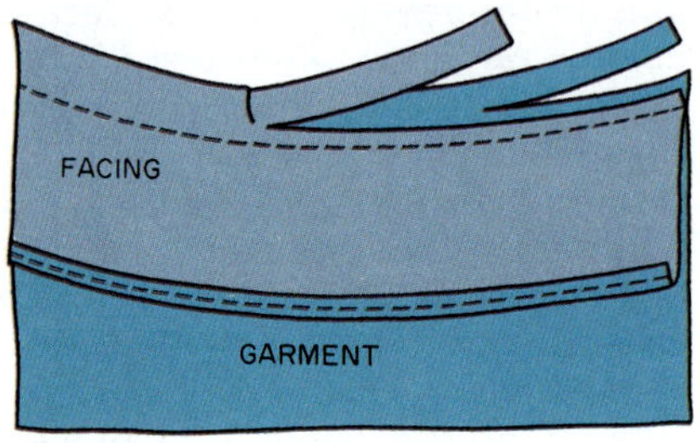

GRADING

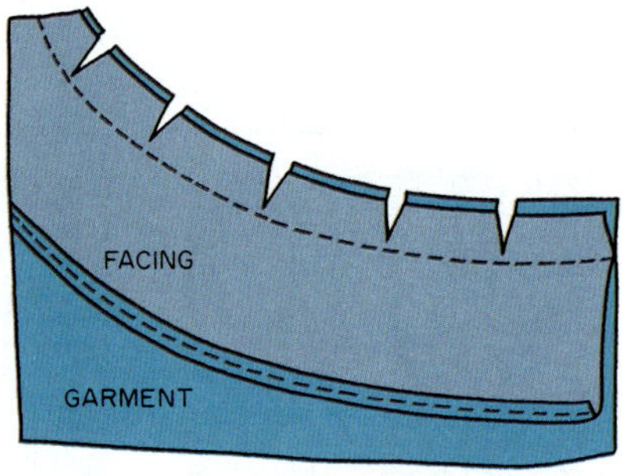

CLIPPING

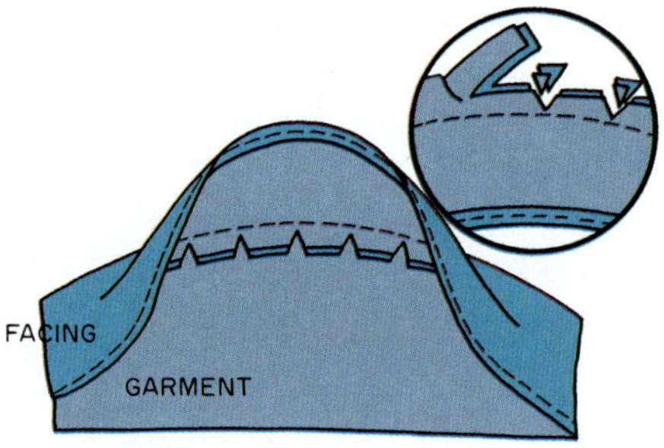

NOTCHING

A facing may also be cut as an extension or a part of the garment. Fold the extended facing to the inside along the foldline. Extended facings are used on straight edges, such as the front openings of shirts and jackets.

To sew a facing, stitch the facing pieces together. Then press the seams open. Finish the outer edge with one of the seam finishes on page 573. Stitch the facing to the garment, with right sides together, matching notches and seams.

For a facing to lie flat and smooth when turned to the wrong side, trim, grade, clip, or notch it as follows.

- Trim the seam allowance to half its width.
- Grade or layer seam allowances if the fabric is thick or if the seams have three or more layers. Trim each layer of a seam allowance slightly narrower than the previous one. Leave at least 1/8–1/4 in. (3–6 mm) of seam allowance to prevent raveling.
- Clip seams that curve inward to let the fabric lie flat. Clip the seam allowance by making small, evenly spaced cuts up to, but not through, the staystitching line.
- Notch the seams that curve outward. To notch, cut V-shaped wedges from the seam allowance. When you press the notched seam allowance open, it will be smooth and the notched edges will meet.

Press the facing seam flat. Then, turn the facing to the inside of the garment and press again.

Emphasize Facings can be extensions of a fabric piece or fitted pieces cut the same shape as the garment area to be faced.

Did You Know? Linings add support to a garment, hide inner construction, add warmth, and increase comfort and ease of movement.

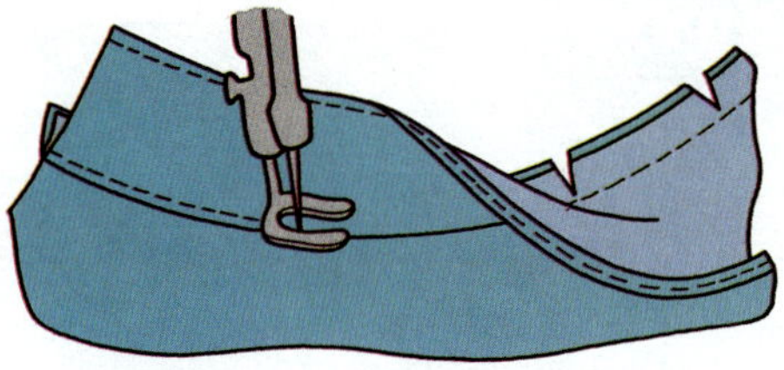

Understitching helps to hold the facing flat and prevent it from showing along the seamline.

- Understitch the facing and seam allowance together. Open out the facing and machine stitch through the facing and seam allowance. Do not stitch through the outer layer of fabric.
- Topstitch from the right side of the fabric through all the layers.
- Tack or stitch the facing to the seam allowances on the inside.

Adding Interfacing

Faced edges are sometimes interfaced to prevent stretching and to give them extra body and shape. Interfacing fabrics are available in a variety of types and weights.

Fusible interfacings are applied to the fabric with an iron. Most fusibles come in plastic wrappers that include specific directions for applying the product.

Sew-in interfacings must be pinned or machine-basted in place and then stitched into the seam. Both types of interfacing are available in woven and nonwoven fabrics.

Pressing

Pressing isn't something you do only when you have finished your garment, although you do that, too. Pressing is an important part of unit construction and guarantees that your seams will lie flat, darts and pleats will be shaped accurately, and facings will lie smooth.

When **pressing** a seam or garment, lift the iron and set it down on the fabric. Do not slide the iron back and forth, which would be ironing the fabric. Ironing can stretch the fabric.

If you're not using a steam iron, use a damp press cloth to create steam. After you've steamed one section, lift the iron just above the fabric and move your press cloth to the next section to press. Then lower the iron again.

To avoid shine, press on the inside of the fabric whenever possible. Do not use heavy pressure. Let the steam do the work.

If you are pressing curved seams and darts, use a tailor's ham so that the curved shape will not be flattened. Press as you finish each unit and before going on to the next.

Press carefully after each step of construction to achieve the best results.

Teaching "Pressing"
(Page 575)

This section explains the importance of pressing at all stages of unit construction and of using the correct pressing technique.

Checking Comprehension

✓ What does pressing guarantee? *That seams will lie flat; darts and pleats will be shaped accurately; facings will lie smooth.*

✓ What can you use if you don't have a steam iron? *A damp press cloth.*

✓ How do you avoid heat shine on your fabric? *By pressing on the inside.*

Activities

Skill Builder: Science
Have students read about and report on the proper care and maintenance of steam irons. How do manufacturers safeguard users from electric shock? What happens when water is left in steam irons? How might minerals in the local water supply affect the performance of steam irons, and what can be done about it?

Reteaching
Have students apply the guidelines in this section to each stage of unit construction in their sewing projects.

Enrichment
Arrange for groups of students to visit a dry-cleaning establishment to find out how industrial pressing machines work and how professional pressing is done.

Emphasize Fabric should be pressed or ironed in the direction of the grain to prevent stretching. Napped fabric, such as corduroy and velvet, can be pressed on the outside with steam alone—without actually touching the iron to the fabric. When pressing on the inside, use very light pressure so as not to flatten the nap.

Did You Know? The bottom, or soleplate, of a steam iron must be cleaned regularly to prevent the buildup of substances from fabrics, such as starches and finishes. Avoid pressing over pins as they can scratch the soleplate. Also take care when using fusible interfacings or fusible webs so the adhesive doesn't touch the iron.

Teaching the Feature
"Serger Applications"

Answers to Feature Questions

1. Different types of stitches are needed to create different types of seams and edges and a variety of designs. In addition, certain fabrics require certain types of stitches.

2. Answers will vary, but most students should feel that this task would be as easy or easier on a serger. With the serger they will finish all the seams as they sew; the fabric is not difficult to handle; there are no facings, buttons, or bottonholes; and it will look like a ready-to-wear item.

Activities

Comparing Time and Skills Demonstrate the serger techniques and have students work in teams to compare several different sewing applications on the conventional machine and on the serger. Have several types of fabrics to compare such as lightweight wovens and knits, sweatshirt knits, and denim. Have each team stitch a seam, finish the seam (if necessary), stitch an edge finish, apply ribbing, and hem. Compare time and skills required for each application. Make a bulletin board showing results. Is the serger a timesaver?

Community Contact Arrange to have a salesperson from a local sewing store demonstrate some of the applications of sergers, showing the various types of stitches described in the feature.

TECHNOLOGY

Serger Applications

Have you ever toured a factory where clothing is mass produced? You would see that each person does a different job on the garment. One person sews only straight seams, another does collars, someone else makes buttonholes. Each person does his or her task on a specific machine designed for the job.

A serger or overlock machine was originally designed for manufacturing, but is now available for home use. It does many of the sewing applications used on ready-to-wear clothing.

Just as there are different machines used in the manufacturing of a garment, some sergers have more capabilities than others. The capabilities depend on the design of the machine—the number of threads the machine uses and the adjustments on the tension dials. Generally, the more capabilities the machine has, the more expensive it is.

Sergers have the capability to create many types of stitches. An overedge stitch finishes the edge of the fabric to prevent raveling but is usually not used for seams. An overlock stitch locks together at the edge of the seam allowance, finishing the edges as it stitches the seam. Some machines make a chainstitch or a safety stitch in addition to the overedge stitch. This gives added strength to the seams. Below are some of the types of stitches and their uses.

- **2-thread overedge stitch.** This stitch is used for lightweight seams and seam finishes on woven fabrics.
- **3-thread overlock stitch.** This is used for stretch seams and durable seams and seam finishes on knit and woven fabrics.
- **2-thread chainstitch.** This is used as a stable basting stitch and for decorative topstitching primarily on woven fabrics.
- **4-thread safety stitch.** This stitch creates stable seams with lightweight seam finishes and is used primarily on woven fabrics. A safety stitch limits the stretch of the material.
- **Wrapped overedge stitch.** This is a decorative stitch for edges and is used on knits or wovens.
- **Flatlock stitch.** This stitch is used for flat, nonbulky stretch seams and decorative stitching primarily on knits.
- **Rolled hem stitch.** This type of stitch is good for narrow hems and seams and decorative stitching. It is used on lightweight knits and wovens.

Think It Through

1. **Why do you think so many different types of stitches are available?**
2. **Would you prefer to make a T-shirt on a serger or on a conventional machine? Explain your answer.**

More About Sergers The numbers used to describe a serger refer to the number of threads that can be used in forming the stitches. A 3-thread serger has one needle and two loopers; on most models three threads are used for all the stitches. A 4/2-thread serger has two needles and two loopers; either two or four threads may be used. A 4/3-thread serger has two needles and two loopers; either three or four threads may be used.

CHAPTER

64 REVIEW

Reviewing the Facts

1. What is unit construction?
2. Why is it important to staystitch around curved or bias-cut edges? How is staystitching done?
3. What purpose do darts, tucks, pleats, and gathers serve? How are darts and tucks different?
4. Name four ways to finish seam allowances.
5. What is the purpose of a facing?
6. Explain the difference between grading and notching. When would you use each?
7. What is the purpose of understitching? How is it done?
8. What is the difference between pressing and ironing?

Thinking Critically

1. What factors influence your choice of interfacing? How would you decide which interfacing to use for a particular fabric?
2. On garments that you are wearing, or with pictures from magazines and catalogs, point out ways in which the garments have been shaped to fit the body.

Applying Your Skills

1. **Writing a Script** Imagine that you are filming a video to help others learn basic sewing techniques. Write a video for one of the following activities: use of gathers in different fashions; use of different seam finishes on various fabrics; decorative stitching. Demonstrate your project to the class, using the script you prepared.

2. **Comparing Techniques** Cut an inward curve (similar to that of a garment facing) through two layers of fabric. Stitch a ⅝ in. (1.6 cm) seam along the curved edge. Press the seam open and note the result. Then, trim and clip the seam. Press the seam again and compare the results.

3. **Creating a Progress Chart** Using the unit construction method, prepare a step-by-step chart for the project you are sewing. Start with preparing the pattern and fabric, laying out the pattern, and cutting and marking the fabric. Use the pattern guide sheet to list each construction step including pressing. As you complete each step, check it off on the chart.

Answers to "Reviewing the Facts"

1. Preparing the separate pieces first, then assembling them in a specific order.
2. To prevent the fabric from stretching as you work with it. To staystitch, stitch through a single layer of fabric, 1/2 in. (1.3 cm) from the edge, in the direction of the grain.
3. To shape a flat piece of fabric to fit the shape of the body. Darts are triangular folds of fabric stitched to a point; tucks are straight folds that don't taper at the end.
4. Any four: pinked; stitched-and-pinked; zigzagged; hemmed; bound; serged or overlocked.
5. To finish a raw edge such as a neckline, armhole, or waistline.
6. Grading is trimming each layer of a seam allowance slightly narrower than the previous one; used for thick fabrics or for three or more layers. Notching is cutting V-shaped wedges from the seam allowance; used for outward curves.
7. To hold the facing flat. Stitch through facing and seam allowance only, not through the outer layer of fabric.
8. Pressing is lifting and lowering the iron from place to place on the fabric; ironing is sliding the iron back and forth.

Answers to "Thinking Critically"

1. Consider fabric weight, interfacing location, the degree of shaping desired, and fabric care requirement. Choices are woven or nonwoven, sew-in or fusible. Hold the fabric and interfacing together to see how they look, feel, and react together. If in doubt as to which interfacing to use, make a test sample.
2. Students should point out darts, pleats, tucks, and gathers. They may also see how seams, belts, and drawstrings are used to shape a garment closer to the body.

COMPLETING THE CHAPTER

Summary

- Garments are sewn and assembled by the unit construction method.
- Before being assembled, fabric pieces are staystitched , and fabric pieces are shaped by sewing darts, tucks, gathers, or pleats, as indicated.
- Fabric pieces are first assembled by sewing, pressing, and finishing the seams.
- Finished seams can be pinked, zigzagged, hemmed, bound, or serged.
- To lie flat, facings can be trimmed, clipped, graded, or notched.
- To be held in place, facings can be understitched, topstitched, or tacked.
- Interfacings for extra body and shape can be sewn or heat-transferred to facings.
- Pressing should be done after each step in unit construction.

For Review

Objective Review Questions Have students complete the "Reviewing the Facts" section on this page.

Study Guide Have students complete the Study Guide from Chapter 64 of their *Student Workbook.*

What Next? Follow-Up Have students revise the lists they made at the beginning of the chapter according to what they have learned. Of what units of construction do their projects actually consist? What steps in unit construction had they omitted or misplaced in sequence?

For Evaluation

Problem Solving Present students with hypothetical situations, and ask them to suggest some solutions, based on chapter content. For example, "Your armhole facing is raveling, and it won't lie flat. What can you do?"

Chapter Test Have students complete the test for Chapter 64 that appears in the *Teacher's Classroom Resources.*

CHAPTER OVERVIEW

Chapter 65 tells students how to add finishing details to sewing projects. Students learn the basic principles for constructing collars, cuffs, sleeves, pockets, and waistbands, and for adding casings, hems, ribbings, closures, and trims. The chapter describes different types of details, such as kimono, raglan, and set-in sleeves, and the different types of closures, including buttons, snaps, hooks and eyes, zippers, and hook-and-loop tapes. A section on trims encourages students to experiment with braid, ruffles, lace, appliques and embroidery to personalize or decorate sewing projects.

INTRODUCING THE CHAPTER

Motivators

What Are Fashion Details? Ask students to brainstorm a list of fashion details—units of construction added to complete a project. Then have them consider several variations of each detail. For example, if students suggest adding pockets, ask, "What kinds of pockets could you add?" Conclude by asking students to list all the ways in which a sewing project might be embellished. Have students save their lists for revision after completing the chapter.

Using the Photograph Refer students to the photograph on this page. Then ask: "What fashion detail is the sewer adding? What other kinds of buttons might have been chosen? What kinds of closures other than buttons might have been used?"

Doll's Dress Continue the demonstration begun in Chapter 63. Consider and choose alternatives for adding special details, and show samples of trims you are considering for decoration. Show how the pattern guide sheet directs your choices but also frees you to make independent decisions about design details. Assemble and sew the chosen details, asking students to explain the reasons for the construction techniques you use. End by dressing the doll and pinning the hem.

CHAPTER

65

Adding the Details

OBJECTIVES

This chapter will help you to:

- Describe the details that give a quality look to sewing.
- Demonstrate techniques used for sewing fashion details.
- Identify common closures and describe how to attach them.
- Select trimmings and trimming techniques to personalize your sewing projects.

WORDS TO REMEMBER

appliqué
sew-through button
shank button

Chapter Resources

Teacher's Classroom Resources
- Lesson Plan
- Life Skills Activity, *You're the Judge*
- Reproducible Master, *A Stitch in Time*
- Extension Activity, *Standards for Details*
- Chapter Test

Student Workbook
- Study Guide
- Worksheet, *Fashion Detail Puzzle*

Fashion details come and go as styles change, but the fundamentals of good sewing can be applied to any design. To achieve a look of quality, you will need to decide on the best techniques for sewing the details you choose. Many of your options depend on your pattern and fabric selection. You may also need to make a choice between finishing something by hand or machine, so your sewing skills will also influence your decisions.

You will be better able to pick out fashion details if you can visualize and evaluate what the finished detail will look like. In this chapter, you will learn some of the sewing techniques needed for:

- Special details such as collars, cuffs, sleeves, pockets, waistbands, casings, ribbings, hems, and trims.
- Closures such as buttons, snaps, hooks and eyes, zippers, and hook and loop tapes.

Special Techniques

If you're just learning to sew, you may want to practice your skills on an easy project before choosing a pattern with several special details. Once you master these techniques, you will have a wider choice of patterns that you will be able to handle.

Collars and Cuffs

You'll find specific instructions on your pattern guide sheet for your garment's collar or cuffs. However, there are some general guidelines for all collars and cuffs.

On a collar, the curved edges should be smooth and the collar points should be even. The undercollar or underside should never show. Interfacing is necessary for some collars and cuffs. Use short reinforcement stitches for the sharp points so fabric threads will not pull out. Trim and grade the seam allowances. Understitch so that they will lie smooth and flat. Press carefully.

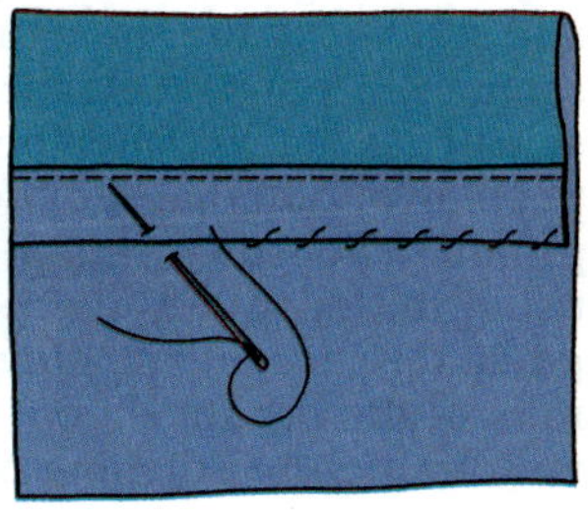

HEMMING STITCH

Most projects require some hand sewing—finishing a hem, attaching fasteners or trims, repairing a seam, or basting fabrics together. These illustrations show how to do four hand stitches. When might you use each stitch?

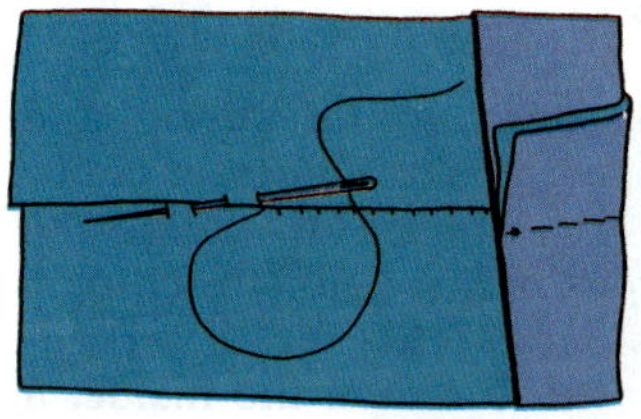

SLIPSTITCH

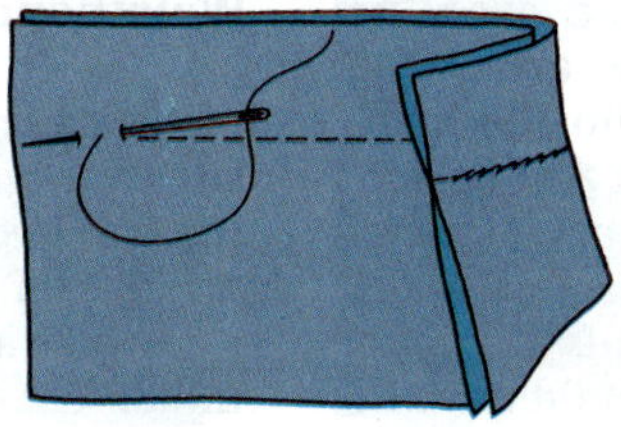

BACKSTITCH

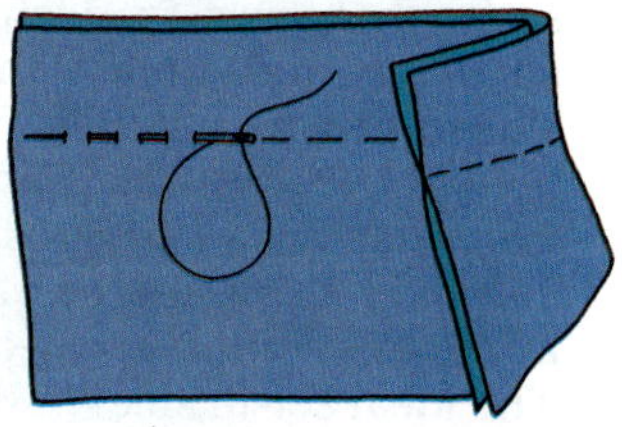

RUNNING STITCH

Did You Know? In sixteenth century Europe, both men and women wore lace collars and cuffs. The size and stiffness of collars was related to status and wealth. Special eating utensils had to be invented for people who wore large ruffs, because the ruffs prevented them from moving their heads even to eat. The term "white-collar worker" derived from upper-class collar fashions, which prevented the mobility needed for most physical labor.

Introducing the Objectives

Discuss the chapter objectives on page 578. Remind students that the objectives focus on important chapter content.

Introducing Vocabulary

Tell students that *applique* comes from a French verb, "to apply," and refers to any cut-out piece of material that is added to the outside of a work made of similar material. For example, paper appliqués appear on greeting cards, wooden appliques on cabinets, and cloth appliqués on sewn fabrics.

TEACHING THE CHAPTER

For convenience, the teaching suggestions for this chapter are arranged according to the following lesson topics:

"Special Techniques," pages 579-582
"Closures," pages 582-584
"Trims," page 584

Teaching "Special Techniques"

(Pages 579-582)

This section gives general instructions for assembling and stitching collars, set-in sleeves, patch pockets, basic waistbands, hems, self-casings, and ribbings. The section also describes variants of these details and procedures for making decisions about hems.

Checking Comprehension

✓ Where can you find out how to construct a collar or cuffs for your sewing project? *The pattern guide sheet tells you.*

✓ What are three general guidelines for all collars and cuffs? *The curved edges should be smooth; collar points should be even; the underside should not show.*

✓ What gives collar and cuffs extra body and shape? *Interfacing.*

Teaching "Closures"

(Pages 582-584)

This section describes sew-through and shank buttons and techniques for sewing buttons and buttonholes. The section also gives general instructions for adding sew-on snaps, hooks and eyes, fly-front and separating zippers, and hook-and-loop tapes.

Checking Comprehension

✓ What is the purpose of a shank? *To leave room for fabric to fit under the button when the garment is buttoned.*

✓ How can you add a thread shank to a sew-through button? *Lay a toothpick or a pin on the button between the holes; sew stitches over the toothpick or pin and through the fabric; remove the device; wrap thread around the lengthened stitches beneath the button.*

✓ What is an important requirement for buttonholes? *They should all be the same length and the same distance from the garment edge.*

✓ How should snaps be sewn? *Sew the ball section to the wrong side of the overlap; align and sew the socket section on the right side of the underlap.*

✓ Where can you use flat, heavy-duty hooks and eyes? *On the waistbands of skirts and pants.*

✓ How does a zipper foot help you to machine stitch a zipper? *By letting you stitch close to the zipper teeth.*

✓ Where are separating zippers used? *In jackets and sweatshirts.*

✓ How do hook-and-loop fasteners work? *Two pieces of nylon tape stick together.*

Activities

Skill Builder: Critical Thinking
Ask students to evaluate the closures described in this section. What are the advantages and disadvantages of each? What other kinds of closures are there? What are the functions of closures, and what other means exist for fulfilling those functions?

Casings

Casings are used for drawstrings or elastic at the waistline of pants, shorts, and skirts, or on one-piece outfits such as dresses and jumpsuits. They are also used at necklines and at hemlines of sleeves and pants.

You can create a self-casing by folding back an extension of the fabric at the edge of the garment and stitching it in place. Some casings—for example those at the waistline of one-piece garments—are made by stitching a strip of bias tape to the inside of the garment.

Leave an opening at the seam to insert the elastic or drawstring. Attach a safety pin to the end of the elastic or drawstring to pull it through the casing.

Ribbings

Ribbing is a knit with lengthwise ridges and crosswise stretch and recovery. Recovery is the ability of a stretch fabric to go back to its original shape. Ribbing may be used instead of a hem to finish necklines, wrists, ankles, armholes, and waistlines. The ribbing provides a snug but comfortable fit for pullover and pull-on garments, such as sweatshirts, sweatpants, and T-shirts.

To maintain stretchability, apply ribbings with a flexible stitch, such as narrow zigzag, overlock stitch, or overedge stretch stitch. Stretch the ribbing to fit the garment edge as you sew.

Closures

Closures include buttons and buttonholes, snaps, hooks and eyes, zippers, and hook-and-loop tapes. Buy your closures when you buy your pattern and fabric. The quantity and size you'll need are listed on the pattern envelope.

Buttons

There are two kinds of buttons: sew-through and shank. A **sew-through button** has two or four holes through it and no shank or loop on the back. You'll need to make a thread shank when you sew the button on. The shank leaves room for the thickness of the buttonhole when the button is closed.

To make a thread shank, lay a toothpick or pin on top of the button between the holes. Use double thread and secure the thread with one or two stitches. Sew several stitches over the toothpick or pin and through the fabric. End stitches with the needle and thread under the button. Remove the toothpick or pin and wind the thread several times around the thread shank under the button. Fasten the thread on the underside of the fabric.

A **shank button** has a built-in shank, or loop, on the back. It does not have any holes through it. Sew it in place with several small stitches through the shank and into the fabric.

For sew-through buttons, you have to make a thread shank. The shank provides room for the fabric to stay smooth beneath the button when the garment is fastened.

Did You Know? On garments needing durable closures, such as coats, two sew-through buttons are sometimes used in place of one. A thread-shanked button on the outside is sewn through another button aligned on the inside.

Emphasize The tool for applying heavy-duty snaps permanently clamps the snap parts to the fabric. Unlike sew-on snaps, heavy-duty snaps usually cannot be removed without damaging the fabric.

Patterns have markings showing the location and length of each buttonhole on the pattern. Buttonholes can be made with a zigzag machine or with a special buttonhole attachment. Well-made buttonholes should all be the same length and the same distance from the edge of the garment. Carefully cut the buttonhole open with the points of a scissors.

Snaps

Sew-on snaps are suitable for areas where there is little strain, such as at the neckline to hold a facing edge flat. Snaps consist of two parts: a ball and a socket. The section of the snap that has the ball should be sewn on the wrong side of the overlap. Then sew the socket on the right side of the underlap so they are perfectly aligned. Make several small stitches through each hole. Secure your thread when you begin and finish your work.

Heavy-duty snaps can be used instead of buttons and buttonholes on jackets and shirts of sturdy, heavyweight fabrics. Each side of a heavy-duty snap is in two sections, applied with a special tool. Follow instruction on the package. Because of their weight, these snaps must be used with at least two thicknesses of fabric reinforced with interfacing.

When sewing on snaps, sew three or four stitches through each hole—carrying the thread under the snap from one hole to the next. Be careful not to have any stitches show on the outside of the garment.

Hooks and Eyes

Hooks and eyes are used on waistbands or above zippers where they are not visible. If the finished edges just meet, use a hook with a round eye. If the edges overlap, use a hook with a straight eye. Attach hooks and eyes with small stitches around each loop. Finish with three or four stitches across the end of the hook to make sure it lies flat. Heavy-duty hooks and eyes, also called skirt or pants hooks, are used on waistbands as a sturdier closure for skirts and pants. The hooks are strong and flat so they will not slide out of the eye.

A straight eye is used for edges that overlap; a round eye for edges that meet. Heavy-duty hooks and eyes are used for waistbands.

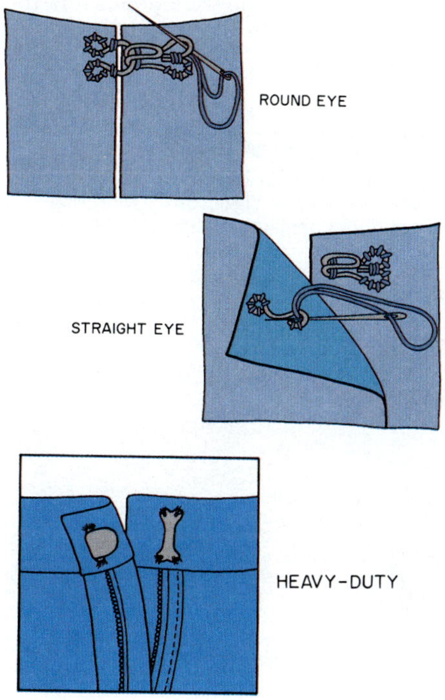

Skill Builder: Critical Thinking
Ask students how closures can be used as key elements in fashion design. Then tell them that closures are sometimes used without regard to their functions. Ask students to use magazine clippings to illustrate these points in a scrapbook or poster.

Skill Builder: Science
Have students examine slide fasteners to determine how they work. Students should observe that zippers function as two rows of gears that are linearly meshed and unmeshed by manipulation of a slider. The slider engages or designates the gears. Have students determine the conditions under which zippers won't work. How can zippers be repaired?

Reteaching
Demonstrate the use of the buttonhole attachment and the zipper foot. Have students sew samplers of sew-through and shank buttons, a buttonhole, a sew-on snap, a hook and eye, a zipper, and a hook-and-loop tape. Then have students follow pattern guide directions to add closures to their sewing projects.

Enrichment
Tell students that button collecting is a popular hobby. Have them find out about the history of buttons and the characteristics of buttons that make them valuable to collectors.

Emphasize In most cases, hooks and eyes should not be visible when the hook and eye is closed. Exceptions include "frogs"—decorative loop closures that mimic the principle of hooks and eyes.

Did You Know? Fly-front pants, closed with buttons, were first worn in the mid-1800s.

Focus on Technology The idea of hook-and-loop fasteners was first proposed in the 1940s by a Swiss engineer, George deMaestral. He observed the clinging power of woodland cocklebers. By examining burs under a microscope, he discovered the hook-and-loop structures that made them cling.

Teaching "Trims"
(Page 584)

This section describes braid, ruffles, lace, appliques, and embroidery as decorative and personal additions to sewing projects.

Checking Comprehension

✔ What are some types of trims? *Braid, ruffles, lace, appliqués, and embroidery.*

✔ How are trims attached to garments? *With straight stitching or fusible webs.*

✔ What is an appliqué? *A fabric cutout sewn to a background fabric.*

✔ How can you make an applique? *By cutting out a chosen design from firmly woven fabric that does not ravel easily.*

✔ How can you use embroidery? *To add initials to pockets, pillows, or tote bags; to decorate T-shirts or place mats.*

Activities

Skill Builder; Writing
Ask students to explain in writing their decisions about trim options for their sewing projects. What did their patterns recommend? What were some possibilities beyond the pattern recommendations? What did students decide to do, and why?

Reteaching
Have students make and attach appliques to fabric samples, or add chosen trims to their sewing projects. Invite students to design and embroider monograms or other decorations for use as trim.

Enrichment
Ask students to survey trims in a fabric store and read information labels on trim bolts or spools. Have students name, describe, and illustrate different trims, and classify them according to general types, specific uses, or some other unifying feature.

Zippers

Detailed instructions for inserting zippers are given on the zipper package. Zippers can be inserted in a seam in two ways—centered, with a row of stitching on each side of the zipper, or lapped, with just one row of stitching showing on the outside. A special zipper foot on the sewing machine makes it easy to stitch close to the zipper teeth.

In fly-front zipper applications the overlap side of the zipper is stitched to a facing, not to the garment. Topstitching holds the facing and zipper in place. On the right front of men's pants, an extension may be a separate piece or cut in one piece with the garment and folded back.

Separating zippers are used in jackets and sweatshirts. They may be inserted to allow the zipper teeth to remain covered or exposed. The method you use for inserting a zipper depends on the garment and the location of the zipper in the garment.

Colorful appliqúes can be attached by machine stitching. Use a close zigzag stitch, covering the edge of the appliqúe completely.

Hook-and-Loop Tapes

Hook-and-loop fasteners consist of two pieces of nylon tape that stick to each other when pressed together. Velcro is the trademark name for hook-and-loop tapes. Though they're too bulky for lightweight fabrics, these closures are common on parkas, jackets, camping equipment, pillows, and totes. They are particularly useful on clothing for people who find it difficult to handle regular closures. Hook-and-loop tape fasteners are available as rectangular strips or circles. Attach the rectangular strips to fabric by machine stitching around all four sides. Attach the circles with a triangle of stitching.

Trims

Trims such as braid, ruffles, lace, and appliqués are wonderful for decorating and emphasizing the lines of garments, accessories, and household items. Almost all can be bought ready-made and can be easily attached with machine stitching or fusible webs.

An **appliqué** (ap-li-KAY) is a cutout fabric decoration sewn onto another fabric background. You can buy appliqués or make them yourself. Use a firmly woven fabric that does not ravel easily. Appliqués can be cut in any shape you choose. Sew on by machine or by hand or use a fusible web.

Embroidery can be used to personalize almost anything that you make or buy. You can add your initials or name to a pocket, pillow, or totebag. You can also use embroidery to create a unique design on a T-shirt or place mat.

Cross-Reference See Teen Tips "T-Shirts—Make It Unique" on pages 614-615.

Did You Know? In ancient Rome the color, design, and width of the trim on hems indicated the wearer's social class and occupation.

More About Trims Beads, sequins, pearls, gemstones, and small mirrors can be sewn on trims or directly on the garment areas to be decorated. More common trims include piping—a narrow cord sewn onto the edges or seams, and rickrack—a woven trim that forms a sawtooth pattern.

INTERPERSONAL SKILLS

Closures to Help People with Disabilities

People with disabilities can gain added independence through clothing adaptations. Being able to manipulate closures is important in maintaining or acquiring self-sufficiency.

Whether a disability is temporary or permanent, a simple task such as opening and closing a zipper can be frustrating. Some disabled people have difficulty grasping the small tab slider, so a zipper pull such as a large metal ring, a tassel, a chain, or a large bead provides something that is easier to grasp. A simple leather thong, large enough to accommodate the thumb, may be looped through the zipper. For separating zippers, knot leather thongs through holes punched in the bottom of the zipper tape. This provides something to hold with one hand while pulling up the zipper with the other.

Zippers may be inserted in leg seams to enable clothing to go over braces or casts. A zipper in a raglan sleeve seam makes clothing easier to pull over the head.

Some people with disabilities find it difficult to handle small buttons. Use large buttonholes and large buttons with raised rims. Toggles may be easier to manage than buttons. Buttons or toggles can be sewn on with elastic thread or with a loop of narrow flat elastic. Horizontal buttonholes are easier to handle than vertical ones.

One of the most adaptable closures is hook-and-loop tape. Because it is easy to open and close with one hand it can replace zippers, buttons, or snaps.

To adapt a garment for hook-and-loop tape, cut the tape in pieces the size of a postage stamp. For the front opening of a shirt, jacket, or dress, sew the buttonholes shut and remove the buttons. Stitch the loop side of the tape behind each buttonhole. Then sew the hook side to where each button was stitched. This method helps prevent the scratchy hooks from irritating the skin. Finish by sewing the buttons on top of the buttonholes.

Think It Through

1. **Do you know anyone who could benefit from some of these suggestions for closures? How can these adaptations be helpful?**
2. **Jason broke his arm playing football and has to keep it in a cast for several weeks. How could his clothing be adapted so that he would be able to dress himself?**

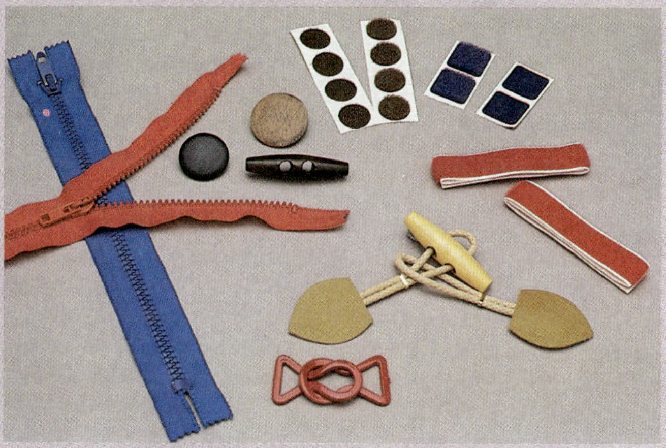

Teaching the Feature

"Closures to Help People With Disabilities"

Answers to Feature Questions

1. Students may answer that they know a person with a disability who is confined to a wheelchair, an elderly person with arthritis, someone who has broken an arm or a leg in an accident, or other disabilities. Discuss specific closures that would help the individual dress easily and comfortably.

2. It would be difficult for Jason to pull anything over his head, so he will want front-opening shirts, jackets, and sweaters. Jason's closures have to be managed with only one hand. Small buttons and buttonholes could be replaced with larger ones; shirt-front openings could be closed with hook-and-loop tape.

Activities

Consciousness Raising Assign students different temporary or permanent disabilities and ask them to put on and take off garments as if their disabilities were real. Have students report on the sources of their frustrations or difficulties. Invite disabled students to a class discussion on clothing aids for people with physical disabilities.

Special-Needs Catalog Have students create a model mail-order catalog with descriptions and illustrations of closures custom designed for individuals with special needs. Students might think of other clothing details to add to the catalog.

Community Contact Have students contact a local or regional service organization or support network for disabled or handicapped persons. Do organization or network self-help programs include clothing workshops? Could students help set up or conduct such a workshop?

Focus on Leadership Suggest that students organize a service project for disabled members of their community. Students might present a custom clothing workshop, distribute a student-made custom catalog, and offer to convert clothing closures or other details as shown in the catalog.

Did You Know? A buttoning instrument called a button aid helps people whose fingers are not agile. It has a thick wooden handle with a wire loop on the end. The wire loop is used to grasp and pull the button through the buttonhole.

COMPLETING THE CHAPTER

Summary

- Fashion details include collars and cuff, sleeves, pockets, waistbands, casings, hems, and ribbings.
- Closures include buttons and buttonholes, snaps, hooks and eyes, zippers, and hook-and-loop tapes.
- Trims, such as braid, ruffles, lace, appliques, and embroidery, emphasize the lines of sewing projects or add decoration.

For Review

Objective Review Questions Have students complete the "Reviewing the Facts" section on this page.

Study Guide Have students complete the Study Guide from Chapter 65 of their *Student Workbook.*

Motivator Follow-Up Ask students to reassess their lists of fashion details in light of what they have learned in this chapter. Have students write essays beginning with the following topic sentence: "The addition of fashion details completes a sewing project."

For Evaluation

Performance Evaluate students' sewing samplers of collars, sleeves, pockets, waistbands, casings, hems, and closures. Have students applied the guidelines set forth in the chapter? Evaluate students' sewing projects. Have they followed pattern guide sheet instructions for adding fashion details?

Self-Appraisal Have students rate their performance on sewing projects in terms of attitude, comprehension, decision-making skills, task organization and management, technical skills, and class participation. Which sewing details did students find easiest and most difficult to master, and why?

Chapter Test Have students complete the test for Chapter 65 that appears in the *Teacher's Classroom Resources.*

CHAPTER 65 REVIEW

Answers to "Reviewing the Facts"

1. The pattern, the fabric, and your sewing skills.
2. Kimono, raglan, and set-in sleeves.
3. Inseam and patch pockets.
4. At the waistline of pants, shorts, skirts, dresses, and jumpsuits; at necklines; at hemlines of sleeves and pants.
5. To finish necklines, wrists, ankles, armholes, and waistlines when you want a snug but comfortable fit.
6. When you attach a sew-through button, you have to make a thread shank; to do this, sew over a toothpick or pin and wrap thread around stitches under the button. A shank button has a built-in shank.
7. Zipper; heavy-duty hook and eye or button above zipper; buttons and buttonholes; heavy-duty snaps; hook-and-loop tapes.
8. Any two: braid; ruffles; lace; appliques; embroidery.

Reviewing the Facts

1. What will influence your decision when choosing a technique to use on special details and closures?
2. What are three basic styles of sleeves?
3. What are two types of easy-to-sew pockets?
4. Where might casings be used?
5. When would you use a ribbing instead of a hem?
6. Describe the difference between attaching a sew-through button and a shank button.
7. What kinds of closures can be used on pants?
8. Name two kinds of decorations that can be added to a sewing project.

Thinking Critically

1. How will well-sewn details on the garments or projects that you sew increase your self-esteem?
2. If you had to decide between finishing something by hand or machine, which would you choose? What are the advantages and disadvantages of each method?

Applying Your Skills

1. **Using Reference Materials.** Visit the library and read about the history and use of embroidery or appliqué. How can embroidery or appliqué be used to personalize everyday items? Suggest five projects anyone could make using these techniques.

2. **Evaluating Alternatives.** Using mail-order or pattern catalogues, select ten garments that use some type of fastener. List alternative types of fasteners that could be used for each design. What would be the advantages and disadvantages of each? How could each garment be adapted for easier use by a person with a physical disability?

3. **Rating Workmanship.** Compare an expensive garment and an inexpensive garment for quality of workmanship. Evaluate details, such as collars, sleeves, cuffs, pockets, waistbands, casings, hems, fasteners, and trims. How does the workmanship differ? Is the best workmanship always on the more expensive garment? Write a report of your findings.

Answers to "Thinking Critically"

1. If details are handled correctly, students are proud of their workmanship and what they have accomplished. They can take pride in wearing something they have made themselves. If the project is made as a gift, the receiver will be impressed with the work that went into making a one-of-a-kind item.
2. Answers will vary. Machine stitching is faster and more durable, but it requires some experience to achieve fine results. Hand stitching is less conspicuous, has a fine "dressmaking" quality, and is easier to remove, such as when changing a hem, but it takes longer to do.

CHAPTER

66

Clothes Care

OBJECTIVES

This chapter will help you to:

- Explain how to care for your clothes.
- Describe different ways to clean clothes.
- Identify some simple clothing repairs.

WORDS TO REMEMBER

detergent
dryclean
mildew
snag
stain
texturizing

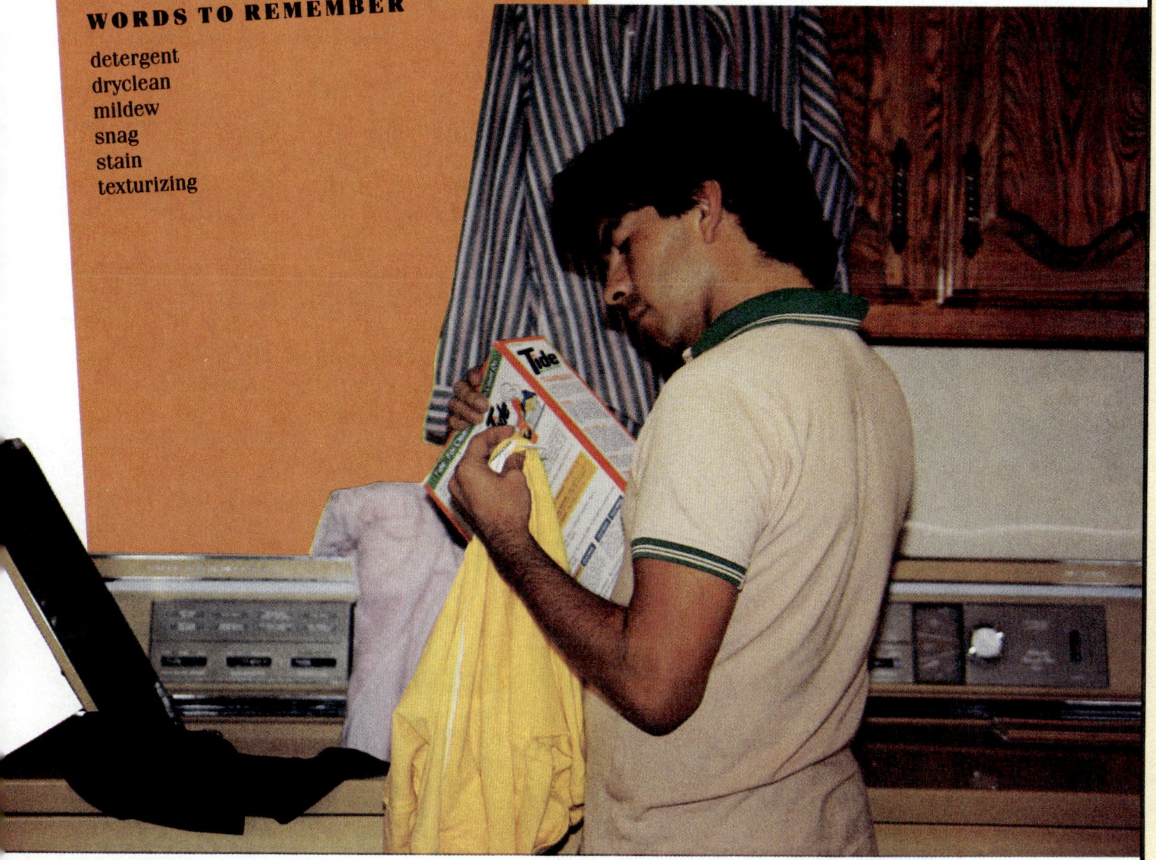

Chapter Resources

Teacher's Classroom Resources
- Lesson Plan
- Life Skills Activity, *Laundry Know-How*
- Reproducible Master, *Read the Care Labels*
- Extension Activity, *Stain Removal Chart*
- Chapter Test

Student Workbook
- Study Guide
- Worksheet, *Clothesline*

CHAPTER OVERVIEW

Chapter 66 offers students suggestions for taking care of their clothes on a daily, occasional, and seasonal basis. Students learn how to remove stains, use laundry products and machines, and sort, wash, and dry clothes. The chapter also explains dry cleaning and simple repairs such as fixing snags, mending seams, patching holes, and replacing fasteners.

INTRODUCING THE CHAPTER

Motivators

What Is Clothing Care? Ask students to list some specific actions that caring for clothes entails. For each action, ask, "Who should be responsible for doing this?" Have students save their lists to revise after completing the chapter.

Using the Photograph Have students examine the photograph on this page. Then ask: "What is this young man doing? Why do you think he is doing that? What are some benefits of reading labels on laundry products?" Ask students if they are responsible for washing their clothes.

What Is Proper? Initiate a class discussion on the reasons for attending to clothing care. What social values support this behavior? Students might note that it is considered desirable to care for one's possessions and to extend the life of clothing. Ask students if they think wearing stained, torn clothes with broken or missing closures is seen as a fashion statement or as a sign of negligence.

Introducing the Objectives

Discuss the chapter objectives on this page. Remind students that the objectives focus on important chapter content.

Introducing Vocabulary

Point out that the root of *detergent* is not *deter,* but *deterge,* a verb meaning "to wash off or cleanse." The verb came into English from French and derives from a Latin verb with the same meaning. *De* is a Latin prefix meaning "off, away."

TEACHING THE CHAPTER

For convenience, the teaching suggestions for this chapter are arranged according to the following lesson topics:

- "General Care," pages 588-589
- "Cleaning Clothes," pages 589-593
- "Simple Repairs," page 593

Teaching "General Care"

(Pages 588-589)

This section describes clothing-care tasks that should be performed daily, and those that need to be done only occasionally or seasonally.

Checking Comprehension

✔ What should you do before putting clothes away in a closet or drawer? *Air them out; brush off lint and dust; check for spots and tears.*

✔ What clothing-care tasks should be done on a weekly basis? *Sewing repairs, hand washing, ironing or pressing.*

✔ How can clothes be damaged in storage? *Dirty clothes can deteriorate and attract insects; wool clothes can become moth-eaten; damp clothes can become mildewed.*

✔ How can you protect woolens? *Treat with moth repellent and seal in airtight bags.*

✔ How can you prevent mildew? *Make sure clothes are completely dry before putting them away.*

Activities

Skill Builder: Critical Thinking
Have students analyze the care guidelines given in this section and determine the reasons for each. For example, why should clothes be aired out before storing? Why should clothes be hung up or folded? Why should closures be partly closed?

Who takes care of household chores in your home? In increasing numbers of families, jobs such as doing the laundry and repairing clothing are shared among several family members. As you accept responsibility for selecting and purchasing your own clothing, you must also accept responsibility for its care.

Caring for clothing rarely takes longer than a few minutes each day, but the results are well worth the effort. Proper care means that you:

- Put on and take off clothes carefully.
- Open zippers and buttons fully to prevent breaking them or ripping seams.
- Bathe daily and use deodorant or antiperspirant.
- Protect clothes by using a napkin while eating and by wearing old clothes when doing messy chores.
- Take care of stains immediately. The longer a stain remains, the harder it is to remove.

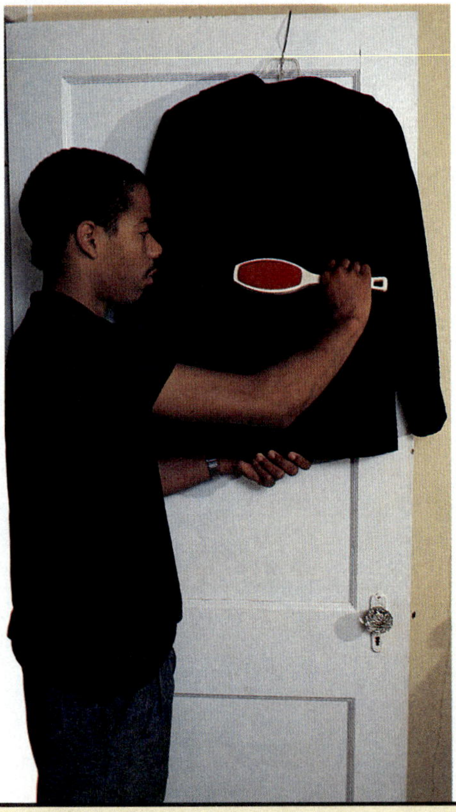

General Care

There are three basic types of clothing care. Keeping clothes in good condition depends on performing some tasks every day, others only occasionally, and still others seasonally.

Daily Care

Take these steps each day to keep your clothes in good condition:

- Before putting clothes away, air them out. Spread them flat on your bed or drape them over a chair.
- Brush off lint and dust. Check each garment to see if it needs repair or has a spot that needs cleaning. A small rip or a loose button takes only a few minutes to fix. If you ignore it, however, the repair may become a major job.
- Set aside any clothes that need to be washed or drycleaned.
- Once your clothes have aired, hang them up or fold them and put them away. Use curved or wooden hangers for jackets and padded hangers for delicate fabrics. Close zippers and one or two buttons on each garment.

Take time to check your clothes before putting them away—brush off lint and remove stains promptly. Set aside clothes that need to be cleaned or repaired.

Focus on Consumer Skills Have students survey the products available for organizing, storing, and caring for clothes. What practical devices for keeping clothes in good condition might students wish to buy or make?

Cross-Reference See Chapter 70 for storage ideas.

Focus on Life Management Have students develop guidelines for protecting clothes while wearing them. Guidelines might refer to taking care with pockets, jewelry, cosmetics, chewing gum, pens, and newspapers, watching where you sit, and so on.

Occasional Care

Set aside some time each week for making sewing repairs. This is also the time to hand wash clothing that can't be put in the machine. If clothes need ironing or pressing, do it all at one time to save effort and energy.

You might also collect all your clothes that need to be fixed and put them in one place, such as a clothes basket or a dresser drawer. Then, when you have a few minutes to spare, make the necessary repairs. You could even repair your clothing while watching television.

Seasonal Care

When the seasons change, people often change their wardrobes and put clothes in storage. A winter coat, for example, may not be worn for several months. When clothes aren't worn for a long time, they can become damaged if not stored properly. To protect stored clothes:

- Make sure that the clothes are clean, dry, and free of stains. If the garments are not cleaned before they are stored, any leftover perspiration and skin oils may weaken the fabric. Insects such as silverfish can attack food stains and damage the fibers, also.
- Treat woolens with moth repellent to prevent moth larvae from eating the fibers. If possible, seal woolens in an airtight bag.
- To prevent **mildew**—a fungus that grows on damp fabric, causing stains—make sure that clothes are completely dry before you put them away. Also, store them where they will remain dry.
- You can also put stored clothes in garment bags or boxes to protect them.

Follow the directions on the care labels when deciding how to clean your clothes.

Cleaning Clothes

All clothes need to be cleaned, but different garments need different types of cleaning. Jeans with a grass stain will require a more thorough washing than will a shirt that is only slightly soiled. Some fabrics require drycleaning, and delicate items need to be washed by hand.

To choose the correct cleaning method, check the care label. It will tell you what procedure to follow, such as machine wash, hand wash, or dryclean. A label will also tell you whether to machine dry or line dry a garment and any cautions about ironing temperatures. The label also tells you what not to do, such as "Do not bleach."

Removing Stains

Sometimes dirt is concentrated in one spot in a garment. Such a spot is a **stain.** You may need to give a stain special treatment before adding the garment to a load of laundry. The chart on page 590 lists removal procedures for some com-

Did You Know? Knits and woven stretch fabrics should be folded and stored flat to maintain shape. Wire hangers, which can leave ridges across the shoulder of some garments, can be decoratively covered with fabric or yarn. Button a jacket or blouse when hanging it up to prevent the front of the garment from sagging on the hanger.

Did You Know? Sachets help keep the air in drawers and closets fresh-smelling. Clothes can be aired with an electric fan, a clothes dryer with the heat turned off, or a vacuum cleaner. A lint remover should be brushed or rolled in the direction of the grain or nap.

Skill Builder: Writing
Ask students to write a description of "a day in the life" of a garment. Students' descriptions should incorporate as many ideas as possible from this section's guidelines.

Skill Builder: Science
Ask students to find out how silverfish, ants, moths, and mildew can live on clothes, and how perspiration, antiperspirants, skin oils, deodorants, and perfumes can weaken fibers.

Reteaching
Draw four columns on the board, headed "Event," "Action," "Procrastination," and "Prevention." In the first column, list the following "events": food spill, body odor, loose button, ripped seam, fallen hem, hair and dandruff, dust and lint, wrinkles, moth-eaten, mildewed. Have students complete the chart for each "event." For example, what action should you take if you find a loose button? What can happen if you neglect a loose button? How can you avoid having loose buttons? And so on.

Enrichment
Have students design a personal clothes-storage and clothing-care system. Ask students to draw layouts and plans for their rooms, closets, and bureau drawers, showing how they would like to organize their wardrobes and spaces for clothing care.

Teaching "Cleaning Clothes"
(Pages 589-593)

This section provides guidelines for using care labels; removing stains; sorting, washing, and drying clothes; ironing or pressing clothes; and drycleaning.

Checking Comprehension

✔ What does a garment's care label tell you? *The care label tells you what kind of washing, drying, or drycleaning steps to follow; how to dry a garment; and any cautions about ironing temperatures. The label also tells you what not to do, such as "Do not bleach."*

✔ How should you initially treat most stains on washable fabrics? *Rinse or soak in cold water.*

✔ How should you clean a grass stain? *Rub in detergent; wash; if stain remains, sponge with alcohol.*

✔ What kinds of clothes should be hand washed? *Delicates, woolens, silks, items labeled "wash separately."*

✔ How does washing make clothes clean? *By dissolving dirt or by lifting particles of soil out of fabric.*

✔ How do soap and detergent differ? *Soap is made from animal or vegetable fat; detergent is made from chemicals or petroleum.*

✔ How do presoaks help clean clothes? *By removing protein stains such as egg, meat juices, and blood.*

✔ What does bleach do? *It acts as a disinfectant and brightens white items.*

✔ What should you do before putting clothes in washer? *Empty pockets; close all fasteners.*

✔ How do you know when to add laundry products to the wash? *The instructions or machine's operating guide tells you.*

✔ What fabrics might be harmed by dry cleaning? *Vinyl, leather, and suede need special handling.*

mon stains. Some stains can be removed by spraying them with a prewash spray, letting the spray set, and then washing the clothing normally.

Always try to treat stains either when they occur or soon afterward. A quick rinse with cold water helps remove many stains from washable fabrics. For nonwashable fabrics, sponge with water or club soda, wetting the fabric as little as possible.

Sorting Clothes

Before washing clothes, you must decide which items can be washed together. First, separate the clothing according to care labels. Put together all clothes that can be machine washed at the same temperature and all those that must be hand washed. Hand washing is best for delicates, woolens, and silks, as well as for single items that should be washed separately.

Next, sort out fabrics that might leave lint, such as terry cloth bath towels and corduroy. Separate bulky items like sheets that might tangle with and tear delicate clothes.

Finally, sort by color. The dye from bright colors may stain whites, so whites should be washed separately. Even if your red cotton T-shirt has the same care instructions as your white cotton underwear, do not wash them together. You may not want pink underwear!

Stain Removal Chart

Stain	Cleaning Method
Blood	Soak in cold water and detergent or presoak. Wash using bleach if safe for fabric.
Candle wax, chewing gum	Harden by rubbing with ice cube, then scrape off with a dull knife or your fingernail.
Chocolate	Soak in cool water. Rub in detergent and wash. If brown stain remains, use bleach if safe for fabric.
Cosmetics	Rub detergent into stain and wash.
Grass, flowers, foliage	Rub detergent into stain and wash. If stain remains, sponge with alcohol. For stains on acetate, dilute alcohol with two parts water.
Grease	Apply prewash soil-and-stain remover, then wash. If stain remains, sponge with cleaning fluid and rinse.
Ink	Sponge with rubbing alcohol or spray with hair spray. Rinse. Rub any remaining stain with detergent and wash.
Nail polish	Do not use polish remover. Sponge with amyl acetate and wash. If necessary, sponge with alcohol mixed with a few drops of ammonia.
Paint, varnish	Rub detergent into stain and wash. If stain is only partially removed, sponge with turpentine or mineral spirits. Rinse.
Perspiration	If garment color has been affected, sponge fresh stains with ammonia, old stains with white vinegar. Rinse and launder.
Soft drinks	Sponge with cold water, or soak in cold water. Wash using bleach if safe for fabric.

More About Stains Catsup or tomato-based stains are treated the same as chocolate stains. Coffee or tea strains are soaked in cold water, then in a presoak, and finally in bleach if safe for the fabric. Mildew can be removed with bleach and ammonia. Rust spots are treated with lemon juice and salt and are placed in the sun before washing.

Cross-Reference For information about grooming see Chapter 3.

Washing will be easier if you sort your laundry into piles of items that can be washed together. You might have quite a few piles: sheets, towels, dark colors, light colors, whites, and delicate fabrics such as laces and sheers.

Washing Clothes

Washing cleans clothes by pushing water between the yarns and fibers. The water either dissolves the soil or lifts the particles of dirt away from the fabric. Cleaning agents are usually used to help remove soil. Two products, soap and detergent, perform the same function but are chemically different. Soap is made from animal or vegetable fat; **detergent** is made from chemicals or petroleum. Sometimes one is preferred over the other. Detergent, for example, is usually recommended for garments treated with a flameproof solution.

It's important to sort your clothes into groups of fabrics and colors that can be washed together.

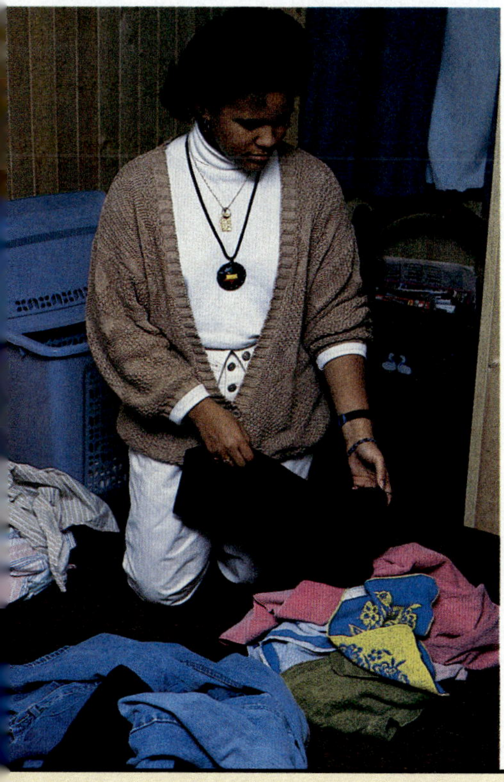

The following laundry products may be used for special purposes:

- Presoak helps remove protein stains like egg, meat juices, and blood.
- Prewash spray helps dissolve or lift out many stains before washing.
- Water softener softens hard water, which has lots of mineral deposits preventing thorough cleaning.
- Disinfectant destroys bacteria. It may be used if the water is not hot, or if there is an illness in the family.
- Bleach removes stains and soil. It acts as a disinfectant, and it brightens white items.
- Fabric softener decreases static electricity and makes fabric feel softer.

You can wash your clothes in two ways—by hand or in a washing machine. The chart on page 592 shows different washing machine settings. Whether the machine is in your home or in a laundromat, you should follow these steps:

1. Check garment pockets to make sure they are empty. Close all fasteners.
2. Select water temperature as directed on the garments' care labels. To save energy, wash with warm or cold water instead of hot water.
3. Add the clothing and the soap or detergent to the machine. (Read the instructions on the machine or in the machine's operating guide first. Some require that you add the soap or detergent before putting the clothing into the machine.) Add bleach if appropriate. If you're using fabric softener, follow package directions.

Focus on Health Laundry products should be carefully measured. Excessive buildups of soap or detergent leave clothes dingy and can harm the skin. Bleaches and cleaning fluids can weaken fibers, remove color, and damage your eyes and skin. Laws require manufacturers to print warning labels on product packaging, which users should heed.

Focus on Health Soil and groundwater can be polluted by chemicals in detergents. In many areas, conservationists recommend using soap rather than detergent. Soap is natural and biodegradable, while detergents often contain high concentrations of phosphate salts that can upset the chemical balance in water and soil.

Activities

Skill Builder: Reading
Have students read evaluations of laundry products in consumer magazines. How are products classified? What are some desirable and undesirable features of laundry products? Which products might be harmful to people or to the environment? Which products are most expensive? Which worked best in independent laboratory tests?

Skill Builder: Science
Have students find out and report on the scientific explanations for three of the following: hard and soft water; static electricity; the setting of stains; club soda as a cleaning agent; effects of disinfectant on bacteria; properties of vinyl; enzymes in presoaks; chlorine and oxygen bleaches; oil-based and water-based stains; properties of fabric softeners; optical brighteners.

Skill Builder: Critical Thinking
Divide the class into groups of 3-5. Give each group a swatch of fabric with a specific stain on it. Instruct students to cut the swatch in half. On one half they are to do nothing; on the other half they are to remove the stain following instructions given with the stained swatch of fabric. Have them compare the two swatches and share findings with the class.

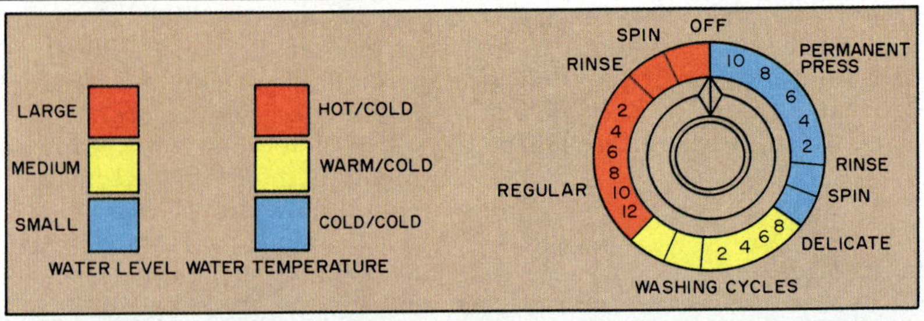

How to Wash Different Loads of Clothes

Water Levels	Water Temperatures	Washing Cycles
Use low for smaller loads, medium for average loads, high for large loads	Use warm and cold temperatures whenever possible for energy conservation	Use a long cycle for heavily soiled fabrics, medium cycle for average, and short cycle for delicate fabrics.

4. Adjust the water level. If you are not washing a full load of clothing, reduce the setting to conserve water.
5. Turn on the wash cycle.
6. When the cycle is over, remove the garments from the washer and clean the filter.

Drying and Ironing

For best results check the care labels again and set the correct temperature on the clothes dryer. Fabrics made of manufactured fibers are usually dried at a lower temperature than cotton fabrics. Be sure to remove your clothes as soon as they're dry. Fold them or hang them up immediately to prevent wrinkling.

Some clothes should not be put in a dryer. The care label will tell you whether you should hang the garment on a clothesline or lay it flat on a towel to dry. Line drying can help give your wash a pleasant, fresh smell. If you only have a few items to dry, hanging them saves energy and avoids shrinkage.

Some fabrics require pressing or ironing to get a smooth finish. Knits and woolens should be pressed, not ironed, to avoid stretching. To iron a woven fabric, be sure to iron with the grainline.

Drycleaning

You will have to **dryclean** some fabrics, that is, they must be cleaned with chemicals rather than soap or detergent and water. After they are cleaned, the clothes are put on forms that are in the shape of a body and steam is blown through them to remove wrinkles. Special touches, such as creases in trousers, are added by a steam-pressing machine or by hand with a steam iron.

Some fabrics and trimmings are harmed by drycleaning. Vinyl, for example, cannot be drycleaned. Leather and suede need special handling. If the care label says not to dryclean, follow the advice. The manager of the drycleaning store will tell you if any trim must be removed before cleaning.

Reteaching
If possible, demonstrate and have students practice the operation of a washer and dryer. Discuss the local condition and supply of water and the cost of energy. Have students develop a personal checklist, for precleaning tasks, sorting practices, and washing and drying reminders. Students' checklists should relate to their own wardrobes and circumstances, as well as to section content.

Enrichment
Ask students to meet at a coin-operated laundromat to wash and dry their clothes. Have students discuss sorting, laundry products, machine operation, and the cost of clothing care. Students might also discuss how different ways of folding clothes become family traditions.

Enrichment
Give each student construction paper, markers, rulers, crayons, and so forth. Have students make an attractive stain removel chart to place in the laundry area of their home. These charts could be laminated for permanent use.

More About Shoes Regular polishing helps shoes and boots maintain their appearance and last longer. Special waxes and oils can be used on leathers to increase water repellency. Suede shoes can be brushed to restore the nap. If shoes or boots get wet, dry them away from direct heat, such as radiator or sunlight. Try to alternate the shoes and boots you wear so they have a chance to air and dry between wearings—they will last longer. When storing shoes or boots, insert shoe trees or stuff with crumpled newspapers. To hold boots upright, insert stiff cardboard folded to fit. To save money, replace worn heels or soles instead of buying a new pair of shoes or boots. A shoe repair store can also restitch seams.

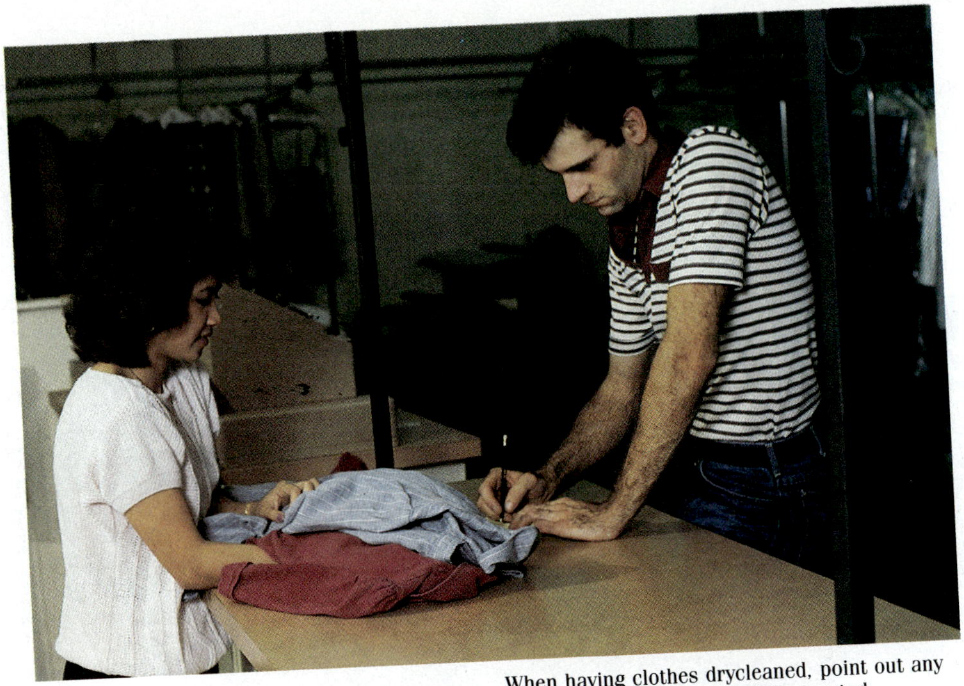

When having clothes drycleaned, point out any stains so they can be specially treated.

Cleaners may miss spots and stains unless you point them out. If you know what caused the stain, tell the drycleaner. Otherwise, it may not be identified correctly. The more information you provide, the better the results.

Some laundromats offer coin-operated drycleaning machines. These cost less than professional drycleaning and remove most soil quite well. They don't, however, provide special treatment for spots and stains.

Simple Repairs

No matter how careful you are you will need to repair your clothing at some point. Here are some ways to make simple repairs.

- **Repairing snags.** Knits often **snag** which means that loops of yarn are pulled out of the knit. To repair these, use a crochet hook or a snag fixer, which can be bought wherever notions are sold. Grasp the snag with the hook and pull it back through to the underside of the fabric. Gently stretch the fabric to smooth out any puckers that the snag caused.
- **Mending seams.** Seams that are coming apart can be stitched by machine or by hand, using a strong backstitch.
- **Patching a hole.** For jeans and casual clothes, use iron-on patches that you can buy in fabric stores. For dressier clothes, matching is important. Cut a piece of fabric from the hem or seam allowance, and place it under the hole. Turn in the torn edges and stitch around the opening with tiny, hardly visible stitches.
- **Replacing fasteners.** You may have to mend the fabric underneath before replacing a fastener.

Did You Know? Darning is another method of repairing tears and holes. New stitches are anchored in the firm area around the tear or hole. Then the sewer copies the knit or weave so that the darned area will be indistinguishable from the surrounding fabric.

Focus on Entrepreneurship Some students might organize and advertise a school-wide mending service, with proceeds to go to school groups.

Focus on Leadership A group of students might offer to help the drama club's wardrobe committee to mend costumes for school theater productions.

Teaching "Simple Repairs"

(Page 593)

This section suggests ways to repair snags, mend seams, patch holes, and replace fasteners.

Checking Comprehension

✔ What are snags? *Loops of yarn that have been pulled out of a knit.*

✔ How should you mend seams by hand? *With a strong backstitch.*

✔ How is the procedure for patching a hole in jeans different from patching a hole in dressy clothes? *When you patch a hole in jeans, you use an iron-on patch. For dressy clothes, you can cut a piece of fabric from the hem or seam allowance, place it under the hole, and stitch around the opening with tiny stitches.*

✔ What might you need to do before replacing a fastener? *Repair the fabric underneath.*

Activities

Skill Builder: Critical Thinking
Ask students to review the chapters on clothing construction and suggest other simple repairs they might add to this section's list. Students might mention resecuring facings, replacing elastic in casings, fixing hems, and the like. Ask students what kinds of sewing tasks they could consider major rather than simple repairs.

Skill Builder: Writing
Ask students to list clothing items in their wardrobes that need repair, and to draw up a schedule for mending them. Suggest that beside each item they write the supplies they will need for the repair.

Reteaching
Show students how to use a crochet hook to repair snags, how to sew a backstitch and a hemming stitch, and how to sew a hole patch. Have students practice these techniques.

Enrichment
Declare a mending day in which each student brings to class a garment to mend. Have students swap garments, discuss the intended repairs, and sit in groups to talk and sew.

Teaching the Feature
"Easy-Care Fabrics"

Answers to Feature Questions

1. Possible answers include: less time spent on clothes care; less money spent on clothes care; more wear from garment; less worry.

2. Students will probably point to such things as people's busy, active lifestyles; less emphasis on housework; and greater emphasis on planned leisure activities.

Activities

Showcase Have students create a display illustrating the theme of the feature. The display might include fabric samples of seersucker and other textured fabrics, nylon-spandex and other manufactured blends, "stone-washed" denim, knits, and the like. The display might also include advertisements and garment labels describing easy-care finishes.

Taking an Opinion Poll Ask students to conduct an opinion poll among their friends and neighbors to find out what people look for in fabrics when buying clothes. Students should develop a standard set of questions to ask in order to find out how people rank fabric qualities in importance. Students can use the data to make generalizations about consumer demand for easy-care fabrics.

Community Contact Arrange to have a fashion designer or sewer talk to the class about working with and caring for easy-care fabrics. Have the person explain what the most popular fabrics are, why, and what they like about them.

TECHNOLOGY

Easy-Care Fabrics

When you want to save time on clothing care, look for garments that don't need ironing. Manufacturers create easy-care garments by using special fibers, special finishes, and special fabric treatments.

- **Fiber content.** The fiber content is generally a very good clue to how much ironing will be needed to maintain a garment's new look. Most manufactured fibers tend to wrinkle less than natural fibers and require relatively little ironing if care instructions are followed. Acrylic, polyester, and nylon are popular manufactured fibers used in garments that need no ironing. These fibers are often blended with natural fibers.

- **Finish.** Crinkles, wrinkles, and puckers are seen in both casual and dressy wear. Ironing would damage these textures. Some fabrics have a permanent heat-set texture. Others may be woven or knit with texturized yarns. **Texturizing** is a process that adds crimp or curl to a normally straight yarn. Knit or woven fabrics may be treated with finishes to create crinkles or a puckered surface, as in seersucker.
- **Fabric manufacture.** Certain fabrics have been prewashed to give them a worn look when you buy them. These fabrics may be called "washed cotton," "laundered sheeting," "prewashed" or "stone-washed" denim. Such fabrics have an uneven surface texture that is desirable in casual sportswear and comfortable activewear. Knits are also manufactured for easy care. Knitted clothes need little ironing, even those that are made of cotton. If you remove them from the dryer immediately they can be hand-smoothed to be wrinkle-free.

Think It Through

1. **Can you think of two specific ways that an easy-care garment affects a person's lifestyle?**
2. **Why do you think there is such a demand today for easy-care garments?**

Focus on Technology Blue denim originated in India, where it was called "dungaree" after the region where it was made. "Jeans" were workclothes made in Genoa, Italy, in the Middle Ages. Later, jeans made of dungaree in France came to be known as "denims," after Nimes, the city where they were made. "Levis," a trademark for jeans made in America out of imported denim in the early 1800s, are named for the man who first made them.

CHAPTER 66 REVIEW

Reviewing the Facts

1. Describe four steps you should take every day to care for your clothes.
2. Why are care labels so important in helping you keep your clothes looking attractive?
3. Explain how clothes should be sorted before you wash them.
4. What do the following laundry products do: presoak, bleach, fabric softener?
5. List three common stains and explain how to treat each.
6. When using an automatic washer, what four steps should you follow before starting the machine?
7. What are two methods of drying clothes?
8. How are clothes drycleaned?

Thinking Critically

1. What sort of impression is given by a person who wears stained or unmended clothing?
2. How does taking care of your clothing show a sense of responsibility?

Applying Your Skills

1. **Classifying Information.** Make a care chart for your clothes. Using the care labels as your guide, classify the different types of care into different columns for your chart. List each item under the appropriate heading.

2. **Computing and Comparing Costs.** Visit a supermarket and write down the prices and sizes of five brands of detergent. Check the package directions and note how much detergent is recommended per wash load. Calculate which brand and size is the least expensive per washload.

3. **Performing Experiments.** Stain separate swatches of fabric with items such as chocolate, lipstick, grass, grease, ink, and soft drinks. Cut each swatch in half. Using the Stain Removal Chart on page 590, try cleaning each stain from one of the fabric halves. Then wash all fabric swatches—both the treated and the untreated—and compare the results.

Answers to "Reviewing the Facts"

1. Any four: air them; brush off lint and dust; check for damage or spots; set aside clothes that need to be mended or cleaned; fold clothes or hang them up.
2. They recommend methods for washing, drying, pressing, and drycleaning clothes, and list any special cautions.
3. Sort by care labels; sort out fabrics that produce lint; separate bulky from delicate items; sort by color.
4. Presoak helps remove protein stains; bleach removes stains and soil, disinfects, and brightens whites; fabric softener decreases static electricity and makes fabric feel softer.
5. Refer to Stain Removal Chart on page 590.
6. Empty pockets and close fasteners; select water temperature; add clothing, soap or detergent, and bleach or fabric softener if desired; adjust water level.
7. Any two: automatic dryer, line drying, laying flat on a towel.
8. They are cleaned with chemicals and then steam is blown through them.

Answers to "Thinking Critically"

1. Students may suggest such impressions as carelessness, poor self-concept and low self-esteem, unfriendliness, and so on.
2. Students may suggest that caring for clothes shows concern about one's appearance, pride, a sense of cooperation with others in the household, and so on.

COMPLETING THE CHAPTER

Summary

- Clothing care involves daily, occasional, and seasonal tasks.
- Different stains require different treatment, but all stains should be treated promptly.
- Sort clothes before washing according to care label instructions and colors.
- Wash clothes with soap or detergent and other laundry aids, such as presoaks, water softeners, disinfectant, bleach, and fabric softener.
- Use washers and dryers according to manufacturer's instructions and the need to conserve water and energy.
- Repair clothes by mending snags and seams, patching holes, and replacing fasteners.

For Review

Objective Review Questions Have students complete the "Reviewing the Facts" section on this page.

Study Guide Have students complete the Study Guide from Chapter 66 of their *Student Workbook.*

Motivator Follow-Up Have students review their lists of proper clothing care they wrote at the beginning of the chapter. Ask students to revise their lists in light of what they have learned.

Class Discussion Write "Care," "Cleaning," and "Repair" on the board. Have students discuss the tasks to be undertaken in each category.

For Evaluation

Checklist Ask students to write ten "dos" and ten "don'ts" covering the main points of this chapter.

Chapter Test Have students complete the test for Chapter 66 that appears in the *Teacher's Classroom Resources.*

CHAPTER OVERVIEW

Chapter 67 offers suggestion for making old or ill-fitting clothes wearable again by redesigning them. Garments can be redesigned by adjusting hems, altering seams, or changing styles. Students learn how they can get more use out of their favorite garments by decorating them with design details, dyes, or paints. The chapter suggests uses for clothes that are no longer worn. Discarded clothes can be donated, sold, or recycled. Recycling ideas include new uses for garments, their fabrics, and even their fibers.

INTRODUCING THE CHAPTER

Motivators

Diagramming Concepts Write *redesign* and *recycle* on the board. Point out that *re* is a Latin prefix meaning "again." Refer students to Chapter 56 for a definition of *design.* Then ask: "What is a cycle? What are some examples of cycles? How might you diagram a cycle to show how it works?" Ask students to create diagrams illustrating the concepts of redesigning and recycling as applied to clothing.

Using the Photograph Have students study the photograph on this page. Then ask: "What is being done? How will this change the look of the garment?"

Evaluating Costs and Benefits Ask students to list all the advantages of redesigning and recycling clothes that they can think of. What resources are expended in the process? What resources are saved? Encourage students to argue the question, "Is it worth it?"

Introducing the Objectives

Discuss the chapter objectives on this page. Remind students that the objectives focus on important chapter content.

CHAPTER

67

Redesigning and Recycling

OBJECTIVES

This chapter will help you to:

- Describe ways to get more use out of your favorite garments.
- Determine how to make old or ill-fitting clothes wearable again.
- Suggest uses for clothes that you can no longer wear.

WORDS TO REMEMBER

patchwork
recycle
redesign

Chapter Resources

Teacher's Classroom Resources
- Lesson Plan
- Life Skills Activity, *Creative Makeovers*
- Reproducible Master, *Patchwork Step-by-Step*
- Extension Activity, *Ideas for Outdated Clothing*
- Chapter Test

Student Workbook
- Study Guide
- Worksheet, *To Tell the Truth*

Think back to the first step of planning your wardrobe, in Chapter 59. You made three piles of clothes:

- Clothes in good condition that you like to wear.
- Clothes that you like, but which need fixing.
- Clothes that you do not wear because you've outgrown them or you don't like them.

In the third pile, you put clothes that no longer appeal to you or that you cannot wear. Did you find some pants that were too short or a dress that was no longer "you"? You don't have to throw those clothes away. You might be able to **redesign** the garment—change it so that it's more in fashion or has an exciting new look. Perhaps you can **recycle** the garment—find a new use for it.

Redesigning and recycling offer many personal rewards. You can use your creativity to alter a poor-fitting pair of pants, redesign a shirt bought at a garage sale, or change a garment in your closet to better suit your tastes. It's a good way to save money by extending the life of your clothes.

Redesigning a Garment

One of the easiest ways to make a garment wearable again is to change the way it fits. You may be able to do this by simply adjusting the hems or seams.

Adjusting Hems

Have you suddenly grown two inches and your clothes are too short or are the newest fashions showing longer or shorter hemlines? If so, you can lengthen or shorten your clothes.

If there is too little fabric for lengthening the garment, stitch a strip of wide hem facing to the bottom edge. Turn the facing to the inside along the new hemline and sew in place. You could also add a fabric band or ruffle.

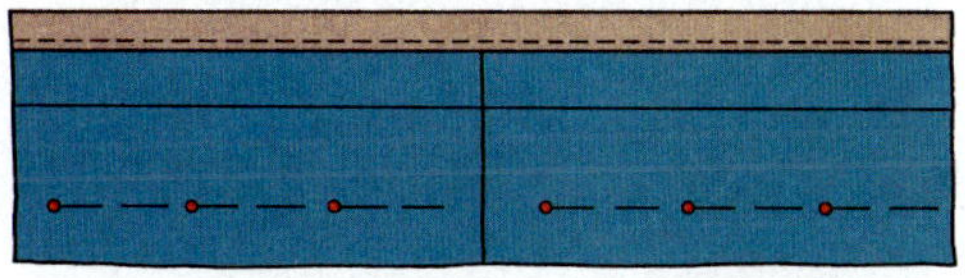

1. To lengthen or shorten a hem, remove stitching and press out old crease. Try on garment and have someone mark the new hem length with pins or chalk.

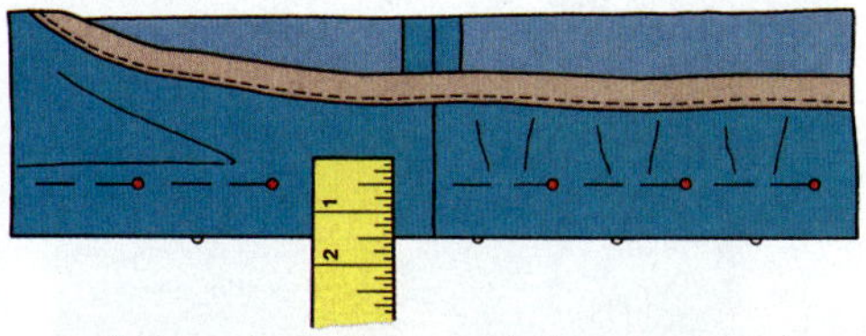

2. Turn up hem along marked line and pin in place. If hem is too wide, cut off extra fabric and finish raw edge with seam tape or stitching. If hem is too narrow, sew on wide hem facing.

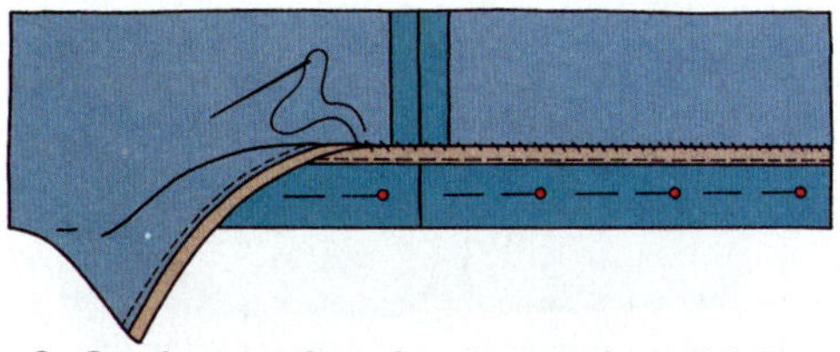

3. Sew hem in place, keeping stitches slightly loose to avoid puckering. Be sure stitches do not show on outside of garment.

More About Alterations Seams and hemlines sometimes show unsightly wear marks or creases when they are let out. These marks can be covered up, using braid or some other type of trim. Some fabrics show needle holes where stitching has been removed. Darts, for example, can be lengthened or shortened to improve a garment's fit, but needle holes in the fabric might show where darts were altered and spoil the effect. In redesigning clothes, you should first check the amount of wear on seamlines and hemlines, and the ability of the fabric to recover from needle holes when seams are ripped out. Such marks are not a problem when you are taking in seams or darts or shortening hemlines.

Introducing Vocabulary

Point out that the compound word *patchwork* means "working with patches." The original expression was "patch work," but in time the two words were spoken and written as one. Ask students for examples of other compound words with *work* or *works* as the suffix. Students might mention paperwork, housework, roadwork, homework, schoolwork, and so on.

TEACHING THE CHAPTER

For convenience, the teaching suggestions for this chapter are arranged according to the following lesson topics:

Teaching "Redesigning a Garment"

(Pages 597-598)

This section explains how to adjust hem and seams. Suggestions for redesigning the style of clothes include changing the use, shape, details, or trimmings of a garment.

Checking Comprehension

✓ What is a disadvantage of serged seams? *Serged seams are usually less than 1/4 inch wide. This makes it difficult to let seams out.*

✓ Give an example of turning a garment from one type to another. *Removing sleeves from sweaters to make a vest, making shorts from pants, making jackets from coats, and so on.*

✔ Give an example of reshaping a garment. *Turning flared pants into straight legs, wide skirts into narrow skirts, and so on.*

✔ Give an example of redesigning by changing a detail. *Shortening sleeves, removing a collar, adding a patch pocket.*

✔ Give an example of redesigning by changing trimmings. *Adding an appliqué, replacing the buttons, and so on.*

Activities

Skill Builder: Critical Thinking
Ask students to evaluate an article of clothing they are wearing. What is the garment's potential for being redesigned? Ask students to think of changes they could make, and to imagine or visualize what the garment would look like after each change. Have students draw a sketch of the redesigned garment.

Reteaching
Ask students to bring a discarded article of clothing to class. Have students lengthen or shorten the hem, take in or let out the seams, and change the style of the garment in one or more of the ways suggested in this section.

Enrichment
Have students write detailed alteration plans for two articles of clothing they have stopped wearing. Plans should include specific goals, alternatives, and priorities for the steps they will take to restore the items to their wardrobes.

Teaching "Creative Measures"
(Page 599)

This section suggests using decorations, dyes, or paints to renew old or damaged clothes.

Checking Comprehension

✔ What kinds of decorations can you use to renew old or damaged clothes? *Patches, appliqués, trims, and embroidery.*

Altering Seams

It is easier to take in seams than to let them out. To take in a seam, put on the garment and pin a new seamline. Baste the new seam, and check the fit by trying on the garment to be sure it feels comfortable. Rip out the old seam as far as necessary. Stitch the new seam, overlapping the old stitching with the new stitching for 1 inch (2.5 cm).

If you want to let out a seam, check the seam allowance to be sure that there is enough fabric to make the change. Many ready-made garments have serged seams that are usually less than 1/4 in. (6 mm) wide. Rip out the old seam as far as necessary. Pin and baste the new seamline, and check the fit. Then stitch the new seam, overlapping the stitching lines.

Changing the Style

You can also change the style of clothes to get more use out of them. Consider making changes in one of the following ways:

- **Use.** You can turn a garment from one type into another. By removing sleeves from a sweater, you make a vest. Shorten pants legs to make cropped pants or shorts; turn sweatshirts into cut-off tops; alter coats to make jackets.
- **Shape.** Reshape a garment. Turn flared pants into straight legs or bring a full garment closer to the body by taking in the side seams. Shortening also changes the shape.
- **Details.** Give a shirt or blouse a new look by shortening the sleeves, removing a collar, or adding patch pockets. Collars or cuffs can be replaced with knitted ribbing.
- **Trimmings.** Add an appliqué, ribbon, buttons, or other trimmings. Replace original buttons or trim to update the design of a garment or accessory.

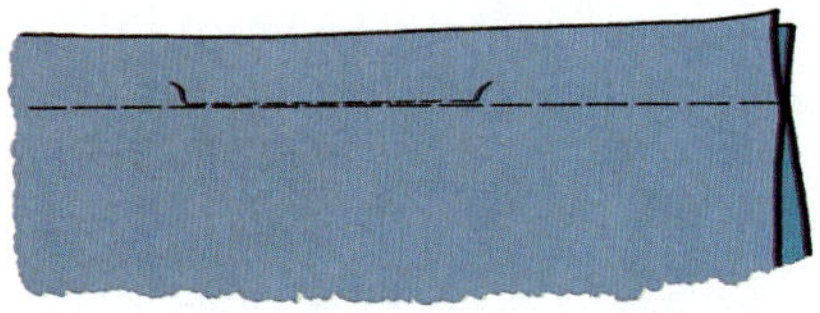

1. When repairing or altering seams, overlap the old stitching lines about 1 in. (2.5 cm) as you start and finish the new stitching.

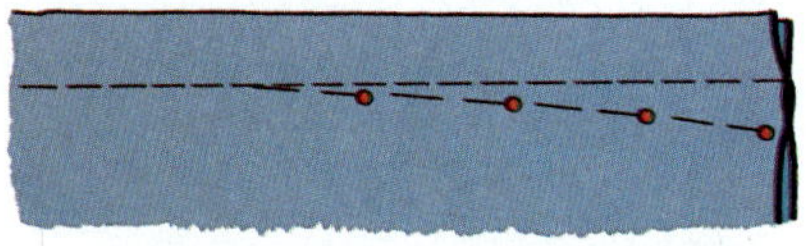

2. To take in a seam, pin new seamline and machine baste. Remove old stitching, and try on garment to check fit. Stitch new seam, overlapping stitches, and press.

3. To let out a seam, check seam allowances for extra fabric. Baste new seam and remove old stitching. Check fit, stitch seam, and press.

Cross-Reference See Teen Tips "T-Shirt—Make It Unique" on pages 614-615.

More About Redesigning To taper pants, restitch both the outer and inner seams. If pants are too short, cut them off to the latest fashion length—cropped, mid-calf, below-the-knee, or shorts—and hem. Or stitch a casing several inches below the knee and insert elastic to make knickers. If shirt cuffs become worn, cut them off, hem bottom of sleeve, and form roll-up cuffs. If a sweater or sweatshirt has lost its shape, stitch casings at the cuffs and bottom edge and insert elastic or cording for a new shape.

Creative Measures

You can make old or damaged clothes bright and lively by adding decorations. Patches, appliqués, trims, and embroidery can cover holes, hide stains, or liven up your clothing. Even if your sweatshirt doesn't have a hole, decorate it with an appliqué, costume jewelry, a painted design, or a sports-team emblem. Use these decorations to make garments that show your individuality.

Dyeing

Perhaps the only thing wrong with a garment is its color. If you don't like the color or it doesn't go with the rest of your clothes, you can consider dyeing, or changing the color of the fabric.

You can dye your clothes at home, or you can have them dyed professionally. For successful home dyeing, follow the directions on the dye package.

Home dyeing works best when a light-colored fabric is darkened. Mix the dye with hot water, and then soak the fabric in a sink, a washing machine, or another container. You must simmer the fabric in the dye if you want it to come out very dark. Natural fibers absorb dye better than manufactured fibers.

In tie-dyeing, parts of the fabric are tightly wrapped or tied, so that the dye penetrates unevenly, producing many different shades of the color. One or several colors may be used in this process.

Dyes may stain containers and other materials, so you should always get permission to use the equipment with which you plan to dye your clothes. Never dye clothes in a laundromat.

Fabric Painting

An old shirt may be given a new look with fabric paint. Acrylic paints, cold-water fabric dyes, tube paints, waterproof markers, and fabric marking pens can be used to cover a stain or reclaim a comfortable old T-shirt, sweatshirt, or skirt.

Wash and dry the garment before painting to soften the fabric and remove any finish that might repel the dye. Then follow instructions for the type of paint or dye that you are using. When the dye dries, cover the painted area with a clean cloth. Use an iron at the proper setting for the fabric and iron over the entire painted area to set the dye.

Give old clothes a new look by dyeing, painting, or adding colorful trims.

Emphasize Dyes stain containers, utensils, range tops, sinks, floors, and skin. Manufacturers recommend wearing rubber or plastic gloves when dyeing. Also, even carefully cold-rinsed, colorfast dyes are not colorfast at first. They can bleed onto other fabrics and should be washed separately several times before being laundered with other clothes.

Focus on Technology Batik is a wax-resist method of dyeing fabric that was developed in Asia in ancient times. Designs are drawn on the cloth with melted wax. After the wax hardens and cools, the cloth is dyed. The dye penetrates only the unwaxed portions of the cloth. The wax is then ironed out, revealing the design.

✓ What guidelines should you follow when dyeing clothing at home? *Carefully follow the directions on the dye package. Mix the dye in hot water, then soak the fabric in this solution. Simmer the fabric in the dye if you want to get very dark colors. Dyes may stain containers and other materials, so you need to get permission to use the equipment.*

✓ What is tie-dyeing? *Parts of the fabric are tightly tied so that dye penetrates unevenly, creating patterns of colors.*

✓ What materials can you use for fabric painting? *Acrylic paints, cold-water fabric dyes, tube paints, waterproof markers, and fabric marking pens.*

Activities

Skill Builder: Reading
Distribute copies of the instructions from a box of fabric dye for students to read. Ask specific questions testing students' reading comprehension. For example: What fabrics are not recommended for dyeing with this product? How much dye should you use per pound of fabric? What should you do to the fabric before putting it in the dye?

Skill Builder: Math
Matt is dyeing two cotton T-shirts dark green. The manufacturer's instructions say he needs 1 package of dye for each dry pound of fabric. Each package should be diluted in 3 gallons (11.4 L) of water. Matt's T-shirts weigh a total of about 8 ounces. How much dye should he use? *(1/2 package)* How much water should he use to dilute the dye? *(1 1/2 gallons [5.7 L])*

Reteaching
Demonstrate dyeing and painting materials and techniques. Have students practice the techniques on articles of their own clothing or on muslin fabric swatches.

Enrichment
Invite students to make a *Creative Living* class banner out of a plain white sheet. Section the sheet into as many equal-size circular positions as there are students. Over a period of time, each student decorates, dyes, or paints his or her portion. Display the banner when it's done.

Teaching the Feature
"Helping the Needy"

Answers to Feature Questions

1. Used clothing donated to charity should be clean, in good repair, and in season. It should not be so out of style that it would embarrass the wearer. In donating clothing, people should take into account the clientele the charity serves.

2. People whose homes have been destroyed by a fire or by a natural disaster such as a hurricane need clothing. Thrift stores operated by charities need clothing donations.

Activities

Identifying Needs On the chalkboard, write different situations in which people might need donations of used clothing. For example, shelter for homeless people in winter, safe house for battered women and their children, job training program for ex-offenders, family whose house burned down, community center for refugees. Have students identify the clothing needs of each group.

Taking Inventory Suggest that students go through their closets at home and identify shoes and clothes that could be donated to charity. Encourage them to follow through. You might set up a used-clothing drop-off site in your classroom.

Personal-Care Kits Suggest that students assemble personal-care kits for families in shelters for the homeless. They might negotiate with local merchants for the best prices on soap, toothpaste, shampoo, and deodorant. Students might sponsor a bake sale or car wash to raise money for these items.

Community Contact Have students identify groups or agencies in your community that distribute used clothing. Suggest that they contact each agency to find out its clothing needs. Students might conduct a school clothing drive for the benefit of a particular agency.

MANAGING RESOURCES

Helping the Needy

On a cold Saturday in December, Meg and Annie hop on a bus and head downtown. They plan to spend the afternoon volunteering at a day shelter for needy people. The director of the shelter had been at their school that week, telling students about the work of the shelter and asking for volunteers.

The volunteer coordinator greets the girls warmly and gives them a tour of the facility. "Most of our guests are street people," the coordinator says, "but we also help low-income families who have trouble making ends meet. About 10,000 people come through our doors each month for food, clothing, and emergency assistance."

The coordinator takes Meg and Annie to the basement. "This is where I'd like you girls to work," he says, opening the door to a room filled with bags and boxes. "This is our clothing donation room. We sort the clothes in here and then put them on shelves in the next room for our guests to look through and take. For now, just put the clothes into piles—women's clothes here, men's clothes over there, children's clothing next to them, and baby clothes right there. Toss out anything you think shouldn't be saved. Okay?"

Meg and Annie nod their heads and begin digging into the bags of clothes. They're impressed with the amount of donations. But they're a little disgusted too. "What's wrong with some people?" asks Annie. "They must think this is the dump. Look at this coat. It's dirty, the buttons are missing, and there's a hole in the sleeve. You can't expect people to wear something like this, even if it is free."

"Right!" agrees Meg. "And look at this—a whole bag of summer shorts and T-shirts. It's the middle of winter!"

Meg rips open another bag. "Yuk! Everything in here is covered with dog hair. I'm not even going to touch this stuff."

"Look at these!" says Annie, as she pulls bellbottom pants and a polyester shirt out of a bag. "My dad wore stuff like this in the seventies. Do you think someone would want these for a Halloween party?"

After working for an hour, the girls stand back and check their progress. The women's pile has heaps of clothing, but there are hardly any clothes in the men's or children's pile. "Men must not give away their clothes," says Meg. "Are there kids our age who need clothes? I don't see anything for them. There aren't many shoes here either."

The girls work for another hour and soon have most of the clothes sorted.

"Well, that wasn't fun," says Meg, "but I do feel that we did something worthwhile. We should come back next week."

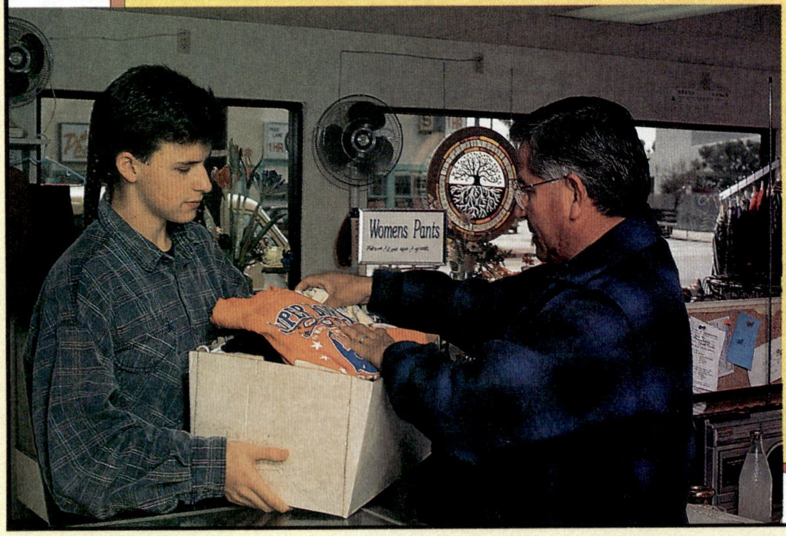

Think It Through

1. **What are some guidelines for donating used clothing to charity?**
2. **Besides homeless shelters, name other situations or places where donations of used clothing are needed.**

Emphasize Donating used clothing to charities is a form of recycling. Recycling clothing is nothing new. Throughout history, families have handed down clothing from child to child. Years ago, when clothing became too worn, it was used for making quilts.

Did You Know? As many as 300,000 people lost their homes to Hurricane Andrew in 1992. Clothing in closets and drawers was shredded, rain soaked, buried under debris, or blown away.

Focus on International Relationships International relief efforts also require clothing donations. Following the earthquake in Armenia in 1988, U.S. relief agencies sent tons of used clothing to the stricken area.

Recycling a Garment

When a garment has reached the end of the road for you, the fabric or its fibers may still be useful for someone else if you recycle it. Here are three ways to recycle clothes.

Passing it On

During your teen years, you're likely to be growing fast. This means you may outgrow garments long before they are worn out. It's wasteful to throw them away because there may be several years' wear left for someone else.

One of the oldest forms of recycling clothing is the hand-me-down. Clothing that you no longer wear or that no longer suits you can be passed on to a younger brother, sister, cousin, niece, or nephew. You might give it to a friend. A shirt or sweater that is no longer right for you may be perfect for someone else. You and your friends could hold a swap meet and trade garments.

If you don't know anyone who can use the clothes you no longer want, look further. You might earn some money by selling these garments through a consignment shop that buys and sells used clothing. You could also give the clothing to a religious organization or a charity such as the Salvation Army. They may repair and fix used clothing and give it to shelters for the homeless or other people in need. Clothes that you give away may help a family that has lost everything in a fire or a flood. Check in your area for organizations that accept used clothing.

Using the Fabric Another Way

Even if only small pieces of the fabric are in good condition, you can save them for patchwork or crafts projects. If you don't use the fabric scraps yourself, there may be a nursery school, retirement home, or community group that can use fabric for projects.

Worn-out garments of soft cotton make good cleaning rags. It's a good idea to remove all fasteners from the rags to protect furniture from being scratched by sharp hooks or button edges. Save trim, decorations, and fasteners for future projects.

Reusing the Fiber

Even if the fabric cannot be redesigned or given away, the fibers may be recycled—to be used as padding, for instance. Fibers are also used as an ingredient in paper. Some cities have organizations that collect old clothes for such recycling.

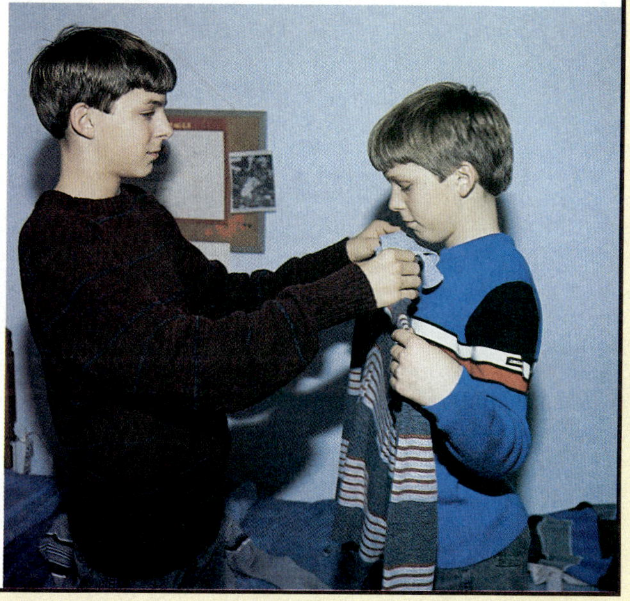

A common method of recycling is to pass garments on to younger family members.

Did You Know? The Salvation Army is an international evangelical and charitable organization founded in England in 1865 by William Booth. The organization, which is operated along military lines, was established in the United States in 1880.

Focus on Leadership Some students might organize a school-wide clothing drive as a public service or for a charitable cause.

Teaching "Recycling a Garment"
(Page 601)

This section describes three ways of recycling garments: passing them on, reusing the fabric, and reusing the fibers.

Checking Comprehension

✓ What is a major benefit of recycling clothing? *Recycling conserves garments, fabrics, and fibers.*

✓ Where can you recycle your discarded clothing? *Pass it on to a relative or friend, sell it through a consignment shop, or give it to a religious organization or charity such as the Salvation Army, homeless shelter and so on.*

Activities

Skill Builder: Writing
Have students write letters to service organizations that redistribute used clothing. Letters should ask for information for a report on the redistribution forces, including any available statistics. Students might then summarize and post the information they receive.

Skill Builder: Science
Have students find out more about how recycling conserves natural resources. For example, what natural resources are used for natural fibers? What natural resources are used to produce manufactured fibers? If fibers were recycled, what ways could natural resources be used?

Reteaching
Ask students to design posters promoting the recycling of clothing, fabrics, and fibers. Students might also develop a fact sheet on the topic to be used for peer education. Have students display their posters and distribute the fact sheets throughout the school or community.

Enrichment
Have students collect and share or swap fabric scraps and discarded clothing. Then have them use the materials to make independent craft projects. Offer awards for the most innovative, most practical, and most artistic craft projects made from recycled clothes.

COMPLETING THE CHAPTER

Summary

- Redesigning or recycling clothes brings many benefits.
- Garments can be redesigned by adjusting hems, altering seams, or changing the style.
- Style can be changed by converting a garment to another use, reshaping a garment, changing the details, or adding trimmings.
- Garments can be renewed through such creative measures as adding decorations, dyeing the garment, or painting the fabric.
- Garments can be recycled by passing them on to someone else, using the fabric in another way, or reusing the fiber.

For Review

Objective Review Questions Have students complete the "Reviewing the Facts" section on this page.

Study Guide Have students complete the Study Guide from Chapter 67 of their *Student Workbook.*

Identifying Alternatives Ask students to describe the sequence of steps and alternatives involved in altering a hem and altering a seam. Have students explain the differences between the three methods of hemming. Then ask students to name four methods of altering a garment's style, with examples of each. Finally, have students name six ways in which garments might be recycled rather than redesigned.

For Evaluation

Performance Test Have students use fabric swatches to show how to alter a hem and how to alter a seam.

Checklist Display a garment to the class. Have students list all the alternatives for redesigning or recycling that garment.

Chapter Test Have students complete the test for Chapter 67 that appears in the *Teacher's Classroom Resources.*

CHAPTER 67 REVIEW

Answers to "Reviewing the Facts"

1. You can use your creativity, and save money.
2. Remove old stitching; press out crease; try garment on; mark new hem length; turn up hem and pin; sew in place. Stitch a strip of wide hem facing to the bottom edge, or add a fabric band or ruffle.
3. Put on the garment; pin new seamline; baste new seam and check fit; rip out old seam; stitch new seam, overlapping the stitching.
4. Any two: change its use or type; change the shape; change the details; add or replace trimmings.
5. Cover holes; hide stains; individualize and add life to clothing.
6. Pass it on; use the fabric in another way; reuse the fiber.
7. Hand clothing down to younger family members or friends; trade with friends; sell at a consignment shop; give to a charity or religious organization.

Reviewing the Facts

1. Why is it useful to know how to redesign and recycle garments?
2. How do you lengthen a hem? What could be used if the hem does not have enough fabric to lengthen?
3. What are the steps for taking in a seam?
4. List two specific ways to change the style of a garment.
5. What are three functions that trimmings, dye, or fabric paint on garments can achieve?
6. What are three ways to recycle clothes?
7. How can you pass on clothing that you no longer wear?

Thinking Critically

1. Have you ever worn used garments, handed down by older brothers or sisters, other relatives, or neighbors? If so, how did you feel about wearing these clothes?
2. Have you ever bought used clothing at a garage sale or rummage sale? What are advantages and disadvantages of buying resale clothing?

Applying Your Skills

1. **Writing Instructions.** Assume you are preparing an article for a crafts magazine. Make up a recycling project that uses everyday objects, such as fabric scraps or old clothing. Include specific cutting and sewing instructions and a sketch of how the finished product should look.

2. **Evaluating Historical Information.** Research the history of patchwork quilts. Find examples of old scrap quilts that were made in America. Report to the class how fabrics were recycled in these traditional quilts.

3. **Performing an Experiment.** Obtain two different fabrics—one made of natural fibers and the other made of manufactured fibers. Dye both fabrics, using fabric dye and following the package directions. What are the results? What might account for any differences?

Answers to "Thinking Critically"

1. Answers may vary. Some may say they were happy to receive and wear hand-me-downs because the clothes expanded their wardrobe, could be worn for a special occasion, looked like new, were of better quality than they could afford, and so on. Others may say they were embarrassed or disliked receiving such items.
2. Advantages include: low prices; finding old or antique styles; being able to dress uniquely or creatively. Disadvantages include: not being able to return items if dissatisfied.

CHAPTER

68

Careers in Clothing and Textiles

OBJECTIVES

This chapter will help you to:

- Identify the interests and skills required for a career in clothing and textiles.
- Give examples of jobs available in design and marketing.
- Give examples of jobs available in clothing construction and care.

WORDS TO REMEMBER

buyer
fashion coordinator
interview
pattern maker

CHAPTER OVERVIEW

Chapter 68 introduces students to career opportunities in the retailing, garment, fashion, and textile industries. Students read about the talents and skills required for a career in clothing and textiles. The chapter gives examples of entry-level jobs, jobs requiring training, and jobs requiring advanced degrees. Specific jobs in the fields of design and marketing include salesperson, stock clerk, buyer, copywriter, artist, personal shopper, fashion coordinator, and fashion or fabric designer. Specific jobs in clothing construction and care include sewing machine operator, drycleaner, pattern maker, textile chemist, textile engineer, and dyer.

INTRODUCING THE CHAPTER

Motivators

Who Made Your Clothes? Ask students to consider all the workers who may have had something to do with the clothes they are wearing. Write students' ideas on the board. Then ask them to suggest a system of classification in terms of fields, industries, occupations, and job titles.

Using the Photograph Direct students' attention to the photograph on this page. Then ask: "What are these workers doing? What do you think is their job title? What other tasks might be part of the job? What kind of interest, talents, skills, and experience are needed?"

Introducing the Objectives

Discuss the chapter objectives on this page. Remind students that the objectives focus on important chapter content.

Introducing Vocabulary

Have students review the "Words to Remember." Point out that *coordinator* is made up of the following parts: *co,* which comes from a Latin prefix for "with, jointly, or together"; *ordinat(e),* which means "to arrange in order"; and *or,* a Latin suffix for the person performing the action of the verb. Ask: "What, then, is a coordinator?"

Chapter Resources

Teacher's Classroom Resources

- Lesson Plan
- Life Skills Activity, *What Skills Do You Have?*
- Reproducible Master, *Do I Want to Work with Clothing and Textiles?*
- Extension Activity, *Careers in Clothing and Textiles*
- Chapter Test

Student Workbook

- Study Guide
- Worksheet, *You Interview the Boss*

TEACHING THE CHAPTER

For convenience, the teaching suggestions for this chapter are arranged according to the following lesson topics:

- "Characteristics for Careers in Clothing and Textiles," pages 604-605
- "Jobs in Design and Marketing," pages 605-607
- "Jobs in Clothing Construction and Care," pages 607-608

Teaching "Characteristics for Careers in Clothing and Textiles"

(Pages 604-605)

This section identifies the general interests and skills required for careers in clothing and textiles.

Checking Comprehension

✓ What kinds of pressures might clothing workers face? *Deadlines, long hours, responsibility for predicting trends.*

✓ What interests and skills do you need for a career in clothing? *A good sense of color, and design; the ability to be organized; attentiveness to detail; interest in the technical aspects of fibers and fabrics.*

✓ Why is being well-organized important? *Clothing jobs involve following many steps and combining many pieces.*

✓ Why is attention to detail important? *People want quality products.*

Activities

Skill Builder: Critical Thinking
Ask students to think of other interests and skills that would be suitable or helpful for careers in clothing. Students might mention mechanical abilities; fine motor skills; good hand-eye coordination; good interpersonal skills for working with supervisors, co-workers, or clients. Problem-solving, decision-making, communication, life management, leadership, and entrepreneurial skills also apply.

Did you ever wonder who designs the spacewear that keeps space shuttle crews safe and comfortable? Who is responsible for the strong and flexible action-wear garments worn by members of Olympic teams from around the world? Experts in fibers, fabrics, and clothing construction work together to outfit astronauts, Olympic athletes, and other people with special clothing requirements. These experts are some of the hundreds of thousands of workers who also put their talents toward meeting the everyday clothing needs of individuals and families.

The clothing and textiles industry is one of the largest industries in the country. Every year new styles and new developments in fibers and technology are introduced. People are needed to manufacture fabrics and sew garments. Others become entrepreneurs—they start new businesses to provide products or services that consumers want.

Careers in clothing and textiles cover a broad range of endeavors, from designing clothing to working in a textile mill or managing a retail store. Jobs are available in all parts of the country. In this chapter, you'll learn about a few of the fascinating careers in clothing and textiles.

For a career in clothing and textiles, you should have an interest in fashion, color, and fabrics.

Characteristics for Careers in Clothing and Textiles

Although many types of jobs exist in this field, several of them attract people with similar characteristics. If you have these traits, a clothing career may be for you.

To be successful in a clothing career, as in any career, you need a strong interest and desire to work in your chosen field. Many of the jobs are demanding and put people under a great deal of pressure. Deadlines must be met, and workers frequently put in long hours. Positions in sales, design, and buying require the ability to predict future trends in styles, colors, and fabrics.

More About Jobs The U.S. Department of Labor lists common job characteristics that job seekers should consider in order to see if their personal talents and skills match the job. For example, job characteristics might include: works with objects, works with ideas, works with people, produces a tangible product, has opportunities for self-expression, works as part of a team, or works independently.

Interests and Skills

- **Do you have a sense of color and design?** Do you also enjoy working with shapes? For almost all clothing careers, a sense of color, design, and shape is essential. Clothing workers combine these elements in their work to create attractive, usable products.
- **Are you well organized?** Clothing jobs often involve following many steps and combining many pieces. To get the job done, you must plan your tasks carefully.
- **Do you pay careful attention to detail?** This trait is very important for a clothing worker, whatever the job. Careful attention to detail results in a quality product—one that people will buy and recommend to friends. Consumers want to be satisfied with how they spend their clothing dollars.
- **Are you interested in the technical side of fibers and fabrics?** Because fibers are the basic building blocks of fabrics, an understanding and knowledge of fiber characteristics are valuable. This information is needed in every area of the garment industry, from the design and manufacture of clothing through clothing care.

If you have the abilities outlined here, you might want to pursue one of these careers.

Jobs in Design and Marketing

Many clothing and textile careers have to do with the design, marketing, and selling of clothes. In any one of these jobs, you could combine an interest in fashion with a career in the world of business.

Entry-Level Jobs

Salespeople in retail stores assist customers in making important decisions about their wardrobes. If salespeople know about fabric and wardrobe planning and have the ability to judge quality in clothing, they can answer questions about the fabrics or garments they sell. This helps build the store's credibility and prestige. The ability to meet and work with the public, a pleasant personality, and a well-groomed appearance are qualities that employers look for in their sales personnel.

Being a salesperson is often the first step in a retail clothing career. Some stores require that a full-time salesperson have a high school diploma, but there are many part-time employment opportunities available for students. A part-time sales job can start you on your career path.

Another entry-level position at a department store is that of a stock clerk. Stock clerks check incoming orders, put price tags on garments, and keep track of how the stock is moving. A stock clerk doesn't need special training, but a good background in math and spelling is helpful. It's also useful to enjoy detailed work and to have good organizational skills.

Jobs That Require Training

Buyers are some of the most important people in the fashion industry. **Buyers** connect designers and garment makers with the stores and shops where clothing is sold. They must be able to spot fashion trends many months in advance as well as have a sense of the colors and styles their customers like. A buyer may work for a large department store, a chain of stores, a mail-order house, or a local specialty store. Large

More About Marketing Reference books list the following job categories: market researcher, manufacturer's representative, salesperson, stockroom person, merchandise manager, display director, and fashion coordinator. Buyers are also called purchasing agents. Related business administration careers include office manager and accountant.

Did You Know? Clothing industry job titles in the fields of communications and advertising include the following: advertising manager, advertising account executive, copywriter, photographer, art director, illustrator, model, fashion stylist, editor, and public relations manager.

Skill Builder: Writing
Divide students into groups. Instruct them to research local opportunities for part-time employment in the field of clothing.

Reteaching
Write the four main section questions on the board. (Do you have a sense of color and design? Are you well organized? Do you pay careful attention to detail? Are you interested in the technical side of fibers and fabrics?) Ask students to rate themselves on each question on a scale from 1 (definitely not) to 5 (yes, very). Ask students to cite a concrete example supporting each rating.

Enrichment
Ask a member of the school guidance department to explain the various tests and inventories people use to find out what their skills and talents are. The visitor might be able to present additional characteristics for careers in clothing, or might be willing to administer and evaluate an interest inventory or career orientation questionnaire.

Teaching "Jobs in Design and Marketing"
(Pages 605-607)

This section describes entry-level, skill-trained, and advance-degree jobs in retailing, merchandising, advertising and promotion, customer services, and designing.

Checking Comprehension

✓ What knowledge and skills can make a salesperson valuable to retailers? *Knowledge of fabrics and wardrobe planning; ability to judge quality in clothing.*

✓ What jobs in design and marketing require training? *Buyer, copywriter, artist, personal shopper.*

✓ For whom might a buyer work? *A department store, a chain of stores, a mail-order house, or a specialty store.*

✔ What is a fashion center? *Buildings housing the sales offices of garment manufacturers.*

✔ What work is done in promotion and publicity departments? *Copywriters and artists prepare ads and displays.*

✔ What are some skills a personal shopper should have? *Good taste; ability to work within a budget; good judgment in selecting clothes for others.*

✔ What jobs in marketing and design require an advanced degree? *Fashion coordinator, designer.*

✔ Why must buyers and fashion coordinators work together? *To make sure that different departments of a store sell clothing and accessories that go well together.*

✔ What does a fashion designer do? *Choose fabrics, plan lines of garments, make sketches or samples from which patterns are made.*

✔ What other kinds of designers work in the textile industry? *Designers of weaves, knits, and fabric designs or prints.*

Activities

Skill Builder: Reading
Have students read clothing and textile job descriptions in career planning resource books. Ask students to report on job titles and job descriptions. Have students discuss the relationship of education, training, and experience to starting wages and salaries.

Skill Builder: Writing
Have students review the information in Chapter 17 on writing resumes. Ask students to write resumes for an entry-level position in a large department store. As another writing assignment, have students design and write employment (help-wanted) advertisements. Ads should include the job title and duties, and the qualities the hirer seeks in an employee.

stores have a number of buyers who travel to fashion centers to select merchandise for their departments. Fashion centers are buildings that house the sales offices of garment manufacturers. In a small specialty store, the owner of the store is often the buyer.

Large clothing stores have promotion and publicity departments where copywriters and artists prepare ads and displays. College writing or journalism courses will help prepare you for a copywriter's job. Artists and display workers should be talented in art. In addition to what they have learned in school, these workers acquire many skills while on the job.

Stores employ stock clerks and salespersons, sometimes on a part-time basis. What skills are needed for these entry-level jobs?

Some department stores offer their customers the services of personal shoppers. A personal shopper selects fashion merchandise that answers a particular customer's needs, saving time and energy for a busy consumer. A personal shopper must have good taste, be able to work within a predetermined budget, and have the ability to choose clothing that is suitable and pleasing to the customer.

Jobs That Require an Advanced Degree

Large stores have **fashion coordinators** who develop advertising themes and plan fashion events that will bring people into the store. The fashion coordinators often involve community groups, such as school clubs, in their projects. You may have attended or modeled at a fashion show put on by a store.

Working closely with the buyers, the fashion coordinators also make sure that different departments of the store sell clothing and accessories that go well together. They keep the buyers informed about the newest colors and styles. They want to make sure, for example, that a customer who selects a suit in a new color can find matching accessories in other departments.

Fashion coordinators are usually college graduates who majored in home economics or art. In addition, they may attend special fashion and merchandising schools where they get work/study experience. They need experience in various positions within a clothing store.

Focus on Entrepreneurship Many opportunities exist in the textiles and clothing fields for entrepreneurs. Some make and sell products such as jewelry, purses, hand-knitted sweaters, children's clothing, toys, pillows, and monogrammed items. Others provide a service such as fashion photographers, illustrators, copywriters, models, alteration experts, wardrobe planners, color consultants, and sewing instructors. Some entrepreneurs work from their homes; some are located in a shop or an office; others run a mail-order business. Successful entrepreneurs must know how to manage a business.

The designer is another important person in the fashion industry. Every piece of clothing that a buyer selects, and every piece that you wear, first takes shape in the mind of a designer. Designers choose the fabrics and plan the lines of new garments. They make sketches, and sometimes samples, from which a pattern can be made.

Designers usually get their training in college programs for fashion design and by working with experienced designers. To be successful, designers must follow fashion trends closely.

In addition to fashion design, job opportunities exist in fabric design, weaving, and knitting. Today, many fabric designers are creating a variety of textures by using computers to weave different kinds of yarn into different patterns. They can quickly color the designs in a variety of combinations and print a copy of each design on paper—all by computer.

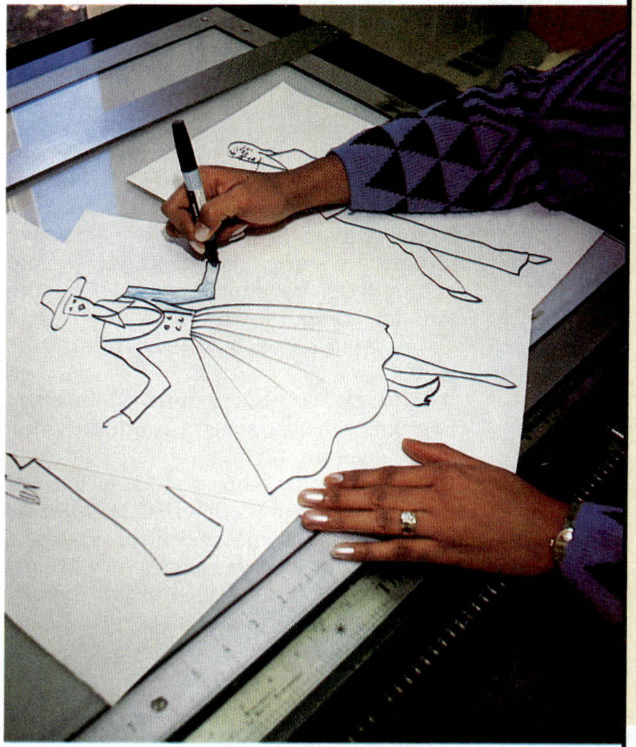

Clothing designers must have a knowledge of art, as well as clothing construction.

Jobs in Clothing Construction and Care

The clothing industry also employs thousands of people who work behind the scenes. These workers are involved in the manufacture of fabrics or garments. They may develop new fibers, dye fabrics, or sew clothes. They also are involved in caring for clothes.

Entry-Level Jobs

The largest number of workers in the garment industry are sewing machine operators. These are the people who do the stitching. Most machine operators are trained on the job to sew on special machines, but they may receive training at a technical or vocational school. Beginners start out stitching the easiest seams. Their wages begin with the legal minimum pay, but they can earn more as they gain skill and responsibility. Operators who show an ability to work with people can become supervisors.

Skilled sewers can work in other businesses. Drycleaning companies employ menders to repair and alter customers' clothing. Resale clothing stores also hire workers with sewing skills for repair work. Many large clothing stores hire alteration workers to alter garments, such as suits, to fit customers.

Reteaching
Ask students if they know anyone who works in the clothing and textile industries. Did they need special training or an advanced degree for their job? What do they do? Do they like their work? Why or why not? Have students discuss possible satisfactions and frustrations of the jobs described in this section.

Enrichment
Visit a fashion design program at a local Vocational Technical Educational Center or invite a representative from the program to present career information to the class.

Teaching "Jobs in Clothing Construction and Care"
(Pages 607-608)

This section describes entry-level, skilled-trained, and advanced degree jobs in manufacturing, drycleaning, and textiles. The chapter concludes with a summary of sources of information for interested students.

Checking Comprehension

✔ Where can skilled alteration workers find jobs? *Drycleaning companies, resale clothing stores, large retail clothing stores.*

✔ Name two jobs in clothing construction and care that require special training. *Drycleaner, pattern maker.*

✔ Why must drycleaners receive training? *They must choose chemicals to remove stains without damaging garments.*

Focus on Technology Textile and apparel industry jobs also include the following categories: textile researcher, machine technician, manufacturing supervisor, industrial engineer, plant engineer, pattern maker, computator, fabric researcher, garment maker, and clothing designer.

More About Care Services Job titles include home counselor, marker, spotter, finisher, sewer, inspector, and assembler. Tailoring is another name for altering, assembling, and sewing clothes.

✓ What are the similarities and differences between a textile chemist and a textile engineer? *Both jobs require advanced degrees. Both the chemist and the engineer develop new things. The chemist, however, develops new fibers and finishes, while the engineer develops new techniques for making yarns and fabrics.*

✓ What knowledge and skills do dyers need? *They need to know about formulas, fibers and fabrics, chemistry, computers.*

Activities

Skill Builder: Critical Thinking
Ask students what manufacturing concerns other than clothing factories are part of the garment industry. Point out that all the tools, equipment, and notions associated with clothing—such as, pins and needles, sewing machines, buttons, threads, and zippers—also have to be manufactured.

Reteaching
Have students list the occupations and professions described in this section. Based on the job descriptions, job prerequisites, and work settings, what do students think are some of the advantages and disadvantages of each job?

Enrichment
Have students read brochures describing courses of study or training programs for jobs described in this chapter. The school library or guidance department has brochures from technical and vocational schools, manufacturer's apprenticeship programs, and colleges offering courses in merchandising, business management, fashion design, textiles, and other careers.

Jobs That Require Training

Drycleaners must know how to choose the right chemicals to remove stubborn spots and stains without damaging a garment. They learn the techniques to use for each type of fabric and stain. Because the job involves making complex decisions, it takes six to twelve months to learn. This training can be obtained in a vocational school or on the job. Drycleaners who own their own shops need some business training as well.

The **pattern maker** holds the highest paid and most important production job in a garment factory. He or she is a skilled worker who makes a pattern from the designer's original sample. All the patterns of a garment are copies of this first one, so accuracy is very important. Many years of on-the-job experience are needed for this career.

Jobs That Require an Advanced Degree

Not all textiles are suitable for making clothing. To find the right types, research is necessary.

Textile chemists develop new fibers and finishes. Manufactured fibers such as nylon and polyester, as well as durable press and water-repellent finishes, are the result of textile research. Textile engineers develop new techniques for making yarns and fabrics. They seek to improve quality yet keep production costs down. These workers must have college degrees and be skilled in math and chemistry.

Dyers are also highly skilled workers. They work in textile mills and choose the formulas used for dyeing the fibers or fabrics. They must know chemistry and understand how the dyes and fibers will react together. They should be familiar with computers, which play a major role in controlling color and dyeing fabrics.

Getting a Job

If you have an interest in a career in the textiles and clothing industry, there are many avenues of experience and study that you can follow. High school diplomas are required for most of the jobs described here. Technical or vocational schools, apprenticeship programs, or some other form of post-high school training may be required for some positions. College or fashion merchandising degrees will help you gain the knowledge and skills necessary for specialized positions offering greater responsibility.

Garment manufacturers need pattern makers, cutters, sewing machine operators, pressers, and inspectors to produce the clothes that people wear.

More About Jobs Manufacturers, schools and colleges, the government, and communities need teachers in the clothing and textile fields. Teachers work as consumer educators, demonstrators and consultants, and extension service specialists of agents in county, state, and federal government. For example, 4-H leaders and home economists are county extension agents. Teachers work in school systems, community colleges, adult education centers, vocational and trade schools, and colleges and universities. They teach home economics, fashion merchandising, sewing construction, textile history, and many other subjects in the fields of clothing and textiles.

INTERPERSONAL SKILLS

What to Wear for an Interview

According to one major university's research, the most common reason that employers give for not hiring an applicant is poor personal appearance. Here are some general grooming tips to help you make a good impression during an **interview**—a meeting between an employer and a job applicant.

- Take a bath or shower before dressing for the interview. Men should shave, if necessary, for a neat appearance.
- Hair should be clean and well-trimmed.
- Fingernails should be clean and trimmed.
- Avoid extremes. Don't dress too casually or too formally.
- Perfume or cologne, if used, should be applied sparingly. A woman should use only a small amount of makeup.

Men can use the following guidelines in dressing:

- Wear a solid-color shirt and a tie. A sports jacket or suit gives a more professional look for offices or stores.
- Choose well-pressed casual or dress pants, not jeans.
- Wear tie shoes or loafers that are polished and neat.

For women, the following guidelines are appropriate:

- Wear a classic dress, a skirt with a sweater, or a skirt-blouse-jacket combination. Pants are not appropriate for an interview.
- Choose sheer or plain-colored pantyhose, coordinated to your outfit.
- Wear classic pumps or flat shoes. Boots are appropriate if they coordinate with your outfit.
- Be conservative in your choice of jewelry.

It is important to make a good impression at a job interview. You're more likely to make that impression if you prepare yourself in advance to look your best.

Think It Through

1. **Why would a neat, well-groomed appearance be especially important for a person employed in the clothing and textile industry?**
2. **Describe in detail an outfit that you now own that would be appropriate for a job interview. What makes the outfit appropriate?**

Teaching the Feature

"What to Wear for an Interview"

Answers to Feature Questions

1. Students should suggest that people who produce and sell clothing need to demonstrate an ability to select appropriate clothing and maintain it well, that a well-groomed appearance shows how garments enhance appearance, and so on.
2. Answers will depend on the individual student's wardrobe, but should demonstrate an understanding of the guidelines given in the text.

Activities

Class Debate Invite students to express their opinions about the suggestions given in the feature. How might they modify the suggestions to better match local or regional expectations and different kinds of jobs or work settings? Designers and artists, for example, might dress more creatively; sewing machine operators might dress casually.

Class Discussion Ask students to extend the feature topic by giving suggestions on how to sit at an interview, where to look, how to talk, and what to say.

Community Contact Arrange to have a personnel director from a local business speak to the class about the importance of proper dress and appearance for an interview. What does the person find appropriate or inappropriate? Ask him or her to cite some examples.

Focus on Decision Making Remind students that when they are choosing clothes for an interview they should avoid presenting an extreme appearance. They should choose comfortable clothes that will help them feel relaxed and self-confident.

Emphasize Clothes worn for an interview should be clean and pressed. Students should avoid clothing that wrinkles easily.

Cross-Reference See Chapter 8 for information about verbal and nonverbal communication and first impressions.

COMPLETING THE CHAPTER

Summary

- The clothing and textile industries employ hundreds of thousands of workers in all parts of the country.
- For a successful clothing career, you need to be able to handle pressure; to have a sense of color, and design; to be well-organized; to pay careful attention to detail; and to have an interest in clothing fibers and fabrics.
- Entry-level jobs in clothing design and marketing include salesperson and stock clerk; jobs requiring training include buyer, copywriter, artist, and personal shopper; jobs requiring advanced degrees include fashion coordinator and designer.
- Jobs in clothing construction and care include garment industry workers, drycleaners, pattern makers, textile chemists, textile engineers, and dyers.

For Review

Objective Review Questions Have students complete the "Reviewing the Facts" section on this page.

Study Guide Have students complete the Study Guide from Chapter 68 of their *Student Workbook*.

Classification Draw three columns on the board, headed "Entry-Level," "Training," and "Degree." Have students complete the chart by listing job categories in the appropriate columns. Ask students to discuss the talents and skills needed for each job.

For Evaluation

Self-Assessment Essay Have students revise their self-assessments, written at the beginning of the chapter, in light of what they have learned. Students should have a broader awareness of their talents and skills, and how these potentially relate to careers in clothing and textiles.

Chapter Test Have students complete the test for Chapter 68 that appears in the *Teacher's Classroom Resources*.

CHAPTER 68 REVIEW

Answers to "Reviewing the Facts"

1. Any three: sense of color and design; well organized; careful attention to detail; interest in fibers and fabrics.
2. The ability to meet and work with the public; a pleasant personality; a well-groomed appearance.
3. Checks incoming orders, puts price tags on garments, and keeps track of how stock is moving.
4. To connect designers and garment makers with stores and shops where clothing is sold; to select clothing for the store.
5. Fashion coordinators are college graduates who majored in home economics or art; they may have work/study experience through fashion and merchandising schools. Designers are trained in college programs for fashion design and by working with experienced designers.
6. Entry-level jobs: (any one) sewing machine operator; alteration worker. Jobs with training: (any one) drycleaner: pattern maker. Jobs with degree: (any one) textile chemist; textile engineer; dyer.
7. Sewing machine operators.

Reviewing the Facts

1. Identify three characteristics useful for careers in clothing and textiles.
2. What are three qualities that an employer looks for when hiring sales personnel in a retail store?
3. Describe the work done by a stock clerk.
4. What is the function of the buyer?
5. What kind of advanced training is usually necessary for a fashion coordinator? A designer?
6. Name three jobs in clothing construction and care, one at each level.
7. In which position in the garment industry are the largest number of workers employed?

Thinking Critically

1. What are some of the ways that you might use your knowledge and skills in clothing and textiles to become an entrepreneur while you are in high school?
2. How can entry-level jobs help prepare you for other jobs within the clothing and textile field?

Applying Your Skills

1. **Forming Questions.** Make up some basic questions you might want to ask on any job interview, as well as a list of questions you think employers will ask you. Compare your lists with those of your classmates. How do they differ?
2. **Comparing Professions.** Select two careers in clothing and textiles that you're interested in finding out more about. Ask your librarian to help you find career books, career encyclopedias, or magazine articles about them. Compare the details of each and explain which you would prefer.
3. **Planning a Product.** Working with two or more classmates, select a textile product that could be made and sold by students. Plan the production steps and estimate the costs of materials and other expenses. Determine a selling price for the product in order to make a profit for the group.

Answers to "Thinking Critically"

1. Students may suggest sewing special garments such as T-shirts, sweatshirts, or shorts to sell to friends or specialty shops. They could use paint, dye, and appliques to personalize the garments. They could design and make gift items, accessories, or room decorations to sell to students. They could make alterations.
2. By starting with an entry-level job, you learn about other positions in the company or industry and gain experience. You may discover the need for additional training and work toward that goal. By demonstrating your abilities, you might be considered for promotions.

TEEN TIPS OVERVIEW

This section focuses on three topics related to students' wardrobes.

Create Your Color Palette

This Teen Tip explains the basic principles of this recent and popular way of matching colors to complexions.

T-Shirt—Make It Unique

In this Teen Tip students discover how some ingenuity and a little work will produce distinctive, individual shirts at a considerable savings over store-bought items.

Designer Jeans—Worth the $$?

This Teen Tip presents the facts behind the high cost of designer jeans. Students have an opportunity to weigh the actual value of these products against their inflated price tags.

These "Teen Tips" support the concepts of "Clothing and Textiles," by presenting ways in which teens can make budget-wise choices about clothes and, at the same time, have fun with their wardrobes.

Introducing "Create Your Color Palette"

(Pages 612-613)

Motivators

Favorite Colors Select a student and ask the other students to state what they think his or her favorite color is, and why they think that. Do this for a few more students, and focus on the fact that people usually know what colors you like at least in part by what you wear. (Be sure to choose students who will not be embarrassed by this attention and who are relatively popular with other students.)

Discussion Question: Ask students: "How do you choose the colors you wear?" Discuss this question. Be sure to bring out that people may choose colors simply because they like them, or because they feel or have been told they look good in them, or because they reflect a certain mood or style. Tell students that this section will suggest a way to choose colors according to one's own skin coloring.

Teaching "Create Your Color Palette"

Checking Comprehension

✔ What kind of skin tones, basically, do "winters" and "summers" have, and what are some colors they look good in? *Their skin has blue undertones. Cool, blue-based colors suit them especially well.*

✔ What kind of skin tones do "autumns" and "springs" have, and what are some colors that suit them? *They have yellow skin undertones and look especially good in warm, yellow-based colors.*

TEEN TIPS

Create Your Color Palette

Have you ever heard people ask each other if they are a "summer" or a "winter?" No, this is not a new horoscope. It's a way of analyzing your skin tone and using this analysis to find the colors that look best on you. Both males and females find that this analysis helps them choose the colors that make them look and feel better.

The basis of the seasonal color system is that skin has blue or yellow undertones. Blue undertones are associated with the cool color seasons—winter and summer. People whose skin has blue undertones look best in cool, blue-based colors. Yellow undertones are associated with the warm color seasons—autumn and spring. People whose skin has yellow undertones look best in warm, yellow-based colors.

Use these steps to choose your best colors:

1. Think about your wardrobe. Which colors do you wear over and over again? Which colors bring compliments from others? Which colors make you look dull or washed-out when you wear them?
2. Look at your skin. Hold a piece of white paper next to the inside of your arm and examine your skin tone. Natural light will give you the truest picture, so stand by a window or go outdoors to do this. If you have a hard time seeing yellow or blue undertones, compare your skin with others to see the differences more clearly.
3. Drape colored fabric beneath your face, or use colored paper—try colors from all four seasons. Your best colors will make your skin look bright and healthy. The wrong colors will make your skin look dull, and any shadows or lines will be more obvious.

Look at the four illustrations of teens as you read the descriptions of the color seasons. Decide in which color you feel each teen looks best. Does each have a color season? Then, put yourself into one of the four color seasons.

WINTER

SUMMER

Did You Know? The concept of seasonal classification of color has become extremely popular. People have become "color consultants" and have developed demonstrations, workshops, and seminars based on these concepts. "Doing your colors" has become a lucrative business. Students might enjoy reading books on the subject and investigating whether there are any local workshops or courses on this topic. They can consider what more they would gain by attending a seminar than they would by simply following the guidelines in this section or by reading.

AUTUMN

SPRING

TEEN TIPS

- **Winter.** This is the most common season type. People in this group have beige, taupe, olive, or brown skin and dark hair. They look best in clear, vivid colors such as royal blue, true red, hot pink, emerald green, purple, and lemon yellow. Primary colors look better on them than pastel or muted colors.

- **Summer.** People in this group also have blue undertones, but they're more delicate in coloring than the winter group. Their skin may be very fair or pink. Soft, cool pastels—especially blue—look great on them, as do pink, lavender, and mauve. Blue-green and light yellow are good, but steer clear of royal blue and yellow-green.

- **Autumn.** People in this group have skin with rich golden tones. Most redheads with freckles and medium-to-deep brunettes with peach, ivory, or golden beige skin belong in this group. These people look best in brown, gold, mustard, rust, and moss green. Ivory and beige look good on them, too.

- **Spring.** People in this group have skin with golden undertones but it is more fair and delicate than people in the autumn group. Clear, delicate colors look better on them than dark, muted, or muddy colors. They look best in ivory, warm beige, peach, apricot, salmon, light aqua, turquoise, and yellow-green.

Remember—most colors can be worn by anyone. You just need to pick the right value and intensity. You can use colors that are not in your season as accents, trims, or accessories.

More About Choosing Colors Have students compare the cost of seminars or courses with that of doing a color analysis themselves. They might also wish to decide whether seminars, courses, or books take a basically simple, if useful, idea and make more of it than is really justified.

Activities

Skill Builder: Science

Have students read about and report on the scientific basis of color: What is color? How is it created? What do the terms *brightness, hue, shade, tones,* and *tint* mean? Are *black* and *white* colors in the strictest sense? If not, what are they?

Reteaching

As a class activity, follow the instructions in this section to determine each student's best colors and what "season" he or she is. Have the students state or jot down what colors they wear often and get compliments for wearing. Have them work in groups of three or four to determine their skin tones, according to step number 2. Bring in or have students bring in fabric samples, and let each student use them to find his or her best colors. (You can use items of clothing instead of fabric samples.) Finally, have each student state what "season" he or she is and what colors suit him or her best.

Enrichment

Ask students to analyze their present wardrobes in terms of what they've learned about colors. Have them determine how much of their wardrobe fits their "season." Have them develop long-range shopping plans for making their wardrobe more closely reflect their best colors (for example replace bright royal parka with one in pastel blue or blue green). Have students include how they might use accessories to use colors in their wardrobe that they like but that do not flatter them.

Introducing "T-Shirt—Make It Unique"

(Pages 614-615)

Motivators

My Favorite T-Shirt One or two days before teaching this section ask students to bring to class their favorite decorated T-shirt. (Alternatively, they can bring a decorated sweatshirt, sleepshirt, pair of jeans, or athletic shoes.) To introduce this lesson, have students show what they've brought in and discuss why they like these items.

Discussion Question: Ask students: "What do people say with their T-Shirts?" Discuss this question, focusing on what people reveal about themselves with their T-shirts. Possible answers include that T-shirts can affirm the wearers' favorite causes, show what sports teams they root for, advertise their membership in a club, promote a favorite singing group, or reflect their sense of humor or values. T-shirts also reveal the wearers' sense of style and design. Ask volunteers to state what the T-shirts they brought to class say about themselves. Tell students that this section will suggest how they can create their own T-shirts.

Teaching "T-Shirt—Make It Unique"

Checking Comprehension

✓ Which of these designs seem most suitable if you wanted to create a "dressy" shirt, with a little "glamour" appeal? Why? *Answers will vary but could include using liquid dyes or acrylic paints to paint designs, tie-dyeing, and using puff paints, jewels, or sequins.*

✓ Which techniques might be most useful if you wanted to create something flashy and fun? Why? *Answers will vary but could include those techniques that involve attaching items to a shirt, such as ribbons, fabric hearts, appliques, or buttons.*

T-Shirt—Make It Unique

TEEN TIPS

You can use T-shirts, sweatshirts, sleepshirts, jeans—even athletic shoes—as a canvas for self-expression. This "art" that you wear can be individualized with designs that vary from the witty to the beautiful. Dare to be different with bright colors and bold designs, or show your more gentle side with soft pastel colors.

1. Stencil or paint a design with liquid dyes.
2. Trim a shirt with ribbons and fabric hearts. Tack on ribbon bows with small hand stitches. Cut out hearts and apply with fusible web.
3. Tie-dye a plain white shirt. Tightly tie or wrap parts of the fabric so the dye will penetrate unevenly, producing many different shades of the color.
4. Use acrylic paints to create a design or write a message.
5. Add a colorful, gathered border to the bottom edge of a shirt. Stitch a seam in 1/2 yard of fabric to make a tube. Hem one edge and gather the other edge. Stitch gathered edge to bottom of shirt.
6. Make appliqués using fabric scraps. Fuse cut-outs to shirt, then outline with closely spaced zigzag stitches on the sewing machine.
7. Collect buttons in different sizes, shapes, and colors. Sew them on a shirt in a sunburst pattern.
8. Use puff paints, sequins, and jewels to add glitter and glamour to ordinary designs.

More About Business Profits The profits manufacturers make, of course, do not simply go into the pockets of top executives. Students can do research, either by reading or by talking with their parents or local business people, about how profits might be used. To start, suggest students consider how businesses grow—where the money comes from to buy new equipment, expand and improve facilities, or develop new products. Have students report on their findings to the class and consider how important "plowing" some of the profits back into a business might be.

Who Are Kidding?

TEEN TIPS

Activities

Skill Builder: Math

Have students choose one technique they would like to try and think about what materials they would probably need. Have them research the cost of these items and calculate the approximate cost of creating a shirt (or other item) using the technique they chose. Remind them not to forget the cost of the basic T-shirt itself!

Reteaching

Invite students to continue planning the T-shirt for which they calculated the cost above. Have them draw a detailed design, write a brief plan for how they'd go about carrying it out, and make a list of materials they would need. Compare the designs in class and critique the plans and shopping lists for thoroughness.

Enrichment

Have students look in stores for T-shirts or other items similar to those they designed. Have them compare the projected cost of their shirts to those in the store and report their findings in class. Discuss whether they think the amount of money they can save justifies the amount of work likely to be involved.

Introducing "Designer Jeans—Worth the $$$?"
(Pages 616-617)

Motivators

Designer Labels Ask students what it means for a piece of clothing to have a designer label. Explain, if they do not know, that it means that a well-known clothing designer, or the company that bears his or her name, has created the design for the product and may have overseen or approved of its manufacture. Ask students what they think a designer label means in terms of the quality of a product.

Discussion Question: Ask students: "What designer jeans are popular and why?" Point out that one very popular designer product is jeans. Ask students which designer jeans are most popular right now. Also ask students to try to tell why those brands are so popular. Tell student that this section will explore the question of whether designer jeans actually represent superior values.

Teaching "Designer Jeans—Worth the $$$?"

Checking Comprehension

✔ Which of the expenses discussed here are actually for the materials and labor that go into a pair of designer jeans? *The costs for fabric, fasteners and thread, and salaries and benefits for sewers and designers.*

✔ Which of all the costs discussed do you think are most likely to vary depending on whether the jeans are designer jeans or just store-brand jeans? *Money paid to the designer or celebrity and money spent on advertising and promotion, public relations, packaging, and labels.*

TEEN TIPS

Designer Jeans—Worth the $$?

American consumers buy about 385 million pairs of jeans a year. You might pay anywhere from $20.00 to $50.00 or more for a pair of jeans, depending upon the brand, the style, and the store where you buy it. Yet an average pair of jeans is worth about $7.00 in materials. Where does the rest of the money go?

Let's take a look at the manufacturer's costs for a pair of jeans:

- $6.00 for denim fabric (about 1¾ yards)
- $1.00 for buttons, rivets, and thread (standard jeans use 5 buttons, 6 rivets, and 213 yards of thread)
- $1.40 in salaries and benefits for designers and sewing machine operators (14 minutes and 40 separate steps for each pair of jeans)
- $2.50 for packaging, shipping, and other overhead costs
- $1.10 for advertising, public relations, and other marketing costs
- $1.30 in salaries and benefits for salespeople and executives
- $1.70 in profits

$15.00 wholesale price to the store

Focus on Consumer Skills Smart consumers take into account the type of store they're shopping in. Have students expand on the "Enrichment" activity by discussing whether shopping in higher-priced stores for products one can also buy in less expensive stores has any advantages. Remind them to include consideration of such factors as return or repair policies, delivery, the cleanliness of the store, and how pleasant it is to shop there.

Styles with certain extras usually cost more to manufacture. For example, stone-washed, acid-washed, or whitewashed jeans must go through an extra manufacturing step, which increases the wholesale cost.

Stores usually sell clothing for twice the wholesale cost, so a pair of jeans that a store buys for $15.00 would sell for $30.00 retail. Stores—just like manufacturers—have many costs, including salaries and benefits for employees, advertising, displays, lighting and heating, markdowns, shoplifting, and security. Some stores have much higher overhead costs than others, depending on their location and services offered. Thus you may pay a higher price at one store than at another for the same brand of jeans.

Why are designer jeans usually more expensive? If a famous designer or celebrity endorses a brand of jeans, he or she receives a fee for each pair of jeans sold. Usually designer labels are widely advertised and promoted—in magazine, newspaper, radio, and television ads—resulting in expensive marketing costs. All of these fees and costs are added to the wholesale and retail prices of designer jeans.

Are you getting a better product with designer jeans? They may be better designed or may fit you better—but not necessarily. It's up to you to decide if they are worth the price.

TEEN TIPS

Activities

Skill Builder: Critical Thinking
Ask students to collect ads for designer jeans from newspapers and magazines and write descriptions of those they see or hear on billboards, radio, and television. Have them analyze these ads, commenting on what they appeal to in the consumer and how they make the appeal. (For example, do they suggest that the designer involved insures greater quality or fashion appeal? Do they use music and dance to suggest that these jeans will make the wearer popular, glamorous, or attractive to the other sex?) Have them also comment on how the advertising claims or suggestions relate to the actual value of the jeans.

Reteaching
Bring in or have the students bring in a pair of store-brand jeans and one or two pairs of designer jeans, noting the cost of each pair and where each was purchased. With the class and using the figures given in the tips, figure out approximately how much each pair cost to manufacture. Calculate the difference between that cost and the retail price and speculate on what the difference in cost was spent for, remembering to include such factors as the manufacturer's overhead, packaging, and the store's costs. Also compare the quality of the fabric and workmanship for each pair of jeans.

Enrichment
Divide the class into small groups and assign each one a local store that sells jeans. Have them visit the store and record the price of as many different brands of jeans as they can. Have the groups share their results and develop a list comparing the cost of various designer and store brand jeans, and showing the variations from store to store. Discuss whether designer jeans are worth the price, and why.

Unit Seven

UNIT PREVIEW

Unit 7 explains how living space reflects one's personality, interests, and values. Students learn that cost, physical layout, and location are factors to consider when choosing housing. They are introduced to the elements and principles of design as a way to organize living space and create a personalized look. Students learn how to show consideration of others when sharing space and how careful planning and proper home maintenance can prevent most home accidents. Conservation measures are explored. The unit concludes with a discussion of careers in the housing area.

CONTENT DEVELOPMENT

Use these lessons to reinforce the following themes:

Content Strands	Chapters
Career Exploration	75
Citizenship/ Leadership	75
Communication	69,71,75,(TT 1)
Consumer Skills	69
Decision Making	69,72,(TT 1,2)
Health and Safety	72,73
Managing Resources	69–72,74,(TT 2,3)
Personal Development	69,(TT 1)
Technology	71,74

UNIT MOTIVATORS

Decision Making Skills

Which Accessories? Have students make a list of the accessories in their room or in one room of their home. Have them decide which accessories they could use to change or to alter the mood or feeling of the room. Ask them to decide the least expensive way that they could create a new design.

Critical Thinking Skills

Analyzing Professions Ask students to look through the classified section of a newspaper to find four job openings related to housing. Have them compare the skills required for each job. Tell them that they will learn about jobs related to the housing area in this unit.

CROSS-CURRICULAR ACTIVITY

Health and Housing Asbestos, radon, and lead-based paint have been cited as potential health hazards in people's homes. Concerns have also been raised about radiation from microwave ovens and televisions. Have students research one of these topics and write a paragraph summarizing their findings.

SPECIAL NEEDS

Strategies for Auditory Learners Have students listen to a radio or television show that features home-improvement ideas or discusses housing issues. Students might also attend a home-improvement seminar or go on a housing tour. Have students share information they learned.

HOUSING AND LIVING SPACE

UNIT SEVEN

Housing and Living Space

CHAPTER

FHA ACTIVITIES

The following activities can be used with your FHA group or as public relation strategies:

Storage Solutions Have students bring in discarded or used items that might be used to make storage items similar to those listed on page 634. Suggest that the students cover or decorate the storage items with wallpaper, wrapping paper, or adhesive-backed paper. Have the students donate the storage items to group homes, shelters, or child care facilities.

Household Hints Have students develop a pamphlet, brochure, or booklet titled, "Helpful Household Hints." Have them survey magazines, newspapers, and homemakers for household hints. Compile the best ideas and have students distribute the hints to parents, faculty, and young adults moving out on their own or going off to college.

UNIT CLOSURE

For Review

Evaluating Design Ask students to choose a room in their home or a room pictured in a magazine. Have them briefly describe the room in writing by analyzing it in terms of basic design elements and principles. Have them read their description to the class.

For Evaluation

Unit Test Have students complete the Unit Test that appears in the *Teacher's Classroom Resources.*

Testmaker Software You may wish to design a unit test using the Testmaker software program.

COOPERATIVE LEARNING

Cooperative Living Divide students into groups of three or four girls and three or four boys. Tell the groups that they have decided to share an unfurnished apartment. Give each group a listing of apartment rentals from the local newspaper. Have group members find an apartment they would like to rent. Then have them list issues that would need to be resolved before they could live together harmoniously. Issues might include splitting the cost of rent and utilities, sharing cleaning and cooking chores, respecting each other's space and personal belongings, and observing hours for entertaining friends. Have groups report on their discussions.

CHAPTER OVERVIEW

Chapter 69 explains the concept of living space and explores the various psychological and physical needs that an individual or family's living space fulfills. A home provides a sense of belonging and reflects a person's values and goals. It also provides shelter, safety, and space. Students learn about the management skills needed to make housing choices and the factors that must be considered in deciding to rent or buy a home.

INTRODUCING THE CHAPTER

Motivators

This Is Where I Belong Have students talk about places where they feel that they belong. Discuss the ways that a home makes people feel safe, both physically and psychologically.

Using the Photograph Have students study the photograph on this page. Then ask: "What is this home providing for these people? How can you tell that they feel as if they belong?"

Home Sweet Home! Explain that most people look forward to returning home after a long or even a short absence. Have students talk about times when they've been glad to return home.

Introducing the Objectives

Discuss the chapter objectives on this page. Remind students that the objectives focus on important chapter content.

Introducing Vocabulary

Explain that living space is often shared among people, but that within that living space individuals need their own personal space that allows them privacy. Discuss other uses of the words *private* and *personal* that help clarify their meanings.

CHAPTER 69

Living Space and You

OBJECTIVES

This chapter will help you to:

- Describe how living space meets psychological needs.
- List the physical needs that housing meets.
- Explain how location, lifestyle, and budget affect housing decisions.

WORDS TO REMEMBER

condominium
facility
location
mortgage
personal space

Chapter Resources

Teacher's Classroom Resources
- Lesson Plan
- Life Skills Activity, *Home for Sale*
- Reproducible Master, *A Home Meets . . .*
- Extension Activity, *Types of Housing*
- Chapter Test

Student Workbook
- Study Guide
- Worksheet, *What Is a Home?*

Have you ever claimed some space on a beach by putting down your towel, sunglasses, and radio? When you did this, you said to all the world, "This is my place. Please do not disturb it." Then you filled up your space with the things that were important to you. For a few hours, you created a home base at the beach—a place where you belonged.

Your home is the place where you always feel that you belong. It is the place where you can meet your needs for warmth, companionship, privacy, safety, and self-expression. It is also the place where you keep your possessions and do the things you want to do. Most importantly, your home is where your family is—where you live with the people you love and the people who love you.

Meeting Psychological Needs

Most of us think of home as a warm, comforting place where we can relax and please ourselves. Our homes fill several emotional needs in us that aren't fulfilled by school or work or other places.

A Sense of Belonging

Your home should provide you with a sense of belonging. You should feel that your home is a place where you can unwind, where you can do things with your family and friends or just be by yourself. A sense of belonging makes you feel that you are a member of the household. You may have to follow certain rules as a member of the family, but you also feel comfortable raiding the refrigerator or participating in family decisions. This is what is meant by a sense of belonging.

Privacy

The need for a place of one's own—**personal space**—is basic to all people. Even if you share your personal space, it's still a place that you feel is your own. You have the privilege of asking people in when you want to and of keeping them out, when that is what you want.

People need private, personal space where they can read, listen to music, study, talk with friends, or just be alone to think and dream.

More About Personal Space To learn when a space is too close for comfort, have students work in pairs. Have each pair stand several feet apart as they begin a conversation. Ask students to move closer as they continue to talk and to notice when they begin to feel uncomfortable with the closeness of the other person. Ask students what this says about privacy and the need for personal space.

More About a Sense of Belonging People often long to return to a place where they feel they belong. Homesickness affects everyone at one time or another—from the child at summer camp to the person on vacation in a foreign country. People miss the sense of belonging and yearn to return to their home and family.

TEACHING THE CHAPTER

For convenience, the teaching suggestions for this chapter are arranged according to the following lesson topics:

- "Meeting Psychological Needs," pages 621-622
- "Meeting Physical Needs," page 622
- "Housing Choices," and "Decisions About Housing," pages 622-626

Teaching "Meeting Psychological Needs"

(Pages 621-622)

This section teaches how housing meets psychological needs by giving people a sense of belonging.

Checking Comprehension

✓ What is meant by a sense of belonging? *It means you feel like a member of the household.*

✓ What is personal space? *A place of one's own.*

✓ How can you make an empty room seem like home? *By putting up your pictures or arranging a few of your mementos.*

✓ If being popular is important to you, how might your home reflect that goal? *You may try to select a home with enough space to have parties and entertain friends.*

Activities

Skill Builder: Writing
Repeat the statement from the text, "This is who I am." Have students write a description of their rooms at home as an expression of who they are and what their values and goals are.

Reteaching
Have students cut out pictures of rooms from magazines and describe what values and goals each room reflects.

Enrichment
Have students interview their parents about how their values and goals are reflected in the family home.

Teaching "Meeting Physical Needs"
(Page 622)

This section teaches how homes meet physical needs by providing shelter, safety, and space for possessions and activities.

Checking Comprehension

✔ How does a home keep you safe? *It protects you and your possessions from inclement weather and from dangers such as accidents, injuries, and crimes.*

✔ What kind of space does a home provide? *It provides space for possessions and activities.*

Activities

Skill Builder: Critical Thinking
Ask students to analyze the way the space in their home is used for different activities. What spaces are used most? Who uses each space and for what activities?

Skill Builder: Math
Ask students to draw a circle graph that shows how the space in their home is allocated. The segments of the graph should indicate the percentages of the total area that are devoted to bedrooms, living area, kitchen, dining area, and so on.

Reteaching
Have students look at floor plans of several homes and identify how the space is used for possessions and activities.

Enrichment
A home provides safety and shelter from the weather. Have selected students find out and report to the class about the features and cost of the following: security systems, smoke alarms, air conditioning, heating systems, insulation.

This privilege allows you to have privacy—the ability to be alone. Everyone needs to get away from others at times, even if it's only for a couple of hours. People use that time away from other people in any way they want to, whether it's to think, to dream, or to make decisions.

Individuality

Just as the way you dress expresses your personality, the way you arrange and use your living space enhances your self-concept. You can put up posters of your favorite rock stars or classical musicians. You can display your collections or work on your hobbies. You can keep your favorite books, tapes, and other possessions around you. All of these things say, "This is who I am."

Later, when you set up your own home, some of these personal possessions will help you feel comfortable in a new place. An empty room quickly becomes yours when you put up your favorite pictures or arrange a few of your mementos.

Values and Goals

How you live also reflects your values. If you value neatness, you will have a well-organized space. If you appreciate family heirlooms, you may have antique furniture that belonged to another generation of your family.

How you live also reflects your goals. If getting a good education is an important goal of yours, you will probably have a comfortable place to study and lots of book shelves. If being popular is important to you, you may want space in your home to have parties and entertain friends.

Your home also reflects the goals of other members of your family. For example, your mother may need room to write or sew, and your brother may need some space to keep his hamster cage.

Meeting Physical Needs

In addition to meeting your psychological needs, a home also meets the following physical needs for you and your family.

- **Shelter.** One important job of a home is to provide shelter from the weather outside, whether it is wind, rain, snow, or extreme heat.
- **Safety.** A home also protects your family and your possessions from dangers such as accidents, injuries, and crimes.
- **Space for possessions.** A home provides you with space for your possessions, such as your books, clothes, and furniture.
- **Space for activities.** A home provides a place for activities, such as cooking, bathing, entertaining, working on hobbies, exercising, and talking. Many of these activity areas can be used by more than one person.

Housing Choices

When your parents chose the home where you now live, they had to ask several important questions about how the home would fulfill their needs and wants:

- How many people are in your household? A large family needs more bedrooms and baths than a small family.

Focus on Relationship Skills Have students role play situations in which siblings who share a room must negotiate for privacy and space for possessions.

Cross-Reference See Teen Tips "Living On Your Own" pages 678-679.

A home provides space for possessions and activities, such as listening to music.

- How old is each member of your family? If there are small children in your family, your parents may have wanted a house with a fenced-in yard. If one or more grandparents live with you, they might want rooms on the first floor to avoid the need to climb stairs.
- What are the special needs of family members? For example, does anyone with disabilities need wheelchair ramps or extra wide doors? Are there other children in the neighborhood? Is the school system a good one? Can you walk to shopping areas?

When making housing choices, people also have to consider four important factors: where the housing is located, what type of housing to choose, whether to rent or buy, and how much to spend on housing.

Where?

The first decision to make when choosing a home is to decide where it will be located. **Location** refers to the region of the country where you will live. The availability of work may be a major factor in determining in what part of the country you will live. For example, if you go to work for an airplane manufacturer in the Pacific Northwest or an oil company in Louisiana, you would have to live where the company is located.

Location also refers to the kind of community you choose to live in—urban, suburban, rural, or small town. People are attracted to a place that offers the lifestyle and the **facilities**, or goods and services available in a community, that they desire. For instance, if they like museums, shopping, and lots of activities, they will choose to live in a city or large suburban area. If they like quiet and the outdoors, they will choose a rural setting for their home.

The facilities and services offered by communities include schools, fire and police protection, parks, libraries, and trash pickup. You might choose a home because it is in a nice neighborhood and has a good school system. Someone else may choose a home that is close to public transportation systems or recreational areas. Others may want to be able to walk to a church or to stores.

Real-Life Situations The homeless are a growing concern in our society. The reasons for the rapidly increasing number of homeless individuals and families are complex and varied: many communities have too few low-cost housing units; housing prices have increased rapidly in some areas; fire or building projects have forced people from their homes; and so on. As a result, the homeless may be "living" in shelters, motels, cars, parks, or on the city streets. Ask students what solutions they may have for the problem of being homeless.

Teaching "Housing Choices" and "Decisions About Housing"

(Pages 622-626)

This section teaches what factors people consider in choosing a home. It focuses on the needs of the family, location, the kind of home and community, cost, and other considerations.

Checking Comprehension

✔ What are some questions a family must ask about how a home would fulfill its needs? *How many people are in the household? How old is each member of the family? What are the special needs of family members?*

✔ What are the different kinds of communities you can live in? *Urban, suburban, rural, or small town.*

✔ What are facilities? *The goods and services available in a community.*

✔ What is the difference between a single-family home and a townhouse? *A single-family house is not attached to any other building, but a townhouse is attached to other units on the sides.*

✔ When is an apartment building considered a high-rise? *When it is very tall.*

✔ Are mobile homes always on the move? *No, they are usually permanently parked in a mobile home park or on an individual's property.*

✔ What is a condominium? *A condominium is one of a group of apartments or townhouses that you buy rather than rent.*

✔ What is the relationship between housing costs and the size of the home? *Usually, the larger the home, the higher the costs.*

✔ What is a mortgage? *A mortgage is a long-term loan that you take out when you buy a home.*

✓ What are two advantages of owning a home? *Any two of the following: It gives you a sense of permanence, it gives you a sense of belonging, the homes may increase in value, you own more of your home as you pay off your mortgage, and you can decorate or remodel it as you like.*

✓ Why can renters move more easily then homeowners? *Because in many cases, renters need only give a month's notice and don't have to go through the time-consuming process of selling a home.*

Activities

Skill Builder: Math
Select students to call area apartment complexes to find out about apartment size, location, facilities, and rental rates. Then have the class discuss the relative values of the apartments.

Skill Builder: Critical Thinking
Have students make a list of the factors that figure into the decision to rent or buy a home. Encourage them to consider such things as financial situation, job security, and ability to maintain property.

A family that enjoys outdoor activities will want housing that has convenient access to recreational facilities and parks.

What Type?

A home can be any size, shape, and style. Here are a few examples:

- **Single-family house.** This home provides living space for one family. It is not attached to any other building. It stands on its own, usually on a separate lot with a lawn and outdoor living space.
- **Townhouse.** This is one of many single-family units attached to other units on its sides. In the city, these may be called row houses. Each family lives in a different unit.
- **Duplex or triplex.** This is a building divided into living spaces for two or three families. The spaces can be side by side or one on top of the other.
- **Apartment building.** This building contains a number of separate living units. The living spaces may range in size from one-room studio apartments to three-bedroom units. If the people who live in each unit have a patio or bit of lawn, the units are called garden apartments. If the building is very tall, it is called a high-rise.
- **Mobile home.** This is a factory-built house that is moved to the home site by truck. It is then usually permanently parked in a mobile home park or on the individual owner's property. Many mobile homes come with furniture and built-in appliances. These homes are very compact, but some owners build porches or decks to add more space.

Rent or Buy?

You can either rent or buy your home. When you rent a house or apartment, you pay a monthly fee—the rent—to the owner in exchange for the right to use that space. When you buy a home, you usually have to take out a long-term

Did You Know? Housing is one of the consumer's largest expenses.

Real-Life Situations Today, many mobile homes are large and creatively designed. A double-width home consists of two units set side by side. Some feature a living room, dining area, kitchen, two or three bedrooms, and two bathrooms. Most mobile homes are financed with loans that span 7 to 10 years, much shorter in length than home mortgages. Mobile homes appeal to young couples, small families, and retired people because of the initial low cost and low monthly finance charges compared to other types of homes. It is one way for a family to own a single-family home.

There are many different types of housing from which to choose. What are the advantages and disadvantages of each of these types?

Reteaching
Use the real estate section of the newspaper to help students identify different kinds of homes. Have students compile a list of the features that the ads focus on to sell homes.

Reteaching
Have students cut out real estate ads that support the assertion that you can rent houses as well as apartments, and buy apartments (condominiums) as well as houses.

Real-Life Situations Low-income families may have several housing options in some communities. Public housing complexes, sometimes called housing projects, are provided by the government for people who have low incomes, are elderly, or are disabled. The rent is usually set as a percentage of the family's monthly income. Urban renewal programs attempt to redevelop run-down urban areas. Rather than tearing down buildings and building new ones, the current emphasis is on renovating existing buildings. Urban homesteading is a program in which families buy old or abandoned houses or apartments at very low prices. They must agree to rehabilitate the home and live in it for a certain number of years.

Enrichment
Ask students to consult area newspapers and the Chamber of Commerce to investigate the facilities that are available in their community that make it a good place to live.

Enrichment
Have students study the real estate section of the local newspaper and prepare a report on new housing developing in the area. What kinds of homes are being built? What price ranges are offered?

Enrichment
Invite a real estate agent to come to the class to explain housing conditions in your area. Have the students prepare a list of questions in advance. Some topics might be the advantages of different kinds of housing, the trade-offs that may be necessary in buying or renting a house, the criteria the realtor uses to appraise a house or other dwelling, current costs and prices in the area, taxes, zoning regulations, and building codes.

loan called a **mortgage**. Then you have 15 to 30 years to pay back the loan.

A **condominium** is one of a group of apartments or townhouses that you buy rather than rent. When you purchase a condominium, you also agree to pay a monthly service fee to pay for things that all of the owners use in common, such as lawns, swimming pools, tennis courts, and hallways.

Owning a home has some advantages and some drawbacks. One advantage is that owning your own home gives you a sense of permanence or belonging. Also, your home may increase in value, and as you pay off your mortgage, you own more and more of your home. Another advantage of home ownership is that you can decorate or remodel it any way you like.

Some of the disadvantages of owning a home include being responsible for all of the maintenance and upkeep and having to sell the home if you move.

Renting also has advantages and disadvantages. If something breaks in a rented apartment or house, such as the plumbing or heating system, the building's owner is responsible for making the repairs. Renters can also move more easily than homeowners. Often, they need to give only a month's notice so the owner can find new occupants.

There are, however, some disadvantages to renting. You probably won't be able to decorate or remodel, and the money you pay every month isn't a part of a larger investment. Also, the building owner can raise the rent.

How Much to Spend?

Another decision you need to make about housing is determined by how much you can afford to pay. Housing prices vary in different areas, such as in a city or a suburban or rural setting, as well as in different parts of the country. When you have a limited amount of money to spend on housing, location is a very important factor in deciding what kind of home you will be able to afford.

Housing costs are also determined by the size of the house or apartment. Usually the larger the space, the higher are the costs.

When choosing housing, many people face trade-offs. They are willing to spend a little more money for a better location, or walk a few blocks more to the bus stop to save on rent. How you make these decisions will depend on what is most important to you.

Decisions About Housing

Even now you make many decisions about your living space, even if you share a room with a brother or sister. Where will you put your tapes or disks? How can you store your clothes? If you want to redecorate, can you use materials you have on hand, or do you need to buy new supplies?

As you read the following chapters, you'll find information that will help you make these decisions and many others.

- You'll find out how to plan and organize your space for your activities and your belongings.
- You'll learn how to use some basic principles and elements of design to give your space the look you want.
- You'll discover ways to care for your space to make it more comfortable.
- You'll learn how to use your knowledge to help keep your home safe and control the energy you use.

The more you learn about housing choices now, the better prepared you'll be to make decisions in the future.

Did You Know? A cooperative apartment (co-op) is different from a condominium. The owner of a co-op owns stock in the corporation that runs the building. Decisions about the building are made by the stockholders as a group. A condominium owner owns the condo and a share of the common ground.

Focus on Consumer Skills Tell students that as they own more and more of their home by paying off the mortgage, the part they own is called equity. Explain that if they need to, they can borrow money on this equity.

INTERPERSONAL SKILLS

Adapting Space for Independent Living

If a family member is disabled, living space can be modified so that the person can live independently. Here are some adaptations that can make a home accessible for everyone who lives there:

- **Special equipment.** People with physical disabilities often require some special equipment to allow them to move about safely at home, especially in the bathroom. They may need grab bars around the tub and toilet, nonskid mats in the tub or shower, and perhaps a tub seat or hand-held shower head. They may also require special faucets if they are unable to turn regular ones.

  If they use crutches or a walker, loose scatter rugs should be removed and objects, such as shoes, books, and toys should be kept off the floor and out of the way. If necessary, have railings installed along hallways or wherever the person has difficulty walking.

  Stairs are a special hazard for people who must use walkers or who have certain heart conditions. Special lifts can be installed that allow them to go up and down the stairs sitting down.
- **Wheelchairs.** People who are confined to wheelchairs need wide, clear paths to allow them to maneuver around the house. It may be necessary to widen doorways and lower light switches and countertops to prepare a home for a wheelchair-bound family member. Also, shelves and clothes poles can be lowered so the disabled person can reach them.

  A family member in a wheelchair will require ramps to go up or down any steps, both indoors and out. In addition, it is difficult to move a wheelchair across deep pile carpets or rugs. Replace thick carpeting with tile, hardwood floors, or flat, tightly woven carpeting.
- **Visual aids.** People who are blind or visually impaired quickly learn where things are located in their homes. Tell them if you move anything so they don't become disoriented, bump into objects, or fall. Special equipment such as braille knobs and control panels can be installed on appliances, as well as braille labels on packaged goods.

Think It Through

1. **How would you prepare a bedroom for a family member who has recently become wheelchair-bound?**
2. **Suggest some ways that you could prepare a kitchen for a person who is blind.**

Teaching the Feature
"Adapting Space for Independent Living"

Answers to Feature Questions

1. Replace carpeting with tile or vinyl flooring, buy a low dresser, lower clothes poles in the closet, make sure there is enough room to maneuver the wheelchair around the furniture, install low shelves and pegs for storage, and lower light switches.
2. Always store the same foods on the same shelves in the cupboards and refrigerator, and keep frequently used foods on low shelves. Always keep cleaning supplies in the same place, and make sure the blind person can identify each kind of cleaning product by the shape of its container. Store mops, brooms, and other cleaning equipment out of the way. Use Braille or raised labels to help the person identify foods and supplies, and use Braille or raised knobs on the range.

Activities

Other Aids for the Disabled Have students brainstorm ways to help disabled people. What special needs might hearing-impaired people have? (A smoke alarm or a telephone would need to have a visual signal, such as a blinking light.) Remind students that a person in a wheelchair cannot reach as high or as low or as far out as non-disabled person. People with arthritis may have little strength in their hands.

Community Contact If there is a senior resource center or nursing home in your area, have students visit it as volunteers. They will gain many valuable insights about the disabled and may form some firm friendships.

Focus on Life Management Point out that handicapped people, those in wheelchairs for example, have special housing needs. Ask students to walk through their homes and compile a list of features that might make things difficult for someone in a wheelchair. When possible, have students propose solutions.

Cross-Reference See "Communication for People with Disabilities" on page 88 and "Closures to Help People with Disabilities" on page 585.

COMPLETING THE CHAPTER

Summary

- Living space should provide a sense of belonging, meet a person's need for privacy and personal space, and reflect the values and goals of the people who live there.
- A home provides shelter, safety, and space for possessions and activities.
- Housing choices are made with the needs of the family in mind. Factors to be decided are location, availability of facilities, the type of home, cost, and whether to rent or buy.
- Types of homes include single-family house, townhouse, duplex or triplex, apartment building, and mobile home. A condominium is an apartment or townhouse that you buy rather than rent.

For Review

Objective Review Questions Have students complete the "Reviewing the Facts" section on this page.

Study Guide Have students complete the Study Guide from Chapter 69 of their *Student Workbook.*

For Evaluation

Class Discussion Have the students talk about the meaning of such adages as "Home is where the heart is" and "A man's home is his castle." Ask the students to think of other adages that indicate our feelings about home.

Chapter Test Have students complete the test for Chapter 69 that appears in the *Teacher's Classroom Resources.*

CHAPTER 69 REVIEW

Answers to "Reviewing the Facts"

1. Sense of belonging, privacy, individuality, values, and goals.
2. Shelter, safety, space for possessions, space for activities.
3. Where it is located, what kind of home it is, whether to rent or buy, and how much to spend.
4. The availability of work, and the type of community.
5. Single-family house, townhouse, duplex or triplex, apartment, mobile home.
6. Advantages of owning: (any two) a sense of permanence; may increase in value; can decorate or remodel. Disadvantages of owning: being responsible for maintenance; having to sell if you move. Advantages of renting: not being responsible for repairs; being able to move easily. Disadvantages of renting: (any two) not being able to remodel or decorate; rent is not an investment; owner can raise rent.
7. A condominium is an apartment (or townhouse) unit that you buy rather than rent.
8. Location and size of home.

Reviewing the Facts

1. What psychological needs does a living space meet?
2. What are the four physical needs that a home can fulfill?
3. List the four basic factors to consider when choosing a place to live.
4. What are two important influences when choosing the location of a home?
5. List five different styles of housing.
6. List two advantages and two disadvantages of owning a home and of renting a home.
7. How do an apartment and a condominium differ?
8. Name two factors that help determine the cost of housing.

Thinking Critically

1. How is your home a reflection of your individuality?
2. Discuss the facilities and services that your community offers. Which of these are the most important to you and your family?

Applying Your Skills

1. **Computing Costs.** Check the real estate ads in your local newspaper. Cut out at least five listings for any one of the following: single-family homes, duplexes, townhouses, or mobile homes. What is the average price? Then cut out five listings for rental housing offering similar space and features. What is the average price of a rental in your area?

2. **Presenting Two Sides of an Issue.** Using your own experience and opinions, list the advantages and disadvantages of renting vs. buying a home. Write a report on the advantages and disadvantages of each, which you would prefer, and why.

3. **Writing a Description.** Find a picture of a home or room in a magazine that clearly shows the interests of the people who live there. Cut out the picture from the magazine. On a separate piece of paper, write a brief description of the people who might live in the room or home.

Answers to "Thinking Critically"

1. Your home reflects your tastes, your preferences, and your needs. The things that are important to you will be evident.
2. A partial list of facilities might include police and fire protection, parks, schools, houses of worship, libraries, public transportation systems, movie theaters, shopping centers and malls, recreational areas, open spaces, closeness to the ocean or the mountains, and camping facilities.

CHAPTER

70

How to Organize Your Space

OBJECTIVES

This chapter will help you to:

- Use floor plans to improve the use of space in rooms.
- Organize specific areas in a room.
- Follow examples of ways to organize and store possessions.

WORDS TO REMEMBER

floor plan
layout
multiple use
scale drawing
traffic pattern

Chapter Resources

Teacher's Classroom Resources
- Lesson Plan
- Life Skills Activity, *Planning Space*
- Reproducible Master, *Storage Solutions*
- Extension Activity, *Arranging a Room*
- Chapter Test

Student Workbook
- Study Guide
- Worksheet, *Find the Hidden Storage Space*

CHAPTER OVERVIEW

Chapter 70 tells how to organize living space to get the best use out of the available space. It explains how to make a floor plan to organize furniture and suggests that furniture be arranged with traffic patterns and activities in mind. Students learn how to organize storage areas by grouping items, keeping them visible and within easy reach, and compartmentalizing space.

INTRODUCING THE CHAPTER

Motivators

Classroom Organization Have students look around the classroom and note the way the furniture and storage areas are organized. Allow students to suggest other possible ways to place classroom furniture and store classroom equipment.

Using the Photograph Have students study the photograph on this page. Then ask: "What is the girl in the photograph doing? Do you see another way she might arrange her possessions?"

Spring Cleaning Point out that many people use spring cleaning as an opportunity to get their living space organized. Ask students when and how often they reorganize closets, rearrange furniture, or clean out drawers.

Introducing the Objectives

Discuss the chapter objectives on this page. Remind students that the objectives focus on important chapter content.

Introducing Vocabulary

Point out that there are traffic patterns in homes as well as on city streets. Instead of cars, it is people who create the traffic. The way people move through living space should be kept in mind when arranging (or laying out) furniture. The layout can be used to alter traffic patterns and ease bottlenecks.

TEACHING THE CHAPTER

For convenience, the teaching suggestions for this chapter are arranged according to the following lesson topics:
- "Organizing Your Furniture," pages 630-631
- "Activity Areas," pages 631-632
- "Storage Areas," pages 632-634

Teaching "Organizing Your Furniture"
(Pages 630-631)

This section teaches how to organize furniture by using a scale drawing to create an effective floor plan and by taking into account traffic patterns and activities.

Checking Comprehension

✓ What is the advantage of starting with a floor plan when rearranging furniture? *You can change your furniture around on paper without having to actually move the furniture.*

✓ What is a *scale drawing*? *One in which the relative size of objects is the same as the relative size of the objects in the actual space.*

✓ Why is it important to indicate closet doors on a floor plan? *So your furniture doesn't get in the way when you open the door.*

✓ How can a floor plan help when you are buying furniture? *You can make sure that your choice is the right size and shape.*

✓ How can you tell if a dresser is in the wrong spot? *If you have to squeeze past a dresser every time you walk into the room, the dresser is interferring with an easy flow of traffic through the room.*

✓ What kind of furniture would be grouped together in a study area? *A desk, chair, bookcase, and desk lamp.*

You probably do more than sleep in your room. You may study, dress, read, listen to music, and perhaps even eat there. You might use your room to have private talks with a friend or for a chance to get away from family noise. Your room is also the place where you keep your clothes, schoolbooks, cassette tapes, and other personal possessions. Your living space, then, provides you with a place to relax and enjoy yourself, perform many activities, and store your things.

Other people use their living spaces in many different ways to meet their own special needs and particular goals. Some people like uncluttered, functional rooms, with a minimum amount of furniture. Other people prefer rooms with lots of furniture and places to display their keepsakes. In this chapter, you will learn how to get the best use out of the space you have, and how to arrange it according to your own tastes and needs.

Organizing Your Furniture

When you open your closet door, does it bang into your desk? Is there a dresser drawer that you can't open because your bed is in the way? Rearranging the furniture in your room could eliminate problems like these and enable you to make better use of the space that you have available.

Making a Floor Plan

A good way to organize your space is to start with a **floor plan,** an illustration of the arrangement of elements in a room or home. With a floor plan, you can change your furniture around on paper without having to actually move the furniture.

A floor plan is a sketch of a room and the furniture drawn to scale. You can try different arrangements to find the best use of the available space.

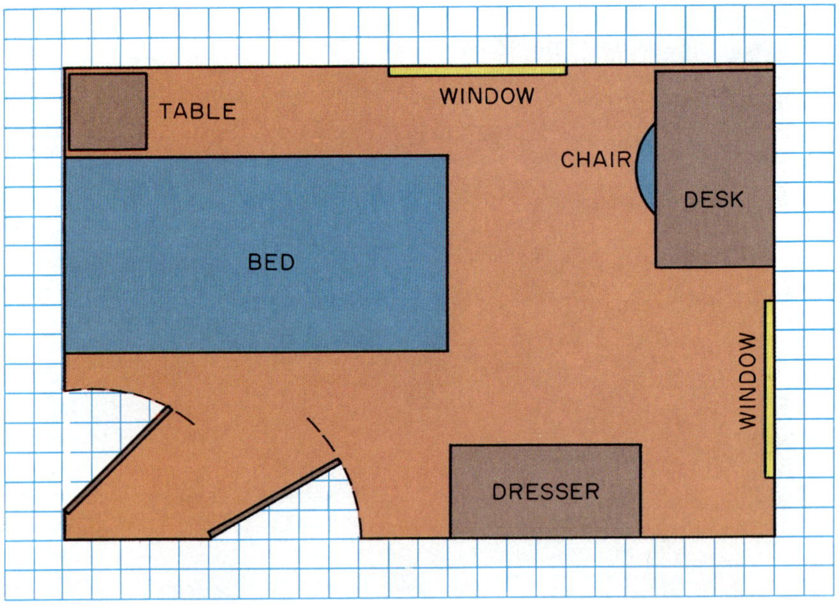

More About Organizing Space When making a floor plan, it's important to allow space for movement. A dresser, for example, takes up more space with the drawers open. Have students think about where else space must be left for movement.

Emphasize Different layouts create different looks in a room. Poorly placed furniture may interfere with the traffic pattern or make a room look cramped and cluttered. Ask students to consider how furniture should be arranged to allow for maximum movement and a neat, spacious look.

To make a floor plan, start by measuring your room and all the furniture in it. Then make a scale drawing of your room on graph paper. A **scale drawing** is one in which the relative sizes of objects are the same as the relative sizes of those objects in that actual space.

Follow these steps:

- Allow a certain number of graph paper squares to equal each foot of space that you measured. For example, if the scale you choose allows two squares per foot, a room measuring 8 ft. x 12 ft. would be drawn as a rectangle 16 squares by 24 squares.
- Indicate features such as doors and windows on the plan. With a dotted line, show which direction the doors open.
- Add your furniture, allowing the correct number of squares per foot for each piece.

By using a floor plan, you can see how furnishings will look in a particular **layout**, or arrangement of furniture. If you want to try another arrangement, draw separate scale drawings of the furniture on graph paper and cut them out. Try several different layouts until you find one you like. This saves you the trouble of having to rearrange your furnishings several times to find the best arrangement. If you are buying furniture, a floor plan can help you make sure that your choice is the right size and shape.

Considering Traffic Patterns

Think about **traffic patterns**, or how people move through the space. Can you move freely from one area of your space to another without tripping over things? If you have to squeeze past a dresser every time you walk into the room, the dresser is interfering with an easy flow of traffic through the room.

You should also think about how an arrangement will look. Depending on how furnishings are placed, a room can look cramped and cluttered or spacious and neat.

Creating Different Areas

One key to organizing space is to group together furnishings and other items that you use together. You can make a special area for each of your activities:

- A study area might include a desk, chair, bookcase, and desk lamp. In your desk drawer would be paper, pens, and pencils.
- A music center would contain all your records or tapes, your cassette tape player or stereo, and a cozy chair.
- A computer area would include your computer, monitor, printer, and storage for disks or computer games, joysticks, and computer projects.
- A science area might include a microscope, magnifying glass, collections of rocks or butterflies, and reference books.
- A game area might include your playing cards, games, puzzles, and a table and chairs.
- A fitness area could include an exercise mat, jump rope, weights, clothes for working out, and a radio or tape player.

Activity Areas

People use living spaces for the activities they enjoy. Whether you sew, build models, read, or program a computer, you want space in your room to pursue your hobby.

Real-Life Situations Many teens have to share a room with one or more siblings. Sharing a room can be fun, but it also takes a lot of consideration and compromise. Each of the people sharing a room must have his or her own personal space and times for privacy. It may help to schedule times when the room is to be used by only one person. It may be possible to divide even a small room so each person has some private space. Furniture can be arranged to create separate sleeping and study areas. Bookcases or screens can be used to divide the room physically. Putting one or two beds up near the ceiling on solid wooden posts allows for the floor space underneath to be used for a study area.

Activities

Skill Builder: Critical Thinking
Have students consider what they need to know in order to make an adequate floor plan. Have them brainstorm until they include such factors as the width and length of the room, the width and height of windows and doors, the location of closets, lights, electrical outlets and switches, ceiling fixtures, plumbing fixtures and drains, registers, radiators, chimneys, alcoves or window seats, and other special features.

Skill Builder: Math
Using the floor plan on page 630, and assuming that the scale is two squares per foot, have students figure out the approximate dimensions of the room, the bed, the desk, and the dresser.

Skill Builder: Reading
Have students read about a make-over of a room in a home magazine and report on how the traffic pattern was improved, what activity areas were created, and how the floor plan gave the room a different look. They might also evaluate how effective they felt the make-over was and what they might have done differently.

Reteaching
To help students understand scale, have them draw a floor plan of their bedroom. Remind them to include all the furniture that is in the room.

Enrichment
Ask students to evaluate the traffic pattern in their homes. They should indicate high and low traffic areas and suggest how rearranging furniture might alter (and perhaps improve) existing traffic patterns

Teaching "Activity Areas"
(Pages 631-632)

This section teaches that there are activity areas in all parts of a home and that some areas are used for several different activities.

Checking Comprehension

✔ What are some possible uses for spare rooms? *They can be used as offices, workrooms, exercise rooms, or sewing rooms.*

✔ How can a desk be used for multiple purposes? *It can be used for doing homework, working with a computer, or building models.*

✔ How can you turn a bed into a couch for daytime use? *Push it against the wall and add large pillows.*

Activities

Skill Builder: Critical Thinking
Basements often serve as multiple use areas in a house. Ask students to think of ways that basement space might be utilized. Which of these uses require that the basement be finished?

Reteaching
A chair is a piece of furniture that allows for multiple uses. Have students sit in their chairs and compile a list of activities that they could do there, such as reading a book, sewing, and so on.

Enrichment
Have students look at floor plans for several homes and identify activity areas. Where can people pursue hobbies, work, listen to music, and so forth? Which areas are suitable for multiple uses?

Teaching "Storage Areas"

(Pages 632-634)

This section teaches how to make effective use of storage space, and how to store items conveniently and efficiently.

Checking Comprehension

✔ What kind of storage helps to keep items visible? *Plastic containers, wire mesh baskets, and open shelves.*

✔ How can you compartmentalize space? *By dividing the space into smaller categories and designating a place for each type of item.*

✔ What kinds of things can you store under the bed? *Sweaters, games, or out-of-season clothes.*

✔ How can you make shelves more attractive? *Paint, stain, or cover the shelves with adhesive-backed paper.*

Not all of your activities are going to be done in your bedroom. Woodworking or staining furniture is best done in a workshop or garage. Some families use spare rooms in their homes for offices, workrooms, exercise rooms, or sewing rooms, and everyone in the family can use the equipment that is kept there.

In most homes, many areas are used for more than one activity. This **multiple use** of space is more efficient than using each area for only one activity. A desk can be used for doing homework, working with a computer, or building models. Your bed can double as a place for playing cards, reading, or listening to music. If you push the bed to the wall and add big, comfortable pillows, you've made a couch that can be used for many activities during the day while still serving as a bed at night.

Some hobbies or activities, such as refinishing furniture, require a space where you can work on the project. Do you have any hobbies that need a special work area or equipment?

Storage Areas

Everyone needs to have space for storing possessions and protecting them from damage. This storage space should be convenient and accessible, and with a little work it can also be attractive.

Solving Storage Problems

Whether you are organizing your closet, your room, the kitchen, or the garage, there are four principles of organization that you should consider:

- **Group similar items together.** Hang or store similar items in the same area so they are easy to find.
- **Keep items within easy reach.** Avoid high shelves or low drawers for items that you use often.
- **Keep items clearly visible.** Use clear plastic storage containers, wire mesh baskets, and open shelves so that you can easily see what you're looking for.
- **Compartmentalize space.** Divide space in the closet or drawers into smaller categories, designating a place for each type of item. For example, hang shirts in one section, and pants in another.

Decide what your storage problem is. You might want a place to store your athletic equipment. Your sister may need a place for her books. Someone else may need a place to put out-of-season clothes.

More About Multiple Use Some furniture is specifically designed for multiple use. The most popular is the sofa bed, which serves as a place to sit during the day and a place to sleep at night. There are also drop-leaf tables, entertainment centers, and studio beds. This type of furniture is particularly useful when space is limited.

More About Furniture When selecting furniture, check these construction features: Chairs should be comfortable and sturdy; legs should rest evenly on the floor; drawers should slide smoothly; handles should be firmly attached; joints (connecting points) should be tight; upholstery should be durable and well-fitted.

MANAGING RESOURCES

Closet Space: The Final Frontier

Is your closet uncharted territory? Do you feel that even an astronaut wouldn't be able to discover the space that lies within your closet?

Here are some storage aids that can expand your closet space:

- Double rods expand the space for hanging clothes in a closet. Raise one pole to 80 in. (200 cm) and install a second pole 40 in. (100 cm) from the floor.
- Plastic-coated wire shelves are lightweight and easy to install for storing sweaters, shorts, T-shirts, and accessories.
- Tubular plastic hangers hold clothes in shape better than wire hangers. Use sturdy wooden hangers for coats and heavy suit jackets. Use padded hangers for lightweight silky blouses and for other garments made of fine fabrics. Use multiple skirt and pants hangers to keep garments accessible and wrinkle-free.
- Plastic hooks can be used to hang hats, belts, bags, robes, and pajamas.
- Kitchen towel racks can be hung on the wall or back of a door to hold scarves and ties.
- Mug racks, used to hold cups, are an easy-to-install way to hold scarves, ties, belts, and bags.
- Clear plastic boxes keep items dust-free and easy to see.
- Shoe racks provide storage for several pairs of shoes and can be used on the wall or on the back of the door.
- Wire basket drawers can eliminate cramped dresser drawers. You can see underwear, socks, and sweaters at a glance. The wire permits air to circulate keeping clothes fresh.
- Open plastic bins can be stacked to hold shoes, accessories, equipment, or games.
- Corkboard is handy for posters, photos, notes, and mementos.
- Modular storage units are versatile for use as shelves and drawers. They can be arranged in interesting ways.
- Fishing tackle boxes and small metal tool chests with see-through plastic drawers can be used to store small items used for a hobby or a collection.

Think It Through

1. **One business that is gaining in popularity is closet planning and organizing. Why do you think this field has become popular?**
2. **If you could redo your closet, how would you change it? If you wouldn't, then what makes it work?**

Teaching the Feature
"Closet Space: The Final Frontier"

Answers to Feature Questions

1. Answers will vary. Students may suggest that people have more possessions to organize, that people have less storage space than they need, that new tubular metal has made closet organization easier and less expensive to do.
2. Answers will vary. Students may suggest using methods to group similar items together or to make better use of space. Others might say their closet already works for these or other reasons.

Activities

The Modular Closet Ask students if they know what a module is. Explain that a module is a standard unit used in the design of buildings or components of buildings. A modular closet consists of individual storage units that can be stacked on top of each other. Ask students to design a modular closet with space for all their closet needs. Have them specify what materials they would need.

Installation Feedback Ask students to discuss any storage aids (rods, hooks, racks, corkboard) that they have helped install in their homes. Have them talk about the difficulty or ease of installation. What were the problems? What would have made the task easier?

Community Contact Encourage students to volunteer to help a nonprofit organization (church, Boy Scouts, school club) organize their storage space. Students could donate inexpensive storage aids (orange crates, cardboard boxes, paper bags) to the group to improve storage capabilities.

More About Closet Space Many older homes do not have built-in closets. Clothes are stored in free-standing wardrobes and other items are stored in furniture, basements, and attics. Home buyers should keep this lack of built-in storage space in mind when considering an older home.

Emphasize The modular closet idea can be expanded to include other kinds of closets or cabinets. Have students suggest other places for modular closet features.

✔ How can you solve storage problems if you don't have much money? *Shop for bargains at garage sales or flea markets; build a room organizer or storage shelves; paint or refinish old furniture; use cardboard boxes.*

✔ Name four places you can store things in your room. *Any four: closet, desk, dresser, bookcase, under the bed, on shelves, or on the wall.*

Activities

Skill Builder: Math
Tell students that they have a $50 budget to buy storage aids that can help them organize a room. Have students use catalogs or go to stores to make a list of what they would buy, and how they would use each item, and the price of each item.

Skill Builder: Critical Thinking
Have students design shelving that would be ideal for a specific purpose (holding stereo and CD equipment, displaying a porcelain collection, or as a kitchen pantry, for example). Then have them figure out what materials (plywood, brackets, door handles, hinges, stain) would be needed to carry out the project.

Skill Builder: Writing
Ask students to write a description of an area in their home in which storage is handled in a particularly effective or unique way. They should tell how it complies with the four principles of organization discussed in this section.

Reteaching
Ask students to look at pictures of rooms in magazines and identify storage areas. Point out the different ways that storage areas are organized.

Enrichment
Divide the class into two groups. Have one group list a hard-to-store item (skis, luggage, folding chairs, ironing board) and the other group suggest possible storage solutions. Then have the groups switch roles.

Before deciding how to store things, ask yourself four questions:

- **How often is the item used?** Something used frequently should be easier to get out than something you rarely need.
- **Do other family members use it?** If so, you'll need to take their use into account when choosing a storage space. You might even want to store the item in a different room.
- **Does it look good on display?** Many objects can be stored and used as decoration at the same time. Chapter 71 offers some ideas.
- **Does it require other tools or supplies?** You don't want to have to go to two or three places to collect the things you need for one activity.

You can store possessions in many different ways. Your closet, dresser, and desk are the obvious places to store your clothes and school supplies.

Here are some suggestions for other storage areas in your room.

- The space under your bed can be used as a storage area. Cut off the upper sections of cardboard boxes so they'll fit under the bed. Use these boxes to store sweaters, games, or out-of-season clothes.
- Bookcases can hold more than just books. If your bookcase holds books that you seldom use, pack them up and use the shelf space for frequently used items instead.
- Wall shelves are good for storing all sorts of items besides books. Shelf storage space can be attractive as well as useful. Mount shelves on the wall with brackets. You might want to paint, stain, or cover the shelves with adhesive-backed paper.
- Walls can be used for storage in other ways. Put up hooks or pegs and use them to hang jewelry, tote bags, jackets, belts, hats, and sporting goods. Baskets of all types can be hung from the wall and ceiling and used for lightweight items.
- Another area that often goes unused is the back of the closet door. Attach shoe racks, belt racks, hooks, and baskets to extend the use of this space for storage.

In choosing between one storage method and another consider your resources, such as money, skill, and time. If your money is limited, shop for bargains at garage sales or flea markets. Perhaps you could build a room organizer out of wood, or make storage shelves out of boards and cement blocks. Paint or refinish an old bookcase, or get cardboard boxes free from stores. Use your imagination to think of other ways to solve your storage problems.

Use boxes for under-the-bed storage to keep items neat and easy to find.

Focus on Life Management Suggest that students use the principles of organization to make more efficient use of desk drawers, purses, backpacks, and briefcases. Ask students to discuss how the principles apply to these different situations.

Focus on Entrepreneurship Have students develop a sales and marketing plan for an inexpensive storage aid (such as a corkboard or storage hooks) that will help other students organize their lockers. Students should create advertising posters and briefly explain how they would go about selling their product.

CHAPTER

70 REVIEW

Reviewing the Facts

1. Why are floor plans a good way to decide how to organize your space?
2. How do you make a floor plan?
3. Why should you think about traffic patterns when organizing your space?
4. List five kinds of activities for which teens might create specific areas in their bedrooms.
5. What is multiple use of space?
6. When solving storage problems, what four questions should you ask?
7. List five kinds of storage items that can help you organize your closet or room.
8. What must you consider when deciding which storage method to use?

Thinking Critically

1. If you wanted to improve your room's organization or appearance, what would you do?
2. What area would you set up in your room if you had the resources? What items would you need for this center?

Applying Your Skills

1. **Planning Space.** Think of an unusual way to store or display a collection. The collection can be anything you think of such as seashells, bottle caps, baseball cards, miniatures, buttons, rocks, and the like. Draw a diagram and write a paragraph explaining your storage/display idea.

2. **Drawing to Scale.** Using graph paper, make a scale drawing of any room in your home. Then, on another sheet of graph paper, rearrange the room to create an entirely new layout.

3. **Researching Ideas.** In the interests of energy and space efficiency, many people are combining spaces in their homes for a single multiuse area. Read several home decorating or home remodeling magazines and report to the class on this or other housing trends.

Answers to "Reviewing the Facts"

1. It is easier to plan a room on paper than it is to move furniture around.
2. Measure the room and furnishings and then draw the room and furniture to scale on graph paper.
3. You need to move freely through the room, without tripping over things or having to squeeze past a piece of furniture.
4. Any five: study area, music center, computer area, science area, game area, fitness area.
5. Using the same area for more than one activity.
6. How often is it used? Do others use it? Does it look good on display? Does it require other tools or supplies?
7. Any five: cardboard boxes, bookcases, wall shelves, hooks or pegs, baskets, shoe or belt racks, double rods, wire shelves, tubular plastic hangers, towel racks, mug racks, clear plastic boxes, wire baskets, plastic bins, corkboard, modular units, fishing tackle boxes, tool chests.
8. Your resources—money, skills, time.

Answers to "Thinking Critically"

1. Answers will vary. Students may suggest that they could paint or refinish furniture; sew closet accessories; use decorative painting to give old furniture a new look; use carpentry skills to build shelves; cover cardboard boxes with wallpaper; use a craft skill to make baskets.
2. Answers will vary. Students may want to set up a craft area (they might need a table to work on), exercise area (stationary bike or mat), sewing area (sewing machine), computer area (computer), or music area (tape or CD player).

COMPLETING THE CHAPTER

Summary

- A floor plan is a good way to organize space and arrange furniture.
- A floor plan starts with a scale drawing of a room and allows a person to change the layout without actually moving the furniture.
- When organizing space, you must consider the traffic patterns and the grouping of furniture into different areas of activity.
- Many areas in a home are used for more than one purpose or activity.
- When storing things, you should group similar items together, keep items visible and within easy reach, and compartmentalize space.
- Many storage aids are available to help people organize space.

For Review

Objective Review Questions Have students complete the "Reviewing the Facts" section on this page.

Study Guide Have students complete the Study Guide from Chapter 70 of their *Student Workbook.*

Take Action One way to organize space more effectively is to discard items. Have students develop a set of criteria for deciding what can be discarded when space is at a premium. One criterion might be: Have I used this item in the last five years?

For Evaluation

Synthesis Ask students to create a floor plan for a room (home office, exercise room, family room). They should indicate the layout of the furniture and the traffic patterns through the room, and should include a plan to store appropriate equipment and other relevant items (computer accessories, weights, board games).

Chapter Test Have students complete the test for Chapter 70 that appears in the *Teacher's Classroom Resources.*

CHAPTER OVERVIEW

Chapter 71 teaches students how to use the five elements of design to create attractive and efficient living space. It explores the use of color, texture, space, shape, and line to produce a pleasing look. The principles of design—unity, contrast, balance, emphasis, proportion, and rhythm—are discussed. Students also learn about the use of accessories as a way of accenting design and making a personal statement about interests and lifestyle.

INTRODUCING THE CHAPTER

Motivators

Describe Your Room Have students describe their room—color scheme, furnishings, wall decorations—and tell what they like about the way it looks. Ask students to think about what their room says about them.

Using the Photograph Have students study the photograph on this page. Then ask: "Did you decorate your own room or would you like to?"

Dress for Success Explain that people apply the elements and principles of design when they dress. Ask students how they go about putting together an outfit that looks good. Have students talk about color, line, accessories, and so forth.

Introducing the Objectives

Discuss the chapter objectives on this page. Remind students that the objectives focus on important chapter content.

Introducing Vocabulary

Read to students the dictionary definitions of the following words: *unity, contrast, balance, emphasis, proportion,* and *rhythm.* Have students discuss how the general meanings of these words are applied to designing a room.

CHAPTER

71

Designing Your Space

OBJECTIVES

This chapter will help you to:

- Describe the elements of design and how to work with them.
- List the principles of design and use examples of each.
- Explain how accessories can be used to add interest to a room.

WORDS TO REMEMBER

accessory
balance
contrast
emphasis
proportion
rhythm
unity

Chapter Resources

Teacher's Classroom Resources
- Lesson Plan
- Life Skills Activity, *Working with the Elements and Principles of Design*
- Reproducible Master, *Design Equation*
- Extension Activity, *Elements and Principles of Design*
- Chapter Test

Student Workbook
- Study Guide
- Worksheet, *"Dream Bedroom"*

Shireen was embarrassed to invite friends to her room. She thought the pink ruffled curtains and pink dresser seemed childish. Although her toy box held sewing supplies, it still looked like a toy box. Her one new possession, a desk, didn't fit in with anything else in the room.

You may feel this way about your own room. What can you do? Shireen and her mother started by buying plaid fabric to make new curtains. Shireen repainted her toy box and dresser. She also made some big pillows to match the curtains and put these pillows on top of the toy box. Next, she rearranged her furniture to make her new desk the center of interest.

Shireen found it didn't take much money to give her room a new look. She applied a knowledge of the elements and principles of design and made creative use of accessories.

The Elements of Design

You can make your personal space more attractive by working with the basic elements, or tools, of design. Those five elements are color, texture, space, shape, and line.

Color

Interior designers give a lot of thought to the colors they use in a room. Color has a powerful, immediate effect on a person's mood. Warm colors, such as red, yellow, and orange, are bold, cheerful, and exciting. Cool colors, such as blue, green, and purple, are quiet, calm, and soothing. If your favorite color is red, but you feel that a whole room in red would be too much, you could use that color for a bedspread or draperies.

When choosing colors for a room, first choose a dominant color. It could be your favorite color, the color of a particular item in the room, or a color that would set the mood you want to create.

Focus on Consumer Skills Have students estimate the costs of the redecorating undertaken by Shireen at the beginning of the chapter.

Cross-Reference See Teen Tips "Four Looks—One Room" on pages 676-677.

Focus on Relationship Skills Decorating decisions are often shared by several people who share a living space. Divide the class into groups of two or three and have them reach a consensus about a decorating plan for a living room. All decisions should be justified by principles of design.

TEACHING THE CHAPTER

For convenience, the teaching suggestions for this chapter are arranged according to the following lesson topics:

- "Elements of Design," pages 637-639
- "Principles of Design," pages 639-640
- "Accessories: The Personal Touch," page 642

Teaching "Elements of Design"
(Pages 637-639)

This section teaches about the five elements of design: color, texture, space, shape, and line. It explores how they can be used to create different looks in a room.

Checking Comprehension

✓ Name three warm colors and three cool colors. *Red, yellow, and orange are warm colors. Blue, green, and purple are cool colors.*

✓ Why are light colors, such as tan, gray, or white, used so often in decorating a room? *Light colors are easily combined with other colors.*

✓ What is texture? *How the surface of an object feels.*

✓ Describe the kind of woods and fabrics that create an informal look in a room. *A more informal look is achieved with deeply grained woods, such as pine and oak, and with nubby fabrics.*

✓ What kind of colors make a room look larger? Smaller? *Bright, light colors make a room appear larger. Darker, rich colors make it look smaller.*

✓ How can you make a room look less cluttered? *Keep items off the floor. Use hanging shelves and sturdy hooks to hold everything from your book bag to your bicycle.*

✓ What kind of effect do curved shapes create in a room? *When you use many curved shapes in a room the result is a soft effect.*

✔ What are three directions that lines can take? *Lines can be vertical, horizontal, or diagonal.*

✔ What are four things in a room that would create a distinctly vertical line? *Any four: tall windows, floor-to-ceiling draperies, vertically striped wallpaper, a tall bookcase, and full-length posters.*

Activities

Skill Builder: Critical Thinking
Manufacturers of consumer products use the elements of design in their packaging. Have students discuss how the use of color, line, and shape on cereal boxes, detergent bottles, and other items are effective in attracting our attention and getting us to buy the product.

Skill Builder: Science
Point out that technology is constantly creating new textures in fabrics. Have students research some of the fibers and finishes used in carpeting and upholstery and report on the properties of these fabrics.

Skill Builder: Writing
Ask students to choose two colors and write a paragraph on each describing the kinds of feelings that the color awakens. Have students suggest possible places to use these colors in the home in view of how they might make people feel.

Reteaching
Using fabric swatches, paint samples, carpet samples, and perhaps wallpaper books, have students create a color scheme for the walls, flooring, and furniture of a living room.

Enrichment
Divide the students into three groups. Each group will design a room with attention to color scheme, textures, line, shape, and space. Then the groups will share their results, noting how the elements of design were applied differently to the different situations.
Room 1: A five-year-old boy's room.
Room 2: A doctor's waiting room.
Room 3: A formal dining room.

You may need to work around colors that are already in your room. Perhaps you can paint the walls, but you can't change the floor color. Choose a light background color for the walls and accent it with colorful accessories. Light colors, such as white, tan, and soft tones of yellow, blue, or green are easily combined with other colors. Many colors work well together, so you'll have quite a few to choose from. Look at the color wheel in Chapter 56 to see how colors can be combined.

Texture

Another important element of design is texture, or how the surface of an object feels. Is it silky or fuzzy? Rough or polished?

For a more formal look, designers use the smooth surfaces of chrome, glass, and polished wood. A formal look is also created with fabrics that have a sheen such as silks and taffetas. A more informal look is achieved with deeply grained woods, such as pine and oak, and with nubby fabrics, woven baskets, and deep pile rugs.

You can also combine textures. A smooth laminated desk contrasts nicely with a woven rag rug, and a knitted afghan accents a smooth comforter.

Space

You can't change the size of your room or the room you share, but you can make it appear larger or smaller with the right use of space. Arranging your furniture along the wall will give the room the feeling of more space. Using one color throughout the room will unify the space. Bright, light colors also make a room appear to be larger.

Space looks larger and less cluttered if you have few items on the floor. Use hanging shelves and sturdy hooks to hold everything from your bookbag to your bicycle.

You can make a room look larger or smaller by your choice of colors and how you arrange the furniture.

Cross-Reference For more information about color and texture, see chapters 56 and 58.

Did You Know? Color is affected by lighting. Daylight gives what is called "true" color, while an ordinary light bulb gives a yellowish cast to objects. Fluorescent light is more blue and gives a slightly cold look to objects.

If your room is large, you can move the furniture toward the center of the room to fill in space and make the room seem cozier. Darker, rich colors make the space look smaller. You could also divide larger spaces into two living areas, one for sleeping and one for activities. A folding screen divider can make one room seem like two smaller ones.

Shape

The shapes of objects in a room can have a strong effect on a room's atmosphere. A matching set of furniture usually repeats certain forms. The arms of a chair, the shape of a headboard, or the frame of a mirror may be curved or straight. Repetition can set a tone for the room.

When you use many curved shapes in a room, the result is a soft effect. If most of the furniture is square or rectangular, the effect will be harder. When many different forms are mixed together, the effect will be informal, or even confusing. It's a good idea to think carefully about how different shapes look together in a room.

Line

Every room has many lines. There is a line at the top of the door, for example, and a line around the base of a lamp. The atmosphere of a room is most affected by the bold lines that stand out and are the most obvious, such as those around windows and moldings.

In a room with tall windows, you could use floor-to-ceiling draperies for the windows and paper the walls with vertically striped wallpaper. If you added a tall bookcase and some full-length posters, the vertical lines would be the boldest element in the room.

Some people feel comfortable in such a vertical room. Others prefer more horizontal lines, because they give the room a more restful effect. These lines could be created with a low bed, a long dresser, and shelves. Still other people like the feeling of motion and excitement that is created by diagonal lines on walls and furniture.

The Principles of Design

Now that you've learned about the elements of design—color, texture, space, shape, and line—it is time to learn about the principles of design. The principles of design are a set of guidelines or rules about how to make color, texture, and the other elements of design work together to create a pleasing appearance. The principles of design are unity, contrast, balance, emphasis, proportion, and rhythm.

Unity and Contrast

Imagine a room with square chairs, curved chairs, tall chairs, and short chairs of many styles and colors. It might be hard to relax in such a room. Designers usually advise clients to choose one color scheme and perhaps one general style of furniture in a room. This helps create a feeling of **unity**, a feeling that all objects in a room look like they belong together.

Unity doesn't mean that a room must have only one color or only one style. You can accent a major color such as beige walls with red and yellow draperies and pillows.

In fact, a room can be more interesting if there is some contrast. **Contrast** is the difference in color and shape among objects. For example, brightly patterned

Emphasize The way furniture is arranged is one way to highlight a feature in a room. Grouping a seating arrangement around a fireplace serves to make it the focal point of the room. Lighting can also help to determine whether or not an object stands out.

More About Shape Another term for shape is "form," and one of the cardinal rules of design is that "form follows function." That means that to be effective, form must fulfill the purpose for which it is planned. A chair's shape should not only be pleasing to the eye, but should also result in a comfortable place to sit.

Teaching "Principles of Design"
(Pages 639-640)

This section teaches about the guidelines that are used to create a pleasing appearance. The principles of design are unity, contrast, balance, emphasis, proportion, and rhythm.

Checking Comprehension

✓ Why do designers advise clients to choose one color scheme and one style of furniture? *Because this helps create a feeling of unity.*

✓ What is contrast? *The difference in color and shape among objects.*

✓ What are the two kinds of balance? *The two types of balance are formal and informal.*

✓ What happens when you emphasize an object? *It becomes the focal point, or center of interest, and it draws the eye to itself.*

✓ When there is a pleasing size relationship among objects, what principle of design is being applied? *A pleasing size relationship among objects is called proportion.*

✓ How is the term *rhythm* used in design? *Rhythm is the regular repetition of line or shape.*

Activities

Skill Builder: Math
Have students work with furniture templates (cutouts) or dollhouse furniture of different sizes. They should match up furniture that demonstrates the principle of proportion in creating furniture arrangements.

Skill Builder: Reading
Have students read about a variety of furniture styles and consider how different styles might be combined and used together, while not violating the principles of unity, rhythm, and balance. How could distinctive styles provide contrast and emphasis? Which styles should never be used together? Why not?

Reteaching
Ask students to look at magazine pictures of rooms and discuss the principles of design that have been applied.

Enrichment
Take students on a bus or walking tour of several neighborhoods in the community. Have students comment on how the principles of design are conformed to or violated in the exterior design of the homes you see.

upholstery can make an interesting contrast with a solid-colored carpet. Similarly, you can contrast shapes by hanging an oval mirror over a rectangular dresser or mixing angular and rounded tables in a room.

Balance and Emphasis

Another effect designers work to achieve is **balance**. Balance means that objects are arranged in even, pleasing ways. Balance can either be formal or informal. When you place identical end tables at each end of a sofa or arrange four photographs in a square on the wall, you are using formal balance. If you were to display several antique bottles of different sizes and shapes in an eye-pleasing arrangement on a table, you would be using informal balance.

An object that stands out in a room receives **emphasis,** or more attention than the other objects. When you emphasize an object, it becomes the focal point, or center of interest, and it draws the eye to itself. For example, a large dramatic painting hung on the wall or a brightly colored rug on a hardwood floor can be used for emphasis in a room.

Proportion and Rhythm

A pleasing size relationship among objects is called **proportion**. A big oak desk that came from your mother's office is out of proportion to the wire ice cream parlor chair you use to sit at the desk. To achieve better proportion, find a larger and more comfortable chair to use at the desk.

The regular repetition of line or shape is called **rhythm**. Rhythm in design is similar to rhythm in music. Striped fabric or pictures hung at regular intervals create a rhythm that can be pleasing in a room. Gathered curtains with a soft gathered valance and a bed with a gathered dust ruffle have a rhythm.

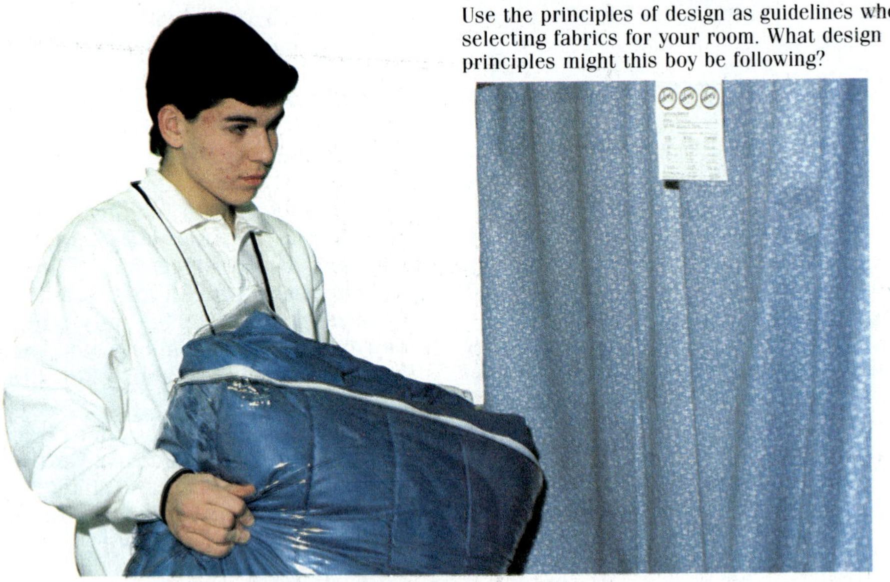

Use the principles of design as guidelines when selecting fabrics for your room. What design principles might this boy be following?

Did You Know? The principles of design are not new ideas. The temples and monuments of ancient civilizations, such as the Greeks, the Romans, and the Incas, show that they were following the same principles when they planned their buildings.

Emphasize Point out or have students identify objects or features within the classroom that illustrate one or more of the principles of design.

TECHNOLOGY

Computers Can Design, Too

Will a computer completely eliminate the pencils and drawing aids used by designers and architects? It seems entirely possible.

Computer graphics use the computer to design or draw an object on a computer screen. It is being used by designers to lay out and plan the interiors of homes and offices.

- **What is it?** The process is computer-aided design (CAD). A CAD system for an interior designer has been compared to what a bulldozer is to a shovel. In a fraction of the time that it would take to hand-draw a floor plan, the computer presents the plan on the screen.
- **What does it do?** After the scale drawing of the room is completed, the computer user goes to a data base, or catalog, of furniture to lay out and plan the space in the room. When the designer gives the computer further instructions, it can show the room three-dimensionally so you are able to "walk" through the space as if it were actually there.

The computer can also display the room in hundreds of color schemes that can be instantly changed. The colors can be shown in a variety of textures, in light and shadow, and from any angle.

The major benefit of computer-aided design is the ability to look at all possible solutions to a problem with amazing speed. Not only is computer-aided design faster, but it is also cheaper and more accurate than hand drawings.

- **Who will use it?** These computer systems are already being used by many high-tech engineering and architecture firms for interior and exterior design. As prices for these systems go down, more designers will be able to own and use these programs. Schools and universities are installing these systems for use by engineering, interior design, and architecture students.

Think It Through

1. **What effect do you think CAD could have on people's jobs?**
2. **Do you think computers take the creativity out of design? Why or why not?**

Teaching the Feature
"Computers Can Design, Too"

Answers to Feature Questions

1. Computers, once users learn how to use them, would make people's jobs faster, easier, and more accurate. The computer could show several solutions to a problem in a short time, so the user could pick the best possible solution without having to spend time figuring. The company might need to develop more projects; otherwise it might not need the workers to work as many hours.

2. Answers will vary. Students would need to look at what the workers would do both before and after they had access to a computer. The computer would give the user a number of design possibilities, but the user can alter them and make the final decisions. The computer can only respond to what the user puts into it.

Activities

Automobile Design Computers are also used to design automobiles. Discuss how the use of computers saves auto manufacturers time and money, and how it may result in better cars.

The Third Dimension A floor plan shows a room in two dimensions—length and width. A computer gives the appearance of adding the third dimension, depth, as well. Have students discuss the advantages of seeing a room three-dimensionally as it is being planned. What could you see that would help you to avoid problems later? What aspects of the principles of design would you be better able to consider?

Community Contact To see how computers aid design, take students to visit a local architectural or interior design firm that uses computers. Encourage students to prepare questions to ask the architect or designer about how the computer affects his or her work.

Did You Know? City planners are now using computer-aided design to help plan the development of buildings. They can see how the building as planned would affect the area around it and evaluate how it fits in with the buildings that are already standing.

Focus on Technology Have students investigate the term *user friendly* and talk about why it is important for computer systems to be easy to use.

Accessories: The Personal Touch

When planning rooms, designers often speak of two things: the major furnishings and the accessories. In a bedroom, the major furnishings may be a bed, a dresser, and a desk. They are expensive items that are not often replaced.

Accessories are the small objects that add visual appeal to a room. They do a great deal to improve the look of a room, are fairly inexpensive, and are easily changed. Posters, for example, don't cost much money and can reflect your interest in music, art, or sports. When your interests change, you can easily get a new poster.

Using Accessories

Accessories add interest to a room, such as a splash of color. They can accent or highlight an area, especially if you keep the room's color scheme in mind when you choose them.

Some accessories are strictly for decoration. A painting, for example, adds beauty to a room. Other accessories have a double purpose. In addition to improving the appearance of a room, accessories can also be useful, such as a calendar that features art prints or colorful baskets that hold craft supplies.

Accessories and You

Your accessories say a lot about you. By looking at them, a stranger might be able to get an idea of the kind of person you are. A ceramic cat, for example, might show your interest in pets and animals. Posters of dirt bikes suggest that you like that sport. By displaying your drawings or sports trophies, you are saying something special about yourself.

Accessories also please your senses. They help satisfy your sense of beauty. Your plants may give you the pleasant feeling of being in a garden. Even on the darkest day, a bright quilt or a cozy afghan may make you feel cheerful.

An accessory can bring back memories of places you've been and people you've known. By looking at a collection of seashells, you can remember the beach where you gathered them. Choose accessories that reflect your own life and have special meaning for you.

Give your room a personal touch by selecting accessories that reflect your interests. What do these items say about the person who lives here?

More About Choosing Accessories Accessories should be chosen to complement the style of the room. Abstract art is most successful if used in a contemporary setting. Baskets and textured tapestries work best in an informal room. Other accessories, such as plants, clocks, and mirrors, fit in with many different styles.

Focus on Decision Making Changing accessories is the least expensive and easiest way to redecorate. Have students talk about the decision to redo a room. How do you know when it is time for a change? What are the factors to be considered in timing the redecoration? Are there good and bad times for making changes?

Teaching "Accessories: The Personal Touch"
(Page 642)

This section teaches what accessories are and how they can be used to add interest to a room and express the personality of its occupant.

Checking Comprehension

✓ Name two purposes of accessories. *They improve the appearance of a room, and some can be useful.*

✓ How are accessories different from major furnishings? *Major furnishings are expensive items that are not often replaced. Accessories are fairly inexpensive and are easily changed.*

Activities

Skill Builder: Writing
Show students several different wall arrangements—some formal, others informal. Each should tell something about the person who designed it. Have students write two paragraphs about each arrangement: the first paragraph detailing the principles of design that apply; the second, describing the person whose wall it is.

Skill Builder: Math
Give students varying budgets and have them "spend" the money to "purchase" accessories for their room which would add interest and also express their personalities. Ask students to discuss how the amount of money they had to spend affected their decisions.

Reteaching
Display 10 to 15 accessories, for example, a painting, a plant, a poster, and antique picture frame. Ask students if they would use these items in their rooms, and have them explain why or why not. Discuss what the accessories say about the owner and where they would be appropriately used.

Enrichment
Restaurants often use accessories (tablecloths, centerpieces, wall decorations) to create an atmosphere. Have students visit two restaurants and compare the atmosphere (formal, informal, cheerful, romantic) that results from the use of accessories.

CHAPTER 71 REVIEW

Reviewing the Facts

1. What are the five elements of design?
2. Give two examples of how colors affect mood.
3. What kind of texture creates a formal look? An informal look?
4. Describe three ways to make a small space look larger.
5. What are the six principles of design?
6. Define unity as a principle of design.
7. What is the most effective way to use emphasis in decorating a room?
8. How can your choice of accessories reflect who you are?

Thinking Critically

1. What other suggestions would you give to Shireen to make her room more "grown-up"?
2. If you could change one element of design in your room, what would it be? How would you change it?

Applying Your Skills

1. **Describing a Design.** Using your own artwork or photos from magazines, put together a picture of your "dream" room. On one page, describe the elements and principles of design you used to get the look you want.

2. **Searching for Ideas.** Look through several issues of craft or decorating magazines. Cut out five simple projects that could be made easily and inexpensively to accessorize a teen's room. Report to the class on one project.

3. **Budgeting a Project.** Describe how you would like to redecorate your room. Establish a cost that the project should not exceed. Then estimate the cost of each specific item or supply that you would have to buy. What is the total estimated cost? If this total exceeds your budget, what changes could you make in your plan? Give specific examples.

Answers to "Reviewing the Facts"

1. Color, texture, space, shape, and line.
2. Warm colors are bold, cheerful, and exciting; cool colors are quiet, calm, and soothing.
3. Formal textures are smooth, shiny, and polished; informal textures are rough and nubby.
4. Arrange the furniture along the wall; use light colors for everything in the room; take things off the floor.
5. Unity, contrast, balance, emphasis, proportion, and rhythm.
6. Unity is a feeling that all the objects look like they belong together.
7. Choose one object to stand out from the rest of the room due to its size or color.
8. They can reflect your interests, experiences, and sense of beauty.

Answers to "Thinking Critically"

1. Students may suggest that Shireen give her toy chest away or put it in the closet and get a sewing table. She could put her sewing supplies in baskets on wall shelves. Instead of curtains, she could hang shades that have been trimmed with appliques or braid. She could coordinate some pillows with the colors in a wallhanging and make the bed the center of interest in the room.
2. Students may answer with personal preferences for color (painting the room or changing fabrics), line (using striped wallpaper or fabric), shape (window treatments, accessories), space (rearranging furniture), and texture (fabric, floor covering, accessories).

COMPLETING THE CHAPTER

Summary

- The elements of design are color, texture, space, shape, and line.
- The elements of design can be used to create an attractive living space.
- The principles of design—unity, contrast, balance, emphasis, proportion, and rhythm—help us to design pleasing rooms.
- Accessories add interest to a room by adding visual appeal or a splash of color.
- Accessories also reflect a person's personality and interests.
- With imagination and creativity, designing or redecorating a room need not cost a lot of money.

For Review

Objective Review Questions Have students complete the "Reviewing the Facts" section on this page.

Study Guide Have students complete the Study Guide from Chapter 71 of their *Student Workbook.*

Chart Have students create a chart with two columns—one representing a formal design, the other an informal design. Students will list the elements and principles of design and contrast the two styles in terms of texture, balance, and so on.

Solving Design Problems Encourage students to share with the class what they don't like about the look of their room, and invite the other students to suggest solutions to the design problems, such as redoing a color scheme, adding or changing accessories, and so on.

For Evaluation

Application Have students formulate a list of ten designing "don'ts," or violations of the principles of design.

Evaluation Have students evaluate a picture of a room, making a statement about each of the elements and principles of design.

Chapter Test Have students complete the test for Chapter 71 that appears in the *Teacher's Classroom Resources.*

CHAPTER OVERVIEW

Chapter 72 explains that taking care of one's home and the things in it avoids waste, makes life easier, and helps people feel good. It suggests ways to establish a cleaning routine to care for personal and shared space. Students learn the management skills needed to schedule daily and weekly chores and maintain a home in good working order.

INTRODUCING THE CHAPTER

Motivators

Neat or Messy? People can be categorized as neat or messy based on the appearance of their personal space. Ask students to think about how their room usually looks and to categorize themselves as neat or messy.

Using the Photograph Have students study the photograph on this page. Then ask: "Is vacuuming one of your household chores? Whose job is it? How often is it done?"

Who Does the Cleaning? Have students analyze who does various chores in their family and note the variety of arrangements that are used to get the cleaning done.

Introducing the Objectives

Discuss the chapter objectives on this page. Remind students that the objectives focus on important chapter content.

Introducing Vocabulary

The verb form of the term *maintenance* is "maintain." *Maintain* comes from the Latin phrase *manu tenere,* literally, "to hold in one's hand." Ask: "When we're talking about home maintenance, what are we trying to maintain around the house?" The verb "prevent" is a form of the term *preventive.* Ask: "When we maintain our homes, what do we *prevent?*"

CHAPTER

72

Caring for Living Space

OBJECTIVES

This chapter will help you to:

- List three reasons why caring for living space is important.
- Describe a routine for keeping your personal and shared space clean.
- Explain how to clean some of the areas in your home.

WORDS TO REMEMBER

maintenance
preventive
routine

Chapter Resources

Teacher's Classroom Resources
- Lesson Plan
- Life Skills Activity, *Time for Cleaning*
- Reproducible Master, *Be Responsible*
- Extension Activity, *Household Cleaning Hints*
- Chapter Test

Student Workbook
- Study Guide
- Worksheet, *Clean-up Kid*

Kirsten always got home from school first. She dumped her schoolbag and her shoes on the floor in front of the TV. Then she made a snack in the kitchen and left the milk, peanut butter, and crackers on the counter.

After she finished her snack, Kirsten called a friend to go skating. When Kirsten couldn't find her skates in the hall closet, she emptied the closet, throwing articles on the floor until she found them. She left 30 minutes later without putting anything back.

When her brother Chad got home later, he put his books in his room. Then he made himself a snack in the kitchen. When he finished he cleaned up the kitchen including the mess left by Kirsten.

In the same amount of time it took Kirsten to create a mess, Chad took responsibility for the comfort and convenience of everyone in the family. He cared for his own space and the space he shares with other family members.

Why Care for Space?

With more family members working outside the home, traditional family roles are changing. Each person in the family now needs to care for the family's living space, not just the adults.

Caring for space means keeping it neat and clean. Possessions should be stored where they belong, and floors, walls, and furniture should be kept clean. There are three good reasons for caring for your living space. Each reason has to do with things you value—your money, your time, and your feelings about yourself.

- **To avoid waste.** If you care for your things, they will last longer and stay in better condition. It is expensive to replace things that have been abused or carelessly treated. If you leave audio cassette tapes on the floor, they can get stepped on and broken.
- **To make life easier.** It is easier to live in a tidy space than in a cluttered one. Whether you want to find a pen, a book, or a baseball mitt, it's easier and less frustrating to find the item if it's where it's supposed to be. With outside work and activities, all family members place more value on their free time. They would rather spend their time doing something they enjoy, instead of searching for a misplaced item.

Get into the habit of putting away your possessions after using them. They will stay in better condition—and you will be able to find them when you need them.

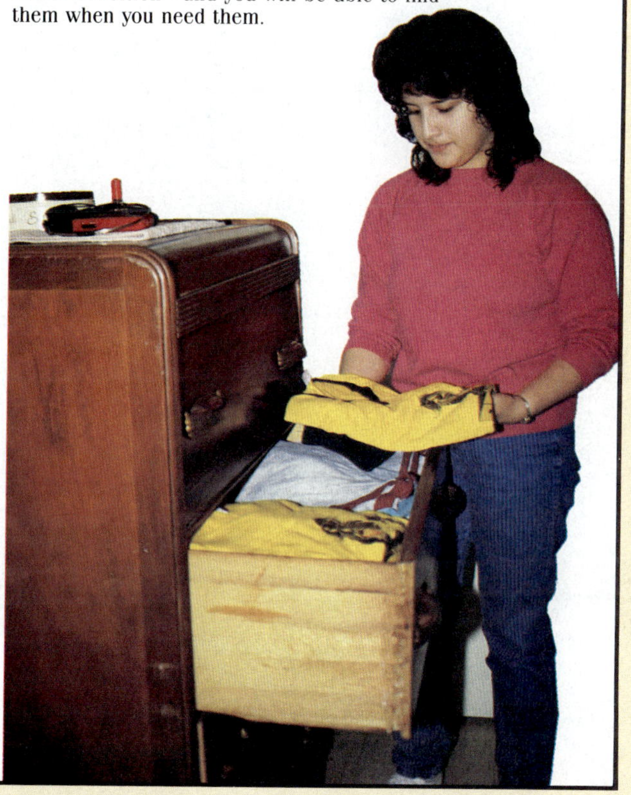

Did You Know? Caring for a home today is much easier than it was 20 years ago, thanks to the development of many maintenance-free materials. No-wax floors, self-cleaning ovens, and frost-free refrigerators have eliminated some household chores altogether and made others much easier.

Real-Life Situations Pets can provide lots of companionship, but they also require care. Dogs must be walked and exercised every day. Cat litter boxes, bird and hampster cages, and aquariums must be cleaned regularly. Fresh food and water must be provided daily for most pets. When choosing a pet, consider how much time is needed for its care.

TEACHING THE CHAPTER

For convenience, the teaching suggestions for this chapter are arranged according to the following lesson topics:

Teaching "Why Care for Space?"

(Pages 645-646)

This section teaches that by caring for space, one can avoid waste, make life easier, and make people feel better.

Checking Comprehension

✓ Why is it important to care for possessions? *They will last longer; be easier to find; and make you feel more organized.*

✓ What can happen to things that are left on the floor? *They can get stepped on and broken.*

Activities

Skill Builder: Math
Have students create a ten-question survey that determines how other students feel about neatness. (Sample questions: Do you categorize yourself as neat or messy? Do you feel anxious when you are in a messy room?) Have students administer the survey and then analyze the results, reporting their findings in percentages.

Reteaching
Show students objects that have deteriorated due to lack of care—a desk, a carpet, a piece of clothing—and ask them to suggest how better care might have prevented the damage.

Enrichment
The text suggests that "traditional family roles are changing." Ask students if that seems to be true in most families and what evidence of changing roles can be seen.

Teaching "Caring for Your Own Space"
(Pages 646-647)

This section teaches that caring for personal space is responsible behavior and gives students ideas on how to establish a routine for doing daily and weekly chores.

Checking Comprehension

✓ List four chores that need to be done every day. *Making the bed, putting school things away when you are finished with them, putting clothes and shoes away, and putting athletic, hobby, or music equipment where it belongs.*

✓ What are two ways of organizing your time to get weekly chores done? *You may do one task each day or set aside a time to do all of them at once.*

✓ What is involved in cleaning up your study area? *Straightening the desk, filing papers, stacking books, and organizing magazines.*

Activities

Skill Builder: Critical Thinking
Ask students to share personal instances in which "what you do in your own space affects other members of your family." Talk about the responsibilities of family members to each other.

Skill Builder: Math
Have students time themselves as they do various daily and weekly chores and then compare their times with other students. Have students give each other suggestions for accomplishing the same tasks in less time. Then have them see how much time they save the next time they do the task.

- **To make you feel better.** A cluttered room can reflect the way you feel about yourself. People who are surrounded by disorder may feel nervous, depressed, or anxious. A neat room, on the other hand, usually makes you feel organized and in control of things.

Even people who say they don't mind clutter would prefer a neat room. There's a feeling of satisfaction and pride that comes when you see that your room is clean and everything has been put away. The reward for your efforts is that you can relax and enjoy your space.

Keeping your room neat and clean is easier if you spend a few minutes each day straightening it up.

Caring for Your Own Space

Even though you probably feel that your room is your personal space, it's still a part of your family's home. How you keep your room is not just a matter of what makes you feel comfortable. It has an effect on the overall condition of your home.

Home furnishings and home repair are expensive. If you don't bother to clean up spilled nail polish, glue, or fruit juice, what will it cost to repair the damage? If you make big holes in the wall when putting up a poster, who will pay to repair the damaged wall? What you do in your own space clearly affects other members of your family.

By caring for your own space and keeping it neat, you are helping the whole family. Money spent on fixing damage caused by carelessness is money that could have been spent on something that could have benefited you and others in your family.

Getting Started

The first step in keeping your living space neat is to find storage space for your possessions. A good system of storage and organization will make it much easier to keep things looking neat. Follow the old adage "A place for everything, and everything in its place."

Establishing a Routine

Once you have found places for the different items in your room, you must see that they all end up there. Putting things away as soon as you finish using them is a big help. It will be easier for you to keep things neat if you get into a **routine**, or set sequence, for cleaning and straightening up your room.

Focus on Life Management Suggest that students reconsider the different kinds of storage described in Chapter 70, keeping in mind what they've learned about caring for space in this chapter. What kinds of storage areas are easy to care for?

Emphasize Each person should care for his or her own space. Children should take on chores as soon as they are able. A three-year-old can be expected to put away toys, a six-year-old can make the bed. Have students review the ages at which they assumed household responsibilities.

Some tasks, such as making the bed, should be done daily, while others need to be done only weekly or occasionally.

- **Daily chores.** You need to do some cleaning chores every day and other chores less often. You might divide up the daily chores like this:

  Make your bed in the morning.
  Put school things away when you get home from school or when you're finished studying.
  Put your clothes and shoes away. Put dirty clothes in the laundry after school or at night.
  Put your athletic, hobby, or music equipment where it belongs when you're done with it.
- **Weekly chores.** Other tasks need to be done only once a week. You may do one of these tasks each day, or set aside a time to do all of them at once. If you do just one thing a day, however, it probably won't take you longer than 10 minutes at a time.

  Straighten your desk and study area.
  File papers, stack books, and organize magazines.
  Empty the wastbasket.
  Straighten drawers and closets.
  Change the sheets on your bed.
  Dust the furniture and other objects in your room.
  Vacuum or sweep the floor.
  Clean or wipe off walls, light fixtures, and windowsills.

Caring for Shared Space

Maintenance of a home, the things that have to be done to keep living space and joint belongings in good working order, is a job for everyone. Each family may have a way of dividing the responsibilities for maintaining the family's living space according to the interests, skills, and time that each family member has to contribute. It's a good idea for the family to get together and talk about the chores that need to be done, who will do them, and when they will be done.

Making a schedule for maintenance of the home may be done differently in each family. Sometimes each family member is made responsible for a particular task. For instance, one person vacuums, and another dusts. The chores

Focus on Leadership Have students work through the following hypothetical situation: Two younger brothers who share a room are constantly arguing about cleaning their room. As the older sibling, suggest a plan that helps them solve their differences.

Did You Know? Some unusual things can be used to clean around the house. Try these out-of-the-ordinary cleaning suggestions:
- Pour a little club soda on fabric and carpet stains and sponge them up.
- Clean windows with newspapers.
- Place an opened box of baking soda in the refrigerator to absorb food odors.

Reteaching
Have students estimate how much time they would need to complete each of the weekly chores listed in the text, then total up the time to determine how long it would take to do all the chores on a Saturday morning.

Enrichment
Have students compare their cleaning routines and discuss how different people schedule chores to meet their own needs. Why might one person decide to do chores at night and another on Saturday afternoon?

Teaching "Caring for Shared Space"
(Pages 647-650)

This section teaches about the different ways that families can divide up household chores and cooperate to maintain the home and prevent accidents and damage.

Checking Comprehension

✓ What factors should be considered when dividing up chores among family members? *The interests, skills, and time that each family member has to contribute.*

✓ What is a good way for families to decide how to maintain shared living space? *The family should get together and talk about the chores that need to be done, who will do them, and when they will be done.*

✓ Describe the system of rotating chores. *A cleaning job is passed around from one family member to another.*

✓ Give two examples of how you can cooperate with other family members to get cleaning chores done. *If your brother is very busy on a particular day, you could volunteer to clean up the living room, even if that's not your job. If your father is working hard, you can offer to give him a hand.*

✔ Why is it important to keep the stove clean? *Because grease can build up and start a fire.*

✔ How can you tell if wallpaper can be washed or not? *Test the wallpaper in an inconspicuous spot.*

✔ What can you use to take care of wooden furniture? *A dust cloth or a duster will do the job. Some people use dusting sprays. You may wish to use furniture polish or wax occasionally.*

✔ How do you clean upholstered furniture? *Upholstered furniture should be vacuumed to remove dust, lint, and pet hair.*

✔ What supplies do you need to clean a toilet? *You'll need a toilet brush and toilet cleaner, and you may want to wear rubber gloves.*

Activities

Skill Builder: Reading
Ask students to read the information on the packaging of several cleaning products to learn how they are used. What precautions, if any, are listed?

Skill Builder: Science
Have the students pool their knowledge and experience to compare commercial window cleaners with the one described in this section. They should compare effectiveness, price, and ease of use.

Skill Builder: Critical Thinking
Have students suggest ways that a person who really hates housework can make cleaning as simple as possible. For example, such people should not decorate with knickknacks because they have to be dusted.

can also be divided on a room-by-room basis. You may clean the bathroom and kitchen, while your brother or sister cleans and straightens up the family room or living room.

Sometimes a cleaning job is passed around from one family member to another. You might be responsible for cleaning the bathroom one week, and the next week your brother or sister would have the job. This kind of system is called rotating chores.

In the spirit of cooperation, if you see that your mother or older brother is very busy on a particular day, you could volunteer to clean up the living room, even if that's not your job. Likewise, if you see your father and sister working hard to clean out the garage or shovel snow off the walk, you can offer to give them a hand.

Prevention

One of the important areas of maintenance in a home is the **preventive** one. This means making sure that accidents and damage do not occur. You can do your part in preventive maintenance by keeping all the shared spaces in the home neat and safe for anyone who wants to use them.

You can keep the range clean so that grease won't build up and start a fire. You can put snack items such as crackers and chips away after you use them so they won't attract insects. You can wax wooden furniture so that spills won't spoil the finish. These are all examples of preventive maintenance.

What to Do

Cleaning isn't difficult; you probably know many of the procedures already. There are certain steps for cleaning each area of a home. If you use commercial cleaning products, follow the directions on the product containers. Misuse of a product can ruin what you're cleaning; it can also be dangerous. Chemicals in cleaning solutions may be very strong, and combinations may be deadly. For example, you should never use ammonia with liquid bleach.

- **Walls.** Check the walls for dirt and fingerprint marks. Use a sponge dampened with a cleaning solution to wipe fingerprints off doors, moldings, switches, drawers, and cabinets. Some paint and wallpaper can be washed, but others cannot, so if you're not sure, test in an inconspicuous spot.

For the most satisfactory cleaning results, follow the instructions on the product containers.

More About Cleaning Products Many cleaning products contain toxic substances such as lye, ammonia, and chlorine so it's important to exercise caution when using them. For example, chlorine bleach should never be mixed with cleaning products containing ammonia—as dangerous fumes would be released. The Consumer Product Safety Commission regulates cleaning products and requires that those containing hazardous substances have warning labels that alert users of the danger.

MANAGING RESOURCES

Who Does the Chores in Your Home?

A popular sign hangs in some offices where a microwave oven and refrigerator are available for use by the employees. It says, "Clean up your mess. Your mother doesn't live here." Most of these people might be surprised to find that even if their mother did live there, she would not clean up the mess.

In many of today's families, because of busy lifestyles, everyone needs to help with the housework. One way for everyone to share these tasks is to use problem-solving techniques to make a family cleaning plan:

- **Define goals.** An order of importance has to be established for each family. Some families have the goal of straightening up the living room before everyone goes to bed. Another goal may be to put the house in order on the weekend.
- **Make decisions.** Decide when and how each person will do his or her part of the cleaning. Will he or she have a specific job to do each week or will the chores be rotated?
- **Adjust your attitude.** If you do the cleaning as willingly and as cheerfully as possible, it will be less of a chore and more of a pleasure. Play music or listen to the radio to get you into a good rhythm for your duties. Think of how good you will feel after you have cleaned a room and everything is neat.
- **Analyze the steps.** The most efficient method for cleaning uses the fewest steps and the least amount of effort. Compare the amount of time that it takes to make a bed with a top sheet, two blankets, and a bedspread, or with only a sheet and a comforter.
- **Use resources.** Look at each job and collect the necessary equipment and cleaning aids. Gather paper towels, dust mop, dust cloth, furniture polish, and anything else that you need, before you begin to work. Try new products that may make your work easier.

Think It Through

1. **What other resource management skills can be applied to doing chores?**
2. **What decisions does your family make together about cleaning in your home? Why do such decisions need to be made?**

Teaching the Feature
"Who Does the Chores?"

Answers to Feature Questions

1. Answers will vary. Students may say they need to manage time, energy, and imagination, as well as helpers. These are all resources that with proper management can get chores done more efficiently.

2. Some of the decisions involve cleaning of shared areas, such as the bathroom, kitchen, and living areas. Other spaces, such as garages or basements, need family cooperation because everyone stores things there. The families may decide on a day or time to clean together, or each person may work at his or her own convenience. The family may agree to give up another luxury and hire someone to do the cleaning. It is not fair for one individual to be responsible for all the work, yet the work must be done. Decisions must be made so the work can get done as efficiently and painlessly as possible.

Activities

Whistle While You Work Ask students to talk about their attitude toward chores. Then discuss whether this attitude might be improved by changing the routines or rotating chores to avoid boredom.

Setting Goals Have students set a cleaning goal for themselves that will improve the way they care for their living space (for example, to make the bed every morning, keep the desk neater, or help with the dinner dishes at night). Have students work at achieving their goals for a week, report on how successful they were, and evaluate the results of their efforts.

Community Contact Have selected students call cleaning services or talk to people who pay to have their homes cleaned. The students should then report to the class about costs and services offered, and answer questions about the advantages and disadvantages of using this kind of service.

Emphasize Point out that a task often seems overwhelming until you get started on it. The problem-solving techniques offered on this page can make a job seem more manageable and help people to take that important first step in getting the task done.

More About Using Resources Cleaning jobs are much easier if you use the right equipment. Tell students that it is important to choose proper cleaning supplies to do a job quickly and correctly.

Reteaching
Have students make a plan for cleaning the classroom. They should define goals, analyze the steps, assign tasks, list needed supplies, and estimate time. You may want to have students carry out the plan and then evaluate the results.

Enrichment
Have students interview several different families to find out how they divide up housecleaning chores. Discuss how the needs of different family members are served by the various plans.

- **Windows.** To clean windows, you can use a cloth or paper towel with a window cleaner. For a cheaper cleaning product, mix four cups of warm water, four teaspoons of baking soda, and one-fourth teaspoon of liquid bleach. Dry the window immediately, using a very dry, lint-free cloth or paper towel, otherwise it will streak.
- **Furniture and other objects.** Wooden furniture needs an occassional dusting. A dust cloth or duster will do the job. Some people use dusting sprays. You may wish to use furniture polish or wax occasionally.

  Upholstered furniture should be vacuumed to remove dust, lint, and pet hair. Use a special vacuum cleaner attachment to pick up dirt and hairs that collect in cracks. Turn cushions over occasionally to let the fabric wear evenly on both sides.

  When you clean the furniture in a room, you should also dust or clean the other objects in the room, such as the pictures, books, knickknacks, and lamps.

Some tasks, such as washing windows, can be rotated among different family members.

- **Floors.** How you clean a floor depends on the type of floor that it is. Carpeted floors can be vacuumed. If you spill something on carpeting, clean it up immediately with a sponge or brush and cold water. Clean smooth floors with a broom or dust mop. Vinyl and tile floors can be washed with a mop and water or with cleaning products designed for these kinds of floors. Hardwood floors may also need to be waxed occasionally with a good floor wax, and vinyl floors can be coated with an acrylic floor finish to shine and protect them.
- **Bathroom.** Use a sponge or cloth and scouring powder or liquid to clean the sink basin and bathtub. Then rinse them carefully. You'll need a toilet brush and toilet cleaner to clean and sanitize inside and outside the toilet. For this kind of cleaning, you may want to wear rubber gloves.

When to Do It

Some cleaning jobs need to be done more frequently than others. Cleaning your room and wiping out the sink and bathtub or shower after using them are routine chores. The kitchen counter needs to be cleaned after every meal.

Other day-to-day considerations will make cleaning easier for everyone. Clean up and put away food that you take out for an afterschool snack. If you take a snack to your room or have it in front of the TV, return your dirty dishes to the kitchen. Rinse them off or put them in the dishwasher.

Clean the floors and dust furniture on a regular basis. Waxing floors and washing windows can be done monthly or even less frequently. No matter how the cleaning chores are divided, it's important that they be done and that each family member does his or her part.

Real-Life Situations Pests such as flies, ants, roaches, silver bugs, and mice can carry germs and damage possessions. To keep pests under control, keep your home as clean as possible. Wipe up crumbs and spills immediately, wash dishes regularly, and remove garbage daily. Store food in sealed containers.

Did You Know? Even household plants need an occasional "cleaning." Wipe the leaves gently with a damp cloth, or place plants in the sink and spray with warm water. Not only will the leaves look shinier, but regular cleaning will help control tiny insects.

CHAPTER 72 REVIEW

Reviewing the Facts

1. Give three reasons for caring for your personal space.
2. How can caring for your own space be beneficial to your whole family?
3. What is the first step in keeping your living space neat?
4. After creating storage space, how can you make sure your room will be neat and clean?
5. What is home maintenance?
6. What are some ways to divide up chores in a home?
7. How can you help in the preventive maintenance of your home?
8. What two things can happen if you misuse a cleaning product?

Thinking Critically

1. Do you think it is OK for one family member to do most of the housework? Why or why not?
2. What do you like and dislike most about cleaning? Can you think of any way to make what you dislike more pleasant?

Applying Your Skills

1. **Making a Schedule.** Set up a weekly time chart that schedules all the routine chores that must be completed at your home. You may set up the chart for yourself only, or for you and other members of your family. Determine how much time you would spend cleaning.

2. **Figuring Costs.** Make a list of cleaning products and supplies you would need to thoroughly clean your home. Then realistically estimate how much you would have to spend. Assume you have *no* supplies at home, such as mops, pails, cleaners, and the like. How long do you think your newly purchased supplies will last?

3. **Looking for Ideas.** Skim a book on household hints for ten helpful ideas on caring for your living space. Write a short paper describing the ideas and explaining why they would be helpful. Be prepared to share the ideas with your class.

Answers to "Reviewing the Facts"

1. To avoid waste, to make life easier, and to make you feel better.
2. It affects the overall condition of the home and prevents unnecessary expenses for repairs and damages.
3. To find storage space for your possessions.
4. Put things away as you use them, and get into a routine for cleaning and straightening your room.
5. Keeping living space and joint belongings in good working order.
6. By task, by room, or on a rotation basis.
7. By keeping your home neat and safe, such as wiping up spills and putting things away.
8. It can ruin what you are cleaning; it can also be dangerous.

Answers to "Thinking Critically"

1. Students should say that they do not feel that it is fair to let one family member do most of the housework. Not helping to share with household responsibilities would be selfish and inconsiderate, as well as unfair.
2. Some may like to clean their room because of the satisfaction they get from seeing how nice it looks when they are finished. Dislikes may include cleaning their room, cleaning the bathroom, or cleaning up after someone else. To make chores more fun, listen to music, make a game of how quickly you can finish, or share chores with a friend.

COMPLETING THE CHAPTER

Summary

- Good home maintenance is the best way to avoid waste, make life easier, and help people feel comfortable in their living space.
- To avoid problems in the family, each person should care for his or her own space within the home.
- A routine for daily and weekly chores should be established to save time.
- Household chores can be shared by family members on a room-by-room or rotating basis.
- Preventive maintenance ensures that accidents and damage do not occur.

For Review

Objective Review Questions Have students complete the "Reviewing the Facts" section on this page.

Study Guide Have students complete the Study Guide from Chapter 72 of their *Student Workbook.*

Develop a Plan Have students develop a spring cleaning plan. Point out that this is the time for home maintenance projects that are done only occasionally, such as washing windows, cleaning carpets, and waxing floors. Students should determine who will do the job (a family member or a cleaning service) and estimate how long it will take. Is special equipment needed?

Role Play Have students work in pairs (couples) or small groups (families) to divide up household chores. Assign students roles (mother of four, working teen) and allow them to develop circumstances that affect their ability to contribute to home maintenance.

For Evaluation

Synthesis Have students make a plan for cleaning a one-bedroom apartment. The plan should include a schedule, a list of cleaning supplies, and an estimate of time.

Chapter Test Have students complete the test for Chapter 72 that appears in the *Teacher's Classroom Resources.*

CHAPTER OVERVIEW

Chapter 73 makes students aware of the dangers that can be present in a home. It assesses the most common causes of home accidents—falls, cuts, poisonings, fires, and electrical problems—and suggests strategies for preventing these mishaps. Students learn about ways to protect their health by making responsible decisions around the house.

INTRODUCING THE CHAPTER

Motivators

Ouch! That Hurts! Have students talk about instances in which they had an accident at home. Ask students to categorize their accidents as falls, cuts, burns, or poisonings.

Using the Photograph Have students study the photograph on this page. Then ask: "What is the woman installing? What is it for? Do you have one or more of them at home?"

Avoiding Accidents Ask students to think about times when they have narrowly avoided being hurt and how the accident was prevented. What safety rules can be formulated from the students' experiences?

Introducing the Objectives

Discuss the chapter objectives on this page. Remind students that the objectives focus on important chapter content.

Introducing Vocabulary

Tell students that when a word ends with the suffix *proof,* it means that "it can't happen." Thus *fireproof* tells us that the item can't catch fire. Ask students to think of other words that end in *proof* (waterproof, mistake-proof, accident-proof, burglar-proof).

TEACHING THE CHAPTER

For convenience, the teaching suggestions for this chapter are arranged according to the following lesson topics:

- "Assessing the Dangers," pages 653-654
- "Preventing Accidents," pages 654-657

CHAPTER

73

Safety in the Home

OBJECTIVES

This chapter will help you to:

- Describe the most common dangers in the home.
- Prevent accidents such as falls, cuts, poisoning, electrical problems, and fire.

WORDS TO REMEMBER

accident
fireproof
pilot light
smoke detector

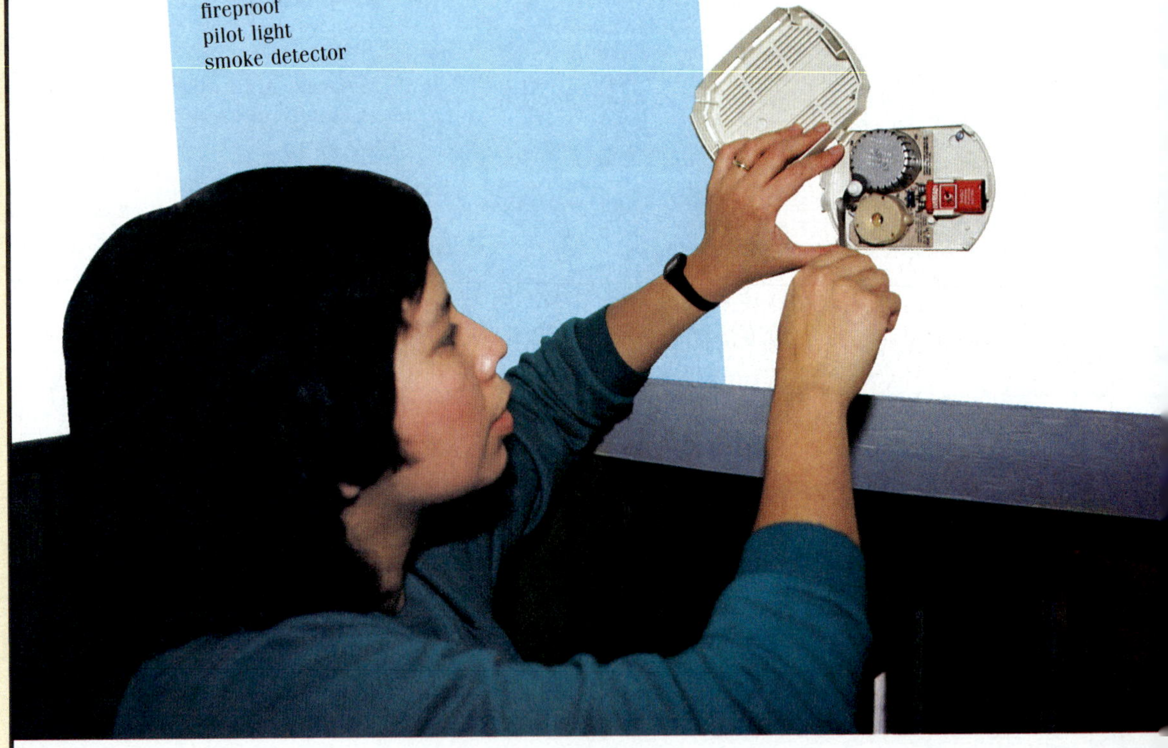

Chapter Resources

Teacher's Classroom Resources
- Lesson Plan
- Life Skills Activity, *All Through the House*
- Reproducible Master, *Prevent Accidents*
- Extension Activity, *First-Aid Kit*
- Chapter Test

Student Workbook
- Study Guide
- Worksheet, *An Ounce of Prevention*

A baseball player dashes from third base to home, trying to score a run. Because she has to take some risks to get home safely, she took some precautions before she left third base. She watched the other players and she got some signals from her coach. Her goal is to get home and hear the umpire yell "Safe!"

We like to think of our homes this way, but the truth is different. Each year in the United States, unexpected falls, fires, drownings, and poisonings injure about 4 million people and claim more than 25,000 lives in the place we like to consider the safest, our homes.

An **accident** is an unplanned, sudden event, and unfortunately, people often have accidents in the most familiar part of their homes. Many accidents don't have to happen if you take steps to make your home safe.

Assessing the Dangers

To prevent accidents from happening in your home, you must make responsible decisions, be aware of the dangers, stay on guard, and plan for prevention.

Before you take steps to avoid accidents, you need to know what the dangers are. Here are the most common causes of home accidents:

- **Falls and bumps.** One-third of all injuries and deaths in the home are the results of falls. Older people and children fall most often, but anyone can fall down a flight of stairs or slip on a wet floor.
- **Cuts.** Knife or scissor cuts may not be as serious as some other injuries, but they are avoidable if sharp objects are stored and used properly. Power tools and equipment such as saws and lawn mowers can cause serious injuries.

Preventing accidents in the home is the responsibility of all family members. What could you do to help make your home safer?

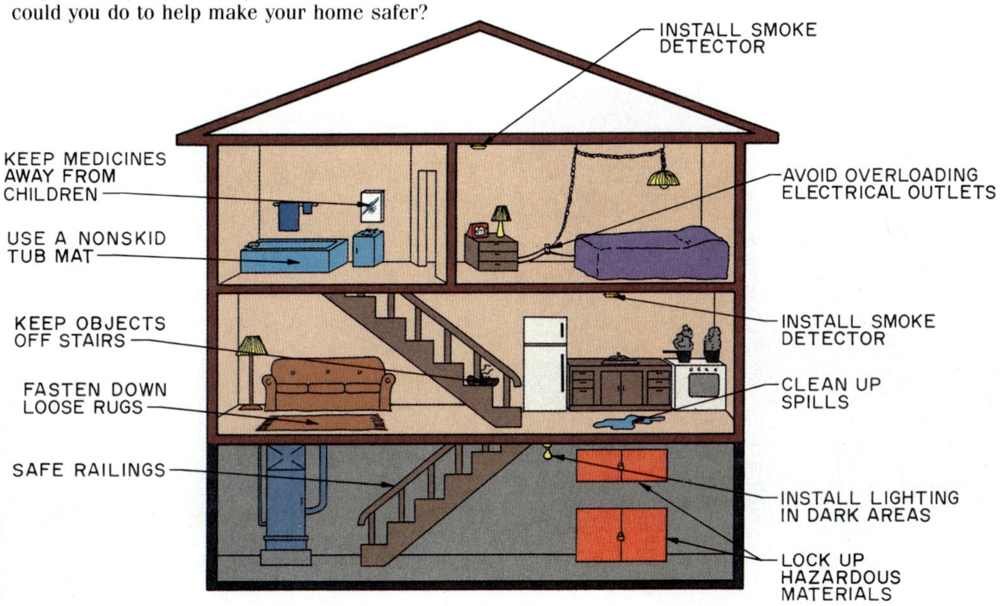

Teaching "Assessing the Dangers"
(Pages 653-654)

This section teaches that the most common causes of home accidents are falls and bumps, cuts, poisonings, and fires and electrical problems.

Checking Comprehension

✔ How can you keep people from getting hurt in the home? *You must make responsible decisions, be aware of the dangers, stay on guard, and plan for prevention.*

✔ How can knife and scissor cuts be avoided? *Sharp objects should be stored and used properly.*

✔ Why are children the most likely victims of poisoning? *Because they can't read labels, they're curious, and they're not likely to know about poisonous substances.*

✔ Name two ways that fires may start. *A lighted match can set a sofa on fire. Grease can start an oven fire.*

Activities

Skill Builder: Math
Have students research current statistics on home accidents. Ask them to report the numbers of accidents and figure out the percentage of injuries and deaths attributed to each category.

Skill Builder: Writing
Ask students to write about a responsible decision that they (or someone in their family) have made that has made their home a safer place to live. Have them hypothesize about what might have happened if the decision had not been made.

Reteaching
Ask students to look at the picture on page 653 and identify the kinds of accidents that might result in each area of the home.

Enrichment
Have selected students interview an emergency room nurse or a paramedic and find out about the kinds of injuries that result from the accidents in the home.

More About Poisonings More accidental poisonings occur in the second year of life. If a child should swallow a poisonous substance, call the poison control center and follow their directions.

Focus on Health Ask students to reread the relevant parts of Chapter 21 to re-emphasize how important safety precautions are when small children are in a home. Have students discuss the ways a home can be childproofed.

Teaching "Preventing Accidents"
(Pages 654-657)

This section identifies the kinds of situations in which falls, cuts, and poisoning are likely to occur and gives suggestions for prevention.

Checking Comprehension

✔ Where are falls most likely to happen? *On cluttered or slippery floors.*

✔ Why is it a good idea to anchor throw rugs? *So they won't skid.*

✔ How can small children be kept safe around stairways? *Small children should never be left around open stairs without gates at the top and bottom. Also, lock basement doors when small children are in the home.*

✔ How should knives be stored to prevent cuts? *Store knives with their handles toward the person opening the drawer.*

✔ What kind of shoes should be worn when mowing the lawn? *Always wear shoes with closed toes when running a lawn mower.*

✔ When are medicines poisonous? *Medicines such as aspirin and prescription drugs are poisonous if taken in excess.*

✔ How should poisonous substances be stored? *In locked cabinets or closets, out of children's reach, in childproof containers.*

✔ What should you do when you see that an electric plug isn't working properly? *If you see any sparks, pull the plug out slowly and don't use it again until it's fixed.*

- **Poisonings.** Little children, who can't read labels, are the most likely victims of poisoning. Children are very curious and not likely to know about poisonous substances.
- **Fires and electrical problems.** Fire is the second biggest killer in the home. A carelessly tossed, lighted match can set a sofa on fire. Grease can start an oven fire. Electrical shock accounts for accidental home deaths.

Preventing Accidents

Human factors should be considered when analyzing the causes and prevention of accidents. If you are alert to these conditions and know how to avoid them, you could save a life.

- **Carelessness.** Many accidents happen when people are under stress or when they are upset. People who are in a hurry or are tired are also more likely to have an accident.
- **Physical needs.** Young children have not developed the physical coordination and awareness to avoid many accidents, whereas elderly people may not be able to react quickly in the face of an emergency. Special cautions may be necessary to keep such family members safe from accidents, especially falls.

Preventing Falls

Falls can happen anywhere, but they're most likely to happen on cluttered or slippery floors. Keep toys, books, and newspapers off the floor, especially where people may be walking, such as from a bedroom to the bathroom. People can slip on freshly scrubbed or waxed floors. Simply putting up a sign—CAUTION: WET FLOORS—will tell others that you've cleaned the floors and warn them to walk carefully.

Six other steps will help you make floors safe:

- Wipe up spills immediately, so people won't slip.
- Keep rooms and hallways well lit, so people can see objects.
- Anchor throw rugs with carpet tape or hook-and-loop tape, so they won't skid.
- Arrange furniture so it will not be in people's way.
- Shorten long electrical cords or speaker wires, or secure them with electrical tape to keep them out of walkways.
- Use stepladders to reach high shelves.

To help prevent falls, secure small rugs with carpet tape.

Emphasize Certain circumstances tend to increase accidents. For example, many accidents happen when people are under stress, upset, or in a hurry. Some accidents can be prevented just by recognizing when we are in one of these states. Remind students to stop what they are doing and take a few deep breaths if they are tense or upset. That way, they are less likely to get hurt.

Cross-Reference See information about first aid on page 207.

Lighting is very important on stairways. Stairways should also be kept clear of clutter; an open stairway is not for storage. Don't put a throw rug at the top of the stairs where someone could slip and fall down the stairs. Stairs should have sturdy handrails, and small children should never be left around open stairs without gates at the top and bottom. Be careful, also, to lock basement doors when there are small children in the home.

Many falls happen in the bathtub and shower because of slippery conditions. Nonskid mats or strips that stick to the bottom can help prevent these falls. Install handrails on the wall near the tub or toilet, and a tub seat for elderly family members who have trouble sitting or standing steadily.

Preventing Cuts

The kitchen, workrooms, and the outdoors are the danger areas where cuts and injuries from tools and equipment most often occur. Proper storage and proper use of knives and other sharp cooking utensils can prevent cuts from occurring in the kitchen. Store knives with their handles toward the person opening the drawer. Keep all knives and scissors out of the reach of children.

Power tools and saws, stored in workrooms and garages, are dangerous objects. These tools should be stored out of children's reach, and their blades should be safely covered.

Care must be taken when operating outdoor tools and machinery. Do not wear jewelry or loose-fitting clothing that could get caught when using these machines. Always wear shoes with closed toes when running a lawn mower. Leather shoes are safer than canvas. Turn off the power before adjusting or fixing any tool.

Preventing Poisoning

Most poisonings occur in the kitchen, bathroom, and bedroom. Many poisonings involve young children, whose curiosity leads them to explore things that they don't know are dangerous.

Closets, medicine chests, cabinets, laundry areas, and other storage areas hold many poisonous substances. Ammonia, bleach, cleansing powders, cosmetics and perfumes, detergents, furniture polish, fertilizers, gasoline, kerosene, paint thinner, and weed killers are all poisonous.

Medicines such as aspirin and prescription drugs are poisonous if they are taken in excess. Children are the most likely to swallow medications that they see adults regularly take. You should never refer to medicine as "candy."

Keep medicines and other dangerous substances high and out of the reach of children. Buy medicines that come in child-proof containers.

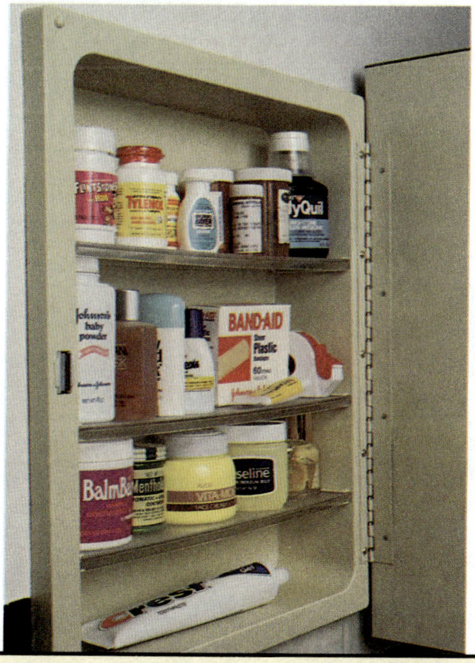

✔ How can the use of extension cords help to prevent electrical problems? *Extension cords that distribute appliances among several outlets prevent circuits from being overloaded.*

✔ What might happen if you use electrical appliances when you are wet? *You could suffer a serious electrical shock.*

✔ What is a pilot light? *A thin stream of gas burned constantly and used to light a gas burner on a range.*

Activities

Skill Builder: Critical Thinking
Have students make a list of safety rules for individuals to follow to avoid falling on stairs and in the bathtub.

Skill Builder: Reading
Ask students to read a first aid manual to learn some ways of dealing with cuts, both minor and serious.

Skill Builder: Writing
Have students make an inventory of where in their homes sharp objects are located and how they are stored. When necessary, students should recommend solutions to storage problems.

Real-Life Situations To protect the home against intruders and theft, always keep doors locked. Replace spring-bolt locks with dead-bolt locks. For added protection, install sliding bolts at the top of doors. Insert a viewer in the front door so you can see who is there before opening the door. To secure sliding glass doors, use restraining rods or chain bolts. Keep all windows closed and locked when away from home. Steel grills can be attached inside windows for protection on the first floor or by fire escapes. However, they should be able to be quickly opened in case of fire. When away, attach timers to lights in two areas of your home.

Skill Builder: Math
Ask students to count the number of electrical appliances in their home (including lamps and televisions) that remain constantly plugged in. Have them determine how the appliances are distributed among outlets and report their findings room by room. Students should identify problem areas and indicate where extension cords could be used.

Reteaching
Visit the technology class and have the teacher talk to students about safety precautions to be taken around power tools. If possible, have selected students try some power tools and ascertain why the safety rules are important.

Preventing poisoning involves these steps:

- Lock all cabinets, closets, or other storage areas that contain poisons.
- Keep dangerous substances high and out of children's reach.
- Warn children not to swallow these products.
- Purchase medicines that come in childproof containers.
- Never place medicine in a container that lacks a warning label.

Preventing Electrical Problems

Most electrical accidents are caused by problems with plugs, outlets, and extension cords and by the improper use of electrical appliances. Here are steps you can take to prevent electrical problems:

- **Plugs and outlets.** Pull furniture away from the wall and inspect electrical cords. Pay special attention to plugs. Unplug and plug them in again while you watch for sparks. If you see any sparks, pull the plug out slowly and don't use it again until it's fixed. When there are small children in the home, cover all unused outlets with plastic safety covers to prevent children from sticking their fingers or other objects into the outlets.
- **Extension cords.** Avoid plugging too many electrical appliances into the same outlet. Otherwise you could overload the circuits and start a fire. Use extension cords to distribute the appliances among several outlets. Keep extension cords out of traffic areas so that no one trips over them, but do not run the cords under rugs or carpeting.
- **Appliances.** Check all appliances for safe wiring. Cords should be well covered with insulation and there should be no fraying. Unplug small appliances and put them away when they're not in use, and clear all dust away from the appliances' motors after you unplug them. Never use electrical appliances when you're wet or have wet hands as you could suffer a serious electrical shock. Also, never use appliances around sinks or bathtubs—they might fall into the water and cause you to be electrocuted.

Learn how to detect electrical hazards. Check electrical cords for broken plugs or exposed wires. Be sure that outlets are not overloaded with too many plugs.

Did You Know? There are four stages in a fire. In the first stage, the fire smolders but there is no smoke, flame, or heat. Smoke appears in the second stage, and in the third stage there is flame. The fourth and final stage is characterized by intense heat. A smoke detector actually detects the fire in the first stage, before there is a considerable amount of smoke. The detector is set off by the invisible gases that are generated as the fire smolders.

Preventing Fire

No home can be made **fireproof**, completely protected from the danger of fire, but steps can be taken to reduce the chances of a fire's occurring. Check electrical outlets and appliances as the first step. Don't store anything near the heater or the furnace. Don't pile papers, wood, or oily rags in a corner, especially near a range, a fireplace, or an electrical source.

Keep the kitchen clean to prevent grease fires. Avoid clutter around the range and check the pilot light on a gas range to be sure that it is working properly. A **pilot light** is a thin stream of gas burned constantly and used to light a gas burner on a range. Because many fires start in the kitchen, keep a fire extinguisher there.

Use matches and candles safely. Always be sure that a burned match is cold and wet before throwing it in the trash. Cigarettes should be completely put out and smokers should never smoke in bed. Finally, use fireplaces and wood stoves carefully.

Sometimes, despite all precautions, a fire occurs. Your family is more likely to survive a fire if it has **smoke detectors**. When they sense smoke, these devices, usually battery-operated, sound an alarm to warn occupants of the home. There should be a smoke detector on each level of your home, and one near the sleeping area. Check the battery regularly to see that the device is working.

A major part of fire safety is knowing how to leave the home if a fire occurs. Be sure that everyone in the home knows an escape route. Home fire drills should be a part of this procedure.

Smoke detectors can save lives by alerting family members to smoke or fire. Is your home protected by smoke detectors?

Enrichment
Have selected students call Poison Control and find out about the service. How many calls do they get? How do they help? What are the most common problems?

Enrichment
Ask students to price home fire extinguishers and find out how they should be used. If possible, demonstrate their use.

Focus on Life Management Have selected students contact insurance companies to find out about homeowner's insurance that would protect a family from the financial devastation of a home fire. Have students discuss the risk/benefit trade-off involved in this kind of insurance.

Focus on Consumer Skills Have students price some of the home safety equipment suggested in this section and figure out how much it would cost to install adequate safety equipment in their own homes.

Teaching the Feature
"Home Fire Drills"

Answers to Feature Questions

1. Students may give several reasons, such as they never think it's going to happen to them in their home, people think that they can easily get out of their home in an emergency, or they may think that having smoke detectors and fire extinguishers are sufficient precautions.

2. Students may answer that there are children or babies in the family who need help. Adults or older children should be responsible for their safety. Elderly persons may need assistance, and special arrangements must be made for people with disabilities. They may need to have bedrooms on a first floor, in addition to another family member to check on their welfare.

Activities

Plan an Escape Have students draw a floor plan for their own home, showing all doors, windows, stairways, porches, and porch roofs, and outside fire escapes. They should then diagram a plan for escaping a fire and indicate *two* ways to reach the ground from each room, especially from bedrooms. Have them mark both routes on their floor plan. Decide where an escape ladder should be kept, if necessary. Ask them to estimate how long it would take to negotiate each escape route.

In Case of Fire Suggest that students write a fire escape plan for their home. They should list all exits and describe the basic fire safety rules. Students might show their plan to their parents, refine it as necessary, then make sure younger siblings are aware of it. Be sure they report results in class and write up the changes they made.

Community Contact Have selected students investigate the fire protection provided by the community. Are the fire fighters full-time employees or volunteers? What is the average response time? What type of equipment do they have?

HEALTH WATCH

Home Fire Drills

Schools have them. Businesses have them. Have you ever had a fire drill in your home? Does everyone in your family know the best exits from the house or apartment in case of fire? Proper planning for a fire emergency can—and does—save lives.

Here are seven steps to follow:

- **Have a planning meeting that everyone in the family must attend.** Discuss safety measures.
- **Establish escape routes.** Everyone should know the best way to get from each room in the home to the outdoors. Determine alternative exits, if the first escape route is blocked. Where should a chain ladder be kept? Does everyone know how to attach it?
- **Set up a buddy system.** If there are small children in the home, determine who could get to them fastest. You may decide that each family member should be responsible for one other family member.
- **Plan a meeting place.** Establish a meeting place outdoors where everyone should come immediately after leaving the home. This way you will know that everyone is safe. Call the fire department from a neighbor's home. Never go back into a burning home to save pets or possessions.
- **Try out each escape route.** Time the route and make changes, if necessary. Draw all the routes on a floor plan and review the plan with the whole family.
- **Hold a fire drill with all family members.** Have it at a time when everyone is home, and preferably when people are in different areas of the house. Set off the smoke detector alarm and check that it can be heard all through the house. Can it be heard in the bathroom when the water is running?
- **Follow up with a meeting to discuss and analyze the results.** If there are changes, have another drill a week or so later.

Think It Through

1. **Why do you think that people do not bother to have home fire drills? Are these valid reasons?**
2. **Do you have any family members who would have difficulty in getting out of the building in case of a fire? What special plans are made for their safety?**

More About Escape Routes Students should discuss escape routes with family members and tell them to stay low or even crawl when escaping a fire. People must also be reminded to feel doors before opening them during a fire; doors that feel hot should be kept closed.

Emphasize Tell students not to panic and run if their clothing catches fire. They should cross their arms over their chests, drop to the floor, and roll over and over slowly. If possible, others should wrap them in a wool blanket, coat, rug, or curtains as they roll on the floor.

CHAPTER

73 REVIEW

Reviewing the Facts

1. Approximately how many home injuries occur yearly in the United States?
2. What are four main types of accidents that occur in the home?
3. List three ways to prevent falls.
4. What can you do to prevent cuts from occurring?
5. Name five common household substances that are poisonous.
6. List two ways to prevent electrical problems.
7. Where should smoke alarms be placed?
8. What is a major part of fire safety?

Thinking Critically

1. What family members live in or visit your home who need to pay special attention to safety features? What have you done to make your home safer for them?
2. Have you ever had an accident because you were in a hurry or upset? What precautions should you have taken so it wouldn't have happened? Why?

Applying Your Skills

1. **Making a Diagram.** Draw a diagram of your home marking the best escape route out of the building from your bedroom in case of fire.

2. **Evaluating Your Home.** Make a safety survey of your own home. List preventive measures that have already been taken in one column, and those that need attention in another column. Compare lists with your classmates.

3. **Researching a Problem.** Read an article or book about a person who is physically disabled. What special modifications would you have to make to your home to accommodate that person's special needs?

Answers to "Reviewing the Facts"

1. Approximately four million people are injured each year.
2. Any four: falls and bumps; cuts; poisonings; electrical problems; fire.
3. Any three: wipe up spills; keep rooms and hallways well lit; anchor throw rugs; keep furniture out of path of traffic; shorten or secure electrical cords; use stepladder; warn of newly washed or waxed floors.
4. Use and store knives and scissors properly.
5. Any five: ammonia; bleach; cleansing powders; cosmetics and perfumes; detergents; fertilizers; furniture polish; gasoline; kerosene; paint thinner; weed killer.
6. Any two: check plugs and outlets; cover unused outlets with caps; check extension cords; don't overload outlets; check appliance cords; unplug appliances after use; never use appliances when you are wet or near water.
7. On each level of the home and in sleeping areas.
8. Knowing how to leave the home if fire occurs.

Answers to "Sharing Your Ideas"

1. Students may answer that they have younger brothers and sisters, a family member who is disabled, or older relatives who live with them or visit. They should mention safety precautions that would help prevent accidents.
2. Students may answer that they slipped on the floor, fell down the stairs, cut their fingers, and so on. The cause may have been a slippery floor, items on the stairs, incorrect use of a knife, etc. Precautions would be to take more time, watch out for hazards, use tools correctly, etc. By taking precautions, you can help prevent accidents to yourself and others.

COMPLETING THE CHAPTER

Summary

- The most common home accidents are falls and bumps, cuts, poisonings, fires, and electrical problems.
- Accidents are often caused by carelessness and lack of physical coordination or quick reactions, especially of young children.
- Accidents can be prevented by making responsible decisions, being aware of the dangers, staying on guard, and planning for prevention.

For Review

Objective Review Questions Have students complete the "Reviewing the Facts" section on this page.

Study Guide Have students complete the Study Guide from Chapter 73 of their *Student Workbook.*

Checklist Have students compile a safety checklist that could be used when renting or buying an apartment or a house. What should people look for? What kinds of things would indicate that the home is not safe?

Do a Safety Check Have students do a safety check of the classroom, checking for fire or electrical hazards, poisonous materials, sharp objects, and other dangers. Also ask students to comment on how preventive measures have created a safe environment.

For Evaluation

Problem Solving Give students a drawing of a home (or a room) with various safety hazards (perhaps the picture on page 653 or one like it). Ask students to identify the hazards and offer appropriate solutions.

Synthesis Have students design a warning label for an electrical appliance that would help the users of the appliance to avoid falls, electrical problems, fires, and cuts.

Chapter Test Have students complete the test for Chapter 73 that appears in the *Teacher's Resource Book.*

Reteaching
Show students some insulation, weather stripping, and a thermostat and demonstrate how they work.

Reteaching
Ask students to try light bulbs of different wattages in their desk lamp or bedside light and evaluate how much wattage is sufficient for various activities (dressing, doing homework, working on hobbies).

Reteaching
To make students aware of how much water they use, have them keep a list, for a day, of all the times they used water. Their list should include their shower or bath, brushing their teeth, drinking water, flushing the toilet, washing the dishes, and so on. Ask students to compare their totals in class.

Enrichment
Have students chart their family's energy bills for a year to see how energy use differs as the seasons changes.

Enrichment
Suggest that students try to do without one or two appliances (toaster, makeup mirror, electric toothbrush) for a week and then report on how much of an inconvenience it was. What kind of adjustments did they have to make? Would they consider doing without the appliance altogether?

Enrichment
Suggest that students try to save water for a week by following the suggestions gleaned from the text and in classroom discussions. Have them report on how it went.

- Turn off electric lights and appliances such as the radio and TV when no one is in the room.
- Replace high-wattage bulbs with low-wattage ones if light isn't needed for reading or close work.
- Use fluorescent bulbs in the kitchen, bathroom, and workroom. They use less energy than incandescent bulbs.

When buying large appliances that use a great deal of energy every day, look for the EnergyGuide labels on many of these appliances. These labels estimate the cost of running the appliance for one year. You can use these labels to find the model that uses energy most efficiently.

You can also check appliances for energy-saving features. Dishwashers should have controls to allow the user to skip the drying cycle. Instant-on TV sets use more energy then those that take time to warm up.

Gas

Four important pieces of home equipment can run on natural or propane gas—the heating system, the water heater, the clothes dryer, and the range. Follow the tips for managing electric energy mentioned earlier.

Another way to save gas is to buy equipment with an electronic ignition. On standard gas equipment, the pilot light burns constantly even when the equipment isn't in use. By lighting the flame electronically, newer models no longer need the pilot light.

Water

Water is an important and increasingly scarce resource. In some parts of the country, water is scarce because of the terrain, and in others, people sometimes have to ration water because of droughts. You can easily save water by following these suggestions:

- Wash clothes and dishes only when the washing machine and dishwasher are full.
- Take showers instead of baths and keep your daily showers short. A typical tub bath uses 10 to 15 gallons of water, whereas a five-minute shower uses 8 to 12 gallons.
- Don't let water run continuously while shaving, brushing your teeth, or working at the sink. Turn faucets off and on as needed, and turn them off completely after you use them.
- If you wash dishes by hand, use a dishpan or put a stopper in the sink. Washing dishes under continually running water wastes about 30 gallons of water per meal.
- Always fix dripping faucets and other water leaks promptly. A faucet that leaks one drop of water per second wastes 192 gallons of clean water per month.

Turn faucets off completely after use. Fix dripping faucets as soon as possible.

Focus on Decision Making Have students role play a situation in which they are the committee that must set priorities for water use in case of severe water rationing.

Cross-Reference See more information about EnergyGuide labels on page 390.

Did You Know? Gas was first used commercially in homes in 1792 when a British engineer named William Murdock heated coal in an iron vessel and conducted gas through 70 feet of tin and copper tubes to light his home.

TECHNOLOGY

The Smart Home

How smart is your home? Can it turn off the lights? Can it lock doors and windows? Can it turn on the water in the bathtub so that your bath is ready when you get home?

The home of the not-so-distant future will be able to do all of these things, and more, through the technology of **home automation.** This technology can automatically control systems in a home using electricity, electronics, and appliances equipped with microchips. The appliances "talk" to each other and to the house. The "smart house" is convenient and energy efficient.

The level of automation can range from a basic on-off system for lights to a fully automated home where the climate, security, entertainment, and all other systems are controlled through a central panel.

The simplest approach to home automation is a product that plugs into any home. Any electric appliance with an on-off switch can be plugged into a module that is controlled by a hand-held cordless device similar to a TV remote control. The system can be programmed to turn heat up or down automatically or to turn TV, stereos, and lights on or off.

The next level of automation is aimed at home security. Window and door sensors respond if they are opened, closed, or tampered with.

The fully automated home requires complete rewiring, or installation at the time the home is built. Any appliance can be plugged into it and activated from any location. It can be controlled from a phone or TV.

Engineers estimate that energy costs can be cut by 20 to 50 percent through the use of this system. It will be able to turn lights out when no one is in the room, automatically control the water temperature and usage in a dishwasher, control the temperature and humidity in the home, as well as choose music and cook meals.

The engineers and architects who are designing these homes are making every effort to make these systems easy for anyone to understand. They believe that today's teens, who are growing up with computers, will have no problem adapting to fully automated homes.

Think It Through

1. **What features of the automated homes appeal to you the most? Why?**
2. **Suggest some ways that your home is automated or could be automated now.**

Teaching the Feature

"The Smart Home"

Answers to Feature Questions

1. Students may answer with any of the illustrations given. Reasons for appeal may be that people in their family forget to turn the lights off when they leave a room; there may be handicapped or elderly people in the home who would appreciate the convenience; a vacation home could be "watched" by the computer; automated homes conserve energy and the money saved could be used on other things.

2. Students may answer that their homes already have automatic timers on lights, electronic appliances such as microwave ovens or coffee makers that can be programmed to come on at a specific time, VCRs to tape programs when they're not at home, remote controls for entertainment appliances, and automated garage-door openers.

Activities

The Automated Kitchen Have students research the ways in which computers can be used in the kitchen. Ask them if a computer can keep track of what food is available and its nutritional content. Which appliances can be run by computer, and what special features do they have?

Home of the Future Have students read about robots and robotics and suggest ways that robots could be used in an automated home.

Community Contact Invite a representative from a home security firm to come in and talk to the students about automated security systems and demonstrate how some of the equipment, including door and window sensors, works.

Emphasize A few years ago, the popular television cartoon show *The Jetsons* introduced audiences to a space-age family living in an automated home. Their home had all the features described here, as well as others. Now engineers say that many of these systems will be available in the next few years.

Focus on Technology Have students consider not only the advantages, but also the disadvantages, of a computer-run home.

COMPLETING THE CHAPTER

Summary

- Energy is the capacity for doing work. We use it to make electricity and produce heat.
- Electricity, oil, coal, and natural gas are all important energy sources. Alternative sources include wood and the sun.
- People can save energy by regulating heating and cooling and by weatherproofing their homes with insulation and weather stripping.
- Energy can be conserved with careful use of appliances and by buying energy-efficient appliances.
- Careful use of water is important to conserve this increasingly scarce resource.

For Review

Objective Review Questions Have students complete the "Reviewing the Facts" section on this page.

Study Guide Have students complete the Study Guide from Chapter 74 of their *Student Workbook*.

Debate an Issue Nuclear energy is a very controversial way of meeting our energy needs. Ask students to research the facts and debate the pros and cons of nuclear energy.

Community Action Have students discuss ways that they can contribute to their community's effort to conserve energy.

For Evaluation

Develop a Plan Have students develop a comprehensive plan that they believe would result in an overall 10 percent reduction in their family's energy bill (including oil, gas, electricity, and water).

Chapter Test Have students complete the test for Chapter 74 that appears in the *Teacher's Classroom Resources.*

CHAPTER 74 REVIEW

Answers to "Reviewing the Facts"

1. The burning of fuel, hydroelectric power, nuclear reactors.
2. Electricity, oil, natural gas. Alternate sources (any two): wood, coal, sun (solar).
3. Climate where you live, size and age of your home, and size of your family.
4. Any four: lower thermostat setting when away or sleeping; put thermostats in different rooms; set air conditioner higher; use fans instead of air conditioners; use drapes; close fireplace damper when not in use; add insulation; add weatherstripping.
5. R-value. The higher the R-value, the better the insulation.
6. Material used to fill gaps between the door and door frame and around windows so less air leaks in and out.
7. Use electricity carefully and buy energy-efficient appliances.
8. Any three: wash clothes and dishes only when you have a full load; take showers rather than baths; don't let water run; wash dishes in dishpan; fix leaks promptly.

Reviewing the Facts

1. What three sources of power can a utility company use to produce electricity?
2. What are three main sources of home-heating energy? What are two alternate sources of heat?
3. List three factors that affect your family's energy use.
4. Suggest four steps a family can take to cut down on its home-heating costs.
5. How can you compare different types of insulation?
6. What is weather stripping?
7. In what two ways can you manage electricity costs better?
8. List three ways that you can save water.

Thinking Critically

1. If you had your own home, what would you do to manage energy efficiently? Explain your answer.
2. What, in your opinion, is the best source of energy for housing? Why?

Applying Your Skills

1. **Writing Directions.** Think of a project you could sew or build yourself that could save energy in your home. Write out instructions and include a diagram.
2. **Evaluating Energy Use.** If you were in charge of maintenance at your school, what actions would you take to conserve energy in the school? Write a detailed description to be shared with the class.
3. **Drawing Conclusions.** Ask several adult relatives, friends, or teachers what type of energy they use to heat their home. Try to find three people who each use a different type of energy—electricity, gas, or oil. Ask each person which factors were involved in the decision to use this type of energy. What are the advantages and disadvantages of using it? How do the three sets of answers compare with one another?

Answers to "Thinking Critically"

1. Students may answer that they would watch the use of lights and appliances, turn thermostats down in the winter, use fans instead of air-conditioners, add insulation and weatherstripping, dress to be comfortable according to the temperature, cover windows with storm windows or plastic film to keep cold out, and so on.
2. Answers will vary. Students might give as reasons the cost and availability of that energy source.

CHAPTER

75

Careers in Housing

OBJECTIVES

This chapter will help you to:

- Develop the interests and skills needed for careers in housing.
- Identify various jobs available in housing.

WORDS TO REMEMBER

architect
blueprint
construction
visualize

Chapter Resources

Teacher's Classroom Resources
- Lesson Plan
- Life Skills Activity, *Write a Job Description*
- Reproducible Master, *Do I Want to Work in Housing?*
- Extension Activity, *Careers in Housing*
- Chapter Test

Student Workbook
- Study Guide
- Worksheet, *On the Job*

CHAPTER OVERVIEW

Chapter 75 makes students aware of the careers that are available in the housing field. It identifies the interests and skills that could lead to a career in housing design, construction, sales, or maintenance. Jobs are described and divided into three categories—entry-level, those that require training, and those that require a degree. Students learn about the decision-making skills needed to get a job and succeed in it.

INTRODUCING THE CHAPTER

Motivators

Interest Survey Review with the students the chapter titles from this unit and ask them to think about which subjects they found most interesting and why. Were they interested enough in the topic to consider a careeer in that area?

Using the Photograph Have students study the photograph on this page. Then ask: "What area of housing are these people involved in? What skills are needed to succeed in this type of job?"

Career List Have students list as many jobs dealing with housing as they can think of.

Introducing the Objectives

Discuss the chapter objectives on this page. Remind students that the objectives focus on important chapter content.

Introducing Vocabulary

Tell students that the word *blueprint* refers to a mechanical drawing that turns color when exposed to ammonia. Originally the process produced white lines on a blue background; hence the name *blueprint*. Today most of these drawings are done on mylar (similar to tracing paper), which is stronger than paper and more stable. Blueprints now consist of blue or black lines on a white background, but the name *blueprint* still holds.

TEACHING THE CHAPTER

For convenience, the teaching suggestions for this chapter are arranged according to the following lesson topics:

- "Characteristics for Careers in Housing," page 668
- "Jobs in Design, Construction and Sales," pages 669-670
- "Jobs in Home Maintenance and Use" and "Getting a Job," pages 672-673

Teaching "Characteristics for Careers in Housing"

(Page 668)

This section provides an overall look at the skills and interests needed for a career in housing.

Checking Comprehension

✔ What must all people who work in the housing business understand? *People in this business must have a feeling for people and their lifestyles.*

✔ Name two housing professionals who must be able to visualize, and explain why visualization is important. *Carpenters must be able to read a blueprint to visualize a room so they can know how to build it. Interior designers look at a floor plan and then picture how carpeting, wall coverings, and window treatments will match the lines of the furniture.*

✔ Why must designers, builders, and salespeople be able to communicate with people? *Because they have to work closely with their clients, learning what the client wants and making him or her feel comfortable.*

✔ Where can people learn about plumbing, heating and air conditioning? *This knowledge is often acquired on the job or in a technical school.*

Shelter is one of the basic human needs. Comfortable, affordable housing must be planned, built, furnished, decorated, maintained, and sold. Because of this, the housing industry provides jobs and careers for hundreds of thousands of people.

The largest segment of careers in housing is in **construction**, the building of homes. Over one and a half million homes are built every year. These homes may be single-family dwellings or multiple family units.

In the building industry, people are needed to become carpenters, masons, plumbers, plasterers, electricians, painters, and paperhangers. Carpenters are by far the largest group in the building industry.

Many people who start in the home building industry move into commercial construction of stores, office buildings, warehouses, restaurants, apartment buildings, and factories.

Characteristics for Careers in Housing

People who work in the housing industry do not work simply with houses. First and foremost, they work with people. Whether they are designing, constructing, selling, or maintaining a house, people in this business must have a feeling for people and their lifestyles.

Interests and Skills

- **Can you see a finished product by looking at a plan?** Housing workers must be able to **visualize**, or see in their minds, how a completed project might look. Carpenters must be able to read a **blueprint**, the architect's plan or mechanical drawing, to visualize a room so they can know how to build it. Interior designers look at a floor plan and then picture how the furniture can be arranged.
- **Do you communicate with people easily and work well with them?** Designers, builders, and salespeople work closely with their clients, learning what the client wants and making him or her feel comfortable. It makes the work satisfying and leads the clients to recommend the expert or worker to their friends.
- **Do you like fixing up your room by selecting new colors or rearranging your furniture?** Do you have fun picking out new posters for your room? Your interest in colors and shapes may mean that you can use your skills in a housing career.
- **Are you interested in learning how buildings are created and how to use the materials that go into construction?** If you're interested in learning how to work with plastics, pipes, concrete, wood, and bricks, there are many jobs that use these abilities. In addition, the knowledge of plumbing, heating, and air conditioning leads to well-paying jobs. This knowledge is often learned on the job or in a technical school that prepares people for a career.
- **Do you pay attention to detail?** Housing workers must be thorough and complete. A cabinetmaker must make the tops of cabinet doors line up perfectly. A building inspector must check carefully for safety hazards. If you are patient and thorough in your work, you have this characteristic.

Focus on Life Management Encourage students to list 15 things that they do well; then have them use the list to evaluate what careers in housing may suit them. What other kinds of jobs might their personal strengths lead them to pursue?

More About Communicating Tell students that housing professionals who work with people need good listening skills. Explain that one way to improve listening skills is to paraphrase what the speaker just said to make sure you got it right. Another is to work at maintaining eye contact with the speaker.

Jobs in Design, Construction, and Sales

You might want to consider being part of the housing business that plans, builds, and sells homes. These jobs are open to men and women who have the interest and have learned the skills that are in demand.

Entry-Level Jobs

Landscape gardeners must like to work with plants, bushes, trees, and flowers. Generally they work outdoors and many jobs in this field are seasonal. However, there is a growing demand for gardeners to work year-round at offices and shopping malls taking care of indoor plants. Some landscape gardeners have their own businesses, working at many different locations during the week. Others work at apartment and office buildings, or on college or government campuses, caring for larger areas.

Construction workers include carpenters, electricians, masons, painters, plumbers, and roofers. These workers are usually good at working with their hands and have learned special skills for their trade. Many begin their work as apprentices, helpers who are trained on the job by the senior workers. Construction workers can work for building contractors or be self-employed.

Jobs That Require Training

Retail wallpaper, fabric, and furniture stores often have decorating consultants to help customers select appropriate colors, fabrics, and furniture for new homes or redecorating projects.

Some people hire an interior designer to help them improve the appearance of their homes. This is a professional who is trained to work with colors, line, form, texture, unity, and composition to design or redesign one room or a whole house. Depending on the client's budget and wishes, an interior designer might decorate new walls or suggest new arrangements of furniture to make the home more functional.

Decorating consultants and interior designers help people plan living space that is comfortable, attractive, and appropriate to their lifestyle.

Activities

Skill Builder: Math
Have students locate the figures on "housing starts" for the past ten years (these are available in the library in *Statistical Abstracts of the United States, Business Statistics,* and other publications). Tell the students to draw a graph or chart to show annual variations, then discuss what this means for people who work in housing careers.

Skill Builder: Science
Ask students to visualize a geometric design. First have them execute the design on paper. Then have them describe the figure to another student who draws it from the description. Have students compare their drawings and talk about the difficulty in visualizing designs.

Skill Builder: Writing
Have students list their hobbies and describe the skills they are developing by pursuing those interests. Do any of the hobbies demonstrate an inclination toward a career in housing?

Reteaching
Show students a plan for a house in various stages: photograph of a site, blueprint, floor plan, pictures of undecorated rooms, finished product. At each stage ask students to visualize the next step.

Enrichment
Have students role play various situations in which a worker deals with a client. Possible situations are: interior designer and home owner; hair stylist and customer; sales clerk and customer. Point out that the purpose of the role play is to underline the need for good communication skills in working with clients.

Did You Know? Before pursuing a career as a real estate salesperson students should be aware that states have different licensing requirements for people who list and sell properties.

Emphasize City planning is an increasingly important field. Towns and cities have to be careful to use their resources wisely, and city planners can make sure that the community gets the most for their money and takes best advantage of natural resources.

Real estate agents help people who want to buy, sell, or rent homes and office space.

Consultants and designers usually take special courses in interior design at a professional school. Most designers are members of the American Society of Interior Designers (ASID). They may work for furniture stores or architects or have their own businesses.

A real estate salesperson helps people buy and sell homes. Buyers consult with a realtor and explain what size home they want, what location they want, and how much they can pay. The real estate salesperson tries to find a house or condominium that matches their needs.

A real estate career requires special training in housing financing and sales. The field is highly competitive, but other sales jobs provide good experience for real estate sales.

Jobs That Require a Degree

Architects actually design buildings and homes. They may design houses for individual families or huge apartment buildings for hundreds. They may create a new house or redesign an older one.

Architects must know about the materials used for building and about people's living patterns. They must also be able to visualize a completed project while it's still on the drawing board. Computer skills and the ability to work with computer-aided design are especially important to architects. A college degree and a license in architecture are required.

City planners work for local governments to guide the growth of an area. First they predict the future population of the area. Then they predict the people's needs for the facilities and services that make the area livable, such as housing, schools, shopping, recreation, and transportation. City planners suggest ways to meet future needs so that the city can grow in pace with the population. A college degree and computer skills are definite assets.

Teaching "Jobs in Design, Construction, and Sales"
(Pages 669-670)

This section describes the sectors of the housing field that plan, build, and sell homes.

Checking Comprehension

- Name six kinds of construction workers. *Carpenters, electricians, masons, painters, plumbers, and roofers.*
- Where do some decorating consultants work? *In wallpaper, fabric, and furniture stores.*
- What is an interior designer trained to work with? *Colors, line, form, texture, unity, and composition.*
- What information must home buyers give to a realtor? *What size home they want, what location they want, and how much they can pay.*

Activities

Skill Builder: Math
Have students investigate and compare the average salaries of people in the jobs discussed in this section.

Skill Builder: Reading
Ask students to read about a famous architect and his or her accomplishments. Then hold a classroom discussion on the impact an architect can have on a community.

Skill Builder: Critical Thinking
Have students think about what kind of classes, hobbies, volunteer activities, and part-time jobs they could pursue in order to prepare themselves for jobs in the housing fields discussed.

Reteaching
Ask students to check the classified ads in the local newspaper to see what opportunities are available in their area for careers in housing. Discuss the other information they can get from the ads.

Enrichment
Invite a city planner to address the class about the "master plan" in their community. Encourage a question-and-answer session.

Focus on Decision Making and Entrepreneurship Many people in housing careers choose to start their own businesses. Have students consider the advantages and disadvantages of doing so, and what decisions must be worked through before a person is ready to become self-employed.

Did You Know? Architects should be able to draw upside down as they sit opposite a client so that the client can understand the drawing.

INTERPERSONAL SKILLS

Success on the Job

What do you think is the key to success on the job? Did you ever take a class that taught that subject? Most people don't realize that they are developing the keys to on-the-job success while they are attending school.

The most important factor is a good attitude toward your work. If you have a positive attitude, you will find satisfaction in your work and in pleasing your employer. Optimistic employees have a positive affect on the attitudes of coworkers and are often looked to for leadership.

Here are some additional skills that contribute to a worker's success:

- **Be reliable.** When given a task, do it willingly and on schedule. Follow directions, and ask questions if you are not entirely sure of what you are to do. Always do quality work.
- **Get along with others.** Whether working as part of a team or independently, be helpful and pleasant to coworkers.
- **Be punctual.** This means coming to work on time everyday, taking breaks and lunches during the time allowed, and trying not to be absent.
- **Work hard.** Don't loaf on the job. Your employer expects you to manage your time and equipment efficiently.
- **Try to do your best.** If you try to do your job better every day, you will feel satisfied that you are doing your best.
- **Be willing to learn.** This includes learning new tasks and improving the math, writing, and communication skills you already have.
- **Follow rules and procedures.** Every organization has safety rules and business procedures. Be sure you know what your employer expects from you so you can act professionally.
- **Learn to deal with stress.** Problems at home affect your work. Work problems can also affect your personal and family life. You can minimize such problems by learning how to deal with stress both at home and at work.
- **Be cooperative.** If you are polite, considerate, and fair towards others, everyone will benefit.
- **Give reasonable notice.** When you leave a job, two weeks notice is usually appropriate.
- **Leave with a good impression.** You may want to return to the company later, or you may ask your employer for a reference in the future.

Think It Through

1. **Which of these skills do you think you're strong in? Which can you learn? How would you go about learning them?**
2. **Why are these skills needed to succeed on the job?**

Teaching the Feature

"Success on the Job"

Answers to Feature Questions

1. Answers will vary. Students may say that they are strong in following directions, being on time, or working hard. They may say that they can learn these skills by simply making an effort or by choosing a role model to pattern their behavior after.

2. These skills are needed to succeed because there is a lot of competition and having certain basic abilities will help people get ahead on the job. Also, these skills can be helpful in other areas of life. For instance, being reliable will help people not only in their jobs but also in their personal relationships.

Activities

Following Directions Give students some rope, then verbally explain how to tie a sailor's knot. This will make students aware of how difficult it can sometimes be to follow directions. Give students a set of written instructions for a different knot and have them evaluate the clarity of the instructions.

Personal Assessment Have students list the characteristics discussed in this feature in the order that represents their own personal strengths, listing their strongest trait first.

Community Contact Have students interview their employers (or parents and friends who are employers) to find out what they think are the most important characteristics of a good employee. Then have students synthesize the results of their interviews and make the results available to other students in the school to help them succeed on the job.

Focus on Relationship Skills Have students work in teams to accomplish a task and then evaluate the dynamics of the group. Did they get along, communicate, interact, and work well as a team? What problems did they have?

Did You Know? In many companies, employers evaluate their employees' performance once a year. During this "annual review," the employer compliments the employee on his or her strengths and offers suggestions for overcoming weaknesses. The annual review is usually the basis on which raises are given.

Teaching "Jobs in Home Maintenance and Use" and "Getting a Job"

(Pages 672-673)

This section teaches about careers in the area of home maintenance—mainly cleaning and repair—and discusses how home economists can work in the extension service or as home service advisers.

Checking Comprehension

✔ What kind of jobs are part of the home maintenance industry? *Repairing broken appliances, leaking roofs, damp basements, faulty heating systems, and others.*

✔ Why do some people hire others to clean and maintain their homes? *As more people work outside the home, time for home maintenance is limited.*

✔ What kind of institutions use maintenance services? *Office buildings, apartment houses, hospitals, day-care centers, nursing homes, senior citizen homes, hotels and motels.*

✔ How can sales clerks help people maintain their homes? *Knowledgeable sales clerks can advise customers on what materials to buy and how to use tools and materials correctly and safely.*

✔ What is the job of an apartment building superintendent? *To keep all the housing units in good repair.*

✔ Why do many superintendents live in the buildings where they work? *Because they may need to be available for emergencies at all hours.*

✔ What is the extension service? *An educational program run by the U.S. Department of Agriculture and county governments.*

✔ How do home economists provide information to the consumer? *They offer suggestions and ideas on how to get the most out of housing. They may run educational workshops, write articles, or give speeches.*

Jobs in Home Maintenance and Use

The home maintenance industry is among the largest in the country. People are needed to repair everything in the home, including broken appliances, leaking roofs, damp basements, and faulty heating systems.

Entry-Level Jobs

As more people work outside the home, time for home maintenance is limited. Many people prefer to hire the services of others to clean and maintain their homes. Positions for private household workers are plentiful. This is a service-oriented business that requires efficiency and organization.

The rising number of office buildings, apartment houses, and hospitals, as well as day-care centers, nursing homes, and senior citizens' homes, increases the demand for maintenance services. These positions also offer good opportunities for part-time and evening hours. Hotels and motels also provide a growing demand for cleaning and maintenance workers.

Many people like to maintain or improve their homes themselves. They need knowledgeable sales clerks to advise them on what materials to buy and how to use tools and materials correctly and safely. These sales clerks work in hardware or in home improvement stores.

Jobs That Require Training

Large apartment buildings have superintendents who keep all the housing units in good repair. They must know how to fix leaks, check furnaces, repair broken windows, and do other similar jobs. Often, these workers live in one of the units in the building. They may need to be available for emergencies at all hours.

The home maintenance industry is among the largest in the country. People are needed to repair everything from water pipes to air conditioners.

Emphasize Jobs in home maintenance are service-oriented positions that require efficiency and organization. When people hire someone to clean their home or do repairs, they want to know that the job will be done on time, efficiently, and economically. An unhappy client will not use the service again and will not recommend it to friends.

People who work for home service and home repair businesses also require special training. They may learn how to repair major appliances, such as air conditioners and refrigerators, or to fix heating, electrical, or plumbing systems. Some businesses provide services such as exterminating insects and rodents or cleaning carpets and upholstery. In most cases, the company or employer provides training courses, on-the-job training, or pays for workers to take special courses.

Jobs That Require a Degree

Home economists with a college degree can work in the field of housing, just as they can in the areas of food or clothing. Some work in the extension service, an educational program run by the U.S. Department of Agriculture and county governments.

Some utility companies have home service advisers who work with the public, helping to manage resources. These workers do many of the same things for businesses that extension home economists do for government agencies.

In both of these jobs, home economists offer suggestions and ideas on how to get the most out of housing. They may run educational workshops, write articles, or give speeches. Whatever the methods, their goal is to provide information to the consumer.

Getting a Job

Did the information in this chapter make you think you would like a career in housing? If so, you might consider a job in this field. There are steps you can take to prepare for such a career.

On-the-job experience is a great help. You can get this by getting a part-time job in a related field while you are going to school or by finding an entry-level job as an apprentice upon graduation. A technical school will help you get the necessary skills. There are many opportunities for college graduates and graduates of specialized schools, such as professional interior design schools. Special training in sales, financing, or computers is very helpful.

Many teens have part-time or summer jobs that give them on-the-job experience in the construction or home maintenance fields. What jobs might be available in your community?

Focus on Entrepreneurship Encourage students to develop plans for a "small business" providing a service around the home, such as a cleaning, lawn mowing, or "handyperson" service. Students should designate specific people to do the work, set rates, list the necessary tools, make advertisements and develop work schedules.

Activities

Skill Builder: Writing
Have students write a job description for one of the following jobs and a classified advertisement that highlights the job and that would attract qualified applicants:

- apartment house superintendent
- air conditioner repairer
- maintenance worker for a child care center
- sales clerk in a home improvement store

Skill Builder: Critical Thinking
Have students decide the process they would use to hire a home maintenance person to perform various tasks around the home (cleaning, appliance repair, a home improvement project). What sources of information could they use? Have them develop a set of criteria for determining who would do a good job.

Skill Builder: Reading
Have students consult the library for brochures from training schools and colleges that prepare people for jobs in home maintenance. Ask students to read the brochures to see what kinds of classes are involved, how long the training takes, and so on. Students might think about whether they would consider attending the school.

Reteaching
Have students discuss with their parents and tell the class about the types of work that home maintenance professionals have done on their home in the past year or two.

Enrichment
Have selected students call the county extension service and find out what kinds of programs are available in the field of housing. If possible, have someone from the service visit the class and bring some of the literature that the service makes available to consumers.

COMPLETING THE CHAPTER

Summary

- People with housing careers must be able to visualize projects, communicate with others, be interested in colors and shapes, be interested in construction and materials, and pay attention to details.
- Entry-level positions in design, construction, and sales include landscape gardeners and construction workers. Positions that require training include decorating consultants, interior designers, and real estate salespeople. Advanced degrees are required for architects and city planners.
- Entry-level positions related to home maintenance include household workers, maintenance workers, and sales clerks. Positions that require training include superintendents and service/repair workers. Home economists must have a college degree.

For Review

Objective Review Questions Have students complete the "Reviewing the Facts" section on this page.

Study Guide Have students complete the Study Guide from Chapter 75 of their *Student Workbook.*

Class Discussion Have students discuss how sex stereotyping may make it difficult for men or women to pursue some housing careers.

Research Project Have students use the Yellow Pages to find out what kind of housing job titles are listed for their community and what services housing professionals advertise.

For Evaluation

Job Levels Have students list as many jobs as possible under the three headings: Entry-Level Jobs, Jobs that Require Training, and Jobs that Require a Degree.

Chapter Test Have students complete the test for Chapter 75 that appears in the *Teacher's Classroom Resources.*

CHAPTER 75 REVIEW

Answers to "Reviewing the Facts"

1. Construction.
2. Any three: ability to visualize a finished project; communicating and working well with others; interest in colors and shapes; interest in construction and materials; attention to detail.
3. Entry-level jobs: (any one) landscape gardener, construction worker. Jobs requiring training: (any one) decorating consultant, interior designer, real estate salesperson. Jobs requiring a degree: (any one) architect, city planner.
4. A helper who is trained on the job by a senior worker.
5. Any two: knowledge of materials; knowledge of people's living patterns; ability to visualize a completed project; computer skills.
6. Guide the growth of an area by predicting future populations and future needs, and suggesting ways that these can be met.
7. Entry-level jobs: (any one) private household worker, cleaning and maintenance worker, sales clerk. Jobs requiring training: (any one) apartment building superintendent, home service and repair worker.
8. County extension services or utility companies.

Reviewing the Facts

1. In what area of housing are the largest number of people employed?
2. List three interests or skills that are important for careers in housing.
3. Identify one career at each job level in home design, construction, and sales.
4. What is an apprentice?
5. Name two special abilities architects must have.
6. Describe the work of city planners.
7. List an entry-level job and a job that requires training in the home maintance industry.
8. Name two areas where home economists and home service advisers can work in the field of housing.

Thinking Critically

1. What effect do you think changes in the way people live will have on careers in housing?
2. If you could have any job described in this chapter, which would you choose? Why?

Applying Your Skills

1. **Researching a Career.** Choose one career in the field of housing. Do library research or conduct an interview with someone in that career. Write a one-page report describing specific characteristics and qualifications necessary for that career.

2. **Researching History.** Use your library and find books about the Middle Ages. Read about the lives of apprentices, or the history of craft unions and guilds. Report to your class.

3. **Analyzing Tools.** Choose three careers in this chapter. List or describe the types of tools each career person would have to work with daily. Do research to guide you in finding the tools of each trade.

Answers to "Thinking Critically"

1. Answers will vary. Students may predict that people will want regular help with maintenance; hi-tech appliances may require more repairs; people may want new designs and materials for living spaces and home furnishings; people may move more frequently and need help buying, selling, or renting; and so on.
2. Answers will vary. Students should acknowledge the skills and interests that are needed to function in that choice of job and have a desire to possess those skills.

TEEN TIPS OVERVIEW

This section focuses on subjects that are important to teens' growing sense of independence.

Four Looks One Room

This Teen Tip discusses how students can make their living space reflect their individuality without too much expense or work.

Living on Your Own

This Teen Tip outlines some of the emotional and practical prerequisites for living alone or with friends. Activities help students evaluate their own readiness for independent living and plan how to move closer to that goal.

Terrific Teenage Tool Kit

This Teen Tip outlines the basic tools teens should know how to use. Directions for six simple but useful "fix-it" projects are also included.

These "Teen Tips" bring the concepts of "Housing and Living Space" to the students by presenting practical approaches to managing their living spaces and their lives.

Introducing "Four Looks—One Room"

(Pages 676-677)

Motivators

Design Ideas A few days before introducing this section, ask students to cut out pictures of rooms that appeal to them from magazines and newspapers. Have them bring their collections to class and discuss what they like about the rooms they chose.

Evaluating Your Own Space Ask students to think about their own room, or the space they live in. Have them make two lists, one of design aspects they like, one of things they'd like to change. Tell students to save their lists. Comment that this section will suggest ways in which they might be able to improve the look of their living space.

Teaching "Four Looks—One Room"

Checking Comprehension

✔ These various "looks" include some simple things that can be done to any room to change its decor. What are some of these common things? *Using fabrics for window or bed coverings, decorating with plants in different containers, putting mirrors and pictures on walls.*

✔ Which of these suggestions might take the most effort and/or money to do? *Anything that involves buying furniture; using built-ins; and stenciling.*

TEEN TIPS

Four Looks—One Room

Using different colors and accessories can change the look of any room. Start by choosing the main color for your room. Then select one or more colors as an accent. Your creativity, plus some time and effort, will help you achieve the unique look that you want.

Here are four possible ways to spruce up a room:

1 To create a country look, use a floral print, lots of ruffles and lace, and soft window treatments. Stencil a design on the walls, woodwork, furniture, or floor. You can buy ready-made stencils or make your own designs.

2 For a tailored look, choose plaid fabric for a bedcover and matching window shades. Select accessories that combine function and form, such as a swing-arm lamp that can light two areas. Highlight only a few carefully chosen items.

Did You Know? According to some recent research, colors have very definite effects upon mood, although the specific effect may vary from person to person. Blue, for example, makes most people feel calm. Red makes many people feel warm, others agitated. Orange makes many people uneasy. Interested students can research findings on color and mood and suggest color schemes they would like to have in their homes. They might also wish to keep track of how colors in various places (such as the doctor's or dentist's office, a favorite restaurant, a sports arena) affect their mood and whether that effect is appropriate to the place.

3 For a natural, outdoor look, add lots of texture to the room. Hang straw mats on the walls, and use baskets in various sizes for storage. Plants—both large and small—help create a feeling of the outdoors.

4 To create a dramatic look, use bold colors and patterns. Group pictures or photos together on the walls to create a gallery. Use mirrors to make the room look larger—look for inexpensive ones at flea markets and garage sales.

TEEN TIPS

Activities

Skill Builder: Math
Ask students to imagine they are going to add new curtains, a rug, and a new bedspread or covering for a couch to some room in their house or apartment. Ask them to measure the area each of these items would cover. If time permits, have them visit a store, find a fabric, rug, or spread they like (or all three), and figure out how much the items would cost for their space.

Reteaching
Have students refer to the evaluations of their own spaces they did earlier in the lesson. Have them choose three or four things they might do fairly easily that would improve the aspects they said they wanted to change. Encourage them to draw out detailed plans for what they might do. Ask them also to consider the pictures of rooms they collected for the first activity in this lesson and think about whether any of the elements in those rooms might be incorporated into their plans. Have students share and critique these plans in class.

Enrichment
Encourage students to carry out (with parental approval) at least one of the plans they made in the "Reteaching" activity. Give them a reasonable amount of time to complete the project, and ask them to keep records of what they do and how much they spend. Be sure to emphasize that even very small and inexpensive changes, such as moving furniture around or changing the lighting, can greatly improve a room. Have students report on their projects and discuss how they liked doing them and how they feel about the end result.

Focus on Self-Expression One's surroundings are a reflection of one's self-esteem and personality. Have students review the concepts of Unit 1, particularly in Chapter 1, "You as an Individual," Chapter 2, "The Teen Years," and Chapter 3, "Your Health and Wellness," and consider specific ways in which their surroundings reflect who they are and how they feel about themselves. Encourage students to write down what they discover and, if they wish, to share their findings in class.

Introducing "Living on Your Own"
(Pages 678-679)

Motivators

Discussion Question: Ask students: "Have you ever imagined living on your own?" Have students discuss this question and describe some of their imagined homes. Focus on details by asking about such factors as where they would live, what their living space would be like, whether they would live alone or with others, and how they would support themselves.

Listing Responsibilities Comment that living independently means taking on many responsibilities, at least some of which will be new. Ask the students to take a few minutes to write down all the responsibilities they presently have. Give a few examples of what you mean, such as managing any money they earn, keeping their room (or their part of it) clean, doing their own laundry, or doing regular chores around the house. Tell students to keep the lists for use later and note that this section focuses on the responsibilities that living alone entails.

Teaching "Living on Your Own"

Checking Comprehension

✓ This tip says that many things are important for living alone, including making mistakes and making your own decisions. Why might those two things be important? *Answers will vary but could include the fact that many decisions accompany independent living, from when to go to bed to what to do about a leaking roof. Mature, independent people aren't afraid of acting just because they might make an incorrect decision. They admit errors and move on, instead of dwelling on past mistakes.*

Living on Your Own

Growing up takes time. Accepting responsibility, learning from mistakes, and making your own decisions are important steps in the transition from being a child to becoming an adult.

You can prepare for your role as an adult while you are a teen. One way is to be a responsible person while you are living at home. This means caring for your own clothing, possessions, and room. You can practice making decisions based on your goals and values—and being flexible, too.

To help you better understand the responsibilities of living on your own, you may want to open your own checking and savings accounts and to take charge of your own appointments. You could earn money to pay for your own expenses—such as clothing, entertainment, car insurance, or telephone bill.

TEEN TIPS

Focus on Relationship Skills Beginning to live independently causes major changes in family relationships. Sometimes the change is smooth and friendly, and sometimes it is traumatic. Have students refer to Unit 2, "Your Family and Friends" and especially to Chapter 10, "Understanding Families", Chapter 11, "Strengthening Families", and Chapter 12, "Adjusting to Changes in Families" and think about the interpersonal dynamics involved when an older teen leaves home to live on his or her own after high school. Have the students consider why leaving can be a difficult time, both for the person leaving and for family members left behind.

Most young people plan to leave home someday and live independently—either by themselves or with friends. When considering leaving home, ask yourself the following questions. If you can answer all of them positively, you might be ready to live on your own.

- Am I earning (or have the ability to earn) a steady living?
- Am I capable of managing my own finances?
- Am I able to provide my own food, clothing, and shelter?
- Can I handle housekeeping?
- Do I enjoy spending time alone, or can I get along with roommates?
- Do I avoid extreme reactions to difficult situations?
- Am I willing to accept the consequences of my actions?

TEEN TIPS

✓ Why does the checklist include questions about your ability to spend time alone and avoid extreme reactions to difficult situations? *Answers will vary but could include the following observations: you will spend much more time alone living independently than you do living with your family, extreme reactions are a mark of immaturity and do not help anyone cope with the difficulties that inevitably accompany adult living.*

Activities

Skill Builder: Writing
Have each student write a letter to himself or herself that objectively evaluates his or her own readiness for living alone, or with friends, taking into account the list of responsibilities prepared earlier and the checklist in this section.

Reteaching
Ask students to identify three steps they need to take to move closer to independent living. These steps could be as basic as learning to handle a checkbook or as advanced as investigating possible places to live. Have the students outline how they could go about taking these steps, and discuss the plans in class.

Enrichment
Divide the class into small groups to investigate how to do the following, and approximately how much each step costs: find an apartment, move their belongings, obtain basic furniture and kitchen equipment, and obtain basic services, such as gas, electricity, telephone, water, and garbage collection. Have groups share their findings and come up with an approximate cost for starting out living alone.

Introducing "Terrific Teenage Tool Kit"
(Pages 680-681)

Motivators

The things I need to do . . . Ask students to think back over the past six months to a year and to write down all the things around their homes that required some work with tools (for example, hanging a picture or rewiring a lamp). Have students share their lists, and ask students to state who did the work involved. Record the responses on the chalkboard for use later.

Discussion Question: Ask students: "Are you handy?" Ask students to discuss this question and point out that doing the kinds of things the students just listed can be important parts of independent living. Tell them that this section will talk about some kinds of home tasks they can do themselves.

Teaching "Terrific Teenage Tool Kit"

Checking Comprehension

✔ Which of the tasks described here seem to be the most difficult, and why? *Answers will vary but might include putting up a curtain rod, taking a door off its hinges, and removing a bicycle wheel, because these activities require several steps and use more than one tool.*

✔ Which of the tasks described do you think is the most useful for you? Why? *Answers will vary.*

✔ What other kinds of "do-it-yourself" tasks would you like to be able to do, and why? *Answers will vary.*

TEEN TIPS

Terrific Teenage  Tool Kit

Are you handy with tools, or must you ask someone to help you when anything needs to be fixed? Could you hang up a picture? Put up a curtain rod? Take a door off its hinges? You could if you knew how to use these basic tools for some simple tasks:

Hammer with claw end
Nails, assorted sizes
Picture hanging hooks
Straight screwdriver
Phillips screwdriver
Pliers
Adjustable wrench

How to put in a nail

Place masking tape over the spot on the wall where the nail will go. To start, hold the nail in place with one hand, and tap gently with the hammer. Be sure to hold the hammer near the end of its handle. Then hit the nail squarely and firmly until it is inserted the desired amount.

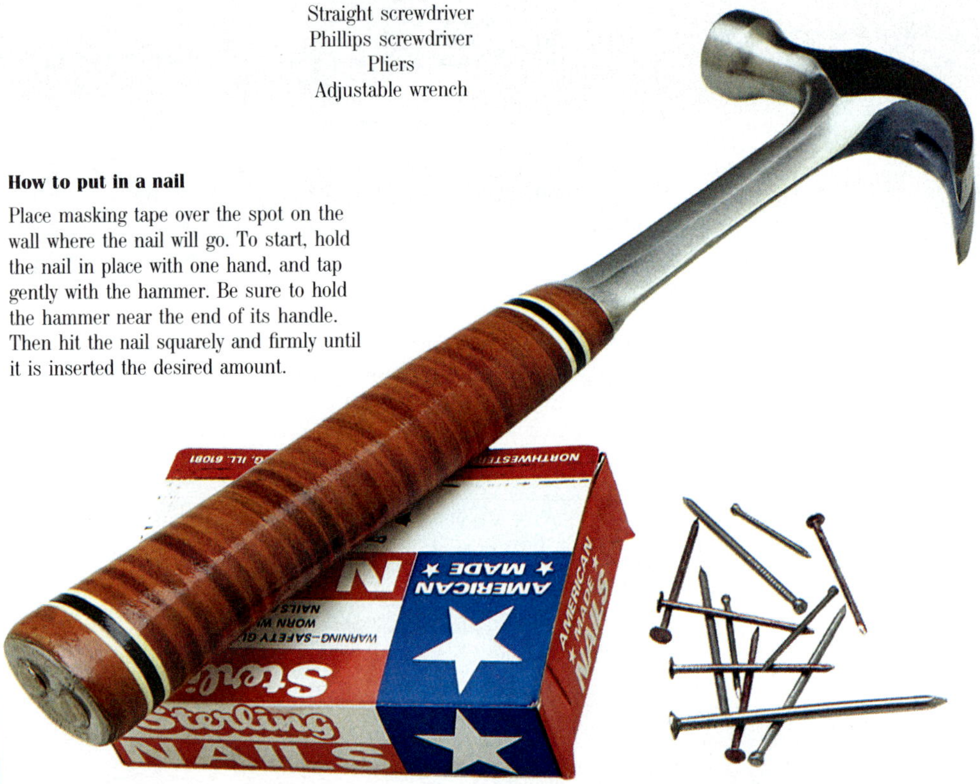

More About Buying Tools There's a wide variation in quality and price among all tools, power and hand, and the wise consumer does research before buying. Interested students can choose one or more tool category (such as drills, wrenches, or hammers). They might talk to knowledgeable sources, such as industrial arts teachers or hardware store personnel, to determine the relative cost and value of different brands. Have students share the results of their comparisons with the class and comment on whether the most expensive tool is necessarily the best.

TEEN TIPS

How to remove a nail

Use the claw end of the hammer to lift out the nail. When the nail is partly removed, place a piece of cloth or wood beneath the head of the hammer to prevent damaging the wall.

How to fill an unwanted hole

If you move a picture or make a mistake pounding in a nail, fill the hole with a bit of spackle or patching compound. Smooth with a putty knife. After it dries, sand with fine sandpaper and touch up the paint.

How to put up a curtain rod

First, measure the window accurately. Then insert the topmost screw part way at each end to hold the rod in place. You can start the screw holes by hammering a nail into the wall about 1/8″; remove nail. Use a straight screwdriver (for screws with a single slot) or a Phillips screwdriver (for screws with an X slot). Fit the screwdriver into the screw slot and push against the head of the screw as you turn it. Next, insert the other screws part way. Finally, tighten all screws.

How to take a door off its hinges

Sometimes a door has to be taken off its hinges in order to move a piece of furniture into a room. To do this, use a straight screwdriver and a hammer. Hold the screwdriver with the edge just underneath the ball top of the hinge bolt. Tap the end of the screwdriver with the hammer to loosen the bolt. Undo the bottom bolt first, then the top one. To replace the door, put it back on the hinges, insert the bolts, and hammer them down.

How to take off a bicycle wheel

Use an adjustable wrench or pliers to remove the nuts and bolts that hold the wheel in place. Put tape or a piece of cloth around each nut to prevent scratches. Then adjust the wrench or the pliers to fit snugly around the nut. Turn counterclockwise to loosen nut. If the bolt is a screw, you can use a screwdriver to hold it as you turn the nut. If the nut is hard to loosen, apply a few drops of oil and let soak for a few hours.

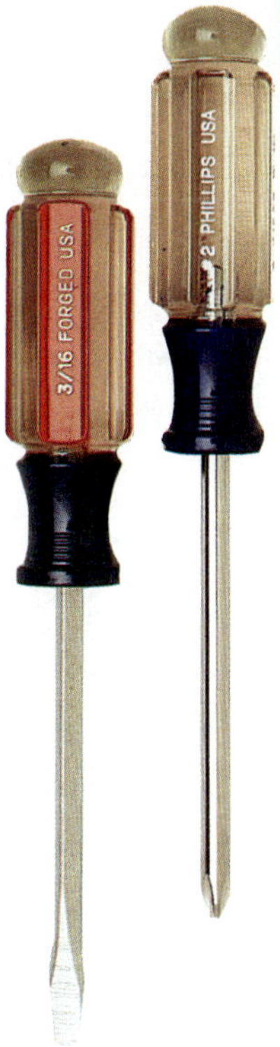

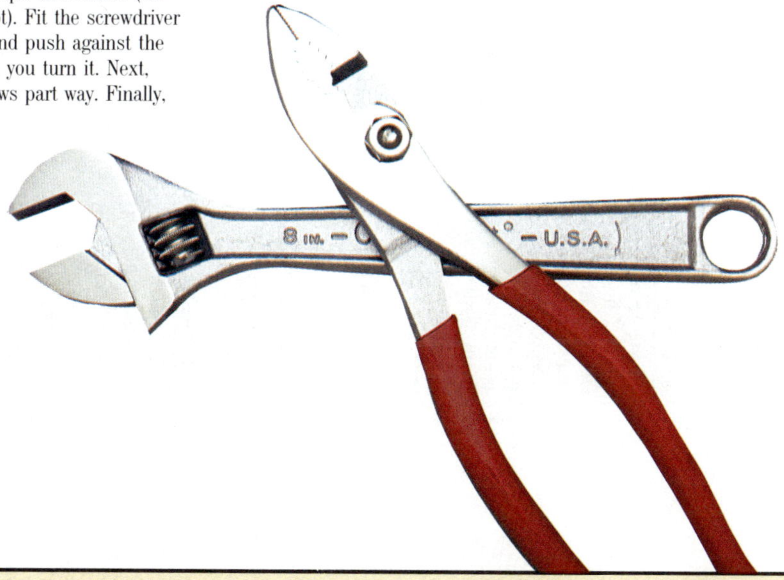

Activities

Skill Builder: Writing
Ask the students to think of one "do-it-yourself" task they would like to teach others to do. They can choose a task outlined here and simply rewrite the instructions, or they can use a different task. (They may need to do some research or talk to someone before writing their instructions.) Have them write clear instructions for doing this task. Students can then share their instructions with the class, which can critique the instructions for clarity and thoroughness.

Reteaching
Ask students to bring in all the tools listed on page 680, and any others they have found useful. (Alternatively, bring in these and other tools yourself.) Have students discuss what tasks these tools are used for. Also have them try using these tools on sample materials, and discuss how comfortable they feel using them.

Enrichment
Have students research the cost of hiring someone to do the tasks described in this section, or any other basic household task that interests them. They might ask parents, apartment building or school superintendents, hardware store personnel, industrial arts teachers, or local repairers. They might also look in the newspaper classified advertisements. Have students share their findings, and discuss how much money learning to be your own "fixer" might save.

Focus on Independent Living Learning to use tools and do household repairs is a vital part of learning to live independently. Have students recall the work done in the other Teen Tips in this Unit, "Four Looks—One Room" and "Living On Your Own," and think about how the basic idea of "do-it-yourself" might relate to these two sections. Have them discuss how being "handy" can save money and also increase their independence. In addition, having the ability to fix things around the home contributes greatly to one's self-esteem. Have students consider why this might be so.

Appendix

Table of Food Values

Milk Group	Amount	Calories	Carbohydrates (g)	Fat (g)	Protein (g)	Calcium (mg)	Iron (mg)	Vitamin A (IU)	Thiamin (mg)	Riboflavin (mg)	Niacin (mg)	Vitamin C (mg)
Cheese, American, process	1 oz/28 g	105	Tr	9	6	174	.1	340	.01	.10	Tr	0
Cheese, Cheddar	1 oz/28 g	115	Tr	9	7	204	.2	300	.01	.11	Tr	0
Cheese, cottage, creamed	½ c/120 ml	117	.1	5	14	67.5	.15	185	.025	.185	.135	Tr
Cheese, cottage, dry	½ c/120 ml	62.5	.5	Tr	12.5	23	.15	20	.02	.10	.1	0
Cheese, cream	1 oz/28 g	100	.2	10	2	23	.3	400	Tr	.06	Tr	0
Chocolate milk	1 c/240 ml	210	26	8	8	280	.6	300	.09	.41	.3	2
Cream, heavy	1 T/15 ml	80	.1	6	Tr	10	Tr	220	Tr	.02	Tr	Tr
Cream, light	1 T/15 ml	30	1	3	Tr	14	Tr	110	Tr	.02	Tr	Tr
Cream, sour	1 T/15 ml	25	1	3	Tr	14	Tr	90	Tr	.02	Tr	Tr
Ice cream 16% fat	½ c/120 ml	175	16	12	2	75.5	.05	445	.02	.14	.5	5
Milk	1 c/240 ml	150	11	8	8	291	.1	310	.09	.4	.2	2
Milk, low fat 2%	1 c/240 ml	121	12	5	8	297	.1	500	.1	.4	.2	2
Milk, skim	1 c/240 ml	85	12	Tr	8	302	.1	500	.09	.34	.2	2
Yogurt, fruit	1 c/240 ml	230	42	3	10	343	.2	120	.08	.4	.2	21
Yogurt, plain, skim milk	1 c/240 ml	125	17	Tr	13	452	.2	20	.11	.53	.3	2
Yogurt, plain, whole milk	1 c/240 ml	140	11	7	8	274	.1	280	.07	.32	.2	1
Meat, Poultry, Eggs, Fish, and Legumes Group												
Beef, lean (roasted)	3 oz/85 g	165	0	7	25	11	3.2	10	.06	.19	4.5	—
Beef, hamburger, 21% fat	3 oz/85 g	235	0	17	20	9	2.6	30	.07	.17	4.4	—
Chicken (broiled)	3 oz/85 g	240	0	7	42	16	3.0	160	.09	.34	15.5	—
Chicken (fried)	3 oz/85 g	160	1	5	26	9	1.3	70	.04	.17	11.6	—
Eggs (hard cooked)	1	80	1	6	6	28	1	260	.04	.13	Tr	0
Fish, bluefish (baked)	3½ oz/100 g	135	0	4	22	25	0.6	40	.09	.08	31.6	—
Ham, boiled	1 oz/28 g	65	0	5	5	3	.8	0	.12	.04	.7	—
Kidney beans (red beans)	1 c/240 ml	230	42	1	15	74	4.6	10	.13	.10	1.5	—
Lamb shoulder (roasted)	3 oz/85 g	285	0	18	23	9	1.0	—	.11	.2	4.0	—
Lentils	1 c/240 ml	210	39	Tr	16	50	4.2	40	.14	.12	.12	0
Peanut butter	2 T/30 ml	190	6	16	8	20	.6	0	.04	.04	4.8	0

Peas, dried, split	1 c/240 ml	230	42	1	16	22	3.4	80	.3	.18	1.8	—
Pork (roast)	3 oz/85 g	310	0	20	26	9	2.6	0	.46	.21	4.1	—
Sardines	3 oz/85 g	175	0	9	20	372	2.5	190	.02	.17	4.6	—
Tuna, canned in oil	3 oz/85 g	170	0	7	24	7	1.6	70	.04	.1	10.1	—
Turkey, dark meat (roasted)	3 oz/85 g	175	0	7	26	—	2.0	—	.03	.2	3.6	—
Veal cutlet	3 oz/85 g	185	0	9	23	9	2.7	—	.06	.21	4.6	—
Fruits and Vegetables Group												
Apple	1 (2¾"/63 mm)	80	20	1	Tr	10	.4	120	.04	.03	.1	6
Apricots	3 med	55	14	Tr	1	18	.5	2,890	.03	.04	.6	11
Banana	1 med	100	26	Tr	2	10	.8	230	.06	.07	.8	12
Beans, green	1 c/240 ml	30	7	Tr	2	63	.8	680	.07	.11	.6	15
Bean sprouts	1 c/240 ml	35	7	Tr	4	20	1.4	20	.14	.14	.8	20
Blueberries	1 c/240 ml	90	22	1	1	22	1.5	150	.04	.09	.7	20
Broccoli	1 c/240 ml	40	7	Tr	5	136	1.2	3,880	.14	.31	1.2	140
Cabbage, shredded	1 c/240 ml	15	4	Tr	1	34	.03	90	.04	.04	.2	33
Cabbage, red, shredded, raw	1 c/240 ml	20	5	Tr	1	29	.6	30	.06	.04	.3	43
Cantaloupe	½ melon	80	20	Tr	2	38	1.1	9,240	.11	.08	1.6	90
Carrots	1	30	7	Tr	1	27	.5	7,930	.04	.04	.4	6
Celery, raw	3 stalks	15	6	Tr	Tr	48	.3	330	.03	.03	.3	12
Corn, sweet kernels	1 c/240 ml	130	31	1	5	5	.3	580	.15	.10	2.5	8
Cranberry sauce	½ c/120 ml	202.5	52	Tr	.5	8.5	.3	30	.015	.015	.5	3
Dates	10	220	58	Tr	2	47	2.4	40	.07	.08	1.8	0
Grapefruit juice[a]	¼ c/60 ml	25	6	Tr	.25	6	.05	5	.01	.01	.1	24
Grapes, seedless	10	81	9	Tr	Tr	6	.2	50	.03	.02	.2	2
Lettuce, iceberg	¼ head	17.5	2.6	Tr	.8	18	.45	297	.05	.05	.3	5
Mustard greens	1 c/240 ml	30	6	1	3	193	2.5	8,120	.11	.20	.8	67
Onions, boiled	½ c/120 ml	30	7	Tr	1.5	25	.4	Tr	.03	.03	.2	7.5
Orange	1 (3"/76 mm)	65	16	Tr	1	54	.5	260	.13	.05	.5	66

Note: Although ice cream is a good source of calcium, it also contains many calories, and may lead to weight problems.
Key: Tr—Nutrient present in trace amounts. [a] Made from concentrate.

Table of Food Values (cont.)

Fruit and Vegetables Group	Amount	Calories	Carbohydrates (g)	Fat (g)	Protein (g)	Calcium (mg)	Iron (mg)	Vitamin A (IU)	Thiamin (mg)	Riboflavin (mg)	Niacin (mg)	Vitamin C (mg)
Orange juice[a]	¼ c/60 ml	30	7.25	Tr	.5	6.25	.1	135	.05	.001	.22	30
Peaches, peeled	1 (2½″/63 mm)	40	10	Tr	1	9	.5	1,330	.02	.05	1.0	7
Pear, Bartlett	1 (2½″/63 mm)	100	25	1	1	13	.5	30	.03	.07	.2	7
Peas, green, frozen	1 c/240 ml	110	19	Tr	.8	30	2.3	960	.43	.14	2.7	21
Pepper, green sweet, raw	1 med	15	4	Tr	1	7	.5	310	.06	.06	.4	94
Pineapple, cubed	1 c/240 ml	80	21	Tr	1	26	.5	110	.14	.05	.3	26
Potato, baked	1 med	145	33	Tr	4	14	1.1	Tr	.15	.07	2.7	31
Potatos, French fried	10 pieces	155	18	7	2	9	.7	Tr	.07	.04	1.8	12
Prunes, dried	4 med	110	29	Tr	1	22	1.7	690	.04	.07	.7	1
Raisins (snack package)	½ oz/14 g	40	11	Tr	Tr	9	.5	Tr	.02	.01	.1	Tr
Spinach	1 c/240 ml	40	6	1	5	167	4	14,580	.13	.25	.9	50
Tomatoes, canned	1 c/240 ml	50	10	Tr	2	14	1.2	2,170	.12	.07	1.7	41
Tomato, raw	1 med	25	6	Tr	1	16	.6	1,110	.07	.05	.9	28
Tomato juice	6 oz/170 g	35	8	Tr	2	13	1.6	1,460	.09	.05	1.5	29
Bread and Cereals Group												
Bread, white enriched	1 slice	70	13	1	2	21	.6	Tr	.08	.06	.8	Tr
Bread, whole wheat	1 slice	65	14	1	3	24	.8	0	.07	.03	.8	Tr
Bread, pumpernickel (⅔% rye)	1 slice	80	17	Tr	3	27	.8	0	.09	.07	.6	0
Corn flakes, fortified (25% RDA)	1 c/240 ml	95	21	Tr	2	V	V	V	V	V	V	13
Crackers, saltines	4	50	8	1	1	2	.5	0	.05	.05	.4	0
Egg noodles, enriched	1 c/240 ml	200	37	2	7	16	1.4	110	.22	.13	1.9	0
Pasta, enriched (macaroni cooked, etc.)	1 c/240 ml	190	39	1	7	14	1.4	0	.23	.13	1.8	0
Rice, instant, enriched	1 c/240 ml	180	40	Tr	4	5	1.3	0	.21	V	1.7	0
Rice, enriched	1 c/240 ml	185	41	Tr	4	33	1.4	0	.19	.02	2.1	0
Rice, puffed, whole grain	1 c/240 ml	60	13	Tr	1	3	.3	0	.07	.01	.7	0
Wheat, farina, quick	1 c/240 ml	105	22	Tr	3	147	V	0	.12	.07	1	0

Wheat flakes, fortified, 25% U.S. RDA	¾ c/180 ml	105	24	Tr	3	12	4.8	1,320	.40	.45	5.3	16
Wheat, puffed, whole grain	1 c/240 ml	55	12	Tr	2	4	.6	0	.08	.03	1.2	0
Wheat, shredded, whole grain	1 large biscuit	90	20	1	2	11	.9	0	.06	.03	1.1	0
Wheat, whole grain cereal	1 c/240 ml	110	23	1	4	17	1.2	0	.15	.05	1.5	0
Other												
Bacon, fried crisp	2 slices	85	Tr	8	4	2	.5	0	.08	.05	.8	—
Butter	1 T/14 g	100	Tr	12	Tr	3	Tr	430	Tr	Tr	Tr	0
Doughnuts, glazed	1	205	22	11	3	16	.6	25	.1	.1	.8	0
Honey	1 T/21 g	65	17	0	Tr	1	.1	0	Tr	.01	.1	Tr
Margarine, regular	1 T/15 g	100	Tr	12	Tr	3	Tr	470	Tr	Tr	Tr	0
Mayonnaise	1 T/15 ml	100	Tr	11	Tr	3	.1	40	Tr	.01	Tr	—
Nuts, peanuts, salted	1 c/240 ml	840	27	72	37	107	3	—	.46	.19	24.8	0
Nuts, walnuts	1 c/240 ml	785	19	74	26	Tr	7.5	380	.28	.14	.9	—
Oil, corn	1 T/15 ml	120	0	14	0	0	0	—	0	0	0	0
Pizza, cheese	1 slice	145	22	4	6	86	1.1	230	.16	.18	1.6	4
Popcorn, plain	1 c/240 ml	25	5	Tr	1	1	.2	—	—	.01	.1	0
Salad dressing, Italian	1 T/15 ml	85	1	9	Tr	2	Tr	Tr	Tr	Tr	Tr	—
Salad dressing, Italian low calorie	1 T/15 ml	10	Tr	1	Tr	Tr	Tr	Tr	Tr	Tr	Tr	—
Seeds, sunflower	½ c/120 g	405	14.5	34.5	17.5	87	5.15	35	1.42	.17	3.9	—
Sugar	1 T/12 g	45	12	0	0	0	Tr	0	0	0	0	0

Note: All fruits and vegetables fresh unless noted. Vegetables fresh cooked unless noted.
Key: [a] Made from concentrate. Tr—Nutrient present in trace amounts. V—Varies by brand; consult label.

United States Recommended Daily Allowances (U.S. RDA)

The U.S. Recommended Daily Allowances (U.S. RDAs) for vitamins, minerals, and protein were developed from the Recommended Dietary Allowances of the Food and Nutrition Board, National Academy of Sciences—National Research Council (NAS-NRC) by the Food and Drug Administration for use in its nutrition labeling, nutritional guidelines, and dietary supplement regulations.

U.S. RDA		
Unit		**Adults and children 4 or more yrs.**
Protein		
High quality g		45
Lower quality g		65
Vitamins		
Vitamin A	IU	5000
Vitamin D	IU	400
Vitamin E	IU	30
Vitamin C	mg	60
Folacin	mg	0.4
Thiamin (B_1)	mg	1.5
Riboflavin (B_2)	mg	1.7
Niacin	mg	20
Vitamin B_6	mg	2
Vitamin B_{12}	mcg	6
Biotin	mg	0.3
Pantothenic acid	mg	10
Minerals		
Calcium	g	1
Iron	mg	18
Phosphorus	g	1
Iodine	mcg	150
Magnesium	mg	400
Zinc	mg	15
Copper	mg	2

IU = International Unit
g = gram
mg = milligram
mcg = microgram

1000 mcg (micrograms) = 1 mg
1000 mg (milligrams) = 1 g

Percentages of U.S. RDA

This chart shows what percentage of the U.S. RDA you need for your age and sex.

Most people do not need 100 percent of the U.S. RDA for every nutrient. Use of 100 percent of the U.S. RDA as a nutritional goal is in no way dangerous. However, it may lead to needless changes in your diet and to spending more money on food than is necessary. It may also cause you unwarranted concern about nutrient shortages in your day's food choices. On the other hand, at certain stages of the life cycle, some people need more than 100 percent of certain nutrients.

For your daily nutrition goal, select the appropriate amounts of nutrients shown in this table. For example, the recommended amount of calcium for a 16-year-old male or female is 120 percent of the U.S. RDA. Therefore daily food choices by 16-year-olds should provide 120 percent or more of the U.S. RDA for calcium, rather than 100 percent.

Age	Food Energy[1]	Protein[2]	Vitamin A	Vitamin C	Thiamin	Ribo-flavin	Niacin[3]	Calcium	Iron
Years	*Calories*	*Percent of U.S. Recommended Daily Allowance*							
Child:									
1–3	1300	35	40	70	50	50	30	80	85
4–6	1800	50	50	70	60	65	35	80	60
7–10	2400	55	70	70	80	75	50	80	60
Male:									
11–14	2800	70	100	75	95	90	55	120	100
15–18	3000	85	100	75	100	110	55	120	100
19–22	3000	85	100	75	100	110	60	80	60
23–50	2700	90	100	75	95	95	45	80	60
51+	2400	90	100	75	80	90	35	80	60
Female:									
11–14	2400	70	80	75	80	80	45	120	100
15–18	2100	75	80	75	75	85	30	120	100
19–22	2100	75	80	75	75	85	35	80	100
23–50	2000	75	80	75	70	75	30	80	100
51+	1800	75	80	75	70	65	25	80	60
Pregnant	+300[4]	+50[4]	100	100	+20[4]	+20[4]	35	120	100+
Nursing	+500[4]	+35[4]	120	135	+20[4]	+30[4]	35	120	100

[1] Calorie needs differ depending on body composition and size, age, and activity of the person.

[2] U.S. RDA of 65 grams is used for this table. In labeling, a U.S. RDA of 45 grams is used for foods providing high-quality protein, such as milk, meat, and eggs.

[3] The percentage of the U.S. RDA shown for niacin will provide the RDA for niacin if the RDA for protein is met. Some niacin is derived in the body from tryptophan, an amino acid present in protein.

[4] To be added to the percentage for the girl or woman of the appropriate age.

Source: *Nutrition labeling, Tools for Its Use,* Agriculture Information Bulletin No. 382, U.S. Department of Agriculture, 1975.

Glossary

Note: Numbers in parentheses indicate the chapter in which the term appears.

abbreviation A shortened form of a word. (44)
abstract thinking A thought process that includes concepts that are difficult to understand. (2)
accessory A small object that adds visual appeal to a room. (71)
accident An unplanned, sudden event. (73)
acquaintance Someone you know, but not as well as you know a good friend. (7)
addictive A substance that is difficult, and sometimes impossible, to stop using. (3)
additive A substance added to food before it is sold. (41)
adolescence The period of life when you grow from being a child to being an adult. (2)
adopted A child who has been legally made a permanent member of a new family (10)
aerobic Any exercise that improves your ability to use oxygen by requiring sustained regular movement for 30 minutes or more, with no rests. (35)
aide Worker who assists higher-level workers with their jobs. (17)
alternative A choice (5)
amino acid Any of the twenty-two chemicals that make up all proteins. (36)
analogous color scheme A color scheme that uses colors that are closely related. (56)
annual percentage rate (APR) The percentage cost of credit on a yearly basis. (28)
anorexia nervosa An eating disorder in which people believe they are overweight even when they are too thin, causing them to diet even more. (39)
appetite The desire to eat. (35)
appliance A piece of kitchen equipment run by electricity or gas. (42)
appliqué A cutout fabric decoration sewn onto another fabric background. (65)
apprentice A helper who is trained on the job by senior workers. (54)
appropriate Suitable for an occasion. (55)
architect A person who designs buildings and homes. (75)
arcing Sparks that can damage a microwave oven and start a fire. (48)
attitude Thoughts and judgments you have about the world around you. (1)
back-up plan An alternative way of doing something if the original plan does not work out. (6)
bait and switch When a store advertises a product at a low price, but then tries to get you to buy a more expensive product. (29)
balance When objects are arranged in an even, pleasing way. (71)
barter The direct exchange of one resource for another. (25)
basal metabolism All the automatic functions of your body, including breathing, tissue repair, blood circulation, and growth. (39)
beat To mix ingredients thoroughly so that air is introduced. (46)
Better Business Bureau An organization formed by businesses that promise to obey business standards; in return, the Bureau tries to resolve consumer complaints against its members. (32)
bias Any curve or angle that is not cut on the lengthwise or crosswise grain of the fabric. (64)
blend To mix two or more ingredients together thoroughly; *also,* a yarn made from two or more different fibers. (46, 58)
blended family A family that joins two separate families through marriage. (10)
blueprint An architect's plan or mechanical drawing. (75)
bobbin A small spool that holds the bottom thread in a sewing machine. (62)
body language Your posture and the way you move, walk, or sit. (8)
bolt-end label A label on a fabric bolt that lists the fiber content, recommended care, fabric width, and price per yard. (61)
brainstorming A free-for-all approach to problem solving that lists as many ideas as people can think of in order to get ideas flowing and promote discussion. (11)
braise To cook food in a small amount of liquid in a pan that has a tight-fitting lid. (47)
brand The particular name of a product. (41)
broil To cook food directly with a glowing heat source. (47)
budget A plan for using your money. (27)
buffet A style of meal service in which all the food is arranged on a serving table for people to select from and make up their own plates. (53)
bulimia An eating disorder in which a person overeats, and then gets rid of the food by using laxatives or vomiting.

buyer A person who connects designers and garment makers with the stores and shops where clothing is sold. (68)

calendar A weekly, monthly, or yearly record of appointments, important events, holidays, birthdays, and other important dates. (26)
calorie An amount of energy; specifically, a measure of heat. (36)
capital The money you invest in a business. (34)
carbohydrate Any of the nutrients that provide your body with ready energy. (36)
caregiver A person who takes care of children or who cares for people who are sick or elderly. (18)
caring The emotional bond that one person feels for another. (13)
casserole A dish which can be used for both cooking and serving. (47)
cereal Any grain. (37)
characteristic A special feature or trait that distinguishes one individual from another. (1)
checking account An account on which you can write checks directing the bank to pay money as directed. (28)
child abuse The physical or emotional mistreatment of children. (21)
child care center A place where children are cared for while their parents work. (22)
childproof Safe for children. (21)
cholesterol A white, waxlike substance that plays a part in transporting and digesting fat. (36)
chop To cut into small pieces. (46)
citizen A member of a group such as a school, a community, or a nation. (16)
classic A style that stays popular for a long time. (57)
clearance sale A sale held by stores to get rid of old stock to make room for new items. (30)
clergy Religious workers such as priests, ministers, rabbis, and mullahs. (17)
client A person who is given help and information by a professional. (17)
clique A small, exclusive group of people within a peer group. (13)
coagulate To change from a fluid state to a thickened mass. (51)
communicating Sending messages from one person to another. (8)
community resource Any person or facility in your community that helps you enjoy your life, improve your skills, or achieve your goals. (25)
comparison shopping Comparing features and prices of different brands and models of the same item before you buy. (31)
complementary color scheme A scheme that uses colors that are direct opposites on the color wheel. (56)
compromise A way of solving a problem in which each person gives up something in order to come to an agreement. (7)
concentrate A juice product from which most of the water has been removed. (50)
condominium One of a group of apartments or townhouses that you buy rather than rent. (69)
confidentiality The complete privacy of a person's business. (11)
conflict A problem that arises in a relationship. (9)
conform To be like the people around you. (55)
conscience Your inner voice that tells you whether what you are doing is right or wrong, according to your values. (15)
conserve To save or use carefully so as not to deplete a resource. (25)
construction The building of homes. (75)
consumer A person who buys and uses things. (30)
contaminated Food containing large amounts of bacteria. (43)
contrast The difference in color and shape among objects. (71)
coordinated piece A piece of clothing that can be worn with another in several different ways. (59)
cost per wearing The total of the purchase price of a garment and the cost of cleaning it, divided by the number of wearings. (60)
counseling Advice and guidance from experts, religious leaders, or support groups. (11)
creativity The ability to use your imagination to do things in new ways. (24)
credit An arrangement for receiving money, merchandise, or a service now and paying for it later. (28)
custody The right of caring for children, granted by a court in case of divorce. (12)
customary system The measurement system that is standard in the U.S. which measures in teaspoons, tablespoons, cups, pints, quarts, ounces, and pounds. (45)
cut A section or part of a meat carcass. (52)

Daily Food Guide A guide, developed by nutritionists, which lists the number and size of servings needed daily from each food group. (37)
danger zone The range of temperatures in which bacteria grow and produce poisons most rapidly—between 60°and 125° F (16° and 52° C). (43)

dart A triangular fold of fabric stitched to a point to shape the fabric to body curves. (64)
day-care center A place where infants and preschool children are cared for during the day while their parents work. (22)
deadline Date by which a task must be completed. (26)
decision The choice you make between different possibilities. (5)
dehydrated Any milk product from which some or all of the water has been removed. (51)
department store A store offering a wide variety of items, often in different price ranges, under one roof. (30)
depression A prolonged feeling of sadness or a serious emotional disorder characterized by hopelessness and an inability to enjoy life. (3)
designer A person who creates new styles. (57)
detergent A cleaning agent made from chemicals or petroleum. (66)
developmental task Any of the skills and abilities that children acquire as they grow. (19)
diet The food and drink you typically consume. (35)
Dietary Guidelines Recommendations for improving eating habits, developed by the U. S. government. (38)
dieting Controlling your food intake for a specific purpose. (39)
dietitian A person who has studied food and nutrition and their relationship to health and fitness. (24)
directional cutting Cutting with the grain of the fabric. (63)
directional stitching Stitching with the grain of the fabric. (64)
direct mail ad Advertisement that is delivered by the postal service. (29)
discount store A store that sells nationally advertised brands at reduced prices. (30)
distract To lead children away from something they should not do by interesting them in another activity. (21)
divorce The legal termination of a marriage. (12)
dovetail To combine tasks in such a way that one overlaps another, saving time. (44)
dryclean To clean fabrics with chemicals rather than detergent or soap and water. (66)
dyeing Changing the natural color of a fiber, yarn, or fabric using a substance. (58)

ease The extra room a pattern allows for clothing to fit comfortably. (63)
electronic funds transfer (EFT) The method of banking and paying bills automatically with the use of computers. (27)
emotional maturity Being secure enough with your own self-image to be able to meet the emotional demands and responsibilities you face. (23)
empathy The ability to understand what someone else is experiencing. (13)
emphasis When one object receives more attention than other objects in the room. (71)
end-of-season sale A sale held to clear out merchandise to make room for the next season's styles. (60)
energy The capacity for doing work. (74)
enriched Processed grain products which have had nutrients replaced. (37)
entrée Main dish. (38)
entrepreneur A person who starts a new business to provide a product or service that they think consumers want. (34)
entry-level job A job for which little or no experience is needed. (17)
environment Everything that surrounds you including your family, friends, teachers, and the neighborhood and society in which you live. (1)
equivalent Any of the comparison facts that help convert one measurement into another. (45)
etiquette Accepted customs of behavior. (53)
evaluate To judge an action or decision by studying it carefully. (5)
expectation What each person wants in a relationship. (9)
expense Any of the things that you spend your money on. (27)
expiration date The last day a product can be used safely. (41)
extended family A family that includes parents, children, and other relatives, such as grandparents, uncles, aunts, and cousins. (10)
eye contact Direct visual contact with another person's eyes. (8)

fabric Material, or cloth, made from yarn. (58)
facility Any of the goods and services available in a community. (69)
facing An extra piece of fabric sewn on the outside and turned to the inside to finish an edge. (60)
factory outlet A store in which a manufacturer sells goods directly to the consumer. (30)
fad A fashion that is very popular for a short time. (57)
family day care A child-care arrangement in which a small number of children are cared for in a person's home. Also called family child care. (22)
family life cycle The stages of life that the average family goes through. (12)

family style A style of meal service in which the food is brought to the table in bowls which are passed from person to person or served from the head of the table. (53)
fashion A style of clothing that is accepted in a society at a given time. (57)
fashion coordinator A person who develops advertising themes and plans fashion events to bring people into a store. (68)
feed Part of the sewing machine that positions the fabric for the next stitch. (62)
fetus An unborn child. (23)
fiber An indigestible threadlike cell that helps to move food through the digestive system; *also,* the basic ingredient of all fabrics, it is the tiny strand that makes up yarn. (36, 58)
figure type Size category determined by height and body proportion. (61)
finance charge The money you pay to the lender for allowing you credit. (28)
financial stability The ability to meet all your everyday living costs. (23)
fine-motor skills Ability to control the small muscles of the body, such as in the hands. (19)
finish A substance added to a fabric to change its appearance, feel, or performance. (58)
fireproof Protected from the danger of fire. (73)
first aid Emergency care or treatment given to an ill or injured person. (21)
first impression The image people have of someone they have just met. (8)
fixed goal A goal that can be met at a certain time. (4)
flatware Knives, forks, and spoons. (53)
flexible Having the ability to adapt to different plans if the original plans don't work out. (6)
flexible goal A goal that has no definite time limit in which it needs to be accomplished. (4)
floor plan An illustration of the arrangement of elements in a room or home. (70)
food poisoning A disease caused by bacteria growing in food until food becomes poisonous. (43)
food preference The food a person likes best. (40)
formal clothes Particularly dressy clothes, such as a tuxedo or long dress. (55)
format The way information is presented. (44)
fortified Given additional nutrients. (37)
foster child A child who is taken into a new family on a temporary basis. (10)

garment industry The many companies involved in manufacturing clothing. (57)
garnish A thin, decorative strip of vegetable used to add color to food. (46)
gathers Soft folds of fabric stitched into a seam. (64)
generic product Product that is plainly packaged and usually the cheapest of all brands. (41)
goal A target you set for yourself to accomplish. (4)
goods Material things, such as clothes or records, that you can use. (31)
grain The direction in which the yarns run in a fabric. (63)
gross-motor skills Ability to control the large muscles of the body, such as the arms and legs. (19)
guidance Advice or assistance that helps children learn what behavior is acceptable and what is not. (18)

hand-eye coordination Ability to get eyes and muscles to work together to make complex movements. (19)
Heimlich maneuver A procedure in which one uses pressure to force an object that is interfering with breathing from the throat. (21)
hem The bottom edge of fabric turned up and sewn to the wrong side of the garment. (60)
heredity The characteristics that you inherit from your parents and ancestors. (1)
home automation Technology that automatically controls systems in a home. (74)
homogenized Milk that has had its creamy fats blended into the liquid. (51)
hormones Substances in your body that trigger physical changes. (2)
hue A specific color name. (56)
human resource A personal resource such as knowledge, skills, imagination, energy, time, family, and friends. (25)
hunger The body's physical signal that it is short of energy and needs food. (35)
hydroelectric power Power generated by the force of falling water. (74)

illusion An image that fools the eye. (56)
image ad Advertisement that attempts to associate a product with a popular image so people will want to try it. (29)
implement To put a project into action and monitor it. (6)
improvise To come up with new ideas when some of your plans don't work out. (6)
impulse buying Buying things that you had not intended to buy. (30)
income The money you take in and have available to spend. (27)
individuality The ways in which you are different from others. (55)

infatuation An intense but usually short-term feeling of love for someone who may not even know the yearnings exist. (14)
information ad Advertisement that provides information about a specific product or service. (29)
ingredient Any one of the individual food items needed to make a recipe. (40)
inseam measurement The length of the pant leg from the bottom to where the two legs meet. (60)
insulation Material put inside walls or ceilings to keep cold out and heat in. (74)
intensity Brightness or dullness of a color. (56)
interest A fee paid for the use of money. (28)
interview A meeting between an employer and a job applicant. (68)
inventory The amount of each product in stock; *also,* a detailed list of everything on hand. (54, 59)

jealous Feeling hurt or resentful when a boyfriend or girlfriend spends time with or pays attention to someone else. (15)

knead To press and fold dough. (49)

layout A diagram included in sewing instructions that shows how to place the pattern pieces on fabric; *also,* the arrangement of furniture. (63, 70)
legume The dried seed of the bean plant. (37)
licensed A business that is given permission by the state government to operate. (22)
location The region of the country where you will live. (69)
lockstitch A sewing machine stitch in which a thread above the fabric meets another thread coming from below the fabric, and the two threads lock in the middle of the fabric layers. (62)
long-term goal Something you plan to accomplish sometime in the future. (4)
looper Part of the serger that performs like a bobbin in a conventional sewing machine. (62)
loyalty Being faithful to others, especially when they need it. (13)

mail order An order for products by mail. (30)
maintenance The things that have to be done to keep living space and joint belongings in good working order. (73)
malnourished A result of not getting enough of the nutrients essential for growth and development. (38)
management Making decisions about the things you want to do, and then accomplishing the goals you have set for yourself. (2)
manners The way you behave toward other people. (8)
manufactured fiber Fiber formed all or in part by chemicals. (58)
marbling Fine streaks and flecks of fat within the lean area of meat. (52)
material resource An object that you can use to provide or make other things. (25)
media The means by which ads are broadcast or displayed (television, radio, magazines, newspapers, direct mail). (29)
menu The list of foods that a restaurant offers. (53)
metric system The measurement system which measures in grams and liters. (45)
microwave A type of energy wave that operates at a very high frequency. (48)
mildew A fungus that may grow on damp fabric, causing stains. (66)
mineral Any of the nutrients that are simple substances form part of many tissues, and are needed to keep body processes operating smoothly. (36)
moderation Neither too much nor too little. (38)
money order A piece of paper that is sold in banks and post offices and can be used like a check. (28)
monochromatic color scheme A scheme that uses variations of the same color. (56)
mortgage A long-term loan that people take out when they buy a home. (69)
multiple use Using the same area for more than one activity. (70)

natural fiber Fiber that comes from plants or the hair of animals. (58)
natural resource Anything found in nature that people can use, such as air, water, and soil. (25)
nonverbal Without words. (8)
notion Any of the sewing supplies—including thread, zippers, buttons, and trimmings needed to complete a project. (61)
nuclear family Two parents and one or more children sharing a household. (10)
nurture To help children learn and develop by providing love, support, attention, and encouragement. (10, 18)
nutrient Any of the nourishing substances food contains. (36)
nutrient density The proportion of nutrients to the calories a food contains. (37)
nutrition The way that your body uses food. (35)

objective The ability to listen without becoming emotionally involved. (17)

parallel play Playing alongside each other, rather than together. (19)
parenting Taking care of children by meeting their physical, emotional, mental, and social needs. (18)
parliamentary procedure A democratic method which involves people voicing their opinions in order to reach a majority decision. (16)
passive activity An activity that a person watches or listens to, but does not join in. (20)
pasteurized Liquid milk that has been heated and cooled to kill harmful germs. (51)
patchwork A method of sewing small fabric shapes together to create a decorative piece of fabric. (67)
pattern A set of written directions and printed paper pieces showing how to put a sewing project together. (61)
pattern catalog A book that shows all the patterns available from one company. (61)
pattern maker A skilled worker who makes a pattern from the designer's original sample. (68)
pediatrician A doctor who cares for children. (24)
peel To remove the skin of fruits and vegetables. (46)
peer group People your own age. (2)
perishable Tending to spoil easily. (42)
personal inventory A review of your interests and skills. (17)
personality The combination of characteristics and actions that makes you different from every other person. (1)
personal space A place of one's own. (69)
pilot light A thin stream of gas burned constantly and used to light a gas burner on a range. (73)
place setting The arrangement of the tableware each diner will need for the meal. (53)
platonic A relationship based on friendship, rather than romance. (14)
poach To simmer in a small amount of liquid so food keeps its original shape. (47)
pollution Waste that has not been disposed of properly. (25)
portion One of the servings that a recipe yields. (40)
prejudice A fixed mental picture about a whole group of people on the basis of an opinion or feeling, not fact. (9)
premature birth A birth that occurs before development is complete. (23)
prenatal Before birth. (23)
preservative A substance added to food to keep it fresh and tasty longer. (41)
press To lift the iron and set it down on fabric, not sliding it back and forth. (64)
preventive Making sure ahead of time that accidents and damage do not occur. (72)
principal The amount of money you have in your account. (28)
prioritize To rank in order of importance. (4)
processed Food that has been changed from its raw form before being sold. (37)
processed meat Meat that has been seasoned, smoked, or prepared in some way before it is brought to the store. (52)
procrastinate To put off doing something. (26)
produce A term used to describe fresh fruits and vegetables. (50)
promoted Advanced to a position of higher rank and greater responsibility. (54)
proportion The relationship between spaces within a garment; *also,* a pleasing size relationship among objects. (56, 71)
protein Any of the nutrients necessary for building and repairing body tissues; it is the basis of all the body's cells and forms the major part of hair, nails, and skin. (36)
pull date The last day a product may be sold. (41)
puree To cut or mash food so fine that no solid pieces remain. (46)

quick bread Bread that uses baking soda or baking powder to rise. (49)

recipe Detailed instructions for preparing food. (40)
recycle To find a new use for a garment. (67)
redesign To change a garment so that it is more in fashion or has an exciting new look. (67)
redress To correct a wrong. (32)
reference A person who is willing to tell an employer more about you. (22)
reflex An automatic, involuntary response. (19)
relationship Any of your connections with other people. (7)
reliability Being a person others can count on. (13)
resource Something that you need to accomplish a goal. (4)
respect Being polite and considerate to a person because you find them worthy. (7)
return policy A store's rules for allowing a customer to return an item in exchange for another item or for cash. (33)
rhythm The regular repetition of line or shape. (71)

role A part you play when you interact with others. (9)
role model A person you admire and whose behavior you use as an example. (16)
role playing Pretending to be someone else. (20)
rotate To turn a dish a quarter or half-turn in a microwave oven. (48)
rotation A system in which newly purchased foods are put behind older foods so the older supplies are used before newer ones. (42)
routine A set sequence of events. (72)

sanitation Storing, washing, and cooking food properly, as well as keeping the kitchen, appliances, tools, and yourself clean. (43)
sauté To cook food slowly in a little fat until it is tender, but not brown. (47)
savings account An account that holds the savings you deposit. (28)
scale drawing A drawing in which the relative sizes of objects are the same as the relative sizes of those objects in the actual space. (70)
schedule A daily or weekly plan showing the time and length of each of your activities. (26)
seam The line of stitching that joins the pieces of a garment together. (60)
seam allowance The fabric between the line for cutting and the line for stitching. (63)
seasonal More plentiful at certain times of the year. (50)
self-concept The particular view that you have of yourself. (1)
self-confident Having confidence in or being sure of yourself. (13)
self-control An inner control over your own behavior. (15)
self-esteem The way you feel about yourself. (2)
selvage The finished edge of fabric. (63)
sensory toys An object that appeals to the senses—it can be touched, listened to, looked at, or put in the mouth. (20)
sequence The order in which steps are to be done. (44)
serger A high-speed overlock machine that trims, sews, and overcasts in one step. (62)
service Work performed for one person by another, such as a haircut. (31)
serving A portion of a food that a person needs to supply daily nutritional needs. (37)
sew-through button Button that has two or four holes through it and no shank. (65)
shank button Button that has a built-in shank, or loop, on the back but no holes through it. (65)
shield To cover parts of food with aluminum foil to protect them from overcooking in the microwave oven. (48)
shoplifting Stealing goods from stores. (33)
short-term goal Something you can accomplish soon. (4)
shred To grate or cut food into fine pieces using a grater. (46)
sibling Another word for brother or sister. (10)
simmer To cook food in liquid at temperatures just below the boiling point. (47)
single-parent family One parent and one or more children living in the same household. (10)
size range A size category. (60)
small claims court A court in which consumers and businesses present their complaints informally, and a judge decides the case. (32)
smoke detector Battery operated device that sounds an alarm when it senses smoke. (73)
snag A loop of yarn pulled out of a knit. (66)
specialty store A store that sells only a certain type of merchandise. (30)
spoilage Damage that happens when food is too old to eat or contains bacteria or mold. (50)
stages Periods during which a child can perform certain tasks. (19)
stain Dirt that is concentrated in one spot in a garment. (66)
stamina Staying power or endurance. (35)
standing time The time you should allow for food to continue to cook after the microwave oven is turned off. (40)
staple Any of the basic food items that are used regularly. (40)
status Favored position within a group. (55)
staystitching A line of machine stitches through just one layer of fabric that keeps the curved edge from stretching and losing its shape as the fabric is handled. (64)
steamer A metal basket which allows steam to pass through it as it holds food above boiling water. (47)
stepparent A person who marries a child's mother or father. (10)
stereotype An unfair label that is automatically given to strangers, based on the belief that all members of a certain group are alike. (9)
stir-fry To cook food very quickly in very little fat until the food is just tender. (47)
stress The physical and emotional tension that is caused by important happenings or changes in your life. (3)

table service Restaurant service in which waiters and waitresses take your order at the table, bring the food, and clean up after the meal. (53)

telecommunication Any electronic system that transmits voices, images, and information from one place to another. (34)
texture The way a fabric looks and feels. (56)
texturizing A process that adds crimp or curl to a normally straight yarn. (66)
tipping Giving extra money to waiters and waitresses for good service. (53)
tolerance The ability to accept people as they are. (9)
traffic pattern How people usually move through a space. (70)
traumatic An experience causing severe emotional shock that may take time to heal. (12)
trimming Any of the decoration sewn on a garment. (60)
tuck A small, stitched fold—which doesn't taper at the end—used to give a garment shape. (64)

Underwriter's Laboratory An agency that tests electrical products for safety. (31)
unit construction Preparation of separate pieces of fabric before assembling them in a specific order. (64)
unit price The price of an item per ounce or by count. (31)
unity A feeling that all objects in a room look like they belong together. (71)
universal product code An emblem of thick and thin black lines that is printed on items so price and product name can be read on an electric scanner. (41)
unrequited love Love that is not returned. (14)
utensil A small kitchen tool, like a knife. (42)

value Lightness or darkness of a color. (56)
values Guidelines you have for living with yourself and others. (4)
vandalism The marring and destroying of someone else's property. (33)
variable Any condition that determines how long a food needs to be cooked in a microwave oven and at what power level. (48)
variety meat Organ meat such as liver, heart, or kidney. (52)
verbal Using words. (8)
versatile Having many different uses. (59)
view A different version of a sewing pattern. (61)
visualize To see in your mind how a completed project might look. (75)
vitamin Any of the nutrients that help the body stay healthy, function properly, and make use of other nutrients. (36)
volume The amount of space taken up by an ingredient. (45)

wardrobe The clothes that you own. (59)
warranty A written statement from a manufacturer or retailer promising to repair or replace a defective product or to refund your money. (31)
weatherstripping Material used to fill gaps around door frames and windows so that less air leaks in and out. (74)
wellness A state of good health that you achieve by making a conscious effort to look after yourself. (3)
work center An organized area where the main kitchen tasks can be performed. (42)
work triangle The arrangement of the three major centers in the kitchen. (42)

yarn Fiber that has been twisted together in order to make fabric. (58)
yeast bread Bread that rises through the action of a tiny plant called yeast. (49)

Credits

Abbott Laboratories, 228
American Egg Board, 469
American Plywood Association, 385
Ballard, Jim, 98, 118 (left center), 182, 196, 203, 232 (bottom), 236 (inset), 600
Bean, Roger B., 108, 111, 118 (center, bottom right), 119, 193, 201, 375, 537, 607, 625 (bottom left), 629, 641, 652, 660
P.A. Bergner, Duane R. Zehr, 603
Bradley University Childcare Center, Roger B. Bean, 177
Bradshaw, Jim, 26, 145 (top)
Burger King, 357
Burlington Coat Factory, Roger B. Bean, 304, 311, 543
Burlington Coat Factory, Todd Carroll, 515
Burlington Coat Factory/Woodruff High School, Roger B. Bean, 506, 517, 519
Byerly's Music Store, Roger B. Bean, 260
California Closet Company, 633
Carroll, Todd, 515 (inset), 530, 588
Certainteed Corp., 667
Chi-Chi's Inc., 331
Chung, Bom Joon (art), 60 (top left), 241
City of Peoria Board of Election Commissioners, Roger B. Bean, 154
Coleco Industries, Inc., 235 (bottom right)
Coleman, Bruce/Goor, Ron, 72-73
Coleman, Bruce/Hennegin, C. 12-13
Council of Better Business Bureaus, Inc., 299
Coventry Creative Graphics, 267, 274, 293, 380, 383 (left), 549, 589
Davis, Howard, 387 (bottom), 446, 556, 557, 559, 564, 567, 568, 571, 572, 573, 574, 575, 579, 581, 582, 583, 592, 597, 598, 630, 653, 656
Denton Bicycle, Ann Garvin, 32
Eagle Cleaners, Todd Carroll, 593
Esser, Stephan, 334
Faull, Donna, Teen Tip page design. Photos: 232, 244, 321 (top, center)
Finast Food Stores, Bob McElwee, 483
Find out Productions, 232 (center)
Fishel, Scott, 625 (bottom right)
Flo & Friends/Morton High School, Roger B. Bean, 545, 548, 552
Fogler's Variety Store/Woodruff High School, Roger B. Bean, 257, 308
Four x Five, 12-13, 72-73, 172-173, 326-327
Ben Franklin's, Roger B. Bean, 306, 606
Frazier, David R., Photofile, Inc., 69 (right center), 146, 243, 378, 451, 458, 482
Frazier, David R., Photofile, Inc./Aaron Haupt, 248
Frisch, Stephen, 172-173, 231, 238-239 (background), 319, 326-327, 496-497, 611, 618-619
Gaffney, Jim, 501
Garvin, Ann, 16, 58, 60 (bottom center), 61, 76, 109, 113, 115, 117, 118 (top left), 134, 161, 166 (bottom right), 185, 194, 195, 209, 219, 221, 253, 254, 258, 264. 269, 282, 337, 338, 340, 341, 345, 346, 347, 348, 349, 351, 358, 359, 370, 371, 373, 381, 387 (top), 389, 394, 398, 409, 410, 412, 413 (right), 415, 417, 418, 419, 420, 421, 422, 423, 424, 425, 427, 428, 429, 430, 431, 432, 434, 437, 438, 439, 441, 443, 445, 447, 448, 449, 453, 454, 455, 456, 459, 460, 462, 463, 464, 466, 467, 468, 470, 471, 472, 475, 476, 477, 478, 486, 511, 533, 541, 550, 560, 584, 585, 587, 604, 615 (top left), 621, 624, 625 (top right), 632, 637, 645, 665
Graphic Associates/Woodruff High School, 67 (left center), 166 (bottom right), 169 (top right), 320 (left, right), 615 (bottom)
Herm, Martha, 625 (left center)
Noah Herman Sons Realtor, House of the 1990s, Roger B. Bean, 388, 623, 625 (top left)
Hofer, Charles, 103, 178, 233 (right center), 322
Hutchings, Richard, 45
Illinois Outdoor, 307
Image Bank/Janeart Ltd., 12-13
Image Bank/Miguel, 12-13
Image Factory, Teen Tip headliners, Art: 170-171, 323 (top right), 492-493, 614 (bottom left), 615 (top right), 617
Impact Communications, 68 (bottom left), 101, 167 (top right), 175, 190, 220, 234-235, 322 (bottom right), 323 (bottom left), 370, 493 (top)
Thomas Jefferson School, Roger B. Bean, 174, 189, 224, 461
K's Merchandise, Roger B. Bean, 288, 292, 536, 539
K's Merchandise/Woodruff High School, Roger B. Bean, 275, 286, 294, 296
Kee, Vicky, 233 (bottom right)
Landmark Recreational Center, Todd Carroll, 367

Living Well Fitness Center, Roger B. Bean, 272
McDonald's, Michael Jenkins, 487
McElwee, Bob, 157, 162, 261, 262, 300, 314, 329, 355, 366, 369, 382, 383, 395, 396, 400, 401, 407, 440, 444, 452, 498, 504, 591, 594, 634, 636, 638, 640, 649, 662
Maloof Realty, Roger B. Bean, 670
Manual High School, Roger B. Bean, 238
Manual High School, David Owen, 312
March of Dimes, 95
Morton High School, Roger B. Bean, 82, 104, 106, 160, 186, 211, 250, 256, 273, 283, 291, 332, 609, 620, 644, 646, 647, 673
Morton Junior High School, Roger B. Bean, 99, 601
Murray's Shoes/Woodruff High School, 281
Owen, David, 17
PCEEO Trewyn Head Start, Roger B. Bean, 225
Pearl's T.V. and Appliance, Bob McElwee, 663
Peoria Area Blind People's Center, Roger B. Bean, 627
Peoria Public Library, Roger B. Bean, 215
Peterson, Norm A., 96, 330
PhotoEdit
  Brenner, Roger, 206
  Denny, Mary Kate, 143
  Ferguson, Myrlene, 217
  McBrady, Stephen, 63, 377
  Oddie, Alan, 102
  Spunberg, W., 18
Proctor New Horizons Employee Child-care Center, Proctor Community Hospital, Charles Hofer, 180
Phelps, Brent, 30, 39, 66 (top left), 67 (top right, bottom right), 69 (bottom left, bottom right), 70 (photo), 71 (photo), 149, 151, 155, 163, 167 (bottom left), 168, 169 (bottom left), 204, 236-237 (background), 268, 280, 324-325, 362, 374, 433, 490, 491, 492, 493 (bottom), 494-495 (center), 614-615 (background), 616, 617, 658, 678, 679 (bottom), 680, 681
Potlatch, 309
Proctor Community Hospital, Charles Hofer, 229
Purcell, Liz (art), 70-71, 184, 325, 510, 612-613, 676, 677
Richwoods High School, Roger B. Bean, 44
St. Francis OB-Gyn Clinic, David Owen, 222
Schaer, Laura, 251, 276, 508, 518, 524, 531, 534, 540, 547, 580
Scotti Bureau of Marketing Research, Inc., Roger B. Bean, 315
The Singer Sewing Company, 558
Slater, David, 69 (left center)
Stephanie's, Roger B. Bean, 474
Strix Pix, David S. Strickler, 33, 41, 55, 192, 336, 363
Suntree Productions Ltd., 75
Taco Bell, 495 (top)
Texas Highways, 198, 522 (top left, top right)
Tien-Tsin, Impact Communications, 480
Utley, Arvella, 321
Vernon, Alice (food stylist), 234-235
Walgreen's, Duane R. Zehr, 277, 290
Wolinsky, Cary, 522 (bottom right)
Woodruff High School, Roger B. Bean, 14, 15, 19, 20, 22, 24, 25, 28, 29, 36, 38, 43, 46, 49, 50, 52, 54, 57, 60 (top, bottom left, bottom right), 62, 66 (bottom right), 74, 77, 78, 79, 83, 84, 85, 86, 87, 90, 92, 110, 118 (top right), 121, 122, 125, 126, 128, 129, 130, 133, 135, 136, 138, 139, 140, 142, 144, 145 (bottom), 147, 153, 158, 167 (center), 200, 227, 240, 241, 245, 266, 267, 328, 333, 339, 343, 353, 354, 361, 392, 405, 406, 413 (left), 436, 499, 503, 512, 514, 526, 528, 554, 563, 566, 570, 576, 578, 596, 642, 664
Woodruff High School, Todd Carroll, 278
Zehr, Duane R., 35, 47, 88, 91, 93, 118 (bottom left), 123, 127, 205, 213, 218, 237 (insets), 249, 285, 317, 320 (center), 365, 393, 521, 532, 599, 648, 654, 655, 669

Contents:
  Garvin, Ann, 9, 10
  Hutchings, Richard, 5
  Owen, David, 7
  Phelps, Brent, 5, 9, 11
  Woodruff High School, Roger B. Bean, 6, 8

Index

D